APA Handbook of
Research Methods in Psychology

APA Handbooks in Psychology

APA Handbook of
Research Methods in Psychology

VOLUME 2

Research Designs: Quantitative,
Qualitative, Neuropsychological,
and Biological

Harris Cooper, *Editor-in-Chief*
Paul M. Camic, Debra L. Long, A. T. Panter,
David Rindskopf, and Kenneth J. Sher, *Associate Editors*

American Psychological Association • Washington, DC

Published by
American Psychological Association
750 First Street, NE
Washington, DC 20002-4242
www.apa.org

To order
APA Order Department
P.O. Box 92984
Washington, DC 20090-2984
Tel: (800) 374-2721; Direct: (202) 336-5510
Fax: (202) 336-5502; TDD/TTY: (202) 336-6123
Online: www.apa.org/pubs/books/
E-mail: order@apa.org

In the U.K., Europe, Africa, and the Middle East, copies may be ordered from
American Psychological Association
3 Henrietta Street
Covent Garden, London
WC2E 8LU England

AMERICAN PSYCHOLOGICAL ASSOCIATION STAFF
Gary R. VandenBos, PhD, *Publisher*
Julia Frank-McNeil, *Senior Director, APA Books*
Theodore J. Baroody, *Director, Reference, APA Books*
Kristen Knight, *Project Editor, APA Books*

Typeset in Berkeley by Cenveo Publisher Services, Columbia, MD

Printer: Maple-Vail Book Manufacturing Group, York, PA
Cover Designer: Naylor Design, Washington, DC

Library of Congress Cataloging-in-Publication Data

APA handbook of research methods in psychology / Harris Cooper,
editor-in-chief.
     v. cm.
   Includes bibliographical references and index.
   Contents: v. 1. Foundations, planning, measures, and psychometrics—
v. 2. Research designs : quantitative, qualitative, neuropsychological,
and biological—v. 3. Data analysis and research publication.
   ISBN-13: 978-1-4338-1003-9
   ISBN-10: 1-4338-1003-4
   1. Psychology—Research—Methodology—Handbooks, manuals, etc. 2.
Psychology—Research—Handbooks, manuals, etc. I. Cooper, Harris M. II.
American Psychological Association. III. Title: Handbook of research
methods in psychology.
   BF76.5.A73 2012
   150.72′1—dc23
                           2011045200

British Library Cataloguing-in-Publication Data
A CIP record is available from the British Library.

Printed in the United States of America
First Edition

DOI: 10.1037/13620-000

Contents

Volume 2: Research Designs: Quantitative, Qualitative,
Neuropsychological, and Biological

Editorial Board

QUALITATIVE RESEARCH METHODS

Overview of Qualitative Methods

VARIETIES OF QUALITATIVE RESEARCH: A PRAGMATIC APPROACH TO SELECTING METHODS

Nancy Pistrang and Chris Barker

Preparing to conduct a qualitative research study for the first time can be a bewildering experience. Diners seating themselves at a table in the Qualitative Research Restaurant are handed a lengthy menu of potential methodological approaches. The ingredients of each are described in the elaborate prose typical of restaurant menus, but lacking is the friendly waiter, fellow diner, or restaurant guide who will help the diner go behind the often-optimistic descriptions on the menu to understand how satisfying each dish ultimately will be.

This chapter attempts to fill such a role. It is an informed guide, advising qualitative researchers on how to make sense of the multiplicity of approaches with which they will be faced and how to choose the one that best fits the needs of their project. It facilitates the process of choosing a particular qualitative approach by highlighting the similarities and differences among a number of popular ones, and articulating what each is trying to do and what each is most and least suited for achieving. The treatment here will necessarily be somewhat superficial: Subsequent chapters in this volume describe a number of specific approaches in much greater depth.

The chapter first considers some background issues, such as why researchers would want to adopt a qualitative approach in the first place. The second section examines a number of prominent approaches to qualitative research, attempting to group them according to a rudimentary taxonomy. The third section looks at how each of the approaches might be used to answer a hypothetical research question, using a running example. The final section addresses some frequently asked questions that arise during the conduct of qualitative studies.

BACKGROUND ISSUES

Why Use Qualitative Methods?

Historically in psychology, qualitative research arrived relatively late. Anthropologists and sociologists had employed qualitative approaches since the inceptions of their disciplines in the 19th and 20th centuries. Psychology, however, pretty much defined itself as an exclusively quantitative enterprise. Graduate schools, at least in the English-speaking world, taught statistics and research design but not qualitative methods, and mainstream journals consisted solely of quantitative papers.

This situation began to change in the 1980s and 1990s. In the United States, Gergen's (1985) *American Psychologist* paper on social constructionism was an early call for psychologists to reevaluate their methodological approach. In the United Kingdom, Potter and Wetherell's (1987) text on discourse analysis was influential, as was Henwood and Pidgeon's (1992) paper on the grounded theory approach. In 1996, the British Psychological Society published a handbook of qualitative methods (Richardson, 1996); the equivalent landmark within U.S. psychology was the American Psychological Association's publication of the Camic, Rhodes, and Yardley (2003) handbook. In 1994, we published the first edition of our clinical psychology research methods text (Barker, Pistrang, & Elliott, 1994),

DOI: 10.1037/13620-001
APA Handbook of Research Methods in Psychology: Vol. 2. Research Designs, H. Cooper (Editor-in-Chief)

which attempted to present a balanced treatment of both quantitative and qualitative methods within a pluralistic framework. At the time, this felt like a novel enterprise. By the time the second edition appeared (Barker, Pistrang, & Elliott, 2002), the picture had changed markedly, and qualitative methods seemed to be much more widely accepted.

So, why use qualitative methods? In a nutshell, the major strengths of qualitative approaches are that they (a) give in-depth, textured data, often called "thick description" (Geertz, 1973, p. 6), and are thus more able to look at nuances and contradictions; (b) are particularly useful for investigating personal meanings; (c) are valuable for inductively generating theory and are therefore often used in underresearched, undertheorized areas in which exploratory work is needed; (d) give research participants freedom to describe their own experiences in their own language and therefore may redress the power imbalance in the researcher–participant relationship; and (e) can give voice to disadvantaged or excluded subpopulations. On the other hand, the strengths of quantitative approaches are (a) greater precision of measurement, tied in with explicit theories of psychological measurement and statistics; (b) the ability to make comparisons, both between participants and across studies; and (c) the ability to test causal hypotheses using experimental designs.

To take a trivial hypothetical example, suppose that we are investigating mood states. The quantitative approach might be to administer a standardized questionnaire, such as the Profile of Mood States (POMS; McNair, Lorr, & Droppleman, 1971). This would give a profile of scores for each participant, for example, 20 on depression, 15 on anger, and so forth. It would enable comparison of mood across groups of participants, the investigation of correlations between mood and other variables, or the tracking of mood fluctuations over time.

A qualitative approach, on the other hand, would involve asking the participant, "How are you feeling right now?" Her response might include a large amount of text, including something like the following:

> Well, not so bad, except that I'm a bit worried about how my daughter is getting on, and my lower back is really stiff this morning, and I'm feeling grouchy because I had a bad night's sleep last night. However, I'm really looking forward to retiring and doing lots of activities in my spare time.

The contrast is clear. The quantitative approach gives a numerical summary, which will enable comparisons to be made with other respondents or with the norms for the instrument. On the other hand, the qualitative approach gives the texture of the person's responses—one feels a much greater acquaintance with the participant hearing her words rather than just knowing her POMS scores; in other words, the data are richer. However, this immediately raises the question of what to do with such a mass of qualitative data. How can the researcher make sense of this unstructured stream of consciousness? What analytic tools are available, and how does one decide which ones to use? It is with such questions that this chapter is concerned.

Other, more personal factors may enter into this choice between qualitative and quantitative approaches. Many people have a preference for working either with numbers or with words, as some people are more drawn to either the sciences or the humanities. It is important to take such preferences into account because it is pointless working within a paradigm one has little aptitude for or sympathy with. However, a word of caution is appropriate: Qualitative approaches are far from an easy option. Although they may seem appealing to researchers who lack statistical ability, they involve hours of painstaking work, reading and rereading transcripts, and arriving at a viable coding system. Practical factors may also be relevant. Qualitative studies tend to have a small sample size and thus may be more appropriate for researchers working on their own or researching a hard-to-recruit population.

Pluralism and Pragmatism

Two main principles underlie our treatment of the material in this chapter: pluralism and pragmatism. *Pluralism*, or more fully *methodological pluralism*, holds that the various approaches to research, qualitative and quantitative, each have their respective strengths and weaknesses—that there is no one best overall method. The pluralist stance in research methodology is allied to the pluralist stance more generally, such as political pluralism, or the valuing of cultural diversity. Elsewhere, we discuss the implications of this stance at greater length, in the context of both clinical (Barker et al., 2002) and community psychology (Barker & Pistrang, 2005).

Allied to the pluralist position is a *pragmatic* perspective. This looks at each method in terms of what questions each can help the researcher answer—a "whatever works" position. In contrast to some authors, who see a fundamental dichotomy between qualitative and quantitative approaches, our pluralist, pragmatic position regards it as entirely unproblematic for a researcher to use multiple methods. It is possible to carry out, say, a discourse analysis and a randomized controlled trial with the same participants, as Madill and Barkham (1997) have done in a large comparative psychological therapy outcome study. Each genre of research (discourse analysis or randomized controlled trial) answers its own specific set of research questions.

Some Philosophical Background

Because we consider pragmatic issues to take precedence over philosophical ones, we will not burden the reader overly much with discussion of epistemological issues. *Epistemology* refers to the theory of knowledge and examines the philosophical basis underlying various approaches to knowledge generation (Bryman, 2004). Epistemological analysis is a valuable enterprise in which research methodologists can engage to clarify the implications of adopting particular methods. However, newcomers to qualitative research are frequently overwhelmed by the amount of philosophical discourse, often expounded in jargon-heavy prose, that it is apparently necessary to assimilate. In our view, novice qualitative researchers, who are this chapter's primary intended audience, can usually subsist on relatively small portions of this discourse. We attempt to outline two essential philosophical concepts that are encountered in the qualitative research literature. These can be expressed in terms of two dichotomies.

The most frequently encountered dichotomy is that between positivism and naturalistic enquiry. *Positivism* is a complex philosophical position, expounded by the 19th-century French philosopher Auguste Comte, which partially underlies quantitative approaches to research. In brief, it holds that the social sciences should model themselves after the physical sciences (which provided the knowledge base underlying the enormous technological development of the 19th century). The key tenets of positivism are that (a) science should restrict its attention only to observable facts, (b) the methods of the physical sciences (quantitative measurement, hypothesis testing, etc.) should be applied in the social sciences, and (c) science is objective and value free.

Followed rigorously, the positivist tenets put severe restrictions on what can be studied (e.g., self-reports of cognitions and emotions are disallowed), and few contemporary psychologists would sign up to the positivist program. Historically, its purest representation in psychology was the 1920s Watsonian behaviorism and Skinner's methodological behaviorism. However, the *hypothetico–deductive* method, which proposes that research progresses by formulating and testing explicit hypotheses, is a legacy of positivism and is central to the received model of psychological research in the English-speaking world. Although positivism in its original form has few advocates, it has become something of a "straw man" for qualitative researchers to define what their approach is not.

The antithesis of the positivist position is called the *naturalistic enquiry* position, which is often regarded as the conceptual basis of qualitative methods (Lincoln & Guba, 1985). It sees the ultimate aim of research as exploring and understanding the phenomenon in question rather than testing theoretically derived hypotheses or predictions, and it is concerned more with inner experience than with observable behavior and with words rather than numbers.

A related dichotomy to that between positivism and naturalistic enquiry is that between realism and constructionism. *Realism* proposes that there is a real world out there and that the task of researchers is to describe it as accurately as possible. *Constructionism*, on the other hand, argues that there is no objective reality independent of human thought, and that participants (and, indeed, researchers) make their own constructions that cannot be independently verified because there is no reality against which to verify them. Quantitative research is placed in the realist camp and qualitative in the constructionist camp. In practice, however, as Willig (2008) argued, the position is more subtle, in that there is a continuum from realist positions through to radical constructionist positions. It is possible for qualitative research to be conducted either from a realist or a constructionist perspective. For example, if the research topic is attitudes to climate change, a researcher taking a realist stance would seek to ascertain information about beliefs and views that could potentially be verified against other sources of information, whereas researchers taking a constructionist stance might focus on how people put together and convey their arguments. Quantitative research, although usually more realist, can also be conducted from a constructionist perspective. For example, the personal construct theory approach uses sophisticated statistical methods to examine participants' idiosyncratic ways of making sense of their world (Winter, 1992).

The remainder of this chapter gives an overview of a number of commonly used methods and attempts to help readers understand when it might be best to adopt each particular one. Although pragmatic issues are to the fore, epistemological and other considerations are also taken into account.

SOME PROMINENT APPROACHES TO QUALITATIVE RESEARCH

This section sets out the essential background to a number of popular qualitative research approaches. As noted, qualitative research is not a unitary entity. There are many different variants, and qualitative researchers may disagree among themselves on fundamental issues. Our aim is to provide thumbnail sketches of each of the approaches covered, pointing the reader toward additional sources of information for each one. In addition to specific references on each particular approach, several useful volumes look in detail at different qualitative approaches (e.g., Camic et al., 2003; Denzin & Lincoln, 2005; Smith, 2008; Willig, 2008; Willig & Stainton-Rogers, 2008), as do the subsequent chapters in this volume.

Brand-Name Versus Generic Approaches

From even a brief perusal of the literature, it becomes apparent that a large number of brand-name approaches to qualitative research exist, alongside more generic approaches advocated in a number of influential texts (e.g., Creswell, 1998; Miles & Huberman, 1994; Silverman, 2000; Taylor & Bogdan, 1998). The position resembles that in the psychotherapy and counseling field, where there are many specific therapeutic orientations, but there is also a body of work on more integrative or eclectic approaches, in addition to research highlighting the common factors that underlie superficially disparate approaches (Messer & Wampold, 2002).

Some powerful forces propel the field toward having brand-name approaches. In the case of both qualitative research and psychological therapy, there is considerable advantage in terms of academic recognition for the proponents of an approach to attach a label to it in order to highlight its unique features. More important, psychology is a field that has been built on careful attention to the replicability and precision of its procedures, and a specific approach with clearly defined steps increases the transparency of the methods. Thus, in our experience, journal editors and reviewers seem more comfortable if authors say that they are following a specific brand-name method because this ensures that an explicit series of methodological steps has been followed. This then feeds the tendency for researchers to label their approach to satisfy reviewers.

Our own position is that there is much more similarity than difference among many of the approaches to qualitative research. Ultimately, what should be important is that the research is done in a systematic way that meets its aims, rather than the particular label that is attached to it. Researchers must make a choice, however, so we will attempt to draw out commonalities among approaches as well as outline the unique features of each one to clarify the basis on which the choice is made.

Data Collection Methods

Data for qualitative research can come from several sources. Probably the most common is the individual semistructured interview in which the interviewer follows a flexible interview guide (often called an *interview schedule* or *protocol*). Interviews are usually audio recorded because the analysis focuses on the speech rather than visual channel. They may be held in a group setting, known as a *focus group* (Kitzinger, 1995). Interviews are normally transcribed before analysis.

Another possibility for data collection is qualitative observation. In the most common form, participant observation, the researcher is present, usually for long periods of time, in the setting under study and takes copious field notes, which then provide the raw material for later analysis. Another form of observation is to directly record naturally occurring conversations, such as medical consultations or calls to a telephone helpline. These conversations are then transcribed verbatim before analysis. A final possibility is to use naturally occurring written texts, such as blogs or newspaper articles.

Families of Approaches

As a heuristic aid, we have grouped various approaches to qualitative research together into families sharing important common features. Like most such taxonomies, this is a rough grouping, and some of the placements may be contentious. An earlier version of this taxonomy (Pistrang & Barker, 2010), which focused on psychological therapy research, differed slightly because of its more specialized content.

The four families of qualitative research approaches that we consider are as follows:

1. *Thematic analysis approaches*, which share the aim of identifying and describing the central ideas (usually referred to as *themes* or *categories*) occurring in the data.
2. *Narrative approaches*, which pay particular attention to the unfolding of events or experiences over time.
3. *Language-based approaches*, which pay close attention to the underlying social rules governing language and how language functions to achieve certain ends for the speaker or writer.
4. *Ethnographic approaches*, which are characterized by extensive data collection in the field, usually including participant observation.

The following sections examine each of these families in turn, outlining their characteristic features and describing a selection of representative approaches.

Thematic Analysis Approaches

Thematic analysis approaches attempt to identify themes or ideas in the material under study. This material can come from any of the data sources discussed thus far, but it is most usual to work with interview data. The researcher normally analyzes the material inductively, that is, the themes are derived from the data, rather than established beforehand. For example, if the research question concerns adolescents' experience of membership in gangs, there may be themes of "looking out for each other," "defending our territory," and so on. Themes may be organized in a hierarchical structure, with higher order themes and subthemes. In a sense, thematic analysis is a qualitative analog of the statistical approaches of factor analysis or cluster analysis, both of which aim to describe a complex data set in terms of a number of dimensions or groupings. In addition to the brand-name versions, some authors (notably Boyatzis, 1998; Braun & Clarke, 2006; see Chapter 4 of this volume) have articulated a generic version of thematic analysis.

Specific thematic analysis methods vary in terms of how structured they are and also in the degree of inference or interpretation they encourage. These two factors tend to go together. The first approaches to be considered, content analysis and framework analysis, are more structured and make fewer inferences during the analysis; the last one, interpretative phenomenological analysis, is less structured and more inferential. Grounded theory lies somewhere in the middle of the spectrum.

Content analysis. Content analysis straddles the quantitative–qualitative boundary. In that it analyzes qualitative data, it can be a considered to be a qualitative method; however, in that its output is quantitative, that is, frequency counts for each content category, it is more akin to a quantitative approach. It is included here both because it illustrates some important boundary issues and because it shares several common features with the other members of the thematic analysis family (Joffe & Yardley, 2003).

The essence of content analysis is to specify a clearly defined set of content categories. These may either be a priori, that is, developed and defined at the start of the study, before the data collection, or they may be post hoc, that is, by induction from the data. In either case, the researchers develop a coding manual to enable the data to be reliably coded. Raters then record instances of occurrences of each content category in the data (Krippendorff, 2004).

Framework analysis.   Framework analysis, developed by Ritchie and Spencer (1994), is another highly structured method of qualitative thematic analysis. It began in the context of social policy research as an applied approach that would generate useful data for policy makers: Ritchie and Spencer give the example of studying people's understanding of the term *disability*. Framework analysis subsequently has become popular in medical research, following Pope, Ziebland, and Mays's (2000) frequently cited *British Medical Journal* paper on qualitative data analysis, in which it has a prominent place.

Framework analysis is in many ways similar to content analysis, although its output is usually purely qualitative. The researcher develops a structured index (i.e., the coding framework) for the data. This framework is usually derived directly from the research questions and from the questions in the interview protocol. In the analysis phase, the researchers systematically record the occurrence of each of the categories in the entire data set. Charts are then used to show the pattern of occurrence of each theme for each participant, thus clearly documenting the interim steps in the analysis. However, a final phase of the analysis may involve more interpretation (e.g., where the researchers develop a typology or generate an explanatory account of the phenomenon; Ritchie, Spencer, & O'Connor, 2003).

Grounded theory.   Grounded theory was developed by two sociologists, Barney Glaser and Anselm Strauss (Glaser & Strauss, 1967), as a reaction to what they saw as the predominantly quantitative bias of the discipline of sociology at that time. Historically, grounded theory was one of the first systematic approaches to qualitative research. Sadly, as Willig

(2008) has related, the two original proponents subsequently disagreed about how grounded theory should be conducted, and the approach is no longer a unitary entity. One influential strand is the social constructionist version of grounded theory, as described by Charmaz (1990; see Chapter 3 of this volume).

Strauss and Corbin (1998) presented a systematic method for conducting a grounded theory analysis, explaining the large number of technical terms associated with this approach. The method is similar to that in generic thematic analysis, although as the name suggests, the ultimate goal is to generate theory that is grounded in the data, that is, there is a clear link between the theory and the observations upon which it rests. Some grounded theory researchers attempt a higher level synthesis to produce one superordinate theme to articulate the principal, underlying theoretical idea.

Interpretative phenomenological analysis. Phenomenological approaches aim to study participants' inner experiences: in other words, how they perceive and make sense of the world. Phenomenological methods have a long history within psychology, being associated with Giorgi and his colleagues at Duquesne University (e.g., Giorgi, 1985) and with client-centered and existential movements in clinical and counseling psychology (Laing, 1959; Shlein, 1963).

One user-friendly version of phenomenology is labeled *interpretative phenomenological analysis* (IPA; Smith, Flowers, & Larkin, 2009). It was developed in the United Kingdom within a health psychology context, but it has subsequently been applied in several other areas of psychology (see Chapter 5 of this volume). It is the most psychological of the methods covered in this chapter in that it is explicitly concerned with inner experiences. It also aims to be more interpretative in that it tries to go beyond participants' words to understand their deeper meanings.

An attraction of IPA for beginning qualitative researchers is that its analytic procedures are clearly laid out. In practice, the steps of the analysis are broadly similar to those in the other thematic analysis methods. Because it also has a more idiographic focus, seeking to understand individuals in depth, it often employs smaller sample sizes than is usual in other thematic analysis approaches (Smith et al., 2009).

Narrative Approaches

Narrative approaches share the feature of focusing on the unfolding of events or experiences over time (Murray, 2003). One criticism of thematic analysis studies is that their results can sometimes seem decontextualized because quotations from different participants are assembled together without a sense of how each quotation fits into a participant's entire account. Narrative approaches, on the other hand, bring chronology to the forefront. They may concern an encapsulated narrative about a particular aspect of experience, such as a child's account of her first day at school, or they may be much broader, such as an individual's account of her whole life history.

Narrative analysis. Narrative analysis arises out of narrative psychology, which gives prominence to how we make sense of things by the stories we tell. There is a persuasive argument that the act of telling stories is a central way for human beings to understand themselves and their world (Murray, 2003; Sarbin, 1986; see Chapter 6 of this volume).

The term *narrative analysis* covers a range of approaches, the common thread being that the narrative, rather than the person, is the object of study. The focus may be on the narrative's literary aspects, such as its plot structure, its predominant themes, its internal coherence, or its social context (Avdi & Georgaca, 2007; Murray, 2003). As an example of a thematically oriented narrative approach, Humphreys (2000) examined the nature of stories that members of Alcoholics Anonymous told within their group meetings. He classified these stories into five fundamental types and examined the characteristics and function of each type within the self-help group context.

Life history research. Life history research (Taylor & Bogdan, 1998) takes one or more individuals and attempts to construct a coherent narrative of salient aspects of their life experiences. This is often assembled via multiple in-depth interviews, but supplementary material, such as diaries, photographs, and recordings, may also be drawn upon. The goal of the investigation is usually to present one or more individual life experiences as exemplars of a broader phenomenon.

One example is Bogdan and Taylor's (1976) classic study of "Ed Murphy," a young man with intellectual disability (at that time referred to as "mental retardation"). He gave a vivid and moving account of his experience of being labeled as "retarded" and of being cared for in various state institutions. Although clearly one should be cautious about generalizing from a single individual's experiences, this narrative has great power in demonstrating the presence of articulate awareness in an often-devalued group of people and in highlighting the undesirable aspects of the way people with intellectual disabilities have been treated.

Language-Based Approaches

The distinguishing feature of the language-based family of qualitative approaches is that they closely examine language, not as an indication of what the speaker or writer might be thinking or feeling, but rather to understand what underlying social rules govern its production or what the language seems to have been used to accomplish. For instance, in a study of parent–teacher interactions, a mother's statement that "I'm very anxious about my son's reading difficulties" would not be regarded as an indication of her psychological state. Instead, it might be analyzed in terms of the picture of herself that is being constructed within that particular social context (e.g., a responsible parent), or what she is responding to in the conversation (e.g., the teacher's attempt to minimize the problem), or the response her statement elicits (e.g., reassurance).

Language-based approaches may also be described as discourse-based or discursive approaches, or as discursive psychology (Hepburn & Wiggins, 2007; Potter, 2003). Because the terms *discourse* and *discursive* tend to be tied to particular research paradigms, we prefer to use the term *language-based* to indicate a broader scope. However, our intention is not to suggest a focus on solely spoken language (these approaches can be used to study both talk and text) or on psycholinguistic features such as grammar or syntax.

Conversation analysis. Conversation analysis originated in sociology, within the branch called *microsociology*, which looks at how social rules are played out in tiny instances of interpersonal interactions (in contrast to *macrosociology*, which examines larger scale entities such as the family or social class). For instance, a seminal conversation analysis study concerned how two people in a conversation manage turn-taking, that is, how they manage to coordinate when one speaker stops talking for another to start (Sacks, Schegloff, & Jefferson, 1974). As with many aspects of interpersonal behavior, this apparently simple phenomenon becomes much more complicated on closer examination. More recently, conversation analysis has been extensively used to study doctor–patient interactions (Heritage & Maynard, 2006); for example, Stivers (2002) examined the subtle interactions between pediatricians and parents of sick children in decisions about prescribing antibiotic medication.

Conversation analysis has close affiliations with *ethnomethodology* (Garfinkel, 1967), which studies the methods that people use to achieve and reproduce an agreed-on social order. Both approaches were developed at the University of California, Los Angeles (UCLA) in the 1970s (incidentally at a time when the present authors had the great fortune to be graduate students in psychology there). Ethnomethodology has remained largely restricted to sociology, whereas conversation analysis has recently been adopted by psychologists within a variety of contexts to understand the implicit rules by which speakers are operating (see Chapter 7 of this volume).

Conversation analysis also has affinities with *psychotherapy process research* (e.g., Elliott, 2010), a set of approaches (both qualitative and quantitative) used to study what happens during psychotherapeutic interactions (in contrast to *outcome research*, which studies whether psychotherapy clients benefit from such interactions). For example, *response mode analysis* (Goodman & Dooley, 1976; Stiles, 1992) examines the antecedents and consequences of various kinds of therapist helping responses (e.g., questions or interpretations). Pistrang and Barker's (2005) research has used process analytic methods to study helping interactions in couples and other lay contexts.

Discourse analysis. The term *discourse analysis* covers a range of approaches (Potter, 2003; see Chapter 8 of this volume). These share an interest in examining how speakers or writers present themselves (not necessarily consciously or intentionally) via the language used: in discourse jargon, the *subject positions* that the speaker is adopting. For example, in a previous paragraph, we mentioned that we both attended graduate school at UCLA. A discourse analyst would ask what subject position is indicated by this statement. Does the statement legitimize our implicit claim to possess expertise about conversation analysis or ethnomethodology?

Another key concept is *discourse repertoires*, the idea that speakers draw on social and cultural resources that then shape how things are talked about. For instance, public announcements in London Underground railway stations currently refer to members of the public making a journey as "customers"; discourse analysts would examine the meanings and implications of employing this term, with its commercial connotations, as opposed to the more traditional alternative of "passengers."

Ethnography

Approaches in this final family all come under the single heading of *ethnography*, which is yet another label that subsumes a variety of methods. Their common feature is that the researcher "goes into the field" to understand the social organization of a given group or culture (Emerson, 2001) and usually develops a profound, sustained, and detailed engagement with the participants. The focus of the study can range from large (e.g., an entire cultural system), to medium (e.g., a single organization, such as a hospital or school), to small (e.g., a few individuals in a youth gang).

The classic studies are in cultural anthropology or urban sociology, where researchers live for months or years in the communities that they are studying. The main research tool is participant observation, recorded via the researcher's field notes. However, the researcher will also supplement this observation with extended conversations with key informants in the setting, either informally, or using more structured interviews.

More recent versions of ethnography are conducted on a smaller scale, in local settings. For instance applied ethnography (Savage, 2000) and focused ethnography (see Chapter 10 of this volume) emphasize using ethnographic methods to address practical problems, such as how health care interventions can be made acceptable to patients from a variety of cultural backgrounds.

CHOOSING AMONG THE VARIOUS QUALITATIVE APPROACHES

As we have discussed, our pragmatic, pluralist position implies that the main determinant of the research method should be the research question. Just as in the overall choice between qualitative and quantitative methods, however, other factors also play a role. Each individual researcher will have their own cognitive style and personal leanings and will inevitably find some methods or approaches more congenial than others. Furthermore, there may also be external constraints, such as the available resources for the project. For students and researchers new to qualitative research, availability of supervision is another important external factor.

Having decided to use a qualitative approach generally, the researcher needs to select a particular qualitative method. This choice can be made in two steps: first to choose the overall family of methods (thematic analysis, language-focused, narrative, or ethnographic) and then to choose the particular method from within the selected family. The first step is usually easier because there are clear differences between the families; the second is harder because, by definition, the family resemblance within each of the groupings tends to be greater.

Running Example

To illustrate how these choices might play out in practice, we will employ a running example, adapted from a current research project of our own (Pistrang, Jay, Gessler, & Barker, 2011). The general topic area is that of *peer support*, in other words, how people obtain psychological help or support from someone who has experienced a similar problem. There is an existing qualitative and quantitative literature on the benefits of peer support, for both

the recipients and the supporters, in a variety of health and clinical psychology contexts (e.g., Davidson et al., 1999; Schwartz & Sendor, 1999). For simplicity's sake, we will look at one common application, in the cancer field, focusing on one-to-one peer support, rather than group approaches.

Choosing a Thematic Analysis Approach

Within our running example, research questions concerning participants' thoughts or feelings about giving and receiving peer support would lend themselves to a thematic analysis approach. Data could be collected using semistructured interviews, for example, asking participants about their expectations for support and their views of the important processes and outcomes.

Suppose that the researcher is interested in understanding the impact of peer support on the recipient. The research question could be, "What are the benefits and drawbacks of having a peer supporter, from the cancer patient's point of view?" *Generic thematic analysis approaches* could then be used to code the respondents' accounts, for example, in terms of the types of benefits described (e.g., "improved mood," "feeling less alone," or "being less dependent on health care professionals"). For a more structured approach, *framework analysis* could be used. This yields detailed charts or tables, allowing mapping of when each theme occurs for each respondent. If the researcher were particularly concerned with how frequently each of the different types of outcome occurred across the sample of respondents, then *content analysis* would be appropriate.

A *grounded theory* approach could also be used. In this approach, the emphasis would be to develop a set of theoretical concepts or overarching ideas that bring some coherence to the data. For example, underlying all of the themes might be a sense that peer support helps patients to become more empowered within the health care system, both by knowing more and by becoming more confident to articulate their preferences. Using the grounded theory approach, the researcher would then identify a central or core category of peer support as facilitating empowerment and illustrate how this might occur.

Alternatively, if the research question were more concerned with individuals' experiences of receiving peer support, then a *phenomenological approach*, such as *interpretative phenomenological analysis*, could be used. This approach would take a more in-depth look at respondents' thoughts and feelings about, and the meanings they attach to, receiving peer support. Although it has similarities to other thematic approaches, a phenomenological approach would place greater emphasis on understanding the respondent's personal world. For example, one theme that might be identified is participants' sense of being profoundly understood by their peer supporter and the impact of this on their identity in terms of feeling "normal" and connected to others.

Choosing a Narrative Approach

Narrative and life history approaches would focus on chronological accounts of the phenomenon. In our running example, a *narrative approach* would focus on the storied aspects of participants' accounts, for example, how she was feeling throughout the whole course of her illness, at what point she was introduced to the peer supporter, what happened next, how they bonded, or failed to bond, and so forth. The analysis could examine how each party made sense of their experiences via the stories that they constructed and whether such stories clustered together in any meaningful way. For example, narratives could concern their coping with the illness, such as "triumph over adversity" or "feeling totally overwhelmed," or they could concern their relationship with their peer supporter, such as "becoming like sisters."

Life history approaches might look at the detailed history of a single patient's encounter with the health care system over time and study how the peer support program affected their trajectory through that system.

Choosing a Language-Focused Approach

Language-focused approaches are concerned with exactly what goes on in interpersonal interactions. In our running example, these approaches would be used to their best advantage in analyzing recordings of the interactions between the patient and the peer supporter. They would then give a detailed picture

of peer support in practice. In contrast to thematic analysis approaches, the focus is not on participants' thought or feelings, but rather on their verbal behavior in the interaction: what, when, and how things are said.

Conversation analysis or *process analysis* approaches might examine some particular aspects of speech. For example, one common verbal response in peer support is the *me-too disclosure*, in which the supporter responds to what the patient has said by saying something like, "Yes, I've been through that, too." The analysis could look at what happens after such disclosures: In what ways do they seem to facilitate or inhibit the subsequent conversation? Are there particular subtypes of disclosure with their own particular consequences? A further possibility might be to use a procedure called tape-assisted recall (Elliott & Shapiro, 1988), which combines the use of recordings with participants' moment-by-moment commentaries on replayed recordings. Using this approach, the researchers could obtain the patient's reactions to specific me-too disclosures made by the peer supporter.

Discourse analysis might examine the linguistic repertoires drawn on by both the peer supporter and the patient, for example, whether the discussion was couched in terms of the military metaphors so often employed in this area—"battling cancer," "fighting spirit," and so on—and what the consequences of such language seem to be. It could further examine which subject positions the peer supporter seemed to be adopting. For example, she could potentially position herself as a "fellow sufferer," a "survivor," or as a "quasi-professional counselor." Discourse analysis could also be used to analyze the interviews between the patient (or the peer supporter) and the researcher, with a similar aim, to examine discourse repertoires and subject positions.

Choosing an Ethnographic Approach

Ethnographic approaches take a broader look at the phenomenon. In contrast to the previous approaches, which were used to address more individual-focused research questions, ethnography focuses on the wider social or cultural system and has a distinctive emphasis on the importance of the environmental context in its analysis. Thus, in terms of our running example, if a focused ethnography were used, the researcher might ask, "What is the role of the peer support program within the medical system in the hospital?" "How is it viewed by the doctors, nurses and other health professionals?" and "Does it, for example, reinforce or destabilize existing working practices or beliefs?"

Summary

We hope this discussion of our running example has given readers a sense of the kinds of thought processes that researchers need to go through when selecting the best qualitative approach for a particular research topic. The central message is that there are many ways to approach a given research area, and the choice of a particular approach to be taken is largely determined by the particular question to be addressed. We say, "largely determined" rather than "completely determined" because there are always other personal and contextual issues to be taken into account, as we have discussed. However, the first question that researchers always need to ask is, "What am I trying to learn, and which method(s) will help me best learn it?" Once that question is answered, the researcher can then evaluate the methods in terms of other criteria.

SOME FREQUENTLY ASKED QUESTIONS ABOUT QUALITATIVE RESEARCH

This last section addresses three frequently asked questions that researchers new to qualitative research often ask: How is it evaluated? Can it be combined with other methods? and What is its impact on the participant?

How Is Qualitative Research Evaluated?

Quantitative researchers can draw on a large body of work on reliability and validity to evaluate their own and other researchers' studies. Qualitative researchers have no analogous framework. This is partly because quantitative research usually relies on a realist epistemology, which implies that there is something against which validity claims can be verified. Qualitative researchers often adopt nonrealist epistemologies, which means that the concepts of

reliability and validity cannot be straightforwardly applied: If the researcher's representations are just one of several constructions, in what sense can they be said to be valid constructions?

That being said, there clearly must be some criteria for evaluating qualitative research. An ethnographer could not go out into the field and make up a fictional story about what she saw there. An interviewer could not totally disregard what her respondent says when she writes up her findings. Qualitative researchers therefore often speak of the *trustworthiness* of their findings. Several scholars (e.g., Elliott, Fischer, & Rennie, 1999; Mays & Pope, 2000; Yardley, 2000) have set out guidelines for how the trustworthiness of research can be evaluated. Some central criteria are (a) *grounding* (that the researchers present some of the raw data upon which their conclusions are based), (b) *transparency* (that the researchers disclose their own leanings and expectations), (c) *coherence* (that the themes or interpretations of the data hang together within a plausible framework), and (d) *credibility checks* (that the researchers engage other sources, such as other researchers or the research participants, to check their conclusions). However, there is some debate about how such criteria should be used and whether they can be applied to all genres of qualitative research (Barbour, 2001; Reicher, 2000).

How Can Qualitative Research Be Combined With Other Methods?

As we said in the introductory section, this chapter has been written from a pluralist point of view, which holds that no one method is superior overall to any other and that it is possible for methods to be used in combination. There is a new and currently rapidly expanding literature on mixed-method research, with its own handbook (Tashakkori & Teddlie, 2002) and the *Journal of Mixed Methods Research*, which was launched in 2007.

Several models for combining qualitative and quantitative research have been proposed (Morgan, 1998). In some investigations, the quantitative study has primacy, for example, where qualitative research is conducted as a pilot study to develop or refine a quantitative interview. In others, the qualitative research has primacy, for example, where extensive qualitative interviews are used to build on the results of a preliminary quantitative survey study. In other studies, the two approaches may be more balanced.

A mixed-methods approach does not have to occur at the level of the individual study or even at the level of the individual researcher. Some researchers may decide that they prefer one type of research or another and want to stick with that approach for the foreseeable future. That is as it should be, and pluralism can still occur at the level of the research area or at the level of the field or discipline generally (Barker & Pistrang, 2005). In our view, a research community has healthy diversity if different researchers are working within different approaches with a general attitude of mutual tolerance and respect.

What Is the Impact of Qualitative Research on the Participant?

The last question is also a central ethical question for investigators: What is the impact of my research on my participants, for good or for bad? This topic has little empirical evidence. Anecdotally, in some of our studies, participants have often mentioned the benefits of being interviewed about aspects of their lives, even when the topics have been sensitive or painful. Receiving an hour's sustained attention from a nonjudgmental and interested listener is a rarity for many people. That this would be beneficial is consistent with the theoretical and empirical literature on the benefits of empathic listening (e.g., Bohart & Greenberg, 1997).

On the other hand, researchers should always be alert to the potential for harmful impacts. Qualitative interviews may take participants into painful territory, and the possibility for this to be temporarily or even permanently distressing must be always at the forefront of the interviewer's mind. Because of the more open-ended nature of qualitative research, the interviews may end up getting into areas that neither party had anticipated. Furthermore, there is the possibility that participants could disclose information that the researcher needs to act upon, such as evidence of abuse. Ethical practice requires that a robust protocol be in place for terminating distressing interviews and supporting participants afterward and also for what to do should the participant reveal evidence of danger to self or others.

CONCLUSION

This chapter has given a flavor of how researchers choose from the plethora of available qualitative research methods. We started out by imagining that readers were diners being handed a menu at the Qualitative Research Restaurant. As we wrote the chapter, however, we realized that space limitations meant that we would only be able to serve up little taster portions of each dish—just *hors d'oeuvres* or *amuse-bouches*. For readers who are now looking for more substantial offerings for their main course, we happily recommend the subsequent chapters of this volume.

References

Avdi, E., & Georgaca, E. (2007). Narrative research in psychotherapy. *Psychology and Psychotherapy: Theory, Research, and Practice, 80*, 407–419.

Barbour, R. S. (2001). Checklists for improving rigour in qualitative research: A case of the tail wagging the dog? *British Medical Journal, 322*, 1115–1117. doi:10.1136/bmj.322.7294.1115

Barker, C., & Pistrang, N. (2005). Quality criteria under methodological pluralism: Implications for doing and evaluating research. *American Journal of Community Psychology, 35*, 201–212. doi:10.1007/s10464-005-3398-y

Barker, C., Pistrang, N., & Elliott, R. (1994). *Research methods in clinical and counselling psychology.* Chichester, England: Wiley.

Barker, C., Pistrang, N., & Elliott, R. (2002). *Research methods in clinical psychology: An introduction for students and practitioners* (2nd ed.). Chichester, England: Wiley. doi:10.1002/0470013435

Bogdan, R., & Taylor, S. (1976). The judged, not the judges: An insider's view of mental retardation. *American Psychologist, 31*, 47–52. doi:10.1037/0003-066X.31.1.47

Bohart, A. C., & Greenberg, L. S. (Eds.). (1997). *Empathy reconsidered: New directions in psychotherapy.* Washington, DC: American Psychological Association. doi:10.1037/10226-000

Boyatzis, R. E. (1998). *Transforming qualitative information: Thematic analysis and code development.* London, England: Sage.

Braun, V., & Clarke, V. (2006). Using thematic analysis in psychology. *Qualitative Research in Psychology, 3*, 77–101. doi:10.1191/1478088706qp063oa

Bryman, A. (2004). *Social research methods* (2nd ed.). Oxford, England: Oxford University Press.

Camic, P. M., Rhodes, J. E., & Yardley, L. (Eds.). (2003). *Qualitative research in psychology: Expanding perspectives in methodology and design.* Washington, DC: American Psychological Association. doi:10.1037/10595-000

Charmaz, K. (1990). "Discovering" chronic illness: Using grounded theory. *Social Science and Medicine, 30,* 1161–l172.

Creswell, J. W. (1998). *Qualitative inquiry and research design: Choosing among five traditions.* Thousand Oaks, CA: Sage.

Davidson, L., Chinman, M., Kloos, B., Weingarten, R., Stayner, D., & Tebes, J. K. (1999). Peer support among individuals with severe mental illness: A review of the evidence. *Clinical Psychology: Science and Practice, 6,* 165–187. doi:10.1093/clipsy.6.2.165

Denzin, N., & Lincoln, Y. S. (Eds.). (2005). *The Sage handbook of qualitative research.* Thousand Oaks, CA: Sage.

Elliott, R. (2010). Psychotherapy change process research: Realizing the promise. *Psychotherapy Research, 20,* 123–135. doi:10.1080/10503300903470743

Elliott, R., Fischer, C. T., & Rennie, D. L. (1999). Evolving guidelines for publication of qualitative research studies in psychology and related fields. *British Journal of Clinical Psychology, 38,* 215–229. doi:10.1348/014466599162782

Elliott, R., & Shapiro, D. A. (1988). Brief structured recall: A more efficient method for studying significant therapy events. *British Journal of Medical Psychology, 61,* 141–153.

Emerson, R. M. (Ed.). (2001). *Contemporary field research: Perspectives and formulations.* Prospect Heights, IL: Waveland Press.

Garfinkel, H. (1967). *Studies in ethnomethodology.* Englewood Cliffs, NJ: Prentice Hall.

Geertz, C. (1973). *The interpretation of cultures.* New York, NY: Basic Books.

Gergen, K. J. (1985). The social constructionist movement in modern psychology. *American Psychologist, 40,* 266–275. doi:10.1037/0003-066X.40.3.266

Giorgi, A. (Ed.). (1985). *Phenomenology and psychological research.* Pittsburgh, PA: Duquesne University Press.

Glaser, B. G., & Strauss, A. L. (1967). *The discovery of grounded theory: Strategies for qualitative research.* Chicago, IL: Aldine.

Goodman, G., & Dooley, D. (1976). A framework for help-intended communication. *Psychotherapy: Theory, Research, and Practice, 13,* 106–117. doi:10.1037/h0088322

Henwood, K. L., & Pidgeon, N. (1992). Qualitative research and psychological theorising. *British Journal of Psychology, 83,* 97–111. doi:10.1111/j.2044-8295.1992.tb02426.x

Hepburn, A., & Wiggins, S. (Eds.). (2007). *Discursive research in practice: New approaches to psychology and interaction.* Cambridge, England: Cambridge University Press. doi:10.1017/CBO9780511611216

Heritage, J., & Maynard, D. W. (Eds.). (2006). *Communication in medical care: Interaction between primary care physicians and patients.* Cambridge, England: Cambridge University Press. doi:10.1017/CBO9780511607172

Humphreys, K. (2000). Community narratives and personal stories in Alcoholics Anonymous. *Journal of Community Psychology, 28,* 495–506. doi:10.1002/1520-6629(200009)28:5<495::AID-JCOP3>3.0.CO;2-W

Joffe, H., & Yardley, L. (2003). Content and thematic analysis. In D. F. Marks & L. Yardley (Eds.), *Research methods for clinical and health psychology* (pp. 56–68). London, England: Sage.

Kitzinger, J. (1995). Introducing focus groups. *British Medical Journal, 311,* 299–302.

Krippendorff, K. (2004). *Content analysis: An introduction to its methodology* (2nd ed.). Thousand Oaks, CA: Sage.

Laing, R. D. (1959). *The divided self: An existential study in sanity and madness.* London, England: Tavistock.

Lincoln, Y., & Guba, E. G. (1985). *Naturalistic inquiry.* Beverly Hills, CA: Sage.

Madill, A., & Barkham, M. (1997). Discourse analysis of a theme in one successful case of psychodynamic-interpersonal psychotherapy. *Journal of Counseling Psychology, 44,* 232–244. doi:10.1037/0022-0167.44.2.232

Mays, N., & Pope, C. (2000). Assessing quality in qualitative research. *British Medical Journal, 320,* 50–52. doi:10.1136/bmj.320.7226.50

McNair, D. M., Lorr, M., & Droppleman, L. F. (1971). *EITS manual for the Profile of Mood States.* San Diego, CA: Educational and Industrial Testing Service.

Messer, S. B., & Wampold, B. E. (2002). Let's face facts: Common factors are more potent than specific therapy ingredients. *Clinical Psychology: Science and Practice, 9,* 21–25. doi:10.1093/clipsy.9.1.21

Miles, M. B., & Huberman, A. M. (1994). *Qualitative data analysis: An expanded sourcebook* (2nd ed.). Thousand Oaks, CA: Sage.

Morgan, D. L. (1998). Practical strategies for combining qualitative and quantitative methods: Applications to health research. *Qualitative Health Research, 8,* 362–376. doi:10.1177/104973239800800307

Murray, M. (2003). Narrative analysis and narrative psychology. In P. M. Camic, J. E. Rhodes, & L.

Yardley (Eds.), *Qualitative research in psychology: Expanding perspectives in methodology and design* (pp. 95–112). Washington, DC: American Psychological Association. doi:10.1037/10595-006

Pistrang, N., & Barker, C. (2005). How partners talk in times of stress: A process analysis approach. In T. A. Revenson, K. Kayser, & G. Bodenmann (Eds.), *Couples coping with stress: Emerging perspectives on dyadic coping* (pp. 97–119). Washington, DC: American Psychological Association. doi:10.1037/11031-005

Pistrang, N., & Barker, C. (2010). Scientific, practical and personal decisions in selecting qualitative methods. In M. Barkham, G. E. Hardy, & J. Mellor-Clark (Eds.), *Developing and delivering practice-based evidence: A guide for the psychological therapies* (pp. 65–89). Chichester, England: Wiley-Blackwell. doi:10.1002/9780470687994.ch3

Pistrang, N., Jay, Z., Gessler, S., & Barker, C. (2011). Telephone peer support for women with gynaecological cancer: Recipient's perspectives. *Psycho-Oncology.* Advance online publication. doi:10.1002/pon.2005

Pope, C., Ziebland, S., & Mays, N. (2000). Analysing qualitative data. *British Medical Journal, 320,* 114–116. doi:10.1136/bmj.320.7227.114

Potter, J. (2003). Discourse analysis and discursive psychology. In P. M. Camic, J. E. Rhodes, & L. Yardley (Eds.), *Qualitative research in psychology: Expanding perspectives in methodology and design* (pp. 73–94). Washington, DC: American Psychological Association. doi:10.1037/10595-005

Potter, J., & Wetherell, M. (1987). *Discourse and social psychology.* London, England: Sage.

Reicher, S. (2000). Against methodolatry: Some comments on Elliott, Fischer, and Rennie. *British Journal of Clinical Psychology, 39,* 1–6. doi:10.1348/014466500163031

Richardson, J. T. E. (Ed.). (1996). *Handbook of qualitative research methods for psychology and the social sciences.* Leicester, England: British Psychological Society.

Ritchie, J., & Spencer, L. (1994). Qualitative data analysis for applied policy research. In A. Bryman & R. G. Burgess (Eds.), *Analysing qualitative data* (pp. 173–194). London, England: Routledge. doi:10.4324/9780203413081_chapter_9

Ritchie, J., Spencer, L., & O'Connor, W. (2003). Carrying out qualitative analysis. In J. Ritchie & J. Lewis (Eds.), *Qualitative research practice: A guide for social science students and researchers* (pp. 219–262). London, England: Sage.

Sacks, H., Schegloff, E. A., & Jefferson, G. (1974). A simplest systematics for the organization of turn taking in conversation. *Language, 50,* 696–735. doi:10.2307/412243

Sarbin, T. R. (Ed.). (1986). *Narrative psychology: The storied nature of human conduct.* New York, NY: Praeger.

Savage, J. (2000). Ethnography and health care. *British Medical Journal, 321,* 1400–1402. doi:10.1136/bmj.321.7273.1400

Schwartz, C. E., & Sendor, M. (1999). Helping others helps oneself: Response shift effects in peer support. *Social Science and Medicine, 48,* 1563–1575. doi:10.1016/S0277-9536(99)00049-0

Shlein, J. M. (1963). Phenomenology and personality. In J. T. Hart & T. M. Tomlinson (Eds.), *New directions in client-centered therapy* (pp. 95–128). Boston, MA: Houghton-Mifflin.

Silverman, D. (2000). *Doing qualitative research: A practical handbook.* London, England: Sage.

Smith, J. A. (Ed.). (2008). *Qualitative psychology: A practical guide to research methods* (2nd ed.). London, England: Sage.

Smith, J. A., Flowers, P., & Larkin, M. (2009). *Interpretative phenomenological analysis: Theory, method and research.* London, England: Sage.

Stiles, W. B. (1992). *Describing talk: A taxonomy of verbal response modes.* Newbury Park, CA: Sage.

Stivers, T. (2002). Participating in decisions about treatment: Overt parent pressure for antibiotic medication in pediatric encounters. *Social Science and Medicine, 54,* 1111–1130. doi:10.1016/S0277-9536(01)00085-5

Strauss, A., & Corbin, J. (1998). *Basics of qualitative research: Techniques and procedures for developing grounded theory* (2nd ed.). Newbury Park, CA: Sage.

Tashakkori, C., & Teddlie, C. (Eds.). (2002). *Handbook of mixed methods in social and behavioral research.* Thousand Oaks, CA: Sage.

Taylor, S. J., & Bogdan, R. (1998). *Introduction to qualitative research methods: A guidebook and resource* (3rd ed.). New York, NY: Wiley.

Willig, C. (2008). *Introducing qualitative research in psychology: Adventures in theory and method* (2nd ed.). Buckingham, England: Open University Press.

Willig, C., & Stainton-Rogers, W. (Eds.). (2008). *The Sage handbook of qualitative research in psychology.* London, England: Sage.

Winter, D. A. (1992). *Personal construct psychology in clinical practice.* London, England: Routledge.

Yardley, L. (2000). Dilemmas in qualitative health research. *Psychology and Health, 15,* 215–228. doi:10.1080/08870440008400302

Yardley, L., & Bishop, F. (2008). Mixing qualitative and quantitative methods: A pragmatic approach. In C. Willig & W. Stainton Rogers (Eds.), *The Sage handbook of qualitative research in psychology* (pp. 352–370). London, England: Sage.

Chapter 2

METASYNTHESIS OF QUALITATIVE RESEARCH

Margarete Sandelowski

The only thing that links them together
is you. You are their thread.

(J. Carroll, 1999, p. 215)

This chapter contains an overview of the historical
context for the issues concerning and methodological approaches distinctive to qualitative metasynthesis. *Qualitative metasynthesis* is defined here as a
form of scientific inquiry in which research findings
about a target event, process, experience, or other
phenomenon contained in written reports of completed qualitative studies are summed up, integrated, or otherwise assembled via qualitative or
quantitative methods so that these research findings
may more usefully serve as a basis for practice or
policy or for future research. In its encompassing
both a family of methodological approaches and the
intention to combine the findings from empirical
research in a systematic, auditable, credible, and
communicable way, qualitative metasynthesis is a
form of systematic review analogous to the synthesis
of quantitative research findings, including the constellation of statistical techniques collectively
referred to as *meta-analysis* (see Cooper, 2010; Volume 3, Chapter 25, this handbook).

OVERVIEW OF QUALITATIVE METASYNTHESIS

The proliferation of qualitative studies in the behavioral and social sciences and practice disciplines (e.g.,
education, medicine, nursing) and the adoption of

evidence-based practice as a paradigm, methodology,
and pedagogy in the practice (especially health care)
disciplines over the past 3 decades have led to the
current spate of interest in qualitative metasynthesis.
Central to evidence-based practice is the systematic
review and integration of findings in a targeted body
of empirical research on which to base practice or
policy. As embodied in institutions such as the
Cochrane Collaboration (http://www.cochrane.org/)
and in conventional hierarchies of research methods,
meta-analysis has typically been considered the gold
standard method for integrating research findings,
whereas the *randomized controlled trial* (see Part II of
this volume) has been considered the gold standard
method for generating those findings.

To counter the view of the randomized controlled trial as yielding the best evidence base for
practice, proponents of qualitative research emphasized the distinctive role it plays in reaching facets of
human experience out of the reach of quantitative
methods, in enhancing the significance of quantitative research, and in fully realizing the goals of
evidence-based practice (Barbour, 2000; Greenhalgh, 2002; Pope & Mays, 1995; Sandelowski,
2004). Emphasized also were the analytic power in
combining idiographic generalizations from a series
of qualitative studies in a common research domain,
the bias in conventional hierarchies of methods, and
the limitations of prevailing conceptions of evidence
and evidence-based practice (Kearney, 1998a;
Morse, Swanson, & Kuzel, 2001; Mykhalovskiy &

The book that serves as a basis for this chapter (Sandelowski & Barroso, 2007) was made possible by National Institute of Nursing Research, National
Institutes of Health Grant R01NR004907 for the methodological study Analytic Techniques for Qualitative Metasynthesis (2000–2005).

Weir, 2004; Timmermans & Berg, 2003; Trinder & Reynolds, 2000). A host of reports of qualitative metasynthesis studies have now been published, but key points of confusion and debate remain concerning their relationship to other kinds of reviews or studies, and their implementation and goals (Barbour & Barbour, 2003; Finfgeld, 2003; Jones, 2004; Thorne, Jensen, Kearney, Noblit, & Sandelowski, 2004; Zimmer, 2006).

Qualitative Metasynthesis Versus Other Reviews and Forms of Inquiry

Qualitative metasynthesis continues to be conflated with secondary analyses of primary qualitative data, narrative overviews or reviews of qualitative research or quantitative research, and other kinds of inquiry in the sciences and humanities in which research reports are used as primary sources of data. In secondary analyses of primary qualitative data, data generated in the course of qualitative studies (typically from interviews and field observations) are reanalyzed to address a research question different from the ones guiding the studies in which they originated (Heaton, 2004). In contrast, the data in qualitative metasynthesis projects are the findings contained in written reports of qualitative studies, or the grounded theories, phenomenological descriptions, ethnographic explanations, and the like that the researchers who conducted these studies produced from the interview, observation, and other data they collected. In qualitative metasynthesis studies, reviewers work with research reports that contain only those excerpts of data that the authors of these reports selected to support the interpretations they present as the research findings. Although some published reports of metasyntheses indicate use of these excerpts as if they were the findings, the value of these data snippets are highly limited; without access to the entire data set from every study reported, reviewers have no way of placing those data snippets in the context of the whole. Reviewers must evaluate whether the data shown in reports support researchers' interpretations, but reviewers are in no position to reanalyze those data. Qualitative metasynthesis does not involve any reanalysis of primary data, but it does provide new interpretive syntheses of the data-based interpretations researchers present as findings in their research reports. Qualitative metasyntheses are composed of reviewers' interpretations of researchers' interpretations of their data, not of those data themselves.

In contrast to narrative overviews of qualitative research directed toward surveying studies addressing a common topic and highlighting their major findings, qualitative metasynthesis studies are directed toward assembling findings about a target phenomenon into a coherent whole to serve as a provisional basis for practice or policy. Such overviews are akin to the he found/she found annotated references constituting nonstatistical summaries of quantitative research reports. Neither of these types of reviews bears any relationship to the explicit use of a narrative method (Elliott, 2005; Riessman, 2008) to synthesize qualitative research findings. The words *narrative* and *qualitative* continue to be inappropriately deployed to designate reviews that are simply nonsystematic or nonquantitative in polemical literature promoting the greater scientific value of systematic reviews of quantitative research, even though a review can be both systematic and involve explicitly narrative or other qualitative methods.

In contrast to other kinds of inquiry in which written documents are also used as primary sources of data, qualitative metasynthesis is targeted toward one particular kind of document (the conventional scientific research report), toward one element in that report (the findings), and toward one goal (to integrate those findings for use in practice or policy). Written documents, such as letters, diaries, household inventories, newspaper and professional articles, and books of a period are key primary sources of data in historical, ethnographic, narrative, discourse, and other social science and humanities studies. The word *primary* designates the closeness of the source to the actual times, persons, and events under study (e.g., in a study of World War II, documents written in that period). Although research reports are among the documents that might be used in these kinds of studies, their treatment will be different from that in qualitative metasynthesis studies. For example, research reports have been treated as if they were artifacts or inscriptions of the culture of scientific research (e.g., Latour & Woolgar, 1986; Law, 2004); as evidence to infer changes in the views of patients, diseases, therapeutics, and research methodologies (e.g., Reiser, 1978; Thorne, Joachim, Paterson, & Canam, 2002); and as rhetoric in studies of reading and writing practices (e.g., Bazerman, 1988; Golden-Biddle & Locke, 1993). None of these studies, however, constitute qualitative metasynthesis studies, even though they involve the use of research reports, because they entail treating the entity referred to as *the research report* differently from the way they are treated in qualitative metasynthesis studies. In the latter studies, the research report is typically treated as if it were an index of the study conducted, whereas the findings in that report are treated as if they were indexes of the phenomena under investigation.

Procedural Objectivity Versus Disciplined Subjectivity

Systematic reviews of quantitative research are typically differentiated from other kinds of literature reviews because of their greater transparency, rigor, and precision. Yet such reviews are as "situated (and) partial" (Lather, 1999, p. 3) as any other kind of review or, indeed, as any other human activity. Although systematic reviews are procedurally objective (i.e., conducted according to an explicit, auditable, and communicable protocol), their outcomes reflect the often hidden and inchoate judgments and choices reviewers made in every phase of the review process, including decisions about how to pose research questions, what research reports and data from them to include or exclude, how to make data comparable enough to be combined, how to combine them, and how to interpret them (Dijkers, 2009; Linde & Willich, 2003; Sandelowski, Voils, & Barroso, 2007; Shrier et al., 2008).

The objectivity of any research synthesis, therefore, inevitably rests on a disciplined subjectivity. Recognizing this disciplined subjectivity requires understanding the research synthesis enterprise as an engagement between resisting readers and resistant texts (Sandelowski, 2008). The object of review in research synthesis projects is the reports of studies, not the studies themselves. Although research reports are treated as if they were mirrors of the studies conducted, they are, in fact, after-the-fact reconstructions or accounts intended to make readers

"virtual . . . (yet) trusting witnesses" to studies, the conduct of which they have not actually observed (Shapin, 1984, pp. 490–491). Decisions made about studies are actually judgments made about accounts of those studies written to conform to the prescribed style for reporting them (i.e., typically the experimental–American Psychological Association style; Bazerman, 1988) and to the preferences of publication venues for the type information to include or exclude. This is especially relevant to reports of qualitative research because a wider range (in comparison to reports of quantitative research) of reporting styles is permissible.

The work of research synthesis requires reviewers to make research reports "docile" to review (Moreira, 2007, p. 8). Information is never simply extracted from reports as given. Instead, information is transformed into data that are then further manipulated, modified, and reconfigured to enable them to be compared and combined. In qualitative metasynthesis studies, themes are discerned and metaphors and concepts are translated into each other. In quantitative meta-analyses, effect sizes are calculated from different statistical expressions of results. The results of these operations must then be further "re-assembled, enumerated, narrated, tabulated, funnel- or forest-plotted" (Sandelowski, 2008, p. 109) or otherwise turned into the outcomes of the review. Reports "do not simply yield their findings; rather reviewers make [reports] yield" them (Sandelowski, 2008, p. 109). Efforts to differentiate qualitative from quantitative research synthesis along the subjective–objective divide fail to take account of the procedural objectivity characterizing the former, the judgments characterizing the latter, and the extent of reviewer intervention entailed in any systematic review.

Comprehensive Versus Purposeful Selection of Research Reports

Valid research syntheses are generally said to depend on the comprehensive retrieval of all research reports—published or unpublished—in any venue relevant to a domain of study. Some proponents of qualitative metasynthesis, however, have argued for a purposeful, as opposed to comprehensive, sampling strategy on the grounds that this is congruent with the sampling imperative of primary qualitative research (e.g., Jones, 2004). The challenge is to identify which of the many purposeful sampling strategies (e.g., maximum variation, stratified, theoretical) will be used and toward what purpose. For example, if a maximum variation sampling strategy is selected, reviewers must state on what specific dimensions the sample of reports will vary and to what extent. Regardless of type, purposeful sampling is likely to be credibly achieved only after an exhaustive search of the literature has been conducted. Without having perused the universe of potentially relevant documents, reviewers can have no analytically defensible basis for a purposeful selection of these documents. One of the criticisms of systematic reviews in general is that they end up conducted on the basis of only a fraction of the relevant documents available (MacLure, 2005; White, 2001). Accordingly, no matter what sampling strategy is chosen, reviewers must communicate the grounds for document selection and deselection.

The Place of Quality Criteria in Qualitative Metasynthesis Studies

Among the most controversial topics concerning qualitative metasynthesis is the place of quality criteria, which remain a bone of contention in qualitative research as a whole and the subject of a voluminous literature. Variously discussing quality in terms of different kinds of validities, rigor, credibility, and trustworthiness and in the context of competing philosophical positions from positivism to relativism, qualitative researchers have yet to agree on quality criteria and on whether such agreement can ever be reached (e.g., Hammersley, 2009; Seale, 1999; Smith & Deemer, 2000; Smith & Hodkinson, 2005). The dilemma is that no "in principle"(Engel & Kuzel, 1992, p. 506) arguments can adequately address quality in the diversity of practices of which qualitative research is composed. Judgments about research quality are historically and culturally contingent, with different communities of scholars sanctioning different criteria at different times. The many checklists and standards that have been proposed to assess the quality of qualitative research oversimplify the evaluation process

and typically conflate the adequacy of reporting (highly dependent on the publication venue) with the appropriate selection and use of methods (highly dependent on disciplinary affiliations and commitments; Barbour, 2001; Eakin & Mykhalovskiy, 2003; Sandelowski & Barroso, 2007). Even when standards are agreed to in the abstract, acceptable inter- and even intrarater reliabilities are difficult to achieve (Dixon-Woods et al., 2007; Sandelowski & Barroso, 2002); if achieved, they may reflect only the ability to induce agreement not the quality of studies per se (Hak & Bernts, 1996). For these reasons, quality appraisal ends up being a largely idiosyncratic affair that operates for the exclusion of many relevant documents and against claims of neutrality and transparency. Quality criteria are, therefore, most wisely used in qualitative metasynthesis projects, not to exclude reports or findings a priori, but rather to characterize them for use in a posteriori analyses: For example, to determine whether the source of a finding is largely from high noise–low signal studies where methodological flaws outweigh informational value, or low noise–high signal studies where informational value outweighs methodological flaws (Edwards et al., 2000).

Aggregation Versus Interpretation as Goals of Research Synthesis

Thematic in the qualitative metasynthesis literature are efforts to align an interpretive approach to synthesis with qualitative metasynthesis and to align an aggregative, enumerative approach with quantitative research synthesis, and to malign the latter as unsuitable for the former. Aggregation is typically rejected as a goal of qualitative metasynthesis because it is seen to be not only in the province of statistical methods but also as an overly simplified view of knowledge development as cumulative (Hammersley, 2001; Noblit & Hare, 1988).

Yet, all modes of synthesis are inescapably interpretive because they consist of reviewers' treatments, that is, rerenderings of the research findings in reports (which consist of researchers' interpretive renderings of information obtained from and about research participants who interpreted their lives in the process of being researched). Although synthesis by aggregation is typically based on a quantitative logic, whereby findings deemed to replicate each other are summed up and the findings with the largest magnitude are considered to have more evidence for their existence, that logic may be entirely appropriate for certain kinds of qualitative research findings. Indeed, as will be discussed later in this chapter, aggregative approaches have been used to synthesize qualitative research findings without compromising their integrity or complexity (Sandelowski & Barroso, 2007). Moreover, just as all efforts to quantify qualitative data entail interpretive judgments (Sandelowski, Voils, & Knafl, 2009) so, too, does aggregation.

CONDUCTING QUALITATIVE METASYNTHESIS STUDIES

Qualitative metasynthesis studies are conducted according to a systematic, explicit, and communicable research protocol, yet this protocol is not fixed in advance. In keeping with the interactive and emergent nature of qualitative research design, and the cyclic and data-derived nature of qualitative analyses, qualitative metasynthesis studies are designed by and in the doing, not by a priori design. The conduct of qualitative metasynthesis studies remains open ended and flexible enough to accommodate the actual nature of the available reports in a targeted domain of research. Research questions are initially conceived as "compasses" as opposed to "anchors" (Eakin & Mykhalovskiy, 2003, p. 190) because they point reviewers to a set of procedures for sampling, searching, analyzing, and synthesizing that, after inspection of the body of literature under review, will likely be revised. As reviewers begin to amass, and immerse themselves in, the research reports in a targeted domain, they iteratively develop the systematic, auditable, and communicable protocol that will ultimately guide the work of review. Exhibit 2.1 summarizes the elements that must be addressed in designing, proposing, conducting, and reporting the results of qualitative metasynthesis studies. The extent to which these elements, and the iterative process of their development, are detailed in reports of such studies will vary with the publication venue.

Setting the Boundaries of a Qualitative Metasynthesis Study

As in any empirical study, reviewers must decide exactly what phenomenon will be studied, with whom and over what time period. For example, if the topic of study is the management of chronic illness, reviewers will ultimately have to define operationally both *management* and *chronic illness*. They will also have to determine and defend their decisions as to whether their study will address (a) any chronic illness or only specified chronic illnesses (e.g., arthritis, diabetes, schizophrenia); (b) management at any point in the chronic illness trajectory or only at certain points (e.g., from diagnosis to first treatment decision, as the disease nears end stage); (c) chronic illness management in persons of any gender, age, race or ethnicity, nationality, social class, or other designation, or only certain of these persons; and (d) the time period extending back to the first report of a qualitative study on the management of chronic illness to the present or to another time frame.

Setting such delimitations is especially challenging in qualitative metasynthesis studies because of the permeable boundaries around the kinds of phenomena toward which these studies are typically directed (e.g., living with chronic illness, becoming resilient, decision making) that defy easy definition and because of the open-ended nature of qualitative studies. A target phenomenon, such as living with chronic illness, encompasses an array of diverse experiences and events, any one or all of which might become the object of a metasynthesis study. For example, as described in Sandelowski and Barroso (2007), it was only after an initial review of all of the reports of research relevant to the topic of women living with HIV infection that we saw how many of the findings in these studies were devoted to motherhood. Moreover, of the research reports of studies with findings pertaining to motherhood, more than half were conducted to address research purposes other than the exploration of motherhood. Had our search been restricted only to reports of studies that had as their explicit research purpose the exploration of motherhood, many of these reports would likely not have been retrieved. Accordingly, reviewers should initially set the boundaries of their metasynthesis studies to enable

---

Exhibit 2.1

Elements of a Qualitative Metasynthesis Study From Design to Dissemination

---

I. Introduction
   a. Research problem generating the study with literature review addressing the problem
   b. Research purpose/questions addressing the research problem

II. Methods
   a. Metasynthesis methods/techniques (e.g., metasummary, grounded theory)
   b. Search and sampling strategies
       1. Goals of search strategy (i.e., comprehensive, purposeful)
       2. Search parameters (i.e., topical/thematic, population, temporal, methodological)
       3. Key definitions and search terms
       4. Inclusion and exclusion criteria
       5. Channels of communication and information sources used
       6. Tools used to conduct searches and track search outcomes
   c. Appraisal strategies
       1. Technique and tools used to extract information from individual reports
       2. Quality criteria used as covariate or to exclude reports
   d. Analysis strategies (e.g., content analysis, thematic analysis, visual displays)
   e. Synthesis strategies (e.g., aggregation, configuration)
   f. Validation strategies (e.g., audit trail, negotiated consensus, expert consultation)

III. Results of review
   a. Profile of reports
       1. Number of relevant primary research reports
       2. Inclusive publication years of reports
       3. Inclusive years of data collection
       4. Primary author disciplinary affiliations
       5. Geographic location of studies
       6. Purpose of studies featured
       7. Theoretical and methodological orientation of studies
       8. Classification of findings
       9. Related reports from same parent study, with identical or overlapping samples
   b. Profile of study participants
       1. Total and mean/median/modal sample size across reports
       2. Age, gender, racial/ethnic, class, national, other relevant background features
       3. Other features relevant to the purpose of the review (e.g., stage of illness or pregnancy, diagnostic tests, treatment modalities)
   c. Synthesis of findings
       1. Delineation of key findings (e.g., metasummary, model, line-of-argument)
       2. Visual displays of findings

IV. Discussion of the synthesis produced
   a. Link to existing scholarship
   b. Implications for research, practice, and policy
   c. Limitations of the study

V. End of text
   a. List of complete citations to primary research reports
   b. Acknowledgments, including grant support

Note. From *Reviewing Research Evidence for Nursing Practice: Systematic Reviews* (pp. 90–91), by C. Webb and B. Roe (Eds.), 2007, London, England: Blackwell. Copyright 2007 by Wiley-Blackwell Publishing. Adapted with permission.

---

retrieval of all reports of studies that are likely to contain findings relevant to their purpose.

Setting time frames for study is challenging too because of historical changes in the phenomena of interest and in the terms used to refer to ostensibly the same phenomena. A case in point is the change from *compliance* to *adherence* to refer to medicine taking and other therapeutics. Such changes in terminology must be interpreted as they reflect major reconceptualizations of patients, health care providers, and the relationships between them, and the location of agency and responsibility for health outcomes. Also contributing to the challenges of setting temporal boundaries for review are ongoing advancements in all practice fields (especially health care) and the need to synthesize findings still relevant to contemporary practice (Barroso, Sandelowski, & Voils, 2006; Shojania, Sampson, Ansari, Doucette, & Moher, 2007). A case in point is the transformation of HIV infection from a fatal to a chronic disease brought about by the advent in 1996 of antiretroviral therapy. Reviewers may decide to set the temporal boundary of their reviews to account for such change.

Locating Reports of Qualitative Studies

Recall, or the percent of potentially relevant documents retrieved, and precision, or the percent of actually relevant documents retrieved, are the most commonly used performance measures in information retrieval (Losee, 2000; Marchionini, 1995). Optimal search strategies are those that achieve the best balance between recall and precision, neither yielding too many documents that are irrelevant, nor failing to yield documents that are relevant. Well-known formal and informal search strategies, such as footnote chasing, backward chaining, or the ancestry approach; citation searching, forward chaining, or the descendancy approach; hand-searching key journals and other documents; and social networking are described in Cooper (2010) and Sandelowski and Barroso (2007).

For several reasons, achieving a balance between recall and precision is especially challenging for reviewers conducting qualitative metasynthesis studies. First, because of the "multidisciplinary pedigree of qualitative research" (Barbour & Barbour, 2003, p. 183), reviewers must know how to search literatures across the behavioral, social, and health sciences, and the humanities. Searching electronic databases, especially, is so intricate and idiosyncratic to each database that reviewers will be wise to include on their research teams information specialists who are expert in the particular scientific or

humanities databases most likely to yield relevant documents (Harris, 2005).

Second, electronic databases may not permit retrieval of reports by method (Littleton, Marsalis, & Bliss, 2004). Even if they permit retrieval by method, there is no uniform way to refer to qualitative research or even to qualitative research of one kind. For example, a report of a grounded theory study may not contain these words anywhere in the title, abstract, or main text, the only signal of method being a citation to a grounded theory methods text. Even when potentially relevant documents are retrieved, the literary nature of titling qualitative reports and the variable information provided in abstracts may make it difficult for reviewers to determine the relevance of reports to the purpose of their study without retrieving the entire document.

Over the past decade, studies have been conducted better to delineate and address the distinctive challenges of electronic searching for qualitative research reports (e.g., Barroso et al., 2003; Evans, 2002; Grant, 2004; Shaw et al., 2004). Notable among these studies are those of the members of the Hedges team who empirically determined the search terms most likely to yield the most precise and accurate outcomes in several databases. Their work highlighted the importance of understanding individual databases so that search strategies will be developed that will improve the precision of outcomes while not wasting the typically limited resources available to reviewers conducting research synthesis studies. Team members Wong, Wilczynski, and Haynes (2004) found that the OVID search terms with the best sensitivity, or proportion of relevant reports retrieved (keeping specificity $\geq$ 50%), specificity, or proportion of irrelevant reports retrieved (keeping sensitivity $\geq$ 50%), and optimization of sensitivity and specificity (on the basis of absolute [sensitivity–specificity] $\leq$26%) for detecting qualitative research reports in MEDLINE in 2000 were *interview:.mp*, *interviews.tw.*, and *interview:.mp.*, respectively. Walters, Wilczynski, and Haynes (2006) found that the OVID search terms with the best sensitivity (keeping specificity $\geq$ 50%), specificity (keeping sensitivity $\geq$ 50%), and optimization of sensitivity and specificity (on the basis of the lowest possible absolute difference between sensitivity and specificity)

25

for detecting qualitative research reports in Embase in 2000 were *interview:.mp*, *qualitative.tw.*, and *exp. health care facilities and services*, respectively. Wilczynski, Marks, and Haynes (2007) found that the best OVID search terms for detecting qualitative research reports in the Cumulative Index to Nursing and Allied Health Literature (CINAHL) in 2000—with the same three parameters Walters et al. (2006) used for Embase—were *exp.interviews*, *audiorecording.sh.*, and *exp. study design*, respectively. McKibbon, Wilczynski, and Haynes (2006) found that the best OVID search terms for detecting qualitative research reports in PsycINFO, also using the same three parameters, were *interview.tw*, *interviews.tw*, and *interview.tw*, respectively.

To increase the likelihood that no relevant texts will be missed, reviewers should hand-search key journals publishing qualitative research and research in the targeted domain of review, in addition to books, anthologies, and theses and dissertations, the contents of which may not be amenable to electronic searching. Reports of qualitative studies are often published in book-length forms, the length of which adds to the labor and complexity of qualitative metasynthesis.

A third factor complicating the search for qualitative research is the permeable line that exists between a qualitative versus a nonqualitative study. Qualitative research is composed of highly diverse methodological traditions each of which is understood and implemented differently by scholars with highly diverse disciplinary affiliations and research agendas. The term *qualitative* is used to refer to entities for generating and analyzing data (such as paradigms, methods, data, and techniques), to entities that are simply deemed to be nonquantitative, and to entities totally irrelevant to qualitative research (such as biochemical and laboratory assays). Moreover, the words-versus-numbers line often drawn between qualitative and quantitative research fails to account for the appropriate use of numbers and statistical methods in qualitative studies and the interpretive acts that characterize any quantitative study (Kritzer, 1996; Sandelowski et al., 2009). Accordingly, reviewers must develop an operational definition of *qualitative research* to

set the methodological parameters for their metasynthesis studies.

Yet, differentiating qualitative from quantitative research may become irrelevant in the search and retrieval phase of a study because it is now increasingly less defensible to limit reviews on the basis of methodology. For example, if the purpose of a research synthesis project is to determine views of, and what accounts for, medicine taking, both qualitative and quantitative observational studies will contribute to that determination. Differentiating studies by methodology may be less relevant also for the analysis and synthesis of findings because such differences may be overemphasized or because they can be methodologically transcended (Pope, Mays, & Popay, 2007; Sandelowski, Voils, & Barroso, 2007).

Appraising Reports

Appraising qualitative research reports involves understanding the nature of the study featured in each report. Evaluating the relevance and worth of a study to address a specific research purpose requires careful reading of reports both to locate research findings and to place them in the substantive and methodological contexts of the studies in which they were produced. The comprehensive reading guide in Sandelowski and Barroso (2007, Chapter 4) helps reviewers to locate this information, regardless of the presentation style of the report.

Finding the research findings. The primary objective in appraising reports of studies is to locate and extract the findings. Findings in qualitative research reports are the data-based interpretations researchers advance about the target phenomenon under investigation (e.g., a grounded theory of a process, a phenomenological description of an experience). The researcher interpretations constituting the findings in these reports are distinguished from the data offered as evidence for these findings (e.g., quotations, field note excerpts, stories, case histories) and from the analytic procedures used to transform these data into findings (e.g., coding schemes, data displays).

This orientation to findings as separable from data and from other elements of the research report and process implies that *findings* can in fact be found. This view contrasts with the constructivist view of *findings* as made, not found: that is, as the cocreated product of a unique, and historically and culturally situated, encounter between researchers and research participants (Sandelowski, 2004). This distinction is important for two reasons. First, qualitative metasynthesis would not be what it was intended to be by its proponents—that is, a means of integrating the results of research about a phenomenon to serve as the provisional basis for practice or policy—if reviewers held a strong constructivist view of knowledge as inseparable from knower, or an extreme postmodern antipathy to any truth claims. Although reviewers will always acknowledge that all findings are inescapably socially constructed in the research process, and the provisional nature of any truth claims, qualitative metasynthesis requires operating "as if truth holds still" (Thorne et al., 2004, p. 1354), that is, as if faithful accounts of a *real* world could be produced. Reviewers maintain contact with the empirical world depicted in research reports, even as they remain cognizant of the series of interpretive acts and discursive practices entailed in any effort to synthesize research findings and of issues involving authority, voice, and representation (Alvesson & Sköldberg, 2000; Sandelowski, 2006). The value of qualitative metasynthesis for practice and policy depends on a stance of *subtle realism* (realism with a dose of constructionism) whereby findings are seen as entities that can be found and that reflect a truth, albeit provisional and partial.

Second, the distinction is important because qualitative reports may have no extractable data-based findings. Typically the unintended result of mistaking "heaped" data (Wolcott, 1994, p. 13) for "thick description" (Geertz, 1973, p. 37), such reports offer only unlinked excerpts of data presented as if they were findings and, therefore, have little value for metasynthesis. The absence of data-based findings in the report of a qualitative study may also, however, be deliberate and appropriate, as in oral histories and testimonials, artistic renderings of ethnographic findings (Richardson, 2000), and other forms of "transgressive writing" (Schwalbe, 1995, p. 394) by qualitative researchers

who deny the possibility of any claim to knowledge or who view any claims to knowledge as disguised claims to power. Such studies may still have value in metasynthesis studies, for example, as sources of concepts or metaphors that may be useful in synthesizing the findings of the other studies under review.

Classifying the findings.   Once findings are located, the second key objective of the appraisal of reports is to classify these findings. The selection of synthesis methods depends on ascertaining the nature of the findings, not on methodological claims about how these findings were produced. Even allowing for the diverse, discipline-specific ways any one qualitative method may be understood and executed, and the inconsistent relationship between methods and findings in qualitative research (Eakin & Mykhalovskiy, 2003), such claims cannot simply be read off the page and accepted as given because this may lead to the unwarranted exclusion of findings or to the selection of synthesis methods unsuitable for the findings. Reviewers must be willing to read against methodological claims in cases in which there is no evidence from the presentation of findings that the methods claimed were used, but for which no other reason to exclude those findings exists. For example, a basic descriptive study misrepresented in a report as a phenomenological study should be read and evaluated as a basic descriptive study. Such a study may still be judged as having produced credible findings worthy of inclusion in a metasynthesis study, that is, as meeting standards for basic descriptive studies.

As fully described in Sandelowski and Barroso (2007), reviewers should classify findings by degree of interpretive transformation. Findings are appraised according to the extent to which data were transformed, ranging from no transformation at all (i.e., read-only data excerpts and, therefore, candidates for exclusion), to transformations that remain closer to data as given (i.e., topical or thematic surveys of the informational contents derived from basic content or thematic analyses of interview data), to transformations farther removed from the data as recorded in interviews and field observations (e.g., a phenomenology of self-transcendence, a grounded theory of decision making under life-threatening conditions, a Foucault-inspired analysis of competing discourses around motherhood in HIV-positive women). For example, a data-near transformation might detail and group the reasons women give for breast- or bottle-feeding their babies. A more interpretive transformation might frame these reasons in the sociology of deviance and show them to be actions whereby women justify their choices (Murphy, 1999). As described in more detail later in this chapter, findings on the data-near end of the data transformation continuum lend themselves to synthesis by aggregation methods, such as metasummary, whereas findings on the data-far end of the continuum lend themselves to synthesis by configuration methods, such as grounded theory and meta-ethnography.

Analyzing Data

Once data are extracted, they must then be made *docile*, or amenable to treatments that will render them comparable and, therefore, combinable. These techniques include variations of (a) qualitative content or thematic analyses (Braun & Clarke, 2006; Hsieh & Shannon, 2005) directed toward distilling the manifest (surface) or latent (underlying) informational contents in the findings (e.g., Thomas & Harden, 2008) and (b) visual displays to *play* with different arrangements of data and the results of these analyses, such as the many case-, time-, variable-, and theme-oriented data displays shown in Miles and Huberman (1994) and Sandelowski and Barroso (2007).

The key objective of analysis is to determine the relationship of findings to each other to ascertain how they might be synthesized. Findings may be seen as replicating and, therefore, as confirming each other. Here, findings within and across research reports are judged to indicate the same thing about the same phenomenon, as when HIV-positive women are repeatedly found to describe children as a reason for adhering to their medication regimen. In contrast, findings may be seen as diverging from and, therefore, as refuting each other. Here findings within and across reports are judged to say contradictory things about the same phenomenon, as when HIV-positive women are found to describe children as a reason both for

adhering and not adhering to their medication regimen. Findings initially viewed as contradictory may, however, upon further comparison with other findings, be subsequently viewed as not contradictory. An example is when reviewers conclude that having children contributes to maternal adherence to medications when children are seen as a reason to live but contributes to maternal nonadherence when their care diverts mothers away from caring for themselves. Finally, findings may be seen to complement or otherwise extend or explain each other. Here findings are judged to be disparate (about different things) and unrelated. Or, they are seen to be disparate and related—neither confirming nor refuting each other but rather extending or explaining each other. An example of findings extending each other is when the finding that nausea interferes with adherence further specifies the finding that side effects favor nonadherence. An example of findings explaining each other is when the finding that certain women were suspicious of health care providers' recommendations offers a potential explanation for the finding that women often did not adhere to their medication regimens. Reviewers would then further search for evidence that supported or refuted this hypothesis.

Determinations of the relationship of findings within and across reports enable reviewers to group them topically and thematically and then to reduce them to their topical or thematic essences, or to produce interim topical and thematic syntheses of them. Reviewers must be careful not to omit any findings, even if appearing in only one report, and to preserve their contradictions and ambiguities. Like data reduction in all qualitative research, reduction of findings in qualitative metasynthesis projects actually entails the amplification and complication of data as reviewers tack back and forth between the findings given in reports and the progressively more abstract renderings of these findings reviewers create as they move through the analysis process. Examples of stages in the analysis process are shown in Sandelowski and Barroso (2007).

Synthesizing Findings

Having classified the findings and having compared them with each other to ascertain their relationships, reviewers will be in a position to determine whether they are synthesizable by aggregation or configuration. In synthesis by aggregation, findings deemed to replicate each other are pooled, summed up, or otherwise assimilated. *Metasummary* is a methodological approach directed toward synthesis of data-near findings by aggregation. In synthesis by configuration, findings deemed to constitute a "mosaic" (Hammersley, 2001, p. 548) of disparate, irreplicable parts are assembled or arranged into coherent theoretical or narrative renderings of them (Campbell et al., 2003; Noblit & Hare, 1988). Whereas aggregated findings are merged, configured findings are "meshed" (Mason, 2006, p. 20). Grounded theory and meta-ethnography are methodological approaches directed toward synthesis of data-far findings by configuration. As all research involves interpretation on the part of researchers, the word *configuration* (connoting pattern, design, and gestalt) arguably better captures what proponents of interpretive research synthesis advocate, that is, a mosaic, big-picture, and novel-whole view of research synthesis.

Although any one or combination of methods and techniques (e.g., phenomenology, narrative, numerical conversion of textual data) may conceivably be used to synthesize qualitative research findings, the methods featured in the following sections are those most used or featured in published reports of, and methodological literature on, qualitative metasynthesis studies as they are defined here. These methods are arranged by the degree of interpretive transformation of the findings targeted for synthesis (i.e., data-near to data-far).

Aggregation via metasummary. As first advanced by and fully described in Sandelowski and Barroso (2007), metasummary is a methodological approach to the synthesis by aggregation of qualitative findings classified as topical or thematic surveys of data that combines familiar qualitative content and thematic analysis techniques with basic computations. Because they are data near, such survey findings do not lend themselves to methods for synthesizing qualitative research requiring data-far findings. Metasummary is based on a preponderance-of-evidence logic, whereby higher frequency findings are taken to be evidence of the relative importance

of a finding and of the replication that is both foundational to validity in quantitative research and to the claim of having discovered a pattern or theme in qualitative research. Metasummaries of findings may serve as end points of qualitative research synthesis studies containing largely survey findings or as empirical foundations for approaches to qualitative metasynthesis by configuration. Because qualitative survey findings are analogous in form and mode of production to the descriptive findings often presented in reports of quantitative observational studies in addition to the results of bivariate and multivariable analyses, metasummary can also be used to synthesize these quantitative descriptive and qualitative survey findings (Sandelowski, Barroso, & Voils, 2007).

Metasummary techniques include the extraction of findings, grouping of findings in shared topical domains via a data-derived form of qualitative content analysis, further reduction of the findings in each topical group into shared thematic domains via basic thematic analysis, and calculation of frequency effect sizes (Onwuegbuzie, 2003) of each of these synthesized findings. Each report is treated as the unit of analysis (and basis for calculating effect sizes) regardless of its length or the number of participants in the study featured. This is because qualitative findings are usually presented at the study level, with the description of themes typically prevailing over frequency counts, and within-participant or between-theme comparisons typically prevailing over between- and cross-participant comparisons. (In contrast, quantitative findings are presented as group-level statistics—e.g., odds ratio—on the basis of participant-level information.) Examples of the use of metasummary are shown in the Draucker et al. (2009) study of healing in sexual abuse victims, Williams's (2006) study of spirituality at the end of life, and in Sandelowski and Barroso (2007).

Configuration via grounded theory. Grounded theory is the oldest of the methodological approaches to metasynthesis by configuration, although it was first advanced as a way of developing theory at least 2 decades before the rise of interest in synthesizing qualitative research findings and before the use of the term *qualitative metasynthesis* to refer to this interest. Early in the history of grounded theory, Glaser and Strauss (1971) warned that continued failure to link local grounded theories into formal theories would relegate the findings of individual studies to "little islands of knowledge" (p. 181), separated from each other and doomed ultimately never to be visited. Accordingly, the ultimate goal of grounded theory is to develop formal theories (a form of metasynthesis) both (a) ethnographically faithful to the specific experiences, events, and the like from which they were derived; and (b) transferable to experiences other than those from which they were derived (a form of analytic generalization). In its neopositivist (Corbin & Strauss, 2008), constructivist (Charmaz, 2006), and postmodern (Clarke, 2005) guises, grounded theory encompasses a set of signature practices for the generation, development, and testing of theory, including theoretical sampling to the point of theoretical saturation and constant comparison analysis.

Using grounded theory as a method for metasynthesis, reviewers typically begin with a broad action-oriented research question (e.g., "How do people manage chronic illness?" "How do organizations accomplish their work?") and with broad inclusion criteria for the selection of research reports to address this question. On the basis of grounds developed in the course of analyzing these reports, reviewers then develop the specific research questions that will guide the plan for the subsequent theoretical sampling of reports and findings in reports. Findings most amenable to synthesis via grounded theory are those with data-far findings classified as conceptual or thematic syntheses or interpretive explanations. Grounded theory may also be used with syntheses of data-near survey findings by metasummary. Metasynthesis by grounded theory will be composed of one or more theoretical renderings of findings (descriptions, explanations) organized around one or more of the grounded theory coding families or templates, such as the popular conditional matrix whereby a core sociocultural process is identified along with its causes, consequences, conditions, and covariates (Corbin & Strauss, 2008). Examples of the use of grounded theory methods for qualitative metasynthesis include the Kearney and

O'Sullivan (2003) metasynthesis of findings on identity and health behavior change, and Kearney's (1998b) study of women's addiction recovery and (2001) study of domestic violence.

Configuration via meta-ethnography. Meta-ethnography is by far the methodological approach most often cited in reports of metasynthesis studies, although its conceptualization and application are as diverse as the reviewers citing it. As Noblit and Hare (1988) first advanced and described it, meta-ethnography combines familiar elements of grounded theory (e.g., constant comparison analysis, conceptual synthesis) with conceptual translation for the explicit purpose of interpretively comparing a highly limited number of ethnographies (as opposed to large numbers of reports of different kinds of qualitative studies). Central to meta-ethnography is the juxtaposition of key metaphors or concepts constituting the findings in individual ethnographies to ascertain whether and how they are like or unlike each other. The results of meta-ethnography may include a reciprocal translation synthesis in cases in which ethnographies are seen to be similar to each other, a refutational synthesis in which they are seen to contradict each other, or a lines-of-argument synthesis in which inferences can be drawn about a whole (i.e., a culture) from disparate studies of its parts. Examples of the adapted use of meta-ethnography include the Campbell et al. (2003) study of experiences with diabetes and diabetes care, the Pound et al. (2005) study of medicine taking, and the Malpass et al. (2009) study of patients' management of antidepressant medication.

Metasynthesis via metastudy. The most encompassing approach to qualitative metasynthesis is what Paterson, Thorne, Canam, and Jillings (2001) first described as metastudy, a program of research directed not only to integrating the findings of qualitative studies in a targeted domain of research (which they referred to as *meta-data-analysis*) but also to the intensive (historical, discursive) study of the research traditions in which these findings are embedded (which they referred to as *metamethod* and *metatheory*). For Paterson et al., the findings cannot be understood apart from intensive study of the theoretical and methodological frameworks that generated them. Accordingly, metastudy involves treating research reports and the findings in them as indexes of the studies conducted and of the phenomena targeted by those studies, and as documentary sources of information about changing research traditions. Examples of components of metastudy include the Paterson, Canam, Joachim, and Thorne (2003) study of the assumptions underlying qualitative studies of fatigue; the Thorne et al. (2002) study of the influence of research frameworks; and the Paterson (2001) study of perspectives of chronic illness.

Other approaches for synthesizing findings. Most published metasynthesis studies are ad hoc combinations of techniques drawn from the methodological literature on qualitative metasynthesis and on qualitative research as a whole (e.g., S. M. Carroll, 2004; Larun & Malterud, 2007; Sim & Madden, 2008). Such techniques include the various domain analyses Spradley (1979) described in his classic text on ethnography, the use of a priori conceptual or theoretical frameworks to arrange research findings, and the use of constant targeted comparison to ascertain the similarities and differences between a target phenomenon and other extrastudy phenomena with apparent resemblances to the target (Sandelowski & Barroso, 2007). Examples of the application of these techniques are shown in the Draucker et al. (2009) study of healing from sexual violence (taxonomic analysis), S. M. Carroll's (2004) study of nonvocal ventilated patients' experiences of being understood (use of a priori theoretical framework to arrange research findings), and Sandelowski and Barroso (2007).

Optimizing the Validity of Qualitative Metasynthesis Studies

The trustworthiness of the results of metasynthesis studies rests largely on the extent to which reviewers can successfully communicate and defend the choices made that constitute their studies. Toward this end, reviewers must show how they addressed the descriptive, interpretive, theoretical, and pragmatic validity of their study procedures and findings (Kvale, 1995; Maxwell, 1992; Seale, 1999). In qualitative metasynthesis studies, *descriptive validity* refers to measures taken to optimize the comprehensiveness of search procedures, identification of all

relevant research reports, and the accurate characterization of information from each report included in the study. *Interpretive validity* refers to measures taken to optimize the full and fair representation of what the researchers who conducted and authored the reports of the studies included in the review intended to convey in their findings. *Theoretical validity* refers to measures taken to optimize the credibility of the methods reviewers developed to produce their metasyntheses and to the metasyntheses themselves. *Pragmatic validity* refers to measures taken to optimize the "applicability, timeliness, and translatability for practice" (Sandelowski & Barroso, 2007, p. 228) of the research syntheses produced. Among these measures are the maintenance of an audit trail (Rodgers & Cowles, 1993); negotiation of consensus among members of the review team (Belgrave & Smith, 1995); consultations with information retrieval, methodological, and practice experts; and, as needed, contact with authors of reports (Sandelowski & Barroso, 2007).

Disseminating the Results of Qualitative Metasynthesis Studies

The outcomes of qualitative metasynthesis studies are typically disseminated according to the guide shown in Exhibit 2.1. For audiences other than the traditional consumers of research reports, alternative forms of dissemination may be warranted. Examples of such departures include a digital library (Barroso, Edlin, Sandelowski, & Lambe, 2006) and dramatization of synthesized findings (Sandelowski, Trimble, Woodard, & Barroso, 2006).

CONCLUSION

In summary, qualitative metasynthesis entails the systematic and comprehensive retrieval of all of the relevant reports of completed qualitative studies in a target domain of empirical inquiry, analytic and interpretive emphasis on the findings in these reports, systematic and appropriately eclectic use of qualitative or quantitative methods to integrate the findings in these reports, and the use of reflexive accounting practices to optimize the validity of study procedures and outcomes. Conducting qualitative metasynthesis studies requires a wide-ranging knowledge of the diversity in qualitative methods and an attitude of openness as opposed to overcommitment to any one method or any one execution of method in appraising reports and synthesizing their findings.

The future of the research synthesis enterprise lies in finding credible ways to integrate qualitative and quantitative research findings in shared domains of inquiry in mixed-research synthesis studies or programs of research. Separate syntheses of findings from reports of qualitative and quantitative studies may be conducted to address complementary research purposes, or qualitative and quantitative findings may be transformed into each other and then integrated as a unit in the same study to address a common research purpose (Crandell, Voils, Chang, & Sandelowski, 2011; Pope et al., 2007; Sandelowski, Voils, & Barroso, 2006; Voils et al., 2009; Voils, Sandelowski, Barroso, & Hasselblad, 2008). The future of research synthesis lies not in preserving artificial divides between qualitative and quantitative research but rather in drawing from and further developing the full repertoire of research synthesis methods to accommodate all of the evidence upon which best practices might be based.

References

Alvesson, M., & Sköldberg, K. (2000). *Reflexive methodology: New vistas for qualitative research.* London, England: Sage.

Barbour, R. S. (2000). The role of qualitative research in broadening the "evidence base" for clinical practice. *Journal of Evaluation in Clinical Practice, 6,* 155–163. doi:10.1046/j.1365-2753.2000.00213.x

Barbour, R. S. (2001). Checklists for improving rigor in qualitative research: A case of the tail wagging the dog? *British Medical Journal, 322,* 1115–1117. doi:10.1136/bmj.322.7294.1115

Barbour, R. S., & Barbour, M. (2003). Evaluating and synthesizing qualitative research: The need to develop a distinctive approach. *Journal of Evaluation in Clinical Practice, 9,* 179–186. doi:10.1046/j.1365-2753.2003.00371.x

Barroso, J., Edlin, A., Sandelowski, M., & Lambe, C. (2006). Bridging the gap between research and practice: The development of a digital library of research syntheses. *CIN: Computers, Informatics. Nursing, 24,* 85–94.

Barroso, J., Gollop, C. J., Sandelowski, M., Meynell, J., Pearce, P. F., & Collins, L. J. (2003). The challenges of searching for and retrieving qualitative studies.

Western Journal of Nursing Research, 25, 153–178. doi:10.1177/0193945902250034

Barroso, J., Sandelowski, M., & Voils, C. I. (2006). Research results have expiration dates: Ensuring timely systematic reviews. *Journal of Evaluation in Clinical Practice, 12,* 454–462. doi:10.1111/j.1365-2753.2006.00729.x

Bazerman, C. (1988). *Shaping written knowledge: The genre and activity of the experimental article in science.* Madison: University of Wisconsin Press.

Belgrave, L. L., & Smith, K. J. (1995). Negotiated validity in collaborative ethnography. *Qualitative Inquiry, 1,* 69–86. doi:10.1177/107780049500100105

Braun, V., & Clarke, V. (2006). Using thematic analysis in psychology. *Qualitative Research in Psychology, 3,* 77–101. doi:10.1191/1478088706qp063oa

Campbell, R., Pound, P., Pope, C., Britten, N., Pill, R., Morgan, M., & Donovan, J. (2003). Evaluating meta-ethnography: A synthesis of qualitative research on lay experiences of diabetes and diabetes care. *Social Science and Medicine, 56,* 671–684. doi:10.1016/S0277-9536(02)00064-3

Carroll, J. (1999). *The marriage of sticks.* New York, NY: Tor.

Carroll, S. M. (2004). Nonvocal ventilated patients' perceptions of being understood. *Western Journal of Nursing Research, 26,* 85–103. doi:10.1177/0193945903259462

Charmaz, K. (2006). *Constructing grounded theory: A practical guide through qualitative analysis.* London, England: Sage.

Clarke, A. E. (2005). *Situational analysis: Grounded theory after the postmodern turn.* Thousand Oaks, CA: Sage.

Cooper, H. (2010). *Research synthesis and meta-analysis: A step-by-step approach* (4th ed.). Los Angeles, CA: Sage.

Corbin, J., & Strauss, A. (2008). *Basics of qualitative research: Techniques and procedures for developing grounded theory* (3rd ed.). Thousand Oaks, CA: Sage.

Crandell, J. L., Voils, C. I., Chang, Y., & Sandelowski, M. (2011). Bayesian data augmentation methods for the synthesis of qualitative and quantitative research findings. *Quality and Quantity, 45,* 653–669.

Dijkers, M. P. (2009). The value of "traditional" reviews in the era of systematic reviewing. *American Journal of Physical Medicine and Rehabilitation, 88,* 423–430. doi:10.1097/PHM.0b013e31819c59c6

Dixon-Woods, M., Sutton, A., Shaw, R., Miller, T., Smith, J., Young, B., . . . Jones, D. (2007). Appraising qualitative research for inclusion in systematic reviews: A quantitative and qualitative comparison of three methods. *Journal of Health Services Research and Policy, 12,* 42–47. doi:10.1258/135581907779497486

Draucker, C. B., Martsolf, D. S., Ross, R., Cook, C. B., Stidham, A. W., & Mweemba, P. (2009). The essence of healing from sexual violence: A qualitative metasynthesis. *Research in Nursing and Health, 32,* 366–378. doi:10.1002/nur.20333

Eakin, J. M., & Mykhalovskiy, E. (2003). Reframing the evaluation of qualitative health research: Reflections on a review of appraisal guidelines in the health sciences. *Journal of Evaluation in Clinical Practice, 9,* 187–194. doi:10.1046/j.1365-2753.2003.00392.x

Edwards, A., Elwyn, G., Hood, K., & Rollnick, S. (2000). Judging the "weight of evidence" in systematic reviews: Introducing rigor into the qualitative overview stage by assessing Signal and Noise. *Journal of Evaluation in Clinical Practice, 6,* 177–184. doi:10.1046/j.1365-2753.2000.00212.x

Elliott, J. (2005). *Using narrative in social research: Qualitative and quantitative approaches.* London, England: Sage.

Engel, J. D., & Kuzel, A. J. (1992). On the idea of what constitutes good qualitative inquiry. *Qualitative Health Research, 2,* 504–510. doi:10.1177/104973239200200409

Evans, D. (2002). Database searches for qualitative research. *Journal of the Medical Library Association, 90,* 290–293.

Finfgeld, D. L. (2003). Metasynthesis: The state of the art—So far. *Qualitative Health Research, 13,* 893–904. doi:10.1177/1049732303253462

Geertz, C. (1973). Thick description: Toward an interpretive theory of culture. In C. Geertz (Ed.), *The interpretation of cultures: Selected essays* (pp. 37–126). New York, NY: Basic Books.

Glaser, B. G., & Strauss, A. L. (1971). *Status passage.* Chicago, IL: Aldine.

Golden-Biddle, K., & Locke, K. (1993). Appealing work: An investigation of how ethnographic texts convince. *Organization Science, 4,* 595–616. doi:10.1287/orsc.4.4.595

Grant, M. J. (2004). How does your searching grow? A survey of search preferences and the use of optimal search strategies in the identification of qualitative research. *Health Information and Libraries Journal, 21,* 21–32. doi:10.1111/j.1471-1842.2004.00483.x

Greenhalgh, T. (2002). Integrating qualitative research into evidence based practice. *Endocrinology and Metabolism Clinics of North America, 31,* 583–601. doi:10.1016/S0889-8529(02)00009-9

Hak, T., & Bernts, T. (1996). Coder training: Theoretical training or practical socialization? *Qualitative Sociology, 19,* 235–257. doi:10.1007/BF02393420

Hammersley, M. (2001). On "systematic" reviews of research literatures: A "narrative" response to Evans & Benefield. *British Educational Research Journal, 27,* 543–554. doi:10.1080/01411920120095726

Hammersley, M. (2009). Challenging relativism: The problem of assessment criteria. *Qualitative Inquiry, 15,* 3–29. doi:10.1177/1077800408325325

Harris, M. R. (2005). The librarian's roles in the systematic review process: A case study. *Journal of the Medical Library Association, 93,* 81–87.

Heaton, J. (2004). *Reworking qualitative data.* London, England: Sage.

Hsieh, H.-F., & Shannon, S. E. (2005). Three approaches to qualitative content analysis. *Qualitative Health Research, 15,* 1277–1288. doi:10.1177/1049732305276687

Jones, M. L. (2004). Application of systematic review methods to qualitative research: Practical issues. *Journal of Advanced Nursing, 48,* 271–278. doi:10.1111/j.1365-2648.2004.03196.x

Kearney, M. H. (1998a). Ready-to-wear: Discovering grounded formal theory. *Research in Nursing and Health, 21,* 179–186. doi:10.1002/(SICI)1098-240X(199804)21:2<179::AID-NUR8>3.0.CO;2-G

Kearney, M. H. (1998b). Truthful self-nurturing: A grounded formal theory of women's addiction recovery. *Qualitative Health Research, 8,* 495–512. doi:10.1177/104973239800800405

Kearney, M. H. (2001). Enduring love: A grounded formal theory of women's experience of domestic violence. *Research in Nursing and Health, 24,* 270–282. doi:10.1002/nur.1029

Kearney, M. H., & O'Sullivan, J. (2003). Identity shifts as turning points in health behavior change. *Western Journal of Nursing Research, 25,* 134–152. doi:10.1177/0193945902250032

Kritzer, H. M. (1996). The data puzzle: The nature of interpretation in quantitative research. *American Journal of Political Science, 40,* 1–32. doi:10.2307/2111692

Kvale, S. (1995). The social construction of validity. *Qualitative Inquiry, 1,* 19–40. doi:10.1177/107780049500100103

Larun, L., & Malterud, K. (2007). Identity and coping experiences in chronic fatigue syndrome: A synthesis of qualitative studies. *Patient Education and Counseling, 69,* 20–28. doi:10.1016/j.pec.2007.06.008

Lather, P. (1999). To be of use: The work of reviewing. *Review of Educational Research, 69,* 2–7.

Latour, B., & Woolgar, S. (1986). *Laboratory life: The construction of scientific facts.* Princeton, NJ: Princeton University Press.

Law, J. (2004). *After method: Mess in social science research.* London, England: Routledge.

Linde, K., & Willich, S. N. (2003). How objective are systematic reviews? Differences between reviews on complementary medicine. *Journal of the Royal Society of Medicine, 96,* 17–22. doi:10.1258/jrsm.96.1.17

Littleton, D., Marsalis, S., & Bliss, D. Z. (2004). Searching literature by design. *Western Journal of Nursing Research, 26,* 891–908. doi:10.1177/0193945903258729

Losee, R. M. (2000). When information retrieval measures agree about the relative quality of document rankings. *Journal of the American Society for Information Science, 51,* 834–840. doi:10.1002/(SICI)1097-4571(2000)51:9<834::AID-ASI60>3.0.CO;2-1

MacLure, M. (2005). "Clarity bordering on stupidity": Where's the quality in systematic review? *Journal of Education Policy, 20,* 393–416. doi:10.1080/02680930500131801

Malpass, A., Shaw, A., Sharp, D., Walter, F., Feder, G., Ridd, M., & Kessler, D. (2009). "Medication career" or "moral career"? The two sides of managing antidepressants: A meta-ethnography of patients' experience of antidepressants. *Social Science and Medicine, 68,* 154–168. doi:10.1016/j.socscimed.2008.09.068

Marchionini, G. (1995). *Information seeking in electronic environments.* New York, NY: Cambridge University Press. doi:10.1017/CBO9780511626388

Mason, J. (2006). Mixing methods in a qualitatively driven way. *Qualitative Research, 6,* 9–25. doi:10.1177/1468794106058866

Maxwell, J. A. (1992). Understanding and validity in qualitative research. *Harvard Educational Review, 62,* 279–300.

McKibbon, K. A., Wilczynski, N. L., & Haynes, R. B. (2006). Developing optimal search strategies for retrieving qualitative studies in PsycINFO. *Evaluation and the Health Professions, 29,* 440–454. doi:10.1177/0163278706293400

Miles, M. B., & Huberman, A. M. (1994). *Qualitative data analysis: An expanded sourcebook* (2nd ed.). Thousand Oaks, CA: Sage.

Moreira, T. (2007). Entangled evidence: Knowledge making in systematic reviews in healthcare. *Sociology of Health and Illness, 29,* 180–197. doi:10.1111/j.1467-9566.2007.00531.x

Morse, J. M., Swanson, J. M., & Kuzel, A. J. (Eds.). (2001). *The nature of qualitative evidence.* Thousand Oaks, CA: Sage.

Murphy, E. (1999). "Breast is best": Infant feeding decisions and maternal deviance. *Sociology of Health and Illness, 21,* 187–208. doi:10.1111/1467-9566.00149

Mykhalovskiy, E., & Weir, L. (2004). The problem of evidence-based medicine: Directions for social science. *Social Science and Medicine, 59,* 1059–1069. doi:10.1016/j.socscimed.2003.12.002

Noblit, G. W., & Hare, R. D. (1988). *Meta-ethnography: Synthesizing qualitative studies.* Newbury Park, CA: Sage.

Onwuegbuzie, A. J. (2003). Effect sizes in qualitative research: A prolegomenon. *Quality and Quantity, 37,* 393–409. doi:10.1023/A:1027379223537

Paterson, B. L. (2001). The shifting perspectives model of chronic illness. *Journal of Nursing Scholarship, 33,* 21–26. doi:10.1111/j.1547-5069.2001.00021.x

Paterson, B., Canam, C., Joachim, G., & Thorne, S. (2003). Embedded assumptions in qualitative studies of fatigue. *Western Journal of Nursing Research, 25,* 119–133. doi:10.1177/0193945902250029

Paterson, B. L., Thorne, S. E., Canam, C., & Jillings, C. (2001). *Meta-study of qualitative health research: A practical guide to meta-analysis and metasynthesis.* Thousand Oaks, CA: Sage.

Pope, C., & Mays, N. (1995). Reaching the parts other methods cannot reach: An introduction to qualitative methods in health and health services research. *British Medical Journal, 311,* 42–45.

Pope, C., Mays, N., & Popay, J. (2007). *Synthesizing qualitative and quantitative health evidence.* Berkshire, England: Open University Press.

Pound, P., Britten, N., Morgan, M., Yardley, L., Pope, C., Daker-White, G., & Campbell, R. (2005). Resisting medicines: A synthesis of qualitative studies of medicine taking. *Social Science and Medicine, 61,* 133–155. doi:10.1016/j.socscimed.2004.11.063

Reiser, S. J. (1978). *Medicine and the reign of technology.* Cambridge, England: Cambridge University Press.

Richardson, L. (2000). Writing: A method of inquiry. In N. K. Denzin & Y. S. Lincoln (Eds.), *Handbook of qualitative research* (2nd ed., pp. 923–948). Thousand Oaks, CA: Sage.

Riessman, C. K. (2008). *Narrative methods for the human sciences.* Los Angeles, CA: Sage.

Rodgers, B. L., & Cowles, K. V. (1993). The qualitative research audit trail: A complex collection of documentation. *Research in Nursing and Health, 16,* 219–226. doi:10.1002/nur.4770160309

Sandelowski, M. (2004). Using qualitative research. *Qualitative Health Research, 14,* 1366–1386. doi:10.1177/1049732304269672

Sandelowski, M. (2006). "Meta-jeopardy": The crisis of representation in qualitative metasynthesis. *Nursing Outlook, 54,* 10–16. doi:10.1016/j.outlook.2005.05.004

Sandelowski, M. (2007). From metasynthesis to method: Appraising the qualitative research synthesis report. In C. Webb & B. Roe (Eds.), *Reviewing research evidence for nursing practice: Systematic reviews* (pp. 88–111). London, England: Blackwell. doi:10.1002/9780470692127.ch8

Sandelowski, M. (2008). Reading, writing, and systematic review. *Journal of Advanced Nursing, 64,* 104–110. doi:10.1111/j.1365-2648.2008.04813.x

Sandelowski, M., & Barroso, J. (2002). Reading qualitative studies. *International Journal of Qualitative Methods, 1*(1). Retrieved from http://ejournals. library.ualberta.ca/index.php/IJQM/article/ view/4615/3764

Sandelowski, M., & Barroso, J. (2007). *Handbook for synthesizing qualitative research.* New York, NY: Springer.

Sandelowski, M., Barroso, J., & Voils, C. I. (2007). Using qualitative metasummary to synthesize qualitative and quantitative descriptive findings. *Research in Nursing and Health, 30,* 99–111. doi:10.1002/nur.20176

Sandelowski, M., Trimble, F., Woodard, E. K., & Barroso, J. (2006). From synthesis to script: Transforming qualitative research findings for use in practice. *Qualitative Health Research, 16,* 1350–1370. doi:10.1177/1049732306294274

Sandelowski, M., Voils, C. I., & Barroso, J. (2006). Defining and designing mixed research synthesis studies. *Research in the Schools, 13,* 29–40.

Sandelowski, M., Voils, C. I., & Barroso, J. (2007). Comparability work and the management of difference in research synthesis studies. *Social Science and Medicine, 64,* 236–247. doi:10.1016/j. socscimed.2006.08.041

Sandelowski, M., Voils, C. I., & Knafl, G. (2009). On quantitizing. *Journal of Mixed Methods Research, 3,* 208–222. doi:10.1177/1558689809334210

Schwalbe, M. (1995). The responsibilities of sociological poets. *Qualitative Sociology, 18,* 393–413. doi:10.1007/BF02404488

Seale, C. (1999). *The quality of qualitative research.* London, England: Sage.

Shapin, S. (1984). Pump and circumstance: Robert Boyle's literary technology. *Social Studies of Science, 14,* 481–520. doi:10.1177/030631284014004001

Shaw, R. L., Booth, A., Sutton, A. J., Miller, T., Smith, J. A., Young, B., . . . Dixon-Woods, M. (2004). Finding qualitative research: An evaluation of search strategies. *BMC Medical Research Methodology, 4*(5). Retrieved from http://www.biomedcentral.com/1471-2288/4/5

Shojania, K. G., Sampson, M., Ansari, M. T., Ji, J., Doucette, S., & Moher, D. (2007). How quickly do systematic reviews go out of date? A survival analysis. *Annals of Internal Medicine, 147,* 224–233.

Shrier, I., Boivin, J., Platt, R. W., Steele, R. J., Brophy, J. M., Carnevale, F., . . . Rossignol, M. (2008). The interpretation of systematic reviews with meta-analyses: An objective or subjective process? *BMC Medical Informatics and Decision Making, 8*(19). Retrieved from http://www.biomedcentral. com/1472-6947/8/19

Sim, J., & Madden, S. (2008). Illness experience in fibromyalgia syndrome: A metasynthesis of qualitative studies. *Social Science and Medicine, 67,* 57–67. doi:10.1016/j.socscimed.2008.03.003

Smith, J. K., & Deemer, D. K. (2000). The problem of criteria in the age of relativism. In N. K. Denzin & Y. S. Lincoln (Eds.), *Handbook of qualitative research* (2nd ed., pp. 877–896). Thousand Oaks, CA: Sage.

Smith, J. K., & Hodkinson, P. (2005). Relativism, criteria, and politics. In N. K. Denzin & Y. S. Lincoln (Eds.), *The Sage handbook of qualitative research* (3rd ed., pp. 915–932). Thousand Oaks, CA: Sage.

Spradley, J. P. (1979). *The ethnographic interview.* Fort Worth, TX: Harcourt Brace Jovanovich.

Thomas, J., & Harden, A. (2008). Methods for the thematic synthesis of qualitative research in systematic reviews. *BMC Medical Research Methodology, 8*(45). Retrieved from http://www.biomedcentral.com/1471-2288/8/45

Thorne, S., Jensen, L., Kearney, M. H., Noblit, G., & Sandelowski, M. (2004). Qualitative meta-synthesis: Reflections on methodological orientation and ideological agenda. *Qualitative Health Research, 14,* 1342–1365. doi:10.1177/1049732304269888

Thorne, S., Joachim, G., Paterson, B., & Canam, C. (2002). Influence of the research frame on qualitatively derived health science. *International Journal of Qualitative Methods, 1*(1). Retrieved from http:// ejournals.library.ualberta.ca/index.php/IJQM/article/ view/4611/3760

Timmermans, S., & Berg, M. (2003). *The gold standard: The challenge of evidence-based medicine and standardization in health care.* Philadelphia, PA: Temple University Press.

Trinder, L., & Reynolds, S. (Eds.). (2000). *Evidence-based practice: A critical appraisal.* Oxford, England: Blackwell Science.

Voils, C. I., Hasselblad, V., Chang, Y. K., Crandell, J., Lee, E. J., & Sandelowski, M. (2009). A Bayesian method for the synthesis of evidence from qualitative and quantitative reports: An example from the literature on antiretroviral medication adherence. *Journal of Health Services Research and Policy, 14,* 226–233. doi:10.1258/jhsrp.2009.008186

Voils, C. I., Sandelowski, M., Barroso, J., & Hasselblad, V. (2008). Making sense of qualitative and quantitative findings in mixed research synthesis studies. *Field Methods, 20,* 3–25. doi:10.1177/1525822X07307463

Walters, L. A., Wilczynski, N. L., & Haynes, R. B. (2006). Developing optimal search strategies for detecting clinically relevant qualitative studies in Embase. *Qualitative Health Research, 16,* 162–168. doi:10.1177/1049732305284027

White, D. G. (2001). Evaluating evidence and making judgments of study quality: Loss of evidence and risks to policy and practice decisions. *Critical Public Health, 11,* 3–17. doi:10.1080/095815900 10028228

Wilczynski, N. L., Marks, S., & Haynes, R. B. (2007). Search strategies for identifying qualitative studies in CINAHL. *Qualitative Health Research, 17,* 705–710. doi:10.1177/1049732306294515

Williams, A.-L. (2006). Perspectives on spirituality at the end of life: A meta-summary. *Palliative and Supportive Care, 4,* 407–417. doi:10.1017/ S1478951506060500

Wolcott, H. F. (1994). *Transforming qualitative data: Description, analysis, and interpretation.* Thousand Oaks, CA: Sage.

Wong, S. S., Wilczynski, N. L., & Haynes, R. B. (2004). Developing optimal search strategies for detecting clinically relevant qualitative studies in MEDLINE. *Studies in Health Technology and Informatics, 107,* 311–316.

Zimmer, L. (2006). Qualitative meta-synthesis: A question of dialoguing with texts. *Journal of Advanced Nursing, 53,* 311–318. doi:10.1111/j.1365-2648-.2006.03721.x

Thematic Approaches

CHAPTER 3

GROUNDED THEORY AND PSYCHOLOGICAL RESEARCH

Antony Bryant and Kathy Charmaz

GROUNDED THEORY

Grounded theory—or more accurately the grounded theory method—burst on to the methodological scene in the mid-1960s with the publication of a trio of books by Barney Glaser and Anselm Strauss: *Awareness of Dying* (1965), *The Discovery of Grounded Theory* (1967), and *Time for Dying* (1968). In these three texts, Glaser and Strauss demonstrated their innovative approach to social research with two specific and detailed examples of the approach (*Awareness of Dying* and *Time for Dying*) plus the more generic and polemical publication *Discovery of Grounded Theory* that argued the cause of the method itself. This latter text can be considered to be the founding trilogy of the method.

Glaser and Strauss were well aware that grounded theory was a highly innovative methodological breakthrough, although they were unaware of how grounded theory would spread across disciplines and professions. *Awareness* (1965) offered a methodological appendix, thereby stressing the importance of their approach, and *Discovery* (1967) took this further, offering a sustained justification and manifesto for their new approach to social research. The key innovations of the method offered a challenge and an alternative to the governing orthodoxy of contemporary social sciences. Glaser and Strauss sought to elevate qualitative research to a level equivalent to that of quantitative research, offering corresponding ways in which qualitative research could be carried out with rigor and diligence. This approach involved a critique of existing methods, supplemented by the articulation of a genuine alternative.

The key point of their critique was that the value of qualitative research was undermined if it was seen largely as descriptive and impressionistic, at best merely preparatory to rigorous quantitative research. Some qualitative research may well achieve no more than this level, hence the need for a rigorous method of carrying out qualitative research. Furthermore, much graduate-level research was highly constrained by choice of topic, level of analysis, and methodological approach. Grounded theory offered a way of breaking away from these limitations. The method advocated entering the research domain without preconceived hypotheses, an avowedly qualitative approach, and an overall objective of conceptual articulation and theoretical development even for relatively inexperienced and junior researchers. The method itself centered on an iterative approach going back and forth between data gathering and analysis; the two activities intimately intertwined, leading to the development of new levels of abstraction in the form of concepts and eventually to theoretical statements that were grounded in the data.

The initial users of the method centered on the doctoral program that Strauss ran at the University of California, San Francisco (UCSF) starting in the 1960s; many of these early adopters became well-known grounded theory theorists and researchers in later years. Moreover the method spread across many graduate schools, but the founding trilogy was not well suited to this audience, many of

DOI: 10.1037/13620-003
APA Handbook of Research Methods in Psychology: Vol. 2. Research Designs, H. Cooper (Editor-in-Chief)

whom were keen to have access to some form of grounded theory primer. Eventually Strauss published *Qualitative Analysis for Social Scientists* (1987), aimed specifically at "a particular style of qualitative analysis of data (grounded theory)" (p. xi). He drew heavily on Glaser's book *Theoretical Sensitivity* (1978), incorporating several extended verbatim extracts, and sought to introduce the approach to those unfamiliar with its precepts. He noted that the method had been derived by and used by sociologists, but it had now spread to "researchers in education, public health, social work, and nursing," arguing that this "general style of doing analysis . . . does not depend on particular disciplinary perspectives" (Strauss, 1987, xi).

A few years later, and partly because the earlier book was seen as not sufficiently accessible to a novice audience, Strauss, together with Juliet Corbin, published *Basics of Qualitative Research: Grounded Theory Procedures and Techniques* (Strauss & Corbin, 1990). This in particular led to the method achieving its current widespread popularity (the book is now in its third edition; Corbin & Strauss, 2008.)

The origins of the method then clearly resided within sociology, but by the 1980s, its popularity had spread across the social sciences and related disciplines—particularly in areas associated with health care, nursing, social work, and education. From the outset grounded theory was linked to what might be termed *practice-based disciplines*, to a large extent the result of the method's origins in the context of nursing and caring for terminally ill patients. In the 1960s, Glaser and Strauss had each had recent experience of bereavement. In their initial studies, they were assisted by Jeanne Quint (later Jeanne Quint Benoliel), a nursing specialist who transformed the practice of care for the terminally and chronically ill in the course of her career (Washington State Nurses Association, 2011). Strauss's academic position at UCSF reinforced this aspect, given the autonomy he had in the School of Nursing and the support from its dean Helen Nahm. As a consequence, its origins and early institutional embodiment indelibly and fortuitously marked grounded theory. The personal and academic experiences of the originators, the influence of professional practice, and the disciplinary focus of UCSF all affected the ways in which the method was taken up and articulated.

In their later individual work, Glaser and Strauss continued to stress grounding theory in data—each in their own way. Strauss sought to link the method to the broader issue of agency and social action, although often in ambiguous and cryptic fashion (see Bryant, 2009). Glaser stressed the centrality of *process*, arguing for identification of *basic social processes* (see his editor's introduction in Glaser, 1996) and also sustaining the clarion call for concepts to be grounded in the data (an invocation of considerable ambiguity, as discussed in a later section).

The Attraction of Grounded Theory for Psychology Research

The attraction of grounded theory for researchers in psychology emanates from two key developments. The first, and more general one, concerns the significant growth in understanding and use of qualitative research methods and techniques in the period starting from around the time that grounded theory first appeared (mid-1960s), a phenomenon that occurred across many disciplines and practices but particularly those associated with the social sciences. As interest in qualitative research grew, so too did the number and range of different qualitative methods (in some senses to a bewildering extent as can be seen from perusal of the successive editions of *The Handbook of Qualitative Research*, Denzin & Lincoln, 1994, 2000, 2005), with grounded theory rapidly becoming the most widely claimed of all.

The second development is more specific to the psychological disciplines and also dates from the 1960s, but it builds on the first one. As Glaser and Strauss were undertaking the research that led to the articulation of grounded theory, the predominant approaches to psychiatric research and practice were the subject of sustained critiques, including those from the likes of Foucault (1967, 1973), Goffman (1961), Laing (1961, 1965), Szasz (1961, 1970), and many others who argued that most orthodox orientations and professional practices were far too slanted toward a *scientistic* (i.e., natural science's ideological belief in itself as the appropriate standard for all kinds of knowledge) and medical model, at best paying only scant attention to the experiences and feelings of those subject to the investigations and treatments of the professionals. Although many of these critiques were predominantly focused on psychiatry rather than psychology, the impact on the wider, and less medically centered, field was almost certainly significant, in part bound up with the "alternative" emanations that characterized the 1960s and 1970s. The consequence was that by the 1980s, as the critiques of positions such as Laing's (1961, 1965) antipsychiatry gathered force, concern remained that research and practice in psychology had not taken on board the issue of the ways in which psychological processes of research and practice needed to consider all those involved and not simply in the form of expert (doctor or nurse) and patient (passive recipient, subject or victim).

The net result was that from the 1980s onward the realization grew that the predominance of quantitative, impersonal methods in psychological research needed to be complemented by more individual-centered, qualitative, and interpretive ones, as the phenomenological tradition in psychology has long exemplified. Madill and Gough (2008) made this point about moving toward interpretive qualitative approaches very clearly, arguing that

> the surge in popularity of qualitative methods in psychology can be traced to dissatisfaction with cognitive–experimental psychology in the 1960s and 1970s. During this period, broadly humanistic qualitative methods were developed as one response to a wider countercultural critique of traditional sources of authority (e.g., empirical phenomenology). A second wave of qualitative methods was then ushered into psychology with the importation of postmodernist and poststructuralist perspectives during the 1980s and early 1990s as well as a central focus on discourse or text (e.g., discourse analysis). The situation in the early 21st century is one of heterogeneity, with qualitative

research best conceptualized as a fuzzy set. (p. 254)

Offering an even earlier starting point for this form of critique, Haverkamp, Morrow, and Ponterotto (2005, p. 123) referred to Sigmund Koch's criticism of psychologists from the period of the 1930s to the 1950s who valued "science and method above psychology's human subject matter and human nature," advocating that they should study "humanly significant problems with methods chosen or devised with intelligent flexibility to fit the problems being pursued."

Glaser and Strauss put forward grounded theory as a challenge to sociological research orthodoxy. The take up of grounded theory by researchers in psychology developed from a similarly critical motivation, simultaneously drawing on the enhanced interest in and foundations for qualitative research and with the aim of offering a more empathic and inclusive form of research and professional practice.

The Groundedness of Psychological Research

Although writers such as Covan (2007) have been correct to point to the parallels between Durkheim's (1938) advocacy of the distinctive nature of sociological forms of explanation and Glaser and Strauss's stress on social research that is grounded in the data, the ramifications of groundedness have specific value for psychological researchers seeking to respond to the sorts of critique mentioned in the section The Attraction of Grounded Theory for Psychology Research. In this sense, striving for groundedness can be seen to alert researchers to the ways in which psychological practices, research, and disciplinary enhancement need to attend to the experiences of individuals, whether or not the specific individuals or research subjects are identified or labeled from the outset as patients or sufferers or are specified in terms of some skill, experience, or inclination.

But this immediately raises a number of concerns regarding the validity and status of such research. In essence it comes down to the extent to which personal accounts actually count—that is, how far can they be relied on and developed into anything more than personalized and partial narratives or descriptions? This has been a perennial issue for all forms of research and investigation involving human subjects. It can be termed the tension between experience and analysis.

What grounded theory offers is a methodical and operational resolution of this tension, but the ways in which resolution is accomplished need to be clearly understood for the method to be effectively applied. Glaser and Strauss carried out their initial grounded theory research in the early 1960s at a number of hospitals where their research team conducted a mixture of interviews and observations, aided and abetted by professional medical practitioners. In the ensuing years, grounded theory has become identified as a method that centers on interviewing, and hence the role of participants and the status of their accounts has become a central feature of the method. Glaser and Strauss started from the data emanating in the context of their research—interviews, observations, discussions, and the like—but they did not merely record and report them. Rather they used these materials as the basis for an iterative process aimed at delivering focused abstractions clearly derived from and appropriate for acting in the contextual sources. The process of doing this involved what they termed *constant comparison*, which initially involves iteration between gathering data and analyzing it, with the outcome of any analysis being the potential basis for further data gathering. Many authors refer to this term when explaining their use of grounded theory, which sometimes goes no further than some form of iterative coding of the data, without the iteration between data gathering and analysis. Fassinger (2005, p. 160) referred specifically to Charmaz (2000) in this regard, offering a fourfold view of the comparison process, including data from different sources, data from the same source at different points in time, incidents against other incidents, and categories against other categories.

This search for groundedness, the extent to which personal accounts can be used analytically, raises issues centered on the tension between insider–participant accounts and outsider–analytic ones. The methods literature often terms this tension as the distinction between *emic* and *etic*, terms that Kenneth Pike (1967) introduced in the 1960s.

As a linguist, Pike derived these terms from *phonemic* and *phonetic*, and although the two are usually characterized as the view from the inside and the view from the outside, respectively a more cogent contrast is that between meaning and structure.

An emic model is one that explains the ideology or behavior of members of a culture according to indigenous definitions. An etic model is one that is based on criteria from outside a particular culture. Etic models are held to be universal; emic models are culture specific (see What-When-How, 2011)

In later years the terms were taken up by anthropologists such as Marvin Harris (see Headland, 1999). In that context, they are now most often taken to refer to the insider and outsider views of a specific culture.

Grounded theory offers a form of resolution to this tension, with researchers encouraged to engage with active participants eliciting from them accounts of the processes and background to the research context. But having then obtained this information, grounded theory outlines ways in which this source material can be rigorously and cogently developed so that the outcome of the analysis, although clearly "grounded" in the context, offers insights and abstractions that rise above mere redescription or echoing of actors' narratives. Glaser and Strauss saw this process of moving from grounded details to explanatory abstractions as one of induction; however, this is somewhat misleading if induction is simply seen as the production of general statements from a group of discrete observations. The outcome of a successful grounded theory study ought to be a conceptual model or grounded theory that incorporates a wide range of emic perspectives into a coherent and convincing whole, producing something ultimately persuasive, with plausible promise, when relayed back to the research participants.

Grounded theory can then be understood to enhance and complement some of the key developments in social analyses that emerged in the 1960s and 1970s. The early grounded theory texts, particularly *Awareness of Dying* (Glaser & Strauss, 1965) and *Time for Dying* (Glaser & Strauss, 1968) can be reread as profound examples of conceptual analyses founded on a context in which all the actors play constitutive and constructing roles. This context also includes the researchers, recognizing that social contexts are socially constructed, and then demanding and expecting conceptualization by the researcher that can be offered as a deeper and more extensive account of the context itself. As early as 1983, Turner understood this point:

> This approach to qualitative data promotes the development of theoretical accounts that conform closely to the situations being observed, *so that the theory is likely to be intelligible to and usable by those in the situations observed* [emphasis added], and is open to comment and correction by them. The approach also directs the researcher immediately to the creative core of the research process and *facilitates the direct application of both the intellect and the imagination* [emphasis added] to the demanding process of interpreting qualitative research data. It is worth noting that the quality of the final product arising from this kind of work is *more directly dependent on the quality of the research worker's understanding of the phenomena under observation* [emphasis added] than is the case with many other approaches to research. (Turner, 1983, pp. 334–335)

A few years after the publication of *Discovery* (Glaser & Strauss, 1967), Clifford Geertz published his essays on *The Interpretation of Cultures* (1973). This text is seen as one of the founding statements of symbolic anthropology, and landmark essays, such as "The Balinese Cockfight," exhibit the sorts of abductive leaps and generation of insights that resonate with the ones in *Awareness* (Glaser & Strauss, 1965) and *Time* (Glaser & Strauss, 1968). Where Glaser and Strauss called for *groundedness*, Geertz called for *thick description*.

The writings of Geertz (1973), together with some of those associated with antipsychiatry, share with Glaser and Strauss's trilogy (1965, 1967, 1968) a common concern that research involving social actors must embody the balance between experience and analysis. In some cases, this search for *balance* was a remedial strategy to correct what was seen as

the impersonal and remote approaches that tended to predominate among academic researchers and many professionals. In the hands of some of its more extreme or provocative proponents, such as Laing (1961, 1965) and also some of the early ethnomethodology writings of Garfinkel (1967), this orientation privileged actors' accounts and often dismissed those of experts and other outsiders or at best treated them simply as mere alternatives.

But grounded theory offered a more productive, promising, and engaging orientation. It provided the beginnings of a rigorous and methodical approach to the study of social contexts and artifacts. The initial trilogy was not developed as a full-fledged method but rather as a manifesto with proven examples that might provide convincing evidence for this new approach. The ensuing decades then witnessed various ways in which the method could be developed—sometimes in divergent ways—and also demonstrated that attempts to balance experience with analysis are never once-and-for-all resolutions, but they usually serve as the next iteration in the development of social understanding both on the part of social actors and those researching social contexts. Grounded theory, with its aim of encouraging the development of *substantive* theories—that is, a "theory developed for a substantive or empirical area of sociological inquiry, such as patient care, geriatric life styles etc." (Glaser & Strauss, 1967, p. 77)—afforded a balance between reason and relativism, aiming to have an impact on practice and action within the substantive area: Something that also lies at the heart of many aspects of psychological research and practice. The challenge that Glaser and Strauss threw down to orthodox sociological research provided a basis for a similar challenge from within the psychological research community, particularly for those who were keen to advocate approaches that treated the individual as the starting point for effective practice, supplementing or remedying impersonal and objectifying medical standpoints.

OUTLINE OF GROUNDED THEORY

Grounded theory includes a systematic, inductive, and comparative approach for conducting inquiry for the purpose of constructing theory. The method is designed to encourage researchers in persistent interaction with their data while remaining constantly involved with their emerging analyses. Data collection and analysis proceed simultaneously and each informs and streamlines the other. Grounded theory builds empirical checks into the analytic process and leads researchers to examine all possible theoretical explanations for their empirical findings. The iterative process of moving back and forth between empirical data and emerging analysis makes the collected data progressively more focused and the analysis successively more theoretical.

Systematic, Inductive, and Comparative

One of the key innovations that Glaser and Strauss offered was the outline of a systematic approach to the conduct of qualitative research. We do not mean to imply that up to that point qualitative research had been an unsystematic endeavor, but publication of *The Discovery of Grounded Theory* (Glaser & Strauss, 1967) set down a challenge for those who contended that qualitative research was incoherent, impressionistic, and descriptive—perhaps at best a potentially useful preparatory phase for "real" quantitative research.

Persistent Interaction, Constant Involvement, and Iterative

This concept of induction is encapsulated in one of the early terms used for grounded theory: *the method of constant comparison*. The idea is that conceptual development occurs through a process of comparison between a range of different research artifacts—statements, findings, characterizations of incidents, and codes. This comparative process relates to the iterative aspect of the method, whereby data collection and analysis are interlinked as simultaneous phases, in contrast to many other qualitative and quantitative approaches in which analysis only starts once the data collection phase has been completed. The researcher engages in persistent interaction with data and analysis, identifying patterns or higher level abstractions as a result of prolonged immersion in, and engagement with, the data.

CONSTRUCTING THEORY

The objective of the method is to develop more refined concepts and theories rather than merely reinforcing or clarifying existing ones. Moreover, the theoretical statements that develop from the use of grounded theory do not claim the status of grand or overarching theories, but rather they are initially offered as substantive ones. This term has a specific meaning in the context of grounded theory writing—that is, statements that draw on a specified context and have theoretical power constrained by that context.

As we have argued elsewhere (but specifically in Bryant, 2009), the meaning of the term *theory* is fraught with ambiguity and ambivalence. For some the term is an accolade, hence citations for Nobel prizes often mention that the winners have made major contributions to some theory or another. Conversely, those wishing to disparage a concept may use the term in precisely the opposite sense, and hence those arguing in favor of intelligent design refer to Darwin's work as only a theory of evolution. So, in one sense, *theory* implies something along the lines of conjecture or supposition, but in another sense, it implies something with an enhanced status, attained only after exhaustive efforts to test and challenge it. This latter meaning is certainly what Glaser and Strauss had in mind in arguing for theories to be grounded. Although when a grounded theory is first developed, it can hardly claim this status, which can only come with time and the attention of others.

To give readers an overview of the method, we will now consider the following key topics in turn: coding and sampling, memo-writing, theoretical saturation, and theoretical sensitivity.

Coding and Sampling

In grounded theory the initial data gathering should be performed within a specific context, but with a wide remit. This approach might sound somewhat inchoate and problematic, but in many instances, it proves an effective starting point, offering researchers the possibility of fairly unconstrained investigation of the domain from the outset of their research. For instance, in Glaser and Strauss's (1965) initial work, they cast their net across the whole spectrum of people and actions in the hospital setting in which they began their research.

Once some initial data has been gathered, it can then be analyzed and configured using the technique of open coding. Unlike earlier forms of coding, which involved application of previously prepared coding structures to the data, grounded theory is formed on the basis of investigation of the data from which potential codes can be derived. Although this method does not start from a clear and specific research question, it certainly does offer a series of more generic questions for the guidance of researchers. This involves asking a subset of questions, such as the following:

- What is this data about?—i.e. the researcher should not assume that the context and import of the data is necessarily apparent; the research orientation should allow for serendipity and surprise;
- What is this data a study of?—i.e. in many instances grounded theory researchers have found that data collected with perhaps one issue in mind often yields more profound analysis with regard to unexpected issues than to those planned at the outset;
- What is going on?—i.e. not simply assuming that what people say or talk about are the core or primary activities;
- What are people doing?—i.e. investigating social processes;
- What is the person saying?—i.e. not merely taking down their utterances, but looking more deeply into these;
- What do these actions and statements take for granted?—i.e. maintaining a constant awareness of the tension between "experience" and "analysis";
- How do structure and context serve to support, maintain, impede or change these actions and statements?

The initial codes are then the result of the context-based interaction between the researcher(s) and the data.

Initial coding begins as soon as the researcher has data because grounded theorists engage in simultaneous data collection and analysis. Coding consists of constructing short-hand analytic labels that define data, synthesize and sort them, and initiate the analytic substance and direction of their study. Grounded theorists aim to make their codes short, incisive, and initially spontaneous (Charmaz, 2006). Through coding early data, grounded theorists direct subsequent data gathering and begin thinking analytically about their data. Essentially, coding means that the researcher breaks the data into fragments and labels these fragments. Each label not only identifies its respective fragment but takes this bit of data apart.

Grounded theory coding forces the researcher to engage with the data, and its inductive character encourages him or her to work from fresh views about what is happening in the data without applying preconceived concepts. The researchers' standpoints and starting points shape but should not determine how they view and code data. Grounded theorists code for actions and, consistent with Glaser's (1978) definitive statement, typically seek to use gerunds, the noun form of the verb, to capture actions and to gain an analytic handle on emerging ideas (see Exhibit 3.1). Note how Kathy Charmaz's codes use gerunds such as "identifying past self," "being a superwoman," and "discovering a creative self."

By coding for actions, grounded theorists can compare what is happening in fragments of data and begin seeing links between data that may foretell the analytic story in these data. During initial coding, the researcher conducts line-by-line coding as a heuristic device to interact with the data and to see it anew. As coding ensues, the grounded theorist compares data with codes, and codes with codes. The aim of the coding exercise is to complete the comparative analytic process in a manageable fashion, allowing the grounded theorist to see and theorize processes in the data. This type of coding fosters constructing successively more abstract theoretical categories.

The iterative nature of grounded theory leads the researcher to gather more data about codes that appear to be pertinent and relevant to the specific research context, and to keep coding these data and writing memos about them. Grounded theorists focus their research questions as they explore a general area; they do not begin with a specific preconceived

---

Exhibit 3.1
Initial Coding: Line-by-Line Coding

Coding	Statement
Identifying past self—an awful martyr; disclaiming martyrdom Feeling badly about past identity; seeing self go through phases	**S:** And I used to be an awful martyr, but I never thought I was a martyr, and I'm not anymore. And that's—and then when I found out I was a martyr, I felt terrible. But then I got over that too, you know, it's funny how you go through the phases.
	I: In which ways did you see yourself as a martyr?
Explaining martyrdom—linking it to complaining Enumerating multiple involvements Redefining involvements Being a superwoman Reducing involvements Rejecting past involvements Seeing a choice Learning from the past Redefining the past Wanting to change the past Recalling earlier negative self-definition Discovering intelligent self Regretting past Acknowledging must start from the present Discovering creative self Having discounted talents Having seen self as ordinary Becoming self-aware Viewing self-awareness as contingent on positive view of self	**S:** Well, I would work hard at things and then complain about it. You know, I may not complain all the time, but it would be like, "Oh, God, you know, I travel a hundred miles a day and put in 40 hours a week and I work 7 days a week, I'm working two jobs and milking two cows and raising three kids, and got a garden and a drill team and a 4-H group—and I did all these things—I belong to five horse clubs and—and it's like, I look back and it's like God, what an idiot. I have to be superwoman, you know. And now I don't belong much to clubs and I don't like crowds of people and I don't have to do all these things. And it's, I don't know, it's just, because it's a learning, it's like I'm 52 years old and it's like, God, you know, and I, all that's happened, it's like I didn't learn anything until I hit my forties. Then you think, "God, if I could go back, I could change so many things." I always thought I was stupid, and I'm finding out I'm really not, you know, I'm really fairly intelligent. I wish I would have got more education and done some different things, but I just have to go on and do what I can do now. I never knew I was creative . . . I'll have other people say that "I can't do that [artwork]." And I always thought, "well, anybody could do that," I never thought it was anything special. You know, but I guess all of that [being aware of her talents] comes with feeling good about yourself.

Note. S = initial of participant's pseudonym; I = interviewer.

---

research question (Charmaz, 1990, 2006, 2008; Glaser, 1978, 1998, 2003; Thornberg & Charmaz, in press). The researcher takes the most frequent or significant codes and investigates how they might work as analysis moves toward more focused coding. Thus, the researcher will seek to use these codes for further analysis: Do they shed light on the context in some manner? Do they provide terms with explanatory power? Are they likely to provide a basis for further conceptual development, investigation, and analysis? The aim is to use these codes as the basis for tentative categories. If necessary, further line-by-line or keypoint-by-keypoint coding is carried out to define other potentially useful codes.

These initial codes are then used to guide later stages of data gathering; thus, there is a gradual development in the targeting and focus of data gathering once the analysis is under way. So, whereas the initial coding is fairly nebulous and unconstrained, later stages of research become more anchored in and directed by the developing analysis. During the early stages of research, grounded theorists who conduct interviews choose their research participants according to whether they have had the relevant experience for the topic of inquiry such as being a mental health client or having been diagnosed with a postpartum depression. But after grounded theorists have raised fruitful codes to tentative categories, their sampling stems from the categories themselves (Charmaz, 2006; Glaser, 1978, 1998, 2003; Glaser & Strauss, 1967; Thornberg & Charmaz, in press). This later form of sampling is termed *theoretical sampling*, which can be defined as

> a type of grounded theory sampling in which the researcher aims to develop

the properties of his or her developing categories or theory, not to sample of randomly selected populations or to sample representative distributions of a particular population. When engaging in theoretical sampling, the researcher seeks people, events, or information to illuminate and define the boundaries and relevance of the categories. Because the purpose of theoretical sampling is to sample to develop the theoretical categories, conducting it can take the researcher across substantive areas. (Bryant & Charmaz, 2007c, p. 611)

In many of the papers in which psychologists evoke or use grounded theory, the initial stage is often more specific and constrained, with the research being explicitly developed from the start to investigate a particular group of people exhibiting specific skills and behaviors. This *purposive* sampling does not invalidate the use of grounded theory provided that it is not undertaken with a particular hypothesis or set of research questions already articulated, in which case, grounded theory would not be an appropriate method to use.

Studies such as those by Abrams, Dornig, and Curran (2009); Jewell (2007); and Harborne, Wolpert, and Clare (2004) used focused or purposive sampling from the outset; some refer to this as convenience sampling. Cagnetta and Cicognani (1999) in their study exemplified a fairly common use of grounded theory, not restricted to psychological research. As the title of their article, "Surviving a Serious Traffic Accident," indicates, they were concerned with studying the different ways in which people had come through a specific experience; hence, they chose sampling that was initially purposive and focused. They also set up interviews with six main issues in mind and completed all interviews before starting the analysis. This might seem to preclude the use of grounded theory, except that the issues were fairly open ended and far nearer to the generic questions specified earlier in this section, than to specific research questions. Although they did not iterate between data collection and analysis, they coded the first five interviews using a

line-by-line strategy, resulting in more than 250 categories, but they realized that one specific aspect—or dimension—was common to all the interviews. This aspect, time, was then used as a guide or heuristic device in the later stages of coding the other interviews.

Similarly, Propp et al. (2010) specified a research question centered on patient-care teams and selected interviewees accordingly, collecting all the interview materials and only later coding them using the procedures recommended by Strauss and Corbin (1998). Again this departs somewhat from initial, full-blown ideas about the implementation of grounded theory, but it seems to have been necessitated by the demands of the relevant ethical review board, a common issue that arises when researchers wish to use grounded theory. Ethics committees often require clear research protocols and targeted ethical practices with clearly specified participants. If such preparatory materials are mandated, this need not preclude use of grounded theory as Propp's research demonstrated.

Memo-Writing

Memo-writing is an intermediate stage of analytic writing that occurs between coding and writing a first draft of a paper or chapter. Memos are a place to record and explore ideas. Because memos consist of analytic conversations with the self, grounded theorists use them to explore ideas, compare data, define gaps in data collection, and develop analytic categories. In the brief memo in Exhibit 3.2, written early in the research project, Kathy Charmaz explored the meaning of the codes in Exhibit 3.1. Note that "Reconciling Past and Present Selves" does not appear as a code in the excerpt. Instead, it is a tentative category that subsumes these codes. In a sense, "Reconciling Past and Present Selves" first emerges as a code of the codes taken together and thus must be put to analytic and empirical test. The memo explores this category, looks at the data and codes accounted by it, and suggests implications of it. Charmaz was beginning to tease out the analytic properties of this tentative category but considerable work needed to be done by comparing it with data from other research participants and defining the conditions under which this category is evident.

Exhibit 3.2
Example of an Early Memo

Reconciling Past and Present Selves

Reconciling past and present selves means that a person accounts for discordant views between the past self and the present self. Such reconciling has a direction, entails definition of past and present selves, and informs present meanings and actions. Many ill people look back with nostalgia and longing for the self that they had been in the past (compare with E. and R.). In this case, however, S. defines her past self in light of her present assumptions and the self she has become. Not only does she see herself as learning from the past but also she separates her present self from her past self and the actions that supported it. The images reflected of this past self are now jarring and thus need to be accounted for and put to rest. By juxtaposing past and present, S. engages in interpretive work to account for shifts and changes that contribute to her present self, one that she defines as vastly preferable to the self of her past. Through identifying her past self as an "awful martyr," "an idiot," and "superwoman," S. distances her present, aware self from the person she was in the past. The codes reflect the comparative process in which she is engaged as she disavows her past. By enumerating, redefining, and rejecting her past multiple involvements, she sees herself learning from the past and realizing that she has choices about who she can become. Through engaging in this comparative process, she validates her present self by rejecting her past self.

This comparative process is not without regrets. S. expresses feeling badly about her past identity, the complaining which she now takes as martyrdom, and the direction her life took in the past. A certain sadness and shame permeates S.'s account, which is then partially counterbalanced by the positive views in discovering a creative and intelligent self.

Are S's reflections accurate? We don't know. What is important is her conviction that she now sees the truth in the pejorative views she holds of the past.

Grounded theorists engage in memo-writing throughout the research process. Successive memos gain analytic precision, conceptual power, and establish theoretical relationships. By raising increasingly abstract questions in memos that inform further empirical checks, grounded theorists use memos as a tool for theory construction.

Theoretical Saturation

Charmaz (2006) defined *theoretical saturation* as "the point at which gathering more data about a theoretical category reveals no new properties nor yields any further theoretical insights about the emerging grounded theory" (Bryant & Charmaz, 2007c, p. 611). Assessment of this saturation is in the hands of the researcher or research team, and thus it can cause concern for both novice and experienced researchers. Sometimes it is fairly clear that new sources of focused data—interviews, observations, and the like—are reinforcing the researcher's earlier analysis of the theoretical category but adding very little that had not already become apparent. If so, then further pursuit of data will bolster confidence, but the researcher's time and other resources can now be better spent on analysis, abstraction, and integration of theoretical categories than on gathering more data.

Bowen (2008) made some important points in his discussion of saturation, noting that it is "rarely evident in research reports" (p. 137), explaining that discussion of the way in which it has been achieved should be made explicit. He referred to an article by Caelli, Ray, and Mill (2003) where they argued that

> evidence of saturation must be given [*by whom*] in the presentation of the data [*to whom*] and discussed [*by and with whom*] via the forms in which it was recognized [*by whom*] during the analysis [*performed by*]. (quoted in Bowen, 2008, p. 137)

Unfortunately, the use of the passive voice in this extract effaces some of the key issues as we have indicated in the italicized inserts. The active role of the researcher—and the fact that even if the research is largely conducted by one person, others are usually involved if only in a supervisory or advisory capacity—is at the heart of recent developments of grounded theory.

Theoretical Sensitivity

In our introduction to *The Sage Handbook of Ground Theory* (Bryant & Charmaz, 2007a), we argued that many aspects of grounded theory were paradoxically both *simple* and *skillful*. Thus many writers on grounded theory, to indicate that the method is ready and accessible for inexperienced researchers, will stress that certain aspects such as coding or memo-writing are simple and straightforward (Holton, 2007), whereas in practice this is often not the case. This paradox or ambiguity is particularly evident in discussions concerning *theoretical sensitivity*. Glaser's book (1978) remains a key source of enlightenment, but development of the skill does not come easily or naturally. Holton (2007) rightly asserted that "theoretical sensitivity requires two things of the researcher—analytic temperament and competence" (p. 275). Kelle (2007) dealt with this issue at some length, and he concluded that "the previously presented two basic rules, (1) to abstain from forcing preconceived concepts, and (2) to utilize theoretical sensibility in this process, are obviously difficult to reconcile" (p. 198). Moreover, he noted that in the years following publication of *Discovery* (Glaser & Strauss, 1967), the "apparent antagonism between emergence and theoretical sensitivity remained a major problem for teaching the methodology of grounded theory" (p. 198). He offered a useful definition of the term: "In developing categories the sociologist should employ *theoretical sensitivity*, which means the ability to *see relevant data* and to reflect upon empirical data material with the help of theoretical terms" (Kelle, 2007, p. 211).

Li and Shyu (2007) referred to theoretical sensitivity being increased by reading literature from such relevant disciplines as psychology, sociology, and nursing as well as from discussions with "nurse researchers, a psychologist, and a physician" (p. 275). Kokotsaki (2007) argued that development of the skill is facilitated by the systematic nature of procedures of grounded theory (p. 645).

Theoretical saturation and theoretical sensitivity necessarily evoke discussion of the active role of the researcher, the nature of research data, and the interaction between the two. This interaction has been at the heart of discussions about grounded theory since the 1990s, and it is the basis of the constructivist articulation of grounded theory, a topic to which we now turn in discussing issues around data and grounded theory.

DATA AND GROUNDED THEORY

The expression "all is data" is constantly used by Glaser in his grounded theory writings, and as it stands it makes perfectly good sense. Although grounded theory is usually associated with interview data, this type of data is not an indelible part of the method. Taking the invocation at face value, grounded theory can be used in conjunction with anything that can be treated as data, including documents, literature, previously published research findings, video and audio recordings, survey findings, field notes, and so on. Glaser has recently written two accounts, one dealing with the use of quantitative data in grounded theory (2008) and the other (2009) applying the method to a specific book—*The Sage Handbook of Grounded Theory* by Bryant and Charmaz (2007c).

In the psychological literature, a similarly broad use of data can be found. Kearney and O'Sullivan (2003) used grounded theory to synthesize a number of studies that were identified as relevant to the general research topic (health–behavior change). The researchers searched through a range of journals, selecting more than 50 articles from which they then chose 14 studies. Johnson and Delaney (2007) gathered data by extended observation, which they reported took more than 400 hours. The researchers met each week "to discuss the observations, the initial coding of the incidents, common themes that were emerging, and the direction that the study was taking" (Johnson & Delaney, 2007, p. 43). Eventually they arrived at an initial scheme and core category. They then moved on to a series of interviews, with potential participants identified on the basis of the initial findings—an example of theoretical sampling. Cooney (2006) used two focus groups and participant observation; the former were "formal field group interviews following a semi-structured question format" (p. 220). Again the questions were open-ended rather than related to a specific hypothesis or research aim: They were related to welfare and work. For example, "Why are people on welfare? What's good about welfare? What's bad about welfare? Why is it important to work? What's bad about work? and What are barriers to working?" (Cooney, 2006, p. 217). Cooney then used the answers in a further step, listing them on posters and asking participants to rank the responses for each question.

Thus, researchers may adapt the method to studies that do not use interviews or may supplement interview sources with others. But concerns arise when the phrase "all is data" is assumed to mean something akin to "data is all." This common misconception derives from statements in *Discovery* (Glaser & Strauss, 1967) along the lines that theories emerge from the data, a trope that can be found in the later, individual writings of both Glaser and Strauss. So although Glaser's critique of Strauss and Corbin's work (1990, 1998) included the accusation that Strauss had replaced "emergence" with "forcing" (see Glaser, 1992), Strauss and Corbin argued that "the researcher begins with an area of study and allows the theory to emerge from the data" (1998, p. 12).

This problematic, or perhaps unsophisticated, idea of data has been critiqued extensively for some time. In our writings, both separately (Bryant 2002, 2003; Charmaz, 2000, 2003, 2006) and more recently in concert (Bryant & Charmaz, 2007a, 2007b), we have argued that Glaser and Strauss's use of the metaphor of *emergence* is misleading and ill founded. Its use effaces the active role played by the researcher—or research team—in interrogating the data and developing codes and categories thereafter: This is the basis of the constructivist view of grounded theory. Glaser and Strauss argued that theory is *discovered*, arising and emerging from data that have an independent existence, distinct to and external from the researcher. For constructivists, neither data nor theories are discovered. Rather, researchers as social actors *construct* grounded theories on the basis of prior experience and current concerns, and interactions with people, perspectives, and research practices. Constructivism, as the term implies, is founded on the argument that social reality is socially constructed, with social actors continually contributing to the maintenance of social order and social change. This focus on the way in which social reality is constructed offers further complementarities between grounded theory and what Madill and Gough (2008) referred to as the "broadly humanistic qualitative methods [that] were developed as one

response to a wider countercultural critique of traditional sources of authority" (p. 254).

The outcome of a constructivist basis for grounded theory has been a plethora of work demonstrating the ways in which grounded theory needs to take account of the positionality and reflexivity of the researcher—Mruck and Mey (2007) and Green, Creswell, Shope, and Clark (2007) offered useful overviews and further reading. It has also led to far clearer understanding of the influence of the philosophy of pragmatism in grounded theory, including the ways in which this can shed new light on grounded theory, qualitative research in general, and arguments about knowledge claims. (This important aspect of grounded theory cannot be developed any further at this juncture, but interested readers should refer to Bryant, 2009; also see Reichertz, 2007; Strubing, 2007.) Some of the key aspects of the constructivist critique of Glaser and Strauss, and an understanding of the divergent ways in which their work developed, can be understood through consideration of the role of codes, concepts, and categories in grounded theory.

Codes, Concepts, and Categories

Researchers using grounded theory often find themselves inundated with codes once they start analyzing their data. Cagnetta and Cicognani (1999) reported more than 500 codes resulting from the analysis of their interviews. A large number of initial codes is not uncommon, and, in some cases, scholars have criticized grounded theory as leading to unwieldy results, impossible for researchers to manage and comprehend. On the other hand, the literature is replete with papers in which the use of grounded theory is claimed, but it goes no further than some preliminary and incomplete attempts at open coding.

The grounded theory literature is the source of confusion regarding the nomenclature around codes, concepts, and categories. Often authors use terms interchangeably, so that there seems to be no difference between codes and concepts for some and between concepts and categories for others. The easiest resolution of this is to regard codes as the most numerous and lowest levels of analysis, with categories at intermediate levels of abstraction and concepts at still higher levels. In the *Sage Handbook* (Bryant & Charmaz, 2007c), we provided a discursive glossary that indicates different authors' use of these, and other, terms. The source of the confusion can be traced to *Discovery* (Glaser & Strauss, 1967), as Dey (2007) has pointed out:

> Glaser and Strauss described categories as "conceptual elements of a theory" (1967: 36). Categories emerge initially from a close engagement with data, but can achieve a higher level of abstraction through a process of "constant comparison" which allows their theoretical elaboration and integration. (p. 168)

As has been mentioned, the process of moving from data to initial codes and then on to concepts and categories is at the heart of grounded theory, yet it is all too often left clouded in mystery—on the one hand, being characterized as easy or obvious, and on the other, explained using equally enigmatic terms such as *saturation* or *theoretical sensitivity*.

Echoes of this perplexity can be found in some writings of researchers who have struggled with grounded theory both successfully and unsuccessfully. According to Kearney (2007) much of Strauss's efforts in the 1980s and 1990s were spent explaining to others how to use grounded theory. He was constantly asked for simple guidelines for using the method, and eventually he published the *Qualitative Analysis for Social Scientists* in 1987. Students demanded still further explication of grounded theory, and the result was *Basics of Qualitative Research* published in 1990 (Strauss & Corbin, 1990).

Many researchers trying to use grounded theory maintained a constant demand for guidance on its basic procedures, such as coding and the development of categories. In part, this may well be because the research community imbues inexperienced researchers with a lack of confidence in their own powers of abstraction and conceptualization. Hence their requests for guidance; but all too often, heuristic guidelines become recipe-like formulae that have the potential to undermine the basic premises of a research approach that was explicitly developed as a free-flowing and flexible response to a far more rigid

orthodoxy. We make the general point that anything offered as a heuristic will rapidly be seen as algorithmic; flexibility and suggestiveness are thrown out in favor of more certain and reassuring mechanistic rules and all too rigid structures.

So we would reinforce and extend Glaser's stress on gerunds and focus not on the researcher, the data, and the concepts but rather on researching, abstracting, and conceptualizing. This lies at the heart of the constructivist account of grounded theory and leads to a discussion of the role of reflexivity in research.

GROUNDED THEORY AND THE RESEARCH PROCESS: REFLEXIVITY

Much of the grounded theory literature gives the impression that the research process involves a lone researcher developing codes, concepts, and perhaps eventually a grounded theory. In fact, from its earliest inception, grounded theory was a team effort; the early work was the result of explicit collaboration between Glaser and Strauss (1965) and Quint (1967). Strauss's later research was also team based, as Wiener (2007) has explained. This team approach implies that discussion and dialogue lie at the heart of the method, and range across all stages of data gathering, analysis, and conceptualization. Moreover the use of memos means that reflection and reflexivity are constant activities, requiring researchers to articulate their thoughts and ideas as the research develops and then to use these statements as data for later stages: again showing the wisdom behind Glaser's dictum "all is data."

The psychology research literature exemplifies these features and also shows the ways in which psychologists have sought to use teamwork and reflexivity for forms of member checking and triangulation. Hall, Long, Bermbach, Jordan, and Patterson (2005) outlined an extensive team project, specifically designed to incorporate varying levels of experience, skills, commitment, and foster interdisciplinary research. Harborne et al. (2004) explained that they worked as a team during the coding phase (using Strauss and Corbin's [1990, 1998] approach), later enhancing their work with "credibility checks" and double coding by a "qualified clinical psychologist" together with "discussion with colleagues . . . to assess whether the data resonated with their experience" (p. 330).

Reflection and reflexivity necessarily lead to the issue of the relationship between the view from the inside and the outside, and as has been explained earlier, grounded theory offers a basis for an iterative dialogue between the two, incorporating the possibility for some form of empathic understanding but upholding the researcher's viewpoint. The latter is the basis for ultimately deciding on such issues as saturation and ensuing conceptualization. Stineman, Rist, and Burke (2009) referred to Schön's concept of "reflection in action" (p. 26) in their discussion of objective and subjective views of disability. Their actual use of grounded theory is restricted to coding, referring to team members each developing "their own taxonomy" (p. 26), which are then combined.

VALIDITY AND USEFULNESS

All qualitative research outcomes and findings have to contend with the issue of validity; in fact so too do quantitative ones, but these outcomes have recourse to a readily available and generally accepted set of procedures and practices for demonstrating validity. For grounded theory, these matters are also bound up with the origins of the method since Glaser and Strauss (1967) specifically took issue with what they termed "verification"—that is, the strategy whereby researchers were encouraged to use existing theories from which they then derived hypotheses to be verified through standard and accepted processes of deduction and test.

In the early statements of the method, researchers were urged to develop theories that met the criteria of *fit*, *grab*, and *modifiability* and that somehow *worked* or *earned their way* (Glaser & Strauss, 1967). These criteria sound vague and nebulous, but the general tenor of such guidance resonates with the pragmatist view of knowledge and theoretical statements, a tradition that was highly influential on Strauss's intellectual formation. For pragmatists such as John Dewey (1938) and William James (1907/1981), knowledge about the world was always an active process. They specifically offered a critique of what they termed the *spectator view of*

knowledge, which implied a contemplative and passive orientation to the world. They argued that theories and concepts are best seen as tools; they should promote our understanding in the sense of helping us act in a more effective or insightful manner. Strauss never fully developed the pragmatist viewpoint in his grounded theory writings (see Bryant, 2009), but in his last book (Strauss, 1993), he defined pragmatism as a "red thread" (p. 22) running continually through his work.

Given this ambiguous tradition within grounded theory, and the continual need to counter the credibility gap between the qualitative and the quantitative camps, it is not surprising to find that many of those using grounded theory in their research go to some lengths to explain how their work meets such criteria as validity, rigor, coherence, and so on. Charmaz offered four criteria for grounded theory studies (2006, pp. 182–183): credibility, originality, resonance, and usefulness. *Credibility* means having sufficient data to support the researcher's theoretical categories and claims. *Originality* relies on bringing new insights to the studied phenomenon. *Resonance* refers to whether the researcher has provided an in-depth portrayal of the phenomenon, and *usefulness* means that research participants can apply the researcher's analysis to their realities and other researchers could build on this analysis.

Psychological researchers have sought to develop similar criteria within their disciplinary and professional domains. Elliott, Fischer, and Rennie (1999) referred to Lincoln and Guba's focus on "trustworthiness" as a criterion, itself centered on a new understanding of traditional criteria, such as credibility, transferability, dependability, and confirmability. This last aspect broaches the question of whose confirmation might be sought (e.g., other researchers, domain experts, social actors, or the research subjects). As a consequence many such *strategies for rigor* include *member checking*, resonating with the quote from Turner (1983). Thus Cooney (2006) referred to this form of verification and claimed that "we did find we achieved clarity on meaning," although she noted that "Glaser argues vehemently against member checking" (p. 221). Harborne et al. (2004) stated that they did not ask participants to review the findings, something that they see as a limitation of the study. Midence and O'Neill (1999) specifically sought verification "by checking the findings with the participants, and asking them to comment on how these categories reflected their experience" (p. 277). Propp et al. (2010) also mentioned face-to-face member checks and inclusion of others with specialist knowledge, something that is seen by some as helping to develop theoretical sensitivity.

Yardley (2000) in a general discussion of the issue of quality in qualitative research argued that the criteria for legitimacy and quality need to be "meaningful to those people for whose benefit the research was intended" (p. 219), but this is not to abdicate the analyst's intellectual independence. She referred to Riessman's criteria of commitment, rigor, transparency, and coherence but stated that the most important issues are impact and utility. Thus, a key theorist's work may be difficult and somewhat inaccessible but highly influential; Yardley herself mentioned Foucault in this regard. In so doing, Yardley raised the issue of something akin to *sensitizing concepts*—a key feature of Chicago sociology—so that the value of research or any other form of insight can be seen in terms of its *sociocultural impact*.

Teram, Schachter, and Stalker (2005) referred to Kvale's threefold view of validity: communicative validity, pragmatic validity, and craftsmanship involving continuous checking, questioning, and theoretical interpretation. This last form they specifically associated with the constant comparative analysis of grounded theory. In this sense, grounded theory appears to offer a form of self-checking self-validation; however, this is to mistake the results of grounded theory, which are far better understood as the basis for *plausible* accounts rather than *validated* ones.

THE CURRENT STATE OF THE METHOD AND GUIDE FOR FURTHER READING

Grounded theory has developed significantly since its emergence in the mid-1960s. Those wishing to find out more about using the method can find a clear introductory account in Charmaz (2006). Glaser continues to develop his thoughts on the

method, and his recent works deal with issues such as formal grounded theories (Glaser, 2006) and the use of quantitative data with the method (Glaser, 2008). His book *Theoretical Sensitivity* (Glaser, 1978) remains one of the key texts in the articulation of the method. Bryant (2009) offered an account of the influence of pragmatism in the development of grounded theory as well as an overview of many of the issues that researchers often encounter when considering use of the method in their work.

The *Sage Handbook of Grounded Theory* (Bryant & Charmaz, 2007c), published to coincide with the 40th anniversary of *Discovery* (Glaser & Strauss, 1967), offered a challenging variety of contributions from researchers seeking to use and develop the method across a wide range of disciplines and contexts. The method is truly international, and Glaser is proud that his mailing list and sales cover more than 50 countries. Given this popularity and growth, it is not surprising that there has been some divergence among those writing about grounded theory—something we have covered in recent writings (Bryant, 2003, 2009; Bryant & Charmaz, 2007a, 2007b, 2011; Charmaz, 2000, 2008). This divergence should be seen as an indication of vitality and growth; the method is flourishing and the ultimate test of this is the range and value of outcomes that are generated by its use by researchers.

References

Abrams, L. S., Dornig, K., & Curran, L. (2009). Barriers to service use for postpartum depression symptoms among low-income ethnic minority mothers in the United States. *Qualitative Health Research, 19*, 535–551. doi:10.1177/1049732309332794

Bowen, G. A. (2008). Naturalistic inquiry and the saturation concept: A research note. *Qualitative Research, 8*, 137–152. doi:10.1177/1468794107085301

Bryant, A. (2002). Re-grounding grounded theory. *Journal of Information Technology Theory and Application, 4*, 25–42.

Bryant, A. (2003). A constructive/ist response to Glaser. *Forum Qualitative Sozialforschung/Forum: Qualitative Social Research, 4*. Retrieved from http://www.qualitative-research.net/index.php/fqs/article/view/757

Bryant, A. (2009). Grounded theory and pragmatism: The curious case of Anselm Strauss. *Forum Qualitative*

Sozialforschung/Forum: Qualitative. Social Research,
10, 1–38.

Bryant, A., & Charmaz, K. (Eds.). (2007a). Editors'
introduction grounded theory research: Methods
and practices. In A. Bryant & K. Charmaz (Eds.),
The Sage handbook of grounded theory (pp. 1–28).
London, England: Sage.

Bryant, A., & Charmaz, K. (Eds.). (2007b). Grounded
theory in historical perspective. In A. Bryant & K.
Charmaz (Eds.), *The Sage handbook of grounded*
theory (pp. 31–57). London, England: Sage.

Bryant, A., & Charmaz, K. (Eds.). (2007c). *The Sage*
handbook of grounded theory. London, England: Sage.

Bryant, A., & Charmaz, K. (2011). Grounded theory. In
M. Williams & W. P. Vogt (Eds.), *Sage handbook of*
innovation in social research methods (pp. 205–227).
London, England: Sage.

Cagnetta, E., & Cicognani, E. (1999). Surviving a serious
traffic accident: Adaptation processes and quality of
life. *Journal of Health Psychology, 4*, 551–564.

Caelli, K., Ray, L., & Mill, J. (2003) "Clear as mud":
Toward greater clarity in generic qualitative research.
International Journal of Qualitative Methods, 2, 1–24.

Charmaz, K. (1990). Discovering chronic illness: Using
grounded theory. *Social Science and Medicine, 30*,
1161–1172. doi:10.1016/0277-9536(90)90256-R

Charmaz, K. (2000). Grounded theory: Objectivist and
constructivist methods. In N. K. Denzin & Y. S.
Lincoln (Eds.), *Handbook of qualitative research* (2nd
ed., pp. 509–535). Thousand Oaks, CA: Sage.

Charmaz, K. (2003). Grounded theory. In M. Lewis-Beck,
A. E. Bryman, & T. Futing Liao (Eds.), *The Sage*
encyclopedia of social science research methods
(pp. 440–444). London, England: Sage.

Charmaz, K. (2006). *Constructing grounded theory a*
practical guide through qualitative analysis. London,
England: Sage.

Charmaz, K. (2008). Grounded theory as an emergent
method. In S. N. Hesse-Biber & P. Leavy (Eds.), *The*
handbook of emergent methods (pp. 155–170). New
York, NY: Guilford Press.

Cooney, K. (2006). Mothers first, not work first: Listening
to welfare clients in job training. *Qualitative Social*
Work, 5, 217–235. doi:10.1177/1473325006064258

Corbin, J., & Strauss, A. (2008). *Basics of qualitative*
research (3rd ed.). Thousand Oaks, CA: Sage.

Covan, E. (2007). The discovery of grounded theory
in practice: The legacy of multiple mentors. In A.
Bryant & K. Charmaz (Eds.), *The Sage handbook of*
grounded theory (pp. 58–74). London, England: Sage.

Denzin, N., & Lincoln, Y. (1994). *The handbook of quali-*
tative research (1st ed.). Thousand Oaks, CA: Sage.

Denzin, N., & Lincoln, Y. (2000). *The handbook of quali-*
tative research (2nd ed.). Thousand Oaks, CA: Sage.

Denzin, N., & Lincoln, Y. (2005). *The handbook of quali-*
tative research (3rd ed.). Thousand Oaks, CA: Sage.

Dewey, J. (1938). *Logic: The theory of inquiry.* New York,
NY: Holt, Rinehart & Winston.

Dey, I. (2007). Grounding categories. In A. Bryant &
K. Charmaz (Eds.), *The Sage handbook of grounded*
theory (pp. 167–190). London, England: Sage.

Durkheim, E. (1938). *The rules of the sociological method.*
New York, NY: Free Press.

Elliott, R., Fischer, C., & Rennie, D. (1999). Evolving
guidelines for publication of qualitative research
studies in psychology and related fields. *British*
Journal of Clinical Psychology, 38, 215–229.
doi:10.1348/014466599162782

Fassinger, R. (2005). Paradigms, praxis, problems, and
promise: Grounded theory in counseling psychology research. *Journal of Counseling Psychology, 52*,
156–166. doi:10.1037/0022-0167.52.2.156

Foucault, M. (1967). *Madness and civilization.* London,
England: Tavistock.

Foucault, M. (1973). *The birth of the clinic.* London,
England: Tavistock.

Garfinkel, H. (1967). *Studies in ethnomethodology.*
Englewood Cliffs, NJ: Prentice-Hall.

Geertz, C. (1973). *The interpretation of cultures.* New
York, NY: Basic Books.

Glaser, B. (1978). *Theoretical sensitivity.* Mill Valley, CA:
Sociology Press.

Glaser, B. (1992). *Basics of grounded theory: Emergence vs.*
forcing. Mill Valley, CA: Sociology Press.

Glaser, B. (Ed.). (1996). *Gerund grounded theory: The*
basic social process dissertation. Mill Valley, CA:
Sociology Press

Glaser, B. (1998). *Doing grounded theory: Issues and dis-*
cussions. Mill Valley, CA: Sociology Press.

Glaser, B. (2003). *The grounded theory perspective II.* Mill
Valley, CA: Sociology Press.

Glaser, B. (2006). *Doing formal theory: A proposal.* Mill
Valley, CA: Sociology Press.

Glaser, B. (2008). *Doing quantitative grounded theory.* Mill
Valley, CA: Sociology Press.

Glaser, B. (2009). *Jargonizing theory.* Mill Valley, CA:
Sociology Press.

Glaser, B., & Strauss, A. (1965). *Awareness of dying.*
Chicago, IL: Aldine.

Glaser, B., & Strauss, A. (1967). *The discovery of grounded*
theory: Strategies for qualitative research. Chicago, IL:
Aldine.

Glaser, B., & Strauss, A. (1968). *Time for dying*. Chicago, IL: Aldine.

Goffman, E. (1961). *Asylums: Essays on the social situation of mental patients and other inmates*. Chicago, IL: University of Chicago.

Hall, W., Long, B., Bermbach, N., Jordan, S., & Patterson, K. (2005). Qualitative teamwork issue and strategies: Coordination through mutual adjustment. *Qualitative Health Research, 15*, 394–410.

Harborne, A., Wolpert, M., & Clare, L. (2004). Children being diagnosed with ADHD. *Clinical Child Psychology and Psychiatry, 9*, 327–339. doi:10.1177/1359104504043915

Haverkamp, B., Morrow, S., & Ponterotto, J. (2005). A time and a place for qualitative and mixed methods in counseling psychology research. *Journal of Counseling Psychology, 52*, 123–125. doi:10.1037/0022-0167.52.2.123

Headland, T. 1999. *Emics and etics: The insider/outsider debate*. Retrieved from http://www.sil.org/~headlandt/eticemic.htm

Holton, J. (2007). The coding process and its challenges. In A. Bryant & K. Charmaz (Eds.), *The Sage handbook of grounded theory* (pp. 265–289). London, England: Sage.

James, W. (1981). *Pragmatism*. Cambridge, MA: Hackett. (Original work published 1907)

Jewell, G. (2007). Contextual empowerment. *Journal of Transcultural Nursing, 18*, 49–56.

Johnson, M., & Delaney, K. (2007). Keeping the unit safe: The anatomy of escalation. *Journal of the American Psychiatric Nurses Association, 13*, 42–52. doi:10.1177/1078390307301736

Kearney, M. (2007). From the sublime to the meticulous. In A. Bryant & K. Charmaz (Eds.), *The Sage handbook of grounded theory* (pp. 127–149). London, England: Sage.

Kearney, M., & O'Sullivan, J. (2003). Identity shifts as turning points in health behavior change. *Western Journal of Nursing Research, 25*, 134–152. doi:10.1177/0193945902250032

Kelle, U. (2007). The development of categories. In A. Bryant & K. Charmaz (Eds.), *The Sage handbook of grounded theory* (pp. 190–212). London, England: Sage.

Kokotsaki, D. (2007). Understanding the ensemble pianist. *Psychology of Music, 35*, 641–668.

Laing, R. D. (1961). *Self and others: The discovery of grounded theory in practice*. London, England: Tavistock.

Laing, R. D. (1965). *The divided self*. London, England: Tavistock.

Li, H. J., & Shyu, Y. (2007). Coping processes of Taiwanese families during postdischarge period for an elderly member with hip fracture. *Nursing Science Quarterly, 20*, 273–279. doi:10.1177/0894318407303128

Madill, A., & Gough, B. (2008). Qualitative research and its place in psychological science. *Psychological Methods, 13*, 254–271. doi:10.1037/a0013220

Midence, K., & O'Neill, M. (1999). The experience of parents in the diagnosis of autism. *Autism, 3*, 273–285. doi:10.1177/1362361399003003005

Mruck, K., & Mey, G. (2007). Grounded theory and reflexivity. In A. Bryant & K. Charmaz (Eds.), *The Sage handbook of grounded theory* (pp. 515–537). London, England: Sage.

Park, R. (1967). *On social control and collective behavior*. Chicago, IL: University of Chicago Press.

Pike, K. L. (1967). *Language in relation to a unified theory of structure of human behavior* (2nd ed.). The Hague, The Netherland: Mouton.

Propp, K. M., Apker, J., Zabava Ford, W., Wallace, N., Serbenski, M., & Hofmeister, N. (2010). Meeting the complex needs of the health care team: Identification of nurse team communication practices perceived to enhance patient outcomes. *Qualitative Health Research, 20*, 15–28. doi:10.1177/1049732309355289

Quint, J. C. (1967). *The nurse and the dying patient*. New York, NY: Macmillan.

Reichertz, J. (2007). Abduction: The logic of discovery of grounded theory. In A. Bryant & K. Charmaz (Eds.), *The Sage handbook of grounded theory* (pp. 214–228). London, England: Sage.

Stineman, M., Rist, P. and Burke, J. (2008). Through the clinician's lens: Objective and subjective views of disability. *Qualitative Health Research, 20*, 816–829.

Strauss, A. (1987). *Qualitative analysis for social scientists*. Cambridge, England: Cambridge University Press. doi:10.1017/CBO9780511557842

Strauss, A. (1993). *Continual permutations of action*. New York, NY: Aldine de Gruyter.

Strauss, A., & Corbin, J. (1990). *Basics of qualitative research*. Thousand Oaks, CA: Sage.

Strauss, A., & Corbin, J. (1998). *Basics of qualitative research* (2nd ed.). Thousand Oaks, CA: Sage.

Strubing, J. (2007). Research as pragmatic problem-solving. In A. Bryant & K. Charmaz (Eds.), *The Sage handbook of grounded theory* (pp. 580–602). London, England: Sage.

Szasz, T. (1961). *The myth of mental illness*. London, England: Paladin.

Szasz, T. (1970). *Ideology and insanity*. London, England: Pelican.

Teram, E., Schachter, C., & Stalker, C. (2005). The case for integrating grounded theory and participatory action research: Empowering clients to inform professional practice. *Qualitative Health Research, 15,* 1129–1140. doi:10.1177/1049732305275882

Thornberg, R., & Charmaz, K. (in press). Grounded theory. In S. Lapan, M. Quartaroli, & F. Riemer (Eds.), *Qualitative research: An introduction to methods and designs.* San Francisco, CA: Jossey-Bass.

Turner, B. (1983). The use of grounded theory for the qualitative analysis of organizational behaviour. *Journal of Management Studies, 20,* 333–348. doi:10.1111/j.1467-6486.1983.tb00211.x

Washington State Nurses Association. (2011). *Jeanne Quint Benoliel, PhD, RN, FAAN.* Retrieved from http://www.wsna.org/Hall-of-Fame/Jeanne-Quint-Benoliel/

What-When-How. (2011). *Emic and etic (anthropology).* Retrieved from http://what-when-how.com/social-and-cultural-anthropology/emic-and-etic-anthropology/

Wiener, C. (2007). Making teams work in conducting grounded theory. In A. Bryant & K. Charmaz (Eds.), *The Sage handbook of grounded theory* (pp. 293–309). London, England: Sage.

Yardley, L. (2000). Dilemmas in qualitative health research. *Psychology and Health, 15,* 215–228.

CHAPTER 4

THEMATIC ANALYSIS

Virginia Braun and Victoria Clarke

Until recently, thematic analysis (TA) was a widely used yet poorly defined method of qualitative data analysis. The few texts (Boyatzis, 1998; Patton, 2002), chapters (Hayes, 1997), and articles (Aronson, 1994; Attride-Stirling, 2001; Fereday & Muir-Cochrane, 2006; Tuckett, 2005) often came from outside psychology and were never widely taken up within the discipline. Instead, qualitative researchers tended to either use the method without any guiding reference or claim some mix of other approaches (e.g., grounded theory and discourse analysis [DA]) to rationalize what essentially was TA. Braun and Clarke (2006) developed TA (in relation to psychology) in a "systematic" and "sophisticated" way (Howitt & Cramer, 2008, p. 341). TA is rapidly becoming widely recognized as a unique and valuable method in its own right, alongside other more established qualitative approaches like grounded theory, narrative analysis, or DA.

TA is an accessible, flexible, and increasingly popular method of qualitative data analysis. Learning to do it provides the qualitative researcher with a foundation in the basic skills needed to engage with other approaches to qualitative data analysis. In this chapter, we first outline the basics of what TA is and explain why it is so useful. The main part of the chapter then demonstrates how to do thematic analysis, using a worked example with data from one of our own research projects—an interview-based study of lesbian, gay, bisexual, and transsexual (LGBT) students' experiences of university life. We conclude by discussing how to conduct thematic analysis well and how to avoid doing it poorly.

WHAT IS THEMATIC ANALYSIS?

TA is a method for systematically identifying, organizing, and offering insight into patterns of meaning (themes) across a data set. Through focusing on meaning *across* a data set, TA allows the researcher to see and make sense of collective or shared meanings and experiences. Identifying unique and idiosyncratic meanings and experiences found only within a single data item is not the focus of TA. This method, then, is a way of identifying what is common to the way a topic is talked or written about and of making sense of those commonalities.

What is common, however, is not necessarily in and of itself meaningful or important. The patterns of meaning that TA allows the researcher to identify need to be important in relation to the particular topic and research question being explored. Analysis produces the answer to a question, even if, as in some qualitative research, the specific question that is being answered only becomes apparent through the analysis. Numerous patterns could be identified across any data set—the purpose of analysis is to identify those relevant to answering *a particular* research question. For instance, in researching white-collar workers' experiences of sociality at work, a researcher might interview people about their work environment and start with questions about their typical workday. If most or all reported that they started work at around 9:00 a.m., this would be a pattern in the data, but it would not necessarily be a meaningful or important one. If many reported that they aimed to arrive at work earlier

DOI: 10.1037/13620-004
APA Handbook of Research Methods in Psychology: Vol. 2. Research Designs, H. Cooper (Editor-in-Chief)

than needed so that they could chat with colleagues, this could be a meaningful pattern.

TA is a flexible method that allows the researcher to focus on the data in numerous different ways. With TA you can legitimately focus on analyzing meaning across the entire data set, or you can examine one particular aspect of a phenomenon in depth. You can report the obvious or semantic meanings in the data, or you can interrogate the latent meanings, the assumptions and ideas that lie behind what is explicitly stated (see Braun & Clarke, 2006). The many forms TA can take means that it suits a wide variety of research questions and research topics.

WHY THEMATIC ANALYSIS?

The two main reasons to use TA are accessibility and flexibility. For people new to qualitative research, TA provides an entry into a way of doing research that otherwise can seem vague, mystifying, conceptually challenging, and overly complex. It offers a way into qualitative research that teaches the mechanics of coding and analyzing qualitative data systematically, which can then be linked to broader theoretical or conceptual issues. For much qualitative research, the relationship is reversed. For example, to do DA, the researcher needs to first be familiar with complex theoretical perspectives on language (see Chapter 8 of this volume), which invert the commonsense view of language as a mirroring reality—instead, language is theorized as *creating* reality. Knowing this background is essential because it guides what the researcher sees in the data, how they code and analyze the data, and the claims that they make. In contrast, TA is *only* a method of data analysis, rather than being an approach to conducting qualitative research. We see this as a strength because it ensures the accessibility and flexibility of the approach.

TA offers a way of separating qualitative research out from these broader debates, where appropriate, and making qualitative research results available to a wider audience. Its accessibility as a method also suits multimethods research being conducted by research teams, where not everyone is a qualitative expert. TA also has a lot of potential for use within participatory research projects—such as

participatory action research (see Chapter 11 of this volume) or memory work (Onyx & Small, 2001)—in which many involved in the analysis are not trained researchers.

FLEXIBILITY AND CHOICES IN THEMATIC ANALYSIS

Linked to the fact that it is just a method, one of the main reasons TA is so flexible is that it can be conducted in a number of different ways. TA has the ability to straddle three main continua along which qualitative research approaches can be located: inductive versus deductive or theory-driven data coding and analysis, an experiential versus critical orientation to data, and an essentialist versus constructionist theoretical perspective. Where the researcher locates their research on each of these continua carries a particular set of assumptions, and this delimits what can and cannot be said in relation to the data as well as how data can and should be interpreted (for a detailed discussion of these positions, see Volume 1, Chapter 1, this handbook). Any researcher doing TA needs to actively make a series of *choices* as to what form of TA they are using and to understand and explain why they are using this particular form (Braun & Clarke, 2006).

An inductive approach to data coding and analysis is a bottom-up approach and is driven by what is *in* the data. What this means is that the codes and themes derive from the content of the data themselves—so that what is mapped by the researcher during analysis closely matches the content of the data. In contrast, a deductive approach to data coding and analysis is a top-down approach, where the researcher brings to the data a series of concepts, ideas, or topics that they use to code and interpret the data. What this means is that the codes and themes derive more from concepts and ideas the researcher brings to the data—here, what is mapped by the researcher during analysis does not necessarily closely link to the semantic data content.

In reality, coding and analysis often uses a combination of both approaches. It is impossible to be purely inductive, as we always bring something to the data when we analyze it, and we rarely *completely* ignore the semantic content of the data when we code for a particular theoretical construct—at the very least, we have to know whether it is worth coding the data for that construct. One tends to predominate, however, and a commitment to an inductive or deductive approach also signals an overall orientation that prioritizes either participant or data-based meaning or researcher or theory-based meaning. For this reason, inductive TA often is experiential in its orientation and essentialist in its theoretical framework, assuming a knowable world and "giving voice" to experiences and meanings of that world, as reported in the data. Deductive TA is often critical in its orientation and constructionist in its theoretical framework, examining how the world is put together (i.e., constructed) and the ideas and assumptions that inform the data gathered. These correspondences are not given, however, or necessary. Consistency and coherence of the overall framework and analysis is what *is* important.

Braun and colleagues' analysis of gay and bisexual men's experiences of sexual coercion provides a good example of a more inductive, experiential, essentialist form of TA, in which different forms or modes of sexual coercion were identified from men's reported diverse experiences (Braun, Terry, Gavey, & Fenaughty, 2009). Clarke and Kitzinger's (2004) analysis of representations of lesbian and gay parents on television talk shows is a good example of more deductive, critical, constructionist TA. This study drew on the concept of *heteronormativity* to examine how participants in liberal talk-show debates routinely invoke discursive strategies of *normalization*, emphasizing lesbian- and gay-headed families' conformity to norms of White, middle-class heterosexuality, as a response to homophobic and heterosexist accounts of lesbian and gay parenting and its impact on children.

Like any form of analysis, TA can be done well, and it can be done poorly. Essential for doing *good* TA are a clear understanding of where the researcher stands in relation to these possible options, a rationale for making the choices they do, and the consistent application of those choices throughout the analysis (further criteria are discussed later in the chapter). We now provide a worked example that lays out how you actually *do* TA.

THEMATIC ANALYSIS: A WORKED EXAMPLE

We illustrate how to do TA using a worked example from an ongoing project that examines sexuality, gender identity, and higher education (Braun & Clarke, 2009; Clarke & Braun, 2009b). Like many research projects, which evolve not just from identified *gaps* in the literature but also from topics that grab us and pique our curiosity, this one developed as a result of our experiences and reflections related to teaching and teaching training as well as from intellectual and political questions about sexuality and gender identity in the classroom.

Part of the project involved interviewing 20 LGBT-identified students in New Zealand (10 students) and Britain (10 students) to understand their experiences of university life. Our worked example of thematic analysis uses data from four of the British students. The students varied on race/ethnicity (one British Asian, three White, one born in Europe), class (working or middle class) and age (one middle-aged student), but they were all studying social science subjects. The scope of *university life* was broadly conceived, including the classroom, the curriculum, and "hidden" curriculum—the norms and ideas implicitly conveyed at university—interactions with course peers and teaching staff, the campus and wider university environment, the local geographic area, and the local gay scene. In the semistructured interviews, which lasted around an hour, participants were all asked about their expectations of university life, whether they were *out* (open) about their sexuality at university, their experiences of the classroom and the curriculum, their views on LGBT lecturers coming out in the classroom, and, if they were studying a people-based discipline (Ellis, 2009), whether LGBT issues were included when relevant. Experiences and perceptions of the wider campus environment and of student housing, interactions with other students, friendship networks and social life, and the best and worst things about university life as a LGBT student were also covered.

The interviews were audio recorded and then transcribed orthographically, reproducing all spoken words and sounds, including hesitations, false starts, cutoffs in speech (indicated by a dash; e.g., thin-), the interviewer's *guggles* (e.g., *mm-hm, ah-ha*), laugher, long pauses [indicated by (pause)], and strong emphasis (indicated by under-score). Commas signal a continuing intonation, broadly commensurate with a grammatical comma in written language; inverted commas are used to indicate reported speech; three full-stops in a row (. . .) signal editing of the transcript. We have mainly edited for brevity, removing any words or clauses that are not essential for understanding the overall meaning of a data extract. There are many different styles of transcription (e.g., Edwards & Lampert, 1993) but if transcribing audio data for TA, this level of detail is more than sufficient. As a general practice, we do not advocate "cleaning up" the transcript (such as making it more grammatical or removing hesitations, pauses, and guggles) when working with data. Depending on your form of TA, such details may be omitted from quoted data (if done, it should be noted); however, because the details can be revealing, we suggest working with a full transcript while doing the analysis.

This topic, research question, and data collection method all suited TA. The research question was experiential and exploratory, so our worked example illustrates a primarily experiential form of TA, within a contextualist framework, which assumes truth can be accessed through language, but that accounts and experiences are socially mediated (Madill, Jordan, & Shirley, 2000). It illustrates a combination of inductive *and* deductive TA: inductive as we mainly code from the data, on the basis of participants' experiences (meaning our analytic lens does not completely override their stories); deductive as we draw on theoretical constructs from feminist and queer scholarship like heterosexism (Adam, 1998), compulsory heterosexuality (Rich, 1980), heteronormativity (Warner, 1991), and the hidden curriculum of heteronormativity (Epstein, O'Flynn, & Telford, 2003) to render visible issues that participants did not explicitly articulate. This means that the data are broadly interpreted within a feminist and a queer (e.g., Clarke & Braun, 2009a; Gamson, 2000) theoretical and ideological framework.

A SIX-PHASE APPROACH TO THEMATIC ANALYSIS

The six phases in our approach to TA (Braun & Clarke, 2006) are outlined and illustrated using worked examples. This is an approach *to* TA and to *learning to do* TA. More experienced analysts will (a) likely have deeper insights into their data during familiarization, (b) find the process of coding quicker and easier and be able to code at a more conceptual level, and (c) more quickly and confidently develop themes that need less reviewing and refining, especially if working with a smaller data set. Writing is also likely to take a more central place throughout analysis with more experience. The point we wish to emphasize is that certain skills of analysis develop only through experience and practice. Even experienced researchers, however, will draw and redraw lots of *thematic maps* when searching for themes and will engage in extensive review processes when working with larger data sets. A thematic map is a visual (see Braun & Clarke, 2006) or sometimes text-based (see Frith & Gleeson, 2004) tool to map out the facets of your developing analysis and to identify main themes, subthemes, and interconnections between themes and subthemes.

Phase 1: Familiarizing Yourself With the Data

Common to all forms of qualitative analysis, this phase involves immersing yourself in the data by reading and rereading textual data (e.g., transcripts of interviews, responses to qualitative surveys) and listening to audio recordings or watching video data. If you have audio data, we recommend listening to them at least once as well as reading the transcript, especially if you did not collect the data or transcribe them. Making notes on the data as you read—or listen—is part of this phase. Use whatever format works for you (e.g., annotating transcripts, writing comments in a notebook or electronic file, underling portions of data) to highlight items potentially of interest. Note-making helps you start to read the data *as data*. Reading data *as data* means not simply absorbing the surface meaning of the words on the page, as you might read a novel or magazine, but reading the words actively, analytically, and critically, and starting to think about what the data mean. This involves asking questions like, How does this participant make sense of their experiences? What assumptions do they make in interpreting their experience? What kind of world is revealed through their accounts? We will illustrate this with a brief example from Andreas's interview:

Andreas: let's say I'm in a in a seminar and somebody a a man says to me "oh look at her" (Int: mm) I'm not going "oh actually I'm gay" (Int: mm [laughter]) I'll just go like "oh yeah" (Int: mhm) you know I won't fall into the other one and say "oh yeah" (Int: yep) "she looks really brilliant"

Our initial observations included (a) Andreas reports a common experience of presumed heterosexuality, (b) coming out is not an obvious option, (c) social norms dictate a certain response, (d) the presumption of heterosexuality appears dilemmatic, and (e) he colludes in the presumption but minimally (to avoid social awkwardness). Looking a bit more deeply, we speculated that (a) Andreas values honesty and being true to yourself, but (b) he recognizes a sociopolitical context in which that is constrained, and (c) walks a tightrope trying to balance his values and the expectations of the context. These initial observations suggest the data will provide fertile grounds for analysis; reading Andreas's answer *as* data reveals the richness that can be found in even brief extracts of text. We did deliberately pick a particularly rich extract, however; not all extracts will be as vivid as this one, and you may have little or nothing to say about some parts of your data.

The aim of this phase is to become intimately familiar with your data set's content and to begin to notice things that might be relevant to your research question. You need to read through your entire data set at least once—if not twice, or more—until you feel you know the data content intimately. Make notes on the entire data set as well as on individual transcripts. Note-making at this stage is observational and casual rather than systematic and inclusive. You are not coding the data yet, so do not agonize over it. Notes would typically be a stream of consciousness, a messy rush of ideas, rather than polished prose. Such notes are written only *to* and

for you to help you with the process of analysis—think of them as memory aids and triggers for coding and analysis. At most, they may be shared among research team members.

Phase 2: Generating Initial Codes

Phase 2 begins the systematic analysis of the data through coding. Codes are the building blocks of analysis: If your analysis is a brick-built house with a tile roof, your themes are the walls and roof and your codes are the individual bricks and tiles. Codes identify and provide a label for a feature of the data that is potentially relevant to the research question (Exhibit 4.1 shows an example of coded data). Coding can be done at the semantic or the latent level of meaning. Codes can provide a pithy summary of a portion of data or describe the content of the data—such descriptive or semantic codes typically stay close to content of the data and to the participants' meanings. An example of this is "fear/anxiety about people's reactions to his sexuality" in Exhibit 4.1. Codes can also go beyond the participants' meanings and provide an *interpretation* about the data content. Such interpretative or latent codes identify meanings that lie beneath the semantic surface of the data. An example of this is the "coming out imperative"; this code offers a conceptual interpretation to make sense of what Andreas is saying (see Exhibit 4.1).

Some codes mirror participants' language and concepts; others invoke the researchers' conceptual and theoretical frameworks. For example, the code "not hiding (but not shouting)" stayed close to the participants' use of language (e.g., John said "I don't make an attempt to hide that I'm gay but at the same time I'm not very forward about it"). In contrast, the code "modifying behavior . . . to avoid heterosexism" invoked our frame of reference: No student spontaneously used the term *heterosexism* to describe their experiences, but we interpret their accounts through this framework (Adam, 1998).

Codes are succinct and work as shorthand for something you, the analyst, understands; they do not have to be fully worked-up explanations—those come later. Codes will almost always be a mix of the descriptive and interpretative. A novice coder will likely (initially) generate more descriptive codes; as noted, interpretative approaches to coding develop

---

Exhibit 4.1
Example of Coded Transcript (Andreas)

Transcript	Codes
Andreas: . . . I sometimes try to erm not <u>conceal</u> it that's not the right word but erm let's say I'm in a in a seminar and somebody- a a man says to me "oh look at her"	Not hiding (but not shouting) Heterosexual assumption Hidden curriculum of heteronormativity
VC: mm	
Andreas: I'm not going "oh actually I'm <u>gay</u>" (Int: mm [laughter]) I'll just go like "oh yeah" (VC: mhm) you know I won't fall into the other one and say "oh yeah" (VC: yep) "she looks really brilliant"	Coming out is difficult (and not socially normative) Dilemmas created by the heterosexual assumption Managing the heterosexual assumption by minimal agreement
VC: yep	
Andreas: but I sorta then and after them you hate myself for it because I I don't know how this person would react because that person might then either not talk to me anymore or erm might sort of yeah (VC: yep) or next time we met not not sit next to me or that sort of thing	Coming out imperative Being a "happy, healthy" gay man It's important to be honest and authentic Fear/anxiety about people's reaction to his homosexuality Heterosexism is a constant possibility Heterosexism = exclusion
VC: yep	
Andreas: so I think these this back to this question are you <u>out</u> yes but I think wherever you go you always have to start afresh	Heterosexual assumption
VC: yep	
Andreas: this sort of li-lifelong process of being courageous in a way or not	Coming out is difficult (and not socially normative)

with experience. This does not mean that interpretative codes are better—they are just harder to "see" sometimes. What is important for all codes is that they are relevant to answering your research question. Coding is something we get better at with practice.

TA is not prescriptive about how you segment the data as you code it (e.g., you do not have to produce a code for every line of transcript). You can code in large or small chunks; some chunks will not be coded at all. Coding requires another thorough read of every data item, and you should code each data item in its entirety before coding another. Every time you identify something that is potentially relevant to the research question, code it. We say "potentially" because at this early stage of analysis, you do not know what might be relevant: Inclusivity should be your motto. If you are unsure about whether a piece of data may be relevant, code it. It is much easier to discard codes than go back to the entire data set and recode data, although some recoding is part of the coding process.

Once you identify an extract of data to code, you need to write down the code and mark the text associated with it. You can code a portion of data with more than one code (as Exhibit 4.1 shows). Some people code on hard-copy data, clearly identifying the code name, and highlighting the portion of text associated with it. Other techniques include using computer software to manage coding (see Volume 1, Chapter 16, this handbook) or using file cards—one card for each code, with data summary and location information listed—or cutting and pasting text into a new word-processing file, created for this purpose (again, ensure that you record where all excerpts came from). An advantage of the latter methods is that you collate your coded text as you code, but there is no right or wrong way to manage the physical process of coding. Work out what suits you best. What *is* important is that coding is inclusive, thorough, and systematic.

After you generate your first code, keep reading the data until you identify the next potentially relevant excerpt: You then have to decide whether you can apply the code you have already used or whether a new code is needed to capture that piece of data. You repeat this process throughout each data item and the entire data set. As your coding progresses, you can also modify existing codes to incorporate new material. For example, our code "modifying behavior, speech, and practices to avoid heterosexism" was initially titled "modifying behavior to avoid heterosexism." Because students also reported modifying speech and things like dress or self-presentation to avoid "trouble," we expanded this code beyond "behavior" to make it better fit what participants said. It is a good idea to revisit the material you coded at the start because your codes will have likely developed during coding: Some recoding and new coding of earlier coded data may be necessary.

This stage of the process ends when your data are fully coded and the data relevant to each code has been collated. Exhibit 4.2 provides some examples of codes we generated from our data, with a few data extracts collated for each code. Depending on your topic, data set, and precision in coding, you will have generated any number of codes—there is no maximum. What you want are enough codes to capture both the diversity, and the patterns, within the data, and codes should appear across more than one data item.

Phase 3: Searching for Themes

In this phase, your analysis starts to take shape as you shift from codes to themes. A theme "captures something important about the data in relation to the research question, and represents some level of *patterned* response or meaning within the data set" (Braun & Clarke, 2006, p. 82). Some qualitative researchers make reference to "themes emerging from the data," as if their data set was a pile of crocodile eggs and analysis involved watching the eggs until each baby crocodile (theme) emerged, perfectly formed, from within. If only it were so easy. Searching for themes is an *active* process, meaning we generate or construct themes rather than discovering them. Although we call this phase "searching for themes," it is not like archaeologists digging around, searching for the themes that lie hidden within the data, preexisting the process of analysis. Rather, analysts are like sculptors, making choices about how to shape and craft their piece of stone (the "raw data") into a work of art (the analysis). Like a piece of stone, the data set provides the material base for analysis and limits the possible end

product, but many different variations could be created when analyzing the data.

This phase involves reviewing the coded data to identify areas of similarity and overlap between codes: Can you identify any broad topics or issues around which codes cluster? The basic process of generating themes and subthemes, which are the subcomponents of a theme, involves collapsing or clustering codes that seem to share some unifying feature together, so that they reflect and describe a coherent and meaningful pattern in the data. In our data, we noticed codes clustering around heterosexism and homophobia. Examining these in more detail, we identified that the codes either focused on experiences of heterosexism and homophobia, or responses to and ways of managing heterosexism and homophobia. We then constructed one theme using *all* the codes relating to the participants' experiences of heterosexism and homophobia (e.g., "incident of (naming) homophobia/heterosexism"; "tensions in relating to straight men") and another using the codes relating to the participants' management of (actual and feared) heterosexism (e.g., "monitoring/assessing people and the environment for the possibility of heterosexism"; "modifying speech, behavior, and practices to avoid heterosexism"). The code "managing the heterosexual assumption by minimal agreement" (see Exhibit 4.1) appeared to be a variation of the code "modifying speech, behavior, and practices to avoid heterosexism," and so it was incorporated into that theme.

A lot of codes also clustered around the issue of identity but did not form one obvious theme. In this case, after exploring lots of different ways to combine these codes into themes and drawing lots of thematic maps, we generated two themes: one around coming out and being out, and one around different versions of being a gay man. These provided the best mapping of the identity data *in relation to our research questions*. A number of codes cut across both themes, such as the notion of *good gays* (who conform to the norms of compulsory heterosexuality as much as possible by being "straight-acting" and "straight-looking"; Taulke-Johnson, 2008) and *bad gays* (who are "politically active and culturally assertive"; Epstein, Johnson, & Steinberg, 2000, p. 19). This example is not a case of undesirable

Exhibit 4.2
Six Codes With Illustrative Data Extracts (Direct Quotes)

Modifying speech, behavior, and practices to avoid heterosexism	Tensions in relating to straight men	Incident of (naming) homophobia/heterosexism	Fear/anxiety about people's reactions to his sexuality	Managing the heterosexual assumption by minimal agreement	Monitoring/assessing people/the environment for the possibility of heterosexism
I'm not somebody that goes out looking for trouble . . . (David)	I know if I go into a lecture hall and I'm like on my own without a group some of the lads are a little bit less inclined to sort of sit with you in a way . . . (David)	This one guy drunk just came along and just started telling me to my face I was sick that there was something wrong with me, there was something wrong with us and we should [f**k] the hell out of there . . . (Asha)	I'd just hate to see what my dad would do (Asha)	I realize and notice that I sometimes try to erm not conceal it, that's not the right word, but erm let's say I'm in . . . seminar and somebody- a a man says to me "oh look at her" I'm not going "oh actually I'm gay" I'll just go "oh yeah" you know I won't fall into the other one and say "oh yeah she looks really brilliant . . ." (Andreas)	just how much I know them . . . there's a lot of people I wouldn't go into great detail with about what I get up to and stuff, whereas other people I would, yeah I suppose I like to feel reasonably safe when telling them stuff like that (John)
so you don't want to necessarily go down that road, so you sort of make up some- not make up some story, but you only tell sort of half the truth (Andreas)	that's the old thing that it's sort of easier in a way to be out with females than with sort of you know blokey blokes (Andreas)	I have once seen a group of lads standing outside one of the [gay] bars like jeering and stuff . . . (John)	I was a little bit worried about how I was treated, I didn't want to go out and start helping them in shoe shops . . . (David)	I don't agree but I don't disagree, I kind of erm , I probably just say"yeah she-" What would I say? Probably something like "oh she looks okay" or "yeah she looks nice" but I wouldn't say "oh yeah like I wanna (laughs) I wanna do her" or something like that (John)	erm I just remember him making some kind of comment to me on the bus to London about Earl's Court and gay art or something and er yeah, and I just didn't think that he'd be the sort of person that'd be that bothered by things like that you know what I mean (John)
I would feel fine going clubbing [to a straight club] with my boyfriend but I'd be very wary of making it obvious (John)	I did have quite a- an interesting conversation with one guy . . . at the end of the conversation . . . he goes. . . "you're an actual really nice guy aren't you? 'Cos I wasn't really over sure about you when we first started, 'cos you could tell you were gay as soon as you walked through the door" . . . my reaction was "get knotted" sort of thing and just walked off 'cos I thought you know that shouldn't be a issue (David)	There's this one person from work who's extremely religious, and I don't mention it [my sexuality] whatsoever, he did mention one story that er gay people were cursed by the god and turned into monkeys (Asha)	I was asked . . . "why did you come from another country to Bristol?" if you er go into this er spiel about "oh there was somebody involved" then you're close to "who was it then?" . . . you never know how people react (Andreas)	I was asked "what are you doing then in Bristol?" . . . "was it a nice girl?" so you don't want to necessarily go down that road so you . . . only tell sort of half the truth (Andreas)	you go to a party where you don't know anybody . . . and "oh let me introduce you to so and so" and then you sort of after a while you start this there's always testi- testing can I not can I tell that- but I mean what will happen if I tell will people then immediately say "oh sorry mate I need a drink" (Andreas)
if I'm out with my boyfriend and it's late at night and we're sort of walking home and we'll sort of holding hands and . . . if it's like mostly girls and stuff and that's okay but if a group of lads were coming like we would loosen up or go via like a different route (David)		I had a couple of incidents where all of sudden when you then say "I'm gay" then it's this (pause) you know erm wink wink nudge nudge thing sort of these jokes (Andreas)	if I came out there I probably would have been lad bait so I decided to keep it to myself . . . I had an idea of what kind of response I would get and so just sensible decision of just keeping my mouth shut (Asha)		
with other Asians as well . . . I wouldn't say probably I would just shut up (Asha)					

overlap between themes; it illustrates that certain concepts or issues may cut across themes and provide a unifying framework for telling a coherent story about what is going on in the data, overall.

Another important element of this stage is starting to explore the relationship between themes and to consider how themes will work together in telling an *overall* story about the data. Good themes are distinctive and, to some extent, stand alone, but they also need to work together as a whole. Think of themes like the pieces of a jigsaw puzzle: Together they provide a meaningful and lucid picture of your data. In your analysis, one central theme or concept may draw together or underpin all or most of your other themes—for our example, this would be heteronormativity.

During this stage, it can also be useful to have a miscellaneous theme, which includes all the codes that do not clearly fit anywhere, which may end up as part of new themes or being discarded. Being able to let go of coded material and indeed provisional themes if they do not fit within your overall analysis is an important part of qualitative analysis. Remember, your job in analyzing the data, and reporting them, is to tell a *particular* story about the data, that answers your research question. It is not to represent everything that was said in the data.

How many themes are enough or too many? For our data set, we generated six themes; for brevity, only four are summarized in Exhibit 4.3. Unfortunately, there is no magic formula that states that if you have X amount of data, and you are writing a report of Y length, you should have Z number of themes. The more data you have, the more codes and thus themes, you will likely generate; if you are writing a longer report, you will have space to discuss more themes. But with more themes, your analysis can lose coherence. What is essential is that your themes are presented in sufficient depth and detail to convey the richness and complexity of your data—you are unlikely to achieve this if you report more than six or seven themes in a 10,000-word report. Your themes will likely be "thin." If you are trying to provide a meaningful overview of your data, one to two themes are likely insufficient; however, they may be sufficient for an in-depth analysis of one aspect of the data. In an 8,000- to 10,000-word article, we typically report two to six themes.

You should end this phase with a thematic map or table outlining your candidate themes, and you should collate all the data extracts relevant to each theme, so you are ready to begin the process of reviewing your themes.

Phase 4: Reviewing Potential Themes

This phase involves a recursive process whereby the developing themes are reviewed in relation to the coded data and entire data set. This phase is essentially about quality checking. It is particularly important for novice researchers and for those working with very large data sets, where it is simply not possible to hold your entire data set in your head. The first step is to check your themes against the collated extracts of data and to explore whether the theme works in relation to the data. If it does not, you might need to discard some codes or relocate them under another theme; alternatively, you may redraw the boundaries of the theme, so that it more meaningfully captures the relevant data. If these tweaks do not work, you might need to discard your theme altogether and start again—you should not force your analysis into coherence. Key questions to ask are as follows:

- Is this a theme (it could be just a code)?
- If it is a theme, what is the quality of this theme (does it tell me something useful about the data set and my research question)?
- What are the boundaries of this theme (what does it include and exclude)?
- Are there enough (meaningful) data to support this theme (is the theme *thin* or *thick*)?
- Are the data too diverse and wide ranging (does the theme lack coherence)?

You may end up collapsing a number of potential themes together or splitting a big broad theme a number of more specific or coherent themes.

Once you have a distinctive and coherent set of themes that work in relation to the coded data extracts, you should undertake the second stage in the review process—reviewing the themes in relation to the entire data set. This involves one final reread of all your data to determine whether your themes meaningfully capture the entire data set or an aspect thereof. What you are aiming for is a set of

---

Exhibit 4.3
Definitions and Labels for Selected Themes

Theme 1. "There's always that level of uncertainty": Compulsory heterosexuality at university. Maps the participants' experiences of (infrequent) homophobia and (*constant*) heterosexism and highlights tensions experienced in relating to (straight) others, particularly people who are common sources of heterosexism and overt homophobia (i.e., straight men; members of religious and non-White groups), and feelings, or fear, of exclusion and not belonging. Heterosexism meant participants negotiated their sexual identities in an uncertain environment and experienced constant (but minimized) fear of people's reactions to their sexuality. They had expected university students to be liberal and open minded and were surprised and disappointed they weren't. But they felt this applied if you were "straight-acting," indicating university is a safe space only if you are a "good gay." Participants' experienced difficulty coming out at university but also internalized and took responsibility for these difficulties rather than viewing coming out as something that is difficult because of compulsory heterosexuality. Although participants expressed some anger about experiences of overt homophobia, some homophobic and heterosexist "banter" (e.g., antigay humor) was acceptable if from friends—an indication that friends were comfortable with their sexuality but wasn't acceptable it from strangers. The heterosexual assumption and compulsory heterosexuality were typically framed as a to-be-expected part of normal life.

Theme 2. "I don't go out asking for trouble": Managing heterosexism. Outlines the ways the participants modified their speech, behavior, and practices to avoid heterosexism and homophobia and continually monitored people and the environment for evidence of potential heterosexism or homophobia. They constantly weighed whether it was safe to come or be out with a particular person or in a particular space. The participants typically assumed responsibility for managing heterosexism (they don't "ask" for trouble) and accepted this as a normal part of life. They seemed to lack a sense of entitlement to live free from heterosexism and a political and conceptual language with which to interpret their experiences of heterosexism and homophobia.

Theme 3. "I'm not hiding, but I'm not throwing it in people's faces": Being out (but not too out) at university. Focuses on the degree to which the participants were out and open about their sexuality at university and the management of sexual identity amid competing pressures to be a "happy, healthy gay" (comfortable with and open about their sexuality, with a "fully realized" gay identity) and a "good gay" (not too "overt"; not "forcing" their homosexuality on others).

Theme 4. Mincing queens versus ordinary guys who just happen to be gay. Focuses on participants' resistance to a gay identity as a "master status" (Becker, 1963), an identity that overrides all other identities—they wanted to be seen as an ordinary guy who just happens to be gay. They took responsibility for carefully managing other people's perceptions of their sexual identity, acutely aware that it takes very little to be judged as "too gay" (a "bad gay"). They felt very limited by popular conceptions of gay men and worked hard to distance themselves from the image of the camp gay man, the "mincing queen," the *Sex and the City* gay best friend, the gay style guru . . .

---

themes that capture the most important and relevant elements of the data, and the overall tone of the data, in relation to your research question. If your thematic map and set of themes does this, good. You can move to the next phase. If not, further refining and reviewing will be necessary to adequately capture the data. A mismatch will most likely occur if selective or inadequate coding has taken place, or if coding evolved over a data set and data were not recoded using the final set of codes. Revision at this stage might involve creating additional themes or tweaking or discarding existing themes.

Phase 5: Defining and Naming Themes

When defining your themes, you need to be able to clearly state what is unique and specific about each theme—whether you can sum up the essence of

each theme in a few sentences is a good test of this (see Exhibit 4.3). A good thematic analysis will have themes that (a) do not try to do too much, as themes should ideally have a singular focus; (b) are related but do not overlap, so they are not repetitive, although they may build on previous themes; and (c) directly address your research question. Each theme identified in Exhibit 4.3 has a clear focus, scope, and purpose; each in turn builds on and develops the previous theme(s); and together the themes provide a coherent overall story about the data. In some cases, you may want to have subthemes within a theme. These themes are useful in cases in which there are one or two overarching patterns within the data in relation to your question, but each is played out in a number of different ways. Themes 3 and 4, for example, could be described as subthemes of a broader theme of "managing gay identity."

This phase involves the deep analytic work involved in thematic analysis, the crucial shaping up of analysis into its fine-grained detail. As analysis now necessarily involves writing, the separation between Phase 5 and Phase 6 is often slightly blurry. This phase involves selecting extracts to present and analyze and then setting out the story of each theme with or around these extracts. What makes good data to quote and analyze? Ideally, each extract would provide a vivid, compelling example that clearly illustrates the analytic points you are making. It is good to draw on extracts from across your data items to show the coverage of the theme, rather than drawing on only one data item (this can be frustrating when one source articulates it all perfectly—the analysis in Exhibit 4.4 quotes Asha because he expressed that part of the theme particularly well).

The extracts you select to quote and analyze provide the structure for the analysis—the data narrative informing the reader of your interpretation of the data and their meaning. In analyzing the data, you use it to tell a story of the data. Data do not speak *for themselves*—you must not simply paraphrase the content of the data. Your analytic narrative needs to tell the reader *what* about an extract is interesting and *why*. Throughout your analytic section, you would typically have at least as much narrative surrounding your data as extracts. Data must be *interpreted* and connected to your broader research questions and to the scholarly fields within which your work is situated. Some qualitative research includes this as a separate discussion section; other research incorporates discussion of the literature into the analysis, creating a Results and Discussion section. Both styles work with TA. An integrated approach works well when strong connections exist with existing research and when the analysis is more theoretical or interpretative. This approach can also avoid repetition between results and discussion sections.

Exhibit 4.4 shows part of the analysis of our theme "managing heterosexism." It starts with a general summary of the theme's core issue, and then expands on this by providing specific examples of different aspects of the theme, illustrated using brief extracts. Once sufficient detail has been provided to show the scope of the theme, the longer extract offers rich and evocative detail of what this actually meant for one participant. Analysis of that extract begins by highlighting some data features that provide the basis for our interpretation around a broader practice of minimization and individualization—a pattern across the data set. There is an interweaving of detailed and specific analysis of what happens in a particular data extract, and more summative analysis that illustrates the broader content of the data set in relation to the theme. This reflects our combination of two broad styles of thematic analysis: (a) *descriptive*, in which data tend to be used in illustrative ways, and (b) *conceptual and interpretative*, in which extracts tend to be analyzed in more detail, often for the latent meanings on which they draw. Both offer important analyses of data and serve different purposes, but they can usefully be combined, as we show. The latter can be a more difficult form of analysis to grasp because it moves from surface or apparent meanings to latent or implicit meanings; it can take experience to learn to *see* these in data.

Even when we present a lot of short extracts of data, however, seemingly reporting quite closely what participants said, the analysis always moves *beyond* the data. It does not just report words—it interprets them and organizes them within a larger overarching conceptual framework. Regardless of what form of TA is done, analysis uses data to make a point. Analysis needs to be driven by the question, "So what?" What is relevant or useful here to answering my question? This process of telling an analytic narrative around your data extracts needs to take place for *all* your themes. Each theme also needs to be developed not only in its own right but also in relation to your research question and in relation to the other themes. Conclusions can and should be drawn from across the whole analysis. So an analysis needs to make interconnections between themes and say something overall about the data set.

The other aspect of this phase is working out what to call each theme. Naming might seem trivial, but this short title can and should signal a lot. A good name for a theme is informative, concise, and

---

Exhibit 4.4
Report of Theme 2: *"I don't go out asking for trouble"*: *Managing heterosexism* [excerpt]

In common with others (e.g., Taulke-Johnson & Rivers, 1999), our participants described monitoring and assessing people and the environment for evidence of potential heterosexism, weighing up whether it would be safe to come and be out. They decided *not* to come out when people made overtly antigay comments. Asha, for instance, took the comment "one thing I just can't understand is gay people" as strong evidence of a potential negative response to his coming out and chose not to. They made decisions *to* come out when people discussed gay-related issues in a broadly positive way, mentioned gay friends, or expressed "gay-friendly" sentiments (e.g., "want[ing] to be the ultimate personal fag hag," Asha).

This monitoring was sometimes a relatively passive process ("I just picked up tell-tale signs about it," Asha); at other times, participants actively "test[ed] the waters" (David) and "tr[ied] and manipulate the conversation to head in that direction and see how to respond to it" (Asha). Asha described this rather evocatively:

 Asha: just basically erm er, does he have a gay friend? Yes or no, is he alright with a gay friend? Yes or no. This person is alright to go out with- you know to come out with and basically if the answers are different the questions are different and the outcomes would be different . . . you're just trying to you know answer all the questions to see what the outcome is and it's kinda a bit of a headache

 VC: It sounds exhausting, and stressful

 Asha: It is, very much so but it's kinda something that I have in the back of my mind . . . I find out you know which box they tick, which box they don't tick and if they tick the right ones or if they tick the wrong ones I know what action to take from there . . .

 VC: Yep yep, god that sounds very hard

 Asha: Well the thing is it's almost kinda- I wouldn't, I don't know it's something that just happens in the background you know- I hardly notice it

 VC: Yeah like this processing that going on and kinda churning away

 Asha: Yeah all these things that you just happens that you're not even completely aware of but it's building up and you know you look back at it you see all these point and you say to my- you say to yourself right "I'm gonna tell this person I'm gay" "I'm gonna" you know and yeah

After initially agreeing with the interviewer, VC's, assessment that this is an "exhausting stressful process" ("It is, very much so"), Asha described it as a more subconscious process, something he "hardly notice[d]." When VC *again* suggested it sounded "very hard," he offered no agreement. Despite his detailed and vivid account, Asha appeared invested in framing this as a mundane rather than negative, and therefore "hard," process. This "minimizing the negative" approach was common: The participants consistently framed phenomena that could be read as evidence of heteronormativity and instances of prejudice (Taulke-Johnson, 2008) as to-be-expected parts of normal life.

Asha earlier vividly described this process in a way that suggested it *was* negative yet implicitly located the problem within his own psychology rather than the environment:

 Asha: constantly monitoring, keeping an eye out, keeping an ear out just you know, the little checklist this worst case- or not a worst case scenario but you're having a list in your mind of all the possible things that can go wrong and you- you're always going over that list of all the things that could go wrong I've kinda built- well personally for me it builds on my paranoia

In describing himself as *paranoid*, Asha suggests his response, rather than a heterosexist context, is at fault. All the participants interpreted difficulties they experienced in navigating a heterosexist world in this way. John, for example, associated his difficulties with coming out with his personality (he got embarrassed, and *feared* getting and looking embarrassed) rather than with the inherent difficulties that can exist around coming out (see DeCrescenzo, 1997; Flowers & Buston, 2001; Markowe, 2002) in heterosexist contexts. In internalizing their response to heteronormative contexts thus, responsibility for change is located *within* the participants, making it a personal rather than a political issue.

The degree to which students implicitly accepted responsibility for *managing* heterosexism to avoid "trouble" (David) by constantly modifying their speech, behavior, and other practices was the most striking feature of how they navigated the university climate. They had a strong sense that behaving or speaking in certain ways (being a "bad gay"; Taulke-Johnson, 2008) invited "trouble" and placed the onus on themselves to avoid it and protect themselves: "you have to sort of be very careful how you sort of came across to people" (David). The participants censored their speech and behavior ("tell . . . half of the truth," Andreas); avoided coming out or making "overt" displays of homosexuality, such as by showing affection to a same-sex partner, being too camp and acting like "a mincing queen" (John), or wearing "obviously gay" clothing; and avoided certain people ("groups of lads," John) and areas. Campus and city were seen as safe "as long as you took the measures—you know as long as you're sensible about it you don't go throwing it in people's faces you don't go down to you know places like [predominantly working class/non-White city suburb]" (Asha). [**analysis continues**] catchy. The name "mincing queens" versus "ordinary guys who just happen to be gay" (see Exhibit 4.3) is memorable and signals both the focus of the theme—different ways of being gay—and something about the content of the analysis—that participants' navigate between two different versions of being a gay man. "Mincing queens" is also a direct quote from the data. Using quotes in titles (also evident in Themes 1–3) can provide an immediate and vivid sense of what a theme is about while staying close to participants' language and concepts.

Phase 6: Producing the Report

Although the final phase of analysis *is* the production of a report such as a journal article or a dissertation, it is not a phase that only begins at the end. Unlike in quantitative research, we do not complete our analysis of the data and *then* write it up. Writing and analysis are thoroughly interwoven in qualitative research—from informal writing of notes and memos to the more formal processes of analysis and report writing. The purpose of your report is to provide a compelling story about your data based on your analysis. The story should be convincing and clear yet complex and embedded in a scholarly field. Even for descriptive TA, it needs to go beyond description to make an *argument* that answers your research question. Good writing comes with practice but try to avoid repetition, paraphrasing, unnecessary complexity, and passive phrasing. In general, qualitative research is best reported using a first-person active tense but check the requirements for your report.

The order in which you present your themes is important: Themes should connect logically and meaningfully and, if relevant, should build on previous themes to tell a coherent story about the data. We decided to use "compulsory heterosexuality at university," which documents the participants' experiences of homophobia and heterosexism, as our first theme because these experiences, particularly the constant possibility, and fear, of heterosexism, shaped almost every aspect of the students' university life and would be referenced throughout the rest of the analysis. From there, it made sense to discuss the participants' experiences of managing heterosexism. We decided the two identity themes

were the logical next step because the theme of coming out and being out closely related to the participants' fear of heterosexism and the ways in which they managed their practices to avoid heterosexism. The second identity theme—which discussed different conceptualizations of gay identity and the participants' desire to be perceived as ordinary guys who just happen to be gay—had a less immediately obvious connection to the first two themes but linked well to the first identity theme.

DOING THEMATIC ANALYSIS WELL

These guidelines lay out the process for producing a good TA that is thorough, plausible, and sophisticated. But like any analysis, TA can be done well, and it can be done poorly. Common errors include providing data extracts with little or no analysis (no interpretation of the data that tells us how they are relevant to answering the research question) or simple paraphrasing or summarizing data (see Braun & Clarke, 2006). Using data collection questions as themes is another common error—themes are better identified across the content of what participants say rather than via the questions they have been asked. "Incidents of homophobia" would be a weak theme, for example, because it would involve simply describing different things participants reported in response to an interview question on the topic. "'There's always that level of uncertainty': Compulsory heterosexuality at university" is a much stronger theme because it captures something more complex about how the participants' constant fear of homophobia and heterosexism shaped their university lives. It also incorporates data from across the whole interviews not just responses to specific questions about homophobia and heterosexism.

On a different level, an analysis can be weak or unconvincing if themes are not coherent or try and do too much. Analysis can also suffer from lack of evidence. You need to provide examples of, and analyze, enough data to convince the reader that this pattern you claim really was evident—consider the balance of data and analysis in Exhibit 4.4. A TA does have to relate to *patterns* found *across* your data set. This does not mean every data item has to evidence each theme, but it has to be more than idiosyncratic. Finally, TA can suffer because of mismatches between the data and analysis, or between the form of TA done, and the theoretical position of the report (for more discussion of these and for a checklist for doing good TA, see Braun & Clarke, 2006). In developing and revising your analysis, make sure data-based claims are justified and that the claims fit within your overall theoretical position (e.g., whether you are using an experiential or critical form of TA).

References

Adam, B. D. (1998). Theorising homophobia. *Sexualities, 1*, 387–404. doi:10.1177/136346098001004001

Aronson, J. (1994). A pragmatic view of thematic analysis. *The Qualitative Report, 2*(1). Retrieved from http://www.nova.edu/ssss/QR/BackIssues/QR2-1/aronson.html

Attride-Stirling, J. (2001). Thematic networks: An analytic tool for qualitative research. *Qualitative Research, 1*, 385–405. doi:10.1177/146879410100100307

Becker, H. (1963). *Outsiders: Studies in the sociology of deviance.* New York, NY: Free Press.

Boyatzis, R. E. (1998). *Transforming qualitative information: Thematic analysis and code development.* Thousand Oaks, CA: Sage.

Braun, V., & Clarke, V. (2006). Using thematic analysis in psychology. *Qualitative Research in Psychology, 3*, 77–101. doi:10.1191/1478088706qp063oa

Braun, V., & Clarke, V. (2009). Special issue: Coming out in higher education. *Lesbian & Gay Psychology Review, 10*, 3–69.

Braun, V., Terry, G., Gavey, N., & Fenaughty, J. (2009). "Risk" and sexual coercion among gay and bisexual men in Aotearoa/New Zealand—key informant accounts. *Culture, Health & Sexuality, 11*, 111–124. doi:10.1080/13691050802398208

Clarke, V., & Braun, V. (2009a). Gender. In D. Fox, I. Prilleltensky, & S. Austin (Eds.), *Critical psychology: An introduction* (2nd ed., pp. 232–249). Los Angeles, CA: Sage.

Clarke, V., & Braun, V. (2009b). Is the personal pedagogical? Sexualities and genders in the higher education classroom. *Feminism & Psychology, 19*, 175–180. doi:10.1177/0959353509102186

Clarke, V., & Kitzinger, C. (2004). Lesbian and gay parents on talk shows: Resistance or collusion in heterosexism. *Qualitative Research in Psychology, 1*, 195–217. doi:10.1191/1478088704qp0140a

DeCrescenzo, T. (Ed.). (1997). *Gay and lesbian professionals in the closet: Who's in, who's out, and why.* Binghamton, NY: Haworth Press.

Edwards, J. A., & Lampert, M. D. (Eds.). (1993). *Talking data: Transcription and coding in discourse research.* Hillsdale, NJ: Erlbaum.

Ellis, S. J. (2009). Diversity and inclusivity at university: A survey of the experiences of lesbian, gay, bisexual and trans (LGBT) students in the UK. *Higher Education, 57*, 723–739. doi:10.1007/s10734-008-9172-y

Epstein, D., Johnson, R., & Steinberg, D. L. (2000). Twice told tales: Transformation, recuperation and emergence in the age of consent debates 1998. *Sexualities, 3*, 5–30. doi:10.1177/136346000003001001

Epstein, D., O'Flynn, S., & Telford, D. (2003). *Silenced sexualities in schools and universities.* Stoke-on-Trent, England: Trentham Books.

Fereday, J., & Muir-Cochrane, E. (2006). Demonstrating rigor using thematic analysis: A hybrid approach of inductive and deductive coding and theme development. *International Journal of Qualitative Methods, 5*, 1–11.

Flowers, P., & Buston, K. (2001). "I was terrified of being different": Exploring gay men's accounts of growing up in a heterosexist society. *Journal of Adolescence, 24*, 51–65. doi:10.1006/jado.2000.0362

Frith, H., & Gleeson, K. (2004). Clothing and embodiment: Men managing body image and appearance. *Psychology of Men & Masculinity, 5*, 40–48. doi:10.1037/1524-9220.5.1.40

Gamson, J. (2000). Sexualities, queer theory, and qualitative research. In N. K. Denzin & Y. S. Lincoln (Eds.), *Handbook of qualitative research* (2nd ed., pp. 347–365). Thousand Oaks, CA: Sage.

Hayes, N. (1997). Theory-led thematic analysis: Social identification in small companies. In N. Hayes (Ed.), *Doing qualitative analysis in psychology* (pp. 93–114). Hove, England: Psychology Press.

Howitt, D., & Cramer, D. (2008). *Introduction to research methods in psychology* (2nd ed.). Harlow, England: Prentice Hall.

Madill, A., Jordan, A., & Shirley, C. (2000). Objectivity and reliability in qualitative analysis: Realist, contextualist and radical constructionist epistemologies. *British Journal of Psychology, 91*, 1–20. doi:10.1348/000712600161646

Markowe, L. A. (2002). Coming out as lesbian. In A. Coyle & C. Kitzinger (Eds.), *Lesbian and gay psychology: New perspectives* (pp. 63–80). Oxford, England: BPS Blackwell.

Onyx, J., & Small, J. (2001). Memory-work: The method. *Qualitative Inquiry, 7*, 773–786. doi:10.1177/107780040100700608

Patton, M. Q. (2002). *Qualitative evaluation and research methods* (3rd ed.). Thousand Oaks, CA: Sage.

Rich, A. (1980). Compulsory heterosexuality and lesbian existence. *Signs: Journal of Women in Culture and Society, 5,* 631–660. doi:10.1086/493756

Taulke-Johnson, R. (2008). Moving beyond homophobia, harassment and intolerance: Gay male university students' alternative narratives. *Discourse: Studies in the Cultural Politics of Education, 29,* 121–133. doi:10.1080/01596300701802813

Taulke-Johnson, R., & Rivers, I. (1999). Providing a safe environment for lesbian, gay and bisexual students living in university accommodation. *Youth & Policy, 64,* 74–89.

Tuckett, A. G. (2005). Applying thematic analysis theory to practice: A researcher's experience. *Contemporary Nurse, 19,* 75–87. doi:10.5172/conu.19.1-2.75

Warner, M. (1991). Introduction: Fear of a queer planet. *Social Text, 29,* 3–17.

Chapter 5

INTERPRETATIVE PHENOMENOLOGICAL ANALYSIS

Jonathan A. Smith and Pnina Shinebourne

Interpretative phenomenological analysis (IPA) is a recently developed qualitative approach to psychology. This chapter describes the core features of IPA and its theoretical underpinnings. It then provides a step-by-step outline to conduct a study using IPA from data collection through analysis to writing up. Each stage is illustrated with examples from a project exploring the experience of women in rehabilitation for addiction problems.

CORE FEATURES

IPA is concerned with lived experience. Experience covers quite a lot of territory. For example, just walking down the road involves experience. Therefore it is useful to consider Dilthey's (1976) distinction between experience and "an experience." Something becomes an experience when it is important to us, and IPA is almost always concerned with this type of experience. Examples of experiential research questions that would lend themselves to the IPA approach are as follows: What is the impact on patients of receiving a positive genetic test result for Huntington's disease? What sense of home do recent immigrants have? How do elite sports performers conceptualize their activity?

IPA has three primary theoretical touchstones: phenomenology, hermeneutics, and idiography. Phenomenology is the philosophical movement primarily concerned with human lived experience. The philosopher Edmund Husserl, founder of the school of phenomenology, argued for an approach that

attended closely to human experience in its own terms, rather than according to a predetermined category system. For the psychologist, this means as far as possible bracketing ones preconceptions and allowing the phenomenon to speak for itself. This philosophical program was extended by the phenomenologists who followed Husserl. Heidegger (1962) was particularly concerned with the way in which our experience always occurs and is made sense of within a situated context. For Merleau-Ponty (1962) a key factor was the importance of our bodies in enabling experience, and for Sartre (1943) a primary concern was our relations with others. One can see how each of these thinkers is making their own contribution to a holistic account of human experience, and IPA draws on this holistic phenomenology as the underpinning for its approach.

Although IPA is concerned with experience and the meaning of experience to people, it recognizes that this experience cannot be transparently extracted from people's heads—rather, it involves a process of engagement and interpretation on the part of the researcher. Therefore IPA is also influenced by hermeneutics, the theory of interpretation. Hermeneutics began by offering guides to the interpretation of religious texts, clearly a major feature of academic pursuit as first constituted. Over time, however, hermeneutics has extended its remit and now engages with all interpretation.

Heidegger (1962) was a student of Husserl's and took on the intellectual mantle of phenomenology. One of the major ways in which

Thanks to two editors of this volume for helpful comments on a previous version of this chapter.

DOI: 10.1037/13620-005
APA Handbook of Research Methods in Psychology: Vol. 2. Research Designs, H. Cooper (Editor-in-Chief)

Heidegger distinguished himself from Husserl was in arguing that the phenomenological project required the type of interpretative process we are describing:

> Phenomenology is seeking after a meaning which is perhaps hidden by the entity's mode of appearing. In that case the proper model for seeking meaning is the interpretation of a text and for this reason Heidegger links phenomenology with hermeneutics. (Moran, 2000, p. 229)

Smith and Osborn (2003) have described the psychological process of examining experience as involving a double hermeneutic. The participant is trying to make sense of what is happening to them. And the researcher is trying to make sense of the participant trying to make sense of what is happening to them. This points to the way in which the researcher is similar to the participant and shares a common humanity, drawing on the same skills and techniques that the participant has. At the same time, the researcher is different from the participant. The researcher only has entrée to the participant's experience through access provided by that participant, and then the researcher engages in a process of interpretation more systematically and fully than the participant usually does.

IPA is an idiographic approach: It is especially concerned with the particular experience of the individual. Although it does not eschew more general claims, such generalizations can only be made after a careful examination of accounts of experience, on a case-by-case basis. Most research, quantitative and qualitative, is by contrast nomothetic—that is, it is concerned with an analysis at the level of the population or group rather than the individual. IPA's commitment to idiography is most obviously demonstrated in the case study, and there is a growing corpus of IPA case study research (e.g., see de Visser & Smith, 2006; Eatough & Smith, 2006). More commonly, however, an IPA study involves a small number of cases each analyzed in turn. The researcher then moves to look for patterns across cases but tries to retain the individual detail and nuance of the case. Therefore, the best IPA presents an analysis of convergence and divergence within its participant sample.

IPA can be used in a wide range of areas. It can be seen to be working at its best with research topics that are relatively new, however, for which we do not know much about or in areas that are inherently complex or ambiguous. Although IPA can be used to ask participants about topics which are not of current import and that therefore involve cool reflection, it is much more effective when engaged in topics involving *hot cognition*—that is, the participant is concerned with something of existential import in the here and now or recent past. In this sort of project, one can often hear, during an interview, the participant wrestling in real time with something important that is happening to them. This significance and currency is then made manifest in the resultant transcript and lends itself to a fuller and richer analysis. For a full account of the philosophical and theoretical foundations of IPA, see Smith, Flowers, and Larkin (2009).

IPA is not the only phenomenological approach. The best known alternative is Giorgi's phenomenological psychology (Giorgi & Giorgi, 2008). IPA differs from Giorgi's method in that Giorgi considers his approach to be operationalizing a descriptive Husserlian procedure, whereas IPA is interpretative and less wedded to a particular phenomenlogical tradition. Giorgi is also more concerned with attempting to ascertain the general structure of a phenomenon, whereas IPA is more concerned with capturing the individual nuance of experience. IPA shares a considerable amount of ground with Benner's (1994) interpretive phenomenology, which is focused particularly on a Heideggarian analysis of caring, and with Van Manen's (1990) phenomenology of pedagogy and writing.

DESIGN

As discussed, IPA research is concerned with an indepth exploration of lived experience and with how people are making sense of that lived experience. The focal point of an IPA study is therefore guided by open and exploratory research questions. Exhibit 5.1 illustrates the research questions guiding a project conducted by the authors exploring the experience of women in rehabilitation for addiction problems (Shinebourne & Smith, 2009).

Exhibit 5.1
Research Questions From Project Exploring the Experience of Women in Rehabilitation for Addiction Problems

---

- How do the participants describe their experiences of addiction and recovery?
- In what contexts do their experiences occur?
- How do the participants understand and make sense of their experiences of addiction and recovery?
- How are individual differences reflected in the participants' accounts of their experiences with alcohol or drug addiction and recovery?

Note. From *Qualitative Research Methods in Psychology: Combining Core Approaches* (p. 54), by N. Frost (Ed.), 2011, Maidenhead, England: Open University. Copyright 2011 by McGraw-Hill. Reprinted with permission.

The questions are broad and open, aiming to explore in detail participants' accounts of lived experience. In this example, the first two questions are descriptive. The third question opens up a space for participants to reflect on how they make sense of their experience. The fourth question encourages the participants and the researcher to stay focused on the particular detail, texture, and nuance of each participant's account.

SAMPLING

In line with the theoretical underpinnings of IPA, participants are selected purposively because they can offer access to a particular perspective on the phenomena being studied. IPA makes a strong case for a single case study. A detailed analysis of a single case would be justified when one has a particularly rich or compelling case. A detailed single case study offers opportunities to learn a great deal about the particular person and their response to a specific situation as well as to consider connection between different aspects of the person's account (Smith, 2004).

More commonly, researchers conduct IPA studies with a small sample of participants rather than just one. IPA research is conducted on a small sample size because the detailed examination of a case-by-case analysis is elaborate and time-consuming. With

a small number of participants, it is sensible to aim for a fairly homogeneous sample. The aim then is to look in detail at psychological similarities and differences within a group that has been defined as similar according to important variables. So, for example, in a study on how well the participants think the U.S. president is performing, one might decide to conduct this particular study on young, first-time voting, working-class, Black women. The aim is to look at this particular group in detail and then bound the claims that can be made. The next study can look at a different group (e.g., young, first-time voting, working-class, Black men) and so forth. Making a decision on the extent of homogeneity is guided partly by interpretative concerns (degree of similarity or variation that can be contained in the analysis of the phenomenon) and partly by pragmatic considerations (ease or difficulty of contacting potential participants, relative rarity of the phenomenon).

Sample size tends to vary according to the research question and the quality of data obtained. For example, the rehabilitation project incorporated two separate studies: a single case study of one participant whose account was particularly detailed and nuanced, and a second study of six participants. In this way, it was possible to develop the analysis of the single case in considerable depth. At the same time, the study of six participants provided sufficient cases for examining similarities and differences between participants but not so many as to overwhelm the researchers by the amount of data generated. In the second study, homogeneity was achieved by using the following inclusion criteria: participants needed to be women, between the ages of 31 and 52, based in the same rehabilitation program, and within 1 to 2 years of starting their rehabilitation program. Potential participants can be reached by approaching relevant groups, agencies, or gatekeepers; through personal contacts; or through snowballing, that is, asking participants as they are recruited whether they know other people who may be interested in participating.

DATA COLLECTION

IPA requires a data collection method that will invite participants to offer rich, detailed, first-person accounts of experiences and phenomena. The majority of IPA studies have used semistructured, in-depth, one-on-one interviews. The advantage of using semistructured interviews is that they enable the researcher and the participant to engage in a dialogue in real time, and they afford a flexibility to follow up important issues that come up in the participant's account. It is possible, however, to use other methods suitable for collecting detailed verbal accounts, for example, diaries (e.g., Smith, 1999), focus groups (e.g., Flowers, Knussen, & Duncan, 2001), and e-mail dialogues (Turner, Barlow, & Ilbery, 2002).

With semistructured interviews, preparing an interview schedule in advance is helpful to keep the focus on the specific research area and to anticipate possible difficulties, for example, in wording sensitive questions. The example in Exhibit 5.2 illustrates an interview schedule that was developed for the rehabilitation project.

The questions are open and expansive, encouraging participants to talk at length. At the same time, it is helpful to prepare specific prompts as participants may find some questions too general or abstract. To reduce potential unease in the interview situation, it is usually helpful to start the interview with a descriptive question about the present before asking questions about potentially sensitive issues and questions inviting reflection.

An IPA interview typically lasts for an hour or longer. It is not necessary to follow the sequence of the interview schedule or to ask all the questions in exactly the same way of each participant. As the dialogue evolves, the researcher may decide to vary the order of the questions or to make space for a novel perspective that has not been anticipated but appears particularly pertinent to the participant. The participant is the experiential expert on this particular topic. The schedule is merely a guide to facilitate the participant giving their account. It is critical that the participant is given considerable leeway in how the interview proceeds, and it is incumbent on the researcher to probe interesting and potentially important issues as they arise.

Because most IPA studies are concerned with significant existential issues for the participants, it is important to monitor how the interview is affecting

---

Exhibit 5.2
Part of the Interview Schedule From Project Exploring the Experience of Women in Rehabilitation for Addiction Problems

1. Can you tell me what place alcohol and drugs have in your life at the moment?
   Possible prompts: What happens? How do you feel? How do you cope?
2. Can you tell me about a recent time when you used alcohol or drugs?
   Possible prompts: What happened? How did you feel? How did you cope?
3. Can you describe how alcohol, drinking, and using drugs affect your relation with other people?
   Possible prompts: Partner, family, friends, work colleagues?
4. Can you tell me how you started drinking or using drugs?
   Possible prompts: How long ago? What do you think brought this about?
5. Have you changed the ways you used alcohol or drugs over time?
   Possible prompts: In what ways? Does anything make it better? Does anything make it worse? How do you feel about these changes?
6. What would be for you a positive development?
   Possible prompts: How can your situation improve? Can you imagine what it would feel like?

Note. From the doctoral dissertation *Women's Experience of Addiction and Recovery* (p. 111), by P. Shinebourne, 2010, London, England: Birkbeck University of London. Copyright 2010 by P. Shinebourne. Adapted with permission.

---

the participant. It may be prudent to proceed gently or to avoid pursuing some questions if the participant appears uncomfortable. In IPA research, it is necessary to audio record the interviews and to transcribe the whole interview verbatim. This means producing a transcript with everything said by the participant and researcher with spaces to mark conversational turns and with wide margins to allow analytic notes.

Conducting good interviews requires a high level of skill. The interviewer needs to establish rapport at the outset, listen attentively to what the participant is saying to judge how to phrase the next question, and manage the interview flow so a calm and reflective atmosphere is created. It may well take a considerable amount of practice before a researcher feels confident that he or she is interviewing well.

ANALYSIS

IPA provides flexible guidelines for analysis that can be adapted by researchers in accordance with their research aims. Analysis in IPA is a complex, iterative, and multidirectional process, but for the purpose of illustrating the process, it is useful to describe distinct stages.

The initial stage consists of becoming immersed in the data through close reading of the transcript a number of times. Each reading may provide some new insights. At this stage, the researcher may note observations and reflections about the interview experience or any other thoughts and comments of potential significance. Notes and comments may focus on content, language use (features such as metaphors and other figures of speech, repetition, pauses), context, and initial interpretative comments. It is useful to highlight distinctive phrases and emotional responses. We illustrate this process in Exhibit 5.3, which contains a short extract from an interview with Alison (name changed), one of the participants in the addiction rehabilitation study, with the initial comments added in the left-hand margin.

The next stage requires the researcher to transform the initial notes into emerging themes.

Although still grounded in the particular detail of the participant's account, the researcher aims to formulate a concise phrase at a slightly higher level of abstraction that may refer to a more psychological conceptualization. At this stage, the researcher will inevitably also be influenced by having already annotated the transcript as a whole. It is an iterative process and, in the movement of the hermeneutic circle, the part is interpreted in relation to the whole and the whole is interpreted in relation to the part. Exhibit 5.4 represents the emergent themes for the same extract from Alison, with the themes added in the right-hand margin.

The next stage consists of looking for connections between the emerging themes, grouping them together according to conceptual similarities and providing a label for each cluster. Sometimes some themes act like a magnet pulling other themes toward them. The emerging themes in this case study can be grouped by different configurations of the relation between Alison and the world: focusing on self in relation to itself, self in relation to alcohol, self in relation to others, and self in relation to recovery. The process is iterative because it is necessary to ensure that the clusters make sense in

---

Exhibit 5.3
Initial Comments

Original transcript

Probably on the way to getting drunk I enjoyed it but it was very short lived because
   I used to drink so much right at the start and I was sort of remembering falling
into this kind of lull of contentment, I suppose for a while, and suddenly feel, oh,
   I feel better now, I feel alright I can actually talk and be sociable and be the person
everyone wants me to be and be happy and, you know, do all that, entertain
   everyone, you know, and I'd start to kind of really entertain everyone being,
feeling very loving towards everyone and hugging everyone and stuff and then
   beyond that stage I never knew how I was, and it's, I would like change personality
   almost and become like I'm I don't know, like a showgirl, I suppose, so I would
   start performing you know, sorts of props, hats, sticks, chairs, whatever I could
   find, ahm, and just be very entertaining, I never upset anyone, ahm, you know,
   I never got aggressive or anything like that at all, I just, it was just almost like
my body was taking over a character from vaudeville or something like that, you know,
   [laughing] which of course everyone loved, you know, so the more I was like that it's
   hard talking about it actually [crying] [pause, recollects herself] so I was, I was that
   character everyone loved, that person, so I suppose I got caught in a trap of being like
   that, and having to drink so much in order to get to that person I did not know sober.

Exploratory comments

short-term enjoyment

"lull"—metaphoric, indicates a sense of foreboding, lull before the storm? pleasing others

change personality—acting out a character

embodying a character feeling loved only when acting out another character—self-esteem issues?
"caught in a trap"—inevitability, passivity, false promises

Exhibit 5.4
Developing Emergent Themes

Original transcript	Emerging themes
probably on the way to getting drunk I enjoyed it but it was very short lived because I used to drink so much right at the start and I was sort of remembering falling into this kind of lull of contentment, I suppose for a while, and suddenly feel, oh, I feel better now, I feel alright I can actually talk and be sociable and be the person everyone wants me to be and be happy and, you know, do all that, entertain everyone, you know, and I'd start to kind of really entertain everyone being, feeling very loving towards everyone and hugging everyone and stuff and then beyond that stage I never knew how I was, and it's, I would like change personality almost and become like I'm I don't know, like a showgirl, I suppose, so I would start performing you know, sorts of props, hats, sticks, chairs, whatever I could find, ahm, and just be very entertaining, I never upset anyone, ahm, you know, I never got aggressive or anything like that at all, I just, it was just almost like my body was taking over a character from vaudeville or something like that, you know, [laughing] which of course everyone loved, you know, so the more I was like that it's hard talking about it actually [crying] [pause, recollects herself] so I was, I was that character everyone loved, that person, so I suppose I got caught in a trap of being like that, and having to drink so much in order to get to that person I did not know sober.	*Escalating drinking*
	Positive drinking experience
	Pleasing others
	Changing self through drink
	Projection of self into another person
	The process of becoming the other self
	Low self-esteem
	Ambivalence

relation to the original transcript. Exhibit 5.5 shows a part of this process for Alison.

Following this, the thematic relationship is presented graphically in a table of themes. Exhibit 5.6 shows the structure of major themes, themes, and subthemes and, for each theme or subtheme, it also includes a relevant short extract from the transcript, followed by the line number, so that it is possible to return to the transcript and check the extract in context. As Eatough and Smith (2006) wrote:

> For the researcher, this table is the outcome of an iterative process in which she/he has moved back and forth between the various analytic stages ensuring that the integrity of what the participant said has been preserved as far as possible. If the researcher has been successful, then it should be possible for someone else to track the analytic journey from the raw data through to the end table. (p. 120)

Exhibit 5.5
Initial Clustering of Themes (Extract)

Perception of self
Low self-esteem
Moral judgments of self
Positive appraisals of self
Metaphors expressing perception of self (e.g., mixture of water and fire)
The self as a process of becoming

Relations with others
Pleasing others
Dysfunctional relationships
Fear of being rejected by others
Family dynamics
Support from others

Experience of self as drunk
Escalating drinking
Positive drinking experience
Harmful experience of being drunk
Metaphoric expressions for the experience of being drunk (wave, the sea)
The self-changing through drinking

We illustrate this process in Exhibit 5.6, which shows the first superordinate theme, *self in relation to alcohol*, and the three interrelated themes comprising it. Exhibit 5.6 represents the analysis of a case study of one participant. And one could proceed from here to write up this case. More usually a project involves more than one case. This involves repeating the whole process for each participant and constructing a table of themes for each transcript. Inevitably, the analysis of the first case will become part of the hermeneutic circle of understanding,

thereby influencing the analysis of the subsequent transcripts. Following from IPA's idiographic commitment, however, it is important to keep an open mind to allow new themes to emerge from each transcript. The process is iterative as earlier transcripts are reviewed in the light of new themes. Finally a table of themes for the study as a whole is constructed. In this process, the individual tables are reviewed and checked again with the transcripts. At this stage, it may be possible to combine some themes or to reduce the data, making decisions

---

Exhibit 5.6
Superordinate Theme 1: Self in Relation to
Alcohol (Including Illustrative Extract for Each Theme and Line Numbers)

A. **The experience of the self as drunk**
Metaphoric expressions of the experience of being drunk
  Big wave 449
  At sea 457
  Even if you were sitting on the beach . . . you'd get caught back in 460
Escalating drinking
  On the way to getting drunk I enjoyed it 28
  It would just spiral and spiral 25
  Beyond that stage I never knew how I was 35
The harmful experience of being drunk
  Completely out of control around alcohol 14
  Having blackouts, memory loss 15
  I could have done myself in by accident 574
The high and the low of the drinking experience
  Creative and energetic and interesting 498
  Feelings of like fun and excitement 495
  Alcohol actually helps me with my general flow 846
  Unlocking some sort of artistic feeling 496
  Washed up and deplete 502
  Very tearful and self-remorseful 503
Ambivalence and dilemmas
  I feel too scared of the blackouts 75
  I am not completely giving up alcohol 3
  If only I could get to that without so much alcohol 488
B. **I created such a character for myself**
The self-changing through drinking
  Having to drink so much in order to get to this person 44–45
  I would change personality 35
  I was that character everyone loved 43
The process of becoming the other self
  My body was taking over a character 40

I could feel myself changing 478
I look very different 1161
Feeling the other self
  It feels a part of me but it does not really feel the whole of me 1094–1095
  Feeling totally in my body 1052
  It feels amazing to kind of connect immediately 1055–1056
The porous body
  When you are drunk you are open to spirits visiting your body 475
  I feel like I am a vessel 477
  Things probably come through me 1106
The self as a process of becoming
  From one day to the next I really do change 1110
  Evolving now 1113
  There needs to be more like a centre to me 1108
C. **Perception of the self**
Metaphors expressing perception of self
  Mixture of water and fire 809
  A bit ground 818
  I don't have metal at all 822
Positive appraisals of self
  I am caring towards hopefully everyone 169 Intuitive 170
  Quiet and contemplative 66
Negative appraisals of self
  I can't really assert myself 1015
  No sense of self-worth 602
  Not valuing myself 224
Moral judgments of self
  Guilt and anxiety you have done something wrong 504
  Feeling remorseful 149–150
  I am like a bad person or I am wasting my life 392–393

Note. This is an expanded version of a table that first appeared in "Alcohol and the Self: An Interpretative Phenomenological Analysis of the Experience of Addiction and Its Impact on the Sense of Self and Identity," by P. Shinebourne and J. A. Smith, 2009, *Addiction Research and Theory, 17,* p. 167. Copyright 2009 by Informa. Adapted with permission.

based not only on the prevalence of data but also on the pertinence of the themes and their capacity to illuminate the account as a whole.

WRITING UP

Next one turns to writing a narrative account of the study. Typically this entails taking the themes established in the final table and writing them up one by one. Each theme needs to be introduced and then illustrated with extracts from the participant, which are in turn followed by analytic comments from the authors. The narrative account may engage several levels of interpretation (see Larkin, Watts, & Clifton, 2006; Smith et al., 2009), which may generate new insights. The narrative account contains relevant extracts in the participants' own words, which not only enables the reader to assess the pertinence of the interpretations but also retains the *voice* of the participants' personal experience. Smith et al. (2009) suggested that one way of looking at the narrative account is to consider the extracts from participants as representing the *P* in IPA, and the accompanying analysis as representing the *I*. In a typical IPA project, the narrative account is followed by a discussion section that considers the themes

---

Exhibit 5.7
Example of Write-Up: Dynamics of Relationships in the Family

The enduring impact of childhood families and relations on their predicament as adults constituted a prevailing theme in all participants' accounts. As discussed, Julia attributed her tendency to suppress emotions to a controlled father in a family where it was not acceptable to express anger. Susie describes her parents as "very strict, quite Victorians" and she suggests that her addictive and obsessive behaviors might have been learned in childhood:

It helps me to understand my family with, how we were brought up 'cause I know today, both my parents are long long dead, but they both were workaholics and perfectionist, both died of heart attacks very young, so and my brothers and sisters were all very much the same even those who don't drink and take drugs still got this you know, um there's no sense of balance, um so I know it's something also that, I could have learnt or picked up on that, to be loved or to have self-esteem I need to prove myself.

Susie recounts that she had to follow everything her parents prescribed for her and, as the oldest daughter, had to take on responsibility at a young age for looking after her younger siblings. Leaving home and forming intimate relationships meant freedom in defiance of her parents:

I did everything my parents wanted but that's when I went, I left home you know I really started drinking and taking, cannabis mainly, cocaine came later at work um, it was freedom, you know[ ] the way I gave myself permission to be naughty was through my drinking and taking drugs [ ] Got in to a relationship, completely against my parents wishes, and he is, he was a drug, a cannabis user.

Similarly, Claire describes how in retrospect she came to understand her upbringing as problematic, although she says she used to believe that "nothing major has ever happened to me":

My childhood wasn't as functional as I thought, you know I had a very, yeah my dad was an alcoholic but I didn't really see him as one because he was a functional and sociable one you know, good job it was all of that kind of thing, he wasn't there a lot so my home life was kind of like that erm and then he left erm so it was just me and my mum and my sister so it's been very much like that ever since it's always been the three of us so it's always been this very intense thing that no men can never penetrate us three, do you know what I mean, we've always been very close like that and I suppose I find it quite hard to trust people.

This extract illustrates, as noted, the significance of the intense bond between Claire and her mother. Elsewhere in the interview she describes her relations with her mother as "codependency," like "a mirror thing when I see my mum doing stuff . . . then I see myself doing it as well." This extract from Claire also points toward possible problematic relations with men ("no men can never penetrate us"), as confirmed when Claire says she had "disastrous relationship with men all my life, you know there's always been like my father" (see the next extract). Mother and sister were also the key figures providing support and bearing the brunt of her addiction:

It would always be my mum would stay and look after me she, she would clear up my flat try and get me to the doctor's and those kind of things but in turn I would then ring them [mother or sister] at three o'clock in the morning drunk, abusive not remembering always threatening to kill myself you know and then coming round.

identified in the analysis in relation to existing literature. The write-up of the case Study of Alison can be seen in Shinebourne and Smith (2009).

Exhibit 5.7 shows an extended example from the write-up of Study 2 of the addiction rehabilitation project. This involved interviews with six women as described earlier. The analysis generated a number of themes and this exhibit presents how part of the theme "dynamics of relationships in the family" is presented in the results section.

This extended section from the write-up shows how the table of themes opens up into a persuasive account that explains to the reader the important experiential things that have been found during the process of analysis. It also shows how each claim is substantiated with verbatim extracts from participants and how extracts are followed by local analytic interpretive comments. For a full description of IPA, including its theoretical origins, guidance on practice, and examples of research, see Smith et al. (2009).

WHERE IPA IS AND WHERE IT IS GOING

IPA is a relative newcomer to the field. The first paper describing it was by Smith (1996). Since then it has been picked up enthusiastically, particularly in health, clinical, and counseling psychology and increasingly in cognate areas (e.g., education, sports science, health research). What does the current corpus look like? Jonathan A. Smith recently conducted a review of the IPA literature (Smith, 2011). Between 1996 and 2008, 293 papers were published in journals tagged in three major databases (*Web of Science*, MEDLINE®, PsycINFO®).

The existence of a substantial corpus now enables us to begin to consider the quality of IPA studies. Smith et al. (2009) used Yardley's (2000) criteria for evaluating qualitative research to consider how an IPA study can meet these criteria. For example, Smith et al. (2009) argued that sensitivity is shown in a good IPA study by sensitivity *to the data*. Extensive extracts from participants are required so that each claim in the study is supported with evidence from the interview corpus. Commitment to IPA is shown by a recognition that experiential qualitative psychology is demanding, requiring a range of skills different from those

acquired during a quantitative training, and by effort directed at honing those skills and making them manifest in interviews. Transparency is addressed by providing a clear presentation, within the constraints of word length set by publishing outlets, of what was done in the study, step by step.

Smith's (2011) review offered a set of more specific criteria for assessing IPA papers and offered detailed summaries of those papers graded well in a critical evaluation of a clearly defined subset of the corpus. Hopefully, this will be helpful both to researchers wishing to improve their skills in IPA and to those required to review IPA work.

References

Benner, P. (Ed.). (1994). *Interpretive phenomenology: Embodiment, caring, and ethics in health and illness.* Thousand Oaks, CA: Sage.

de Visser, R., & Smith, J. A. (2006). Mister in-between: A case study of masculine identity and health-related behaviour. *Journal of Health Psychology, 11,* 685–695. doi:10.1177/1359105306066624

Dilthey, W. (1976). *Selected writings.* Cambridge, England: Cambridge University Press.

Eatough, V., & Smith, J. A. (2006). I feel like a scrambled egg in my head: An idiographic case study of meaning making and anger using interpretative phenomenological analysis. *Psychology and Psychotherapy: Theory, Research, and Practice, 79,* 115–135.

Flowers, P., Knussen, C., & Duncan, B. (2001). Re-appraising HIV testing among Scottish gay men: The impact of new HIV treatments. *Journal of Health Psychology, 6,* 665–678. doi:10.1177/135910 530100600605

Frost, N. (Ed.). (2011). *Qualitative research methods in psychology: Combining core approaches.* Maidenhead, Berkshire, England: Open University Press.

Giorgi, A., & Giorgi, B. (2008). Phenomenology. In *Qualitative psychology: A practical guide to methods* (2nd ed., pp. 26–52). London, England: Sage.

Heidegger, M. (1962). *Being and time.* Oxford, England: Blackwell.

Larkin, M., Watts, S., & Clifton, E. (2006). Giving voice and making sense in interpretative phenomenological analysis. *Qualitative Research in Psychology, 3,* 102–120. doi:10.1191/1478088706qp062oa

Merleau-Ponty, M. (1962). *Phenomenology of perception.* London, England: Routledge & Kegan Paul.

Moran, D. (2000). *Introduction to phenomenology.* London, England: Routledge.

Sartre, J. P. (1943). *Being and nothingness.* New York, NY: Washington Square Press.

Shinebourne, P. (2010). *Women's experience of addiction and recovery* (Unpublished doctoral thesis). Birkbeck University of London, England.

Shinebourne, P., & Smith, J. A. (2009). Alcohol and the self: An interpretative phenomenological analysis of the experience of addiction and its impact on the sense of self and identity. *Addiction Research and Theory, 17,* 152–167. doi:10.1080/16066350802245650

Smith, J. A. (1996). Beyond the divide between cognition and discourse: Using interpretative phenomenological analysis in health psychology. *Psychology and Health, 11,* 261–271. doi:10.1080/0887044960 8400256

Smith, J. A. (1999). Towards a relational self: Social engagement during pregnancy and psychological preparation for motherhood. *British Journal of Social Psychology, 38,* 409–426. doi:10.1348/01446669 9164248

Smith, J. A. (2004). Reflecting on the development of interpretative phenomenological analysis and its contribution to qualitative research in psychology. *Qualitative Research in Psychology, 1,* 39–54.

Smith, J. A. (2011). Evaluating the contribution of interpretative phenomenological analysis. *Health Psychology Review, 5,* 9–27.

Smith, J. A., Flowers, P., & Larkin, M. (2009). *Interpretative phenomenological analysis: Theory, method, and research.* London, England: Sage.

Smith, J. A., & Osborn, M. (2003). Interpretative phenomenological analysis. In J. A. Smith (Ed.), *Qualitative psychology* (pp. 51–80). London, England: Sage.

Turner, A., Barlow, J., & Ilbery, B. (2002). Play hurt, live hurt: Living with and managing osteoarthritis from the perspective of ex-professional footballers. *Journal of Health Psychology, 7,* 285–301. doi:10.1177/1359105302007003222

Van Manen, M. (1990). *Researching lived experience.* New York: State University of New York Press.

Yardley, L. (2000). Dilemmas in qualitative health research. *Psychology and Health, 15,* 215–228. doi:10.1080/08870440008400302

Narrative- and Language-Based Approaches

CHAPTER 6

NARRATIVE ANALYSIS

Michael Bamberg

A number of different connotations are commonly connected to the use of the terms *narrative research*, *narrative inquiry*, and *narrative analysis*—connotations that intersect and often contribute to the impression of narrative research as complex and multilayered, if not confusing. One of the most central ways this complexity plays out is in what can be taken as the most basic intersection, namely, that between research *on* narratives, in which narratives are the object of study, and research *with* narratives, in which narratives are the tools to explore something else—typically aspects of human memory or experience. One of the goals of this chapter is to work through some of this complexity and to make recommendations for how to follow methodical procedures when working *with* narratives—procedures that are built on, and follow insights gained from, work *on* narratives.

The chapter is divided into two parts, which are followed by a summary and reflection. The first part presents an overview on the topic of narrative methods with the aim to show how different research questions and research traditions have informed and led to what falls broadly under the purview of narrative methods. The second part of the chapter features an analysis of a story that illustrates how traditions and questions sampled in the first part of the chapter can be applied and how they contribute to answer a number of research questions. Thus, in contrast to the traditional approach of starting with a question and from there using the methodologically appropriate toolbox to answer the question, this chapter proposes an alternative route: It presents a sampling of methods to reveal a variety of strategies for how to pose interesting research questions. In essence, the reader is not given a recipe for how to arrive at good narrative research; rather, if the reader's insight is along the lines of "oh, now I know how to pose my research question that can be followed by use of narrative methods," the goal of this chapter has been accomplished.

PART 1: THE PROJECT OF NARRATIVE ANALYSIS

Why Narrative?

An examination of narrative analysis must begin with a definition of what we mean by *narrative*. Let me start with a provisional definition of *narrative* that is revisited throughout this chapter: When narrators tell a story, they give *narrative form* to experience. They position characters in space and time and, in a broad sense, give order to and make sense of what happened—or what is imagined to have happened. Thus, it can be argued that narratives attempt to *explain* or *normalize* what has occurred; they lay out why things are the way they are or have become the way they are. Narrative, therefore, can be said to provide a portal into two realms: (a) the realm of experience, where speakers lay out how they as individuals experience certain events and confer their subjective meaning onto these experiences; and (b) the realm of narrative means (or devices) that are put to use to make (this) sense. In the first instance, we typically encounter

DOI: 10.1037/13620-006
APA Handbook of Research Methods in Psychology: Vol. 2. Research Designs, H. Cooper (Editor-in-Chief)

research *with* narrative and in the second, we encounter research *on* narrative. At this point, we have not specified whether narrators employ narrative means to make sense to others in communicative and interactive settings or whether narrators attempt to make sense to themselves, as when writers write for themselves, or clients speak in search of their selves in a therapeutic setting. We have further left unspecified whether narrators talk about themselves, that is, tell personal experiences they imagined or underwent in person (first-person experiences) or whether they talk about the experiences of others—even fictionally invented others (third-person experiences). Furthermore, we also look more closely into the kinds of experiences or themes that are configured into meaningful units by use of different narrative means. Although all these issues are important, we start with a closer characterization of narrative analysis.

Narrative Means and Narrative Meaning

It is perfectly reasonable to collect narratives of people's experiences and archive them in textual, audio, or video format so they can be accessed later by those who are interested in them, but the project of narrative analysis involves more. Starting again from a provisional and broad definition, which requires more specification, narrative analysis attempts to systematically relate the narrative means deployed for the function of laying out and making sense of particular kinds of, if not totally unique, experiences. Narrative analysts can place more weight on analyzing the narrative means, or the intention may be to extrapolate and better understand particular experiences. In the best of all worlds, both approaches inform each other, that is, learning more about narrative means improves our analysis of what narratives are used for and vice versa. Narrative analysts are required to lay out the relationship between narrative means and the experience that is constituted by such means to make transparent and document how they arrive at their interpretive conclusions.

Whenever the analytic focus is on the narrative means, qualitative and quantitative approaches have been employed side by side with little joint consideration. Explorations of how children learn to use narrative means that establish characters in a story,

how to tie clauses together into meaningful episodes, or how to evaluate what is going on from an overarching perspective, have turned up elaborate coding systems that allow cross-age and cross-linguistic quantitative comparisons, delivering insights into the acquisition of narrative competencies. Further research into comparisons between first- and second-language learners' narrative means and the means and strategies used in atypical populations (e.g., individuals with Down syndrome and autism) have led to interesting applied fields, such as literacy education and parental training in narrative intervention programs.

Narrative inquiry that is more interested in how meaning is conferred onto experience, especially in narratives of personal experience about concrete life situations (ranging from experiences such as menarche or first romantic involvements to larger research questions such as divorce and professional identity and continuing up to aging and life satisfaction), has traditionally leaned more toward the employment of qualitative research procedures. The relationships among the use of concrete narrative means to construct highly subjective and specific life situations as well as retrospective evaluations of life courses are open to both quantitative and qualitative analytic procedures. In the next section, I focus more strongly on narrative analysis as a qualitative research method, pointing toward possibilities for other research practices whenever appropriate.

The Emergence of Narrative Analysis

Having clarified that narrative analysis is invested in both the means and the way these means are put to use to arrive at presentations and interpretations of meaningful experiences, we can turn to a brief genealogy of the emergence of narrative analysis in the social sciences and, more specifically, in the discipline of psychology. To get a clearer conception of what spurred the recent surge of interest in narrative and narrative methods as well as to better understand debates among proponents of different analytic practices, it is worthwhile to distinguish among (a) how it was possible that narratives have become accepted as a genre that seems to closely reflect people's sense-making strategies—particularly narratives of lives, as in (auto-)biography, life writing, confessions, and other disclosures of identity; (b) how narrative could catapult into the role of a method—one that is said to be the main portal into individual and communal sense making, experience, and subjectivity; and (c) how differences (and commonalities) among a variety of narrative methods seemingly compete with one another as analytic tools. I briefly consider these distinctions in the sections Narrative as Genre, Narrative as Method, and Narrative Methods.

Narrative as genre. Stories and storytelling practices are assumed to be closely tied to with the phylogenesis of language, human social formations, and the historically emerging vision of individuality and the modern person. Early narrative forms, reaching back as far as 1500 B.C.E., reflect forms of recorded historical experience in epic formats and are argued to be instrumental in the creation of communal (tribal) education. In the course of sociogenesis, the epic form is joined and partly replaced by folk tales, fables, and travelogues—all foreshadowing the rise of the romantic fiction and the novel, starting around 1200 and culminating in Europe between 1600 and 1750. The new and innovative narrative techniques put to use in these genres—in concert with the development of the print culture—gave rise to the writing (and reading) of letters, confessions, and memoirs. This in turn fed readers' interest in personal histories, the biography, life history, and autobiographies—all making use of temporal sequences of lived events for a systematic and self-reflective quest of the (authentic) self. Notably, the character in these quests, the person the story is centrally about, is becoming more and more open to be construed in terms of change and personal development. En route from the epic via the novel to the biography, narrative has emerged as a new but central formatting device for the organization of self and (modern) identity. It successfully fed the commonly shared belief that who we are, or who we think we are, is realized in the stories we tell about ourselves; everyone not only *has* a story but also has a right to tell their story (Bamberg, 2011). Thus, not only is the quest for the modern self in the form of the "who-am-I" question deeply rooted in the history of narrative, but, in addition, the story actually becomes the very data to be analyzed when seeking answers to the who-am-I question.

The realization that the (modern) self is open to change, and that the means for actual change have to work through the narrative, has led to a second wave of interest in narrative. In keeping with the "therapeutic narrative of selfhood" and its injunction "that we become our 'most complete' and 'self-realized' selves" (Illouz, 2008, p. 172), we are continuously urged to seek out the "problem" in our narrative, the one that is causing our lack of fulfillment and the suffering that comes in its wake. Grounding the problem in some previous events, often reaching back into childhood experiences, and establishing a narrative connection that has led to the problem, not only is said to enhance self-reflection but also is regarded the first step in a healing exercise that is supposed to free the narrator of the problem and the suffering it causes. Narrative self-reflection in conjunction with narrative self-disclosure are taken to form the cornerstones of a narratively grounded approach to a rational and reflexive self-monitoring.

Narrative as method. Although the relationship between narrative and identity has been theorized by philosophers, historians, literary critics, and psychologists (among others), credit for moving the narrative mode of sense making into a special status belongs to Bruner (1986, 1991) and Lyotard (1984). Lyotard and Bruner have argued cogently that there are two kinds of sense-making modes, which stand in opposition to one another: one best characterized as a *logico-scientific* mode, and the other, often underrated and neglected, as a *narrative* mode of ordering experience and making sense. Both methods of knowing rely on different procedures for verification, with narrative knowing centering around the particularity and specificity of what occurred and the involvement (and accountability or responsibility) of human agents in bringing about these specific and incidental events. Thus, viewing narrative as a basic human method to make sense of experience is more than sharing how this sense has been made in the form of stories. The term *narrative as method* implies a general approach that views individuals within their social environments as actively conferring meaning onto objects in the world, including others and selves; the way this happens in everyday situations as well as in interviews or surveys, is necessarily subjective and interpretive. If narrative is elevated into "the primary form by which human experience is made meaningful" (Polkinghorne, 1988, p. 1), then it makes sense to argue that the stories we tell are such because they reflect "the stories we are" (McAdams, 1993; Randall, 1995).

Tapping into these narrative processes of meaning making is not unproblematic. For one, there are different stories about ourselves (or what we tell our experience to be) at different occasions. And the ways these occasions are conducted affect the internal organization of what is being told, its content matters, and the meaning that both teller and audience may take from them. Another problem is the often-claimed assumption that the sharing of narratives about situations in which narrative meaning has been conferred onto others and selves is open to reflection and seemingly transparent to both narrator and audience (see Hollway & Jefferson, 2008, for a critique of this assumption). Although narratives can become, and in particular settings can be used as, reflective means, there is no a priori reason to render stories unanalyzed as reflections of subjectivities or presentations of participants' *own* voices (Gubrium & Holstein, 2009). A more dangerous stance may be lurking in the narrative-as-method metaphor when life and experience are leveled as narrative so that not only human knowledge but also interactive practices, particularly interviews, become narrative inquiry and blur the boundaries between us as living our stories and us as analyzing the stories of others. Even if narrative is elevated into a central or primary method of sense making, it still needs to be open to interpretation and reinterpretation. This interpretation requires laying open the angles and perspectives from where meaning is being conferred and scrutinizing the methods employed by narrators in arriving at their stories (and lives).

Narrative methods. Although the argument for narrative as method was instrumental for a great number of inquiries into the personal sense making of experience (in different disciplines and on different experiential topics), narrative as method should be kept separate from what has traditionally been held under the purview of *narrative methods*. Narratives, whether acquired through particular elicitation techniques, such as interviewing, or found in natural (private, public, or institutionalized) interactional settings, typically are the result of a research stance or orientation. Critical in relation to traditional survey practices, the narrative interview was designed to overcome the common tendency to radically decontextualize and disconnect the respondents' meaning-making efforts from the concrete setting for which they originally were designed and from the larger sociocultural grounds of meaning production (Mishler, 1986, p. 26). In recent years, a number of qualitative, in-depth interviewing techniques have been designed to elicit explicitly narrative accounts—some open-ended and unstructured, others semistructured and guided. These techniques include the *free association narrative interview method* (Hollway & Jefferson, 2008); the *biographic-narrative interpretive method*, an interview technique that leads into personal experience, lived situations, and life-histories (Wengraf, 2006); or *narrative-oriented inquiry* (Hiles & Cermák, 2008), to name a few.

Although the focus on different methods in narrative interviewing has led to interesting insights into the relationships between narrative form and content in the face of different elicitation strategies, others have taken this focus to push more in the direction of carefully considering the conditions under which narrative means are employed in narrative practices. The notion of narrative practices here incorporates interviewing practices of all kinds, including focus or brainstorming groups, and also opens up the field for narrative inquiry into institutional and everyday storytelling practices, such as during dinnertime, at sleepovers, on schoolyards, in courtrooms, at Alcoholics Anonymous meetings, or during medical anamnesis.

One way to differentiate among narrative methods is to rely on the distinction between structure and performance (Bamberg, 1997). Gubrium and Holstein (2009) suggested a similar bipartite division, one that draws on narratives as texts and narratives as practice. The study of the textual properties of narratives typically is concerned with the textual structural properties as well as with content in terms of themes and the ways characters are presented in (narrated) time and space. The focus on narrative practice "takes us outside such accounts and their transcripts to varied storytelling occasions" (Gubrium & Holstein, 2009, p. 210). Riessman (2008) suggested a tripartite division with regard to different analytic stances regarding narratives: She differentiated between thematic, structural, and dialogic–performative approaches. Thematic approaches are primarily interested in what topically and thematically surfaces in the realm of a story's content, whereas analysts concerned with a story's structure orient more strongly toward the linguistic phenomena as well as the story's overall sequential composition. Analysts who fall into the dialogic–performative group combine aspects of the thematic and structural analytic orientations but also ask "who an utterance may be directed to, when, and why, that is, for what purposes?" (Riessman, 2008, p. 105).

In the next section, I briefly work through three analytic traditions that differ in terms of their background assumptions, their basic units of analysis, and their procedural analytic steps. These three analytic traditions are grounded in different disciplinary orientations and also ask distinct questions and have different purposes. This next section aims to show more clearly what kinds of questions open up when adopting different analytic procedures. The first analytic orientation is textual in the sense that it focuses on the linear sequence of clauses—the way narratives are forming cohesive sequences of referred-to events. The second orientation centers around the overall conceptual structure of the text—the way events are conceived as parts of episodes, which in turn are parts of larger thematic structures such as plots. Both of these traditions typically deal with texts but with two different orientations: The first one deals with texts in terms of a bottom-up formation process, and the second one deals with texts in terms of a top-down formation process. In addition, both analytic orientations are dealing with what can best be characterized as monologues. A third orientation comes close to Gubrium and Holstein's (2009) analytic focus on narrative practice and

Riessman's (2008) suggestion to foreground the dialogic–performative features of the act of telling in the analytic process. I am calling this kind of analytic focus *interactive–performative* (Bamberg, 1997, 2011).

Narrative Methods and Analytic Concepts

In working through various approaches a tripart distinction will be made, although in actual narrative research, the three different approaches that follow are often not clearly distinguishable. Nevertheless, as ideal types they follow particular principles and guidelines. The purpose of the next sections is to be able to conceptually move within each of these frameworks toward their different goals.

Texts as linguistic structure: Words, sentences, and topical cohesiveness. The preferred definition within this first method is that a narrative consists of minimally two narrative (event) clauses, such as "The king died. Then the queen died of grief." Both referred-to happenings result in the second event, not only temporally following each other, but seen as connected by some form of causal contingency. This approach to narrative assumes that events do not happen *in* the world. The flow of continuously changing time needs to be stopped and packaged into bounded units: events and event sequences. This is done by use of particular verb-type predicates in conjunction with the kinds of temporal marking that particular languages have at their disposal. Stringing these events together forms the backbone or skeleton of a story (Labov, 1972). Whenever speakers step out of the sequence of stringing events into their story, they usually pursue other business (e.g., summarizing or evaluating what happened) by way of adopting a more overall or evaluative perspective.

Temporality is only one among several options to make a story cohesive. Other means include the use of spatial markers and the marking of character continuity. Taken together, narrators make use of linguistic devices to move characters through the spatial and temporal contiguity of what happened and, in doing so, *build* characters and position them in relationships with one another. In English, for example (as in most Indo-European languages), there are intricate options to employ shifts from proper names (*Jennie*) to nominal forms (*this girl*) to pronouns (*she*) to simply not mentioning the referent (zero-pronoun). A narrator employs these shifts skillfully, in conjunction with temporal and spatial devices, to build small thematic units, those that resemble paragraphs or episodes, when it comes to sequencing of otherwise-random clauses into larger units that ultimately surmount to the narrative and what it is about.

This way of approaching narratives starts from the clause and its lexical–syntactic makeup as the basic analytic unit and assumes that tying clauses cohesively together follows the language-specific practices and norms of cohesion building. In following these procedures, a fuller, episodic structure emerges—one that resembles and is typical for stories. Stories, according to this view, come into existence by use of lexical and syntactic devices that speakers put to use as indexes for story formations. The devices continuously signal (contextualize) where the narrator is in the construction of the overarching unit. Thus, on the basis of the smallest unit of analysis, the clause, the linguistic devices employed mark, and as such are interpreted as, what the speaker assembles as a given narrative to be *about*. This approach can be stretched into the semantic organization of cohesion building: Shifts between lexical devices that seemingly refer to the same character also can be significant. Referring to a female character by use of gendered terms, such as *great body* or *slut*, places her in membership categories that obviously mark different positions in regard to this female character but also locate a different sense of self of the speaker in regard to the audience (Bamberg, 2004).

Texts as cognitive structure: Plots, themes, and coherence.   Although it is possible, as Labov (1972) suggested, to describe the units that emerge in the course of narrative cohesion building in terms of elements that ultimately result in some structural whole, the emergent whole is more than its linguistic components. In other words, the emerging units are as much products or outcomes of bottom-up construction processes as they are reflections of an overall structure that organizes its components from the top to the bottom. Typically, this top-down kind of process is conceived of in terms of conceptual units that have their origins in (universally) shared story grammars. These kinds of conceptual units have found support in cognitive research on story comprehension and story retellings (cf. Mandler & Johnson, 1977; Thorndyke, 1977). The argument is that these units are more conceptual and less linguistic in nature. They are units that speakers and story comprehenders bring to the telling situation as templates to embed or make fit the story particulars. These units typically include an (optional) *abstract*, followed by an *orientation* (or *setting* or *exposition*), followed by the *complication* (also called *problem* or *crisis*), maybe an action or action orientation toward a resolution, resulting in the *resolution* (or occasionally *failure*), which then is ultimately followed by a *coda* (or *closure*). The *orientation* takes the listener into the there-and-then where actions take place, and the *coda* takes the audience back to the here-and-now of the telling situation.

The characters in the story are the exponents of intentionality (and emotions), and it is their action orientation—on the basis of the interiority of their minds and emotions—that leads up to what action (or nonaction) unfolds. However, not unlike actions and action orientations in the epic, individual actions in story grammar approaches are held together and called out by larger motivational scripts that resemble plots, if not aspects of the human drama. Take for instance a story that is played out in the movie *Stand by Me* that involves a vomiting incident during a pie-eating contest, which actually figures as an intentional part within a revenge plot. Although the characters in these plot configurations engage in the same kind of activities—they all vomit while competing in (and watching) the contest and act (unknowingly) within the revenge scheme of the protagonist—they offer different options for identifications for teller and audience (cf. Bamberg, 2003).

Thus, in spite of story characters conceived of as intentional agents, the cognitive orientation in regard to narrative research integrates the sequence of events (as intended or not-intended) into more or less coherent configurations that contain a purpose. Purpose here, in a top-down fashion, gains its meaning from the narrative whole. The whole lends meaning to the components of the story and their sequential arrangement. And the way the components are arranged is to be viewed as a function of the whole. Consequently, the analysis within this analytic frame proceeds from the whole to its parts. The general theme of a narrative is established through the examination of this part–whole relationship typically through multiple readings of the narrative and often as part of a team exercise. Through this process, the components of a narrative can be divided and undergo their individual analytic scrutiny in addition to relating them to a larger whole.

Both the linguistic–cohesive and cognitive–coherence approaches focus on monologic texts. Although for both approaches striving for stronger cohesive ties and better coherence are in the service of easier and better comprehension, the purpose of the story according to these approaches is to encode information, and the way the information is structured is relevant for the effect of the story on the audience. The linguistic and conceptual structures of the story are functions in the service of the theme, the overall plot, and the content. It is as if the content and its organization are central to the narrator's concern, and he or she follows the linguistic and cognitive conventions that are appropriate to encode this content. Consequently, any research interest that is primarily concerned with content and thematic structuring will gravitate toward these methods.

Beyond the text: Why this story here and now?
In contrast to the previous two more monologic and textually oriented approaches, an interactive–performative orientation works with narratives as situated in dialogue (we use the term *interaction*; cf. Chapters 7 and 8 of this volume) and is performed—not only with linguistic means but also with *other* bodily means.[1] The focus is on storytelling as activity, including what has been going on before the speaker enters the floor and what happens thereafter (e.g., the story's uptake). Thus,

we see a clear shift in terms of what enters into the focus of analyzing such narratives: Examining stories in terms of their cohesive and coherence (thematic) components and analyzing the means that are taken to be the building blocks simply is not sufficient. Such stories, irrespective whether they are small and short or whether they constitute a lengthy turn in the form of a full-blown life story, have antecedents and consequences in situations in which they emerge. These situations are taken to be part of narrative practices that heavily affect how a story is told and what their thematic and structural makeup turns out to be. This, however, does not imply that an interactive–performative approach to narrative analysis is oblivious to content and structure. According to this third performance-type approach, linguistic and cognitive structuring is part of what speakers accomplish with their narratives. But what speakers do with their stories may serve multiple purposes—and most of them often cannot be read directly off of the stories' structure or content, necessitating appeals to larger contextual issues and their analysis.

What narrators accomplish with their stories is first of all highly local business. They may claim to *explain* but simultaneously engage in acts of apologizing, gaining their audience's empathy or attempting to regain their trust, for example, to be reelected (see the analysis of former U.S. Senator John Edward's confession to having had an extramarital affair and repeatedly lying about it; Bamberg, 2010). According to an interactive–performative approach to narrative, although narrators often may *appeal* to their core identity, who speakers *really* are is most often not what a close analysis of their stories reveals. Thus, the analysis of narratives-in-interaction is limiting its focus to answer two questions: "Why this story here and now?" and more concretely, "What is being accomplished with this story?"

The interactive–performative approach to narrative has not gone without critique. For one, it has been noted that an approach that views such narratives as concrete activities in local interactions places limits on what can be generalized. A second,

---

[1] The implication that language is *another* bodily means of expression and communication is purposely used in this context. One of the reasons is to take language out of the (purely) cognitive realm and place it in the realm of interactive activities in which we make sense and display a sense of self. Analytically, we place language at the same level as other bodily means.

and as such potentially further limiting aspect of this approach to narratives and narrative analysis, is its focus on other–than-textual components of storytelling. Inquiry, for instance, into narrators' use of intonation and gaze to navigate their activity on the floor, and how this is in the service of the actual story performed, are questions that are only possible to review by close and time-consuming analytic procedures. Nevertheless, an analytic stance that dismisses this type of approach as only local and irrelevant with respect to the larger questions (such as identity issues behind the stories told) may do so prematurely and confer interpretations that are difficult to follow and thus may not hold if greater scrutiny was considered. At this point, the issue is not one of which approach is best or correct. In laying out these approaches, the perspective presented is that each comes from a distinct tradition, focuses on different forms of narrating, and usually pursues different types of research questions.

PART 2: THE JENNIE STORY

To exemplify the methodological procedures discussed thus far, a *small* story was chosen that demonstrates the multiple layers of narrative analysis. The story emerged in a group discussion among four 10-year-old boys (Billie, Martin, Victor, and Wally) and an adult male moderator. The boys are in the same grade of an inner-city elementary school, spread across different classrooms. They know each other but do not consider each other to be friends. The story itself is short but complex. It is embedded in Victor's turn but does not have a clear beginning, and, as we will see, it does not have a clear ending. Its plot and theme also are ambiguous, and why this story may have been shared, at least initially, is unclear. The story nevertheless is what we would consider a typical story that emerged in relatively mundane multiparty talk—here about girls—and is a perfect example to demonstrate how narrative analysis proceeds in an attempt to make transparent how narrators operate in their narrative practices.

The study started as an exploratory project with the aim to follow up twenty 10-year-old boys in their interactions in and outside school for a period of 5 years. They were audio- and videotaped at different occasions engaged in talk so that we as researchers could participate in their narrative practices. The overall frame of the research project fits Potter's characterization of attempts to work up the narrative repertoires of 10- to 14-year-old males (although I analyze them as *positioning strategies*; Bamberg, 2003, 2004) and their sequential and conversational occasionings (Chapter 8 of this volume). The particular topic chosen for the purpose of illustration in this chapter comes from a larger stretch of talk on the topic of girls. Although the original intent was to simply develop a large archive of records of interaction in which we could identify storied accounts, we specified our research questions in the early process of collecting records of their interactive practices, and one of our questions was formulated as the representation of self and the other around issues of gender and sexuality. In this example, the original guiding question was how the male 10-year-old (Victor) positions his sense of self in relation to a particular girl named Jennie.[2] I begin by analyzing the story out of context and, in a second step, expand the transcript to include previous and subsequent thematic information as well as extratextual modalities that disambiguate the story told. The first transcript follows a division into clauses that make transparent the cohesive linkages between lexical choices and clause linkages and that shows how they contribute to the thematic buildup of the underlying plot.

Turning to the question of transcribing narrative data, it should be kept in mind that transcripts attempt to manage three general and complex tasks: (a) rendering reality, (b) transforming (as in actually changing) reality, and (c) picking out and communicating what is considered relevant about that reality to the reader and to the interpretive task at hand. Placing the task of transcription at this intersection requires managing the claims of realism to represent faithfully what is happening in an objective reality

---

[2]*Jennie*, like all other names of participants in this chapter, is a pseudonym. The study was approved by the institutional review board of Clark University, and consent was given by the participants and their guardians that granted us permission to use excerpts from their interactions for educational purposes.

with the requirement of transforming what is assumed to be happening into lines on paper by the use of conventions that not only reduce but also enrich the complexity of reality and make visible what is considered relevant. This transformation is by necessity one that simultaneously veils and unveils, makes the strange familiar and the familiar strange. It is comparable to the task of describing what happens in slow motion or in fast-forward modalities of watching actions and events emerge. Transcribing further requires decisions regarding what is being picked from the universe of observables and made communicable. Therefore, there is no right or wrong transcription. And transcription systems, definitive and principled or not, always are prescriptions of interpretive procedures.

The following transcript represents what is transmitted verbally in a clause-by-clause format. *Clauses* are units that include a predicate and its satellites (subject, object, etc.) and capture the syntactic and lexical makeup of these clauses. Displaying each clause as a separate line orients the analytic eye to the language-specific word order—such as in English subject-verb-object, German subject-object-verb, or Maori verb-subject-object—so that parallel constructions or syntactic shifts come to the fore. Transcripts that highlight the syntactic constructedness and linkages between clauses make transparent how characters are introduced and followed up and how the sequential arrangements of spatial locations and temporal connections are constructed—in short, they lay open how characters are given shape in space and time.

A transcript of this sort is still relatively reader friendly, in contrast, for instance, to transcripts that use the international phonetic alphabet or incorporate an overload of symbols that readers first have to learn to follow. Not all prosodic information (stress and intonation) is captured in the transcript. When the accent or voice quality is accentuated, however, this is indexed as contextual information ≪high pitch≫. Arrows are used to index rising ↑ or falling ↓ intonation, CAPITALS are used for special stress on syllables or words, and short breaks are indexed by dots (.).

(91) Jennie used to call me her little honey

(92) for some STRANGE REASON

(93) we used to go to preschool together (.) right ↑

(94) and there was that big mat

(95) like it was a big pillow

(96) in the little in the reading area

(97) and I used to like to get there wicked early

(98) cause my Dad used to work for the city (.) right ↑

(99) and I used to hide in that pillow

(100) so Jennie couldn't find me (.) right ↑

(101) and she used to run up there

(102) and she used to pounce on the ball

(103) she said VICTOR I'M GONNA FIND YOU ≪in high pitch≫

(104) and then I just sit there going oughhhh ↓ ≪ducking down – shaking hands≫

When taking a first stab at a transcript like this, I suggest taking a number of highlighters and starting by marking the different actors by use of different colors from start to end (including so-called *zero-pronouns*). In a second step, the predicates will be marked for their temporal sequence—those that move the action forward in a different color from those that encode stative information; followed by marking locations that are being referred to—again with an eye on changes and movements. This first level of analysis seems to approach the transcript in excessive detail, particularly for those who are in good native command of (English) literary (narrative) conventions. However, imagine someone who speaks Maori as her first language (or Chinese, a language that has no tense marking) and thus is familiar with different narrative conventions to weave characters into their spatial and temporal relationships. In addition, this level of transparency further enables us to make initial assumptions as to where the story begins and what it consists of in terms of delineating main (Jennie and Victor) from secondary characters (father) and probably even to tackle the question how the two main characters (Jennie and Victor) are positioned in relation one another. In the following sequence, I lay out this first stab and take the reader through this kind of (dry) exercise.[3]

Words and Sentences and Their Linkage to Topical Cohesiveness

The example begins with a person reference in turn- and sentence-initial position (line 91) in the form of a name: *Jennie*. Three other referents in the subject position follow: *we* (line 93), *I* (lines 97 and 99 and again in line 104), and *my Dad* (line 98). Jennie is reintroduced in the subject position in lines 100 to 103, and reference to the speaking self reappears in object position (*me*) in lines 100 and 103. The cohesive flow of the participating characters in this segment is indexed by the shifts between proper names and pronouns: from *Jennie* to *us* (me and Jennie), with *my Dad* briefly intersecting, then returning to *Jennie* as the main character, ending with the speaker referring to himself in the subject position (who previously was positioned in object position, subjected to Jennie's actions).

In terms of the temporal flow, all actions and events are clearly marked as having taken place in the past—except for Vic's action in line 104, which is stated in the present tense. However, most actions are marked as having habitually occurred (*used to*), not clearly establishing event boundaries to the left and right of each singular event, as for example in *"one day I hid in the pillow, she ran up, pounced on the ball, and said . . ."*—in which case, we have three clear temporal boundaries between four events so that they would be read in sequence. Nevertheless, an implied temporal and contiguous sequence of habitual occurrences of actions resembles a hide- and-seek scheme, where the *hiding* action has to be completed so that *running up* to the location and the *pouncing* can follow and establish what can be considered the overall activity frame of hide-and-seek.

In terms of the spatial layout, the first orientation to space is implied in line 93 by mentioning their *preschool*. Lines 94 to 96 remain within this location and add descriptive detail. With lines 97 to 98, the speaker remains at the same location (*there*), adding a temporal marking (*wicked early*) but from a different perspective. Although the description of the schoolroom's interior seemed to have come from within this room (both speaker and audience are visualizing it from within), the mentioning that it was *wicked early* came from an outside perspective, setting up an earlier temporal reference frame: He had been dropped off by his father, with reasons added as to why this was the case (line 98). With line 99, the speaker returns to the focalization point inside the room, hides behind the pillow, and remains there until the end of the story (line 104).

Each of these three characters are positioned in two relational setups: the father as the agent dropping off his son, who in turn is positioned in the object position as undergoer. The relational positions between Jennie and Victor are spelled out similarly: Jennie is positioned as agent (line 91) and reappears in this position in lines 100 to 104. Intermittently, there is the *I* that *got* (not *went*) to preschool early (not through his agency) and the *I* that went into hiding (line 99). Hiding itself is an agentive move, although requiring another agent with respect to whom going into hiding is a reaction. It also implies the intention of not wanting to be seen or found—resulting in line 104 in a self-positioning as put, not moving, with the unspoken agenda to remain in a nonagentive position for the rest of this narrative.

Let us reflect on the analytic procedure thus far. We have tried to trace the way cohesive ties are put to use so the characters could be identified and viewed as relating to one another and have tried to do so in line with the temporal and spatial arrangements in which the characters are situated. Remaining within the analytic layer of words and sentences and focusing on the emergence of cohesion, it can be noted that the narrator positions himself as undergoer, if not victim, of the actions of others. The presentation of these actions as having taken place about 5 years ago, as having happened repeatedly, and as not under his control can be read as designed to downplay his agency and eschew accountability. This much we can assert from a bottom-up scrutiny of how clauses are presented as following each other and from how the cohesive ties between them are set up. And although there seems

---

[3]I am not suggesting that these analytic procedures have to be laid out in this kind of detail when published. However, if a decision is necessary with regard to what the narrative consists of, as in the case of the transcript under investigation, the analyst has to be able to draw on this analytic procedure.

to be some overarching temporal sequence, the actual narrative skeleton, existing of a sequence of event clauses, is thin. The description of the pre-school's interior (lines 94–96) as well as the aside about his father dropping him off early on his way to work (lines 97–98) do not contribute to any plot development and neither do the first two opening lines (line 91–92).

Summarizing the examination of spatial, temporal, and character references and tying them together, the local orientation and by implication also a temporal setting come to the fore in line 93, marking the start of a story. From here an action orientation, and with it a particular character constellation, can unfold and move forward (lines 101–103), resulting in an outcome (line 104). The first two lines (91–92) are marked off as a different incident, although one that may thematically be related to the story that starts in preschool. According to Labov's (1972) definition, the first two lines do not establish a narrative because with line 92, by use of a free clause, the speaker removes himself from the event formation. Thus, having established line 93 as the orientation (with lines 94–96 further detailing the setting) and lines 99 to 100 as the establishment of an action frame for this setting, lines 101 to 103 can then be taken as a possible complication, although not resulting in a resolution (line 104). In case we did not know that we were in a here-and-now 5 years later, one could assume that Victor may have stayed in hiding or, symbolically speaking, may be interpreted as "still in hiding."[4]

The choice of particular formulations will become more relevant when analyzed in terms of their interactive functions. At this point, however, it is noteworthy that the narrative starts with an attribution that originated from the person who will subsequently be developed into the main character (at least in terms of her agency) of the story. The specific formulation that is attributed to him (*honey*), further elaborated by a diminutive (*little*), and claimed to be owned (*my*)—*my little honey*—draws on a semantic field that is typically connoted to lovers' talk or parental (most likely mother–child)

terms of endearment. The fact that Victor claims that this formulation was a habitual attribution by Jennie, and that Jennie's pursuits also happened habitually, point to the interpretation that he neither views these categorizations as accidental nor motivated by anything he did to encourage her. To the contrary, Jennie's actions are marked off not only as repetitive and therefore extreme but also as unreasonable—clearly underscored in his evaluative stance expressed in line 92. The aside in lines 97 to 98 that establishes the events as taking place in the morning before school was in session (with little supervision present) also may add to his overall evaluative stance of not being agentively involved, that is, not protected by the normal frame of adult supervision, with his father gone, and subjected to the mercy of a female protagonist who is his age.

Plots and Themes: Toward the Production of Story Coherence

Having started working through the narrative with a focus on the sequence of clauses and their lexical and syntactic makeup, we were able to sort through some of the eventive (the temporal sequence of what happened) and evaluative (where Victor gave insight into his evaluative stance regarding what happened) components of the story. Separating the events that reportedly happened from evaluative stances left us with the question: What functions do the particular lexical and syntactic choices of the speaker serve (in service of the larger question, what this story means)? We now analyze the segment of discourse from the perspective of the second layer that pursues the question of story coherence, linking the plot with its contents.

In terms of its overall structure, the first two lines (91–92) need to be dealt with separately. The story starts with an orientation into the there and then with line 93. Topically, the story focuses on Jennie—with the narrator positioned in recipient role—and its theme is her (habitual) pursuit of him. This theme is not marked as a typical hide-and-seek gamelike activity in the life space of 5-year-olds but as an activity that did not result (at the time) in play

---

[4]The question that is looming already at this level of analysis is, what is the point of telling this story? What is it that telling this story contributes and makes relevant for the situation speaker and audience are currently in? Is it (more) about Jennie? (More) about me? Or is it about our relationship? Back then? Here and now?

and fun for the sake of play. Moving from this overall interpretation of lines 93 to 104 back to the first two lines, the thematic link becomes more transparent: The two structural segments speak to the (same) issue of Jennie's habitual actions, and both are strongly characterized from the same evaluative orientation. In the first segment (lines 91–92), the evaluation of Jennie's actions (*for some strange reason*) is marked off by stepping out of the there-and-then and giving Victor's evaluative position from the here-and-now of speaking time. In the second segment (lines 93–99), the speaker's evaluative position is more implicit and signaled by the use of lexical and grammatical choices that characterize him not only as uninvolved but also as not approving of the position into which he is placed by Jennie. To support this interpretation, we may take additional (performative) means into account, such as using his *telling body* (both expressing his emotion [*oughhh*] and his bodily display of posture and hands): Both can be taken to index what it must have looked and felt like hiding behind the pillow. In this last line of his story (line 104), in which he highlights his affect, he also switches from the use of past tense to the present tense (*sit*). This can further be taken to index the relevancy of this part of his story—not necessarily the high point but something that has enduring relevance.

At this point, it is relevant to keep in mind that Jennie is a girl and Victor is positioned as a boy. In English, this distinction most commonly is implied by names culturally typifying boys and girls, and, of course, by the marking of personal pronouns (*he* vs. *she*). Note, however, that Jennie simply could have been referred to as *a friend* (or *my friend*), leaving her gender less accentuated. Focusing on this categorical distinction, the question can be asked whether this story is at its core *about* girl–boy relationships (i.e., heterosexuality). At the same time, this story is about something that happened in preschool—a long time ago, which can be interpreted in two ways: (a) as still currently relevant or (b) as something that happened in the remote past, with no or only little relevance to the state of affairs in the present. In the first instance, picking up on the theme of heterosexuality, Jennie's thematic role was to make the point that the narrator views himself as still having to go into hiding: Nowadays, although twice their age, Jennie, or other girls, position Victor (as a male) in the same plotlike configuration. In this latter case, we are dealing with an account that characterizes the actions of a female child in the distant past, and how these past actions have affected a male child. If this is not being made explicit, why then tell the story?

Having conducted a thematic analysis of the underlying plot configuration of Victor's story, we end up with at least two options for what kind of plot is in circulation. According to a first option, Victor could be heard as configuring the particulars of what happened as part of a general conflict between males and females. Being called "my little honey" and being physically pursued are examples of intrusion and therefore unwanted actions of females into what is being constructed symbolically as male space. In this type of plot configuration, the reasons for these kinds of actions are inscrutable and enigmatic and thus potentially result in conflict. Whatever Victor's motives may have been to borrow this kind of plot—maybe Victor is heard as a young boy for whom girls still have "cooties," maybe he is heard as speaking from the position of "male angst" in regard to women in general, or maybe Jennie's attempts (cumulatively or one of her approaches in particular) have left Victor traumatically scarred—the way the characters are positioned in the there and then may invite these kinds of interpretation.[5] In a second option, another interpretation suggests that Jennie is configured as a member of the category of females who pursue males as part of a romantic or heterosexual plot configuration. Within this interpretive scenario, Victor presents himself back there and then as declining but borrowing this kind of stance to be relevant and potentially still holding in the here and now. Within this plot configuration, he could be read as borrowing the persona of someone who is popular but uninvolved— the mainstay of "male cool." And maybe it is this

---

[5]These three interpretive conclusions were suggested by colleagues and students after watching and having worked through the first two analytic layers: (a) the words and sentences and (b) the themes and plots.

feature in the way he constructs his relationship to the other gender that is foregrounded and made relevant for the here and now of the telling situation. At this point, the analysis of the layer of story coherence does not resolve whether either of these two thematic configuration attempts is appropriate.

Interaction and Performance: Why This Story Here and Now?

Having started with a close look at the actual wording and its composition into a linear and cohesive text that was feeding into a common topical theme, followed by an analysis of the overarching thematic organization of the plot of the story, we will now expand our analytic focus to incorporate the third layer outlined in the section Beyond the text: Why this story here and now? Here, the excerpt is examined in terms of the following question: What does the story mean to the participants in their ongoing negotiation of what is topically and interactionally relevant? With this layer, we are opening the analysis to more contextual information, such as how the participants are trying to signal what they consider relevant and how this is being negotiated. As noted, the goal is to continue to disambiguate what thematically is being negotiated and to make the cues that are used by the participants transparent to the analytic eye. We not only go beyond the (original) text by considering previous and subsequent textual elements but also draw on other bodily cues such as gaze, gestures, and posture.

One of the cues we had spotted earlier in the analysis was Victor's abrupt introduction of Jennie by the use of her name in line 91. Starting a turn, narrative or not, by use of a referential form that is highly specific indexes a context in which the referred-to character is taken as presupposed; in other words, this form pointed the participants toward previous mentionings of Jennie as thematically relevant. Other cues are to be uncovered in how Victor has picked up on what had been said immediately before and how others are picking up on his story after his turn completion.

Beginning with the two plot configurations revealed in the analysis in the first two layers in Victor's overall structuring, we can see that both plot configurations correlate with two different types of speech activities at the interactive–performative layer: Although the configuration in which females make unexplainable and unwanted moves in relation to males lends itself to the speech activity of complaining, the plot in which female approaches contribute to a gain in social status and popularity, and consequently are likely to fall into the "wanted category," can translate into speech acts of boasting or flaunting a male (heterosexual) identity.

Starting from a slightly expanded transcript,[6] we can see that Victor (line 91) cuts into Billie's turn (line 98). However, at the exact moment when Victor's and Billie's turn begin to overlap, Billie's complaint story is not fully developed. Instead, at that point, Billie just had claimed to have had a girlfriend and that this girlfriend seemed to have been very experienced with boys. From the visual cues available (particularly his gaze orientation), Victor does not hear Billie out and his turn seems to deliberately interrupt. In light of these observations, it remains unclear whether Victor is telling his story about Jennie as boasting about girlfriends or whether Victor is contributing to a theme that lends itself more for a complaint, namely, that girls intrude male territory. Furthermore, to better understand why Jennie was made relevant in response to Billie's conversational contribution, we are forced to look further for

			≪everyone sitting≫ ≪gaze distributed around≫
(96)	Bil	my ex-girlfriend had like twelve ex-ex-ex-ex boyfriends	≪all gaze at Billie≫
(97)		she had twelve of them	
(98)		and she takes the [good stuff	≪Vic gazes at moderator≫

[6]The contextual information on the right-hand side of the transcript is shaded so it can be distinguished from the textual information. In addition, square brackets [are used to mark the beginnings of overlapping speech.

(90)		and she breaks up	≪Vic continues gaze at mod≫
(91)	Vic	[Jennie used to call me her little honey for some STRANGE REASON	
		we used to go to preschool together (.) right ↑	
		and there was that big mat	
(95)		like it was a big pillow	≪gestures outlining pillow≫
		in the little in the reading area	≪everyone tuned to Vic – posture + gaze≫
		and I used to like to get there wicked early	
		cause my Dad used to work for the city (.) right ↑	
		and I used to hide in that pillow	≪participants gaze at Victor≫
(100)		so Jennie couldn't find me (.) right ↑	
		and she used to run up there	
		and she used to pounce on the ball	
		she said VICTOR I'M GONNA FIND YOU	≪high pitch≫ ≪everyone smiling≫
(104)		and then I just sit there going oughhhh ↓	≪ducking down – shaking hands≫
			≪pause + little laughter≫ ≪gaze + body postures reorienting≫
(105)		she was tall when she was in preschool	
(106)		she was like [	≪Vic gesturing tall≫
	Bil	[she is short now	
	Vic	no she is huge (.)Jennie Thompson ↑	≪Vic standing up≫
	Bil	yes to YOU ↓	≪gesturing small≫
(110)	Wal	she is taller she is shorter than [me	
	Bil	[she's shorter than me	
	Mar	[shorter than me	
	Vic	no she isn't Billie↓	
		she is taller than you	
(115)	Bil	neh	
	Vic	I know I know one girl who is taller than ALL of you	≪topic change≫

earlier mentions of Jennie in the conversation and will return to this shortly.

Victor's story (ending in line 104) is taken up in the form of laughter conjoined with everyone moving their bodies back to a more relaxed position and a reorientation of gaze from Victor to other orientation points in the room. These bodily reactions typically signal the recognition of the end of the story and open the floor for someone else to follow up—often with an evaluation or a second story. This, however, does not happen. Victor reenters the floor with a brief descriptive claim regarding Jennie's size when she was in preschool. This claim, although

topically cohesive, is postnarrative. With line 104, he had marked his turn (and thus his story) as completed. So the question is what his continuance is supposed to accomplish. The subsequent argument among the participants about Jennie's present-day size reconfirms that everyone knows Jennie, but it does not necessarily answer questions raised by Victor's story about Jennie.

Another way of providing thematic continuity between the topic of Victor's story and his postnarrative claims to Jennie's size can be provided by moving out of the textual representation and into Victor's bodily self-representation: going into hiding and ducking down, that is, making himself purposely small and invisible. When playing hide-and-seek, this may be an appropriate move, although when boasting about being approached or pursued by a girl, this may be construed as a form of anxiety or unreadiness for the challenge of (mature) sexuality. If this thematic strand is woven, or emerging at one or another point in the interaction, Victor's postnarrative comment on Jennie's size is most likely to be heard as an inoculation attempt against this kind of interactive positioning by the present participants. Standing up from his chair when challenged on his size and making himself oversee the other participants (see transcript, line 108) is likely to be read in support of this interpretation.

Reevaluating where we are in our attempt to disambiguate the thematic relevance of Victor's story from a contextual–interactive vantage point, and entering the contextualization of his story from an analytic angle that is grounded in the conversational–interactive fabric of relational work between the participants, opens up new questions originating from the expansion of the text and its interactional embedding as the new unit of analysis: Where and how was Jennie originally made topically relevant? How did this topic progress from that point and how is Jennie positioned in this topical progression? What is interactively accomplished between the participants of the conversation? Questions like these, and maybe others, are central to the analytic layer of the performance approach under investigation, although there is not enough space to lay this out in detail. So let me describe how the story emerged at this point in the conversation among the participants.

Earlier, in a discussion of how long one has to know someone to count as best friend, Victor had mentioned Jennie whom he had known from when he was born. Later on, this statement was recalled, and Victor claimed her as a "best friend." Challenged by Wally who objected, "you can't trust girls," a new topic emerged, namely, whether you can trust moms and sisters. At this point, Victor sided clearly with those who trust. Over the next turns, initiated by a (small) story from Billie on the topic of his mom always showing his baby pictures, a number of additional stories were called up by all participants, including the moderator, which all shared experi-

ences in which mothers embarrassed their children by taking and showing their pictures. Dads were explicitly excluded from and positioned as strictly opposing if not undermining such practices. Wally summed up the discussion with the words, "you can't trust your girlfriend either 'cause they tell their friends"—with Victor agreeing, "yeah, you're right it's nuts"—thereby overtly calling into question his earlier claim that he trusted his mom and sister. It is at this point that Billie joined the conversation with his story about his ex-girlfriend who had broken up with him, followed by the Jennie story.

In light of the unfolding topics in the form of complaint stories, Victor's Jennie story oscillates between two orientations. On the one hand, Victor can be heard as flaunting his authority of knowing about girls' pursuit of boys. And presenting himself as uninvolved and unresponsive in response to such attempts, he brings off a certain stance of (typically masculine) cool. On the other hand, he can be interpreted as joining the chorus of second stories that complain about girls' (and mothers') tendencies to embarrass them. Within this version, he presents himself—just as Billie did in his turn—as subjected to the actions of the generalized female other and simultaneously as deeply vulnerable. Note that this latter interpretation goes beyond the interpretation of Victor's story as a complaint. In the sharing of their stories, the singular and unique experiences of the five participants have gained the status of generalizable knowledge that is collectively disclosed. Telling these personal experiences in storied forms is vulnerable territory—and this seems to be highly reflected in Victor's story about Jennie and his postnarrative attempt to negotiate Jennie's size. In spite of the fact that these stories are carefully navigated territories, sharing such stories is relational work that has the potential to build trust and intimacy among the participants. To sum up, in our attempts to disambiguate the Jennie story and figure out what this story means and why it was shared at this particular point in the interaction, we entered the viewpoints and values of the local culture of 10-year-olds as a community of story-sharing practices, a *narrative reality* (Gubrium & Holstein, 2009) that goes far beyond the text, its form and content, and into the world of narrative practice.

CONCLUSION

We started this chapter with the assumption that narrative analysis lays open, in the sense of making transparent, how narrators use narrative means to give (narrative) form and thereby make sense of events and experiences. To do this, this chapter drew on three approaches to work with narratives: (a) a linguistic-based approach that works through the lexical and syntactic configurations of texts and follows their buildup into the topical organization of the text, (b) a cognitive-based approach that works from the assumption that the story segments are held together by an overarching structure of the plot organization, and (c) an interactive-based approach that views stories (and their meanings) as local accomplishments among participants. Although all three approaches work with different assumptions of what people do when they engage in storytelling activities, and although each begins from different units of analysis as analytic givens and is likely to ask different types of research questions, we took these three approaches and applied them to a particular instance of storytelling.

The particular instance of storytelling was deliberately one in which there are different ways of making sense of the story: what the story is about and the purpose it can be argued to serve interactively. We first used the methods available to identify whether a story actually is being shared, and where this story starts and ends. From there we made transparent the different layers of topical consistency and thematic coherence to address the question of what interactive purposes the telling of this story may have had. Ending up with no definitive answer may be viewed as a shortcoming of the methods employed. Rather than giving definitive answers to particular research questions, however, it was the declared purpose of this chapter to raise questions to which narrative approaches may be used in search for answers.

Turning back to the overarching goal of the research project from where this small interactive narrative had originated, which was the investigation of 10- to 15-year-old boys' positioning strategies (also called *discursive* or *interpretive repertoires*), we nevertheless were able to take away some important insights from this kind of analysis. What can be interpreted as ambivalence between hearing Victor as both complaining *and* boasting may be nothing more than navigating dilemmatic positions that pull into different directions. One pull that we could identify in similar narratives within this age-group of boys is taking shape in a plot orientation (also called *master narrative*), within which young boys seek to differentiate a (male) sense of self from the female other, whereas the other plot orientation pulls for a more integrated approach of (male) self and (female) other. Both are different in terms of relational investments in others, that is, those who are placed in membership categories different from self and in-group. At the same time, both plot orientations do different discursive work in different situations (cf. Bamberg, 2011; Bamberg & Georgakopoulou, 2008). Indeed, findings like this led us to realize the potential of storytelling practices as the field par excellence in which different narrative plot orientations are tried out and navigated as what my colleagues and I have called *identity projects* (Bamberg, 2011; Bamberg, De Fina & Schiffrin, 2011). Having started at the onset of this contribution from a definition according to which narratives "give narrative form to experience," we now are able to refine this definition: Apart from exactly doing that, narratives in the way they are practiced in everyday interactions also are the testing grounds for compliance and resistance to dominant versions, in which ambivalence can interactively be displayed and tried out in different communities of practices and in which these narrative practices are the grounds in which identities and sense of self can constantly be innovated and redefined.

The attempt has been made to show that each of the three approaches laid out in this chapter has its own merits and shortcomings. Making transparent what cohesive ties feed the buildup of what the text is topically about forms a first and necessary step in cuing the audience into what activity is going on and what the potential purposes may be for making that particular experience from 5 years ago relevant to the here and now of the telling situation. Analyzing the part–whole relationships in terms of their top-down conceptual integration into plot organizations presents a second layer of analytic work that points toward some overarching thematic relevance that the story may have for the narrator—again tied into the local situation of sharing. Both analytic procedures remain fixated on texts, either in terms of their linguistic or conceptual structuring. They both form starting points to be complemented by scrutiny of a third analytic layer that turns more closely to the functions of the textual means analyzed in the preceding two layers. In addition, this approach also suggests investigating the intertextual embeddedness of the text (the *before* and *after*) along with the use of *other* bodily means that are brought to bear in the telling of the narrative. As documented, this layer of interpretive analysis takes the interpreter into the realm of narrative practices as the place to analyze the purpose and the accomplishment of what is happening.

Reconceptualizing the three narrative methods (texts as words and sentences, texts as plots and themes, and going beyond the text and asking why this story here and now) as analytic layers that offer insights into narratives as texts-in-interactions is not straightforward. On the one hand, it needs to be emphasized that the analytic orientations start from different assumptions about the person, language, and narrative. The three orientations are inspired by different research traditions, asking different (research) questions. Against this backdrop, the use of three approaches as matrixes for different analytic layers should not be construed as a ticket to (randomly) mix methods or to triangulate in order to find out *more* about narrative texts or practices. Nevertheless, and this is a topic worth following up elsewhere, seeing the three different approaches applied next to one another—modifying the data continuously so that these three approaches can speak to the data (and the data to the different questions being pursued)—helps seeing them as practices that are not necessarily only in competition but also employable together.

References

Bamberg, M. (1997). Positioning between structure and performance. *Journal of Narrative and Life History, 7(1–4)*, 335–342.

Bamberg, M. (2003). Stories, tellings, and identities. In C. Daiute & C. Lightfoot (Eds.), *Narrative analysis: Studying the development of individuals in society* (pp. 135–157). London, England: Sage.

Bamberg, M. (2004). Form and functions of "slut bashing" in male identity constructions in 15-year-olds: "I know it may sound mean to say this, but we couldn't really care less about her anyway." *Human Development, 47*, 331–353. doi:10.1159/000081036

Bamberg, M. (2010). Blank check for biography? Openness and ingenuity in the management of the "Who-Am-I-Question." In D. Schiffrin, A. De Fina, & A. Nylund (Eds.), *Telling stories* (pp. 181–199). Washington, DC: Georgetown University Press.

Bamberg, M. (2011). Who am I?–Narration and its contribution for self and identity. *Theory and Psychology, 21*, 3–24.

Bamberg, M., De Fina, A., & Schiffrin, D. (2011). Discourse and identity construction. In S. Schwartz, K. Luyckx, & V. Vignoles (Eds.), *Handbook of identity theory and research* (pp. 177–199). Berlin, Germany: Springer-Verlag.

Bamberg, M., & Georgakopoulou, A. (2008). Small stories as a new perspective in narrative and identity analysis. *Text and Talk, 28*, 377–396.

Bruner, J. S. (1986). *Actual minds, possible worlds.* Cambridge, MA: Harvard University Press.

Bruner, J. S. (1991). The narrative construction of reality. *Critical Inquiry, 18*, 1–21. doi:10.1086/448619

Gubrium, J. F., & Holstein, J. A. (2009). *Analyzing narrative reality.* Thousand Oaks, CA: Sage.

Hiles, D. R., & Cermák, I. (2008). Narrative psychology. In C. Willig & W. Stainton-Rogers (Eds.), *Sage handbook of qualitative research in psychology* (pp. 147–164). London, England: Sage.

Hollway, W., & Jefferson, T. (2008). The free association narrative interview method. In L. Given (Ed.), *The Sage encyclopedia of qualitative research methods* (pp. 286–315). Thousand Oaks, CA: Sage.

Illouz, E. (2008). *Saving the modern soul. Therapy, emotions, and the culture of self-help.* Berkeley: University of California Press.

Labov, W. (1972). *Language in the inner city.* Philadelphia: University of Pennsylvania Press.

Lyotard, J. F. (1984). *The postmodern condition: A report on knowledge* (G. Bennington & B. Massumi, Trans.). Minneapolis: University of Minnesota Press.

Mandler, J., & Johnson, N. (1977). Remembrance of things parsed: Story structure and recall. *Cognitive Psychology, 9*, 111–151. doi:10.1016/0010-0285(77)90006-8

McAdams, D. (1993). *The stories we live by: Personal myths and the making of the self.* New York, NY: Guilford Press.

Mishler, E. G. (1986). *Research interviewing: Context and narrative.* Cambridge, MA: Harvard University Press.

Polkinghorne, D. E. (1988). *Narrative knowing and the human sciences.* Albany: State University of New York Press.

Randall, W. L. (1995). *The stories we are: An essay on self-creation.* Toronto, Ontario, Canada: University of Toronto Press.

Riessman, C. K. (2008). *Narrative methods for the human sciences.* London, England: Sage.

Thorndyke, P. W. (1977). Cognitive structures in comprehension and memory of narrative discourse. *Cognitive Psychology, 9,* 77–110. doi:10.1016/0010-0285(77)90005-6

Wengraf, T. (2006). *Interviewing for life-histories, lived situations and personal experience. The biographic-narrative interpretive method (BNIM) on its own and as part of a multi-method full spectrum psychosocial methodology.* Retrieved from http://www.uel.ac.uk/cnr/Wengraf06.rtf

CHAPTER 7

ETHNOMETHODOLOGY AND CONVERSATION ANALYSIS

Paul ten Have

Ethnomethodology (EM) and conversation analysis (CA) are the somewhat confusing names of two related research traditions that were developed in the 1960s in the United States by Harold Garfinkel and by Harvey Sacks (with his coworkers Emanuel Schegloff and Gail Jefferson), respectively. The contexts for their initiatives were the theoretical and methodological debates in sociology that were current at the time. Since then, EM and CA have become more or less established paradigms that have attracted researchers from a range of disciplines around the world. As a first characterization, one can note their interest in the detailed ways in which members of society collaboratively constitute the situations in which they find themselves and the (inter)actions that take place in those situations. The general sociological issue of social order is reconsidered as a local achievement of members in situations, and the research objective is to explicate *how* this is done in an accountable way. CA can be seen as a specialized form of EM, originally focusing on verbal interaction and later also considering nonvocal aspects. It has developed a rather specific, relatively conventionalized research style using audio or video recordings and detailed transcripts as basic data. Other forms of EM use a much wider range of data types, such as ethnographic observations, while the approach is closely fitted to the chosen topic and the properties of the research site.

THE EMERGENCE OF THE ETHNOMETHODOLOGICAL PROGRAM

To summarize a rather complex net of influences and inspirations, it can be said that Harold Garfinkel's initiative started with his critical confrontation with the theories of his dissertation supervisor, Talcott Parsons at Harvard, from a phenomenological perspective informed by the work of Schutz, Gurwitsch, and Husserl (Garfinkel, 1967; Heritage, 1984b; Rawls in Garfinkel, 2002). When he was involved with a study of jury deliberations and listened to the tapes of those discussions, he was struck by the carefulness of the jury members' commonsense reasoning: their serious "lay methodology." So, in line with anthropological disciplines like ethnomedicine and ethnobotany, he coined the term *ethnomethodology* for the study of the methods that ordinary members of society use and take for granted. As a professor in sociology at the University of California, Los Angeles, he undertook a series of empirical studies to further develop EM as a research program. Some of these studies used a procedure of breaching commonsense background expectancies as demonstrations of their importance in everyday sense making. It turned out that such breaches were often experienced as upsetting and that they led to instant efforts to normalize the situation (Garfinkel, 1967, pp. 35–75).

These background expectancies are part of an immense collection of taken-for-granted, "seen but

The author thanks Paul Camic, Harrie Mazeland, and Jonathan Potter for their remarks on earlier versions of this chapter.

DOI: 10.1037/13620-007
APA Handbook of Research Methods in Psychology: Vol. 2. Research Designs, H. Cooper (Editor-in-Chief)

unnoticed," and silently presupposed capacities and understandings that can be taken as foundational for both ordinary and specialized forms of social life. Imagine trying to make a dish by following a recipe from a cookbook without understanding what the terms used meant, how to handle a knife to cut the vegetables, how to boil water, and so on. It is this level of presupposed, ordinarily unnoticed but essential capacities and understandings that is of interest to ethnomethodologists. Of course, they do not limit their attention to things like following a recipe. They have, indeed, studied this level of unnoticed phenomena for a very wide range of activities.

A critical point in all this is that the level of concrete capacities and understandings is not only ignored in instructions such as recipes but also in all sorts of plans; reports; and scientific analyses of various sorts, including, of course, sociology. In that discipline, social life is generally investigated in terms of pregiven concepts or preelaborated theories, on the basis of data gathered in terms of pregiven categories and methods. In fact, Talcott Parsons was a champion of this approach of first elaborating an extensive, rationally organized category system, *before* doing any empirical work. In contrast to this external top-down approach, Garfinkel maintained that members of society should not be treated as "dopes" whose task it was to act according to some theories but rather as actually capable of "doing social life," which can be investigated "from within actual settings" (Garfinkel, 1967, p. 68).

To explicate the specifics of his approach, Garfinkel developed a complex writing style, which tends to be rather incomprehensible to the uninitiated, and which, in combination with the breaching procedures, led quite often to strongly negative reactions from other sociologists. I discuss a key excerpt from the preface to *Studies in Ethnomethodology* (Garfinkel, 1967) to present Garfinkel's general ideas and to familiarize readers with his style and basic concepts.

> Ethnomethodological studies analyze everyday activities as members' methods for making those same activities

visibly-rational-and-reportable-for-all-practical-purposes, i.e., "accountable," as organizations of commonplace everyday activities. The reflexivity of that phenomenon is a singular feature of practical actions, of practical circumstances, of common sense knowledge of social structures, and of practical sociological reasoning. By permitting us to locate and examine their occurrence the reflexivity of that phenomenon establishes their study. (Garfinkel, 1967, vii)

The first sentence tells us that EM studies focus on the fact that members in their ordinary actions in various ways make the sense and purpose of those actions recognizable for other members. Accountability refers to the moral obligation among members to produce their actions in ways that are recognizably reasonable in the situation in which they are done. By using reflexivity, Garfinkel stresses the self-explicating and self-referencing aspect of practical actions. What is made clear in the doing of an action is its *local* and *situated* meaning, what anthropologists might characterize as *emic* in contrast to *etic*. The frequent use of words like *everyday*, *practical*, and *common sense* further stresses the EM focus on the achieved ordinariness of actions. It is the local sense displays rather than some theorized general sense of actions that is of interest to ethnomethodologists. The last sentence in the excerpt formulates the methodological basis of EM studies. To conduct EM studies, the ethnomethodologist has to immerse himself or herself in the situation of interest, mentally if not physically. One has to acquire "membership knowledge" to become what Garfinkel has elsewhere called "vulgarly competent" in the setting (Garfinkel & Wieder, 1992).

In later work, Garfinkel elaborated the ethnomethodological program in various ways, but most often in terms of the contrast between EM and the established sociological approach characterized as *constructive* or *formal analysis*. The general theme of these elaborations is that in EM studies the phenomena that established approaches study in terms of predefined concepts of social order are *respecified* as members' methods for creating a locally account-able order. In their search for analytic generalities, mainstream sociologists ignore or gloss over the specific, locally required concrete details of actions, which are the phenomena of interest for ethnomethodologists (cf. Garfinkel, 2002).

Ethnomethodology's Methods

As the phenomena of interest for an ethnomethodologist occur on a level of seen but unnoticed or used but taken for granted, a first practical problem for EM is how to make those phenomena noticeable. Garfinkel's own efforts, as reported in his *Studies in Ethnomethodology* (Garfinkel, 1967), were quite strongly oriented to this problem of noticeability, or rather as an effort to demonstrate the existence and relevance of phenomena of this type. His so-called breaching experiments were part of a pedagogy, a strategy to convince his students and colleagues that he was after something relevant, not just for sociology but for everyday life. By breaching expectancies, or having them breached by his students, such as asking for the meaning of ordinary expressions, he did two things. He made noticeable their relevance and moral quality in the production of everyday situations, and he provoked extra sense-making activities to repair the experienced disturbances. The people exposed to the breaches showed they were puzzled and shocked, but they immediately made efforts to normalize the situation, by taking it as a joke or finding some other motive or explanation for the breach. In addition to these provocative interventions, Garfinkel also studied what might be called *natural breaches*, such as the efforts by a biological male to pass as a natural female.

Later ethnomethodologists turned to other means to study the details of situated practices, most often intense ethnography supplemented with audiovisual recordings of in situ activities (cf. Chapter 10 of this volume). This serves two purposes. On the one hand, it allows researchers to acquire a certain measure of membership knowledge by immersing themselves in the social life of the setting under study. In this way, they gain access to relevant local understandings and even some competence to act as a member. And on the other hand, the ethnographic fieldwork (and especially the audiovisual recordings) gives them access to the fine details of the verbal and visible activities in ordinary settings of the specific form of life.

In their *Invitation to Ethnomethodology*, Francis and Hester (2004) formulated the process of EM research in the following summary way:

> Doing ethnomethodology involves taking three methodological steps: 1. Notice something that is observably-the-case about some talk, activity or setting. 2. Pose the question "How is it that this observable feature has been produced such that it is recognizable for what it is?" 3. Consider, analyse and describe the methods used in the production and recognition of the observable feature. (pp. 25–26)

And they added,

> In other words, then, ethnomethodology starts out with what might be called the "common-sense appearance of the social world" and then seeks to describe how they will have been produced "from within" such that they do indeed have the appearances they have. (p. 26)

Some Examples of Ethnomethodological Study

Scanning any list of ethnomethodological studies, one may be struck by the enormous variety of topics, or rather of settings and activity types studied. There are, for instance, studies of the ways in which both staff and inmates used a so-called convict code to explain situations in a halfway house for former drug users (Wieder, 1974), of laboratory practices focusing on the identification of artifacts (Lynch, 1985), of the art of piano improvization (Sudnow, 1978), of the interactions of users with a complex copy machine (Suchman, 1987, 2007), or of the reasoning practices of Tibetan monks (Liberman, 2004).

These examples can be invoked to illustrate several of the methodological aspects of EM research. Wieder (1974) has done intensive ethnography, which Lynch (1985) and Liberman

(2004) have also used, together with recordings. Sudnow (1978) has studied his own actions. Wieder, in his report, referred to a tradition of ethnography in which a local subculture, such as the convict code, is invoked to explain the actions of a local gang of people. In contrast to this tradition, he described the ways in which such a subculture is actually used by its members to account for the situation in which they have to act as they do, as a "folk sociology." Here access was mainly gained by his experience in the setting, by seeing and hearing the inmates and staff members telling the code, and also in accounting for their actions in dealing with him.

In the study by Suchman (1987, 2007), a special setup was created in which two subjects were asked to carry out some tasks at the copier, with one having to read out the instructions and the displays, while the other had to handle the practical actions at the machine. In this way, she gained access to the users' situated reasoning, which she could confront with the preplanned reasoning implemented in the machine, as part of an artificial intelligence project. In her analysis she contrasted the plans implemented in the machine with the observed situated actions. She stressed the inability of such plans to foresee the local circumstances and ad hoc practical reasonings that guide the actual actions of the users at the machine in situ.

In whatever way access to the phenomena of interest is acquired, the researcher will have to produce a record in one way or another, as ethnographic notes, audio or visual recordings, or transcriptions thereof, as an aid to the process of *noticing* in the sense of the quote from Francis and Hester (2004). These records constitute the material the researcher works on, fixing what has happened, in a way objectifying these happenings to help make them "anthropologically strange" rather than just to be taken for granted (Garfinkel, 1967, p. 9). Almost always, EM research reports contain quotes, longer fragments or pictures from such records, inviting the readers to check what is reported with the data as rendered in such quotes and excerpts. So recordings serve a double purpose: as research materials to explore and as demonstrations to support the arguments.

The studies by Lynch (1985, 1993), Sudnow (1978), and Liberman (2004) illustrated the fact that to do an ethnomethodological study of some specialized activity, the researcher has to have or acquire a sufficient level of competence in doing that activity (Garfinkel & Wieder, 1992; Lynch, 1993, pp. 265–308). This is a special case of the more general, noted requirement that an ethnomethodologist has to have the relevant membership knowledge to understand, in the sense used earlier, members' practical activities (ten Have, 2002). So Lynch had to have some competence in reading images produced by the electronic microscope, Sudnow had to be able to play the piano, and Liberman had to learn the Tibetan language as well as acquire a basic understanding of Tibetan Buddhist philosophy. The practical issue, of course, is how far the researcher should go in this matter.

A persistent theme in both the programmatic statements of EM as well as most if not all ethnomethodological studies is the discrepancy between, on the one hand, general statements and ideas about practical activities, like plans, instructions, protocols, and formal accounts, and on the other, the activities to which they refer in their actual, particular, and methodic detail. This theme has surfaced in the discussions of Wieder's and Suchman's studies, but is also discernable in the others mentioned. As Heap (1990, pp. 42–43) has noted, ethnomethodological studies can bring different kinds of "news": In a "critical news approach," the researcher claims that things are *not* as they appear or are presented, whereas in a "positive news approach," the message is that something *is* organized in a particular way, which is of interest in itself. I return to these issues in a later section on applied studies.

A MAJOR OFFSHOOT: CONVERSATION ANALYSIS

Garfinkel's (1967) explorations quite soon became a source of inspiration for a number of other sociologists of younger generations. A prominent one was Sacks, who came to focus on spontaneous talk, that is, conversation. Both Sacks and his close colleague Schegloff had studied with Goffman, who was already famous for his studies of interaction, although in a different framework than the one Sacks came to develop. At first, Sacks explored various aspects of verbal interaction, including the use of categorization of persons, in what later became known as *membership categorization analysis* (MCA; see the section A Minor Offshoot), but gradually he concentrated on the actual organization of talking together, in collaboration with Schegloff and later Jefferson. This became what is now known as CA. Since their publication of a paper on the organization of turn-taking in 1974, CA became a recognizable paradigm in the Kuhnian sense, a research tradition with its own approach to data and analysis, with a prominent exemplar, and a growing set of people working along the lines set out by the originators.

The relations between EM and CA can be characterized as ambivalent (cf. Clayman & Maynard, 1995). Like EM, CA also studies the ways in which members of society organize their dealings with each other with an eye on the local circumstances in which they find themselves and with a stress on the local achievement of a social order. But whereas EM tended more and more to stress the local specificity of these methods, CA would often formulate those in more general terms, as is clearly the case in the paper on turn-taking. Furthermore, whereas ethnomethodologists have studied many aspects of an immense variety of situations, CA concentrated, at least originally, on the organization of talking together in itself, whatever the situation. Later, many conversation analysts turned to studying how the specifics of talk related to aspects of the situation in which it occurred, quite often an institutional setting. Although the expression CA is well established, at the initiative of Schegloff (1987), CA's object is now mostly termed *talk-in-interaction*. And although CA originally was conducted almost exclusively on the basis of audio recordings, video is now in general use. In a way, this seems to have brought EM and CA closer together again, as current studies of multimodal activities often combine inspirations from both EM and CA, as I illustrate later in this chapter.

The specificity of CA's analytic perspective can be characterized in terms of a restricted set of organizations, including most prominently those of turn-taking and sequence. The basic idea of turn-taking

organization is that a turn-at-talking consists of one or more units, such as sentences or single words like *yes*, called *turn-constructional units* (TCUs). When one such unit comes to a possible end, the turn might go to another participant; this moment is called a *transition-relevance place* (TRP). Then the current speaker may select another to take over, or another may self-select to speak, or the current speaker may continue, either immediately or a bit later (see Sacks, Schegloff, & Jefferson, 1974, for details and illustrations).

The organization of sequences, more or less coherent sets of subsequent turns, is rather more complicated, as can be seen in a recent book-length overview by Schegloff (2007b). The core idea is that a sequence can minimally consist of a pair of turns, one acting as an initiative such as a question, to be followed immediately by a response such as an answer. The technical term for such a two-part sequence is *adjacency pair* (Schegloff & Sacks, 1973, pp. 295–296), and other examples besides question–answer are *invitation–acceptance/decline, greeting–greeting,* and so forth. In sequences consisting of more than two parts, the core of such sequences quite often consists of one basic adjacency pair to which other parts are added in a *sequence expansion*. The first speaker may, for instance, react to the second part with a *third-turn response*, such as a thanks or an evaluation of the response. The core sequence may also be prepared in some way by a so-called *presequence*, such as, "May I ask you a question?" Another possibility is that the response to the first part of the pair is delayed, for instance, by an inquiry like "Now or tomorrow?" which starts an *inserted sequence*. And, of course, the core sequence may be followed up in many ways by *postexpansions*.

A few more technical terms deserve to be explicated, if only to show the kinds of complexities of sequences considered in CA. First-pair parts like invitations, requests, proposals, or accusations have possible second-pair parts that can be divided into two *alternate types*, such as acceptance or declination. The ways in which responses of these two types are designed tend to differ: Some are relatively short and produced promptly, whereas others may be much more elaborated, delayed in various ways, and accounted for in often a rather complex manner. The first type has been called a *preferred* response and the latter *dispreferred*. Accepting an invitation tends to be done using the first, preferred format, whereas a declination will be done in the second, dispreferred way. This is one example of what more generally is called *preference organization,* which can be observed in many other sequential environments as well. It should be stressed that preference here does not refer to any psychological entity, such as the willingness or not to accept an invitation, but just to the conventional formatting of turns. It has been suggested that these various forms of preference have to do with an underlying very general *preference for progressivity*, that is, to get on or to move forward in any interactive activity (Schegloff, 1979; Stivers & Robinson, 2006).

Insertion sequences are quite often initiated to clarify the meaning and purpose of a first-pair part. In that case it can also be called a *repair sequence.* Repair can be initiated any time a speaker decides to do something about a preceding utterance, the so-called *trouble source*, which is in some way problematic. And, of course, a repair can be initiated and done by the speaker of that trouble source, which is called *self-initiated self-repair.* That is in fact the preferred way of doing repair (Schegloff, Jefferson, & Sacks, 1977), compared with *other-initiated self-repair* or *other-repair.* Here also, the preference for progressivity can be seen at work; self-repair, especially when done quickly, is the least disturbing to the flow of the conversation of these alternatives.

Whereas the original concepts of CA, like the ones noted thus far, have been mainly developed on the basis of audio recordings, it has become clear by analyzing videos that visual impressions also may impact heavily on the social organization of face-to-face interactions. Goodwin (1981), who initiated the use of video for CA study, has shown, for instance, that speakers may adapt their utterances-in-course in response to visual displays of attention, agreement, disagreement, puzzlement, and so forth.

Doing CA: Recordings and Transcriptions

EM tends to use two kinds of data-gathering methods: intensive ethnography or recordings. For CA the use of recordings is absolutely required, whereas ethnography may be used as an adjunct way of gathering background data. It is only through the observation of the details of interaction that CA can be convincingly done. As in EM generally, CA prefers naturally occurring situations, that is, situations in which the impact of the researcher is minimal or absent. This, of course, is an important contrast with other types of social and behavioral sciences, but it fits EM's and CA's situationalist interests and their generally observational approach.

The most important aspect of working with recordings is that it allows repeated inspection, listening, or viewing, as the case may be. The results of this observational process are laid down in a transcript, in which the words spoken are rendered in a way that suggests *how* this was done, partly with a specialized use of typographical symbols. Jefferson has developed a set of conventions for this job, which is now in general use (cf. Jefferson, 2004). The example in Extract 7.1 may illustrate some of the complexities involved.

Extract 7.1
Coworkers on the Phone

(Coworkers Maggie and Sorrell went to a wedding reception where Maggie had some sort of momentary blackout and felt ill. Next morning she phones Sorrell at work to say that she will not be coming to work, is going to the doctor)

1	Maggie:	.hh because I (.) you know I told Mother what"d ha:ppened yesterday
2		there at the party,
3	Sorrell:	[° Yeah.°]
4	Maggie:	[a::] n d uh, .hhhhh (0.2) uh you know she asked me if it was
5		because I'd had too much to dri:nk and I said no=
6	Sorrell:	=[No ::::::.]
7	Maggie:	=[because at the t]i:me I'd only ha:d,h you know that drink "n
8		a ha:lf when we were going through the receiving line.
9	Sorrell:	Ri:ght.

Note. From "Is 'No' an Acknowledgment Token? Comparing American and British Uses of (+)/(–) Tokens," by G. Jefferson, 2002, *Journal of Pragmatics, 34*, p. 1346. Copyright 2002 by Elsevier. Reprinted with permission.

The extract is introduced, within double brackets, with a description of the interactional context, to assist the reader in understanding the episode. In the actual transcript a number of special symbols are used to render the specific, hearable details of the speech production. Underlining indicates stress; square brackets ([]) are used to indicate those parts that were spoken in overlap; when one utterance follows another very quickly, this is indicated by an equal sign (=); and a marked prolongation of a sound is indicated by the colons (:). Punctuation marks are used to indicate intonation: a question mark indicates a rising tone, a comma indicates a nonfinal flat tone, and a dot indicates a downward falling tone. The dot-preceded .hhh, finally, renders an inbreath. In interaction the shaping of an utterance and the timing of one in relation to others is essential, therefore such details have to be noted as exactly as possible.

CA as a Data-Driven Approach

It has often been noted that CA uses a *data-driven* approach. This means that at first the researcher takes an attitude that has been characterized as *unmotivated looking*, that is, without a prespecified problem or question in mind. This does not deny the fact that one has a broadly focused interest in CA in the *how* of interactional organization. Furthermore, now that there is a well-defined and elaborate tradition, the CA is structured by an extensive conceptual apparatus, which would be silly to ignore (see the section A Major Offshoot). So although much is already known about the organization of interactive talk, the interest in much current CA work is still to discover previously unnoticed phenomena. At the same time, one would also want to extend and refine what is known or to apply CA to new substantive areas. The news that CA can offer to existing non-CA knowledge is often that the latter is too simple in the sense that it ignores or glosses over the *actual* details of interactive talk or that it starts from and is limited by current cultural, mostly individualistic and mentalistic, preconceptions. Like EM more generally, it demonstrates in detail that persons act in more intersubjectively responsible ways than is recognized in most other approaches in the human sciences (Button, 1991).

In a typical CA approach (see ten Have, 2007, for a more extensive treatment), the researcher starts with inspecting some recordings or transcripts looking for episodes that seem somehow interesting, maybe puzzling or especially apt. That episode should be analyzed in depth using CA's conceptual repertoire. As argued elsewhere (ten Have, 2007), such an analysis essentially takes two steps, which I call *understanding* and the *analysis* proper. Listening to the recording and reading the transcript, the analyst first tries to understand what the interactants are doing organizationally when they speak as they do. They may, for instance, be requesting information, offering to tell a story, changing the topic, and so forth. Such understandings will be based, at first, on the researcher's own membership knowledge, as, one might say, a *cultural colleague* of the speakers. Second, however, the analyst will check the sequential context and especially the uptake of the utterances in question in subsequent talk, immediately following or later in the conversation, for instance, by granting a request. Understanding the actions, although not the purpose of the research, is a necessary requirement for the next step, the analysis proper, which is to formulate the procedures used to accomplish the actions as understood. Because CA's interest is organizational and procedural, the ultimate object of CA research is what Schegloff (1992) has called the *procedural infrastructure of interaction*, and, in particular, the practices of talking in conversation. This means that conversational practices are not analyzed in terms of individual properties or institutional expectations, but as situated collaborative accomplishments.

Such an analysis results in an analytic formulation of a device, a typical sequence, or whatever may be reported as such in a single-case study. Most of the time, however, the researcher will go on to inspect other cases, which may be relevantly compared with the first one. This may lead to a confirmation, a reformulation, a specification, or a differentiation into types. The researcher may formulate conditions for, and effects of, the device or sequence, in general, its functions. This more extended type of research is often called a *collection study*. The idea is that the analysis of a first case can be used as a starting point for a more systematic exploration of an emerging analytic theme. The researcher searches an available data set of newly collected data for instances that seem to be similar to the candidate phenomenon, the first formulation of the theme as well as data that seem to point in a different direction, the so-called *deviant case analysis*. In short, the researcher builds a collection of relevant cases in search of patterns that elucidate some procedural issues. This may seem to suggest a kind of principled independence of a single research project from existing knowledge, but this is not the case for all of CA reports. An investigation may take off from an issue internal to the CA tradition, or even from some problem or idea external to it, but all the same each and every piece of data should be first analyzed in its own terms.

This stress on analyzing each instance in its own terms is, of course, at odds with a general preference for quantification, which is dominant in the social sciences at large. Whether quantification makes sense in CA has been debated by some of its major practitioners, notably Schegloff (1993) and Heritage (1999). The general upshot seems to a need for caution and a limitation of sensible quantification to some of the most easily differentiable aspects, such as the choice of a word in an identical position or a clearly defined (yes–no) outcome (cf. examples in Heritage, 1999, and an experiment reported in Heritage, Robinson, Elliott, Beckett, & Wilkes, 2007; see also the discussions in Chapter 8 of this volume contrasting discursive psychology with mainstream methods).

Later Developments in CA

A particular aspect of the development of CA is that during the first 15 years of its existence, its basic approach and its core concepts had been developed by a very small number of people, mainly Sacks, Schegloff, and Jefferson (1974). So everything coming after that could be seen as extensions, additions, or applications, in one or another direction. The CA as it emerged in the 1960s and 1970s might be characterized as *CA-in-general*, or *pure CA*, in the sense that it took as its core task to study talk-in-interaction as such, without taking into account its particular setting or interactional genre. In their turn-taking paper, Sacks et al. had already hinted at

the possibility to compare conversation to other kinds of speech-exchange systems (1974, pp. 729–731). Some years later, CA researchers began to take up the implied challenge and started to study interactional talk in a variety of settings, such as law courts, medical consultations, new interviews, and many others. Such studies can be characterized as *applied CA* and I will discuss some examples in a later section. But at the same time, pure CA continued to be elaborated, by the originators, like Schegloff and Jefferson, and by others who started doing CA later, many of whom had a background in functional or interactional linguistics (cf. Ford, Fox, & Thompson, 2002; Ochs, Schegloff, & Thompson, 1996). One of the interests that this strand of CA has added to the earlier ones is the issue of *linguistic resources* that speakers have at their disposal as members of a speech community. By comparing findings on the basis of the study of English-speaking interactants with data on conversations in Finnish or Japanese, it became clear that the devices actually used partly depend on what particular linguistic systems allow or facilitate (cf. Hayashi, 2005; Sidnell, 2009; Sorjonen, 2001; Tanaka, 1999). The English system, for instance, facilitates the early projection of the action an utterance will be doing, whereas in Japanese the verbs that embody the action tend to be produced in sentence final positions. So Japanese speakers can still change the action in their talk at a relatively late moment, but they may also at times use an early placeholder word if they need to inform their recipients on what they are up to (Hayashi, 2005).

A MINOR OFFSHOOT: MEMBERSHIP CATEGORIZATION ANALYSIS

As noted, apart from the approach that later became known as CA, Sacks also for some time worked on a rather different enterprise that is currently called MCA. He noted that a large part of the knowledge that people use and rely on in their interactions is organized in terms of categories of people, either in general terms (as in *children*) or in reference to a particular person (as in *my husband*). These insights and their elaborate explication was at first part of his doctoral research on calls to a suicide prevention center (cf. Sacks, 1972a; also a number of lectures in

Sacks, 1992) in which callers explained their life situation and their feeling that they had "no one to turn to." What Sacks noted, among other things, was that people use person-categories as part of *sets* of categories, which he called *membership categorization devices* (MCDs; Sacks, 1972a, 1972b). For instance, within the MCD *sex*, people use two basic categories, female and male, whereas the MCD *age* does not have a fixed number of categories because their use depends on situational considerations. Sometimes two categories suffice, *old* and *young*, but often more subtle differentiations are called for.

Categories are not just named or implied, they also carry a number of different associated properties, later called *category predicates*, like the one that Sacks used a lot: *category-bound activities*. So, for instance, he noted that the activity *crying* may be considered bound to the category *baby*, and the activity *picking up (a child)* is typical of the category *mother* (Sacks, 1972b). Other kinds of predicates might involve properties like rights and responsibilities, specialized knowledge, and competencies. Sacks (1972a) also made an effort to explicate "rules of application," such as an *economy rule* (one category is often sufficient) and a *consistency rule* (once a category from a specific MCD is used, other categories from that device tend to be used also). Although many different categories may be *correct*, there are most often only a few that are also *relevant* in the situation at hand.

It is remarkable, as can be seen by reading Sacks's (1992) *Lectures on Conversation* in chronological order, that his interest in these matters became less prominent after about 1967, being more strongly focused on issues of turn-taking and sequence. He did, however, publish some of these mid-1960s explorations of categorization much later (Sacks, 1972a, 1972b), so apparently he did not disavow them. In his introduction to the first volume of Sacks's (1992) *Lectures*, Schegloff commented on this shift as mainly a methodological one. Although the work on membership categorization tended to stress the recognizability of expressions such as category terms, for any member of the culture, Sacks later sought to substantiate such claims in terms of the demonstrable understanding by the participants, as visible in their uptake.

Although MCA more or less disappeared from the CA enterprise, it was later taken up again by more ethnomethodologically inclined authors, including Hester and Eglin (1997), Jayyusi (1984), and Watson (1997). In the introduction to a volume collecting some of these later MCA studies, Hester and Eglin (1997, pp. 11–22) commented on an ambiguity in Sacks's observations on membership categorization. Some of his formulations suggest a decontextualized model of membership categories and collections of categories as preexisting any occasion of use, whereas at other times, he stresses the occasionality of any actual usage. Hester and Eglin (1997, p. 21) stressed that for EM "membership categorization is an *activity* carried out in particular local circumstances." It should be seen as "in situ achievements of members' practical actions and practical reasoning." In recent years MCA continues to be used and debated (cf. Carlin, 2010; Schegloff, 2007a, 2007c).

Currently, MCA is often used to analyze written texts (Watson, 2009), but the underlying theme of MCA, namely, the social organization of knowledge, emerges regularly in CA proper, for instance, in a series of papers by Heritage (1984a) on the use of *Oh* as a marker of a change of knowledge of the speaker and more recently on what he has called *epistemics*, or more particularly *epistemic rights* and *epistemic authority* (Heritage, 2005; Heritage & Raymond, 2005; Raymond & Heritage, 2006). As he wrote, "Interactants not only keep score on who knows what, they also keep rather close watch over the relevant rights that each may have to know particular facts" (Heritage, 2005, p. 196), and that they do can be shown in the details of their actions and reactions, when analyzed in sequential terms. In my view, then, terms like EM, CA, and MCA denote variants of one big enterprise to study the local organization of human action or even of human sociality.

APPLIED STUDIES

As used in this section, the notion of *application* can refer both to projects in which the insights and methods of EM and CA are applied to specific substantive themes or areas and ones in which EM and

CA insights are used to criticize or educate specific practices, although the first is much more frequent than the second. The basic idea is that the detailed attention that EM and CA give to everyday practices can be used to extend or correct available, often quantitative, knowledge about such practices. Established knowledge about some practice is often too general to cover the details of such practices in the situations in which they occur. Therefore such knowledge, as available in theories, plans, or reports, is quite often not able to effectively predict or understand the relative success or failure of practical projects. This theme was already discernable in Suchman's work (1987, 2007), as the instructions provided by an "intelligent" copier were misunderstood by the users, while the machine also misunderstood some of the users' actions, together leading to various type of practical troubles.

In the past 3 decades an increasing number of studies in EM and CA have been of an applied character. For reasons of space only a few themes can be developed at some length, and only a small number of topical areas are mentioned in this chapter. Most applied CA studies deal with interactions between institutional agents and their clients of some sort, such as patients, defendants, interviewees, and so on. In line with the remarks by Sacks et al. (1974) about the comparison of speech-exchange systems, these studies quite often (especially in the 1980s) used a comparison between the institutional interaction studied with informal conversation as an implicit or explicit frame of reference. Early studies of doctor–patient interaction, for instance, noted the restrictions on turn-taking opportunities and turn-type selection to which patients seemed to be subjected (cf. Frankel, 1984, 1990; West, 1984). They also made it clear that such encounters tended to be organized in a restricted number of phases, such as history taking, examination, diagnosis, and treatment. What was discernable then, and confirmed later (cf. Beach, 2001; Heritage & Maynard, 2006; Stivers, 2007), was that the speaking opportunities for patients depend very much on the phase of the encounter. One can note a shift, in these later studies, from a somewhat moral noting of restrictions to a more diversified description of the uses by patients of their speaking opportunities, and the ways in which physicians do react to (or anticipate) patients' moves. In other words, whereas at first it was the asymmetry that was noted, it was later seen that the asymmetry-prone context of medical interaction also allowed for half-hidden negotiations, especially about treatment options. Application in the second, practical sense also seems to be on the rise in recent years, as CA-based insights and studies are used in medical education and professional training (Maynard & Heritage, 2005; Stein, Frankel, & Krupat, 2005).

When CA emerged in the 1960s, some psychotherapists were already recording their sessions with patients. Sacks, for instance, used some recordings, in his case of group therapy with teenagers, to explore conversation (cf. Sacks, 1992). That these interactions were not just conversations but rather therapy sessions was largely ignored in his comments. Later, the tendency was to use data from ordinary interactions. It was only since about the turn of the century that CA researchers turned to psychotherapy as a topic for the application of CA. Since then, a substantial number of papers and a book (Peräkylä, Antaki, Vehviläinen, & Leudar, 2008) have been published. Of course, therapists use quite a varied set of the verbal practices that, for them, constitute therapy. The challenge for CA is to explicate these practices in greater detail than has been done before and to point out and describe features of interaction that are part of psychotherapy but that psychotherapeutic theories have not recognized or discussed (Peräkylä et al., 2008). A major difference between CA research and previous studies of psychotherapy lies in CA's stress on sequence organization: how one utterance relates to previous and subsequent utterances in detail.

A major characteristic of psychotherapy sessions, in contrast to physician–patient encounters, is their lack of an overall structural organization in phases. Therefore, CA studies in this field tend to focus on local sequential relations, for instance, the ways in which a therapist's comments relate to previous utterances by the patient, or the ways in which a patient reacts to such a recipient action. In psychotherapy, recipient actions are among the major means at the therapist's disposal to influence the patient is a more or less subtle manner.

Peräkylä et al. (2008) distinguished different types of such actions. A therapist may (a) propose a different, probably more focused term for one used by the patient, (b) extend a patient's sentence as a display of understanding, (c) reformulate what was just said, or (d) offer a different interpretation than the one suggested by the patient. In so doing, the therapists may be seen as "stretching the boundaries of ownership of knowledge" (Peräkylä et al., 2008, pp. 192–193), suggesting that they know the patient better than the individual. Such reworkings are mostly selective and thus reshape what was said by the other party. Therapists' questioning initiatives and patients' responses to therapist sayings are also discussed. CA studies of psychotherapy offer a detailed sociological account of therapeutic processes rather than a psychological one. CA foregrounds the collaborative and negotiative character of such interactions. What therapists do is a specialized use of quite ordinary conversational means.

From the mid-1990s onward, there have been quite a number of CA-based studies of interaction in which at least one of the participants is communicatively impaired in one way or another. In Goodwin's edited book *Conversation and Brain Damage* (2003), he collected work by the major contributors to this area, focusing on aphasia. The core message that is stressed in all of these contributions is that whatever communicative success is achieved in the encounters under study has to be seen as a collaborative achievement. It depends on the use of quite ordinary conversational methods, adapted to the particularities of the impairment in the case at hand, in which both the aphasics and their interlocutors have to be creative. In this way, the book's essays have a polemical subtheme in relation to conventional psycholinguistic and neurological approaches, which are oriented to individual failings rather than collective communicative successes.

A number of contributions deal explicitly with the contrast between ordinary, real-life interactions with an aphasic and formal tests. In the latter type of situations, an aphasic may be asked, for instance, to tell a story on the basis of a set of cartoon drawings, or to answer standardized questions, at the request of a tester who has only a professional interest in the performance displayed in those tellings or answers.

This situation is contrasted with naturally occurring situations in which an aphasic wants to tell the story of a personal experience to a close relative, for instance, or participate in the arrangement of eating out with a family group. In such situations it is the achievement of shared understanding that matters and not the objective assessment of the linguistic quality of an individual performance.

The concept of aphasia covers a range of impairments, and the patients whose speech is exemplified and analyzed in the various chapters suffer from a variety of types of linguistic insufficiencies, including quite prominently the inability to find the right word in time. In such cases, the speakers often use general terms instead of a more specific ones, requiring a more specific interpretation or (implicit or explicit) guess made on the basis of shared knowledge or situational cues. This also accounts for the fact that mutual understanding is best achieved in active collaboration with intimates.

Although these three types of applied studies mostly applied CA concepts and methods and based their findings in most cases just on audio or video recordings, a different type of applied studies emerged in the late 1980s that, in addition to video recordings, also used ethnographic fieldwork. I have mentioned the early work of Suchman (1987) on users' work on an advanced copier, which she carried out as part of a research job in an industrial firm. She continued her studies there focusing on specialized work activities involving complex technological support devices like computers and various communication technologies. Later, other researchers were able to start similar projects, so now one can speak of a tradition of "workplace studies." Apart from Suchman, important contributions have been made by Button, Heath, and Whalen (cf. collections edited by Button, 1993; Heath & Luff, 2000; Luff, Hindmarsh, & Heath, 2000). Heath has led a particularly successful Work, Interaction and Technology Research Group at King's College in London, which has studied a wide range of settings, including control rooms for the London Underground system, museums, and art galleries as well as journalists working in a news agency.

In these studies, the use of video is crucial because the activities often take place in a group setting involving team members and the extensive use of various technological artifacts. Analyzing such activities requires, on the one hand, visual access to the local environment to study bodily actions and nonvocal exchanges in situ, and, on the other, a deeper, locally specialized understanding of the activities under study than is generally used for agent–client interactions. Some participant observation—as well as studying relevant documents and interviewing experts—is used to acquire the necessary background to really understand what is going on. To mention one example, Nevile (2004), from Australia, collected the core data for his studies of talk-in-interaction in the airline cockpit by video-recording the activities of flight crews on scheduled flights by commercial airlines. But before he even approached the airlines to ask for their cooperation, he prepared his research by extensively reading whatever he could find about the operation of commercial airlines, training and operations manuals, official accident reports, and so on. He also watched available information videos showing pilots at work, visited conferences, and talked to research psychologists working with flight crews and accident investigators.

In such workplace studies, the concepts, findings, and methods of CA are applied as part of a wider undertaking that is broadly inspired by EM. I mention a few general insights that can be gained from these studies. First, such specialized (team)work requires an experience-based practical knowledge that goes far beyond what can be acquired through formal instruction in a nonwork setting. Second, effective teamwork not only requires the individual worker's understanding of the task at hand but also an understanding *at a glance* of what others are doing. A lot of actual coordination of activities occurs in an implicit fashion, often by seeing in peripheral vision or by overhearing talk and adapting one's own activities accordingly. So, for instance, the worker in a London Underground control room who is tasked with making announcements to the traveling public knows from observing and overhearing his colleagues at work on some crisis situation what to announce, to whom, and when without getting a request to do so (see Heath & Luff, 2000). Third, formal accounts of work activities cannot make this

hidden work and the competencies involved in it visible to outsiders, including the overseeing management (cf. Whalen & Vinkhuyzen, 2000).

To illustrate how CA can figure in this more encompassing endeavor, let me refer shortly to some of Nevile's (2004) findings when studying airline cockpits. In the first part of his book, he analyzed the use of personal pronouns: *I, you,* and *we.* Some of these uses are officially prescribed in the relevant manuals, and others are voluntary and impromptu, chosen on the spot. They function, in any case, as designators of local and momentary cockpit identities, with associated tasks and responsibilities. In the second part of the book, Nevile, by discussing a range of concrete examples, examined how pilots coordinate their talk and nontalk activities as they perform the routine tasks necessary to fly their plane. Such coordination is essential to maintain a shared understanding of where they are in the flight and what has to be done then and there, as pilots have to perform their tasks with split-second precision and strictly in sequence, one after the other. In doing this work, talk is just one of the resources that participants use and orient to; others include gaze direction, gesture, and placement and movement of parts of the body, such as head, arms, hands, legs, and eyebrows. In the third and final part of his book, Nevile widened his perspective on talk *in* the cockpit to investigate how it is coordinated with talk to participants *outside* the cockpit, such as air traffic controllers and cabin crew members. Again, the issue is that the two pilots have to attain and demonstrate a shared understanding of the local consequences of the outside talk, which they can do by internal talk or nonvocal but visible activities. Investigation of such fine-tuned activities requires finely detailed transcriptions of talk with descriptions of the associated activities.

To give an impression of how this is done, I quote one of Nevile's examples in Extract 7.2, which in the original text is accompanied by a picture of the pointing finger that is mentioned.

The arrows indicate the moment in the talk at which the nonvocal activities start or stop. Workplace studies are a rather demanding kind of study, but they are also extremely rewarding and necessary because they reflect the subtle but too often ignored complexity of specialized work.

Extract 7.2
In the Cockpit

```
C = Captain
PNF = Pilot not flying
FO = First officer
PF = Pilot flying
1                   (50.3)
2    C/PNF:         one thousand to altitude.
                    ↑————-↑
2a   C/PNF:         ((moves right hand up from lap, then left
                    to right, at chest height, with index finger
                    extended))
                             ↑————↑
2b   C/PNF:                  ((holds right hand still, just to
                             the right of own chest, index
                             finger points to FO/PF's side of
                             main instrument panel))
                                      ↑
2c   C/PNF:                           ((moves right hand
                                      down and left, back to
                                      right leg))
3                   (3.2) = (0 > 1.4 > 2.4 > 3.2))
                    ↑——————↑
4                            ((sound of altitude alert buzzer))
5    FO/PF:         >alert (.) for level (.) two fi::ve zero
6                   (27.5)
```

Note. From *Beyond the Black Box: Talk-in-Interaction in the Airline Cockpit* (p. 131), by M. Nevile, 2004, Aldershot, England: Ashgate. Copyright 2004 by Maurice Nevile. Reprinted with permission.

There are many other types of applied studies using EM, CA, or MCA. In all these it has been proven that it is useful to explicate the ways in which (inter)action and communication depend on the local application of *infrastructural* practices. The stress on restrictions that are operative in institutional settings, which was stressed in early applied CA, can now be broadened in saying that task-oriented interactions basically depend on *general* interactional capacities, which in the setting at hand get a specialized application.

CONCLUSION

Within the limits of the space available, I have offered a summary characterization of EM and its offshoots CA and MCA. Contrary to most of the human sciences and Western culture at large, EM does not take off from the individual and his or her mind. Instead, ethnomethodologists observe human action as inherently social and situated. Therefore they largely abstain from precategorized and researcher-provoked ways of collecting data but rather use intense ethnography and audio or video recordings. In so doing, they can reveal news about human life that was previously unavailable. Quite often this can lead to what has been called a respecification of previously developed concepts in the human sciences, including sociology and psychology, as *members' situated practices* (Button, 1991; Garfinkel, 2002). This kind of work as applied to psychological concepts has been taken up by discursive psychology, which is discussed in Chapter 8 of this volume. That chapter also provides an exemplary sketch of the different stages of a research project, including an analysis of some interactional episodes that clearly demonstrate the impact of sequentiality in human interaction.

References

Beach, W. A. (Ed.). (2001). Introduction: Diagnosing "lay diagnosis." *Text: Interdisciplinary Journal for the Study of Discourse, 21,* 13–18.

Button, G. (Ed.). (1991). *Ethnomethodology and the human sciences.* Cambridge, England: Cambridge University Press.

Button, G. (Ed.). (1993). *Technology in working order: Studies of work, interaction and technology.* London, England: Routledge.

Carlin, A. P. (2010). Discussion note: Reading "A tutorial on membership categorization" by Emanuel Schegloff. *Journal of Pragmatics, 42,* 257–261. doi:10.1016/j.pragma.2009.06.007

Clayman, S. E., & Maynard, D. W. (1995). Ethnomethodology and conversation analysis. In P. ten Have & G. Psathas (Eds.), *Situated order: Studies in the social organization of talk and embodied activities* (pp. 1–30). Washington, DC: University Press of America.

Ford, C. E., Fox, B. A., & Thompson, S. A. (Eds.). (2002). *The language of turn and sequence.* New York, NY: Oxford University Press.

Francis, D., & Hester, S. (2004). *An invitation to ethnomethodology: Language, society and interaction.* London, England: Sage.

Frankel, R. M. (1984). From sentence to sequence: Understanding the medical encounter through micro-interactional analysis. *Discourse Processes, 7,* 135–170. doi:10.1080/01638538409544587

Frankel, R. M. (1990). Talking in interviews: A dispreference for patient-initiated questions in physician–patient encounters. In G. Psathas (Ed.), *Interactional competence* (pp. 231–262). Washington, DC: University Press of America.

Garfinkel, H. (1967). *Studies in ethnomethodology.* Englewood Cliffs, NJ: Prentice-Hall.

Garfinkel, H. (2002). *Ethnomethodology's program: Working out Durkheim's aphorism.* Lanham, MD: Rowman & Littlefield.

Garfinkel, H., & Wieder, D. L. (1992). Two incommensurable, asymmetrically alternate technologies of social analysis. In G. Watson & R. M. Seiler (Eds.), *Text in context: Studies in ethnomethodology* (pp. 175–206). Newbury Park, CA: Sage.

Goodwin, C. (1981). *Conversational organization: Interaction between speakers and hearers.* New York, NY: Academic Press.

Goodwin, C. (Ed.). (2003). *Conversation and brain damage.* New York, NY: Oxford University Press.

Hayashi, M. (2005). Referential problems and turn construction: An exploration of an intersection between grammar and interaction. *Text: Interdisciplinary Journal for the Study of Discourse, 25,* 437–468.

Heap, J. L. (1990). Applied ethnomethodology: Looking for the local rationality of reading activities. *Human Studies, 13,* 39–72. doi:10.1007/BF00143040

Heath, C., & Luff, P. (2000). *Technology in action.* Cambridge, England: Cambridge University Press. doi:10.1017/CBO9780511489839

Heritage, J. (1984a). A change-of-state token and aspects of its sequential placement. In J. M. Atkinson & J. Heritage (Eds.), *Structures of social action: Studies in conversation analysis* (pp. 299–345). Cambridge, England: Cambridge University Press.

Heritage, J. (1984b). *Garfinkel and ethnomethodology.* Cambridge, England: Polity Press.

Heritage, J. (1999). CA at century's end: Practices of talk-in-interaction, their distributions and their outcomes. *Research on Language and Social Interaction, 32,* 69–76. doi:10.1207/S15327973RLSI321&2_9

Heritage, J. (2005). Cognition in discourse. In H. te Molder & J. Potter (Eds.), *Conversation and cognition* (pp. 184–202). Cambridge, England: Cambridge University Press. doi:10.1017/CBO9780511489990.009

Heritage, J., & Maynard, D. W. (Eds.). (2006). *Communication in medical care: Interaction between primary care physicians and patients.* Cambridge, England: Cambridge University Press. doi:10.1017/CBO9780511607172

Heritage, J., & Raymond, G. (2005). The terms of agreement: Indexing epistemic authority and subordination in assessment sequences. *Social Psychology Quarterly, 68,* 15–38. doi:10.1177/019027250506800103

Heritage, J., Robinson, J. D., Elliott, M. N., Beckett, M., & Wilkes, M. (2007). Reducing patients' unmet concerns in primary care: The difference one word can make. *Journal of General Internal Medicine, 22,* 1429–1433. doi:10.1007/s11606-007-0279-0

Hester, S., & Eglin, P. (Eds.). (1997). *Culture in action: Studies in membership categorization analysis.* Washington, DC: University Press of America.

Jayyusi, L. (1984). *Categorization and the moral order.* Boston, MA: Routledge & Kegan Paul.

Jefferson, G. (2002). Is "no" an acknowledgment token? Comparing American and British uses of (+)/(–) tokens. *Journal of Pragmatics, 34,* 1345–1383. doi:10.1016/S0378-2166(02)00067-X

Jefferson, G. (2004). Glossary of transcript symbols with an introduction. In G. H. Lerner (Ed.), *Conversation analysis: Studies from the first generation* (pp. 13–31). Amsterdam, the Netherlands: Benjamins.

Liberman, K. (2004). *Dialectical practice in Tibetan philosophical culture: An ethnomethodological inquiry into formal reasoning.* Lanham, MD: Rowman & Littlefield.

Luff, P., Hindmarsh, J., & Heath, C. (Eds.). (2000). *Workplace studies: Recovering work practice and informing systems design.* Cambridge, England: Cambridge University Press. doi:10.1017/CBO9780511628122

Lynch, M. (1985). *Art and artifact in laboratory science: A study of shop work and shop talk.* London, England: Routledge & Kegan Paul.

Lynch, M. (1993). *Scientific practice and ordinary action: Ethnomethodology and social studies of science.* New York, NY: Cambridge University Press.

Maynard, D. W., & Heritage, J. (2005). Conversation analysis, doctor–patient interaction and medical communication. *Medical Education, 39,* 428–435. doi:10.1111/j.1365-2929.2005.02111.x

Nevile, M. (2004). *Beyond the black box: Talk-in-interaction in the airline cockpit.* Aldershot, England: Ashgate.

Ochs, E., Schegloff, E. A., & Thompson, S. A. (Eds.). (1996). *Interaction and grammar.* Cambridge, England: Cambridge University Press. doi:10.1017/CBO9780511620874

Peräkylä, A., Antaki, C., Vehviläinen, S., & Leudar, I. (Eds.). (2008). *Conversation analysis and psychotherapy.* Cambridge, England: Cambridge University Press.

Raymond, G., & Heritage, J. (2006). The epistemics of social relationships: Owning grandchildren. *Language in Society, 35,* 677–705. doi:10.1017/S0047404506060325

Sacks, H. (1972a). An initial investigation of the usability of conversational data for doing sociology. In D. Sudnow (Ed.), *Studies in social interaction* (pp. 31–74). New York, NY: Free Press.

Sacks, H. (1972b). On the analyzability of stories by children. In J. J. Gumperz & D. Hymes (Eds.), *Directions in sociolinguistics: The ethnography of communication* (pp. 325–345). New York, NY: Rinehart & Winston.

Sacks, H. (1992). *Lectures on conversation* (Vols. 1–2). Oxford, England: Basil Blackwell.

Sacks, H., Schegloff, E. A., & Jefferson, G. (1974). A simplest systematics for the organization of turn taking for conversation. *Language, 50*, 696–735. doi:10.2307/412243

Schegloff, E. A. (1979). The relevance of repair to syntax-for-conversation. In T. Givon (Ed.), *Syntax and semantics 12: Discourse and syntax* (pp. 261–286). New York, NY: Academic Press.

Schegloff, E. A. (1987). Analyzing single episodes of interaction: An exercise in conversation analysis. *Social Psychology Quarterly, 50*, 101–114.

Schegloff, E. A. (1992). Repair after next turn: The last structurally provided defense of intersubjectivity in conversation. *American Journal of Sociology, 97*, 1295–1345. doi:10.1086/229903

Schegloff, E. A. (1993). Reflections on quantification in the study of conversation. *Research on Language and Social Interaction, 26*, 99–128. doi:10.1207/s15327973rlsi2601_5

Schegloff, E. A. (2007a). Categories in action: Person-reference and membership categorization. *Discourse Studies, 9*, 433–461. doi:10.1177/1461445607079162

Schegloff, E. A. (2007b). *Sequence organization in interaction: A primer in conversation analysis* (Vol. 1). Cambridge, England: Cambridge University Press. doi:10.1017/CBO9780511791208

Schegloff, E. A. (2007c). A tutorial on membership categorization. *Journal of Pragmatics, 39*, 462–482. doi:10.1016/j.pragma.2006.07.007

Schegloff, E. A., Jefferson, G., & Sacks, H. (1977). The preference for self-correction in the organization of repair in conversation. *Language, 53*, 361–382. doi:10.2307/413107

Schegloff, E. A., & Sacks, H. (1973). Opening up closings. *Semiotica, 8*, 289–327. doi:10.1515/semi.1973.8.4.289

Sidnell, J. (Ed.). (2009). *Conversation analysis: Comparative perspectives*. Cambridge, England: Cambridge University Press. doi:10.1017/CBO9780511635670

Sorjonen, M.-L. (2001). *Responding in conversation: A study of response particles in Finnish*. Amsterdam, the Netherlands: Benjamins.

Stein, T., Frankel, R. M., & Krupat, E. (2005). Enhancing clinician communication skills in a large healthcare organization: A longitudinal case study. *Patient Education and Counseling, 58*, 4–12. doi:10.1016/j.pec.2005.01.014

Stivers, T. (2007). *Prescribing under pressure: Parent–physician conversations and antibiotics*. New York, NY: Oxford University Press.

Stivers, T., & Robinson, J. D. (2006). A preference for progressivity in interaction. *Language in Society, 35*, 367–392. doi:10.1017/S0047404506060179

Suchman, L. (1987). *Plans and situated action: The problem of human–machine communication*. Cambridge, England: Cambridge University Press.

Suchman, L. A. (2007). *Human–machine reconfigurations: Plans and situated actions* (2nd ed.). Cambridge, England: Cambridge University Press.

Sudnow, D. (1978). *Ways of the hand: The organization of improvised conduct*. London, England: Routledge & Kegan Paul.

Tanaka, H. (1999). *Turn-taking in Japanese conversation: A study in grammar and interaction*. Amsterdam, the Netherlands: Benjamins.

ten Have, P. (2002, September). The notion of member is the heart of the matter: On the role of membership knowledge in ethnomethodological inquiry. *Forum: Qualitative Social Research, 3*(3). Retrieved from http://www.qualitative-research.net/fqs/fqs-eng.htm

ten Have, P. (2007). *Doing conversation analysis: A practical guide* (2nd ed.). London, England: Sage.

Watson, R. (1997). Some general reflections on "categorization" and "sequence" in the analysis of conversation. In S. Hester & P. Eglin (Eds.), *Culture in action: Studies in membership categorization analysis* (pp. 49–76). Washington, DC: University Press of America.

Watson, R. (2009). *Analysing practical and professional texts: A naturalistic approach*. Farnham, England: Ashgate.

West, C. (1984). *Routine complications: Trouble with talk between doctors and patients*. Bloomington: Indiana University Press.

Whalen, J., & Vinkhuyzen, E. (2000). Expert systems in (inter)action: Diagnosing document machine problems over the telephone. In P. Luff, J. Hindmarsh, & C. Heath (Eds.), *Workplace studies: Recovering work practice and informing systems design* (pp. 92–140). Cambridge, England: Cambridge University Press.

Wieder, D. L. (1974). *Language and social reality: The case of telling the convict code*. The Hague, the Netherlands: Mouton.

CHAPTER 8

DISCOURSE ANALYSIS AND DISCURSIVE PSYCHOLOGY

Jonathan Potter

Extract 8.1 captures some talk taken from partway through an evening meal in a U.K. family. Anna, who is 3, has not been eating and is increasingly fractious. She has been fed a forkful of food by Mum (although she normally feeds herself). She is still not eating.

This is the kind of material that discursive psychologists work with. It is interaction between people that is happening naturally. It is not staged by the researcher. It is recorded on digital video (allowing us to see the spitting on line 8) and transcribed in a way that captures delay, overlap, intonation, and volume (see Chapter 7 of this volume). This is the stuff of real life. It is a recording of how the interaction unfolds for the participants—it does not have functional magnetic resonance imaging recordings of Mum's or Anna's brain, and participants have not been interviewed about what is going on. Participant actions are

intelligible to one another, however, and are redolent with psychological matters. For example, in the unfolding interaction, Mum's summons in line 1 is inflected with a prosodic contour that we might describe as warning; Anna's sob in line 3 is a display of upset. Moreover, the display of upset follows the warning that Anna is likely to hear as pressing her to eat.

These materials allow us to consider how the interaction unfolds, and each bit of the interaction is relevant to what came before and what came after. It is after Anna's sob (in the slot where she should be eating according to Mum's warning) that Mum produces an explicit threat: "If you don't eat your dinner there will be no pudding." Note that this is an interesting and somewhat intensified attempt at social influence. And yet threats make hardly any appearance in the literature on social influence. Discursive psychologists look at materials like this not only to address classic psychological issues but also to be stimulated into new thinking on new issues.

Note also that the threat is built so that the agency for producing the unpleasant upshot (no pudding) is embedded rather than exposed. This may soften the appearance of autocratic control (relevant to family dynamics), and it may produce eating as subject to general impersonal rules rather than parental whim (in line with a classic project of socialization). All of this is occasioned by Anna failing to act on Mum's implicit directive on line 3.

The threat has an orderly place—but it is not the first action used for encouraging eating in these mealtimes. It is delayed and only comes after requests, directives, cajoling, and other actions take

---

Extract 8.1
Mum and Anna

01	Mum:	[An]na?
02		(1.6)
03	Anna:	U↑hhuh ((more of a sob than a response))
04		(0.6)
05	Mum:	If you don' eat your di̱nner:, (0.4)
06		there'll be ̱no pudding.
07		[(1.2)]
08	Anna:	[((spits mouthful onto her plate))]
09	Mum:	That's horrible.

DOI: 10.1037/13620-008
APA Handbook of Research Methods in Psychology: Vol. 2. Research Designs, H. Cooper (Editor-in-Chief)

place. This gives the child space to produce the appropriate behavior as generated by her volition.

There is something fascinating about what happens after the threat. Anna spits out her food. This is not just random food spitting—food is being ejected just in the slot where Mum has produced the strongest push for food to be ingested. That is, in just this slot, Anna is doing something that counts as defiance. Once a threat has been issued, compliance is a relevant next action but so is defiance. We can see in these concrete, readily researched materials some of the big issues of social relations played out, in particular, the sociological truism that power and resistance go together. These are basic concerns of discursive psychology (for more detail, see Craven & Potter, 2010; Hepburn & Potter, 2011b). Let me now lay these out more systematically.

This chapter introduces and overviews the use of discourse analysis to study psychological questions and, in particular, the perspective known as discursive psychology (DP). DP begins with psychological matters as they arise for people as they live their lives. It studies how psychological issues and objects are constructed, understood, and displayed as people interact in both everyday and institutional situations. It focuses on such questions as the following:

- How does one of the parties in a relationship counseling session build a description of troubles that indirectly blames the other party and places the onus on them to change (Edwards, 1997)?
- How does a speaker show that they are not prejudiced while developing a damning version of an entire ethnic group (Wetherell & Potter, 1992)?
- How do narratives in sex offender therapy sessions manage issues of blame, and how can this be misidentified as a "cognitive distortion" (Auburn, 2005)?

Questions of this kind involve a focus on matters that are psychological for people as they act and interact in particular settings—in families, in workplaces, in schools, and so on.

The nature and scope of psychology is understood very differently in discourse analytic work compared with other approaches, such as social cognition. Instead of starting with inner mental or cognitive processes, with behavioral regularities, or

with neural events that are happening below and behind interaction, it starts with the public displays, constructions, and orientations of participants.

DP starts with discourse because discourse is the primary arena for human action, understanding, and intersubjectivity. We communicate with one another, express our desires and fears, and come to understand others feelings and concerns primarily though talking. DP, however, is a very different project to the psychology *of* language. What might someone be *doing* by saying they are "angry" or that they "like" that cheesecake?

Contemporary DP is a domain of naturalistic study. That is, it works from audio and video records of people interacting with one another within their everyday and institutional settings. A central feature of discourse analytic work on psychological topics in the past few years has been the excitement of working directly on action and interaction as it unfolds in real time in real situations. Indeed, a case could be made that an empirical program that started with life as it is lived is long overdue and ought to be foundational to other kinds of psychological perspective (Edwards, 1997). The conclusion of this program of work is that social life is organized with an extraordinary degree of granularity and orderliness, which is best seen as it unfolds in real time as people respond to one another's talk and display, moment by moment, a subtle practical understanding of one another. In real life, psychology is in motion; DP is an approach that attempts to capture that motion.

DP is an approach rather than a method. It starts with discourse not because of an interest in the psychology of language per se but because discourse is the fundamental medium for human action. Rather than seeing its fundamental analytic aim as an attempt to open up the mythic black box in which psychology has been thought to be hiding since Descartes and Locke developed their arguments, it is focused on the public realm to which people have access when they are dealing with other people. Its basic methodological and analytic principles follow from its metatheoretical, theoretical, and conceptual arguments, although these are further supported through the empirical fruitfulness in particular studies (Potter, 2003).

This chapter first provides a review of the development of discursive psychology, outlines some of its basic features, and then overviews its core methodological stages and procedures. This review is illustrated by examples from a connected program of work on interaction on a child protection helpline; it ends with a discussion of prospects and debates.

THE DEVELOPMENT OF DISCURSIVE PSYCHOLOGY

Discourse analysis is a broad interdisciplinary field that has evolved in different forms and with different assumptions within linguistics, sociology, cultural studies, and psychology. Even systematic overviews often have widely different contents—compare, for example, the coverage in Phillips and Jørgensen (2002) with Schiffrin, Tannen, and Hamilton (2003). Even the more specific field of DP has considerable complexity and has seen a range of internal debates; this is a sign of its continuing vitality. For simplicity, the coverage in this chapter will highlight three main strands of work that in the past 20 years have progressively engaged with a different set of problematics.

Strand 1: Interviews and Repertoires

Starting in the mid-1980s, the focus of discourse analytic work in psychology was on identifying the different *interpretative repertoires* that are used to build social action (Potter & Wetherell, 1987). An interpretative repertoire is a cluster of terms, categories, and idioms that are closely conceptually organized. Repertoires are typically assembled around a metaphor or vivid image. In most cases, interpretative repertoires are identified by analyzing a set of open-ended interviews in which participants address a set of different themes.

The repertoire notion is derived from Gilbert and Mulkay's (1984) pioneering study of the different repertoires that scientists use to construct their social world when they are writing research papers and arguing with one another. It was further developed in Wetherell and Potter (1992) in a major study of the way *Pākehā* (White) New Zealanders constructed versions of social conflict and social organizations to legitimate particular versions of relations between groups. Much of the interest was

in ideological questions of how the organization of accounts, and the resources used in those accounts, could be used to understand the reproduction of broad patterns of inequality and privilege. Put simply, how did White Europeans undermine Maori land claims and other grievances without appearing self-interested or racist?

This strand of work was closely allied to, and influenced by, Billig's (1996) rhetorical psychology and incorporated the central notion of ideological dilemmas (Billig et al., 1988), which itself builds on the notion of interpretative repertoires from Potter and Wetherell (1987). For example, Billig (1992) found in talk about the British royal family a web of arguments and assumptions that work to sustain the familiar social hierarchies and avoid questioning privilege.

This work was largely based on the analysis of open-ended interviews, or group discussions, that provided the ideal environment for generating the kinds of ideological themes or interpretative repertoires that were a key topic of study. This has been a continuing and productive theme in discourse research on such topics as gender and nationalism (for many examples from social psychology, see Augoustinos, Tuffin, & Rapley, 1999; Condor, 2006; Reynolds & Wetherell, 2003). This work has been particularly effective in tackling ideological questions that are not easily addressed by more mainstream social cognition perspectives (Augoustinos, Walker, & Donaghue, 2006). Part of its continuing momentum comes from its critical opposition to mainstream social cognitive accounts of human action.

Strand 2: Discursive Psychology and Constructionism

From the early 1990s, the strand of discourse work that focused on the analysis of repertoires was joined by a further distinct strand of work. A crucial and distinctive feature of this new strand of work was its focus on records of naturalistic interaction such as conversations, legal argument, newspaper reports, parliamentary debates, and news interviews rather than on the transcripts of open-ended interviews. Its focus was on the role that descriptions of the world and of psychological states play in the formation of particular actions, such as criticisms of other persons, and how speakers use them to manage their accountability.

Whereas the earlier strand of work was developed under the title of discourse analysis and only subsequently became described as DP, this strand of work for the first time used the explicit title *discursive psychology* (Edwards & Potter, 1992, 1993). DP moved to a more explicit style of discursive constructionism focused on texts and talk, with different analytic and epistemic consequences to the cognitive of constructionism found in Berger and Luckmann (1966) and other forms of social construction (see Potter, 1996; Potter & Hepburn, 2008). The continuing momentum of this work comes from its critical engagement with mainstream cognitive psychological work, shown in particular through studies that respecify notions, such as memory, scripts, emotion, attribution, and perception in interactional terms (Edwards, 1997; Hepburn, 2004; Stokoe & Hepburn, 2005). For an overview of these first two strands of discourse work see Hepburn (2003, Chapter 7).

Strand 3: Discursive Psychology and Sequential Analysis

From around the middle of the 1990s these two strands of DP started to be joined by a third strand of work. The specific characteristics of this strand reflect a continuing and deeper engagement with conversation analysis (see Chapter 7 of this volume). Indeed, at times these two fields blur together. This engagement with conversation analysis is reflected in a series of characteristics:

- Working with a corpus of conversational materials;
- Close use of both the recording and a careful Jeffersonian transcript;
- The use of existing conversation analytic studies as analytic resources;
- Attention to psychological phenomena in institutional settings; and
- Integration of lexical analysis with attention to prosody, delivery, and embodied action.

For a range of examples in this strand of DP, see papers in Hepburn and Wiggins (2005, 2007).

This strand of work sustained the interest in the way facts are built as factual and the way conduct is made accountable. It increasingly exploited the sophisticated understanding of sequence, position, and turn design provided by conversation analysis. Indeed, there has been a convergence of issues in both conversation analysis and DP as both focus on concerns with how shared knowledge is displayed and how intersubjectivity is established or contested (compare Edwards, 1999b; Heritage & Raymond, 2005). This is a field of mundane epistemics (Potter & Hepburn, 2008).

This strand of work also provides a further nuanced approach to categories and how they are conversationally and sequentially occasioned. This is an evolving concern within discursive psychology (compare Antaki, 1998; Edwards, 1998; Potter & Wetherell, 1987, Chapter 6; Stokoe, 2009; Widdicombe & Wooffitt, 1995). This strand of DP is still engaged in a debate with cognitivism and its problems in different arenas (e.g., Antaki, 2004; chapters in te Molder & Potter, 2005). However, it has started to address new topics. There is a major interest in taking the administration of psychological methods as a topic in its own right, studying how particular interactional practices in experiments, surveys, focus groups, and so on contribute to the methodical production of psychological findings (e.g., Antaki, Houtkoop-Steenstra, & Rapley, 2000; Maynard, Houtkoop-Steenstra, Schaeffer, & van der Zouwen, 2002; Puchta & Potter, 2002). There is also a growing concern with considering how psychological matters become parts of institutional practices such as therapy (Peräkylä, Antaki, Vehviläinen, & Leudar, 2008), counseling (Kurri & Wahlström, 2001), mediation (Stokoe & Edwards, 2009), gender reassignment assessments (Speer & Parsons, 2006), peer evaluation (Cromdal, Tholander, & Aronsson, 2007), and others. This is an area in which conversation analytic work and DP have converged.

Although there has been considerable change and development in discursive psychology over the past 20 years, it has not been a linear progression; much of the development involved broadening and deepening. This overview has traced the bare contours of the different themes and traditions that make up the fast-evolving and somewhat contested terrain of contemporary DP. Ultimately, the field is defined by its studies and achievements.

THE GENERAL THEORETICAL ORIENTATION OF DISCURSIVE PSYCHOLOGY

Discursive research treats discourse as having four key characteristics.

Characteristic 1: Discourse Is Action Oriented

Discourse is a practical medium and the primary medium for action. Actions may be relatively discrete objects associated with speech act verbs—an *admonishment*, say, or a *compliment*. Yet they can also be complex and embedded within institutional practices without a clear speech act verb. Consider the use of questions to indirectly deliver advice in person-centered counseling, for example (Butler, Potter, Danby, Emisson, & Hepburn, 2010). There is no lay term for this practice; even the semitechnical description *person centered* is only a global catch-all for a range of discrete practices. As work in the second strand of DP has shown, actions are often done indirectly via descriptions. Practices of this kind offer the speaker a different kind of accountability than an on-the-record speech act. The fundamental point that distinguishes discourse analytic work from the mainstream psychology of language is that discourse is studied for how action is done rather than treating discourse as a pathway to putative mental objects. This also distinguishes it from a range of humanistic and qualitative approaches (see other chapters in Part I of this volume).

Characteristic 2: Discourse Is Situated

It is a central observation of discursive psychology that actions are situated in three senses. First, action is situated *sequentially*. That is, actions are situated within the here and now of unfolding conversation. They are located in time, orienting to what has just happened and building an environment for what happens next. For example, when an invitation is issued this sets up an ordered array of possible next actions, of which accepting or turning down are most relevant. It is not possible to simply ignore the invitation without this being, potentially, hearable as the action of ignoring the invitation. Moreover,

when the recipient accepts or rejects an invitation, the recipient is locally displaying an understanding that that is precisely what has been issued, so the turn by turn unfolding of talk provides an ongoing check on understanding (Schegloff, 1992). The explication of this order of interaction has been the central project of conversation analysis that has highlighted an extraordinary level of specificity and organization (Schegloff, 2007).

Second, action is situated *institutionally*. Institutions often embody special identities that are pervasively relevant—news interviewer, therapist, patient—such that actions will be understood in relation to those identities. And they often involve collections of local interactional goals to which all parties orient (Drew & Heritage, 1992; Heritage & Clayman, 2010). These institutional goals are often themselves dependent on broader everyday practices that are refined for the institutional setting (compare Edwards, 2008, on *intention* with Potter & Hepburn, 2003, on *concern*). The specific analytic relevance here is how psychological matters are introduced, constructed and made relevant to the setting's business (Edwards & Potter, 2001).

Third, action is situated *rhetorically*. Billig (1996) has emphasized the pervasive relevance of rhetorical relations, even where there is an absence of explicit argument (e.g., he has explicated the rhetorical underpinning of *opinion* discourse; see Billig, 1989; see also Myers, 2004). Discourse research highlights, for example, the way descriptions are built to counter actual or potential alternatives, and they are organized in ways that manage actual or possible attempts to undermine them (Potter, 1996). A major theme in DP is the way epistemic issues are managed using a wide range of conversational and rhetorical resources (Potter & Hepburn, 2008). This theme cuts right across the conventional psychological topics of memory, attribution, attitudes, and persuasion.

Characteristic 3: Discourse Is Both Constructed and Constructive

Discourse is constructed from a range of resources—grammatical structures, words, categories, rhetorical commonplaces, repertoires, conversational practices, and so on—all of which are built and delivered in real time with relevant prosody, timing, and so on. These resources, their use, and their conditions of assembly can become topics of discursive study.

Discourse is constructive in the sense that it is used to build versions of psychological worlds, social organizations, action, and histories and broader structures. Such versions are an integral part of different actions. Discursive research can be focused on the way constructions are built and stabilized, and how they are made neutral, objective, and independent of the speaker. People are skilled builders of descriptions; they have spent a lifetime learning how to do it. Part of the discourse analytic art is to reveal the complex and delicate work that goes into this seemingly effortless building.

Characteristic 4: Discourse Is Produced as Psychological

Discursive psychologists are focused on the way what counts as psychological is a central concern of participants. People can construct their own and other's dispositions, assessments, and descriptions as subjective (psychological) or objective. For example, an assessment of a minority group can be couched in the language of attitudes (I am generally positive about Polynesian Islanders) or built as an objective feature of this social group using a range of descriptive procedures (Potter & Wetherell, 1988).

Edwards (2007) has distinguished *subject-side* from *object-side* descriptions and has highlighted the way producing discourse in either of these ways can be a central element in a range of practices. A person can be described as having a legitimate complaint about something in the world (an object-side description) or as moaning and whining (a subject-side description that highlights things wrong with the speaker rather than the world; Edwards, 2005). One of the features of the normative organization of interaction is that it provides a baseline calibration for marking out psychological investment.

SEVEN STAGES IN THE EXECUTION OF DISCURSIVE RESEARCH

The discussion of the different stages in the execution of discursive research are illustrated by examples from a program of research conducted by Alexa Hepburn and myself with the National Society for the Prevention of Cruelty to Children (NSPCC), Britain's largest child protection charity.

Let me start with the broadest of considerations. In terms of the politics and ethics of research, we chose this study site because of our prior interest in child protection. We also hoped to provide support for the important work of the NSPCC. One possibility that we envisaged was that we could use discourse methods to explicate the practices of the call takers on the child protection helpline and highlight the delicate underlying orderliness of how they were doing a job that seemed, at times, superficially more haphazard (Hepburn & Potter, 2003).

I have chosen this program of work to illustrate DP because it shows how some of the background concerns in the way questions and analysis develop as well as how studies can accumulate progressively. It will also illustrate the way classic psychological topics (emotion, shared knowledge) can be addressed and reworked in discourse work. For simplicity the process will be broken into seven stages: obtaining access and consent, data collection, data management, transcription, developing research questions, corpus building and preliminary analysis, and developing and validating analysis. In practice, these stages are somewhat overlapping—transcription, data management, and question development tend to come and go at all stages of the research process.

Stage 1: Obtaining Access and Consent

One of the features that makes contemporary DP distinctive from most other psychological methods is that it works primarily with audio or video records of interaction happening in natural settings. This makes the process of gaining access and consent, developing appropriate ethics scripts, and working closely with participants in a way that sustains and merits a strong degree of trust an integral part of the research process. Gaining access and consent can be a challenge. And it is likely that researchers sometimes use other forms of data generation—questionnaires, say, or open-ended interviews—because they expect that access will be refused. However, experience shows that with the right approach and an proportionate commitment of time and effort, trust can be developed and consent can be obtained for working in the most sensitive of sites—family therapy, police interrogation, neighbor mediation, physiotherapy for stroke patients, and social work assessments of parents whose children are in care (to list some recent examples).

Initial contact is often through a key institutional member—a medical practitioner, school teacher, or parent—who can provide an authoritative link for the researchers. A key feature of this contact is often to identify the participants' anxieties about the research process. These are often focused on the possibility that the research will evaluate their practice. Ironically it is the professionals rather than clients that often have more doubt about the research process (although the professionals often suggest that the clients will not agree). It is striking that many professionals are doubtful that their practice will stand up to analytic scrutiny, perhaps because many of the training materials use unrealistic and simplified idealizations of what interaction should look like. Silverman (1997) referred to this as the problem of the Divine Orthodoxy. Practitioners feel they are condemned to fail because they are compared with an idealized, normative standard completely removed from actual practice.

Let me develop this topic with the research on the NSPCC child protection helpline. This helpline receives around 100,000 calls a year from across the United Kingdom. It is legally mandated to pass credible reports of abuse to either social services or the police, whether the caller wishes them to or not. The hotline also provides counseling, information, and advice to anyone concerned about the risk to a child of ill treatment, neglect, or abuse. All call takers are trained social workers, called child protection officers (CPOs) at the time of the data collection, each with at least 3 years' field experience working on child protection.

Access negotiations started with a letter to the head of the helpline that was intended to target the worries that potential research participants have: How will issues of ethics and anonymity be managed? What extra work will be involved? How might the research benefit the organization? The letter was also used to head off the idea that the research might criticize the organization or its workers. This letter was followed up by a series of face-to-face meetings that were crucial in establishing trust. These meetings included not only senior management but also individual CPOs who would be in control of recording and obtaining consent from callers.

In this case, the organization opted for the CPOs using their own skills to make judgments about consent. They asked callers at the start of calls whether they would be willing to take part in the research and offered the possibility for them to ask questions about the research. We provided the CPOs with a basic script, developed in the light of British Psychological Society (BPS) guidelines about consent, but the CPOs would tailor what they asked to individual callers. Ethical issues, then, satisfied both the NSPCC and the BPS. For a detailed account of how this process of gaining access and the development of ethics procedures played out, see Hepburn and Potter (2003).

Stage 2: Data Collection

In terms of data collection, the main aim is to develop an archive of records of interaction in the setting under study. There are no hard and fast rules for the size of such a collection. Even small amounts of material can provide the basis for useful research; but the more material there is and the more appropriate the sampling then more questions will become analytically tractable and more confidence can be placed in the research conclusions.

Some considerations are paramount here. First, the quality of recording has a powerful effect on the time taken in transcription and analysis. Time and resources devoted to getting high-quality recordings will pay off handsomely when it comes to transcribing the recordings and working with them in data sessions. Hours are wasted relistening to a key piece of talk against a loud recording hum and attempting to work out whether a child has taken a mouthful of food or just put the fork near her mouth. Solid-state recorders with good microphones and digital video cameras with large hard disc drives are both effective. Make sure voice activation is disabled.

Second, if embodied activities are available to participants, then they are certain to be a live part of the interaction. That means that it will be important to have video records of face-to-face interaction (or non-face-to-face interaction that is technologically mediated with a visual modality). High-quality digital video is inexpensive, simple, and easy to manipulate so this is not an insurmountable problem.

Third, once the whole process has been put into place, actually making recordings is almost always simpler and easier than analyzing and transcribing them. This means that researchers should err on the side of collecting more recordings than planned. Digital recordings can be easily stored, and they provide an important resource for future research.

Fourth, a characteristic feature of contemporary DP is that participants collect the data themselves. This is designed to minimize the reactivity generated by extended researcher involvement and allows the participants to manage ethical issues in a way that suits them best. This means that simplicity is a key consideration—it minimizes what the participants have to learn and the effort they have to put into the collection. Current recorders are ideal as they often have large storage, long battery life, and a simple press and record function.

In the case of our child protection research, we spent some time setting up a system that allowed easy recording without interfering with the CPOs work. The CPOs used a hot desk system, so we set up two desks so that calls could be recorded on MiniDisk. Different technical systems have different requirements—some organizations already collect full digital recordings for auditing purposes so it is a matter of satisfying ethics requirements and downloading the appropriate set of calls onto a portable hard drive. When CPOs who had signed up for the research took shifts, they used these desks.

Stage 3: Data Management

As research projects evolve, data management becomes increasingly important. Much of this is focused on systems of folders that collect together recordings in different forms, different forms of transcript, and analytic notes. Such a system can facilitate data sharing—discourse research is often collaborative—and can assist full backup of data and analysis. Encryption and secure storage may be required depending on the agreements with participants and the sensitivity of the materials. This is also a prelude for data reduction and involves the systematic building of a particular corpus that is small enough to be easily worked with but large enough to be able to make appropriate generalizations.

The precise pattern depends on the research. In the NSPCC study, we assigned a two-letter code to each CPO who took part; each had their own folder. This code was taken from their pseudonym. Within each folder, each call had its own folder with a memorable name—"neighbor black eye," say. Within this folder, was a high-quality recording in WAV format as well as a smaller MP3 version that could be sent via e-mail and easily backed up. Each folder often also contained two versions of the transcript (as we describe in the next section) and sometimes further transcript and analytic observations.

Stage 4: Transcription

Contemporary discourse research works continuously with both the original audio or video recordings and the transcript. It is no longer the case that after transcription the recordings are put into storage. Nevertheless, the transcript is an essential element in the research.

It is common to use two forms of transcript. A basic first-pass transcript is often generated by a transcription service. This has just the words (not broken up by the colons, arrows, etc., that capture features of delivery) rendered as effectively as the service can hear them. This kind of transcript has two uses:

1. It allows the researcher to quickly go through a stretch of interaction and get an overall feel for what is there. This can be a particularly important shortcut where there are many hours of recordings.
2. It is searchable, allowing one to sift through an entire set of materials very quickly for particular phenomena that can be identified through individual lexical items or transcriber descriptions.

The second form of transcription is an attempt to capture on the page features of the delivery of talk that participants treat as relevant for understanding the activities that are taking place. The standard system used in DP and conversation analysis was developed by Jefferson (2004; see also Hepburn & Bolden, in press). It was designed to be easy to learn and simple to produce, using mainly standard keyboards. It encodes features such as overlaps and pauses, volume and emphasis, features of prosody such as rising and falling intonation, and features of the speed of delivery (for a summary, see Chapter 7 of this volume). It was developed in parallel to the broader evolution of conversation analysis and is specifically designed to support analysis of interaction. Other sorts of questions (about speech accommodation, say, or speech production disorders) will require a different kind of transcript.

Jeffersonian transcript is extremely labor intensive. The ratio of record time to transcription time can be anything above 1:20, with key factors being the quality of the recording, the complexity of the interaction, and whether there are nonvocal elements that need to be represented. It also takes time to learn to do good quality transcription. It is necessary to both understand the roles of the different symbols and learn to apply them consistently. This is facilitated by listening to the audio that goes with high-quality transcript—examples are available on various websites.

Because of the time investment required to produce quality transcript, there are rarely resources for completely transcribing a full set of recordings. Various criteria can be used to decide what to transcribe and in what order.

Stage 5: Developing Research Questions

It has been common in psychological research to stress the importance of formulating a clear research question before starting the research. And there are often good reasons for such a rule because it can help avoid confusion and sloppiness when doing a wide range of psychological studies, particularly when utilizing experimental designs, questionnaires, or open-ended interviews. However, with discursive research, much of the discipline comes from working with a set of naturalistic materials—records of people living their lives in a particular setting. And many of the questions formulated for more traditional research have a causal form—what is the effect of *X* on *Y*—which is rarely appropriate for discourse work. Rather than posing a question, the focus is often on attempting to explicate the workings of some kind of social practice that is operating in the setting, perhaps with the ultimate aim of making broader sense of the setting as a whole. And this often means that questions are continually refined in the course of a program of work and a study within that program.

One of the benefits of working with naturalistic materials is that they present their own challenges that lead to novel questions. They often feature actions or occurrences that are unexpected or not easily understood with the repertoire of explanatory concepts available in contemporary psychology. This can provide an exciting start point for analytic work. A common practice in the discursive community is to use different levels of engagement with the materials to generate questions. A key part of this often includes data sessions with analytically minded colleagues.

In the NSPCC program, we had a range of broad interests from our prior work that we brought to the study: How is bullying and violence reported? How are descriptions built as factual? How do ethnic and gender categories figure in assessments? However, we tried not to become too focused on these and instead open up to new possibilities. We did ask the CPOs what they found difficult about their jobs and what they were interested in. Out of a range of possibilities, they noted that they found it to be a problem when callers became very upset and that closing calls could present difficulties. These, too, we noted but put aside as we worked toward a deeper engagement with the materials.

We started with a number of intensive data sessions with colleagues and a range of broader discussions. As these evolved, a number of themes of interest emerged. We will illustrate this chapter with two different ones.

One theme was focused on crying and how it is noticed and how it is responded to. This topic emerged out of three background interests. First, crying was one of the issues that the CPOs had told us was challenging to deal with. So this focus satisfied our concern to do research that might be socially useful to our participants. Second, the then-current literature on transcription did not give a clear idea of how to transcribe crying. This made the basic issue of how to represent different features of crying and upset in Jefferson-style transcript practically relevant. Third, the broad topic of emotion has been theoretically interesting in discourse work. It is sometimes picked out as the kind of issue that is not susceptible to interaction analysis because it is so bound up with bodily states. Emotion is often treated as a causal variable that has a distorting effect on cognition (Park & Banaji, 2000). It was thus a theoretically important analytic challenge. We felt it would be interesting to contribute to the small but growing discourse literature on talk and emotion (Buttny, 1993; Edwards, 1997, 1999a; Locke & Edwards, 2003; Ruusuvuori, 2005).

One of the features of specific psychological work on crying is that it has overwhelmingly worked with participants' reports of crying (in questionnaires or rating scales). There is no work that uses direct observation, or attempts to provide situated descriptions of crying.

In fact, the crying literature provides a microcosm of the broader practices in psychology where, instead of starting by directly studying crying as it happens (in families with young children, in relationship disputes), the standard work is based around scales where people make retrospective reports about crying on a questionnaire that has a series of Likert-style items all of which use the category "crying." A central feature of DP is its cutting out of these retrospective self-reports with their constructions and categories. The recent interactional literature on questions and question design in news interviews and other settings shows that questions are complex social actions (Clayman & Heritage, 2002; Raymond, 2003; and chapters in Freed & Ehrlich, 2010). They set up a range of subtle constraints and response requirements far beyond the more standard questionnaire design injunctions about bias and leading questions. This literature complements the already challenging (for psychologists) interactional literature that highlights the complex role of questions within psychological methods (Antaki & Rapley, 1996; Puchta & Potter, 1999; Schegloff, 1999). A basic feature of DP is that it sidesteps these problems.

A second theme emerged rather differently. One of us had been doing work on core conversation analytic issues and in particular on the topic of tag questions. These had been subject to a wide range of linguistic and sociolinguistic analysis, but relatively little work had approached tag questions as part of an interaction analytic study. Moreover, there is a particularly interesting class of tag questions for which the interrogative element does not come at the end of the turn but in the middle (*turn-medial tag questions*). Thus, "but it is the case, isn't it, that Labor is doing poorly in the polls" has the tag interrogative ("isn't it?") in the middle of the sentence rather than the end. And note that as the turn unfolds, at the point at which the speaker issues the interrogative ("isn't it?"), the recipient is treated as if he or she is going to respond yes but is not in a position to respond because the declarative ("Labor is doing poorly in the polls") has not yet been delivered. This initially rather dry technical interest occasioned a search through the entire set of NSPCC calls for turn-medial tag questions. When a collection of such questions had been identified, then full Jeffersonian transcript of the extended sequences in which they arose was performed.

This focus became progressively broader as it became clear that the turn-medial tags regularly appeared in sequences where the recipient was being advised to do something by the NSPCC CPO and was resisting the advice. The analysis started to focus on advice resistance from callers and how it, in turn, could be resisted by CPOs (picking up from existing work on advice and advice resistance; for a review, see Hepburn & Potter, 2011a). Again, this had the attractiveness of focusing on something at the heart of the services that the NSPCC were delivering. At the same time, tag questions have a major theoretical interest with respect to how issues of knowledge become live in interaction because tag questions are commonly used to mark the recipient of the question as knowing more on the specific topic than the speaker who issues the tag. This theme of *mundane epistemics* has become an increasingly important element in DP.

Stage 6: Corpus Building and Preliminary Analysis

In DP, the analytic stage of work is often the most time consuming and the most crucial. The same materials may be subject to different analyses that identify different practices or highlight different themes. Indeed, once a high-quality data set has been collected, it may be used by different researchers in different studies. The success of these studies is down to the rigor and sophistication of the analysis.

Discursive psychological analysis often uses a systematic trawl through the materials to build a corpus of examples. This early trawl is typically inclusive rather than exclusive with the aim of including central examples and borderline cases. It is expected that such a corpus will be refined. When analytic understanding has been improved, it is likely that some of the cases will be dropped from the corpus and new cases will be seen as appropriately part of the corpus.

The process of analysis will involve increasingly precise attempts to specify what is going on and how some practice or practices are unfolding. This stage is akin to hypothesis testing as the researcher often has a number of initial ideas that cannot survive a careful exploration of cases that accounts for the specific details of what is there. I show this in operation with the two examples from the NSPCC study. In each case, I try to show how the analysis builds to a particular account of the actions that occurring in the material.

Crying and crying receipts.   The analysis of crying and crying receipts started by identifying all the calls in which crying appears and then transcribing the full sequence. This generated a corpus of 14 crying sequences—some were quite brief (just a few turns) whereas some went on for many minutes and many pages of transcript. One of the first research tasks was to build an extension of the Jeffersonian transcription scheme that would enable the different features of crying such as sobs, whispers, wet and dry sniffs, and tremulous voice to be represented. This extension is described in detail in Hepburn (2004) along with a detailed account of the limitations of the contemporary psychological literature on crying for dealing with it as an interactional object. This fine-grained description of crying is extremely time consuming— yet its value is that it provides a way of seeing how delicately the different activities in crying and crying recipiency are organized together. The architecture of this interaction is complex with each participant carefully monitoring the other and showing the result of this monitoring in the turns of talk that they take.

We can illustrate this with Extract 8.2. Various characteristic elements of crying on the helpline are highlighted, such as caller apologies (A), and CPO actions such as "right-thing" descriptions (RT), "take-your-times" (TYT), and what we have termed "empathic receipts" (ER). Note also the characteristic layout of the kinds of materials used in discourse research with the extract number, the code for particular data source, the anonimized participant descriptions (CPO, Caller), and the line numbers that allow specific reference to parts of the extract. The identification and characterization of the different elements of crying allows the analyst to see how they are consequential for the unfolding interaction.

First, note the way the TYT in line 2 is occasioned by the caller's sobbing that starts in line 1 and continues through to line 4. We can see how delicate the mutual attention in this interaction is as, despite the sobbing, the caller responds to the TYT with a whispered "khhay" (line 8). One of the interesting features we found with interaction and crying is there is a considerable amount of *live silence*—that is, silence that the recipient would normally expect to be filled by specific sorts of turns (Hepburn & Potter, 2007). Ironically, perhaps, interaction work shows that silence is a major part of crying.

Second, note further on in the sequence the caller's tremulously voiced apology (line 35). We might think that the caller is apologizing for the transgressive nature of sobbing over the phone to a stranger. However, a careful examination of where apologies appear in crying sequences suggests that they are more likely to be apologies for disruption of ongoing actions or failing to provide normatively expected contributions. That is, they are explicated better by understanding the consequences of crying for basic conversational organization. For example, in this case, the CPO's assessment in lines 26 through 28 is followed by an extremely quiet and very disrupted second assessment on line 31 (the normatively expected turn). The following delay from the CPO would allow the turn to be recycled, and the apology could be specifically apologizing for the absence of this recycling.

Third, note the RT descriptions on lines 26 through 28 and through lines 36 through 45. These

Extract 8.2
JK Distraught Dad

01	Caller:	>.Hhih .hhihhh<	
02	CPO:	D'you want- d'y'wann'ave [a break for a] moment.=	←TYT
03	Caller:	[Hhuhh >.hihh<]	
04		=>hhuhh hhuhh<	
05		(0.6)	
06	Caller:	.shih	
07		(0.3)	
08	Caller:	°°k(hh)ay°°	
09		(1.8)	
10	Caller:	.shih > hhuh hhuh[h]<	
11	CPO:	[S]'very har:d when	←ER
12		they're not there with you isn't it.=	←ER
13		and [you're-] (.) you're tal:kin about it.	←ER
14	Caller:	[>.hhih<]	
15		(0.8)	
16	Caller:	>.Hhuh .HHuh<	
17		(2.1)	
18	Caller:	.shih	
19		(0.2)	
20	Caller:	°.shih° (.)°° (Need) hhelp(h) °°	
21		(2.5)	
22	Caller:	.HHhihh° hh°	
23		(0.5)	
24	Caller:	HHhuhh >.hih .hih<	
25		(0.7)	
26	CPO:	.Htk.hh Well you're doing what you can now to	←RT
27		actually offer them protection and help though	←RT
28		are:n't you.	←RT
29	Caller:	.Skuh (.) Huhhhh	
30		(0.5)	
31	Caller:	°°I:'m not the(hehheh)re. Hh°°	
32		(3.2)	
33	Caller:	.Shih	
34		(0.4)	
35	Caller:	~↑I'm ↑sorry.~	←A
36	CPO:	An they als- well E-E-Eddie obviously al- thought	←RT
37		you were the person to contact to get he:lp.	←RT
38	Caller:	Yeh. hh	
39	CPO:	F'which (.) ye know he turned to you: .hh	←RT
40		(0.7)	
41	Caller:	.Hh[h°hhh°]	
42	CPO:	[T'help 'im.]=didn't he.	←RT
43	Caller:	°°Yhhehhh°°	
44	CPO:	So 'e saw you as a person who could help in this	←RT
45		situa[tion] for him:.	←RT
46	Caller:	[.Shih]	
47		(0.9)	
48	Caller:	.Hdihhhh hhhuhh	
49		(0.2)	
50	Caller:	H↑oh: s(h)orry.	←A
51		(0.4)	
52	CPO:	.Htk s'↑oka:y. kay.	

```
53                (1.3)
54    Caller:      .SKUH
55                (0.3)
56    CPO:         It's distressing but it's also quite a shock        ←ER
57                isn't it I guess [ (for you) ]                       ←ER
58    Caller:                      [.HHHHhih]hh HHHhuhhhh
59                (1.7)
60    Caller:      ((swallows)) °Hhhoh dhear.°
```

are constructed from information already provided by the caller, redescribed to present him having done the right thing. Such descriptions seem designed to reassure the caller and move him out of the crying sequence. These descriptions are often accompanied by tag questions (e.g., lines 28 and 42), which may be designed to lead away from crying by encouraging agreement with the RT description.

Finally let us consider the topic of empathy. This has been a notion in areas of psychology since the early 1900s—but it tends to be conceptualized in terms of a cognitive image of one mind sharing the experiences of another. However, we have focused on how empathy is built, as a practice, in real time in live situations, where each party has available to them the talk of the other (Hepburn & Potter, 2007). We found ERs to be built by combining two elements:

1. A formulation of the crying party's mental or psychological state.
2. A marker of the contingency, doubt, or source of the mental state formulation.

The mental state formulations (e.g., it's distressing but it's also quite a shock) are typically derivable from local features of the talk such as the amount of sobs and wet sniffs, combined with the caller's own prior formulations of their state. That is, the empathic moment is not a magical one of mind reading but a mundane and practical one involving responding to what is in the immediate talk and, in doing so, displaying close monitoring. The mental state formulation is combined with a second element that involves the recipient marking their formulation as limited ("I guess"), dependent on what is hearable, or using a tag question ("isn't it?") to mark the speaker as the one with authority over the correctness of the formulation. In each of

these ways, the CPO defers to the caller who is crying as the party who has the right to define the nature of their own psychological state. What we have here is a procedural account of empathy grounded in the perspectives of the participants as displayed in their talk.

More generally, although emotion is often thought of as something that is beyond the purchase of discourse research (probably because of its early emphasis on people talking about things in open-ended interviews), studies of this kind show the way that issues and actions that we understand as emotional can be tractable to interaction analysis (cf. Edwards, 1997, 1999a). This is not surprising once we remind ourselves of the practical and communicative role that emotions play in social life (Planalp, 1999). Indeed, by carefully listening to these materials and carefully transcribing the interaction, the analysis starts to highlight precisely how the *emotional* issues become live, are noticed, attended to, managed, and how both parties mutually coordinate in fine ways in what initially seems like a highly chaotic strip of interaction.

In this case, the patterning may reflect one institutional setting and its goal orientations—much more work will be needed to develop an understanding of the complex patterning in which speakers are familiars, babies and young children are involved, and there is an immediate physical or psychological cause of the crying (Hepburn & Potter, 2011b). More broadly, discursive work offers the possibility of understanding the various phenomena that are loosely glossed as emotion in terms of what they are doing and where they appear in peoples' lives.

Resisting advice resistance.   I have noted in this extract how the topic of tag questions, and particularly turn-medial tag questions, in advice resistance sequences came to the fore. This involved a search for calls in which advice was resisted and transcription of those sequences (Hepburn & Potter, 2011a). We became interested in a related collection of practices used by the CPO when the caller resisted the advice they were offering over an extended period of time. These resistance sequences were in turn typically occasioned by the CPO rejecting a caller's request for action or for some kind of alternative project. Typically the main element of the advice was that the caller her- or himself should initiate some course of action. In the resistance sequences, the CPO has reissued advice, often on several occasions during the call, and the caller has indicated in a number of direct or indirect ways that they are unlikely to follow the advice.

Again, this study draws heavily on the methods of conversation analysis (see Chapter 7 of this volume), but it is particularly focused on psychological themes. As before, analysis works back and forth between the collection of full calls, individual full calls, the ongoing corpus of examples, and the

details of specific instances. There is also a strong analytic emphasis on the institutionality of what is going on; this is shown in the orientations of the participants and is central in the analytic conclusions.

In the call transcribed in Extract 8.3, the Caller is expressing concern about a neighbor's possibly abusive actions toward her child and is wondering if Social Services should become involved. Simplifying considerably, as discussion continues, it becomes clear that Social Services will be unlikely to act and the CPO advises the caller to communicate directly with the neighbor ("drop her a note," "get her side of the story"). The caller repeatedly resists this advice—probably as it would involve abandoning her project of passing on the problem to Social Services on behalf of which the call was made in the first place.

The extract starts with the CPO reissuing advice from earlier on in the call to talk directly to the neighbor (combined with a sympathetic stance on the neighbor's behavior). At this point, the caller displays more of what Heritage and Sefi (1992) have identified as characteristic advice resistance—delays

---

Extract 8.3
JX Neighbor and Son

01	CPO:	↑Well perhaps↑ you need to extend that hand of
02		friendship an if she really is: .hhhh ↑ye know
03		if she is finding it a bit tough with the new baby
04		an everything she might really welcome (0.2) .hhh
05		you making ↑contact with her again.=If you have been
06		friendly in the pa:st,
07		(0.2)
08	Caller:	Yeah::.
09		(0.2)
10	CPO:	Ye know,
11		(0.9)
12	CPO:	°°Ehr:
13		(0.3)
14	Caller:	[Y:eah.]
15	CPO:→	[.hh #a-]#It sounds as though the grown ups
16	→	have got to be grow:n u:p.=Doesn'it.=Really:,
17	Caller:	Ye- Oh ye[ah because I mean the girls get o:n]:,
18	CPO:	[u- FOR THE CHILDREN'S POINT is (it)]
19	Caller:	She told one o' my neighbours recently, that
20		(.) she ws gunna move anyway after chrissmas

with unmarked acknowledgments, and no commitment to act on the advice appears. It is what is (relevantly and normatively) absent here, rather than what is present, that allows the CPO as participant, and Hepburn and I as analysts, to identify what is going on as advice resistance. Note that the delays here may seem small in the abstract, but they are highly hearable and consequential for the parties to the conversation. Indeed, a delay of less than two tenths of a second is regularly quite sufficient to show that a recipient is not going to agree to an invitation (Drew, 2005). That is why such delays are measured so carefully in Jeffersonian transcription.

The way the CPO responds to this resistance has a number of interesting features, but let me focus on three features of what the CPO does on lines 15–16.

First, the advice is repacked in this construction in an idiomatic form: The grownups have got to be grow:n u̲:p. As Billig (1996), Sacks (1992), and others have noted, idioms have a self-sufficient quality that makes them tricky to resist. And Drew and Holt (1988, 1998) have shown that idioms are recurrently used in situations in which speakers are making complaints that are not being affiliated with. The construction in the third extract repackages the advice in a harder to counter form. In this way the CPO is both orienting to, and countering, the caller's advice resistance.

Second, the repackaged advice is combined with an interrogative (a tag question): =Doesn'it. The striking thing about this is that it treats the recipient as both knowing the content of the advice (knowing that grownups have to be grown up) and treats her agreement as the expected or preferred response (Hepburn & Potter, 2010; Heritage & Raymond, 2005). Put another way, the recipient is treated as able to both confirm and agree with the course of action that they should follow and that they have, up to this point, been resisting. Instead of continuing to try to *persuade* the recipient of the virtues of a course of action, they are sequentially positioned as *already* supporting it. This is not so much social influence as interactional rebuilding. It highlights the possibility of a sequential politics of intersubjectivity.

The third observation is about what happens after the tag—the increment = Really:, is latched to

it. The technical literature of conversation analysis helps us with what is going on here:

> This continuation past the point of possible turn transition leaves the interrogative in a turn-medial position. The consequence of this is to dampen the response requirement, and close what might have been a stretched gap between turns, indicating further disagreement. Hence the interrogative projects a "yes" but does not wait for it to be delivered. (Hepburn & Potter, 2011a, pp. 224–225)

In what has turned into a tussle between Caller and CPO over what the Caller should do, the subjectivity of the Caller has been conversationally redesigned—moment by moment—as supporting a course of action and they are immediately—and delicately—held off both signaling up-and-coming disagreement and actually forming the disagreement. This is a joint action in which intersubjectivity is a contested space, as both parties draw on the normative resources of talk and the institutional affordances of Caller and CPO.

This study explicated a familiar and yet subtle practice of offering advice, which is part of a broader social landscape of families, abuse, and social support. It used the careful analysis of conversation to get at joint action, intersubjectivity, and the (contested) forming of subjectivity. The analysis is grounded in detailed records of this institution unfolding, which provides both its empirical basis and the opportunity for other researchers to audit the claims made and to refine alternative accounts of what is going on. This is the exciting zone in which contemporary DP is working, and the potential is only just being realized. Again, this analysis was designed to contribute to both applied issues (how to manage advice resistance) and theoretical issues (how is intersubjectivity something that can be contested).

Stage 7: Developing and Validating Analysis

In practice there is not a clear-cut distinction between analysis and validation. Building a successful analysis that works and is attentive to all the details of the materials that are being studied is already a major part of validating the findings. Nevertheless, some themes are worth highlighting. They are not typically separate operations, but they are common across much discursive research. Individually or together, they contribute to establishing the adequacy of particular analyses.

Participants' orientations. One of the enormous virtues of working with open-ended, naturally occurring materials is that they provide a major resource in validating findings that is absent in most other psychological methods. That resource is the turn-by-turn nature of interaction. Any turn of talk is oriented to what came before and sets up an environment for what comes next (Heritage, 1984). At its simplest, when someone provides an acceptance it provides evidence that what came before was an invitation. If an analyst claims that some conversational move is an indirect invitation, say, we would want to see evidence that the recipient is orientating (even indirectly) to its nature as an invitation. Close attention to this turn-by-turn display of understanding provides one important check on analytic interpretations (Chapter 7 of this volume; Heritage & Clayman, 2010). In these examples orientations are central to building the analysis and confirming its success.

In the crying work, for example, we were able to confirm the various features of crying as actually features of crying by considering how they are treated by CPOs. However, this focus on orientation is at the center of every stage of analysis; it does not make sense to pick out one feature on its own. The point is that interaction unfolds in real time with each participant producing their turn on the basis of what has happened up until that point, and most important, what has happened immediately before (Schegloff, 2007). Each turn provides, in its orientation to what came before, a display that is central to the intelligibility of interaction. One of the limitations of most psychological methods is that they cut across this kind of display.

Deviant cases. Deviant cases are often analytically and theoretically informative. They can show whether a generalization is robust or breaks down. For example, studies of media interviews show that interviewees rarely treat interviewers as accountable

for views expressed in their questions. As Heritage & Greatbatch (1991) have shown, this is the normal (indeed, normative, pattern). There are occasional deviant cases, however, in which a news interviewer is treated as responsible for some view. However, rather than showing that this pattern is not normative, they show up precisely that it is normative. Cases of departure can lead to considerable interactional trouble, which interferes with the interviewee making their point (Potter, 1996).

In the crying research, for example, there is a deviant case in which the CPO holds off making ERs as the caller starts to show signs of crying. Instead they pursue a somewhat skeptical line about how the caller knows about the specific abuse they are reporting. It is notable that the caller terminates the call very soon after this failure. Such a case helps us understand precisely the role of ERs in the management of crying.

Coherence. The accumulation of findings from different studies allows new studies to be assessed for their coherence with what comes before. For example, work on the organization of food assessments in mealtime conversations (Wiggins, 2002) builds on, and provides further confirmation of, earlier work on assessments and compliments (Pomerantz, 1984). Looked at the other way round, a study that clashed with some of the basic findings in discourse work would be treated with more caution—although if its findings seemed more robust, it would be more consequential.

The analytic work on crying and on resisting advice resistance builds on, and meshes with, work on the organization of phone calls, work specifically on calls to helplines, work on tag questions, work on sequence organization and delay, work on advice, and work on the nature of advice resistance. In each case the studies move the literature on and generate a larger web of understanding.

Readers' evaluation. One of the most fundamental features of DP compared with other psychological perspectives is that its claims are accountable to the detail of the empirical materials and that the empirical materials are presented in a form that allows readers, as far as possible, to make their own checks and judgments. Discourse articles typically present a range of extracts from the transcript alongside the interpretations that have been made of them. This form of validation contrasts with much traditional experimental and content analytic work, where it is rare for anything close to raw data to be included or for more than one or two illustrative codings to be provided. Sacks's (1992) ideal was to put the reader as far as possible into the same position as the researcher with respect to the materials. Such an ideal is unrealizable in practice, but discourse work is closer than many analytic approaches in psychology.

CONCLUSION

For much of the past 100 years, psychology has developed as a hypothetico–deductive science that has conceptualized the world in terms of the effects and interactions of variables on one another that can best be assessed using experiments analyzed using multivariate statistics. This methodological apparatus has been combined with a cognitivist form of explanation for which the causes of human action are seen to lie within individuals. In some ways, this has been a hugely impressive and successful enterprise. Yet this has had a number of unintended consequences that restrict its approach to human action.

First, the search for general relationships that underlie behavior has the consequence of moving research away from the specifics of human action. Action is typically modeled, restricted, or reported and transformed into the kind of counts that are amenable to multivariate analysis. On the extremely rare occasion that records of actual interaction in natural settings are used, it is quickly transformed into counts (using content analysis, say). Second, this search for general relationships combined with the need for simple controlled designs means that little attention has been paid to the nature and organization of the rich local and institutional settings in which human conduct invariably takes place.

Third, the hypothetico–deductive approach has led researchers away from careful descriptive studies in favor of studies that start with some kind of relationship or model to be tested. This combines with the legacy of the distinction drawn between competence and performance that has become foundational in cognitivist psychology and that treats performance data as enormously messy and something to be bypassed by focusing, via hypothetical models, directly on competence.

In contrast to this, DP starts with the concrete particulars of human action recorded in specific settings with minimal researcher interference. In many ways it is a classically empiricist enterprise. Its analytic approach is focused on the way practices are built in real time and how their organization and intelligibility is dependent on the normative organization of talk. Psychological matters come into DP study through their emergence as issues that are relevant for participants. Instead of attempting to capture underlying competence, it is focused on how psychological matters are public and intelligible.

Thus the study of crying (a) started with materials collected as parts of actions that the participants would do irrespective of their researched status; (b) first involved a descriptive project that bracketed the category "crying" and started to explicate the form and nature of features of behavior, such as wet sniffs and sobs; and (c) focused on crying as something that is displayed and communicated, unfolding in real time with different stages. The key interest for discursive work is in the public practices, how upset is displayed, understood, and receipted. That is, the focus is on what crying and upset is for these participants, and its role in this very specific institutional setting. Likewise in the study of resisting advice resistance, psychological matters—and in particular what the caller knows about the appropriate course of action they need to follow—are managed by a cluster of practices operating in real time with a scale of relevance to participants in the order of tenths of a second. These are not played out in the abstract as psychological processes but rather in terms of the goals and affordances of the institution of the helpline.

Both of these studies explicate the orderliness of specific, institutionally bounded realms of human action. This orderliness is not something that is statistical and causal, but normative and voluntaristic. Thus, elements of crying such as delays and wet sniffs do not cause particular crying receipts; however, they make relevant a restricted set of next actions as well as providing a context for understanding what the CPO does next.

The program of DP offers an alternative analytic approach that respecifies core psychological notions, such as cognition, perception, embodiment, and emotion and places the situated understandings of the participants at the core of the research. Its focus on peoples' practices makes it distinct from both mainstream experimental psychology and from a range of alternative qualitative methods (e.g., narrative psychology, interpretative phenomenological analysis, ethnography) that typically use open-ended interviews as their main technique of data generation.

References

Antaki, C. (1998). Identity-ascriptions in their time and place: "Fagin" and "the terminally dim." In C. Antaki & S. Widdicombe (Eds.), *Identities in talk* (pp. 71–86). London, England: Sage.

Antaki, C. (2004). Reading minds or dealing with psychological implications? *Theory and Psychology, 14*, 667–683. doi:10.1177/0959354304046178

Antaki, C., Houtkoop-Steenstra, H., & Rapley, M. (2000). "Brilliant. Next question . . .": High-grade assessment sequences in the completion of interactional units. *Research on Language and Social Interaction, 33*, 235–262. doi:10.1207/S15327973RLSI3303_1

Antaki, C., & Rapley, M. (1996). "Quality of life" talk: The liberal paradox of psychological testing. *Discourse and Society, 7*, 293–316. doi:10.1177/0957926596007003002

Auburn, T. (2005). Narrative reflexivity as a repair device for discounting "cognitive distortions" in sex offender treatment. *Discourse and Society, 16*, 697–718. doi:10.1177/0957926505054942

Augoustinos, M., Tuffin, K., & Rapley, M. (1999). Genocide or a failure to gel? Racism, history and nationalism in Australian talk. *Discourse and Society, 10*, 351–378. doi:10.1177/0957926599010003004

Augoustinos, M., Walker, I., & Donaghue, N. (2006). *Social cognition: An integrated introduction.* London, England: Sage.

Berger, P. L., & Luckmann, T. (1966). *The social construction of reality.* Garden City, NY: Anchor.

Billig, M. (1989). The argumentative nature of holding strong views: A case study. *European Journal of Social Psychology, 19*, 203–223. doi:10.1002/ejsp.2420190303

Billig, M. (1992). *Talking of the royal family.* London, England: Routledge.

Billig, M. (1996). *Arguing and thinking: A rhetorical approach to social psychology* (2nd ed.). Cambridge, England: Cambridge University Press.

Billig, M., Condor, S., Edwards, D., Gane, M., Middleton, D. J., & Radley, A. R. (1988). *Ideological dilemmas: A social psychology of everyday thinking.* London, England: Sage.

Butler, C., Potter, J., Danby, S., Emisson, M., & Hepburn, A. (2010). Advice implicative interrogatives: Building "client centred" support in a children's helpline. *Social Psychology Quarterly, 73*, 265–287.

Buttny, R. (1993). *Social accountability in communication.* London, England: Sage.

Clayman, S., & Heritage, J. C. (2002). *The news interview: Journalists and public figures on the air.* Cambridge, England: Cambridge University Press.

Condor, S. (2006). Temporality and collectivity: Diversity, history and the rhetorical construction of national entitativity. *British Journal of Social Psychology, 45*, 657–682. doi:10.1348/014466605X82341

Craven, A., & Potter, J. (2010). Directives: Contingency and entitlement in action. *Discourse Studies. 12*, 1–24. doi:10.1177/1461445610370126

Cromdal, J., Tholander, M., & Aronsson, K. (1997). "Doing reluctance": Managing delivery of assessments in peer evaluation. In A. Hepburn & S. Wiggins (Eds.), *Discursive research in practice: New approaches to psychology and interaction* (pp. 203–223). London, England: Sage.

Drew, P. (2005). Is confusion a state of mind? In H. te Molder & J. Potter (Eds), *Conversation and cognition* (pp. 161–183). Cambridge, England: Cambridge University Press.

Drew, P., & Heritage, J. C. (Eds.). (1992). *Talk at work: Interaction in institutional settings.* Cambridge, England: University of Cambridge Press.

Drew, P., & Holt, E. (1988). Complainable matters: The use of idiomatic expressions in making complaints. *Social Problems, 35*, 398–417. doi:10.1525/sp.1988.35.4.03a00060

Drew, P., & Holt, E. (1998). Figures of speech: Figurative expressions and the management of topic transition in conversation. *Language in Society, 27*, 495–522. doi:10.1017/S0047404598004035

Edwards, D. (1997). *Discourse and cognition.* London, England: Sage.

Edwards, D. (1998). The relevant thing about her: Social identity categories in use. In C. Antaki & S. Widdicombe (Eds.), *Identities in talk* (pp. 15–33). London, England: Sage.

Edwards, D. (1999a). Emotion discourse. *Culture and Psychology, 5*, 271–291. doi:10.1177/1354067X9953001

Edwards, D. (1999b). Shared knowledge as a performative and rhetorical category. In J. Verschueren (Ed.), *Pragmatics in 1998: Selected papers from the sixth International Pragmatics Conference* (Vol. 2, pp. 130–141). Antwerp, Belgium: International Pragmatics Association.

Edwards, D. (2005). Moaning, whinging and laughing: The subjective side of complaints. *Discourse Studies, 7*, 5–29. doi:10.1177/1461445605048765

Edwards, D. (2007). Managing subjectivity in talk. In A. Hepburn & S. Wiggins (Eds.), *Discursive research in practice: New approaches to psychology and interaction* (pp. 31–49). Cambridge, England: Cambridge University Press. doi:10.1017/CBO9780511611216.002

Edwards, D. (2008). Intentionality and mens rea in police interrogations: The production of actions as crimes. *Intercultural Pragmatics, 5*, 177–199. doi:10.1515/IP.2008.010

Edwards, D., & Potter, J. (1992). *Discursive psychology*. London, England: Sage.

Edwards, D., & Potter, J. (1993). Language and causation: A discursive action model of description and attribution. *Psychological Review, 100*, 23–41. doi:10.1037/0033-295X.100.1.23

Edwards, D., & Potter, J. (2001). Discursive psychology. In A. W. McHoul & M. Rapley (Eds.), *How to analyse talk in institutional settings: A casebook of methods* (pp. 12–24). London, England: Continuum International.

Freed, A. F., & Ehrlich, S. (Eds.). (2010). *"Why do you ask?": The function of questions in institutional discourse*. Oxford, England: Oxford University Press.

Gilbert, G. N., & Mulkay, M. (1984). *Opening Pandora's box: A sociological analysis of scientists' discourse*. Cambridge, England: Cambridge University Press.

Hepburn, A. (2003). *An introduction to critical social psychology*. London, England: Sage.

Hepburn, A. (2004). Crying: Notes on description, transcription and interaction. *Research on Language and Social Interaction, 37*, 251–290. doi:10.1207/s15327973rlsi3703_1

Hepburn, A. (in press). Transcription. In J. Sidnell & T. Stivers (Eds.), *Routledge handbook of conversation analysis*. London, England: Routledge.

Hepburn, A., & Potter, J. (2003). Discourse analytic practice. In C. Seale, D. Silverman, J. Gubrium, & G. Gobo (Eds.), *Qualitative research practice* (pp. 180–196). London, England: Sage.

Hepburn, A., & Potter, J. (2007). Crying receipts: Time, empathy and institutional practice. *Research on Language and Social Interaction, 40*, 89–116.

Hepburn, A., & Potter, J. (2010). Interrogating tears: Some uses of "tag questions" in a child protection helpline. In A. F. Freed & S. Ehrlich (Eds.), *"Why do you ask?": The function of questions in institutional discourse* (pp. 69–86). Oxford, England: Oxford University Press.

Hepburn, A., & Potter, J. (2011a). Designing the recipient: Some practices that manage advice resistance in institutional settings. *Social Psychology Quarterly, 74*, 216–241.

Hepburn, A., & Potter, J. (2011b). Threats: Power, family mealtimes, and social influence. *British Journal of Social Psychology, 50*, 99–120.

Hepburn, A., & Wiggins, S. (Eds.). (2005). Developments in discursive psychology [Special Issue]. *Discourse and Society, 16*(5). doi:10.1177/0957926505054937

Hepburn, A., & Wiggins, S. (Eds.). (2007). *Discursive research in practice: New approaches to psychology and interaction*. Cambridge, England: Cambridge University Press. doi:10.1017/CBO9780511611216

Heritage, J. C. (1984). *Garfinkel and ethnomethodology*. Englewood Cliffs, NJ: Prentice-Hall.

Heritage, J. C., & Clayman, S. (2010). *Conversation analysis and institutional interaction*. Cambridge, England: Cambridge University Press.

Heritage, J. C., & Greatbatch, D. (1991). On the institutional character of institutional talk: The case of news interviews. In D. Boden & D. H. Zimmerman (Eds.), *Talk and social structure: Studies in ethnomethodology and conversation analysis* (pp. 93–137). Cambridge, England: Polity Press.

Heritage, J. C., & Raymond, G. (2005). The terms of agreement: Indexing epistemic authority and subordination in assessment sequences. *Social Psychology Quarterly, 68*, 15–38. doi:10.1177/019027250506800103

Heritage, J. C., & Sefi, S. (1992). Dilemmas of advice: Aspects of the delivery and reception of advice in interactions between health visitors and first time mothers. In P. Drew & J. Heritage (Eds.), *Talk at work* (pp. 359–419). Cambridge, England: Cambridge University Press.

Jefferson, G. (2004). Glossary of transcript symbols with an introduction. In G. H. Lerner (Ed.), *Conversation analysis: Studies from the first generation* (pp. 13–31). Amsterdam, the Netherlands: Benjamins.

Kurri, K., & Wahlström, J. (2001). Dialogic management of conflict in domestic violence counselling. *Feminism and Psychology, 11*, 187–208. doi:10.1177/0959353501011002009

Locke, A., & Edwards, D. (2003). Bill and Monica: Memory, emotion, and normativity in Clinton's grand jury testimony. *British Journal of Social Psychology, 42*, 239–256. doi:10.1348/014466603322127238

Maynard, D. W., Houtkoop-Steenstra, H., Schaeffer, N. C., & van der Zouwen, J. (Eds.). (2002). *Standardization and tacit knowledge: Interaction and practice in the survey interview*. New York, NY: Wiley.

Myers, G. (2004). *Matters of opinion: Talking about public ideas*. Cambridge, England: Cambridge University Press. doi:10.1017/CBO9780511486708

Park, J., & Banaji, M. R. (2000). Mood and heuristics: The influence of happy and sad states on sensitivity and bias in stereotyping. *Journal of Personality and Social Psychology, 78,* 1005–1023. doi:10.1037/0022-3514.78.6.1005

Peräkylä, A., Antaki, C., Vehviläinen, S., & Leudar, I. (Eds.). (2008). *Conversation analysis of psychotherapy.* Cambridge, England: Cambridge University Press. doi:10.1017/CBO9780511490002

Phillips, L. J., & Jørgensen, M. W. (2002). *Discourse analysis as theory and method.* London, England: Sage.

Planalp, S. (1999). *Communicating emotion: Social, moral, and cultural processes.* Cambridge, England: Cambridge University Press.

Pomerantz, A. M. (1984). Agreeing and disagreeing with assessments: Some features of preferred/dispreferred turn shapes. In J. M. Atkinson & J. Heritage (Eds.), *Structures of social action: Studies in conversation analysis* (pp. 57–101). Cambridge, England: Cambridge University Press.

Potter, J. (1996). *Representing reality: Discourse, rhetoric and social construction.* London, England: Sage.

Potter, J. (2003). Discursive psychology: Between method and paradigm. *Discourse and Society, 14,* 783–794. doi:10.1177/09579265030146005

Potter, J., & Hepburn, A. (2003). I'm a bit concerned—Early actions and psychological constructions in a child protection helpline. *Research on Language and Social Interaction, 36,* 197–240. doi:10.1207/S15327973RLSI3603_01

Potter, J., & Hepburn, A. (2008). Discursive constructionism. In J. A. Holstein & J. F. Gubrium (Eds.), *Handbook of constructionist research* (pp. 275–293). New York, NY: Guilford Press.

Potter, J., & Wetherell, M. (1987). *Discourse and social psychology: Beyond attitudes and behaviour.* London, England: Sage.

Potter, J., & Wetherell, M. (1988). Accomplishing attitudes: Fact and evaluation in racist discourse. *Text, 8,* 51–68. doi:10.1515/text.1.1988.8.1-2.51

Puchta, C., & Potter, J. (1999). Asking elaborate questions: Focus groups and the management of spontaneity. *Journal of Sociolinguistics, 3,* 314–335. doi:10.1111/1467-9481.00081

Puchta, C., & Potter, J. (2002). Manufacturing individual opinions: Market research focus groups and the discursive psychology of attitudes. *British Journal of Social Psychology, 41,* 345–363. doi:10.1348/014466602760344250

Raymond, G. (2003). Grammar and social organisation: Yes/no interrogatives and the structure of responding. *American Sociological Review, 68,* 939–967. doi:10.2307/1519752

Reynolds, J., & Wetherell, M. (2003). The discursive climate of singleness: The consequences for women's negotiation of a single identity. *Feminism and Psychology, 13,* 489–510. doi:10.1177/09593535030134014

Ruusuvuori, J. (2005). Empathy and sympathy in action: Attending to patients' troubles in Finnish homeopathic and GP consultations. *Social Psychology Quarterly, 68,* 204–222. doi:10.1177/019027250506800302

Sacks, H. (1992). *Lectures on conversation* (Vols. 1–2, G. Jefferson, Ed.). Oxford, England: Basil Blackwell.

Schegloff, E. A. (1992). Repair after next turn: The last structurally provided defense of intersubjectivity in conversation. *American Journal of Sociology, 97,* 1295–1345. doi:10.1086/229903

Schegloff, E. A. (1999). Discourse, pragmatics, conversation, analysis. *Discourse Studies, 1,* 405–435. doi:10.1177/1461445699001004002

Schegloff, E. A. (2007). *Sequence organization in interaction: Vol. 1. A primer in conversation analysis.* Cambridge, England: Cambridge University Press. doi:10.1017/CBO9780511791208

Schiffrin, D., Tannen, D., & Hamilton, H. E. (Eds.). (2003). *Handbook of discourse analysis.* Oxford, England: Blackwell. doi:10.1111/b.9780631205968.2003.x

Silverman, D. (1997). *Discourses of counselling: HIV counselling as social interaction.* London, England: Sage.

Speer, S. A., & Parsons, C. (2006). Gatekeeping gender: Some features of the use of hypothetical questions in the psychiatric assessment of transsexual patients. *Discourse and Society, 17,* 785–812. doi:10.1177/0957926506068433

Stokoe, E. (2009). Doing actions with identity categories: Complaints and denials in neighbor disputes. *Text and Talk, 29,* 75–97.

Stokoe, E., & Edwards, D. (2009). Accomplishing social action with identity categories: Mediating neighbour complaints. In M. Wetherell (Ed.), *Theorizing identities and social action* (pp. 95–115). London, England: Sage.

Stokoe, E., & Hepburn, A. (2005). "You can hear a lot through the walls": Noise formulations in neighbour complaints. *Discourse and Society, 16,* 647–673. doi:10.1177/0957926505054940

te Molder, H., & Potter, J. (Eds.). (2005). *Conversation and cognition.* Cambridge, England: Cambridge University Press. doi:10.1017/CBO9780511489990

Wetherell, M., & Potter, J. (1992). *Mapping the language of racism: Discourse and the legitimation of exploitation.* Hemel Hempstead, England: Harvester/Wheatsheaf.

Widdicombe, S., & Wooffitt, R. (1995). *The language of youth subcultures: Social identity in action.* London, England: Harvester/Wheatsheaf.

Wiggins, S. (2002). Talking with your mouth full: Gustatory mmms and the embodiment of pleasure. *Research on Language and Social Interaction, 35,* 311–336. doi:10.1207/S15327973RLSI3503_3

Multilayered Approaches

CHAPTER 9

CASE STUDY METHODS

Robert K. Yin

INTRODUCTION: WHAT IS THE CASE STUDY METHOD AND WHY USE IT?

Case study research continues to be poorly understood. In psychology, as in sociology, anthropology, political science, and epidemiology, the strengths and weaknesses of case study research—much less how to practice it well—still need clarification.

To start, case study as a research method differs from case studies as a teaching tool[1] or from case records maintained by service agencies.[2] As a second broad distinction, especially pertinent to psychology, case study research differs from at least two other types of like-sounding research methods: (a) single-subject research, found both in neuropsychology (e.g., see Chapter 33 of this volume) and in behavioral research more generally (e.g., see Kratochwill, 1984; Morgan & Morgan, 2009; Tawney & Gast, 1984; see also Chapter 31 of this volume); and (b) case-control studies (e.g., see Schlesselman, 1982; see also Chapter 15 of this volume). Figure 9.1 explains the main differences and compares them to conventional experimental group designs. The four choices also can overlap, hence Figure 9.1 only depicts an ideal classification.

Figure 9.1 points to the two key dimensions in distinguishing among the four methods. For instance, between the two types of methods emphasizing individual data (Figure 9.1, Row 2), single-subject research calls for some formal manipulation, such as a repeated trial type of pattern. Conversely, between the two types of methods not involving any manipulation (Figure 9.1, Column 2), case-control studies usually collect data from groups of individuals who already have exhibited the condition of interest (e.g., tobacco users). The studies then proceed to estimate the differences between the group's mean and that of a retrospectively selected control group (e.g., nontobacco users). Given Figure 9.1's two dimensions, case study research focuses on individual-level data and is limited by the inability or unwillingness to manipulate any intervention.

Having differentiated case study research in this approximating manner, the following chapter reviews the main aspects of case study research—its definition, design, data collection procedures, and analytic techniques. The chapter serves readers who may want to refresh their understanding of case study research, but the chapter also informs those who might want to overcome their skepticism about the method.[3]

Case Studies: A Brief Definition

All case study research starts from the same compelling feature: the desire to derive a(n) (up)close or

---

[1]The teaching tools are invaluable, but a teaching case's data can be manipulated for instructional purposes, and the cases are not part of the research literature. In contrast, research cases must adhere strictly to methodological procedures, linking all findings to explicit evidence. For a broad discussion of teaching cases in business, law, and medicine, see Garvin (2003). For examples of teaching cases in psychology, see Dunbar (2005) and Golden (2004).

[2]Bromley (1986) noted that such records, although otherwise appearing to be case studies, can be influenced by "expectations regarding accountability rather than factual data" (p. 69) and are therefore "liable to a variety of accidental or deliberate omissions and distortions" (p. 90).

[3]For instance, even devoted supporters of *gold standard* research have found some benefit from doing their own published research using the case study method (e.g., Cook & Foray, 2007).

DOI: 10.1037/13620-009
APA Handbook of Research Methods in Psychology: Vol. 2. Research Designs, H. Cooper (Editor-in-Chief)

	Intervention(s) Manipulated by a Researcher	
	YES	**NO**
GROUPED DATA	Conventional Experimental Designs	Case-Control Studies
INDIVIDUAL DATA	Single-Subject Research	Case Study (single or multiple)

FIGURE 9.1.   Case study research compared with three other kinds of behavioral research.

otherwise in-depth understanding of a single or small number of "cases," set in their real-world context (e.g., Bromley, 1986, p. 1). The closeness aims to produce an invaluable but complex understanding—an insightful appreciation of the "case"—hopefully resulting in new learning about real-world behavior.

In technical terms, the likely complexity translates into a broad array of variables. Assuming that each "case" is a single data point, the situation then leads to the following brief definition of the case study as a research method: "In case studies, the number of variables of interest will far outstrip the number of available data points" (Yin, 2009, p. 18).

Three Conditions Leading to Large Number of Variables of Interest in a Case Study

Three conditions contribute to the large number of variables: conditions over time, in-depth inquiry, and contextual conditions.

Conditions over time.   The first and most common condition comes from the fact that interest in a case covers multiple conditions extending over time. Analyzing the temporal pattern can be the explicit subject of a case study, as in the unfolding of key events that might explain some culminating event—or as in a developmental case study that could track human or animal behavior (e.g., Denenberg, 1982).

Even if a temporal pattern is not a direct topic of inquiry or is fairly short (e.g., Bromley, 1986, p. 5), it can create a continual flow of variables that may

be relevant and that cannot be ignored. In this sense, and regardless of the brevity of the time period, case studies rarely serve as literal *snapshots*—as if everything occurred at the same exact moment. Important events, including the repetition of seemingly but not precisely like behavior, occur at different points in time and may become an essential part of understanding a case.

In-depth inquiry of the case.   Second, a case study involves an in-depth inquiry into the case. The multiple features of a case translate into another large number of variables.

In psychology, the case is likely to focus on some individual's behavior. At an earlier time, such an individual might have served as both the investigator and the subject of study, producing the famous studies on memory, perception, and learning by Ebbinghaus, Stratton, and Galton, respectively (e.g., Garmezy, 1982) as well as the folklore created by the Phase I safety trials in medicine, during which medical scientists' first commitment has been to test newly created medical remedies on their own bodies. These kinds of studies, in which the cases were either the researchers or their friends and relatives, also appear to have been an integral part of the tradition in doing case study research in applied linguistics (Duff, 2008, p. 37).

In contemporary settings, the individuals of interest can come from a wide range of situations, including clinical cases, studies of individual development or learning as in a Piagetian study of cognitive development, and single animal preparations in comparative psychology.[4] One of the most notable

---

[4]For instance, individual development is a common topic of inquiry in comparative psychology, where independent variables are deliberately manipulated at different ages of a life cycle (Denenberg, 1982). The significant findings then often lie with the interactions among the independent variables, producing yet more variables, challenging the assumed independence of the variables, and therefore also requiring "a more complicated model than causality as a framework for interpreting [the] findings" (Denenberg, 1982, p. 22).

case studies in neurology, referenced by one analyst as "the most famous neurological case in the world" (Rolls, 2005, p. 51),[5] involved the case of "H. M.," about whom more than 30 articles had been published between 1957 and 1968 alone (Scoville & Milner, 1957; Sidman, Soddard, & Mohr, 1968).

Alternatively, other psychology fields (e.g., social, educational, management, occupational, environmental, and community psychology) as well as related fields outside of psychology may focus on organizations or other entities, rather than on individuals. The in-depth study of such entities also will translate into a large number of variables. Research on collaborative care clinics, involving the coordination of medical and behavioral health services (e.g., Kessler & Stafford, 2008), would be an illustrative example of such case studies.

Contextual conditions.   A third set of conditions comes from outside of the case. Thus, in addition to investigating the case over time and in depth, a case study will include the collection of data about the contextual conditions surrounding the case. Indeed, one of the strengths of case study research is its ability to examine contextual conditions to the fullest extent that might appear relevant. For instance, if the case is an individual, data about the individual's family, work, and peer environments could be common components of a full case study. If the case is a small group or an organization, data about cultural, economic, social, and political conditions and trends would be counterpart components.

Moreover, the boundary between a case and its context may not be sharp because real-world affairs do not readily fall within clear-cut categories. The ability to appreciate any such blurring as part of a case study is considered a strength of case study research. The likely benefit will be an ensuing study that enriches later understandings of the original case.

By comparison, other methods will likely treat any blurring between the focus of study and its context as, at best, an annoyance. In fact, most other methods do not address contextual conditions with great ease. For instance, other than a small number of covariates, experiments minimize the role of contextual conditions by controlling them out.

Similarly, surveys cannot include too many contextual questions because of the limitations on the degrees of freedom.

Summary of three conditions.   These three conditions help to explain why the number of variables of interest in a case study is likely to be enormous. In contrast, the number of data points, as represented by the individual cases, is likely to be small. As a practical matter, no single case study, even if consisting of multiple cases, will be able to have the number of cases that would match, much less exceed in any realistic multiple, the number of variables.

This situation has far-reaching implications for case study design and analysis. The designs belong to a family of their own and cannot be considered part of some other family of designs, such as experimental or quasi-experimental designs. Likewise, the analytic methods cannot employ most of the statistical methods conventionally used with these other types of methods because the case study's data points will have little or no variance.

Motives for Using the Case Study Method

Given the preceding constraints, case study research might at first appear to have limited value. In fact, however, case studies have been a common part of research in psychology and related fields for a long time. Why is this?

Exploration.   A quick but overly narrow response to this question calls attention to case studies in an *exploratory* mode—that is, to collect some data to determine whether a topic is indeed worthy of further investigation, and if so, the research questions or hypotheses that might be most relevant in the subsequent research. In this exploratory mode, case study research appears only as a prelude to the use of other methods, such as surveys and experiments. However, such an outdated hierarchy of research methods is surely incorrect (e.g., Bromley, 1986, p. 15).

Description and explanation.   Among other problems with the hierarchical view is the fact that surveys and experiments also have exploratory modes. Conversely, case study research can be used

---

[5]Rolls's (2005) book consists of 16 chapters, each covering a famous case in psychology.

in *descriptive*, *explanatory*, and *evaluative* modes, in addition to its use in an exploratory mode. Descriptive case studies can serve many purposes, such as presenting a rarely encountered situation or one not normally accessible to researchers. For instance, a famous case study of a small group of youths from a White, urban, and low-income neighborhood focused on their interpersonal relationships (Whyte, 1943/1955). Among other findings, the study described how the youths' ability (or inability) to break away from their neighborhood ties helped (or hindered) their likely job mobility. Although such a revelation would strike us in the 21st century as a commonly understood (and possibility still recurring) phenomenon, few researchers had produced such an intimate portrayal of specific youths up to that time.

As for the explanatory mode of case studies, a common example comes from the field of educational psychology and the complementary relationships among different methods: The effectiveness of a specific education curriculum might be determined by conducting an experiment, assessing student outcomes under treatment and control conditions. An explanation of how the learning took place, however, would require a complementary case study, focusing on implementation, classroom observations, and interviews of students about their learning strategies (Shavelson & Towne, 2002). Many other descriptive and explanatory examples, whether the subjects of study are individuals, small groups, organizations, or more abstract cases such as *decisions*, can be cited.

Evaluation.   Evaluation may be considered a fourth motive for doing case studies (Yin, 1994). For instance, a case study of an academic or medical program can describe the context, evolution, and operations of the program. An expected component of such a study includes evaluative data about how well the program has been working. For one program that had integrated mental health services into primary care for more than 15 years, the data covered a variety of (quantitative) outcome measures determined on the basis of scales that measured patients' functioning as well as their symptoms (Kates, 2008).

In fact, in academic environments, such evaluative case studies are commonly conducted, although they are not formally organized or labeled as case study research. These case studies take the form of the assessments conducted by visiting committees who periodically review individual academic departments. The visiting committee focuses on the well-being and progress being made by a department and collects a variety of evidence (observations, interviews, and reviews of pertinent documents such as the department's publications) to arrive at both formative and summative judgments.

The preceding illustrations show how using case studies in any of these exploratory, descriptive, explanatory, or evaluative modes highlight the potential value of case studies as an important part of a researcher's full methodological repertoire.

Caveats and Concerns in Doing Case Study Research

Despite its apparent applicability for studying many relevant real-world situations and addressing important research questions, case study research nevertheless has not achieved widespread recognition as a method of choice. Some people actually think of it as a method of last resort. Why is this?

Part of the method's notoriety comes from a lack of trust in the credibility of a case study researcher's procedures, which do not seem to protect sufficiently against such biases as a researcher seeming to find what she or he had set out to find. Another factor contributing to the method's reputation comes from the use of qualitative data, which are presumed to be based on less robust measures than those used to collect quantitative data. Yet another factor comes from the perceived inability to generalize the findings from a case study to any broader level.

When case study research is done poorly, all of these challenges can come together in a negative way, potentially reinforcing the prejudices against the method. In contrast, more systematic and careful use of case study research can begin to overcome, if not dissipate, the concerns. For instance, and as will be shown later in this chapter, when relevant, some case studies can be conducted *entirely* on the basis of quantitative data. Many case studies will and should rely on qualitative data, however, and procedures such as establishing a *chain of evidence* or an *audit trail* will increase the reliability of such data.

The preceding recommendation is just one example of the ways in which case study research practices can address the general concerns associated with the method. The remainder of this chapter briefly reviews many other ways to address these concerns. At the same time, the limited length of this chapter precludes a full rendition of how to deal with all of the challenges—such as addressing concerns regarding construct validity, internal validity, external validity, and reliability in doing case study research (for a fuller discussion, see Yin, 2009, pp. 40–45).

CASE STUDY RESEARCH DESIGNS

Doing case study research does not mean going immediately into a field setting and collecting data. Beyond the inevitable need to define one's own research questions, researchers may first want to consider certain research design choices as being pertinent to case studies.[6] Using these designs will help to make the ensuing case study more methodic, while still leaving room for appropriate discovery and openness to unanticipated findings in the field.[7]

Regarding research designs, an initial misconception, created years ago, was the idea that case study research did not have a design of its own but simply was one of many of the designs used in quasi-experiments. Thus was born the idea of the "one-shot post-test-only case study" and its seemingly defenseless status as a design to be avoided at all costs (e.g., Campbell & Stanley, 1966).

Only gradually has this misconception been overcome, mainly on the basis of a heightened awareness that the seeking and testing of rival explanations is an essential part of empirical research and that case study research can pursue this objective in its own way, although not necessarily with the efficiency of a tightly controlled experiment. Thus, in 1984, Campbell (1984/2009) wrote: "More and more I have come to the conclusion that the core of the scientific method is not experimentation per se but rather the strategy connoted by the phrase 'plausible rival hypotheses'" (p. vii).

Campbell's fuller thinking and explanation was spelled out in greater detail in an unfortunately little-known article on "degrees of freedom and the case study" (Campbell, 1975). Later, in the revised edition of his work on quasi-experimental designs, Campbell liberated the case study method from its earlier status. Although the original one-shot design was still to be avoided as a quasi-experimental design, he wrote that "certainly the case study as normally practiced should not be demeaned by identification with the one-group post-test-only design" (Cook & Campbell, 1979, p. 96).

Defining a Case

The case study method's own research designs begin by identifying, even on a tentative basis, the case that is to be the subject of study (Yin, 2009, pp. 29–33, 46). The case serves as the main unit of analysis in a case study, although case studies also can have nested units within the main unit (see the section Embedded Designs). A case is generally a bounded entity (a person, organization, behavioral condition, event, or other social phenomenon), but the distinction between the case and its contextual conditions—in both spatial and temporal dimensions—may be blurred, as previously discussed.

Single- Versus Multiple-Case Studies

Any specific case study can consist of a single case or of multiple cases, leading to the first distinction in case study designs—that between a single-case study and a multiple-case study; the latter sometimes is called an "extended case study"

---

[6]Some qualitative research can rightfully value start-up procedures that deliberately avoid any initial research questions, much less research design, because either might undesirably influence the interpretation of the real-world setting, behavior of interest, or the meanings thereof as accorded by participants (e.g., Van Manen, 1990). Those who follow this sequence are likely to be highly experienced investigators, and those having little or no qualitative research experience should only adopt such a sequence with great care.

[7]For instance, a case study might have started with a certain design, only to find it either unworkable or less promising than originally thought, following some initial data collection. As with laboratory experiments, the remedy would be to cease collecting data under the original design and to revise it, then to restart data collection afresh. The common criticism of case studies, unfortunately, is that the investigator may not later have ignored the original data but might have reused them, thereby creating an unwanted bias and flaw.

(see Bromley, 1986, p. 8; Burawoy, 1991). In single-case studies, the selected case may be a rare; critical;[8] or, paradoxically, ordinary case. This last variant is illustrated by a famous community case study: *Middletown* was deliberately chosen as an average U.S. small town in the Midwest during the early 20th century (Lynd & Lynd, 1929). The case study showed how the town transitioned from an agricultural to an industrial economy and thereby provided important information and insights about a significant era in all of U.S. history.

Multiple-case studies provide additional options in comparison to single-case studies. The multiple-case design is usually more difficult to implement than a single-case design, but the ensuing data can provide greater confidence in a study's findings. The selection of the multiple cases might be considered akin to the way that one might define a set of multiple experiments—each case (or experiment) aiming to examine a complementary facet of a larger research question. A common multiple-case design might call for two or more cases that deliberately try to test the conditions under which the same findings might be *replicated*. For instance, seven teachers, separately assigned to seven students with *developmental coordination disorder*, were the subject of a multiple-case study (Miyahara & Wafer, 2004). Each teacher–student pair was a case, and a between-pair replication logic was used to determine the relationship between systematically alternating teaching strategies and a student's performance assessed with a variety of psychometric measures over time.

As an important note, the use of the term *replication* in relation to multiple-case designs deliberately mimics the same principle as used in multiple experiments (e.g., Hersen & Barlow, 1976). Thus, the cases for a multiple-case study, as in the experiments in a multiple-experiment study, might have been selected to either predict similar results (*direct replications*) or to predict contrasting results but for anticipatable reasons (*theoretical replications*).

In neither situation would a tallying of the cases (or the experiments) provide a feasible way to decide whether the group of cases (or experiments) supported an initial proposition. Thus, some investigators of multiple-case studies might think that a cross-case analysis would largely consist of a simple tally (e.g., five cases supported the proposition but two did not) to arrive at a cross-case conclusion. The numbers in any such tally, however, are likely to be too small and undistinguished to support such a conclusion with any confidence.

An adjunct of the replication parallelism is the response to the age-old question of "how many cases" should be included in a multiple-case study—an issue that continues to plague the field to this day (e.g., Small, 2009). Students and scholars appear to assume the existence of a formulaic solution, as in conducting a *power analysis* (e.g., Lipsey, 1990), to determine the needed sample size in an experiment or survey.[9] For case studies (again, as with multiple experiments) no such formula exists. Instead, analogous to the parallel question of "how many experiments" need to be conducted to arrive at an unqualified result, the response is still a judgmental one: the more cases (experiments), the greater confidence or certainty, and the fewer the cases (experiments), the less confidence or certainty.

Holistic Versus Embedded Case Studies

Either single- or multiple-case study designs can have a secondary or embedded unit of analysis nested *within* each case being studied. The possibility therefore leads to four main types of case study designs. These, together with the dashed lines representing the blurred boundary between a case and its context, are illustrated in Figure 9.2.

As an example, an embedded arrangement would arise when the main case is a single organization, and the organization's employees are a secondary unit of analysis. Data about the main case might come from largely qualitative methods, whereas data about the employees might come from a sample survey (or the tallying and analysis of employee records). The nested arrangement is relevant as long

---

[8]This would be directly akin to a critical experiment, where the single case (or experiment) represents an opportunity to compare two directly competing or rival hypotheses.

[9]Quantitative analysts readily recognize that statistically significant differences also might not equate with findings of any practical or clinical significance. Thus, even in experimental research, the issue of the desired sample size entails discretionary judgments.

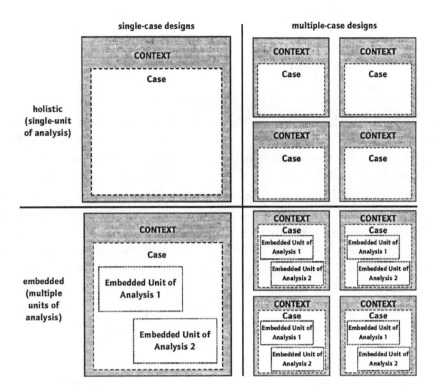

single-case designs | multiple-case designs

holistic (single-unit of analysis)

embedded (multiple units of analysis)

FIGURE 9.2. Basic types of designs for case studies. From *Case Study Research: Design and Methods* (p. 46), by R. K. Yin, 2009, Thousand Oaks, CA: Sage. Copyright 2009 by COSMOS Corporation. Reprinted with permission.

as the entire study and its main research questions are still about the organization in its entirety (e.g., the employee survey data are used as a further corroboration of the organization's overall condition). If the findings about employee (but not organization) characteristics become the main findings of the entire study, however, the original data about the organization as a whole would likely become merely a contextual condition for what, in the end, would be a piece of survey research about employee characteristics and not a case study.

Among the four types of designs, the embedded, multiple-case studies are the most complex. Such studies would resemble the hypothetical study just described but cover two or more organizations, with survey data coming from the employees of each of the organizations. In contrast, the holistic single-case study appears to be the most straightforward of the four types.

The Role of Theory

The role of theory in design work. A case study that starts with some theoretical propositions will

be easier to implement than one having no initial research questions, much less propositions. The theoretical propositions should by no means be considered with the formality of grand theory in social science but mainly need to suggest a simple set of relationships such as "a [hypothetical] story about why acts, events, structures, and thoughts occur" (Sutton & Staw, 1995, p. 372). More elaborate theories will (desirably) point to a more intricate pattern that will (paradoxically) add precision to the later analysis, yielding a benefit similar to that of having more complex theoretical propositions in quasi-experimental research (Rosenbaum, 2002, pp. 5–6, 277–279).

This desired role of theory serves as one point of difference between case study research and related qualitative methods such as ethnography (Van Maanen, 1988; see also Chapter 10 of this volume) and grounded theory (Corbin & Strauss, 2007; see also Chapter 3 of this volume). These other qualitative methods also can differ in other respects, including their basic epistemological assumptions (see Volume 1, Chapter 1, this handbook). For instance, other qualitative research may not necessarily focus on any case in the first place, may not be concerned with any theoretical propositions, and may not engage in formal design work.

The role of theory in generalizing from case studies.   For case study research, the availability of theoretical propositions not only serves the design function well but also helps to explain how one might generalize from a completed case study. The procedure even applies well to the holistic, single-case study, which has been commonly criticized for having no generalizability value.

To understand the process requires distinguishing between two types of generalizing: *statistical generalizations* and *analytic generalizations* (Yin, 2009, pp. 38–39). For case study research, the latter generalization is appropriate.

Unfortunately, most scholars, including those who do case study research, are imbued with the former type of generalization. They think that each case represents a sample of some known and larger universe, and they do not understand how a small set of cases can generalize to any larger universe. The simple answer is that a single or small set of cases cannot generalize in this manner, nor are they intended to. Furthermore, the incorrect assumption is that statistical generalizations, from samples to universes, are the only way to generalize findings from social science research.

In contrast, analytic generalizations depend on using a study's theoretical framework to establish a logic that might be applicable to other situations. Again, an appealing parallel exists in experimental science, in which generalizing about the findings from a single or small set of experiments does not usually follow any statistical path to a previously defined universe of experiments.[10] Rather, for both case studies and experiments, the objective for generalizing the findings is the same two-step process. The first step involves a conceptual claim whereby investigators show how their study's findings have informed a particular set of concepts, theoretical

constructs, or hypothesized sequence of events. The second step involves applying the same theoretical propositions to implicate other situations, outside of the completed case study, for which similar concepts might be relevant. For example, political science's best-selling work has been a single-case study about the Cuban missile crisis of 1962 (Allison, 1971; Allison & Zelikow, 1999). The authors did not generalize their findings and theoretical framework to U.S.–Cuban relations or to the use of missiles. They used their theoretical propositions to generalize their findings to the likely responses of national governments that might be confronted by other types of international crises.

As another example, Neustadt and Fineberg's (1983) single-case study of "the epidemic that never was"—a swine flu vaccination program launched by the federal government in 1976—retrospectively attracts continuing policy attention. Their case study covered the early spread of an influenza, the mass inoculation of people, and the subsequent cancellation of the vaccine program. In the face of threats by newer flu epidemics, such as the H1N1 strain of 2008–2010 in the United States and abroad, the study has been of contemporary interest in the search for clues about the quandaries of policy actions in public health crises.

Making analytic generalizations requires carefully constructed claims (Kelly & Yin, 2007), again whether for a case study or for an experiment. The argument is not likely to achieve the status of *proof* as in geometry,[11] and the claims must be presented soundly and be resistant to logical challenge. The relevant theory may be no more than a series of hypotheses or even a single hypothesis. Cronbach (1975) further clarified that the sought-after generalization is not that of a conclusion but rather more like a "working hypothesis" (also see Lincoln & Guba, 1985, pp. 122–123). Confidence in such hypotheses can then build as new case studies, again as in the case of new experiments, continue to produce findings related to the same theoretical propositions. To the extent that any study concerns

---

[10]Experimental psychology has had to overcome the fear that from a sampling standpoint, the main generalization from any experiment using college sophomores as subjects could only be to the universe of college sophomores. However, the characteristics of the subjects in an experiment always will lurk as a rival explanation.

[11]To be noted is that statistical generalizations also do not achieve the status of "proof" in geometry but by definition are probabilistic statements. The "working hypotheses" as analytic generalizations also are probabilistic statements, just not expressed in numerical terms.

itself with generalizing, case studies will tend to generalize to other situations (on the basis of analytic claims), whereas surveys and other quantitative methods tend to generalize to populations (on the basis of statistical claims).

CASE STUDY DATA COLLECTION

The complexity of any case study and its large number of variables also implicates the data-collection process. The different variables are likely to come from different sources of field-based evidence, and case study researchers therefore need to know how to collect data from these multiple sources.

The space constraints of this chapter preclude discussing field data (for additional information, see Chapter 10 of this volume). However, four data-collection procedures transcend all fieldwork: using a *protocol* to guide data collection, preserving a *chain of evidence*, *triangulating* data from different sources of evidence, and appealing to *rival explanations* throughout the data-collection process. All four procedures are essential parts of any data collection and will markedly strengthen a case study's later findings and claims. Brief descriptions follow.

Case Study Protocol

The protocol guides researchers in collecting all case study data. The questions in the protocol are directed at the researcher, *not* any field informant, and in this sense a protocol differs entirely from any *instrument* used in a conventional interview or survey. The protocol's questions in effect serve as a mental framework, not unlike similar frameworks held by detectives when investigating crimes. In those situations, the detectives may privately entertain one or more lines of inquiry (including rival hypotheses), but the specific questions posed to any informant are tuned to each specific interview situation. The questions as actually verbalized in an interview derived from the line of inquiry (i.e., mental framework) but do not come from a verbatim script (i.e., questionnaire).

Chain of Evidence

The principle underlying the use of a chain of evidence comes directly from forensics, in which law enforcement officials are careful to preserve evidence in an untainted manner, from a distinct origin at the crime scene to the final laboratory testing of the evidence. In doing case studies, the parallel process is more conceptual than physical. The principle is to allow an external observer—in this situation, the reader of the case study—to follow the derivation of any evidence from initial research questions to ultimate case study conclusions. As with criminological evidence, the process should be tight enough that evidence presented in a case study is assuredly the same evidence that was collected during data collection. Conversely, no original evidence should have been lost, through carelessness or bias, and therefore fail to receive appropriate attention in the case study analysis. Relevant evidence, likely to assume a narrative rather than numeric nature, might be displayed as a question-and-answer narrative, directly aligning the original protocol questions with the field evidence.

For instance, a multiple-case study of 40 neighborhood organizations used a protocol with 49 questions. Each of the 40 case studies consisted of responses to all 49 questions, with the field team integrating and citing (with footnotes) the specific observational, interview, and documentary (narrative and numeric) evidence that had been collected (for one of the case studies, see Yin, 2012, pp. 69–87). The organization of these 40 case studies actually facilitated a reader's own cross-case analysis because the reader could turn to the same numbered question in each case and judge the extent to which the responses appeared to be parallel or contrasting.

Triangulation

The principle of *triangulation* comes from navigation, where the intersection of three different reference points is used to calculate the precise location of an object (Yardley, 2009, p. 239). In research, the principle pertains to the goal of seeking at least three ways to verify or corroborate a particular event, description, or fact being reported by a study. Such corroboration is another way to strengthen the validity of a study.

Triangulation can be applied throughout a study, although the practice has tended to be associated with a study's data collection phase. In collecting data, the ideal triangulation would not only seek confirmation from three sources but also would try to find three contrasting sources (e.g., seeing an event with one's own eyes, a direct observation; recording the words of someone else who was there, a verbal report; and citing a description in a report written by yet a third person, a document).

Rival Explanations

Rival explanations are not merely alternative interpretations. True *rivals* compete directly with each other and cannot coexist. Research findings and their interpretations may be likened to combatants that can be challenged by one or more rivals. If one of the rivals turns out to be more plausible than an original interpretation, the original interpretation would have to be rejected, not just footnoted.

Case study research demands the seeking of rival explanations throughout the study process. Interestingly, the methodological literature offers little inkling of the substantive rivals that should be considered by researchers, either in doing case study or any other kinds of social science research (Rosenbaum, 2002; Yin, 2000). The only rivals to be found are methodological but not substantive ones, such as those involving the null hypothesis, experimenter effects, or other potential artifacts created by the research procedures. In contrast, in detective work, a substantive rival would be an alternative explanation of how a crime had occurred, compared with the explanation that might originally have been entertained.

The desired rival thinking should draw from a continual sense of *skepticism* as a case study proceeds. During data collection, the skepticism should involve worrying about whether events and actions are as they appear to be and whether informants are giving candid responses. Having a truly skeptical attitude will result in collecting more data than if rivals were not a concern. For instance, data collection should involve a deliberate and vigorous search for "discrepant evidence" (Patton, 2002, p. 553), as if one were trying to establish the potency of the plausible rival rather than seeking to undermine it (Rosenbaum, 2002, pp. 8–10). Finding no such evidence despite diligent search again increases confidence about a case study's later descriptions, explanations, and interpretations.

CASE STUDY ANALYSIS

Case study analysis takes many forms, but none yet follow routine procedures as may exist with other research methods. The absence of any cookbook for analyzing case study evidence has only partially been offset by the development of prepackaged software to code large amounts of narrative text. The software will follow an analyst's instruction in coding and categorizing the words found in a text, as might have been collected from interviews or documents. Unlike quantitative software, whereby an analyst provides input data and the computer uses an algorithm to estimate some model and produces the output data, there is no automated algorithm when doing qualitative analysis.

Instead, the analyst must logically piece together the coded evidence into broader themes and, in essence, create a unique algorithm befitting the particular case study. Thus, in case study research, the analytic course still depends on a marshaling of claims that use evidence in a logical fashion. Strong case study claims will thoroughly cover all relevant evidence, combined with the explicit entertaining of rival explanations.

Case study analysis can begin by systematically arraying qualitative data (narratives and words) into hierarchical relationships, matrixes, or other arrays (e.g., Miles & Huberman, 1994). The logic underlying the arrays may not differ from that used in the arrays that might start a quantitative analysis, an observation also made by others (e.g., Bernard & Ryan, 2010). For instance, quantitative analysis often starts with preliminary correlations or even chi-squares (both of which are arrays) before moving to more complex modeling.

In case study analysis, a simple array might be a word table, organized by some rows and columns of interest, that presents narrative data in the cells of the table. Given this or other arrays, several different analytic techniques can then be used, including pattern matching, explanation building, and time-series analysis. Multiple-case studies, in addition to using these several techniques within each single case, would then follow a replication logic. All these techniques are briefly discussed in the next sections.

Pattern Matching

A pattern-matching logic compares an empirically based pattern with a predicted one. For instance, analogous to a "non-equivalent dependent variables" design (Cook & Campbell, 1979, p. 118), the prior prediction in a community study might stipulate that the patterns of outcomes in many different sectors (e.g., retail sales, housing sales, unemployment, and population turnover) will be adversely affected by a key event (e.g., the closing of a military base in a single-employer small town—see Bradshaw, 1999). The analysis then examines the data in each sector, comparing pre–post trends with those in other communities and statewide trends. The pattern matching then includes a detailed explanation of how and why the intervention had (or had not) affected these trends. By also collecting data on and then examining possible rival explanations (e.g., events co-occurring with the key event or other contextual conditions), support for the claimed results is strengthened even further.

Explanation Building

A case study may not have started with any predicted patterns but in fact started with a rather open-ended research question. For instance, a case study might have been conducted after the outcome of interest already had occurred (analogous to *case-control studies*)—in this case, the demise of a high-tech firm that only a few years earlier had been a Fortune 50 firm (see Schein, 2003). The purpose of the Schein (2003) case study was to build an explanation for the demise, again deliberately entertaining rival explanations. The strength of the main explanation was reflected by the depth, intensity, and logic in assembling the case study data, which in this illustration consumed an entire book.

Time-Series Analysis

This technique mimics the time-series analyses in quantitative research (see Chapter 32 of this volume). In case study research, the simplest time-series can consist of assembling key events into a *chronology*. The resulting array (e.g., a word table consisting of time and types of events as the rows and columns) may not only produce an insightful descriptive pattern but also may hint at possible

causal relationships because any presumed causal condition must precede any presumed outcome condition. Assuming again the availability of data on rival hypotheses, such information would be included as part of the chronological pattern and its rejection would strengthen any claims considerably.

If the case study includes a major intervening event in the midst of the chronological sequence, the array could serve as a counterpart to an *interrupted time-series*. For instance, imagine a case study in which a new executive assumed leadership over an organization. The case study might have tracked sales, personnel, and other organizational characteristics for multiple periods of time, both before and after the executive's ascendance. If all the trends were in the appropriate upward direction, the case study could begin to build a claim crediting the new leader with these accomplishments. Again, attention to rival conditions (such as the organizational foundations that might have been put into place by the new executive's predecessor), and making them part of the analysis, would further strengthen the claim.

When Sufficient Quantitative Data Are Relevant and Available

These examples were deliberately limited to those situations in which a case study did not attempt any statistical analysis, mainly because of a lack of data points other than some simple pre–post comparison. Each of the three techniques can assume a different posture when more time intervals are relevant and sufficient data are available. In education, a common single-case design might focus on a school or school district as a single organization of interest (e.g., Supovitz & Taylor, 2005; Yin & Davis, 2007). Within the single case, considerable attention might be devoted to the collection and analysis of highly quantitative student achievement data.

For instance, a study of a single school district tracked student performance over a 22-year period (Teske, Schneider, Roch, & Marschall, 2000). The start of the period coincided with a time when the district was slowly implementing an educational reform that was the main subject of the study. Figure 9.3 shows that at the outset, students were performing at about half the city average; however, 9 years later, they eventually approached the city

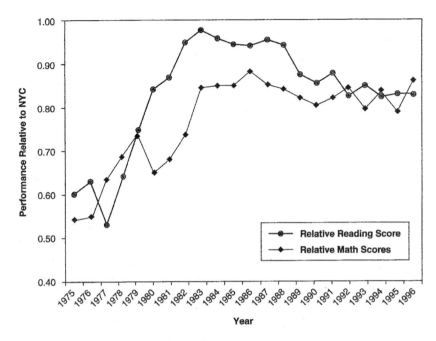

FIGURE 9.3. Performance by students in one school district. From *City Schools: Lessons From New York* (p. 322), by D. Ravitch and J. P. Viteritti (Eds.), 2000, Baltimore, MD: Johns Hopkins University Press. Copyright 2000 by Johns Hopkins University Press. Graphics redrawn with permission.

average. The available data permitted the study to use ordinary least-squares models (in reading and in mathematics) to test the correlation between reform and performance and also accounted for important covariates (each covariate representing a rival of some sort). The analysis was but one of several complementary and important quantitative and qualitative analyses reported fully in the cited work, including in-depth examination of the reform. All of the evidence supported the conclusion that the district's reform had led to the improved performance.

Quantitative data also may be relevant and available when a case study uses an embedded design. Although the main conclusions will deal with the case being studied, within a single organization, employees might have been surveyed (e.g., Lipset, Trow, & Coleman, 1956). Likewise, an evaluation of a revitalization strategy in a single neighborhood might have used regression models to analyze an extensive data set on housing sales in the neighborhood (e.g., Galster, Tatian, & Accordino, 2006).

Finally, an evaluation of a comprehensive children's mental health reform initiative can involve a highly complex mix of qualitative and quantitative data analyses (e.g., Bickman & Mulvaney, 2005).[12]

Replication Logic for Multiple-Case Studies

This chapter has discussed the desire to apply a replication or corroboratory logic to interpret findings across the cases in a multiple-case study. This logic emulates that used to address whether the findings from a set of multiple experiments—too small in number to be made part of any meta-analysis—support any broader pattern of conclusions.

The replication or corroboratory frameworks can vary. In a *direct* replication, the single cases would be predicted before the study started to arrive at similar results. In a *theoretical* replication, each single case's ultimate disposition also would have been predicted beforehand, but they might have been predicted to vary or even to contrast on the basis of

[12]The authors of the neighborhood revitalization and children's mental health studies did not label their studies as "case studies." Nevertheless, the main topic of both studies was a single entity (a neighborhood and an initiative), and in this sense the studies fit the definition of case studies used in this chapter.

preconceived propositions. Even more complex could be the stipulation and emergence of a typology of cases on the basis of the multiple-case study.

ADDITIONAL COMMENTS ABOUT THE POSITIONING OF THE CASE STUDY METHOD

Case Studies as a Partner to Qualitative Research

The sections thus far have provided an overview of case study research methods, but at least one more topic needs to be addressed. This topic derives from the observation that this chapter is included in Part I, Qualitative Research Methods, of this volume, suggesting that the case study method represents one of the strands within qualitative methods. Why is this?

On the contrary, some people would counterclaim that the present discussion of case study methods has largely assumed a postpositivist rather than hermeneutic or otherwise qualitative orientation—largely because of the rationalistic approach to the definition and design of case studies.

Complicating the debate, and as a reaction to the counterclaim (i.e., to "counter" the counterclaim), case studies are nevertheless found as part of several if not most strands of qualitative research, such as ethnographies (see Chapter 10 of this volume), life histories, narrative analysis (see Chapter 6 of this volume), and participatory action research (see Chapter 11 of this volume). The case study method may indeed serve well as an integral partner to each of these strands of qualitative research. The partnership mainly appears to be based on shared fieldwork practices (such as the use of participant observation to collect field data and the desire to triangulate among sources of evidence). Case studies also can be an accommodating partner for capturing other highly valued concerns in qualitative research, such as rendering participants' meanings of their own

real-world experiences, attending to self-reflexivity, and integrating contextual conditions.

This partnership role suggests that the case study method actually may not be a strand of qualitative research, any more so than case studies are to be regarded as one of the designs in quasi-experimental research. Thus, even the use of the label "qualitative case study" may be misleading, both by implying that the case study method is itself a strand within qualitative research[13] and by inadvertently underplaying the actual strand of qualitative research (ethnography, life history, grounded theory, etc.) within which the case study method is being used.

Case Studies as a Separate Research Method

Rather than being another strand, case study research may involve a separate research method. As a separate method, it would embrace both qualitative and quantitative research but not be a creature of either. If so, this would serve as a significant realization for research in psychology. The case study's shared heritage includes the early work in psychology previously cited, the studies by the Chicago school of sociology in the early 20th century, and anthropological studies also conducted in that era. The case study method, within and outside of psychology, seems to have its own design, data-collection, and analytic procedures. They set case study research apart from qualitative research. Nor should case studies be confused with any of the designs in quasi-experimental research. Freed from these associations, the separate procedures for case study research finally may have become easier to develop and recognize.[14]

As an indicator of the separateness of the method, contemporary students and scholars are now able to start and complete their own case studies, using qualitative or quantitative techniques as indicated throughout this chapter. The possible existence of a separate craft may be readily acknowledged every

---

[13]One popular textbook on qualitative research indeed treats case studies as a separate strand within qualitative research, along with four other qualitative strands—narrative research, phenomenology, grounded theory, and ethnography (Creswell, 2007).

[14]For instance, Platt's (1992) review of case study research in sociology revealed a hiatus, from 1970 to 1979, when 18 of 30 methodological texts did not mention much less describe the case study method *at all*, and of the remaining 12, five used the term "in such a limited sense that one might question whether it should have been counted" (Platt, 1992, p. 18). Platt then went on to explain how case study research resurfaced after this period, mainly on the basis of the articulation of distinct case study research designs and augmented data collection procedures. Since Platt's article was published, an even fuller methodological understanding of case study research, including its analysis procedures, has emerged and is still emerging.

time someone says she or he would like to do a case study as the *main* method for a new study—not unlike the alternative choices of saying one wants to do an experiment, a survey, or an ethnography. At the same time, the case study method is still evolving. New contributions are still needed to improve the method's design, data-collection, and analytic procedures. Such tasks pose the ongoing challenge of doing case study research.

References

Allison, G. T. (1971). *Essence of decision: Explaining the Cuban Missile Crisis.* Boston, MA: Little, Brown.

Allison, G. T., & Zelikow, P. (1999). *Essence of decision: Explaining the Cuban missile crisis* (2nd ed.). New York, NY: Addison Wesley Longman.

Bernard, H. R., & Ryan, G. W. (2010). *Analyzing qualitative data: Systematic approaches.* Los Angeles, CA: Sage.

Bickman, L., & Mulvaney, S. (2005). Large scale evaluations of children's mental health services: The Ft. Bragg and Stark County studies. In R. Steele & M. Roberts (Eds.), *Handbook of mental health services for children, adolescents, and families* (pp. 371–386). New York, NY: Kluwer Academic/Plenum. doi:10.1007/0-387-23864-6_24

Bradshaw, T. K. (1999). Communities not fazed: Why military base closures may not be catastrophic. *Journal of the American Planning Association, 65,* 193–206. doi:10.1080/01944369908976047

Bromley, D. B. (1986). *The case-study method in psychology and related disciplines.* Chichester, England: Wiley.

Burawoy, M. (1991). The extended case method. In M. Burawoy et al. (Eds.), *Ethnography unbound: Power and resistance in the modern metropolis* (pp. 271–287). Berkeley: University of California Press.

Campbell, D. T. (1975). Degrees of freedom and the case study. *Comparative Political Studies, 8,* 178–193.

Campbell, D. T. (2009). Foreword. In R. K. Yin (Ed.), *Case study research: Design and methods* (4th ed., pp. vi–vii). Thousand Oaks, CA: Sage. (Original work published 1984)

Campbell, D. T., & Stanley, J. (1966). *Experimental and quasi-experimental designs for research.* Chicago, IL: Rand McNally.

Cook, T. D., & Campbell, D. T. (1979). *Quasi-experimentation: Design and analysis issues for field settings.* Chicago, IL: Rand McNally.

Cook, T. D., & Foray, D. (2007). Building the capacity to experiment in schools: A case study of the Institute

of Educational Sciences in the U.S. Department of Education. *Economics of Innovation and New Technology, 16,* 385–402. doi:10.1080/10438590 600982475

Corbin, J., & Strauss, A. (2007). *Basics of qualitative research: Techniques and procedures for developing grounded theory* (3rd ed.). Thousand Oaks, CA: Sage.

Creswell, J. W. (2007). *Qualitative inquiry and research design: Choosing among five approaches* (2nd ed.). Thousand Oaks, CA: Sage.

Cronbach, L. J. (1975). Beyond the two disciplines of scientific psychology. *American Psychologist, 30,* 116–127. doi:10.1037/h0076829

Denenberg, V. H. (1982). Comparative psychology and single-subject research. In A. E. Kazdin & A. H. Tuma (Eds.), *Single-case research designs* (No. 13, pp. 19–31). San Francisco, CA: Jossey-Bass.

Duff, P. A. (2008). *Case study research in applied linguistics.* New York, NY: Routledge.

Dunbar, G. (2005). *Evaluating research methods in psychology: A case study approach.* Malden, MA: Blackwell. doi:10.1002/9780470776537

Galster, G., Tatian, P., & Accordino, J. (2006). Targeting investments for neighborhood revitalization. *Journal of the American Planning Association, 72,* 457–474. doi:10.1080/01944360608976766

Garmezy, N. (1982). The case for the single case in research. In A. E. Kazdin & A. H. Tuma (Eds.), *Single-case research designs* (No. 13, pp. 5–17). San Francisco, CA: Jossey-Bass.

Garvin, D. A. (2003). Making the case: Professional education for the world of practice. *Harvard Magazine, 106,* 56–107.

Golden, L. B. (2004). *Case studies in marriage and family therapy.* Upper Saddle River, NJ: Pearson.

Hersen, M., & Barlow, D. H. (1976). *Single-case experimental designs: Strategies for studying behavior.* New York, NY: Pergamon.

Kates, N. (2008). Integrating mental health services into primary care: The Hamilton FHT mental health program. In R. Kessler & D. Stafford (Eds.), *Collaborative medicine case studies: Evidence in practice* (pp. 71–82). New York, NY: Springer. doi:10.1007/978-0-387-76894-6_7

Kelly, E. A., & Yin, R. K. (2007). Strengthening structured abstracts for education research: The need for claim-based structured abstracts. *Educational Researcher, 36,* 133–138. doi:10.3102/0013189X07300356

Kessler, R., & Stafford, D. (Eds.). (2008). *Collaborative medicine case studies: Evidence in practice.* New York, NY: Springer.

Kratochwill, T. R. (Ed.). (1984). *Single subject research: Strategies for evaluating change.* New York, NY: Academic Press.

Lincoln, Y. S., & Guba, E. G. (1985). *Naturalistic inquiry.* Thousand Oaks, CA: Sage.

Lipset, S. M., Trow, M., & Coleman, J. (1956). *Union democracy: The inside politics of the International Typographical Union.* New York, NY: Free Press.

Lipsey, M. W. (1990). *Design sensitivity: Statistical power for experimental research.* Thousand Oaks, CA: Sage.

Lynd, R. S., & Lynd, H. M. (1929). *Middletown: A study in modern American culture.* New York, NY: Harcourt.

Miles, M. B., & Huberman, A. M. (1994). *Qualitative data analysis: An expanded sourcebook.* Thousand Oaks, CA: Sage.

Miyahara, M., & Wafer, A. (2004). Clinical intervention for children with developmental coordination disorder: A multiple case study. *Adapted Physical Activity Quarterly, 21,* 281–300.

Morgan, D. L., & Morgan, R. K. (2009). *Single-case research methods for the behavioral and health sciences.* Thousand Oaks, CA: Sage.

Neustadt, R. E., & Fineberg, H. (1983). *The epidemic that never was: Policy-making and the swine flu affair.* New York, NY: Vintage.

Patton, M. Q. (2002). Two decades of developments in qualitative inquiry. *Qualitative Social Work: Research and Practice, 1,* 261–283. doi:10.1177/147332500 2001003636

Platt, J. (1992). Case study in American methodological thought. *Current Sociology, 40,* 17–48. doi:10.1177/001139292040001004

Rolls, G. (2005). *Classic case studies in psychology.* Abingdon, England: Hodder Education.

Rosenbaum, P. (2002). *Observational studies* (2nd ed.). New York, NY: Springer.

Schein, E. (2003). *DEC is dead, long live DEC: Lessons on innovation, technology, and the business gene.* San Francisco, CA: Berrett-Koehler.

Schlesselman, J. J. (1982). *Case-control studies: Design, conduct, analysis.* New York, NY: Oxford University Press.

Scoville, W. B., & Milner, B. (1957). Loss of recent memory in bilateral hippocampal lesions. *Journal of Neurology, Neurosurgery, and Psychiatry, 20,* 11–22. doi:10.1136/jnnp.20.1.11

Shavelson, R. J., & Towne, L. (Eds.). (2002). *Scientific research in education.* Washington, DC: National Academies Press.

Sidman, M., Soddard, L. T., & Mohr, J. P. (1968). Some additional quantitative observations of immediate memory in a patient with bilateral hippocampal lesions. *Neuropsychologia, 6,* 245–254. doi:10.1016/0028-3932(68)90023-7

Small, M. L. (2009). "How many cases do I need?" On science and the logic of case selection in field-based research. *Ethnography, 10,* 5–38. doi:10.1177/1466138108099586

Supovitz, J. A., & Taylor, B. S. (2005). Systemic education evaluation: Evaluating the impact of systemwide reform in education. *American Journal of Evaluation, 26,* 204–230. doi:10.1177/1098214005276286

Sutton, R. I., & Staw, B. M. (1995). What theory is not. *Administrative Science Quarterly, 40,* 371–384. doi:10.2307/2393788

Tawney, J. W., & Gast, D. L. (1984). *Single subject research in special education.* Columbus, OH: Merrill.

Teske, P., Schneider, M., Roch, C., & Marschall, M. (2000). Public school choice: A status report. In D. Ravitch & J. P. Viteritti (Eds.), *Lessons from New York City schools* (pp. 313–338). Baltimore, MD: Johns Hopkins University Press.

Van Maanen, J. (1988). *Tales of the field: On writing ethnography.* Chicago, IL: University of Chicago Press.

Van Manen, M. (1990). *Researching lived experience: Human science for an action sensitive pedagogy.* Albany: State University of New York Press.

Whyte, W. F. (1955). *Street corner society: The social structure of an Italian slum.* Chicago, IL: University of Chicago Press. (Original work published 1943)

Yardley, L. (2009). Demonstrating validity in qualitative psychology. In J. A. Smith (Ed.), *Qualitative psychology: A practical guide to research methods* (pp. 235–251). Los Angeles, CA: Sage.

Yin, R. K. (1994). Discovering the future of the case study method in evaluation research. *Evaluation Practice, 15,* 283–290. doi:10.1016/0886-1633(94)90023-X

Yin, R. K. (2000). Rival explanations as an alternative to 'reforms as experiments. In L. Bickman (Ed.), *Validity and social experimentation: Donald Campbell's Legacy* (pp. 239–266). Thousand Oaks, CA: Sage.

Yin, R. K. (2009). *Case study research: Design and methods* (4th ed.). Thousand Oaks, CA: Sage.

Yin, R. K. (2012). *Applications of case study research* (3rd ed.). Thousand Oaks, CA: Sage.

Yin, R. K., & Davis, D. (2007). Adding new dimensions to case study evaluations: The case of evaluating comprehensive reforms. *New Directions for Evaluation, 113,* 75–93. doi:10.1002/ev.216

CHAPTER 10

USING FOCUSED ETHNOGRAPHY IN PSYCHOLOGICAL RESEARCH

Laura M. Simonds, Paul M. Camic, and Andrew Causey

This chapter provides a basic introduction to ethnographic methodology and explores its implementation in settings relevant to psychologists, arguing that its use potentially can give researchers insight into human experiences that are otherwise difficult to access. After describing some of the basic tools of this methodology (such as participant observation, map-making, census, informal interview, and object- or photo-elicitation), we make a case for considering and using a number of the key features underlying this approach to research, including sustained contact, attention to place, pansensory investigation, and emergent theory generation. We then discuss how psychologists can engage with a concentrated version of ethnographic methodology—focused ethnography—and provide two brief examples to illuminate its practical use.

DEFINITION

Focused ethnography (sometimes referred to as *microethnography* [Spradley, 1980, p. 30] or *applied ethnography*) is a methodological approach to understanding human behaviors in social contexts that examines the lived experiences of the researcher and individuals of specific subsets or segments of a group in limited contexts, usually for limited amounts of time, and with a specific predetermined topic in mind (Morse & Field, 1995, p. 154). The aim is to gather extensive bodies of data from a

variety of sensory impressions and using different methods that will be analyzed and interpreted by the researcher to understand the character of social interactions, often with the broader interest in exposing or explaining an existing problem and ways that it might be addressed (Roper & Shapira, 2000, p. 8). Researchers interested in this methodology would be well served by reading Muecke's "On the Evaluation of Ethnographies" (1994) to consider how their work might fare in critical academic arenas before starting their research.

HISTORICAL BACKGROUND AND RATIONALE

What is the aim of ethnographic research? Briefly, it is to examine closely social experiences and interactions by a particular group of people over a long period of time and in a defined and described environmental[1] context. This examination should attend to the perspectives of those who are the focus of the research: The ethnographer is trying to see and understand the world from the insiders' viewpoint, taking extensive careful notes and then documenting (publishing or otherwise making public) the observations, often in written form.

Before the 1890s, ethnographers, those researchers interested in documenting and describing the life-ways of other groups, tended to obtain their data by compiling facts and anecdotes from reports,

---

[1]*Environment* is broadly defined here to refer to a range of perceived or recognized surroundings such as the natural world, the human-made world (e.g., objects, buildings, infrastructures), the social world of relationships, the conceptual world of thoughts and theories, and the numinous world (e.g., dreams, hallucinations, beliefs).

DOI: 10.1037/13620-010
APA Handbook of Research Methods in Psychology: Vol. 2. Research Designs, H. Cooper (Editor-in-Chief)

diaries, and newspaper and magazine articles written by government officials, missionaries, merchants, and travelers (Wax, 1986, p. 28). These early ethnographers' compilations were necessarily fragmentary and their synthesis problematic because the information they gathered together was incomplete or inaccurate. People such as Edward Tylor (1832–1917) were primarily interested in addressing broad issues, such as race or religion, and used their collected data to discover wide-ranging views and broad connections. Because much of the data they were amassing were derived from the observations of individuals involved in colonizing projects, the Western slant and politically partisan perspectives of their observations were not overt to many early ethnographers.

With the publication of Malinowski's *Argonauts of the Western Pacific* in 1922, the field of ethnography changed. In his introduction, Malinowski described his work in the Trobriand Islands and stated that the only way to do effective cultural investigation was through what has come to be known as *participant observation*, that is, to camp

> right in their villages . . . (to) seek out
> the natives' society. And by means of this
> natural intercourse, you learn to know
> him, and you become familiar with his
> customs and beliefs far better than when
> he is a paid, and often bored, informant.
> (1961, p. 7)

Since then, participant observation has been the primary investigative tool of ethnographers, and it is the method most closely associated with the work of cultural anthropologists, although the approach is not without its critics.

For the past several decades, anthropologists have realized that the ethnographic endeavor is a mix of both objective and subjective observations (some would say only the latter), and by its very nature is interpretivist (e.g., see Clifford & Marcus, 1986; Geertz, 1973). In addition, ethnography has been critiqued as a dominating and colonializing project, an observation that cannot be simply brushed away.

To avoid becoming entangled in epistemological arguments and postmodern critiques, most contemporary ethnographers both embrace the subjectivity

of their work, by making honest reflexive note of their personal or theoretical assumptions as well as any limitations to their research. At the same time, they are enhancing the scientific aspects of data collection whenever possible, such as verifying information through various means and from multiple viewpoints. In the end, ethnographers are content to recognize that their observations are at once subjective interpretations of a mere fragment of their constrained perceptions of social experiences and, at the same time, sensitive and intensively engaged but fleeting glimpses of life as it is lived by others.

To make up for limitations resulting from subjectivity or interpretation, ethnographers try to write reflexively—that is, by taking careful note of themselves as researchers (Denzin, 1997, p. 217) and by focusing on the scope and depth of their observations (see Robben & Sluka, 2007). Ethnography is less about discovering cultural *truths* than it is about exploring individual behaviors, cultural artifacts, and social relationships. As Spradley said, "Rather than *studying people*, ethnography means *learning from people*" (1980, p. 3).

In ordinary ethnographic methodology, two aspects of data gathering are particularly important: extensive immersion in a cultural setting, and an interest in the insiders' perspectives (for a detailed discussion, see LeCompte & Schensul, 1999, pp. 9–21). In usual circumstances, a cultural anthropologist will prepare for research by learning appropriate languages spoken by the group or used to write about the group and then will read as many previous primary sources as possible; fieldwork is informed, not overwhelmed, by these prior investigations. The anthropologist then lives, works, and learns with the group for an uninterrupted period of time, usually at least a year (the amount of time usually allotted by funding agencies) but often longer. The assumption is that this longitudinal, or diachronic, study will provide the researcher with the time necessary to sense and record a broad enough range of experiences to begin seeing patterns in the group's social behaviors. Added to the longitudinal nature of the research is the anthropologist's desire to understand the *emic*, or insiders', point of view (Pike, 1967). This is not to suggest that a researcher can become of one mind with the group being studied, of course. Rather, it is assumed that human beings share the most basic abilities to sense the world, and that the outsider–ethnographer can make a concerted effort to empathize with, and consciously consider, the insiders' notions of their perceived world.

The ethics of ethnographic research require that researchers always make known their position and their intent (Spradley, 1980, pp. 20–25). Although one does not want to unduly influence the ordinary workings in a social setting, one also does not want to obtain data by any but transparent means. Each researcher choosing the ethnographic approach should follow the human subjects protocols of their discipline (for general information on institutional review boards and ethics committees, see Roper & Shapira, 2000, pp. 56–61). Privacy and protection of those researched is essential; in some cases, informants should be referred to by pseudonyms, and informed consent forms are almost always appropriate (see Morse & Field, 1995, pp. 54–64).

The ethnographer creates notes, in any media considered appropriate to the project but ordinarily in the form of written, sound, and visual recording, of the extensive experiences within the group. Analysis and synthesis of the data are often addressed once the researcher has returned from the field site. Much ethnographic work is interested in what has come to be known as grounded theory (Glaser & Strauss, 1967; also see Chapter 3 of this volume), that is, developing explanatory theories of social interactions on the basis of the data gathered rather than testing a preexisting theory (Morse & Field, 1995).

FOCUSED ETHNOGRAPHY

Long-term, in-depth ethnographic projects often contain within them instances of microethnography, and it is no doubt these that provided the foundation for focused ethnographic work. In such instances, ethnographers doing fieldwork for a year or more might find themselves in a new locale or with a different group or subgroup than that being

examined daily. Experiences from this temporary interaction are often fleeting yet felt to be of some potential value to the larger project and so must be intensely observed and recorded in detail. For example, in a research project among the Toba Bataks of North Sumatra, Causey (2003) centered on interactions with international tourists in the souvenir marketplace. The researcher also had the opportunity to travel with his carving teacher several miles inland to get advice from a spiritual healer on increasing the carving teacher's business. Causey only had 7 hours to gather as much information as possible about the lifeways of Bataks living beyond the tourist center as well as the practices of a traditional shaman and used the approach of focused ethnography to do so.

Focused ethnography, as a research methodology, by its very nature truncates some aspect of ordinary ethnographic research, whether it is the longitudinal aspect of the investigation, the scope of the topic, or the extent of social sphere or social subset to be studied. Because of this more focused interest, the researcher must enhance the intensity of data gathering, not simply of quantity but of quality as well, and does so primarily via documentation of enriched sensory experiences (see Knoblauch, 2005). The researcher's field notes must reflect the more focused nature of the project: They must become a detailed account of all that is sensed, not just the visual (Clifford, 1986, p. 11), realizing that the individuals living in the social context being studied will also be sensing whole environmental circumstances even if they may not be fully aware of it.[2]

Focused ethnographies often address particular structural questions when making observations (Spradley, 1980, p. 107)—that is, rather than simply observing social interactions in the context of a general subject, they attend to a specific question or problem. Even though the issue is more defined or the time more limited, the researcher should make note of the most wide-ranging sensory experiences to avoid allowing certain aspects—those outside of the structural question—to be ignored. This is done precisely because those other aspects may offer the

---

[2]Assumptions made in anthropology are that human beings are very much the same physiologically and as such can have an understanding of others and can decipher cultural patterns.

clue to understanding the complexity of the social situation. One should be attentive not simply to what is being said but also to the special jargons and inflections used. A focused ethnography is not created from the amassing of a collection of rushed interviews performed in a social setting but rather is built upon diverse impressions, interpretations, interventions, and observations gathered from a variety of different methods (what Geertz, 1973, referred to as "thick description").

Once a research site has been identified, it is important to document the environment thoroughly and sensitively (Spradley, 1980, p. 55). Because focused ethnographic projects often limit expenditures of time, they must expand sensory experience and the breadth of data-collection measures deployed (Marion & Offen, 2009, p. 13). Before designing a focused ethnography, researchers might consider how far in their everyday life they are aware of all senses and how this informs their thoughts, reactions, and experiences: not just the basic five senses but also the senses of apprehension, of curiosity, of being watched, of fear, of wonder, of delight—in short, any sense that is honestly felt or consciously identified. Acknowledging the full panoply of sensory experiences momentarily in familiar settings will assist investigations in new socioenvironmental contexts. For many psychologists, this approach may be seen as the antithesis of years of research training that sought to make them objective scientists, yet it is because of the positivistic epistemology underlying much of psychological inquiry that sensory and reflective experiences become discarded and highly suspect (Camic, Rhodes, & Yardley, 2003, pp. 4–7).

The ethnographic approach, therefore, requires the researcher to become hyperaware of the subtleties of existence and attuned to the potentially informative nature of these. For example, are the background sounds from a heating duct and a computer hum actually in harmony? Does the situation make the researcher feel at ease or vulnerable? Is the light soft, warm, sterile, or deadening? Does the physical layout of space engender cooperation or defensiveness? The researcher should recognize and store as many sense impressions as possible. If it is not possible for researchers to fully document sense impressions in the field site, they must try to recreate their experiences with words as soon as possible once returning from the field. Notes at this preliminary stage of research must be written in as much detail and with as precise vocabulary as possible because such first impressions of environment will fade quickly with repeated exposure. First impressions are often strong and should be recorded in detail because they may have bearing on the researcher's ability to empathize with the individuals being studied; it is better to have too much such data documented in the notes than too little.

A NOTE ON NOTES

The methodology of a focused ethnographic approach to research is not unlike other participatory social science projects that hinge for their validity on sharp observations, precise definitions, and extensive notetaking. In the case of focused ethnography, however, time is usually short. To compensate, notes must be meticulous and detailed, encompassing aspects of life and environment that are sometimes dismissed. If circumstances allow, the researcher should carry a small (well-bound) booklet and mechanical pencil at all times and, perhaps, an electronic notebook; this is how the researcher records memorable or evocative experiences that are fleeting, or words and terms that are uttered—or muttered—in the social setting (Morse & Field, 1995, p. 111; Spradley, 1980, p. 63). Taping thoughts and observations with a small recorder might work in certain situations, but researchers should recognize that such behavior might attract unwanted, perhaps even suspicions, attention.

If note-taking in the research site is obtrusive, then the researcher must practice developing short-term memory to mentally record all experiences, words, smells, sights, and events for later documentation: Reliving the day from the moment of waking to the moment of typing observations in a quiet setting will enable the researcher to tap into the remembered, or mental, notes as well as more sensory experiences. As is the case with other scientific research, notes should be duplicated for safety and protected for integrity, particularly if personal or private information of human participants is included.

METHODOLOGY

Ethnographic methodology includes a complex spectrum of methods of which only a few are discussed here. Because of this limitation, we might refer to the focused project as an "ethnographic approach" rather than an example of "doing ethnography" (Blum Malley & Hawkins, 2010). Metaphorically, the different methods are perhaps better thought of as complementary tools in a toolbox rather than stacked bricks in a foundation: They can be used independently and freely; they are not necessarily contingent upon each other. Each focused ethnographic project is unique, so the researcher must carefully examine which aspects of the investigation are being limited to decide which methods are appropriate and useful in obtaining a thorough picture of the circumstances under investigation. The data obtained by any one method are often supported by that derived by other methods. This process of triangulation of methods not only creates diversity in the data pool but also helps validate observations (Roper & Shapira, 2000, p. 24). With that said, the researcher should also realize that the brief list of methods presented here is incomplete and that the first one—participant observation—is the most essential, most complex, and oftentimes the most informative.

Participant Observation

As noted, participant observation is perhaps the most fundamental method associated with the ethnographic approach. Extensive general information on this method is available (e.g., see LeCompte & Schensul, 1999; Spradley, 1980), so the goal here is to address its use in focused ethnographic projects. One of the attractive aspects of this method is its seeming naturalness: One simply lives in the social context of interest, experiencing what it is like to be an insider, and then produces copious notes. Sometimes, it is precisely this easy: The researcher locates a cultural setting, integrates within it by finding a social place, takes extensive notes on both personal experiences and observed behaviors, and all the while documents details of the physical environment. More often, however, the researcher's efforts to fit in are stymied, essential observations are hidden from view, and note-taking is continuously

interrupted. To get the most out of this method, one must be socially, intellectually, and methodologically flexible, resisting the urge to allow the project's outcome to depend on its data exclusively. One of the difficulties is the persistent need to hover somewhere in and around various positionings: participant–observer (Morse & Field, 1995, pp. 107–111), insider–outsider (Berreman, 2007), and subject–object (Crapanzano, 1986). Serious issues can be averted as long as any identity dilemmas are carefully noted in the record. In general, the more socially thorough, contextually detailed, and honestly reflexive the participant–observation notes are, the more useful they will be.

Mapping

Once the first impressions of the field site have been recorded in detail, and recognizing that sensory rich notes should continue throughout the project, the researcher should make use of other ethnographic methods. A particularly useful tool is the simple map (Morse & Field, 1995, p. 115), a line drawing of the field site from a bird's-eye view based on the researcher's experience of space (i.e., not traced from an existing map) and including such things as geographic edges, boundaries, paths, intersections, and landmarks (Lynch, 1977). The map can be photocopied and shown to individuals in the research group for corrections and additions, but the researcher should also make a mental note of how the corrections or additions are made (with irritation? in anger?) and what is added. Researchers might consider asking respondents to draw their own maps of the area of concern and then use these revisions to gain an understanding of the insiders' differing perspectives and uses of the space.

Making a Census and Creating a Genealogy

Knowing who is involved (directly, indirectly, peripherally) in the social interactions of a field site often is crucial to understanding unfolding of events and behaviors there. For this reason, many researchers will make a census of the site. Ordinarily, simple headcounts can provide the data required. In other cases, a more thorough door-to-door or desk-to-desk census must be created, detailing such things as gender, age, or job or marital status, whatever general demographic information is useful to the project. If details about social connections are needed, then *genealogies*—a term used in its broadest sense including not only kin reckonings but also such things as business flow charts of employment histories and hierarchies—should be collected as well.

Informal Interview

Informal, or conversational, interviews can elicit detailed and thorough information about a social context. As opposed to a formal interview, during which the researcher has specific written questions to be answered, the informal interview is more relaxed and follows the ordinary flow of conversation, which helps to create a natural connection with the respondent (Spradley, 1980, p. 23). Before engagement with a conversant, the researcher may have developed a number of talking points that are memorized; these are raised in any order they might occur in a conversation primarily to encourage the individual to speak freely on the focal topics. Although notes might be taken at the time, the researcher should be aware that a precise mental recording of the conversation may be less likely to disrupt the flow of words and may still provide solid data, as long as the conversation is recorded as quickly as possible afterward.

Object or Photo Elicitation

In some research settings, individuals are unwilling or unable to speak freely on the issues being investigated. In situations such as these, the researcher might consider using physical prompts to encourage a person to speak (Morse & Field, 1995, p. 119). These prompts, whether in the form of an actual object, a document, or a photograph, can be provided by the researcher (e.g., a photograph of a building or person) or can be requested from the respondent, such as asking to see a favorite object (Wallendorf & Arnould, 1988). The purpose is to give individuals an anchor for personal reflection: a focus for their attention that will inspire them to speak or, in some cases, write about their thoughts, feelings, impressions, and opinions. Documentation of the physical prompt, such as a photograph of the

object or photocopy of the image, must be kept with the rest of the data.

FOCUSED ETHNOGRAPHY IN PSYCHOLOGICAL RESEARCH

Thus far, our description of the characteristics and practice of focused ethnography as an approach to research might seem rather alien to psychologists, perhaps even to those who situate themselves within what might broadly be termed the qualitative tradition. So, why might psychologists consider using focused ethnography? Put simply, our suggestion would be that this approach to research allows the psychologist to gain insight into human behavior and experience that otherwise might be difficult to access. Consequently, adopting this approach as part of a research repertoire invites consideration of different types of research question and, as a result, potentially allows access to a broader range of understandings. By way of illustrative examples, we aim to make a case that focused ethnography provides a way for students and established researchers to engage with the principles of ethnography to answer important psychological questions. Given the truncation of standard ethnographic procedures, the focused approach allows consideration of smaller scale issues over more limited periods of time than is the case for more traditional approaches to ethnography, making the approach relevant for both masters and doctoral students in psychology. We also hope to make a case for the approach's appeal to applied psychologists who want to understand the context of their (inter)action in a contextualized and time-effective way. Finally, we might also consider that the focused ethnographic approach could be relevant to psychologists as educators in expanding the skills, repertoire, and critical faculty of students as apprentice researchers. Its methods and epistemology invite curiosity, critique, and rigor and challenge long-held assumptions. In this respect, if nothing else, ethnography encourages an approach that treats the familiar as strange, thus increasing a sense of engagement with the psychosocial and cultural world and a questioning frame of mind. An additional benefit would be the appreciation of how qualitative and quantitative methods might be blended within a research project. This is not to say that all focused ethnographies would do so and, given that what we are describing here is an *approach to* rather than a prescriptive *way of doing* focused ethnography, the old maxim holds that the data collection methods need to be chosen on the basis of their appropriateness in addressing the questions of enquiry. To this end, mixed methods cannot be precluded from the outset. Furthermore, like other methods, focused ethnography has limits to its application. It is certainly challenging to consider the application of this approach to the realm of psychological enquiry, generally, because its methods are quite different than those psychologists typically deploy. Additionally, the central requirements of sustained contact and participant observation will limit its range of application. Engaging with the possibilities afforded by focused ethnography, however, raises the potential of turning our attention toward overlooked areas.

If we are to state that focused ethnography involves a close examination of social experience and interaction by members of a particular group, then what does this mean for psychological research? First and foremost, it should be obvious that this approach to research takes a contextualist epistemology. That is, emphasis is placed on the importance of understanding the context in which meaning is situated and constructed as revealed through action, thought, signs, symbols, and other ways of communicating, or the absence of these, but crucially emphasis is placed on a detailed analysis of the real-world context of meaning and not some contrived setting (although an ethnography of the real world of the laboratory could well be the focus of an ethnographic study). Context can denote historical time, location, groups, and individuals. Given the centrality of the social world in shaping perceptions, attitudes, and experience and how these are conveyed to the researcher, it is evident that a one-time interview with a respondent that is devoid of the contextual factors pertinent to the issue at hand is also a contrived setting. Thus, it should also be clear that focused ethnography does not entail looking at a single data source, such as narratives gained from interviews, divorced from their context of production. Instead, the approach

attempts to document how meaning is constructed in social contexts using a range of data-collection methods, drawing on diverse modalities, to accumulate a rich corpus of data that is then analyzed and patterned by the researcher to illuminate an issue and, more important, to make unknown issues apparent.

Mixed methods and triangulation of data sources are not concepts that are unusual for psychologists. But perhaps what is not so customary is the use of the range of the diverse methods and modalities described here. In this sense, focused ethnography might seem for many psychologists to be unacceptably subjective and interpretative. It does indeed involve subjectivity, but this does not mean that careful observation and recording of the context gives way to ungrounded and fanciful interpretation. As Clifford and Marcus (1986) observed, "to recognize the poetic dimensions of ethnography does not require that one give up facts and accurate accounting for the supposed free play of poetry" (p. 26). To put this another way, social interactions are dynamic and multifaceted and, as such, can be witnessed and documented only partially regardless of the research method at hand. But, recognition that a single *truth* position is untenable does not inevitably imply a postmodern stance toward research enquiry. Our contention would be that the psychologist wishing to apply focused ethnography does so recognizing that the glimpse is partial, as it is with any data-collection and enquiry method, and that the rejection of a single truth position does not give way to research methods that lack rigor or the rejection of empirical science.

To the extent that the methods of focused ethnography require considered use, rigorous application, diligent recording techniques, and grounded data analysis, this is entirely congruent with psychology as an empirical science. We would suggest that focused ethnography allows the researcher to document partial realities with greater depth and breadth precisely because it attempts to access multiple and differing viewpoints. As such, in the context of focused ethnography, this partiality relates to the necessary selection of a slice of time and place, but the attempt to understand this segment of culture aims for comprehensiveness. As such, the obvious strength of this approach for psychologists lies in its encouragement of blending a multiplicity of data sources. As Silverman (2007) observed, the endeavor of qualitative research has become equated with asking people questions, most often in interview or focus group formats, with its attendant implication that we need to get inside people's heads to find out what they experience, as if knowing that experience were the most important thing and assuming that it could be accessed reliably. Silverman cautioned researchers not to "assume people's experiences are your most reliable source of data and that this always means you need to ask people questions" (p. 145). Indeed, it is evident to psychological science that there is little reliable correlation between what people say they do and what they actually do. Past behavior, on the other hand, is a robust predictor of future behavior. As part of an ethnographic approach, one may ask people questions and, indeed, this is often the case whether done by way of interviews, focus groups, or psychometric instruments or surveys. But Silverman also urged us to consider how much in our routine contexts are taken for granted and invited us to "treat 'obvious' actions, settings and events as potentially remarkable" (p. 146). Doing so does not require us to ask but to look.

Having attempted to describe the approach of focused ethnography and its potential relevance for psychologists, the chapter now sketches two brief case studies of how focused ethnography can be used. In the examples, one of a completed ethnography and one in which we consider how focused ethnography might be used, we emphasize key features enunciated earlier in this chapter, such as sustained contact, attention to place, pansensory investigation, and emergent theory generation. Some of the tools outlined earlier are applied to the case studies.

A word on the use of theory: As we have noted, focused ethnographies tend to address particular structural questions—that is, a focus on a specific question or problem within the general context of study. In this way, an enquiry at the outset would be guided by theoretical frameworks as this would shape the focus for enquiry. During the course of the work, however, problems and issues may also be uncovered by ethnographic enquiry and, indeed, the appeal of the approach is most persuasive when this

is the case. As such, starting questions do not entirely shape the enquiry. Instead, observation and description of the culture allow questions to emerge and hence, the emphasis on emergent theory generation.

FOCUSED ETHNOGRAPHY WITHIN EXPERIMENTAL AND QUASI-EXPERIMENTAL RESEARCH

Experimental and quasi-experimental designs, both large and small scale, are generally not considered likely arenas in which to undertake a focused ethnography. Yet these research designs offer a compelling opportunity to extend our understanding of how meaning is structured by members of a group (e.g., understanding the response of different socioeconomic groups to curbside recycling) within an intervention designed by the researcher. One of the significant advantages of ethnography is its flexibility to engage in a wide range of settings, participant groups, time frames, and financial budgets. A focused ethnography, rather than a longer and less purposeful traditional ethnography, is likely to be more appropriate to the research aims of many psychologists (Camic & Simonds, 2006). In particular, within a focused ethnography, participants are linked by location, such as within a hospital unit (Smallwood, 2009), clinic (Neal, Brown, & Rojjanasrirat, 1999), school (Rhodes & Camic, 2006), or neighborhood health care center (Macfarlane, 2008). These locations are "not a place of residence or culture in the anthropological sense, but share behavioural norms and a common language" (Waltz, Strickland, & Lenz, 2005, p. 217) as do sports (Krane & Baird, 2005) and virtual worlds (Hine, 2000).

As we have stated, a focused ethnography provides a set of methodological tools to look at specific roles and behaviors within a highly contained and limited context, such as the complex day-to-day interactions, for example, that occur in a cardiac care unit (Smallwood, 2009), thus allowing the clinical researcher and service manager to obtain a greater understanding of implicit, subtle, and systemic factors often impossible to measure quantitatively. Within experimental and quasi-experimental studies, this approach can also be used to examine detailed components or parts of a multifaceted intervention to answer different subquestions embedded within large-scale research projects. This can be particularly useful if the research seeks to gain an in-depth understanding of how participants (a) engage with a specific intervention, (b) interact with other participants in a defined setting, and (c) negotiate the group culture that, in part, forms how the intervention is applied and interpreted. Although psychologists are not the only social scientists to ignore contextual elements when reporting research findings—sometimes writing lablike accounts of research even when it is not taking place under controlled conditions of experimentation—much of psychological research treats the research context as nonconsequential: a venue to be controlled and manipulated without regard to the values, emotions, cognition, or motivation of participants' lived lives.

The School and Community Climate Project

The School and Community Climate Project is an example of a longitudinal, mixed-methodological study that employed an overarching quasi-experimental, matched-group design to investigate the impact of teacher-designed interventions on the social and emotional climate of public middle schools in suburban Chicago (Rhodes & Camic, 2006; Rhodes, Camic, Milburn, & Lowe, 2009). Approximately 2,600 students in Grades 6 to 8 (ages 12–14) and 180 teachers participated in the study. Three of the five schools involved in the 5-year project were intervention schools where teachers joined teacher-led working groups (TWG) to design and complete intervention projects within their specific schools. To carry out particular projects, teachers were provided with consultant and financial resources as well as political support from building and district administrations.

The aim of the project was to ascertain whether the social and emotional climate of middle schools could be improved through teacher-led innovation and change initiatives rather than the usual state board of education, U.S. Department of Education, or researcher-designed interventions that dominate school improvement strategies within U.S. public schools. Although this study used a rigorous and

well-respected matched-group design, along with reliable and valid psychometric measures, the design could not provide researchers with insight into key issues, such as how teachers worked together within TWGs, how innovations were decided on, the perceptions teachers held toward building and district administrators, teachers' relationship with parents, factors that led to participation and nonparticipation among teachers in developing school improvement projects, and the challenges teachers experienced in having new roles as "change agents" within school systems that had not previously consulted teachers about innovation and school improvement issues other than to decree that they were to carry out state and national initiatives.

To address these issues, a decision was reached in the early design stages of the study to conduct multiple, focused ethnographies in the three intervention schools. The researchers wanted to know whether teacher-led school improvement projects were effective, with standard measures and quantification being used to make this determination, but they also wanted to know *how* teachers engaged with this new and radical concept that placed them at the center of designing, implementing, and assessing school improvement. To know the answer to the latter question, focused ethnographies were undertaken within 20 of the 29 TWGs that were in operation at the three intervention schools. One of those is briefly discussed in the next section as an illustrative example of a focused ethnography within a large-scale experimental study.

The Respecting Differences TWG. The Respecting Differences TWG set out to assess and reduce bullying and teasing within School A in the study. "This group was established in response to student and teacher concerns about aggressive student behaviour" (Rhodes & Camic, 2006, p. 46) toward other students. Six teachers in School A participated in this TWG. Planning meetings to discuss the issue of student bullying occurred after school in five 90-minute meetings over 3 months. Issues addressed during these meetings included how to accurately determine the incidence and influence of bullying, the social impact of bullying on all students, the effect bullying has on the learning process, the emotional risk it places on vulnerable students, and the role of teachers in intervening to change student behavior and attitudes. One of the authors (PC), also a coprincipal investigator of the study, attended these meetings and observed the sites where bullying was reported to occur (in hallways between class periods, at school sports events, in classrooms when a teacher was not present, in the lunchroom, at bus stops). The author negotiated his involvement in this TWG by offering to share his field notes with members, agreeing to actively participate in discussions about bullying as requested by TWG members, and to support teachers as coresearchers as they developed their interventions.

Data that emerged from working with this group included the following: an initial TWG survey of students and staff to determine the extent of bullying, a physical map of the school and separate maps of geographic areas within and near the school where bullying was reported to occur, and field notes from meetings and from observations of student interactions in the noted geographic areas. A key initial issue was the negotiation of the researcher's role in the Respecting Differences TWG. Teachers were not reluctant to allow a participant observer but in return they wanted a favor of sorts, and that favor was help to put their plans into action. For this focused ethnography to be effective, the role of the researcher had to change from the more usual neutral, distanced, and objective outsider, typical of most psychological research, to that of a coworker helping out. Although the researcher definitely did not maintain a leadership or organizational role, he was also not a bystander. He informally interviewed teachers and students, made maps, and took copious notes of meetings and observations and shared these with TWG members.

What was learned from a focused ethnography?
The work of this TWG resulted in a significant reduction in reported bullying episodes in School A as compared with other intervention or control schools. A focused ethnography, however, was not needed to demonstrate this outcome because standardized measures and incidence reporting would have been sufficient. The focused ethnography provided additional information not accessible through standardized measurements and an experimental design that centered on determining effectiveness of the overarching teacher-led school improvement intervention. A particularly noteworthy finding that came about from the addition of a focused ethnography was the surprising ambivalence teachers had toward the concept of bullying. Although policies to reduce bullying had been mandated by state law, the uncertainty of what was bullying, how to define it, and whether it was just part of normal development were issues that both divided and united teachers in this school. Competing cultural norms clashed, as some teachers believed student aggressiveness toward each other was part of the usual school experience, whereas others believed it was possible to eradicate it entirely. The conversations teachers had with each other mirrored some of the issues being played out in the larger U.S. society, namely, what is the role of government and government institutions to modify and control the behavior of citizens. In regards to understanding why some social experiments (interventions) fail or succeed more so than others, a focused ethnography can, such as this one did, provide added information about the issues being played out behind the scenes of standardized questionnaires and quantified findings. In this study, the subtle and not so subtle debate among teachers regarding teasing and bullying interventions provides strong evidence that the attitudes, motivations, and cultural beliefs of the people who are charged with carrying out an intervention (e.g., teachers) needs to be better understood and taken into account to more correctly understand why a social intervention succeeds or fails. The scientific merit or social worth of an intervention may be thwarted by social and cultural factors; appreciating these factors provides additional insight into why some large-scale intervention experiments may succeed whereas others do not. A focused ethnography, embedded within an experimental design, can provide the researcher with additional information about distinctive components of an intervention and the experience participants had undertaking that intervention.

Using Focused Ethnography to Study Clinical Settings

This example focuses on challenging behavior in adults with intellectual disabilities[3] and, more specifically, care staff's responses to these behaviors and what might underpin these. Challenging behaviors can be described in various ways but studies have typically focused on aggression toward others and self-injurious behavior. Research has focused on the ways in which care staff respond to these (typically a focus on their propensity to help). A body of research has assessed Weiner's (1986) theory of attribution as a model for predicting the helping behavior of care staff toward people with intellectual disabilities who exhibit challenging behavior. A review by Willner and Smith (2008) of 10 studies testing the principles of attribution theory, published between 1990 and 2006, presented the conclusion that the evidence for attribution as an explanatory model for staff helping behavior is, at best, mixed. Willner and Smith proposed that the use of vignettes in these studies and failure to define robustly what constitutes helping behavior might be reasons for mixed findings. Some evidence, however, suggests that even when *real* instances of staff behavior are the focus of investigation, attribution theory still fails to provide a coherent understanding (e.g., Bailey, Hare, Hatton, & Limb, 2006; Wanless & Jahoda, 2002).

The attribution theory approach involves seeing whether theoretically derived factors help explain variance in helping behavior (that might be defined in various ways) often on the basis of hypothetical vignettes. As such, these studies attempt to predict what a person might do given (a) their perception of the stability of the behavior (low stability means optimism for change and hence the perceived value and likelihood of helping increases), and (b) their perception of the controllability of the behavior (low controllability engenders sympathy and decreases anger, thus increasing the likelihood of helping; see Willner & Smith, 2008). Studies in this area focusing on attribution theory take a model-driven,

hypothesis-testing approach to understanding and, ultimately, predicting helping behavior. As indicated, the predictive power of this model is variable and, in some studies, findings are counter to those hypothesized. How might focused ethnography be used in the attempt to understand staff responses, particularly helping behavior, in this context?

Revealing contextualized meanings. Members of care staff that work with challenging behavior operate in a complex and emotive environment. Research studies in this area that do use observational methods often focus on recording staff responses (e.g., the types of responses and how these might reinforce challenging behavior and hence be construed as instances of unhelpful behavior). Naturally, underpinning any response are cognitive, emotional, and motivational factors and, by drawing on the theoretical framework of attribution theory, researchers have attempted to understand underpinning factors such as causal beliefs, anger, and optimism. Taking a different approach to elucidating beliefs that might influence reactions, Wilcox, Finlay, and Edmonds (2006) used a discourse analytic approach to understand the constructions of aggressive challenging behavior by care staff and the functions of these. As well as finding an individual pathology discourse that construed causes of challenging behavior as being internal and stable, what was also evident was a context discourse in which challenging behavior is seen as an understandable reaction to environmental conditions. As such, the context discourse is more optimistic of change, whereas the individual pathology discourse is not. Crucially, staff were shown to hold both discourses simultaneously. The work of Wilcox et al. helped provide a rationale for focused ethnography because these authors drew attention to structural and contextual factors that likely influence discourses—a position of relative powerlessness (either when comparing themselves with professionals or in their ability to effect change), poor pay, and perceptions of being blamed or seen to be ineffective. As the authors noted, "It may be fruitful in the future to consider which contexts encourage care staff to construct

---

[3]In times past and in different locations, the terms *mental retardation* and *mental handicap* have been used. In the United Kingdom, the term *learning disability* is used and, increasingly it seems, in both the United Kingdom and the United States the term *intellectual disability* is used.

challenging behaviour in particular ways. The care staff's own context may be an influential factor in such an analysis" (Wilcox et al., 2006, p. 212).

Example application of focused ethnography. A focused ethnography, then, would attempt to take a holistic approach to understanding the context in which direct care staff work; that is, how the meaning of challenging behavior and working with it is understood and negotiated *within* context. This would be achieved primarily by sustained engagement with the environment, by way of time-limited but intensive participant observation (e.g., in an inpatient setting or community facility) and mapping of the environment. The resources available for observation will vary from study to study, but, as an example, it might take place for 1 or 2 days a week over a 2- to 3-month period, varying the days of the week when the participant observer is present. As indicated, dense and detailed field notes of this observational work are essential in focused ethnography and these might, for example, include sketches, impressions, and details of interactions, relationships, and events. In aiming to apprehend direct care staff's viewpoint from the inside, one might ask, "What are the customs, beliefs, and practices that give meaning for care staff working in this environment?" Observation would focus on actors, places, and activities to understand what is done, when, by whom, and why. In observing the environment, several aspects might be focused on, such as the following: How are the contexts of interaction between staff and clients structured? What are the cultural markers of this group (e.g., physical space, time, documentation, procedures, rules, policies, beliefs, expectations, etc.)? Are some markers implicit and others explicit—which ones and why?

In documenting the environment in field notes, the researcher might make note of access to the setting, geographic situation, age and style of facility, level and type of environmental noise and pollution, lighting, the physical layout of the space, how staff and clients occupy the space, signage or injunctions, signals of hospitality, comfort levels (furniture, heating levels), interactive spaces between staff and clients, and spaces where the staff are "off work." All these will give the researcher a rich sense of place

and will allow detailed contextualization of the study findings. Staff might also map their environment as this could give insight into social and spatial relationships. Marking of important features of the environment could give a sense of how participants experience their environment. For example, are there sites of intense activity, anxiety, and respite? The taking of a census might also be used to map the context. This might involve asking staff to delineate all those who are involved in the daily work and interactions in the setting. Hierarchies may be a particularly important aspect to map as these might reveal how the actions of others impinge on care staff and the level of control they have. This could illuminate influences on the day-to-day behavior and perceptions of care staff. Such interdisciplinary relationships might also be observed within team meetings and in interactions between staff and clients' family members. In this context, participant observation can be a persuasive approach given that beliefs and expectations about work, relationships, and responsibilities, especially in contexts in which individuals may be sensitive to criticism and blame, might remain hidden in verbal accounts.

An additional way in which the context of care staff might be apprehended and documented is via the use of photo elicitation. Staff might either be provided with images or be asked to document their work via photographs, either ones they have taken or other images that seem important to them. Additionally, the photographs could be used as a helpful anchoring tool for an interview that aims to delve deeper into staff experience, to engage respondents in more sensitive topics, or to provide a structure for their written accounts (e.g., in the form of daily diaries). Although this might raise some ethical and practical complexities and constraints when taking photographs in context, photographs may provide a bridge between the physical realities of an environment and the psychological effects of them. Images captured, for example, might depict interactions between staff and clients or staff engaged in particular activities that might give access to views of the work done in this context.

In addition to these data sources, informal conversations and more formal interviews with care staff would be conducted. To complement observational data, these might focus on perceptions of factors that influence responses to challenging behavior but all the while being mindful that the focus would be on understanding how these different perceptions might be influenced by the environmental context, organizational structural factors, and the theories, feelings, beliefs, and expectations of care staff. This information, combined with the other data sources, might allow a broader perspective on the circumstances, individual and contextual, that influence care staff responses to challenging behavior.

APPLICATION TO PRACTICE TRAINING CONTEXTS

We suggested earlier in this chapter that the ethnographic approach may be used as a research methods educational tool. Cobb and Hoffart (1999) described participant observation, taking field notes, and interviewing (and critiques of these) in real-world contexts as part of doctoral-level qualitative methods training for nurses, arguing that this allows strengths and gaps in expertise to be identified and competences expanded. The methods of focused ethnography outlined in this chapter, along with the examples, not only provide novel research strategies but also are offered to stimulate thinking regarding research methods training.

CONCLUSION

We hope we have been able to interest readers to consider the merits of integrating a focused ethnographic approach in their research. It is a powerful tool to contextualize the how, where, and why aspects of quantitative research that is often absent from reports. For those who use qualitative methods, it equally helps to illuminate aspects of research that are ignored. Research with human participants takes place in a specific location with specific people who are interacting with each other; understanding more about this interaction and how *participants* understand their participation, within the context of research ranging from randomized controlled trials to single-case studies, will help to contextualize and humanize psychological research and provide, we argue, urgent and important information.

References

Bailey, B. A., Hare, D. J., Hatton, C., & Limb, K. (2006). The response to challenging behaviour by care staff: Emotional responses, attribution of cause and observations of practice. *Journal of Intellectual Disability Research, 50,* 199–211. doi:10.1111/j.1365-2788.2005.00769.x

Berreman, G. D. (2007). Behind many masks: Ethnography and impression management. In A. C. G. M. Robben & J. A. Sluka (Eds.), *Ethnographic fieldwork: An anthropological reader* (pp. 137–158). Malden, MA: Blackwell.

Blum Malley, S., & Hawkins, A. (2010). Translating cultures: Ethnographic writing in the composition classroom. Retrieved from http://www.engagingcommunities.org

Camic, P. M., Rhodes, J. E., & Yardley, L. (2003). Naming the stars: Integrating qualitative methods into psychological research. In P. M. Camic, J. E. Rhodes, & L. Yardley (Eds.), *Qualitative research in psychology: Expanding perspectives in methodology and design* (pp. 3–15). Washington, DC: American Psychological Association. doi:10.1037/10595-001

Camic, P. M., & Simonds, L. M. (2006, November). *Focused ethnography: A methodology for clinical psychology research.* Paper presented at the Group of Trainers in Clinical Psychology Annual Conference, Cardiff, Wales.

Causey, A. (2003). *Hard bargaining in Sumatra: Western travelers and Toba Bataks in the marketplace of souvenirs.* Honolulu: University of Hawaii Press.

Clifford, J. (1986). Introduction: Partial truths. In C. James & G. E. Marcus (Eds.), *Writing culture: The poetics and politics of ethnography* (pp. 6–11). Berkeley: University of California Press.

Clifford, J., & Marcus, G. E. (1986). *Writing culture: The poetics and politics of ethnography.* Berkeley: University of California Press.

Cobb, A. K., & Hoffart, N. (1999). Teaching qualitative research through participatory coursework and mentorship. *Journal of Professional Nursing, 15,* 331–339. doi:10.1016/S8755-7223(99)80063-5

Crapanzano, V. (1986). Hermes' dilemma: The masking of subversion in ethnographic description. In C. James & G. E. Marcus (Eds.), *Writing culture: The poetics and politics of ethnography* (pp. 51–76). Berkeley: University of California Press.

Denzin, N. K. (1997). *Interpretive ethnography: Ethnographic practices for the 21st century.* Thousand Oaks, CA: Sage.

Geertz, C. (1973). *The interpretation of cultures: Selected essays.* New York, NY: Basic Books.

Glaser, B. G., & Strauss, A. L. (1967). *The discovery of grounded theory: Strategies for qualitative research.* Chicago, IL: Aldine.

Hine, C. (2000). *Virtual ethnography*. London, England: Sage.

Knoblauch, H. (2005). Focused ethnography. *Forum: Qualitative Social Research, 6*. Retrieved from http://www.qualitative-research.net/fqs/

Krane, V., & Baird, S. M. (2005). Using ethnography in applied sport psychology. *Journal of Applied Sport Psychology, 17*, 87–107. doi:10.1080/10413200590932371

LeCompte, M. D., & Schensul, J. J. (1999). *Designing and conducting ethnographic research, Part 1, ethnographer's toolkit*. Walnut Creek, CA: AltaMira Press.

Lynch, K. (1977). *Image of the city*. Cambridge, MA: MIT Press.

Macfarlane, J. E. (2008). A focused ethnography about treatment-seeking behaviour and traditional medicine in the Nasioi area of Bougainville. *Papua and New Guinea Medical Journal, 51*, 29–42.

Malinowski, B. (1922). *Argonauts of the Western Pacific: An account of native enterprise and adventure in the archipelagoes of Melanesian New Guinea*. New York, NY: Dutton.

Marion, J. S., & Offen, J. L. (2009). Translating multisensory experience: An introduction. *Anthropology News, April*.

Morse, J. M., & Field, P. A. (1995). *Qualitative research methods for health professionals* (2nd ed.). Thousand Oaks, CA: Sage.

Muecke, M. (1994). On the evaluation of ethnographies. In J. M. Morse (Ed.), *Critical issues in qualitative research methods* (pp. 187–209). Thousand Oaks, CA: Sage.

Neal, J., Brown, W., & Rojjanasrirat, W. (1999). Implementation of a case-coordinator role: A focused ethnographic study. *Journal of Professional Nursing, 15*, 349–355. doi:10.1016/S8755-7223(99)80065-9

Pike, K. L. (1967). Etic and emic standpoints for the description of behavior. In D. C. Hildum (Ed.), *Language and thought: An enduring problem in psychology* (pp. 32–39). Princeton, NJ: Van Nostrand.

Rhodes, J. E., & Camic, P. M. (2006). Building bridges between universities and middle schools: A teacher-centred collaboration. *Educational and Child Psychology, 23*, 42–51.

Rhodes, J. E., Camic, P. M., Milburn, M., & Lowe, S. R. (2009). Improving middle school climate through teacher-centered change strategies. *Journal of Community Psychology, 37*, 711–724. doi:10.1002/jcop.20326

Robben, A. C. G. M., & Sluka, J. A. (2007). *Ethnographic fieldwork: An anthropological reader*. Malden, MA: Blackwell.

Roper, J. M., & Shapira, J. (2000). *Ethnography in nursing*. Thousand Oaks, CA: Sage.

Silverman, D. (2007). *A very short, fairly interesting and reasonably cheap book about qualitative research*. London, England: Sage.

Smallwood, A. (2009). Cardiac assessment teams: A focused ethnography of nurses' roles. *British Journal of Cardiac Nursing, 4*, 132–138.

Spradley, J. P. (1980). *Participant observation*. New York, NY: Holt, Rinehart & Winston.

Wallendorf, M., & Arnould, E. (1988). "My favorite things": A cross-cultural inquiry into object attachment, possessiveness, and social linkage. *Journal of Consumer Research, 14*, 531–547. doi:10.1086/209134

Waltz, C. H., Strickland, O., & Lenz, E. R. (2005). *Measurement in nursing and health research* (pp. 215–228). New York, NY: Springer.

Wanless, L. K., & Jahoda, A. (2002). Responses of staff towards people with mild to moderate intellectual disability who behave aggressively: A cognitive emotional analysis. *Journal of Intellectual Disability Research, 46*, 507–516. doi:10.1046/j.1365-2788.2002.00434.x

Wax, R. H. (1986). *Doing fieldwork: Warnings and advice*. Chicago, IL: University of Chicago Press.

Weiner, B. (1986). *An attributional theory of motivation and emotion*. Berlin, Germany: Springer.

Wilcox, E., Finlay, W. M., & Edmonds, J. (2006). "His brain is totally different": An analysis of care-staff explanations of aggressive challenging behaviour and the impact of gendered discourses. *British Journal of Social Psychology, 45*, 197–216. doi:10.1348/135910705X43589

Willner, P., & Smith, M. (2008). Attribution theory applied to helping behaviour towards people with intellectual disabilities who challenge. *Journal of Applied Research in Intellectual Disabilities, 21*, 150–155. doi:10.1111/j.1468-3148.2007.00390.x

CHAPTER 11

CRITICAL PARTICIPATORY ACTION RESEARCH AS PUBLIC SCIENCE

María Elena Torre, Michelle Fine, Brett G. Stoudt, and Madeline Fox

Cultivated within the long history of psychological research dedicated to social action, this chapter traces one stream of action research, critical participatory action research (critical PAR), across the 20th and the 21st centuries in the field of psychology. Rooted in notions of democracy and social justice and drawing on critical theory (feminist, critical race, queer, disability, neo-Marxist, indigenous, and post-structural), critical PAR is an epistemology that engages research design, methods, analyses, and products through a lens of democratic participation. Joining social movements and public science, critical PAR projects document the grossly uneven structural distributions of opportunities, resources, and dignity; trouble ideological categories projected onto communities (delinquent, at risk, damaged, innocent, victim); and contest how "science" has been recruited to legitimate dominant policies and practices.

In the following pages, we sketch an intentional history of the seeds of critical participatory research as they have been nurtured, buried, and then rediscovered throughout the past century of social psychology. We then turn, in some detail, to Polling for Justice, a contemporary piece of quantitative and qualitative social inquiry, designed as a participatory survey of and by youth in New York City with adult researchers, poised to track social psychological circuits of injustice and resistance as they affect the educational, criminal justice, and health experiences of urban youth (Fox et al., 2010). We purposely focus on a very traditional psychological method—the self-completed questionnaire—to illustrate how methods, analyses, and products shift when engaging critical PAR as an epistemology. The chapter closes with a discussion of critical science to make explicit the validity claims of critical PAR.

The history of critical PAR has been told through different legacies. Within education studies, critical PAR is associated with the tradition of liberation theology and Paulo Freire. Within postcolonial studies, critical PAR's lineage stretches back to the revolutionary praxis of Orlando Fals Borda in South America and Anisur Rahman in Asia. Within psychology, critical PAR is typically linked to the intellectual legacy of Kurt Lewin. In the first section of this chapter, we review a set of equally significant yet shadowed scholars, particularly women, and men of color, who helped carve the scientific path toward critical PAR as practiced within psychology in the 21st century. Each of these scholars invented social psychological methods to contest what Ignacio Martín-Baró (1994) called the "collective lie" of prevailing ideological constructions of social problems and to awaken a sense of injustice—through research—to mobilize everyday people for change. Our intent in excavating this scholarship is to create an intellectual genealogy for contemporary PAR through a line of critical science projects in which engaged social scientists have collaborated with communities to interrogate the gap between dominant ideologies and human lives, using deeply participatory methodologies accountable to the goals of social justice.

ON THE GROUNDS OF HISTORY

As many scholars have documented (Cherry, 2008; Cherry & Borshuk, 1998; Danziger, 1990; Finison,

DOI: 10.1037/13620-011
APA Handbook of Research Methods in Psychology: Vol. 2. Research Designs, H. Cooper (Editor-in-Chief)

1978; Harris, 2009; Torre & Fine, 2011), from the discipline's beginning one can find psychologists, philosophers, and educators who have argued for epistemological and methodological approaches to social inquiry that incorporate complex human activity within social political contexts, include multiple levels of analysis, allow for human diversity, and speak with a sense of social responsibility. Over time, however, narrow understandings of expertise, logics, and experimentalism have prevailed. Much of the early critical scholarship was pushed to the margins, relegated to footnotes, or lost from textbooks altogether.

Writing in the 1800s, Wilhelm Dilthey called for the budding field of psychology to distinguish itself as a holistic science that situated the study of human experience in a social historical context. Wary of the growing trend toward natural "scientific" thinking and positivism that resulted in fracturing the human condition into disconnected, measurable parts, Dilthey proposed methodologies that would iterate back and forth between the relations of the part and the whole, crafting a complex, contextualized understanding of humans, human thought, and experience (Dilthey, 1883/1989; Fox, 2010).

Firm in his belief in the importance of context and that no two human thoughts or experiences could be the same, Dilthey argued that causal explanations had limited applicability in understanding human beings and social relations (Fox, 2010). Dilthey was not alone in his concerns about experimentalism and reductionist practices in psychology. Wilhelm Wundt, the much-heralded father of modern experimental psychology, expressed similar concerns about the limits of experimentation (Danziger, 2000). Perhaps drawing from his often-overlooked work in social psychology and anthropology, Wundt called for a psychology that included social historical context and a use of what we now would call qualitative methods (Danziger, 1990; Harris, 2009).

Several years later, W. E. B. Du Bois, a student of William James, launched a series of studies based in history and focused on the social conditions of African Americans in the United States at the Sociological Laboratory at Atlanta University, where he was director and professor of economics and history from 1896 to 1914. The most famous of these

studies—the Philadelphia Study; the Farmville, Virginia Study; and the Atlanta University Studies—investigated the impact of racial inequalities and structural racism on urban and rural African Americans, documenting and analyzing regional economics and history, birth and death rates, conjugal relations, occupations, wages and class distinctions, businesses and trades, and communal organizations and experiences of group life (Green & Driver, 1978).

Du Bois's (1898) scholarship signifies an early analysis of social psychological and political dynamics that shape social problems. Du Bois's studies were designed intentionally to locate the "Negro Problem," not in African Americans as individuals or a group but *in the conditions under which they live.* Taking the relationship between human experience and context seriously, Du Bois's studies represent some of the first large-scale community surveys in the United States. With teams of undergraduates, he documented the impact of social and economic conditions on African American communities and in turn created a detailed account of structural racism at the turn of the century (Du Bois, 1898). Thus, we see in Du Bois an early example of positioning social science as a method for social change. The Atlanta Sociological Laboratory became a center for social inquiry, producing historically informed research with both qualitative and quantitative methods. Du Bois's laboratory studies, presented annually at the Atlanta University Conferences, demonstrated his belief that empirical research when joined with structural analyses could affect social change and that policy could be grounded in scientific fact rather than opinion and ideology (Wortham, 2005), a belief that undergirds critical PAR in the 21st century.

With parallel intellectual commitments, Jahoda, Lazarsfeld, and Zeisel (1931/2003) undertook a social psychological analysis of everyday life in Marienthal, a community outside of Vienna, Austria, circa 1930, where villagers suffered individually and collectively from what was then called the Worldwide Economic Crisis. Using ethnography and time charts, conversations with and observations of everyday people, Jahoda et al. refused academic language that would distance them from their informants. They relied instead on the words and metaphors of people in the community to demonstrate the devastating material, psychological, and existential consequences of severe and collective unemployment in Central Europe.

Carrying these progressive, critical intellectual commitments forward into the 1940s and early 1950s, social research experienced a vibrancy with the action-oriented studies and writings of researchers such as Benedict and Weltfish (1943), Watson (1947), Williams (1947), and Selltiz and Wormser (1949). Motivated by the atrocities of World War II and lingering racial segregation in the United States, these scholars sought to unite theory and action to better understand and respond to the potential extremes of racial and ethnic hatred. During this period, there was a palpable urgency in the social scientific literature around using social research to build and protect democracy.

In the 1940s, housing activist Wormser and researcher Selltiz, both research associates at Lewin's Center for Community Interrelations (CCI), formalized a method called the Community Self-Survey as a "tool of modern democracy" (Allport, 1951, p. vii). CCI was the research department of the American Jewish Congress and served as the "activist arm" of Lewin's Center for Group Dynamics at the Massachusetts Institute of Technology (Cherry & Borshuk, 1998; Marrow, 1969). Within CCI, Wormser and Selltiz led the effort to systematize the self-survey approach reflecting the Center's dual desire to positively affect group dynamics and keep method and action in constant conversation. Their work marked an important period in the history of social science, whereby engaged research was understood to have a key role in democratic nation-building (Torre, 2006)—in other words, that social psychology in its most "scientific" form had a responsible and active role to play in interrupting injustice and in helping people understand their relationships to each other.

The community self-survey was introduced as a strategy to provoke individuals and communities to examine their individual lived experiences within a broader understanding of (the denial of) civil rights in their community on the basis of *facts*, or "objective evidence about the total situation" (Wormser & Selltiz, 1951a, p. 1). Echoing the work of Du Bois (1898) and Jahoda et al. (1931/2003), the desire and

continual design for facts that undergirds the survey work speaks to the somewhat uncritical belief of the time that an objective *fact-based* understanding of social issues would be instrumental in solving social problems.

The self-surveys departed from past research approaches in their dedication to participation. The hallmark of the method was its use of large-scale community participation and democratic education practices throughout the research process and particularly in data collection. The method was initially developed by future Fisk president Charles S. Johnson and colleagues at the Race Relations Department (later Institute) established by the American Missionary Association at Fisk University. Throughout the 1940s and 1950s, self-surveys, sometimes referred to as community audits, were conducted in cities across the United States, providing some of the first opportunities for people of different racial and ethnic backgrounds to engage in meaningful integrated work, in this case, social research for social justice.

Typically, researchers were invited into a community by a "sponsoring committee" made up of traditional community leaders as well as those already interested in race relations. Diverse committees and subcommittees of researchers and community members were formed in the areas of housing, schools, employment, churches, social welfare, and health services to conduct the research. They employed traditional and innovative methods, which were based in the local knowledge of the *fact-finders* (or what we would call *co-researchers*). At times, the methods explicitly relied on the diversity of the research partners, pairing Black and White investigators. Research findings were disseminated widely and resulted in the formation of municipal Fair Employment Practices laws, local councils on race relations, and the ending of discriminatory bans against African Americans in housing.

Building on the work of Johnson (1943), Wormser and Selltiz (1951a, 1951b) made early arguments for what might be called radical inclusion within the research process. The theory behind self-surveys was that through *participation*, large numbers of *community members* become *invested* in the issues and outcomes of the research—in *documenting and*

173

challenging the discrimination and inequalities of their own community. CCI was particularly careful about selecting sampling sites that would deepen understandings of intergroup relations:

> A self-survey differs from other surveys in its change-producing potential only to the extent that a representative cross section of the community participates. It is important, therefore that the sponsors should include as many *different elements* in the community as possible as well as the *largest number* of people possible. Participation by a representative cross section of the community necessarily means participation by people who have not previously been concerned with problems of discrimination and intergroup relations as well as those who have. Unless previously unconcerned people take part, one of the basic principles underlying self-surveys—the concept that participation in fact-finding is likely to develop a feeling of responsibility to do something about the facts found—becomes inoperative. (Wormser & Selltiz, 1951a, p. 615)

The self-survey work reveals an early example of a social psychology for social justice that foreshadows 21st-century PAR commitments to the ongoing interrelationship between research and action. An inclusive participatory approach challenged taken-for-granted practices of government, housing, and education; extended boundaries of expertise by legitimating traditionally unrecognized knowledge; and recognized that those most intimately involved in the practices of the community would have the keenest insight into the questions asked, where evidence lay and what methods would be most appropriate. In addition, Wormser and Selltiz (1951b) wrote to popularize the method far and wide, hoping communities across the nation would launch self-surveys and audits, "making available to communities a basic pattern which they could adapt to their own situations" (p. 13). It is refreshing to re/member a history of activist social science ideas that insisted, at once, on engaging

cross-site macro patterns of injustice while being of use to local communities.

Traveling ahead 30 years and into El Salvador, psychologist and Jesuit priest Martín-Baró (1994) used public opinion polls to wedge open public debate on the experiences of disenfranchised Salvadorans. Like Wormser and Selltiz, Martín-Baró developed research methods to explore social injustice with the hope of inspiring social change. His work departed, however, in its explicit call for a liberatory praxis within science.

In *Writings for a Liberation Psychology*, Martín-Baró (1994) argued,

> Thus to acquire a new psychological knowledge it is not enough to place ourselves in the new perspective of the people; *it is necessary to involve ourselves in a new praxis* [italics added], an activity of transforming reality that will let us know not only about what is, but also about what is not, and by which we must try to orient ourselves toward what ought to be. (p. 29)

Although the public opinion polls were designed to systematically reveal social conditions and the concrete inequalities of the lives of Salvadorans, Martín-Baró was also strategic about their potential as *social mirrors*, scientific instruments designed to reflect back lived realities that were being denied by dominant ideologies and "official" definitions of Salvadoran life. Interrupting the distorted social narratives, or *collective lie* as Martín-Baró termed it, with aggregated data from everyday people not only eased what he referred to as the "schizophrenia" of living one experience while being told you are or should be having another, but also allowed people to reunderstand their individual experiences through a collective lens. In other words, the experience of seeing the reality of one's life in the mirror alongside others creates openings for new levels of analysis of one's experience, of connections to larger social–political frameworks, and of transformative thought (Martín-Baró, 1994).

Before he was killed by government soldiers in 1989, Martín-Baró outlined a framework for liberation psychology. He argued that for psychology to understand and contribute to interrupting injustice, it needs to attend to the ways the production of knowledge is shaped by social, historical, and political systems. In other words, researchers must challenge the designs of their studies to answer questions about the purpose of research, who benefits, who is made vulnerable, and how might the research facilitates social transformation. He put forth a science *of* the oppressed rather than *for* the oppressed that called for research designed from the perspective of those most affected by injustice.

Martín-Baró (1994) articulated three urgent tasks for the field that have since been built upon by participatory action researchers (Brydon-Miller & McGuire, 2009; Fine & Torre, 2004; Lykes & Mallona, 2008): recovering historical memory, de-ideologizing everyday experience, and utilizing people's virtues. Critical PAR takes on these tasks because it makes central underrecognized knowledges and virtues; validates expanded notions of expertise; and develops research designs and methods that unearth forgotten alternatives in the history of science and fight for social justice, that connect past and contemporary struggles for equal rights, and that "interrupt consistency" (Arendt, 1958) or what has become normal (e.g., Anand, Fine, Surrey, & Perkins-Munn, 2002).

Steeped in transformative practices, theorizing and researching with those most marginalized in an effort to mobilize for social justice, critical PAR enjoys a long, but too often forgotten, lineage in psychology. These projects of social research for the public good can easily be seen as precursors to what we now call critical PAR. We turn now to consider a contemporary PAR project, Polling for Justice (PFJ).

POLLING FOR JUSTICE

To demonstrate how one might pursue a critical PAR project, the next section of the chapter describes PFJ, one of our recent projects and a present-day embodiment of this historical lineage. There is no single way to conduct critical PAR. Rather, we believe critical participatory researchers are bound by a set of critical and participatory commitments throughout the research process, such as finding

ways to harness varying forms of expertise; coconstructing what questions most need asking; collaborating to develop both theory and method; coanalyzing data; and creating ongoing and multiple forms of dissemination with a principled purpose of working against unjust, oppressive structures. The next four sections describe how the researchers of PFJ addressed these commitments.

PFJ is a PAR project designed to examine the extent to which urban youth (ages 16–21) experience injustice across sectors of education, criminal justice, and health. An interdisciplinary collaboration among faculty and students at the City University of New York, a committed group of youth researchers, and youth-centered community organizations,[1] the primary methodological instrument was a text-based and Internet-based survey coconstructed by youth and adults. With participation at the heart of theory, methods, crafting questions, and analyzing the data, PFJ gathered data from more than 1,110 New York City youth.

As a multigenerational research collective, we have produced scholarly and activist, empirical and performative products, including academic articles, political testimony, and youth-organizing pamphlets. Additionally, in the spirit of Du Bois's pageants, we have developed a process we call "Performing the Evidence."

Deep Participation of Varied Forms of Expertise in Coconstructing Research Questions

PFJ began with a 2-day intensive research camp for New York City young people, university faculty, graduate students, community organizers, and public health professionals. We posed a single, simple challenge to the group: to collectively design a large-scale, citywide research project, creating a youth survey of standardized and home-grown items and conducting a series of focus groups, to document youth experiences across various public sectors of the city. We explained that the youth and adults were recruited because of their distinct experiences, knowledge, and forms of expertise. The young people and adults formed groups to pool

---

[1]Organizations include the Urban Youth Collaborative and the Annenberg Institute for School Reform.

what they knew about prisons and their impact on youth, foster care, immigration and deportation, homeless shelters, educational experiences, peer relationships, access to health education, worries about feeling safe, exposure to and involvement with violence, and their concern for communities. We created a graffiti wall where anyone could jot down the questions they would want to ask of other New York City teens.

Signs with different topics printed on them were hung on doors, and each participant chose the room where they wished to contribute their expertise. In one room, people were working on issues of education and schooling; in another, safety and violence; in a third, youth experiences with the criminal justice system; and in a fourth, the focus was on public health. These rooms were filled with experts from many perspectives—youth from New York City more knowledgeable than any about the daily experiences of their own lives, scholars from the academy, and experts from the community—as well as findings and tools from published studies. In these rooms, various kinds of expertise blended, clashed, and ultimately heightened the expert validity of the survey we collaboratively produced.

In one room, a group gathered to take on the task of deciding how the PFJ survey should ask New York City youth about experiences with the criminal justice system. After scouring existing instruments and surveys, the group found the questions largely inadequate. They found little that reflected their own knowledge and experiences inside and at the gateways of the criminal justice system. They wanted to ask questions about school; *and* public space; *and* police, school safety agents, and transit authority employees. This group decided they needed to generate original questions. In collaboration with Sarah Zeller-Berkman (2010), they developed a matrix of detailed questions about both positive and negative experiences with police. Items included "In the last six months: I was helped by a police officer"; "I was given a summons/ticket"; "I was arrested"; "I was stopped for the clothes I was wearing"; and "I was touched inappropriately by police."

Following the first days of intensive work by the four expert groups, the survey went through countless revisions with input from the broad group of youth researchers, graduate students, faculty, youth organizers, community members, public health professionals, and city officials. Through the lengthy survey revision process, where we reworded and reworked the survey over 6 months, the questions about youth interactions with the police remained unchanged.

In the final version, 17 questions assessed youth experiences with specific social policies of dispossession that disrupt social and institutional relationships: in education (e.g., "Have you ever dropped out or been pushed out of high school?"), family and home life (e.g., "Have you ever been homeless?"), and policing and prison (e.g., "Have you ever been in jail or prison?"). We also decided to measure youths' experience of *human insecurity* by asking the extent to which money, health, housing, education, and police cause stress in youth lives.

Collaboratively Building Theory: Circuits of Dispossession and Privilege

Listening to conversations among the youth during initial meetings and since, it was easy—and painful—to hear the uneven distribution of *human security* across race, ethnicity, class, gender, immigration status, sexuality, and ZIP code. For low-income youth of color and for lesbian, gay, bisexual, transsexual, and questioning (LGBTQ) youth, a palpable sense of human insecurity contaminates growing up.

The PFJ survey was designed to document the ways in which key social policies, institutions, and practices systematically facilitate or deny youth human rights and opportunities and the ways in which youth mobilize to resist, negotiate, and challenge collectively technologies of dispossession. We intended to investigate how urban youth experience, respond to, and organize against the profoundly uneven opportunities for development across three sectors: education, health care, and criminal justice within the five boroughs of New York City. That is, the PFJ researchers set out to theoretically and empirically examine what we call *circuits of dispossession* (Fine & Ruglis, 2009) and *pools of youth resistance* in New York City.

Our partnerships were strategic. Like the collaborations of Wormser and Selltiz (1951b), Kenneth

Clark (Cherry, 2004), and Martín-Baró (1994), PFJ was explicitly designed to gather and funnel social science evidence into organizing campaigns for justice—violence against girls and women, police harassment, college access, high-stakes testing, and access to comprehensive sexuality education, to name just a few.

Participatory Analysis: "Stats-n-Action"

As data analysis began, we found we needed to devise participatory methods to engage the youth researchers in quantitative analysis. When we first experimented with working through the data with high school researchers, we found the process engaged the group unevenly. We shifted analytic strategies and started running analyses in real time, inductively. In a series of seminars we call "Stats-n-Action," our research team of high school youth and academics have waded through, understood, and analyzed statistical output together. This engagement with quantitative data across age and comfort with mathematics became crucial as we generated theories on the basis of a participatory process from our findings.

To illustrate, in the preliminary data, after more than 400 responses had come in, we were noticing young people reporting high numbers of interactions with the police. The PFJ survey asked about racial and ethnic identity via the following categories: Black or African American, African Caribbean, Asian, South Asian or Pacific Islander, White, Middle Eastern, Latino/a, Native American or American Indian, Alaskan Native, Other (with room to specify). Survey-takers could check as many boxes as they needed to describe their identity, and any survey-taker who checked more than one box was coded "multiracial." In the preliminary findings, we were puzzled because the data showed that youth who reported the highest level of interaction (positive and negative) with the police were youth who identified as multiracial. These youth were reporting more interactions than youth who identified singularly as Latino/a or African American/Black/African Caribbean. The PFJ youth researchers generated a theory to explain this finding, suggesting that we look more closely at the category multiracial to see which specific boxes were checked. Several youth

researchers hypothesized that many in that category would identify as "Black and Latino/a." We ran the analysis in real time during the research meeting and found that youth who checked both Latino/a *and* African American/Black/African Caribbean were indeed the most likely to report interactions with the police. The youth researchers were, in general, not surprised by this finding and additionally wondered how skin tone might play a factor. We came to our understanding of Black, Latino/a, and Black and Latino/a youth experience of police through our cross-generational, participatory analysis of quantitative data. Furthermore, the youth researchers' speculation about skin color raised interesting potential questions for further research.

PFJ now sponsors a regular Stats-n-Action series for high school researchers, undergraduates, doctoral students, community activists, and junior faculty. Our multigenerational participatory quantitative analysis sessions have been inspired by Tukey's (1977) statistical techniques, particularly his theoretical approach. In the mid-1970s, Tukey developed exploratory data analyses (EDA), an inductive, iterative, descriptive, graphical approach to statistics. EDA emphasizes looking at variation and outliers, taking seriously sample participants on their own terms, rather than standing in as representatives for a larger population. Our experiences confirm Tukey's belief that "exploratory data analysis is detective work—numerical detective work—or counting detective work—or graphical detective work" (Tukey, 1977, p. 1). Our budding efforts to merge participatory action research and exploratory data analysis (PAR-EDA) have proven a surprising and fruitful methodology for doing multigenerational research.

Performing the Evidence: Insisting on Audience Participation in Action

In 1915, Du Bois produced *The Star of Ethiopia*, a pageant of African American history, with a cast of hundreds of everyday people performing a rich counterstory about the history and culture of African Americans. With pageantry, performance, journalism, and circus theater, Du Bois challenged the *collective lies* being told about African Americans by circulating new stories of injustice and resistance, and provoking alternative possibilities about "what could be" into the public African American imagination. In a similar spirit, PFJ has also taken a performative turn. Eager to twin society inquiry and theater, we have collaborated with performing artists to creatively present our evidence to varied audiences. Our performative work and engagement with embodied methods builds on scholars such as Gallagher (2008) and Pratt (2000), who have written provocatively about using theater and role-play in research and youth spaces, as well as Kip Jones (2006) and Norm Denzin (2003), who have encouraged social scientists to experiment with performance as a means to share research in a multimedia world.

As we analyzed the data, the PFJ youth researchers decided to develop skills in community theater, including Playback Theatre (Fox, 1994; Salas, 2007) and Theatre of the Oppressed (Boal, 2002), as a methodology for collaborative analysis and dissemination of our findings. Over the course of 1 year, youth learned improvisational theater skills, collaborated with guest artists from various traditions, and used an embodied approach to analysis and dissemination of the PFJ study.

The PFJ performances were conceived as an extension of the *ethic of participation*. The audiences included teachers, parents, school administrators, young people, social scientists, community members, police, Department of Education officials, and policymakers—viewers, listeners, and observers as well as thinkers, learners, and those who will effect change. To activate the participation of audience members, the performances had three phases. In the first phase, the researchers started with a presentation of largely quantitative data in embodied, visual, storied ways that employed metaphor, humor, maps, graphs, and numbers. In the second phase, audience members were invited to respond and react to the data using a form of improvisation called Playback Theatre (Fox, 1994; Salas, 2007) to transform the audience members' affective responses into theater on the spot. Finally, in the third phase, the PFJ researchers invited audience members to contribute their own expertise and experience in generating knowledge and visions for action in light of the PFJ data.

If we consider the PFJ survey as an instance of Martín-Baró's (1994) social mirror, one that provides a critical reflection of the lived realities of urban youth of color, then with performances of the data, the PFJ researchers held up a "social mirror-in-the-round," creating a visual and lived link between researcher and audience, and between youth, adults, and structural inequalities. Through action and performance, the PFJ researchers asked audiences to think critically about their own position in the social arrangements that produce (and can possibly interrupt) negative youth experiences with police, education, and public health. The move to performance reflects a desire to challenge a social psychological dissociation from the evidence, to interrupt and incite the passive audiences and bystanders, to refuse diffusion of responsibility (Darley & Latané, 1968), and to engage a dynamics of political solidarity (Subasic, Reynolds, & Turner, 2008).

In keeping with a commitment to use research findings to support ongoing organizing and advocacy within New York City, PFJ collaborated with youth activist groups (such as the Brotherhood/Sister Sol and Girls for Gender Equity), published academic articles from the PFJ data in scholarly journals and books (Fox et. al, in press), participated in community speak-outs, sponsored workshops for youth, testified in city-sponsored hearings, sent op-ed pieces to national and daily newspapers, and presented papers at professional conferences. In other words, PFJ quite deliberately circulated PFJ evidence through the academy, communities, youth organizing, and policy institutions.

THE COMMITMENTS OF CRITICAL PAR AS A PUBLIC SCIENCE

This chapter has journeyed through history and method, recuperating buried commitments that have been central to some of the most progressive works within social psychology, and has elaborated through the example of PFJ these commitments for critical PAR in the 21st century. Although we will not dwell on the nature of the erasures, we do recommend that readers consult the writings of Tuana (2006) on the production of epistemological ignorance to understand how distinct threads of psychological research have been stitched into the canon, whereas others have been dropped (see also Cherry,

2008; Jackson, 2004; Rutherford & Pickren, 2008). We end by bridging the intellectual genealogy of critical PAR to key decisions of theory and design used in PFJ to make explicit how critical PAR carries forward and expands intellectual legacies embedded in the recesses of psychology's history and contributes to a responsible framework of scientific validity.

Any discussion about epistemology and methodology should include a focus on validity. For many, approaching research methods through a critical PAR framework is, in itself, thought to be a move toward stronger validity. Although we recognize and respect the importance of traditional notions of validity, the commitments essential to critical PAR as an epistemological stance raise certain tensions with conventional validity. The commitments to democratic participation and action force us to explicitly contend with issues that may remain hidden in more traditionally conducted psychological research. Sometimes the tensions suggest a need to redefine familiar notions of validity, whereas other times they require new types of validity. To illustrate, we close this chapter by outlining these negotiations in the PFJ project. We consider each epistemological commitment on its own terms, as elaborated in Table 11.1.

As we sketch key decisions made in PFJ, we heed Harding's notion of "strong objectivity" (1993), taking seriously the very concepts that lie at the heart and arguably the "soul" of social inquiry. Furthermore, we echo Du Bois's (1898) call for the integration of science and ethics, placing issues of objectivity, validity, generalizability, and justice at the center of the scientific enterprise.

Critical Theory

Critical inquiry deliberately shifts the gaze from "what's wrong with that person?" to "what are the policies, institutions, and social arrangements that help to form and deform, enrich and limit, human development?" and "how do people resist the weight of injustice in their lives?" Du Bois (1898) struggled to reframe the "Negro problem" by analyzing racialized patterns of housing, education, access to health care, and criminal justice. Jahoda et al. (1933) told the story of making lives and meaning in an Austrian community by interrogating how people live in communities infected by massive unemployment. Clark collaborated with Ellis (E. Ellis, personal communication, May 14, 2004) and other men in prison to refract the origins of the "crime problem" off of the individual men deemed criminals and back onto state neglect of communities long abandoned by the economy and quality schooling. Wormser and Selltiz (1951b) engaged everyday people from different racial groups to track the economic, social, and psychological impress of discrimination on community life and public institutions.

In line with these works, critical PAR lifts responsibility for social problems off the backs of individuals who have paid the greatest price for injustice and exposes the social and political conditions that produce and justify injustice. As displayed in the top row of Table 11.1, critical PAR purposefully theorizes how these conditions enter the bodies, aspirations, and relationships of people by documenting the geography of injustice and by chronicling the varied forms of resistance.

In this spirit, PFJ has been designed explicitly to understand youth experiences as negotiated within the uneven geography of opportunities: to document how race, class, gender, sexuality, and community map onto education, health, criminal justice, and psychological outcomes. We believe working with interdisciplinary teams of adults and youth as co-researchers has strengthened our understandings of key constructs in youth development, such as resilience, critical consciousness, and resistance. This iterative exchange from theory to participatory deconstruction of the data back to theory strengthens our construct validity and creates an opportunity to theorize adolescent development from the vantage point of marginalized youth.

Our participatory knowledge-building also enhances what we would consider our *ecological validity*, borrowing from Bronfenbrenner (1979). With youth on the research team, we learned intimately about the ways in which circuits of dispossession operate across levels: embedded in state policy (e.g., high-stakes testing and finance equity), traversing through institutional relations between youth and educators, and penetrating young people's educational aspirations and achievements. We then learned how these educational outcomes spill

TABLE 11.1			

Epistemological Commitments of Critical Participatory Action Research (PAR)

Epistemological commitments of critical PAR	Intellectual legacy	Theory and design decisions in polling for justice	Validities for a critical participatory science
Reframing the problem through critical theory	Du Bois (1898); Jahoda, Lazarsfeld, & Zeisel (2003); Ellis & Clark (E. Ellis, personal communication, May 14, 2004); Fine et al. (2005); Martín-Baró (1994)	Integrated critical race, feminist and queer theory into our framing of youth problems Analyzed urban youth experiences in the context of racialized history, policies, institutional practices and race/gender/sexuality/class arrangements Resisted victim blaming analyses by assessing outcomes in the macro, meso, and micro context of power, uneven opportunities and varied forms of dispossession Traced the dialectics of circuits of dispossession and human rights over space and contexts	Construct validity—to ensure that analyses recognize the impact of history and structures of injustice on individuals and communities Ecological validity—to document the multiple levels of the "problem," including macro, meso, and micro
Deep and broad participation	Wormser & Selltiz (1951a, 1951b); Fine & Torre (2004); Lykes & Mallona (2008); Brydon-Miller & McGuire (2009)	Blended local youth knowledge (privileged and marginalized) in conversation with varied forms of "legitimated" expertise, e.g., lawyers, public health researchers, social psychologists, judges, educators, and so forth Organized the research team to ■ Craft questions ■ Consult/challenge dominant literatures in the field ■ Shape methods ■ Design the research to be in conversation with prevailing policies and academic arguments ■ Determine sample strategies ■ Gather evidence ■ Analyze data ■ Determine research products	Expert validity—to value and democratically bring together varied bases of knowledge including local, critical, professional, and outside perspectives
Action and accountability to social change and social movements	Du Bois (1898); Lewin (1946); Martín-Baró (1994); Torre & Fine (2006); Lykes & Mallona (2008)	Built theory through producing scholarly and youth-friendly writings, performances, and other research products Established a network of allies to engage the data for greatest social impact	Impact validity—to ensure that the research is designed as action, for action, and in solidarity with movements for social change

into physical and mental health and criminal justice outcomes. Working across vertical levels of analysis (policy—institution—lives) and across horizontal sites of development (education, health, and criminal justice) strengthens the conceptual and political reach of the work, reflecting a heightened measure of ecological validity.

Deep Participation

Looking across the history of critical psychology, we can see that researchers have experimented with varied forms of participation. In the community self-surveys, community members were core data gatherers such that diverse groups of citizens banded together to jointly investigate the racial distributions in employment, housing, and education. Pioneers in bringing together White and Black community researchers, Wormser and Selltiz (1951a, 1951b) encouraged those who had benefited and those who had been disadvantaged by local injustices to collaborate in the expectation that joint labor would help them realize their shared fates. They believed such collaborations would strengthen the validity and utility of the research; cultivate informed, diverse, and skilled community leaders; and build elite allies in the struggle against racial discrimination.

This commitment to deep participation speaks to another aspect of validity criteria—in this case *expert validity* (see Table 11.1, second row). Critical participatory work contests and expands traditional views of expertise, recognizing situated knowledges and systemic relationships. An example is in research that shifts the unit of analysis to *circuits of dispossession* (Fine & Ruglis, 2009) and *human rights*. Although some may benefit, others suffer, witness, sacrifice, feel empathy, guilt, or responsibility or believe it is not their problem. Postcolonial theorists recognize that we are all engaged in and (differentially) affected by these circuits (MacLeod & Bhatia, 2008). Torre's (2005, 2006) use of participatory contact zones extends this framework to epistemology and method, such that those individuals who reflect these varied positions are recruited onto the research team to collaboratively construct research questions, settle on methods, engage analysis, and determine products. In the shared analytical space of the research team, difficult, power-sensitive conversations ensue across varied forms of expertise, as questions are deliberately framed to document the broad and uneven impact of injustice.

RESEARCH AS/FOR ACTION: ACCOUNTABILITY TO SOCIAL MOVEMENTS AND CHANGE

Finally, we draw wisdom and inspiration from those who have designed science to serve the interests of social justice. Drawing on the thinking of Barreras and Massey (in press), critical participatory projects are crafted toward *impact validity,* anticipating from the start how to produce evidence that can be mobilized for change. In this vein, PFJ has been designed to generate four kinds of actions and to be accountable to varied communities of action:

- *Building theory*—Research collectives of adult and youth are collaboratively writing scholarly and youth-friendly popular documents about our findings on dispossession, privilege, and resistance.
- *Contributing to social policy*—Focused on educational, criminal justice, school safety, and high-stakes testing, PFJ researchers have spoken at City Council meetings, been involved in class action suits, sent our data to newspapers, and gone to Albany for lobbying data. One subproject within PFJ, undertaken by children of incarcerated parents, has involved research and a video produced by youth affected by mass incarceration. The film is being viewed by varied audiences of youth, advocates, and incarcerated parents—and has been sent with a policy brief to more than 200 legislators in Albany (Munoz Proto, in press).
- *Performing data*—Following in the footsteps of Du Bois's (1915) *Star of Ethiopia,* the PFJ researchers have been working with improvisational, visual, and other artists to perform the data for varied audiences throughout New York City, across the United States, and internationally. We are piloting participatory performance, designed to invite audiences to see themselves not as witnesses, nor as empathetic, but rather as deeply engaged agents within dialectical systems of dispossession and privilege, which we are all responsible to interrupt (Fox, 2010).

- *Distributing evidence to organizing allies*—In collaboration with a series of youth organizing groups, public interest lawyers, and journalists, we have created a clearinghouse of youth justice data to be integrated into city council testimony for ethical policing in schools; youth–parent–community organizing against school closings and high-stakes testing; and community education against sexual and sexuality harassment of youth by police and peers. We consider this a form of generalizability for organizing.

CONCLUSION

Critical PAR stands on the broad shoulders of 20th-century women and men who dared to design research for justice. Today we collaborate with youth who confront 21st-century assaults on their dignity, humanity, and human securities in a society increasingly defined by huge wealth and opportunity gaps (Wilkinson & Pickett, 2009). We offer this chapter to sketch critical PAR as public science grounded in epistemologies that value the messy participation of various forms of knowledge and expertise. Critical PAR challenges hegemonic conceptions of where social problems originate, cultivates deep participation, produces evidence designed to awaken a sense of injustice (Deutsch & Steil, 1998), and seeks to provoke collective engagement. Refusing the distinctions between theoretical and applied, and science and advocacy, critical PAR commits at once to human rights, social justice, and scientific validity.

References

Allport, G. W. (1951). Foreword. In M. H. Wormser & C. Selltiz (Eds.), *How to conduct a self-survey of civil rights* (pp. v–vii). New York, NY: Association Press.

Anand, B., Fine, M., Surrey, D., & Perkins-Munn, T. (2002). *Keeping the struggle alive: Studying desegregation in our town*. New York, NY: Teachers College Press.

Arendt, H. (1958). *The human condition*. Chicago, IL: University of Chicago Press.

Barreras, R., & Massey, S. (in press). Impact validity as a framework for advocacy-based research. *Journal of Social Issues*.

Benedict, R., & Weltfish, G. (1943). *The races of mankind* (Public Affairs Pamphlet No. 85). New York, NY: Public Affairs Committee.

Boal, A. (2002). *Games for actors and non-actors* (2nd ed.). New York, NY: Routledge.

Bronfenbrenner, U. (1979) *The ecology of human development: Experiments by nature and design*. Cambridge, MA: Harvard University Press.

Brydon-Miller, M., & McGuire, P. (2009). Participatory action research: Contributions to the development of practitioner inquiry in education. *Educational Action Research, 17*, 79–93.

Cherry, F. (2004). Kenneth B. Clark and social psychology's other history. In G. Philogene (Ed.), *Racial identity in context: The legacy of Kenneth B. Clark* (pp. 17–33). Washington, DC: American Psychological Association.

Cherry, F. (2008). Social psychology and social change. In D. Fox, I. Prilleltensky, & S. Austin (Eds.), *Critical Psychology* (pp. 93–109). Los Angeles, CA: Sage.

Cherry, F., & Borshuk, C. (1998). Social action research and the Commission on Community Interrelations. *Journal of Social Issues, 54*, 119–142.

Darley, J. M., & Latané, B. (1968). Bystander intervention in emergencies: Diffusion of responsibility. *Journal of Personality and Social Psychology, 8*, 377–383.

Danziger, K. (1990). *Constructing the subject: Historical origins of psychological research*. New York, NY: Cambridge University Press.

Danziger, K. (2000). Making social psychology experimental: A conceptual history, 1920–1970. *Journal of the History of Behavioral Sciences, 36*, 329–347.

Denzin, N. (2003). *Performance ethnography: Critical pedagogy and the politics of culture*. Thousand Oaks, CA: Sage.

Deutsch, M., & Steil, J. (1988). Awakening the sense of injustice. *Social Justice Research, 2*, 3–23.

Dilthey, W. (1989). *Introduction to the human sciences* (R. A. Makkreel & F. Rodi, Eds.). Princeton, NJ: Princeton University Press. (Original work published 1883)

Du Bois, W. E. B. (1898). The study of the Negro problems. *Annals of the American Academy of Political and Social Science, 11*, 1–23.

DuBois, W. E. B. (1915). The star of Ethiopia: A pageant. *Crisis Magazine, 11*, 91–93.

Fine, M., Bloom, J., Burns, A., Chajet, L., Guishard, M. Y., Payne, Y. A., ... Torre, M. E. (2005). Dear Zora: A letter to Zora Neal Hurston fifty years after Brown. *Teachers College Record, 107*, 496–529.

Fine, M., & Ruglis, J. (2009). Circuits of dispossession: The racialized and classed realignment of the public sphere for youth in the U.S. *Transforming Anthropology, 17*, 20–33. doi:10.1111/j.1548-7466.2009.01037.x

Fine, M., & Torre, M. E. (2004). Re-membering exclusions: Participatory action research in public institutions. *Qualitative Research in Psychology, 1*, 15–37.

Finison, L. J. (1978). Unemployment, politics, and the history of organized psychology. *American Psychologist, 31*, 747–755.

Fox, J. (1994). *Acts of service: Spontaneity, commitment, tradition in the non-scripted theatre.* New York, NY: Tusitala.

Fox, M. (2010). *Animating adolescence: Engaging responses to the historical institutional construction of adolescence.* Unpublished manuscript.

Fox, M., Mediratta, K., Ruglis, J., Stoudt, B., Shah, S., & Fine, M. (2010). Critical youth engagement: Participatory action research and organizing. In L. Sherrod, J. Torney-Puta, & C. Flanagan (Eds.), *Handbook of research and policy on civic engagement with youth* (pp. 621–650). Hoboken, NJ: Wiley.

Fox, M., Calliste, N., Greene, C., Francis, D., Pearson, J., Ramsey, D., . . . Fine, M. (in press). Embodied evidence: Youth participatory action research on circuits of dispossession and pools of resistance in New York City. *Rethinking Schools.*

Gallagher, K. (2008). *The theatre of urban: Youth and schooling in dangerous times.* Toronto, Ontario, Canada: University of Toronto Press.

Green, D. S., & Driver, E. D. (Eds.). (1978). *Du Bois: On sociology and the Black community.* Chicago, IL: University of Chicago Press.

Harris, B. (2009). What critical psychologists should know about the history of psychology. In D. Fox, I. Prilleltensky, & S. Austin (Eds.), *Critical psychology: An introduction* (pp. 20–35). London, England: Sage.

Harding, S. (1993). Rethinking standpoint epistemology: "What is strong objectivity?" In L. Alcoff & E. Potter (Eds.), *Feminist epistemologies* (pp. 49–82). New York, NY: Routledge.

Jackson, J. (2004). "Racially stuffed shirts and other enemies of mankind": Horace Mann Bond's parody of segregationist psychology in the 1950s. In A. S. Winston (Ed.), *Defining difference: Race and racism in the history of psychology* (pp. 261–283). Washington, DC: American Psychological Association.

Jahoda, M., Lazarsfeld, P., & Zeisel, H. (2003). *Marienthal: The sociography of an unemployed community.* New Brunswick, NJ: Transaction. (Original work published 1931)

Johnson, C. S. (1943). *To stem this tide: A survey of racial tension areas in the United States.* Boston, MA: The Pilgrim Press.

Jones, K. (2006). A biographic researcher in pursuit of an aesthetic: The use of arts-based (re)presentations in "performative" dissemination of life stories. *Qualitative Sociology Review, 2*, 66–85.

Lewin, K. (1946) Action research and minority problems. *Journal of Social Issues, 2*, 34–46.

Lykes, M. B., & Mallona A. (2008). Towards a transformational liberation: Participatory action research and activist praxis. In P. Reason & H. Bradbury (Eds.), *The Sage handbook of action research* (pp. 260–292). Thousand Oaks, CA: Sage.

MacLeod, C., & Bhatia, S. (2008). Postcolonial psychology. In C. Willig & W. Stainton-Rogers (Eds.), *Handbook of qualitative research in psychology* (pp. 576–590). London, England: Sage.

Martín-Baró, I. (1994). *Writings for a liberation psychology.* Cambridge, MA: Harvard University Press.

Marrow, Alfred F. (1969). *The practical theorist: The life and work of Kurt Lewin.* New York, NY: Basic Books.

Munoz Proto, C. (in press). In research of critical knowledge: Tracing inheritance in the landscape of incarceration. In S. Steinberg & G. Canella (Eds.), *Critical qualitative research reader.* New York, NY: Peter Lang.

Pratt, G. (2000). Research performances. *Environment and Planning D: Society and Space, 18*, 639–651. doi:10.1068/d218t

Rutherford, A., & Pickren, W. E. (2008). Women and minorities. In S. Davis & W. Buskist (Eds.), *Handbook of twenty-first century psychology* (pp. 35–49). Thousand Oaks, CA: Sage.

Salas, J. (2007). *Improvising real life: Personal story in Playback Theatre* (3rd ed.). New York, NY: Tusitala.

Selltiz, C., & Wormser, M. H. (Eds.). (1949). Community self-surveys: An approach to social change [Special issue]. *Journal of Social Issues, 5*(2).

Subasic, E., Reynolds, K., & Turner, J. (2008). The political solidarity model of social change: Dynamics of self-categorization in intergroup power relations. *Personality and Social Psychology Review, 12*, 330–352.

Torre, M. E. (2005). The alchemy of integrated spaces: Youth participation in research collectives of difference. In L. Weis & M. Fine (Eds.), *Beyond silenced voices* (pp. 251–266). Albany: State University of New York Press.

Torre, M. E. (2006). *Beyond the flat: Intergroup contact, intercultural education and the potential of contact zones for research, growth and development.* Unpublished manuscript.

Torre, M. E., & Fine, M. (2006). Researching and resisting: Democratic policy research by and for youth. In S. Ginwright, J. Cammarota, & P. Noguera (Eds.), *Beyond resistance: Youth activism and community change: New democratic possibilities for policy and practice for America's youth* (pp. 269–285). New York, NY: Routledge.

Torre, M. E., & Fine, M. (2011). A wrinkle in time: Tracing a legacy of public science through community self-surveys and participatory action research. *Journal of Social Issues, 67,* 106–121.

Tuana, N. (2006). The speculum of ignorance: The women's health movement and epistemologies of ignorance. *Hypatia, 21,* 1–19.

Tukey, J. W. (1977). *Exploratory data analysis.* Reading, MA: Addison-Wesley.

Watson, G. B. (1947). *Action for unity.* New York, NY: Harper & Brothers.

Wilkinson, R., & Pickett, K. (2009). *The spirit level: Why greater equality makes societies stronger.* New York, NY: Bloomsbury Press.

Williams, R. M. (1947). *The reduction of intergroup tensions: A survey of research on problems of ethnic, racial and religious group relations.* New York, NY: Social Science Research Council.

Wormser, M. H., & Selltiz, C. (1951a). Community self-surveys: Principles and procedures. In M. Jahoda, M. Deutsch, & S. W. Cook (Eds.), *Research methods in social relations: Selected techniques* (pp. 611–642). New York, NY: Dryden Press.

Wormser, M. H., & Selltiz, C. (1951b). *How to conduct a self-survey of civil rights.* New York, NY: Association Press.

Zeller-Berkman, S. (2010). *Critical developments: What the field of youth development can learn from the life histories of adults and young people involved in activism* (Unpublished doctoral dissertation). The Graduate Center, City University of New York, New York, NY.

CHAPTER 12

VISUAL RESEARCH IN PSYCHOLOGY

Paula Reavey and Jon Prosser

The aim of this chapter is to review and make clear the variety of ways in which psychologists use visual images to address research questions. Visual research has been developed mainly by qualitative researchers as a way to study human experiences and to engage participants more fully in the research process. In contemporary culture more generally, visual images have become an important means by which we express our feelings and how we communicate with one another using emerging technologies (mobile phones, social networking sites, and virtual reality Internet fora). It should then come as no surprise that psychologists have seized the opportunity to study the impact of these developments on the way we experience our worlds. This chapter discusses the range of possibilities for researching the visual and reviews the implications for the way in which we study human experience more generally.

To address these aims, we have structured the chapter as follows. First, we outline exactly what we mean by visual research as it has developed in psychological research methods. Second, we provide a brief history of how visual techniques have previously been used to study psychological phenomena. We then explain how qualitative researchers have initiated the use of visual approaches to study experience via a broader range of modalities (the means by which we communicate, i.e., written, spoken, visual, touch, and sound). This has entailed a shift from a monomodal position (where language only is studied) to a multimodal one (where language *and* images are studied together). Next, we introduce

five main ways in which qualitative researchers have used visual techniques to study people's experiences. This includes reviewing how qualitative researchers have sought to bring emotions to the foreground of research, exploring the role of the environmental setting in making sense of experience, examining the role of the body and appearance in making sense of self and identity, using visual images in the study of social memory, and using the visual to study communication and interaction. After this section, we concentrate on how visual research methods can alter the context of the research setting by increasing a sense of collaboration between the researcher and participant. Following this, we set out a number of ways in which qualitative researchers have analyzed visual material, almost always alongside verbal data, generated through interviews, focus groups, diaries, or observations. Finally, we provide some guidance on the ethical issues that inevitably arise when conducting visual research and then conclude the chapter.

WHAT IS VISUAL RESEARCH?

Visual research focuses on what can be seen. How humans *see* is part nature, part nurture, being governed by perception, which, like other sensory modes, is mediated by physiology, culture, and history. Visual researchers use the term *visible* ontologically in referring to imagery and a naturally occurring phenomena that can be seen, emphasizing the physiological dimension and disregarding meaning or significance. *Visual*, on the other hand, is not

DOI: 10.1037/13620-012
APA Handbook of Research Methods in Psychology: Vol. 2. Research Designs, H. Cooper (Editor-in-Chief)

about an image or object in of itself but is more concerned with the perception and the meanings attributed to these images or objects. *To visualize* and *visualization* refer to researchers' sense-making attributes that are epistemologically grounded and include concept formation, analytical processes, and modes of representation (Wagner, 2006).

There are two basic approaches to undertaking qualitative visual research. In the first approach, researchers create or manufacture visual artifacts during the research process (Banks, 2001; Pink, 2007). The second approach has its origins in the *visual turn* (Mirzoeff, 2009) during which researchers explore visual artifacts in terms of their mode, production, interpretation, and application (Emmison & Smith, 2000; Rose, 2007). Increasingly, researchers have combined these approaches to enhance analytic insights (Stanczak, 2007).

Empirically oriented visual researchers frame their work theoretically or pragmatically to meet their needs, which may be shaped by research questions, disciplinary norms, or analytical frameworks. Banks (2007), a visual anthropologist, organized his fieldwork into three basic strands. The first is concerned with documentation and researcher-created imagery that may include photographs, moving images, sketches, and concept maps, which are collected and stored along with the usual hand-written field notes and voice recordings. Visual researchers may then analyze the visual data using concept maps or flow diagrams and represent their findings using particular images, graphs, or diagrams. Throughout this process, the researcher is pivotal to creating images. The second strand involves the collection and study of images produced, consumed, or used by the subjects or respondents of the research. Here the emphasis is on understanding the participant's engagement with differing types of media, their mode of production, and the context in which visual data are set because they are important in determining the meaning the participant ascribes to imagery. Banks's third strand is a combination of the first two and is currently the preferred approach. Here researchers collect visual data (e.g., video of complex interpersonal interaction) and combine this information with the subject's insights and the meaning making of imagery they employ or adapt.

The mix of researcher and researched insights represents an epistemological shift towards a more collaborative mode of knowledge production.

A complementary question to, "What is visual research?" is "Why is visual research currently so popular in the social sciences more generally?" A simple answer is because there has been a general awakening to the significance and ubiquity of imagery in contemporary lives:

> All around us are screens on computers, game consoles, iPods, handheld devices and televisions . . . where the internet was once held to be the revival of text, there are already over 100 million video clips on YouTube, more than 3 billion photos on the file-sharing Flickr, and over 4 billion on the social networking site Facebook. (Mirzoeff, 2009, p. 2)

The term *visual culture* is now commonly used to reflect a combination of visuality (generalized insights into the visual in everyday spaces not merely as entities or visual texts) and meaning making through taken-for-granted practices and habitus. Visuals are pervasive in public, work, and private space, and we have no choice but to look. Qualitative psychologists are no longer acting as though they were sightless and are increasingly taking up the challenge to understand the behavior of individuals and groups within a society dominated by visual culture.

A visual approach has gained prominence among sensory research methods. It is argued that because visual culture is dominant, visual methods are of primary importance. However, others argue that anatomically modern humans appeared about 200,000 years ago, and it was their highly developed visual and sensory acuity rather than language skills (which appeared much later) that were central to their survival. The possibility that the ability to interpret and represent visually are innate and central to the human psyche is echoed in Harper's (2002) statement: "The parts of the brain that process visual information are evolutionarily older than the parts that process verbal information" (p. 13). Older does not mean superior, but it does suggest that visual capacity is deeply ingrained, and evolutionary psychologists, drawing on Darwinism, argue that multiple generations of people (including researchers) have innate and unchangeable visually oriented natures (Buss, 2005). Despite a continual evolution marked by instinctual deprivation, humans never lost their visual insight. The upsurge in interest in visuality by psychologists reflects a deep need to see closer and higher and to see what is hidden that remains implicit to the human condition.

PSYCHOLOGY AND THE VISUAL: A BRIEF HISTORY

Psychology has a longstanding concern with the visual and with technologies of visualization. This goes way beyond the specialized subdiscipline of the psychology of perception; it is instead part of the conceptual roots of the discipline as a whole. The emerging visual technology of photography was after all a central part of how the nascent discipline of psychology established its scientific credibility in the late 19th century—through the visual recording of scientific observation. For example, in *The Expression of Emotions in Man and Animals*, Darwin (1872/1999) made comparisons across photographs and illustrations of children and animals as the evidential base for his theory of universal emotional expressions. This approach greatly influenced the growth of comparative psychology in the late 19th century (Richards, 2002). Moreover, photographs and minute observations of his son William Erasmus Darwin, which Darwin and his wife collected as a "developmental diary" from his birth, are arguably the template from which developmental psychology was established (Fitzpatrick & Bringmann, 1997).

The use of visual records to differentiate species and meticulously categorize plants and animals into various types and subtypes became the hallmark of 19th-century natural science. It marked the systematization of observation, indicating accuracy, evidential recording, and careful attention to detail. What is measurable, therefore, is assumed to be what is observable. In the case of psychology, the fledgling discipline sought to separate itself from philosophy, and the myriad metaphysical difficulties that appeared to prohibit a "science of mind," by emulating the natural sciences such as functional physiology as far as possible (Richards, 2002). Recent successes at that time in physiology had arisen from mapping functional connections between anatomy and behavior. This same logic was applied to what Fechner (1860/1966) called "an exact theory of the functional relationships between body and soul and between the bodily, mental, somatic and physiological world" (cited in Meischner-Metge & Meischner, 1997, p. 102).

Photography also greatly influenced the development of psychopathology and clinical psychology. Visual categorization of different personality types and the categorization of the *mad*, *subnormal*, or *criminal* were performed by assembling photographic arrays in which purported mental differences could be made legible to the trained eye (Jackson, 1995). Photographs were also commonly used to lend visual credibility to diagnostic categories of mental defects or "feeblemindedness." Through careful visual recording, the spaces between a person's eyes, the size of a forehead, or the body posture of an asylum inmate could provide direct evidence for an observable and thus categorical difference in the person under study. The multiple exposure technique used by Marey—in which a series of images are exposed on the same photographic plate—was also used by Francis Galton (cited in Draaisma, 2000). Galton argued that his "compound photographs" of criminals and of "consumptives" taken one by one onto the same photographic plate showed their common features because individual or noncommon features would be effectively washed out during the process. The technique was, Galton claimed, a sort of "pictorial statistics" where norms of human development and diversity could be visually represented. This idea fed into popular notions of normality and abnormality around mental health, which gained currency in the late 19th and early 20th century (Porter, 2003). Visual techniques such as the Rorschach ink blot tests—surely one of the most recognizable representations of psychology—and the Thematic Apperception Test (see Cramer, 1996) were and still are used to provide insight into a person's personality type, to identify their unconscious motivational state, or to detect signs of mental illness.

Social psychology has throughout its history used film and photography to document research and shore up the face validity of its claims. Milgram's (2005) images of participants presented in the infamous studies on obedience in the early 1960s appear to leave little room for doubting the validity of his claims. Close analyses of the statistical evidence and the ecological validity of the experimental setup about the tendency for *ordinary* people to follow orders that can lead to the harming of others is somewhat overshadowed by these powerful images.

Similarly the video recordings taken by Zimbardo, Maslach, and Haney (2000) of the Stanford Prison Experiment (SPE) have been promoted as powerful testimony as to the ease with which people take on the aggressive or passive behavior in their respective roles as prisoner or guard. This material was captured using the sort of hidden camera techniques that have become the mainstay of reality-television shows such as *Candid Camera*, or more recently, *Big Brother* (where people are secretly filmed and thus observed—a team of psychologists was involved in providing an analysis of subsequent changes in behavior or mental state). Interestingly Zimbardo has claimed that Alan Funt, creator of the first reality-television show *Candid Camera*, was "one of the most creative, intuitive social psychologists on the planet" (Zimbardo et al., 2000, p. 197). Lewin also used hidden camera techniques to make a series of films that focused on the spaces of child development, the best known being the 1935 film *The Child and the World* (see van Elteren & Luck, 1990). To summarize, a historical analysis of the role of visual within psychology can reveal its instrumental effects in providing the context for *the psychological* to become observable and, therefore, measurable and more *scientific*. In using visual images as evidence, and in employing visual technologies to increase the accuracy and thus the status of psychological observations, the discipline of psychology has also made its findings more publicly accessible. Despite these noteworthy uses of visual images throughout psychology, very little in the way of methodologies has attempted to accommodate the visual in making sense of how people experience the world. This is especially difficult to understand with regards to qualitative methodologies that claim to capture more readily meaning making in everyday experience (see Chapter 1 of this volume).

MOVING FROM THE MONO- TO THE MULTIMODAL IN QUALITATIVE RESEARCH

Qualitative research is now well established in certain subdisciplines of psychology (critical, community, social, clinical, educational), even though as a methodology it remains on the margins of psychology's mainstream. Rather than searching for generalizable laws (which is psychology's ultimate aim), qualitative researchers are concerned with uncovering the variety of ways in which people make and interpret meaning, experience the world, tell stories about their lives, and communicate with others (Parker, 2004; Stainton, Rogers, & Willig, 2008; Willig, 2008). At the center of qualitative research perhaps is the question of *how people experience the world and make sense of that experience*. The participant, and not the researcher, therefore, is the focus of meaning generation within the research process. In recent years, several publications have emerged that meticulously charter the best way to collect, store, and analyze qualitative data in systematic and logical fashion. And yet, it was not until the publication of Ratcliff's chapter on video methods in APA's first handbook on qualitative methods (Ratcliff, 2003) that any publication included chapters on visual approaches. Furthermore, 2011 witnessed the first-ever publication of a psychology-based volume of visual methods, signaling the relatively late uptake of visual approaches in psychology (Reavey, 2011).

The majority of qualitative work still continues to use verbal data only, in the form of semistructured and unstructured interview data, natural conversations, focus groups discussions, diaries, or written reports. What these approaches share in common is a focus on either the broad sense-making patterns contained in transcripts, or the minute detail of the way in which the language is structured and performed in social interactions. What they also share, however, is a reliance on the spoken or written word as a source of data—a fundamentally *monomodal approach*. Many visual researchers (Pink, 2007; Radley, 2009) have pointed to the limitations of looking at people's life narratives and experiences using language alone, and through their work, have pointed to a number of neglected areas that would benefit from a *multimodal* approach—that is, an approach that attends to extradiscursive modalities such as visual stimuli. After all, if qualitative researchers want to make sense of experience, they must surely acknowledge that a variety of modalities—verbal, visual, sound, touch—make up a person's experience of the world.

The Potential for Multimodal Approaches.

To date, visual research in psychology has addressed a number of psychology relevant topics, including the role of the body and embodiment (Del Busso, 2009; Gillies et al., 2005), health and illness (Radley, 2009; Radley & Taylor, 2003a, 2003b), the process of remembering (Brookfield, Brown, & Reavey, 2008; Middleton & Brown, 2005; Middleton & Edwards, 1990; Radley, 1990), identity and appearance (Gleeson & Frith, 2006), and mental health difficulties (Silver & Reavey, 2010). This multimodal work has combined visual (photography, drawing, and painting) and verbal or written (interview, focus group discussions, and diaries) data to create a richer picture of the topic under study. Photographs are perhaps the most popular visual medium to be used in psychology. They have been used for a variety of techniques, ranging from the use of existing images to *elicit* or *trigger* discussion in an interview or focus group (here referred to as *photo-elicitation*) to the use of photographic images generated by participants within the context of the research (here referred to as *photo-production*[1]). Regardless of the specific technique being used, what all visual researchers in psychology share is the acknowledgment that (a) individuals *experience* the world not only through narrative but also through setting (space) and embodiment and (b) individuals are *already* using multimodal forms of expression and communication when (re)presenting their experiences in everyday life. As people become more proficient in using new communication technologies

to convey ideas and feelings and engage in new forms of social interaction, relationality, and subjectivity, it is ever more vital that researchers in psychology engage with these everyday forms of communication and representation.

A further acknowledgment by visual researchers in psychology is how images can successfully act to disrupt well-rehearsed participant accounts and generally enliven the interview (Brookfield, Brown, & Reavey, 2008; Gillies et al., 2005; Reavey, 2008; Silver & Reavey, 2010). Participants, when faced with a photograph from their past, for example, can suddenly be confronted with and are able to *imagine* the emotions or their embodied states from that time, such that the past can enter into the present moment and create new narratives or more complex accounts (especially if the reemergence of the past collides with narratives of the present). This is not to say that somehow the visual dupes the person or compels them to tell the truth about the past, but it can nevertheless serve to provide a more complex and layered account, and one that is more seeped in emotional resonances and reminders, and one in which the setting (the actual place) of the experience is brought into sharper view. Collier (1957), the founder of photo-elicitation in anthropology and sociology, in comparing nonvisual interviews with visual interviews has also noted that the latter tend to be more focused, detailed, and precise:

> The material obtained with photographs was precise and at times even encyclopedic; the control interviews were less structured, rambling, and freer in association. Statements in the photo interviews were in direct response to the graphic probes and different in character as the content of the pictures differed. (Collier, 1957, p. 856)

A REVIEW OF FIVE PSYCHOLOGICAL TOPICS USING VISUAL RESEARCH

Emotions

A noteworthy feature of using images is their ability to speak to the often unspeakable or to evoke

---

[1]Sometimes authors refer to *photo-elicitation* to describe both approaches. However, we have separated the two terms to distinguish between two very different approaches.

emotions that could otherwise be put to one side. This is the reason why so many charity campaigns use powerful visual cues, such as starving children, to incite an emotional reaction and encourage people to dig deep into their pockets. Without those cues, it is difficult to see how many charities would survive as they need potential donors to *witness* the difficulties their benefactors endure. In visual research, images have also been used to incite emotion, especially in situations in which participants may need to be reminded of how they felt because they have perhaps chosen to move on from or have actively forgotten an experience that was difficult (Frith, 2011). In everyday life, however, individuals also use images to deliberately engage with their feelings. A video of a wedding, or a child's first steps, for example, may be played to activate difficult to reach memories. It is not surprising that photographic and video footage is now part of so many households in industrial societies as the impetus to remember how things feel is intrinsic to our sense of well-being (see Middleton & Brown, 2005).

Visual researchers in psychology have embraced the power of the visual to incite emotion and bring it to the conversational fore in an interview or focus group. A powerful example of this can be found in Radley and Taylor's (2003a) photo-production study of medical and surgical patients' recovery on a hospital ward. The study involved participants taking pictures of the hospital spaces where they were recovering as well as an interview 1 month after they had left the hospital, using the photographs as a way to maneuver the interview discussion. Radley and Taylor have argued that an image itself can provoke participants to try to explain aspects of their experience that are not immediately accessible to them. Radley and Taylor also argued that the photographic images put participants in the position of having to examine issues that they may not have chosen to or did not wish to explore in the first instance.

A photo-elicitation study (using participants' domestic photographs) by Kunimoto (2004), with Japanese Canadians interned during the World War II, revealed different kinds of memories and emotions to the ones initially spoken. Kunimoto, for example, noted how the photographs introduced

accounts that were far more emotional, specific, and rich and how they contrasted significantly with the dry accounts the participants offered previous to their introduction.

In a study examining issues of selfhood for individuals diagnosed with body dysmorphic disorder (BDD; a condition marked by a distressing preoccupation with an imaginary or minor defect in a facial feature or a localized part of the body), Silver and Reavey (2010) used both drawing and photo-elicitation to explore with participants aspects of their appearance across different time periods. What Silver and Reavey found particularly interesting was the way in which participants moved away from accounting for their BDD in the present and brought to the fore an intensely emotional account of their idealization of their childhood self, on which present judgments about facial disfigurement were grounded (Silver & Reavey, 2010). This emotional connection between past and present in the clinical literature on BDD had been absent up until this point, and Silver and Reavey argued that the visual methods in the study were particularly useful as a means to examine the emotional connection between past and present because participants had a visible portrait of the self physically (and thus emotionally) changing over time.

Space and Objects

Another aspect of using visual methods is the manner in which this modality succeeds in widening the focus of participants' accounts of their experience to attend to the setting in which they take place. Almost all qualitative methods involve asking participants to recall and reflect on experiences, using purely verbal methods, which can lead to an account that is overwhelmingly organized in terms of time sequences only (Goodwin, 2008). A number of studies incorporating visual methods have, on the other hand, succeeded in disrupting such narratives, encouraging participants to also reflect on the social and material contexts (spaces and places) out of which their experiences emerge (Bowes-Catton, Barker, & Richards, 2011; Hodgetts, Chamberlain, & Groot, 2011; Hodgetts, Chamberlain, & Radley, 2007; Majumdar, 2011). Objects also form part of the setting and can be used by individuals to anchor or bring alive a discussion, or to reminisce. In a

FIGURE 12.1.   Homeless man with ninja sign. From *Visual Methods in Psychology: Using and Interpreting Images in Qualitative Research* (p. 310), by P. Reavey (Ed.), 2011, London, England: Routledge. Copyright 2011 by D. Hodgetts; all rights reserved. Adapted with permission.

photo-production study on homelessness by Hodgetts et al., for example, one of the participants had taken photos of a board he used to write amusing messages, which successfully captured the attention of passers-by (see Figure 12.1; Hodgetts, Chamberlain, & Groot, 2011).

In the broad discipline of memory studies, photographs of objects and spaces, for example, are commonly used to bring a topic to life. It is much easier to start with a familiar object when recollecting, than it is to begin with a sometimes unmanageable and entangled set of memories. If we can take a visual record at the time at which we experience something or can gather together existing visual images of an event (e.g., our existing personal photographs), we can bring the space and setting of the experience explicitly into an interview, focus group, or diary.

In a photo-production diary study by Del Busso (2009, 2011) on young women's experiences of embodiment,[2] participants were asked to take pictures of objects or spaces that reflected experiences of embodied pleasure (eating, having sex, exercise, etc., and the places in which these occurred; see Figure 12.2). The data analyzed were people's verbal accounts rather than the photographs themselves, and the analytical approach was hermeneutic phenomenological analysis (see Langdridge, 2007).

In a follow-up interview, participants used the photos and written diaries to organize the discussion. And from this, it became clear that the manner in which participants experienced embodied pleasure was integral to the setting in which those experiences occurred. In other words, it was not only the *what* they experienced but also the *where* that was important. In sum, visual research in psychology can bring to the fore the spaces and objects through which people experience themselves so that the various forms of selfhood reported (verbally) and shown (visually) are fully understood.

Embodiment and Appearance

The role of our outward appearance and the felt sensation of our bodies in making sense of emotions, identity, and selfhood have become increasingly noted in social psychological accounts of experience (Brown, Reavey, Cromby, Harper, & Johnson, 2008; Frost, 2001; Gillies et al., 2004, 2005; Howarth, 2011). How we feel in our bodies, how we see ourselves, and how others see us has thus become acknowledged as one of the key ways in which we make sense of who we are and how we experience the world (Stam, 1998). Many researchers in this field have long documented the difficulties in accessing people's embodied experiences and appearances using language-based methodologies alone. One

[2]By *embodiment*, we mean how it feels to be in one's body—the physical and emotional sensation.

FIGURE 12.2. Ann's photograph of the woods. From *Being in Motion: Femininity, Movement, and Space in Young Women's Narratives of Their Embodied Experiences in Everyday Life* (p. 154), by L. Del Busso, 2009 (Unpublished doctoral dissertation), London South Bank University, London, England. Copyright 2009 by L. Del Busso; all rights reserved. Reprinted with permission.

obvious problem facing researchers studying appearance and embodiment is the difficulty with which participants recall information relating to their bodies, especially if they are having to recall events or changes over significant periods of time. A photo-production study (using interview methodology and photographs produced by patients over a period of time) by Frith and Harcourt (2007), found that gradual changes in appearance sometimes went unnoticed by patients until they were able to look at a series of photographs in the interview discussion. For example, on looking at the photographs, some patients noticed they looked older or had put on weight; something they had not picked up before viewing the visual material. As one participant remarked:

> One of the things that I've been aware of is the fact that over a period of a couple of months I put on quite a lot of weight when I was having my chemo, and I can see from the start of the chemo to the end, that I actually found that quite upsetting. I feel I look so much older and looking at those photographs and when I see photographs of myself just a couple

of months before, or even after I'd had the operation before I lost my hair, I feel like I've aged a lot. . . . I mean I always had lines on my forehead but I used to, my fringe used to cover them, do you know what I mean, in a sense I used to hide a bit behind my longer hair and now I can't. (Frith & Harcourt, 2007, p. 1345)

In a study attempting to research embodied experiences, Gillies et al. (2005) (using the researchers as participants) found that language-based methodologies alone were insufficient as a means to generate rich enough accounts. Not only did their previous language-based work (Gillies et al., 2004) tend to reproduce the traditional separation of *mind* and *body* but also it was difficult to escape cultural and stereotypical accounts of the body and sensations. To overcome these past difficulties, the research group used painting as a means to circumvent them. Using the trigger *aging* and attending to the physical and emotional sensations accompanying this, the group painted pictures of their experiences (feelings, thoughts, and sensations) of aging, without thinking or trying to justify their picture (see Figure 12.3).

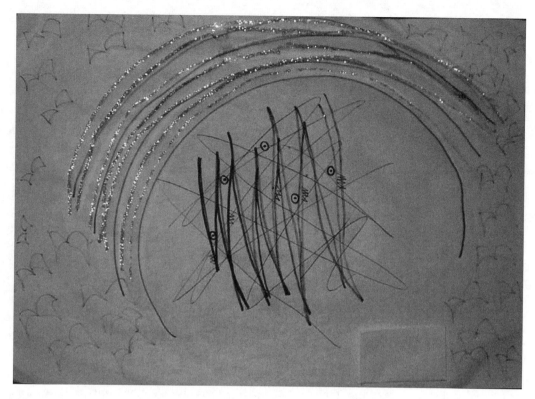

FIGURE 12.3.   A painting of an experience of aging.

Furthermore, there were no rules associated with painting; the painting could be literal or entirely abstract.

The painting of the pictures was followed by a series of focus group discussions about the paintings as well as emerging themes. These discussions were transcribed and used as the main verbal data set and were analyzed thematically (see Gillies et al., 2005; Reavey & Johnson, 2008). The group found that, on the whole, the visual data afforded a less culturally stereotypical and less dualistic (where mind and body were split) representation of the embodied experience of aging. The paintings also evoked more in-depth descriptions of physical sensations and emotions and dramatically disrupted the narrative of aging on which the group members had previously drawn. Partly this was because the paintings started from a more personal account—of what the painting was about, the feelings it evoked, or the experience or event on which it was based.

Remembering

Much of the qualitative research (and cognitive research; see Conway, 1997) conducted in the area of memory has highlighted how individuals reconstruct the past to fit with their present concerns (Middleton & Brown, 2005). Who we are in the present (our present self) thus helps us organize and structure our recollections of the past. As a result of this "reconstructive turn" in the study of memory, many qualitative researchers, interested in the rich accounts individuals offer of their past, use detailed verbal transcripts to examine the various ways in which individuals make sense of and interpret the past in relation to the present (Haaken & Reavey, 2009).

Despite the rich pickings contained in verbal data, a number of researchers have highlighted how remembering in everyday life is often facilitated via the use of visual images, whether this is personal video or photographic images or wider cultural images (e.g., the traditional and "ideal" nuclear family). Looking through a photo album or watching a home video of ourselves as children, or seeing our own children as they grow up, is a key way in which we are able to keep the past alive. Such activities can also serve as useful memory prompts when we have forgotten the specific details of an event, a particular phase in life, or any feelings associated with them. It is also worth noting, however, which photographs participants actively choose to forget and leave out of a research study: Participants' discussions of absent images can be just as interesting and illuminating as the images they focus on (see Frith, 2011; Radley & Taylor, 2003b).

Visual researchers in psychology have made use of the visual precisely to allow participants the opportunity to recollect, using familiar images. For example, in a photo-elicitation study by Brookfield et al. (2008), participants were asked to bring photographs of their adopted children's past families or any items belonging to their children before their adoption (e.g., teddy bears given to them by their biological parents) to a focus group discussion. The data analyzed were the verbal discussions of the photographs, and a discourse analytic approach informed the theoretical perspective. In the United Kingdom, adopted parents are strongly encouraged to keep any (verbal and visual) records of their adopted children's previous families to be able to create a coherent story about the past. These so-called life-story books are used to establish for the child a version of the past that they can understand. Visual images form a very large part of this process, so the participants were familiar with the technique of using images to talk about their children in their everyday lives. The process by which any family photographs are managed and integrated into the process of remembering, however, is far from straightforward and involves possible tensions between different individuals' versions as well as dilemmas associated with how to speak to images that evoke difficult feelings.

Visual images are not only an aid to memory but form part of how we piece together the relevance of the past to our present concerns. This is a complex and multilayered activity, and it goes far beyond treating visual images as simple reminders or evidence of past events or experiences.

Communication and Interaction

The study of communication in the context of interaction, in the discipline of social psychology, has grown significantly in the past 3 decades. Psychologists within this tradition have wanted to learn more about what people are *doing* when they speak to one another (blaming, justifying, withdrawing) rather than merely *what* they are saying. Rather than treating language as a window onto the mind's activities, language is treated as *actively* producing psychological states in the context of interactional exchanges (e.g., conversations). Psychologists interested in how language is used in interactions can be referred to as discursive psychologists and the mode of analysis as discourse analysis. And in recent years, those who analyze various forms of *discourse* (conversations, counseling sessions, help-line calls, Internet dialogue, etc.) have become increasingly interested in *nonverbal data* (expression, eye contact, gesture, gaze, etc.) and the role it plays in mediating the discursive exchange (Goodwin, 1994, 2000; Speer & Green, 2007). A defiant look or a roll of the eyes, for example, can successfully disrupt a conversational exchange and potentially change the course of the interaction. Increasingly sophisticated video technology has also facilitated this shift toward examining *seen phenomena* (gaze, facial expression, eye movement, and gesture) to advance research practice in this area. Goodwin has also examined a number of ways in which professionals (including archeologists as well as police officers) are taught to read visual information in particular ways, resulting in a professional gaze that structures their interactions greatly (see Goodwin, 1994, 2000, 2008). In sum, video and Internet technologies have been adopted to analyze the visual and textual (what is said or written) in combination to illustrate how both produce particular social and psychological acts.

INCREASING COLLABORATION BETWEEN RESEARCHER AND PARTICIPANT

All qualitative researchers go through a process of establishing rapport with subjects, but a participatory approach is far more radical. There is a fundamental belief that respondents should be treated as participants or collaborators because they are capable of providing expert testimony in their own lives and because they offer unique and specific insights. Contemporary participatory visual methods in psychology are employed explicitly to promote research that is *authoritative* in that it speaks on behalf or individuals or groups, *critical* in that it challenges the status quo, and *therapeutic* in that it enables difficult experiences to be explored (Thomson, 2008).

Throughout the evolution of visual studies, researchers have been the instigator, designer, collector, interpreter, and producer in the empirical process. Post-1960 attention broadened to include external narratives and combine researcher and participant insights. One of the earliest documented examples of this genre in qualitative visual research was Chalfen, Worth, and Adair's (1997) project Through Navajo Eyes, conducted in the mid-1960s. The aim was to investigate the Whorf-Sapir hypothesis (language is a guide to social reality) by providing the Navajo with film cameras and basic instruction in using and editing film they made of their customs and traditions. Chalfen et al.'s approach was an alternative to maintaining a distinct separation between outsider researchers and their subjects by providing the Navajo with the means to visually depict their own culture and a capacity to provide what is in essence an emic (insider/qualitative) perspective.

A visual approach to researching participant's experiences and behaviors has become established worldwide, whereby researchers seek out ways of giving voice by *close listening* and engaging them in the research process. Words, particularly when framed in technical or academic language, are the domain of researchers and therefore can be disempowering to many participants. This is especially pertinent in cases where language skills are limited or in which images and their mode of production are more central to participants' everyday culture. Put simply, participants may feel more confident in creating drawings, photographs, and videos than articulating their experiences through words alone. Their creative enthusiasms, aesthetic capacity, and understanding of visualizing, mobile technology, doodling, graffiti, sketching, dreaming, blogging, video, and digital photography can be harnessed to express views to mutual benefit.

Qualitative visual methods inherently emphasize research *with* rather than *about* or *on* participants. Visual-elicitation, involving using photographs, drawings, or diagrams in a research interview to stimulate a response, is the most common method in participatory visual research. Experienced practitioners think very carefully before exploring the meaning of images or objects with the interviewee. Although photo-elicitation is commonly used as an icebreaker, it is the capacity of the photograph or video to act as a neutral third party when the power differential between researcher and researched is considerable that this approach is particularly valued. Radley and Taylor (2003a) provided sound exemplars of image-elicitation from a social psychologist's perspective within a broad health framework (Radley, 2009). Although some evidence exists of its effectiveness in decreasing the power differential (Packard, 2008; Warren, 2005), the method is not researcher-proof and the biggest danger to the democratization of the research process remains when researchers arrive at an interview with too many preconceptions in terms of focus, process, or direction the visual-elicitation should take.

Participants feel less pressured when discussing sensitive topics through intermediary artifacts. Because they do not speak directly about a topic on which they feel vulnerable but work through a material go-between (e.g., a doll, toy, line drawings, mobile phone images, or memorabilia), they are perhaps more able to express difficult memories and powerful emotions. This approach has gained in popularity because visual researchers believe that transitional objects have the capacity to be the locus of corporeal embodied memories (Reavey & Brown, 2010). There is longstanding belief that the strength of image- and artifact-elicitation lies in its capacity to evoke as well as create collective and personal memory. Past studies of the meaning of family photographs (Chalfen 1998; Cronin, 1998) challenged the dichotomy between realism and symbolism. Current studies of the relationship between photography and memory, in relation to familial dynamics and interpersonal relationships, draw on family collections, public archives, museums, newspapers, and art galleries for source material (Kuhn, 2007). Used injudiciously, without sensitivity, and under certain conditions, however, apparently innocuous visual stimuli and material culture can evoke inaccurate, distorted, unexpected, and even painful memories.

Arts-based approaches are particularly participant-friendly and invoke beyond-text sensations employed to access sensory phenomena that are highly meaningful in ways that are ineffable and invisible using conventional text-based methods. *Art-based research* is defined by McNiff (2008) as

> the systematic use of artistic process, the actual making of artistic expressions in all of the different forms of the arts, as a primary way of understanding and examining experience by both researchers and the people that they involve in their studies. (p. 29)

The *Handbook of the Arts in Qualitative Research* (Knowles & Cole, 2008) covered a range of arts-based research methods promoting the notion that art should be regarded as a participatory-sensitive form of knowledge and not merely an ornamental product of human experience. Higgs's (2008) chapter in the *Handbook of the Arts,* "Psychology: Knowing the Self Through the Arts," provided an example of a burgeoning and important link between psychology, arts-based research, and participatory qualitative visual research. This work is part of a distinctive movement toward using creative approaches that improve the quality and trustworthiness of data and findings by drawing on participants' resourcefulness and ingenuity. Gauntlett (2007) used what he termed "creative research methods" and asked participants to make things with collage, by drawing, or by making a video to help them represent themselves and their thinking. In his book *Creative Explorations,* Gauntlett explained how, by adopting the methodological middle-ground between on the one hand method-sparse postmodern and cultural studies thinking and on the other method-limiting word-dominated approaches, fresh and insightful data and findings about people's experiences are gained. In his current work, participants are invited to spend time playfully and creatively making something metaphorical or symbolic about their lives and then reflecting on their creation (see http://www.artlab.org.uk). Gauntlett noted that a more hands-on minds-on approach by participants makes for more trustworthy results and draws on an eclectic array of theories and disciplines from neuroscience to philosophy to provide the theoretical underpinning for his methods. His approach is far removed from psychotherapists

and art therapists of a past era who asked their subjects to construct or make something and then referred to a diagnostic manual to gain the expert insight into what a patient's artwork *actually* meant. Gauntlett expressed the belief that

> pictures or objects enable us to present information, ideas or feelings simultaneously, without the material being forced into an order or a hierarchy. Language may be needed to *explain* the visual, but the image remains primary and shows the relationships between parts most effectively. (p. 15).

His critique of orthodox verbal interviews rests on the perspective that interviewers have unreasonable expectations of interviewees. According to Gauntlett (2007), people's brains do not usually contain ready-made lists of "what I think" about topics such as identity, which gives rise to participants generating "instant answers" that are imprecise and inaccurate. A caveat to art-based participatory visual methods, however, is that the process of creating artwork entails a sensual experience, and analysts need to take account of participant's enthusiasm to create an artistic rendition of events rather than communicate personal insights.

Often changes in research reflect changes in technology and vice versa. Tools and techniques for seeing more and differently are key factors in step changes in visual research, including participatory approaches. Advances like the telescope, microscope, X-ray, ultrasound, magnetic resonance imaging (MRI) scanner, photography, and computers reflect our innate capacity to *see, store, organize,* and *represent* knowledge. Technological innovations have, and always will, bring new ways of researching especially for those employing a visual dimension to social science and science. Current participatory visual research and method owes much to Steven Sasson's invention of the digital camera in 1975. Qualitative visual researchers in psychology are aware of the speed at which technology is changing what and how they study. This is an exciting time to be a visual researcher, and the capacity to communicate where communication was once thought impossible is changing. We provide one example here: Improvements in intensive care have led to an increase in the number of patients who survive severe brain injury. Some of these patients go on to have a good recovery, but others awaken from the acute comatose state and do not show any signs of awareness. Those who yield no evidence of purposeful sensory response are given a diagnosis of a vegetative state. Monti et al. (2010) reported a study giving credibility to the possibility that some patients classified as vegetative are actually conscious, and a few may be able to communicate and actively participate in research on their lived experiences. They used functional MRI (fMRI) to scan 54 patients' brains to record any activity generated in the patients' brains following verbal prompts and questions from the doctors. They found signs of awareness in five patients who demonstrated the ability to generate willful, neuroanatomically specific responses during two established mental-imagery tasks, one of whom was able to answer basic "yes" or "no" to questions by activating different parts of his or her brain. The results show how much we still have to learn about visual evidence, sensory consciousness, and participatory methods. Researchers can potentially communicate with people diagnosed as in a vegetative state through auditory or other sensory stimuli, record responses visually (through fMRI), and ask simple yes–no questions. The study illustrates the power of applied technology to question assumptions of what is possible in participatory research.

ANALYTICAL APPROACHES

In this section, we provide a brief overview of the kinds of analyses used by qualitative researchers to examine visual data, including the following:

- The study of images only.
- The study of images produced by participants, alongside their verbal description and interpretation of them.
- The use of the image only as a "trigger" to elicit discussion and not as part of the analysis.
- The co-study of visual and verbal data as they occur in real time, such as the study of nonverbal and verbal communication in a video recording of an interaction.

The Study of Images Only

In cultural studies and sociology, it is not unusual to find research based on analyses of visual images only, especially within the semiotic tradition. Often the aim of such research is to study how cultural and social phenomena are represented through visual images, asking such questions as what and how are certain values communicated through them (van Leeuwen, 2008). This is not to say that images have a transparent or fixed meaning, as they must be always be understood in relation to shifting cultural contexts (Hall, 1997). In psychology, there is a greater reluctance to study images only, as psychologists tend to be more interested in not just what or how images communicate but also *how* people mobilize, interpret, and use them in everyday life. As Goodwin noted, "The focus of analysis is not . . . representations or vision per se, but instead the part played by visual phenomena in the production of meaningful action" (2008, p. 157). There are examples, however, of psychologists analyzing images to study social psychological phenomena. Gleeson, a social psychologist interested in learning disabilities, for example, has studied the range of identities available to individuals with disabilities by analyzing portraits of disability produced by U.K. charities. Her "polytextual thematic analysis" of these images involves 11 clear stages of data analysis (for details, see Gleeson, 2011). The general principle is to identify themes relevant to the main research question and involves (a) identifying themes across a whole data set of images, (b) describing the features of each theme and providing a justification for why an image can be categorized under this theme, (c) viewing the description of all themes in relation to one another, highlighting any similarities and differences, and (d) seeing whether any themes cluster together to provide a higher order theme that connects them. Results are written up and presented verbally, but it is recommended that the images are central to the presentation to illustrate the emerging themes.

The Study of Images Produced by Participants, Alongside Their Verbal Description and Interpretation of Them

Researchers who invite participants to produce their own photographs or artworks see the images produced as central to the analytical process. The images people have produced are not relegated to the status of a trigger for further discussion, but they are analyzed with the participant as key analytic objects. To provide an illustrative example, we turn to the photo-production work of Radley and Taylor (2003b), who invited participants to take 12 photographs of their hospital environment during a period of recovery after surgery or illness. The participants were then interviewed immediately after taking the photographs and 1 month later, with the photographs forming the central part of the interview procedure.

In the interview, participants were asked to talk about and explain five aspects of the photography, including the following (see Reavey & Johnson, 2008, p. 310):

1. What the picture showed;
2. What the focus of the image was;
3. Their response to the objects and places in the photograph;
4. The most significant image that captured the experience of their hospital stay; and
5. Reflections on the choice of images, the act of taking pictures, and whether they had taken the pictures they would have liked to (i.e., potential limitations).

In short, the ways in which the participants responded to images at the moment of taking the picture as well as their subsequent descriptions and memories emerging from a discussion of them, were argued to be indicative of feelings or tendencies toward their world (Radley & Taylor, 2003a). The final images, therefore, represented patients' prior engagements with the objects and spaces captured, their act of selecting significant features of the space, and a comment on their experiences of their stay. This approach called for a continued reflexive process by participants, who were invited to comment on all aspects of the production of images as well as the associated meanings discussed in relation to the final photographic image. During this process, the researchers commented that many of the images were not interesting or aesthetically pleasing but fairly banal—of interest, however, were the associated meanings contained within them.

The Image Is Used Only as a "Trigger" to Elicit Discussion and Does Not Form Part of the Final Analysis

Ready-made images, whether domestic or mass produced, have been used in a number of qualitative research projects to *elicit* discussion or encourage debate within interviews and focus groups. The images used can be photographs, film, cartoons, graffiti, advertising billboards, and art in general (including objects; Harper, 2002). Individuals may find it easier to talk about aspects of identity and the self or body image via images relating to those topics. Pictures of differently shaped bodies, for example, can make it easier for participants to start with larger cultural themes before focusing in on their own experiences. Starting with the general can put participants at ease and enable them to make comparisons between themselves and others. In studies of memory, the use of family photographs may be used as a way to access the joint process of remembering among family members, although the content of the photographs may not form part of the final analysis—only the conversational exchange (the *discourse*) is presented (see Middleton & Brown, 2005).

The Study of Visual and Verbal Data as They Occur in Real Time

As noted, a growing number of researchers are using visual phenomena, mainly video recordings, to study the processes of communication, cognition, and interaction, as they occur in real time (e.g., discursive psychologists). Rather than asking participants to reflect on an image to produce data, their experiences are studied as they occur. Thus, video data can capture what is being said, gestures and gazes, *and* the spatial environment wherein the actions unfold. The researcher may also use additional materials, such as the use of graphs, charts, and tables, if they are studying how professionals communicate ideas and facts (see Goodwin, 1994).

The visual data are studied alongside other sources that make up meaning-making practices in interactions, namely, talk. In terms of visual phenomena, the researcher may be interested in identifying a number of activities that all form part of the interaction (Goodwin, 2008):

- gaze;
- body posture or movement;
- gesture; and
- setting, including background objects or objects handled by participants.

The analysis of video data will begin with some form of transcription, as it does for verbal qualitative data. It is, therefore, vital that the researcher is able to adequately transcribe visual phenomena in conjunction with the verbal data. Academic journals do not yet accommodate alternative modes of presentation, so transcripts are often the only way to provide concrete examples from a data set. Goodwin (2008), for example, has used a range of transcription symbols (e.g., a hand to signal pointing) and diagrams (see Figure 12.4) to denote gaze, body movement, and gesture to indicate how an interaction unfolds. In research presentations, which are much less constrained by academic convention, the researcher should consider accompanying the presentation of

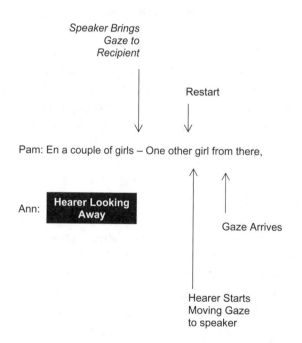

FIGURE 12.4.   Gaze between speakers and hearers: transcript of Pam and Ann. From *Handbook of Visual Analysis* (p. 158), by T. van Leeuwen and C. Jewitt (Eds.), 2008, London, England: Sage. Copyright 2008 by Sage. Adapted with permission.

data from transcripts alongside the video material to better illustrate the analytic points.

ETHICS AND THE VISUAL

Conducting research ethically is viewed as the cornerstone of good practice and increasingly regarded as a professional necessity. Following a surge of interest in research ethics globally, there is an expectation that visual researchers will act reflexively and critically to protect respondents and participants. Making sound ethical decisions during research projects to fulfill this expectation will depend on researchers' personal moral frameworks, disciplinary or paradigm alliance, compliance with legal requirements, and an acceptance of regulations governing research ethics frameworks from funding bodies, professional body guidelines, and institutional ethical committees.

A range of approaches to research ethics in psychology are closely aligned to medical research ethics (Alderson, 2004, p. 98; Israel & Hay, 2006). Consideration of these is important in helping to guide researchers in thinking through the ethical challenges that confront them. An ethics-of-care approach is an important but less common model that challenges the deontological framework underpinning biomedical ethics (Gilligan, 1982). Here, ethical decisions are made on the basis of care, compassion, and a desire to act in ways that benefit the individual or group who are the focus of research rather than following universalist principles or absolute norms and rules that may govern ethical decision making. Qualitative visual researchers seek to implement collaborative relationships in their research relationships, which bear some commonality with an ethics-of-care approach (e.g., Banks, 2001; Harper, 1998; Pink, 2007; Rose, 2007).

The most common principles that underpin ethical approaches and codes of practice have been referred to as mutual respect, noncoercion and nonmanipulation, and support for democratic values and institutions. Similar themes are raised by Papademas (2004):

> Respect for person and the moral
> requirement to respect autonomy and

the requirement to protect those with diminished autonomy; Beneficence and complementary requirement to do no harm and to maximise possible benefits and minimise possible harms; Justice and the fair distribution of the benefits and burdens of research. (p. 122)

Wiles et al. (2008) provided a useful list of key practical issues following the principles outlined by Papademas:

- researchers should strive to protect the rights, privacy, dignity and well-being of those that they study;
- research should (as far as possible) be based on voluntary informed consent;
- personal information should be treated confidentially and participants anonymized unless they choose to be identified;
- research participants should be informed of the extent to which anonymity and confidentiality can be assured in publication and dissemination and of the potential reuse of data. (p. 8)

Visual Ethics and the Law

There is an unspoken assumption that psychologists using visual methods comply with national and international law. Cultural and community pluralism added to technical legal language makes this area difficult for researchers using imagery. Although laws provide a basic framework and minimum standards by themselves they do not necessarily equate with what the research community would consider to constitute acceptable ethical or moral practices. Indeed for many the law represents a minimalist requirement for visual researchers' ethics and more is expected.

Generic laws apply to citizens and researchers and effectively span national laws. The general rule in the United States and the United Kingdom, for example, is that anyone may take photographs in public places or places where they have permission to take photographs. Problems may occur in determining what constitutes a public and semipublic space, such as shopping precincts, schools, or railway stations, but we assume that usually researchers will seek prior permission from owners or managers.

New laws may cause researchers to interpret their relevance to the research environment. The U.K. Data Protection Act 1998, for example, may affect photography. An image of an individual may be considered personal data for the purpose of the act requiring consent to be obtained, which is impractical when videoing people's behavior in busy public spaces. Most researchers consider the spirit of the law is not contravened if consent is not obtained in these circumstances.

Copyright is an aspect of the law that few psychologists using visual methods take into account. For copyright purposes, images come under "artistic works" and include, for example, paintings, cartoons, sketches, graphs, diagrams, sketches, photographs, and moving images such as films. Copyright of artistic works is an automatic right given to creators of original material that allows them to control copying, adaptation, issuance of copies to the public, performance, and broadcasting. Researchers wishing to retain control of images they have created (and own the copyright) or to use images made by others (who own the copyright) by, for example, publishing them should be aware of laws that safeguard copyright. Often visual researchers will ask participants to assign copyright to them at the onset of a study if they intend to ask respondents to create artistic works, such as web pages, drawings, or photographs, as part of the data collection process. Intellectual property rights such as data protection and copyright are convoluted and are continually modified to meet changing circumstances. The rights are analogous throughout Western countries, and although images are normally covered by the particular copyright law of the country in which they are made, copyright owners will automatically be protected in many other countries because most are signatories to the Berne Convention for the Protection of Literary and Artistic Works, which provides reciprocal protection. Banks (2007), a visual anthropologist, reminded us that visual researchers should be vigilant to two important issues: "The first is legal: are they producing, reproducing or altering an image that someone else might claim to own? The second is moral, by what right (legally enforceable or otherwise) are they producing, reproducing or altering an image?" (p. 89).

Banks (2007) also suggested an intellectual rather than legal-ethical resolution to ethical decision making. He proposed that the best way to avoid problems is awareness of context: "The researcher should know enough about the society or community through her research, both in the library and in the field, to anticipate what the likely response will be" (p. 88).

Contemporary societies feature a mix of religions and ethnicity and visual researchers should be aware of the significance of this. It is important, for example, that visual researchers seeking to photograph women of Islamic faith negotiate consent *before* taking a photograph and, if married, they in turn may seek their husband's approval before agreeing. Sharia law deals with Islamic law and is concerned with day-to-day aspects of life, including social issues, family, dress, and behavioral codes, but it is not explicit on the topic of photography. There are multiple interpretations of Sharia law and different countries and communities have different understandings of the use of photography.

Critical Issues

In this section we consider two issues relevant in conducting ethical research, which pose particular challenges in visual research: informed consent, and anonymity and confidentiality.

Obtaining informed consent entails not only gaining agreement or permission to take or produce visual images but also to reproduce or display those images to different audiences and in different contexts. In providing informed consent, participants are expected to not be deceived or coerced into taking part in research, to be informed of the purpose of the research and the research process, and to understand the uses to which the research will be put (Wiles, Crow, Charles, & Heath, 2007). In ethnographic research, detailed discussion of the research, its purpose, and its plans for dissemination all might be part of the consent-gaining procedure (Rose, 2007). On other occasions, for example, if an image is required for illustration purposes, then a simple request to take a photograph with an explanation as to the purpose may be sufficient (Banks, 2001). The process requires careful consideration and there are a number of epistemological as well as

ethical benefits of obtaining informed consent to collect and use visual images (Banks, 2007; Pink, 2007). Chief among these is the argument that obtaining consent is a requisite of obtaining quality data. Visual data alone may provide limited understandings of the meanings and experiences that are recorded within that data, and it is through negotiation with participants that visual data are produced that can appropriately reflect the realities and experiences of participants (Banks, 2001; Harper, 1998). The public display, publishing, or wider dissemination of visual data without the consent of individuals pictured has been described as ethically questionable (Pink, 2007; Prosser & Schwartz, 1998). Gaining consent is also important for maintaining rapport and a relationship of trust between researchers and individuals in the field and to avoid a detrimental impact on the success of ongoing or subsequent research (Prosser, 2000). Like other visual researchers, Chaplin (2004) was clear in her advice to "always ask permission before photographing someone, and always get written permission before publishing the photograph" (p. 45). However, although this is good ethical practice, obtaining informed consent is not always straightforward. Attaining consent for photographing children, for example, requires careful deliberation because of the particular difficulties that this poses. Parental consent is needed if a child is not viewed as having the capacity to consent (Masson, 2004). In some circumstance, both the parents and the children are asked for their consent to photograph or video regardless of the child's capacity to consent. The notion of a person's capacity to give consent is a judgment that relates to vulnerable members of a society, for example, the young, older people, and those with disabilities.

Another challenging dilemma concerns what participants are consenting to. There are differences between consenting to take part in visual research and consenting for an image to go in a book. For example, consent may be required not only to produce a photograph or film footage but also for the specific formats and contexts in which the image is displayed, such as books, conference papers, and exhibitions, or for general illustrative purposes (Pink, 2007; Prosser & Loxley, 2008). Although participants might give consent to having their photograph taken, they may not be consenting to subsequent display of those images. The question of what participants are consenting to becomes more complex if visual data are to be archived, resulting in unknown further reuses of data. It is increasingly common for visual researchers to seek blanket consent to use the images collected as part of a project to be used in any way they (the researcher) deem fit which does not in their view endanger participant.

Visual data presents particular challenges to the anonymity and confidentiality of individuals particularly when photography is employed. The benefits of collaborative research, in which participants are encouraged to take part in the production, analysis, and dissemination of visual research are well documented (Banks, 2001; Pink, 2007). The close relationships established between researchers and participants in such instances enables discussion of the implications of showing images and films to be undertaken. However, participants who engage in the research process because they see benefits in terms of voice and agency may question the need to be anonymized—indeed, they object if they are *not* seen (Wiles et al., 2008). If an aim of participatory visual research is to empower and give voice to marginalized groups and individuals, but those individuals and groups are anonymized against their wishes, this raises important questions about power relationships in research and control of the research.

Given that visual data reveals important information that text- or word-based methods cannot uncover, attempting to disguise visual data can remove the very point of including the data in the first place. Hence, visual researchers tend to favor gaining consent from participants to display their images unchanged. An alternative is partial anonymization in which decisions are made about what to anonymize in an image because, for example, clothing, jewelry, tattoos, and the environments where individuals are photographed can all potentially breech confidentiality. Barrett (2004), on the other hand, took a minimalist approach in her photographic essay of a needle exchange facility in an U.S. city by showing photographs only of hands or people with backs turned. Clark, Prosser, and Wiles (2010) illustrated how overanonymizing data can

also be a danger with a photograph showing the distinctive feature of a building, a car number plate, and an adult and a child that were all anonymized, rendering the image almost meaningless. Researchers adopt a range of techniques when anonymizing participants and respondents. These may include using actors and reenacting events, using software packages that render photographs in the form of a cartoon-style graphic, or various forms of pixilation for the blurring of faces (Wiles et al., 2008). However, it has been argued that pixelating images can dehumanize the individuals in them, and because of its widespread use on television, can invoke associations with criminality (Banks, 2001).

Maintaining internal confidentiality (between members of a specific group) can give rise to anonymity problems from media other than photographic rendition. Clark, Prosser, and Wiles (2010) located various ways in which family members and the creator could be identified by members of a school or neighborhood community (see Figure 12.5). They pointed out that

> the author's name, although hidden by a black pen, can be guessed by the size of the first and second name, and be seen when the paper on which the original is made, is held up to the light and the drawing shows all the information required to identify a family of four, of mixed race, comprising two adults and two children of each gender and a mother with one leg. (2010, p. 87)

The digitization of data and the growth of the Internet to display, store, and exchange visual data, have created further ethical challenges (Pauwels, 2006). Assurance to participants that visual data once disseminated in the academic domain and therefore potentially made public will be used appropriately is no longer possible. Once in the public realm, participants and researchers have no control over how images might be interpreted by audiences, or may be used for different purposes by others. This means particular care should be taken to ensure that participants understand the implications of consenting to the displaying of images used in research given that they may be

FIGURE 12.5. Example of participant's drawing. From "Ethical Issues in Image-Based Research," by A. Clark, J. Prosser, and R. Wiles, 2010, *Arts and Health, 2*, p. 407. Copyright 2010 by Routledge of the Taylor & Francis Group. Reprinted with permission.

placed online. The flip side is that visual researchers may access and use visual data from the Internet in their own research. Lee (2000) suggested that images appropriated in this way should still "fall within the scope of existing guidelines on ethical research practice in respect of informed consent, privacy and confidentiality and the need to protect research participants from harm" (p. 135). Although empirical visual researchers may support this position (Godel, 2007; Pauwels, 2006), those adopting a critical or sociosemiotic analysis of "found" visual data are less enamoured with the prospect of seeking approval of copyright owners or those depicted.

Visual psychologists feel vulnerable and unprepared to field the ethical probes of nonvisual methodologists. Evidence of the relationship between visual researchers and institutional ethics committees is rare and often anecdotal. Pauwels (2008) recounted that

> a recent conference session on ethics in visual research and in particular on the role of ethics review committees (IVSA [International Visual Sociology Association] Annual Conference, New York, August 2007) revealed the urgent need to address these (ethical) issues and also the

willingness of most parties involved to improve the situation. Many participants testified about IRBs [institutional review boards], which worked strictly by the book and were ignorant of the specific demands of visual research, and thus in good faith provided obstacles to innovative and well thought through research. But there were also examples of review boards that did include people experienced in visual research, and which succeeded in making headway. (p. 256)

This provides indicative rather than substantive data but nonetheless suggests that there are important issues to be explored by consulting members of ethics review boards and applicants to those boards. Visual psychologists, like their qualitative cousins in sociology and anthropology, are uneasy with the difficulties posed by acquiescing to various regulatory mechanisms and are nervous about the complexity of applied moral decision making. Although negotiating informed consent and applying appropriate strategies of anonymity and confidentiality make for ethical complexity, this should not be taken to mean the endeavor should be avoided.

CONCLUSION

Psychology has a long and complex historical relationship with the visual. Although a qualitatively driven visual dimension has not featured prominently methodologically in psychology as it has in other social science disciplines, a distinctive and robust body of work has emerged that bodes well for the future (Reavey, 2011). There are many excellent ways of undertaking visual research and applying visual methods within psychology, and what is prescribed here represents just one. Our advice is to ignore or at the very least treat with caution any visual researchers who claim theirs is the only, proper, or best way without a clear rationale. We recognized that in attempting to provide a resource useful to a cross-section of psychologists and applied researchers we would necessarily sacrifice depth for breadth.

Over the past decade the qualitative visual methodological landscape has changed. There has been a general awakening to the significance and ubiquity of imagery in contemporary lives. Visuals are pervasive in public, work, and private spaces, and we have no choice but to look. Qualitative psychologists have taken up the challenge to understand the behavior of individuals and groups within a society dominated by visual culture using visual methodologies. Although a paucity of insightful exemplars of remains, the richness of possibilities that once constrained visual studies in psychology appears to be dissipating fast. The visual and other sensory approaches have opened up possibilities for understanding individual embodied and emotional experiences. The most significant challenge facing visual researchers in the 21st century lies in developing the capacity to be sufficiently flexible, creative, and critical to provide solutions to problems facing humanity. The past 2 decades have witnessed an exponential growth in interest in visual research, which has contributed to the robustness and complexity in visual studies and is to be welcomed. As one would expect given the rate and nature of change, this has brought unmitigated diversity and methodological problems such as visual analysis and complex ethical considerations. However, there is every reason to be positive. A methodologically framed, qualitatively driven, visually orientated, mixed-method, interdisciplinary approach to examining overarching and substantive psychological themes and research questions that are central to understanding the nature of everyday individual's existence is being developed. An interdisciplinary mixed-methods approach encourages the establishment of flexible and diverse research teams capable of a contrastive and reflexive rhetoric. Visual-centric qualitatively driven research is widely practiced across a range of disciplines and it is timely and appropriate to apply these approaches to the study of all forms of psychology. Our hope is that during the next decade studies in visual psychology will become a world movement and a means to attaining long overdue internationalization and global recognition of image-based methodologies.

References

Alderson, P. (2004). Ethics. In S. Fraser, V. Lewis, S. Ding, M. Kellett, & C. Robinson (Eds.), *Doing research with children and young people* (pp. 97–112). London, England: Sage.

Banks, M. (2001). *Visual methods in social research*. London, England: Sage.

Banks, M. (2007). *Using visual data in qualitative research*. London, England: Sage.

Barrett, D. (2004). Photo-documenting the needle exchange: methods and ethics. *Visual Studies, 19*(2), 145–149. doi:10.1080/1472586042000301647

Bowes-Catton, H., Barker, M., & Richards, C. (2011). "I didn't know that I could feel this relaxed in my body": Using visual methods to research bisexual people's embodied experiences of identity and space. In P. Reavey (Ed.), *Visual methods in psychology: Using and interpreting images in qualitative research* (pp. 255–271). London, England: Routledge.

Brookfield, H., Brown, S. D., & Reavey, P. (2008). Vicarious and post-memory practices in adopting families: The re-production of the past through photography and narrative. *Journal of Community and Applied Social Psychology, 18*, 474–491. doi:10.1002/casp.960

Brown, S. D., Reavey, P., Cromby, J., Harper, D., & Johnson, K. (2008) On psychology and embodiment: Some methodological experiments. In J. Latimer & M. Schillmeier (Eds.), *Knowing/unknowing bodies* (pp. 197–215). Oxford, England: Blackwell.

Buss, D. (2005). *The evolutionary psychology handbook*. Hoboken, NJ: Wiley.

Chalfen, R. (1998). Interpreting family photography as a pictorial communication. In J. Prosser (Ed.), *Image-based research: A sourcebook for qualitative researchers* (pp. 214–234). London, England: Falmer Press.

Chalfen, R., Worth, S., & Adair, J. (1997). *Through Navajo eyes: An exploration in film communication and anthropology* (2nd ed. rev.). Albuquerque: University of New Mexico Press.

Chaplin, E. (2004). My visual diary. In C. Knowles & P. Sweetman (Eds.), *Picturing the social landscape: Visual methods and the sociological imagination* (pp. 34–48). London, England: Routledge.

Clark, A., Prosser, J., & Wiles, R. (2010). Ethical issues in image-based research. *Arts and Health, 2*, 81–93. doi: 10.1080/17533010903495298

Collier, J., Jr. (1957). Photography in anthropology: A report on two experiments. *American Anthropologist, 59*, 843–859. doi:10.1525/aa.1957.59.5.02a00100

Conway, M. (Ed.). (1997) *Cognitive models of memory*. Hove, England: Psychology Press.

Cramer, P. (1996). *Storytelling, narrative, and the Thematic Apperception Test*. London, England: Guilford Press.

Cronin, O. (1998). Psychology and photographic theory. In J. Prosser (Ed.), *Image-based research: A sourcebook for qualitative researchers* (pp. 69–83). London, England: Falmer Press.

Darwin, C. (1872/1999). *The expression of the emotions in man and animals: Definitive edition.* Waukegan, IL: Fontana Press.

Del Busso, L. (2009). *Being in motion: femininity, movement, and space in young women's narratives of their embodied experiences in everyday life* (Unpublished doctoral dissertation). London South Bank University, London, England.

Del Busso, L. (2011). Capturing embodied experience: The use of photographs in research on young women's embodied experiences in everyday life. In P. Reavey (Ed.), *Visual methods in psychology: Using and interpreting images in qualitative research* (pp. 43–55). London, England: Routledge.

Draaisma, D. (2000). *Metaphors of memory: A history of ideas about the mind.* Cambridge, England: Cambridge University Press.

Emmison, M., & Smith, P. (2000). *Researching the visual.* London, England: Sage.

Fechner, G. T. (1966). *Elements of psychophysics.* Orlando, FL: Holt, Rinehart & Winston. (Original work published 1860)

Fitzpatrick, J. F., & Bringmann, W. G. (1997). Charles Darwin and psychology. In W. G. Bringmann, H. E. Lück, R. Miller, & C. E. Early (Eds.), *A pictorial history of psychology* (pp. 51–52). Chicago, IL: Quintessence Books.

Frith, H. (2011). Narrating biographical disruption and repair: Exploring the place of absent images in women's experiences of cancer and chemotherapy. In P. Reavey (Ed.), *Visual methods in psychology: Using and interpreting images in qualitative research* (pp. 55–69). London, England: Routledge.

Frith, H., & Harcourt, D. (2007). Using photographs to capture women's experiences of chemotherapy: Reflecting on the method. *Qualitative Health Research, 17,* 1340–1350.

Frost, L. (2001) Theorizing the young woman in the body. *Body Society, 11,* 63–85.

Gauntlett, D. (2007). *Creative explorations: New approaches to identities and audiences.* London, England; New York, NY: Routledge.

Gillies, V., Harden, A., Johnson, K., Reavey, P., Strange, V., & Willig, C. (2004). Women's collective constructions of embodied practices through memory work. *British Journal of Social Psychology, 43,* 99–112. doi:10.1348/014466604322916006

Gillies, V., Harden, A., Johnson, K., Reavey, P., Strange, V., & Willig, C. (2005). Painting pictures of embodied experience: The use of nonverbal data production for the study of embodiment. *Qualitative Research in Psychology, 2,* 199–212. doi:10.1191/1478088705qp038oa

Gilligan, C. (1982). *In a different voice: Psychological theory and women's development.* Cambridge, MA: Harvard University Press.

Gleeson, K. (2011). Polytextual thematic analysis for visual data—pinning down the analytic. In P. Reavey (Ed.), *Visual psychologies: Using and interpreting images in qualitative research* (pp. 314–340). London, England: Routledge.

Gleeson, K., & Frith, H. (2006). Deconstructing body image. *Journal of Health Psychology, 11,* 79–90. doi:10.1177/1359105306058851

Godel, M. (2007). Images of stillbirth: Memory, meaning, and memorial. *Visual Studies, 22,* 253–269. doi:10.1080/14725860701657159

Goodwin, C. (1994). Professional vision. *American Anthropologist, 96,* 606–633. doi:10.1525/aa.1994.96.3.02a00100

Goodwin, C. (2000). Action and embodiment within situated human interaction. *Journal of Pragmatics, 32,* 1489–1522.

Goodwin, C. (2008). Practices of seeing visual analysis: an ethnomethodological approach. In T. van Leeuwen & C. Jewitt (Eds.), *Handbook of visual analysis* (pp. 157–183). London, England: Sage.

Haaken, J., & Reavey, P. (2009). *Memory matters: Contexts of understanding sexual abuse recollections.* London, England: Routledge.

Hall, S. (1997). Introduction. In S. Hall (Ed.), *Representation: Cultural representations and signifying practices.* London, England: Sage.

Harper, D. (1998). An argument for visual sociology. In J. Prosser (Ed.), *Image-based research: A sourcebook for qualitative researchers* (pp. 24–42). London, England: Falmer Press.

Harper, D. (2002). Talking about pictures: a case for photo elicitation. *Visual Studies, 17,* 13–26. doi:10.1080/14725860220137345

Higgs, G. E. (2008). Psychology: Knowing the self through the arts. In J. G. Knowles & A. L. Cole (Eds.), *Handbook of the arts in qualitative research* (pp. 545–557). London, England: Sage.

Hodgetts, D., Chamberlain, K., & Groot, S. (2011). Reflections on the visual in community research and action. In P. Reavey (Ed.), *Visual methods in psychology: Using and interpreting images in qualitative research* (pp. 299–313). London, England: Routledge.

Hodgetts, D., Chamberlain, K., & Radley, A. (2007). Considering photographs never taken during photo-production project. *Qualitative Research in*

Psychology, 4, 263–280. doi:10.1080/14780880 701583181

Hodgetts, D., Chamberlain, K., Radley, A., & Hodgetts, A. (2007). Health inequalities and homelessness: Considering material, relational, and spatial dimensions. *Journal of Health Psychology, 12,* 709–725. doi:10.1177/1359105307080593

Howarth, C. (2011). Towards a visual social psychology of identity and representation: photographing the self, weaving the family in a multicultural British community. In P. Reavey (Ed.), *Visual methods in psychology: Using and interpreting images in qualitative research* (pp. 241–255). London, England: Routledge.

Israel, M., & Hay, I. (2006). *Research ethics for social scientists: Between ethical conduct and regulatory compliance.* London, England: Sage.

Jackson, M. (1995). Images of deviance: Visual representations of mental defectives in early twentieth-century. *British Journal for the History of Science, 28,* 319–37.

Knowles, J. G., & Cole, A. L. (Eds.). (2008). *Handbook of the arts in qualitative research.* London, England; Los Angeles, CA: Sage.

Kuhn, A. (2007) Photography and cultural memory: a methodological exploration. *Visual Studies, 22,* 283–293.

Kunimoto, N. (2004). Intimate archives: Japanese-Canadian family photography, 1939–1949. *Art History, 27,* 129–155. doi:10.1111/j.0141-6790.2004.02701005.x

Langdridge, D. (2007). *Phenomenological psychology: Theory, research, and method.* London, England: Pearson Prentice Hall.

Lee, R. (2000). *Unobtrusive methods in social research.* Buckingham, England: Open University Press.

Majumdar, A. (2011). Using photographs of places, spaces, and objects to explore South Asian Women's experience of close relationships and marriage. In P. Reavey (Ed.), *Visual methods in psychology: Using and interpreting images in qualitative research* (69–85). London, England: Routledge.

Masson, J. (2004). The legal context. In S. Fraser, V. Lewis, S. Ding, M. Kellett, & C. Robinson (Eds.), *Doing research with children and young people* (pp. 43–58). London, England: Sage.

McNiff, S. (2008). Art-based research. In J. G. Knowles & A. L. Cole (Eds.), *Handbook of the arts in qualitative research* (pp. 29–41). London, England; Los Angeles, CA: Sage.

Meischner-Metge, A., & Meischner, W. (1997). Fechner and Lotze. In W. G. Bringmann, H. E. Lück, R. Miller, & C. E. Early (Eds.), *A pictorial history of psychology* (pp. 101–106). Chicago, IL: Quintessence Books.

Middleton, D., & Brown, S. D. (2005). *The social psychology of experience: Studies in remembering and forgetting.* London, England: Sage.

Middleton, D., & Edwards, D. (Eds.). (1990). *Collective remembering.* London, England: Sage.

Milgram, S. (2005). *Obedience to authority: An experimental view.* New York, NY: Pinter & Martin. (Original work published 1974)

Mirzoeff, N. (2009). *An introduction to visual culture* (2nd ed.). London, England: Routledge.

Monti, M. M., Vanhaudenhuyse, A., Coleman, M. R., Boly, M., Pickard, J. D., Tshibanda, Owen, A. M., & Laureys, S. (2010). Willful modulation of brain activity in disorders of consciousness. *New England Medical Journal, 362,* 579–589.

Packard, J. (2008). "I'm gonna show you what it's really like out there": The power and limitation of participatory research methods. *Visual Studies, 23,* 63–77.

Parker, I. (2004). *Qualitative psychology: Introducing radical research.* Buckingham, England: Open University Press.

Papademas, D. (2004). Editor's introduction: ethics in visual research. *Visual Studies, 19,* 122–126. doi:10.1080/1472586042000301610

Pauwels, L. (2006). Discussion: Ethical issues in online (visual) research. *Visual Anthropology, 19,* 365–369. doi:10.1080/08949460600656691

Pauwels, L. (2008) A private practice going public? Social functions and sociological research opportunities of web-based family photography. *Visual Studies, 23,* 34–49.

Pink, S. (2007). *Doing visual ethnography* (2nd ed.). London, England: Sage.

Porter, R. (2003). *Madness: A brief history.* Oxford, England: Oxford University Press.

Prosser, J. (2000). The moral maze of image ethics. In H. Simons & R. Usher (Eds.), *Situated ethics in education research* (pp. 116–132) London, England: Routledge.

Prosser, J., & Loxley, A. (2008). *Introducing visual methods* (National Centre for Research Methods Review Paper 010). Retrieved from http://eprints.ncrm. ac.uk/420/1/MethodsReviewPaperNCRM-010.pdf

Prosser, J., & Schwartz, D. (1998). Photographs within the sociological research process. In J. Prosser (Ed.), *Image-based research: A sourcebook for qualitative researchers* (pp. 115–130). London, England: Falmer Press.

Radley, A. (1990). Artefacts, memory, and a sense of the past. In D. Middleton & D. Edwards (Eds.), *Collective remembering* (pp. 46–59). London, England: Sage.

Radley, A. (2009). *Works of illness: Narrative, picturing, and the social response to serious disease.* Ashby-de-la-Zouch, England: InkMen Press.

Radley, A., & Taylor, D. (2003a). Images of recovery: a photo-elicitation study on the hospital ward. *Qualitative Health Research, 13*, 77–99. doi:10.1177/1049732302239412

Radley, A., & Taylor, D. (2003b). Remembering one's stay in hospital: a study in photography, recovery, and forgetting. *Health: An Interdisciplinary Journal for the Social Study of Health, Illness, and Medicine, 7*, 129–159.

Ratcliff, D. (2003). Video methods in qualitative research. In P. M. Camic, J. E. Rhodes, & L. Yardley (Eds.), *Qualitative research in psychology: Expanding perspectives in methodology and design* (pp. 113–129). Washington, DC: American Psychological Association. doi:10.1037/10595-007

Reavey, P. (2008). *Back to experience: Material subjectivities and the visual.* Keynote address at the Visual Psychologies Conference, University of Leicester, England.

Reavey, P. (2010) Spatial markings: memory and child sexual abuse. *Memory Studies, 3*, 314–329.

Reavey, P. (2011). The return to experience: Psychology and the visual. In P. Reavey (Ed.), *Visual methods in psychology: Using and interpreting images in qualitative research* (pp. 1–14). London, England: Routledge.

Reavey, P., & Johnson, K. (2008). Visual approaches: Using and interpreting images. In C. Stainton, W. Rogers, & C. Willig (Eds.), *The Sage handbook of qualitative research* (pp. 296–315). London, England: Sage.

Richards, G. (2002). *Putting psychology in its place: A critical historical overview* (2nd ed.). London, England: Routledge.

Rose, G. (2007). *Visual methodologies* (2nd ed.). London, England: Sage.

Silver, J., & Reavey, P. (2010). "He's a good looking chap, ain't he?": Narrative and visualisations of self in body dysmorphic disorder. *Social Science and Medicine, 70*, 1641–1647.

Speer, S. A., & Green, R. (2007). On passing: The interactional organization of appearance attributions in the psychiatric assessment of transsexual patients. In V. Clarke & E. Peel (Eds.), *Out in psychology: Lesbian, gay, bisexual, trans, and queer perspectives* (pp. 335–369). Chichester, England: Wiley.

Stam, H. (Ed.). (1998). *The body and psychology.* London, England: Sage.

Stanczak, G. (Ed.). (2007). *Visual research methods: Image, society, and representation.* London, England: Sage.

Stainton, C., Rogers, W., & Willig, C. (Eds.). (2008). *The Sage handbook of qualitative methods in psychology.* London, England: Sage.

Thomson, P. (Ed.). (2008). *Doing visual research with children and young people.* London, England, and New York, NY: Routledge.

van Elteren, M., & Luck, H. (1990). Lewin's films and their role in field theory. In S. A. Wheelan, E. A. Pepitone & V. Abt (Eds.), *Advances in field theory* (pp. 38–61). New York, NY: Sage.

van Leeuwen, T. (2008). Semiotics and iconography. In T. van Leeuwen & C. Jewitt (Eds.), *Handbook of visual analysis* (pp. 92–119). London, England: Sage.

van Leeuwen, T., & Jewitt, C. (Eds.). (2008). *Handbook of visual analysis.* London, England: Sage.

Wagner, J. (2006). Visible materials, visualised theory, and images of social research. *Visual Studies, 21*, 55–69. doi:10.1080/14725860600613238

Warren, S. (2005). Photography and voice in critical qualitative management research. *Accounting, Auditing, and Accountability Journal, 18*, 861–882. doi:10.1108/09513570510627748

Wiles, R., Crow, G., Charles, V., & Heath, S. (2007). Informed consent in the research process: following rules or striking balances? *Sociological Research Online, 12.* Retrieved from http://socresonline.org.uk/12/2.html

Wiles, R., Prosser, J., Bagnoli, A., Clark, A., Davies, K., Holland, S., & Renold, E. (2008). *Visual ethics: Ethical issues in visual research* (National Centre for Research Methods Review Paper 011). Retrieved from http://www.ncrm.ac.uk/research/outputs/publications/methodsreview/MethodsReviewPaperNCRM-011.pdf

Willig, C. (2008). *Introducing qualitative methods in psychology: adventures in theory and method.* Buckingham, England: Open University Press.

Zimbardo, P., Maslach, C., & Haney, C. (2000). Reflections on the Stanford prison experiment: Genesis, transformations, consequences. In T. Blass (Ed.), *Obedience to authority: Current perspectives on the Milgram paradigm* (pp. 193–238). London, England: Erlbaum.

CHAPTER 13

RESEARCHING THE TEMPORAL

Karen Henwood and Fiona Shirani

This chapter showcases methodologically innovative work in the psychological and social sciences that is qualitative and longitudinal in its research approach and for which questions about time and temporal experience are of significant interest. It considers the case for conducting qualitative inquiries longitudinally and for putting concern for the significance of time and temporality in people's lives at the heart of empirical, interpretive studies (Neale & Flowerdew, 2003). Time is useful to social researchers as a *vehicle of study*, because it provides a means of designing studies around key moments, transitions, trajectories, and periods of elapsed time of longer duration so that significant change is more likely to have occurred. It can also be treated as a *topic of study*, for which the substantive research focus is on how people think about and relate to time, to open up to scrutiny the range of ways in which life is experienced and made sense of temporally (Salmon, 1985). Time is a multidimensional construct and, for this reason, needs to be approached not just biographically but generationally and historically (Neale, 2007).

There is a longstanding commitment in the United Kingdom and in the United States, as well as in other countries, to investing in large-scale quantitative longitudinal (or panel) studies in which the same group of people is interviewed repeatedly with standardized questions. Such research is meant to measure consistency or change in people's beliefs and attitudes over time. In comparison, qualitative longitudinal studies that seek to understand processes of change dynamically have remained small

scale and piecemeal (Henwood & Lang, 2005; Mason, 2002). Moreover, whenever there has been sustained methodological discussion of how to generate, maintain, and analyze longitudinal data sets, this has generally focused exclusively on large-scale *quantitative* methods. When *qualitative* longitudinal (QLL) study has been discussed, it has appeared to be an intriguing but minority interest among the possibilities that such methods offer for studying time and change (Saldaña, 2003).

To sharpen and clarify understanding that there are different forms taken by longitudinal studies, Elliott, Holland, and Thomson (2008) have addressed both the shared and distinctive contributions of quantitative and qualitative approaches to long-term study. They have portrayed longitudinal study generically as the means of generating "unique insights into process, change and continuity in time in phenomena ranging from individuals, families and institutions to societies" (p. 228), while also pointing firmly to the way that each of the two established traditions of longitudinal study produce "different types of data, privileging particular forms of understanding and pursuing different logics of inquiry" (p. 228). Other researchers have explicitly advocated the merits of QLL study within predominantly quantitative research communities. For example, social policy researchers have pointed to the need for attentiveness to the ways in which the same experiences are recounted differently at different time points to study people's experiences and perceptions before, during, and after an intervention (Corden & Millar, 2007; Lewis, 2007). QLL research

DOI: 10.1037/13620-013
APA Handbook of Research Methods in Psychology: Vol. 2. Research Designs, H. Cooper (Editor-in-Chief)
Copyright © 2012 by the American Psychological Association. All rights reserved.

addressing the complexity of transitions, and how they are differently experienced by the people involved, has been portrayed as a complementary method to the narrative study of lives (Miller, 2000).

This chapter is written in the spirit of pursuing what lies behind the different logic of the qualitative inquiry tradition, while accepting that there is also value in integrating quantitative and qualitative studies in ways that may be qualitatively or quantitatively led (Mason, 2006). The chapter starts with coverage of some of the key ideas and arguments providing the theoretical and methodological background to temporal study and then illustrates these discussions by drawing on a QLL inquiry into the dynamics of men's identities, relationships, and personal lives. Known as the Men as Fathers Project, (see http://www.cardiff.ac.uk/sosci/researchprojects/menasfathers/index.html) it is part of the Timescapes network (see http://www.timescapes.leeds.ac.uk), the first major large-scale QLL study in the United Kingdom. The network has been designed to scale up the reach and impact of hitherto cottage industry–style QLL studies in a number of ways. One involves linking together projects exploring continuities and changes in people's lives over the full life course. Hence, it includes studies of young lives, midlife transitions, and the oldest generation. Our concern in this chapter is to highlight some of the core methodological and analytical issues that are being addressed in the men-as-fathers study relating to its use of QLL methodology and commitment to researching the temporal more generally.

INTELLECTUAL BACKGROUND

The intellectual background to the research developments that are of interest in this chapter is provided by a set of discussions that are multi- and interdisciplinary. Some of the key theoretical and methodological issues at stake are encapsulated in biographical or life course methods (e.g., Chamberlayne, Bornat, & Wengraf, 2000; Heinz & Krüger, 2001; Rosenthal, 2004). According to Chamberlayne et al. (2000), the burgeoning of life course methods across the social sciences has to do with their capacity to offer an antidote to commonly adopted research approaches (positivism, determinism, and social constructionism) that divorce researchers from understanding the lived realities of people's lives. These authors advocate paying attention to the meanings people attach to the events they encounter in their daily lives and giving them prominence as the basis for their actions.[1] Collecting life stories, often in the form of oral histories, and understanding them in ways that see interconnections between personal meanings and wider patterns of sociohistorical change is a particularly emphasized feature of life course study (Thompson, 1975), and one that corresponds closely with more qualitative, cultural, and psychological perspectives on the narrative study of lives (Andrews, Day Schlater, Squire, & Treacher, 2000; Squire, 2008).

Family studies are another field of inquiry that has built the case for developing principles and practices of temporal inquiry. Such inquiries generate knowledge about family formation and function in the context of wider societal organization and change, and include the study of personal lives.[2] As with life course research, there is a conviction that social theorizing at a macroscopic level fails to address the complex patterns of people's lived lives on the ground, and a particular concern is that theories overstate the extent of changes over continuities in people's relationships in (post)modern times (Smart, 2007).[3] Out of this field, methodological initiatives have developed to counter researchers'

---

[1]In this way, life course research recapitulates two of the most long-established principles in qualitative inquiry: studying ordinary meanings in ways that make them interesting and useful objects of study (Charmaz, 2006; Charmaz & Henwood 2008) and taking seriously participants' meaning frames (also known as the *actors' perspective*) as the basis for understanding why they do what they do (Henwood, 2008; Henwood, Pidgeon, Sarre, Simmons, & Smith, 2008).

[2]Although family studies research employs theoretical analysis and invokes social theory, it a highly empirical field of inquiry, involving both quantitative and qualitative studies. It concerns many issues with a direct relevance to social and welfare policy (e.g., impact of divorce, transnational adoption, singledom).

[3]*Postmodernity* refers to the condition of societies that have undergone a fundamental shift to a mode of organization characterized by technological advance, information technology, and a culture skeptical of absolute truth claims; it also applies where economies are underpinned by consumption rather than industrial production.

preoccupation with theoretical abstractions and the lack of engagement with the vitality and bedrock of people's lives (see http://www.socialsciences.manchester.ac.uk/realities). The Timescapes QLL study of identities and relationships across the life course is one of these initiatives; its particular concern is with providing an alternative to family researchers' static, atemporal focus so that is possible to study the *dynamics* of personal lives. QLL study is adopted as a means of walking alongside people through time as their lives unfold (Neale, 2007; Neale & Flowerdew, 2003). This leads to a focus on continuities and changes occurring in daily life—called *microtemporal processes*—that are unlikely to follow single or linear trajectories because the phenomena under study are in the making and so may, themselves, be changing. This is where a definitive contrast is set up between quantitative and QLL study because the former measures discrete variables, at specific moments in time, on a linear metric so that their intrinsic (and hence unchanging) qualities can be reliably counted and validly compared.

By drawing on the work of the temporal theorist Barbara Adam (1990), the Timescapes program has further underpinned its conceptualization of what she has called the extraordinary temporal dimensions of everyday life. Clock, or quantitative time, is represented by calendars and timetables; it is a dominant form of time, often central to adult life, and it operates according to the logic of commodities and markets (it is not to be wasted, it rushes past us, and it can run out). Equally important are the other times that are intricate, are multiple, and join us to our worlds of lived, everyday experience—our lifeworlds[4]—in many and varied ways: as normative times (e.g., socially approved timings and sequences), synchronization and timeliness, expectancy and anticipation, prioritization, pace and duration, personal time (my time), and task times—each with their own boundaries. These times are produced at moments in everyday living, providing us with experiential modes that extend beyond the visible present. For example, they can affirm the durability of what we hold deeply significant; create

a sense of security; alter or change; bridge or create distance between who we think we are at different times; and, through imagination, bring the future into the present (Salmon, 1985). As the temporal processes that engage us most in our lifeworlds may be invisible to research participants and researchers alike, making them visible requires an awareness of temporal process and movement of time that is not available to us in the realm of the everyday. The name of the QLL network Timescapes derives from the concept in Adam's (1998) work referring to the multiple vantage points for looking in and across time that bring our lives and worlds into view. The extent to which looking at the world through Timescapes, and the space–time horizons they create, can be made accessible to qualitative analysts remains a matter of ongoing study within the network.

ILLUSTRATIVE STUDY

The Men as Fathers Project is considered in this chapter to illustrate an innovative methodological approach, combining an interest in subjective experiences of everyday life, continuity and change, and time and temporal process. The study began in 1999, lay dormant for a period, and was then reactivated 8 years later in 2008. During both phases of the project, we have been researching how men's identities come to be formed—not in isolation but in a relational and contextual way; accordingly, we have been cognizant of how their lives involve relationships—how they are linked with the lives of others. Our investigative approach has involved asking how men who become fathers experience and make sense of this major life transition over the short and longer term. Their personal sense and identity making is also embedded within a broader set of sociopolitical contestations and cultural possibilities over what the lives of men who are fathers, and their significant others, should and can be (Edley & Wetherell, 1999; Wetherell & Edley, 1999).

In describing the context of contemporary lives and times in which our study participants became

---

[4]*Lifeworlds* is a term used in the philosophy of social science to refer to our pregiven, directly apprehended experiences of the world; they are pregiven rather then being known through any particular theory or scientific interpretation (e.g., Hughes, 1990).

fathers, a salient issue is the way that individuals appear to be living out their lives in rapidly changing times, involving a fundamental questioning of the identities and relationships that are necessary now, and will be in the future, to sustain human sociality and personal life (Henwood, Gill, & Mclean, 2002; Hollway & Featherstone, 1997). Over time, we have come to see particular value in asking questions about whether such changes have implications for how people move through life course transitions, their timing, people's temporal experiences more generally, and their orientations to past, present, and future (Shirani & Henwood, 2011b). In this chapter, we are concerned primarily with the varied lines of exploration we have conducted into a key subjectively and culturally meaningful issue, paternal involvement. Paternal involvement is a currently predominant signifier of good fatherhood, and interrogating men's ways of relating to it can help inform sociopolitical and scientific understanding of the practices and meanings of fatherhood and masculinity today (Dermott, 2008; Doucet, 2007; Henwood & Procter, 2003).

In research such as ours, which uses qualitative and temporal research strategies to understand people's personal lives in times of change, it is useful to appreciate how our own inquiries may be intertwined with a number of linked social transformation agendas. One of these is *detraditionalization*. Analysts of this phenomenon (Beck & Beck-Gernsheim, 1995) hold that in contemporary society people are increasingly disembedded from traditions of family, class, and culture and burdened by the proliferation of individual choice through processes of deindustrialization and consumerisation. There is also an emphasis on the fragmentation of identities and loosening of relational ties, as found in analyses of how people are living in postmodern times more generally. Another perspective on social transformation highlights the phenomenon of *destabilization* (Frosh, 1995). A main observation here is that previously predominant cultural frameworks (including ones that define masculinity and paternity) no longer imbue established ways of life with such exclusivity, privilege, or socially valued meaning. Following critiques of research that is excessively preoccupied by theory for obscuring understanding

the vital processes of everyday life, it is important that these frameworks have not driven our analytical work on the dynamics of men's personal lives. Nonetheless, it is important to acknowledge the important backcloth these analyses can provide to understanding what might be at stake as we seek to understand men and fathers' sense and identity making—and ways of living out their lives with others—in times that can involve uncertainty and change.

The first analysis we describe deploys the well-honed techniques of qualitative thematic analysis (see Chapter 4 of this volume), developed in ways appropriate to meeting the challenges and potentials of QLL study. In this line of work, we have also engaged in the construction and comparison of carefully crafted case data (Shirani & Henwood, 2011a). The second has pursued a more specialized, psychosocial analysis of how men identify themselves as modern fathers—in ways that may be imagined as much as real—to deal with some of the dynamics of identities and relationships in and through time (Finn & Henwood, 2009). Before presenting these analyses, we first address some methodological concerns relating to our QLL interview study and to our use of supplementary methods and data, including our use of visual data (Henwood, Finn, & Shirani, 2008).

QLL Design, Interviewing, and Ethics

Longitudinal study has the unique potential of allowing for planning in data collection, including in the long term, making it possible to follow through an interest in topics through times of change. In QLL interview studies it is also possible to take advantage of initially unforeseen opportunities and serendipity; the flexible approach to devising actual questions and interviewing style means that adaptations can be made to meet the needs of research situations as they are encountered at moments in time (Farrall, 2006; Holland, Thompson, & Henderson, 2006; Saldaña, 2003).

When the first phase of the study was undertaken in 1999–2000, we followed the design that is often preferred in studies of parenting transitions: three waves of interviews—the first before the birth of the first child, the second after a suitable period of time has elapsed after the birth for basic routines around care of the child to be established, and a third later in the first year (see also Hollway, 2010). Subsequently, when we again used this pattern with our second sample of first-time fathers in 2008–2009, the third interview was convened around the time of the child's first birthday to incorporate issues to do with the celebration of a significant family event into the interviewing strategy.

Our own experience of using three, sequentially organized interviews throughout 1 year as our core study design was that it enabled us to track participants at a level of intensity (Thomson, 2010) that was not overburdening or overly intrusive. We were aware, however, of having to weigh up practical and ethical issues that encouraged us to pursue less intensive modes of data collection with our interest to maximize opportunities to generate rich[5] qualitative data that are replete with personal and social meanings regarding the men's subjective responses and the circumstances of their fathering. We dealt with these tensions by making reference to guidance on relational research ethics that is appropriate for this kind of research (Mauthner, Birch, Jessop, & Miller, 2002) and especially to the need for careful attentiveness to situational demands (Edwards & Mauthner, 2002).

When recruiting and retaining participants, we followed the common practice in QLL studies of making and maintaining contact between researchers and the researched more regularly than is strictly required to setup the research encounters and conduct the interviews and other data-collection activities. This is important to avoid attrition in long-term studies through geographic mobility of participants and loss of up-to-date contact details on the part of the research team. When we have contacted our study participants with updates and offers of occasional research briefings, this has been a convenient moment to prompt for the minimal but necessary information exchanges to update research records.

More regular communications also build a stronger sense of participants' involvement in the study through their sense of familiarity with the research

and acceptance of it as a routine part of their life activities and commitments. In contrast to other QLL studies, such routine acceptance has not become a feature of our study, probably because researchers and the researched have shared fewer common experiences and were not undergoing similar life transitions at the time of the interviews. This means that our study has not really followed the reported tendency in the methodological literature for formal, contractual relationships to be replaced entirely with ones that are more similar to a shared commitment and friendship (McLeod & Thomson, 2009; Miller & Boulton, 2007).

Nonetheless, our own practice has been informed by guidance on how to manage this shift away from contractual to more shared interests and intimacy in the researcher–researched relationship. Such guidance suggests a need for adjustment on the part of researchers given the possibility in QLL study of a significant intensification of relationship risks (Miller & Boulton, 2007; Morrow, 2009). It is known, for example, that such shifts can create new obligations for researchers to respond to multiple communications from participants on matters unrelated to the study itself and that, in some circumstances, this can become an extra burden (Grime, 2010).

The major additional researcher burden accruing because of the long-term nature of our study has occurred because of the sustained efforts we have had to make with some consistently difficult-to-contact participants to offset the risk of them becoming disconnected from the study, leading to passive withdrawal. In our experiences, this situation occurs in situations in which participants' lives are unstable, gatekeepers do not support their participation, and their life circumstances mean that their involvement in the research can be unmanageable and even threaten their identity. Developing strategies to counteract such problems has been a priority for some QLL researchers (Hemmerman, 2010). For our part, we have found that awareness of, interest in, and notetaking about such matters can provide a potentially useful research resource in the form of relevant contextual information and

---

[5]The term *rich* as used here refers specifically to the desired qualities of qualitative data that need to open up and allow for possibilities for depth of interpretation, understanding of symbolization, and appreciation of the local situations and broader contexts of activity and meaning making. Properties of richness in quantitative data, by contrast, relate to having sufficient measures of variables to manipulate using statistical methods.

metadata (data about primary data), which can be of assistance in broadening understanding of pertinent circumstances and situations beyond the interviews. In some circumstances, this understanding can have a bearing on how to interpret and understand the men's lives and relationships by ourselves and other users of the data.[6]

Having a second phase to our research provided us with an opportunity to revisit our data-collection strategy and to adapt it to take into account what had transpired in the intervening 8 years. Although we had not anticipated doing this in the earliest phase of the study, we were able to serendipitously increase our aspirations to include studying men and fathers across the life course and to make researching the temporal a more explicit strategy for studying personal and social change in our study. In QLL studies that are seeking to combine regularity of contact, intensity of involvement in the research encounter, and the generation of insight by making comparisons over longer time frames (McLeod & Thomson, 2009; Thomson & Holland, 2003), it is often assumed that interviewer continuity is especially advantageous. In particular, maintaining relationships between researcher–researched and between the members of a research team over extended time periods is deemed to be a key part of the QLL method for researching the long view. In our study, of necessity, different interviewers were involved as members of the research team changed. Yet, we found that different team members brought complementary interests and specialist commitments with them, expanding the possibilities of study (Shirani, 2010).

In 2008, when we undertook our second main data collection phase, we decided to repeat the initial intensive study design, carrying out three waves of interviews over a period of transition with a second cohort of first-time fathers, this time in Wales. The aim was to further mine the possibilities inherent in intensive QLL design that involves a high frequency of data collection and enables rapid alterations in the pace of daily life to be studied, along with experiences of irreversible change over a specified time period. At the same time, because change can take time to occur, our second phase featured a set of interviews with our original participants from the east of England 8 years after their first child was born, by which time their lives had changed in a variety of ways. This combination of intensive observation (frequently over a short time period) and extensive observation (after a significant period of time has elapsed) is fit for generating insights about dynamic processes, for example, through making comparisons of vertical and horizontal cross-sections of data. By looking at data vertically (i.e., across waves of data collected at a single time point), patterns can be identified, and these patterns can be studied further by making horizontal comparisons (across data collected at different time intervals) for how they continue or change and involve movement though different time periods (Holland et al., 2006; Neale, 2007).

Our study has adopted an in-depth, qualitative interviewing strategy to elicit from interviewees their expectations and experiences of fathering as well as any changes over time in their way of engaging in fathering along with its implications for other spheres of life, including relationships with significant others. Interviewees were encouraged to indicate how they construed fatherhood in relation to salient social models, whether such models had changed over time, and how they positioned themselves and other people in relation to them. Participants were asked about their aspirations and hopes for family life and the future. Utilizing the reinterviewing possibilities that are inherent in QLL study, some key issues raised in earlier interviews were reintroduced by the researcher or followed up in later interviews. In this way, interviewees' responses could be traced through, including how they reflected on earlier remarks.

During the second phase of the study, the kinds of strategies that worked best for generating temporal data were worked on and temporal questioning became a more prominent feature. Where appropriate, interviewees were asked to talk about issues from the perspectives of past, present, and future.

---

[6]The latter point is important given our commitment within Timescapes to data sharing among projects and data archiving to promote its reuse.

Questions were asked directly about key milestones in their lives so far and the timing of significant events. The implications of such issues were asked about more indirectly, in ways that took account of where interviewees were now in their own life course. In an attempt to directly elicit temporal data, interviewees were asked about the meaning of the word *time* with mixed results: Although some interviewees engaged with the questions at length, others found it too abstract and philosophical to engage with easily. How men looked back on previous moments and thought about the future, in the short and long term, was addressed—for example, by asking them to reflect on or envisage fathering their children at different ages. How they reacted to their own parents becoming grandparents, and to themselves moving a generational position within their families, provided other insight about how they engaged with temporal questions—in this case, about biographical and generational time.

Supplementary Methods and Data

To assist in the collection of temporal data, before interviews were conducted, participants were asked to complete a timeline of significant events in their lives thus far to generate some initial data on the past. To provide data on the future, they were also asked, "Where do you see yourself in 10 years' time?" For the most part, the timeline proved useful as a prompt to facilitate further discussion of how such questions were answered in subsequent interviews. In temporal terms, it was possible using this technique to ask interviewees about futures they had envisaged on a range of occasions during which they were situated differently within an ever-shifting present. The timeline also served as a device in later interviews for participants to rework the past from the perspective of the present or to comment on its continuing relevance.

One of the prime developers of QLL methodology Saldaña (2003) has advocated on the inclusion of visual methods within QLL studies, as "visual images, whether still or in motion, provide some of the richest and most tangible data for accessing change through time" (p. 25; also see Chapter 12 of this volume). Visual images, and especially photographs, can be uniquely informative about time and place because their particular properties (e.g., facial expressions, gestures, clothes) evoke an era, linking people to historical epochs about which they have no experience. On other occasions, where people do see themselves in an image, or describe themselves as being unlike the person in the image (i.e., disidentifying with the person they see depicted in it), this can help them talk about their personal lives and engage with larger social realities. Photoelicitation techniques offer a way for the researcher to enable people to speak of thoughts, hopes, and fears that may otherwise be difficult and of things that have not actually happened but that may operate as part of their imaginary worlds (Barthes, 1981; Henwood, Shirani, & Finn, 2011; Smart 2007).

Our approach to using visual images has been experimental. While following the early example of visual methods as an aid in interpretive qualitative research (Beloff, 1997), we have drawn more extensively on contemporary developments in visual psychology (Reavey, 2011) and have tried a number of different ways of generating and presenting photographic images. We have found that, although each has its own merits, there are reasons to critique each one for its usefulness for our specific study and beyond, as we now will briefly illustrate (for more lengthy discussion, see Henwood et al., 2010).

One of our study techniques has been to present interviewees with a sequence of images depicting how social representations of fatherhood have altered through historical time.[7] It was developed as an alternative to a collage technique in which multiple images from magazines and the Internet were presented to interviewees at once, and interviewees chose to talk about the ones they most wished to emulate or avoid. Although this made the collage a useful technique, it failed to elicit extended narratives about each of the images in terms of ideas they potentially encoded about change through time.

---

[7]The sequence started with a black-and-white image of Victorian vintage depicting a distant, formal father figure, while the final image was a contemporary depiction of father and child face to face and in mutual gaze to represent the latest idea of a relational father (Dermott, 2008). In between were images from the 1950s and 1980s. At each subsequent point in the sequence, fathers appeared in less gender role–bound activities and poses. The famous Athena "man and baby" image was included to depict a cultural turning point in depictions of fatherhood and masculinity.

Therefore, we needed a different methodological tool that would enable interviewees to engage with each presented image.

With the technique of presenting a sequence of images depicting sociocultural change in ideas of fatherhood and masculinity over time, interviewees were invited to comment on each individual image before being presented with the next. In addition, because each image appeared in succession, the sequence presented a simulation of a moving image. Accordingly, the technique can be described as involving a narratively organized set of images, presented in visual mode, of time and change in fatherhood ideals. The technique proved valuable as it enabled men to make temporal comparisons more easily than they otherwise were able to do. One result of this method was that it showed how our participants could reconfigure their thoughts about fatherhood and re-represent themselves in relation to the flow of the images. It proved possible for the interviewees, when speaking in this way, to articulate their shifting and coexisting identifications with ideas of masculinity encoded in more traditional and modern representations of fatherhood, and it elicited some sense from them of their experiences of how masculine identities may be changing and, crucially, not changing in and through time (Henwood, Finn, & Shirani, 2008).

In visual methodology (Rose, 2001), it is often said that limitations are imposed by using researcher-generated images because their framing of responses in cultural terms may or may not have relevance in the context of someone's lived life. In the second phase of our study, during which we conducted a long-term follow-up with our English sample, participants were asked to select favorite photographs from their own family pictures. They were initially asked why they had chosen the pictures, which led to further discussion about family life. For example, one participant described liking the picture representing his happy, smiling children as it was removed from his experience of day-to-day family life, which was often overshadowed by family disagreements. This method offered some temporal data as participants discussed family resemblances between them and their child, which often led them to reflect on their childhood experiences. Fathers in the Welsh sample were asked to discuss personal photographs from the first year of their child's life, with detailed questioning around temporal experiences. Participants were asked questions such as "Did you think about what the child would be like before s/he was born?" and "Do you have any thoughts on what the child will be like as s/he gets older?" to temporally extend their talk about fatherhood. It proved challenging for these men to reflect on past or future in relation to the images; instead, they preferred to focus on the present joys of fatherhood. The success of using personal photographs to elicit temporal data appeared to be dependent on the age and gender of the child, working best with older sons as the men could more easily identify resemblances and recall their own childhood memories with this age-group than with babies.

This method also has its limits in that not all fathers considered themselves to be part of photographic culture[8] or were able to engage in tasks involving reading images in such imaginative ways. Of those who could provide an abundance of images, some related quite restricted cultural scripts about those images that were devoid of personal meaning. Nonetheless, some of the participant-generated images proved to be extraordinarily rich in personal and cultural meanings associated with different dimensions of time and the ways in which they interpenetrated one another. For example, one man chose an image taken at a family wedding of his child sitting on a war memorial with people passing by. In light of his recent house move and a time of significant change, the image represented to him the significance of life constantly changing, as indicated by the juxtaposition of the memorial (depicting the end of life), his child (at the beginning of life), and passers-by (only there for a fleeting moment).

Inclusion of visual methods has strengthened our methodological project of using QLL methods to study the personal and cultural processes of men and fathers' identities in the making. Our visual strategies added possibilities for following through on our Timescapes commitments to develop a more

---

[8]Some took or collected very few pictures.

fine-grained understanding of how masculine and paternal identities are worked up and worked out in relation to time in everyday life. Our experience is that such methods are useful because they enable people to make temporal comparisons more easily than they would otherwise be able to do and to show their awareness and consideration of diverse temporalities (generational or historical as well as biographical). As a result, people are able to talk about issues that are less visible when spoken about outside a questioning framework designed to highlight matters of time and change. More generally, lessons have been learned about when and why deploying visual, especially visual narrative, photo-elicitation methods is likely to be fruitful.

QLL and Data Analysis

Initially, our approach to data analysis involved carefully reading men's accounts and interpreting their significance to understand how men's lives, and aspects of paternal subjectivity, are and are not changing in the context of sociopolitical transformations in gender relationships and family life. A much-discussed issue is whether the emergence of a model of new fatherhood and new men can be taken to indicate that new forms of masculinity are being produced and reproduced in the context of changing expectations of fatherhood. Accordingly, our earliest line of data analysis (Henwood & Procter, 2003) addressed this issue, centering on the common theme of *paternal involvement* that we identified as featuring throughout the data. Our analysis went on to point to the tensions this aspiration generated in their personal lives and opened up different ways to frame the meanings of paternal involvement. What follows are two examples of our efforts to conduct temporally focused data analysis in this vein.

Analysis: Example 1. Our first example analysis looks explicitly at continuities and changes in the men's accounts by comparing them across the different waves of QLL/temporal data. Coming to the data for the first time, the analyst could see that the theme of paternal involvement, which had emerged from the data and been analyzed in the initially published analysis (Henwood & Procter, 2003), unfolded and changed over time as a set of

relationships developed with two further linked, emergent themes of—in the participants' own terms—exclusion (from involvement) and redundancy (from a fathering role).

Some of the men who had strongly invested in the ideal of full involvement in their child's life before the birth expressed very different sentiments 8 years later, looking forward to a time when they would no longer be so responsible for their child. Furthermore, other interviewees, who had earlier acknowledged the ideal of involvement but retained a stronger practical and emotional investment in more traditional models of fathers as breadwinners, raised the issues of responsibility and dependency as problematic much earlier than those investing in involvement. Our analytical work established the overarching theme that became the centerpiece of the developing QLL analysis and eventual research article focusing on relevance without responsibility (Shirani & Henwood, 2011a).

Working up a full analysis of the data involved carefully inspecting the initially established pattern. To this end we tabulated each interviewee's articulation of the three interlinked themes of involvement, exclusion, and redundancy: This was our first attempt at representing our interviewee's data sequentially or narratively in case study format. This is demonstrated in Table 13.1 with data from one participant.

The tabulation clearly documented changes in talk about involvement and exclusion or redundancy and contained a brief summary of how these issues were discussed in each interview and contributory circumstances (e.g., child being breastfed). This made it possible to see change and continuity in the accounts over time and also highlighted those cases in which the issues were discussed in most depth. From this, a one-page summary document was produced to provide background information about four selected cases to illustrate diagrammatically the changes and continuities in these men's accounts (see Figure 13.1).

Case study construction and analysis (see Chapter 9 of this volume) is strongly advocated as a way of handling longitudinal and temporal data and to capture lived experiences of transition, time, and change. Thomson (2007) has offered a range of

TABLE 13.1

Representing Key Themes

Psuedonym	Before birth	Feeding	Round 2	Round 3	Round 4
Simon	Some exclusion from embodied experience of pregnancy, not really happening to him. Does not mind at this stage.	Breast	Helpless during labor although more involved as it was a home birth. Feels powerless at not being able to feed baby and this is more frustrating than anticipated.	Is a marginal part of the threesome. Partner's attention has been diverted.	Balances periods of high involvement with time away traveling by self. Happy with this balance although difficult for relationship with partner.

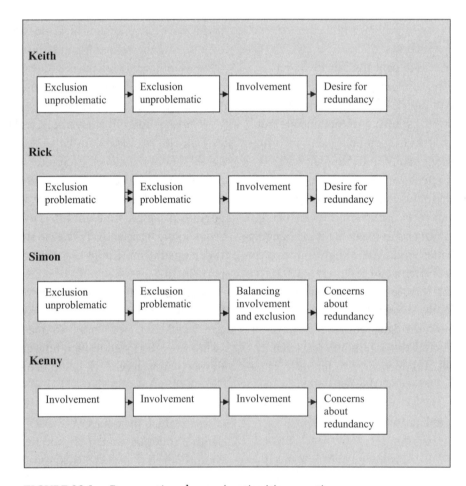

FIGURE 13.1.   Representing changes/continuities over time.

specific ideas about how to enrich and thicken the construction of case study data to gain insight into the subjective experience of social change and to be able to study how processes of wider sociocultural change are played out through the trajectories of people's lives as both narrated and as lived. A summary of the main points involved in her QLL case study method are as follows: (a) Narratively and temporally represent accounts of linkages between emergent themes, (b) embed linkages in contextual details of lives and worlds, (c) bring complexity of subjective experiences to the fore, and (d) carefully select cases and bring them into dialogue to highlight the dynamics of continuities and change over time and to identify insights with wider relevance across the sample in ways that further strengthen the developing analysis.

These ideas have helped us to conduct our analysis so that it was possible to bring out the significance of the three interlinked themes: involvement, exclusion, and redundancy. A small set of carefully selected and detailed individual case studies (Figure 13.1) were constructed focusing on the men's accounts of these themes, along with the contextual details of their personal lives and social worlds, in the form of subjectively rich, contextually detailed, extended temporal narratives. These case studies were subsequently put into dialogue with one another to identify and magnify themes with wider relevance across the sample.

As a result of following these steps in our "relevance without responsibility analysis" (Shirani & Henwood, 2011a), we were able to show important commonalities within the data regarding fathers' greater involvement over time. This illustrated how often the paternal involvement ideal does not play out in men's lives in ways that follow their anticipated trajectories because of alterations in their lived experiences, emergent concerns about dependency, and changing work and family circumstances. These men adopted a temporal strategy of deferment to the future; at each interview, they were looking forward to a life course stage that they felt would be preferable to their current situation. Exhibit 13.1 gives a summary account of our analytical work.

Analysis: Example 2. This analysis in its published form (Finn & Henwood, 2009) takes as data the connections and disconnections men in the study made with their own fathers and explores what we have called the men's fluctuating *identificatory imaginings* as involved fathers. The analysis points to fluctuations in men's accounts across the interviews, during which they invested in similar and different ways of managing fatherhood and being a man that were both similar to and different from those of their own fathers and men of that

---

> **Exhibit 13.1**
> **Relevance Without Responsibility (RWR)–QLL Analysis Process**
>
> ---
>
> - Comparative analysis: noticing how paternal involvement—an emergent theme from the data—unfolded and changed over time as a set of relationships developed with exclusion and redundancy
> - Initial tabulation of linked themes (careful inspection of the pattern) to:
>   see change and continuity in accounts over time, and
>   select cases where issues are discussed in most depth
> - QLL case construction and presentation

generation. It shows how to understand such biographical and generational imaginings and how these need to be seen as dynamically mediated by cultural discourses (of the modern father), the men's social conditions (making it more or less difficult for them to spend time in the home), and processes of intergenerational transmission (as they involve flows of meaning and affect).

This form of analysis is not only informed by a Timescapes agenda but also is shaped in specific disciplinary ways by a psychosocial research perspective (e.g., Hollway, 2006; Walkerdine, 2010). In the case of our own study, its dual focused agenda is marked out in three main ways: (a) investigating the specific ways in which our participants come to live out cultural ideals of fatherhood and paternal involvement socially and psychically, (b) bringing into view the dynamics of masculine and paternal subjectivity, and (c) asking questions about the significance of shifting cultural ideas about what it means to be a man and a father in contemporary times. By building on this earlier analysis, we are continuing with the psychosocial aspects of our work analytically and theoretically (Henwood & Finn, 2010) to open up further ways of investigating intergenerational transmissions between fathers and their own fathers (and mothers).

REFLECTIONS AND CONCLUDING REMARKS

In this chapter we have discussed programmatic statements that have been made in favor of taking a

QLL and temporal approach to researching identities and relationships in changing lives and times. We have also shown how these statements have translated into the methodological and analytical work of our specific inquiries into men and fathers' identities and relationships through the life course. Our inquiries have been conducted amid a growing awareness of the importance of possible sociocultural transformations in the meanings and practices of fatherhood and of the heterogeneity and plurality of masculine identities and subjectivities. These inquiries are being taken forward as part of a unique experiment—the Timescapes study—one that is aimed at scaling up the undoubted insights that can be generated from carefully crafted qualitative and case study research focused on understanding the personal, social, and cultural meanings that are at the center of people's everyday activities and life changes—their identities, relationships, and lives-in-the-making.

A major excitement—but also a challenge—has become apparent to us in the Men as Fathers Project: the sense of how many possibilities are being opened up for inquiring into the dynamics of identities and relationships in and through time. Taking up the Timescapes way of dealing with this challenge (Adam, 2008; Neale, 2007), we have adopted a QLL design capable of generating microtemporal data that are both qualitative (i.e., they articulate people's everyday subjective experiences and understandings of contextual and sociocultural meanings) and biographical, dynamic, or temporal (rather than fixed in particular moments in time). This way of working has brought into view the times and textures of people's everyday lives, making it possible to investigate the dynamic ways in which people experience, negotiate, and work out the significance and meanings of their relationships, identities, and lives in and through time (Neale & Flowerdew, 2003). Hence, adopting this approach represents one way in which we have set ourselves up to be able to study the ways in which everyday experiences, ideas, understandings, and issues of masculinity and fathering are implicated in the dynamic processes of men's identity and subjectivity formation.

When researching people's lives temporally, it is not enough simply to track them as they make their way through significant moments, episodes, and transitions that are part of the life course. It is also necessary to inquire how they live out their lives within historical periods or epochs and as members of particular generations or cohorts. Focusing on the three key dimensions of time—historical, generational, and biographical—is another distinctive feature of the QLL approach that is under development across the Timescapes network, and one to which our own study into paternal and masculine subjectivities and identities contributes. In our study we see men and fathers' identities as being constituted not just biographically but in the context of change in (post)modern times. This does not mean that we are setting up a singular, linear model of progressive change with categories such as pre- and postmodern necessarily preceding sequentially from one to the other. Rather, we are seeking to bring out the (usually invisible) multidimensionalities and directionalities, pluralities, and complexities of time and change associated with the shift to modernity, as they are experienced and created by people (Salmon, 1985), and to explore their dynamic involvement in the unfolding of varied life forms and social processes (Adam, 2008).

Embedded in our approach to QLL study is an interest in being able to pursue questions of continuity and change within the multiple conditions and flows of time. We specifically wish to avoid the implication that any one modality alone (such as the discursive, as opposed to other experiential, phenomenological, or sensory modes) is constitutive of men and fathers' subjectivities (Henwood, Finn, & Shirani, 2008). In developing our interest in the conditions and flows of time, we have used visual methods alongside the pursuit of a psychosocial QLL and temporal research perspective (Finn & Henwood, 2008; Henwood & Finn, 2010). Thus far, our efforts in this research have involved studying participants alignments with, or distancings from, one's own father's personal and generational ways of doing masculinity and fathering. This has allowed us to open up to inquiry the resultant tensions and adaptations that are apparent in study participants' aspirations or desires as men and as fathers, the ways in which men reflect on these from various vantage points in time, and how their meaning and significance alter in the processes of reworking and reflection.

References

Adam, B. (1990). *Time and social theory*. Cambridge, England: Polity.

Adam, B. (1998). *Timescapes of modernity*. London, England: Routledge.

Adam, B. (2008). The Timescapes challenge: Engagement with the invisible temporal. In R. Edwards (Ed.), *Researching lives through time: Time, generation and life stories* (Timescapes Working Paper Series No. 1, ISSN: 1758-3349, pp. 7–12). Leeds, England: University of Leeds.

Andrews, M., Day Sclater, S., Squire, C., & Treacher, A. (Eds.). (2000). *Lines of narrative: Psychosocial approaches*. London, England: Routledge. doi:10.4324/9780203471005

Barthes, R. (1981). *Camera lucida: Reflections on photography*. New York, NY: Hill & Wang.

Beck, U., & Beck-Gernsheim, E. (1995). *The normal chaos of love*. Cambridge, England: Polity.

Beloff, H. (1997). Making and unmaking identities: A psychologist looks at artwork. In N. Hayes (Ed.), *Doing qualitative analysis in psychology* (pp. 55–58). Hove, England: Psychology Press.

Chamberlayne, P., Bornat, J., & Wengraf, T. (Eds.). (2000). *The turn to biographical methods in social science: Comparative issues and examples*. London, England: Routledge. doi:10.4324/9780203466049

Charmaz, K. (2006). *Constructing grounded theory*. London, England: Sage.

Charmaz, K., & Henwood, K. L. (2008). Grounded theory. In C. Willig & W. Stainton-Rogers (Eds.), *Handbook of qualitative research in psychology* (pp. 240–260). London, England: Sage.

Corden, A., & Millar, J. (2007). Time and change: A review of the qualitative longitudinal research literature for social policy. *Social Policy and Society, 6*, 583–592. doi:10.1017/S1474746407003910

Dermott, E. (2008). *Intimate fatherhood*. London, England: Routledge.

Doucet, A. (2007). *Do men mother?* Toronto, Ontario, Canada: University of Toronto Press.

Edley, N., & Wetherell, M. (1999). Imagined futures: Young men's talk about fatherhood and domestic life. *British Journal of Social Psychology, 38*, 181–194. doi:10.1348/014466699164112

Edwards, R., & Mauthner, M. (2002). Ethics and feminist research: Theory and practice. In M. Mauthner, M. Birch, J. Jessop, & T. Miller (Eds.), *Ethics in qualitative research* (pp. 14–31). London, England: Sage.

Elliott, J., Holland, J., & Thompson, R. (2008). Longitudinal and panel studies. In P. Alasuutari, L. Bickman, & J. Brannen (Eds.), *Handbook of social research methods* (pp. 228–248). London, England: Sage.

Farrall, S. (2006). *What is qualitative longitudinal research?* (Papers in Social Research Methods: Qualitative Series No. 11). London, England: London School of Economics and Political Science Methodology Institute.

Finn, M., & Henwood, K. (2009). Exploring masculinities within men's identificatory imaginings of first-time fatherhood. *British Journal of Social Psychology, 48*, 547–562. doi:10.1348/014466608X386099

Frosh, S. (1995). Unpacking masculinity: From rationality to fragmentation. In C. Burck & B. Speed (Eds.), *Gender, power and relationships* (pp. 218–231). London, England: Routledge.

Grime, J. (2010, January 20). *Ethical issues and qualitative longitudinal study*. Presentation at Timescapes Conference: The Craft of Qualitative Longitudinal Research, Cardiff University, Cardiff, England.

Heinz, W. R., & Krüger, H. (2001). The life course: Innovations and challenges for social research. *Current Sociology, 49*, 29–45. doi:10.1177/0011392101049002004

Hemmerman, L. (2010). Researching the hard to reach and the hard to keep: Notes from the field on longitudinal sample maintenance. In F. Shirani & S. Weller (Eds.), *Conducting qualitative longitudinal research: Fieldwork experiences* (Timescapes Working Paper Series No. 2, ISSN: 1758-3349, pp. 7–19). Leeds, England: University of Leeds.

Henwood, K. L. (2008). Qualitative research, reflexivity and living with risk: Valuing and practicing epistemic reflexivity and centring marginality. *Qualitative Research in Psychology, 5*, 45–55. doi:10.1080/14780880701863575

Henwood, K., & Finn, M. (2010). Researching masculine and paternal subjects in times of change: Insights from a qualitative longitudinal (QLL) and psychosocial case study. In R. Thomson (Ed.), *Intensity and insight: Qualitative longitudinal methods as a route to the psycho-social* (Timescapes Working Paper Series No. 3, ISSN: 1758-3349, pp. 34–45). Leeds, England: University of Leeds.

Henwood, K., Finn, M., & Shirani, F. (2008). Use of visual methods to explore parental identities in historical time and social change: Reflections from the 'men-as-fathers' project. *Qualitative Research, 9*, 112–115.

Henwood, K. L., Gill, R., & Mclean, C. (2002). The changing man. *The Psychologist, 15*, 182–186.

Henwood, K., & Lang, I. (2005). Qualitative social science in the UK: A reflexive commentary on the "state of the art." *Forum: Qualitative Social Research, 6.* Retrieved from http://www.qualitative-research.net/ index.php/fqs/article/view/16

Henwood, K. L., Pidgeon, N., Sarre, S., Simmons, P., & Smith, N. (2008). Risk, framing and everyday life: Epistemological and methodological reflections from three socio-cultural projects. *Health, Risk and Society, 10,* 421–438. doi:10.1080/13698570802381451

Henwood, K., & Procter, J. (2003). The "good father": Reading men's accounts of paternal involvement during the transition to first-time fatherhood. *British Journal of Social Psychology, 42,* 337–355. doi:10.1348/014466603322438198

Henwood, K., Shirani, F., & Finn, M. (2011). So you think we've moved, changed, the representation got more what? Methodological and analytical reflections on visual (photo-elicitation) methods used in the men-as-fathers study. In P. Reavey (Ed.), *Visual methods in psychology: Using and interpreting images in qualitative research* (pp. 330–345). London, England: Routledge.

Holland, J., Thompson, R., & Henderson, S. (2006) *Qualitative longitudinal research: A discussion paper.* (Families and Social Capital ESRC Research Group Working Paper No. 2.1, ISBN 1 874418-62-4). London, England: Families and Social Capital Research Group.

Hollway, W. (2006). *The capacity to care: Gender and ethical subjectivity.* London, England: Routledge.

Hollway, W. (2010). Preserving vital signs: The use of psychoanalytically informed interviewing and observation in psycho-social longitudinal research. In R. Thomson (Ed.), *Intensity and insight: Qualitative longitudinal methods as a route to the psycho-social* (Timescapes Working Paper Series No. 3, ISSN: 1758-3349, pp. 19–33). Leeds, England: University of Leeds.

Hollway, W., & Featherstone, B. (Eds.). (1997). *Mothering and ambivalence.* London, England: Routledge. doi:10.4324/9780203284018

Hughes, J. (1990). *The philosophy of social research* (2nd ed.). London, England: Longman.

Lewis, J. (2007). Analysing qualitative longitudinal research in evaluations. *Social Policy and Society, 6,* 545–556. doi:10.1017/S1474746407003880

McLeod, J., & Thomson, R. (2009). *Researching social change.* London, England: Sage.

Mason, J. (2002). *Qualitative research resources: A discussion paper.* Swindon, England: ESRC.

Mason, J. (2006). Mixing methods in a qualitatively-driven way. *Qualitative Research, 6,* 9–25. doi:10.1177/1468794106058866

Mauthner, M., Birch, M., Jessop, J., & Miller, T. (2002). *Ethics in qualitative research.* London, England: Sage.

Miller, T. (2000). Narrative construction and childbirth. *Qualitative Health Research, 10,* 309–323. doi:10.1177/104973200129118462

Miller, T., & Boulton, M. (2007). Changing constructions of informed consent: Qualitative research and complex social worlds. *Social Science and Medicine, 65,* 2199–2211. doi:10.1016/j.socscimed.2007.08.009

Morrow, V. (2009). *The ethics of social research with children and families in young lives: Practical experiences* (Working Paper 53). Oxford, England: Department of International Development, University of Oxford.

Neale, B. (2007, June). *Timescapes: Changing Relationships and Identities Through the Life Course. A study funded under the ESRC Changing Lives and Times Qualitative Longitudinal Initiative. Feb 2007–Jan 2012. RES 347 25 000. Study overview.* University of Leeds, Leeds, England. Available at http://www.timescapes.leeds. ac.uk/events-dissemination/publications.php

Neale, B., & Flowerdew, J. (2003). Time, texture and childhood: The contours of longitudinal qualitative research. *International Journal of Social Research Methodology: Theory and Practice, 6,* 189–199. doi:10.1080/1364557032000091798

Reavey, P. (Ed.). (2011). *Visual methods in psychology: Using and interpreting images in qualitative research.* London, England: Routledge.

Rose, G. (2001). *Visual methodologies.* London, England: Sage.

Rosenthal, G. (2004). Biographical research. In C. Seale, G. Gobo, J. F. Gubrium, & D. Silverman (Eds.), *Qualitative research practice* (pp. 48–64). London, England: Sage.

Saldaña, J. (2003). *Longitudinal qualitative research: Analyzing change through time.* Walnut Creek, CA: AltaMira.

Salmon, P. (1985). *Living in time: A new look at personal development.* London, England: Dent.

Shirani, F. (2010). Researcher change and continuity in a qualitative longitudinal study. In F. Shirani & S. Weller (Eds.), *Conducting qualitative longitudinal research: Fieldwork experiences* (Timescapes Working Paper Series No. 2, ISSN: 1758-3349, pp. 49–59). Leeds, England: University of Leeds.

Shirani, F., & Henwood, K. (2011a). Continuity and change in a qualitative longitudinal study of fatherhood: Relevance without responsibility. *International Journal of Social Research Methodology, 14,* 17–29.

Shirani, F., & Henwood, K. (2011b). Taking one day at a time: Temporal experiences in the context of unexpected life course transitions. *Time and Society, 20,* 49–68.

Smart, C. (2007). *Personal life: New directions in sociological thinking.* Cambridge, England: Polity.

Squire, C. (2008). *Approaches to narrative research.* (ESRC National Centre for Research Methods Review Paper NCRM 009). Retrieved from http://eprints.ncrm.ac.uk/419/

Thompson, P. (1975). *The Edwardians: The remaking of British society.* London, England: Weidenfeld & Nicolson.

Thomson, R. (2007). The qualitative longitudinal case history: Practical, methodological and ethical reflections. *Social Policy and Society, 6,* 571–582. doi:10.1017/S1474746407003909

Thomson, R. (2010). Creating family case histories: Subjects, selves and family dynamics. In R. Thomson (Ed.), *Intensity and insight: Qualitative longitudinal methods as a route to the psycho-social* (Timescapes Working Paper Series No. 3, ISSN: 1758-3349, pp. 6–18). Leeds, England: University of Leeds.

Thomson, R., & Holland, J. (2003). Hindsight, foresight and insight: The challenges of longitudinal qualitative research. *International Journal of Social Research Methodology: Theory and Practice, 6,* 233–244. doi:10.1080/1364557032000091833

Walkerdine, V. (2010). Communal beingness and affect: An exploration of trauma in an ex-industrial community. *Body and Society, 16,* 91–116. doi:10.1177/1357034X09354127

Wetherell, M., & Edley, N. (1999). Negotiating hegemonic masculinity: Imaginary positions and psycho-discursive practices. *Feminism and Psychology, 9,* 335–356. doi:10.1177/0959353599009003012

SAMPLING ACROSS PEOPLE AND TIME

Chapter 14

INTRODUCTION TO SURVEY SAMPLING

Roger Tourangeau and Ting Yan

One of the many things that distinguishes psychology from the other social sciences is its reliance on experiments as a key methodological tool and its relative neglect of surveys of members of well-defined populations (e.g., see Presser, 1984). Political scientists and sociologists are more likely than psychologists to use data from survey samples, although developmental, educational, and organizational psychologists do sometimes analyze data from population surveys, often taking advantage of data sets that are publicly available. Relative to laboratory experiments, surveys based on large, representative samples are expensive to conduct and are getting more expensive all the time. In part, these costs reflect the size and geographic scope of survey samples. For example, the monthly employment figures released by the Bureau of Labor Statistics are derived from the Current Population Survey (CPS), a survey carried out each month by the U.S. Census Bureau. The CPS is carefully designed to represent the civilian noninstitutional population of the United States (15 years old or older), and it collects information from more than 60,000 households each month. These households are clustered in more than 824 sites around the country. (In the survey literature, a *household* is a group of people living together; the place they live in is referred to as a *housing unit* or *dwelling unit*.) Each state and the District of Columbia are represented by one or more sample sites and by numerous households in the monthly CPS samples. National surveys involving face-to-face interviews (like the CPS) can cost $1,000 per case.

PROBABILITY SAMPLING

Sampling statisticians who work on surveys like the CPS distinguish between different types of samples. A fundamental distinction is the one between probability and nonprobability samples. A *probability sample* (what is often called a *random sample*) is a sample in which each element of the population has a known (or at least calculable) and nonzero probability of selection. Our focus in this chapter is on probability samples—more specifically, on probability samples of households rather than of businesses or other institutions. *Nonprobability samples* (which encompass all other kinds of samples) are ones in which it is impossible to assign a probability of selection to every unit in the population. The main subtypes of nonprobability sample are *samples of convenience* (such as the samples of volunteers that figure so prominently in psychological research), *purposive samples* (which are selected deliberately to meet some goal, often nonstatistical), and *quota samples* (in which interviewers recruit and interview an assigned number of cases from each of several subgroups).

The concept of probability sampling is sufficiently unfamiliar to most psychologists that it will be useful to unpack the standard definition. First of all, the requirement that a selection probability could be assigned to every element in the population presupposes that there *is* a well-defined population from which the sample is being drawn and that it attempts to represent. Sampling statisticians

We are very grateful to Rick Valliant for his comments on an earlier version of this chapter.

DOI: 10.1037/13620-014
APA Handbook of Research Methods in Psychology: Vol. 2. Research Designs, H. Cooper (Editor-in-Chief)

refer to this population as the *target population* for the survey.[1] The target population for the CPS is the civilian household population (age 15 and older) for the 50 states of the United States and the District of Columbia at a given time period (the calendar week that includes the 12th day of the month). All surveys that use probability sampling have (sometimes only implicitly) a well-defined target population that the survey is trying to characterize via its sample. For example, in a telephone survey, the target population consists of all persons living in households that can be reached by telephone (or sometimes households that can be reached by a landline telephone). Often the sampling or survey procedures consistently omit some portion of the target population, a problem referred to as *undercoverage*. Telephone surveys omit the portion of the household population that does not have a telephone, plus those households that do have a telephone but are nonetheless excluded from sampling (as we will explain later). Many telephone surveys also omit cellular telephones and thus miss the growing proportion of the household population that is cell only.

The definition of probability sampling also requires that the sample be selected using some clearly defined sampling procedure that allows the assignment of a selection probability to each member of the population. This requirement is most easily met when there is a list of all the members of the population. Although some surveys use *list* samples (e.g., researchers conducting a survey of employees at a firm may select the sample from a complete list of the firm's employees), most surveys rely on more complicated sampling strategies that are needed when, as is typically the case, there is no list of the entire target population. Still, regardless of whether the sampling procedure is relatively simple or complicated, the sampling procedure must consist of some objective but random method for selecting a portion of the full population as members of the sample.

Apart from a well-defined population and an objective selection procedure, probability sampling means that (a) it must be possible to calculate a selection probability for each sample member (and for the nonsample members as well, although this is rarely done in practice) and (b) the selection probability must be nonzero for every element in the target population. With sample designs that allow multiple pathways into the sample, it may be difficult or impossible to determine the selection probability for a specific unit. For example, many people now have more than one telephone number through which they can be reached, and this may give them multiple chances of being selected into a telephone sample. Calculating the selection probabilities for a given member of a telephone sample thus requires finding out the number of different telephone numbers a sample member is linked to by virtue of which he or she could have been selected into the sample. High-quality telephone surveys include the questions needed to determine that number, allowing the researchers to calculate each respondent's selection probability. Besides the requirement that the selection probability can, in principle, be calculated for every member of the target population, that probability must be greater than zero. If the selection probabilities for some portion of the population are zero, this means that that portion of the population has been excluded by design and that the sample estimates may be biased.

It is often thought that probability samples have to give every member of the target population the same selection probability, but unequal probability samples are probably the rule rather than the exception among federal and other high-quality surveys. There are many reasons for selecting different elements with different probabilities. One of the most common is to increase the samples size for small, but analytically important, subgroups of the population. By giving the members of these subgroups higher selection probabilities, the sample design

---

[1]Some sampling texts distinguish between the target and the *survey* population (e.g., Kalton, 1983). The target population is the ideal population given the survey's objectives, whereas the survey population is the smaller population that it is actually possible to survey. The distinction reflects various practical constraints reflected in the implementation of the survey. Ideally, the CPS would cover members of the armed forces, people living in institutions, and residents of Puerto Rico and other U.S. territories—that is, the entire U.S. population 15 years old or older—but, as a practical matter, it is restricted to persons of that age living in noninstitutional settings in the 50 states and the District of Columbia. This distinction is often of little practical consequence, and we use the term *target population* to refer to the population that the survey is attempting to characterize.

increases their representation in the sample and allows analysts to produced reasonably precise estimates for these *oversampled* subgroups.

NONPROBABILITY SAMPLES

Most empirical social science studies do not use probability samples but instead rely on less rigorous methods for recruiting respondents. The bulk of psychological studies involve experiments with student samples. These samples are typically self-selected samples of volunteers, meeting some course requirement or lured by a cash payment. In the language of survey sampling, such samples are *samples of convenience*, and they lack all the earmarks of probability samples. They are not drawn from any well-defined population of interest, they are not selected through some objective and random procedure, and it would be impossible to calculate the probability that any given participant would end up in any particular study.

The use of probability sampling is relatively new—probability sampling only won widespread acceptance among statisticians in the 1930s or so—and at least one alternative to it has had considerable intuitive appeal over the years. That alternative—*purposive* or *judgment* sampling—involves selecting a set of units deemed to be typical or representative of the target population (at least in the aggregate). It often seems counterintuitive that a randomly selected sample can really capture the diversity of a large population; it might seem more sensible to construct a microcosm of the population by having experts handpick a representative sample. As late as the 1920s, there was controversy about the relative merits of purposive and probability sampling (e.g., Jensen, 1926) and it was not until some years later that the advantages of probability sampling were clearly demonstrated (Neyman, 1934).

One final method of nonprobability sampling is worth mentioning because it persisted for some time after the adoption of probability sampling by statistical agencies around the world. That method is *quota sampling*, which attempts to achieve a sample that represents the target population by recruiting fixed numbers of respondents in each of a set of cells. For example, targets might be given to the interviewers

for each sex, age category, and employment status. That is, each interviewer would be told to complete interviews with so many males and so many females, so many young people and so many older people, and so on. The General Social Survey (GSS), carried out by the National Opinion Research Center and funded by the National Science Foundation, used a combination of probability sampling and quota sampling through the 1970s. The GSS used probability sampling to select geographic areas down to the level of blocks and then assigned quotas to the interviewers, who recruited respondents from their blocks to fill these quotas. Stephenson (1979) reported the results of a study comparing this block-quota sampling with a full probability sample (see also Stephan & McCarthy, 1958, for an earlier comparison of probability and quota sampling). He found biases in a few estimates from the block-quota sample, but in general the results from the two samples were similar.

Although nonprobability samples are now largely shunned by the federal statistical agencies that sponsor most of the large-scale surveys conducted in the United States, they have made something of a comeback with the advent of Web surveys. Many online survey firms offer samples selected from panels of volunteers that may number into the millions; the panels themselves are just very large samples of convenience (see Couper, 2000, for a discussion of Web surveys and the types of samples they use). As survey costs have risen and survey response rates have fallen (Tourangeau, 2004), the appeal of these online panels has increased dramatically. Getting a thousand completed interviews with members of a nationally representative probability sample can easily cost $1 million or more; a thousand completed surveys from members of an online panel can cost less than $10,000. The popularity of these online panels has prompted concern among organizations of survey professionals, such as the American Association for Public Opinion Research (AAPOR), which has recently issued a report examining the issues raised by nonprobability Web panels (AAPOR, 2010).

In the remainder of this chapter, we cover probability sampling for household surveys in detail. We start by describing the different types of lists (or *frames*) from which samples are selected. The next two sections of the chapter then turn to the major classes of sample design. The simplest probability sample design is the *simple random sample*, which is rarely used in practice but provides a convenient mathematical foundation for discussing the more complex sample designs covered in the next section of the chapter. The final two sections discuss the methods for weighting sample data (a step needed in part to compensate for the use of sample designs that give unequal selection probabilities to different portions of the population) and for measuring the sampling errors associated with statistics derived from surveys with complex samples.

SAMPLING FRAMES

Major Types of Sampling Frames

Survey samples start with a sampling frame, a list or procedure that identifies all the elements making up the target population. Lessler and Kalsbeek's (1992) more detailed definition provides a useful starting point for our discussion of sampling frames:

> The frame consists of materials, procedures, and devices that identify, distinguish, and allow access to the elements of the target population. The frame is composed of a finite set of units to which the probability sampling scheme is applied. Rules or mechanisms for linking the frame units to the population elements are an integral part of the frame. The frame also includes auxiliary information (measures of size, demographic information) used for (1) special sampling techniques such as stratification and probability proportional to size sample selections, or (2) special estimation techniques, such as ratio or regression estimation. (p. 44)

The ideal frame would be a list of all members of the population, along with addresses and telephone numbers that could be used to locate and contact them. Although many European countries do have population registries, the United States lacks a list of its residents. As a result, for general population surveys in the United States, households are usually the sampling units. Households are typically identified and sampled through either their addresses or telephone numbers; thus, the two major types of sampling frames used for general population surveys in the United States are *area frames* and *telephone frames*. As we shall see, both strategies rely on a set of rules that link households (i.e., persons who live together) to frame elements (addresses in the case of area frames, telephone numbers in the case of telephone frames).

Area frames. Many surveys sample addresses rather than directly selecting households. The frame for such samples typically begins with a list of areas that encompass the target addresses, or an *area frame*. Area frames, together with area probability sampling, were widely used in the early stages of survey research (see Kish, 1965) and this combination is still used in many federal surveys, including the CPS. With area probability samples, the sample is often selected in stages, beginning with relatively large areas (such as counties or metropolitan areas), then proceeding to progressively smaller areas at successive stages (U.S. Census Tracts or blocks), and finally to individual addresses.[2]

Separate frames are needed for each stage of sampling. The frame for the first stage of selection is typically a list of counties and metropolitan areas, along with population figures and geographic definitions for each. Once a sample of counties or other first-stage units has been selected, frames for the sampling units at the next stage must be obtained. In many surveys, the second-stage frame consists of lists of Census Tracts or blocks. Information about counties, metropolitan areas, Census Tracts, and blocks is available from the U.S. Bureau of the Census. Once relatively compact areas like blocks have been selected, the next step is to compile a list of addresses within those areas.

There are two main options for developing these address lists. The traditional approach is to send field staff (or *listers*) to compile a list of the

---

[2]The Office of Management and Budget is charged with defining official metropolitan areas, which consist of a central city (with at least 50,000 residents) and one or more adjacent counties or countylike units (such as parishes or boroughs).

addresses for the housing units in the sample areas, following a strict protocol. For instance, the listers may be trained to canvass each selected area, starting at a specific spot (typically, the northwest corner) noted on the map for the area and continuing clockwise; the lister is supposed to write down an address or description of every housing unit he or she finds. The lists are sent back to a central office for further processing and compilation before sampling is carried out. Thus, the frame at this stage consists of a set of area maps along with the lists of addresses for the housing units in each one. This listing process is referred to as *traditional listing*, *field listing*, or *on-site enumeration*, and it is commonly employed in conventional area probability sampling. The other option is relatively new; it involves using the address list maintained by the U.S. Postal Service (USPS), which is available through various commercial firms. The USPS address list is called the *delivery sequence file* (DSF); it is a list of residential addresses that mail carriers follow (and update continually). The list is ordered by zip code, carrier route, and walk sequence number. This sequence of codes uniquely identifies every delivery point in the country.

Evaluation studies suggest that for a survey of the general population, the DSF may offer coverage as high as 97% of U.S. households (Iannacchione, Staab, & Redden, 2003; O'Muircheartaigh, Eckman, & Weiss, 2002). Comparisons of address lists based on the DSF with those developed through conventional listing tend to show a high match rate between the two (Dohrmann, Han, & Mohadjer, 2006; O'Muircheartaigh, Eckman, & Weiss, 2002; O'Muircheartaigh, English, & Eckman, 2002), suggesting that DSF address list frame is a viable alternative to the field listing for general population surveys. This conclusion is, however, restricted to urban areas; in rural areas, the DSF addresses tend to be rural route numbers or general delivery and thus of little help for sampling purposes. As a result, surveys that use an address list originally based on the DSF typically use it only for urban areas and rely on traditional listing for any rural areas that are included in the sample. Apart from this limitation, the DSF has a second drawback. It is not directly available from the USPS but is

available only through private vendors. The completeness and accuracy of the address lists obtained from these private vendors varies across vendors, who differ in how often they update the addresses and in what additional data they provide (Link, Battaglia, Frankel, Osborn, & Mokdad, 2006, 2008).

Although the jury is still out on the relative accuracy of traditional listing versus commercial address lists, for urban areas, the trend seems to be in favor of the commercial lists. For the present, traditional listing seems to be needed for rural areas.

Frames for telephone samples. To construct a sampling frame of household telephone numbers, one can either use an existing list of telephone numbers (such as a telephone directory) or adopt a random-digit-dial (RDD) methodology (Wolter, Chowdhury, & Kelly, 2009). Telephone directories can provide a list of telephone numbers located in a certain geographic area; however, it is known that not all households list their telephone numbers and not all listed telephone numbers are linked to an occupied household. Thus, RDD methodology represents the preferred alternative for constructing a sampling frame of household telephone numbers.

RDD makes use of the structure of U.S. telephone numbers, which can be represented as 1-NPA-NXX-abcd. The first digit "1" is the international country code for the United States and is the same for all U.S. telephone numbers; in the remainder of this section, we ignore this portion of the number. The next three digits (NPA) represent number plan areas or, to use more familiar terminology, area codes; these tend to be nested within states but do not have a straightforward correspondence with any other unit of geography. The three digits represented by NXX are called exchange codes or prefixes. Finally, the last four digits (abcd) are the suffix. Most forms of RDD sampling are based on a unit called the *100-bank*. A 100-bank consists of the 100 possible telephone numbers that begin with a given combination of the first eight digits (i.e., NPA-NXX-ab). With any given 100-bank, it is possible that all 100 numbers have been assigned to landline telephone numbers, to cellular telephone numbers, or to a mix of landline and cell telephones. It is also possible that only a fraction of the 100 numbers have been assigned and the rest are yet to be assigned. It is possible to obtain a list of all the active NPA-NXX combinations either from Telcordia or through such vendors as Survey Sampling, Inc., or Marketing Systems Group.

Telephone sampling faces two important but conflicting challenges. On the one hand, many of the potential numbers within active area code–prefix combinations are not working residential numbers (WRNs); in fact, the overall proportion of WRNs is less than 10 percent and falling (see Boyle, Bucuvalas, Piekarski, & Weiss, 2009, Table 5). Thus, a good deal of time and money can be wasted in dialing numbers that are unassigned or assigned to businesses. The unassigned numbers are not necessarily linked to a recorded message and thus can be hard to identify. On the other hand, sampling only listed telephone numbers, which would yield a much higher hit rate of WRNs, would also omit a substantial portion of the telephone population—around 30% (Brick, Waksberg, Kulp, & Starer, 1995).

Survey researchers have developed two strategies for coping with the linked problems of low hit rates and low population coverage. One sampling strategy was developed in the late 1970s and is called the *Mitofsky-Waksberg method* (Waksberg, 1978). This strategy selects a sample of 100-banks and, within each one, generates a random two-digit ending that is added to the eight digits defining the bank to give a full telephone number. That number is dialed, and if it turns out to be a WRN, additional numbers are generated from that bank and are added to the sample until a fixed number of WRNs is contacted within the bank. As Waksberg (1978) showed, this two-stage procedure produces an equal-probability sample of WRNs; it also sharply increased the proportion of sample numbers that turn out to be WRNs. Still, the Mitofsky-Waksberg procedure has two major drawbacks. Operationally, it is complicated because the status of the initial numbers in a sample of 100-banks has to be determined before additional numbers can be selected from those banks and it is not always easy to tell whether any given number is a WRN. In addition, statistically, the clustering of the sample within 100-banks increases the variance of the estimates derived from the sample.

The Mitofsky-Waksberg method increases the hit rate of WRNs because many 100-banks contain *no* WRNs, and the method restricts the second stage of sampling to 100-banks with at least one WRN (i.e., to banks in which the first number generated turned out to be a WRN). Within those banks, the hit rate of WRNs is relatively high. In 1993, Casady and Lepkowski (1993) explored the properties of another potential method for filtering out 100-banks with no WRNs. They examined the statistical properties of *list-assisted* sampling and, in particular, of a method of sampling that generates random numbers only within 100-banks associated with at least one listed residential number. Listed-assisted sampling became a practical possibility once databases that included all the listed telephone numbers throughout the United States were commercially available. Subsequent empirical work by Brick et al. (1995) showed that the exclusion of 0-banks (those associated with no residential listings) from list-assisted RDD samples led to little bias, in part because the 0-banks included so few WRNs—less than 4% of the total. List-assisted sampling of 1+-banks (that is, 100-banks with at least one residential listing) is now the most widely used method of sampling in government and academic surveys and has largely supplanted the Mitofsky-Waksberg method.

Still, like area sampling, telephone sampling is currently in a state of flux. Telephone service is undergoing a sea change as cellular telephones supplant landline telephones and as new forms of telephone service (such as Voice over Internet Protocol, or VoIP) supplant more traditional forms. The population coverage of list-assisted samples appears to be declining for two reasons. First, the 1+ banks appear to include a shrinking proportion of WRNs, with one study (Fahimi, Kulp, & Brick, 2009) suggesting that as many as 20% of all WRNs may be in 0-banks (for a more optimistic assessment of the current coverage of 1+ banks, see Boyle et al., 2009, who estimated that these banks still include about 95% of all WRNs). The second issue is the growing proportion of the population with only cellular telephone service; as of 2009, more than 22% of U.S. households were cell only (Blumberg & Luke, 2009; Blumberg, Luke, Cynamon, & Frankel, 2008). In addition, one of every seven U.S.

homes (14.7%) had a landline telephone but received all or almost all of their calls on wireless telephones. Although RDD samples can include cell telephone numbers, the response rates for these numbers are often very low (e.g., Brick et al., 2007). Thus, even when they are included in the sample, cell-only households are likely to be underrepresented among the respondents in a telephone survey. It is not clear how telephone surveys will adjust to these new realities, and some researchers have suggested using the mail instead of the telephone for surveys with relatively small budgets (Link & Mokdad, 2005).

Frame Problems and Coverage Errors

The perfect sampling frame would satisfy four requirements: (a) Every population element would appear on the frame; (b) every population element would appear as a separate frame element; (c) every population element would appear on the frame only once; (d) and the frame would contain nothing but population elements (Kish, 1965; see also Lessler & Kalsbeek, 1992). That is, with a perfect frame, there would be a one-to-one correspondence between the frame elements and the elements in the target population. Any departures from such a one-to-one correspondence between the sampling frame and target population create potential coverage problems. Kish (1965) provided a good summary of the statistical issues raised by each of these departures; these are undercoverage, ineligibility, duplication, and clustering.

Undercoverage.   *Undercoverage* refers to the omission of some members of the target population from the sampling frame. No frame is perfect, but area frames are thought to provide the best coverage of the general population, with some undercoverage because of the exclusion of the homeless population, missed housing units, and within-household omissions. This last form of undercoverage reflects the failure to include all members of the household on household rosters, either because of deliberate concealment (Tourangeau, Shapiro, Kearney, & Ernst, 1997) or confusion about who should be included (Martin, 1999). Even the CPS, which has very high levels of coverage overall, has relatively high rates of undercoverage (20–25%) among some demographic subgroups, such as young Black or Hispanic males (see Fay, 1989). Higher levels of undercoverage are likely with telephone surveys, owing to the exclusion of households without any telephone service at all, those linked only with numbers in zero banks, and those with cell-only service (at least in telephone surveys that sample only landline numbers).

For means and proportions, coverage bias results when the population elements that are included on the sampling frame differ from those that are not on the frame on the characteristic of interest:

$$Bias = P_{Exc}(\overline{Y}_{Cov} - \overline{Y}_{Exc}), \qquad (1)$$

in which P_{Exc} is the proportion of the target population that is excluded from the frame, $\overline{Y}_{Cov}$ is the mean (or proportion) among the portion of the population that is covered, and $\overline{Y}_{Exc}$ is the mean (or proportion) among those who are excluded. Intuitively, the bias gets worse as the proportion of the population that is left out gets larger and as the excluded portion differs more markedly from the portion that is represented on the variable of interest.

Coverage bias is obviously not desirable, and survey researchers do their best to reduce the extent of undercoverage—that is, to reduce the P_{Exc} term in the bias equation—to a minimum. For example, when one frame is clearly inadequate, the survey researchers may sample from a second frame to improve coverage; telephone surveys may thus include samples of both landline and cell telephone numbers. Or, interviewers assigned to cases in an area sample may be instructed to look for missed units linked to the sample addresses (a method known as the *half-open interval* procedure) and to add some portion of these omitted addresses to the sample.

Ineligible, blank, or foreign elements.   Thus, the first potential problem is that the frame may not include enough elements, excluding some members of the target population. But the opposite problem can also occur—that is, the frame can include too many elements, including some that do not belong to the target population. We have already mentioned one important example of such ineligible elements, the nonworking numbers in a frame of telephone numbers. Survey researchers attempt to purge such elements from the frame before sampling or at least before fielding the sample. For example, the vendors of telephone samples often put the sample numbers through auto-dialers that can identify unassigned numbers by their rings; this allows them to cull out some of the unassigned numbers before the sample is fielded. Unoccupied dwellings are the analogue to unassigned numbers in the context of area samples, but it is difficult to identify them without actually knocking on the door.

Ineligible units are generally less of a problem than undercoverage because they do not contribute to error if they are excluded from the sample. The presence of a large number of ineligibles in a sample can lead to smaller-than-expected sample sizes and add to the data-collection costs. It is best to allow for ineligibility by selecting a bigger initial sample if the rate of ineligibility is known or if it can be estimated at the time the sample is drawn.

Duplication (or multiplicity). When a population element is associated with more than one element on the sampling frame, the frame is said to have duplicates. *Duplication* (or *multiplicity*) is quite common in surveys. For example, in RDD surveys, households with two or more telephone lines have two or more chances for inclusion in the sample. Similarly, in area frames, households with more than one residence constitute duplicates. A population element linked to two frame elements has twice the probability of being selected as the other population elements. This can bias the survey estimates if there is a correlation between the rate of duplication and the variables of interest.

Multiplicity can be handled in several ways. Sometimes the frame can be deduplicated before sampling. Or rules can be adopted to identify and remove duplicate elements at the time of sample selection or data collection. For instance, a rule can be imposed to accept only the first eligible element and treat the later frame elements as ineligibles. (Of course, this in turn requires a rule for defining one of the frame elements as the first.) The most common solution is to apply weights after data collection to compensate the overrepresentation of population units linked to two or more frame elements. The weighting factor is the inverse of the number of frame elements linked with the population element. Thus, in a telephone survey, questions are administered to identify the number of telephone numbers through which the respondent might have been selected into the sample and this information is used in constructing the weight for the respondent.

Clustering. The final frame problem is clustering, when a frame element corresponds to multiple population elements. For instance, a telephone number is usually shared by all members of the household. Therefore, if the survey samples adults via their telephone numbers, it runs into the problem of the clustering of household members who share the same telephone number. Although it is possible to select all of the eligible elements within the cluster, this is often difficult operationally, especially if each member is supposed to respond for himself or herself. Still, some surveys (including the CPS) gather information about all sample household members.

The alternative is to subsample within the household. In the case of household surveys, within-household respondent selection procedures can be used to select (randomly or nonrandomly) one eligible member of the household. As noted, this can lead to coverage problems, when household members are left off of the rosters that are used to select a single member as the respondent (Martin, 1999; Tourangeau et al., 1997). Streamlined within-household selection procedures are often used in telephone surveys (such as asking for the adult with the most recent birthday) and these can also lead to undercoverage problems (Gaziano, 2005).

To conclude our discussion of frames, we note that coverage problems are problems with sampling frames. As a result, they exist *before* the sample is drawn. Any biases that might be produced would still arise even if we did a census of the frame elements rather than drawing a sample. Thus, they are not problems with any specific sample, but are likely to affect all samples selected from the frame.

SIMPLE RANDOM SAMPLING

Most discussions of sampling procedures start with a description of simple random sampling because it is mathematically the simplest procedure and it provides the key building blocks for other designs that are more common in practice. Sampling texts usually follow certain notational conventions that we also adopt here. The sampling texts usually represent population values and parameters by capital letters and the corresponding sample quantities by lower case letters. For example, the population size is N and the sample size is n. Likewise, the vector of population values for a given variable is represented by $Y_1, Y_2, Y_3, \ldots Y_N$; the vector of sample values is represented by $y_1, y_2, y_3, \ldots y_n$. In general, we follow the notation used by Kalton (1983).

A simple random sample is a sample with a fixed size, n, in which each element has the same probability of selection (n/N) and each *combination* of n elements has the same probability of selection as every other combination of n elements. Sometimes, selection procedures are used that allow the same population element to be selected more than once, a design referred to as unrestricted random sampling or simple random sampling with replacement (*srswr*). We focus on simple random sampling without replacement (or *srswor*).

The population mean ($\overline{Y}$) and sample mean ($\overline{y}$) are defined in the usual way:

$$\overline{y} = \sum_{i=1}^{n} y_i$$
$$\overline{Y} = \sum_{i=1}^{N} Y_i. \tag{2}$$

And the sample element variance is also defined in the familiar way:

$$s^2 = \frac{\sum_{i=1}^{n}(y_i - \overline{y})^2}{n-1}. \tag{3}$$

But, in the sampling literature, the expression for the population element variance typically uses $N - 1$ rather than N in the denominator:

$$S^2 = \frac{\sum_{i=1}^{N}(Y_i - \overline{Y})^2}{N-1}. \tag{4}$$

When N is used in place of $N - 1$, the population element variance is denoted by σ^2 rather than by S^2.

The statistical properties of a given statistic depend both on the form of the estimator and the sample design; reflecting this, sampling texts often use subscripts to denote statistics from a particular sample design. Thus, the sample mean from a simple random sample is denoted $\overline{y}_0$. With a sample random sample, $\overline{y}_0$ is an unbiased estimator of the population mean.

Because the sample is drawn from a finite population with a fixed population total (denoted by Y), there is a slight negative covariance among the elements in a simple random sample. This covariance is reflected in the sampling variance for the mean:

$$V(\overline{y}_0) = (1 - n/N)\frac{S^2}{n}$$
$$= (1 - f)\frac{S^2}{n}. \tag{5}$$

Equation 5 is similar to the formula for the variance of a mean that most psychologists are familiar with, but introduces a new element—the factor $1 - f$, or the *finite population correction*. (In addition, Equation 5 uses S^2 in place of σ^2.) The variance in Equation 5 measures the variance of the means from all possible simple random samples drawn from the population. According to the equation, the variance depends on the variance of the elements, the size of the sample, and the portion of the population that is selected into the sample. It seems intuitive that the mean would vary less across samples as the samples included larger and larger proportions of the population; f, the *sampling fraction*, represents the proportion of the population that is included in the sample and $1 - f$ represents the reduction in variance that results from selecting a non-negligible share of the population. At the limit, there will be no variation across samples when the sample includes the entire population so that the survey is a complete census (that is, when $f = 1$). When population is infinite or when the sample is selected with replacement, the finite population correction term drops out (since $f = 0$) and $S^2 = \sigma^2$ so that Equation 5 reduces to the more familiar σ^2/n.

The sample element variance is an unbiased estimate of S^2 (not of σ^2), so that the expression in Equation 6 gives an unbiased estimator of the variance of a mean derived from a simple random sample:

$$v(\overline{y}_0) = (1-f)\frac{s^2}{n}. \qquad (6)$$

Again, the lower case v indicates that the quantity in Equation 6 is a sample estimate. Similarly, an estimator for the standard error of $\overline{y}_0$ is given by the square root of the quantity in Equation 6):

$$se(\overline{y}_0) = \left[(1-f)\frac{s^2}{n}\right]^{1/2}. \qquad (7)$$

When the variable of interest (y) is dichotomous, the mean becomes a proportion. The sample proportion (p_0) provides an unbiased estimate of the population proportion (P). An unbiased estimator of the sampling variance of p_0 is given by

$$v(p_0) = (1-f)\frac{p_0(1-p_0)}{n-1}. \qquad (8)$$

Relative to other sampling designs, simple random samples have a number of noteworthy properties:

- The samples are element samples, that is, they are samples selected in a single stage directly from a list frame for the target population;
- The selection probabilities for any one population element do not depend on those of any other population member;
- No special effort is made to represent the members of different subpopulations (or, in sampling parlance, members of different *sampling strata*);
- The samples are equal probability samples (i.e., every element in the population has the same selection probability);[3] and
- Because the samples are equal probability samples, the resulting data do not require any weighting to produce unbiased estimates of population means or proportions.

As we shall see, most or all of these properties of simple random sampling tend to be absent from the sample designs that are used to draw large national samples in practice. Still, simple random samples provide a useful starting point for discussing more complex designs and the efficiency of statistics from other sampling designs is often compared with that of sample random samples (as in our discussion of design effects).

In those instances in which simple random sampling can be used, the simplest practical method (assuming that the frame exists as an electronic data file) is to (a) generate a random variable for each element on the frame, (b) sort the file by this file by this randomly generated variable, and (c) select the first n cases from the sorted frame file. In an earlier era, tables of random numbers would have been used in place of random number generators to select the sample of cases from the frame.

MORE COMPLEX SAMPLE DESIGNS

Most actual samples depart from simple random sampling for three main reasons. The first has to do with the absence of sampling frames that provide adequate coverage of the target population. In the United States, for example, there is no complete list of individuals or households that could be used to cover the general population and the costs of developing such a list frame would be prohibitive.[4] Instead, most samples are compiled on the basis of frames for *clusters* of people, such as lists of counties or smaller geographic units, like blocks. A second reason for the relative popularity of cluster samples is that they can sharply reduce the cost of data collection. Even if one could select a simple random sample of adults in the United States or, say, of high school students, it would be extremely expensive to interview the members of the sample because they would be scattered at random across the United States. It is a lot more cost effective to carry out in-person interviews with sample cases that are clustered—within a number of sample blocks or sample high schools. The final reason that simple random samples are seldom selected in practice is

---

[3]The class of equal probability sampling designs is often referred to as *epsem* designs in the sampling literature (e.g., Kish, 1965); epsem is an acronym for equal probability of selection methods.

[4]The closest thing to such a frame in the United States is the master address file (MAF) compiled by U.S. Census Bureau; the MAF is the list of residential addresses used to mail out the questionnaires for the decennial census of the population. It is thought to have nearly complete coverage, but by law, it is not available to researchers outside the U.S. Census Bureau.

that they are not just expensive but can be statistically inefficient as well. Because simple random samples do not ensure representation to key population subgroups, the estimates derived from them can have higher variances than similar estimates from stratified sample designs. Simple random samples guarantee unbiased estimates in the long run, but other designs that build in greater control over subgroup sample sizes offer greater intuitive appeal (the sample *looks* more like a cross-section of the population) and they can produce unbiased estimates with lower standard errors.

Stratification

Stratification refers to dividing the population into nonoverlapping subgroups and then selecting separate samples within each of the subgroups (or *strata*). It makes sense that stratified samples would produce less variability than simple random samples of the same overall size because stratified samples control the stratum sample sizes. This means that certain unrepresentative samples become impossible in a stratified design rather than just unlikely (e.g., all the samples in which no cases are selected from one or more of the strata). The reduced sampling variance relative to simple random sampling reflects this feature of stratified sampling (e.g., see Neyman, 1934). Another way of looking at the gains from stratification is to think of the overall sampling variance in a survey estimate as consisting of two components—one reflecting random fluctuations across samples in the mix of cases by stratum and the other reflecting random fluctuations in the sample means within each stratum. Stratified sampling eliminates the first component of the sampling variance.

Most sampling texts use the subscript h to denote a specific stratum; we follow that convention here. We denote the size of the stratum population by N_h, the stratum sample size by n_h, the stratum population mean by $\bar{Y}_h$, the stratum mean by $\bar{y}_h$, and so on. The proportion of the overall population in stratum h is denoted by W_h ($= N_h/N$). The overall sample estimate (for a mean or proportion) is a weighted sum of the stratum means (or proportions):

$$\bar{y}_{str} = \sum_{h=1}^{H} W_h \bar{y}_h. \tag{9}$$

Because the samples in each stratum are selected independently from each other, the variance of $\bar{y}_{str}$ is given by Equation 10:

$$V(\bar{y}_{str}) = \sum_{h=1}^{H} W_h^2 V(\bar{y}_h). \tag{10}$$

If the samples within each stratum are selected via simple random sampling, the variance becomes

$$V(\bar{y}_{str}) = \sum_{h=1}^{H} W_h^2 (1 - f_h) \frac{S_h^2}{n_h}, \tag{11}$$

in which f_h is the sampling fraction in stratum h (that is, n_h/N_h) and S_h^2 is the within-stratum element variance. The latter quantity can be estimated by the sample within-stratum variance, s_h^2, leading to Equation 12:

$$v(\bar{y}_{str}) = \sum_{h=1}^{H} W_h^2 (1 - f_h) \frac{s_h^2}{n_h}. \tag{12}$$

There are two major types of stratified sample—proportionate and disproportionate. In a proportionate stratified sample, the proportions of the sample in each stratum are the same as the population proportions (i.e., $\frac{n_h}{n} = \frac{N_h}{N} = W_h$). A proportionate allocation thus yields a sample that is a microcosm of the population in the sense that the sample contains the same mix by stratum that the population does. It also means that the sample is selected with equal probabilities (since $f_h = \frac{n_h}{N_h} = \frac{W_h n}{W_h N} = \frac{n}{N} = f$). When the sample follows a proportionate stratified design, the estimator for the sampling variance given in Equation 12 simplifies even further:

$$v(\bar{y}_{str}) = \frac{(1 - f)}{n} \sum_{h=1}^{H} W_h s_h^2. \tag{13}$$

The expression in Equation 13 is quite similar to the one in Equation 6, except that the weighted sum of the within-stratum element variances replaces the overall element variance. Because the overall variance is the sum of the within and between components, it follows that the variance of a mean from a proportionate stratified cannot be larger than that from a simple random sample and can be considerably smaller. The gains from stratification will vary from variable to variable and depend on the ratio of the within-stratum element variance for that variable ($S_w^2 = \sum_{h=1}^{H} W_h S_h^2$) to the total element variance (S^2).

Given the clear advantages of proportionate allocation—greater apparent representativeness, increased precision of the estimates, and greater computational ease (because weights are not needed)—one might wonder why anyone would use disproportionate allocation across strata. There are two main reasons that disproportionate allocation is often used in practice. First, additional sample cases are sometimes needed to increase the precision of estimates involving one of the strata. For example, the CPS sample design might allocate more than the proportionate sample size for a particular state so that the unemployment rate figures for that state meet a specified precision goal. A related purpose for departing from proportionate allocation is to improve the precision of estimates of the *difference* between the means for two of the strata ($\bar{y}_1 - \bar{y}_2$). Difference estimates tend to achieve maximum efficiency when the two strata have near-equal sample sizes (for a more thorough discussion, see Kalton, 1983, p. 25).

The second reason for using a disproportionate allocation is that it can lower the variance of an estimate for the entire population even more than a proportionate allocation can. The proportionate allocation puts the sample cases where the population is—that is, $n_h \propto W_h$. The optimal allocation takes into account uncertainty and costs per case as well:

$$\frac{n_h}{n} = \frac{W_h S_h / \sqrt{c_h}}{\sum_{h=1}^{H} W_h S_h / \sqrt{c_h}}, \qquad (14)$$

in which S_h is the within-stratum standard deviation and c_h is the cost per case for data collection within stratum h. Equation 14 says that optimal allocation allots cases where the population is largest, where the uncertainty is greatest, and where the costs per case are lowest. When the data collection costs do not differ by stratum, then the stratum sample sizes are proportional to the product of the stratum weight and the within-stratum standard deviation ($n_h \propto W_h S_h$), an allocation often referred to as the

Neyman allocation (after Neyman, 1934). And when the stratum standard deviations are also the same, then the proportionate allocation is also optimal.

Regardless of whether the allocation of sample cases to the strata is proportionate or disproportionate, the best stratification variables are those for which there is substantial variation across strata (and minimal variation within strata) on the key survey variables. There are several practical limitations on the effectiveness of stratification. First, the stratification variables need to be available for all members of the population; this means that the stratification variables are usually limited to variables available on the sampling frame. In addition, most surveys involve multiple variables, and the stratification variables (and the allocation of sample cases by strata) that are best for one survey variable may not be best for another. Thus, in practice, the variables that are used to stratify the sample tend to be ones that are weakly related to all the variables in the survey. For example, in an area probability sample, the sample areas are likely to be stratified geographically (by Census region or finer levels of geography) and by level of urbanization (e.g., urban versus rural). Similarly, in a telephone survey, the stratification variables are also likely to be geographic variables, reflecting information that is available about the area covered by the area code or prefix of the sample numbers. In a business survey, it is sometimes possible to find better stratification variables because richer data tend to be available for businesses. Because the frame data may offer only limited choices for stratification variables, surveys sometimes select a large initial sample and conduct short screening interviews with the members of that initial sample. These screening data are used to classify the cases by strata, and a stratified subsample is selected for more detailed data collection. The screening interviews allow the researchers to collect better stratification data than are available on the frame. This technique is referred to a *two-phase* or *double* sampling.

Systematic Sampling

Before the era of high-speed computers, it was often necessary to select samples by hand and one method that reduced the labor involved was systematic sampling. *Systematic sampling* entails selecting every

kth element on the list, beginning with an element selected at random from among the first k (Madow & Madow, 1944) When the sampling interval (the value of k) is not an integer, it is still easy to use systematic sampling. One method is simply to truncate the result obtained by successively adding k to previous sums beginning with the random starting value. For example, suppose the goal is to select a sample of 100 students from a population of 1,623 students at specific high school. The sampling interval is then 16.23 (= 1,623/100). A random start is selected (i.e., a random number is generated in the range from 0.01 to 16.23); let us say that this starting value is 2.55. The first selection is the second student on the list (the integer portion of 2.55); the next selection is the 18th student on the list (corresponding to the truncated value of 2.55 plus 16.23, or the integer portion of 18.78); the third student selected is the 35th student on the list (corresponding to the truncated value of 2.55 plus 16.23 plus 16.23, or the integral portion of 35.01); and so on down the list until 100 students are selected. If the integer portion of the initially selected random start is zero, then one just adds the sampling interval to that random start and begins over from there. For example, had the initial random start been 0.35, the new random start would be 16.58 (i.e., 0.35 plus 16.23) and the first selection would be the 16th student on the list.

Even though computational burden is no longer much of a consideration, many sampling statisticians still use systematic sampling to select samples. One reason is that this selection algorithm is easy to program and easy to check. Another consideration is the flexibility of this method. One way to select a simple random sample is to generate a random variable for each element on the list, sort the elements by this random value, and then select a systematic sample. The first two steps put the elements into a random order and the third step selects an equal probability sample of them. Systematic sampling also offers a simple method for selecting a proportionate stratified sample; just sort the elements by the stratum variables and then select a systematic sample from the sorted list. (When the strata are formed by sorting the file in this way, the strata are said to be *implicit*.) This eliminates the need to select separate samples from each stratum.

Systematic sampling also provides a simple way to build relatively complex stratification into a sample design. After the elements have been sorted into their respective strata, they can be further sorted within the strata by some continuous variable. For example, a population of high schools can be sorted into strata on the basis of whether they are public or private and by their Census region (Northeast, Midwest, South, or West); the schools can then be sorted further within these eight strata according to the percentage of students who are minority group members. It is often easier to take advantage of the frame variables in this way than to group the schools into refined explicit strata. Systematic sampling can also be used to select samples that give unequal selection probabilities to the population elements and is a common method for carrying out probability proportional to size (PPS) sampling, in which the selection probabilities for the elements are proportional to their size.

The major drawback to systematic sampling is that is sharply reduces the number of possible samples that can be selected and sometimes those samples can be highly unrepresentative. Suppose the sampling interval is an integer, say, 100. This means that, no matter how large the population is once the frame file has been sorted, only 100 distinct samples can be selected. If the order of the elements on the frame follows some underlying periodicity, this can also create problems. Consider a list in which husbands and wives alternate, with the wife always preceding her husband; then when k is an even integer, such as 100, half of the possible samples will consist exclusively of wives and the other half will consist exclusively of husbands. The limited number of potential samples means that it can be difficult to find an unbiased estimator of the variance for statistics derived from systematic samples; Wolter (2007) provided a good discussion of these difficulties. Making the last variable used to sort the frame file a randomly generated value helps alleviate these problems by increasing the number of potential samples.

Cluster Sampling

As we noted at the outset of this section, it is often more cost effective to pick geographically linked bunches of cases rather than individuals. For example, the members of a sample may be clustered within a set of sample blocks or sample schools. The advantage of selecting the sample in this way is that it can lead to large reductions in the data collection costs, allowing the survey to have a much larger sample than would otherwise be possible.

The simplest version of cluster sampling involves selecting a set of clusters and then including all of the individuals within that cluster as part of the sample (e.g., Hansen, Hurwitz, & Madow, 1953, Volume 1, Chapter 6) More complicated versions involve subsampling units within the selected clusters. Large national samples often involve multiple levels of clustering; the sample is selected in several stages, with smaller clusters selected at each successive stage. The CPS sample is an example. It is selected in three stages. The first-stage units are metropolitan areas and individual counties; a total of 824 such areas are included in the CPS sample. Within the sample first-stage areas, clusters of housing units are then selected; these second-stage units typically consist four nearby housing units. Sometimes these clusters are larger than expected and a third stage of sampling is carried out to select a subsample of the housing units. Data are gathered for all of the residents at the sample housing units (U.S. Department of Labor, 2006). Many national area probability samples follow similar strategies, selecting counties or metropolitan areas in the first stage, blocks in the second, addresses in the third, and individuals in the final stage of selection.

The clustering of the sample can complicate the estimation of even simple statistics, like means or proportions. Let us start with the simplest possible case, in which the sample consists of a clusters, selected from a population of A clusters via simple random sampling; let us further assume that all of the clusters include the same number of elements (B). Under these assumptions, the mean for the population is as follows:

$$
\begin{aligned}
\bar{Y} &= \frac{\sum\limits_{\alpha=1}^{A} \sum\limits_{\beta=1}^{B} Y_{\alpha\beta}}{AB} \\
&= \frac{\sum\limits_{\alpha=1}^{A} \bar{Y}_{\alpha}}{A}.
\end{aligned}
\tag{15}
$$

in which $\bar{Y}_{\alpha}$ represents the population mean for the cluster. If there is no subsampling within clusters (so that the cluster sample size, b, equals B), then the overall sample mean ($\bar{y}_{clu}$) is an unbiased estimator of the population mean:

$$
\begin{aligned}
\bar{y}_{clu} &= \frac{\sum\limits_{\alpha=1}^{a} \sum\limits_{\beta=1}^{B} y_{\alpha\beta}}{aB} \\
&= \frac{\sum\limits_{\alpha=1}^{a} \bar{y}_{\alpha}}{a}.
\end{aligned}
\tag{16}
$$

In effect, this design selects a simple random sample of a clusters out of a population of A clusters and the estimator for the overall mean is an average of the means for the clusters in the sample; the sample means for those clusters are also their *population* means since no subsampling was done and all B elements were included in the sample for the cluster (i.e., $\bar{y}_{\alpha} = \bar{Y}_{\alpha}$). This implies that the variance of $\bar{y}_{clu}$ can be estimated using a variant of Equation 6:

$$
\begin{aligned}
v(\bar{y}_{clu}) &= (1-f)\frac{s_a^2}{a} \\
s_a^2 &= \frac{\sum\limits_{\alpha=1}^{a} (\bar{y}_{\alpha} - \bar{y}_{clu})^2}{a-1}.
\end{aligned}
\tag{17}
$$

In Equation 17, the sample estimate of the variation in the cluster means (s_a^2) replaces the estimate of the element variance in Equation 6 because, in effect, the sample observations are cluster means rather than individual data points. By the same logic, the number of sample clusters (a) replaces the overall sample size (n, or in this case aB). The sampling fraction (f) can be seen either as the proportion of clusters included in the sample (a/A) or the proportion of individuals (n/N, since $n = aB$ and $N = AB$).

The relative efficiency of this whole-cluster design can be compared with that of a simple random sample by comparing the estimated variances for the same statistic (such as the sample mean), assuming the same sample sizes:

$$
Deff_{clu} = \frac{V(\bar{y}_{clu})}{V(\bar{y}_0)}
$$

$$= \frac{(1-f)\frac{S_a^2}{a}}{(1-f)\frac{S^2}{n}} = B\frac{S_a^2}{S^2}. \tag{18}$$

The design effect (or *Deff*) is the ratio of the expected variances under the two designs, and its value depends on the amount of between-cluster variation expressed as a proportion of the total variation in the survey variable y.

The design effect because of the clustering of the sample can also be expressed in terms of the similarity of the elements from the same cluster as measured by the intraclass correlation statistic, or ρ:

$$Deff_{clu} = 1 + (B-1)\rho. \tag{19}$$

Roughly speaking, ρ is the expected correlation between any two elements from the same cluster. If subsampling is used to select elements from the sample clusters, the subsample size (b) replaces the cluster size (B) in Equation 19. Either way, the loss of efficiency because of clustering reflects the degree to which the data provided by different members of the same cluster are redundant with each other (with the redundancy indexed by ρ) and the number of sample cases per cluster. At the limit—if every sample member selected from a cluster provides the same information—the design effect is b, or the mean from the clustered sample is b times more variable than the mean from a simple random sample of the same overall size, where b is the number of sample cases per cluster. This consequence of Equation 19 seems reasonable because the sample includes only a independent data points to characterize the population, not n.

Although whole cluster sampling is sometimes used in practice (as when students are sampled via the selection of intact classrooms), it is more common to subsample the elements in a cluster, in a two-stage or multistage design. And, of course, most naturally occurring populations come in clusters of unequal sizes rather than clusters of the same size. We deal briefly with each of these complications.

The simplest multistage design features two stages of sampling—the first selects a simple random sample of a clusters and the second stage

selects simple random subsamples consisting of b elements apiece from each of the sample clusters. The overall sample size is then ab. The sample mean ($\bar{y}_{2s}$) still provides an unbiased estimator of the population mean:

$$\bar{y}_{2s} = \frac{\sum_{\alpha=1}^{a}\sum_{\beta=1}^{b} y_{\alpha\beta}}{ab}$$
$$= \frac{\sum_{\alpha=1}^{a} \bar{y}_\alpha}{a}, \tag{20}$$

but the sample cluster means ($\bar{y}_\alpha$) are now estimates, based on the b sample elements from the cluster, not on all B elements in the cluster. The overall estimate of the mean is subject to sampling error both in the selection of the clusters and in the selection of elements within the sample clusters. The expected variance of a mean from a two-stage sample reflects both sources of these sources of sampling error:

$$V(\bar{y}_{2s}) = (1-\frac{a}{A})\frac{S_a^2}{a} + (1-\frac{b}{B})\frac{S_b^2}{ab}$$
$$S_b^2 = \frac{\sum_{\alpha=1}^{A}\sum_{\beta=1}^{B}(Y_{\alpha\beta} - \bar{Y}_\alpha)^2}{A(B-1)}. \tag{21}$$

The new term is the within-cluster variance (S_b^2), averaged across all clusters. When whole-cluster sampling is used, the second term in the variance equation drops out, leading to the variance estimator presented in Equation 17.

Because the variation in the *sample* means for the clusters itself reflects both sources of sampling error, the unbiased estimator for the variance of $\bar{y}_{2s}$ does not fully parallel the expression in Equation 21:

$$v(\bar{y}_{2s}) = (1-\frac{a}{A})\frac{s_a^2}{a} + \frac{a}{A}(1-\frac{b}{B})\frac{s_b^2}{ab}. \tag{22}$$

The second term in Equation 22 involving the within-cluster variation (s_b^2) is multiplied by the sampling fraction at the first stage of selection (a/A); because this factor is often quite small, $v(\bar{y}_{2s}) \approx \frac{s_a^2}{a}$ is often used instead of the expression in Equation 22. Kalton (1983, pp. 34–35) gave a fuller justification for the use of this approximation to estimate the variance of a mean from a two-stage sample.

When there is subsampling at the second stage of a two-stage sample design, the question naturally arises as to how many elements should be selected from each cluster—that is, how large should b be? On the basis of a simple cost model in which the total data-collection costs for the survey reflects the costs per cluster, or C_a, and the costs per element, or C_b, we can derive the optimal cluster size (b'):

$$b' = \sqrt{\frac{C_a(1-\rho)}{C_b\rho}}. \tag{23}$$

If the cost of adding a new cluster is 10 times that of adding a case within an existing cluster (i.e., $C_a/C_b = 10$) and if the value of ρ is .05, then the optimal sample size for a cluster is about 14. If the cost ratio drops to 5, then the optimal cluster size drops to about 10. For a fixed ratio of costs, the higher the value of ρ, the smaller the optimal cluster sample size. With a cost ratio of 10, the optimal cluster size is about 15 when $\rho = .04$, but is about 31 when $\rho = .01$.

Unequal Cluster Sizes

In all of the designs we have discussed so far, the sample size is fixed and is not itself subject to sampling fluctuations. One complication introduced by clusters of unequal sizes is that it becomes more difficult to control the final size of the sample, which typically depends at least in part on which clusters are selected in the various stages of sampling. In situations in which both the numerator and denominator of the sample mean are subject to sampling error, it is common to use a ratio estimator (r) in place of the simple mean to estimate the population mean ($\overline{Y}$):

$$r = \frac{y}{x}. \tag{24}$$

In Equation 24, y represents the sample total and x the sample size (which is a random variable). In practice, both y and x are typically weighted totals. An estimator of the variance of the ratio mean (based on Taylor series approximation) is as follows:

$$v(r) \approx \frac{1}{x^2}[v(y)+r^2v(x)-2r\,\mathrm{cov}(x,y)], \tag{25}$$

in which $\mathrm{cov}(x,y)$ represents the covariation between the sample totals and the sample sizes. The variance terms ($v(y)$ and $v(x)$) are estimated from the variation in the clusters totals around the average cluster total; the covariance term is estimated in the same way. For example, in a stratified design, the estimator for $v(y)$ is as follows:

$$v(y) = \sum_{h=1}^{H} a_h s_{yh}^2$$
$$s_{yh}^2 = \sum_{\alpha=1}^{a_h} \frac{(y_{h\alpha} - y_h/a_h)^2}{a_h - 1}, \tag{26}$$

in which a_h is the number of first-stage units selected in stratum h, $y_{h\alpha}$ represents the sample total for the survey variable y in a first-stage unit from that stratum, and y_h is the stratum total. In many sampling textbooks, the first-stage units are referred to as primary sampling units (or PSUs), the second-stage units as secondary sampling units (or SSUs), and so on.

PPS Sampling

One of the implications of Equation 25 is that fluctuations in the cluster sizes increase the overall variance of a ratio mean; the more the cluster sizes vary, the more the estimates vary. That is the significance of the $v(x)$ term in the equation. Moreover, the ratio mean is biased (though it is consistent) and the size of the bias also depends on the variation in the cluster sample sizes (see Kish, 1965, pp. 208–209). As a result, it is important to try to control the fluctuations in the size of the samples across the different clusters in a two-stage or multistage sample.

One method for accomplishing this is to make the selection probabilities for all but the final stage units proportional to the size of the unit; typically, the size measure is an estimate of the number of elements in the cluster. In a two-stage sample, a first-stage units are selected, but their selection probabilities vary, depending on their estimated size:

$$\Pr_1(FS_i) = \frac{a}{A}\frac{M_i}{\overline{M}}, \tag{27}$$

in which M_i is the estimated size of first-stage unit i, $\overline{M}$ is the average size of all the first-stage units in the population, and A is the total number of first-stage units. Equation 27 boosts the selection probabilities for larger than average clusters and reduces them for smaller than average units. At the second stage of sampling, within each of the sample first-stage units, an equal probability sample of elements is drawn; the sample size for the second-stage units (b) is the same within every sample first-stage unit:

$$\Pr_2(FS_i) = b / M_i. \tag{28}$$

It is apparent from Equations 27 and 28 that the overall selection probabilities across both stages of sampling are constant across all the elements in the population ($= \dfrac{ab}{A\overline{M}} = \dfrac{n}{N}$). In addition, the sample sizes in each cluster are also constant; they are all equal to b. Thus, PPS sampling simultaneously accomplishes two important goals—it reduces (or, ideally, eliminates) variability in the cluster sample sizes and it achieves an equal probability sample.

PPS sampling can easily be extended to more than two stages of sampling. For example, in a three-stage sample, the first-stage units would be selected according to Equation 27 and the units at the second stage of selection would also be selected with probabilities proportional to size:

$$\Pr_2(SS_{ij}) = \frac{b}{B_i} \frac{M_{ij}}{\overline{M}_i}, \tag{29}$$

in which M_{ij} is the size of the jth second-stage unit within first-stage unit i, $\overline{M}_i$ is the average size of all the second-stage units in that first-stage unit, and B_i is the total number of second-stage units within that first-stage unit. At the final stage of selection, c elements are selected at random from among the M_{ij} elements in that second-stage unit, yielding an equal probability sample of abc elements, with c sample elements selected within each second-stage cluster.

A couple of complications arise in practice. Equation 27 can yield selection probabilities that are greater than one. When that happens, the unit is taken with probability 1 and is referred to as a *certainty* or *self-representing* selection. Sample sizes within these certainty selections may have to be adjusted to produce an equal probability sample overall. The second complication is that the measures

of size are typically only estimates. For example, the measure of size for an area sample might be housing unit counts from the most recent census. The actual number of housing units found at the time the survey is fielded is likely to vary from that figure; as a result, the relevant equation (e.g., Equation 28) would be used to set the sampling *rates* (i.e., the sampling fraction within unit ij would be c/M_{ij}), but the actual sample sizes might vary somewhat from one area to the next, depending on how close the size estimate is to the actual count of elements.

WEIGHTING

Survey data are often weighted to make inferences from the sample to the population as close as possible. The weights are used for three main purposes—to compensate for unequal selection probabilities, to adjust for the effects of nonresponse, and to correct for discrepancies between the sample characteristics and known population figures. These discrepancies from population benchmarks can reflect random sampling error or more systematic problems, like undercoverage. Often, the weights are computed in three steps, first adjusting for differential selection probabilities, then for nonresponse, and finally to bring the sample into line with population benchmarks.

Base Weights

Under a probability sampling design, each sampled element has a known probability of selection whether or not the element eventually responds to the survey. The base weights (W_1) are simply the inverses of the selection probabilities:

$$W_{1i} = 1 / \pi_i. \tag{30}$$

The differences in selection probabilities are sometimes present by design, as when a disproportionate allocation is used. Groups sampled at higher than average rates are said to be *oversampled*; those sampled at lower than average rates are said to be *undersampled*. The overrepresented groups get relatively small weights and the underrepresented groups get relatively large ones. Another source of variation in the weights is the selection of a single respondent from households with more than one eligible member. Often, samples are equal probability (or nearly equal probability) down to the household level but then select a single person to respond from among several eligible household members. Persons living alone have a higher final selection probability than those living in households with two or more members of the target population, and the base weights correct for this. When the weights are calculated according to Equation 28, the sum of the weights provides an estimate N, the population size.

It is easy to show that the weighted sum of the sample observations yields an unbiased estimate of the population total:

$$\hat{Y} = \sum_{i=1}^{n} W_{1i} y_i. \tag{31}$$

The estimate for the population mean usually takes the form of a ratio estimator (compare Equation 24):

$$r = \frac{\sum_{i=1}^{n} W_{1i} y_i}{\sum_{i=1}^{n} W_{1i}}. \tag{32}$$

Compensating for Nonresponse

Unfortunately, the sample of cases that actually provide data (the *responding* cases) are generally only a subset of the cases that were selected for the sample. If the nonrespondents are missing completely at random (MCAR; Little & Rubin, 2002), then the respondents are simply a random subsample of the initial sample and nonresponse does not introduce any bias into the estimates. In most situations, however, it is obvious that nonresponse is not a purely random phenomenon; for example, response rates are almost always noticeably higher within some subgroups than within others. This implies that the mix of cases by subgroup is different for the respondents than it was for the sample as a whole; members of some groups are unintentionally overrepresented or underrepresented relative to members of other groups.

The basic method for compensating for this differential nonresponse involves estimating the probability that each case will become a respondent. There are two main approaches for estimating these

response propensities. The first method is to group the cases (both respondents and nonrespondents) into nonresponse adjustment cells and to use the observed response rate within each cell as the estimated response propensity for the cases in that cell (see Oh & Scheuren, 1983, for an early discussion of this approach). The second approach is to fit a logistic regression (or similar) model, predicting which cases will become respondents (versus nonrespondents) on the basis of some set of covariates available for both (Ekholm & Laaksonen, 1991). Whichever method is used to estimate the response propensities, the adjusted weights for the responding cases (W_{2i}) are just the base weights defined in Equation 28 divided by the estimated response propensity ($\hat{p}_i$):

$$W_{2i} = W_{1i} / \hat{p}_i. \tag{33}$$

The nonrespondents are dropped at this point (i.e., they are assigned adjusted weights of zero). The sum of the adjusted weights for the respondents should equal (exactly in the case of the nonresponse cell approach, approximately in the logistic regression approach) the sum of the unadjusted weights for the whole sample ($\sum_{i=1}^{r} W_{2i} = \sum_{i=1}^{n} W_{1i}$, where the first summation is across the r respondents and the second is across all n cases in the initial sample).

Nonresponse adjustments are effective at reducing bias to the extent that the variables used to form the adjustment cells (or the variables included in the logistic regression model for estimating propensities) are actually related to both the response propensities and to the survey variables of interest (Little & Vartivarian, 2005). With the adjustment cell approach, the nonresponse bias is completely removed when the respondents and nonrespondents within each adjustment cell have the same distribution on the survey variables. Both methods for computing nonresponse adjustments require information on both the respondents and nonrespondents. Thus, the calculation of nonresponse weights is often limited by what is available for both, typically data from the frame or data collected in the process of attempting to carry out the survey (such as the number of calls made to the sample household). As a result, the nonresponse adjustments are unlikely to be fully successful at compensating for the biasing effects of nonresponse.

Adjusting to Population Totals

As a final step in developing weights, the weights assigned to the survey participants may be adjusted to bring them into line with external population figures (e.g., estimates from a recent census or from the American Community Survey [ACS]; the ACS is the largest survey done by the Census Bureau between decennial censuses). For example, the researchers may want to ensure that the weighted sample figures match the population in terms of the mix by gender or region. These same methods are also sometimes used to compensate for nonresponse bias (Kalton & Flores-Cervantes, 2003).

The first method for adjusting to population totals is known as *ratio adjustment*, *poststratification*, or *cell weighting*. It adjusts "the sample weights so that the sample totals conform to the population totals on a cell-by-cell basis" (Kalton & Flores-Cervantes, 2003, p. 84). The procedure is quite simple—the weight for each respondent (e.g., W_{2i} above) in a weighting cell (or poststratum) is multiplied by an adjustment factor:

$$W_{3ij} = \left(\frac{N_i}{\sum\limits_{j=1}^{r_i} W_{2ij}} \right) W_{2ij}, \qquad (34)$$

in which W_{3ij} is the adjusted or poststratified weight and the adjustment factor (the factor in parentheses on the right side of Equation 34) is the ratio between the population total for cell i (N_i) and the sum of the current weights (the W_2's) for the respondents in that cell. Sometimes the *population* total is actually an estimate based on a large survey. After adjustment, the weighted sample totals for each cell exactly match the population totals. The adjustment factors are sometimes based on the population proportions rather than population totals; for example, the sample proportions by gender for the respondents may be aligned with the population proportions.

The other popular adjustment procedure is called *raking* (or *rim weighting*; see Deming & Stephan, 1940). It adjusts the sample weights so that sample totals line up with external population figures, but the adjustment aligns the sample to the *marginal* totals for the auxiliary variables, not to the cell totals. For example, if population figures are available for males and females and for people living in cities and those living in rural areas, the adjusted sample weights would bring the sample totals into line with the population figures for males and females and for city dwellers and residents of rural areas, but not for males with living in cities or females living in rural areas. Raking might be preferable to poststratification when population figures are not available for every adjustment cell formed by crossing the auxiliary variables. Or there may be few participants in a given cell so that the adjustment factors become extreme and highly variable across cells. Or, finally, the researchers may want to incorporate too many variables in the weighting scheme for a cell-by-cell adjustment to be practical.

Raking is carried out using iterative proportional fitting (the same algorithm used to fit log-linear models). First, the sample weights are adjusted to agree with the marginal totals for one of the auxiliary variables, say, the gender of the respondents. The adjustment factor is computed in the same way as the one described in Equation 34, only the population targets are based on marginal totals (the total number of males and females). Then, the weights are adjusted to agree with the marginal totals for the next auxiliary variable (level of urbanization) and so on until adjustments have been made for each of the auxiliary variables. The adjustment process for later variables (urbanization) may have thrown off the totals for the earlier variables (gender) so the process is repeated until the weights no longer change. (Convergence is usually rapid but need not be; see the discussion in Kalton & Flores-Cervantes, 2003, p. 86.)

Occasionally, more sophisticated adjustments are applied to survey weights, such as generalized regression (or GREG) weighting, that take further advantage of the external data (e.g., Lee & Valliant, 2009). All three of these methods for adjusting weights to external figures—poststratification, raking, and GREG weighting—are members of a single family of techniques called *calibration estimation* (Deville & Sarndal, 1992).

There can be drawbacks to weighting adjustments like the ones described here. As the weights become more variable, the variance of the resulting estimates can increase. Consider, for example, a sample that consists of several hundred cases each with a weight of one and a single case with a weight of 10,000. Clearly, the estimates will largely reflect the value for the high weight observation; effectively, the sample size is close to one. Sampling statisticians sometimes attempt to gauge the impact of the weights of the variability of the estimates by calculating a design effect due to weighting. A popular approximation is that the weights increase the variance of means and proportions by a factor equal to $1 + L$ (where L is the relative variance of the weights). To reduce this impact, extreme weights may be scaled back or *trimmed* (Potter, 1990). *Trimming* refers to establishing maximum weight and setting any weights that exceed this value to the maximum. Of course, the $1 + L$ formula is only an approximation and, as Little and Vartivarian (2005) noted, sometimes weighting adjustments actually reduce the variance of the estimates at the same time as they increase the variance of the weights.

VARIANCE ESTIMATION

Because they depart from simple random sampling in various ways (such as unequal selection probabilities, clustering, and the use of stratification), survey samples require different procedures for estimating sampling errors from the procedures outlined in introductory statistics texts. Those texts for the most part assume simple random sampling without replacement. Earlier we discussed the notion of a design effect, or the ratio of the sampling variance of a statistic from a more complex design to the variance under a simple random sample (e.g., see Equation 19). Clustering, unequal-size clusters, and unequal selection probabilities all tend to increase the sampling variances of survey statistics relative to a simple random sample; stratification tends to reduce the variances. The net effect of these features of most national samples is to increase the variability of the estimates, generally substantially, relative to the corresponding estimates from a simple random sample. National samples often produce statistics with design effects ranging from 2 to 3 or higher. Clearly, treating data from a survey sample

as though they came from a simple random sample can produce very misleading conclusions.

Because the usual formulas cannot be used to estimate variances, sampling statisticians have developed several alternative approaches for use with survey data instead. We briefly describe the five main approaches—Taylor series approximation, the random groups procedure, balanced repeated replication, jackknife repeated replication, and bootstrapping.

Taylor series approximation. The estimators used in surveys are often nonlinear combinations of the observations, such as the ratio mean in Equation 24 or correlation and regression coefficients, and unbiased estimators of their sampling variance are not always available (Wolter, 2007). The Taylor series approach (or delta method) is to replace the nonlinear estimators with linear approximations of them; variance estimators are then applied to the linear approximation (Hansen et al., 1953, Volume 2, Chapter 4). Sometimes exact variance expressions are available for the linear approximation (as with Equation 25) or sometimes another approach must be used to estimate the variance of the approximation. Linear approximations have been worked out for many standard survey statistics and many of the software packages available for estimating variances for survey data from complex samples are based on these approximations.

Random Groups

Conceptually, a straightforward method for estimating the variation from one sample to the next would be to select multiple samples and observe the actual variation across samples. This insight is the basis for another approach for estimating the variance of statistics from survey samples—the random group approach. As Wolter (2007) noted:

> The random group method of variance estimation amounts to selecting two or more samples from the population, usually using the same sampling design for each sample; constructing a separate estimate of the population parameter of interest from each sample and an estimate from the combination of all samples; and

computing the sample variance among the several estimates. Historically, this was one of the first techniques developed to simplify the variance estimation for complex sample surveys. (p. 21)

The different samples are variously referred to as *interpenetrating samples*, *replicated samples*, or *random groups* (Mahalanobis, 1946). The simplest situation is when the random groups are selected independently. In that case, a reasonable estimator for the combined sample is the unweighted average of the estimates from the random groups:

$$\bar{\hat{\theta}} = \sum_{\alpha=1}^{k} \hat{\theta}_\alpha / k, \tag{35}$$

in which $\bar{\hat{\theta}}$ is the overall estimate for some parameter and $\hat{\theta}_\alpha$ is the estimate for that parameter from random group α. The variance estimator for $\bar{\hat{\theta}}$ reflects the variation across the random group estimates:

$$v(\bar{\hat{\theta}}) = \frac{1}{k} \sum_{\alpha=1}^{k} \frac{(\hat{\theta}_\alpha - \bar{\hat{\theta}})^2}{k-1}. \tag{36}$$

Sometimes an overall estimate ($\hat{\theta}$) is calculated by combining the random groups into a single large sample and this estimate is used instead of the average of the estimates from each random group; the expression in Equation 36 is still used as the variance estimator. (The two overall estimators—$\hat{\theta}$ and $\bar{\hat{\theta}}$—are sometimes identical but do not have to be.) The random groups may be selected as independent samples but more commonly a single large sample is selected and then divided at random into subsamples; these random subsamples are the random groups for variance estimation purposes. The subsamples must be formed to preserve the key features of the original sample design (see Wolter, 2007, pp. 31–32). Typically, each subsample includes one or more first-stage units randomly selected from each stratum in the full sample design.

Balanced and Jackknife Repeated Replication

A limitation of the random groups approach is that the number of random groups available for variance estimation is typically quite small; the stability of the variance estimate depends in part on k, the

number of random groups. Some sample designs attempt to gain the maximum possible benefits from stratification by including just two first-stage selections in each stratum. (Any fewer selections would make it impossible to come up with an unbiased estimator of the sampling variance.) At this lower limit, only two subsamples can be created, each a half-sample that includes one of the two selections from each stratum.

Balanced repeated replication (BRR) is an attempt to get around this limitation. With a total of H strata in the design, each with two first-stage selections, one could in principle form a total of $2H$ different half-samples. The squared difference between the estimate from each half-sample and the corresponding full-sample estimate is an unbiased estimate of the variance of the full-sample estimate (see Wolter, 2007, p. 110). The trick is to improve the stability of this variance estimate by computing multiple half-sample estimates. This is what BRR does. With BRR, multiple half-samples are formed in a balanced way, so that the estimates from the different half-samples are uncorrelated (McCarthy, 1969).

The basic procedure for constructing an estimate and estimating its variance is similar to the procedure in the random group method. First, a number of half-samples are formed. (To maintain full balance, the number of half-samples has to be a multiple of four greater than or equal to the number of strata.) For each one, an estimate is computed on the basis of the elements included in that half-sample ($\hat{\theta}_\alpha$). This typically involves doubling the weights of the cases in the half-sample. Next, the overall estimate is computed as an average of the half-sample estimates ($\bar{\hat{\theta}}$). Finally, the variance of the overall estimate is computed as follows:

$$v(\hat{\theta}) = \sum_{\alpha=1}^{k} \frac{(\hat{\theta}_\alpha - \hat{\theta})^2}{k}. \tag{37}$$

Typically, the full-sample estimate ($\hat{\theta}$) rather than the mean of the half-sample estimates ($\bar{\hat{\theta}}$) is used to calculate the variance. Forming a half-sample necessarily entails forming a complementary half-sample at the same time and alternative versions of the BRR variance estimator in Equation 37 make use of the data from the complementary half-sample.

Jackknifing follows an approach similar to BRR (Durbin, 1959). It forms replicates by dropping a sample first-stage unit within each stratum and then weighting up the remaining first-stage selections to maintain the overall stratum weight. If there are two first-stage selections in each stratum (as BRR assumes), this amounts to forming a replicate by dropping one of the selections from a stratum and then doubling the weight for the other selection in that stratum. Typically, 2H replicates are formed, with each first-stage unit dropped from the sample in turn. The jackknife variance estimator for a stratified sample takes this form:

$$v_J(\hat{\theta}) = \sum_{h=1}^{H} \frac{m_h-1}{m_h} \sum_{\alpha=1}^{m_h} (\hat{\theta}_{h\alpha} - \hat{\theta})^2, \qquad (38)$$

in which m_h is the number of first-stage selections in stratum h (often two) and $\hat{\theta}_{h\alpha}$ is the estimate that results when unit α is dropped from stratum h.

Bootstrapping

Random groups, BRR, and jackknife repeated replication (JRR) are all examples of replication procedures for variance estimation. That is, they assess the variation in the estimates derived from the one sample that was actually selected by mimicking the selection of multiple samples and measuring the variation across these pseudo-samples, or *replicates*. The random groups procedure forms the replicates by dividing the original sample into subsamples that preserve the stratification and clustering in the original. BRR forms half-samples by repeatedly taking one selection from each stratum; it attempts to make the estimates from these half-samples orthogonal to each other. JRR forms replicates by deleting one first-stage selection from each stratum in turn.

With bootstrapping (Efron, 1979), the replicate samples are formed by taking simple random samples *with replacement* from the full sample. If the full sample is a stratified multistage sample, then the bootstrap involves repeatedly selecting samples including m_h of the a_h first-stage sample units within each stratum. The units selected into the bootstrap sample are reweighted. In the simplest case, the bootstrap sample includes a_h-1 selections from stratum h (i.e., $m_h = a_h-1$), some of which may be

selected more than once. The new weight for a given selection is as follows:

$$w_{hi}^* = w_{hi} \frac{a_h}{a_h-1} d_{hi}, \qquad (39)$$

in which d_{hi} represents the number of times the unit was selected; units that were not selected in a given bootstrap sample thus get a weight of zero. The new weights for a given bootstrap replicate are used to generate an estimate ($\hat{\theta}_\alpha$). As in Equation 37, the variance estimate for the full-sample estimate is the average squared deviation of the bootstrap estimates from the full-sample estimate across the k bootstrap replicates. The performance of the bootstrap improves as k gets larger.

Software for Variance Estimation

At least three general statistical analysis packages (SAS, SPSS, and STATA) allows users to take into account complex sample design features, like clustering and unequal selection probabilities, using the Taylor series approach. Most of the packages also allow users to use replication methods. For example, the SAS survey procedures allow both BRR and jackknifing as well as Taylor series estimates of variances for survey statistics, such as means, proportions, and logistic regression coefficients. In addition, at least two specialized packages were developed specifically for the analysis of survey data—SUDAAN developed at RTI International and WesVar developed at Westat. (RTI International and Westat are two of the largest survey firms in the United States.) All of these packages are well documented and handle most statistics that analysts are likely to use (means, proportions, regression coefficients, logistic regression coefficients, etc.).

Empirical comparisons of the different variance estimation approaches (and of the different software packages) have not revealed major differences across the approaches for many types of statistics. For example, in an early comparison of Taylor series, JRR, and BRR, Kish and Frankel (1974) found similar results for the three methods. BRR is often thought to be relatively inflexible (because it assumes two sample first-stage units per stratum), but many real samples come close enough to this requirement that BRR gives reasonable results. Now that computational resources are cheap, bootstrapping has become a more attractive option—it does well with all types of estimates and all types of sample design—but for the present many of the existing analysis packages do not yet allow for this method. Still, the era when analysts had difficulty locating software for analyzing survey data is long past. There is little excuse for not using appropriate methods to estimate the variances in survey statistics because using an inappropriate procedure can lead to biased results.

CONCLUSION

Although the mathematics of survey sampling are mostly well established, important changes still are taking place in the practice of sampling. The frames used in area surveys and telephone surveys are in a state of flux, as commercial address lists complied on the basis of the DSF provide an alternative to the traditional field listing of addresses and as more of the population moves away from traditional landline telephone services. It is not yet clear how samplers will adjust to either of these new realities. Falling response rates (and lower rates of coverage) have encouraged samplers to use more sophisticated weighting procedures, such as calibration estimation, to reduce the biases in survey statistics. On a more positive note, analytical packages like SAS and SPSS have incorporated modules that allow analysts to more accurately estimate the variance of survey statistics ranging from descriptive statistics, like means and proportions, to more analytic statistics, like regression coefficients. And more sophisticated model-based estimation procedures are constantly being developed, including procedures based on Bayesian methods, to improve the estimates derived from survey data. These new methods are likely to play an increasingly important role as the costs of surveys continues to rise and the representativeness of survey samples continues to decline.

References

American Association for Public Opinion Research. (2010). *AAPOR report on online panels*. Retrieved from http://www.aapor.org/AM/Template. cfm?Section=AAPOR_Committee_and_Task_ Force_ Reports&Template=/CM/ContentDisplay. cfm&ContentID=2223

Blumberg, S. J., & Luke, J. V. (2009). *Wireless substitution: Early release of estimates from the National Health Interview Survey, July–December 2008*. Retrieved from http://www.cdc.gov/nchs/data/nhis/ earlyrelease/wireless200905.pdf

Blumberg, S. J., Luke, J. V., Cynamon, M. L., & Frankel, M. R. (2008). Recent trends in household telephone coverage in the United States. In J. M. Lepkowski, C. Tucker, J. M. Brick, E. De Leeuw, L. Japec, P. J. Lavrakas, . . . R. L. Sangster (Eds.), *Advances in telephone survey methodology* (pp. 56–86). New York, NY: Wiley.

Boyle, J., Bucuvalas, M., Piekarski, L., & Weiss, A. (2009). Zero banks: Coverage error and bias in RDD samples based on hundred banks with listed numbers. *Public Opinion Quarterly, 73*, 729–750. doi:10.1093/poq/nfp068

Brick, J. M., Brick, P. D., Dipko, S., Presser, S., Tucker, C., & Yuan, Y. (2007). Cell phone survey feasibility in the U.S.: Sampling and calling cell numbers versus landline numbers. *Public Opinion Quarterly, 71*, 23–39. doi:10.1093/poq/nfl040

Brick, J. M., Waksberg, J., Kulp, D., & Starer, A. (1995). Bias in list-assisted telephone samples. *Public Opinion Quarterly, 59*, 218–235. doi:10.1086/269470

Casady, R. J., & Lepkowski, J. M. (1993). Stratified telephone survey designs. *Survey Methodology, 19*, 103–113.

Couper, M. P. (2000). Web surveys. A review of issues and approaches. *Public Opinion Quarterly, 64*, 464–494. doi:10.1086/318641

Deming, W. E., & Stephan, F. F. (1940). On a least squares adjustment of a sample frequency table when the expected marginal totals are known. *Annals of Mathematical Statistics, 11*, 427–444. doi:10.1214/ aoms/1177731829

Deville, J.-C., & Sarndal, C.-E. (1992). Calibration estimators in survey sampling. *Journal of the American Statistical Association, 87*, 376–382. doi:10.2307/ 2290268

Dohrmann, S., Han, D., & Mohadjer, L.(2006). Residential address lists vs. traditional listing: Enumerating households and group quarters. In R. Harter (Chair), *Proceedings of the Survey Research Methods Section, American Statistical Association, Session 106: Sample Survey Quality II* (pp. 2959–2964). Retrieved from http://www. amstat.org/sections/srms/Proceedings/

Durbin, J. (1959). A note on the application of Quenouille's method of bias reduction to the estimation of ratios. *Biometrika, 46*, 477–480.

Efron, B. (1979). Bootstrap methods: Another look at the jackknife. *Annals of Statistics, 7*, 1–26. doi:10.1214/ aos/1176344552

Ekholm, A., & Laaksonen, S. (1991). Weighting via response modeling in the Finnish Household Budget Survey. *Journal of Official Statistics, 7,* 325–337.

Fahimi, M., Kulp, D., & Brick, J. M. (2009). A reassessment of list-assisted RDD methodology. *Public Opinion Quarterly, 73,* 751–760. doi:10.1093/poq/nfp066

Fay, R. E. (1989). An analysis of within-household undercoverage in the Current Population Survey. In *Proceedings of the U.S. Bureau of the Census Annual Research Conference* (pp. 156–175). Washington, DC: U.S. Bureau of the Census.

Gaziano, C. (2005). Comparative analysis of within-household respondent selection techniques. *Public Opinion Quarterly, 69,* 124–157. doi:10.1093/poq/nfi006

Hansen, M. H., Hurwitz, W. N., & Madow, W. G. (1953). *Sample survey methods and theory.* New York, NY: Wiley.

Iannacchione, V. G., Staab, J. M., & Redden, D. T. (2003). Evaluating the use of residential mailing addresses in a metropolitan household survey. *Public Opinion Quarterly, 67,* 202–210. doi:10.1086/374398

Jensen, A. (1926). The representative method in practice. *Bulletin of the International Statistical Institute, 22,* 359–380.

Kalton, G. (1983). *Introduction to survey sampling.* Newbury Park, CA: Sage.

Kalton, G., & Flores-Cervantes, I. (2003). Weighting methods. *Journal of Official Statistics, 19,* 81–97.

Kish, L. (1965). *Survey sampling.* New York, NY: Wiley.

Kish, L., & Frankel, M. R. (1974). Inference from complex samples. *Journal of the Royal Statistical Society. Series B. Methodological, 36,* 1–37.

Lee, S., & Valliant, R. (2009). Estimation for volunteer panel web surveys using propensity score adjustment and calibration adjustment. *Sociological Methods and Research, 37,* 319–343. doi:10.1177/0049124108329643

Lessler, J. T., & Kalsbeek, W. D. (1992). *Nonsampling error in surveys.* New York, NY: Wiley.

Link, M. W., Battaglia, M. P., Frankel, M. R., Osborn, L., & Mokdad, A. H. (2006). Address-based versus random-digit-dial surveys: Comparison of key health and risk indicators. *American Journal of Epidemiology, 164,* 1019–1025. doi:10.1093/aje/kwj310

Link, M. W., Battaglia, M. P., Frankel, M. R., Osborn, L., & Mokdad, A. H. (2008). A comparison of address-based sampling (ABS) versus random-digit dialing (RDD) for general population surveys. *Public Opinion Quarterly, 72,* 6–27. doi:10.1093/poq/nfn003

Link, M. W., & Mokdad, A. H. (2005). Alternative modes for health surveillance surveys: An experiment with web, mail, and telephone. *Epidemiology, 16,* 701–704.

Little, R. J., & Rubin, D. B. (2002). *Statistical analysis with missing data* (2nd ed.). New York, NY: Wiley.

Little, R. J., & Vartivarian, S. (2005). Does weighting for nonresponse increase the variance of survey means? *Survey Methodology, 31,* 161–168.

Madow, W. G., & Madow, L. H. (1944). On the theory of systematic sampling. *Annals of Mathematical Statistics, 15,* 1–24. doi:10.1214/aoms/1177731312

Mahalanobis, P. C. (1946). Recent experiments in statistical sampling in the Indian Statistical Institute. *Journal of the Royal Statistical Society, 109,* 325–378.

Martin, E. (1999). Who knows who lives here? Within-household disagreements as a source of survey coverage error. *Public Opinion Quarterly, 63,* 220–236. doi:10.1086/297712

McCarthy, P. C. (1969). Pseudoreplication: Half-samples. *Review of the International Statistical Institute, 37,* 239–264. doi:10.2307/1402116

Neyman, J. (1934). On the two different aspects of the representative method: The method of stratified sampling and the method of purposive selection. *Journal of the Royal Statistical Society, 97,* 558–625. doi:10.2307/2342192

Oh, H. L., & Scheuren, F. (1983) Weighting adjustments for unit nonresponse. In W. G. Madow, I. Olkin, & D. Rubin (Eds.), *Incomplete data in sample surveys: Vol. 2. Theory and bibliographies* (pp. 143–184). New York, NY: Academic Press.

O'Muircheartaigh, C., Eckman, S., & Weiss, C. (2002). Traditional and enhanced field listing for probability sampling. In *Proceedings of the Section on Survey Research Methods, American Statistical Association,* 2563–2567.

O'Muircheartaigh, C., English, N., & Eckman, S. (2002, May). *Predicting the relative quality of alternative sampling frames.* Paper presented at the 57th Annual Conference of the American Association for Public Opinion Research & World Association for Public Opinion Research, St. Pete Beach, FL. Retrieved from http://www.amstat.org/sections/srms/Proceedings/

Potter, F. J. (1990). A study of procedures to identify and trim extreme sampling weights. In R. P. Moore (Chair), *Proceedings of the Survey Research Methods Section, American Statistical Association: II. Sample Weighting and Design Issues* (pp.225–230). Retrieved from http://www.amstat.org/sections/srms/Proceedings/

Presser, S. (1984). The use of survey data in basic research in the social sciences. In C. F. Turner & E. Martin (Eds.), *Surveying subjective phenomena* (Vol. 2, pp. 93–114). New York, NY: Russell Sage.

Stephan, F., & McCarthy, P. J. (1958). *Sampling opinions.* New York, NY: Wiley.

Stephenson, C. B. (1979). Probability sampling with quotas: An experiment. *Public Opinion Quarterly, 43,* 477–495s. doi:10.1086/268545

Tourangeau, R. (2004). Survey research and societal change. *Annual Review of Psychology, 55,* 775–801. doi:10.1146/annurev.psych.55.090902.142040

Tourangeau, R., Shapiro, G., Kearney, A., & Ernst, L. (1997). Who lives here? Survey undercoverage and household roster questions. *Journal of Official Statistics, 13,* 1–18.

U.S. Department of Labor. (2006). *Design and methodology: Current population survey* (Technical Report 66).

Washington, DC: U.S. Department of Labor and U.S. Department of Commerce.

Waksberg, J. (1978). Sampling methods for random digit dialing. *Journal of the American Statistical Association, 73,* 40–46. doi:10.2307/2286513

Wolter, K. (2007). *Introduction to variance estimation* (2nd ed.). New York, NY: Springer.

Wolter, K., Chowdhury, S., & Kelly, J. (2009). Design, conduct, and analysis of random-digit dialing surveys. In D. Pfeffermann & C. R. Rao (Eds.), *Handbook of statistics: Vol. 29A. Sample surveys: Design, methods and applications* (pp. 125–154). Holland, the Netherlands: Elsevier. doi:10.1016/S0169-7161(08)00007-2

CHAPTER 15

EPIDEMIOLOGY

Rumi Kato Price

Epidemiology is a broad discipline that investigates the distributions of health and illness in populations and factors affecting these conditions. *Distributions* can be defined as a range of observable, and sometimes latent, measures of how a specific health or illness condition is spread or contained; relevant factors include both etiological and confounding factors that mask the true etiology. In modern epidemiology, surveillance and prevention of diseases are also considered as applications of epidemiology (Last, 2001). Health and illness encompass a wide range of phenotypes (outcomes), including clinically defined diseases and injuries, various types of health-related problems, and normal behaviors as well. The study population is most frequently the human population. However, depending on the types of phenotype and topic areas, the unit of analysis (observation) may be nonhuman species, such as a rat (e.g., effect of chronic stress on the size of a rat's hippocampus density), or the unit can be any quantifiable unit, such as a geographic unit (alcohol outlet density in segment unit affecting the rate of motor vehicle accidents). Because epidemiology often serves as a foundation for providing the evidence base and logic for both treatment and preventive intervention, epidemiology is considered to be an integral part of both medicine and public health.

Epidemiologic methods, including biostatistics, provide basic tools for biomedical and public health research. As seen in this chapter, the modern origin of epidemiology is usually traced to infectious diseases that involved identification of infectious agents (e.g., West Nile virus) and vectors (e.g., culex mosquitoes) that carry these agents. However, contemporary epidemiology has expanded in scope to include a large number of chronic noninfectious conditions, such as diabetes mellitus, obesity, and most psychiatric disorders. Epidemiology as a discipline, in fact, has proliferated so much that it is difficult to think of a phenotype to which epidemiology is irrelevant and is probably best thought of as a multidisciplinary science that allows studies in many applied fields within public health (Ahrens, Krickeberg, & Pigeot, 2005). This chapter, however, is written primarily for psychologists and other behavioral and social scientists, teachers, and students who are interested in psychosocial studies that employ epidemiological methods.

The first section of this chapter provides a brief history of epidemiologic research. Next, we provide basics of epidemiologic methods. The methods include main concepts of epidemiology and note how they relate to contemporary epidemiologic methods; commonly used measures, including measures of occurrence, association, impact, predictive utility, and disease burden; traditional and hybrid study designs; and selected topics in sampling methods. Fuller descriptions of some topics introduced here are provided in other chapters (e.g., for genetic epidemiology, see Chapter 36 of this volume; for sampling, see Chapter 14 of this volume; for question order effects, see Volume 1, Chapter 13, this

Preparation for this chapter was supported in part by National Institutes of Health Grants R01DA09281 and R01MH060961 to the author. Greg Widner provided editorial assistance.

DOI: 10.1037/13620-015
APA Handbook of Research Methods in Psychology: Vol. 2. Research Designs, H. Cooper (Editor-in-Chief)

handbook). Although this chapter provides basic information on measures of association, more elaborate quantitative data analysis strategies are given separately over several commonly used methods in Volume 3, this handbook. For excellent further in-depth reading and reference books on epidemiology, readers may also consult with Ahrens and Pigeot (2005), Bhopal (2002), Morabia (2004a), Oakes and Kaufman (2006), and Susser and Stein (2009).

BRIEF HISTORY OF EPIDEMIOLOGY

The word *epidemic* means "something that falls upon people" in ancient Greek (*epi*, upon, and *demos*, the people). This original meaning still is in evidence in contemporary epidemiology because the essence of epidemiology involves examining diseases and conditions at the population level. The second basic idea, studying disease distribution may stem from Hippocrates' distinction of *epidemic* (diseases that are visited upon) from *endemic* (reside within). The third idea of *etiology* or *causes* can also be traced back to such early writings by ancient Greek and Roman philosophers and practitioners of medicine, including Hippocrates (ca. 460–375 B.C.) and Galen (or Galenus; 129–199/217) (see Ahrens et al., 2005; Susser & Stein, 2009).

A modern use of the term *epidemiology* is believed to have first appeared in Madrid circa 1802 (Greenwood, 1932). Throughout the 19th century and up to middle of the 20th century, however, use of this term was restricted to studies of epidemics of infectious disease origin (Greenwood, 1932). The most well-known example of the practice of epidemiology in this regard is the work on the 1854 London cholera outbreak by a British physician, John Snow. Snow identified the source of transmission for the cholera outbreak as the Broad Street water pump by plotting fatal attacks and deaths during a short span of approximately 45 days. This example illustrates several basic concepts such as incident cases, ratios, relative risk, and case-control design (see the Fundamentals of Epidemiologic Methods section for details of these measures and designs). Modifying a cause (removing the handle of the suspected water pump), further illustrated the connection of epidemiology to etiology that leads to intervention and

prevention and public health. It was 17 years later, however, when the causative agent *Vibrio cholerae* was finally identified and publicized (Brock, 1999; Snow, 1854; see also the John Snow website created by the UCLA School of Public Health: http://www.ph.ucla.edu/epi/snow.html). The fact that effective action can be taken even in the absence of knowledge of a specific etiological factor is an important concept in modern public health.

The connection of epidemiology to statistics originates in population thinking. In England and France, devastating plague epidemics stimulated the interest for population data collection. The etymology of the word *statistics* shows the word was derived from New Latin *statisticum collegiums* (council of state), Italian *statista* (statesman), and German *Statistik*, or in a contemporary term *population statistics* (Morabia, 2004b; Rosen, 1958). The occurrence of disease in populations were first measured in ratios, proportions, and a rudimentary mortality ratio, as early as late 17th century (e.g., Graut's plague statistics). William Farr, superintendent of the England General Register Office, is often credited for advancing epidemiologic statistics at the time multiple epidemics of infectious diseases such as cholera and phthisis (tuberculosis) plagued England (Farr, 2004; Susser & Adelstein, 1975; Susser & Stein, 2009). The development of later, more refined epidemiologic measures reflect the evolution of methodology for studying diseases and conditions over the past two centuries and will be introduced in the section Commonly Used Basic Epidemiologic Measures.

Emergence of large-scale epidemiologic studies examining psychiatric or psychological outcomes coincided with the emergence and dominance of chronic disease epidemiology in the latter half of 20th century. Psychosocial or psychiatric epidemiology became a subfield of epidemiology and contributed to advances of chronic disease epidemiology methods over the past 60 years. It is usual to separate landmark studies to first generation (before World War II), second generation (after World War II to about 1980), third generation (1980–2000), and current fourth generation (Tohen, Bromet, Murphy, & Tsuang, 2000). Most of the commonly used epidemiologic measures and study designs were developed and refined with second- and third-generation studies. Because this chapter focuses on epidemiologic methods, I provide a summary of four landmark psychosocial and psychiatric epidemiology studies in Appendix 15.1. Social Class and Mental Illness (Faris & Dunham, 1939, 1960) provided an example of pre–World War II record examination study. The Epidemiologic Catchment Area (ECA) study (Robins & Regier, 1991) was a classic general population psychiatric epidemiology study carried out in 1980s. The International Study of Schizophrenia (ISoS) was an example of clinical-sample-based multicountry series carried out in Europe) (Hopper, Harrison, Janca, & Sartorius, 2007; Leff, Sartorius, Jablensky, Korten, & Ernberg, 1992). The National Vietnam Veterans Readjustment Study (NVVRS) (Kulka et al., 1990; Schlenger et al., 1992) provided an example of another classic study but focused on a special population (U.S. veterans).

FUNDAMENTALS OF EPIDEMIOLOGIC METHODS

In the remainder of this chapter, I describe fundamentals of epidemiologic concepts, frequently employed epidemiologic measures, epidemiologic study designs, and common sampling methods. Because statistical techniques have proliferated in 21st-century psychological research, other chapters in Volume 3, this handbook, detail a variety of current analysis techniques.

Concepts of Epidemiology

Epidemiology is often not thought of as a distinctive scientific discipline (such as medicine) but as an allied methodological field based heavily in statistics. However, several epistemological concepts distinguish epidemiology from other fields (e.g., clinical medicine). As noted, population thinking is the foundation of epidemiology, and study populations include individuals, dyads, families, groups, communities, states, and nations at macro levels.

The second fundamental concept is variation. Examining variations is an essential aspect of inquiry in most science fields; epidemiology focuses on patterns of diseases and other health conditions. Variations can be across time, between subgroups, or across place. The importance of this concept

rests on the assumption that understanding such variations lead to new knowledge on the etiology of a disease or health condition, thus in turn leading to intervention and prevention of disease (Bhopal, 2002). Early emphasis on natural history (observational study of disease process) is related to the history of epidemiology being tied to disease epidemics. Thus, by understanding the disease epidemic pattern, one hoped to identify the causative agent (e.g., vibreo cholera) or source of transmission (e.g., water pump in John Snow's case). As the field expanded to endemic or chronic diseases, interest in natural history shifted toward identifying underling factors that yield the observed patterns of disease over time, that is, developmental or life course perspectives (Ben-Shlomo & Kuh, 2002; Berkman & Kawachi, 2000).

The third fundamental concept is causal inference. Although not unique to epidemiology, historically epidemiology is considered the discipline that "discovered" and further articulated the concept of causal relationship (Rothman & Greenland, 2005) in the area of health and disease. Epidemiology contributed to establish distinctions such as necessary and sufficient conditions (Greenwood, 1932) and association and causation (Hill, 1961). Epidemiologists also elaborated multiple causation models (Morris, 1964) and web of causation mechanisms (MacMahon & Pugh, 1970) and introduced the notion of interaction (MacMahon & Pugh, 1970) and moderator effects (Susser, 1973).

The fourth fundamental concept is sometimes referred to as the epidemiologic triangle (Ahrens et al., 2005; Bhopal, 2002) of agent, host, and environment. The model can be crudely considered as corresponding to "what" (agent), "who" (host), and "where" (environment), which are the key variables in understanding the spread of disease. An additional factor is time, which is often placed in the center of the triangle. Agents are necessary for diseases to occur (biological, physical, chemical); host factors are those that influence the chance for the disease to express or affect the severity of the disease; and, finally, environments are external conditions that contribute to the disease process. The idea is that an epidemic occurs when three factors are not in balance (homeostasis). This model is most suitable for studying outbreaks of epidemics such as infectious diseases. However, the model may not be well suited for use when host factors are complex and the disease process is chronic (endemic) (Ahrens et al., 2005; Songer, 2010).

These fundamental concepts are summarized in Table 15.1. Each concept is summarized with respect to its meaning, historical origin, and role for methodological development. Several other and related concepts not listed in Table 15.1 are often found in introductory textbooks of epidemiology. For example Zhang and colleagues (2004) analyzed eight textbooks on epidemiology published over the past century and summarized the evolution of six concepts of epidemiology: confounding, bias, cohort, case-control, causal inference and interaction. Other concepts involving study designs

(cohort, case control) and sampling (that would create statistical bias) are more fully discussed in the section Study Designs and the section Sampling Methods and Issues.

Commonly Used Basic Epidemiologic Measures

I now introduce some basic measures of occurrence, association, impact, predictive utility, and disease burden used in a wide range of epidemiologic research. These measures provide different ways in which associations (relationship between cause, risk factor, and outcome) are quantitatively assessed. Aimed as an introductory section, measures specific to multivariate analysis are omitted here. However, some measures such as risk ratio and odds ratio are

---

TABLE 15.1

Basic Concepts in Epidemiology

Concept	What it means	Historical origin	How they relate to methodological methods
Population thinking	Finding a cause of disease requires examining the whole population, not just individuals	Can be traced back to Hippocrates (Buck, Llopis, Najera, & Terris, 1998); modern origins can be traced to British epidemiologists such as William Farr and John Snow (examined by Susser & Stein, 2009, Chapter 7)	Sampling techniques, study designs, prevalence, incidence
Stochastic variation	Disease expression is not constant but varies by groups, place, and time; and that expression is not perfect and comes with a random element	Modern origin in epidemiology can be traced to John Snow with comparisons of rates across three places	Measures of occurrence, association, and multivariate modeling are based on the notion of random error; modern-day statistics used in epidemiology are almost always stochastic
Causal inference	Identifying the relationship between factors (causes) and disease occurrence	Can be traced back to Aristotle (384–322 B.C.), Hippocrates (ca. 460–375 B.C.), and Galen (ca. 129–199/217); modern prototypes, Lind's report on scurvy (ca. 1753) (from Carpenter, 1986) and Snow's study on cholera (1854)	Necessary vs. sufficient causes, confounding, interaction, mediators, statistical controls
Epidemiologic triangle	Disease expression depends on three factors of agent (what), host (who), and environment (where) and considered a basic model of causation	19th-century microbiologists such as Robert Koch and Louis Pasteur (examined by Susser & Stein, 2009, Chapters 10 and 11)	Multilevel, multivariate, and interaction analysis; prevention models

also applicable in the context of multivariate statistics. Also it should be noted that a majority of this discussion involves dichotomous measures reflecting a disease orientation of epidemiologic outcomes.

Measures of occurrence. Prevalence and incidence measures are the most commonly used measures of occurrence. Prevalence rate can be classified into point prevalence and period prevalence. Point prevalence is calculated as follows:

(Number of existing cases on a specific date) / (Population number in the particular date).

Psychiatric epidemiology most frequently uses period prevalence, which is the frequency of occurrence during a given time period. Lifetime prevalence is the cumulative prevalence up to the point of assessment and is often asked by *ever* questions (i.e., "Have you ever . . . ?"). A shorter period prevalence can be 30 days, past month or year, or some other unit of time. Incidence rate (cumulative incidence) is calculated as follows:

(Number of new cases in a given period) / (Population at risk for the given period).

When the denominator is the product of Person × Time of at-risk population (e.g., Person × Number of Years Disease Free), this is usually called the *incidence density rate*. The latter measure may be more suitable when individuals in populations are observed for varying durations over time in a cohort-based study. In a fixed population, (Prevalence) = (Incidence) × (Average Duration of Disease). However, in a dynamic population (such as a human population over time), this equivalence cannot be assumed. Although they are not identical and serve different purposes, hazard rate, $h(t)$, is considered synonymous with incidence, therefore, hazard rate is sometimes called the incidence intensity. It is the instantaneous rate of developing disease in a short interval Δ around time t, thus, as a shorthand, it can be written nonmathematically as follows (cf. Bhopal, 2002, p. 168):

Hazard rate = (Probability that disease-free person at t will develop disease between t and Δt) / (Time from t to Δt), where Δt is a small change in t.

If time interval is assumed to be constant, incidence rate is an estimate of the hazard rate. One might prefer the use of incidence for acute and short-duration diseases, whereas prevalence may be more preferable for chronic and noncyclical diseases. Use of incidence cases is better suited for studying causes of disease, because it is not confounded with factors that could affect the course of illness independent of etiology. Hazard rate is an essential function for estimating failure time as in death and treatment studies (Benichou & Palta, 2005; Bhopal, 2002; Mausner & Kramer, 1985).

Measures of association. Relative risks (RR) and odds ratio (OR) remain the most frequently used measures of association. In a prospective cohort study, RR is defined as the ratio of incidence rate in the exposed group as compared with incident rate in the unexposed group. Using a standard 2 × 2 table (see Table 15.2), RR is as follows:

$$RR = [a / (a + b)] / [c / (c + d)].$$

A retrospective study (e.g., case control) is usually able to estimate RR of prevalent cases. OR is theoretically more appropriate in case-control or cross-sectional studies, although RR and OR are often used interchangeably and distinctions depend on a number of design factors (Knol, Vandenbroucke, Scott, & Egger, 2008). In the epidemiological context, OR estimates the probability of being diseased (or exposed) compared with not diseased (or exposed). Using the same 2 × 2 table, OR is typically reported in the format of $(a \times d) / (b \times c)$, but this does not show its intended meaning because its

TABLE 15.2

Risk Ratio and Odds Ratio Computation Table

Exposure classification	Disease cases	Nondiseased (or controls)	Total
Present	a	b	M1 (a + b)
Absent	c	d	M2 (c + d)
Total	M3 (a + c)	M4 (b + d)	N = M1 + M2 = M3 + M4 = = a + b + c+ d

equivalent forms are more intuitive to understand the meanings of ORs:

$$OR = (a \times d) / (b \times c) = (a/c) / (b/d)$$
$$= (a/b) / (c/d).$$

The formula $(a/c) / (b/d)$ is the exposure probably in cases as compared with nondiseased controls; the formula $(a/b) / (c/d)$ shows the disease probability among exposed as compared with nonexposed. In a simple two-by-two table, the confidence interval of the $Ln(OR)$ is easily computed:

$$Ln\ (OR) \pm 1.96\ SE[Ln\ (OR)] = Ln(OR)$$
$$\pm\ (1/a + 1/b + 1/c + 1/d)^{1/2}.$$

ORs asymptotically approach the RR for a rare disease (less than 10% incidence rate). When certain assumptions are met, an OR can be adjusted to provide an estimate of RR using the following:

$$RR = OR / [(1 - P^0) + (P^0 \times OR)],$$
where P^0 is the incidence rate.

Cautions are needed, however, when making inferences from the confidence intervals (or standard errors) using this adjustment because confidence intervals appear to be substantially narrower than the true values (McNutt, Wu, Xue, & Hafner, 2003; Zhang & Yu, 1998). It is not entirely clear why OR has become a standard measure of association. One reason may be the symmetric nature (with respect to disease and nondisease), although such symmetry is only true if there are no additional covariate in the model. The ease of interpretation of ORs in multiple logistic regression may have contributed substantially to the current wide use of OR in epidemiologic and psychosocial studies (Benichou & Palta, 2005; Bhopal, 2002; Kahn & Sempos, 1989).

Measures of impact. Traditional epidemiologic measures of association are useful for pinpointing a relative effect of exposure and or any risk factors. *Attributable risk* (AR), sometimes called *attributable fraction*, was originally intended to quantify the impact of a well-known cause on disease outcome (e.g., smoking and cancer; Levin, 1953). AR measures the proportion of risk in the exposed group that is attributable to the risk factor of interest. In a general term, $AR = [Pr(D) - Pr(D/E)]$ $Pr(D)$, where $Pr(D)$ is the population probability of a disease; $Pr(D/E)$ is the probability conditioned on the nonexposed group, so the intent is to measure the fraction of the difference between overall average risk of the population and average risk in the unexposed group. AR can be interpreted in several ways, for example, proportion of excess risk or proportion of a preventable disease; consequently, a number of derived formulas are used with each with some different interpretation (Levin, 2007; Rockhill, Newman, & Weinberg, 1998). To see the connection with RR, the original formula can be rewritten as (cf. Bhopal, 2002, p. 209):

$$AR = \text{(Incidence in exposed)} - \text{(Incidence in unexposed)} / \text{(Incidence in exposed)}$$
$$= RR_{(exposed)} - RR_{(unexposed)} / RR_{(exposed)}$$
$$= (RR - 1) / RR.$$

Population attributable risk (PAR), sometimes called *population attributable fraction*, measures the proportion of disease in the population as a whole that is attributable to exposure or a risk factor:

$$PAR = [\text{(Incidence in total population)} - \text{(Incidence in unexposed population)}] / \text{(Incidence in total population)}$$
$$= P_{(exposed)} (RR - 1) / [1 + P_{(exposed)} (RR - 1)].$$

Thus, RR or OR, when appropriate, can be used even for a cross-sectional study to obtain PAR (e.g., Prigerson, Maciejewski, & Rosenheck, 2002). The PAR has gained popularity as an alternative or an addition to traditional measures of association because in part PAR allows making a choice of prevention(s) targeted to specific risk factor(s) and choice of disease, in cases in which a prevention should have the greatest reduction in the future if that prevention were to be implemented. Nonetheless, AR and PAR rates are estimates of the amount of risk reduction that could potentially be achieved. Data do not usually allow confirming the causality of a risk factor, thus AR and PAR should be considered the theoretical upper-limit estimates. An experimental trial is needed to assess the validity of a specific estimate. More extensive discussion on usefulness and potential pitfalls of AR and PAR is found in Benichou and Palta (2005) and Bhopal (2002).

Predictive utility. More relevant for performance of a screening test, sensitivity and specificity relate to basic epidemiologic concepts of error specifications (Type I error concerns false positive rate and Type II error concerns false negative rate). An exposure or a risk factor can be equated with a screening test (positive and negative). Sensitivity (true positive rate) and specificity (true negative rate), respectively are as follows:

Sensitivity = [Number of true positives (diseased)] / { [Number of true positives (diseased)] + [Number of false negatives (screen/exposure/ risk factor negatives who are/ became diseased)] }
= a / (a + c);

Specificity = [Number of true negatives (nondiseased)] / { [Number of true negatives (nondiseased)] + [Number of false positives (screen/ exposure/risk positives who are/ remain nondiseased)] }
= d / (d + b),

where a, b, c, and d are the cell numbers used identically to those in Table 15.2.

Although they can be applied to cross-sectional results, the concepts are designed to predict the future outcomes. Associated measures include positive predictive value (PPV) = (Number of true positives) / [(Number of true positives) + (Number of false positives)] = a / (a + b); negative predictive value (NPV) = (Number of true negatives) / [(Number of true negatives) + (Number of false negatives)] = d / (d + c); and the false discovery rate (FDR) drives from a simple formula b / (b + a) = 1 – PPV (Bhopal, 2002). FDR is often used in multiple-hypothesis testing in genetic analysis, although one would need to replace the screening measure with hypothesis testing and disease classification with significance determination.

For use as a clinical screening tool, one would want to maximize the value of sensitivity (pick up all who become diseased), but as a cost-efficiency screening device, one would want to maximize the value of specificity (screen out those who are likely to be disease free). To counterbalance sensitivity and specificity, the receiver (relative) operating characteristic (ROC) curve has been used for a wide range of topics, including radiology; psychology; medicine (Weinstein & Fineberg, 1980); and, most recently, machine learning. ROC can be used to determine the optimal utility of a predictive measure, for example, finding the best cutoff of dimensional symptom measures (Robins & Price, 1991), optimal choice and recode for biomarkers (Perkins & Schisterman, 2006), or choosing an optimal screening instrument for the general-population survey (Kessler et al., 2003). The ROC curve plots the sensitivity (true positives, y-axis) and 1 – specificity (false positives, x-axis), which provides a visual aid in deciding the optimal screening tool or cutoffs.

The most commonly used summary statistic is the area under the curve (AUC), which varies between .5 and 1 (where .5 is random prediction). This can be computed by constructing trapezoids under the curve as an approximation; however, a maximum likelihood estimator is also available. The AUC contains some attractive features, such as its close relationship to Wilcoxon test of ranks and Gini coefficients (Hand & Till 2001). Another related statistics is the sensitivity index, d', which gives the distance from the means of the signal (curve) and the noise distribution (for ROC, this is the diagonal straight line) and can be used as an approximation of AUC. Although this index is derived from the signal detection theory in that it is the difference in the right-trail probabilities of detection present versus random noise under the normal distribution assumption. More simply, however, this can be estimated as follows:

$$d' = \text{(Hit rate or Sensitivity)} - \text{(False alarm rate)}$$
$$= \text{(True positive rate)} - \text{(False positive rate)}.$$

Unlike sensitivity, specificity, PPV, and NPV, AUC and d' are independent of cutscore, which contributes to their utility for comparing predictive power across instruments Because AUC and d' are nonparametric statistics, they are suitable for evaluating nonparametric or semiparametric modeling approaches to decision making (e.g., Price et al., 2000).

Disease burden. For public health and health impact assessment for multifactorial chronic illnesses, traditional epidemiologic measures geared toward association and etiology may not provide the needed tools for priority assessment of intervention and prevention. Potential years of life lost (PYLL) is a simple measure for premature mortality and estimates the average number years a person would have not died prematurely. PYLL for a particular population in the given year is a summation over all deaths in the population in that year. With cause of death information, PYLL can be computed for cause-specific mortality, such as PYLL attributable to alcohol (Rehm, Patra, & Popova, 2006). Slow-progressing chronic diseases are likely to produce some excess mortality, but the personal and societal impacts may be greater during life. Such may be the case for a number of debilitating psychiatric disorders, such as depression (unless it leads to suicide). Disability-adjusted life years (DALY), developed by the World Health Organization (Murray, 1996), take into account both premature deaths and the impact of disability during years alive. DALY is a measure of overall disease burden and is expressed as follows:

$$DALY = (YLL) + (YLD),$$

where YLL is life years lost because of premature mortality, $YLL = \Sigma \, d \times e$, where d is fatal case, e is individual life span, and summation is over the health outcomes of the disease; and YLD is years lived with disability adjusted for severity, $YLD = \Sigma \, n \times t \times w$, where n is a case, t is the duration of the disease, w is the disability weight, and summation is again over all health outcomes (Murray, 1994).

Both PYLL and DALY, unlike the measures described thus far in the chapter, are derived within the tradition of mortality and morbidity statistics with the use of life tables. Critics of DALY point out that the underlying assumption that disability means loss of productivity may not be appropriate. Methodologically, computation of DALY requires several assumptions, such as age weighting and discount rate (discount coming

from health benefit in the same sense that financial investment now is worth more in the future). The need to make such assumptions makes DALY estimates sensitive to values of assumptions (Fox-Rushby & Hanson 2001). That said, a major finding demonstrating the societal costs of psychiatric illnesses, such as depression, suicide attempts, and alcoholism (Murray & Lopez, 1997), is a major contribution of DALY.

Study Designs

Five basic study designs are most frequently used in epidemiological research: case series, cross-sectional, case-control, cohort, and trial studies (Bhopal, 2002). In contemporary research, case series—an observational study using medical records for a given outcome or tracking a small number of patients with a known exposure—are mostly used for surveillance by government or health care sectors (hospital case surveillance) and thus are omitted here. Clinical trials and other experimental designs are enormously important for medication development and environmental prevention research. The clinical trial design can be considered a combination of case-control and cohort design with experimental manipulation. (Details are found in Chapters 25–30 of this volume and thus are omitted here.)

Cross-sectional study. This design is conceptually most simple. A population is defined at a particular point in time and, most frequently, in a geographically or politically defined boundary (e.g., contiguous states of the United States). Once the population is defined and the sample is drawn (or the whole population is studied such as in the example of the U.S. Census), counting cases will provide prevalence rates. Cross-sectional studies also allow examinations of differences in rates among subgroups and associations between the outcomes and risk factors (in some cases, protective factors). These comparisons and correlational examinations enable researchers to generate hypotheses regarding underlying etiology of disease expression. Natural history of an illness can be examined in a limited way in a cross-sectional study by retrospectively assessing the timing of onset and recurrence. Incidence rates can also be obtained in theory if the population is assumed to be closed (no population attrition or migration). For psychosocial conditions and psychiatric illnesses, however, obtaining incidence rates from a cross-sectional study is problematic. If they are arrived at on the basis of self-report, the accuracy of timing is questionable. If they are arrived at on the basis of archival data, record searches are often incomplete and case definitions may vary across various record sources. Moreover, a cross-sectional study is not suitable for measuring changes over time. By design it is a snapshot in which it is difficult to discern causal relationships. Thus, hypothesis testing for multiple potential explanations in cross-sectional studies is difficult, if not impossible (Bhopal, 2002; Kelsey, Whittemore, Evans, & Thompson, 1996). Despite these disadvantages, most large-scale surveys use a cross-sectional design in large part because of relative cost-efficiency. When the prevalence is expected to be low, cross-sectional studies afford accurate and reliable estimates of population prevalence, which is useful for policy purposes.

Cohort study. Believed to be first introduced by Frost (1935), a *cohort study* is designed to examine the study population, usually at the time of exposure to one or more risk factors, and track that population over a period of time to observe differences in outcomes. This type of study is also called a *follow-up*, *longitudinal*, or *prospective* study. In contrast to a cross-sectional study, data are collected at least at two time points from the same individuals in a cohort study. A prospective cohort study is the most commonly used design in contemporary epidemiology. Use of a retrospective cohort study has not been uncommon, however, and they are advantageous when historical records are available for the defined cohort (e.g., occupational group; Bhopal, 2002; Comstock, 2004; Doll, 2004; Mausner & Kramer, 1985). In reality, most prospective cohort studies use some historical records, such as medical records, that existed before baseline data collection. Retrospective cohort studies can easily be expanded to prospective studies after baseline data are collected to test the hypothesis developed from the retrospective data. Most prospective cohort studies collect data in a follow-up period over a preceding

period. In short, the retrospective–prospective dichotomy, although conceptually important, share more features than may be superficially obvious. A clear advantage of prospective cohort studies is the ability to observe outcomes via self-report or direct medical examinations or assay collection. When case definition is well established, incidence rates can be obtained as part of examining the natural history of the disease in question. Disadvantages include the labor-intensive nature of data collection, various forms of attrition that can bias results, and the inability to assess cohort-specific effects, for example, a youth cohort established in the Depression era may be different from a youth cohort of the same age range established during the 1960s with respect to illicit drug use, even though individual risk factors may be similar (Bhopal, 2002; Mausner & Kramer, 1985; Miller, Goff, Bammann, & Wild, 2005).

Case-control study. The *case-control study*, sometimes called a *retrospective study*, examines the association between disease and hypothesized risk factors of past exposure by comparing diseased cases and unaffected control samples at risk of developing disease. The case-control design arose in the context of infectious diseases in 19th-century England. Doll and Hill's (1950) classic study on the relationship between cigarette smoking and lung cancer is considered a model case-control investigation. Although this design has a number of strengths (e.g., relative ease and cost-efficient data collection, straightforward data analysis scheme, clinical relevance of results), it has several major limitations, including results being more dependent on accurate case definition, incomplete case records, adequacy of control selection, and selection bias in prevalent cases (Breslow, 2005; Mausner & Kramer, 1985). For those reasons, a cohort study design is usually considered superior by many epidemiologists and the case-control design has fallen out of favor in recent years. Nevertheless, a study of a rare disorder or condition would require an extremely large cohort studies. For such a disorder, practically only a case-control design may be feasible. The case-control design has become a preferred design for genetic epidemiology of psychiatric disorders (Andrieu & Goldstein, 1998) compared with the family-based association study or general-population cohort study. This is in part because cost containment is necessary, which is required for large sample sizes, and extreme cases are preferable to identify gene variants with modest effect size. In fact, the case-control design is a standard in the genome-wide association study, which is currently considered the most advanced genetic epidemiology approach for gene identification (e.g., see Wellcome Trust Case Control Consortium, 2007).

Hybrid designs. Many hybrid study designs that combine elements of different designs have been developed. An obvious motivation is to improve design efficiency and reduce disadvantages associated with each of the major basic designs described thus far. For example, the repeated cross-sectional design repeats a cross-sectional data collection multiple times on, in principle, different individuals. This design is used in government-sponsored annual surveys (Johnston, O'Malley, Bachman, & Schulenberg, 2009; Substance Abuse and Mental Health Services Administration, 2009) and is usually designed *not* to include the same respondents. This design is not only helpful for monitoring trends over time but also for separating developmental or age effects from cohort and period effects (Yang & Land, 2008). Use of the repeated cross-sectional design may be more advantageous than a longitudinal cohort design when the population is in flux because a cohort design is restricted to the initial sample recruited at the baseline survey. However, this design still does not allow making inferences regarding changing behaviors over time (Yee & Niemeier, 1996).

In a classic paper, Mantel and Haenszel (1959) discussed the interconnectedness of different study designs. In fact they argued that studies using different designs should reach the same conclusions. For example, case-control and cohort studies can be seen as two sides of the same coin: Whereas the case-control study selects cases and controls by which to associate exposure in the past to risk factors, the cohort-study sample may be ascertained on the basis of exposure and risk factors by which to

estimate disease incidence and prevalence in the future (Mausner & Kramer, 1985, p. 158). Thus, a hybrid study design can be chosen from a large cohort or cross-sectional study to a case-control substudy (Doll, 2004). This is referred to as a *nested case-control study* or sometimes called *two-stage sampling* (Breslow, 1996; White, 1982). For example, I studied differences in coping behaviors in midlife between those who had a suicide attempt or suicidal ideation (cases) and those who scored very low in the combined risk scale for suicidality obtained in preceding years (controls) from a cohort of Vietnam veterans who had been followed up since 1972 (Price et al., 2009). Because those veterans were all at higher risk of psychological problems in middle age, to get contrasting results in coping behaviors, we considered a nested case-control design to be scientifically better and more economical than following up all of the cohort members. As in this case, an obvious advantage of a cohort-based nested case-control design is the knowledge of all cohort members. This design may be particularly efficient for a rare disorder or condition (e.g., suicide attempt). It is also an efficient strategy when the budget is limited and the outcome is a rare event or disorder. For example, it would not be economical to obtain data on all cohort members when omitted members may not provide information that is as informative as selected cases and controls (Tager, 2000). A potential problem with a nested case-control design is that the choice of a control group is often dependent on the choice of cases, especially when selecting matched controls. When multiple phenotypes are of interest, drawing several matched control groups would defeat the merit of a nested case-control design because a case may be a case for one phenotype but may be a control for another phenotype, or an uninformative sample for yet another phenotype. In such a case, it may be more scientifically sound to follow up all cohort members.

An alternative is the *case-cohort design* (also called *case-base design*), in which the control group is randomly selected from the entire cohort, thus serving as a control for multiple outcomes (Prentice, 1986). This is an unmatched nested case-control design in which a control is drawn at the onset of cohort study. The choice between a case-cohort and nested case-control design should be made on the basis of the purpose of the study (e.g., narrowly defined single outcome versus need to investigate multiple outcomes). For some measures (e.g., incidence rate ratio), analysis becomes more complex and requires variance adjustments. An apparent lack of consensus for correct variance estimators appears to hinder a wider use of this hybrid design (Barlow, Ichikawa, Rosner, & Izumi, 1999; Kass & Gold, 2005; Langholz & Thomas, 1990; Wacholder, 1991) despite the potential to assess incidence of comorbid psychiatric disorders.

Although the case-cohort or nested case-control designs try to retain the advantage of the cohort study design without the costs required for following up all cohort members, a hybrid design can be developed to reduce scientific weaknesses of a cohort design, even though it may increase the costs and labor. A *sequential cohort design* (sometimes referred to as an *accelerated longitudinal design*) is particularly labor intensive by combining cross-sectional and longitudinal cohort sampling (Schaie, 1965). *Cohort* usually refers to age cohort; this design is aimed at measuring samples of multiple ages at multiple times of measurements. This design is thus suitable for developmental studies in which age-related changes are considerable, a large age span needs to be studied, and potential period and cohort effects could complicate interpretations of simple cohort designs. Such a design allows separating environmental and sociocultural changes from normative age changes. Age-graded changes are in part biological and can be considered under genetic control. In such a situation, a cohort-sequential design can be informative and time efficient as in studies of behavioral genetics (Heath et al., 1999).

The *case-crossover design* is another relatively recent hybrid design first introduced in 1991 to study transient effects on the risk of acute events, using only cases (Maclure, 1991). The idea is to capture a case's exposure immediately before or during the case-defining event within the same person (i.e., the person serving as his or her matched control; Lu & Zeger, 2006). It is a variation of repeated-measures longitudinal design and can be considered

as an alternative to the case-control design. The crossover design is often associated with clinical trial studies or pharmacoepidemiology because of its ability to measure the association of drug exposure with acute outcomes (Delaney & Suissa, 2009). The design can be applied, however, to observational epidemiology—for example, effect of alcohol consumption on injury within a defined time after consumption (Spurling & Vinson, 2005). An advantage of this design is its ability to remove the effect of unmeasured time-invariant (between-subject) confounders. It is a conceptually attractive alternative to a case-control study, for which obtaining controls are logistically or theoretically difficult, or ethically undesirable. A disadvantage is its "carry-over" effect. For example if the past drinking affects the drinking on the day of injury, the results would be biased, which would be applicable to heavy drinkers (Kass & Gold, 2005).

Table 15.3 summarizes the aims of each design (types of knowledge gain), advantages, disadvantages, and example studies for the three basic study designs introduced thus far (for more detailed comparisons of several designs, see Bhopal, 2002; Kass & Gold, 2005).

Sampling Methods and Issues

Covering all aspects of sampling techniques is beyond the scope of this review. For those readers interested in further detail, see comprehensive and introductory books on sampling, including Fuller (2009) and Kalton (1983) as well as Chapter 14 of this volume. Within the traditional sampling techniques, systematic sampling techniques are most applicable to cross-sectional design and its variations. Cohort study sampling uses the same sampling technique as a cross-sectional design at baseline data collection. Follow-up sampling is dependent on design and attrition scheme and others that are study specific. For case-control design, matching methods become more important. Simple random sampling is possible for a reasonably well-defined small population or sampling frame (such as a class of university). Most large-scale psychiatric epidemiology survey sampling applies more complex survey techniques.

TABLE 15.3

Basic and Hybrid Epidemiological Designs: Advantages, Disadvantage, and When to Use

Design	Knowledge gain	Advantages	Disadvantages	Example studies
Cross-sectional	■ Prevalence ■ Disease burden ■ Group difference ■ Association with risk factors (odds ratios) ■ Generate hypotheses	■ Relatively cost-effective ■ Ability to provide generalizable estimates ■ Allows analysis of many different outcomes ■ Data collection commitment short	■ Access to sampling frame needed ■ Data collection time frame short ■ Difficult to make causal inference ■ Selection bias due to nonresponse ■ Analytical adjustments most likely needed to provide generalizable results	■ Major landmark psychiatric epidemiology studies ■ Epidemiologic Catchment Area (ECA) Wave 1; (Robins & Regier, 1991) ■ National Comorbidity Study [NCS] Wave 1; Kessler et al., 1994) ■ National Epidemiologic Survey on Alcohol and Related Conditions [NESARC] Wave 1; Grant, 1997) ■ National Vietnam Veterans Readjustment Study (Kulka et al., 1990; Schlenger et al., 1992)
Cohort	■ Incidence ■ Burden of disease ■ Risk factor analysis (relative risks) ■ Temporal or causal analysis	■ Ability to observe changes ■ Ability to discern cause-effect better than cross-sectional ■ Complete information on all members of the sample ■ Allow analysis of many different outcomes	■ Labor intensive ■ Costs high ■ Long-term research commitment ■ Confidentiality issues high with small sample size ■ Selection bias due to differential attrition ■ Difficult to change measures over the course of study ■ Results are cohort specific ■ May not be suitable for rare diseases ■ Complex analysis to adjust within-individual correlations	■ Classical life course studies (e.g., Oakland Growth Study; Elder, 1974) ■ Follow-up surveys of general-population cross-sectional studies (e.g., NESARC longitudinal) ■ Special population longitudinal (e.g., Millennium cohort study; Ryan et al., 2007) ■ Genetic epidemiology (e.g., Vietnam Era Twin Registry, Goldberg, True, Eisen, & Henderson, 1990; Denedin Longitudinal Study, Caspi et al., 2003)
Case-control	■ Clinical knowledge ■ Risk factor analysis (odds ratios) ■ Generate hypothesis ■ Potential discovery of agent	■ Cost-effective ■ Straightforward analysis	■ Sensitive to case definition ■ Not suitable for dimensional outcomes ■ Criteria for appropriate control often difficult to assess ■ Greater risk for confounding ■ Difficult to make causal inferences ■ Results potential bias due to stratification	■ Earlier clinical epidemiology studies ■ Early generation genetic association studies

TABLE 15.3

TABLE 15.3

Basic and Hybrid Epidemiological Designs: Advantages, Disadvantage, and When to Use

Repeated cross-sectional	■ Same as single-point cross-sectional ■ Allows multipoint trend analysis	■ Same advantages of cross-sectional	■ Same disadvantages of single-point cross-sectional ■ Difficult to change conceptual and analytical framework corresponding to paradigmatic or cultural changes	■ Large-scale trend monitoring surveys (National Survey on Drug Use and Health)
Nested case-control (two-stage sampling)	■ Same as case-control ■ Potential for discovery greater (e.g., gene variants) ■ Causal inference potential greater with knowledge of cohort as a whole	■ More cost-effective than collecting data from all cohort members or the whole original case-control sample members	■ Same disadvantage as case-control ■ Ability to make population causal inference substantially reduced	■ Based on large hospital or agency records (Graham et al., 2005) ■ Genetic epidemiology (e.g., genome-wide association study; Bierut et al., 2008)
Case-cohort	■ Same as case-control	■ Control drawn from the whole cohort reduce costs for drawing cases for multiple substudies ■ Results not dependent on definition of control ■ Multiple outcomes can be studied simultaneously	■ Variance estimation technique complex for some measures ■ Models of multiple outcomes still under development (Kang & Cai, 2009)	■ Incidence study of large cohort studies (Salomaa et al., 1999) ■ Genetic epidemiology (Kulathinal, Karvanen, Saarela, & Kuulasmaa, 2007)
Cohort-sequential	■ Able to document nonmonotonic and relatively rapid changes (e.g., age graded)	■ Combined advantage of cohort and repeated panel data collection ■ Shorter duration of data collection commitment ■ Ability to separate cohort effects from developmental changes	■ Labor and cost intensive ■ Shorter term research commitment than long-term cohort study ■ Normative history graded influence still a confounder	■ Normal developmental studies in behavior genetics (e.g., early to adolescent development) ■ Child developmental studies
Case cross-over	■ Disease burden ■ Impact of short-term exposure ■ Ability to draw causal inference greater than regular cohort studies	■ Cost-effective ■ No control needed (within-subject control) ■ Remove time-invariant confounding	■ Carry-over effect contaminate results ■ Suitable only for transient types of exposure	■ Phamacoepidemiologic applications (e.g., acute drug effect) ■ Injury prevention (e.g., alcohol intoxication and resultant injuries)

Note. These are commonly used designs in observational epidemiology. Clinical case series (uncommon research design) and clinical trial (experimental design) are not included.

Multistage sampling for large cross-sectional surveys. We briefly describe here the steps involved in complex sampling and the analytical consequences of complex survey design. As an illustration of arguably the most complex sampling design, the National Survey on Drug Use and Health (NSDUH) defines the population as civilian, non-institutionalized, ages 12 or older, and residing in the United States and the District of Columbia. The basic sampling scheme (simplified version) is that the first-level stratum is U.S. states with different target sample sizes. Each state is partitioned into roughly equal-size regions called *state sampling regions*, which totaled 900 in the 2005 NSDUH sampling strata. The first-stage sampling was U.S. Census tracts, which were partitioned into compact clusters of dwelling units (DUs) in the second stage, which was termed *segments*. Each segment was selected within each sampled census tract with probability proportionate to size. It is this segment for which a complete list of all eligible DUs was compiled to determine the minimum number of DUs in each segment. Using a random start point and interval-based selection, sample DUs were selected and a roster of all persons residing in DUs were compiled. For NSDUH, multiple persons are selected from the DUs to obtain the required numbers for age-groups and the state (Morton, Chromy, Hunter, & Martin, 2006.)

This example shows that both multiple strata (state, region) and multiple sampling stages (census tracts, segment, DUs, and selection of person in DU) affect the probability of a person being chosen. Sampling weights are derived accordingly and include nonresponse adjustment. Thus weights are used to adjust for unequal probability selection in that weighted data correspond to the data as if simple random sampling had been applied. Remaining problems relate to variance estimates because the weighted number of observations is different from actual sample size and complex sampling produces correlated data. Most commonly used in the 21st century is the Taylor series linearization method, which uses an infinite sum of terms calculated from the values of its derivatives at a single point (Lohr, 1999). This method derives a linear approximation of variance estimates on the basis of the variance of

the linear terms of the Taylor expansion for a particular statistic of interest. Other well-known replication methods (such as jackknife and balanced repeated replication) also regained popularity in part because of the simplicity of statistics based on repeated resampling (Rust & Rao, 1996; Wolter, 1985). Corrections on standard errors are customarily done thanks to the availability of easy-to-use software (e.g., Brick & Morganstein, 1996; Research Triangle Institute, 2001; Westat, 2008) that can handle more than two strata and are particularly suitable for multistage sampling used in large-scale government annual surveys. When sample stratification structure is relatively simple, other estimators (such as the Huber-White estimator) provide consistent variance estimates (Rogers, 1993). In recent years, major statistical packages such as SAS Institute's survey procedures (e.g., An & Watts, 1998) and Mplus (Muthén & Muthén, 1998–2010) now allow for the inclusion of complex sampling weights and variance adjustments.

Sampling controls in the case-control design. Three basic principles for control selection are to reduce ascertainment, confounding, and information biases (Wacholder et al., 1992). The study-base principle is to randomly select controls from disease-free sample members of the sample (if no random control is possible, an appropriate control can be selected to ensure representativeness of the exposure); the deconfounding principle is to choose controls to be as similar as the cases with respect to the distribution of one or more confounders by stratification or matching (Breslow, 2005) and comparable accuracy refers to uniform exposure and outcome measures between cases and controls. Of those principles, methods to achieve the deconfounding principle by matching are perhaps the most controversial. The basic justification for matching is that underlying factors used for matching are hypothesized to be associated with exposure. Thus, ideal matching should result in the distribution of exposure in the matched control group to be similar to that of the case group. Several justifications can be made for the necessity of matching. For example, matching can improve efficiency, and certain matching such as cotwin control or sibling control are intended to control for multiple factors that are difficult to measure (such as quantitative genetics). Matching introduces several problems, however. Matching on underlying risk factors may reduce the variability in exposure variables of interest and thus reduce efficiency. Such is the case with overmatching. Overmatching is more serious beyond loss of efficiency when an intermediate confounder, which is affected by exposure and is an etiological factor, is used for matching. Such intermediate confounders mask the true nature of the causal relationship and lead to statistical bias (Breslow, 2005; Kupper, Karon, Kleinbaum, Morgenstern, & Lewis, 1981). In general, stratification of the control sample with broad demographics (e.g., age-group, gender) should be sufficient to achieve comparability of cases and controls without unnecessary matching.

Sampling bias. Sampling bias, which is also called *ascertainment* bias in genetic epidemiology, arises when sampling is not random. Numerous sources contribute to selection bias, but examples include self-selection such as using only volunteers without the use of a sampling frame, nonresponse, and refusal. In epidemiology, a classic example of Berkson's bias (Berkson, 1946) involved a retrospective study examining a risk factor for a disease in a hospital in-patient sample. If a control group is also obtained from the in-patient population, a difference in hospital admission rates for the case versus control sample can result in a spurious association between the disease and the risk factor. In a more general term, Berkson bias occurs when the sampling fractions depend jointly on exposure and disease. Another example is the healthy worker effect and is often found in occupationally defined follow-up or case-control studies for which controls or unexposed groups come from different occupational or nonworking groups (Li & Sung, 1999). For example, veterans are in general healthier than their general population counterpart because of military eligibility criteria. Thus even though they may have suffered from combat-related psychological injuries, their morbidity and mortality may not be significantly different from those among a civilian-matched control. In genetic epidemiology, ascertainment (sampling) bias often resides in

specific sampling strategies. For example, sampling of affected (diseased) probands to obtain pedigree data would produce an upward bias favoring positive familial association with the trait of interest. Another ascertainment bias more akin to genetic association studies is population stratification bias in which estimates of genetic effect are subject to confounding when cases and controls differ in their ethnic backgrounds. Potential bias by population stratification appears pronounced when allele frequencies and phenotypes both vary by ethnicity (such as DRD2 and alcoholism; Thomas & Witte, 2002).

Sampling for Internet surveys. Issues with sampling for Internet-based surveys are not very different from sampling for more traditional surveys. Some distinct characteristics need to be mentioned, however. Most notable is that the population is restricted to those with access to the Internet. Another, compared with in-person interview, is self-completion; however, this is also applicable to self-administered mail surveys. Another distinction of the Internet survey is less controlled access to participation. There is a general consensus that Internet and e-mail surveys will lower costs and eliminate interviewer bias. Disadvantages include substantial margin for sample bias and lower response rates even compared with mail surveys. It is not clear whether the quality of data is better or worse compared with mail surveys. Detailed interviews that would require interviewers, such as for a psychiatric diagnostic assessment, are not suitable for Internet-based surveys (Fricker & Schonlau, 2002). Focusing on sampling, Zhao and Jin (2006) listed a dozen sampling approaches. Among those that are unique to the Internet include hypertext links, pop-up surveys, and banner invitations (others, such as harvested addresses, have a telephone equivalence). These methods are useful in drawing a random sample, although the sampling frame is restricted to site visitors. When a closed population is appropriate (e.g., organization, company), drawing a probability sample for an e-mail or web survey is no different from sampling for use with more conventional survey media. Currently, probability sampling for a general population for Internet surveys still depends on preexisting conventional lists like the base random-digit dialing list, such as those used by KnowledgePanel (Schonlau, Fricker, & Elliott, 2002). Although these methods have been widely available for more than a decade and half, comprehensive reviews on the methodology and assessment of e-mail and Internet surveys are lacking.

CONCLUSION

This chapter has introduced epidemiologic concepts and basic methods. A brief history of epidemiologic research and main concepts of epidemiology has shown that the development of methods was historical in nature, reflecting the historical focus of diseases of the time. Method development was closely tied to basic concepts; major studies contributed greatly to development and refinement of the contemporary study design and methods. Many of basic epidemiologic measures are linked with each, conceptually and often mathematically, and serve different purposes for stages of epidemiologic inquires. Use of particular measures requires knowledge of advantages and disadvantages of study designs as well as the properties of the measures. Considerable confusions still exist even for basic measures with respect to how to use particular measures in the most appropriate fashion. Careful consideration is needed for choosing the most appropriate measure among those that have similar properties.

APPENDIX 15.1: EXAMPLES OF LANDMARK PSYCHOSOCIAL AND PSYCHIATRIC EPIDEMIOLOGIC STUDIES IN 20TH CENTURY

Name	Why landmark?	Epidemiologic methods used	Major findings and impacts
Social Class and Mental Illness	Represents the first generation psychiatric epidemiology studies; application of Chicago school ecological perspective to mental illness	Used record examination; ecological analyses by developmental zones; no individual data	Downward drift hypothesis supported; spurred a generation of studies examining social causation vs. social selection theory to explain the association between socioeconomic status and mental illness
Epidemiologic Catchment Area	Then the largest general-population psychiatric epidemiology study; first major multisite study; development of standardized psychiatric assessment to arrive at diagnostic criteria; all major Axis I disorders assessed	General population cross-sectional and 1-year follow-up design; multistage cluster sampling; several oversample schemes; subset clinical samples; Diagnostic Interview Schedule (Robins et al., 1981) used by lay interviewers; built-in mental health services assessment	Psychiatric disorder is common (one third of U.S. adult population experience a clinical psychiatric syndrome sometime in their lifetime); comorbidity rates are high; standardized instrument, careful cluster sampling, assessment of comorbidity became norms of subsequent large-scale studies such as National Comorbidity Study (Kessler et al., 1994) and National Epidemiologic Survey on Alcohol and Related Conditions (Grant et al., 2004)
International Study of Schizophrenia (ISoS)	World Health Organization initiatives in instrument development and multination coordination; focus on cross-cultural similarities and differences; focus on schizophrenia, an extreme spectrum of psychiatric disorders	A total of 12 counties involved; use of clinical samples utilizing existing clinical infrastructure; admission-based ascertainment; careful cross- cultural equivalence examination; follow-up assessments	The International Pilot Study of Schizophrenia and the ISoS both confirm differences in long-term prognosis of schizophrenia; recovery rates better in developing than industrial countries; focus on prognosis and disability in contrast to accurate prevalence/incidence estimation continues to enlighten mainstream U.S. psychiatric epidemiology
National Vietnam Veterans Readjustment Study	The then-largest special population (veteran) study; first major attempt to accurately assess the rates of post- traumatic stress disorder (PTSD) among Vietnam veterans	Cross-sectional; cluster sampling to obtain representative samples; three comparison groups—deployed, nondeployed era veteran, and civilian control	Lifetime prevalence rate of PTSD 31% among veterans; war-zone exposure definite risk factor; a majority appear to have adjusted relatively well to civilian lives; study spurred a generation of studies on war and other traumas and PTSD; became customary to assess psychological stress in military research

References

Ahrens, W., Krickeberg, K., & Pigeot, I. (2005). An introduction to epidemiology. In W. Ahrens & I. Pigeot (Eds.), *Handbook of epidemiology* (pp. 1–40). Berlin, Germany: Springer. doi:10.1007/978-3-540-26577-1_1

Ahrens, W., & Pigeot, I. (Eds.). (2005). *Handbook of epidemiology*. Berlin, Germany: Springer. doi:10.1007/978-3-540-26577-1

An, A., & Watts, D. (1998). *New SAS procedures for analysis of sample survey data*. Cary, NC: SAS Institute. Retrieved from http://support.sas.com/rnd/app/papers/survey.pdf

Andrieu, N., & Goldstein, A. (1998). Epidemiologic and genetic approaches in the study of gene–environment interaction: An overview of available methods. *Epidemiologic Reviews, 20,* 137–147.

Barlow, W. E., Ichikawa, L., Rosner, D., & Izumi, S. (1999). Analysis of case-cohort designs. *Journal of Clinical Epidemiology, 52,* 1165–1172. doi:10.1016/S0895-4356(99)00102-X

Benichou, J., & Palta, M. (2005). Rates, risks, measures of association and impact. In W. Ahrens & I. Pigeot (Eds.), *Handbook of epidemiology* (pp. 89–156). Berlin, Germany: Springer. doi:10.1007/978-3-540-26577-1_3

Ben-Shlomo, Y., & Kuh, D. (2002). A life course approach to chronic disease epidemiology: conceptual models, empirical challenges and interdisciplinary perspectives. *International Journal of Epidemiology, 31,* 285–293. doi:10.1093/ije/31.2.285

Berkman, L., & Kawachi, I. (2000). A historical framework for social epidemiology. In L. Berkman & I. Kawachi (Eds.), *Social epidemiology* (pp. 3–12). New York, NY: Oxford University Press.

Berkson, J. (1946). Limitations of the application of fourfold table analysis to hospital data. *Biometrics Bulletin, 2,* 47–53. doi:10.2307/3002000

Bhopal, R. (2002). *Concepts of epidemiology: An integrated introduction to the ideas, theories, principles, and methods of epidemiology*. Oxford, England: Oxford University Press.

Bierut, L. J., Stitzel, J., Wang, J., Hinrichs, A., Grucza, R., Xuei, X., . . . Goate, A. M. (2008). Variants in nicotinic receptors and risk for nicotine dependence. *American Journal of Psychiatry, 165,* 1163–1171. doi:10.1176/appi.ajp.2008.07111711

Breslow, N. E. (1996). Statistics in epidemiology: the case-control study. *Journal of the American Statistical Association, 91,* 14–28. doi:10.2307/2291379

Breslow, N. E. (2005). Case-control studies. In W. Ahrens & I. Pigeot (Eds.), *Handbook of epidemiology* (pp. 287–319). Berlin, Germany: Springer. doi:10.1007/978-3-540-26577-1_7

Brick, J. M., & Morganstein, D. (1996). WesVarPC: Software for computing variance estimates from complex designs. In *Proceedings of the 1996 Annual Research Conference* (pp. 861–866). Washington, DC: U.S. Bureau of the Census.

Brock, T. (1999). *Robert Koch: A life in medicine and bacteriology*. Washington, DC: ASM Press.

Buck, C., Llopis, A., Najera, E., & Terris, M. (Eds.). (1998). *The challenge of epidemiology: Issues and selected readings* (Scientific Publication No. 505). Washington, DC: Pan American Health Organization.

Carpenter, K. (1986). *The history of scurvy and vitamin C*. Cambridge, England: Cambridge University Press.

Caspi, A., Sugden, K., Moffitt, T., Taylor, A., Craig, I., Harrington, H., . . . Poulton, A. (2003). Influence of life stress on depression: moderation by a polymorphism in the 5-HHT gene. *Science, 301,* 386–389. doi:10.1126/science.1083968

Comstock, G. (2004). Cohort analysis: W. H. Frost's contributions to the epidemiology of tuberculosis and chronic disease. In A. Morabia (Ed.), *A history of epidemiologic methods and concepts* (pp. 223–230). Basel, Switzerland: Birkhaser Verlag.

Delaney, J. A., & Suissa, S. (2009). The case-crossover study design in pharmacoepidemiology. *Statistical Methods in Medical Research, 18,* 53–65. doi:10.1177/0962280208092346

Doll, R. (2004). Cohort studies: History of the method. In A. Morabia (Ed.), *A history of epidemiologic methods and concepts* (pp. 243–274). Basel, Switzerland: Birkhaser Verlag.

Doll, R., & Hill, A. (1950). Smoking and carcinoma of the lung; preliminary report. *British Medical Journal, 2,* 739–748. doi:10.1136/bmj.2.4682.739

Elder, G. (1974). *Children of the great depression: Social change in life experience*. Chicago, IL: University of Chicago Press.

Faris, R., & Dunham, H. (1939). *Mental disorders in urban areas: An ecological study of schizophrenia and other psychosis*. Chicago, IL: University of Chicago Press.

Faris, R., & Dunham, H. (1960). *Mental disorders in urban areas: An ecological study of schizophrenia and other psychosis* (2nd ed.). New York, NY: Hafner.

Farr, W. (2004). On prognosis. In A. Morabia (Ed.), *A history of epidemiologic methods and concepts* (pp. 159–178). Basel, Switzerland: Birkhaser Verlag.

Fox-Rushby, J. A., & Hanson, K. (2001). Calculating and presenting disability adjusted life years (DALYs) in cost-effectiveness analysis. *Health Policy and Planning, 16,* 326–331. doi:10.1093/heapol/16.3.326

Fricker, R., & Schonlau, M. (2002). Advantages and disadvantages of Internet research surveys: Evidence from the literature. *Field Methods, 14,* 347–367. doi:10.1177/152582202237725

Frost, W. (1935). The outlook for the eradication of tuberculosis. *American Review of Tuberculosis, 32,* 644–650.

Fuller, W. (2009). *Sampling statistics.* Hoboken, NJ: Wiley. doi:10.1002/9780470523551

Goldberg, J., True, W., Eisen, S., & Henderson, W. (1990). A twin study of the effects of the Vietnam war on posttraumatic stress disorder. *JAMA, 263,* 1227–1232. doi:10.1001/jama.263.9.1227

Graham, D. J., Campen, D., Hui, R., Spence, M., Cheetham, C., Levy, G., . . . Ray, W. A. (2005). Risk of acute myocardial infarction and sudden cardiac death in patients treated with cyclo-oxygenase 2 selective and non-selective non-steroidal anti-inflammatory drugs: nested case-control study. *Lancet, 365,* 475–481.

Grant, B. F. (1997). Prevalence and correlates of alcohol use and DSM-IV alcohol dependence in the United States: Results of the National Longitudinal Alcohol Epidemiologic Survey. *Journal of Studies on Alcohol, 58,* 464–473.

Grant, B. F., Stinson, F. S., Dawson, D. A., Chou, S. P., Dufour, M. C., Compton, W., . . . Kaplan, K. (2004). Prevalence and co-occurrence of substance use disorders and independent mood and anxiety disorders. *Archives of General Psychiatry, 61,* 807–816. doi:10.1001/archpsyc.61.8.807

Greenwood, M. (1932). *Epidemiology: Historical and experimental.* Baltimore, MD: Johns Hopkins Press.

Heath, A. C., Madden, P., Grant, J., McLaughlin, T., Todorov, A., & Bucholz, K. (1999). Resiliency factors protecting against teenage alcohol use and smoking: Influences of religion, religious involvement and values, and ethnicity in the Missouri Adolescent Female Twin Study. *Twin Research, 2,* 145–155. doi:10.1375/136905299320566013

Hand, D. J., & Till, R. J. (2001). A simple generalization of the area under the ROC curve for multiple class classification problems. *Machine Learning, 45,* 171–186. doi:10.1023/A:1010920819831

Hill, A. (1961). *Principles of medical statistics.* New York, NY: Oxford University Press.

Hopper, K., Harrison, G., Janca, A., & Sartorius, N. (2007). *Recovery from schizophrenia: An international perspective—A report from the WHO Collaborative Project, the International Study of Schizophrenia.* New York, NY: Oxford University Press.

Johnston, L., O'Malley, P., Bachman, J., & Schulenberg, J. (2009). *Monitoring the future: National survey results on drug use, 1975–2008: Vol. 1. Secondary school students.* Bethesda, MD: National Institute on Drug Abuse.

Kahn, H., & Sempos, C. (1989). Relative risk and odds ratio. In *Statistical methods in epidemiology* (pp. 45–71). New York, NY: Oxford University Press.

Kalton, G. (1983). *Introduction to survey sampling.* Newbury Park, CA: Sage.

Kang, S., & Cai, J. (2009). Marginal hazards model for case-cohort studies with multiple disease outcomes. *Biometrika, 96,* 887–901. doi:10.1093/biomet/asp059

Kass, P., & Gold, E. (2005). Modern epidemiologic study designs. In W. Ahrens & I. Pigeot (Eds.), *Handbook of epidemiology* (pp. 321–344). Berlin, Germany: Springer. doi:10.1007/978-3-540-26577-1_8

Kelsey, J., Whittemore, A., Evans, A., & Thompson, W. (1996). *Methods in observational epidemiology* (2nd ed.). New York, NY: Oxford University Press.

Kessler, R. C., Barker, P. R., Colpe, L. J., Epstein, J. F., Gfroerer, J. C., Hiripi, E., . . . Zaslavsky, A. M. (2003). Screening for serious mental Illness in the general population. *Archives of General Psychiatry, 60,* 184–189. doi:10.1001/archpsyc.60.2.184

Kessler, R. C., McGonagle, K. A., Zhao, S., Nelson, C. B., Hughes, M., Eshleman, S., . . . Kendler, K. S. (1994). Lifetime and 12-month prevalence of DSM-III-R psychiatric disorders in the United States: results from the National Comorbidity Survey. *Archives of General Psychiatry, 51,* 8–19.

Knol, M. J., Vandenbroucke, J., Scott, P., & Egger, M. (2008). What do case-control studies estimate? Survey on methods and assumptions in published case-control research. *American Journal of Epidemiology, 168,* 1073–1081. doi:10.1093/aje/kwn217

Kulathinal, S., Karvanen, J., Saarela, O., & Kuulasmaa, K. (2007). Case-cohort design in practice: Experiences from the MORGAM Project. *Epidemiologic Perspectives and Innovations, 4*(15). doi:10.1186/1742-5573-4-15

Kulka, R., Schlenger, W., Fairbanks, J., Hough, R., Jordan, B., Marmar, C., . . . Grady, D. A. (1990). *Trauma and the Vietnam War generation: Report of findings from the National Vietnam Veterans Readjustment Study.* New York, NY: Brunner Mazel.

Kupper, L. L., Karon, J., Kleinbaum, D., Morgenstern, H., & Lewis, D. (1981). Matching in epidemiologic studies: Validity and efficiency considerations. *Biometrics, 37,* 271–291. doi:10.2307/2530417

Langholz, B., & Thomas, D. (1990). Nested case-control and case-cohort methods of sampling from a cohort: A critical comparison. *American Journal of Epidemiology, 131,* 169–176.

Last, J. (2001). *A dictionary of epidemiology* (4th ed.). New York, NY: Oxford University Press.

Leff, J., Sartorius, N., Jablensky, A., Korten, A., & Ernberg, G. (1992). The International Pilot Study of Schizophrenia: Five-year follow-up findings. *Psychological Medicine, 22,* 131–145. doi:10.1017/S0033291700032797

Levin, B. (2007). What does the population attributable fraction mean? *Preventing Chronic Disease, 4,* 1–5.

Levin, M. L. (1953). The occurrence of lung cancer in man. *Acta-Unio Internationalis Contra Cancrum, 9,* 531–541.

Li, C.-Y., & Sung, F.-C. (1999). A review of the healthy worker effect in occupational epidemiology. *Occupational Medicine, 49,* 225–229. doi:10.1093/occmed/49.4.225

Lohr, S. L. (1999). Variance estimation in complex surveys. In *Sampling: Design and analysis* (pp. 289–318). Pacific Grove, CA: Duxbury Press.

Lu, Y., & Zeger, S. (2006). On the equivalence of case-crossover and time series methods in environmental epidemiology. *Biostatistics, 8,* 337–344. doi:10.1093/biostatistics/kxl013

Maclure, M. (1991). The case-crossover design: A method for studying transient effects on the risk of acute events. *American Journal of Epidemiology, 133,* 144–153.

MacMahon, B., & Pugh, T. (1970). *Epidemiology: Principles and methods.* Boston, MA: Little, Brown.

Mantel, N., & Haenszel, W. (1959). Statistical aspects of the analysis of data from retrospective studies of disease. *Journal of the National Cancer Institute, 22,* 719–748.

Mausner, J., & Kramer, S. (1985). *Epidemiology: An introductory text* (2nd ed.). Philadelphia, PA: Saunders.

McNutt, L.-A., Wu, C., Xue, X., & Hafner, J. (2003). Estimating the relative risk in cohort studies and clinical trials of common outcomes. *American Journal of Epidemiology, 157,* 940–943. doi:10.1093/aje/kwg074

Miller, A., Goff, D., Bammann, K., & Wild, P. (2005). Cohort studies. In W. Ahrens & I. Pigeot (Eds.), *Handbook of epidemiology* (pp. 253–285). Berlin, Germany: Springer. doi:10.1007/978-3-540-26577-1_6

Morabia, A. (2004a). *A history of epidemiologic methods and concepts.* Basel, Switzerland: Birkhaser Verlag.

Morabia, A. (2004b). Part I: Epidemiology: An epistemological approach. In A. Morabia (Ed.), *A History of epidemiologic methods and concepts* (pp. 1–124). Basel, Switzerland: Birkhaser Verlag.

Morris, J. (1964). *Uses of epidemiology.* Edinburgh, Scotland: Livingtone.

Morton, K., Chromy, J., Hunter, S., & Martin, P. (2006). *2005 National Survey on Drug Use and Health: Sample design report.* Research Triangle Park, NC: RTI International.

Murray, C. J. L. (1994). Quantifying the burden of disease: the technical basis for disability-adjusted life years. *Bulletin of the World Health Organization, 72,* 429–445.

Murray, C. J. L. (1996). Rethinking DALYs. In C. J. L. Murray & A. D. Lopez (Eds.), *The global burden of disease* (pp. 1–98). Cambridge, MA: Harvard School of Public Health on behalf of the World Health Organization and the World Bank.

Murray, C. J. L., & Lopez, A. (1997). Global mortality, disability, and the contribution of risk factors: Global Burden of Disease Study. *Lancet, 349,* 1436–1442.

Muthén, L. K., & Muthén, B. O. (1998–2010). Mplus. *Statistical analysis with latent variables. User's guide.* (6th ed.) Los Angeles, CA: Muthén & Muthén. Available at: http://www.statmodel.com/ugexcerpts.shtml

Oakes, J., & Kaufman, J. (Eds.). (2006). *Methods in social epidemiology.* San Francisco, CA: Jossey-Bass.

Perkins, N. J., & Schisterman, E. (2006). The inconsistency of "optimal" cutpoints obtained using two criteria based on the receiver operating characteristic curve. *American Journal of Epidemiology, 163,* 670–675. doi:10.1093/aje/kwj063

Prentice, R. (1986). A case-cohort design for epidemiologic cohort studies and disease prevention trials. *Biometrika, 73,* 1–11. doi:10.1093/biomet/73.1.1

Price, R. K., Spitznagel, E. L., Downey, T. J., Meyer, D. J., Risk, N. K., & El-Ghazzawy, O. G. (2000). Applying artificial neural network models to clinical decision making. *Psychological Assessment, 12,* 40–51. doi:10.1037/1040-3590.12.1.40

Price, R. K., Chen, L.-S., Risk, N. K., Haden, A. H., Widner, G. A., Ledgerwood, D. M., & Lewis, C. L. (2009). Suicide in a natural history study: Lessons and insights learned from a follow-up of Vietnam veterans at risk for suicide. In D. Buchanan, C. Fisher, & L. Gable (Eds.), *Research with high-risk populations: Balancing science, ethics, and law* (pp. 109–132). Washington, DC: American Psychological Association. doi:10.1037/11878-005

Prigerson, H. G., Maciejewski, P., & Rosenheck, R. (2002). Population attributable fractions of psychiatric disorders and behavioral outcomes associated with combat exposure among US men. *American Journal of Public Health, 92,* 59–63. doi:10.2105/AJPH.92.1.59

Rehm, J., Patra, J., & Popova, S. (2006). Alcohol-attributable mortality and potential years of life lost in Canada, 2001: Implications for prevention and policy. *Addiction, 101,* 373–384. doi:10.1111/j.1360-0443.2005.01338.x

Research Triangle Institute. (2001). *SUDAAN user's manual* (Release 8.0). Research Triangle Park, NC: Author.

Robins, L. N., Helzer, J., Croughan, J., & Ratcliff, K. (1981). The National Institute of Mental Health Diagnostic Interview Schedule. Its history, characteristics, and validity. *Archives of General Psychiatry, 38,* 381–389.

Robins, L. N., & Price, R. K. (1991). Adult disorders predicted by childhood conduct problems: Results from the NIMH Epidemiologic Catchment Area project. *Psychiatry: Interpersonal and Biological Processes, 54,* 116–132.

Robins, L. N., & Regier, D. (1991). *Psychiatric disorders in America: The Epidemiological Catchment Area Study.* New York, NY: Free Press.

Rockhill, B., Newman, B., & Weinberg, C. (1998). Use and misuse of population attributable fractions. *American Journal of Public Health, 88,* 15–19. doi:10.2105/AJPH.88.1.15

Rogers, W. (1993). Regression standard errors in clustered samples. *Stata Technical Bulletin, 13,* 19–23.

Rosen, G. (1958). *A history of public health.* New York, NY: MD Publications. doi:10.1037/11322-000

Rothman, K., & Greenland, S. (2005). Basic concepts. In W. Ahrens & I. Pigeot (Eds.), *Handbook of epidemiology* (pp. 43–88). Berlin, Germany: Springer. doi:10.1007/978-3-540-26577-1_2

Rust, K. F., & Rao, J. (1996). Variance estimation for complex surveys using replication techniques. *Statistical Methods in Medical Research, 5,* 283–310. doi:10.1177/096228029600500305

Ryan, M. A. K., Smith, T., Smith, B., Amoroso, P., Boyko, E., Gray, G., . . . Hopper, T. I. (2007). Millennium cohort: Enrollment begins a 21-year contribution to understanding the impact of military service. *Journal of Clinical Epidemiology, 60,* 181–191. doi:10.1016/j.jclinepi.2006.05.009

Salomaa, V., Matei, C., Aleksic, N., Sansores-Garcia, L., Folsom, A., Juneja, H., . . . Wu, K. K. (1999). Soluble thrombomodulin as a predictor of incident coronary heart disease and symptomless carotid artery atherosclerosis in the Atherosclerosis Risk in Communities (ARIC) Study: A case-cohort study. *Lancet, 353,* 1729–1734. doi:10.1016/S0140-6736(98)09057-6

Schaie, K. W. (1965). A general model for the study of developmental problems. *Psychological Bulletin, 64,* 92–107. doi:10.1037/h0022371

Schlenger, W. E., Kulka, R. A., Fairbank, J. A., Hough, R. L., Jordan, B. K., Marmar, C. R., & Weiss, D. S. (1992). The prevalence of post-traumatic stress disorder in the Vietnam generation: A multimethod, multisource assessment of psychiatric disorder. *Journal of Traumatic Stress, 5,* 333–363. doi:10.1002/jts.2490050303

Schonlau, M., Fricker, R., & Elliott, M. (2002). *Conducting research surveys via e-mail and the web.* Santa Monica, CA: RAND. Retrieved from http://www.rand.org/pubs/monograph_reports/MR1480/

Snow, J. (1854). *On the mode of communication of cholera.* London, England: Churchill.

Songer, T. (2010). *Introduction to the fundamentals of epidemiology.* Retrieved from http://www.pitt.edu/~super1/lecture/lec19061/001.htm

Spurling, M. C., & Vinson, D. (2005). Alcohol-related injuries: evidence for the prevention paradox. *Annals of Family Medicine, 3,* 47–52. doi:10.1370/afm.243

Substance Abuse and Mental Health Services Administration. (2009). *Results from the 2008 National Survey on Drug Use and Health: National findings.* Rockville, MD: Office of Applied Studies. Retrieved from http://www.oas.samhsa.gov/nsduh/2k8nsduh/2k8Results.cfm

Susser, M. (1973). *Causal thinking in the health sciences: Concepts and strategies of epidemiology.* New York, NY: Oxford University Press.

Susser, M., & Adelstein, A. (1975). An introduction to the work of William Farr. *American Journal of Epidemiology, 101,* 469–476.

Susser, M., & Stein, Z. (2009). *Eras in epidemiology: The evolution of ideas.* New York, NY: Oxford University Press.

Tager, I. B. (2000). Current view of epidemiologic study designs for occupational and environmental lung diseases. *Environmental Health Perspectives, 108,* 615–623. doi:10.2307/3454397

Thomas, D. C., & Witte, J. (2002). Point: Population stratification: A problem for case-control studies of candidate-gene associations? *Cancer Epidemiology, Biomarkers, and Prevention, 11,* 505–512.

Tohen, M., Bromet, E., Murphy, J., & Tsuang, M. (2000). Psychiatric epidemiology. *Harvard Review of Psychiatry, 8,* 111–125.

Wacholder, S. (1991). Practical considerations in choosing between the case-cohort and nested case-control designs. *Epidemiology, 2,* 155–158. doi:10.1097/00001648-199103000-00013

Wacholder, S., McLaughlin, J., Silverman, D., & Mandel, J. (1992). Selection of controls in case-control studies. *American Journal of Epidemiology, 135,* 1019–1028.

Weinstein, M. C., & Fineberg, H. V. (1980). *Clinical decision analysis.* Philadelphia, PA: Saunders.

Wellcome Trust Case Control Consortium. (2007). Genome-wide association study of 14,000 cases of seven common diseases and 3,000 shared controls. *Nature, 447,* 661–678. doi:10.1038/nature05911

Westat. (2008). WesVar, Version 5.1 [Computer software]. Retrieved from http://www.westat.com/westat/statistical_software/WesVar/wesvar_downloads.cfm

White, J. E. (1982). A two stage design for the study of the relationship between a rare exposure and a rare disease. *American Journal of Epidemiology, 115,* 119–128.

Wolter, K. (1985). *Introduction to variance estimation.* New York, NY: Springer-Verlag.

Yang, Y., & Land, K. (2008). Age-period-cohort analysis of repeated cross-section surveys: Fixed or random effects? *Sociological Methods and Research, 36,* 297–326. doi:10.1177/0049124106292360

Yee, J., & Niemeier, D. (1996). *Advances and disadvantages: Longitudinal vs. repeated cross-section surveys.* Retrieved from http://ntl.bts.gov/data/letter_am/bat.pdf

Zhang, F. F., Michaels, D. C., Mathema, B., Kauchali, S., Chatterjee, A., Ferris, D. C., . . . Morabia, A. (2004). Evolution of epidemiologic methods and concepts in selected textbooks of the 20th century. *Social and Preventive Medicine, 29,* 97–104.

Zhang, J., & Yu, K. (1998). What's the relative risk? A method of correcting the odds ratio in cohort studies of common outcomes. *JAMA, 280,* 1690–1691. doi:10.1001/jama.280.19.1690

Zhao, W., & Jin, Y. (2006). A study of sampling method for Internet survey. *International Journal of Business and Management, 1,* 69–77.

CHAPTER 16

ISSUES IN COLLECTING LONGITUDINAL DATA

Emilio Ferrer and Kevin J. Grimm

Collecting repeated measures from individuals is one of the most common forms of data collection in psychological research. Although these data are highly informative and, in many cases, necessary for studying psychological processes, their collection are not always straightforward. The goal of this chapter is to provide a review of some important issues regarding the collection of data in longitudinal studies. Some of these issues concern the planning required before the data collection; other issues are related to the actual gathering of information. In addition to reviewing these issues, we will provide a number of recommendations that facilitate data collection in longitudinal studies.

LONGITUDINAL DATA: DEFINITION

There is a long advocacy for longitudinal data in psychological research. This is particularly the case when the goal is to study psychological processes as they unfold over time. In those instances, repeated measures from the same individuals are needed to accurately infer change over time. More specifically, longitudinal data can be described as those data exhibiting a number of features. First, some of the same entities are observed at repeated occasions. As we will describe in the following sections, not all the entities are required to be observed at each occasion. Second, the measurement and scaling of observations are known. For example, it is important to

understand the measurement properties of the variables and factors, so it can be determined that the same construct is being measured at all occasions. In this way, changes over time can be interpreted as quantitative changes in the construct of interest rather than qualitative changes in the nature of the construct, or changes in the measuring instrument, as when the meaning of words changes over time. Third, the ordering and metric of the time underlying the observations is known. Such time will depend on the research question and can range from milliseconds to decades. Whatever the metric, it needs to be well characterized to make appropriate inferences about time sequences and time-related changes.

Objectives of Longitudinal Research

Although it is commonly agreed on that investigating any changing phenomenon requires longitudinal data, collecting good longitudinal data presents a number of important challenges. One of the first challenges concerns the purpose of the study. In other words, what kind of longitudinal data are most relevant to answer the desired research questions? Or, alternatively, what types of questions can one address with longitudinal data? One helpful way to conceptualize these issues is through Nesselroade and Baltes's (1979) objectives of longitudinal research. Put forth more than 30 years ago, these objectives are still highly relevant and can be useful in determining the

This work was supported in part by National Science Foundation Grants BCS-05-27766 and BCS-08-27021 and by National Insitutes of Health–National Institute of Neurological Disorders and Stroke Grant R01 NS057146-01 to Emilio Ferrer, and by National Science Foundation Grant DRL-0815787 and the National Center for Research on Early Childhood Education, Institute of Education Sciences, U.S. Department of Education Grant R305A06021 to Kevin J. Grimm.

DOI: 10.1037/13620-016
APA Handbook of Research Methods in Psychology: Vol. 2. Research Designs, H. Cooper (Editor-in-Chief)

types of questions to investigate and, as a consequence, the types of data to be collected.

The first objective is the identification of intraindividual change. An apparently obvious goal in longitudinal research is examining change at the individual level. This is not always the case, however, because some longitudinal research is focused on the group and does not always apply to a given individual (e.g., Molenaar, 2004). Change at the individual level can take different forms, such as systematic long-term trends or short-term fluctuations. The interest centers on the individual, however, and how change is manifested for each person. Examining this goal requires multiple occasions of measurement—data with high density if the questions pertain to fluctuations—and statistical models specified at the individual level or, in some cases, models that consider the individual to be the unit of analysis. In subsequent sections, we describe various research designs, statistical models, and issues associated with each of the objectives.

Related to the first goal, the second objective is the direct identification of interindividual differences in intraindividual change. That is, not only do we examine change for each person, but we also inspect such changes across individuals and detect differences in those changes. Such differences can be systematic and possibly associated with—or explained by—other important variables. Addressing questions related to this objective would require collecting repeated measures data from multiple individuals and, possibly, employing multiple variables.

The third objective concerns the analysis of interrelationships in change. Imagine, for example, that one is interested in studying the development of fluid reasoning and processing speed. Pertinent questions here would include how each of these processes unfolds over time, say, during childhood and adolescence, and whether they are related to each other. It is possible that one process helps the other develop over time (e.g., Kail, 2007). It is also possible that both cognitive processes influence each other over time. Alternatively, they can develop in a parallel way or both can be influenced by a third mechanism. Whatever the dynamics, this third objective centers on the interrelations between changes in two or more variables.

To accomplish this third objective, longitudinal data over time needs to be collected on two or more variables. Of particular importance is the choice of statistical models because different models will focus on different aspects of the interrelations at work. For example, some models (e.g., correlated growth curves) allow researchers to identify associations between changes (e.g., slopes) in two variables, whereas other models (e.g., latent difference score models) specify such interrelations in terms of lead-lag dynamic sequences. For this, the researcher will need to decide what type of question to address and then specify a model according to the hypothesis of change (e.g., Ferrer & McArdle, 2010; Grimm, 2007; McArdle, 2009).

The fourth objective refers to the analysis of causes (or determinants) of intraindividual change and the fifth concerns the analysis of causes (or determinants) of interindividual differences in intraindividual change. These goals refer to the identification of mechanisms (i.e., time-related associations, dynamic sequences) that explain within-person changes and differences in such changes across people. Examining research questions with these goals requires collecting repeated data in both the outcomes and the covariates of interest. In addition, identifying the desired mechanisms entails the use of specific models of change, typically dynamic models.

These objectives of longitudinal research help researchers in the selection of questions to be examined. Such questions will, in turn, guide the type of research design to be employed, the data to be collected, and statistical model.

Benefits and Challenges of Longitudinal Data

There is a strong agreement about the benefits of longitudinal designs and their preference over cross-sectional studies (e.g., Hertzog & Nesselroade, 2003; Nesselroade & Baltes, 1979). This is particularly the case when the research question involves the study of processes that unfold over time. Studying such processes, their growth or decline, and their association with other relevant dimensions requires longitudinal designs with repeated measures over time.

The advantages of longitudinal designs over cross-sectional designs are many and varied. As described in the previous sections, they allow the researcher to address multiple questions about change, examining such questions with cross-sectional data is limited in some cases and not plausible in many other instances. For example, longitudinal data allow the direct estimation of within-person change as well as variability in such change across individuals, as some persons may show larger change than others. Moreover, longitudinal data permit estimating associations between within-person changes and other covariates of interest (e.g., development of reading achievement as related to parental education) and the interrelations between two processes as they unfold over time (e.g., depressed mood and sleep disorders; e.g., see, Ferrer & Ghisletta, 2011; Schaie & Hofer, 2001, for discussions about benefits of longitudinal over cross-sectional data).

The advantages of longitudinal designs over cross-sectional designs are many and varied but most center on capturing variation in change. Nesselroade and Baltes's (1979) five rationales concerned the collection of longitudinal, as opposed to cross-sectional, data. Longitudinal data are necessary to study change. Often, change is approximated by cross-sectional differences (e.g., Grimm & Ram, 2009). For example, cognitive development between ages 3 and 4 can be studied longitudinally by measuring a sample of 3-year-olds, waiting a year, and measuring them again at 4 years old. Cross-sectionally this can be approximated by measuring a group of 3-year-olds and another group of 4-year-olds simultaneously. The cross-sectional differences between these two groups can approximate the longitudinal changes if the sample of 4-year-olds represents what the 3-year-old sample would be in 1 year. The extent to which this is not the case, cross-sectional differences are a poor approximation of longitudinal changes. Furthermore, even when the conditions are met and cross-sectional differences are a good approximation of longitudinal changes, they are only a good estimate of the average amount of change and do not provide any information regarding variation (or covariation) in changes across individuals.

A second limitation of cross-sectional data as an estimate of longitudinal change concerns its lack of information about the mechanisms underlying the observed change. Often, such change process is being driven by many factors, with different external variables influencing those factors. For example, some important factors in a given developmental process include a set of initial conditions, how quickly the process changes, how acceleration and deceleration influence the change process, and how the process enters and leaves different phases of change (Grimm, Ram, & Hamagami, 2010). In these situations involving complex developmental processes with multiple change aspects, cross-sectional data simply average over these important aspects of change, thus missing the complexity of the process.

Although the advantages of longitudinal data are obvious, such data present a number of challenges and issues. Some of these issues are logistic, such as deciding the time interval between assessments and how to best allocate one's budget to optimize sample size and measurement occasions. These issues can be evaluated before data collection begins. Other issues need to be dealt with while the data are being collected, such as maximizing retention of participants. Yet others are of a methodological nature and need to be addressed once the data have already been collected. Some of these issues include attrition, cohort effects, and retest effects.

Selection of Occasions, Variables, and Persons

In all longitudinal designs, perhaps the main challenge concerns the selection of data regarding variables, persons, and occasions. Cattell (1988) illustrated this idea with the so-called basic data relations box (see Figure 16.1), a hypothetical sample space containing all dimensions of experimental designs. The challenge for the researcher is to select which individuals (how many and who) should participate in the study, which variables should be measured, and on how many occasions (see Nesselroade, 1988, for an extensive discussion on these issues).

With regard to the participants, researchers will need to consider issues related to statistical power and sampling bias. These issues will determine how

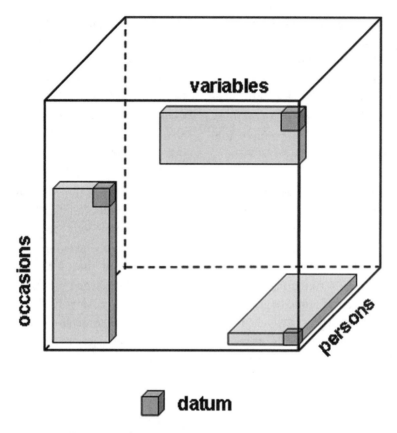

FIGURE 16.1.   Data box containing all hypothetical variables, persons, and measurement occasions.

many persons are necessary (or desirable) in the study and which persons ought to be selected from the population of interest. Similar thought should be given to the selection of variables. Here, the researcher will face issues related to multivariate representation and modeling as well as proper measurement of the constructs of interest. Finally, with regard to the measurement occasions, critical decisions will involve the number of assessments necessary to examine change together with the interval between occasions. We elaborate on each of these aspects of data collection in subsequent sections of the chapter.

Number and Frequency of Assessments

One of the main issues to consider when planning a longitudinal study is cost. In fact, this issue often prevents researchers from collecting longitudinal data. Acquiring measures from multiple participants at multiple occasions requires time as well as funds. In the absence of one of the two, researchers

may opt for a cross-sectional design with just one measurement occasion. But given a budget that allows the collection of repeated measures, investigators still need to decide a number of important questions before proceeding with the study, such as the number of measurement occasions, the time interval between occasions, sample size—sometimes in combination with number of assessments— duration of assessment period, and extent of the battery of measures or experimental protocol.

The minimum number of data points for a longitudinal design is two. Often, two time points are chosen because of budget constraints. But such a two-occasion design can also be chosen because of the research question, such as in pre–post tests experiments. Although two occasions of data might sound limiting, they can be highly informative of change and processes, especially in designs that allow inferences across a wide range of time (e.g., age in cohort-sequential or accelerated longitudinal designs; see McArdle & Bell, 2000; McArdle, Ferrer-Caja,

Hamagami, & Woodcock, 2002; McArdle & Woodcock, 1997). For example, a researcher interested in the development of reading skills from age 7 to 16 may employ a cohort-sequential design with two or three measurement occasions per individual. In such a study, individuals between ages 7 and 16 are measured twice or three times within a 5-year period (see Figure 16.2) and, possibly, with different time intervals. Instead of focusing on changes across the two (or three) measurement occasions, the goal is to examine change across age in all participants, from 7 to 16 years (see Figure 16.3), even though no one person is measured across all ages (we elaborate on this design in subsequent sections; see McArdle et al., 2002, for an example with two-occasion data covering the life span).

Years	Time/Ages	7	8	9	10	11	12	13	14	15	16
1-2	*Wave* 1	50	50	50	50	50	50	-	-	-	-
3-4	*Wave* 2	-	-	50	50	50	50	50	50	-	-
5	*Wave* 3	-	-	-	-	50	50	50	50	50	50
Total	*W*1–*W*3	50	50	100	100	150	150	100	100	50	50

FIGURE 16.2. Data collection plan: A cohort-sequential design. At Wave 1 (Years 1–2 of the study), 300 participants ages 7 to 12 are assessed. At Wave 2 (Years 3–4), they are assessed for a second time (at ages 9–14). At Wave 3 (Year 5), the participants (now ranging in age from 11–16) are assessed for a third time. The last row represents the total number of unique data points available at each age from 7 to 16 years. Additional participants could be assessed during the empty cells for (a) ensuring enough data are available at each age, (b) building balanced sample sizes at each age, and (c) increasing the data density at particular ages when more data are needed (e.g., when changes occur more rapidly).

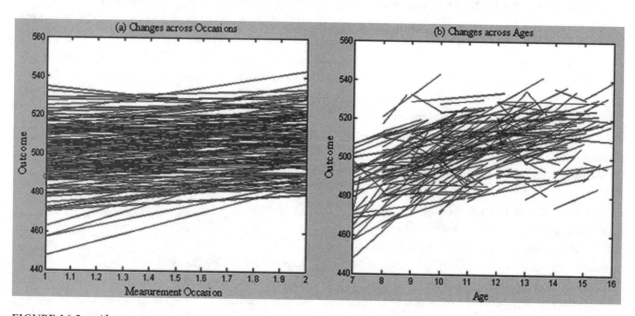

FIGURE 16.3. Alternative ways to conceptualize data: (a) by measurement occasion and (b) by age.

If possible, however, more than two occasions are preferable. In fact, much has been written on the limitations of two-occasion data as a longitudinal design (e.g., Duncan, 1975; Rogosa, 1988) and the problems associated with the study of change, pertaining particularly to two-occasion data (Cronbach & Furby, 1970). Most of these problems relate to the unreliability of change scores and no longer apply when the data include three or more occasions of measurement. In addition, having more than two occasions increases the data density, and this improves the estimation precision, especially with sparse data.

Deciding on the specific number of occasions will mostly depend on the characteristics of the process to be studied (see Nesselroade & Boker, 1994). A process that changes rapidly will necessitate frequent measurements to capture the features of the process (e.g., trend and amplitude). In this case, sparse measurement will miss the important aspects of the signal. In contrast, a process that is stable or shows slow change will require fewer measurements. In this case, frequent assessments are not needed but would add in the estimation of true change. When information about the change features is available, this can be used to select the number of occasions as well as the intervals between assessments. In many instances, however, this information is not available, and researchers might need to collect pilot data to get a sense of how quickly the process is changing.

Sample Size and Statistical Power

More than 3 decades ago, Schlesselman (1973a, 1973b) addressed the issue of frequency of measurement and study duration as well as sample size. With regard to frequency of measurement and study duration, Schlesselman offered a number of simple statistical techniques for determining these two factors with linear and quadratic models of age-related change. In particular, he tabled the precision of growth estimates as a function of number of repeated observations and years of duration of the study. With regard to sample size, he focused on two different goals of longitudinal investigations: (a) determining means and average rates of change on a number of variables for designated age groups and detecting differences among these age groups;

and (b) determining individual levels and rates of change for study participants and characterizing the magnitude of individual differences. For each of these two goals, Schlesselman offered a number of simple statistical techniques.

Currently, the number and frequency of assessments, study duration, and sample size in longitudinal studies is commonly determined in the context of statistical power (e.g., Basagaña & Spiegelman, 2010; Fan, 2003; Hedeker, Gibbons, & Waternaux, 1999; Hertzog, Lindenberger, Ghisletta, & von Oertzen, 2006; Maxwell, Kelly, & Rausch, 2008; Muthén & Curran, 1997; Raudenbush & Xiao-Feng, 2001; Tu et al., 2007; Winkens, Schouten, van Breukelen, & Berger, 2006; Zhang & Wang, 2009; see also Volume 1, Chapter 11, this handbook). For example, Hedeker et al. (1999) developed a general framework for determining sample size in longitudinal studies with the goal of detecting group differences, in the context of mixed models. Muthén and Curran (1997) provided guidelines for power analysis in longitudinal randomized trials using latent growth curve models. Raudenbush and Xiao-Feng (2001) studied power to detect group differences in polynomial growth models as a function of sample size per group, duration of the study, and total number of assessments. Winkens et al. (2006) studied the effects of sample size and the number of measurement occasions on the statistical power for group comparisons in longitudinal data analysis. In addition, they included a cost function to determine the balance between sample size versus measurement occasions. Similar effects were studied by Yan and Su (2006) but also including nonlinear models. Finally, studies of statistical power for longitudinal designs with discrete data are scarce. Some exceptions include Jung and Ahn's (2003) power analyses for comparing group differences in change models with binary variables and Rochon's (1998) work with discrete, binary, and Poisson variables.

MEASUREMENT ISSUES

Selection of Variables for Measuring Change

Another consideration when planning a longitudinal study concerns the measures. The selection of the measures is made on the basis of the types of questions to be answered. In this regard, the measures need to capture the construct under study and be sensitive to change. Important aspects concern the measurement and psychometric properties of variables and their underlying constructs, including various forms of validity and reliability (e.g., Little, Lindenberger, & Nesselroade, 1999; see also Volume 1, Chapter 32, this handbook). In many situations, techniques such as factor analyses, structural equation modeling with latent variables and item response models may be required to guarantee that the measures are psychometrically sound. Another issue regarding the measures concerns their sensitivity to capture changes in the construct over time. For this, in addition to the standard psychometric criteria, other indexes are needed to evaluate whether the selected variables are adequate to capture the intended change. Some of these criteria include the sensitivity to measure systematic change with precision (e.g., for within-person reliability, see Cranford et al., 2006; see also Volume 1, Chapter 31, this handbook).

In some instances, measures selected to assess a given construct need to be changed over the course of a study. This could be due to several reasons. For example, imagine a study on reasoning spanning childhood and adolescence. Because of the developmental maturation of the participants (and education, experience, etc.) the measures to assess reasoning will need to be changed to be appropriate for the specific ages (or the specific developmental stages). This situation often exists when researchers decide to add new variables or change scales during a study because of refinements in testing or changes in the meaning of a construct for the population under study. That is, although the focus on the construct (i.e., reasoning) remains intact, instruments used to capture such constructs change over the course of the study. These situations present an interesting challenge when measuring change over time because the variables are not the same across all occasions. To deal with this issue, linkage using factor or item response models and ideas behind factorial invariance (to be described in subsequent sections) are typically required to ensure the intended construct is equivalent across time (see McArdle, Grimm, Hamagami, Bowles, & Meredith, 2009).

Factorial Invariance Over Time

A critical aspect of longitudinal data related to measurement is factorial invariance over time. *Factorial invariance* (Meredith, 1964, 1993) refers to the equivalence in the measurement of a given construct. In longitudinal designs, factorial invariance—or measurement invariance across time—refers to the situation in which the numerical values across measurement occasions are obtained on the same measurement scale (Meredith, 1993). Although this issue is typically addressed at the phase of data analysis, understanding the underpinnings and implications of factorial invariance can help during study planning and data collection. In this type of invariance, each observed variable must relate to the underlying construct in the same fashion over time. This condition ensures that the latent construct has an equivalent definition across measurement occasions (Ferrer, Balluerka, & Widaman, 2008; Hancock, Kuo, & Lawrence, 2001; Sayer & Cumsille, 2001; Widaman, Ferrer, & Conger, 2010). Such equivalence guarantees that the same construct is being measured at all occasions and that the scale of the construct is also the same at all occasions, which are necessary conditions to identify quantitative changes in the construct over time (cf. Nesselroade, Gerstorf, Hardy, & Ram, 2007).

A practical approach to factorial invariance was proposed by Widaman and Reise (1997). On the basis of the work by Meredith (1993; Meredith & Horn, 2001), Widaman and Reise distinguished a number of increasingly restrictive models for assessing invariance. The first of such models was *configural invariance*, indicating that the same observed variables of the latent construct are specified at each occasion, independent of the numerical values. The second model was *weak metric invariance*, indicating that the factor loading of each indicator has the same value across all occasions. The third model was *strong factorial invariance*, in which the restriction is further increased by specifying an invariant intercept for each indicator across all occasions. The last model, *strict factorial invariance*, requires invariant unique variances for each manifest variable over time.

Meeting the criteria of strong or strict invariance is necessary to identify changes in the construct over time. Often, however, such criteria are difficult to meet with empirical data. Because of this difficulty, some investigators occasionally free restrictions and allow some of the parameters in the model not to be invariant across occasions (e.g., some of the factor loadings are not invariant across all occasions). This type of invariance, often called *partial invariance*, is not always considered a sufficient compromise of proper measurement. To overcome this difficulty, Nesselroade, Gerstorf, Hardy, and Ram (2007) proposed that invariance be met at the level of the interfactor relationships instead of at the level of indicators.

Longitudinal invariance has significant implications for the planning of studies and data collection. Because factorial invariance permits examining change at the level of the construct—as opposed to the manifest variable—researchers should collect measures with multiple indicators (e.g., scales with several items) at each occasion. These measures allow specifying models of change that involve latent variables as opposed to composites or single indicators (e.g., Ferrer et al., 2008; Hancock et al., 2001; McArdle, 1988; Widaman et al., 2010). These second-order growth models increase precision and power of change estimates (e.g., see Hertzog et al., 2006). In addition to being able to formally assess factorial invariance and adequately assess quantitative change in the construct over time, such a latent variable approach has important advantages over single indicators.

A final consideration regarding factorial invariance and data collection concerns those situations in which the measures need to be changed across assessments. As described in previous sections, this is sometimes the case when a measure is no longer appropriate to assess a given construct (e.g., becomes obsolete, is no longer age appropriate) or when researchers are trying to reduce practice effects. If situations like this are foreseeable during the planning of the study, it is recommended that variables overlap measurement occasions when transitioning or measurement invariance studies are conducted outside of the longitudinal study. Having such *transition* across occasions in which the different measures are present allows the testing of longitudinal invariance and, if the criteria are met, the

definition of a single construct across all occasions (see McArdle et al., 2009).

Figure 16.4 illustrates the idea of using different measures to represent the same construct across occasions. In particular, this figure is a path diagram of a second-order linear growth curve (Ferrer et al., 2008; Hancock et al., 2001; McArdle, 1988) with observed variables changing across time (as in McArdle et al., 2009). At the first order, the level of the measurement model, a single factor is specified at each of the four measurement occasions. At each measurement occasion, observed variables considered to be age appropriate were chosen to represent the construct. At the first measurement occasion, only X_1 was appropriate; at the second occasion, X_1 and X_2 were appropriate; at the third measurement occasion, X_2 and X_3 were appropriate; and at the fourth occasion, X_3 was the only age-appropriate measure. With this type of data, examining change over the four measurement occasions at the level of observed variables is not possible. Under certain conditions of measurement invariance, however, the use of a measurement model enables the evaluation of change at the factor level. Examining change at the factor level is possible because the transition occasions where one observed variable is being transitioned out and another is being transitioned in. In Figure 16.4, the measurement Occasions 2 and 3 can be seen as transition occasions.

The conditions that need to be met to examine change at the factor level are related to measurement invariance. In the path diagram, the factor loadings are given the same label to denote they are invariant over time. Similarly, measurement intercepts (not presented in the diagram for clarity) need to be constrained to be equal across time. This level of measurement invariance—*strong metric invariance*—is necessary to model change at the factor level regardless of whether there are changes in the measurement protocol.

Longitudinal data that are structured in this way can be useful when studying change over ages across which the manifestation of a construct changes over time. Even though the manifestation changes, the construct remains. Furthermore, as in McArdle et al. (2009), it is possible to do this at the item level. Thus, instead of having measures that transition in

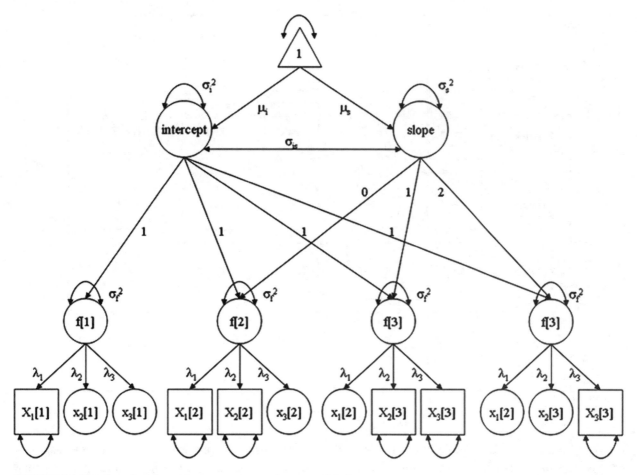

FIGURE 16.4. Plot of study with measurement change and linkage across occasions.

and out, items can transition in and out (see also Edwards & Wirth, 2009). A few drawbacks should be noted, however. Strong metric invariance, the invariance of factor loadings and measurement intercepts, cannot be fully examined and tested, and if strong metric invariance does not hold, the examination of change will be compromised. In cohort-sequential and accelerated longitudinal designs, these types of models can be difficult to fit (see McArdle et al., 2009, Appendix).

Planned Incomplete Data of Measures, Persons, and Occasions

Ideally, a longitudinal study would involve multiple measures on multiple individuals at multiple occasions. This, however, is not always possible because of time and budgetary constraints. For example, many studies involve an extensive battery of measurements that participants cannot reasonably complete because of fatigue or lack of time. In these

situations, instead of having every participant complete all the measures at all times, the design of the study can include a random selection of persons, measures, and occasions. For example, given a battery of measures that takes about 4 hours to complete, certain sections of the battery could be randomly assigned to each participant, instead of asking all participants to complete the entire battery.

Figure 16.5 illustrates the idea of planned incomplete data of measures. This figure represents a study design in which the overall sample is divided into four groups. Each group is then randomly assigned to a number of variables. For example, in the illustrative design, the battery of measures consists of five tests. Squares denote tests completed and circles represent tests not completed. Of the measures, Test A is considered the strongest marker of the construct under study so it is decided that all groups complete this measure. The others, however, are randomly assigned in a way that each group completes three

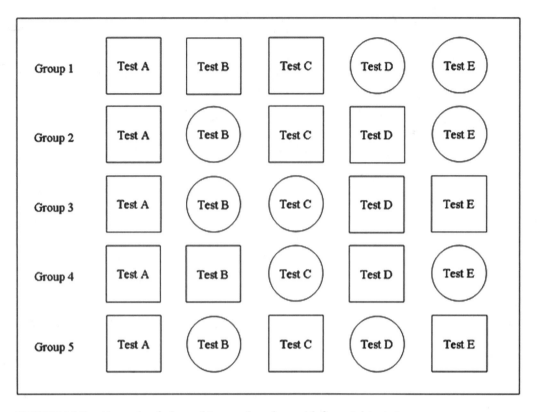

FIGURE 16.5. Example of planned incomplete data with factorial invariance.

tests only, but all tests are completed by at least two groups. This design could then be balanced at the next measurement occasion, and so on (for an example of such design across different studies and waves of measurement, see McArdle et al., 2009).

The idea behind this approach is that not all participants need to be assessed on all variables, but all variables are being completed by some participant. In these situations, researchers will want to ensure that all permutations in the random selection are considered. The resulting incomplete data would be missing in a random fashion, by design (Graham, Taylor, Olchowski, & Cumsille, 2006; McArdle, 1994; McArdle & Hamagami, 1991). This random nature of the incomplete data enables the use of statistical techniques dealing with data that are *missing at random* (see Volume 3, Chapter 2, this handbook). In these cases, however, measurement invariance is often assumed because it cannot be statistically tested.

Planned incomplete data can also be applied to the number of measurement occasions and to the interval across occasions (see Bell, 1954; McArdle & Woodcock, 1997; Thorndike, 1933). There are

situations in which it is not possible to assess all participants at all times. In many instances, participants do not need to be assessed at all times to obtain reliable estimates of change (Bell, 1953, 1954). Yet in other situations, assessing participants at all time points may not be desirable. In these instances, researchers may arrange to have participants measured at different times and at different intervals between measurement occasions, for example, to examine retest effects (e.g., Ferrer, Salthouse, Stewart, & Schwartz, 2004; McArdle & Woodcock, 1997). Researchers will want to consider this when planning the study and decide the number of occasions and the spacing between them. Simulation work exists to help determine the number of occasions required to optimally assess change and growth (e.g., Hamagami & McArdle, 2001). For example, Hamagami and McArdle (2001) studied this issue with complex multivariate dynamic models. They showed that two random data points per person were sufficient to examine change in dynamics in a sample with an age span of 20 years. Other work has focused on power analysis to determine sample size in longitudinal studies considering differing degrees and patterns of missing data (Hedeker et al., 1999; Jung & Ahn, 2003). In spite of the benefits of planned incomplete data, these ideas remain underused in the planning of longitudinal studies.

ISSUES DURING COLLECTION OF LONGITUDINAL DATA

Attrition

In previous sections we have described the possibilities of planned incomplete data to maximize resources. In contrast to this type of benign incomplete data, other types of incomplete data can bias the results of the study. In some instances, good planning before and during data collection can help minimize the loss of data. In other situations, especially when the data are already collected, statistical models are needed to account for the types and patterns of missingness in the data.

One of the most prevalent issues in longitudinal studies is incomplete data. Almost invariably in such studies, data are lost, especially as the study progresses. The first phase during which missing data can occur is during the initial sampling and contact of participants. Lack of representativeness in the sampling, lack of response, and refusal by participants are all significant forms of incomplete data that are often overlooked and unstudied, and perhaps more so than in other social science disciplines, such as sociology, demography, and political science. These factors ought to be considered during the planning of the study before data collection.

The main mechanism leading to missing data in longitudinal studies is attrition. Attrition can be due to the participants' refusal to complete parts of a questionnaire or take part in an experimental task. More important, participants can decide to drop out from the study, either temporarily or permanently. Reasons for dropout include fatigue, aversion to or dissatisfaction with the study, relocation, health, and, in studies involving older individuals, death. Many of these issues are difficult to prevent and avoid. Other aspects, however, can be thought out before data collection to minimize the loss of data.

The main problems associated with attrition are the reduction in statistical power and bias of parameter estimates. The former is associated with data loss. The latter is particularly worrisome when the dropout is nonrandom—that is, those individuals who continue in the study are systematically different from those who withdraw. This is particularly problematic in studies involving older populations. Those who tend to remain in the study are typically healthier, more motivated, and more highly functioning than those who drop out (see Ferrer & Ghisletta, 2011; Schaie & Hofer, 2001).

When attrition is not related to the study in any systematic way, the missing data can be ignored. When, however, data loss is related to variables in the study (e.g., participants in a study about health cannot take part in an assessment because of illness), accounting for the incompleteness is more complicated. Sometimes information about the reasons for missing data is related to measured variables and can be taken into consideration in the statistical analyses. Other times, although the missing data are related to variables in the study, such information is not available so statistical models are limited—or ineffective—in accounting for the missing data (for comprehensive reviews on analyses of incomplete data, see Graham, 2009; Schafer & Graham, 2002).

One fundamental question for researchers collecting longitudinal data is how to minimize attrition. For this, tracking the participants over time and keeping them involved in the study is essential. Some common techniques to track participants over time include collecting contact information from the participants as well as from two or three other contact individuals. These other contacts can help locate the participants in case, say, they move from their original residence. It is always useful, particularly in studies that last several years, to check from time to time to ensure that the records are up to date.

Retention can also be improved by keeping participants involved and engaged in the study. Some methods to facilitate this include periodical contact with the participants via newsletters, postcards, birthday cards, and the use of various incentives. In most longitudinal studies, participants are paid or offered some incentives for their continued participation. Incentives—monetary or not—often increase over time, so participants receive higher incentives the longer they stay in the study. In addition to such payments, it is a good idea to regularly send information about the findings and progress of the study to the participants. This can be done, for example, through newsletters or summary reports that contain key findings written in nontechnical language so that participants can see the application of the research and the relevance of their participation.

Retest Effects

Another important issue associated with the collection of longitudinal data concerns the retest effects. Together with cohort, selection, and maturation, retest effects represent a major threat to validity in longitudinal studies (e.g., see Baltes, Cornelius, & Nesselroade, 1979; Schaie, 1977, 1986). Many studies involve measurement occasions that are not related to the attribute in question. This is the case, for example, when measuring physical growth. Assessment will indicate how much participants grow irrespective of the number of measurement occasions or the method used. In many other studies, however, the repeated measurement may interfere with the assessment of the attribute.

One plausible example is the assessment of memory. Imagine a sample of individuals responding to a battery of measures related to memory at repeated occasions. The mere completion of the tests at a given occasion may influence the participants' performance at the next assessment. This could be due to a number of factors, such as familiarity with the setting, practice, the number of repeated assessments, time between assessments, and the nature of the attribute being measured (e.g., Cattell, 1957; McArdle & Woodcock, 1997). In these situations, the repeated measurement is contaminating the assessment of the process under investigation. That is, in the illustration, improvements in memory could be due to both developmental maturation and practice effects. Empirical findings of this phenomenon indicate that performance in cognitive tests tend to improve over repeated occasions, varying in degree across variables (e.g., Rabbitt, Diggle, Smith, Holland, & McInnes, 2001; Wilson et al., 2002; cf. Schaie, 1988), across persons (Ferrer et al., 2004; Ferrer, Salthouse, McArdle, Stewart, & Schwartz, 2005), and across occasions (Lövdén, Ghisletta, & Lindenberger, 2004; Rabbitt et al., 2001).

When collecting longitudinal data, researchers will want to be aware of retest effects, especially with regard to the specific attribute being studied. The goal is to minimize these effects and, if this is not plausible, to include in the design ways to account for them. Typically, longitudinal studies are used to investigate the development (e.g., time-course, age-related changes) of a given attribute. It is important that the changes related to development or maturation are separated from the changes related to retest (i.e., reflecting practice and experience).

Two possible ways to separate such effects are via design, during the planning of the study, or statistical methods, after the data have been collected. The design approach involves the planning of the study and data collection. For example, a researcher can use so-called refreshment samples at the repeated assessments. These are samples with the same characteristics and structure with respect to important variables (e.g., age, gender, socioeconomic status) as the main sample at the initial assessment and are included at any repeated occasion. With this approach, the researcher can now compare equivalent samples that differ only with respect to the number of assessments. If the samples are certainly equivalent with respect to important sampling characteristics, differences in the scores in such comparisons can be attributed to retest effects (cf. Schaie 1988). Because including refreshment samples is costly and not always feasible, researchers sometimes need to deal with the issue of retest effects via statistical models. Such an approach takes place in the phase of data analysis, after the data have been collected. The idea behind this approach is to estimate separately the effects resulting from the time-course of the study (e.g., age-related changes) from the effects resulting from retest (e.g., practice, experience). Interested readers are referred to the existing literature in the area (e.g., Ferrer et al., 2004; McArdle & Woodcock, 1997; Rabbitt et al., 2001).

A final comment regarding retest effects is that it can be confounded with other important factors in longitudinal studies, such as attrition and cohort effects (Schaie, 1988). For example, the presence of cohort effects in a study may compromise the estimation of retest effects. The reason for this is because any approach, either design or statistical analyses, relies on the assumption of equivalence across samples. That is, the compared samples should only differ with respect to number of measurement occasions and age (or other time-related variable). When cohort effects accentuate the differences between the samples, the estimation of retest effects is confounded.

RECOMMENDATIONS AND PRACTICAL GUIDELINES

The venture into longitudinal data collection and analysis is not a small one, especially given the necessary resources of both time and money. Ideally, longitudinal studies are planned before any data collection begins in order to optimize resources; however, many plans for longitudinal data collection come after an initial cross-sectional study, which should guide subsequent data collection. As in all studies, appropriate power analyses should be conducted to determine how much data are really needed to have adequate power to study hypothesized relations. Power analyses for longitudinal studies must be specific to the types of models that will be fit to answer specific research questions. Additionally, the following questions should guide data collection:

1. How rapidly does the construct change? How quickly the construct changes influences how often the construct needs to be measured and the length of the time intervals between measurement occasions. At one extreme, a construct that fluctuates rapidly, such as physiological measures and mood, requires many measurement occasions and short time intervals between assessments to adequately capture the process. At the other extreme, a construct that does not change (if this exists is a question in itself) only requires one measurement occasion; however, more measurement occasions would lead to a more accurate measure of the construct and a test of whether the construct actually changes.

2. What major time metrics guide the change process? In most change processes there are several time metrics that influence when, how much,

and how quickly change unfolds. Possible time metrics include measurement occasion (an important time metric when considering practice effects), chronological age, grade in school, maturational or pubertal age, time until death, and time since diagnosis, surgery, and so on. One major issue when considering several time metrics is their high degree of colinearity. Thus, to study multiple time metrics, an innovative study design is crucial to lower the degree of colinearity (e.g., see McArdle & Woodcock, 1997).

3. What are the important aspects of the change process? Often, researchers are interested only in two aspects of change—an initial status and a rate of change. However, many developmental processes do not follow such simple linear models, and nonlinear models with multiple aspects of change are necessary to adequately understand the change process (see Grimm et al., 2010; Nesselroade & Boker, 1994). Aspects of change that might be of interest include the rate of change, timing (location) of changes, lower and upper asymptotes, transitions to different phases of development, and period of acceleration. If additional aspects of change are practically and theoretically important, then it is necessary to sample time when these aspects of change are present.

4. How can the construct best be measured at each occasion, age, and so on? In many longitudinal studies, the same battery of tests (or scales) is administered throughout the study with the idea that using the same battery will lead to a more accurate (and simpler) study of individual change. The battery may not measure the same constructs in the same way at all occasions or ages, and without multivariate assessment, studying factorial invariance is limited. Researchers should consider how to best represent the construct at each occasion or age and design a study that enables the measures to be equated or linked over time. Additionally, it is important that the full range of abilities (attitudes, proficiencies, and so on) are covered at each measurement occasion because studying change becomes difficult when data have floor and ceiling issues.

CONCLUSION

Longitudinal data are a necessary aspect of studying developmental process, change, and intraindividual variability and dynamics. The appropriate planning of longitudinal studies can alleviate some difficulties that would otherwise limit or be dealt with during analysis. Longitudinal data collection carries a heavy cost and thus should be given appropriate time to plan and optimize resources.

References

Baltes, P. B., Cornelius, S. W., & Nesselroade, J. R. (1979). Cohort effects in developmental psychology. In J. R. Nesselroade & P. B. Baltes (Eds.), *Longitudinal research in the study of behavior and development* (pp. 61–88). New York, NY: Academic Press.

Basagaña, X., & Spiegelman, D. (2010). Power and sample size calculations for longitudinal studies comparing rates of change with a time-varying exposure. *Statistics in Medicine, 29,* 181–192.

Bell, R. Q. (1953). Convergence: An accelerated longitudinal approach. *Child Development, 24,* 145–152. doi:10.2307/1126345

Bell, R. Q. (1954). An experimental test of the accelerated longitudinal approach. *Child Development, 25,* 281–286. doi:10.2307/1126058

Cattell, R. B. (1957). *Personality and motivation structure and measurement.* New York, NY: World.

Cattell, R. B. (1988). The data box: Its ordering of total resources in terms of possible relational systems. In J. R. Nesselroade & R. B. Cattell (Eds.), *Handbook of multivariate experimental psychology* (2nd ed., pp. 69–130). New York, NY: Plenum Press.

Cranford, J. A., Shrout, P. E., Iida, M., Rafaeli, E., Yip, T., & Bolger, N. (2006). A procedure for evaluating sensitivity to within-person change: Can mood measures in diary studies detect change reliably? *Personality and Social Psychology Bulletin, 32,* 917–929. doi:10.1177/0146167206287721

Cronbach, L. J., & Furby, L. (1970). How we should measure "change": Or should we? *Psychological Bulletin, 74,* 68–80. doi:10.1037/h0029382

Duncan, O. D. (1975). Some linear models for two-wave, two-variable panel analysis with one-way causation and measurement errors. In H. M. Blalock (Ed.), *Quantitative sociology: International perspectives on mathematical and statistical modeling* (pp. 285–306). New York, NY: Academic Press.

Edwards, M. C., & Wirth, R. J. (2009). Measurement and the study of change. *Research in Human Development, 6,* 74–96.

Fan, X. (2003). Power of latent growth modeling for detecting group differences in latent growth trajectory parameters. *Structural Equation Modeling, 10,* 380–400. doi:10.1207/S15328007SEM1003_3

Ferrer, E., Balluerka, N., & Widaman, K. F. (2008). Factorial invariance and the specification of second-order latent growth models. *Methodology: European Journal of Research Methods for the Behavioral and Social Sciences, 4,* 22–36.

Ferrer, E., & Ghisletta, P. (2011). Methodological issues in the psychology of aging. In K. W. Schaie & S. L. Willis (Eds.), *Handbook of the psychology of aging* (7th ed., pp. 25–39). San Diego, CA: Elsevier.

Ferrer, E., & McArdle, J. J. (2010). Longitudinal modeling of developmental changes in psychological research. *Current Directions in Psychological Science, 19,* 149–154.

Ferrer, E., Salthouse, T. A., McArdle, J. J., Stewart, W. F., & Schwartz, B. S. (2005). Multivariate modeling of age and practice in longitudinal studies of cognitive abilities. *Psychology and Aging, 20,* 412–422. doi:10.1037/0882-7974.20.3.412

Ferrer, E., Salthouse, T. A., Stewart, W. F., & Schwartz, B. S. (2004). Modeling age and retest processes in longitudinal studies of cognitive abilities. *Psychology and Aging, 19,* 243–259. doi:10.1037/0882-7974.19.2.243

Graham, J. W. (2009). Missing data analysis: Making it work in the real world. *Annual Review of Psychology, 60,* 549–576. doi:10.1146/annurev.psych.58.110405.085530

Graham, J. W., Taylor, B. J., Olchowski, A. E., & Cumsille, P. E. (2006). Planned missing data designs in psychological research. *Psychological Methods, 11,* 323–343. doi:10.1037/1082-989X.11.4.323

Grimm, K. J. (2007). Multivariate longitudinal methods for studying developmental relationships between depression and academic achievement. *International Journal of Behavioral Development, 31,* 328–339. doi:10.1177/0165025407077754

Grimm, K. J., & Ram, N. (2009). A second-order growth mixture model for developmental research. *Research in Human Development, 6,* 121–143. doi:10.1080/15427600902911221

Grimm, K. J., Ram, N., & Hamagami, F. (2010). *Nonlinear growth curves in developmental research.* Manuscript submitted for publication.

Hamagami, F., & McArdle, J. J. (2001). Advanced studies of individual differences: Linear dynamic models for longitudinal data analysis. In G. Marcoulides & R. Schumacker (Eds.), *Advanced structural equation modeling: New developments and techniques* (pp. 203–246). Mahwah, NJ: Erlbaum.

Hancock, G. R., Kuo, W., & Lawrence, F. R. (2001). An illustration of second-order latent growth models. *Structural Equation Modeling, 8*, 470–489. doi:10.1207/S15328007SEM0803_7

Hedeker, D., Gibbons, R. D., & Waternaux, C. (1999). Sample size estimation for longitudinal designs with attrition: Comparing time-related contrasts between two groups. *Journal of Educational and Behavioral Statistics, 24*, 70–93.

Hertzog, C., Lindenberger, U., Ghisletta, P., & von Oertzen, T. (2006). On the power of multivariate latent growth curve models to detect correlated change. *Psychological Methods, 11*, 244–252. doi:10.1037/1082-989X.11.3.244

Hertzog, C., & Nesselroade, J. R. (2003). Assessing psychological change in adulthood: An overview of methodological issues. *Psychology and Aging, 18*, 639–657. doi:10.1037/0882-7974.18.4.639

Jung, S. H., & Ahn, C. (2003). Sample size estimation for GEE method for comparing slopes in repeated measurements data. *Statistics in Medicine, 22*, 1305–1315. doi:10.1002/sim.1384

Kail, R. V. (2007). Longitudinal evidence that increases in processing speed and working memory enhance children's reasoning. *Psychological Science, 18*, 312–313. doi:10.1111/j.1467-9280.2007.01895.x

Little, T. D., Lindenberger, U., & Nesselroade, J. R. (1999). On selecting indicators for multivariate measurement and modeling with latent variables: When "good" indicators are bad and "bad" indicators are good. *Psychological Methods, 4*, 192–211. doi:10.1037/1082-989X.4.2.192

Lövdén, M., Ghisletta, P., & Lindenberger, U. (2004). Cognition in the Berlin Aging Study (BASE): The first ten years. *Aging, Neuropsychology, and Cognition, 11*, 104–133. doi:10.1080/13825580490510982

Maxwell, S. E., Kelley, K., & Rausch, J. R. (2008). Sample size planning for statistical power and accuracy in parameter estimation. *Annual Review of Psychology, 59*, 537–563. doi:10.1146/annurev.psych.59.103006.093735

McArdle, J. J. (1988). Dynamic but structural equation modeling of repeated measures data. In J. R. Nesselroade & R. B. Cattell (Eds.), *The handbook of multivariate experimental psychology* (Vol. 2, pp. 561–614). New York, NY: Plenum Press.

McArdle, J. J. (1994). Structural factor analysis experiments with incomplete data. *Multivariate Behavioral Research, 29*, 409–454. doi:10.1207/s15327906mbr2904_5

McArdle, J. J. (2009). Latent variable modeling of differences in changes with longitudinal data. *Annual Review of Psychology, 60*, 577–605. doi:10.1146/annurev.psych.60.110707.163612

McArdle, J. J., & Bell, R. Q. (2000). Recent trends in modeling longitudinal data by latent growth

curve methods. In T. D. Little, K. U. Schnabel, & J. Baumert (Eds.), *Modeling longitudinal and multiple group data: Practical issues, applied approaches, and scientific examples* (pp. 69–108). Mahwah, NJ: Erlbaum.

McArdle, J. J., Ferrer-Caja, E., Hamagami, F., & Woodcock, R. W. (2002). Comparative longitudinal structural analyses of the growth and decline of multiple intellectual abilities over the life-span. *Developmental Psychology, 38*, 115–142. doi:10.1037/0012-1649.38.1.115

McArdle, J. J., Grimm, K. J., Hamagami, F., Bowles, R. P., & Meredith, W. (2009). Modeling lifespan growth curves of cognition using longitudinal data with multiple samples and changing scales of measurement. *Psychological Methods, 14*, 126–149. doi:10.1037/a0015857

McArdle, J. J., & Hamagami, E. (1991). Modeling incomplete longitudinal and cross-sectional data using latent growth structural models. In L. M. Collins & J. L. Horn (Eds.), *Best methods for the analysis of change: Recent advances, unanswered questions, future directions* (pp. 276–304). Washington, DC: American Psychological Association. doi:10.1037/10099-017

McArdle, J. J., & Woodcock, R. W. (1997). Expanding test–retest design to include developmental time-lag components. *Psychological Methods, 2*, 403–435. doi:10.1037/1082-989X.2.4.403

Meredith, W. M. (1964). Notes on factorial invariance. *Psychometrika, 29*, 177–185. doi:10.1007/BF02289699

Meredith, W. M. (1993). Measurement invariance, factor analysis, and factorial invariance. *Psychometrika, 58*, 525–543. doi:10.1007/BF02294825

Meredith, W., & Horn, J. (2001). The role of factorial invariance in modeling growth and change. In L. M. Collins & A. G. Sayer (Eds.), *New methods for the analysis of change* (pp. 203–240). Washington, DC: American Psychological Association. doi:10.1037/10409-007

Molenaar, P. C. M. (2004). A manifesto on psychology as idiographic science: Bringing the person back into scientific psychology—this time forever. *Measurement: Interdisciplinary Research and Perspectives, 2*, 201–218.

Muthén, B. O., & Curran, P. J. (1997). General longitudinal modeling of individual differences in experimental designs: A latent variable framework for analysis and power estimation. *Psychological Methods, 2*, 371–402. doi:10.1037/1082-989X.2.4.371

Nesselroade, J. R. (1988). Sampling and generalizability: Adult development and aging research issues examined within the general methodological framework of selection. In K. W. Schaie, R. T. Campbell, W. Meredith, & S. C. Rawlings (Eds.), *Methodological issues in aging research* (pp. 13–42). New York, NY: Springer.

Nesselroade, J. R., & Baltes, P. B. (1979). *Longitudinal research in the study of behavior and development*. New York, NY: Academic Press.

Nesselroade, J. R., & Boker, S. M. (1994). Assessing constancy and change. In T. Heatherton & J. Weinberger (Eds.), *Can personality change?* (pp. 121–147). Washington, DC: American Psychological Association. doi:10.1037/10143-006

Nesselroade, J. R., Gerstorf, D., Hardy, S., & Ram, N. (2007). Idiographic filters for psychological constructs. *Measurement: Interdisciplinary Research and Perspectives, 5*, 217–235.

Rabbitt, P., Diggle, P., Smith, D., Holland, F., & McInnes, L. (2001). Identifying and separating the effects of practice and of cognitive ageing during a large longitudinal study of elderly community residents. *Neuropsychologia, 39*, 532–543. doi:10.1016/S0028-3932(00)00099-3

Raudenbush, S. W., & Xiao-Feng, L. (2001). Effects of study duration, frequency of observation, and sample size on power in studies of group differences in polynomial change. *Psychological Methods, 6*, 387–401. doi:10.1037/1082-989X.6.4.387

Rochon, J. (1998). Application of GEE procedures for sample size calculations in repeated measures experiments. *Statistics in Medicine, 17*, 1643–1658.

Rogosa, D. (1988). Myths about longitudinal research. In K. W. Schaie, R. T. Campbell, W. Meredith, & S. C. Rawlings (Eds.), *Methodological issues in aging research* (pp. 171–209). New York, NY: Springer.

Sayer, A. G., & Cumsille, P. E. (2001). Second-order latent growth models. In L. M. Collins & A. G. Sayer (Eds.), *New methods for the analysis of change* (pp. 179–200). Washington, DC: American Psychological Association. doi:10.1037/10409-006

Schafer, J. L., & Graham, J. W. (2002). Missing data: Our view of the state of the art. *Psychological Methods, 7*, 147–177. doi:10.1037/1082-989X.7.2.147

Schaie, K. W. (1977). Quasi-experimental research designs in the psychology of aging. In J. E. Birren & K. W. Schaie (Eds.), *Handbook of the psychology of aging* (pp. 39–58). New York, NY: VanNostrand Reinhold.

Schaie, K. W. (1986). Beyond calendar definitions of age, cohort, and period: The general developmental model revisited. *Developmental Review, 6*, 252–277. doi:10.1016/0273-2297(86)90014-6

Schaie, K. W. (1988). Internal validity threats in studies of adult cognitive development. In M. L. Howe & C. J. Brainard (Eds.), *Cognitive development in adulthood: Progress in cognitive development research* (pp. 241–272). New York, NY: Springer-Verlag.

Schaie, K. W., & Hofer, S. M. (2001). Longitudinal studies in aging research. In J. E. Birren & K. W. Schaie (Eds.), *Handbook of the psychology of aging* (5th ed., pp. 53–77). San Diego, CA: Academic Press.

Schlesselman, J. J. (1973a). Planning a longitudinal study: 1. Sample size determination. *Journal of Chronic Diseases, 26*, 553–560. doi:10.1016/0021-9681(73)90060-X

Schlesselman, J. J. (1973b). Planning a longitudinal study: 2. Frequency of measurement and study duration. *Journal of Chronic Diseases, 26*, 561–570. doi:10.1016/0021-9681(73)90061-1

Thorndike, R. L. (1933). The effect of the interval between test and retest on the constancy of the IQ. *Journal of Educational Psychology, 24*, 543–549. doi:10.1037/h0070255

Tu, X. M., Zhang, J., Kowalski, J., Shults, J., Feng, C., Sun, W., & Tang, W. (2007). Power analyses for longitudinal study designs with missing data. *Statistics in Medicine, 26*, 2958–2981. doi:10.1002/sim.2773

Widaman, K. F., Ferrer, E., & Conger, R. D. (2010). Factorial invariance within longitudinal structural equation models: Measuring the same construct across time. *Child Development Perspectives, 4*, 10–18. doi:10.1111/j.1750-8606.2009.00110.x

Widaman, K. F., & Reise, S. P. (1997). Exploring the measurement invariance of psychological instruments: Applications in the substance use domain. In K. J. Bryant, M. Windle, & S. G. West (Eds.), *The science of prevention: Methodological advances from alcohol and substance abuse research* (pp. 281–324). Washington, DC: American Psychological Association. doi:10.1037/10222-009

Wilson, R. S., Beckett, L. A., Barnes, L. L., Schneider, J. A., Bach, J., Evans, D. A., & Bennett, D. A. (2002). Individual differences in rates of change in cognitive abilities of older persons. *Psychology and Aging, 17*, 179–193. doi:10.1037/0882-7974.17.2.179

Winkens, B., Schouten, H. J. A., van Breukelen, G. J. P., & Berger, M. P. F. (2006). Optimal number of repeated measures and group sizes in clinical trials with linearly divergent treatment effects. *Contemporary Clinical Trials, 27*, 57–69. doi:10.1016/j.cct.2005.09.005

Yan, X., & Su, X. (2006). Sample size determination for clinical trials in patients with nonlinear disease progression. *Journal of Biopharmaceutical Statistics, 16*, 91–105. doi:10.1080/10543400500406579

Zhang, Z., & Wang, L. (2009). Statistical power analysis for growth curve models using SAS. *Behavior Research Methods, Instruments, and Computers, 41*, 1083–1094. doi:10.3758/BRM.41.4.1083

CHAPTER 17

USING THE INTERNET TO COLLECT DATA

Ulf-Dietrich Reips

The Internet is not one single monolithic medium. It consists of many services with different functions and needs for input, even more so than the medium *telephone* varies between clunky devices made from wood that we sometimes see in old movies, the iPad, smartphones, and Voice over Internet Protocol.[1]

Using the Internet can mean writing and receiving e-mails that may be purely text based or rich in media. It can mean to "surf" using a web browser on a desktop computer, laptop, or smartphone. Driving a car often automatically means using the Internet because information about the location of the car is sent to satellites and databases connected via the Internet. The *Internet of Things*, one of the next steps in the Internet revolution, will connect more and more of the world to the Internet. This connection can be made by the average person with the help of various services (e.g., http://www.touchatag.com). According to the Gartner Group, by the end of 2012, physical sensors will generate 20% of nonvideo Internet traffic: "The extent and diversity of real-time environmental sensing is growing rapidly as our ability to act on and interpret the growing volumes of data to capture valuable information increases" (Plummer et al., 2009).

Universal addressability of things and people (sometimes called the *Semantic Web*; Berners-Lee, Hendler, & Lassila, 2001; World Wide Web Consortium [W3C], 2010) allows Internet-based data collection even about people and things that are not connected to the Internet.[2] Other agents refer to them by sending their location, images, and so on. A case vividly demonstrating this principle is Google Street View: Combining location information with panoramic images creates a highly informative and immersive tool to explore the world at a human scale (i.e., with the eyes of a traveler). The future combination of visual location information with the Internet of Things will create an increasingly tightly meshed representation of the world on the Internet.

This chapter shows the major steps in collecting data on the Internet. The first section, Internet-Based Research, narrates the short history of Internet-based data-collection methods in psychological research, describes their characteristics, and presents a systematic overview of the four basic types of methods. Some notions about planning Internet-based research lead to the second section, Generating a Web Experiment. The section describes an example and provides the reader with the opportunity to become active and experience Internet-based data-collection methods by creating and conducting a web experiment in a step-by-step fashion. The example introduces the important concepts of client-side versus server-side processing and illustrates a number of important techniques. The third section, Pretesting, emphasizes the need to take extra care in preparing the materials and procedure

---

[1]Examine some images of phones at http://www.sparkmuseum.com/TELEPHONE.HTM and http://www.lisisoft.com/imglisi/4/Utilities/137414mla_xp_main_thumb.png.

[2]From the definition favored by the W3C (2010), you may gather that the semantics of the Semantic Web are not generally agreed upon: "The term 'Semantic Web' refers to W3C's vision of the Web of linked data. Semantic Web technologies enable people to create data stores on the Web, build vocabularies, and write rules for handling data."

DOI: 10.1037/13620-017
APA Handbook of Research Methods in Psychology: Vol. 2. Research Designs, H. Cooper (Editor-in-Chief)

and evaluating their usability. Useful procedures in pretesting of Internet-based data collection are introduced, and the section explains how these procedures prevent methodological problems. In the fourth section, Recruitment, the pros and cons of various ways of attracting participants to Internet-based studies are explained, concluding with the use of games as research environments on the Internet. The Data Analysis section explains a number of important issues such as raw data preservation, paradata, inclusion criteria, and technical variance. Furthermore, the section introduces several specific methods, including log file analysis. The concluding section looks at future trends and the continuing evolution of Internet-based methods and their use in behavioral and social research.

INTERNET-BASED RESEARCH

General Issues and History

The first psychological questionnaires on the World Wide Web (WWW) appeared in 1994 following the introduction of interactive form elements in the scripting language HTML that underlies the WWW (Musch & Reips, 2000). Krantz, Ballard, and Scher (1997) and I (Reips, 1997) conducted the first Internet-based experiments in the summer of 1995, and I opened the first virtual laboratory for Internet-based experiments in September 1995 (Web Experimental Psychology Lab: http://www.wexlab.eu).[3] Their results had also been presented at the Society for Computers in Psychology (SCiP) conference in Chicago in 1996 (see http://psych.hanover.edu/SCiP/sciprg96.html; also see Smith & Leigh, 1997). Several studies in most areas of Internet-based data collection—surveying, web experimentation, data mining, and social network analysis online—were presented at the German Online Research conference in Cologne in 1997 (see http://www.gor.de/gor97/abstracts.htm). The number of studies conducted via the Internet has grown exponentially since then.

To find examples of psychological studies archived or currently in progress on the web, the reader may visit studies linked at the Web Experimental Psychology Lab or at the following websites:

- Web experiment list at http://wexlist.net/ (Reips & Lengler, 2005; see Figure 17.1)
- Web survey list at http://www.wexlist.net/browse.cfm?action=browse&modus=survey
- Psychological Research on the Net by John Krantz at http://psych.hanover.edu/research/exponnet.html
- Online Social Psychology Studies by Scott Plous at http://www.socialpsychology.org/expts.htm
- Decision Research Center by Michael Birnbaum at http://psych.fullerton.edu/mbirnbaum/decisions/thanks.htm

Types of Internet-Based Research

Generally speaking, there are four types of Internet-based data collection (Reips, 2006). It can take the forms of nonreactive Internet-based methods, Internet-based surveys and interviews, Internet-based tests, and Internet-based experiments.

Nonreactive Internet-based methods and data mining. These types of research involve the use and analysis of existing databases and collections of materials on the Internet (e.g., open forum contributions, server log files, or picture repositories). The Internet provides many opportunities for nonreactive data collection. The sheer size of Internet corpora multiplies the specific strengths of this type of methods: Nonmanipulable events can be studied as they happen in natural behavior on the Internet (navigating, searching, selecting, chatting, reading, timing of these behaviors, and so on), facilitating the examination of rare behavioral patterns or integrating behavioral traces in useful ways (e.g., for television program recommendations; Van Aart et al., 2009). Many of these *user behaviors* are stored in server log files or data bases. Thus, log file analysis is an important example of a nonreactive web-based method (Reips & Stieger, 2004).

Nonreactive methods have a long tradition in psychological research (e.g., see Fritsche & Linneweber, 2006), and they were used early on in the Internet. In 1996 and 1997, Stegbauer and Rausch (2002)

---

[3]Because web addresses (URLs) may change, the reader may use a search engine like Google (http://www.google.com) to access the web pages mentioned in this chapter if a link does not work. In the present case, typing "Web Experimental Psychology Lab" into the search field will return the link to the laboratory as the first result listed.

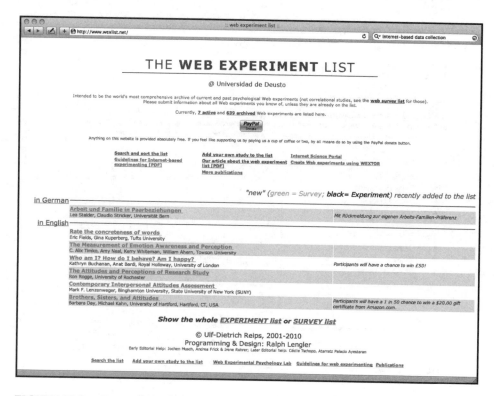

FIGURE 17.1.   Front page of the web experiment list. Retrieved from http://wexlist.net

studied the communicative behavior among members of several mailing lists. In this early example of the use of nonreactive data on the Internet, the authors were interested in the so-called *lurking behavior* (i.e., passive membership in mailing lists, newsgroups, forums, and other social Internet services). They analyzed the number and time of postings and the interaction frequencies pertaining to e-mail headers in contributions (without much need for filtering: It certainly helped that spam was a rare phenomenon at the time). Several questions regarding the lurking phenomenon could thus be clarified empirically. For example, about 70% of subscribers to mailing lists could be classified as lurkers, and "among the majority of users, lurking is not a transitional phenomenon but a fixed behavior pattern [within the same social space]" (Stegbauer & Rausch, 2002, p. 267). However, the behavioral pattern is specific to a mailing list: The analysis of individuals' contributions to different mailing lists showed a sizeable proportion of people may lurk in one forum but are active in another. "With this result, Stegbauer and Rausch empirically supported the notion of so-called 'weak ties' as a basis for the transfer of knowledge between social spaces" (Reips, 2006, p. 74).

The most widely used services on the Internet are search engines. With billions of searches performed every day, it is obvious that these searches contain much information about many aspects of human life. A simple measure is *search engine count estimates* (SECEs) that you may have seen as an opener of a slide presentation ("Googling *X* returns 1.2 million links"). Janetzko (2008) has shown good quality (objectivity, validity, reliability) for SECEs as estimates of relative importance of searched items. Several search engine providers have recently moved beyond frequencies and subjected their data to higher order algorithms for mining, as the following examples show.

With the knowledge about new search-based prediction services still not having disseminated widely to the population, it is possible to generate relatively manipulation-free (and thus accurate) predictions. For example, Google's Eurovision site (Google Eurovision, 2010) generates a prediction from searches for performers in the yearly Eurovision song contest, which correctly predicted the winner in 2009. Figure 17.2 shows the prediction for the 2010 contest at the time of this writing, May 12, 2010. The reader may visit the Eurovision song

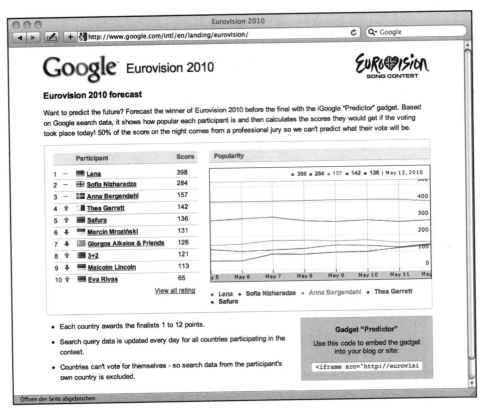

FIGURE 17.2.   Using Google Analytics to predict the results of the Eurovision Contest. As in 2009, the prediction correctly identified the winner. Retrieved from http://www.google.com/intl/en/landing/eurovision

contest site at http://www.eurovision.tv/page/home to confirm whether the prediction was accurate. Similar approaches from Google Trends (http://www.google.com/trends) and Google Insights (http://www.google.com/insights) have been used to predict a rise in influenza (Ginsberg et al., 2009) and local unemployment rates (Askitas & Zimmermann, 2009). Psychologists working in health care, social services, or advertising may benefit directly from these new intelligent data mining tools. They can get more time for preparing the events predicted for their area, psychological researchers may use the tools to mine searches for certain terms or combinations of terms, in combination with filters like geolocation or time frame (Reips, 2009). One freely available tool that was developed for researchers to mine messages sent on the social networking platform Twitter is iScience Maps (http://tweetminer.eu). My colleague and I (Reips & Garaizar, 2011), who developed and published the tool, were able to replicate an older study on personality characteristics associated with first names and discover the frequencies

of first names as a confound that explains the results of the original study. Using iScience Maps, conducting the study took only about 2 hours even though the replication was conducted for both the Western part of the United States and the United Kingdom plus Ireland, compared with weeks for the original study, which was conducted in Los Angeles only. Data from websites for psychologists may also be mined to discover mega trends, for example, changes in the topics studied in psychological research (Reips & Lengler, 2005).

Social websites have become valuable sources for social behavioral research that is based on nonreactive data collection. David Crandall and colleagues from Cornell University (http://www.cs.cornell.edu/~Crandall) created detailed maps by analyzing the location information of approximately 35 million geo-tagged photos that had previously been uploaded to Flickr, a website dedicated to photo sharing. The locations of the motifs show the relative interest in places, and because the sea is always an attractive motive, the shapes of continents appeared on the maps (see Figure 17.3; Barras, 2009). This information may lead to applications in tourism, city planning, ecology, and economics. For example, city planners may trace the location maps over long periods and thus identify areas to be developed or to be made accessible via public transportation.

Internet-based surveys and interviews. The most commonly used Internet-based assessment method is the web survey. The frequent use of surveys on the Internet can be explained by the apparent ease with which web questionnaires can be constructed, conducted, and evaluated. web survey methodology is a difficult matter, however, if one aims at generalizing results from a sample to a particular population. Work by Dillman and his group (Dillman & Bowker, 2001; Dillman, Smyth, & Christian, 2008; Smyth, Dillman, Christian, & Stern, 2006), among others, has shown that many web surveys are plagued by problems of usability, display, coverage, sampling, nonresponse, or technology. Joinson and Reips (2007) have shown through experiments that the degree of personalization and the power

attributable to the sender of an invitation to participate in the survey can affect survey response rates. Data quality can be influenced by degree of anonymity, and this factor as well as information about incentives also influence the frequency of dropout (Frick, Bächtiger, & Reips, 2001). The impression of anonymity on the Internet is particularly helpful in the investigation of sensitive topics. Mangan and Reips (2007) described two web surveys on the sensitive and rare condition sexsomnia that reached more than five times as many participants from the target population than all nine previous studies from 20 years of research combined.

Design factors like the decision whether to apply a "one screen, one question" procedure may trigger context effects that turn results upside down (Reips, 2002a, 2010). Any aspect of a web survey that may annoy participants, such as forcing a response, will likely create psychological reactance (Brehm, 1966) and subsequently lead to an increase in random answering behavior, nonresponse, and possibly even dropout (Stieger, Reips, & Voracek, 2007). Despite these findings, converging evidence shows that

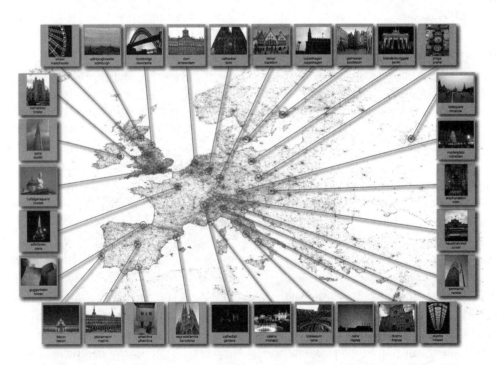

FIGURE 17.3. Map of Europe generated from information embedded in Flickr photographs. From "Gallery: Flickr Users Make Accidental Maps," by G. Barras, April 27, 2009, *New Scientist*. Image created by David Crandall. Reprinted with permission. Retrieved from http://www.newscientist.com/article/dn17017-gallery-flickr-user-traces-make-accidental-maps.html

web-based survey methods result in qualitatively comparable results to traditional surveys, even in longitudinal studies (Hiskey & Troop, 2002). Recently, survey researchers have begun to explore options of mixed-mode surveys (e.g., De Leeuw, 2005; also see the meta analysis by Shih & Fan, 2007). A very good source for research on web surveying is the web survey methodology website (http://websm.org).

Web-based psychological testing. One specific subtype of web surveying involves psychometric measurement. Buchanan (2001, 2007), Buchanan and Smith (1999), Preckel and Thiemann (2003), and Wilhelm and McKnight (2002), among others, have shown that web-based testing is possible if the particularities of the Internet situation are considered (e.g., computer anxiety may keep certain people from responding to a web-based questionnaire) and tests are used that were *validated for use on the Internet*. Buchanan and Smith found that an Internet-based self-monitoring test not only showed similar psychometric properties to its conventional equivalent but also compared favorably as a measure of self-monitoring. Similarly, Buchanan, Johnson, and Goldberg (2005) modified an International Personality Item Pool (http://ipip.ori.org/ipip) inventory. In their evaluation it showed to have satisfactory psychometric properties as a brief online measure of the domain constructs of the Five Factor model. Across two studies using different recruitment techniques, they observed acceptable levels of internal reliability and significant correlations with relevant criterion variables. Psychometric equivalence of paper-and-pencil versions of questionnaires with their web-based counterparts is not always the case, however. For instance, Buchanan et al. (2005) could recover only two of four factor-analytically derived subscales of the Prospective Memory Questionnaire with a sample of $N = 763$ tested via the Internet. Buchanan and Reips (2001) showed that technical aspects of how the web-based test is implemented may interact with demography or personality and, consequently, introduce a sampling bias. In their study they showed that the average education level was higher in web-based assessment if no JavaScript was used to code survey and website, and that Mac users scored significantly higher

on the personality dimension *Openness to Experience* (appreciation for art, adventure, curiosity, emotion, unusual ideas, and variety of experience) than Windows users.

Via the iScience server at http://iscience.eu the author of this chapter offers the Five Factor personality test for use on the Internet. Researchers may append the test to their own study by redirecting participants to a study-specific URL. The English and German versions of the test were previously validated for use on the Internet by Buchanan et al. (2005) and Hartig, Jude, and Rauch (2003); validation of the version in Spanish is under way.

Web experiments. *Web experiments* show several basic differences from experiments conducted in the laboratory or in the field (Reips, 2000, 2002d; Reips & Krantz, 2010). However, the underlying logic is the same as that in the other experimental methods. Hence, the definition of *experiment* used here requires manipulation of the independent variable(s), repeatability, and random assignment to conditions. Likewise, a quasi-web experiment would involve nonrandom assignment of subjects to conditions (see Campbell & Stanley, 1963; Kirk, 1995). Birnbaum (2007) further discusses representative and systextual experiment designs.

Web experiments offer a chance to validate findings that were acquired using laboratory experiments and field experiments. The number of participants is notoriously small in many traditional studies because researchers set the Type I error probability to a conventional level (and therefore the power of these studies is low; Faul, Erdfelder, Buchner, & Lang, 2009). One of the greatest advantages of web research is the ease with which large numbers of participants can be reached. The Web Experimental Psychology Lab, for instance, is visited by several thousand people per month (Reips, 2001, 2007). On the Internet the participants may leave a survey at any time, and the experimental situation is usually free of the subjective pressure to stay that is often inherent in experiments conducted for course credit with students. Because web experiments are often visible on the Internet and remain there as a documentation of the research method and material, overall transparency of the research process is increased.

Planning an Internet-Based Study

In planning an Internet-based study, many of the topics covered in this handbook are of importance. For example, regarding the measurement of psychological constructs (Volume 1, Chapters 12–31, this handbook) on the Internet we need to consider measurement scales, behavior observation (Volume 1, Chapter 12, this handbook), and use of computers (Volume 1, Chapter 16, this handbook). Regarding psychological tests we need to consider the various subtypes of tests (Volume 1, Chapters 17–19, this handbook) and brief instruments and short forms (Volume 1, Chapter 20, this handbook). In the next section I focus on planning and generating a web experiment, but many of the issues apply to all types of Internet-based data collection.

GENERATING A WEB EXPERIMENT

Important Techniques

For anyone using the Internet for research purposes it is important to know that there is a growing body of research on newly developed techniques (*tricks*) (e.g., Reips, 2002d, 2007) and the impact of design features of web-based studies. For example, when choosing a response format for questions one has many options, some of which are not available in paper-and-pencil format (Reips, 2002a, 2010). Figure 17.4 shows a radio button scale, a slider scale, and a visual analogue scale. Funke, Reips, and Thomas (2011) found slider scales to lead to significantly higher break-off rates than radio button scales (odds ratio 6.9) and also to substantially higher response times. Problems with slider scales were especially prevalent for participants with less than average education, suggesting the slider scale format is more challenging in terms of previous knowledge needed or cognitive load. The finding resonates well with the general principle that low-tech solutions are to be preferred for the design of web-based data collection (Buchanan & Reips, 2001; Reips 2007, 2010).

In an earlier work (Reips, 2002c), I proposed 16 standards or guidelines that may help researchers and reviewers of manuscripts that are based on Internet-mediated research. The proposed standards that refer to techniques are explained in the following sections.

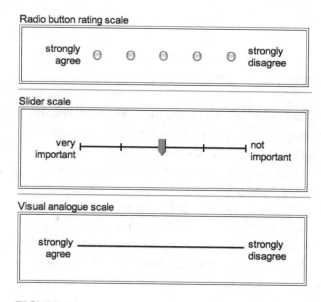

FIGURE 17.4. From top to bottom: A radio button scale, a slider scale, and a visual analogue scale.

Standard 5: Link your study to other sites. Consider linking your web study to several Internet sites and services (*multiple-site entry* technique) to determine effects of self-selection or sampling and estimate generalizability. The multiple-site entry technique is implemented by identifying each source for participants by using a slightly modified link, for example

- http://wextor.org:8080/yourname/yourstudy/index.html?so=clinic1ar (patients from clinic 1—note that two random characters were added after the "1" so as to not allow anyone to change the URL to a real existing link like "_clinic2")
- http://wextor.org:8080/yourname/yourstudy/index.html?so=clinic2gi (patients from clinic 2)
- http://wextor.org:8080/yourname/yourstudy/index.html?so=psstudents (psychology students)
- http://wextor.org:8080/yourname/yourstudy/index.html?so=frfam (friends and family)
- http://wextor.org:8080/yourname/yourstudy/index.html?so=onr (a forum for online researchers)

The resulting data table will contain a column named "so" containing the values "clinic2," "frfam," "onr," and so on, so analyses can be done by source. Following Standard 5, a win–win situation usually results: Either the results are replicated for all sources and samples, thus strengthening the argument that both do not play a role in obtaining these specific results, or some sources and samples may deviate systematically (maybe even theoretically predictable) from the rest—opening up interesting investigations into the reasons for the deviation.

Standards 7 to 9: Possible strategies to deal with dropout.   If dropout is to be avoided, Standard 7 suggests the use of a *warm-up technique*, that is, the actual experimental manipulation only happens several pages deep into the material, after the typical initial spike in dropout, so a high compliance is already established. Any dropout or other nonresponse behavior occurring before the experimental manipulation cannot be attributed to the manipulation. Thus, the results are immune to dropout-related criticisms.

For example, in a web experiment on list context effects by Reips, Morger, and Maier (reported in Reips, 2002c, 2003b) the target category "number" was experimentally manipulated in a categorizing task only after 31 other items had been categorized to the nonmanipulated categories "flower," "female," and "vegetable," resulting in a dropout of only about 2% (usually, dropout rates are at about 35% in web experiments; Musch & Reips, 2000).

Standard 8 says to use dropout to determine whether there is *motivational confounding*, that is, the confounding of the motivation to continue participating in the experiment with levels of the independent variable(s). For example, in the case of one experimental condition being more boring than another, a difference in results from the two conditions could simply come from the difference in "boringness" (Reips, 2007).

Standard 9 suggests the use of the high-hurdle technique, incentive information, and requests for personal information to influence time and degree of dropout. The *high-hurdle* technique seeks to provoke an early drop in participants who likely would have dropped later during a study (Reips, 1997, 2000; but see discussion between Frauendorfer & Reips, 2009, and Göritz & Stieger, 2008). *Incentive information* is known to have an influence on response rates and dropout (Frick et al., 2001; Göritz, 2006; Musch & Reips, 2000)—a small amount or a chance to win a raffle in the sense of a

token of appreciation seems to be the optimal strategy. *Requests for personal information* at the beginning of a study were shown to increase compliance with study instructions, including a reduction in dropout and other nonresponse (Frick et al., 2001). This is in line with Standard 10.

Standard 10: Ask filter questions (seriousness of participation, expert status, language skills, etc.) at the beginning of the experiment to encourage serious and complete responses.   The "seriousness check" (Diedenhofen et al., 2010; Reips, 2000) has become one of the most successful techniques to increase the quality of data in Internet-based data collection. In a simple albeit very effective strategy, participants are asked at the very beginning of the study whether they "are intending to seriously participate now" or whether they "just want to take a look." Including only the data of those who chose the first option dramatically improves the quality of data. For example, in Reips (2005), I repeatedly found dropout rates to differ markedly between serious (about 15% dropout) and other (about 75% dropout) participants. Diedenhofen, Aust, Ullrich, and Musch (2010) found that restricting analyses to serious participants allowed a more valid forecast of election results. Moreover, serious participants answered attitudinal questions in a more consistent manner than other participants.

Standard 11: Check for obvious naming of files, conditions, and, if applicable, passwords.   During the process of creating a study, many researchers tend to use names for files and folders that help them remember the meaning of conditions and files or sequences of screens. However, these names are visible to participants via the browser's location window. Consider, for example, a URL like http://somesite.edu/psych/survey3/controlcond/page4.html. Participants in this study would be able to jump pages by exchanging the 4 in "page4" for a different number; similarly, they could investigate previous surveys by changing "survey3." From "controlcond," they could think they were sent to the control condition (Reips, 2002b). Using web services for scientists that were constructed with these issues in mind (e.g., WEXTOR) will support the scientist in avoiding such frequent errors, for example, by mixing logical with random sequences of characters.

Standard 12: Consider avoiding multiple submissions by exclusively using participant pools and password techniques. Multiple submissions are a rare phenomenon—who would like to repeatedly fill in a questionnaire, after all? Internet scientists observed that repeated submissions mostly happen right after the first submission (Birnbaum, 2000; Reips & Birnbaum, 2011). To ensure that each participant joins the study only one time, one can send out e-mails to a predefined list of participants. Each of the e-mails contains a unique URL to the study that works only a single time. Furthermore, by building and maintaining a participant pool (or "online panel"; Göritz, 2007) for recurring participation requests to the same pool of people, one exerts a higher degree of control of participation than in open recruitment on the Internet.

Standard 13: Perform consistency checks. For example, items with slightly different wording but identical meaning should be answered in the same way, and participants claiming to have a high educational degree should be of a certain age.

Meta Tagging

Meta tags are information snippets in the headers of web pages that inform web browsers, caches, and proxy servers about various issues related to the page. Exhibit 17.1, for example, shows several meta tags suitable for pages following the entry page in Internet-based research studies. The "robots" tag tells search engines not to process the content of the page, so no participant will enter the study via this page. The "pragma" tag tells caches and proxy servers not to save the content (so no outdated content is served). The "expires" tag tells caches and proxy servers to consider the content expired (the date lies in the past); thus, it is not stored.

Client Versus Server

Reactive data-collection techniques on the Internet can be categorized into server-side and client-side processing (Schmidt, 2000, 2007).

Server-side processing means that all necessary computing is done at the researcher's web server,

---

Exhibit 17.1

Use of Meta Tags for Internet-Based Research Studies in Pages Following the Entry Page

```
<HTML>
<HEAD>
<meta name="author" content="Experimenter">
<meta name="robots" content="none">
<meta http-equiv="pragma" content="no-cache">
<meta http-equiv="expires" content="Thursday, 1-Jan-1991
   01:01:01 GMT">

<TITLE> </TITLE>
</HEAD>
(insert the body of the web page here)
```

---

including receiving and sending hypertext transfer protocol (HTTP) requests (communication with participant computers), recording and computing of data, communicating with a database application, writing logs, and dynamically selecting and creating materials that may depend on a user's input. Because dynamic procedures are performed on the server, server-side processing is less subject to platform-dependent issues. Sometimes, however, the server may resemble a bottleneck, causing delays.

Client-side methods distribute most tasks to the processing power of the participants' computers. Therefore, time measurements do not contain error from network traffic and problems with server delays are less likely. Server-side processing relies on the participants' computer configurations, however, and thus is subject to issues of technical variance (Schmidt, 2007). Server-side and client-side processing methods can be combined, and they can be used to estimate technical error variance by comparison of measurements.

WEXTOR

WEXTOR (available at http://wextor.org) was developed by Reips and Neuhaus (2002). It is a web-based tool that can be used to design laboratory and web experiments in a guided step-by-step process. It dynamically creates the customized web pages and JavaScript needed for the experimental procedure and provides experimenters with a print-ready visual display of their experimental design. WEXTOR flexibly supports complete and incomplete factorial designs with between-subjects, within-subjects, and quasi-experimental factors as well as mixed designs. It implements server- and client-side response time measurement and includes a content wizard for creating interactive materials as well as dependent measures (graphical scales, multiple-choice items, etc.) on the experiment pages.

Many of the methodological solutions discussed in this chapter were built into WEXTOR. As a web service, WEXTOR can be used to design and manage experiments from anywhere on the Internet using a login and password combination. For support, there are tutorials, a frequently asked questions page, feedback and bug report forms, and an associated mailing list, all linked at the site. Figure 17.5 shows WEXTOR's entry page. The reader is encouraged to download the step-by-step-tutorial available from http://wextor.org/wextor_docs/WEXTOR_tutorial. pdf and re-create a web experiment as explained.

The process of creating an experimental design and procedure as a self-contained folder of all materials and scripts for an experiment with WEXTOR involves 10 steps. An experimenter logs on to WEXTOR, clicks on the link to "Create/modify an experimental design," and then enters number and names of within- and between-subjects and quasi-experimental factors and their levels. The experimenter then specifies the number of web pages (screens) and adds information about the type of design (e.g., complete or incomplete), the assignment to conditions, counterbalancing, and so on. Text, stimuli (for a discussion of stimulus delivery, see Krantz, 2001), and measures of various kinds can be added, including visual analogue scales that were shown to produce better measurements than radio button scales (Funke & Reips, in press; Reips & Funke, 2008). Any object can be integrated with the experimental materials, including, for example, videos or Flash content (for more information on using media in Internet-based research, see Krantz & Williams, 2010).

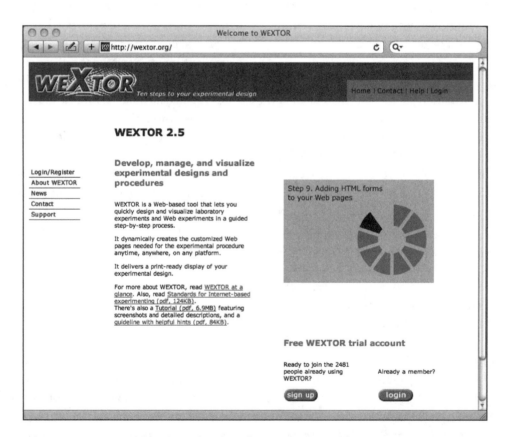

FIGURE 17.5.   WEXTOR is a web service for generating and hosting experiments that can be conducted in the lab or on the Internet. Retrieved from http://wextor.org

WEXTOR produces an organized visual and textual representation of the experimental design and the web pages and associated JavaScript and cascading style sheet (CSS) files required to implement that design. Furthermore, a code sheet is generated. In the final step, one can then download the experimental materials in a compressed archive that contains all directories (folders), scripts, and web pages.

After decompressing the archive, the resulting web pages created in WEXTOR can be viewed and tested for their functionality, even when not connected to the Internet. After further editing in a hypertext markup language (HTML) editor, the whole folder with all experimental materials can be uploaded onto the WEXTOR server or to a personal web server. Then the experiment is ready to go.

Many techniques for Internet-based experimenting mentioned in this chapter were built into WEXTOR to automatically avoid common errors found in Internet-based data collection. Among these techniques are meta tags, the seriousness check technique, the multiple site entry technique, and the high-hurdle technique discussed in the section Important Techniques. Flexible timing out of individual pages and soft form validation can be applied to the web pages. Skins are available to flexibly change the appearance of all web pages in the entire experiment at once. Figure 17.6 shows options for the implementation of the high-hurdle technique (Reips, 2000, 2002c), response time measurement, session identification, and form validation in Step 9 in WEXTOR.

For experiments hosted at the WEXTOR website, data preparation can optionally be done on the server, so that data can then be downloaded and opened in spreadsheet programs like Excel or SPSS. The downloaded data file contains a column showing the path taken by each participant (e.g., to see use of the back button) and both server-side and client-side measurements of response time for each page that was accessed.

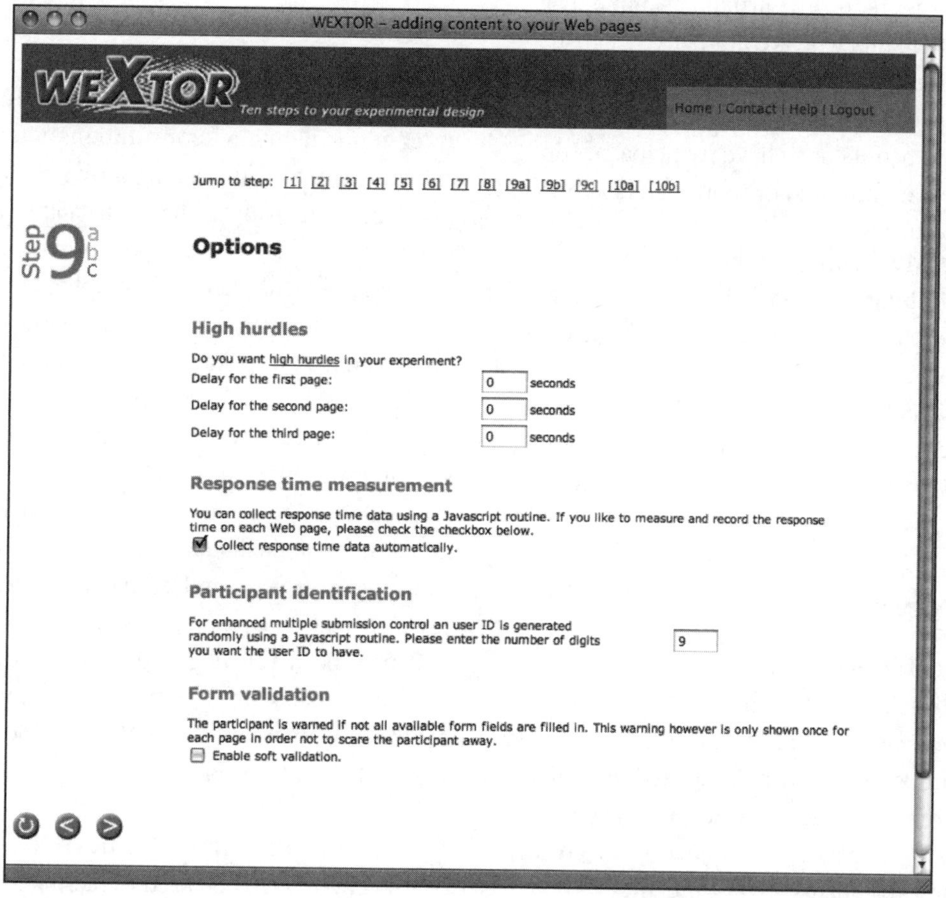

FIGURE 17.6. Step 9c in WEXTOR, showing implementation of the high hurdle, double collection of response times, session ID, and soft validation.

PRETESTING

Pretesting for an Internet-based study involves gathering information about several aspects that combine to make the study materials accessible and understandable to participants, for example, the usability of the websites involved.

Steps and Procedures

It is best to follow several steps during a pretest phase: First, test your study offline on your own computer and read the form entries in the location window. Second, test the study online and remember to mark the entries or record the time for later exclusion of test data. Third, ask a few colleagues and friends to test the study, and possibly observe some of them to see where they seem to have problems or get stuck. A good procedure is to ask participants to think aloud (speak out what they are thinking, while they are thinking), which often reveals the worst usability problems.

In studies that require a particular sample (e.g., children, participants who are not native English speakers), pretest a few people from the target population. Finally, check comments and data after the first two dozen people or so have participated (do not recruit several hundred or more testers at once).

Preventing Methodological Problems

To prevent running into methodological problems, ask experts for advice (e.g., see the website of the Society for Computers in Psychology, http://scip.ws). Internet-savvy colleagues may help detect technical issues, whereas those trained in Internet-based research may be able to give advice on designs and procedures.

RECRUITMENT

Portals and Lists

Portals and list sites such as the Web Experiment List and others mentioned in this chapter are a good way to recruit people who are interested in taking part in research. These sites are accurately referred to by many other places on the web as research sites that welcome participants. Over time, they have gained a stable reputation and are used and recommended by many universities around the world.

Mailing Lists, Forums, and Newsgroups

An effective way to recruit participants is to send e-mails to mailing lists, newsgroups, or forums (newsgroups were popular in the early days of the Internet, whereas forums are more of a recent development) of people who, in principle, are open to receiving invitations to participate in studies. Of course, this openness depends on a number of factors, for example, whether the study is related to the topic or membership and clientele of the mailing list, newsgroups, or forum and whether the invitation is endorsed by the moderator. In 2003, I heard an interesting paper on the 1st day of a conference and decided to replicate the study overnight. Within 8 hours, complete data sets from 162 participants (compared with 64 in the original study) were recorded in the web experiment, most of which were recruited via three mailing lists of which I am a member. I included the results in my talk on the 2nd day of the conference to demonstrate how efficient Internet-based data collection can be in comparison with the methods used by the original authors (Reips, 2003a).

Participant Pools and Online Panels

A recruitment option for institutions and for researchers who want to follow a long-term strategy in managing one's participants is the *participant pool technique*. People who sign up for this pool provide the web experimenter with their demographic data and can be paid for participation. The technique thus is attractive for researchers who want to know much about their participants, including who participated in which web experiments. Consequently, the technique allows for drawing stratified samples (Reips, 2000). Following a naming tradition in survey research, participant pools are in much of the literature on online research now called *online panels*—unfortunately suggesting to reviewers that the participants in the research at hand may have been a small group of experts discussing an issue in a small group meeting. Göritz has published extensively on online panels (Göritz, 2007, 2009; Göritz, Reinhold, & Batinic, 2002).

Search Engines and Banners

Search engines may be used to recruit participants to studies that remain on the Internet for lengthy periods of time, for example, when testing an item pool for the development of a new test, or for the recruitment of people who are interested in a particular phenomenon. Exhibit 17.2 shows how meta tags can be used to inform search engines, in this case, the study entrance page (and it should be only that one—because the researcher does not want to have participants enter a study later). In the example, the study will appear high in searches for "micronations" associated with terms like *ruler*, *survey*, *head of state*, *psychology*, and *research*. The meta tag <META NAME="description" CONTENT="""> informs searches that "research psychologists invite rulers of micronations to complete a survey of experiences that we hope will contribute to understanding the needs of micronations," so this very particular audience will receive an invitation by search, but not many others.

A supplementary option to guide search engines for proper handling of web-based studies is the Sitemaps protocol that was introduced by Google in 2005 (Sitemaps, 2010). Like the robots.txt file, it allows a webmaster to inform search engines about URLs on a website that are available for crawling. Improving on the robots.txt file, Sitemap allows for the inclusion of additional information about each URL: last update, frequency of changes, and relative importance to other URLs in the site. This information allows search engines to crawl the site more intelligently. According to the Wikipedia article on the subject, "Sitemaps are particu-

larly beneficial on websites where . . . some areas of the website are not available through the browsable interface, or webmasters use rich Ajax, Silverlight, or Flash content that is not normally processed by search engines" (Sitemaps, 2010).

Sitemaps containing all accessible URLs on a site can be submitted to search engines. Because the major search engines use the same protocol, having a Sitemap would let these search engines have the updated pages and links information. However, the Sitemaps protocol does not guarantee that web pages will be included in search indexes.

Banners ads were shown to generate only few responses despite their cost, and thus this method is not recommended (Tuten, Bosnjak, & Bandilla, 2000). Furthermore, any recruitment that takes the form of commercial ads may throw a negative light on the research, even on research in general.

Offline Recruitment

One way to recruit participants for Internet-based data collection is often overlooked: traditional media and other offline routes. Simply handing out fliers or printing a study URL in documents accessed by potential participants from the desired population can be very successful. The case of the BBC Internet study (Reimers, 2007) illustrates just how successful recruitment via mostly traditional media like radio and television can be in terms of large numbers: Reimers and the BBC collected data from around 255,000 participants.

Other Sources and Techniques in Recruitment

To assess Internet users' privacy concerns Paine, Reips, Stieger, Joinson, and Buchanan (2007) used a Dynamic Interviewing Program (Stieger & Reips, 2008) to survey users of an instant messaging client (ICQ, "I seek you") using both closed and open question formats. Even though their final analysis was conducted only on the basis of data from 530 respondents, the Dynamic Interviewing Program automatically contacted 79,707 ICQ users who indicated in the instant messaging service that they were open to being contacted.

Figure 17.7 shows Clickworker.com, a crowdsourcing job market. The largest of such websites is

---

Exhibit 17.2

Use of Meta Tags to Recruit via Search Engine

```
<HTML>
<HEAD>
<META NAME="keywords" CONTENT="micronations,ruler,
    survey,head of state,psychology,research,">
<META NAME="description" CONTENT="research
    psychologists invite rulers of micronations to complete
    a survey of experiences that we hope will contribute to
    understanding the needs of micronations">
<TITLE>Survey of Rulers of Micronations</TITLE>
</HEAD>
<BODY>
(Further information on the study and a link to the study
    would be placed here)
</BODY>
</HTML>
```

Amazon's Mechanical Turk. Mechanical Turk is a large job market that equally values and shows job seekers and job openings. Because the jobs can be very small and short-term, the site is an ideal place to recruit participants and have the payment arranged via Amazon's well-established and trusted services. However, results from a recent study by Reips, Buffardi, and Kuhlmann (2011) show that participants recruited via mechanical turk provide lower quality data than participants from traditional sources for Internet-based data collection: for example, shorter and less variable response times per item (which one would expect to vary widely, if participants think about the items) and more responses to the middle of scales in 50 out of 64 items. At the root of these findings may be that "Mturkers" sign up as workers. Workers respond to be paid, whereas other research participants respond to help with research. A second reason why Mturkers provide lower quality data may be tied to the forums they have established where jobs are discussed, including online studies. It may well be that rumors and experiences shared in these forums lead to a decrease in data quality.

Many potential participants of research studies are more easily recruited if they believe that participating will be fun. Consequently, a way to create Internet-based research is to use game scenarios as covers or design feature. The iScience server at http://iscience.eu includes one link to a web service named *idex*—on it, researchers and students can create their own Stroop-like web experiments, then invite participants, and later download the data from the site (Figure 17.8).

DATA ANALYSIS

Scientific investigation relies on the principle of preserving raw data. Raw data need to be saved for investigations by other researchers from the community

FIGURE 17.7. Clickworker.com, an online job market for small- and large-scale jobs that can be used in recruiting and paying participants. Retrieved from http://www.clickworker.com/en/

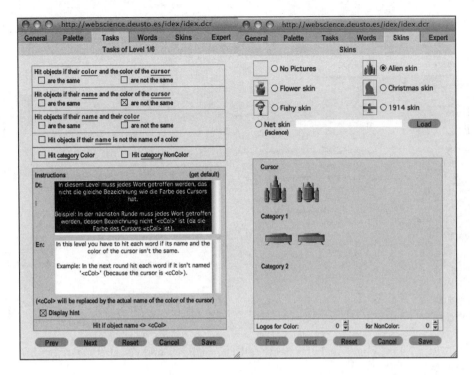

FIGURE 17.8.   Two of the panels in idex needed to configure Stroop-like web experiments as arcade-style games. Retrieved from http://webscience.deusto.es/idex

(American Psychological Association, 2010), for example, to aid in deeper understanding of the research, reanalysis, or meta-analysis. This principle applies to Internet-based data collection as well. Raw data in Internet-based data collection can include results from searches, server log files, or whole databases (Reips, 2007; Reips & Stieger, 2004).

It may be difficult to retain raw data if data collection or parts thereof are delegated to web services, especially those that may not allow easy download of all data. Figure 17.9 shows Google Analytics, a useful free service for collecting, analyzing, and visualizing statistics about visitors to websites. Collecting data with Google Analytics may be difficult, however, because Google follows a strategy that requires the owner of a Google Analytics account to log in frequently to view and save the data.

Paradata

Stieger and Reips (2010) have developed a tool, the UserActionTracer, that allows the recording and later reconstruction of paradata, such as timing, clicks, scrolling, and so on, as a reconstructed video sequence. They applied UserActionTracer to a large web sample ($N = 1,046$) in an online questionnaire of average length and found that 10.5% of participants showed more than five single behaviors (out of 132 theoretically possible) that have a clearly negative impact on data quality.

Inclusion Criteria

Data collected on the Internet in their raw form usually contain a number of entries that resemble noise and are not to be included in data analysis, for example, accesses from automatic scripts that are used by search engines to assess the content of web pages. Also, because participants on the web exert much more freedom to withdraw their participation, criteria should be preset in each Internet-based data-collection effort as to which entries are to be included and which not. For example, a preset inclusion criterion may be that at least half of all items in a questionnaire have to be answered. The following is a typical series of inclusion–exclusion steps in an Internet-based study.

The number of hits is taken of the very first page. Then, all cases are excluded that ended here, that is, when no further pages were accessed.[4] This exclusion

[4]If the meta tags for the exclusion of search engine spiders are used as advised elsewhere in this chapter, then no one will enter the study materials after the first page.

FIGURE 17.9.   Google Analytics freely collects, analyzes, and visualizes statistics about visitors to websites.

step may also be defined with a different threshold, for example, the first major point in the study was not reached. Such major points can be agreeing to having read an informed consent page, providing demographic information (e.g., so a minimum age can be assumed), distributing to experimental conditions, displaying the instructions, and so on. Next, only those participants are included who answered positively to the seriousness check (possibly also excluding those who did not respond at all to the check). Exclusions to avoid data from multiple submissions can conservatively be determined on the basis of Internet protocol numbers, even though two or more different participants may be assigned the same number by a large provider. Further criteria for inclusion or exclusion may include the following: whether the browser back button was used, whether a certain proportion of items was answered, whether particularly important items were answered, whether a certain minimum or maximum time was reached, or whether a longer break was taken.

Checking for Technical Variance

In a typical Internet-based study, the participants will access the materials using hundreds of combinations of computers, operating systems, versions and types of web browsers, and network speeds. Information about these can be gathered, many are part of the HTTP (operating systems, version, and type of web browsers), and others can be computed (network speeds) or gathered via JavaScript (e.g., size and resolution of screen used).

The impact of technical variance can then be checked by analyzing the data via analysis of variance, using the technology parameters as factors. Often, one will find well-established differences, such as different results on personality tests for Mac versus PC users and JavaScript turned on or off depending on level of education (Buchanan & Reips, 2001). It will depend on the aim of the study whether any other differences that may appear are a challenge or an asset to the hypothesis at hand.

CONCLUSION

Even though Internet-based data collection has been around for more than 15 years and is widely accepted, there are still ongoing debates in some fields about whether this new method should be accepted (e.g., Kendall, 2008 vs. Honing & Reips, 2008, for the field of musicology). In the meantime, numerous articles appear that report data from Internet-based data collection, even in areas in which the technique is still debated (such as Egermann, Nagel, Altenmüller, & Kopiez, 2009, in the case of musicology research).

The Internet of Things will spread and become more of a topic for the general public as well as for researchers over the coming years. It will be a question of whether and when issues of privacy with various Internet services that recently have been discussed more broadly will lead to a compromise between Internet penetration of daily life and the desire and legal requirement for anonymity and privacy.

With this chapter, I hope to have contributed to the spreading of helpful information that counters two popular misconceptions (Reips, 2002c): that Internet-based data collection is neither just like offline data collection nor is it completely different from offline data collection.

References

American Psychological Association. (2010). *Publication manual of the American Psychological Association* (6th ed.). Washington, DC: Author.

Askitas, N., & Zimmermann, K. F. (2009). Google econometrics and unemployment forecasting. *Applied Economics Quarterly, 55*, 107–120. doi:10.3790/aeq.55.2.107

Barras, G. (2009). Gallery: Flickr users make accidental maps. *New Scientist*. Retrieved from http://www.newscientist.com/article/dn17017-gallery-flickr-user-traces-make-accidental-maps.html

Berners-Lee, T., Hendler, J., & Lassila, O. (2001). The Semantic Web: A new form of web content that is meaningful to computers will unleash a revolution of new possibilities. *Scientific American, 284*(6), 34–35. doi:10.1038/scientificamerican0501-34

Birnbaum, M. H. (2000). Decision making in the lab and on the web. In M. H. Birnbaum (Ed.), *Psychological experiments on the internet* (pp. 3–34). San Diego, CA: Academic Press. doi:10.1016/B978-012099980-4/50002-2

Birnbaum, M. H. (2007). Designing online experiments. In A. N. Joinson, K. Y. McKenna, T. Postmes, & U.-D. Reips (Eds.), *The Oxford handbook of Internet psychology* (pp. 391–403). Oxford, England: Oxford University Press.

Brehm, J. W. (1966). *A theory of psychological reactance.* New York, NY: Academic Press.

Buchanan, T. (2001). Online personality assessment. In U.-D. Reips & M. Bosnjak (Eds.), *Dimensions of Internet science* (pp. 57–74). Lengerich, Germany: Pabst Science.

Buchanan, T. (2007). Personality testing on the Internet: What we know, and what we do not. In A. N. Joinson, K. Y. McKenna, T. Postmes, & U.-D. Reips (Eds.), *The Oxford handbook of Internet psychology* (pp. 447–459). Oxford, England: Oxford University Press.

Buchanan, T., Johnson, J. A., & Goldberg, L. R. (2005). Implementing a five-factor personality inventory for use on the Internet. *European Journal of Psychological Assessment, 21*, 115–127. doi:10.1027/1015-5759.21.2.115

Buchanan, T., & Reips, U.-D. (2001, October 10). Platform-dependent biases in Online Research: Do Mac users really think different? In K. J. Jonas, P. Breuer, B. Schauenburg, & M. Boos (Eds.), *Perspectives on Internet research: Concepts and methods.* Retrieved from http://server3.uni-psych.gwdg.de/gor/contrib/buchanan-tom

Buchanan, T., & Smith, J. L. (1999). Research on the Internet: Validation of a World-Wide Web mediated personality scale. *Behavior Research Methods, Instruments, and Computers, 31*, 565–571. doi:10.3758/BF03200736

Campbell, D., & Stanley, J. (1963). *Experimental and quasi-experimental designs for research.* Boston, MA: Houghton, Mifflin.

De Leeuw, E. D. (2005). To mix or not to mix data collection modes in surveys. *Journal of Official Statistics, 21*, 233–255.

Diedenhofen, B., Aust, F., Ullrich, S., & Musch, J. (2010, May). *Seriousness checks are useful to improve data validity in online research.* Poster presented at 12th General Online Research Conference, Pforzheim, Germany.

Dillman, D. A., & Bowker, D. K. (2001). The web questionnaire challenge to survey methodologists. In U.-D. Reips & M. Bosnjak (Eds.), *Dimensions of Internet science* (pp. 159–178). Lengerich, Germany: Pabst Science.

Dillman, D. A., Smyth, J. D., & Christian, L. M. (2008). *Internet, mail, and mixed-mode surveys: The tailored design method.* New York, NY: Wiley.

Egermann, H., Nagel, F., Altenmüller, E., & Kopiez, R. (2009). Continuous measurement of musically-induced emotion: A web experiment. *International Journal of Internet Science, 4*, 4–20.

Faul, F., Erdfelder, E., Buchner, A., & Lang, A. G. (2009). Statistical power analyses using G*Power 3.1: Tests for correlation and regression analyses. *Behavior Research Methods, 41*, 1149–1160. doi:10.3758/BRM.41.4.1149

Frauendorfer, D., & Reips, U.-D. (2009, April 6–8). *Investigating the high hurdle technique.* Paper presented at 11th General Online Research conference, Vienna.

Frick, A., Bächtiger, M. T., & Reips, U.-D. (2001). Financial incentives, personal information, and drop-out in online studies. In U.-D. Reips & M. Bosnjak (Eds.), *Dimensions of Internet science* (pp. 209–219). Lengerich, Germany: Pabst Science.

Fritsche, I., & Linneweber, V. (2006). Nonreactive methods in psychological research. In M. Eid & E. Diener (Eds.), *Handbook of multimethod measurement in psychology* (pp. 189–203). Washington, DC: American Psychological Association. doi:10.1037/11383-014

Funke, F., & Reips, U.-D. (in press). Why semantic differentials in web-based research should be made from visual analogue scales and not from 5-point scales. *Field Methods*.

Funke, F., Reips, U.-D., & Thomas, R. K. (2011). Sliders for the smart: Type of rating scale on the web interacts with educational level. *Social Science Computer Review, 29*, 221–231.

Ginsberg, J., Mohebbi, M. H., Patel, R. S., Brammer, L., Smolinski, M. S., & Brilliant, L. (2009). Detecting influenza epidemics using search engine query data. *Nature, 457*, 1012–1014. doi:10.1038/nature07634

Google Eurovision. (2010). *Eurovision 2010 forecast.* Retrieved from http://www.google.com/intl/en/landing/eurovision

Göritz, A. S. (2006). Incentives in web studies: Methodological issues and a review. *International Journal of Internet Science, 1*, 58–70.

Göritz, A. S. (2007). Using online panels in psychological research. In A. N. Joinson, K. Y. McKenna, T. Postmes, & U.-D. Reips (Eds.), *The Oxford handbook of Internet psychology* (pp. 473–485). Oxford, England: Oxford University Press.

Göritz, A. S. (2009). Building and managing an online panel with phpPanelAdmin. *Behavior Research Methods, 41*, 1177–1182. doi:10.3758/BRM.41.4.1177

Göritz, A. S., Reinhold, N., & Batinic, B. (2002). Online panels. In B. Batinic, U.-D. Reips, & M. Bosnjak (Eds.), *Online social sciences* (pp. 27–47). Göttingen, Germany: Hogrefe & Huber.

Göritz, A. S., & Stieger, S. (2008). The high-hurdle technique put to the test: Failure to find evidence that increasing loading times enhances data quality in web-based studies. *Behavior Research Methods, 40*, 322–327. doi:10.3758/BRM.40.1.322

Hartig, J., Jude, N., & Rauch, W. (2003). *Entwicklung und Erprobung eines deutschen Big-Five-Fragebogens auf Basis des International Personality Item Pools (IPIP40)* [Development and testing of a German Big Five questionnaire that is based on the International Personality Item Pool (IPIP40)]. Frankfurt, Germany: Arbeiten aus dem Institut für Psychologie der Johann Wolfgang Goethe-Universität.

Hiskey, S., & Troop, N. A. (2002). Online longitudinal survey research: Viability and participation. *Social Science Computer Review, 20*, 250–259.

Honing, H., & Reips, U.-D. (2008). Web-based versus lab-based studies: A response to Kendall (2008). *Empirical Musicology Review, 3*(2), 73–77.

Janetzko, D. (2008). Objectivity, reliability, and validity of search engine count estimates. *International Journal of Internet Science, 3*, 7–33.

Joinson, A. N., & Reips, U.-D. (2007). Personalized salutation, power of sender, and response rates to web-based surveys. *Computers in Human Behavior, 23*, 1372–1383.

Kendall, R. (2008). Commentary on "The potential of the Internet for music perception research: A comment on lab-based versus web-based studies" by Honing & Ladinig. *Empirical Musicology Review, 3*(1), 8–10.

Kirk, R. E. (1995). *Experimental design: Procedures for the behavioral sciences* (3rd ed.). Pacific Grove, CA: Brooks/Cole.

Krantz, J. H. (2001). Stimulus delivery on the web: What can be presented when calibration isn't possible? In U.-D. Reips & M. Bosnjak (Eds.), *Dimensions of Internet science* (pp. 113–130). Lengerich, Germany: Pabst Science.

Krantz, J. H., Ballard, J., & Scher, J. (1997). Comparing the results of laboratory and World-Wide Web samples on the determinants of female attractiveness. *Behavior Research Methods, Instruments, and Computers, 29*, 264–269. doi:10.3758/BF03204824

Krantz, J. H., & Williams, J. E. (2010). Using graphics, photographs, and dynamic media. In S. Gosling & J. A. Johnson (Eds.), *Advanced methods for conducting online behavioral research* (pp. 45–61). Washington, DC: American Psychological Association. doi:10.1037/12076-004

Mangan, M. A., & Reips, U.-D. (2007). Sleep, sex, and the web: Surveying the difficult-to-reach clinical population suffering from sexsomnia. *Behavior Research Methods, 39*, 233–236. doi:10.3758/BF03193152

Musch, J., & Reips, U.-D. (2000). A brief history of web experimenting. In M. H. Birnbaum (Ed.), *Psychological experiments on the Internet* (pp. 61–87). San Diego, CA: Academic Press. doi:10.1016/B978-012099980-4/50004-6

Paine, C., Reips, U.-D., Stieger, S., Joinson, A., & Buchanan, T. (2007). Internet users' perceptions of "privacy concerns" and "privacy actions." *International Journal of Human-Computer Studies, 65*, 526–536. doi:10.1016/j.ijhcs.2006.12.001

Plummer, D. C., Hafner, B., Hill, J. B., Redman, P., Brown, R. H., Dulaney, K., . . . Rosser, B. (2009). *Gartner's top predictions for IT organizations and users, 2009 and beyond: Where is the money?* Stamford, CT: Gartner Group. Retrieved from http://www.gartner.com/DisplayDocument?id=874312

Preckel, F., & Thiemann, H. (2003). Online versus paper-pencil version of a high potential intelligence test. *Swiss Journal of Psychology, 62,* 131–138. doi:10.1024//1421-0185.62.2.131

Reimers, S. (2007). The BBC Internet study: General methodology. *Archives of Sexual Behavior, 36,* 147–161. doi:10.1007/s10508-006-9143-2

Reips, U.-D. (1997). Das psychologische Experimentieren im Internet. [Psychological experimenting on the Internet]. In B. Batinic (Ed.), *Internet für Psychologen* (pp. 245–265). Göttingen, Germany: Hogrefe.

Reips, U.-D. (2000). The web experiment method: Advantages, disadvantages, and solutions. In M. H. Birnbaum (Ed.), *Psychological experiments on the Internet* (pp. 89–117). San Diego, CA: Academic Press. doi:10.1016/B978-012099980-4/50005-8

Reips, U.-D. (2001). The web Experimental Psychology Lab: Five years of data collection on the Internet. *Behavior Research Methods, Instruments, and Computers, 33,* 201–211. doi:10.3758/BF03195366

Reips, U.-D. (2002a). Context effects in web surveys. In B. Batinic, U.-D. Reips, & M. Bosnjak (Eds.), *Online social sciences* (pp. 69–79). Göttingen, Germany: Hogrefe & Huber.

Reips, U.-D. (2002b). Internet-based psychological experimenting: Five dos and five don'ts. *Social Science Computer Review, 20,* 241–249.

Reips, U.-D. (2002c). Standards for Internet-based experimenting. *Experimental Psychology, 49,* 243–256. doi:10.1026//1618-3169.49.4.243

Reips, U.-D. (2002d). Theory and techniques of conducting web experiments. In B. Batinic, U.-D. Reips, & M. Bosnjak (Eds.), *Online social sciences* (pp. 229–250). Seattle, WA: Hogrefe & Huber.

Reips, U.-D. (2003a, August 25–27). *Seamless from concepts to results: Experimental Internet science.* Paper presented at the symposium "Decision Making and the Web," 19th biannual conference on Subjective Probability, Utility, and Decision Making (SPUDM), Swiss Federal Institute of Technology (ETH), Zurich, Switzerland. Retrieved from http://iscience.deusto.es/archive/reips/SPUDM_03/index.html

Reips, U.-D. (2003b). Web-Experimente: Eckpfeiler der Online-Forschung [Web experiments: Cornerstones in online research]. In A. Theobald, M. Dreyer & T. Starsetzki (Eds.). *Online-Marktforschung: Beiträge aus Wissenschaft und Praxis* (Rev. ed., pp. 73–89). Wiesbaden, Germany: Gabler.

Reips, U.-D. (2005, November). *Collecting data in surfer's paradise: Internet-based research yesterday, now, and tomorrow.* Paper presented at the Society for Computers in Psychology (SCiP) conference, Toronto, Ontario, Canada.

Reips, U.-D. (2006). Web-based methods. In M. Eid & E. Diener (Eds.), *Handbook of multimethod measurement in psychology* (pp. 73–85). Washington, DC: American Psychological Association. doi:10.1037/11383-006

Reips, U.-D. (2007). The methodology of Internet-based experiments. In A. N. Joinson, K. Y. McKenna, T. Postmes, & U.-D. Reips (Eds.), *The Oxford handbook of Internet psychology* (pp. 373–390). Oxford, England: Oxford University Press.

Reips, U.-D. (2009). Schöne neue Forschungswelt: Zukunftstrends [Beautiful new world of research: Future trends]. *Nicht-reaktive Erhebungsverfahren* (pp. 129–138). Bonn, Germany: GESIS Schriftenreihe, Band 1.

Reips, U.-D. (2010). Design and formatting in Internet-based research. In S. D. Gosling & J. A. Johnson (Eds.), *Advanced methods for conducting online behavioral research* (pp. 29–43). Washington, DC: American Psychological Association.

Reips, U.-D., & Birnbaum, M. H. (2011). Behavioral research and data collection via the Internet. In R. W. Proctor & K.-P. L. Vu (Eds.), *The handbook of human factors in web design* (2nd ed., pp. 563–585). Mahwah, NJ: Erlbaum.

Reips, U.-D., Buffardi, L., & Kuhlmann, T. (2011, March). *Using Amazon's mechanical turk for the recruitment of participants in Internet-based research.* Paper presented at the 13th General Online Research Meeting, University of Düsseldorf, Germany.

Reips, U.-D., & Funke, F. (2008). Interval level measurement with visual analogue scales in Internet-based research: VAS Generator. *Behavior Research Methods, 40,* 699–704. doi:10.3758/BRM.40.3.699

Reips, U.-D., & Garaizar, P. (2011). Mining Twitter: Microblogging as a source for psychological wisdom of the crowds. *Behavior Research Methods, 43,* 635–642. doi:10.3758/s13428-011-0116-6

Reips, U.-D., & Krantz, J. H. (2010). Conducting true experiments on the web. In S. D. Gosling & J. A. Johnson (Eds.), *Advanced methods for conducting online behavioral research* (pp. 193–216). Washington, DC: American Psychological Association.

Reips, U.-D., & Lengler, R. (2005). The Web Experiment List: A web service for the recruitment of participants and archiving of Internet-based experiments. *Behavior Research Methods, 37,* 287–292. doi:10.3758/BF03192696

Reips, U.-D., & Neuhaus, C. (2002). WEXTOR: A web-based tool for generating and visualizing experimental designs and procedures. *Behavior Research Methods, Instruments, and Computers, 34,* 234–240. doi:10.3758/BF03195449

Reips, U.-D., & Stieger, S. (2004). Scientific LogAnalyzer: A web-based tool for analyses of server log files in psychological research. *Behavior Research Methods, Instruments, and Computers, 36,* 304–311. doi:10.3758/BF03195576

Schmidt, W. C. (2000). The server-side of psychology web experiments. In M. H. Birnbaum (Ed.), *Psychological Experiments on the Internet* (pp. 285–310). San Diego, CA: Academic Press. doi:10.1016/B978-012099980-4/50013-7

Schmidt, W. C. (2007). Technical considerations when implementing online research. In A. N. Joinson, K. Y. McKenna, T. Postmes, & U.-D. Reips (Eds.), *The Oxford handbook of Internet psychology* (pp. 461–472). Oxford, England: Oxford University Press.

Shih, T.-H., & Fan, X. (2007). Response rates and mode preferences in web-mail mixed-mode surveys: A meta-analysis. *International Journal of Internet Science, 2*, 59–82.

Sitemaps. (2010). Retrieved May 5, 2010, from http://en.wikipedia.org/wiki/Sitemaps

Smith, M. A., & Leigh, B. (1997). Virtual subjects: Using the Internet as an alternative source of subjects and research environment. *Behavior Research Methods, Instruments, and Computers, 29*, 496–505. doi:10.3758/BF03210601

Smyth, J. D., Dillman, D. A., Christian, L. M., & Stern, M. J. (2006). Effects of using visual design principles to group response options in web surveys. *International Journal of Internet Science, 1*, 6–16.

Stegbauer, C., & Rausch, A. (2002). Lurkers in mailing lists. In B. Batinic, U.-D. Reips, & M. Bosnjak (Eds.), *Online social sciences* (pp. 263–274). Seattle, WA: Hogrefe & Huber.

Stieger, S., & Reips, U.-D. (2008). Dynamic Interviewing Program (DIP): Automatic online interviews via the instant messenger ICQ. *CyberPsychology and Behavior, 11*, 201–207. doi:10.1089/cpb.2007.0030

Stieger, S., & Reips, U.-D. (2010). What are participants doing while filling in an online questionnaire? A paradata collection tool and an empirical study. *Computers in Human Behavior, 26*, 1488–1495. doi:10.1016/j.chb.2010.05.013

Stieger, S., Reips, U.-D., & Voracek, M. (2007). Forced-response in online surveys: Bias from reactance and an increase in sex-specific dropout. *Journal of the American Society for Information Science and Technology, 58*, 1653–1660. doi:10.1002/asi.20651

Tuten, T. L., Bosnjak, M., & Bandilla, W. (2000). Banner-advertised web surveys. *Marketing Research, 11*(4), 17–21.

Van Aart, C., Siebes, R., Buser, V., Aroyo, L., Raimond, Y., Brickley, D., . . . Mostarda, M. (2009, October). *The NoTube beancounter: Aggregating user data for television programme recommendation.* Paper presented at 8th International Semantic Web Conference (ISWC2009), Washington, DC. Retrieved from http://ceur-ws.org/Vol-520/paper01.pdf

Wilhelm, O., & McKnight, P. E. (2002). Ability and achievement testing on the World Wide Web. In B. Batinic, U.-D. Reips, & M. Bosnjak (Eds.), *Online social sciences* (pp. 151–180). Seattle, WA: Hogrefe & Huber.

World Wide Web Consortium. (2010). *Semantic Web.* Retrieved from http://www.w3.org/standards/semanticweb

PART III

BUILDING AND TESTING MODELS

CHAPTER 18

STATISTICAL MEDIATION ANALYSIS

David P. MacKinnon, JeeWon Cheong, and Angela G. Pirlott

Mediating variables are central to psychology because they explain the processes of psychological phenomena. As a field, psychology focuses on how an organism is intermediate in the link between a stimulus and the response to that stimulus. This focus on the organism that intervenes between stimulus and behavior was recognized early in psychology in the stimulus to organism to response (S-O-R) model (Woodworth, 1928). In this model, the organism, a person for example, translates a stimulus into a response by means of mediating processes within the individual. For example, when a list of words (S) is presented, the person (O) memorizes them and then later recalls (R) the words. This S-O-R model has been extended to understand mediating processes for other units besides individuals—such as schools, teams, and communities—and is now widely used to develop and refine prevention and treatment programs (Kazdin, 2009; MacKinnon, 2008).

Psychological theories specify mediating mechanisms that may explain psychological phenomena. For example, the theory of reasoned action (Fishbein & Ajzen, 1975) in social psychology postulates that attitudes cause intentions, which in turn cause behavior. Applying this theory to intervention research for smoking, an intervention must first change the attitudes toward the consequences of smoking, intentions to smoke, and perceptions of efficacy toward quitting, so that the person can eventually stop smoking. In cognitive psychology, memory processes mediate the transmission of information into a response. When a number of

words are presented, using pictorial cues may be more effective for word recall than memorizing the words in the presented order. Social learning theory describes how various behaviors are learned in social settings. For example, when a child watches a model being reinforced for performing a certain behavior, the child will later produce the same behavior under the same circumstances as a result of this learning process (Bandura, Ross, & Ross, 1963). In clinical psychology, a cognitive theory of depression suggests that changing cognitive attributions about the self or the world reduces depression (Beck, Rush, Shaw, & Emery, 1979). In developmental psychology, a theory of attachment postulates that deprivation at birth leads to developmental deficits, which lead to poor subsequent parenting behavior (Arling & Harlow, 1967).

In the simplest mediation theory, the investigation of mediation specifies a chain of relations by which an antecedent variable affects a mediating variable, which in turn affects a dependent variable. Mediating variables can be behavioral, biological, psychological, or social constructs that transmit the effect of one variable to another variable. There are two overlapping applications of mediation theory. One major application of mediating variables is after an effect is observed and researchers investigate how this effect occurred. This application arises from Hyman's (1955) and Lazarsfeld's (1955) outlines of elaboration methodologies. In this framework, a third variable is inserted into the analysis of an $X \rightarrow Y$ relation to improve the understanding of the relation, that is, to determine whether the relation is

DOI: 10.1037/13620-018
APA Handbook of Research Methods in Psychology: Vol. 2. Research Designs, H. Cooper (Editor-in-Chief)

due to a mediator or is spurious. The most notable citation for this approach to mediation theory is the classic Baron and Kenny (1986) article, which clarified the steps to assess mediation described in earlier references (Hyman, 1955; Lazarsfeld, 1955). Another type of application of mediation theory is selecting the mediating variables for intervention on the basis of theories specifying the causes of the dependent variable or on prior research demonstrating that these are candidate causal variables of the dependent variable. If the mediating variables are causally related to the dependent variable, then changing the mediating variables will change the dependent variable. For example, in drug prevention programs, mediating variables such as social norms or expectations about drug use are targeted to change a dependent variable such as drug use. Many researchers have emphasized the importance of considering mediation in treatment and prevention research (Baranowski, Anderson, & Carmack, 1998; Judd & Kenny, 1981a, 1981b; Kazdin, 2009; Kraemer, Wilson, Fairburn, & Agras, 2002; MacKinnon, 1994; Weiss, 1997). Evaluating mediation to explain an observed effect is probably more susceptible to chance findings than evaluating mediation by design because the mediators in the former case are often selected after the study, whereas the mediators in the latter case are selected in advance on the basis of theory and prior empirical research. Most programs of research investigating mediating variables employ both mediation by design and mediation for explanation approaches (MacKinnon, 2008, Chapter 2).

Because of the importance of identifying mediating variables in psychological research, methods to assess mediation are an area of active research. The purpose of this chapter is to outline current thinking about mediation analysis in psychology, but the length of the chapter precludes addressing all new developments, which can be found in other sources (MacKinnon, 2008; MacKinnon, Fairchild, & Fritz, 2007). This chapter first defines mediation and other third-variable effects. Statistical mediation methods using a single mediator case are then described to clarify the extensions of the single mediator model discussed in the rest of the chapter. Assumptions of the single mediator model are then

addressed, followed by sections on the latest research on statistical testing of mediated effects, such as longitudinal mediation models, mediator and moderator models, and causal inference for mediation models. Last, directions for future research are discussed.

DEFINITIONS

The simplest mediation model involves an independent variable, X, a mediating variable, M, and dependent variable, Y. As described elsewhere (MacKinnon, 2008), there are several different types of third variable effects. In its simplest form, mediation represents the addition of a third variable to an $X \rightarrow Y$ relation so that the causal sequences can be modeled such as X causes the mediator, M, and M causes Y, that is, $X \rightarrow M \rightarrow Y$. Although the mediation relation may appear simple it has several complications. One of these complications is that mediation is one of several relations that may be present when a third variable is included in the analysis of a two-variable relationship. The third variable is a confounding variable if it causes both X and Y; ignoring the third variable leads to an inaccurate inference about the relation of X and Y. If the third variable is related to X or Y so that information about the third variable improves prediction of Y by X, but including the third variable in the analysis does not substantially alter the relation of X to Y, the third variable is a covariate. If the third variable modifies the relation of X to Y such that the X to Y relation differs at different values of the third variable, the third variable is a moderator. A mediator differs from each of these other third variable effects in that the mediator is in a causal sequence such that X causes M and M causes Y (Kraemer et al., 2002; MacKinnon, Krull, & Lockwood, 2000; Robins & Greenland, 1992, for more information on the third variable effects).

MEDIATION REGRESSION EQUATIONS

The single mediator model or $X \rightarrow M \rightarrow Y$ is shown in Figure 18.1 and in Equations 1 to 3:

$$Y = i_1 + c\,X + e_1, \tag{1}$$

$$Y = i_2 + c' X + b M + e_2, \qquad (2)$$

$$M = i_3 + a X + e_3, \qquad (3)$$

where Y is the dependent variable, X is the independent variable, and M is the mediator; the coefficients i_1, i_2, and i_3 are intercepts in each equation; and e_1, e_2, and e_3 are residuals. In Equation 1, the coefficient c represents the total effect (i.e., the total effect that X can have on Y). In Equation 2, the coefficient c' denotes the relation between X and Y controlling for M, representing the direct effect (i.e., the effect of X on Y that is not intervened by M). The coefficient b denotes the relation between M and Y controlling for X. Finally, in Equation 3, the coefficient a indicates the relation between X and M. Equations 2 and 3 are represented in Figure 18.1, which shows how the total effect of X on Y is separated into a direct effect relating X to Y and a mediated effect where X has an indirect effect on Y through M. The current practice of statistical mediation analysis can be grouped into three approaches: (a) causal steps, (b) difference in coefficients, and (c) product of coefficients (MacKinnon, Lockwood, et al., 2002), which are all based on the information from the regression equations for testing the single mediator model.

The first approach to statistical mediation analysis, called the *causal steps approach*, is based on the influential work of Baron and Kenny (1986; Kenny, Kashy, & Bolger, 1998) and Judd and Kenny (1981a, 1981b), originating in Hyman (1955) and Lazarsfeld (1955). In this approach, a researcher conducts four steps of analyses to establish mediation and estimate Equations 1 to 3. First, the independent variable X should be significantly related to the dependent variable Y, resulting in the significant coefficient $\hat{c}$ in Equation 1. Second, the independent variable X should be significantly related to the hypothesized mediating variable M, producing a significant coefficient $\hat{a}$ in Equation 3. Third, the mediating variable M must be significantly related to the dependent variable Y, controlling for the independent variable X, thus finding a significant coefficient $\hat{b}$, in Equation 2. Finally, the relation between the independent variable X and the dependent variable Y should be weaker when the mediating variable M is added to the model. Thus, the coefficient $\hat{c}'$ should be smaller than the coefficient $\hat{c}$ (i.e., $\hat{c} - \hat{c}' > 0$). In the causal steps approach, the conditions by which a potential mediator is identified as a significant mediator are clearly established, but the mediated effect is not directly estimated.

The other two approaches, the *difference in coefficients* and the *product of coefficients* approaches, involve estimation of the mediated or indirect effect and its standard error, allowing formal tests for significance of the mediated effects. In the difference in coefficients approach, the mediated effect is estimated by comparing the relations between the independent variable X and the dependent variable Y from Equations 1 and 2, where the effect of X on Y is estimated with and without adjusting for the mediator M. The idea is that the mediated effect can be estimated by the difference between the total effect

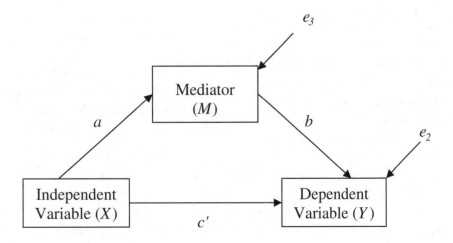

FIGURE 18.1.   Single mediator model.

and the direct effect that is not attributable to the mediator, $\hat{c} - \hat{c}'$. In the product of coefficients approach, the mediated effect is estimated by the product of $\hat{a}$ and $\hat{b}$, $\hat{a}\hat{b}$ (Alwin & Hauser, 1975), from Equations 2 and 3. Thus, the mediated effect reflects the extent to which the independent variable X changes the mediator M and the extent to which the mediator changes the dependent variable Y. The quantities in Equations 1 to 3 can also be presented in a plot as described elsewhere (MacKinnon, 2008).

The mediated effect estimated in the difference in coefficients approach, $\hat{c} - \hat{c}'$, is algebraically equivalent to the mediated effect obtained in the product of coefficients approach, $\hat{a}\hat{b}$, under the normal theory ordinary least squares and maximum likelihood estimation, as long as the same sample is used for Equations 1 to 3 (MacKinnon, Warsi, & Dwyer, 1995). When the mediated effect is assessed in multilevel models (Krull & MacKinnon, 1999) and logistic or probit regression (MacKinnon & Dwyer, 1993), the two estimates of the mediated effect, $\hat{a}\hat{b}$ and $\hat{c} - \hat{c}'$, are not always equivalent.

Although the statistical mediation analysis is straightforward under the assumption that the model is correctly specified, the identification of mediation relations has several complications which can only be addressed in a program of research (MacKinnon, 2008). For example, like all statistical analyses, it is often helpful to consider two models, the population or true model and the sample model. The population model represents the true relations among variables, those relations that we would see if we had the entire population. As a sample of data represents one of many different samples from the population, sample estimates of population parameters vary from sample to sample. Generally, it is assumed that the equations and variables specified in the sample model are the same equations in the population model. There are qualifications even to this sample–population dichotomy. For example, causal inference approaches to mediation suggest another superpopulation model that represents the true causal relations among variables with all assumptions validated, similar to the theoretical mediation model described by MacCorquodale and Meehl (1948). The challenge of using sample data to uncover mediation relations is that evidence for

mediation must come from a program of research, including a variety of designs and approaches to uncovering true mediation relations.

Standard Error of the Mediated Effect

One of the most frequently used standard errors of the mediated effect is the first-order solution derived by Sobel (1982, 1986) using the multivariate delta method (Bishop, Fienberg, & Holland, 1975) as follows:

$$\sigma_{\hat{a}\hat{b}} = \sqrt{\sigma_{\hat{a}}^2 \hat{b}^2 + \sigma_{\hat{b}}^2 \hat{a}^2}, \tag{4}$$

where $\hat{a}$ and $\hat{b}$ are estimated regression coefficients and $\sigma_{\hat{a}}^2$ and $\sigma_{\hat{b}}^2$ are the squared standard error of $\hat{a}$ and $\hat{b}$ from Equations 2 and 3. The formula shown in Equation 4 is implemented in various structural equation modeling programs, such as EQS (Bentler, 1997) and Mplus (L. K. Muthén & Muthén, 1998–2007), for testing significance of mediated or indirect effects. Alternative formulas for the standard error for different approaches can be found in MacKinnon (2008) and MacKinnon, Lockwood, Hoffman, West, and Sheets (2002).

Confidence Limits for the Mediated Effect

Confidence limits of the mediated effects can be constructed using the estimated mediated effect and its standard error. The upper and lower confidence limits are as follows:

Upper confidence limit (UCL) = mediated effect + $z_{Type\,I\,error}(\sigma_{\hat{a}\hat{b}})$. (5)

Lower confidence limit (LCL) = mediated effect − $z_{Type\,I\,error}(\sigma_{\hat{a}\hat{b}})$. (6)

For example, when the mediated effect is calculated by the product of the coefficients, $\hat{a}\hat{b}$, and the standard error is estimated by Equation 4, the confidence limits are obtained as follows:

$$\hat{a}\hat{b} \pm z_{Type\,I\,error} * \sigma_{\hat{a}\hat{b}}. \tag{7}$$

As the mediated effect is the product of two regression coefficients, its distribution most closely follows the distribution of the product of two normally distributed random variables, which may not be normally distributed (Springer, 1979). As a result, more accurate confidence limits can be obtained by using the distribution of the product of the two random variables to obtain critical values (MacKinnon, Fritz, Williams, & Lockwood, 2007). PRODCLIN (MacKinnon, Fritz et al., 2007) is a new program that provides critical values of the distribution of the product of the two random variables and computes confidence intervals for the mediated effects (PRODCLIN can be found at http://www.public.asu.edu/~davidpm/ripl/Prodclin/).

Alternatively, resampling methods such as bootstrapping can be used to compute confidence intervals that adjust for the nonnormal distribution of the product of coefficients (Bollen & Stine, 1990; MacKinnon, Lockwood, & Williams, 2004; Preacher & Hayes, 2004; Shrout & Bolger, 2002). From the original sample data, repeated samples are obtained, and on the basis of the mediation effects estimated from these repeated samples, an empirical sampling distribution is formed to determine the significance of the mediated effect and to construct the confidence intervals (Efron & Tibshirani, 1993; Manly, 1997). Resampling methods are also useful when assumptions of statistical methods are not met, such as data with nonnormal distributions, and also provide confidence limits for more complex mediation models. More on resampling methods for mediation is described in MacKinnon (2008, Chapter 12).

Significance Testing

A statistical significance test for the mediated effect can be conducted in several ways. One way to test the mediated effect is to assess whether the confidence interval includes zero. When zero is not included in the confidence interval, the mediated effect is statistically significant or the hypothesized mediator is considered a statistically significant mediator. Another way to test the significance of the mediation effect is to obtain the ratio of the estimated mediated effect to its standard error and compare the ratio with the critical values under the normal distributions. For example, $\hat{a}\hat{b}$ is divided by the standard error in Equation 4 and this ratio is compared with ± 1.96. If the ratio is greater than 1.96 or smaller than -1.96, the mediated effect is significantly different from zero. In simulation studies (MacKinnon, Lockwood et al., 2002; MacKinnon et al., 2004) of the statistical performance of 14 commonly used methods for testing the significance of mediation, the most widely used causal step methods showed quite low power and low Type I error rates. Power was also low for the methods that assume the normal distribution of mediated effect, in which the estimated mediated effect ($\hat{a}\hat{b}$ or $\hat{c} - \hat{c}'$) is divided by its respective standard error and the ratio is compared with the critical values of z or t distribution. A method testing the significance of $\hat{a}$ and $\hat{b}$ and considering there to be significant mediation if both tests are statistically significant (i.e., joint significance test) showed a good balance between Type I and Type II errors, as did methods based on the distribution of the product of two regression coefficients or bootstrap resampling.

The low power of most methods for testing mediation can be explained in several ways. The low power of the causal steps approach results from the requirement of the first step that the relation between X and Y be significant, especially in the case of complete mediation (i.e., direct effect c' is zero). There are cases in which the mediated effect is statistically significant, even if the relation between X and Y in Equation 1 is not significant, such as in inconsistent mediation, in which the direction of the mediated effect is the opposite of the direction of the direct effect. Investigating the overall relation of X and Y provides useful information for some research; however, requiring the significant relation between X and Y for mediation to exist substantially reduces power to detect real mediation effects for the causal steps approach. The low power of the methods using the product of the coefficients and the difference in the coefficients is due to the nonnormality of the distribution of the mediated effects (MacKinnon et al., 2004). This nonnormality issue can be resolved with resampling methods and the methods based on the distribution of the product of ab described earlier.

Complete Versus Partial Mediation

The total effect c is the sum of the mediated effect (ab or $c - c'$) and the direct effect c'. Complete mediation is defined as a case where the total effect is completely explained by the mediator. In sample data, complete mediation is observed when the mediated effect is statistically significant (i.e., $\hat{a}\hat{b} \neq 0$) and the direct effect is not statistically significant (i.e., $\hat{c}' = 0$), implying that for the population model the mediated effect and total effect are equal (i.e., $ab = c$). Partial mediation refers to the case where the relation between the independent and the dependent variables is not completely accounted for by the mediator. In sample data, both the mediated effect and the direct effect are statistically significant (i.e., $\hat{a}\hat{b} \neq 0$ and $\hat{c}' \neq 0$), indicating that the mediator significantly accounts for part of the relation between the independent and the dependent variables, consistent with mediated and direct effects in the population model (i.e., $ab \neq 0$ and $c' \neq 0$). Considering the complexity of the behaviors studied in social science research, there may be a variety of causes of those behaviors, and thus it is often more realistic to expect that a single mediator would only partially explain the relation between the independent and the dependent variables (Baron & Kenny, 1986). James, Mulaik, and Brett (2006) argued for the specification of complete or partial mediation prior to study and first testing for complete mediation. The test for complete mediation does not include the c' parameter in the model, and as a result, inadequate model fit in covariance structure analysis suggests incomplete mediation. If theory predicts complete mediation, this approach provides a straightforward way to test mediation.

MEDIATION EQUATIONS WITH TWO MEDIATORS

The two-mediator model helps to compare the causal steps, difference in coefficients, and product of coefficients approaches to testing mediation in more complicated models. When the mediation model includes two mediators, the regression equations can be expanded as follows (MacKinnon, 2008):

$$Y = i_1 + c X + e_1, \tag{8}$$

$$Y = i_2 + c' X + b_1 M_1 + b_2 M_2 + e_2, \tag{9}$$

$$M_1 = i_3 + a_1 X + e_3, \tag{10}$$

$$M_2 = i_4 + a_2 X + e_4, \tag{11}$$

where X is the single independent variable, M_1 and M_2 are two mediators, and Y is the dependent variable. The coefficients a_1 and a_2 represent the relations between the independent variable and the two mediators, respectively. The coefficients b_1 and b_2 represent the relations between each mediator and the dependent variable controlling for the independent variable and the other mediator. Again, an estimator of the mediated effect can be obtained by the difference between the total effect and the direct effect, that is, $\hat{c} - \hat{c}'$ or by the product of the relevant coefficients (i.e., $\hat{a}_1\hat{b}_1$ and $\hat{a}_2\hat{b}_2$). The estimator of $\hat{c} - \hat{c}'$ is the total mediated effect, that is, the mediated effect via both M_1 and M_2. On the other hand, the estimators of $\hat{a}_1\hat{b}_1$ and $\hat{a}_2\hat{b}_2$ are the mediated effects uniquely attributable to M_1 and M_2, respectively.

The two-mediator Equations 8, 9, 10, and 11 demonstrate the superiority of the product of coefficients approach compared with the causal steps and difference in coefficients tests. Each method is relatively easily applied to the case of a single mediator; however, only the product of coefficients method is directly applicable to more complicated models. Causal steps and difference score methods could be applied but are more cumbersome. With two mediators, there are now three mediated effects, the effect of X on Y through M_1, the effect of X on Y through M_2, and the total mediated effect of X on Y through M_1 and M_2, called the total indirect effect. With the causal steps method, it is possible to test the significance of the $\hat{a}$ and $\hat{b}$ paths corresponding to each mediated effect, but there is not a direct test of the total mediated effect, the sum of $\hat{a}_1\hat{b}_1$ and $\hat{a}_2\hat{b}_2$. The other limitation of the causal steps method is that there is not a direct point estimate and standard error useful for confidence limits and effect size calculation. In the product of coefficients method, however, it is much more straightforward to test whether the total mediated effect, the sum of $\hat{a}_1\hat{b}_1$ and $\hat{a}_2\hat{b}_2$, is statistically significant either by forming the ratio of the estimate to estimated standard error or by creating confidence limits via a resampling method. The difference score method is appropriate to test the total indirect effect because it is the difference between the relation of X on Y before and after adjustment for both mediators, $\hat{c} - \hat{c}'$. The standard error of this difference for the total indirect effect is given in MacKinnon (2008). However, the difference in coefficients method is quite cumbersome for testing the specific indirect effects, $\hat{a}_1\hat{b}_1$ or $\hat{a}_2\hat{b}_2$, because it is not clear which coefficients would be compared. These problems with causal steps and difference in coefficients methods are magnified in more complicated models. These quantities can be obtained in a straightforward manner with the product of coefficients method.

CONSISTENT AND INCONSISTENT MODELS

Consistent or inconsistent mediation models are determined by the signs of the mediated and the direct effects. For consistent mediation models, all the mediated and the direct effects in a model have the same sign. Inconsistent mediation models, on the other hand, include at least one mediated effect having the opposite sign to the other mediated or direct effects in the model (Blalock, 1969; Davis, 1985; MacKinnon et al., 2000). When the signs of the mediated effect(s) and the direct effect are inconsistent, the overall relation between the independent and the dependent variables (i.e., the total effect) may not be statistically significant, as described in MacKinnon et al. (2000).

The two-mediator model also is helpful to demonstrate inconsistent mediation effects. Sheets and Braver (1999) hypothesized that an overall relation between social dominance and sexual harassment would be zero because of opposing mediated effects via the harasser's power (M_1) and desirability (M_2). There are other hypothetical examples of possible counterproductive effects. For example, an abstinence program may increase intentions to abstain but participating in the program may also increase interest in sexual activity leading to a null program effect because of opposing mediators. For another example, incarceration in prison may lead to rehabilitation, which reduces recidivism, but exposure to fellow inmates in prison may also engender a norm more favorable toward criminal activity, which then increases recidivism. It is possible that any intervention would have opposing mediation effects when the program is composed of multiple components designed to change the outcome. The

opposing mediation relations would be observed more easily if multiple mediator models are estimated.

EFFECT SIZE MEASURES OF MEDIATION

Effect size in mediation models can be specified for each path involved in the mediation pathway and for the entire mediated effect. To specify the effect size of each path, correlations, partial correlations, and standardized coefficients are used. There are several ways to define effect size of the entire mediated effect. One of the most commonly used effect size measures is the proportion mediated, which is obtained by the ratio of the mediated effect to the total effect, that is, $\hat{a}\hat{b}/(\hat{a}\hat{b}+\hat{c}')$. The proportion mediated has heuristic value, in that researchers can gauge the effect size in terms of the proportion of the total effect that is mediated. Limitations of the proportion mediated effect include the large sample size requirements (MacKinnon et al., 1995), ambiguity when effects are small, and ambiguity in interpretation for inconsistent mediation models when the mediated and the direct effects have the opposite signs (taking absolute values of all the effects before calculating the proportion mediated may be helpful in this case; see Alwin & Hauser, 1975). Other measures of effect size for the entire mediated effect are the ratio of the mediated effect to direct effect, $\hat{a}\hat{b}/\hat{c}'$, R^2 measures (Fairchild, MacKinnon, Taborga, & Taylor, 2009), and effect standardized by variance of the dependent variable (see MacKinnon, 2008, for information on mediation effect size measures).

ASSUMPTIONS OF THE SINGLE MEDIATOR MODEL

Most current developments in mediation analysis address statistical and inferential assumptions of the mediation model. For the $\hat{a}\hat{b}$ estimator of the mediated effect, several simultaneous regression analysis assumptions are required, including that the mediator and the residual in Equation 2 are independent and also that the residuals in Equations 2 and 3 are independent (MacKinnon, 2008; McDonald, 1997). It is also assumed that there is not an interaction between X and M in Equation 3, although this interaction can be tested and in some cases may be expected on the basis of the theory outlined in the next section. The temporal order of the variables in the model is also assumed to be correctly specified (e.g., $X \rightarrow M \rightarrow Y$ rather than $X \rightarrow Y \rightarrow M$). Several other types of model specification are assumed to be correct, including self-containment—that no variables related to the variables in the mediation equations are left out of the estimated model and that coefficients estimate causal effects. It is also assumed that the model has minimal errors of measurement (Holland, 1988; James & Brett, 1984; McDonald, 1997).

Assumption of No Interaction Between X and M

The $X \times M$ interaction could be included in Equation 2, which would suggest a moderator effect such that the b coefficient differs across the levels of X. Different b coefficients across levels of X may reflect that an experimental manipulation may have changed the relation of M to Y. For example, a smoking prevention program may remove a relation between offers to use tobacco (M) and subsequent tobacco use (Y) in the program group but not for participants in the control group, because persons exposed to the program learned skills to refuse offers of tobacco so that offers are not significantly related to tobacco use (Judd & Kenny, 1981a). Significant XM interactions may also be obtained when there are other nonlinear relations in the model. If a program increases M to a value so that the relation between M and Y differs from the relation at other levels of M, the XM interaction would be statistically significant because of a nonlinear relation between X and Y. If there is some other variable that is an important mediator it is possible that this variable may predict both M and Y, leading to a statistically significant XM interaction.

Assumption of Correct Model Specification

There have been many important recent extensions to address limitations of the standard mediation analysis described thus far. First, more complicated models are often hypothesized. These models may include multiple independent variables, multiple mediators, and multiple outcomes. With these more comprehensive models, the relations among variables in the mediation model may be more explicitly specified and the mediation effects may be more accurately estimated. Second, when the data are clustered, methods for testing mediation within and across levels have been developed to accommodate the statistical issues in multilevel analysis and also to explore the rich information in multiple levels of analysis (Krull & MacKinnon, 1999, 2001; Preacher, Zyphur, & Zhang, 2010). Third, mediation effects may differ by subgroups defined by moderator variables both within (such as M or Y) the mediation model and outside (variables other than M or Y) the mediation model (Fairchild & MacKinnon, 2009; Muller, Judd, & Yzerbyt, 2005; Preacher et al., 2010). Fourth, mediation requires temporal precedence clarifying that X affects M that affects Y in a longitudinal or temporal order (Gollob & Reichardt, 1991; Kraemer et al., 2002; MacKinnon, 2008). Finally, developments in the causal interpretation of mediation studies (Holland, 1988; Robins & Greenland, 1992) provide a useful framework to describe the strengths and limitations of possible causal inferences from a mediation study.

MEDIATION WITH CATEGORICAL OUTCOMES

In some mediation studies the dependent variable is categorical, such as whether a person suffered a heart attack or died or not. In such cases, Equations 1 and 2 must be rewritten for logistic or probit regression, so that the dependent variable is a latent continuous variable that has been dichotomized for the analysis. Because the residual variances in logistic or probit regression are fixed, the parameters c, c', and b depend on the other predictor variables in the model. So, the differences in coefficients across models could reflect real differences, but they could also be artificial effects caused by the fixed error variance (MacKinnon, 2008). For example, the estimator $\hat{c} - \hat{c}'$ for mediation may be incorrect because the parameter estimate of $\hat{c}'$ depends on the true relation of the mediator to the outcome and the scaling of Equations 1 and 2 (MacKinnon & Dwyer, 1993). A solution to this discrepancy is to standardize regression coefficients before estimating mediation (MacKinnon, Lockwood, Brown, Wang, & Hoffman, 2007; Winship & Mare, 1983), which will bring the two estimates of the mediated effect closer in value.

LONGITUDINAL MEDIATION MODELS

When the same variables are measured repeatedly, researchers can examine more complex questions regarding mediating mechanisms. The time ordering of X, M, and Y can be specified in the mediation model with longitudinal data and researchers can be more confident in the causal sequence of the mediation effect than in cross-sectional studies. Longitudinal data also allow researchers to investigate mediation in terms of within-individual changes. For example, mediation can be modeled as X causes changes in M between pre- and post-test, which, in turn, causes changes in Y between pre- and post-test. In addition, one can examine the stability of effects across time, such as whether the effect of X on M or the effect of M on Y are stable across time, and test the stability of the mediation effect across time. However, it is challenging to determine the optimal timing of measurements to accurately assess when longitudinal relations occur. Also, researchers need to pay more attention to the potential misspecification of the model, such as omitted variables or paths, and hypothesizing correct mediation pathways (Cheong, 2011; Cole & Maxwell, 2003; Collins, Graham, & Flaherty, 1998).

Although there are various ways to model longitudinal mediation relations (MacKinnon, 2008), we present four approaches: autoregressive models, latent growth curve models, latent difference scores models, and person-oriented longitudinal models. Besides these approaches, one can combine the autoregressive model and latent growth curve model (Bollen & Curran, 2004) or specify the model parameters in a continuous time metric to reflect different time intervals between measurements (Boker & Nesselroade, 2002; Fritz, 2007).

Autoregressive Mediation Model

In the typical autoregressive mediation model, relations among X, M, and Y one measurement occasion apart are specified. When the mediation is evaluated in autoregressive models, researchers have several options for modeling mediation. First, one can focus only on the relations consistent with longitudinal mediation, such as $X_{T1} \rightarrow M_{T2} \rightarrow Y_{T3}$, assuming that mediation would not occur within the same wave. Another possibility is to add contemporary mediation relations (e.g., $X_{T2} \rightarrow M_{T2}$, $M_{T2} \rightarrow Y_{T2}$) to the longitudinal autoregressive mediation model and estimate the contemporary mediation effect within each wave, except the first wave, for which the relations among X, M, and Y are typically specified as correlated. A third type of autoregressive mediation model includes any possible relations among X, M, and Y, including longitudinal relations based on time ordering (e.g., $M_{T1} \rightarrow X_{T2}$, $Y_{T2} \rightarrow M_{T3}$), which may be counterintuitive in that the directions of the relations among X, M, and Y are the opposite to the hypothesized mediation model. This type of model, however, may be more realistic, considering that X, M, and Y are interrelated. It is possible that M_{T2} is predicted by Y_{T1} because Y_{T1} is related to M_{T1}.

Regardless of the type of autoregressive model, the estimated mediation effect and its standard error can be obtained in the usual way, using the relevant path coefficients and their estimates of standard errors, to test the significance of the point estimate of mediation and construct confidence intervals. More details on autoregressive mediation models can be found in MacKinnon (2008) and Gollob and Reichardt (1991).

Autoregressive mediation models are beneficial because they can provide information about time-specific mediation effects, such as when the mediation effects start to occur or when they stop working. It is a common practice, however, to estimate autoregressive models only using covariance structure without mean structure, resulting in reliance on the order of individuals in the variables and ignoring the level of longitudinal changes (see also Dwyer, 1983; Rogosa, 1988). In addition, as with many potential mediation effects, it may not be easy to determine which mediation relation represents the true model.

Latent Growth Mediation Model

When latent growth modeling (LGM) is applied for testing mediation, the mediation process is typically modeled using parallel process models (see B. O. Muthén & Curran, 1997; Singer & Willett, 2003, for more on LGM), where the growth trajectories of X, M, and Y are estimated in three distinctive growth trajectories and the mediation is hypothesized in the relations among the growth factors. Typically, researchers examine whether the slope of X affects the slope of M and whether the slope of M, in turn, affects the slope of Y. Alternatively, mediation can be evaluated in the relations among the initial level of X, the slope of M, and the slope of Y. As in the mediation models described in earlier sections, the relation between the trajectory of X and the trajectory of Y has two sources: the indirect effect via the trajectory of M and the direct effect on the trajectory of Y. The unique aspect of testing mediation in the LGM framework is that the mediation is modeled for individual changes, rather than the levels of individuals on the variables. Thus, one can examine whether the greater changes in Y are the results of the greater or smaller changes in M.

When the mediated effect is examined on the basis of the relations of the slope factors of X, M, and Y that are measured across the same time periods, a causality explanation is limited because the relations among the slopes of the three trajectories are correlational. When the variable X represents randomized group status, the effect of X on the slope of M can be interpreted as causal, but the relation between the slope of M and the slope of Y is still correlational. One way to improve causal explanation in the LGM mediation model is using the two-stage piecewise parallel process model (Cheong, MacKinnon, & Khoo, 2003), in which X affects the growth of M at an earlier phase, which then affects the growth of Y at a later phase. Measures are very important in LGM mediation models. If the measures change over time, the interpretation of the change will be confounded. For example, if the items measuring aggression are modified to measure aggressive behaviors that are age appropriate, it is difficult to determine whether the observed change is due to the changes in aggression or due to the changes in measures. For this reason, measurement invariance across time may need to be tested before modeling the mediational process in LGM framework.

Latent Change Score Model

As in the LGM approach to mediation, latent change score (LCS) models also examine the relations among the changes in X, M, and Y. Although the changes in the LGM approach are estimated on the basis of several waves across time, the changes in the LCS approach are estimated on the basis of pairs of adjacent waves (Ferrer & McArdle, 2003; McArdle, 2001; McArdle & Nesselroade, 2003). Again, the relation between the change in X and the change in Y are composed of two parts (i.e., the indirect effect via the change in M and the direct effect) and the interpretation of mediation is similar to the LGM approach: the change in X affects the change in M, which then affects the change in Y.

In the LCS modeling, the true scores at each wave and the change scores between waves are estimated using latent variables and fixed parameters. Once the change scores are obtained, these change scores are then analyzed using the same equations as for cross-sectional models. LCS mediation models with more than two waves of data are particularly informative when researchers expect different mediation mechanisms for changes at different waves of measurement. For example, the treatment program may change adolescent drug use via change in parental monitoring at early adolescence but via change in peer norms at later adolescence. In addition, researchers can test time-specific mediation, as in autoregressive mediation models, by investigating when the changes in X start to affect the changes in M or when the program effects start to decay. In addition, one can examine the change in the difference scores in LCS models and specify the models to represent moving averages.

Person-Oriented Longitudinal Models

Several different approaches have been suggested to identify subgroups of persons on the basis of their values of the independent variable, mediating variable, and dependent variable. Typically, binary latent variables are created to indicate individuals' status, that is, to signify whether the individual's responses are consistent with hypothesized mediation pattern or not. Two of these original approaches are based on trajectory classes (L. K. Muthén & Muthén, 1998–2007) and staged responses across trials (Collins et al., 1998). These models represent several new ways to understand mediational processes at both the individual level as well as the group level (von Eye, Mun, & Mair, 2009). A related approach to identifying mediational processes is to focus on single-subjects data with repeated measures. In this approach, mediation relations observed with one subject are tested with future subjects to provide cumulative evidence for a mediation relation. In some research areas where sample sizes are small, such as some clinical populations, single-subject methods may be the only reasonable approach.

MODERATION AND MEDIATION

The strength and form of mediation relations may depend on other variables. For example, the relation of X to M (a path) or M to Y (b path) may differ across levels of a moderator variable, resulting in different mediated effect (ab) across levels of moderator variable. The moderator variable may be either an experimentally manipulated factor or a naturally occurring variable, such as gender or ethnicity. These types of models have been an active area of research in the past few years (Fairchild & MacKinnon, 2009; MacKinnon, 2008; Muller et al., 2005). One way to organize the different types of mediation analysis with moderator variables is to consider two different types of cases: (a) moderation of a mediated effect and (b) mediation of a moderator effect.

Moderation of a Mediated Effect

In the first case, moderation of a mediation relation, the X to M, M to Y, or the entire mediation relation may differ across levels of a moderator variable, such as subgroups of participants (e.g., cohorts, ages, or sexes). For a single mediator case, the application of moderation of a mediation analysis consists of estimating the same mediation model for each subgroup and then comparing the X to M relation, the M to Y relation, and the mediated effect across subgroups. The equivalence of the mediated effect across groups can be tested (MacKinnon, 2008). Tests of the equality of $\hat{a}$, $\hat{b}$, and $\hat{c}'$ coefficients provides information about the invariance of action theory (how the program changes mediators) and the invariance of conceptual theory

(how mediators are related to the outcome) across groups. The moderation of a mediated effect is more complex when the moderator variable is continuous. Although the regression equations are the same as for the categorical moderator case, the interpretation of results may be complicated for the continuous moderator case because of the large number of values of the moderator at which mediation relations may potentially differ. One approach is to apply a multilevel mediation model to these data (Asparouhov & Muthén, 2008; L. K. Muthén & Muthén, 1998–2007).

Mediation of a Moderator Effect

In a second type of mediation and moderation analysis, mediation of a moderator effect may be investigated. In this situation, a mediating variable is sought to explain how an interaction between two variables is related to a dependent variable, that is, to investigate evidence that the mediator transmits the relation from an interaction to a dependent variable. One common example from the treatment and prevention literature is that program effects are greater for high-risk subjects so that the interaction effect is of program exposure and risk status. In this case, the interaction may affect a mediating variable of social norms that then affects drug use. The purpose of mediation of a moderator analysis is to assess whether the mediating variable(s) explains the interaction effect. Investigation of these effects consists of estimating a series of regression equations for which the main effect of a covariate and the interaction of the covariate and the independent variable are included in both Equations 2 and 3.

To date, models investigating mediation and moderation have been largely independent, which is not surprising given the complexity of investigating mediation and moderation alone. This separation in the theory and statistical testing between moderation and mediation has contributed to some ambiguity regarding the substantive motivation and statistical testing of these models. A critical goal of future research for mediation and moderation models will be to further develop and evaluate a general model in which each of the models is a special case (Fairchild & MacKinnon, 2009; MacKinnon, 2008; Muller et al., 2005).

CAUSAL INFERENCE

Methods for testing mediation that are based on regression and structural equation modeling approaches have been criticized from the perspective of counterfactual approaches to causal analysis of the relations among variables (MacKinnon, 2008, Chapter 13). Limitations to mediation models in particular and structural equation models in general have been outlined in the social science (Holland, 1988; James et al., 2006; Morgan & Winship, 2007) and epidemiological literature (Robins & Greenland, 1992). One widely known limitation of these models is the equivalent model criticism. Applied to the mediation model, if X, M, and Y are measured at the same time, other equivalent models (e.g., $M \rightarrow X \rightarrow Y$ or $M \rightarrow X \leftarrow Y$) would explain the data equally well and are often indistinguishable without more information (Spirtes, Glymour, & Scheines, 1993). Another limitation is the temporal precedence assumption. Cross-sectional data require additional assumptions if they are to be interpreted in a causal fashion. A third limitation is the aforementioned assumption of no omitted variables. When X represents randomization to conditions, inference regarding X to M and X to Y relations is less problematic. With randomization of a sufficient number of units to levels of X, all unmeasured covariates are assumed to be balanced between groups at baseline and, thus, the relation of X to M and the relation of X to Y (that is not adjusted for M) can be attributed to the randomized manipulation. However, inference regarding the M to Y and X to Y adjusted for M relations is problematic because individuals are not randomly assigned to the levels of M and thus omitted variables may seriously affect the interpretation of the $\hat{b}$ and $\hat{c}'$ coefficients.

Modern causal inference approaches suggest strategies for investigating assumptions of the statistical methods, especially the ambiguity regarding the interpretation of the M to Y relation. When X represents random assignment to conditions, causal interpretation of mediating variables is improved (Holland, 1988; Robins & Greenland, 1992) because X must causally precede M and Y. Holland showed that under some assumptions, the regression coefficient for the intervention effect on Y, $\hat{c}$, and the intervention effect on M, $\hat{a}$, are estimators of the true causal effect because of the randomization of units to treatment. In contrast, the regression coefficient, $\hat{b}$, is not an accurate causal effect estimator because this relation is correlational—participants are not directly randomized to scores on the mediator. Along the same logic, the estimator, $\hat{c}'$, is also not an accurate causal estimator of the direct effect because this relation is also correlational. These approaches provide an instrumental variable approach, whereby an estimate of the true causal relation between M and Y is the extent to which the predicted scores in the X to M relation, M', are related to Y, assuming a linear additive relation of M to Y and assuming that there is no direct effect of X on Y (i.e., complete mediation). Several new approaches to causal inference for mediation have added to this original work. These methods use additional information, such as covariates or specifying types of persons on the basis of their response to any intervention, to improve causal inference of mediation effects. One of these promising alternatives is based on ways in which participants could respond to an intervention and estimates the mediated effect within these stratifications (Angrist, Imbens, & Rubin, 1996; Frangakis & Rubin, 2002; Jo, 2008). For example, different types of persons are identified, such as persons who would acquire the mediator if exposed to the intervention and persons who would not get the mediator whether exposed to it or not. Sobel (2007) enhanced the Holland (1988) instrumental variable method to further investigate assumptions of the method. Other alternatives use randomization approaches on the basis of covariates to model observed and counterfactual data (Lynch, Cary, Gallop, & Ten Have, 2008; Pearl, 2009; Robins, 1994; Ten Have et al., 2007).

One of the most important contributions of these causal inference approaches is that they provide alternative ways to improve causal interpretation in mediation analysis especially for the M to Y relation. However, the fact that the M to Y relation in the mediation model is considered the weakest link is interesting from the perspective of theories in psychology. In most psychological studies, the M to Y relation is specified on the basis of theory, extensive prior research, and a variety of information besides statistical analysis, and mediators are selected because of this information. The emphasis on ambiguity of the M to Y relation may be reduced in psychology because it is generally much easier to conduct replication and extension experiments in psychology compared with some other disciplines, such as medicine, for which conducting studies is often more expensive and requires extensive follow-up for disease processes to emerge. The application of causal inference approaches in psychology will remain an important and active area of research in part because it illuminates untested assumptions in mediation theory. Regarding the causal interpretation of mediation relations, researchers have several options based on current research practice. First, new models of causal inference can be applied to mediation analysis, although this may be difficult given the paucity of clear, concrete examples of their application in psychology. Second, one can treat the results of the mediation analysis as descriptive information, rather than true underlying causal mediation relations, especially for the M to Y relation, and address the variety of limitations of such a mediation analysis. Third, one can plan future experimental studies to provide evidence for the consistency and specificity of mediation relations as described in the next section. These future studies may also include qualitative methods and clinical observations. In particular, a program of research that repeatedly tests mediator theory, including testing mediation theory in other contexts, provides the most convincing evidence for mediation.

EXPERIMENTAL DESIGNS TO INVESTIGATE MEDIATION

Most mediation designs in psychology use random assignment of participants to experimental conditions with the goal of obtaining results consistent with one theory and inconsistent with another (MacKinnon, Taborga, & Morgan-Lopez, 2002; Spencer, Zanna, & Fong, 2005; West & Aiken, 1997). In these studies, group mean differences in the outcome are then attributed to the experimental manipulation of the mediator, without measuring these mediators. Experimental results in conjunction with theoretical predictions provide support for mediation hypotheses and recommend further studies to specify and validate the

mediating process. In this section, we first discuss *double randomization* designs and describe two domains of experimental mediation: *specificity* and *consistency*. More examples of these designs can be found in MacKinnon (2008).

Double Randomization Design

A double randomization design involves two separate randomized studies for investigating mediation relations. In Study 1, participants are randomized to the levels of X to determine the causal relation of X to M. On the basis of the results of Study 1, the levels of M are defined and participants are then randomly assigned to these levels in Study 2. If a significant relation of M to Y exists in Study 2, there is more evidence for causality in the mediation relations (MacKinnon, Lockwood et al., 2002; Spencer et al., 2005; West & Aiken, 1997).

Double randomization experiments provide useful information about the mediation relations and reduce the plausibility of alternative explanations; however, the practicality of implementing double randomization experiments is often limited. The greatest drawback is the requirement of random assignment of participants to the levels of the mediator so that the $M \rightarrow Y$ relation can be experimentally tested, although there may be cases in which the mediator is external so this may be more feasible. The extent to which the manipulation can directly change the mediator is an important aspect of these designs as well. If a manipulation is able to change a mediator such that the relation between X and M is close to perfect, then the manipulation does indeed directly change the mediator. As the dependency between X and M approaches perfection, however, there will be statistical problems owing to multicollinearity between X and M.

Specificity Designs

Mediation studies with specificity designs focus on observing the hypothesized mediation relations only for certain predicted variables or groups to ascertain that the mediation relations are unique or specific to those target variables or groups. For example, experimental mediation designs assessing the *specificity* of X examine the extent to which the mediation relation between X and M is specific to certain manipulations of X but not others. Thus, different versions of X are manipulated to determine which specific component of X is responsible for the change in M. Similarly, studies assessing the *specificity of Y* examine whether the mediation relation is observed for some dependent measures (Y) but not others. Experimental designs focusing on the *specificity of moderators* examine the extent to which the mediation relations are observed for certain groups but not others (e.g., culture, ethnicity or race, socioeconomic status, region, and gender). The specificity of a moderator could also examine specific levels of a continuous moderator or individual difference variable, such as the need for cognition or level of depression.

Experimental designs examining the *specificity of the mediator* demonstrate that mediation relations are observed for some mediators (M) but not others, therefore providing evidence that the specific components of the mediator drive the relation. Three major types of specificity of mediator designs are *multiple mediator*, *blockage*, and *enhancement designs*. *Multiple mediator designs* test multiple mediators within an experiment to determine which mediator is responsible for the change in Y. These designs provide evidence of the specificity of M to determine what mediating component drives the mediation relation. *Blockage designs* involve manipulations that block the mediator from operating. To determine whether a certain variable actually mediates the relation between X and Y, one would block the mediator and examine whether the X to Y relation still occurs. If the X to Y relation no longer exists, this provides evidence that the X to Y relation is causally dependent on the mediator. *Enhancement designs* involve interventions that enhance the effects of a hypothesized mediator, thus providing further support for the mediational process. To determine whether a certain variable actually mediates the X to Y relation, one would include a manipulation that would enhance the mediator and examine whether the X to Y relation occurs in greater magnitude.

Consistency Designs

Consistency designs replicate mediation relations in new settings, groups, species (animals, humans),

and times to provide evidence that the mediation relation is consistently observed across many domains and variables. *Consistency designs for X* seek to replicate the mediation relation with alternative independent variables. This provides evidence of the generalizability of the $X \rightarrow M$ relation across settings, time, and populations. *Consistency designs for M* seek to replicate the mediation relation with alternative mediators. *Consistency designs for Y* replicate the mediation relations with alternate dependent variables. Again, this provides support of the generalizability of the X and M variables in the mediation relation. Consistency designs replicate the mediation relation across different groups, for example, across race and ethnicity, socioeconomic status, regions, gender, and individual difference measures. These designs would also hint at evidence for the universality of psychological phenomena.

Statistical tests of mediation relations are needed in all of the experimental designs. For example in the double randomization design, the manipulation of M in the M to Y study may not be perfect, so this model is again a mediator model with the manipulation of X, the mediator M, and the dependent variable Y. Statistical analysis of mediation relations are needed in this design as they are in other research studies. Similarly, tests of moderation of a mediation relation are important in specificity designs to demonstrate different mediation relations across groups. Consistency designs are also improved with analyses demonstrating failure to reject the hypotheses that effects are consistent across groups.

GUIDELINES FOR REPORTING MEDIATION ANALYSIS

The purpose of this section is to provide a number of guidelines for reporting the research study on mediation relations in psychology. Most of the characteristics of mediation studies are the same as for any research study in psychology. First, describe the theoretical and empirical basis for hypothesized mediation relation before conducting the study. Describing the mediation theory will clarify the overall purpose of the study and will likely force consideration of alternative interpretations of the results of the study, leading to better research design. If the mediation theory is complex, explicitly indicate which mediated effect or combinations of mediated effects will be investigated in the study as well as the pattern of effects in the mediation model. Discuss how the mediators targeted for study are the critical mediators on the basis of prior research. Second, describe results of each link in the mediation chain and report the estimated mediated effect, standard errors, and confidence limits as well as effect size measures. If there are more links in the chain, then significance tests for each link in the chain clarify the accuracy of mediation theory. Calculations of confidence limits and significance tests for the mediated effect should be conducted using a method that incorporates the nonnormal distribution of the product, either on the basis of the distribution of the product or the resampling methods. Third, clear discussion of how the study assessed the specified temporal relation among variables is necessary. If longitudinal data are not available, defense of the ordering in the analysis may be more difficult but potentially more important both to bolster evidence for a mediation relation and to guide the design of future longitudinal studies. Fourth, discuss how omitted variables may alter conclusions and provide some indication of the sensitivity of the observed results to additional confounding variables. Fifth, directly address problems with interpreting the M to Y relation. As emphasized in causal inference approaches, randomization is central to defending a hypothesized mediation relation. Thus, the extent to which M can be considered randomized should be addressed by considering counterfactual cases, such as how the relation between M and Y may differ across experimental groups. Also, detailed discussion of the mediator investigated in the study is useful. Is the mediator you measured the actual mediator? Is there a more fine-grained mediator that may actually be the most important in changing Y? Similarly, if you could measure additional mediators what would they be? Sixth, describe additional designs and research findings that could be used to clarify a mediation relation. In particular, future experimental studies to investigate the consistency and specificity of the mediation relation are necessary to provide more convincing evidence for mediation. Overall, the identification of

mediation relations requires a sustained program of research, including many different types of information including qualitative, quantitative, and clinical information. During this process, it may be useful to incorporate prior information on mediation relations in a Bayesian perspective (Yuan & MacKinnon, 2009).

CONCLUSION

Extensive interest in statistical analysis of mediation relations is understandable considering that psychological theories focus on the process by which phenomena occur. Mediation relations are also of interest in many other fields, including epidemiology, public health, and medicine. Mediating processes are critically important for intervention and prevention research because they provide information that can be used to make these interventions more efficient and powerful. Demonstration of mediation relations is a difficult and challenging process, but there has been considerable recent development in methods to assess mediation. Significance tests for mediation on the basis of the nonnormal distribution of the product are most accurate, including tests directly based on the distribution of the product and methods that model the distribution of the product, such as the bootstrap or resampling methods. Multiple mediator and more comprehensive models allow for consideration of omitted and additional variables that may be central to test mediation. Alternative longitudinal mediation models provide important opportunities to test temporal relations among variables in the mediation model. Complementary investigation of mediation relations with person-oriented models provides more evidence for true mediation relations. Developments in causal inference for mediation relations are rapidly increasing, thereby providing an accurate assessment of the limitations and strengths of contemporary mediation methods. Approaches to test the sensitivity of tests of mediation to violations of assumptions should add greatly to the identification of true mediation relations. An important characteristic of psychological research is that it is often easier to conduct randomized replication studies than in other fields, such as sociology or epidemiology.

This opportunity for replication is ideal for testing mediation theory in the variety of applications necessary to demonstrate the consistency and specificity of theoretical mediating process.

References

Alwin, D. F., & Hauser, R. M. (1975). The decomposition of effects in path analysis. *American Sociological Review, 40,* 37–47. doi:10.2307/2094445

Angrist, J. D., Imbens, G. W., & Rubin, D. B. (1996). Identification of causal effects using instrumental variables (with commentary). *Journal of the American Statistical Association, 91,* 444–472. doi:10.2307/2291629

Arling, G. L., & Harlow, H. F. (1967). Effects of social deprivation on maternal behavior of rhesus monkeys. *Journal of Comparative and Physiological Psychology, 64,* 371–377. doi:10.1037/h0025221

Asparouhov, T., & Muthén, B. O. (2008). Multilevel mixture models. In G. R. Hancock & K. M. Samuelsen (Eds.), *Advances in latent variable mixture models* (pp. 27–51). Charlotte, NC: Information Age.

Bandura, A., Ross, D., & Ross, S. A. (1963). Vicarious reinforcement and imitative learning. *The Journal of Abnormal and Social Psychology, 67,* 601–607. doi:10.1037/h0045550

Baranowski, T., Anderson, C., & Carmack, C. (1998). Mediating variable framework in physical activity interventions: How are we doing? How might we do better? *American Journal of Preventive Medicine, 15,* 266–297. doi:10.1016/S0749-3797(98)00080-4

Baron, R. M., & Kenny, D. A. (1986). The moderator–mediator variable distinction in social psychological research: Conceptual, strategic, and statistical considerations. *Journal of Personality and Social Psychology, 51,* 1173–1182. doi:10.1037/0022-3514.51.6.1173

Beck, A. T., Rush, A. J., Shaw, B. F., & Emery, G. (1979). *Cognitive therapy of depression.* New York, NY: Guilford Press.

Bentler, P. M. (1997). *EQS for Windows (Version 5.6).* Encino, CA: Multivariate Software.

Bishop, Y. M. M., Fienberg, S. E., & Holland, P. W. (1975). *Discrete multivariate analysis: Theory and practice.* Cambridge, MA: MIT Press.

Blalock, H. M. (1969). *Theory construction: From verbal to mathematical formulations.* Englewood Cliffs, NJ: Prentice-Hall.

Boker, S. M., & Nesselroade, J. R. (2002). A method for modeling the intrinsic dynamics of intraindividual variability: Recovering the parameters of simulated oscillators in multi-wave panel data. *Multivariate Behavioral Research, 37,* 127–160. doi:10.1207/S15327906MBR3701_06

Bollen, K. A., & Curran, P. J. (2004). Autoregressive latent trajectory (ALT) models: A synthesis of two traditions. *Sociological Methods and Research, 32,* 336–383. doi:10.1177/0049124103260222

Bollen, K. A., & Stine, R. A. (1990). Direct and indirect effects: Classical and bootstrap estimates of variability. *Sociological Methodology, 20,* 115–140. . doi:10.2307/271084

Cheong, J. (2011). Accuracy of estimates and statistical power for testing mediation in latent growth modeling. *Structural Equation Modeling, 18,* 195–211.

Cheong, J., MacKinnon, D. P., & Khoo, S. T. (2003). Investigation of mediational processes using parallel process latent growth curve modeling. *Structural Equation Modeling, 10,* 238–262. doi:10.1207/S15328007SEM1002_5

Cole, D. A., & Maxwell, S. E. (2003). Testing mediational models with longitudinal data: Questions and tips in the use of structural equation modeling. *Journal of Abnormal Psychology, 112,* 558–577. doi:10.1037/0021-843X.112.4.558

Collins, L. M., Graham, J. W., & Flaherty, B. P. (1998). An alternative framework for defining mediation. *Multivariate Behavioral Research, 33,* 295–312. doi:10.1207/s15327906mbr3302_5

Davis, J. A. (1985). *The logic of causal order.* Beverly Hills, CA: Sage.

Dwyer, J. H. (1983). *Statistical models for the social and behavioral sciences.* New York, NY: Oxford University Press.

Efron, B., & Tibshirani, R. J. (1993). *An introduction to the bootstrap.* Boca Raton, FL: Chapman & Hall/CRC Press.

Fairchild, A. J., & MacKinnon, D. P. (2009). A general model for testing mediation and moderation effects. *Prevention Science, 10,* 87–99. doi:10.1007/s11121-008-0109-6

Fairchild, A. J., MacKinnon, D. P., Taborga, M. P., & Taylor, A. B. (2009). R2 effect size measures for mediation analysis. *Behavior Research Methods, 41,* 486–498. doi:10.3758/BRM.41.2.486

Ferrer, E., & McArdle, J. J. (2003). Alternative structural models for multivariate longitudinal data analysis. *Structural Equation Modeling, 10,* 493–524. doi:10.1207/S15328007SEM1004_1

Fishbein, M., & Ajzen, I. (1975). *Belief, attitude, intention, and behavior: An introduction to theory and research.* Reading, MA: Addison-Wesley.

Frangakis, C. E., & Rubin, D. B. (2002). Principal stratification in causal inference. *Biometrics, 58,* 21–29. doi:10.1111/j.0006-341X.2002.00021.x

Fritz, M. S. (2007). *An exponential decay model for mediation* (Unpublished doctoral dissertation). Arizona State University, Tempe.

Gollob, H. F., & Reichardt, C. S. (1991). Interpreting and estimating indirect effects assuming time lags really matter. In L. M. Collins & J. L. Horn (Eds.), *Best methods for the analysis of change: Recent advances, unanswered questions, future directions* (pp. 243–259). Washington, DC: American Psychological Association. doi:10.1037/10099-015

Holland, P. W. (1988). Causal inference, path analysis, and recursive structural equation models. *Sociological Methodology, 18*, 449–484. doi:10.2307/271055

Hyman, H. H. (1955). *Survey design and analysis: Principles, cases, and procedures.* Glencoe, IL: Free Press.

James, L. R., & Brett, J. M. (1984). Mediators, moderators, and tests for mediation. *Journal of Applied Psychology, 69*, 307–321. doi:10.1037/0021-9010.69.2.307

James, L. R., Mulaik, S. A., & Brett, J. M. (2006). A tale of two methods. *Organizational Research Methods, 9*, 233–244. doi:10.1177/1094428105285144

Jo, B. (2008). Causal inference in randomized experiments with mediational processes. *Psychological Methods, 13*, 314–336. doi:10.1037/a0014207

Judd, C. M., & Kenny, D. A. (1981a). *Estimating the effects of social interventions.* Cambridge, England: Cambridge University Press.

Judd, C. M., & Kenny, D. A. (1981b). Process analysis: Estimating mediation in treatment evaluations. *Evaluation Review, 5*, 602–619. doi:10.1177/0193841X8100500502

Kazdin, A. E. (2009). Understanding how and why psychotherapy leads to change. *Psychotherapy Research, 19*, 418–428. doi:10.1080/10503300802448899

Kenny, D. A., Kashy, D. A., & Bolger, N. (1998). Data analysis in social psychology. In D. T. Gilbert, S. T. Fiske, & G. Lindzey (Eds.), *The handbook of social psychology* (4th ed., Vol. 1, pp. 233–265). Boston, MA: McGraw Hill.

Kraemer, H. C., Wilson, T., Fairburn, C. G., & Agras, S. (2002). Mediators and moderators of treatment effects in randomized clinical trials. *Archives of General Psychiatry, 59*, 877–883. doi:10.1001/archpsyc.59.10.877

Krull, J. L., & MacKinnon, D. P. (1999). Multilevel mediation modeling in group-based intervention studies. *Evaluation Review, 23*, 418–444. doi:10.1177/0193841X9902300404

Krull, J. L., & MacKinnon, D. P. (2001). Multilevel modeling of individual and group level mediated effects.

Multivariate Behavioral Research, 36, 249–277. doi:10.1207/S15327906MBR3602_06

Lazarsfeld, P. F. (1955). Interpretation of statistical relations as a research operation. In P. F. Lazarsfeld & M. Rosenberg (Eds.), *The language of social research: A reader in the methodology of social research* (pp. 115–125). Glencoe, IL: Free Press.

Lynch, K. G., Cary, M., Gallop, R., & Ten Have, T. R. (2008). Causal mediation analyses for randomized trials. *Health Services and Outcomes Research Methodology, 8*, 57–76. doi:10.1007/s10742-008-0028-9

MacCorquodale, K., & Meehl, P. E. (1948). On a distinction between hypothetical constructs and intervening variables. *Psychological Review, 55*, 95–107. doi:10.1037/h0056029

MacKinnon, D. P. (1994). Analysis of mediating variables in prevention intervention studies. In A. Cazares & L. A. Beatty (Eds.), *Scientific methods for prevention intervention research* (pp.127–153). Washington, DC: U.S. Department of Health and Human Services.

MacKinnon, D. P. (2008). *Introduction to statistical mediation analysis.* New York, NY: Erlbaum.

MacKinnon, D. P., & Dwyer, J. H. (1993). Estimation of mediated effects in prevention studies. *Evaluation Review, 17*, 144–158. doi:10.1177/0193841X9301700202

MacKinnon, D. P., Fairchild, A. J., & Fritz, M. S. (2007). Mediation analysis. *Annual Review of Psychology, 58*, 593–614. doi:10.1146/annurev.psych.58.110405.085542

MacKinnon, D. P., Fritz, M. S., Williams, J., & Lockwood, C. M. (2007). Distribution of the product confidence limits for the indirect effect: Program PRODCLIN. *Behavior Research Methods, 39*, 384–389. doi:10.3758/BF03193007

MacKinnon, D. P., Krull, J. L., & Lockwood, C. M. (2000). Equivalence of the mediation, confounding, and suppression effect. *Prevention Science, 1*, 173–181. doi:10.1023/A:1026595011371

MacKinnon, D. P., Lockwood, C. M., Brown, C. H., Wang, W., & Hoffman, J. M. (2007). The intermediate endpoint effect in logistic and probit regression. *Clinical Trials, 4*, 499–513. doi:10.1177/1740774507083434

MacKinnon, D. P., Lockwood, C. M., Hoffman, J. M., West, S. G., & Sheets, V. (2002). A comparison of methods to test mediation and other intervening variable effects. *Psychological Methods, 7*, 83–104. doi:10.1037/1082-989X.7.1.83

MacKinnon, D. P., Lockwood, C. M., & Williams, J. (2004). Confidence limits for the indirect effect: Distribution of the product and resampling methods. *Multivariate Behavioral Research, 39*, 99–128. doi:10.1207/s15327906mbr3901_4

MacKinnon, D. P., Taborga, M. P., & Morgan-Lopez, A. A. (2002). Mediation designs for tobacco prevention research. *Drug and Alcohol Dependence, 68,* S69–S83. doi:10.1016/S0376-8716(02)00216-8

MacKinnon, D. P., Warsi, G., & Dwyer, J. H. (1995). A simulation study of mediated effect measures. *Multivariate Behavioral Research, 30,* 41–62. doi:10.1207/s15327906mbr3001_3

Manly, B. F. J. (1997). *Randomization and Monte Carlo methods in biology* (2nd ed.). New York, NY: Chapman & Hall.

McArdle, J. J. (2001). A latent difference score approach to longitudinal dynamic structural analysis. In R. Cudeck, S. du Toit, & D. Sörbom (Eds.), *Structural equation modeling: Present and future. A Festschrift in honor of Karl Jöreskog* (pp. 341–380). Lincolnwood, IL: Scientific Software International.

McArdle, J. J., & Nesselroade, J. R. (2003). Growth curve analysis in contemporary research. In J. A. Schinka & W. F. Velicer (Eds.), *Handbook of psychology: Vol. 2. Research methods in psychology* (pp. 447–480). New York, NY: Wiley.

McDonald, R. P. (1997). Haldane's lungs: A case study in path analysis. *Multivariate Behavioral Research, 32,* 1–38. doi:10.1207/s15327906mbr3201_1

Morgan, S. L., & Winship, C. (2007). *Counterfactuals and causal inference: Methods and principles for social research.* New York, NY: Cambridge University Press.

Muller, D., Judd, C. M., & Yzerbyt, V. Y. (2005). When moderation is mediated and mediation is moderated. *Journal of Personality and Social Psychology, 89,* 852–863. doi:10.1037/0022-3514.89.6.852

Muthén, B. O., & Curran, P. J. (1997). General longitudinal modeling of individual differences in experimental designs: A latent variable framework for analysis and power estimation. *Psychological Methods, 2,* 371–402. doi:10.1037/1082-989X.2.4.371

Muthén, L. K., & Muthén, B. O. (1998–2007). *Mplus user's guide* (5th ed.). Los Angeles, CA: Authors.

Pearl, J. (2009). *Causality: Models, reasoning, and inference* (2nd ed.). New York, NY: Cambridge University Press.

Preacher, K. J., & Hayes, A. F. (2004). SPSS and SAS procedures for estimating indirect effects in simple mediation models. *Behavior Research Methods, Instruments, and Computers, 36,* 717–731. doi:10.3758/BF03206553

Preacher, K. J., Zyphur, M. J., & Zhang, Z. (2010). A general multilevel SEM framework for assessing multilevel mediation. *Psychological Methods, 15,* 209–233.

Robins, J. M. (1994). Correcting for non-compliance in randomized trials using structural nested mean models. *Communications in Statistics Theory and Methods, 23,* 2379–2412. doi:10.1080/03610929408831393

Robins, J. M., & Greenland, S. (1992). Identifiability and exchangeability for direct and indirect effects. *Epidemiology, 3,* 143–155. doi:10.1097/00001648-199203000-00013

Rogosa, D. R. (1988). Myths about longitudinal research. In K. W. Schaie, R. T. Campbell, W. M. Meredith, & S. C. Rawlings (Eds.), *Methodological issues in aging research* (pp. 171–209). New York, NY: Springer.

Sheets, V. L., & Braver, S. L. (1999). Organizational status and perceived sexual harassment: Detecting the mediators of a null effect. *Personality and Social Psychology Bulletin, 25,* 1159–1171. doi:10.1177/01461672992512009

Shrout, P. E., & Bolger, N. (2002). Mediation in experimental and nonexperimental studies: New procedures and recommendations. *Psychological Methods, 7,* 422–445. doi:10.1037/1082-989X.7.4.422

Singer, J. D., & Willett, J. B. (2003). *Applied longitudinal data analysis: Modeling change and event occurrence.* London, England: Oxford University Press.

Sobel, M. E. (1982). Asymptotic confidence intervals for indirect effects in structural equation models. *Sociological Methodology, 13,* 290–312. doi:10.2307/270723

Sobel, M. E. (1986). Some new results on indirect effects and their standard errors in covariance structure models. *Sociological Methodology, 16,* 159–186. doi:10.2307/270922

Sobel, M. E. (2007). Identification of causal parameters in randomized studies with mediating variables. *Journal of Educational and Behavioral Statistics, 33,* 230–251. doi:10.3102/1076998607307239

Spencer, S. J., Zanna, M. P., & Fong, G. T. (2005). Establishing a causal chain: Why experiments are often more effective than mediational analyses in examining psychological processes. *Journal of Personality and Social Psychology, 89,* 845–851. doi:10.1037/0022-3514.89.6.845

Spirtes, P., Glymour, C., & Scheines, R. (1993). *Causation, prediction, and search.* New York, NY: Springer-Verlag.

Springer, M. D. (1979). *The algebra of random variables.* New York, NY: Wiley.

Ten Have, T. R., Joffe, M. M., Lynch, K. G., Brown, G. K., Maisto, S. A., & Beck, A. T. (2007). Causal mediation analyses with rank preserving models. *Biometrics, 63,* 926–934. doi:10.1111/j.1541-0420.2007.00766.x

von Eye, A., Mun, E. Y., & Mair, P. (2009). What carries a mediation process? Configural analysis of mediation. *Integrative Psychological and Behavioral Science, 43,* 228–247. doi:10.1007/s12124-009-9088-9

Weiss, C. H. (1997). How can theory-based evaluation make greater headway? *Evaluation Review, 21,* 501–524. doi:10.1177/0193841X9702100405

West, S. G., & Aiken, L. S. (1997). Toward understanding individual effects in multicomponent prevention programs: Design and analysis strategies. In K. Bryant, M. Windle, & S. West (Eds.), *The science of prevention: Methodological advances from alcohol and substance abuse research* (pp. 167–209). Washington, DC: American Psychological Association. doi:10.1037/10222-006

Winship, C., & Mare, R. D. (1983). Structural equations and path analysis for discrete data.

American Journal of Sociology, 89, 54–110. doi:10.1086/227834

Woodworth, R. S. (1928). Dynamic psychology. In C. Murchison (Ed.), *Psychologies of 1925* (pp. 111–126). Worchester, MA: Clark University Press.

Yuan, Y., & MacKinnon, D. P. (2009). Bayesian mediation analysis. *Psychological Methods, 14*, 301–322. doi:10.1037/a0016972

CHAPTER 19

PATH ANALYSIS AND STRUCTURAL EQUATION MODELING WITH LATENT VARIABLES

Rick H. Hoyle

The focus of this chapter is a family of statistical methods and strategies collectively referred to as *structural equation modeling* (SEM), of which path analysis is a special case. These range from the relatively straightforward and familiar to the complex and new. My goal in the current treatment is threefold and reflected in the structure of the presentation: In the first section of the chapter, I develop a context for understanding the origins of SEM by tracing its emergence and positioning it within the constellation of statistical methods that are familiar to many psychological scientists. In the second section, which constitutes the core of the chapter, I describe and illustrate the steps involved in using SEM. In the third and final section, I present an array of prototypic models that illustrate the range of structures and processes that could be modeled using SEM. A firm grasp of material presented in the chapter will prepare readers to understand most published reports of SEM analysis in psychological science and position them to make an informed decision about whether their own research agenda could benefit from using SEM.

BACKGROUND AND CONTEXT

SEM is a growing family of multivariate statistical methods for modeling data. SEM is substantially more flexible than statistical methods that have dominated data analysis in psychological science since the early 20th century. It allows for multiple independent and dependent variables, which may be observed or implied by the pattern of associations among observed variables. Directional relations, as in analysis of variance (ANOVA) and multiple regression analysis, can be modeled *between* independent variables and *between* dependent variables. Complex models of the latent structure underlying a set of observed variables (i.e., unmeasured sources of influence and their interrelations) can be evaluated. These models can be estimated from continuous or ordered categorical data and include correlations between variables, direct and indirect effects, and focus on both relations between variables and patterns of means across group or over time. The flexibility of SEM permits modeling of data in ways that are not possible with other, more commonly used, statistical methods. For this reason, SEM both facilitates tests of hypotheses not adequately tested by other methods and suggests hypotheses that might not otherwise be considered for lack of a framework within which to venture them.

Historical Context

The roots of contemporary SEM can be traced to the earliest form of path analysis, Wright's (1934) method of path coefficients. Wright, a geneticist, developed path analysis for the purpose of modeling the relative influence of heredity and environment on the color of guinea pigs (Wright, 1920). These influences were assumed to be causal, and Wright

While writing this chapter, the author was supported by National Institute on Drug Abuse (NIDA) Grant P30 DA023026. Its contents are solely the responsibility of the author and do not necessarily represent the official views of NIDA.

DOI: 10.1037/13620-019
APA Handbook of Research Methods in Psychology: Vol. 2. Research Designs, H. Cooper (Editor-in-Chief)
Copyright © 2012 by the American Psychological Association. All rights reserved.

referred to his use of path analysis as a means of testing causal effects when "more direct attempts" (i.e., randomized experiments) were not feasible. The unfortunate result of this co-occurrence of non-experimental design and causal inference is that from the outset, path analysis and SEM have been associated with causal inference (Denis & Legerski, 2006). Although such inferences could be defended for many of Wright's models, given their focus on genetic influences, such is not the case for the lion's share of models that are tested using path analysis and SEM in the social and behavioral sciences.

Wright also is credited with the invention of the path diagram, the widely used graphic means of representing models. His (and therefore *the*) first path diagram was a stylized depiction of the concurrent influences of the genetic contribution of a sire and a dam, environmental factors, and chance on the color of guinea pig offspring (Wright, 1920). From this stylized depiction, Wright developed a more formal and general diagram that could be used to depict the full array of relations between variables in a "system of causes and effects" (p. 330). Wright's *system* corresponds to the contemporary notion of a model. An important feature of Wright's diagram was the inclusion of path coefficients (a term coined by Wright) on paths indicating the magnitude and direction of statistical relations in the system. In a description that captures well the activity of SEM as elaborated later in the chapter, Wright (1920) characterized path analysis as the activity of "expressing the known correlations in terms of unknown path coefficients" (p. 330).

Although there is evidence that social and behavioral scientists were aware of Wright's innovation relatively soon after his seminal publications (e.g., Burks, 1928), it was not until the 1960s that a wave of interest began to build. The stimulus was an important book by Blalock (1964), *Causal Inferences in Nonexperimental Research*, which seemed to underscore the inference that researchers drew from Wright's work—that path analysis/SEM could be used to test causal hypotheses using data from correlational research (a misinterpretation of both Wright's and Blalock's writing). Sociologists extended the use of path analysis to longitudinal models and, though the methodology for including

latent variables (i.e., unmeasured sources of influence) had not yet been fully developed, sociologists indicated an awareness of the importance of accounting for unmeasured variables (Tomer, 2003). It was a sociologist who published the first article in a psychology journal highlighting the potential of path analysis/SEM for psychological research (Duncan, 1969). By 1970, there was evidence that path analysis had begun to find traction in psychological science (Werts & Linn, 1970). Preceding and overlapping developments by methodologists in sociology were important developments by econometricians. Perhaps the most important of these concerned the method by which parameters (e.g., regression coefficients) were estimated. As early as the 1940s, it became evident that ordinary least squares was inadequate for estimating parameters in multiequations systems and that maximum likelihood could be used effectively (e.g., Mann & Wald, 1943). Goldberger and Duncan (1973) integrated the sociological approach to path analysis with the simultaneous equations approach in economics and the factor analytic approach in psychology (e.g., Duncan, 1975; Goldberger, 1971), yielding the generalization of path analysis now known as SEM (described by Bentler, 1986b, as "the literal grafting of a factor analytic model upon a simultaneous equation model," p. 41). This general model was formalized and extended in the 1970s by Jöreskog (1973), Keesling (1972), and Wiley (1973), producing what became known as the LISREL (*LI*near Structural *REL*ations) model.

Bentler (1986b) credited the "spread from the methodology laboratory to the research laboratory with unusual rapidity" to the fact that SEM allows researchers "to effectively study substantive problems that could not easily be investigated using alternative approaches" (p. 35). The effectiveness of SEM was introduced to psychologists primarily by Bentler and colleagues in an early set of publications that used SEM to evaluate complex multivariate hypotheses in a unified and efficient matter (e.g., Bentler & Speckart, 1979; Huba & Bentler, 1982). These and other compelling demonstrations (e.g., Maruyama & McGarvey, 1980) coupled with the growing accessibility of LISREL, the primary computer program for implementing SEM, and the introduction of Bentler's (1985) EQS fueled the early growth in the use of SEM in psychological science.

By the late 1980s developments in SEM methods and reports of substantive research using SEM were appearing with increasing frequency. During the period from 1987 to 1994, the overall number of such publications increased from 80 to 185. During the period, the number of SEM methods-focused articles remained steady, whereas the number of substantive articles increased nearly threefold (Tremblay & Gardner, 1996). This pattern of growth continued during the period from 1994 to 2001, with the number of substantive publications almost doubling and the number of different psychology journals in which a report of research using SEM appeared increasing as well (Hershberger, 2003). Importantly, across the period of these reviews, substantive publications reporting results from analyses using other multivariate methods (e.g., multivariate analysis of variance, factor analysis, cluster analysis) remained steady or declined (Hershberger, 2003; Tremblay & Gardner, 1996). Within a relatively short period of time, SEM has moved from relative obscurity and use by a small number of methodologically minded researchers to its current status as well-known multivariate method used by researchers across the spectrum of psychological science.

Statistical Context

An effective way to begin developing an understanding of SEM is to compare and contrast it with more familiar statistical methods, each of which can be viewed as a special case of SEM. An overly simplistic, but useful, view of SEM is as a hybrid of multiple regression analysis and factor analysis. Some readers will be familiar with the two-step strategy of using factor analysis to determine the latent influences in a set of variables, and then using factor scores or unit-weighted composites to focus the data analysis on the latent influences. In SEM, these two steps are accomplished simultaneously in such a way that actual scores for the latent influences are not needed. Instead, those influences in the form of latent variables (i.e., factors) are estimated from the data when they are included as

predictors or outcomes in a set of regression-like equations. Importantly, however, unlike multiple regression analysis, for which outcomes are addressed one at a time, multiple, possibly latent, outcomes can be included in a single model. Moreover, predictive relations between the outcomes can be modeled if there is reason to do so.

With this general idea in mind, we can see how SEM is a generalization of a host of narrower, more familiar, statistical methods. For example, the *t* test is a special case of ANOVA, which is, in turn, a special case of multiple regression analysis. As noted, multiple regression analysis is a special case of SEM. Focusing on the latent variable component of SEM, covariances (unstandardized zero-order correlations) also are a special case of SEM, though they also are the building blocks for factor analysis. SEM can be used to model categorical latent variables (i.e., latent classes), which are an extension of methods based on contingency tables as well as latent class and latent transition analysis (e.g., Kaplan, 2008; Marsh, Lüdtke, Trautwein, & Morin, 2009). To this set of capabilities can be added the modeling of patterns of means as in trend analysis in ANOVA. And, when the means are from repeated assessments of a sample of individuals, these patterns of means can be treated as predictors or outcomes in multilevel models (e.g., Curran, 2000). The end result for SEM is a very general model that includes components of many narrower statistical models with which psychological scientists are familiar but, bringing them together in a single framework, allows for models and hypothesis tests not possible using those narrower models.

BASIC CONCEPTS

An initial understanding of a number of features of SEM will set the stage for a somewhat more detailed description of the steps involved in using SEM. In each of the short sections that follow, I juxtapose a feature of SEM against a comparable feature typical of statistical methods commonly used by psychological scientists. The goal is not to show that one is superior to the other, but rather to highlight the features of SEM that are likely to be unfamiliar to most readers.

Modeling Versus Analyzing Data

Psychological scientists are accustomed to analyzing data. By *analyze*, I mean test specific differences (e.g., *t*-test, ANOVA) and coefficients (e.g., correlation, regression), typically against zero, using tailored methods that involve relatively little concern for the full array of influences apparent in the data. Modeling data, on the other hand, involves accounting for features of the research design and substantive influences that explain the pattern of relations across a set of variables (for a fuller treatment of this distinction, see Rodgers, 2010). Whereas the outcome of analysis typically is evidence for or against a posited difference or coefficient, the outcome of modeling is a statement about the correspondence between a system of relations between variables specified by the researcher and a set of observed data on those variables. Psychological scientists occasionally engage in modeling, as in factor analysis, in which the goal is to discover a plausible model to explain the relations between a set of variables, or hierarchical multiple regression analysis, in which the goal is to incrementally build a model of the relations that produce variance in single outcome; however, psychological scientists, in the main, are data analysts. As is evident from its name, SEM is a strategy and set of methods for modeling. Thus, its use requires a shift in thinking about hypothesis testing.

Covariances Versus Raw Scores as Data

Whether analyzing or modeling data, the goal of most statistical methods is to account for variability in observed data. The degree to which the difference or relation tested by the model does not account for the data typically is termed error; thus, the goal of data analysis or modeling might be conceptualized as an exercise in minimizing error. SEM differs from methods to which psychological scientists are accustomed in its definition of error. In least squares methods such as multiple regression analysis, the goal is to find the set of coefficients that minimize the difference between each individual's observed value on the outcome variable and the value predicted for them by the regression line on the basis of their scores on the predictor variables. The focus, then, is on the correspondence between observed and predicted case-level data. In SEM, the data of interest typically are the observed variances and covariances of the variables (although means are sometimes of interest). The adequacy of a model is judged by the correspondence between the observed variances and covariances and those predicted by the model. For this reason, SEM is sometimes referred to as covariance structure analysis. The interpretation and use of SEM requires a shift in focus from accounting for individual scores to accounting for covariances.

Specification of a Model Versus Running an Analysis

Most of the data-analytic strategies with which psychological scientists are familiar are, to use a computer analogy, plug and play. All that is required to run an analysis is choosing the variables, in some cases indicating which are independent and which are dependent variables, and identifying them as such in the computer program of choice. Because of the narrow and tailored nature of the methods, relatively few, if any, decisions need to be made beyond which variables to include and where to include them. The execution of an SEM analysis is substantially more involved. This is, in part, a by-product of the high degree of flexibility afforded by the method. In SEM, there is no default model. The selection and designation of variables is just the first in a series of steps involved in specifying a model. As will become apparent as you work your way through the chapter, any number of models might be specified for a set of variables. Indeed, for a large number of variables, the number of models that might be specified is extremely large. The important point is that computer programs for running SEM analyses are not "plug and play." Rather, the researcher must make a potentially large number of decisions about which variables in a set are related to each other and how. Collectively, these decisions are referred to as model specification. Psychological scientists occasionally engage in specification (without using the label), as in choosing how many factors to extract and how to rotate them in a factor analysis, or deciding how to group variables and the order in which groups are entered in hierarchical multiple regression analysis. In SEM, all analyses require specification.

All Parameters Versus a Select Few

In commonly used methods such as ANOVA and multiple regression analysis, the researcher typically is provided with, or elects to attend to, only a subset of the parameters that are estimated. This is because many of the parameters involved in the analysis are neither under the control of, nor typically of interest to, the researcher. Thus, for example, the variances of predictors and the covariances between them in multiple regression analysis are rarely seen when that analysis is run, except during diagnostics for colinearity. The uniquenesses, variance in variables not accounted for by the factors in a factor analysis are not routinely provided in computer output. In SEM, every parameter in a model is "in play." In fact, a decision must be made about how every parameter will be handled in the estimation of the model. Although this requirement adds to the work required before a model can be estimated using SEM, it suggests a potentially large number of hypotheses that might be tested but routinely are not formally considered.

Goodness of Fit Versus Difference From Zero

As noted, the typical focus of data analysis in psychological science is the question of whether a particular difference or coefficient differs from zero. Although these differences and coefficients may be thought of as continuous variables that vary in magnitude, it remains the case that, in many quarters of the discipline, they are categorical variables that can take on two values—significant or nonsignificant. Furthermore, although some statistical methods allow for testing of a set of relations, as in tests of R^2 in multiple regression analysis, most focus on individual relations (e.g., main effects and interactions in ANOVA). In SEM, the primary focus is a system of relations as specified in a model. Tests of specific coefficients are consulted only after the question of whether the model provides an acceptable account of the data has been addressed. By "acceptable account," I mean the degree to which the covariances predicted by the researcher's specified model mirror the observed covariances. When the two *sets* of covariances are statistically equivalent, the model *fits* the data. Thus, a key difference between methods

to which psychological scientists are accustomed and SEM, is that SEM focuses on the collective adequacy of the system of relations in a model. The magnitude of specific coefficients within the model, although related to the adequacy of the model as a whole, typically is of secondary interest.

Latent Versus Observed Variables

A hallmark of SEM is the ability to specify relations between latent variables, or factors. Latent variables are unobserved sources of influence that typically are inferred from the pattern of relations between a set of observed variables, referred to as indicators. Although, as noted, relations between latent variables sometimes are approximated by a piecemeal strategy using factor or principal components analysis followed by ANOVA or multiple regression analysis using factor scores, this combination is implemented seamlessly in SEM. As illustrated in the final section of the chapter, the ability to model and test hypotheses about latent variables is the basis for a number of rigorous and sophisticated strategies for decomposing variance in observed variables. The most straightforward benefit, however, is the ability to estimate relations between variables from which unreliability has been removed. This approach not only results in larger coefficients indexing relations between variable but also, because of the dependency between coefficients in a model, it sometimes results in smaller coefficients (e.g., as in mediation models). In both cases, the coefficients are assumed to better approximate the true relation between constructs than coefficients between fallible observed variables.

STEPS IN THE USE OF STRUCTURAL EQUATION MODELING

Although many types of models can be evaluated using SEM, the steps involved in applying SEM are virtually always the same. These steps are used to implement SEM in the service of one of three goals (Jöreskog, 1993). In a *strictly confirmatory* use of SEM, the goal is to evaluate the degree to which a single, a priori model accounts for a set of observed relations. Alternatively, instead of focusing on a single model, SEM might be used to compare two or more competing models in an *alternative models* strategy. Finally, a use of SEM might have a *model-generating* focus. If, for example, an a priori model does not adequately account for the observed data, rather than abandoning the data, the researcher might use it to generate an explanatory model (McArdle, in press). Of course, using the data to generate a model of the data is inferentially risky (MacCallum, Roznowski, & Necowitz, 1992); however, careful modification of a poor-fitting a priori model with the goal of finding a model that accounts for the data can lead to discoveries that, if replicated, increase understanding of a psychological structure or process. Regardless of the goal, an application of SEM follows an ordered set of steps that begins with specification and concludes with interpretation.

I illustrate those steps with an empirical example. The data are from two waves of a longitudinal study of problem behavior among middle school students (Harrington, Giles, Hoyle, Feeney, & Yungbluth, 2001). A total of 1,655 students from 14 schools participated in the study. Students first completed the self-report survey by early during the academic year when they were from 11 to 13 years old. They completed the survey a second time near the end of the academic year, about 8 months later. (An intervention and a third wave of data detract from the illustrative benefits of the data set and are therefore ignored for this example.) The analysis data set includes 10 observed variables measured at two occasions and assumed to reflect three latent variables. The focal outcome is *problem behavior*, for which indicators are drug use (composite of the number of days out of the past 30 that each of a set of illicit substance were used), sexual activity (ranging from affectionate physical contact to sexual intercourse), and interpersonal aggression (ranging from teasing to physical fighting). One predictor is *risk*, indicated by scores on three individual differences: impulsive decision making, sensation seeking, and (low) self-esteem. The other predictor, *protection*, is reflected by four composite scores on scales designed to tap values and lifestyle variables assumed to be incompatible with problem behavior. These variables include bonding to school, a personal and public commitment to avoid problem behavior, an assumption that prevailing norms are

not to engage in problem behavior, and the view that problem behavior interferes with a productive and otherwise desirable lifestyle. Data from all students on these 10 indicators were available at both time points. Additional information about the data set, including the management of missing data, can be found in the published report (Harrington et al., 2001).

MODEL SPECIFICATION

All applications of SEM begin with the specification of a model. Model specification involves three sets of decisions that stem from questions about a model:

1. Which variables will be included and in what form (observed or latent)?
2. Which variables will be interrelated and how?
3. Which parameters (i.e., coefficients) will be estimated and which will be set to specific values?

Before detailing how these questions are addressed in SEM, let us consider how they are addressed in familiar methods such as ANOVA, multiple regression, and factor analysis. Although each of these statistical methods, when applied to research questions, involve specification, most aspects of specification in these are established by convention and imposed by computer programs used to analyze data. The exception would be the first question, which typically is addressed directly by the researcher without consulting the data, although some data-reduction and data-mining methods involve consulting the data to decide which variables are to be included in a model. A decision about variables that is key in SEM is whether latent variables will be included and, if so, how many. In factor analysis, the decision to extract factors is a decision to include latent variables, and the decision about how many to extract is a decision about how many to include. As with data-reduction and data-mining methods, this decision about including latent variables typically is made on the basis of patterns in the data. In SEM, the decision about whether to include latent variables and how many can be made before data have been collected and certainly should be made before the data have been consulted.

The second question involved in model specification is which variables will be interrelated and how they will be interrelated. Again, restricting our discussion to methods familiar to psychological scientists, these decisions often are part and parcel of using a particular statistical method. For instance, a 2×2 factorial design yields 3 degrees of freedom for specifying a model that will capture the pattern of means. In the default specification, one degree of freedom is used for each main effect, and one is used for the interaction. The remaining $(n - 1) - 3$ degrees of freedom is the divisor in the error term. Even with this simple design, other specifications are possible. These alternative specifications would require defining sets of contrasts that differ from those implied by the standard main-effects-and-interaction specification. With more complex designs, the number of sets of such contrasts is large. In factor analysis, the decision to use an orthogonal rotation method is a decision to not allow factors to correlate with each other; the use of an oblique rotation allows those correlations. A final component, one that is particularly salient in SEM, is the direction of influence between variables that are directionally related. In analyses of data from randomized experiments, this decision is straightforward: Influence runs from the manipulated variables to variables assessed in the experimental context after the manipulation. In data from quasi- or nonexperimental studies, the decision is not straightforward. In its simplest form, it involves deciding, for instance, whether a particular variable will be positioned on the predictor or outcome side of a multiple regression equation. Such decisions constitute model specification within the rather restrictive data-analytic frameworks of methods such as ANOVA and multiple regression analysis.

The final question is which parameters in the model will be estimated and which will be set to a specific value and, therefore, not estimated. This aspect of specification is less apparent than identifying variables and their interrelations, but it is no less important in defining models. Examples of parameters that are estimated include regression coefficients and factor loadings. Parameters that are set are less obvious. For example, in exploratory factor analysis, the uniqueness components of indicators

are independent; that is, the covariances between them are set to zero. As noted, an orthogonal rotation specifies uncorrelated factors, which is equivalent to setting the covariances between the factors to zero. There is relatively little room to fix parameters in the standard statistical methods used by psychological scientists, but every parameter in a model to be estimated and tested using SEM can be set to a particular value, or fixed, given certain mathematical constraints.

Before discussing and illustrating model specification in SEM, it is worth considering what constitutes a *model* in SEM. This consideration is particularly important when drawing inferences from the results from estimating and testing a model in SEM. One interpretation of a model is as a literal reflection of reality as captured by the data. Of course, "reality" is remarkably complex, impossible to fully grasp, and, on some counts, simply uninteresting, rendering this idea of a model less than appealing. An alternative interpretation of a model is as an account anchored in reality, but one that includes only those aspects relevant to a research question (although accounting for salient features of research design). This view of a model assumes that the models of interest to psychological scientists will never fully account for a set of data. Rather, the models will provide a parsimonious account of relations evident in a set of data with reference to an interesting and potentially useful set of constructs and theoretical relations. Consistent with this idea, Box (1979) famously quipped, "All models are wrong, but some are useful" (p. 201). In other words, the goal of model specification is the identification of a model that is testable and useful, even if it fails to account for all aspects of the reality that produced the data. Pearl (2000) offered a definition that will guide our thinking in the remainder of the chapter. A model is "an idealized representation of a reality that highlights some aspects and ignores others" (p. 202).

Now, let us focus specifically and concretely on model specification in SEM by returning to the example introduced at the beginning of this section. Recall that a large sample of middle-school students provided information on 10 observed variables at each of two occasions. All of the variables are relevant to the research question, which concerns the role of certain risk and protective factors in adolescent problem behavior. Although the research question might focus on the contribution of each of the three risk and four protective factors to each of the three problem behaviors, the focus is broader: To what extent do risk and protection evident in certain dispositional, perceptual, and attitudinal constructs, contribute to problem behavior, broadly defined? To address this question, I need three additional variables that reflect the general constructs of risk, protection, and problem behavior. In fact, because the variables are assessed at two points in time, I need to include these constructs twice. Thus, in terms of identifying variables, I will include 26 variables—10 observed variables and three latent variables observed on two occasions.

Having designated the variables to be included in the model, I now need to specify the relations between variables. I will provide additional detail later in this section, but for now I can describe the set of relations in general terms. I intend to explain the commonality among impulsive decision making, sensation seeking, and low self-esteem with a latent variable I label risk. A second latent variable, protection, will account for the commonality among bonding to school, commitment to avoid problem behavior, belief that problem behavior is not the norm, and belief that problem behavior interferes with success. And I will model the commonality

among drug use, sexual activity, and interpersonal aggression as a third latent variable, problem behavior. These relations and any correlations between latent variables constitute a subcomponent of the model referred to as the *measurement model*. As outlined in Table 19.1, the measurement component of the model links measured indicators to latent variables and includes three types of parameters: loadings, variances of latent variables, and unexplained variance in indicators, or uniquenesses. Each of these parameters must be designated as fixed (i.e., set at a specific value) or free (i.e., to be estimated from the data). I outline considerations involved in these designations in the next section.

In the model of interest, the measurement model is not an end in itself. Although I need to establish empirically that the observed variables reflect the latent variables in the pattern I have proposed, my ultimate goal is estimating the directional relations between the latent variables. Because this is a longitudinal model, I am particularly interested in the directional relation between each variable at Time 1 and the other variables at Time 2. These paths and the correlations between the latent variables at Time 1 and unexplained variance in the latent variables at Time 2 constitute the *structural model*. The parameters included in the structural model are listed and described in the lower portion of Table 19.1. These include all directional paths, variances of predictor variables, unexplained variance in outcomes, and

---

TABLE 19.1

Parameters to Be Considered When Specifying a Model

Parameter	Description
Measurement component	
Loading	Coefficient resulting from the regression of an indicator on a latent variable
Variance, latent variable	Variance of a latent variable
Variance, uniqueness	Variance in the indicator not attributable to the latent variables on which it loads
Structural component	
Variance, independent variable	Variance of a measured or latent variables that is not predicted by other variables in the model
Variance, disturbance	Unaccounted for variance in a measured or latent variable that is predicted by other variables in the model
Nondirectional path	Covariance between two variables
Directional path	The amount of change in a dependent variable attributable to an independent variable controlling for other relations in the model

covariances between predictors and unexplained variance in outcomes. As with the measurement model, each of these parameters must be designated as fixed or free.

The specification of a model for estimation requires considerably more detail than offered in the written description that I have provided. For that reason, different strategies and conventions have emerged to formalize the aspects of model specification that I have presented. I describe three strategies, using components of the example model to illustrate.

Path Diagrams

One means of formalizing the specification of a model to be analyzed using SEM is the path diagram. A path diagram of a portion of the example model is shown in Figure 19.1. This example includes all of the components necessary to fully specify all but a few highly specialized models. First, note the squares, labeled using Bentler–Weeks notation (Bentler & Weeks, 1980) as v_1 to v_{10}. These represent observed variables, in this case, the 10 variables described earlier as assessed at one occasion. Next, notice the three large ovals, labeled $F1$ to $F3$, which include the names of the constructs on which the model is focused. These ovals designate latent variables, or factors. Smaller circles indicate variances of two types. Attached to each indicator, and labeled e_1 to e_{10}, are uniquenesses. These, too, are latent influences on the indicators. The uniquenesses reflect both variance attributable to random

processes and variance attributed to processes specific to that indicator. A lone small circle, labeled d_3, is attached to the problem behavior latent variable. Typically referred to as a *disturbance*, this latent influence reflects all processes that contribute to variance in $F3$ that is not attributable to $F1$ and $F2$. The straight lines indicate directional influence, either among latent variables and indicators or between independent and dependent latent variables. The curved arrow between $F1$ and $F2$ indicates a nondirectional path, or covariance. The sharply curved, double-headed arrows pointing to the uniquenesses, the disturbance, and the independent latent variables indicate variances. Finally, notice that associated with each path is either an asterisk or a number. The asterisks indicate free parameters, whose values will be estimated from the data. The numbers indicate fixed parameters, whose value does not change as a function of the data.

Some readers might be surprised to see paths in the measurement component of the model running from the latent variables to their indicators. This specification corresponds to the common factor model, which assumes that the commonality among a set of variables is attributable to one or unmeasured influences. These influences are assumed to account for a portion of the variance in the indicators. In SEM terms, indicators related to latent variables in this way are referred to as reflective indicators; they are fallible reflections of the underlying variable of interest. Virtually all latent variables in psychological science are related to their

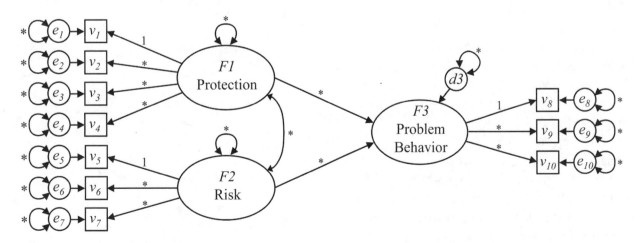

FIGURE 19.1. Path diagram illustrating the components of path diagrams using a portion of the empirical example.

indicators in this way. Nonetheless, it bears mention that an alternative specification reverses the direction of the arrows so that the latent variables are assumed to be caused by its indicators. In this case, the observed variables are referred to as formative indicators. In that alternative specification each measured indicator is assumed to represent a unique component that, when added to the other components, yields the latent variable. Such models pose significant estimation challenges and this, coupled with their rarity in psychological research, justifies my focus solely on reflective indicators in the remainder of the chapter (for an informative discussion of this distinction, see Edwards & Bagozzi, 2000).

Although it is evident from the path diagram that a loading on each latent variable has, for reasons detailed in the section on estimation, been fixed to one, it is not evident that many other parameters have been fixed. There are no paths between uniquenesses, implying that the covariances between them have been fixed to zero. Each indicator is specified to load on only one latent variable, meaning that its loadings on the other two latent variables have been fixed to zero. Thus, although the path diagram is an appealing means of presenting a model, a significant weakness in terms of model specification is that parameters fixed at zero are generally not shown. Of course, the paths I have identified could be added to the model with coefficients of zero associated with them; however, such a diagram would be too cluttered (e.g., imagine a path running from $F3$ to v_1) to effectively communicate the basic features of the model.

Equations

An alternative means of specifying a model is through equations. A straightforward means of doing so is based on the work of Bentler and Weeks (1980) and implemented in the EQS computer program for SEM analyses (Bentler, 1989). In addition to using regression-like equations to specify directional paths in a model, the approach uses an intuitive labeling scheme, a portion of which is used to label variables in the path diagram presented earlier. As shown in the path diagram, observed variables are labeled v, and all latent variables are labeled F. Uniquenesses are labeled e, and disturbances d. In

addition to identifying variables in a model, these labels can be used to identify nondirectional paths and specific parameters using double-label notation. For instance, the loading of v_1 on $F1$ would be labeled, $F1,v_1$. The effect of $F1$ on $F3$ would be labeled, $F1,F3$. Variances are denoted by double reference to the variable in question. Thus, the variance of $F1$ is labeled $F1,F1$, the variance of d_3 as d_3,d_3, and so on. Finally, as in Figure 19.1, free parameters are denoted by asterisks.

Using these labels and a series of simple equations, I can specify the model shown in Figure 19.1. The relations between the indicators and their latent variables are characterized in a series of measurement equations:

$$v_1 = 1F1 + e_1 \tag{1}$$
$$v_2 = *F1 + e_2$$
$$v_3 = {}^*F1 + e_3$$
$$v_4 = *F1 + e_4$$
$$v_5 = 1F2 + e_5$$
$$v_6 = *F2 + e_6$$
$$v_7 = *F2 + e_7$$
$$v_8 = 1F3 + e_8$$
$$v_9 = *F3 + e_9$$
$$v_{10} = *F3 + e_{10}.$$

With the exception of d_3, which is part of the structural component of the model, all of the variables in the path diagram are represented in these equations. Missing from these equations are the variances for the 10 uniquenesses and the two factors that are predicting the third latent variable.

$$e_1, e_1 = * \tag{2}$$
$$.$$
$$.$$
$$.$$
$$e_{10}, e_{10} = *$$
$$F1, F1 = *$$
$$F2, F2 = *.$$

The measurement component of the model is completed by specifying the covariance between $F1$ and $F2$:

$$F1, F2 = *. \tag{3}$$

The remaining paths and parameters in the model constitute the structural model. The paths between latent variables are specified in structural equations:

$$F3 = *F1 + *F2 + d_3. \tag{4}$$

The model is completed by specifying the variance of the disturbance:

$$d_3, d_3 = *. \tag{5}$$

As with the path diagram, free parameters are easily detected in the specification. Some fixed parameters, such as the fixed loading on each latent variable are evident as well. As with the path diagram, however, parameters fixed at zero are not explicitly noted. The covariances between uniquenesses that are fixed at zero would be denoted, for example,

$$e_1, e_2 = 0. \tag{6}$$

Cross loadings fixed at zero (by implication because of their omission from the model) could be included in the measurement equations. For example,

$$v_2 = 1F1 + 0F2 + 0F3 + e_1.$$

Matrix Notation

Another approach to model specification is matrix notation, which is most closely associated with the LISREL computer program (though no longer required for using it). Although it is more tedious and intimidating for those who are new to SEM, model specification using matrix notation has two significant advantages over path diagrams and equations. First, except for certain shortcuts, every parameter, fixed and free, is explicitly shown. Second, matrix notation is the means by which new developments in SEM typically are communicated. As such, an understanding of how models are communicated using matrix notation is essential for keeping abreast of the new developments. Of importance to individuals working on research questions that cross disciplinary boundaries is the fact that matrix notation is used to communicate specifications and findings from substantive research in some disciplines.

Using matrix notation, model specification requires addressing elements in one or more of three matrix equations. A distinction is made within the measurement component between latent variables that are not explained within the model (*F1* and *F2*

in our example) and those explained within the model (*F3*). A third matrix equation specifies the relations between latent variables.

Using matrix notation, indicators of latent variables not explained within the model are labeled as *x* and the latent variables as ξ. Loadings are denoted as λ. Thus, the matrix equation for those latent variables is,

$$x = \lambda_x \xi + \delta. \tag{8}$$

Unpacking the equation yields an equation in which specific parameters are made explicit.

$$
\begin{bmatrix} x_1 \\ x_2 \\ x_3 \\ x_4 \\ x_5 \\ x_6 \\ x_7 \end{bmatrix} =
\begin{bmatrix} 1 & 0 \\ \lambda_{21} & 0 \\ \lambda_{31} & 0 \\ \lambda_{41} & 0 \\ 0 & 1 \\ 0 & \lambda_{62} \\ 0 & \lambda_{72} \end{bmatrix}
\begin{bmatrix} \xi_1 \\ \xi_2 \end{bmatrix} +
\begin{bmatrix} \delta_1 \\ \delta_2 \\ \delta_3 \\ \delta_4 \\ \delta_5 \\ \delta_6 \\ \delta_7 \end{bmatrix}. \tag{9}
$$

When presented in this way, it is apparent that all of the equations for *F1* and *F2* presented in the previous section are included. (Note that *x*s are the *v*s, the ξs are *F*s, the δs are *e*s, and the λs are **s.) Importantly, it is apparent that, as before, for each indicator, one loading is fixed to zero.

The measurement model for the independent variables is completed by specifying the variances for the latent variables and uniquenesses and any covariances between them. The variances and covariances for the latent variables are specified in the matrix, Φ, which for our model takes the form,

$$
\begin{bmatrix} \phi_{11} & \\ \phi_{21} & \phi_{22} \end{bmatrix}. \tag{10}
$$

The diagonal elements are variances and the off-diagonal element is the covariances. The variances and covariances for the uniquenesses are specified in Θ_δ.

$$
\begin{bmatrix}
\delta_{11} & & & & & & \\
0 & \delta_{22} & & & & & \\
0 & 0 & \delta_{33} & & & & \\
0 & 0 & 0 & \delta_{44} & & & \\
0 & 0 & 0 & 0 & \delta_{55} & & \\
0 & 0 & 0 & 0 & 0 & \delta_{66} & \\
0 & 0 & 0 & 0 & 0 & 0 & \delta_{77}
\end{bmatrix}. \tag{11}
$$

Because uniquenesses typically are not allowed to covary, this matrix often is written as a vector including only the diagonal. For our purposes, the advantage of providing the matrix is that it makes clear that a host of model parameters are fixed at zero in the specification.

For the latent variable explained within the model, *F3*, the matrix equation is,

$$y = \lambda_y \eta + \varepsilon. \tag{12}$$

In expanded form, the equation is,

$$\begin{bmatrix} y_1 \\ y_2 \\ y_3 \end{bmatrix} = \begin{bmatrix} 1 \\ \lambda_{21} \\ \lambda_{31} \end{bmatrix} \begin{bmatrix} \eta_1 \end{bmatrix} + \begin{bmatrix} \varepsilon_1 \\ \varepsilon_2 \\ \varepsilon_3 \end{bmatrix}. \tag{13}$$

Note in the path diagram that no variances are associated with *F3* (η_1 in the matrix equation). This is because variance in such latent variables—that is, latent variables that reflect outcomes in a model—is accounted for by paths directed at them and their disturbance terms. Because their variances are not parameters in the model, when there is more than one latent outcome variable in the model their covariances are not parameters in the model either.

Relations between latent variables specified in these matrices are specified in the structural equation,

$$\eta = B\eta + \Gamma\xi + \zeta. \tag{14}$$

For our example, this equation is expanded to reveal individual parameters and their status in the model. (The 0 reflects the fact that variance of η_1 is not estimated. It is partitioned between the paths from ξ_1 and ξ_2 and the disturbance, ζ_1.)

$$\begin{bmatrix} \eta_1 \end{bmatrix} = \begin{bmatrix} 0 \end{bmatrix} \begin{bmatrix} \eta_1 \end{bmatrix} + \begin{bmatrix} \gamma_{11} & \gamma_{12} \end{bmatrix} \begin{bmatrix} \xi_1 \\ \xi_2 \end{bmatrix} + \zeta_1. \tag{15}$$

The only remaining parameter to be specified is the variance of the disturbance (ζ_1 here, but d_3 in the equation and path diagram approaches). Variances of disturbances and any covariances between them are specified in the matrix Ψ, which in the example model, is simply

$$\begin{bmatrix} \Psi_{11} \end{bmatrix}. \tag{16}$$

Either of these strategies, path diagrams, equations, or matrix notation, allow for specification of a model. Each indicates the observed and latent variables to be included in the model, their relative positions in the model, the relations among them, and the various fixed and free parameters that characterize those relations. Regardless of the method used, once a model has been formally specified, assuming data are available for the observed variables, it can be estimated.

ESTIMATION OF PARAMETERS

The goal of estimation is finding the optimal set of estimates for free parameters in a model given the observed data and the relations specified in the model. By "optimal," I mean a statistical criterion targeted by an estimator. As an example, consider the ordinary least squares estimator, which is typically used to find the optimal, or best-fitting, regression line in multiple regression analysis. The criterion targeted by that estimator is the minimization of the average squared distance between the observed value on the dependent variable for each case and the value predicted for them given the regression line. Although the least squares estimator could be used for SEM, the nature of parameter estimation in SEM is such that least squares is not well suited to finding the parameter estimates best suited to testing the model against the data. A number of alternative estimators are available. These generally fall into one of two categories. Normal theory estimators assume multivariate normality and, typically, continuous measurement. Alternative estimators relax one or both of these assumptions.

Because of the complexity of models in SEM, the degree to which the data satisfy the assumptions of the estimator to be used is of even greater concern than is typical. Of course, data rarely are ideal. Consequently, the relevant question is how robust a given estimator is to violations of its assumptions. For instance, the assumption of continuous measurement is virtually never met in psychological research, in which ordered-categorical response options (e.g., Likert-type scales) are the norm. Fortunately, most normal-theory estimators are reasonably robust to violations of the assumption of continuous measurement, producing acceptable results with measures that include five or more categories (Johnson & Creech, 1983; Wirth & Edwards, 2007). The assumption to which most attention has been directed is multivariate normality. Note that the assumption concerns *multivariate*, not univariate, normality. In other words, the joint distribution of all observed variables in the model must be normal (see DeCarlo, 1997, for a discussion of multivariate kurtosis). Because evaluating multivariate normality, especially when the number of observed variables is large, is not straightforward, evaluation typically focuses on univariate distributions. The practical payoff of focusing on univariate distributions is evident; however, it is important to keep in mind that normal univariate distributions do not guarantee multivariate normality. In either case, normal theory estimators seem to be robust to modest departures from multivariate normality, and relatively straightforward corrections are now available to account for consequential departures from multivariate normality.

The most widely used estimator in SEM is maximum likelihood (ML). In the same way that ordinary least squares is assumed in most uses of multiple regression analysis, ML is assumed in most applications of SEM. It is the default estimator in most SEM computer programs. The goal of ML estimation is to find a set of estimates for the free parameters that, when the data and fixed parameters are taken into account, maximize the likelihood of the data given the specified model (Myung, 2003). ML estimation is an iterative procedure that begins with a somewhat arbitrary set of start values for the free parameters and updates these values until the difference between the observed data and the data implied by the model is minimized. At this point, the estimation procedure is said to have converged, and the adequacy of the resultant model is evaluated.

The use of estimators other than ML usually is motivated by one or more characteristics of the data that do not meet the assumptions of ML estimation. For categorical or coarsely categorized data, robust weighted least squares (Flora & Curran, 2004) and the categorical variable methodology (B. O. Muthén, 1984) are appropriate. For data that are, practically speaking, on continuous scales but nonnormally distributed, asymptotic distribution-free (ADF) methods (Browne, 1984) or postestimation corrections to normal-theory estimates (Satorra & Bentler, 1994) are available. ADF methods, though appealing in theory, typically are impractical given the large sample sizes required for them to evidence theoretical properties. The latter method, typically described as a scaling correction, is particularly promising and is illustrated with our example later in this section of the chapter. Because the validity of model evaluation rests most fundamentally on the integrity of estimates, determined in part by an appropriate estimator choice, a critical concern for researchers is whether ML estimation is appropriate and, if it is not, which alternative estimator overcomes the limitations of ML without introducing additional concerns about the integrity of estimates.

Before returning to the example, I briefly treat an important consideration in estimation: identification. Although identification is evaluated and addressed as part of model specification, I address it here because its consequences are most evident during estimation. In general, identification concerns the degree to which a unique estimate can be obtained for each parameter in a model. Although identification typically is discussed at the global level (i.e., for the model as a whole), if any parameter in a model is not identified (i.e., local identification status), then the model is not identified. Importantly, if it is not identified, attempts at estimation will not meet the criterion inherent in most estimators—minimizing the difference between the observed data and the data implied by the model.

With regard to identification, the status of a model is referred to in one of three ways. An identified model is one in which a single, unique value can be obtained through at least one set of manipulations of other parameters in the model given the data. If the value of one or more parameters can be obtained in more than one way, then the model is *overidentified* and subject to testing for model fit. If the value of each parameter can be obtained in exactly one way, then the model is *just identified*. Although the parameter estimates in just identified models are valid, such models cannot be tested. Finally, a model in which a single, unique value for each parameter cannot be obtained is underidentified, or simply, *unidentified*.

Determining the identification status of a specified model can be a challenge, sometimes requiring the determination of whether the specification meets one or more technical criteria. Those criteria are detailed in comprehensive treatments of SEM (e.g., Bollen, 1989). In some instances, those criteria manifest as relatively straightforward rules of thumb. For instance, for the variance of a latent variable to be defined, it must either be fixed either to a specific value (e.g., 1.0) or to the value of the common portion of one of the indicators, which typically is accomplished by fixing the loading for that indicator to a value of 1.0 (Steiger, 2002). Another rule of thumb concerns the number of indicators per latent variable. If a latent variable is modeled as uncorrelated with other variables in a model (e.g., a one-factor model or a model with orthogonal factors), it must have at least three indicators to be identified. This is because of the general identification rule that a model cannot have more free parameters than the number of nonredundant elements in the observed covariance matrix. For present purposes, it is important only to understand that, although SEM is flexible in terms of the kinds of relations between variables that can be specified, that flexibility can be limited somewhat by technical considerations having to do with how parameters are estimated.

Returning now to the example model and ML estimation, I illustrate the estimation process and describe, in context, additional considerations. When illustrating model specification, to simplify the presentation, I made use of only a portion of the full model to be estimated from the data described earlier. Recall that a relatively large sample of middle school students provided data on 10 variables at two points in time. I hypothesized that the 10 observed variables were indicators of three latent variables of interest at two points in time. My interest is whether variability in a latent variable for problem behavior is prospectively predicted by latent variables for personal characteristics that reflect risk for and protection from problem behavior. Displayed in Figure 19.2 is a path diagram depicting the set of relations in the model. Notice that the observed variables are omitted from the diagram. The reason for their omission is twofold: (a) Their inclusion would yield a figure too cluttered to be of use, and (b) although the measure-

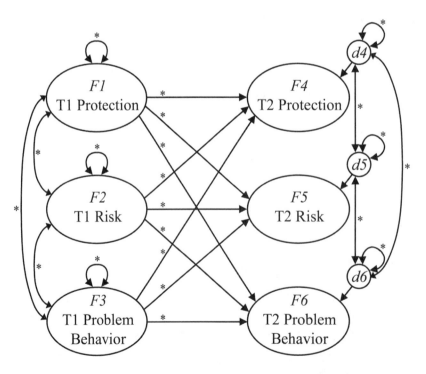

FIGURE 19.2. Structural component of the full example model. T1 and T2 refer to the first and second waves of data collection, respectively. Indicators of the latent variables are not shown.

ment model is a component of the model, for this specific model, it is not the component of greatest interest. The structural component, which specifies the direction relations between the latent variables is of primary substantive interest, and it is this component shown in the figure.

Because the figure shows only the structural component of the model to be estimated, it does not provide full detail regarding model specification. The part of the model not shown concerns the relations and parameters in the measurement component. In our model, these fall into three categories: (a) the relations between indicators and latent variables; (b) uniquenesses associated with indicators; and (c) covariances between uniquenesses. Referring to Figure 19.1, it is apparent that the 10 observed variables at each time point are arrayed so that four reflect protection, three reflect risk, and three reflect problem behavior. It also is evident that a uniqueness is associated with each indicator. What cannot be seen in Figure 19.1, because it does not include repeated assessments of the variables, are nonzero covariances between selected uniquenesses in the model. These are illustrated for indicators of one of the latent variables, protection, in Figure 19.3. Notice the curved arrow and accompanying asterisk between each indicator measured at the two waves of data collection. These autocorrelations are neither substantively interesting nor require justification. They reflect the fact that any unique, nonrandom

variance in an observed variable at one point in time should be evident at other points in time. Imposing Figure 19.3 over the top portion of Figure 19.2 gives a sense of what the full model would look were the path diagram complete.

As noted, the goal of estimation is to obtain values for the free parameters that, when coupled with the fixed parameters, minimize the discrepancy between the observed data and the data implied by the model. Moreover, these values are obtained iteratively, beginning with a guess based on convention and values in the data and culminating in the optimal estimates. The processes of estimation are best understood by dissecting an example.

First, it is useful to pinpoint all of the free parameters to be estimated in a model. In our model there are 65. Their locations in the model are as follows:

- 7 loadings at Time 1 (recall that one is fixed on each latent variable)
- 7 loadings at Time 2
- 10 uniquenesses at Time 1
- 10 uniquenesses at Time 2
- 10 covariances to reflect autocorrelated errors (as in Figure 19.3)
- 3 variances, one for each latent variable, at Time 1
- 3 covariances between the latent variables at Time 1
- 9 paths from Time 1 to Time 2 latent variables
- 3 disturbances at Time 2
- 3 covariances between disturbances at Time 2

In Table 19.2, I provide details from the iteration history only for *F1*, the protection latent variable at Time 1. That part of the model includes nine parameters: four loadings, four uniquenesses, and one latent variable variance. These are shown under the headings "Loadings" and "Variances" in Table 19.2. In the leftmost column is iteration number. The first line is labeled "Start," indicating that values in this line were those with which iteration began. Although these can be specified by the researcher, they typically are inserted automatically by the computer program used for estimation. Note that, for the loadings and the variance of the latent variable, the default start value is 1.0. For the EQS program, used here, the default for variances of the uniqueness terms is 90% of the variance of the observed variables

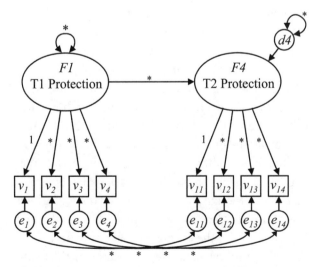

FIGURE 19.3. Portion of the example model illustrated autocorrelated uniquenesses.

TABLE 19.2

Iteration History From Start Values to Convergence (Parameter Estimates for Protection Latent Variable in Example Model)

Iteration	Loadings				Variances					
	v_1	v_2	v_3	v_4	e_1	e_2	e_3	e_4	F1	F_{ML}
Start	1.000	1.000	1.000	1.000	.300	.248	.345	.294	1.000	
0	1.000	.674	.734	.706	.235	.185	.282	.231	.329	11.996
1	1.000	.805	.967	.779	.231	.148	.193	.219	.217	6.070
2	1.000	.913	1.191	.831	.216	.129	.130	.216	.177	3.231
3	1.000	.973	1.317	.844	.199	.119	.096	.216	.165	1.783
4	1.000	1.039	1.443	.838	.176	.105	.062	.218	.156	1.227
5	1.000	1.040	1.405	.812	.173	.100	.065	.220	.161	.645
6	1.000	1.055	1.438	.833	.177	.101	.061	.219	.156	.630
7	1.000	1.055	1.433	.829	.176	.100	.062	.220	.157	.630
8	1.000	1.056	1.436	.830	.177	.100	.061	.220	.156	.630

Notes. Tabled values are unstandardized maximum likelihood estimates. F_{ML} = maximum likelihood fitting function. Loading for v_1 fixed to identify variance of F1.

(e.g., the .300 for e_1 is 90% of the observed variance of .331 for v_1). Importantly, the value in the Start line for v_1, although it is the same as for v_2 to v_4, is not a start value. As shown in the specifications, this is a fixed value, which is evident because its value does not change from one iteration to the next.

Before discussing the pattern of parameter estimates as the estimator moves from start values to convergence, I draw your attention to the final column in Table 19.2. The values in this column are values of the maximum likelihood fitting function. They basically reflect the difference between the observed data in the form of the covariance matrix and the covariance matrix implied by the model given the data at each iteration. The goal of estimation is to minimize that difference and, as can be seen working from top to bottom in the column, the values decrease with each iteration until they stabilize at a minimum value. Although I have rounded those values to three decimal places, minimization is evaluated at the fifth decimal place (unless the computer program is instructed to do otherwise). When the value of F_{ML} does not change at the first five decimal places from one iteration to the next, iteration stops. At this point, the estimation process has converged on a solution; that is, it has produced the set of parameter estimates that maximize the likelihood of the data given the model.

Let us turn now to the columns for loadings and variances. Notice that there is no value for F_{ML} on the Start line. This is because no value has been generated at that point. The next row contains values for the parameters returned when the fixed and start values are substituted into the equations and values for free parameters produced when taking the data into account. It is at this point that the iterative attempt to minimize F_{ML} begins. Notice that, except for the fixed value of the loading for v_1, all of the parameters have changed from their start values. Relative to other values in the F_{ML} column, the value for the model at this point is very large, indicating a relatively poor fit of the model to the data. After a single iteration, the values are updated to produce a substantial drop in the value of F_{ML}. Although subsequent updates result in smaller values of F_{ML}, the decrease is smaller after each update to the parameter estimates. This pattern is reflected in the parameter estimates as well, which change relatively little after the fourth iteration. Notice the pattern of change in the different parameters. For instance, although the start value for the v_2 loading was relatively close to the optimal estimate, the first iteration moved the estimate farther away rather than closer to that estimate. The value for the loading of v_2 had moved close to its optimal value after only two iterations.

Estimation in this case was smooth. Eight is a relatively small number of iterations, and there is nothing in the iteration history to cause hesitation in moving to evaluation of fit. Such is not always the case. For instance, sometimes estimation fails to converge. A failure to converge is a relative term, because an upper bound ordinarily is imposed on the number of iterations to be attempted. The value for that number is 30, and although it is possible that an attempt at estimation would converge if allowed additional iterations (which can be done by overriding the computer program's default), this typically is not the case. A failure to converge can result from the presence of one or more unidentified parameters in a model or ill-conditioned data. In some cases, a model may be identified in terms of specification, but because a parameter estimate is in effect zero (equivalent to having fixed the path to zero in the specification), it is not. Such models are empirically unidentified. Otherwise, failures to converge often occur in complex models or with data that are not normally distributed. A failure to converge is a signal to reevaluate the model specification and, if no problems are identified there, to reexamine the scaling and distribution of variables in the data set.

Computer Programs

Models typically are estimated by computer programs written specifically for SEM. In the early history of SEM, the only computer program for this purpose was LISREL (Jöreskog, & Sörbom, 2006). Early versions of LISREL (first released in 1970) were challenging to use, requiring at least some knowledge of matrix notation to specify models. Despite these challenges, LISREL became (and, in some quarters, remains) synonymous with SEM. The release of EQS (Bentler, 1985) offered an appealing alternative to LISREL, exchanging matrix notation for a simpler specification approach on the basis of equations similar in form to multiple regression equations. By the early 1990s, statistical computing had begun the transition from mainframe to desktop, and SEM programs followed suit. Early desktop versions of LISREL and EQS were, for the most part, direct translations of the mainframe programs. AMOS (Arbuckle, 1995) was the first fully

featured SEM program written to run in the desktop environment, offering the option of model specification by drawing path diagrams. LISREL and EQS have evolved to take full advantage of the desktop environment and, with AMOS, have been joined by other programs for estimating and testing models. A subset of these programs are stand-alone; that is, they do not require another resident program to run. Others are a module within a general purpose statistical analysis program such as IBM SPSS, SAS, or Statistica. In the remainder of this section, I list the alternatives currently available for running SEM analyses and reference relevant websites and publications.

The computer programs one might use for running SEM analyses can be divided into three categories. Perhaps best known are the commercial stand-alone programs, of which LISREL is the prototype. I have mentioned three of these: AMOS, EQS, and LISREL. An increasingly influential addition to this group is M*plus* (L. K. Muthén & Muthén, 1998). Early versions of these programs did not interface well with popular data manipulation programs (e.g., Microsoft Excel) and did not, themselves, offer much in the way of data manipulation, thus requiring the preparation and exporting of data from other programs prior to use. Now, to varying degrees, the programs allow data manipulation and viewing within a spreadsheet format. A critical advantage of these programs is that behind each is a methodologist who contributes regularly to the technical literature on SEM. For that reason, new capabilities are added frequently and, as a result, new versions are released significantly more often than would be typical of statistical software. AMOS (Blunch, 2008; Byrne, 2010) is distributed by SPSS (now IBM SPSS); a basic description is provided at http://www.spss.com/amos/ (see also http://www.spss.com/media/whitepapers/SEMEB.pdf). Although the program runs, and can be purchased, as a stand-alone program (Windows operating system only), it typically is bundled with the SPSS software and often is included in enterprise licenses at education institutions. EQS (Byrne, 2006; Mueller, 1999) is available for multiple computing platforms (detailed information is available at http://www.mvsoft.com/). LISREL (Byrne, 1998; Kelloway, 1998; Mueller,

1999), now in Version 8, includes SIMPLIS, which allows for simple, intuitive specification of models, and PRELIS, which can be used for data manipulation before analysis. Information, including examples, references, and announcements of workshops can be found at http://www.ssicentral.com/lisrel/. M*plus* (Byrne, 2011) is particularly well suited for categorical data and offers the most wide ranging array of modeling capabilities, including multilevel and mixture models. The website for M*plus* (http://www.statmodel.com/), includes extensive information about the program as well as an active discussion list, copies of technical reports, and access to published articles about or using M*plus*. Although not a stand-alone program, I include STREAMS (Structural Equation Modeling Made Simple) in this section, because it features an appealing user interface for manipulating data, specifying models, and presenting results (information at http://www.mwstreams.com/). It does not include the capacity to estimate models, instead using an instance of EQS, LISREL, or M*plus* installed on the same computer.

A second category of SEM computer programs includes those that are integrated into comprehensive commercial programs for quantitative data analysis. A significant strength of these programs is access to the full range of data manipulation and description capabilities offered by the programs. A significant drawback is that the programs typically are slow to incorporate new technical developments compared with the stand-alone commercial programs. Also, documentation, particularly third-party books of the sort available for the stand-alone programs, is sparse. The oldest of the programs in this category are RAMONA, offered by Systat (http://www.systat.com/) and SEPATH, available in Statistica (http://www.statsoft.com/products/statistica-advanced-linear-non-linear-models/itemid/5/#structural). TCALIS is the successor to the CALIS procedure in the powerful SAS System (http://support.sas.com/documentation/cdl/en/statugtcalis/61840/PDF/default/statugtcalis.pdf). Finally, SEM analyses can be done in Stata with GLLAMM (http://www.gllamm.org/; Rabe-Hesketh, Skrondal, & Pickles, 2004).

A final category of computer programs for SEM analyses are no-cost, often open-access, stand-alone programs. As might be expected, these programs do not offer an impressive user interface and provide little or no data manipulation capability. Aside from the fact that they can be obtained at no cost, a subset of these programs allows for modification by users. Perhaps the most widely used from this category is OpenMx (http://openmx.psyc.virginia.edu/), which is particularly well suited to SEM analyses of heredity. The R sem package (http://cran.r-project.org/web/packages/sem/index.html; Fox, 2006) is a good choice for researchers already familiar with data analysis using R. The AFNI *1dSEM* package (http://afni.nimh.nih.gov/sscc/gangc/PathAna.html) is offered as C source code by the National Institute of Mental Health. Finally, SmartPLS (http://www.smartpls.de/forum/), which allows for estimation by the method of partial least squares only, runs on the JAVA platform. These programs make good use of online discussion forums to announce new developments and provide for community-based user support.

Beyond availability, key considerations in choosing a computer program for SEM analyses are as follows:

- What options are available for specifying models (e.g., matrix notation, equations, path diagrams)?
- Does the program have the capabilities needed for the models I will evaluate (e.g., multilevel and multigroup designs)?
- Does the program offer an estimator appropriate for my data (e.g., noncontinuous measurement scales, nonnormal distributions, and missingness)?
- Does the program provide the data manipulation and output control I desire? If not, does it offer straightforward transfer of manipulated data and output to the programs I intend to use for these purposes?

Trial versions (i.e., limited number of variables or cases) of a number of the programs can be obtained, allowing for a firsthand evaluation of their interface and capabilities.

EVALUATION OF FIT

Once a set of optimal parameter estimates have been obtained, the fit of a model can be evaluated.

In theory, this evaluation can be done in a standard null hypothesis statistical testing framework. That is, a null hypothesis can be posed and either be rejected or not using some test statistic. In the case of structural equation modeling, the null hypothesis is,

$$H_0: \Sigma = \Sigma(\hat{\Theta}), \qquad (17)$$

where Σ is the population covariance matrix, estimated by the observed covariance matrix, and $\Sigma(\hat{\Theta})$ is that matrix written as a function of the model parameter values, or the implied covariance matrix. The goal is to fail to reject this null hypothesis or, in statistical test terms, to find a probability *greater* than .05 associated with the test statistic. The minimized value of the ML fitting function can be used to produce a value that, under certain circumstances, is distributed as a χ^2 statistic with degrees of freedom equal to the difference between the number of nonredundant elements in the covariance matrix and the number of free parameters in the model. In theory, using this value and the appropriate reference distribution, one can conclude that a specified model either fits or does not fit the data.

For two principal reasons, this hypothesis test is, in practice, not useful. Most fundamentally, the conditions necessary for the value on the basis of the minimized value of the fit function to approximate a χ^2 statistic are never met in substantive applications of SEM. These conditions include multivariate normal data, a sample large enough to ensure that the asymptotic properties of the estimator are realized, and a model that is correct in the population. Even if the conditions were met in typical applications, the test suffers from the shortcoming of all null hypothesis statistical tests: Unless the implied and observed covariance matrixes are identical, the null hypothesis can, with enough power, be rejected. Conversely, the implied and observed covariance matrices can be nontrivially different but, if power is sufficiently low, the null hypothesis cannot be rejected. Thus, the statistical test, even if valid on theoretical grounds, is as much a reflection of power as it is of meaningful difference between the implied and observed covariance matrices.

Because of these limitations, alternative means of evaluating model fit have been developed. A prevalent strategy, pioneered by Bentler and Bonett

(1980), involves comparing the fit of a specified model against the fit of a model that specifies no relations among the variables (referred to as the null, baseline, or independence model). These comparisons typically yield a value between 0 and 1 that is interpreted as a proportion. The resultant values are indexes, not statistics, and therefore are descriptive rather than inferential. A widely used index is the comparative fit index (CFI; Bentler, 1990). An alternative strategy is to index the absolute fit of a model by summarizing the differences between corresponding elements in the implied and observed covariance matrixes (i.e., the residuals). The root-mean-square error of approximation (RMSEA) is a commonly used index of this sort (Steiger & Lind, 1980). The RMSEA has the additional benefits of including a correction for model complexity and an interpretation that allows for tests of close, rather than exact, fit (Browne & Cudeck, 1993).

Returning now to the running example, I illustrate the general activity of evaluating fit and the use of these specific indexes of fit. Although I have shown the iteration history and parameter estimates only for the Time 1 protection latent variable in Table 19.2, the value of the fitting function is for the full model, which includes six latent variables and the relations between them. As noted, the value of F_{ML} can be used to produce a value that often is interpreted with reference to the χ^2 distribution. That value is computed as the product of F_{ML}, .630 in the current case, and the sample size minus one (1,654 in this case), which yields a value of 1,042.02. This value is referenced against the χ^2 distribution for the number of degrees of freedom in the model. That value, as noted, corresponds to the difference between the number of elements in the covariance matrix (computed as $p(p + 1)/2$, where p is the number of observed variables) and the number of free parameters the model. For our example, there are 210 observed variances and covariances and 65 free parameters in the model, yielding 145 degrees of freedom. The critical value for $p < .05$ for 145 degrees of freedom is 174.1, well below our observed value of χ^2. Assuming the unrealistic assumptions described earlier are met, this outcome indicates that the data implied by our model do not match the observed data within the sampling error.

Before moving to alternative means of evaluating fit, it will be useful to look more closely at the values reflected in this summary statistic. Again, for illustrative purposes, focusing only on that portion of the model relevant to the Time 1 protection latent variable, I have included two covariance matrixes in Table 19.3. On the left is the portion of the observed covariance matrix indicating the variances of, and covariances between, the indicators of the latent variable in question. Our model accounts for those covariances through the specification of the latent variable $F1$. If this specification is sufficient to explain the pattern of covariances, the parameter estimates should yield an implied, or reproduced, covariance matrix very close to the observed matrix. The implied covariance matrix for these variables is shown on the right in Table 19.3. Looking first to the diagonal, the values are, within rounding, identical. This reflects the fact that we fully account for variance in the variables in the model, either by the influence of the latent variable or the influence of a uniqueness component. The values of most interest are the off-diagonal elements, the observed and implied covariances between the variables. Note that some values in the implied matrix are higher and some are lower than their counterparts in the observed matrix; however, on the whole, the values are quite similar. The differences between corresponding elements in the two matrixes yield a third matrix, the residual matrix. For models that do not provide an acceptable account of the data as reflected in the values of fit indexes, examination of the residual matrix can be useful in pointing to specific relations that are over- or, more typically, underestimated in the specified model.

Returning now to the evaluation of fit, given the well-documented concerns about the validity of the χ^2 variate, I could consult one of a number of alternative indexes that have been proposed and evaluated and that generally have found support for most modeling circumstances. The typical recommendation is to choose at least two, each from a different class of index. As noted earlier, I favor CFI, which indexes incremental, or comparative fit, and RMSEA (with confidence intervals), which reflects absolute fit. Values of CFI can range from 0 to 1, with higher values indicating better fit. The value for a specified model is interpreted as the proportionate improvement in fit of the specified model over the null, or independence, model. Although values of .90 and higher are commonly interpreted as indicative of acceptable fit, simulation studies indicate that .95 is a more appropriate lower bound, with values between .90 and .95 interpreted as marginal fit (Hu & Bentler, 1999). The value of CFI for the example model is .952, indicating that the specified model provides an acceptable account of the data.

RMSEA indexes the degree of misspecification in a model per degree of freedom. To explain, a model can only imply data different from the observed data if it is more parsimonious than the unstructured data. To wit, a just identified model, which has the same number of free parameters as elements in the observed covariance matrix will perfectly reproduce the observed data. Such a model has zero degrees of freedom. Fixing a parameter yields a degree of freedom, but it also requires introducing an assumption in the model that is not born out in the data. To the extent the value of the fixed parameter is incorrect, it will result in a poorer fit of the model to the data

TABLE 19.3

Values in Observed and Implied Covariance Matrices for Indicators of One Latent Variable in the Example Model

Variable	Observed matrix				Implied matrix			
	V_1	V_2	V_3	V_4	V_1	V_2	V_3	V_4
V_1	.331				.333			
V_2	.149	.274			.165	.275		
V_3	.219	.244	.384		.224	.237	.383	
V_4	.141	.132	.183	.327	.130	.137	.186	.327

because of misspecification. RMSEA captures this property across the model. Thus, as noted, our example model has 65 degrees of freedom, which can be interpreted as 65 ways in which an assumption was imposed on the model that could be incorrect. RMSEA addresses the question of whether, on average, these assumptions are tenable given the data. If the assumptions imposed by fixed parameters are perfectly consistent with the observed data, they will result in no misspecification and yield a value for RMSEA of zero, indicating perfect model fit. Unlike χ^2, RMSEA typically is interpreted with reference to a criterion of close fit. Thus, values of .08 or less are viewed as indicative of acceptable model fit. Values from .08 to .10 indicate marginal fit, and values greater than .10 indicate poor fit. The standard error of RMSEA is known, and therefore a confidence interval can be put on the point estimate. It is customary to report the upper and lower limits of the 90% confidence interval. In such cases, the focus is on the degree to which the upper limit falls beneath the .08 and .10 criterion values. For the example model, the point estimate of RMSEA is .061, and the 90% confidence limits are .058 and .065. Because the upper confidence limit falls below .08, RMSEA indicates a close fit of the model to the data.

My use of ML implies that the data are multivariate normal; however, as might be assumed given the behaviors under study and the age of the participants, distributions for several of the measures are highly skewed. Indeed, the normalized value of 289.50 for Mardia's coefficient, a test of the correspondence of the distribution in the observed data to the multivariate normal distribution is very high. Examination of the observed variables indicates significant kurtosis in all three of the problem behaviors, particularly polydrug use. As noted in the section on estimation, normal theory estimates such as those produced by ML can be adjusted by a scaling correction that accounts for departure of the data from normality (Satorra & Bentler, 2001). This adjustment yields new values of fit indexes and adjusted standard errors for parameter estimates that, in simulation studies, closely approximate their values when estimated using distribution-free estimators. When this scaling correction is imposed on the ML solution for our example, it results in a

substantially smaller value of $\chi^2 = 679.35$. The ratio of the normal theory χ^2 (1,042.02 in this case) to the scaled χ^2 is an informal index of the degree of non-normality in the data. The value of about 1.5 for the ratio in our example indicates that the non-normality results in a normal theory χ^2 that is about 50% larger than it should be. Because the scaling adjustment affects both the specified and independence model fits, it is not necessarily the case that the value of CFI will increase with the adjustment. In fact, the CFI value drops slightly to .942, just below the cutoff, following the scaling adjustment. RMSEA declines so that the point estimate is .047 and the 90% confidence limits are .044 and .051. In this instance, the statistics to report and interpret are the scaled statistics, which suggest that the model offers an acceptable account of the data.

If, as in the present case, support for the overall fit of a model is obtained, then attention turns to the values of the parameter estimates. It is possible for a model to provide acceptable fit to the observed data but not yield parameter estimates that are consistent with expectation. The most basic question about model parameter estimates is whether they differ from zero, a hypothesis tested, as in other contexts, by the ratio of the parameter estimate to its standard error. The resulting statistic, the critical ratio, is interpreted as a z statistic. Other questions that can be addressed about parameter estimates are their difference from other assumed values (e.g., .30) and their difference from each other.

Because of the number of free parameters in the example model, I present parameters in the measurement and structural components separately. Parameter estimates for the measurement component are presented in Table 19.4. I have chosen to identify parameters using double-label notation; however, I might have used matrix notation or verbal descriptions depending on the audience. For each parameter, I include the estimated (or fixed) value, the critical ratio, and the standardized estimate. The estimate is an unstandardized value, the equivalent of an unstandardized regression coefficient or a covariance (an unstandardized correlation coefficient). The critical ratio is formed by dividing the estimate by its standard error—in this case, robust standard errors that have been scaled to

TABLE 19.4

Parameter Estimates and Test Statistics for Measurement Component of Example Model

Parameter	Time 1				Time 2		
	Estimate	Critical ratio	Standardized estimate		Estimate	Critical ratio	Standardized estimate
Loadings							
$F1,v_1$[a]	1.00		.69	$F4,v_{11}$[a]	1.00		.66
$F1,v_2$	1.06	19.92	.80	$F4,v_{12}$	1.35	27.79	.88
$F1,v_3$	1.44	26.41	.92	$F4,v_{13}$	1.58	27.86	.92
$F1,v_4$	0.83	18.10	.57	$F4,v_{14}$	0.82	18.40	.51
$F2,v_5$[a]	1.00		.40	$F5,v_{15}$[a]	1.00		.40
$F2,v_6$	1.96	12.01	.54	$F5,v_{16}$	2.00	11.83	.55
$F2,v_7$	1.55	12.96	.78	$F5,v_{17}$	1.51	11.88	.77
$F3,v_8$[a]	1.00		.64	$F6,v_{18}$[a]	1.00		.63
$F3,v_9$	4.61	16.29	.77	$F6,v_{19}$	4.42	17.64	.70
$F3,v_{10}$	0.60	10.41	.67	$F6,v_{20}$	0.70	10.42	.65
Unique variances							
e_1,e_1	0.18	24.09	.73	e_{11},e_{11}	0.18	22.77	.75
e_2,e_2	0.10	6.96	.60	e_{12},e_{12}	0.08	17.67	.48
e_3,e_3	0.06	10.38	.40	e_{13},e_{13}	0.06	13.15	.38
e_4,e_4	0.22	22.56	.82	e_{14},e_{14}	0.26	24.24	.86
e_5,e_5	0.24	26.70	.92	e_{15},e_{15}	0.25	27.23	.92
e_6,e_6	0.42	20.94	.84	e_{16},e_{16}	0.42	21.60	.83
e_7,e_7	0.07	13.10	.63	e_{17},e_{17}	0.07	11.76	.63
e_8,e_8	0.07	13.52	.77	e_{18},e_{18}	0.08	11.40	.77
e_9,e_9	0.73	13.36	.64	e_{19},e_{19}	1.08	16.15	.72
e_{10},e_{10}	0.02	5.76	.74	e_{20},e_{20}	0.04	4.79	.76
Latent variable variances[b]							
$F1,F1$	0.16	14.28	1.00				
$F2,F2$	0.05	7.04	1.00				
$F3,F3$	0.05	6.97	1.00				

Notes. Parameter estimates obtained using maximum likelihood. The standard errors for critical ratios were robust standard errors, rescaled to account for non-normality in the data. All estimates are significantly different from zero at $p < .001$. v_1 and v_{11} = protective normative beliefs, v_2 and v_{12} = realization of conflict between problem behavior and ideals, v_3 and v_{13} = commitment to avoid problem behavior, v_4 and v_{14} = bonding to school, v_5 and v_{15} = low self-esteem, v_6 and v_{16} = sensation seeking, v_7 and v_{17} = impulsive sensation seeking, v_8 and v_{18} = interpersonal aggression, v_9 and v_{19} = sexual activity, v_{10} and v_{20} = polydrug use. $F1$ and $F4$ = Protection. $F2$ and $F5$ = Risk. $F3$ and $F6$ = Problem Behavior.
[a]Value in unstandardized estimate column is fixed value of parameter, for which there is no standard error and, therefore, no critical ratio. [b]Time 2 latent variable variances are not estimated directly.

account for nonnormality in the data. This value is distributed as a z statistic; thus, critical values are 1.96, 2.58, and 3.33 for $p < .05$, $p < .01$, and $p < .001$, respectively. The standardized estimate is the value psychological scientists are inclined to present and interpret from multiple regression analysis and factor analysis. The standardized estimates for loadings are the equivalent of factor loadings in exploratory factor analysis. As is apparent from the

large values for the critical ratio, all factor loadings at both time points are significantly different from zero. The standardized values range from .40 for the loading of low self-esteem (v_5 and v_{15}) on risk ($F2$ and $F5$) to .92 for the loading of commitment to avoid problem behavior (v_3 and v_{13}) on protection ($F1$ and $F4$). The moderate-to-large loadings indicate that the observed variables for each construct share considerable commonality, which is presumed to reflect the construct of interest. Moreover, the equivalent values for corresponding loadings at the two time points suggest that the latent variables are similarly defined across this period of time, a point to which I return later in this section.

The estimates of greatest interest are those that index the relations between latent variables. Those estimates, and other estimates within the structural component of the model, are provided in Table 19.5. Although the autocorrelations between uniqueness might have been presented with estimates from the measurement component of the model, they span the two waves of data collection and therefore are included as part of the structural component. The estimates of these covariances are highly significant, suggesting that, had these paths been omitted from the specification, the fit to the data would have been poor. The standardized estimates are correlation coefficients, and their magnitudes make clear that there is considerable and stable nonrandom variance in the indicators not explained by the latent variables. Moving toward the bottom of Table 19.5 and continuing the focus on covariances, the expected high correlations between the latent variables at Time 1 are apparent. Similarly, the covariances between unexplained variances in the latent variables at Time 2 are significant and strong.

These ancillary estimates appear in order, so our attention can now move to the directional relations between the latent variables at Time 1 and Time 2. First, I consider the autoregressive paths, which reflect the stability of the latent variables over the period of time covered by the study, about 8 months. It is no surprise that there is a high degree of stability in risk-related personality. The standardized estimate suggests that, once stability is taken into account, there is relatively little variance in Time 2 risk to be predicted by the other Time 1 latent variables. The stability of protection as reflected in attitudes, values, and perceptions also is quite high. Somewhat surprising is the nonsignificant autoregressive path for problem behavior, suggesting that the behaviors included do not necessarily reflect stable characteristics of individuals or situations at this age. Moreover, the weak stability coefficient indicates that the majority of variance in problem behavior at Time 2 could be predicted from variables at Time 1.

TABLE 19.5

Parameter Estimates and Test Statistics for Structural Component of Example Model

Parameter	Estimate	Critical ratio	Standardized estimate
Uniqueness autocorrelations			
e_1, e_{11}	.09	16.04***	.49
e_2, e_{12}	.02	5.98***	.21
e_3, e_{13}	.02	5.11***	.28
e_4, e_{14}	.12	14.25***	.51
e_5, e_{15}	.14	18.26***	.58
e_6, e_{16}	.22	15.01***	.51
e_7, e_{17}	.02	4.88***	.29
e_8, e_{18}	.03	9.18***	.46
e_9, e_{19}	.55	12.30***	.62
e_{10}, e_{20}	.01	4.55***	.28
Autoregressive paths			
$F1, F4$	.64	5.16***	.68
$F2, F5$	.83	9.83***	.81
$F3, F6$	.28	1.70	.27
Cross-lagged paths			
$F1, F5$	.05	0.81	.08
$F1, F6$	−.27	−2.79**	−.46
$F2, F4$	−.24	−2.43*	−.13
$F2, F6$	.06	0.75	.05
$F3, F4$	−.02	−0.13	−.01
$F3, F5$	.07	0.82	.08
Variances, disturbances			
d_4, d_4	.05	9.75***	.60
d_5, d_5	.02	6.07***	.60
d_6, d_6	.02	5.58***	.66
Covariances, latent variables			
$F1, F2$	−.07	−11.09***	−.77
$F1, F3$	−.08	−11.22***	−.88
$F2, F3$	.03	9.77***	.68
Covariances, disturbances			
d_4, d_5	−.02	−7.76***	−.67
d_4, d_6	−.03	−7.51***	−.82
d_5, d_6	.01	5.93***	.54

Notes. Parameter estimates obtained using maximum likelihood. The standard errors for critical ratios were robust standard errors, rescaled to account for non-normality in the data. $F1$ = Time 1 Protection. $F2$ = Time 1 Risk. $F3$ = Time 1 Problem Behavior. $F4$ = Time 2 Protection. $F5$ = Time 2 Risk. $F6$ = Time 2 Problem Behavior.
*$p < .05$. **$p < .01$. ***$p < .001$.

Moving now to the cross-lagged paths, we find that only two coefficients are significantly different from zero. The effect of Time 1 protection on Time 2 problem behavior is significant and negative. The standardized estimate indicates that, for each standard deviation increase in Time 1 protection, there is almost half a standard deviation decrease in problem behavior at Time 2, controlling for other paths in the model. A second significant path is between Time 1 risk and Time 2 protection. The negative coefficient, in standardized terms, indicates that for each standard deviation increase in risk-related personality at Time 1, there is a modest decrease in protective attitudes, values, and perceptions at Time 2. These findings, coupled with the nonsignificant cross-lagged paths suggest that these protective factors exert a directional, potentially causal, influence on problem behavior and that problem behavior neither begets problem behavior during this period of time nor erodes protective attitudes, values, and perceptions. The addition of a third time point would allow the test of an intriguing hypotheses suggested by the findings: risk-related personality is associated with less protective attitudes, values, and perceptions, which results in greater problem behavior.

I began the section by outlining Jöreskog's (1993) discussion of the different approaches to using SEM. To this point, it would appear that I am using SEM in a strictly confirmatory manner. I could, however, consider alternatives to the specified model that might serve to increase my confidence that the model affords the best account of the data. Use of this alternative models approach is most effective when the models to be compared are nested. One model is nested in another when its free parameters are a subset of the free parameters in another model. I can produce a model nested in our example model by fixing some of its parameters. To illustrate this process, I consider two alternatives. In one alternative, I include only the autoregressive, or stability, paths; this model assumes no directional relation between the variables. To produce this model, I would fix the six cross-lagged paths in the model to zero. In so doing, I reduce the number of free parameters from 65 to 59, thereby increasing the degrees of freedom from 145 to 151. Adding restrictions always increases the value of the fitting function and, therefore, the value of χ^2 for a model. As with comparisons between R^2s in hierarchical multiple regression, the question is whether the increase is significant given the increase in degrees

of freedom. Like R^2s, χ^2s are additive; thus, I can subtract the value for the less restrictive model from the value for the nested model and test it by referring to the χ^2 distribution for the difference in degrees of freedom. When normal theory estimates and statistics can be used, this test is as simple as subtracting the two χ^2s to produce $\Delta\chi^2$. When the scaling adjustment for non-normality is used, as in the present case, the subtraction is a bit more involved because the influence of non-normality is not identical for the two models (Satorra & Bentler, 2001). The scaled χ^2 for the model with no cross-lagged paths is 705.75. The scaled difference between this value and the scaled value of 679.35 for the specified model (computed using a executable file downloaded from http://www.abdn.ac.uk/~psy086/dept/sbdiff.htm) is highly significant, $\Delta\chi^2 = 26.79$, $p < .001$, indicating that (as we know), one or more of the cross-lagged paths is necessary to account for the data.

An alternative means of producing a nested model is through the use of equality constraints. Equality constraints are used in SEM as a means of testing whether two parameter estimates are significantly different. If, for example, I constrain two loadings to equality in a measurement model, I reduce the number of parameters to be estimated because the parameters constrained to be equal are treated as one parameter. This results in an increase in the number of degrees of freedom by one and allows for a statistical comparison of the two models using the χ^2-difference test. As noted, for the measurement component of the example model, corresponding loadings on the factors at the two time points appear to be equivalent. Indeed, it is important for hypothesis testing using the measures that I show their relation to the latent variables of interest remains constant across the 8-month period of time of the study. I can use equality constraints and a nested model comparison to test for this property of the indicators. Although there are 10 indicators, the loadings for three (one on each latent variable) are fixed and therefore not estimated. I can produce a nested model by constraining loadings for the remaining seven to be equal at the two time points. This yields seven degrees of freedom for testing the difference. The χ^2-difference test was highly significant, $\Delta\chi^2 = 43.27$, $p < .001$, indicating that at least one of the equality constraints was inconsistent with the data. Returning to the parameter estimates in Table 19.4, it appears that the loading of the second indicator of protection varies more from Time 1 to Time 2 and any of the other loadings. Relaxing this constraint yields a model with six more additional degrees of freedom than the original model and nested in it. Although the comparison between these two models yields a significant χ^2 difference, $\Delta\chi^2 = 13.72$, $p = .033$, the remaining differences are, practically speaking, trivial and would only be found different because of the high level of statistical power resulting from the large sample size.

MODEL MODIFICATION

Specified models, including the alternatives to which they are compared do not always provide an acceptable account of the data. That is, they yield values for the fit indexes of choice that fail with reference to a priori criteria (e.g., CFI < .95, RMSEA > .10). In such cases, if the researcher is using SEM in a strictly confirmatory or alternative models manner, the analysis is completed and the model or models declared inadequate as a description of the processes that produced the observed data. Yet, data typically are acquired at considerable effort and expense, leading most researchers to respond to evidence of unacceptable fit by asking, "What if?" which shifts them to using SEM for model generation. The what-if question might concern the observed variables: What if certain variables were dropped from the model or new variables added to it? It is generally the case, however, that the variables in a model are of sufficient interest that dropping one or more would leave a set that does not map well onto the original research question or conceptual model guiding the research. Typically, the what-if question concerns the relations between variables in a model and can be phrased in terms of fixed and free parameters. What if certain parameters that were originally fixed are freed? Or, what if one or more free parameters were fixed?

The consideration of whether model fit might be improved by changing the status of parameters in a model is termed specification searching. As the term

indicates, the goal of specification searching is to find and address the misspecification in the original model that resulted in its lack of acceptable fit to the data. Specification searching typically takes one of two forms, each of which involves consulting the results from the initial estimation and testing. In *manual specification searching*, the researcher consults the tests of specific parameter to determine whether parameters that were free in the model could be fixed to zero or consults the residual matrix to determine whether one or more observed covariances were not sufficiently accounted for by the free parameters in a model. In *automated specification searching*, a computer program evaluates all fixed or free parameters and returns a list of those parameters that are contributing to the size of the model χ^2 relative to its degrees of freedom

Although the example model fits the data at an acceptable label, you will recall that the value of CFI, when scaled, dropped just below the criterion of .95. Although the value of RMSEA indicates a close fit, it might nonetheless prove useful to evaluate whether any adjustments to the model would result in a better account of the data. I first examine tests of individual parameters. Referring to Table 19.5, four of the six cross-lagged paths were nonsignificant, suggesting that fixing them to zero would simplify the model without significantly reducing fit. The resultant model does not affect the value of CFI but results in a slightly reduced value of RMSEA (which rewards parsimony). In addition to the trivial improvement in fit, these adjustments to the model result in the autoregressive path for problem behavior achieving statistical significance. This result illustrates the fact that parameters in a model are dependent. As such, changing the status of one will likely change the estimate of others. For this reason, post hoc adjustments are best made one at a time. Because the adjustments do not substantially improve the fit of the model, the model already offers a suitable account of the data, and there is a good chance the modifications would not replicate (MacCallum et al., 1992), I do not retain them. Although the final value of CFI falls just short of the ideal value of .95, the value of .942 for a model that includes no post hoc modifications is more impressive than a value greater than .95 for a model that includes modifications based on specification searching.

I next consult the residual matrix to determine whether there is evidence that any covariances have been underestimated because certain parameters were fixed at zero. Recall that the residual matrix is constructed by subtracting corresponding elements in the observed and implied covariance matrixes. Relatively large values raise the value of the fitting function and, thereby, reduce the favorability of fit indexes. Manually evaluating the residuals can be relatively straightforward for small models; however, for a model based on 20 observed variables, scanning the 190 residual covariances, even their more readily interpretable standardized form, often does not suggest obvious ways in which a model might be modified to improve its fit. Indeed, the only thing clear from scanning the residuals is that the relation between low self-esteem and a number of the remaining observed variables is underestimated. Given the number of these residuals and the position of relevant parameters across the model, I see no obvious fixed parameters that, if freed, would provide the maximum improvement in the fit of the model.

An alternative strategy, one better suited to larger models such as our example, is automated specification searching. Automated searching typically focuses on fixed parameters in a model (although some computer programs allow a focus on free parameters as well). The computer program, in effect, frees each fixed parameter and returns, in the form of a *modification index*, the amount by which the model χ^2 would be reduced if the parameter were freed (Bentler, 1986a; Sörbom, 1989). Some programs order these from highest to lowest, allowing a quick determination of which modifications would produce the greatest improvement in fit. As noted, however, each modification ripples through the model, affecting estimates of some, if not all, of the other parameters. Thus, for example, it may appear that model fit would improve if two fixed parameters were freed; however, freeing the first yields a model in which freeing the second offers no additional improvement in fit. Because of the dependency among parameters, a better approach is to use the multivariate approach to automated searching, in which the full set of modification indexes is

evaluated in search of the set of modifications that, together, would produce the maximum improvement in fit. Although automated specification searching for the example models suggests a number of fixed parameters that, if freed, would improve the fit of the model, one stands out as particularly influential. Referring back to the covariance matrixes, the observed covariance between bonding to school and low self-esteem at Time 2 is –.328, but the value implied by the model is only –.051. Thus, the model only accounts for about 16% of the covariance between these variables. One means of accounting for the residual covariance in the model is to allow the uniquenesses for these two variables to covary. Indeed, the automated search indicates that freeing this parameter would result in a drop in the χ^2 for the model of 143.51. And respecifying the model to include this parameter results in a value of CFI that now exceeds the criterion, .952, and an improved value of RMSEA, .043. The improvement can be seen in the residual covariance matrix, for which the value of this covariance falls to zero (i.e., it is fully accounted for by the model).

Because adjustments to the original specification were made with reference to the data, the likelihood of Type I error is unacceptably high, and therefore fit statistics and indexes cannot be taken at face value (MacCallum et al., 1992). Thus, although researchers working in model generation mode might be tempted to confidently interpret the results from estimation of respecified models that produce acceptable values of fit indexes, they should instead proceed with caution because the likelihood is unacceptably high (i.e., > .05) that the model that fits the data in hand would not fit another set of data from the same population. As such, the results can only be interpreted with reference to the current sample. To infer with confidence that the parameter I freed on the basis of consulting the data applies to the population and not just my sample, I would need to demonstrate satisfactory fit of the modified model to data from a cross-validation sample from the same population.

INTERPRETATION

Once support has been obtained for an interesting and useful model, the focus moves to the final step in using SEM—interpretation and reporting. Interpretation begins with presentation. Although what is presented and, to some extent, how it is presented will be constrained by the medium and forum, a number of principles apply whether the findings are presented in a journal article, a book, or an oral presentation. Particularly when the findings are presented in written format, the observed data should be provided either in the form of a covariance matrix or a correlation matrix with standard deviations (which computer programs can use to derive the variances and covariances). For small data sets, this information can be presented in a table in the text of the document. For larger data sets, the information can be included in an appendix or a public access computer, typically accessed through a website (the covariance matrix for the example used in this chapter can be accessed at http://www.duke.edu/~rhoyle/data/Hoyle_HRM_chapter.dat). In addition, an accurate accounting of the focal model as well as any alternatives and modifications should be included. For many models, a path diagram will suffice. Regardless of the format in which the model is presented, a thorough accounting for degrees of freedom should be offered. The estimation method should be made explicit and its use justified. A set of fit indexes and criteria for their interpretation should be offered (see Hu & Bentler, 1999, for a useful overview). Parameter estimates should be provided. For simple models, these can be included on a path diagram and flagged for statistical significance. For more complex models, a table such as Tables 19.4 and 19.5 should be used. In my presentation of findings from the example analysis, I listed all parameters and provided unstandardized and standardized values as well as statistical test information. I would be unlikely to provide that level of detail in a journal article; however, the estimates and tests of the focal parameters (e.g., the autoregressive and cross-lagged paths) should be given in full. When multiple alternative models are specified a priori, it is useful to table the fit statistics for each model, which facilitates comparisons between models. Finally, if modifications are made to the originally specified model or an alternative specified alternative, it should be made clear to the reader the basis on which the model was modified, including how many consultations of the data were required to produce the model to be interpreted. Additional detail regarding these aspects of presentation can be found in a number of articles and chapters focused specifically on the presentation of results from SEM analyses (e.g., Boomsma, 2000; Hoyle & Panter, 1995; McDonald & Ho, 2002).

The substantive interpretation of SEM results refers to information provided in the presentation. Care should be taken to distinguish between comparative and absolute fit, unstandardized and standardized parameters estimates, and a priori and post hoc components of a model. As with any multivariate model, specific relations should be described with reference for other relations in the model.

Beyond these specific guidelines for presenting and interpreting the statistical results of an SEM analysis, two broader considerations should receive attention. A key consideration in interpretation is the extent to which a statistically defensible model provides a *uniquely* satisfactory account of the data. That is, for many well-fitting models, it is possible to generate one or more alternative models that are, statistically speaking, equivalent to the specified model (Breckler, 1990; MacCallum, Wegener, Uchino, & Fabrigar, 1993). For example, in a simple study involving two variables, x and y, the model that specifies x as a cause of y cannot be distinguished in terms of fit from a model that specifies y as a cause of x or x and y as simply correlated. A set of basic respecification rules can be used to generate possible alternatives to a specified model when they are less obvious (e.g., Stelzl, 1986). Sometimes the inferential conundrum produced by equivalent models can be resolved through design (e.g., x is manipulated) or a consideration of what the variables represent (e.g., x is a biological characteristic). Otherwise, the researcher can only infer that the results provide necessary, but not sufficient, support for the focal model.

Perhaps the most controversial aspect of interpreting results from SEM analyses is the inference of causality (e.g., Baumrind, 1983). Although the judicious application of SEM can strengthen causal inferences when they are otherwise warranted, SEM cannot overcome the significant limitations of non-experimental designs, particularly when all data are gathered at one point in time. Because of its capacity for isolating putative causal variables and modeling data from longitudinal designs, SEM offers a stronger basis for inferring causality than commonly used statistical techniques. In the end, however, statistics yield to design when it comes to causal inferences, and therefore data generated by experimental or carefully designed quasi-experimental designs with a longitudinal component are required (Hoyle & Robinson, 2003).

PROTOTYPIC MODELS

Except for limitations associated with research design (e.g., temporal order of variables in longitudinal models) and model identification, there is considerable flexibility in model specification for SEM analyses. Indeed, as the number of observed variables increases, the number of models one might construct from them increases dramatically (e.g., Raykov & Marcoulides, 2001). For that reason, it is not possible to review all, or even a substantial proportion, of the models psychological scientists might construct and evaluate using SEM. Rather, to give a sense of the sort of models psychological scientists might evaluate using SEM, I briefly describe a number of prototypic models. These generally fall into one of two categories: (a) models focused primarily on latent variables without particular concern for how they relate to each other, and (b) models focused primarily on structural paths, whether they involve observed or latent variables.

At several points in the presentation of these models, I refer to comparisons between groups. Because such comparisons can be undertaken for any model evaluated using SEM, I describe the basic strategy for making such comparisons before presenting the models. In multigroup SEM, data are available on all of the observed variables for two or more groups of cases for which a comparison would be of interest. For instance, the example data set referenced throughout the chapter includes female and male middle-school students in sufficient numbers that parameters in the model could be estimated separately for the two groups and compared individually or in sets. To compare a model across groups, I first need to divide the data according to group

membership and produce (or allow the computer program to produce) separate covariance matrices. A single model is simultaneously fit to these matrixes, permitting the use of equality constraints to compare parameters between groups. For example, I could fit the example model to data from female and male students, constraining corresponding autoregressive and cross-lagged paths to be equal. That model is nested in and has nine more degrees of freedom than a model in which the parameters are free to vary between groups. The χ^2-difference test evaluates whether the set of constraints are consistent with the data. If the difference is significant, adding one or more of the equality constraints resulted in a decline in fit—that is, one or more parameters differ between the groups. Such multiple group comparisons are the equivalent of tests of statistical interaction because a significant between-group difference indicates that the relation between two variables differs across levels of a third variable—in this case, the grouping variable (for a general treatment of between-group comparisons, see Hancock, 2004).

MODELS FOCUSED ON LATENT VARIABLES

Although the model used to illustrate the steps involved in using SEM included latent variables, the primary focus of the model was the directional relations between variables from Time 1 to Time 2. Such is not always the case. For example, it might be the case the latent variables—protection, risk, and problem behavior—are not sufficiently well-defined to warrant tests of hypotheses about the relations between them. Or perhaps the constructs are generally well-defined, but there is reason to believe the relations between the indicators and latent variables differ across groups or time. These and a host of additional questions of potential interest to psychological scientists can be addressed using the measurement model. I illustrate the possibilities by describing two latent-variable focused models.

Measurement Invariance

When latent variables are included in a model and mean levels on those variables or their relations with other variables are to be compared across samples or within a sample across time, a key concern is whether the meaning of the latent variables is consistent across the units to be compared. To the extent that the measurement model for a latent variable is consistent across samples or time, it is *invariant* with respect to measurement.

SEM is an appealing strategy for evaluating measurement invariance, because of the flexibility with which models can be specified and estimated, and the ease with which parameters can be compared across groups or time. For instance, consider the question of measurement invariance with respect to the risk construct in the example used throughout the chapter. Perhaps our concern is the degree to which dispositional risk influences problem behavior for young women and men. A meaningful comparison of this influence assumes that the indicators of risk function similarly for females and males. We can simultaneously estimate the measurement model for risk for females and males, using equality constraints to compare any or all parameters in the model. For instance, it would be important to show that responses on the indicators (e.g., impulsive decision making) are influenced by the latent variable to a similar degree for the two groups (i.e., the factor loadings are comparable). This evaluation is done within a multigroup context in which the models are simultaneously fit to separate covariance matrixes. If we constrain all of the factor loadings to be equal for females and males, and the fit is equivalent to the fit of a model in which the loadings are allowed to vary, we infer that the loadings are equivalent. The same strategy could be used to compare uniquenesses, the variance of the latent variable, or any parameter in the measurement model. Although it would involve a single covariance matrix, the same strategy would be used to evaluate the invariance of the construct for a given sample at two or more points in time as in the example. This form of invariance would be particularly important for indicators measured on multiple occasions across a period of development during which considerable change is expected (e.g., puberty).

The evaluation of measurement invariance can extend beyond the parameters estimated in standard measurement models. Specifically, the invariance of

parameters that implicate the means of the observed variables can be included in the evaluation. This focus on metric invariance (Widaman & Reise, 1997) requires expanding the observed covariance matrix to include the observed means (which typically are zero because variables are mean centered), producing the *augmented moment matrix*. The specification expands as well to include intercepts in the measurement equations, which in the standard application included only the slopes as well as the means of the latent variables. Thus, in addition to the typical covariance structure, the model includes the mean structure (Curran, 2003). The addition of the mean structure allows for the comparison of additional aspects of the measurement model that are relevant to the question of consistency across groups or time and allows for the comparison of *structured means* on the latent variables even when the measurement model is not fully invariant (Byrne, Shavelson, & B. Muthén, 1989).

Latent Growth Models

The addition of the mean structure to a model makes possible another class of specialized models of relevance to phenomena studied by researchers in psychological scientists—latent growth models. Like trend analysis in repeated measures ANOVA, latent growth models focus on modeling patterns of means over time. For instance, returning to the illustrative example, if a sample of adolescents completed our bonding to school measure at the beginning of each of their last 2 years in middle school and their first 2 years of high school, we could examine the trajectory, or growth curve, of school belonging during these transitional years. As in repeated measures ANOVA, we can evaluate the first $k - 1$ order curves, with k indicating the number of repeated assessments.

A virtue of latent growth curve modeling in the SEM context is the ability to focus on individual growth (Singer & Willett, 2003; Willett & Sayer, 1994). For instance, in the school-bonding example, let us assume that, generally speaking, the trajectory during the period we are studying is linear. This outcome would be determined by observing acceptable fit of relevant portions of a model in which the means are fit to a straight line. If estimation yields support for this model, then the focus turns to variability in growth parameters—the slope and intercept of the linear trajectory. These growth parameters are modeled as variances of latent variables, hence, the label *latent* growth modeling. If, for instance, there is in effect no variability in the slope parameter, we might infer that the observed trajectory is normative. If there is variability in this parameter or the intercept parameter, then we can move to an interesting set of questions that concern the explanation or consequences of this variability. At this point, the model is referred to as a conditional growth model, because we are acknowledging that the growth parameters vary across individuals as a function of some characteristic of those individuals or the circumstances in which they live. This general strategy—determining the shape of the trajectory of change in a construct over time and then attempting to explain individual variability in trajectories—is particularly useful for studying development or the time course of a process.

MODELS FOCUSED ON STRUCTURAL PATHS

As with the example used throughout the chapter, SEM frequently is used to model the relations between variables, Although, as in path analysis, the relations can involve only measured variables, the most beneficial use of SEM is to model directional relations between latent variables. I illustrate the benefits of modeling relations in this way.

Cross-Lagged Panel Models

Panel models are those in which the same variables are assessed at multiple points in time. Our example is an instance of this type of model. The simplest case, two variables and two waves of data, illustrates the logic and benefits of cross-lagged panel models as analyzed using SEM. Modeling the two variables as latent variables ensures that no path coefficients are attenuated because of measurement error. This is a particular advantage in this context because path coefficients are to be compared, and it is important that any observed differences in coefficients be attributable to differences in the actual strength of the relations between constructs as opposed to

differential attenuation of path coefficients because of measurement error. Another concern is that the cross-lagged path coefficients are estimated controlling for autoregression. By controlling for autoregression, we ensure that the cross-lagged paths do not reflect the covariation between stable components of the two constructs.

In the prototypic application of SEM to cross-lagged panel designs, we are interested in the absolute and the relative magnitudes of the coefficients associated with the cross-lagged paths. In absolute terms, we are interested in whether, after controlling for stability in the constructs, there is evidence of an association between them. This is determined by testing the departure of the estimates of the path coefficients from zero. In relative terms, we are interested in whether one cross-lagged path coefficient is larger than the other. This is determined by constraining the coefficients to be equal and determining whether the fit of the model declines significantly. If it does, then the constraint must be relaxed and the inference is that the two coefficients differ. If one cross-lagged coefficient is larger than the other, particularly if the smaller coefficient is not significantly different from zero, then the evidence supports a causal relation in the direction of the path associated with the larger coefficient. Thus, for instance, although it is not clear a priori whether problem behaviors influence, or are influenced by, protective attitudes, values, and perceptions, the findings in our example provide strong evidence that the effect is directional and, during the developmental period covered by the study, runs from protection to problem behavior.

Mediation

A distinguishing feature of theories in psychological science is their prescription of the processes or mechanisms by which one construct exerts a causal influence on another. Competing theories may agree about the causal relation but offer differing accounts of the process or mechanisms, prompting research focused specifically on the explanation for the effect. Variables that capture the putative explanations are mediators, and models in which their explanation of an effect is estimated are mediation models. Although such models can be estimated and tested by a series of multiple regression equations (Baron & Kenny, 1986), the inability to deal effectively with measurement error in multiple regression analysis, although always a concern, is of particular problematic for tests of mediation.

The simplest mediation model includes three directional effects: the direct effect of a causal variable on an outcome, the direct effect of the cause on a mediator, and the direct effect of the mediator on the outcome. The latter two effects, together, constitute the indirect effect of the cause on the outcome. The product of the path coefficients for these two paths indexes the indirect, or mediated, effect. In this simple model, the direct and indirect paths are perfectly correlated. As one increases, the other decreases. Moreover, the strongest evidence in support of a putative mediator is a significant indirect effect and a nonsignificant direct effect of the cause on the outcome. Although a number of conditions might lead to the underestimation of the indirect effect, one that is addressed well by SEM is unreliability in the mediator (Hoyle & Kenny, 1999). As the degree of unreliability in the mediator increases, the indirect effect is increasingly underestimated and the direct effect is overestimated. SEM offers a means of estimating these effects with unreliability removed from the mediator. When multiple indicators are available, this is accomplished by modeling the mediator as a latent variable. When only one indicator is available, unreliability can be removed from the mediator by modeling it as a latent variable with a single indicator whose uniqueness is fixed to reflect an estimate of unreliability in the indicator. Using either strategy ensures that the indirect effect is not underestimated, the direct effect is not overestimated, and, as a result, evidence for mediation by the proposed process or mechanism is not missed when it should be found.

Latent Interaction

Measurement error is similarly problematic for tests of moderation, or interaction, in which the effect of one variable on another is assumed to vary across levels of a third variable. The effects of measurement error are compounded in tests of moderation because those tests often involve the product of two variables, each of which may be measured with error. The reliability of the product term typically is lower than the reliability of either of the individual variables, increasing the likelihood that a model that includes the main effects and interaction will yield support only for the main effects. Fortunately, unreliability can be effectively removed from the individual variables and their product by modeling them as latent variables using SEM.

Although the basic approach to using SEM in this way was documented in the mid-1980s (Kenny & Judd, 1984), it has seen limited use. In part, this is due to the fact that specification of the latent interaction variable is complex—increasingly so as the number of indicators of each individual variable increases beyond two. This complexity stems from the fact that indicators of the latent interaction variable are the cross-products of the indicators of the two variables (e.g., two latent variables with three indicators each yields nine indicators of the latent interaction variable) and their relation to both the latent variable and their uniqueness term is nonlinear. It is now apparent that this complexity can be substantially reduced with little or no impact on the integrity of the estimate of the interaction effect. One approach involves fixing most of the parameters (i.e., loadings and uniquenesses) in the latent interaction variable using values calculated from parameter estimates obtained from a model that includes only the individual latent variables (i.e., no latent interaction variable; Ping, 1995). The nonlinearity is conveyed in the fixed parameters, substantially simplifying its specification and estimation. Recent work supports the use of an even simpler approach to specifying the latent interaction term that yields results that differ trivially from those obtained using the full specification. In this approach, each indicator of the two variables is used in only one product variable (e.g., two latent variables with three indicators each—x_1, x_2, x_3, and y_1, y_2, y_3—yield only three indicators of the latent interaction variable—x_1y_1, x_2y_2, x_3y_3), and the relation of these products to their uniqueness and the latent variable is modeled as linear (Marsh, Wen, Nagengast, & Hau, in press). By extracting unreliability from the interaction term, these methods significantly increase the likelihood of detecting moderation when it is present.

CONCLUSION

The flexibility and increasing generality of SEM make it an attractive alternative to traditional statistical methods such as ANOVA, multiple regression analysis, and exploratory factor analysis for psychological scientists. Although those methods have been, and will continue to be, well suited to many hypothesis tests in psychology, they significantly limit the range of hypotheses than can be considered. SEM, with its focus on modeling rather than simply analyzing data, affords new ways of studying the measurement of complex constructs and the relations between them. The ability to embed latent variables in any model is perhaps the most important feature of SEM and, as I have demonstrated, can be used to considerable benefit when the observed variables are measured with error. If the possibilities described and illustrated in this chapter have piqued your interest, I recommend building on the foundation provided here by consulting one or more of the detailed treatments offered in the growing array of textbooks (e.g., Bollen, 1989; Kaplan, 2009; Kline, 2010; Schumacker & Lomax, 2004) and edited volumes (e.g., Hancock & Mueller, 2006; Hoyle, 1995, 2012; Marcoulides & Schumacker, 1996).

References

Arbuckle, J. L. (1995). AMOS for Windows Analysis of Moment Structures (Version 3.5) [Computer software]. Chicago, IL: SmallWaters Corp.

Baron, R. M., & Kenny, D. A. (1986). The moderator–mediator variable distinction in social psychological research: Conceptual, strategic, and statistical considerations. *Journal of Personality and Social Psychology, 51*, 1173–1182. doi:10.1037/0022-3514.51.6.1173

Baumrind, D. (1983). Specious causal attribution in the social sciences: The reformulated stepping-stone theory of heroin use. *Journal of Personality and Social Psychology, 45*, 1289–1298. doi:10.1037/0022-3514.45.6.1289

Bentler, P. M. (1985). *Theory and implementation of EQS: A structural equations program.* Los Angeles, CA: BMDP Statistical Software.

Bentler, P. M. (1986a). *Lagrange multiplier and Wald tests for EQS and EQS/PC.* Los Angeles, CA: BMDP Statistical Software.

Bentler, P. M. (1986b). Structural equation modeling and Psychometrika: An historical perspective on growth and achievements. *Psychometrika, 51*, 35–51. doi:10.1007/BF02293997

Bentler, P. M. (1989). *EQS: Structural equations program manual.* Los Angeles, CA: BMDP Statistical Software.

Bentler, P. M. (1990). Comparative fit indexes in structural models. *Psychological Bulletin, 107*, 238–246. doi:10.1037/0033-2909.107.2.238

Bentler, P. M., & Bonett, D. G. (1980). Significance tests and goodness-of-fit in the analysis of covariance structures. *Psychological Bulletin, 88*, 588–606. doi:10.1037/0033-2909.88.3.588

Bentler, P. M., & Speckart, G. (1979). Models of attitude–behavior relations. *Psychological Review, 86*, 452–464. doi:10.1037/0033-295X.86.5.452

Bentler, P. M., & Weeks, D. G. (1980). Linear structural equations with latent variables. *Psychometrika, 45*, 289–308. doi:10.1007/BF02293905

Blalock, H. M. (1964). *Causal inferences in nonexperimental research.* Chapel Hill: University of North Carolina Press.

Blunch, N. J. (2008). *Introduction to structural equation modelling using SPSS and AMOS.* Thousand Oaks, CA: Sage.

Bollen, K. A. (1989). *Structural equations with latent variables.* New York, NY: Wiley.

Boomsma, A. (2000). Reporting analyses of covariance structures. *Structural Equation Modeling, 7*, 461–483. doi:10.1207/S15328007SEM0703_6

Box, G. E. P. (1979). Robustness in the strategy of scientific model building. In R. L. Lawner & G. N. Wilkinson (Eds.), *Robustness in statistics* (pp. 199–217). New York, NY: Academic Press.

Breckler, S. J. (1990). Applications of covariance structure modeling in psychology: Cause for concern? *Psychological Bulletin, 107*, 260–273. doi:10.1037/0033-2909.107.2.260

Browne, M. W. (1984). Asymptotic distribution-free methods in the analysis of covariance structures. *British Journal of Mathematical and Statistical Psychology, 37*, 62–83.

Browne, M. W., & Cudeck, R. (1993). Alternative ways of assessing model fit. In K. A. Bollen & J. S. Long (Eds.), *Testing structural equation models* (pp. 136–162). Thousand Oaks, CA: Sage.

Burks, B. S. (1928). The relative influence of nature and nurture upon mental development: A comparative study of foster parent–foster child resemblance and true parent–true child resemblance. In G. M. Whipple (Ed.), *The twenty-seventh yearbook of the National Society for the Study of Education* (pp. 219–316). Bloomington, IL: Public School Publishing Company.

Byrne, B. M. (1998). *Structural equation modeling with LISREL, PRELIS, and SIMPLIS: Basic concepts, applications, and programming.* New York, NY: Psychology Press.

Byrne, B. M. (2006). *Structural equation modeling with EQS: Basic concepts, applications, and programming* (2nd ed.). Mahwah, NJ: Erlbaum.

Byrne, B. M. (2010). *Structural equation modeling with AMOS: Basic concepts, applications, and programming* (2nd ed.). New York, NY: Taylor & Francis.

Byrne, B. M. (2011). *Structural equation modeling with Mplus: Basic concepts, applications, and programming.* New York, NY: Psychology Press.

Byrne, B. M., Shavelson, R. J., & Muthén, B. (1989). Testing for the equivalence of factor covariance and mean structures: The issue of partial measurement invariance. *Psychological Bulletin, 105,* 456–466. doi:10.1037/0033-2909.105.3.456

Curran, P. J. (2000). A latent curve framework for studying developmental trajectories of adolescent substance use. In J. Rose, L. Chassin, C. Presson, & J. Sherman (Eds.), *Multivariate applications in substance use research* (pp. 1–42). Mahwah, NJ: Erlbaum.

Curran, P. J. (2003). Have multilevel models been structural equation models all along? *Multivariate Behavioral Research, 38,* 529–569. doi:10.1207/s15327906mbr3804_5

DeCarlo, L. T. (1997). On the meaning and use of kurtosis. *Psychological Methods, 2,* 292–307. doi:10.1037/1082-989X.2.3.292

Denis, D. J., & Legerski, J. (2006). Causal modeling and the origins of path analysis. *Theory and Science, 7.* Retrieved from http://theoryandscience.icaap.org/content/vol7.1/denis.html

Duncan, O. D. (1969). Some linear models for two-wave, two-variable panel analysis. *Psychological Bulletin, 72,* 177–182. doi:10.1037/h0027876

Duncan, O. D. (1975). *Introduction to structural equation models.* New York, NY: Academic Press.

Edwards, J. R., & Bagozzi, R. P. (2000). On the nature and direction of relationships between constructs and measures. *Psychological Methods, 5,* 155–174. doi:10.1037/1082-989X.5.2.155

Flora, D. B., & Curran, P. J. (2004). An empirical evaluation of alternative methods of estimation for confirmatory factor analysis with ordinal data. *Psychological Methods, 9,* 466–491. doi:10.1037/1082-989X.9.4.466

Fox, J. (2006). Structural equation modeling with the SEM package in R. *Structural Equation Modeling, 13,* 465–486. doi:10.1207/s15328007sem1303_7

Goldberger, A. S. (1971). Econometrics and psychometrics: A survey of commonalities. *Psychometrika, 36,* 83–107. doi:10.1007/BF02291392

Goldberger, A. S., & Duncan, O. D. (Eds.). (1973). *Structural equation models in the social sciences.* New York, NY: Academic Press.

Hancock, G. R. (2004). Experimental, quasi-experimental, and nonexperimental design and analysis with latent variables. In D. Kaplan (Ed.), *The handbook of quantitative methodology for the social sciences* (pp. 317–334). Thousand Oaks, CA: Sage.

Hancock, G. R., & Mueller, R. O. (Eds.). (2006). *Structural equation modeling: A second course.* Greenwich, CT: Information Age.

Harrington, N. G., Giles, S. M., Hoyle, R. H., Feeney, G. J., & Yungbluth, S. C. (2001). Evaluation of the All Stars Character Education and Problem Behavior Prevention Program: Effects on mediator and outcome variables for middle school students. *Health Education and Behavior, 28,* 533–546. doi:10.1177/109019810102800502

Hershberger, S. L. (2003). The growth of structural equation modeling: 1994–2001. *Structural Equation Modeling, 10,* 35–46. doi:10.1207/S15328007SEM1001_2

Hoyle, R. H. (Ed.). (1995). *Structural equation modeling: Concepts, issues, and applications.* Thousand Oaks, CA: Sage.

Hoyle, R. H. (Ed.). (2012). *Handbook of structural equation modeling.* New York, NY: Guilford Press.

Hoyle, R. H., & Kenny, D. A. (1999). Sample size, reliability, and tests of statistical mediation. In R. H. Hoyle (Ed.), *Statistical strategies for small sample research* (pp. 195–222). Thousand Oaks, CA: Sage.

Hoyle, R. H., & Panter, A. T. (1995). Writing about structural equation models. In R. H. Hoyle (Ed.), *Structural equation modeling: Concepts, issues, and applications* (pp. 158–176). Thousand Oaks, CA: Sage.

Hoyle, R. H., & Robinson, J. I. (2003). Mediated and moderated effects in social psychological research: Measurement, design, and analysis issues. In C. Sansone, C. Morf, & A. T. Panter (Eds.), *Handbook of methods in social psychology* (pp. 213–233). Thousand Oaks, CA: Sage.

Hu, L.-T., & Bentler, P. M. (1999). Cutoff criteria for fit indexes in covariance structure analysis: Conventional criteria versus new alternatives. *Structural Equation Modeling, 6,* 1–5. doi:10.1080/10705519909540118

Huba, G. J., & Bentler, P. M. (1982). On the usefulness of latent variable causal modeling in testing theories of naturally occurring events (including adolescent drug use): A rejoinder to Martin. *Journal of Personality and Social Psychology, 43,* 604–611. doi:10.1037/0022-3514.43.3.604

Johnson, D. R., & Creech, J. C. (1983). Ordinal measures in multiple indicator models: A simulation study of categorization error. *American Sociological Review, 48,* 398–407. doi:10.2307/2095231

Jöreskog, K. G. (1973). A general method for estimating a linear structural equation system. In A. S. Goldberger & O. D. Duncan (Eds.), *Structural equation models in the social sciences* (pp. 85–112). New York, NY: Academic Press.

Jöreskog, K. G. (1993). Testing structural equation models. In K. A. Bollen & J. S. Long (Eds.), *Testing structural equation models* (pp. 294–316). Thousand Oaks, CA: Sage.

Jöreskog, K. G., & Sörbom, D. (2006). LISREL 8.8 for Windows [Computer software]. Lincolnwood, IL: Scientific Software International.

Kaplan, D. (2008). An overview of Markov chain methods for the study of stage-sequential developmental processes. *Developmental Psychology, 44*, 457–467. doi:10.1037/0012-1649.44.2.457

Kaplan, D. (2009). *Structural equation modeling: Foundations and extensions* (2nd ed.). Thousand Oaks, CA: Sage.

Keesling, J. W. (1972). *Maximum likelihood approaches to causal analysis* (Unpublished doctoral dissertation). University of Chicago, Chicago, IL.

Kelloway, E. K. (1998). *Using LISREL for structural equation modeling: A researcher's guide.* Thousand Oaks, CA: Sage.

Kenny, D. A., & Judd, C. M. (1984). Estimating the nonlinear and interactive effects of latent variables. *Psychological Bulletin, 96*, 201–210. doi:10.1037/0033-2909.96.1.201

Kline, R. B. (2010). *Principles and practice of structural equation modeling* (3rd ed.). New York, NY: Guilford Press.

MacCallum, R. C., Roznowski, M., & Necowitz, L. B. (1992). Model modifications in covariance structure analysis: The problem of capitalization on chance. *Psychological Bulletin, 111*, 490–504. doi:10.1037/0033-2909.111.3.490

MacCallum, R. C., Wegener, D. T., Uchino, B. N., & Fabrigar, L. R. (1993). The problem of equivalent models in applications of covariance structure analysis. *Psychological Bulletin, 114*, 185–199.

Mann, H. B., & Wald, E. (1943). On the statistical treatment of linear stochastic difference equations. *Econometrica, 11*, 173–220. doi:10.2307/1905674

Marcoulides, G. A., & Schumacker, R. E. (Eds.). (1996). *Advanced structural equation modeling: Issues and techniques.* Mahwah, NJ: Erlbaum.

Marsh, H. W., Lüdtke, O., Trautwein, U., & Morin, A. J. S. (2009). Classical latent profile analysis of academic self-concept dimensions: Synergy of person- and variable-centered approaches to theoretical models of self-concept. *Structural Equation Modeling, 16*, 191–225. doi:10.1080/10705110902751010

Marsh, H. W., Wen, Z., Nagengast, B., & Hau, K.-T. (in press). Latent-variable approaches to tests of interaction effects. In R. H. Hoyle (Ed.), *Handbook of structural equation modeling.* New York, NY: Guilford Press.

Maruyama, G., & McGarvey, B. (1980). Evaluating causal models: An application of maximum-likelihood analysis of structural equations. *Psychological Bulletin, 87*, 502–512. doi:10.1037/0033-2909.87.3.502

McArdle, J. J. (in press). Some ethical issues in factor analysis. In A. T. Panter & S. Sterba (Eds.), *Handbook of ethics in quantitative methodology.* New York, NY: Taylor & Francis.

McDonald, R. P., & Ho, M.-H. R. (2002). Principles and practice in reporting structural equation analyses. *Psychological Methods, 7*, 64–82. doi:10.1037/1082-989X.7.1.64

Mueller, R. O. (1999). *Basic principles of structural equation modeling: An introduction to LISREL and EQS.* New York, NY: Springer.

Muthén, L. K., & Muthén, B. O. (1998). *Mplus user's guide.* Los Angeles, CA: Authors.

Muthén, B. O. (1984). A general structural equation model with dichotomous, ordered, categorical and continuous latent variable indicators. *Psychometrika, 49*, 115–132. doi:10.1007/BF02294210

Myung, J. (2003). Tutorial on maximum likelihood estimation. *Journal of Mathematical Psychology, 47*, 90–100. doi:10.1016/S0022-2496(02)00028-7

Pearl, J. (2000). *Causality: Models, reasoning, and inference.* Cambridge, England: Cambridge University Press.

Ping, R. A., Jr. (1995). A parsimonious estimating technique for interaction and quadratic latent variables. *Journal of Marketing Research, 32*, 336–347. doi:10.2307/3151985

Rabe-Hesketh, S., Skrondal, A., & Pickles, A. (2004). Generalized multilevel structural equation modeling. *Psychometrika, 69*, 167–190. doi:10.1007/BF02295939

Raykov, T., & Marcoulides, G. A. (2001). Can there be infinitely many models equivalent to a given covariance structure model? *Structural Equation Modeling, 8*, 142–149. doi:10.1207/S15328007SEM0801_8

Rodgers, J. L. (2010). The epistemology of mathematical and statistical modeling: A quiet methodological revolution. *American Psychologist, 65*, 1–12. doi:10.1037/a0018326

Satorra, A., & Bentler, P. M. (1994). Corrections to test statistics and standard errors in covariance structure analysis. In A. von Eye & C. C. Clogg (Eds.), *Latent variables analysis: Applications for developmental research* (pp. 399–419). Thousand Oaks, CA: Sage.

Satorra, A., & Bentler, P. M. (2001). A scaled difference chi-square test statistic for moment structure analysis. *Psychometrika, 66*, 507–514. doi:10.1007/BF02296192

Schumacker, R. E., & Lomax, R. G. (2004). *A beginner's guide to structural equation modeling* (2nd ed.). Mahwah, NJ: Erlbaum.

Singer, J. D., & Willett, J. B. (2003). *Applied longitudinal data analysis: Modeling change and event occurrence.* New York, NY: Oxford University Press.

Sörbom, D. (1989). Model modification. *Psychometrika, 54*, 371–384. doi:10.1007/BF02294623

Steiger, J. H. (2002). When constraints interact: A caution about reference variables, identification constraints, and scale dependencies in structural equation modeling. *Psychological Methods, 7*, 210–227. doi:10.1037/1082-989X.7.2.210

Steiger, J. H., & Lind, J. C. (1980, May). *Statistically based tests for the number of common factors.* Paper presented at the Annual Meeting of the Psychometric Society, Iowa City, IA.

Stelzl, I. (1986). Changing a causal hypothesis without changing the fit: Some rules for generating equivalent path models. *Multivariate Behavioral Research, 21*, 309–331. doi:10.1207/s15327906mbr2103_3

Tomer, A. (2003). A short history of structural equation models. In B. H. Pugesek, A. Tomer, & A. von Eye (Eds.), *Structural equation modeling: Applications in ecological and evolutionary biology* (pp. 85–124). Cambridge, England: Cambridge University Press. doi:10.1017/CBO9780511542138.005

Tremblay, P. F., & Gardner, R. C. (1996). On the growth of structural equation modeling in psychological

journals. *Structural Equation Modeling, 3*, 93–104. doi:10.1080/10705519609540035

Werts, C. E., & Linn, R. L. (1970). Path analysis: Psychological examples. *Psychological Bulletin, 74*, 193–212. doi:10.1037/h0029778

Widaman, K. F., & Reise, S. P. (1997). Exploring the measurement invariance of psychological instruments: Applications in the substance use domain. In K. J. Bryant, M. Windle, & S. G. West (Eds.), *The science of prevention: Methodological advances from alcohol and substance abuse research* (pp. 281–324). Washington, DC: American Psychological Association. doi:10.1037/10222-009

Wiley, D. E. (1973). The identification problem for structural equation models with unmeasured variables. In A. S. Goldberger & O. D. Duncan (Eds.), *Structural equation models in the social sciences* (pp. 69–83). New York, NY: Academic Press.

Willett, J. B., & Sayer, A. G. (1994). Using covariance structure analysis to detect correlates and predictors of individual change over time. *Psychological Bulletin, 116*, 363–381. doi:10.1037/0033-2909.116.2.363

Wirth, R. J., & Edwards, M. C. (2007). Item factor analysis: Current approaches and future directions. *Psychological Methods, 12*, 58–79. doi:10.1037/1082-989X.12.1.58

Wright, S. (1920). The relative importance of heredity and environment in determining the piebald pattern of guinea-pigs. *Proceedings of the National Academy of Sciences, 6*, 320–332. doi:10.1073/pnas.6.6.320

Wright, S. (1934). The method of path coefficients. *Annals of Mathematical Statistics, 5*, 161–215. doi:10.1214/aoms/1177732676

CHAPTER 20

MATHEMATICAL PSYCHOLOGY

Trisha Van Zandt and James T. Townsend

Mathematical psychology is not, per se, a distinct branch of psychology. Indeed, mathematical psychologists can be found in any area of psychology. Rather, mathematical psychology characterizes the approach that mathematical psychologists take in their substantive domains. Mathematical psychologists are concerned primarily with developing theories and models of behavior that permit quantitative prediction of behavioral change under varying experimental conditions. There are as many mathematical approaches within psychology as there are substantive psychological domains. As with most theorists of any variety, the mathematical psychologist will typically start by considering the psychological phenomena and underlying structures or processes that she wishes to model.

A mathematical model or theory (and we do not distinguish between them here) is a set of mathematical structures, including a set of *linkage* statements. These statements relate variables, equations, and so on with components of the psychological process of interest and possibly also aspects of the stimuli or environment. Regardless of the domain, then, the first step in a mathematical approach is to quantify the variables, both independent and dependent, measured to study a psychological process. Quantification permits variables to be represented as parameters in a mathematical equation or statistical expression, the goal and defining feature of the mathematical psychology enterprise.

Mathematical psychologists, then, construct mathematical and statistical models of the processes they study. Some domains, such as vision, learning and memory, and judgment and decision making, which frequently measure easily quantifiable performance variables like accuracy and response time, exhibit a greater penetration of mathematical reasoning and a higher proportion of mathematical psychologists than other domains. Processes such as the behavior of individual neurons, information flow through visual pathways, evidence accumulation in decision making, and language production or development have all been subjected to a great deal of mathematical modeling. However, even problems like the dynamics of mental illness, problems falling in the domains of social or clinical psychology, have benefited from a mathematical modeling approach (e.g., see the special issue on modeling in clinical science in the *Journal of Mathematical Psychology* [Townsend & Neufeld, 2010]).

The power of the mathematical approach arises when unrealized implications of particular model structures become obvious after the mathematical representation of the model has been written down. By contrast, although verbal models might possess logical structure, the inability to interpret concepts in a mathematical fashion means that we cannot derive their logical implications. The ability to make such derivations for mathematical representations leads to better testability of theories, improved experimental designs targeting specific model predictions, and better data analyses—such analyses frequently being rooted in the statistical properties of the model variables.

This work was supported by National Science Foundation Grant BCS-0738059, National Institutes of Mental Health Grant 57717-04Al, and Air Force Office of Special Research Grant FA9550-07-1-0078.

DOI: 10.1037/13620-020
APA Handbook of Research Methods in Psychology: Vol. 2. Research Designs, H. Cooper (Editor-in-Chief)

Mathematical modeling is the foundation of many of the physical sciences. In comparison to these, psychology is often described as a "young" science; as Laming (1973) described several decades ago, psychologists are still often focused on the questions of *what* is happening rather than *why* it is happening. Mathematical psychologists, pointing to the role that mathematics has played in the advancement of the physical sciences, have argued that advancement in psychology (and other social sciences) will depend on the extent to which mathematical theorizing is applied to psychological issues. A testament to this argument is the fact that although not all *important* psychological models are mathematical, a great many of them are.

Psychology differs from a physical science in more than its age, and the use of mathematical models will not, on its own, carry psychology forward. First, the systems studied by psychologists are far more complex than comparable systems in the physical sciences; and second, relationships between psychological variables are obscured by intrinsic variability in these complex systems. Thus, progress in psychology is tied to progress in statistics as well as technological developments that improve our ability to measure behavior. Even the best mathematical tools may not improve our understanding of some quirk of human behavior if we are unable to measure that behavior or discriminate between changes in that behavior and random fluctuations— fluctuations in either our measurements or the cognitive system we are studying.

The remainder of this chapter consists of three sections. The first outlines the history of mathematical psychology. The second describes its influence in modern experimental psychology (i.e., all those empirically driven and nonapplied fields of psychological study). The third discusses some ongoing issues in the field.

HISTORY

Foundations

Mathematical psychology traces its roots to before the beginning of experimental psychology, the latter usually dated from the 1879 establishment of Wilhelm Wundt's (1832–1920) laboratory in Leipzig, Germany. Eighteenth-century astronomers were well aware of the "personal equation" that characterized variations in observers' times to estimate when celestial objects moved past wires on a grid. These estimates were made with the assistance of a metronome. Thus, the estimates depended on the time the astronomer needed to refocus attention from the visual to the auditory modality. Clearly, the reliability of astronomical measurements were therefore heavily dependent on the degree to which observers differed from each other or, indeed, from one observation to the next.

Many astronomers were thus naturally concerned about precisely measuring the personal equation so that equipment could be appropriately recalibrated for different observers. Astronomer and mathematician Friedrich Bessel (1784–1846), however, was further interested in why such timing issues arose. He formulated a hypothesis that a second stimulus (whether the auditory click of the metronome or visual movement of the star) produced a disturbance in the perceptual system already processing the first stimulus (the visual movement of the star or the auditory click of the metronome; Duncombe, 1945). This was perhaps the first formalization of what was later to be known as the *psychological refractory period* (Rabbitt, 1969) or the *doctrine of prior entry* (Shore & Spence, 2005).

Psychophysics. Although the interesting question of the personal equation focused on the speed with which people can perform a task, a different historical branch began with how frequently people make different kinds of responses. Physiologist Ernst Weber (1795–1878) asked people to make yes–no judgments about whether the perceived weights of two objects were different. Holding the mass of the first object constant, he gradually increased the mass of the second object until people said "yes" ("different"). He was then able to define the *just noticeable difference*, the smallest increase in weight ΔI that a person could detect, and found that it was not a constant but instead a function of the weight I of the first object, or

$$\Delta I = kI. \tag{1}$$

Weber found that the value of k, which determined the just noticeable difference, was a constant for most values of *I*, establishing what we now refer to as *Weber's law*. This law holds for a wide range of intensities *I* and across different stimulus modalities.

Gustav Theodor Fechner (1801–1887), founder of the field of psychophysics and the first true mathematical psychologist, was inspired by Weber's work (Fechner, 1860/1889). Although trained as a physicist, Fechner yearned to solve one of philosophy's central and longstanding puzzles, namely, the relationship of the mind to the outside world and the physiological body itself. This giant of philosophical enigmas is known as the *mind–body problem*, which continues even now to attract attention from philosophers and cognitive scientists. Fechner tried to solve the mind–body problem by establishing a connection, via an equation, between events in the physical world and the psychological experience they evoked. In modern mathematical psychology, this problem is one of foundational measurement: How can psychological experience be quantified and related to physical intensity? Although Weber's work proposed a relationship between physical intensity and a person's *report* of their experience, Fechner sought a lawful and mathematical relationship between physical intensity and the experience itself.

Fechner (1860/1889) had the clever idea of employing Weber's law by making the assumption that the psychological experience of a just noticeable difference is the same for all values of *I*. That is, if the change in the psychological effect $\Delta S = c$ is equal to the same constant *c* for all just noticeable differences ΔI, then

$$\frac{\Delta S}{\Delta I} = \frac{c}{kI},\tag{2}$$

or, in the limit,

$$dS = \frac{c}{kI}\,dI.\tag{3}$$

Applying the rules of calculus to solve this differential equation leads to the expression we now call *Fechner's law*: Psychological effects *S* are a logarithmic function of physical intensity *I*, or

$$S = K\log I,\tag{4}$$

for some constant *K*. Perhaps because of the slow decaying links with philosophy, no one thought at the time of experimentally testing the logarithm

function prediction of Fechner's law. It was not until much later that Stevens (1957, 1961) tried and tested other formulas for the relation of sensation to stimulation.

Mental chronometry. While Weber and Fechner were laying the foundations of psychological measurement and psychophysics, Hermann von Helmholtz (1821–1894) was busy measuring the speed of nerve conduction in a frog's leg (Helmholtz, 1850). The realization that neural events take measureable time spurred F. C. Donders (1818–1889) to develop a system for mental chronometry, the measurement of the time required to perform cognitive tasks (Donders, 1868/1969). Donders asked people to perform three tasks involving two lights. Each task required three different cognitive components. We now refer to these tasks as *simple reactions* (respond when any light is perceived), *go–no go reactions* (respond when one specific light is perceived), and *choice reactions* (respond one way when one light is perceived, and a different way when the other light is perceived).

The cognitive components involved are perception, stimulus discrimination, and response selection. For simple reactions, only perception is required; for go–no go reactions, perception and stimulus discrimination are required; for choice reactions, perception, stimulus discrimination and response selection are required.

Donders (1868/1969) measured the response times for each task and then estimated the duration of the stimulus discrimination and response selection components by subtraction. The difference between simple reaction and go–no go reaction times gave an estimate of stimulus discrimination time. The difference between go–no go reaction and choice reaction times gave an estimate of response selection time. Donders's *method of subtraction* was the foundation of the idea, now fundamental in cognitive psychology, that differences in response time provide information about cognitive architecture—how the brain structures tasks to achieve different levels of performance. It has been used in a variety of experimental paradigms over the past 150 years and set the stage for such techniques of analysis as Sternberg's (1969) *additive factors method*.

Sternberg's (1969) approach proposed to determine whether two subprocesses involved in a psychological task were arranged in a strict series with one starting and finishing before the other (a serial process). Subsequent mathematical work extended the additive factors method in such a way that a very large class of potential mental architectures (including parallel processing in which task subprocesses are executed simultaneously) could also be directly tested (Schweickert, 1978; Schweickert & Townsend, 1989; Townsend, 1984).

Psychometrics. Experimental psychology took a sharp turn in 1914 with the publication of a landmark book by John B. Watson (1878–1958). This book heralded the dominance of the psychological school of behaviorism, which holds that behavior can be explained without reference to mental events. The school of behaviorism was beneficial to psychology by helping the nascent field break away from its sometimes murky philosophical roots. However, it relegated Fechner's (1860/1889) psychological measurement and Donders's (1868/1969) mental chronometry to the realm of pseudoscience and inhibited developments in the study of cognition for several decades. This did not entirely stop the growth of mathematical psychology as it was applied to behavior, however. In fact, one of the later so-called neobehaviorists, Clark Leonard Hull (1884–1952), used mathematics in his mission to form a general theory of learning and motivation (see Hull, 1952).

Applied concerns also required the development of psychologically motivated quantitative methods to solve problems in human engineering and measurement. The desire of colleges and the military to measure human intelligence and aptitude led to the rise of standardized testing and psychometrics just as the behaviorism movement was getting off the ground. Using tests to assess knowledge and aptitude has a history that extends back to ancient China (Elman, 2000). At the turn of the 20th century, the first intelligence tests were published (e.g., Binet, 1905/1916), and the College Entrance Examination Board (now the College Board) was founded, providing colleges and universities with a way to test fitness of applicants to complete their curriculum. Similarly, the military has always been concerned about fitting soldiers to jobs for which they are well-suited, and the demand for large-scale answers to problems of psychological measurement began at the beginning of World War I.

L. L. Thurstone (1887–1955), founder and first president of the Psychometric Society, made significant contributions to the theory of measurement and psychophysics. His work was concentrated on the problem of quantifying human ability—intelligence, primarily—and he worked closely with the Army and the Institute for Government Research writing civil service exams (Thurstone, 1952). His *Law of Comparative Judgment* (Thurstone, 1927) was the first work to establish the concept of a psychological continuum, a range of quantifiable psychological experience that could be used as the basis for psychophysical judgments. He later expanded this continuum to attitudes and ability, and it became the forerunner to the Bradley–Terry–Luce and Rasch models of psychometrics as well as signal-detection theory.

The Rise of Modern Mathematical Psychology

Modern mathematical psychology stems from three innovations in psychology and engineering: the first application of signal-detection theory to human performance (Swets, Tanner, & Birdsall, 1961), the application of information theory to encoding and decoding messages in the human cognitive system (Attneave, 1954), and two milestone publications in mathematical learning theory (Bush & Mosteller, 1955; Estes, 1950). Together these three areas of research laid the groundwork for the idea that remains central in cognitive psychology in the 21st century: The human being, as she makes her way through the world, operates like an information-processing device. Information from the external world is encoded by sensory transducers; this information is operated upon by various brain mechanisms to produce her perception of the world and to allow her to select appropriate responses to the world; finally, if necessary, she can activate her response effectors to manipulate the state of her external world.

Signal-detection theory, born from the problems of communications engineers during World War II, borrows its fundamentals from statistical decision theory. An observer is presented with a low-amplitude signal tone in a burst of white noise and must determine whether the signal is present. This stimulus gives rise to some sensory effect (perceived intensity), which varies randomly each time it is presented. This randomness is attributed to the inherent variability of sensory transduction or noise in the cognitive channel. Randomness means that signals (in which a tone is present) may sometimes have the same sensory effect as noise alone. Signal or noise decisions are made by evaluating either the likelihood that a particular sensory experience resulted from a signal or noise stimulus, or by evaluating the magnitude of the sensory effect relative to some minimum criterion required to call a stimulus a signal. The important contribution of signal-detection theory, which now forms the heart of many modern models of cognition, is that it provided a method for separating effects of response bias (how the likelihood or magnitude of experience is evaluated) from the discriminability of the stimulus.

Information theory also derived from work in statistics and communications engineering (see, e.g., Shannon & Weaver, 1949). It is a way of quantifying the information or uncertainty of a signal from the probabilities associated with each possible stimulus for that signal. Communications engineers were concerned with how signals could be compressed and how much information could be transmitted over a noisy communications channel; the analogy to the human decision maker was immediately obvious to psychologists (e.g., Attneave, 1954; Garner, 1974). Information theory not only could be used to quantify sets of stimuli and collections of responses but also could be used to measure how much information the cognitive system could transmit.

Information theory contributed to the "intelligent machine revolution," represented best perhaps by Wiener's influential 1948 book *Cybernetics; or, Control and Communication in the Animal and the Machine.* Cybernetics, the science of feedback control systems applied to biological systems, influenced our treatment of the human as an information processor but had its greatest impact on research in artificial intelligence. It also encouraged the application of general systems theory (and nonlinear dynamics) in cognitive modeling (see the section Neural Modeling).

From information theory came a tremendous amount of research exploring the processing limitations of humans, and this led to one of the first links between the dependent variables of response frequency and response time. The *Hick-Hyman law* of response time states that response time *RT* is a linear function of the amount of information *H* (measured in *bits*) transmitted through the system, or

$$RT = a + bH, \tag{5}$$

where *b* is called the *channel capacity* of the human (Hick, 1952; Hyman, 1953). Later, Miller (1956) reviewed the channel capacity literature that encompassed a number of different tasks. In his classic paper "The Magic Number Seven Plus or Minus Two: Some Limits on Our Capacity for Processing Information," he argued that people were limited in their ability to process and transmit information to approximately 2.5 bits.

An outcome of Miller's (1956) work was the realization that information contained in a set of items might be less important than the size of the set itself. This, together with other work demonstrating that information theory did not provide a useful explanation for how information was processed (e.g., Leonard, 1959), arguably led to a decline in the use of information theory in cognitive modeling (see also Luce, 2003). However, it still remains a useful way to quantify psychological and behavioral concepts (e.g., Strange, Duggins, Penny, Dolan, & Friston, 2005). In addition, the general concept that humans can be studied as perceptual, cognitive, and action systems through which information flows led to the rise of the "information processing approach," which continues to dominate much of experimental psychology in the 21st century.

Signal detection and information theory both suggested ways that stimuli could be quantified. Furthermore, signal-detection theory suggested what a perceptual representation of stimuli might look like, pointing the way to a cognitive theory of stimulus discrimination. At this same time, new theories of learning were presented (Bush & Mosteller, 1955; Estes, 1950, 1957). Bush and Mosteller's (1955) work derived from the prevailing behavioristic view of animal learning. Their theories focused solely on changes in the observer's response probability over time. For example, Bush and Mosteller's approach employed a simple difference equation for learning. Consider a task in which an animal must learn to make one particular response. Letting $q(n)$ be the probability of an error on trial n, the simplest Bush and Mosteller model specified that $q(n) = aq(n - 1)$, where a is greater than 0 and less than 1. This means that the likelihood of an error decreases over trials—learning.

Consistent with behavioristic dogma, Bush and Mosteller's (1955) learning models did not speculate about the internal mental states of the observer. However, Estes's (1950, 1957) stimulus sampling theory, like signal-detection theory, diverged from this philosophy by representing stimuli as being composed of smaller "elements" that could be sampled and possibly conditioned (i.e., learned) by the observer (e.g., Atkinson & Estes, 1963). In contrast to Bush and Mosteller's approach, Estes's models made a large impact not only on research in learning, but also in memory. Many modern memory models have taken advantage of his conception of stimulus elements and the idea that stimulus elements become associated to various components of a task structure (e.g., Shiffrin & Steyvers, 1997).

The following decades saw the publication of several books that established mathematical psychology as a formal discipline. The first were the three volumes of the *Handbook of Mathematical Psychology* (Luce, Bush, & Galanter, 1963–1965a), followed by two volumes of *Readings in Mathematical Psychology* (Luce, Bush, & Galanter, 1963–1965b). These volumes were targeted primarily toward researchers active in the field. Atkinson, Bower, and Crothers published the more elementary *An Introduction to Mathematical Learning Theory* in 1966, but it was not until the 1970 publication of Coombs, Dawes, and Tversky's *Mathematical Psychology* that there existed an introductory textbook suitable for undergraduates. This text covered a broad set of topics, including signal detection, information, and learning theory as well as judgment and decisions, psychological measurement, and game theory. In 1973, Laming published a more advanced *Mathematical Psychology* text, but this text focused on

models that could predict response times, a neglected domain in texts up until that time.

The *Journal of Mathematical Psychology* and the Society for Mathematical Psychology

By 1960, there were at least a large handful of truly mathematical psychologists. As Estes (2002) described, some of these psychologists regularly participated in what are now called the Social Science Research Council's Knowledge Institutions. These particular institutions were held at Stanford University for the purposes of training social scientists in mathematical and statistical techniques. In 1963, the idea was proposed to begin a new journal devoted to the publication of theoretical, mathematical articles in psychology; in 1964, the first issue of the *Journal of Mathematical Psychology* was published. Richard C. Atkinson, Robert R. Bush, Clyde H. Coombs, William K. Estes, R. Duncan Luce, William J. McGill, and George A. Miller served on the journal's first editorial board.

Several years later, mathematical psychologists began meeting informally in the summer to give papers and symposia. After a number of years, in 1976, the journal's editorial board organized the Society for Mathematical Psychology. Bylaws were drafted by Estes and Luce, together with William H. Batchelder and Bert F. Green; in 1977, the Society was formally incorporated. The Society has now, for more than 40 years, hosted an annual meeting each summer at which students and researchers from a wide range of disciplines have presented papers, posters, and symposia highlighting the application of mathematical and statistical models to problems in psychology, cognitive science, neuroscience, and cognitive engineering.

By the time the Society was getting under way in the United States, a similar organization had already been formed in Europe called the European Mathematical Psychology Group. The Group, although never formally incorporated, has met every year since it was founded by Jean-Claude Falmagne in 1971. The British Psychological Association began publishing the *British Journal of Mathematical and Statistical Psychology* in 1965, which was an offshoot of the *British Journal of Psychology: Statistical Section*

(1947–1952) and later the *British Journal of Statistical Psychology* (1953–1964). The papers appearing in the *British Journal* are from researchers in both psychometrics and mathematical psychology, and so it is in these pages that we can see most strongly the links between these two branches of quantitative psychology.

MODERN MATHEMATICAL PSYCHOLOGY

If one sampled a mathematical psychologist at random, one would find that she could be roughly categorized along four (nonorthogonal) dimensions. First of all, we might determine whether her modeling is strictly axiomatic or more loosely formulated. Next, we could determine whether she takes primarily a deterministic or a stochastic modeling approach. Then, we could ask whether her approach is primarily analytic or computational. Finally, her work may be primarily empirical or theoretical.

At the risk of oversimplification, an axiomatic approach is one in which the modeler writes down some primary definitions and then statements (axioms) about what should be true. For example, the modeler may specify mathematical definitions on the basis of the desire to represent situations in which people are presented with stimulus pairs and that their task is to choose the stimulus in the pair with the greatest perceived magnitude. An axiom might then be that, when presented with two tones (the stimulus pair), people should be able to identify correctly the one that is louder with probability greater than or equal to 0.5. These axioms, then, permit the association of mathematical variables and formulas to psychological concepts. Given a set of axioms, the modeler can go on to make logical inferences about what people should do under different conditions.

Axiomatic theorems do not usually address issues of intrinsic randomness—they tend to be deterministic. Given fixed-model parameters and a fixed stimulus, the model produces one and only one result. A stochastic model, by contrast, might produce very different results even when the parameters and the stimulus are fixed. Models of cognitive processing are frequently stochastic. Sequential sampling models, such as those reviewed by Ratcliff and

Smith (2004), are a perfect example of the stochastic approach. Predictions about behavior are often focused on how dependent variables are distributed, and how the parameters of those distributions change with changes in experimental procedures.

An analytical approach is one in which dependent variables Y can be written as analytical expression involving independent variables X, or $Y = g(X)$ for a function g that does not require any messy numerical calculations (like taking a limit or integrating). The general linear model employed in regression is one example of an analytic expression. The expressions providing finishing time distributions for serial and parallel processing systems (e.g., Townsend, 1972, 1976; also see the section Model Testing, Evaluation, and Comparisons) are other examples.

In contrast, a nonanalytic expression does not allow one to write $Y = g(X)$ and generate predictions for Y algebraically; instead, a computer must be used to simulate the model or solve for Y. Often, the more complex the issue being addressed, the more likely it is that a computational approach will be necessary. Techniques for model comparison (Pitt, Myung, & Zhang, 2002), Bayesian model fitting (Lee, 2008), and models devoted to particularly intractable problems like text comprehension or language processing (e.g., Dennis & Kintsch, 2007) often require a computational approach.

Finally, many mathematical psychologists are also empiricists: They collect data to test their models. However, there is a subset of mathematical psychologists who rarely or never collect data; their work is primarily theoretical. When theoretical work suggests a certain empirical approach, they either collaborate with empiricists or, if it is available, they reanalyze already published data. These mathematical psychologists make theoretical contributions that suggest new mathematical representations of different psychological problems, or methodological contributions that provide new techniques of analysis. They are rather akin to theoretical physicists, some of whom had remarkable insights about the nature of things but were notoriously inept in the laboratory.

Foundational Measurement

Work in foundational measurement has followed the tradition established by Fechner (Falmagne,

1986). It is axiomatic, analytic, deterministic and, for the most part, theoretical. Its goal is to find measurement systems capable of quantifying psychological experience—to measure such experience. In the physical world, we measure objects frequently. We weigh ourselves, we compute distance, we mark time. Such physical quantities are based in extensive measurement, which requires the existence of a ratio scale (one with a true zero). We are so accustomed to making measurements of this sort that it seems natural to extend this kind of logic to psychological problems. However, the axioms of extensive measurement may not be justified for the measurement of psychological experience (cf. Narens, 1996).

Foundational measurement represents the first and oldest approach to applying mathematical reasoning to psychological problems. In many ways, foundational measurement set the tone for mathematical work in psychology, especially in psychophysics and decision making. The pioneering research of Patrick Suppes and R. Duncan Luce is especially notable. Suppes, although officially a philosopher, was perhaps the first, along with Dana Scott, to put a mathematical foundation under the psychological scales proposed by Stevens (1961; Scott & Suppes, 1958; Suppes & Zinnes, 1963). Luce brought the mathematics developed for foundational measurement to bear on problems both in psychophysics and decision making, leading to some of the field's most impressive contributions extending from the 1950s until the present day (Luce, 1959, 2004; Narens & Luce, 1986; Steingrimsson & Luce, 2005a, 2005b, 2006, 2007).

Psychophysics is amenable to a measurement approach because the physical quantity of interest is usually easy to measure (e.g., frequency of a tone) and there is a corresponding continuum of psychological experience (e.g., pitch). A fairly large body of beautiful mathematics has been developed to represent the psychological experience of magnitude in detection and discrimination tasks (e.g., Colonius & Dzhafarov, 2006; Falmagne, 1985; Krantz, Luce, Suppes, & Tversky, 1971; Luce, Krantz, Suppes, & Tversky, 1990; Suppes, Krantz, Luce, & Tversky, 1989).

For decision making, the goal of foundational measurement has been to derive scales of preference for objects on the basis of the frequency with which people choose one object over another. An axiomatic approach provides a basis for predicting what people should prefer in various circumstances. Violations of these predicted preferences point to incorrect axioms, which in turn leads to a greater understanding of how people make decisions. Tversky and Kahneman's work (e.g., Tversky & Kahneman, 1974, 1981) demonstrated above all that perfectly sensible axioms, such as those underlying expected utility theory, do not apply in many decision-making environments. Their work led to Kahneman's Nobel prize in Economics in 2002.

Work in foundational measurement is generally deterministic, meaning that it deals primarily with the algebraic properties of different measurement systems. This fact means that, although mathematically quite elegant, measurement theories are often quite removed from empirical treatments and, indeed, may be difficult or impossible to empirically evaluate because the variability of real data obscure and distort the relationships predicted by the theories (Luce, 2005; Narens & Luce, 1993). Although there have been several promising inroads to formulating stochastic approaches to foundational measurement over the past decade or so (Falmagne, Reggenwetter, & Grofman, 1997; Heyer & Niederée, 1989; Myung, Karabatsos, & Iverson, 2005), as yet there is no completely satisfactory solution.

Cognitive Modeling

Mathematical approaches to modeling cognitive processes are now fairly well ingrained in mainstream cognitive psychology. These approaches are equally balanced between analytic and computational models, but they are primarily stochastic and almost always empirical. It will not be possible for us to give a comprehensive treatment of every area in cognitive psychology for which mathematical modeling is important because this task would require many books. We focus on memory, categorization, choice response time, and neural modeling.

Memory. Nowhere else in experimental psychology has mathematical work had a greater impact than in the development of models for memory. Mathematical models of recognition and recall now set the standard for theoretical developments in this area and have driven empirical research before them. Memory models no longer follow the early examples set by statistical learning theory and models of information processing. It became obvious in the late 1960s and early 1970s that the complexity of the process to be modeled was not adequately captured by linearly decomposing it into a sequence of subtasks (e.g., Sternberg, 1966). This led to the development of connectionist models (see below) and machine-learning-inspired models that incorporate learning, problem solving, and language comprehension (e.g., Dennis, 2005; Jilk, Lebiere, O'Reilly, & Anderson, 2008; Kintsch, McNamara, Dennis, & Landauer, 2007).

Signal-detection theory still plays a very important role in most memory models. Older strength theories (Atkinson & Juola, 1973; Murdock, 1965; Parks, 1966) relied on the signal-detection framework as the basis for the old–new judgment. Newer global memory models—such as those proposed by Murdock (1982), Hintzman (1988), and Gillund and Shiffrin (1984), and even more recent models such as retrieving effectively from memory (Shiffrin & Steyvers, 1997)—develop encoding, storage, and retrieval architectures explaining how memory traces are established, maintained, and decay over time as well as how different memory traces become associated with each other and to the context in which they were experienced. Each of these models requires, however, an evaluation of memory strength for a recognition decision, and this evaluation is assumed to be performed within a signal-detection framework.

Although global memory models go some way toward explaining how memory strength contributes to recognition performance, many researchers have explored the contributions of other memory processes, often lumped together under the term *recall*. In this sense, recall is the ability to remember specific details of the remembered item, and this ability requires conscious effort. In contrast, recognition is based only on perceived strength, which happens effortlessly. Some memory work is focused on separating these different cognitive contributions to recognition decisions (e.g., Wixted, 2007). The receiver operating characteristic curve from signal detection is used to try and separate the signal-detection recognition component from the recall component. Dual-process memory theories thus combine the signal-detection approach with a less-quantitatively specified recall component.

Another theoretical avenue to multiprocess memory models are the multinomial processing-tree models explored by Batchelder and Riefer (1999). This general approach provides a way to explore many different structures producing categorical measurements of behavior. The multinomial processing tree model considers how different components of a task depend on each other (e.g., if recall fails, evaluate familiarity) but does not explain the mechanisms by which each component operates. So whereas signal-detection theory might explain the probability that a subject calls an item *old*, the multinomial approach only assumes that such a probability exists. The approach allows for a consideration of different latent structures and comparisons between different model architectures. It has been applied to a wide range of problems, most recently in the evaluation of cognitive deficits (e.g., Batchelder & Riefer, 2007). It lends itself well to Bayesian analysis and is closely linked to measurement problems in psychometrics (Batchelder, 2010).

Categorization. Categorization tasks ask observers to classify stimuli according to their types. These types may be quite concrete (e.g., chairs, dogs, diseases) or they may be very abstract. As in memory research, several influential mathematical models of categorization have set a standard for explanations of categorization behavior, and much of the empirical work in categorization over the past few decades has been driven by these models.

The first class of these models assumes that subjects construct a mental representation of different categories and that categorization decisions are made on the basis of the psychological distances (often referred to as similarities) between a stimulus and other objects (exemplars) in the mental space (Nosofsky, 1988; Nosofsky & Palmeri, 1997). These models take much inspiration from early work in multidimensional scaling (Torgerson, 1958), which was used to derive scales that could measure multidimensional stimuli and place them in relation to each other.

The second class of these models assumes that categories of stimuli can be represented as probability distributions in multidimensional space (Ashby, 1992; Ashby & Gott, 1988). Categorization judgments are made on the basis of a stimulus's location in that space relative to multidimensional discriminant functions (lines, planes, hyperplanes) that divide the space into categories. These models are called *decision-bound models*, and they are closely related to signal-detection models. They preserve the ideas of discriminability, bias, optimality, and so forth from signal detection, but the interest is more on how different stimulus dimensions are perceived and how those perceptions influence the placement of decision bounds.

Choice response time. Signal-detection theory also motivated most of the current, most successful mathematical models of simple choice, including Ratcliff's diffusion model (e.g., Ratcliff & Smith, 2004), Usher and McClelland's (2001) leaky competing accumulator model, the Poisson race model (Pike, 1973; Van Zandt, Colonius, & Proctor, 2000), Vickers's accumulator model (Smith & Vickers, 1988; Vickers, 1979), and (most recently) the linear ballistic accumulator (Brown & Heathcote, 2008). These models address how simple choices are made in most cognitive experiments. The theory from which all these *sequential sampling* models derive is quite simple: To make a decision, an observer engages a process of information gathering. Information is obtained by repeated sampling from the stimulus (if it is present) or from its mental representation (if it is not). Information is modeled as a continuum of sensory effect, and the stimulus representation from which information is sampled is provided by the signal-detection framework.

Each sample of information supports one of the two possible responses and is stored appropriately. The characteristics of this information (discrete or continuous), the time course of the sampling process (discrete or continuous), and the nature of the storage mechanisms (separate as in a race model or combined as in a random walk or diffusion) define the differences between the sequential sampling models. The important contribution of these models is their explanation of the speed–accuracy trade-off,

an explanation that pulls the dependent variables of response time and frequency together within the same mechanism. To make a decision requires *enough* information—a threshold. If a decision must be made quickly, it must be made on the basis of less information, which will lead to less accurate decisions.

Not only do these models explain changes in both response time and response frequency but also the stochastic processes upon which they are based are (usually) simple enough that we can write down analytic expressions for the response time distributions and the response probabilities as functions of the parameters of the process. These models presently stand as the most successful explanations of response selection in simple tasks. We have some neurophysiological evidence that the brain uses neural modules as information collectors (Schall, 2003), which has encouraged continued application of these models across cognitive, clinical, and developmental psychology (Ratcliff, 2008; White, Ratcliff, Vasey, & McKoon, 2009).

In addition, these models are being brought to bear on classic problems in judgment and decision making (Busemeyer & Diederich, 2002; Merkle & Van Zandt, 2006; Pleskac & Busemeyer, 2010; Ratcliff & Starns, 2009; Van Zandt, 2000). In particular, the sequential sampling framework is being extended to judgments of confidence, leading to the simultaneous prediction of three dependent measures. This body of research, together with other models for judgment and decision making, has been named *cognitive decision theory*.

Neural modeling. One development of the 1980s was the advent of computational models inspired by neural processing mechanisms: parallel-distributed processing (McClelland & Rumelhart, 1986; Rumelhart & McClelland, 1986). The computational tools provided by connectionism have been widely applied to complex cognitive problems, such as speech and pattern recognition (e.g., Norris & McQueen, 2008), and are used in engineering applications including computer vision, handwriting recognition, textual analysis, and quality control.

There was a backlash in the late 1980s against the use of connectionist models for cognition, a backlash rooted in the argument that connectionist models were simply associationism (à la behaviorism) in disguise (Pinker & Mehler, 1988). Also, many cognitive psychologists argued that connectionist models, although they may provide good explanations of how the brain performs computations, do not necessarily make predictions about overt behavior (Fodor & Pylyshyn, 1988). Consequently, although neural modeling is an important and rapidly advancing enterprise, it does not look much like the cognitive connectionism of the early 1980s.

To model the brain well requires a deeper understanding of neuroanatomy than most cognitive psychologists possess, a set of skills that might include animal laboratory work that cognitive psychologists do not usually possess, and measuring devices (such as multiprobe electrode arrays and functional magnetic resonance imaging that were not available at the advent of connectionism. These deficiencies inspired new training programs designed to provide future researchers with these skills and to encourage collaboration between neuroscientists and behavioral scientists. There is now a huge body of research exploring neural models of cognition and brain function, models that are fundamentally quantitative in nature (e.g., Hasselmo, 2009; Howard & Kahana, 2002; O'Reilly & Frank, 2006), published in journals such as the *Journal of Computational Neuroscience* and *Neural Computation*.

At the time connectionist models became popular, there was a wave of enthusiasm for nonlinear dynamics as applied to problems in experimental psychology. This enthusiasm was driven not only by the obvious nonlinear dynamics of connectionist models, but also by *ecological psychology*, which is motivated by the idea that the human brain operates not only within the head but also within the environment (Gibson, 1950). The complex interactions between neural modules and the ever-changing external world can be modeled with general systems theory (Klir, 1969).

General systems theory encompasses the mathematics of catastrophe and chaos theory, which were the focus of much excitement and many symposia in the 1980s, but catastrophe and chaos theory never led to a revolution in mathematical cognitive

modeling. The nonlinear dynamics approach, however, has led to an important bridge between mathematical biology and cognitive science, and to the focus on complex systems in psychology represented by the important work of Turvey (1990, 2009), Kelso (1995), and others (e.g., Large & Jones, 1999; Schmidt, Carello, & Turvey, 1990).

CURRENT ISSUES IN MATHEMATICAL MODELING

As mathematical psychology continues to mature, with the inevitable growing pains that process engenders, there has been some navel-gazing about where the discipline is headed (Luce, 1999, 2005; Townsend, 2008). In the heady 1950s and 1960s, mathematical psychology seemed the road toward a physical science of psychology, but perhaps the road did not go to the places the field's founders anticipated it would. If true, there might be several reasons for this, one being that (of course) one's children never grow up to become what one thought they would. Mathematical psychology prospers, even though it hasn't quite followed in its parents' footsteps.

Mathematical psychology is currently tackling two major issues, and both are focused primarily on methodology: How to distinguish between different models of the same process, and constructing Bayesian methods for the analysis of behavioral data. We discuss each of these before closing the chapter.

Model Testing, Evaluation, and Comparisons

One very important area in mathematical psychology addresses the problem of how to discriminate between different models. This is a long-standing problem in any field that constructs mathematical and statistical models, including statistics, where this issue is dealt with by considering issues of goodness of fit, variance accounted for, information criteria, Bayes factors, and so forth. In addition, the possibility that models based on very different psychological principles or mechanisms might be mathematically similar or even identical, the challenge of *model mimicking*, can generate a formidable threat to the uncovering of psychological laws. These and other important topics are outlined in this section.

Mathematical psychologists have recently focused on the issue of model complexity. That is, one model may fit data better than another not because it is a better model but only because it is more complex. Complexity is not just a question of how many parameters a model has. Two models may have the same number of parameters yet one of them (the more complex one) may be able to accommodate a wider range of data patterns than the other. Dealing with this issue borrows ideas from computer science and has its roots in information theory. Computer scientists have developed numerical techniques for quantifying complexity, opening the way for a different perspective on model selection. Pitt, Myung, and colleagues (Pitt, Kim, Navarro, & Myung, 2006; Pitt, Myung, Montenegro, & Pooley, 2008) are applying these techniques to a number of different problems, including the optimization of experimental designs for model testing and explorations of model parameter spaces.

Another method for model testing and selection is the powerful *state-trace analysis* methodology invented by Bamber (1979) and recently made popular by Dunn (2008). This technique is applied to problems for which the goal is to determine how many processes are contributing to the performance of a task (see the discussion of dual-process memory models). Many empirical pursuits try to answer the question of "how many processes" by looking for dissociations in patterns of data. That is, situations in which one experimental variable moves a dependent variable in the opposite direction (or not at all) of another variable. This finding is sometimes called *selective influence*, and it is used to argue that one variable affects one process whereas another variable affects a different process independent from the first. State trace analysis is a simple technique based on minimal assumptions. In particular, no particular probability distributions, other mathematical functions, or parameters are required. On the basis of this technique, Dunn and colleagues have argued that, in many situations, dissociations do not provide strong evidence for multiple processes (e.g., Dunn, 2004, 2008; Newell & Dunn, 2008).

Another approach to model testing uses the *strong inference* philosophy described by Platt (1964). The fundamental idea requires the scientist to set up a series of two or more juxtaposed hypotheses, rather than the more typical "there is a (predicted) effect" versus "there is no effect." For example, we might first test whether a psychological phenomenon takes place within short-term versus long-term memory and then follow that with a test of whether the coding system in that memory is verbal or spatial. Or, we might formulate two or more entire classes of models that obey contrasting fundamental principles. The scientist first tests among these models and, in a second stage of research, begins to test among more specific models within the *winning* class.

Research on serial versus parallel processing of elements in visual and memory search illustrates the challenges of model mimicking (e.g., Townsend, 1972, 1974) as well as the opportunity for implementation of strong inference (e.g., Townsend, 1984). For instance, parallel and serial models can, for some popular experimental designs, produce exactly the same predictions and thus be totally indiscriminable (e.g., Townsend, 1972). However, Townsend and Wenger (2004) presented mathematical formulations for large classes of parallel and serial models, formulations that highlight empirically distinguishable aspects of the different structures. They then use these class differences as assays to test the models. The strategies we mentioned earlier for identification of even more complex architectures (Schweickert, 1978; Schweickert & Townsend, 1989) also adhere to this strategy. With these assays, juxtaposed models can be refined to be more and more specific so that, for example, if the assays suggest that processing is parallel, then we might go on to test, say, a diffusion process (e.g., Ratcliff, 1978) versus a counting mechanism (e.g., Smith & Van Zandt, 2000).

The issue of how to select among different mathematical models of a process will never be considered "solved" any more than the perfect statistical procedure for all circumstances will be discovered. As models change over the years, techniques for testing and selecting them will necessarily evolve.

The Independent and Identically Distributed Problem and Bayesian Modeling

When subjects participate in a psychological experiment, they are usually asked to make more than one response. This is because one measurement does not allow the researcher to make inferences; intrinsic variability makes the measurement unreliable. A large number of responses from (usually) a large number of subjects across different conditions is collected to overcome this problem.

Although multiple observations solve the problem of statistical power, from a scientific perspective, they create another, entirely different problem. The measurement we obtain from a subject at one point in time is a function of all that has happened to that subject in the past. In particular, it is a function of the other measurements the subject has provided in our experiment. It is not possible to obtain repeated measurements under exactly the same conditions, even if the stimulus conditions remain exactly the same from trial to trial.

Nonetheless, we treat our data as independent and identically distributed (IID) observations from the same data-generating mechanism. Often, we assume the data are IID even if the observations are coming from different subjects. We blithely average, combine and collapse, even knowing that such operations can distort the shape of any underlying function relating independent to dependent variables (Estes & Maddox, 2005).

This is the IID problem, and it is presently being tackled by the application of hierarchical Bayesian modeling techniques to established processing models (Craigmile, Peruggia, & Van Zandt, 2011; Lee, 2008; Peruggia, Van Zandt, & Chen, 2002; Rouder & Lu, 2005; Rouder, Lu, Speckman, Sun, & Jiang, 2005). As in most Bayesian analyses, the goal is to determine the posterior distribution of some model parameters given a specified prior distribution and the model itself (the likelihood). In a hierarchical model, the parameters for each subject are assumed to be drawn from common hyperdistributions, so that the posterior hyperdistributions are informed by all the data from all the subjects. Thus, each subject's data are fit in a way that allows for individual differences, but inferences about effects of independent variables are made on the hyperparameter posteriors, which have "learned" from all the subjects' data combined.

Bayesian modeling has the potential to eliminate the problem of individual differences as well as

order and other confounding effects (e.g., Craigmile et al., 2011), but it is a computationally difficult issue to address. There is currently a great deal of interest in treating response time data as time-series (e.g., Thornton & Gilden, 2005; Van Orden, Holden, & Turvey, 2005), an approach that recognizes that repeated observations from a single subject are correlated. At this time, however, the techniques usually employed for such analyses, as well as the conclusions that result from them, can be criticized (Wagenmakers, Farrell, & Ratcliff, 2004).

CONCLUSION

Modern mathematical psychology is a critical component of modern experimental psychology. From its earliest inception, mathematical psychology has made important contributions to our understanding of learning, memory, perception, and choice behavior; mathematical models continue to guide research in these areas as well as language acquisition and comprehension, problem solving, categorization, and judgment. Although modest in number, mathematical psychologists appear as leaders in many psychological disciplines, especially in cognition and neuroscience. They have been elected to the most esteemed societies in experimental psychology as well as the elite National Academy of Sciences. Several mathematical psychologists (Herbert Simon, Patrick Suppes, William K. Estes, and R. Duncan Luce) have received the highest scientific honor in the United States, that of receiving the National Medal of Science.

As experimental psychology matures, it is likely that our current definition for what constitutes mathematical psychology will change. Eventually, we hope, experimental psychologists will all use mathematical reasoning and develop mathematical models, and thus everyone will be mathematical psychologists under the definition we have provided in this chapter. However, just as there remain specifically mathematical subdisciplines in the physical and life sciences (e.g., physics, chemistry, and biology), we anticipate that mathematical psychology will endure as a unique endeavor among the different subdisciplines that make up the science of psychology.

References

Ashby, F. G. (Ed.). (1992). *Multidimensional models of perception and cognition*. Hillsdale, NJ: Erlbaum.

Ashby, F. G., & Gott, R. E. (1988). Decision rules in the perception and categorization of multidimensional stimuli. *Journal of Experimental Psychology: Learning, Memory, and Cognition, 14*, 33–53. doi:10.1037/0278-7393.14.1.33

Atkinson, R. C., Bower, G. H., & Crothers, E. J. (1966). *An introduction to mathematical learning theory*. New York, NY: Wiley.

Atkinson, R. C., & Estes, W. K. (1963). Stimulus sampling theory. In R. D. Luce, R. R. Bush, & E. Galanter (Eds.), *Handbook of mathematical psychology* (Vol. 2, pp. 121–268). New York, NY: Wiley.

Atkinson, R. C., & Juola, J. F. (1973). Factors influencing the speed and accuracy of word recognition. In S. Kornblum (Ed.), *Attention and performance IV* (pp. 583–612). New York, NY: Academic Press.

Attneave, F. (1954). *Applications of information theory to psychology: A summary of basic concepts, methods, and results*. New York, NY: Holt, Rinehart & Winston.

Bamber, D. (1979). State-trace analysis: A method of testing simple theories of causation. *Journal of Mathematical Psychology, 19*, 137–181. doi:10.1016/0022-2496(79)90016-6

Batchelder, W. H. (2010). Cognitive psychometrics: Using multinomial processing tree models as measurement tools. In S. E. Embretson (Ed.), *Measuring psychological constructs: Advances in model-based approaches* (pp. 71–93). Washington, DC: American Psychological Association. doi:10.1037/12074-004

Batchelder, W. H., & Riefer, D. M. (1999). Theoretical and empirical review of multinomial process tree modeling. *Psychonomic Bulletin and Review, 6*, 57–86. doi:10.3758/BF03210812

Batchelder, W. H., & Riefer, D. M. (2007). Using multinomial processing tree models to measure cognitive deficits in clinical populations. In R. W. J. Neufeld (Ed.), *Advances in clinical cognitive science: Formal modeling of processes and symptoms* (pp. 19–50). Washington, DC: American Psychological Association. doi:10.1037/11556-001

Binet, A. (1916). New methods for the diagnosis of the intellectual level of subnormals. In E. S. Kite (Ed. & Trans.), *The development of intelligence in children*. Vineland, NJ: Publications of the Training School at Vineland. (Original work published 1905)

Brown, S. D., & Heathcote, A. (2008). The simplest complete model of choice reaction time: Linear ballistic accumulation. *Cognitive Psychology, 57*, 153–178. doi:10.1016/j.cogpsych.2007.12.002

Busemeyer, J., & Diederich, A. (2002). Survey of decision field theory. *Mathematical Social Sciences, 43*, 345–370. doi:10.1016/S0165-4896(02)00016-1

Bush, R. R., & Mosteller, F. (1955). *Stochastic models for learning*. New York, NY: Wiley.

Colonius, H., & Dzhafarov, E. N. (Eds.). (2006). *Measurement and representation of sensation*. Mahwah, NJ: Erlbaum.

Coombs, C. H., Dawes, R. M., & Tversky, A. (1970). *Mathematical psychology: An elementary introduction*. Englewood Cliffs, NJ: Prentice-Hall.

Craigmile, P. F., Peruggia, M., & Van Zandt, T. (2011). An autocorrelated mixture model for sequences of response time data. *Psychometrika, 75*, 613–632.

Dennis, S. (2005). A memory-based theory of verbal cognition. *Cognitive Science, 29*, 145–193. doi:10.1207/s15516709cog0000_9

Dennis, S., & Kintsch, W. (2007). The text mapping and inference rule generation problems in text comprehension: Evaluating a memory-based account. In F. Schmalhofer & C. A. Perfetti (Eds.), *Higher level language processes in the brain: Inference and comprehension processes* (pp. 105–132). Mahwah, NJ: Erlbaum.

Donders, F. C. (1969). On the speed of mental processes (W. G. Koster, Trans.). *Acta Psychologica, 30*, 412–431. (Original work published 1868)

Duncombe, R. L. (1945). Personal equation in astronomy. *Popular Astronomy, 53*, 2–13, 63–76, 110–121.

Dunn, J. C. (2004). Remember-know: A matter of confidence. *Psychological Review, 111*, 524–542. doi:10.1037/0033-295X.111.2.524

Dunn, J. C. (2008). The dimensionality of the remember-know task: A state-trace analysis. *Psychological Review, 115*, 426–446. doi:10.1037/0033-295-X.115.2.426

Elman, B. (2000). *A cultural history of civil examinations in late imperial China*. Berkeley: University of California Press.

Estes, W. K. (1950). Toward a statistical theory of learning. *Psychological Review, 57*, 94–107. doi:10.1037/h0058559

Estes, W. K. (1957). Of models and men. *American Psychologist, 12*, 609–617. doi:10.1037/h0046778

Estes, W. K. (2002). Traps in the route to models of memory and decision. *Psychonomic Bulletin and Review, 9*, 3–25. doi:10.3758/BF03196254

Estes, W. K., & Maddox, W. T. (2005). Risks of drawing inferences about cognitive processes from model fits to individual versus average performance. *Psychonomic Bulletin and Review, 12*, 403–408. doi:10.3758/BF03193784

Falmagne, J.-C. (1985). *Elements of psychophysical theory*. New York, NY: Oxford University Press.

Falmagne, J.-C. (1986). Psychophysical measurement and theory. In K. R. Boff, L. Kaufman, & J. P. Thomas

(Eds.), *Handbook of perception and human perfor-mance: Vol. 1. Sensory processes and perceptions*. New York, NY: Wiley.

Falmagne, J.-C., Reggenwetter, M., & Grofman, B. (1997). A stochastic model for the evolution of preferences. In A. A. J. Marley (Ed.), *Choice, decision, and measurement: Essays in honor of R. Duncan Luce* (pp. 111–130). Mahwah, NJ: Erlbaum.

Fechner, G. T. (1889). *Elemente der psychophysik* [Elements of psychophysics] (W. M. Wundt, Ed.). Leipzig, Germany: Breitkopf & Härtel. (Original work published 1860)

Fodor, J. A., & Pylyshyn, Z. (1988). Connectionism and cognitive architecture: A critical analysis. *Cognition, 28*, 3–71. doi:10.1016/0010-0277(88)90031-5

Garner, W. R. (1974). *The processing of information and structure*. Potomac, MD: Erlbaum.

Gibson, J. J. (1950). *The perception of the visual world*. Boston, MA: Houghton Mifflin.

Gillund, G., & Shiffrin, R. M. (1984). A retrieval model for both recognition and recall. *Psychological Review, 91*, 1–67.

Hasselmo, M. E. (2009). A model of episodic memory: Mental time travel along encoded trajectories using grid cells. *Neurobiology of Learning and Memory, 92*, 559–573. doi:10.1016/j.nlm.2009.07.005

Helmholtz, H. (1850). Vorläufiger Bericht über die Fortpflanzungsgeschwindigkeit der nervenreizung [Preliminary report on the propagation velocity of nerve innervation]. *Archiv für Anatomie, Physiologie und Wissenschaftliche Medizin*, 71–73.

Heyer, D., & Niederée, R. (1989). Elements of a model-theoretic framework for probabilistic measurement. In E. E. Roskam (Ed.), *Mathematical psychology in progress* (pp. 99–112). Berlin, Germany: Springer.

Hick, W. E. (1952). On the rate of gain of information. *Quarterly Journal of Experimental Psychology, 4*, 11–26. doi:10.1080/17470215208416600

Hintzman, D. L. (1988). Judgments of frequency and recognition memory in a multiple-trace mem-ory model. *Psychological Review, 95*, 528–551. doi:10.1037/0033-295X.95.4.528

Howard, M. W., & Kahana, M. J. (2002). A distributed rep-resentation of temporal context. *Journal of Mathematical Psychology, 46*, 269–299. doi:10.1006/jmps.2001.1388

Hull, C. L. (1952). *A behavior system; an introduction to behavior theory concerning the individual organism*. New Haven, CT: Yale University Press.

Hyman, R. (1953). Stimulus information as a determinant of reaction time. *Journal of Experimental Psychology, 45*, 188–196. doi:10.1037/h0056940

Jilk, D. J., Lebiere, C., O'Reilly, R. C., & Anderson, J. R. (2008). SAL: An explicitly pluralistic cog-nitive architecture. *Journal of Experimental and*

Theoretical Artificial Intelligence, 20, 197–218. doi:10.1080/09528130802319128

Kelso, S. J. A. (1995). *Dynamic patterns: The self-organization of brain and behavior*. Cambridge, MA: MIT Press.

Kintsch, W., McNamara, D. S., Dennis, S., & Landauer, T. K. (2007). LSA and meaning: In theory and application. In T. K. Landauer, D. S. McNamara, S. Dennis, & W. Kintsch (Eds.), *Handbook of latent semantic analysis* (pp. 467–479). Mahwah, NJ: Erlbaum.

Klir, G. J. (1969). *An approach to general systems theory*. New York, NY: Van Nostrand Reinhold.

Krantz, D. H., Luce, R. D., Suppes, P., & Tversky, A. (1971). *Foundations of measurement* (Vol. I). New York, NY: Academic Press.

Laming, D. R. (1973). *Mathematical psychology*. London, England: Academic Press.

Large, E. W., & Jones, M. R. (1999). The dynamics of attending: How people track time-varying events. *Psychological Review, 106*, 119–159. doi:10.1037/0033-295X.106.1.119

Lee, M. D. (2008). Three case studies in the Bayesian analysis of cognitive models. *Psychonomic Bulletin and Review, 15*, 1–15. doi:10.3758/PBR.15.1.1

Leonard, J. A. (1959). Tactile choice reactions. *Quarterly Journal of Experimental Psychology, 11*, 76–83. doi:10.1080/17470215908416294

Luce, R. D. (1959). *Individual choice behavior: A theoreti-cal analysis*. New York, NY: Wiley.

Luce, R. D. (1999). Where is mathematical modeling in psychology headed? *Theory and Psychology, 9*, 723–737. doi:10.1177/0959354399096001

Luce, R. D. (2003). Whatever happened to information theory in psychology? *Review of General Psychology, 7*, 183–188. doi:10.1037/1089-2680.7.2.183

Luce, R. D. (2004). Symmetric and asymmetric match-ing of joint presentations. *Psychological Review, 111*, 446–454. doi:10.1037/0033-295X.111.2.446

Luce, R. D. (2005). An open measurement problem of interest. *Journal of Mathematical Psychology, 49*, 440–442. doi:10.1016/j.jmp.2005.05.001

Luce, R. D., Bush, R. R., & Galanter, E. (Eds.). (1963–1965a). *Handbook of mathematical psychology* (Vols. 1–2). New York, NY: Wiley.

Luce, R. D., Bush, R. R., & Galanter, E. (Eds.). (1963–1965b). *Readings in mathematical psychology* (Vols. 1–2). New York, NY: Wiley.

Luce, R. D., Krantz, D. H., Suppes, P., & Tversky, A. (1990). *Foundations of measurement* (Vol. 3). New York, NY: Academic Press.

McClelland, J., & Rumelhart, D. (1986). *Parallel distrib-uted processing: Explorations in the microstructure of cognition: Vol. 2. Psychological and biological models.* Cambridge, MA: MIT Press.

Merkle, E. C., & Van Zandt, T. (2006). An application of the Poisson race model to confidence calibration. *Journal of Experimental Psychology: General, 135,* 391–408. doi:10.1037/0096-3445.135.3.391

Miller, G. A. (1956). The magic number seven plus or minus two: Some limits on our capacity for processing information. *Psychological Review, 63,* 81–97. doi:10.1037/h0043158

Murdock, B. B. (1965). Signal detection theory and short-term memory. *Journal of Experimental Psychology, 70,* 443–447. doi:10.1037/h0022543

Murdock, B. B. (1982). A theory for the storage and retrieval of item and associative information. *Psychological Review, 89,* 609–626. doi:10.1037/0033-295X.89.6.609

Myung, J. I., Karabatsos, G., & Iverson, G. J. (2005). A Bayesian approach to testing decision making axioms. *Journal of Mathematical Psychology, 49,* 205–225. doi:10.1016/j.jmp.2005.02.004

Narens, L. (1996). A theory of ratio magnitude estimation. *Journal of Mathematical Psychology, 40,* 109–129. doi:10.1006/jmps.1996.0011

Narens, L., & Luce, R. D. (1986). Measurement: The theory of numerical assignments. *Psychological Bulletin, 99,* 166–180. doi:10.1037/0033-2909.99.2.166

Narens, L., & Luce, R. D. (1993). Further comments on the "nonrevolution" arising from axiomatic measurement theory. *Psychological Science, 4,* 127–130. doi:10.1111/j.1467-9280.1993.tb00475.x

Newell, B. R., & Dunn, J. C. (2008). Dimensions in data: Testing psychological models using state-trace analysis. *Trends in Cognitive Sciences, 12,* 285–290. doi:10.1016/j.tics.2008.04.009

Norris, D., & McQueen, J. M. (2008). Shortlist B: A Bayesian model of continuous speech recognition. *Psychological Review, 115,* 357–395. doi:10.1037/0033-295X.115.2.357

Nosofsky, R. M. (1988). Exemplar-based accounts of relations between classification, recognition, and typicality. *Journal of Experimental Psychology: Learning, Memory, and Cognition, 14,* 700–708. doi:10.1037/0278-7393.14.4.700

Nosofsky, R. M., & Palmeri, T. (1997). Comparing exemplar-retrieval and decision-bound models of speeded perceptual classification. *Perception and Psychophysics, 59,* 1027–1048. doi:10.3758/BF03205518

O'Reilly, R. C., & Frank, M. (2006). Making working memory work: A computational model of learning in the prefrontal cortex and basal ganglia. *Neural Computation, 18,* 283–328. doi:10.1162/089976606775093909

Parks, T. E. (1966). Signal-detectability theory of recognition-memory performance. *Psychological Review, 73,* 44–58. doi:10.1037/h0022662

Peruggia, M., Van Zandt, T., & Chen, M. (2002). Was it a car or a cat I saw? An analysis of response times for word recognition. In C. Gatsonis, R. E. Kass, A. Carriquiry, A. Gelman, D. Higdon, D. K. Pauler, & I. Verdinelli (Eds.), *Case studies in Bayesian statistics* (Vol. 6, pp. 319–334). New York, NY: Springer.

Pike, R. (1973). Response latency models for signal detection. *Psychological Review, 80,* 53–68. doi:10.1037/h0033871

Pinker, S., & Mehler, J. (Eds.). (1988). *Connections and symbols.* Cambridge, MA: MIT Press.

Pitt, M. A., Kim, W., Navarro, D. J., & Myung, J. I. (2006). Global model analysis by parameter space partitioning. *Psychological Review, 113,* 57–83. doi:10.1037/0033-295X.113.1.57

Pitt, M. A., Myung, I. J., & Zhang, S. (2002). Toward a method of selecting among computational models of cognition. *Psychological Review, 109,* 472–491. doi:10.1037/0033-295X.109.3.472

Pitt, M. A., Myung, J. I., Montenegro, M., & Pooley, J. (2008). Measuring model flexibility with parameter space partitioning: An introduction and application example. *Cognitive Science: A Multidisciplinary Journal,* 1285–1303.

Platt, J. R. (1964). Strong inference. *Science, 146,* 347–353.

Pleskac, T. J., & Busemeyer, J. R. (2010). *Two stage dynamic signal detection theory: A dynamic and stochastic theory of confidence, choice, and response time.* Manuscript submitted for publication.

Rabbitt, P. (1969). Psychological refractory delay and response-stimulus interval duration in serial, choice-response tasks. *Acta Psychologica, 30,* 195–219. doi:10.1016/0001-6918(69)90051-1

Ratcliff, R. (1978). A theory of memory retrieval. *Psychological Review, 85,* 59–108.

Ratcliff, R. (2008). Modeling aging effects on two-choice tasks: Response signal and response time data. *Psychology and Aging, 23,* 900–916. doi:10.1037/a0013930

Ratcliff, R., & Smith, P. L. (2004). A comparison of sequential sampling models for two-choice reaction time. *Psychological Review, 111,* 333–367. doi:10.1037/0033-295X.111.2.333

Ratcliff, R., & Starns, J. (2009). Modeling confidence and response time in recognition memory. *Psychological Review, 116,* 59–83. doi:10.1037/a0014086

Rouder, J. N., & Lu, J. (2005). An introduction to Bayesian hierarchical models with an application in the theory of signal detection. *Psychonomic Bulletin and Review, 12,* 573–604. doi:10.3758/BF03196750

Rouder, J. N., Lu, J., Speckman, P., Sun, D., & Jiang, Y. (2005). A hierarchical model for estimating response time distributions. *Psychonomic Bulletin and Review, 12,* 195–223.

Rumelhart, D., & McClelland, J. (1986). *Parallel distributed processing: Explorations in the microstructure of cognition: Vol. 1. Foundations.* Cambridge, MA: MIT Press.

Schall, J. D. (2003). Neural correlates of decision processes: neural and mental chronometry. *Current Opinion in Neurobiology, 13,* 182–186. doi:10.1016/S0959-4388(03)00039-4

Schmidt, R. C., Carello, C., & Turvey, M. T. (1990). Phase transitions and critical fluctuations in the visual coordination of rhythmic movements between people. *Journal of Experimental Psychology: Human Perception and Performance, 16,* 227–247. doi:10.1037/0096-1523.16.2.227

Schweickert, R. (1978). A critical path generalization of the additive factor methods analysis of a Stroop task. *Journal of Mathematical Psychology, 18,* 105–139. doi:10.1016/0022-2496(78)90059-7

Schweickert, R., & Townsend, J. T. (1989). A trichotomy method: Interactions of factors prolonging sequential and concurrent mental processes in the stochastic PERT networks. *Journal of Mathematical Psychology, 33,* 328–347. doi:10.1016/0022-2496(89)90013-8

Scott, D. S., & Suppes, P. (1958). Foundational aspects of theories of measurement. *Journal of Symbolic Logic, 23,* 113–128. doi:10.2307/2964389

Shannon, C. E., & Weaver, W. (1949). *The mathematical theory of communication.* Urbana: University of Illinois Press.

Shiffrin, R. M., & Steyvers, M. (1997). A model for recognition memory: REM—retrieving effectively from memory. *Psychonomic Bulletin and Review, 4,* 145–166. doi:10.3758/BF03209391

Shore, D. I., & Spence, C. (2005). Prior entry. In L. Itti, G. Rees, & J. K. Tsotsos (Eds.), *Neurobiology of attention* (pp. 89–95). New York, NY: Elsevier. doi:10.1016/B978-012375731-9/50019-7

Smith, P. L., & Van Zandt, T. (2000). Time-dependent Poisson counter models of response latency in simple judgment. *British Journal of Mathematical and Statistical Psychology, 53,* 293–315.

Smith, P. L., & Vickers, D. (1988). The accumulator model of two-choice discrimination. *Journal of Mathematical Psychology, 32,* 135–168. doi:10.1016/0022-2496(88)90043-0

Steingrimsson, R., & Luce, R. D. (2005a). Evaluating a model of global psychophysical judgments: I. Behavioral properties of summations and productions. *Journal of Mathematical Psychology, 49,* 290–307. doi:10.1016/j.jmp.2005.03.003

Steingrimsson, R., & Luce, R. D. (2005b). Evaluating a model of global psychophysical judgments: II. Behavioral properties linking summations and productions. *Journal of Mathematical Psychology, 49,* 308–319. doi:10.1016/j.jmp.2005.03.001

Steingrimsson, R., & Luce, R. D. (2006). Empirical evaluation of a model of global psychophysical judgments: III. A form for the psychophysical function and intensity filtering. *Journal of Mathematical Psychology, 50,* 15–29. doi:10.1016/j.jmp.2005.11.005

Steingrimsson, R., & Luce, R. D. (2007). Empirical evaluation of a model of global psychophysical judgments: IV. Forms for the weighting function. *Journal of Mathematical Psychology, 51,* 29–44. doi:10.1016/j.jmp.2006.08.001

Sternberg, S. (1966). High-speed scanning in human memory. *Science, 153,* 652–654.

Sternberg, S. (1969). The discovery of processing stages: Extensions of Donders's method. In W. G. Koster (Ed.), *Attention and performance II* (pp. 276–315). Amsterdam, the Netherlands: North-Holland.

Stevens, S. S. (1957). On the psychophysical law. *Psychological Review, 64,* 153–181.

Stevens, S. S. (1961). To honor Fechner and repeal his law. *Science, 133,* 80–86. doi:10.1126/science.133.3446.80

Strange, B. A., Duggins, A., Penny, W., Dolan, R. J., & Friston, K. J. (2005). Information theory, novelty and hippocampal responses: Unpredicted or unpredictable? *Neural Networks, 18,* 225–230. doi:10.1016/j.neunet.2004.12.004

Suppes, P., Krantz, D. H., Luce, R. D., & Tversky, A. (1989). *Foundations of measurement* (Vol. II). New York, NY: Academic Press.

Suppes, P., & Zinnes, J. (1963). Basic measurement theory. In R. D. Luce, R. R. Bush, & E. Galanter (Eds.), *Handbook of mathematical psychology* (pp. 1–76). New York, NY: Wiley.

Swets, J., Tanner, W. P., & Birdsall, T. G. (1961). Decision processes in perception. *Psychological Review, 68,* 301–340. doi:10.1037/h0040547

Thornton, T. L., & Gilden, D. L. (2005). Provenance of correlations in psychological data. *Psychonomic Bulletin and Review, 12,* 409–441. doi:10.3758/BF03193785

Thurstone, L. L. (1927). A law of comparative judgement. *Psychological Review, 34,* 273–286. doi:10.1037/h0070288

Thurstone, L. L. (1952). L. L. Thurstone. In E. G. Boring, H. S. Langfeld, & H. W. R. M. Yerkes (Eds.), *A history of psychology in autobiography* (Vol. IV, pp. 295–321). Worcester, MA: Clark University Press. doi:10.1037/11154-014

Torgerson, W. S. (1958). *Theory and methods of scaling.* New York, NY: Wiley.

Townsend, J. T. (1972). Some results concerning the identifiability of parallel and serial processes. *British Journal of Mathematical and Statistical Psychology, 25,* 168–199.

Townsend, J. T. (1974). Issues and models concerning the processing of a finite number of inputs. In B. H. Kantowitz (Ed.), *Human information processing: Tutorials in performance and cognition* (pp. 133–168). Hillsdale, NJ: Erlbaum.

Townsend, J. T. (1976). Serial and within-stage independent parallel model equivalence on the minimum completion time. *Journal of Mathematical Psychology, 14,* 219–238. doi:10.1016/0022-2496(76)90003-1

Townsend, J. T. (1984). Uncovering mental processes with factorial experiments. *Journal of Mathematical Psychology, 28,* 363–400. doi:10.1016/0022-2496(84)90007-5

Townsend, J. T. (2008). Mathematical psychology: Prospects for the 21st century. *Journal of Mathematical Psychology, 52,* 269–280. doi:10.1016/j.jmp.2008.05.001

Townsend, J. T., & Neufeld, R. J. (Eds.). (2010). Contributions of mathematical psychology to clinical science and assessment [Special issue]. *Journal of Mathematical Psychology, 54*(1).

Townsend, J. T., & Wenger, M. J. (2004). The serial-parallel dilemma: A case study in a linkage of theory and method. *Psychonomic Bulletin and Review, 11,* 391–418. doi:10.3758/BF03196588

Turvey, M. T. (1990). Coordination. *American Psychologist, 45,* 938–953.

Turvey, M. T. (2009). On the notion and implications of organism-environment system: Introduction. *Ecological Psychology, 21,* 97–111. doi:10.1080/10407410902877041

Tversky, A., & Kahneman, D. (1974). Judgment under uncertainty: Heuristics and biases. *Science, 185,* 1124–1131. doi:10.1126/science.185.4157.1124

Tversky, A., & Kahneman, D. (1981). The framing of decisions and the psychology of choice. *Science, 211,* 453–458. doi:10.1126/science.7455683

Usher, M., & McClelland, J. L. (2001). On the time course of perpetual choice: The leaky competing accumulator model. *Psychological Review, 108,* 550–592. doi:10.1037/0033-295X.108.3.550

Van Orden, G. C., Holden, J. G., & Turvey, M. T. (2005). Human cognition and 1/ƒ scaling. *Journal of Experimental Psychology: General, 134,* 117–123. doi:10.1037/0096-3445.134.1.117

Van Zandt, T. (2000). ROC curves and confidence judgments in recognition memory. *Journal of Experimental Psychology: Learning, Memory, and Cognition, 26,* 582–600. doi:10.1037/0278-7393.26.3.582

Van Zandt, T., Colonius, H., & Proctor, R. W. (2000). A comparison of two response time models applied to perceptual matching. *Psychonomic Bulletin and Review, 7,* 208–256. doi:10.3758/BF03212980

Vickers, D. (1979). *Decision processes in visual perception.* New York, NY: Academic Press.

Wagenmakers, E.-J., Farrell, S., & Ratcliff, R. (2004). Estimation and interpretation of 1/f α noise in human cognition. *Psychonomic Bulletin and Review, 11,* 579–615.

Watson, J. B. (1914). *Behavior: An introduction to comparative psychology.* New York, NY: Henry Holt.

White, C., Ratcliff, R., Vasey, M., & McKoon, G. (2009). Dysphoria and memory for emotional material: A diffusion model analysis. *Cognition and Emotion, 23,* 181–205

Wiener, N. (1948). *Cybernetics; or, control and communication in the animal and the machine.* Cambridge, MA: MIT Press.

Wixted, J. T. (2007). Dual-process theory and signal-detection theory of recognition memory. *Psychological Review, 114,* 152–176. doi:10.1037/0033-295X.114.1.152

CHAPTER 21

COMPUTATIONAL MODELING

Adele Diederich and Jerome R. Busemeyer

Over the past 40 years or so, computational modeling has become a rapidly growing approach in many scientific disciplines. In some fields, it has become a subdiscipline with its own journals such as *PloS Computational Biology*, *Journal of Computational Biology*, *Journal of Computational Neuroscience*, *Journal of Computational Physics*, *Journal of Computational and Applied Mathematics*, *Journal of Computational Methods in Sciences and Engineering*, *Journal of Computational Chemistry*, *Journal of Computational Finance*, and many others. Computational modeling in psychology has been applied predominantly in cognitive psychology, in particular in learning, memory, categorization, pattern recognition, psycholinguistics, vision, and decision making; lately, it is becoming increasingly important in developmental psychology and social psychology. Recently, an entire handbook was devoted to computational modeling in psychology (Sun, 2008a). What is computational modeling? Is there something like computational psychology? Is it different from mathematical modeling and mathematical psychology?

In general, a *model* is an abstraction representing some aspects of a complex phenomenon or situation in the real world. A formal model applies mathematical and statistical methods, formal logic, or computer simulation to establish a correspondence between a particular set of empirical phenomena and a formal system reflecting the assumptions about specific entities or objects and their relations to each other. The model thereby may take on various structures such as algebraic or geometric, and forms such as axiomatic, systems of equations,

algorithms, networks, and so on. They are static or dynamic, deterministic or probabilistic, linear or nonlinear in nature, and so forth. They are designed to describe internal presentations, processes, functions, mechanisms, and structures. The goal of the formal model is to derive predictions, which can connect to data observed in the real world. These data are often obtained in experiments. Interpreting data in light of the model's prediction is crucial for the modeling process and often leads to a modification of the model. This entire process is referred to as mathematical modeling. When the phenomena of interest stem from psychological questions, the area is called *mathematical psychology* (see Chapter 20 of this volume) and the process often is called *cognitive modeling*. We provided a tutorial (Busemeyer & Diederich, 2010) that reviewed the methods and steps used in cognitive modeling.

Sometimes a mathematical model representing the phenomena or situations is so complex that an analytical solution is not readily available or a closed form solution does not even exist. Other times experiments are too expensive or may not even be feasible to conduct. For those cases, a computational approach is considered to be a valuable alternative. Computational approaches develop computer algorithms and programs, and implement them on a computer; computer simulations derive the predictions of the model and also generate data. Instead of deriving a mathematical analytical solution to the problem, a computer simulation—that is, changing the parameters of the system in the computer—provides the basis for studying and evaluating the

DOI: 10.1037/13620-021
APA Handbook of Research Methods in Psychology: Vol. 2. Research Designs, H. Cooper (Editor-in-Chief)

model by comparing the simulated data to the outcome of the experiments. Many of the neural network models are like this.

Coming back to the aforementioned questions: With this description of a computational approach in mind, is computational modeling in psychology different from mathematical psychology? Are mathematical models a subset of computational models as Sun (2008b) has claimed? Or, is it merely a tool in mathematical psychology, one of many methods that can be applied in the modeling process, with the advantage that data can be simulated easily and extremely quickly? After all, computational models require a mathematically and logically formal representation of the problem and could therefore be considered as a subset of mathematical models.

In light of the many disciplines involved in computational modeling research, it seems to be impossible to come up with an agreed-upon definition. There is an interesting discussion going on in some disciplines. Indeed, an entire subfield of computer science studies the relationships and differences between computational and mathematical models. Fisher and Henzinger (2007), for instance, discussed the position of computational and mathematical models in biology. According to them, a mathematical model is a formal model whose primary semantics is denotational, that is, equations relate different numerical quantities to each other and describe how they change over time. The equations do not determine an algorithm for solving them. A computational model is a formal model whose primary semantics is operational, that is, describing a sequence of instructions or steps implemented on a computer (Fisher & Henzinger, 2007, p. 1240). The main difference between both classes of models is seen in their formalism. Hunt, Ropella, Park, and Engelberg (2008) vehemently objected to this view. They saw the main difference in (a) the intent and the approach a scientist uses, (b) the computer's performance when implemented models are executed, and (c) why the computer behaves as it does (Hunt et al., 2008, p. 737). Whereas mathematical models focus on formulating hypotheses about relations, variables, and magnitudes, computational models focus on formulating hypotheses about mechanisms and processes and try to understand the interaction between the

system components (Hunt et al., 2008, p. 738). This discussion has not started yet in psychology to a large extent (but see Boden & Mellor, 1986). Investigating the theoretical status of computational modeling in cognitive science, Sun (2009) described the significance of computational cognitive modeling as it provides "detailed descriptions of mechanisms (i.e., static aspects) and processes (i.e., dynamic aspects) of cognition" (p. 125) and "computational modeling contributes to general, theoretical understanding of cognition through generating mechanistic and process-based descriptions that match human data" (p. 126). These statements also apply to mathematical psychology and, indeed, for both quotes Sun referred to Luce (1995) on his perspective on mathematical modeling in psychology. The word *computational* is not mentioned in that article at all.

Many computational models are computer simulations of complex mathematical equations that cannot be solved in a simple form and must be simulated by the computer. Some other computational models are simply based on if–then production rules and are harder to see as mathematical models. Technically they are finite state machines, or if a probabilistic selection of rules is applied, they technically become Markov models in a large state space. However, these types of computational models are never expressed mathematically even though they could. Models such as Act-R (Lebière & Anderson, 1993; see also the section Symbolic Modeling) or Clarion (Sun, 2009) use some mathematical equations like power function decay, linear combinations of inputs to produce activation values, and mathematical reinforcement learning rules. But they are also heavily reliant on production rules. That is, technically, they could be formalized as mathematical models (dynamic systems, stochastic dynamic systems, finite state machines, Markov processes); however, in practice, it is difficult to see the mathematics in some of them, such as pure production rule systems.

Most computational models in psychology are functional in nature. They are built to describe and explain psychological mechanisms and processes and to predict (human) performance, that is, what can be expected to happen under various conditions. The (cognitive) architecture of a model reflects its structure and computational rules, that is, its functional organization. Cognitive architectures are classified as symbolic, subsymbolic (connectionist), and hybrid depending on the assumed properties of the models and the rules applied to the system.

Symbolic modeling has its origin in computer science, in particular, in artificial intelligence, which focuses on building enhanced intelligence into computer systems. Patterns of reasoning, such as logical operations or processing systems with their respective specified rules, operate by using symbols. From early on these models have attracted a broad range of disciplines from philosophy to engineering. They have been applied to semantic representation, language processing, knowledge representation, reasoning, speech recognition, computer vision, robotic, various expert systems, and many more disciplines (see Nilsson, 2010, for a history and achievement of artificial intelligence with a focus on engineering; and Boden, 2006, for a comprehensive work on a history of cognitive science that also includes the philosophical perspective of computational approaches).

Subsymbolic or *connectionist* models use the analogy of neural networks as observed in the human brain. Activation patterns among large numbers of processing units (neurons) encode knowledge and specific content. The basic assumptions are outlined in the section Subsymbolic Modeling. Connectionist models are developed in many scientific disciplines from computer science to neuroscience, natural science, cognitive science, and behavioral sciences. They have been applied to speech recognition and speech generation, predictions of financial indexes, identification of cancerous cells, automatic recognition to handwritten characters, sexing of faces, and many more. *Hybrid* architectures combine both types of processing and become more interesting for cognitive modelers. More recently, Bayesian models (see Chapter 24 of this volume) and dynamic systems theory (see Volume 3, Chapter 16, this handbook) have been added to the methodological repertoire of computational modeling.

THE ADVANTAGE OF FORMAL MODELING

Formal modeling has several advantages. First, it forces the researcher to give precise definitions and clear statements. This requires a high degree of abstraction: Assumptions about underlying processes, relations between entities, interactions between variables, and so on, all need to be mapped onto mathematical objects and operations. The language of mathematics minimizes the risk of making contradictory statements in the theory. Second, formal modeling allows deriving precise predictions from the underlying assumptions, thereby enabling empirical falsification of these assumptions. Furthermore, deriving predictions is particularly important and useful when they are not obvious. Testable predictions may be useful for deciding between competing theories of a given phenomenon. They are not necessarily quantitative but can also reflect qualitative patterns, which can be observable in the data. Third, mathematical modeling brings together theory and data; it facilitates the analysis and interpretation of complex data and helps generate new hypotheses. Fourth, even rather simple mathematical models often describe data better and are more informative than a statistical test of a verbally phrased hypothesis. Finally, formal models can provide a unifying language and methodology that can be used across disciplines ranging from experimental psychology to cognitive science, computer science, and neuroscience.

SYMBOLIC MODELING

The symbolic approach was put forward by Allen Newell and Herbert A. Simon, starting in the late 1950s and 1960s. In the *Handbook of Mathematical Psychology* (Luce, Bush, & Galanter, 1963), Newell and Simon described "how computers can be used to formulate and test psychological theories without the mediation of mathematical models" (Newell & Simon, 1963, p. 373). According to the authors, a computer is a general-purpose device that is capable of all kinds of manipulations of all kinds of symbols. The meaning of a symbol is determined by the program that performs operations such as recognizing it, comparing it with other symbols, and processing it (Newell & Simon, 1963, p. 375). Symbol manipulation is accomplished by a set of elementary processes together with appropriate combinations of them. These include *reading* symbols (i.e., transforming external patterns into internal representation); *writing* symbols (i.e., transforming internal patterns into external symbols); *comparing* symbols and behaving conditionally on the outcome of comparison (i.e., determining whether two patterns are different or identical and proceeding according one way or the other), *copying* symbols (i.e., creating patterns isomorphic to given patterns), and *associating* symbols (i.e., storing with a symbol information that identifies other symbols; Newell & Simon, 1963, p. 375).

A *symbol system* is a machine that consists of a *memory*, a set of *operators*, a *control*, an *input*, and an *output* (Newell, 1980). The memory is composed of a set of symbol structures that in turn contains abstract symbols, $\{S_1, S_2, \ldots, S_n\}$, called *symbol tokens*. Memory structures persist over time, hold information and can be modified independently. Symbol tokens are patterns in symbol structures that provide access to distal memory systems. Each symbol structure is of a specific *type*, T, and has a number of specific *roles*, $\{R_1, R_2, \ldots\}$, and is written as $(T: R_1 S_1, R_2 S_2, \ldots R_n S_n)$. Operations on symbol structures compose new symbol structures or modify old structure. They are often called *condition–action production rules*; if a condition is present or satisfied, then an action is taken, producing changes in memory. They take symbol structures as input and produce symbol structures as output. The operations are similar to the ones described thus far and include a few more that are closely related to computer language commands, such as if-then-do, exit-if, continue-if, and so on. For an entire list with detailed descriptions, see Newell (1980). The control navigates the behavior of the system and communicates between input and output and interprets its components. Figure 21.1 shows a simplified example of this architecture.

This approach inspired many cognitive scientists. For instance, ACT* (Adaptive Control of Thought [pronounced "act–star"]; Anderson, 1983), a revision of ACT (Anderson, 1976), which in turn has its roots in HAM (Human Associative Memory; Anderson & Bower, 1973), is an information processing model that integrates declarative knowledge (*declarative memory*), procedural knowledge (*procedural knowledge*), and working memory. The model has been extended further into ACT-R (R for Rational)

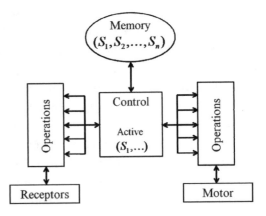

FIGURE 21.1. The structure of a symbolic system. The operations on the left-hand side are "Assign," "Copy," "Write," "Read," and "Input." The operations on the right-hand side are "Do," "Exit–if," "Continue–if," "Quote," and "Behave." From "Physical Symbol Systems," by A. Newell, 1980, *Cognitive Science, 4*, p. 143. Copyright 1980 by Cognitive Science Society, Inc. Adapted with permission.

to include rational analysis (Anderson, 1990). Lebière and Anderson (1993) implemented a connectionist component to the ACT-R production system. That is, declarative knowledge is stored in chunks of the procedural knowledge for each type, T, and procedural knowledge is represented by the connectivity pattern between the various type memories and the central memory. This version of the model may be considered as a hybrid model in which symbolic and subsymbolic components are combined. The symbol approaches usually are implemented by list-processing languages such as Lisp. For further symbolic cognitive architectures (e.g., Soar [States, Operators, And Reasoning]; Executive Process/Interactive Control [EPIC]; Collaborative Activation-Based Production System [CAPS]), see Polk and Seifert (2002) and Sun (2008a).

SUBSYMBOLIC MODELING

Artificial neural networks (also known as *connectionist models* and *parallel distributed processing* [PDP]) or *neural networks* for short, draw on the analogy of biological neural networks. Biological neural networks are composed of neurons (including cell body, axon, and dendrites) and their synaptic connections. Artificial neural networks are mathematical or computational models that try to simulate the structure or functional aspects of biological neural networks (Grossberg, 1982). Processing units (or computational units or artificial neurons) are interlinked by a system of connections to form a complex network. Neurons can be activated by inputs from other neurons and can likewise stimulate other neurons. Information processing within the neural network is characterized by patterns of activation.

Different from the symbolic approach in which the elements are symbols held in one or more memory systems, the elements here are highly simplified units interconnected in a network.

The general framework for connectionist processing is defined by seven key features (Rumelhart, McClelland, & the PDP Research Group, 1986; Thomas & McClelland, 2008).

1. A set of processing units u_i, organized in layers and often distinguished into input units, which receive the information to be processed, output units, which provide the results of the processing, and hidden units, in which specific computations necessary for the entire process may be performed. The units can be interpreted as natural and artificial neurons and groups of neurons. For instance, describing the Mach Band illusion on the level of the retina (lateral inhibition), the input neurons would be the photoreceptors absorbing photons, the hidden units the bipolar cells, and the output units the ganglion cells. For cognitive models, the input units may represent perceptual features, letters, faces, and so on, and output units may represent words, phonemes, and ethnic groups. The representation of cognitive elements by units is discussed further in the section Representation of Cognitive Elements by Units. All the processing is carried out by these units. The system is parallel as many simple operations are carried out simultaneously. Units in a computer simulation are virtual entities and usually presented by circles.

2. A state of activation for each unit, a_i, at a given time t, $a_i(t)$. The state of a set of units at time t are organized in a vector, $a(t) = (a_1(t), a_2(t), \ldots, a_i(t) \ldots, a_n(t))$. The activation values can be any numeric value, but often they are real numbers bounded between 0 and 1. The analogy to neural activity is the neuron's firing rate (rate of action potentials). A zero would indicate the least possible activity and a one the most possible activity of a neuron.

3. The pattern of connectivity. To make it a network, units need to be connected. If units are analogous to neurons, connections are analogous to synapses. Connections are represented with lines, and arrows indicate the flow of information from one unit to the next. In a standard, three-layer feedforward network, activation is sent from all input units to all hidden units to all output units in a single direction, that is, a directed graph with nodes and intermodal connections. The strength or weakness of a connection between any two units determines the extent to which the activation state of one unit can affect the activation state of another unit and can be measured by a connection weight, w. The connections weights of all units are organized in a matrix $W = \|w_{ij}\|$. Often connection weights are real numbers between −1 and 1. High connection weights represent a strong connection, whereas low weights represent a weak connection, analogous to excitatory and inhibitory synapses.

4. The propagation rule. This rule determines how activation is propagated through the network. The activation values of the sending units are combined with the connections weights to produce the net input into the receiving units, usually by a linear function. That is, the inputs from all sending units are multiplied by the connection weights and summed up to get the overall input of the receiving units, that is, the net input for the receiving units is $net(t) = W \cdot a(t)$. The net input for a specific unit, i, is therefore, $net_i(t) = \sum_j w_{ij} a_j(t)$.

5. The activation rule. This rule specifies how the combined or net input of a given unit is transformed to produce its new activation state $a_i(t + 1)$ and is expressed in terms of a function F, such that $a_i(t + 1) = F(net_i(t))$. Typically, the activation F is chosen from a small selection of functions, including $F(x) = sgn(x)$, producing binary (± 1) output; $F(x) = (sgn(x)+1)/2$, producing binary (0/1) output; $F(x) = (1 + e^{-x})^{-1}$, the

sigmoidal (logistic) nonlinearity, producing output between 0 and 1; $F(x) = tanh(x)$, producing output between −1 and 1; and some other forms are also possible. The net input can take on any value and the function F ascertains that the new activation state does not exceed the maximum or minimum activation values (e.g., above 1 or below 0).

6. The learning rule. Learning in a neural network involves modifying the connection weights and finding the right weights is at the heart of connectionist models. The learning rule is an algorithm and specifies how the connectivity changes over time as a function of experience, that is, data. For instance, the simplest learning rule assumes that the weight w_{ij} between two units u_i and u_j changes proportional to the respective activation values, that is, $\Delta w_{ij} = w_{ij}(t + 1) - w_{ij}(t) = \eta a_i a_j$, where the constant η is called *learning rate*.

There are a variety of learning algorithms. They differ from each other in the way in which the adjustment of the connection weights of a unit is formulated (e.g., see Haykin, 1999, for a detailed description of several algorithms). Specific learning rules depend on the architecture of the neural network. In addition, various learning paradigms refer to models of the environment in which the neural network operates. Any given network architecture can usually be employed in any given learning paradigm.

Network Architectures

There are three fundamentally different classes of network architectures: single-layer feedforward networks, multilayer feedforward networks, and recurrent networks.

Single-layer feedforward networks. The input layer of source nodes projects on an output layer of computational nodes but not vice versa. It is strictly feedforward. The notion *single-layer* refers to the output layer of the computational nodes. The input layer is not counted because no computation takes place.

Multilayer feedforward networks. One or more hidden layers or hidden units are sandwiched between the input layer and the output layer. The hidden units intervene between the external input

and the network output in some way. Typically the units in each layer of the network have as their inputs the output signals of the preceding layer. If every node in each layer of the network is connected to every other node in the adjacent forward layer, the neural network is fully connected. If a connection is missing the neural network is partially connected.

Recurrent networks. The network has at least one feedback loop. The feedback loops may be self-feedback loops, that is, the output of a neuron is fed back into its own input or no self-feedback loops, for instance, when the output is fed back to the inputs of all the other neurons.

Learning Paradigms

There are three major learning paradigms: supervised learning, unsupervised learning and reinforcement learning.

Supervised learning. In *supervised learning* (also referred to as *learning with a teacher*), there is given a set of data, the training set, which includes the input (e.g., object patterns) and the desired output (e.g., classification). That is, the input is given together with the correct output, also called the *target*. The parameters of the network are gradually adjusted to match the input and desired output by going through the training set many times. The aim of the supervised neural network is to predict the correct answer to new data that were not included in the training set. That is, the network is expected to learn certain aspects of the input–output pairs in the training set and to apply to it new data.

Unsupervised learning. In *unsupervised learning* (also referred to as *self-organized learning* or *learning without a teacher*), a correct or desired output is not known, that is, there is no input–output pair. This type of learning is often used to form natural groups or clusters of objects on the basis of similarity between objects.

Reinforcement learning. In reinforcement learning the only information given for each input–output pair is whether the neural network produced the desired result and the total reward given for an output response. The weights are updated solely on this global feedback (that is, the Boolean values true or false or the reward value; for details, see Rojas, 1996).

Example

As an example for a learning rule, take the *single-unit perceptron* (Figure 21.2), which is the simplest version of a feedforward neural network and classifies inputs into two distinct categories. That is, it maps a real-valued input vector *a* (e.g., describing visual objects) to a binary output value *y* (e.g., Category A or B). Furthermore, the neural network applies a reinforcement paradigm. The architecture of this model in the previously introduced notation is

$$y = F[\Sigma_{j=1}^n w_j a_j(t) + w_0)] = \text{sgn}[\Sigma_{j=1}^n w_j a_j(t) + w_0], \quad (1)$$

where w_0 is a bias factor. The bias has the effect of increasing or lowering the net input of the activation function, depending on whether it is positive or negative, respectively. Setting $a_0 \equiv 1$, Equation 1 can be written as

$$y = \text{sgn}[\Sigma_{j=0}^n w_j a_j(t)] = \text{sgn}[w'a(t)]. \quad (2)$$

Denote the set of training or learning data as $D = \{[a(t), z(t)], t = 1, \ldots, m\}$, where $\{z(t)\}$ contains the binary classification variables ±1, the desired activation state at time *t* and $a(t) = [a_0(t), a_1(t), \ldots, a_n(t)]$ is the state activation vector for the observation at time *t* as before. Learning is modeled by updating the weight vector *w* during *m* iterations for all

training examples. That is, for each pair in *D* and for each iteration *t* the weight is updated according to

$$\Delta w_j = w_j(t+1) - w_j(t) = \eta(z - y)a_j, \quad (3)$$

where the constant η (>0) is called the *learning rate*, and the learning rule is called the *delta rule*. The delta rule is related to a gradient descent type of method for optimization.

NEUROBIOLOGICAL PLAUSIBILITY

Almost all textbooks on neural network models start with an introduction to the anatomical parts of a biological neuron and to the electrophysiological–biochemical mechanisms of neurons and neuron assemblies. Units are related to neurons (neuron = soma plus dendrites plus axon plus terminal buttons), connections to synapses, activation values to firing rates, connection weights to inhibitory and excitatory synaptic potentials, propagation to neural integration, activation functions somehow to threshold of excitation to trigger an action potential (however, often not according to the all-or-none law; see the section Subsymbolic Modeling), and so on. However, there is some controversy whether connectionist models are neurally plausible. For instance, many connectionist models include properties that are neurally not plausible (e.g., backpropagation) or omit properties that a neural system does have (e.g., hormones, enzymatic deactivation of neurotransmitters, oscillation).

Thomas and McClelland (2008) argued that the primary focus for considering connectionist models should be not neural plausibility but rather the advantage of providing better theories of cognition (p. 29). Cognitive modelers, interpreting basic elements of connectionist models only in abstract functional terms, evaluate a connectionist cognitive model on how well they explain and predict behavioral data obtained in psychological experiments. Evidence from neuroscience is not necessary to develop cognitive models, and they need not be evaluated on neurophysiological criteria (e.g., Broadbent, 1985). Not all cognitive scientists share this view, however. Contrarily, Houghton (2005) is convinced that many cognitive scientists believe

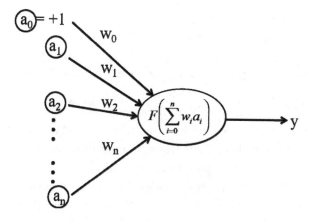

FIGURE 21.2.   A simple single-unit perceptron, also known as McCulloch-Pitts neuron (McCulloch & Pitts, 1943).

that a neurally grounded cognitive psychology is both desirable and achievable. Given that the brain is the main actor in cognition and behavior it is desirable to have neurally and cognitive-based theories that are not only compatible but also translatable one into the other (Houghton, 2005, p. 9). Similarly, Bowers (2009) argued that considering the rapid developments in neuroscience, cognitive theories can and should be constrained by biology (p. 221).

REPRESENTATION OF COGNITIVE ELEMENTS BY UNITS

One of the key properties of connectionist models is the assumption of distributed presentation. Cognitive elements are presented by the pattern of activation over a set of units not by single units. For instances, the 95 printable ASCII characters, that is, the ones on a U.S. keyboard without the control characters are presented by specific patterns of ones and zeros. To be more specific, each character is represented by a vector of length 8, examples of which are presented in Table 21.1.

Each element of the vector stands for one unit and each unit is either in state 1 or 0. A single character, however, can be identified only by the set of units, not by a single unit because three units, that is, those at positions 1, 2, and 4, carry the same information across all four vectors. An alternative representation is that each unit represents one character. Obviously, this requires many more units (95, in this case). The latter representation is known as *local*, *localist*, or *specific* coding and is also dubbed as *grandmother* cell. Whereas distributed coding is well founded in neuroscience (for neural tuning, see

the section Connectionist Version of the Prototype Model), localist representations are considered to be biologically implausible. However, because units in a connectionist model represent the cognitive elements applicable in the respective research domain, both representations are frequently used. Page (2000), for instance, developed a localist model that is embedded in a connectionist model with many properties of a fully distributed model (see also Kruschke's, 1992, ALCOVE model). Bowers (2009) reviewed a range of data and came to the conclusion that localist models provide a better account of single-cell recording distributed approaches and argued that rejections of localist models in neuroscience is due to a misunderstanding about how localist models behave.

NEURAL NETWORKS AS STATISTICAL MODELS

A rather different perspective of neural network models is the statistical approach. Biological and neurophysiologic plausibility is of minor concern and the focus is instead on statistical methodology (see Cheng & Titterington, 1994, and Titterington, 2010, for examples and derivations). The structure or architecture of the neural network model is related to unknown parameters in the statistical framework, the training of the network to parameter estimation. Consider for instance Equation 1. If there is no restriction on y to be binary—that is, instead of taking the activation function $F(x) = sgn(x)$, let $F(x) = x$—then it is a multiple linear regression model. The a_j, typically denoted as x_j, are the covariates or predictors and the w_j are the parameters of the regression model. With the observed outcomes, y, of an experiment and the covariates x_j available to the parameter estimation is equivalent to supervised learning. If the model is as stated in Equation 1, the statistical name is Fisher's linear discriminant function. In more complicated architectures, hidden units are the analog to latent variables. Feedforward networks are regarded as a class of flexible, nonlinear regression or classification functions. To train a network, nonlinear least squares estimates are the standard approach with a gradient descent

TABLE 21.1

Distributed Coding for the Letters *a*, *D*, *j*, and *B*

Character	ASCII
a	01100001
D	01000100
j	01101010
B	01000010

algorithm to handle the optimization problem (for details and more examples, see Cheng & Titterington, 1994; Kay & Titterington, 1999; Ripley, 2006).

EXAMPLE OF A MODELING PROCESS

The following simple example demonstrates how the modeling process is performed. To illustrate the advantage of formal modeling, the focus is on two reasonably simple connectionist types of models for categorical learning. Categorizing (perceptual) objects or patterns in distinct classes is important to many real life situations. Does the functional magnetic resonance imaging scan indicate disease A or B or none? Are these cells cancerous or not? Is this a female or male face? What ethnical group do these people belong to? Often people are successful in performing these and similar tasks, sometimes not. How do we learn to categorize objects, and how do we generalize our knowledge to objects we have not seen before?

Step 1

The first step in the modeling process to answer these questions is to come up with a conceptual theoretical framework. This requires creativity on the part of the researcher and involves hard work. For our demonstration, we take two existing and competing theoretical frameworks for categorization: a prototype model and an exemplar model. According to the prototype model, some members of a category are more central than others. The person extracts the central tendency (sometimes referred to as characteristic features) of the examples presented during a learning phase und uses these characteristic features to form a prototype that serves as basis for categorizing new objects. That is, when a new object, the target, is presented, it is compared with the prototypical object of each category, and the category with the most similar prototype is chosen. According to the exemplar model, the learner stores specific instances (*exemplars*) for each category. When a new target stimulus is presented, the similarity of the target to each stored example is computed for each category, and the category with the greatest total similarity is chosen.

Step 2

The second step is to describe the objects in an abstract formal way, translate the assumptions into equations, and describe the response also in a rigorous form. Here, we take a connectionist version of a prototype model and a connectionist version of an exemplar model (e.g., Nosofsky, Kruschke, & McKinley, 1992). There has been a long debate about which of these two models (prototype vs. exemplar) best represents category learning, and some question whether it is possible to empirically distinguish them. Methods for qualitative comparisons of models are helpful to decide those questions.

For simplicity, assume very simple objects are characterized by only two dimensions. These could be saturation and brightness, length and orientation, distance between eyes and length of mouth, and so on. The stimuli are conveniently described in the form of vectors. A stimulus is denoted $S = (s_1, s_2)$, where s_1 represents the value of the stimulus on the first dimension and s_2 represents the value of the stimulus on the second dimension. Consider the connectionist version of the prototype model first.

Connectionist version of the prototype model.

The model assumes that a stimulus is represented by two sets of input units: One set, u_1, is activated by the value of the stimulus on the first dimension, s_1; and the other set, u_2, is activated by the value of the stimulus on the second dimension, s_2. The number of units in each set is p, $u_i = \{u_{i1}, \ldots, u_{ip}\}$, $i = 1, 2$, and so there are a total of $2 \cdot p$ units. Obviously, this can be written as $u_1 \cup u_2 = \{u_1, \ldots, u_p, u_{p+1}, \ldots, u_{2p}\}$. Each unit within a set is designed to detect a particular stimulus value, which is called the *ideal point* of the unit. This may be considered in analogy to neuronal tuning. Neurons responding best to specific orientation, movement direction, disparity, frequency, and the like are said to be tuned to that orientation, movement direction, disparity, and frequency. The ideal point value of each unit is not naturally given but needs to be defined. These additional detailed assumptions (called *ad hoc assumptions*) are necessary to complete the model. That is, for the prototype model, assumptions about what features should be used to represent the stimuli to be categorized need to be added and also formulated in an abstract way.

The jth unit in the first set is designed to detect a stimulus value, z_1j, that is, the ideal point of that unit and the activation of this unit, denoted $a_1j(t)$, is determined by the similarity of s_1 presented at trial t to the ideal point z_1j. Analogously, the jth unit in the second set is designed to detect a stimulus value, z_2j, and the activation of this unit, denoted $a_2j(t)$, is determined by the similarity of the ideal point z_2j to s_2 presented at trial t.

How large the set U is depends on how many specific features are to be coded. For instance, LeCun et al. (1989) developed a network for zip-code recognition. In their study, 7,291 hand-written zip-code digits were processed such to fit into a 16 × 16 pixel image with grey levels in the range of –1 to +1. Thus, the dimensionality of each input is 256.

The similarity between the current stimulus value s_i and the ideal point z_{ij}, for each unit j is determined by the following function:

$$f_{sim}(z_{ij}, s_i) = \exp\left(-\left(\frac{z_{ij} - s_i}{\sigma}\right)^2\right), \quad i = 1, 2 \quad j = 1,...,p. \quad (4)$$

Note that the choice of this function is another ad hoc assumption. Indeed, there are a variety of similarity functions one can choose from. The proposed one is related to Shepard's (1987) so-called universal law stating that the perceived similarity between two entities is an exponential decay function of their distance. In the present example the similarity function is Gaussian (exponent is 2).

The parameter σ is called the *discriminability parameter*, and it determines the width or spread of the activation around the ideal point. A low discriminability parameter (large σ) makes it hard to discriminate differences between the stimulus value and the ideal point, and a high discriminability parameter (small σ) makes easy-to-discriminate differences between the stimulus value and the ideal point. That is, it determines the rate at which similarity declines with distance. The values of the function range between 0 and 1. If the stimulus value s_i and the ideal point z_{ij} are identical, the function takes on the value 1. If the stimulus value s_i and the ideal point z_{ij} are very far apart, the function approaches 0. The input activation $a_{ij}(t)$ generated at the jth unit is determined by the similarity of that unit relative to the sum of the similarity of all the units:

$$a_{ij}(t) = \frac{f_{sim}(z_{ij}, s_i)}{\sum_{j=1}^{p} f_{sim}(z_{ij}, s_i)}, \quad i = 1, 2, \ j = 1,...,p. \quad (5)$$

The input units are connected to two output units, one for each category. The activation of the two category units are denoted $c_1(t)$ and $c_2(t)$ for category C_1 and C_2, respectively. The connection weight, w_{ijk}, connects the input activation $a_{ij}(t)$ to the kth output unit, $k = 1,2$. The propagation rule, that is, the function that combines the input activation with the connections weights to produce the input to the output units is

$$c_k(t) = \sum_{j=1}^{p} w_{1jk} a_{1j}(t) + \sum_{j=1}^{p} w_{2jk} a_{2j}(t), k = 1, 2. \quad (6)$$

Note that this is the net input for unit, k, that is, $c_k(t) = net_k(t)$. The set of weights $\{w_{11}k, . . ., w_{1p}k; w_{21}k, . . ., w_{2p}k\}$ connecting the inputs to the output for category C_k forms a representation of the prototype pattern for category C_k. The more similar the input activation pattern is to these weights, the more likely the stimulus matches the prototype for category C_k.

The connection weights are updated according to the delta learning rule:

$$\Delta w_{ijk} = w_{ijk}(t + 1) - w_{ijk}(t) = \eta \cdot [h_k(t) - c_k(t)] \cdot a_{ij}, \quad (7)$$

where $h_k(t)$ is the indicator function with $h_k(t) = 1$ for the desired category and 0 otherwise.

The whole learning process begins with some initial weights, and usually these are randomly assigned to represent a state of ignorance at the beginning of the learning process. Alternatively, if some prior knowledge or training exists, then the initial weights can be set to values that represent this prior knowledge or training. The architecture of the connectionist version of the prototype model is presented in Figure 21.3.

One essential step in computational modeling is to implement the model onto the computer, that is, writing codes and algorithms for training the model and estimating the parameters. To do so it is convenient to rewrite the equations in matrix format. Computer languages such as Matlab, Mathematica, and R have built-in matrix operators that allow

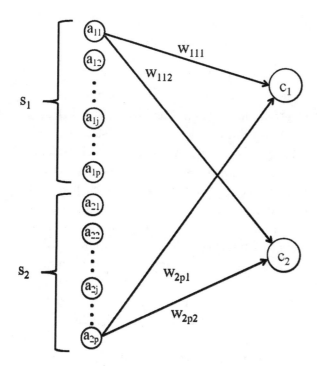

FIGURE 21.3. Architecture of the connectionist version of the prototype model.

effective programming leading to fast computations. The deviation between the p ideal points and the stimulus value s_i in Equation 4 can be written as p-dimensional vector d_i, $i = 1,2$ with

$$d_i = \frac{1}{\sigma}(z_i - s_i O), \qquad (8)$$

where z_i is a vector of length p with the p ideal points for dimension i and O is a p-dimensional vector containing ones. The similarity function is

$$f_{sim}(z_i, s_i) = \exp(-d_i^2), \qquad (9)$$

where $.2$ means the elementwise square of the vector.

The activation function in Equation 3 is a p-dimensional vector with

$$a_i(t) = \frac{1}{O^T \cdot f_{sim}(z_i, s_i)} f_{sim}(z_i, s_i), \quad i = 1,2, \quad (10)$$

where O^T is the transposed vector with ones, that is, a row vector. Note that $\dfrac{1}{O^T \cdot f_{sim}(z_i, s_i)}$ is the inner product that produces a scalar.

Obviously, the activation for both stimulus dimensions can be expressed in one vector of length $2p$

with $a(t) = \begin{pmatrix} a_1(t) \\ a_2(t) \end{pmatrix}$. The weights for each category are arranged in a $2 \times p$ matrix $W = \begin{bmatrix} w_1^T \\ w_2^T \end{bmatrix}$. The propagation rule in Equation 6 can be written as

$$c(t) = Wa(t), \qquad (11)$$

where $c(t) = \begin{pmatrix} c_1(t) \\ c_2(t) \end{pmatrix}$ is a vector of length 2 with the activation of the two category units for categories C_1 and C_2, respectively.

Finally, the delta rule (Equation 7) can be written as

$$\Delta W = W(t+1) - W(t) = \eta \cdot [h(t) - c(t)] \cdot a, \quad (12)$$

where $h(t) = \begin{pmatrix} h_1(t) \\ h_2(t) \end{pmatrix}$ is the two-dimensional vector of the indicator function with 1 for the desired category and 0 otherwise.

There are numerous ways to write the algorithms and programs for the model. A convenient method is to divide the program in several subprograms and address only those necessary for a specific purpose. For instance, estimating parameters from data requires different steps than simulating predictions of the model over a set of predefined parameters. However, both routines involve the computational model. An example of the model written in Matlab code is found in Table 21.2. Subprograms in Matlab are called *functions* and receive input from and provide output to other parts of the program. For demonstrational reasons the expressions are taken apart. For experienced programmers, they can be written more compactly. These functions are embedded in a larger frame where parameters such as the delta and sigma are defined, stimuli vectors are read, ideal points are defined, and so forth. For an example of a complete program, see Busemeyer and Diederich (2010).

Connectionist version of the exemplar model.
The model assumes that the inputs to the network form a square grid with p rows and p columns, that is, a $p \times p$ matrix. Each point on the grid, that is, each cell of the matrix, represents a single input unit. Each unit on the grid is designed to detect a pair of stimulus values. In particular, the unit on the grid point

TABLE 21.2

Matlab Codes for Determining the Similarity Function and Weights for the Prototype Model

Program command	Comment
function[a] = protoac(Z,S, sigma,j);	Input and output of function
fsim=exp(–((Z–S(j))./sigma).^2);	Calculating similarity
a=fsim/sum(fsim);	Calculation activation
function[W] = prototype(eta,p)	
W = zeros(2,p)	Initial connection weights
for j=1:p	Loop for stimuli
[a1]=protoac(Z1,S1,sigma,j);	Activation for category 1
[a2]=protoac(Z2,S2,sigma,j);	Activation for category 2
c=W*[a1;a2];	Propagation
W1=eta*([1;0]–c)*a1;	Adjusting weights for C_1
W2=eta*([0;1]–c)*a2;	Adjusting weights for C_2
W=W+W1+W2;	Updating the weights
End	End of loop

corresponding to row i and column j is designed to detect the value $z_{ij} = [z_i, z_j]$, which is the ideal point for this unit. The difference between the assumptions of the prototype model and the exemplar model is obvious. For the prototype model a unit is tuned to exactly one feature, but the exemplar model assumes that a unit is tuned to two (or possibly more) features. The stimulus $S = (s_1, s_2)$ activates a circular receptive field of grid points. Note that the analogy to neural structures in the brain is drawn including the same terminology. A receptive field of a neuron in the visual system, for instance, is a restricted area of the retina that influences the firing rate of that neuron because of light. Receptive fields of ganglion cells have a concentric form with a center-surround organization. A receptive field in the context of artificial neural networks is a restricted network with local connections that may or may not be concentric. The centroid of the receptive field is located at the pair of stimulus values (s_1, s_2). The amount of activation of a nearby input unit declines as a function of the distance of the unit from this center. The activation of this unit, $a_{ij}(t)$, is determined by the similarity of the stimulus S to the ideal point z_{ij}, denoted as $f_{sim}(z_{ij}, S)$ and defined as

$$f_{sim}(z_{ij}, S) = \exp\left(-\left(\frac{z_i - s_1}{\sigma}\right)^2\right)\exp\left(-\left(\frac{z_j - s_2}{\sigma}\right)^2\right),$$
$$i = 1,...,p \quad j = 1,...,p. \quad (13)$$

This is a type of a bivariate Gaussian distribution and is used to form the receptive field. As for the prototype model, the values of the function range between 0 and 1. If the stimulus values of both dimensions (s_1, s_2) and the ideal point (z_i, z_j) are identical, the function takes on the value 1. If the stimulus value of at least one dimension, s_i, $i = 1,2$, is far apart from its ideal point, z_i, $i = 1,2$, the function approaches 0, regardless of the difference between the stimulus value and its ideal point of the other dimension.

The parameter σ is interpreted as the discriminability parameter and has the same effect as it had before for the prototype model. Low discriminability (large values of σ) produces a large receptive field, which makes it hard to detect differences among stimuli. High discriminability (small values of σ) produces a small receptive field, which makes it easy to detect differences among stimuli.

The input activation $a_{ij}(t)$ generated at the unit in the ith row and jth column is determined by the similarity of that unit relative to the sum of similarity of all the units:

$$a_{ij}(t) = \frac{f_{sim}(z_{ij}, S)}{\sum_{i=1}^{p}\sum_{j=1}^{p} f_{sim}(z_{ij}, S)}, \ i = 1,...,p, \ j = 1,...p. \quad (14)$$

A stimulus produces a bivariate distribution of input activations on the grid, which is centered around the pair of stimulus values. As before, the input units are connected to two category units, one for each category, and the activation of the two category units is $c_k(t)$, $k = 1,2$, for category $C_k(t)$, $k = 1,2$. Each unit on the grid has a connection weight, w_{ijk}, which connects the input activation $a_{ij}(t)$ to the kth output unit, $k = 1,2$. The propagation rule for the exemplar model is

$$c_k(t) = \sum_{i=1}^{p}\sum_{j=1}^{p} w_{ijk} a_{ij}(t), \ k = 1,2. \quad (15)$$

This model is called an exemplar model because each receptive field of a training stimulus is associated with the output category units through a separate set of connection weights. Thus, the model simply associates each region of the stimulus space with a response, and similar examples get mapped to similar responses.

As for the prototype model, the connection weights are updated according to the delta learning rule:

$$\Delta w_{ijk} = w_{ijk}(t+1) - w_{ijk}(t) = \eta \cdot [h_k(t) - c_k(t)] \cdot a_{ij}, \quad (16)$$

where $h_k(t)$ is the indicator function with $h_k(t) = 1$ for the desired category and 0 otherwise. The architecture of the connectionist version of the exemplar model is presented in Figure 21.4.

The matrix form of the exemplar model is derived as follows. The deviations between the ideal points and the stimulus values on each dimension are the same as in Equation 8. The similarities for these deviations are the same as in Equation 9. The function in Equation 13 is one point on the grid (one input unit); all the elements on the $p \times p$ grid of input units can be computed by the Kronecker product $\otimes$:

$$f_{sim}(z,S) = f_{sim}(z_1, s_1) \otimes f_{sim}(z_2, s_2). \quad (17)$$

Note that $f_{sim}(z, S)$ is a p^2 vector with elements as defined in Equation 14. This could have been arranged differently as a $p \times p$ matrix by setting $f_{sim}(Z, S) = f_{sim}(z_1, s_1) \cdot f_{sim}(z_2, s_2)^T$. It depends on what is more convenient for the remaining steps in the calculation, but is also a matter of taste of the individual researcher.

The input activations for all the input units on the $p \times p$ grid are

$$a(t) = \frac{1}{O^T \cdot f_{sim}(z,S)} f_{sim}(z,S), \quad (18)$$

where $a(t)$ is a p^2 vector with elements as defined in Equation 15. The propagation rule and the delta rule are analogous to Equation 11 and Equation 12, respectively. The algorithm for this part of the model can be found in Table 21.3.

TABLE 21.3

Matlab Codes for Determining the Similarity Function and Weights for the Exemplar Model

Program command	Comment
function[a] = exempac(Z1,Z2, S1,S2, sigma,j);	Input and output of function
fsim1=exp(-((Z1-S1(j))./ sigma).^2);	Calculating similarity
fsim2=exp(-((Z2-S2(j))./ sigma).^2);	
fsim=kron(fsim1,fsim2);	
a=fsim/sum(fsim);	Calculation activation

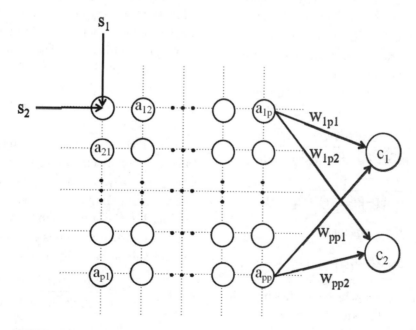

FIGURE 21.4. Architecture of the connectionist version of the exemplar model.

Step 3

The third step of the modeling process is to derive the predictions of the models. The predictions can be qualitative and quantitative. Although qualitative predictions do not require specific parameter values of the model (the predictions hold for all possible parameter values), quantitative predictions do require specific values for the free parameters of the model. Probing the model includes both qualitative and quantitative tests. For a qualitative test, the model predicts characteristic patterns that are compared with patterns observed in data. For the quantitative test, the free parameters of the model are estimated from data, and a goodness-of-fit measure (e.g., Pearson χ^2, Akaike Information Criterion, Schwartz Bayesian Criterion, and many more) provides information about how well the model describes the data in a statistical sense. (For a broader discussion on qualitative versus quantitative tests see also Busemeyer & Diederich, 2010).

Both models make predictions with respect to two different transfer tests: a generalization test and a recognition test. For the generalization test, new stimuli, not previously presented in the training set are classified. For the recognition test, new and old stimuli, that is, those presented in the training set are mixed and classified as *new* and *old*.

For the generalization test, the models assume that the probability of choosing category C_k for a new stimulus S_{new} (i.e., not an element of the training set) is based on a ratio of strength of the output activations. After t trials of training, the output for category $k = 1$ is $c_1(t)$ and the probability for choosing C_1 is

$$\Pr[C_1 \mid S_{now}] = \frac{\exp[\beta \cdot c_1(t)]}{\exp[\beta \cdot c_1(t)] + \exp[\beta \cdot c_2(t)]}$$

$$= \frac{1}{1 + \exp\{-\beta[-c_1(t) + c_2(t)]\}} \quad (19)$$

and the probability for choosing C_2 is

$$\Pr[C_2 \mid S_{now}] = 1 - \Pr[C_1 \mid S_{now}]. \quad (20)$$

That is, the activation rule, which specifies how the net input of a given unit produces its new activation state, is the logistic function $F(x) = (1 + e^{-x})^{-1}$, where $x = \beta(-c_1(t) + c_2(t))$. The coefficient, β, is called a *sensitivity* parameter. Increasing the sensitivity parameter decreases the value for $\exp(-\beta)$ and therefore increases the $F(x)$. That is, increasing the sensitivity increases the slope of the function that relates the choice probability to the activation of a category. Here it increases the probability for choosing C_1 with activation $c_1(t)$.

The predictions of both models over a range of parameters are presented in Figure 21.5. In particular, the sensitivity parameter β ranged from 0 to 15 in unit steps, the learning parameter η from 0 to 1 in steps of .04, and σ in Equation 4 and Equation 13 is set to 5. Suppose the stimuli are defined by two dimensions, and let H and L be sets containing all possible values within the described dimensions. Stimuli belonging to category C_1 have either low values, L, on both dimensions, $(S_1 \in L, S_2 \in L) = (l, l)$, or high values, H, on both dimensions, $(S_1 \in H, S_2 \in H) = (h, h)$. Stimuli belonging to category C_2 have low values on the first dimension and high values on the second dimension, $(S_1 \in L, S_2 \in H) = (l, h)$, or high values on the first dimension and low values on the second dimension, $(S_1 \in H, S_2 \in L) = (h, l)$. For the simulation, the stimuli are realizations from Gaussian distributions, $N(\mu, \varphi^2)$. In particular, stimuli belonging to category C_1 have low values on both dimensions with mean $\mu_1 = 1$ for the first and $\mu_2 = 1$ for the second dimension or high values on both dimensions with mean $\mu_1 = 10$ for the first and $\mu_2 = 9$ for the second dimension; stimuli belonging to category C_2 have either a low and a high value on both dimensions with $\mu_1 = 2$ for the first and $\mu_2 = 10$ for the second dimension, or with $\mu_1 = 9$ for the first and $\mu_2 = 1$ for the second dimension. For all conditions, φ^2 is set to 1.

For a recognition task, the models assume that the probability of classifying a stimulus as *old*, that is, as previously presented in the training set is an increasing function of the total amount of activation produced by the stimulus to both output units. Again, a logistic function is used to relate total activation to old–new recognition response probability:

$$\Pr[old \mid S_{now}] = \frac{\exp\{\gamma \cdot [c_1(t) + c_2(t)]\}}{\delta + \exp\{\gamma \cdot [c_1(t) + c_2(t)]\}} \quad (21)$$

$$= \frac{1}{1 + \exp\{-[\gamma \cdot (c_1(t) + c_2(t)] + \ln(\delta)\}}$$

Prototype: Generalization Predictions

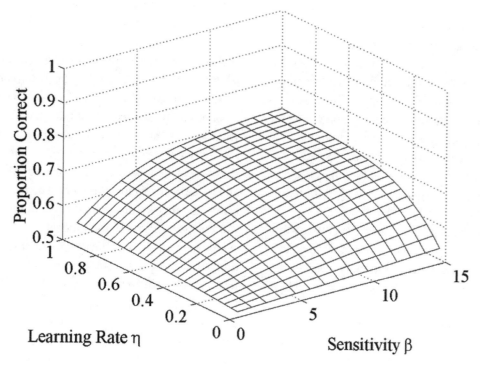

Exemplar: Generalization Predictions

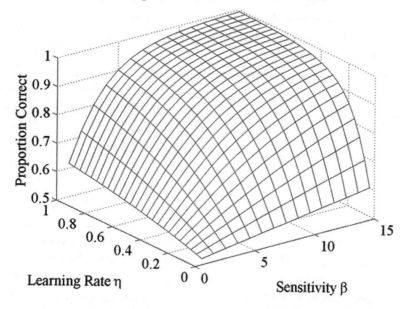

FIGURE 21.5. Prediction of the prototype model (a) and the exemplar model (b) with respect to a generalization task.

and the probability for choosing *new* is

$$\Pr[new \mid S_{new}] = 1 - \Pr[old \mid S_{new}]. \qquad (22)$$

The sensitivity parameter γ determines the recognition probability to the category activations. Increas-

ing the sensitivity parameter causes the recognition probability to be more strongly influenced by the category activations.

The parameter δ is a background-noise constant (Nosofsky et al., 1992). Here, it can be interpreted as a response bias parameter representing the tendency to say *new* to any stimulus, and increasing δ increases the tendency to respond *new*.

Both models have five model parameters: The discriminability parameter σ, which determines the width of the generalization gradients; the learning rate parameter η for the delta learning rule; the sensitivity parameter β for the categorization choice rule; and two parameters for the recognition response rule, the sensitivity parameter γ and the response bias parameter δ. The main difference between the two models is the input representation. The prototype model uses two univariate sets of input units, whereas the exemplar model uses a single bivariate grid of input units. The latter is plausible as many neurons are tuned to more than one feature. For instance, neurons in MT are tuned both to direction and spatial frequency or neurons in V1 and V2 are tuned both to orientation and spatial frequency (e.g., De Valois & De Valois, 1990; Mazer, Vinje, McDermott, Schiller, & Gallant, 2002).

Step 4

The fourth step is to test the predictions of the model with data and to compare the predictions of competing models with respect to their ability to explain the empirical results. However, as Roberts and Pashler (2000) pointed out, showing that a model fits the data is not enough. A major concern is that if a model is too flexible (fits too much) and does not constrain possible outcomes, then the fit is meaningless; if it is too flexible, it is necessary to penalize it for its complexity (Myung, 2000).

All models are an abstraction from a real-world phenomenon, and they focus only on essential aspects of a complex system. To be tractable and useful, models only reflect a simple and limited representation of the complex phenomenon. That is, a priori, all models are wrong in some details, and a sufficient amount of data will always prove that a model is not true. The question is which among the competing models provides a better representation of the phenomenon under question. Within the present context, the question is which of the two models, the prototype model or the exemplar model, provide a better explanation of how objects are categorized.

To empirically test competing models, it is crucial to design experiments that challenge the models. For instance, designing experimental conditions that lead to opposite qualitative predictions (categorical or ordinal) is an essential step in the model testing process. For example, the prototype model predicts that stimulus S is categorized in category C_1 most often, but the exemplar model predicts that stimulus S is categorized in category C_2 most often. Qualitative tests are parameter free in the sense that the models are forced to make these predictions for any value of the free parameters. The following briefly describes a design and shows a qualitative test for the two competing models.

Experiments in categorical learning typically are divided in two phases: a learning or training phase followed by a transfer test phase. During the training phase, the participants categorize objects in distinct classes and receive feedback about the performance. The transfer test is either a generalization test or a recognition test, both without feedback (see Step 3).

Assume that the participants accurately learned the category assignments for each of the four clusters of stimuli, $(S_1 \in L, S_2 \in L) = (l, l)$, $(S_1 \in H, S_2 \in H) = (h, h)$, $(S_1 \in L, S_2 \in H) = (l, h)$, and $(S_1 \in H, S_2 \in L) = (h, l)$, during the training phase. According to the exemplar model, for the transfer test, when fixing the first dimension at a high value $(h, \cdot)$, the probability of choosing category C_2 decreases as the value of the second dimension increases, $(h, l \rightarrow h)$; however, fixing the first dimension at a low value $(l, \cdot)$, the probability of choosing category C_2 increases as the value of the second dimension increases $(l, l \rightarrow h)$. Thus, according to the exemplar model, the value of the second dimension has the opposite effects on response probability, depending on the value of the first dimension (Nosofsky et al., 1992). This crossover interaction effect is critical for a qualitative test of the two competing models. As it turns out, the prototype model cannot predict the crossover effect when fixing one dimension and varying only the second; the exemplar model, however, predicts this crossover for a wide range of parameter values (see Busemeyer & Diederich, 2010). For demonstration, we take the same parameters for β, η, Σ as in Step 3. The means for the stimuli values, however, are set to $\mu_1 = 1$ and $\mu_2 = 1$ or

$\mu_1 = 10$ and $\mu_2 = 10$ for category C_1 and to $\mu_1 = 1$ and $\mu_2 = 10$ or $\mu_1 = 10$ and $\mu_2 = 1$ for category C_2. Figure 21.6 shows the simulation results. A dot indicates a combination of parameters that successfully reproduced the crossover. If the parameters are sufficiently large, the exemplar model predicts the crossover, here, in 337 out of 375 possible cases.

When we take the previous parameters $\mu_1 = 1$ and $\mu_2 = 1$ or $\mu_1 = 10$ and $\mu_2 = 9$ for category C_1 and $\mu_1 = 2$ and $\mu_2 = 10$ or $\mu_1 = 9$ and $\mu_2 = 1$ for category C_2, the simulation reproduces the crossover for both models as shown in Figure 21.7. The exemplar model (A) reproduces the correct pattern in 325 out of 375 possible cases, and the prototype model (B) reproduces it in 191 cases.

This example shows how crucial it is to design a proper experiment to distinguish between two competing models that make, in general, similar predictions. It is not always possible to construct qualitative tests for deciding between competing models. For instance, a model may predict increasing or decreasing functions depending on the specific parameter values. Furthermore, a model might be so complex that is it impossible to identify general qualitative patterns. For example, an arbitrarily large

hidden unit nonlinear neural network model can approximate a wide range of continuous functions, and thus it is not constrained to predict a general pattern that can be tested. Sometimes it is also important to interpret specific parameter values, for example, when comparing patients and healthy adults or younger and older participants. For those cases, a quantitative test of the model or a quantitative comparison of competing models is appropriate. It is also necessary for a model to make quantitative

(A)

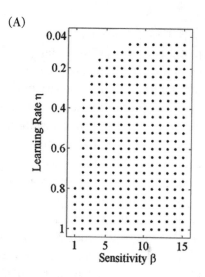

(B)

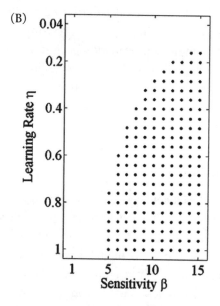

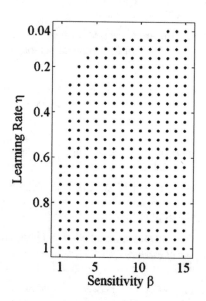

FIGURE 21.6.   Predicted patterns of results for the exemplar model. Each dot indicates a combination of parameters that correctly reproduced the crossover interaction.

FIGURE 21.7.   Predicted patterns of results for the exemplar model (a) and the prototype model (b). Each dot indicates a combination of parameters that correctly reproduced the crossover interaction.

predictions that are more accurate than its competitors. Quantitative predictions of a model are evaluated on the basis of an optimal selection of parameters. Otherwise, a perfectly good model could be rejected because of poor selection of parameters. Parameter estimation and model selection procedures are important topics in formal modeling approaches but go far beyond this chapter. There is an extensive literature on it (see Busemeyer & Diederich, 2010).

Step 5

The last step is in the modeling process is to modify the model in light of the data. Sometimes it is sufficient to make some adjustments to account for the observed data; sometimes it is necessary to reformulate the theoretical framework—for instance, modifying assumptions or by adding new assumptions; sometimes it is inevitable to abandon the model and construct a completely new model on the basis of feedback obtained from new experimental results. That is, new experimental findings pose new challenges to previous models. New models trigger new experiments. Modeling is a cyclic process and progress in the empirical and experimental sciences is made via this cycle: theorizing about the phenomenon and developing a model, deriving predictions from the model, testing the model, revising the model in light of empirical findings, testing the model again, and so on. Thus the modeling process produces an evolution of models that improve and become more powerful over time as the science in a field progresses.

CONCLUSION

What are the advantages of having a computational model? What can they offer to the modeling cycle? D'Mello and Franklin (2009) pointed to two benefits. First, the process of model development is highly instrumental in obtaining a deep understanding of the phenomenon under consideration. It involves deciding on the functional requirements and goal of the model, separating the various individual components of the model, and inventing schemes that bring all this together to obtain the desired behavior. Second, insights can be obtained

from basic computational principles that underlie the model. That is, any decision on a design made in the model-building process can be interpreted as a hypothesis that can be tested empirically.

References

Anderson, J. R. (1976). *Language, memory, and thought.* Mahwah, NJ: Erlbaum.

Anderson, J. R. (1983). *The architecture of cognition.* Cambridge, MA: Harvard University Press.

Anderson, J. R. (1990). *The adaptive character of thought.* Mahwah, NJ: Erlbaum.

Anderson, J. R., & Bower, G. H. (1973). *Human associative memory.* Washington, DC: Winston & Sons.

Boden, M. A. (2006). *Mind as machine: A history of cognitive science.* Oxford, England: Clarendon Press.

Boden, M. A., & Mellor, D. H. (1986). What is computational psychology? *Proceedings of the Aristotelian Society, 58*(Suppl.), 17–35, 37–53.

Bowers, J. S. (2009). On the biological plausibility of grandmother cells: Implications for neural network theories in psychology and neuroscience. *Psychological Review, 116,* 220–251. doi:10.1037/a0014462

Broadbent, D. (1985). A question of levels: Comments on McClelland and Rumelhart. *Journal of Experimental Psychology: General, 114,* 189–190. doi:10.1037/0096-3445.114.2.189

Busemeyer, J. R., & Diederich, A. (2010). *Cognitive modeling.* New York, NY: Sage.

Cheng, B., & Titterington, D. M. (1994). Neural networks: A review from a statistical perspective. *Statistical Science, 9,* 2–54.

De Valois, R. L., & De Valois, K. K. (1990). *Spatial vision.* New York, NY: Oxford University Press.

D'Mello, S., & Franklin, S. (2009). Computational modeling/cognitive robotics compliments functional modeling/experimental psychology. *New Ideas in Psychology, 29,* 217–227.

Fisher, J., & Henzinger, T. A. (2007). Executable cell biology. *Nature Biotechnology, 25,* 1239–1249. doi:10.1038/nbt1356

Grossberg, S. (1982). *Studies of mind and brain: Neural principles of learning, perception, development, cognition, and motor behavior.* Hingham, MA: Reidel.

Haykin, S. (1999). *Neural networks: A comprehensive foundation* (2nd ed.). Upper Saddle River, NJ: Prentice Hall.

Houghton, G. (2005). Introduction to connectionist models in cognitive psychology: Basic structures, processes, and algorithms. In G. Houghton (Ed.),

Connectionist models in cognitive psychology (pp. 1–41). London, England: Psychology Press.

Hunt, C. A., Ropella, G. E. P., Park, S., & Engelberg, J. (2008). Dichotomies between computational and mathematical models. *Nature Biotechnology, 26,* 737–738. doi:10.1038/nbt0708-737

Kay, J. W., & Titterington, D. M. (Eds.). (1999). *Statistics and neural networks.* New York, NY: Oxford University Press.

Kruschke, J. K. (1992). ALCOVE: An examplar-based connectionist model of category learning. *Psychological Review, 99,* 22–44. doi:10.1037/0033-295X.99.1.22

Lebière, C., & Anderson, J. R. (1993). A connectionist Implementation of the ACT-R production system. In *Proceedings of the 15th Annual Conference of the Cognitive Science Society* (pp. 635–640). Mahwah, NJ: Erlbaum.

LeCun, Y., Boser, B., Denker, J. S., Henderson, D., Howard, R. E., & Jackel, L. D. (1989). Backpropagation applied to handwritten ZIP code recognition. *Neural Computation, 1,* 541–551. doi:10.1162/neco.1989.1.4.541

Luce, R. D. (1995). Four tensions concerning mathematical modeling in psychology. *Annual Review of Psychology, 46,* 1–27. doi:10.1146/annurev.ps.46.020195.000245

Luce, R. D., Bush, R. R., & Galanter, E. (Eds.). (1963). *Handbook of mathematical psychology* (Vol. 1). New York, NY: Wiley.

Mazer, J. A., Vinje, W. E., McDermott, J., Schiller, P. H., & Gallant, J. L. (2002). Spatial frequency and orientation tuning dynamics in area V1. *Proceedings of the National Academy of Sciences of the United States of America, 99,* 1645–1650. doi:10.1073/pnas.022638499

McCulloch, W. S., & Pitts, W. (1943). A logical calculus of ideas immanent in nervous activity. *Bulletin of Mathematical Biophysics, 5,* 115–133. doi:10.1007/BF02478259

Myung, I. J. (2000). The importance of complexity in model selection. *Journal of Mathematical Psychology, 44,* 190–204. doi:10.1006/jmps.1999.1283

Newell, A. (1980). Physical symbol systems. *Cognitive Science, 4,* 135–183. doi:10.1207/s15516709cog0402_2

Newell, A., & Simon, H. (1963). Computers in psychology. In R. D. Luce, R. R. Bush, & E. Galanter (Eds.), *Handbook of mathematical psychology* (Vol. 1, pp. 361–428). New York, NY: Wiley.

Nilsson, N. J. (2010). *The quest for artificial intelligence: A history of ideas and achievements.* Cambridge, England: Cambridge University Press.

Nosofsky, R. M., Kruschke, J. K., & Mc Kinley, S. (1992). Combining exemplar-based category representations and connectionist learning rules. *Journal of Experimental Psychology: Learning, Memory, and Cognition, 18,* 211–233. doi:10.1037/0278-7393.18.2.211

Page, M. (2000). Connectionist modeling in psychology: A localist manifesto. *Behavioral and Brain Sciences, 23,* 443–467. doi:10.1017/S0140525X00003356

Polk, T. A., & Seifert, C. M. (2002). *Cognitive modeling.* Cambridge, MA: MIT Press.

Ripley, D. B. (2006). *Pattern recognition and neural networks.* Cambridge, England: Cambridge University Press.

Roberts, S., & Pashler, H. (2000). How persuasive is a good fit? A comment on theory testing. *Psychological Review, 107,* 358–367.

Rojas, R. (1996). *Neural networks. A systematic introduction.* Berlin, Germany: Springer.

Rumelhart, D. E., McClelland, J. L., & the PDP Research Group. (1986). *Parallel distributed processing: Explorations in the microstructure of cognition: Vol. 1. Foundations.* Cambridge, MA: MIT Press.

Shepard, R. N. (1987). Toward a universal law of generalization for psychological science. *Science, 237,* 1317–1323. doi:10.1126/science.3629243

Sun, R. (2008a). *The Cambridge handbook of computational psychology.* New York, NY: Cambridge University Press.

Sun, R. (2008b). Introduction to computational cognitive modeling. In R. Sun (Ed.), *The Cambridge handbook of computational psychology* (pp. 3–19). New York, NY: Cambridge University Press.

Sun, R. (2009). Theoretical status of computational cognitive modeling. *Cognitive Systems Research, 10,* 124–140. doi:10.1016/j.cogsys.2008.07.002

Thomas, M. S. C., & McClelland, J. L. (2008). Connectionist models of cognition. In R. Sun (Ed.), *The Cambridge handbook of computational psychology* (pp. 23–58). New York, NY: Cambridge University Press.

Titterington, M. (2010). Neural networks. WIRE's. *Computational Statistics, 2,* 1–8.

CHAPTER 22

BOOTSTRAPPING AND MONTE CARLO METHODS

William Howard Beasley and Joseph Lee Rodgers

Frequently a researcher is interested in a theoretical distribution or characteristics of that distribution, such as its mean, standard deviation, or 2.5 and 97.5 percentiles. One hundred or even 50 years ago, we were restricted practically by computing limitations to theoretical distributions that are described by an explicit equation,[1] such as the binomial or multivariate normal distribution. Using mathematical models of distributions often requires considerable mathematical ability, and also imposes rather severe and often intractable assumptions on the applied researchers (e.g., normality, independence, variance assumptions, and so on). But computer simulations now provide more flexibility specifying distributions, which in turn provide more flexibility specifying models.

One contemporary simulation technique is Markov chain Monte Carlo (MCMC) simulation, which can specify arbitrarily complex and nested multivariate distributions. It can even combine different theoretical families of variates. Another contemporary technique is the bootstrap, which can construct sampling distributions of conventional statistics that are free from most (but not all) assumptions. It can even create sampling distributions for new or exotic test statistics that the researcher created for a specific experiment.

The field of simulation is a large one, and we try to cover only the aspects that have an immediate benefit for applied behavioral researchers. The field is very wide and extends into almost every area of statistics. It even extends beyond statistics; several influential techniques were developed by physicists in the 1940s and 1950s. The field also has a history that itself is almost as long as modern statistics. Many of the founders of modern statistics conceptually described the benefits and justifications of simulation before they were pragmatically possible. The bootstrap and some useful simulation terminology are introduced in the chapter's first section. General simulations and MCMC simulations are covered in the second section.

R code for the chapter's examples is available at http://dx.doi.org/10.1037/13620-022.supp and can be viewed with a simple text editor. The first example has two versions. The first listing is intended to be a clear and direct translation of the described steps; the second listing is optimized for efficiency and produces the graphs used in this chapter.

THE BOOTSTRAP

The bootstrap is a resampling technique that uses an observed sample to construct a statistic's sampling distribution. Many fathers of modern statistics actively developed and promoted resampling, such as William Gosset (also known as Student), R. A. Fisher, and John Tukey.

Bootstrapping Univariate Observations
Example 1a: Standard error of the median. A psychologist collects waiting times in a sample of $N = 5$

---

[1]Our present definition of *explicit equation* includes exact equations and well-defined series. An analytic solution relies only on explicit equations, although the definition's boundaries are fuzzy.

DOI: 10.1037/13620-022; Supplemental material: DOI: 10.1037/13620-022.supp
APA Handbook of Research Methods in Psychology: Vol. 2. Research Designs, H. Cooper (Editor-in-Chief)

subjects to gain insight into the larger population of people.[2] He believes the population's distribution is likely skewed and decides his research question is best addressed by the median and its variability. Unfortunately, the median does not have a closed-form equation for a standard error. One convenient solution is to use a bootstrap, which has five stages.

Stage 1: Collect the sample and calculate the observed median, MD_{Obs}, from the N scores.

Stage 2: Prepare the sampling frame, which can be thought of as a pool of scores. In this example, all five observed scores are placed in the sampling frame.

Stage 3: Draw N scores with replacement from the sampling frame; this creates one *bootstrap sample*. Repeat this process many times, say $B = 9,999$.

Stage 4: The *bootstrap distribution* is formed by calculating the median of each bootstrap sample. Each bootstrapped statistic is denoted with an asterisk. The bootstrap distribution is the collection of B bootstrapped medians: $MD*_1$, $MD*_2$, . . ., $MD*_{9999}$.

Stage 5: The standard error of the median is estimated by the standard deviation of the bootstrap distribution.

$$\overline{se}_{MD} = \frac{1}{B-1}\sqrt{\sum_{b=1}^{B}(MD_b^* - MD_{Obs}^*)^2},$$

$$\text{where } MD_{Obs}^* = \frac{1}{B}\sum_{b=1}^{B}MD_b^*. \quad (1)$$

Suppose the observed scores were 1, 4, 10, 50, and 80 s, and the summaries are $MD_{Obs} = 10$ and $\overline{X}_{Obs} = 29$. Table 22.1 illustrates possible simulation outcomes. In the first bootstrap sample, the values 4 and 50 were drawn twice, whereas 1 and 80 were never drawn. In the second-to-last sample, the five drawn scores were coincidentally the same as the observed sample. In the last sample, 4 was drawn almost every time.

In Stages 2 and 3, a *sampling frame* was formed and five scores were randomly drawn from it repeatedly. The goal was to mimic the median's variability that would occur if additional samples of

TABLE 22.1

Illustration of Bootstrapped Scores and Statistics

Bootstrap index	Bootstrapped sample (stage 3)	Bootstrapped statistic (stage 4)
1	4, 4, 50, 10, 50	$MD_1^* = 10$
2	10, 80, 10, 50, 80	$MD_2^* = 50$
3	50, 4, 4, 1, 80	$MD_3^* = 4$
. . .		
9,998	1, 4, 10, 50, 80	$MD_{9998}^* = 10$
9,999	4, 4, 4, 4, 50	$MD_{9999}^* = 4$

$N = 5$ were drawn from the *population*. For many types of bootstraps, the best sampling frame is simply the observed sample.

In Stage 4, a bootstrap distribution of medians was built to make an inference about the median of the population. Using a sample's statistic to estimate a population parameter follows the *plug-in principle*; the median is the *plug-in statistic* in this example (Efron & Tibshirani, 1993, Chapter 4).

A statistic's standard error quantifies the variability in its sampling distribution. Instead of calculating the spread of a *theoretical* sampling distribution (closed-form mathematical solutions that exist for statistics like $\overline{X}$, r, and t, but not for MD), we calculate the spread in an *empirical* sampling distribution in Stage 5.

Example 1b: Standard error of the mean. The researcher later reused the collected sample to address a different question—one that is better suited by the mean. The algorithm proceeds as in Example 1a, except the plug-in statistic is now the mean instead of the median. The three necessary changes are bolded in the following stages.

Stage 1: Collect the sample and calculate the observed **mean**, $\overline{X}_{Obs}$, from the N scores.

Stage 2: Prepare the sampling frame, which are the five observed scores in this example.

Stage 3: Draw N scores with replacement from the sampling frame; this creates one bootstrap sample.

---

[2]For a discussion of how to select a worthy research question, see Volume 1, Chapter 7, this handbook.

Repeat this process many times, say $B = 9,999$.

Stage 4: A bootstrap distribution is formed by calculating the mean of each of the B bootstrap samples. The bootstrap distribution is the B bootstrapped means: $\overline{X}_1^*, \overline{X}_2^*, ..., \overline{X}_{9999}^*$.

Stage 5: The standard error of the mean is estimated by the standard deviation of the bootstrap distribution.

$$\overline{se}_{\overline{X}} = \frac{1}{B-1}\sqrt{\sum_{b=1}^{B}(\overline{X}_b^* - \overline{X}_{\text{Obs}}^*)^2},$$

$$\text{where } \overline{X}_{\text{Obs}}^* = \frac{1}{B}\sum_{b=1}^{B}\overline{X}_b^*. \tag{2}$$

The bootstrap samples from Example 1a can be reused to calculate the bootstrapped means.[3] The last column in Table 22.1 would be replaced with the values $\overline{X}_b^* = 23.6, 46, 27.8, ..., 29, 13.2$. Stage 5 then calculates the standard deviation of these 9,999 statistics (the reason for choosing $B = 9,999$ is discussed briefly in the section Bootstrap Sample Size).

There are many types of bootstraps, and the two just described are *nonparametric* in the sense that it requires no assumptions about the sampling distributions (however, it does assume that the observed scores are drawn independently from the population of interest). A procedure is *parametric* when it relies on assumptions about the population distribution. The typical parametric standard error of the mean relies on the central limit theorem; the estimator is

$$\text{Parametric } \overline{se}_{\overline{X}} = \frac{1}{\sqrt{N}}\sqrt{\frac{\sum_{i=1}^{N}(X_i - \overline{X})^2}{(N-1)}} = \frac{s}{\sqrt{N}}. \tag{3}$$

The conventional standard error of the mean measures the variability in a sample (i.e., the standard deviation, s) to estimate the variability in the population of means.[4] It uses the central limit theorem to relate s to the $\overline{se}_{\overline{X}}$. Unfortunately, many useful statistics do not have a convenient theoretical relationship such as this. And for the statistics that do, the required assumptions can be unreasonable in some applied scenarios. The bootstrap can help in both cases; calculating the standard error is simple even for complicated plug-in statistics. The choice of the plug-in statistic is very flexible, and this will be discussed later.

Example 1c: Confidence interval for the mean.
A 95% confidence interval (CI) for the mean[5] can be estimated from the bootstrap distribution created in Stage 4. The bootstrap samples and bootstrap distribution can be reused. Only the final stage is different.

Stages 1 to 4: Proceed as in Example 1b.
Stage 5: Order the $B = 9,999$ bootstrapped statistics from smallest to largest. The CI bounds are marked by the 250th smallest value and the 250th largest value (i.e., the .025 and .975 quantiles). The number of scores in each tail is calculated by $\alpha(B + 1) / 2$; α is .05 with a 95% CI.

A CI determined from this type of bootstrap distribution has an additional advantage over a CI determined from a parametric, theoretical normal distribution. The parametric distribution relies on the central limit theorem for normality, and thus the tails are an equal distance from $\overline{X}$; the CI is defined by $\overline{X} \pm 1.96 \times \overline{se}_{\overline{X}}$. The parametric procedure can be justified as N grows infinitely large, but it can be misleading when a small sample is drawn from a skewed distribution. In fact, the parametric CI in this example is (–1.4, 59.4), which produces a nonsensical negative value for waiting time.

This bootstrap CI method has the appealing feature that it is *range-preserving*; in this case, the CI for waiting time will never be negative. The bootstrap CI is (4.0, 58.8); its boundaries are guaranteed to be values that could be observed in a sample (because they were calculated from values that were actually observed in a sample; Efron & Tibshirani, 1993, Section 13.7). The bootstrap distribution is shown in Figure 22.1, along with the CI.

---

[3] We want to emphasize that this process is unaffected by the choice of plug-in statistic.

[4] When a large sample is drawn from a normally distributed population, the bootstrap standard error will be very close to the conventional standard error of the mean.

[5] A frequentist 95% CI is built so that 95% of similarly constructed CIs will contain the population parameter value.

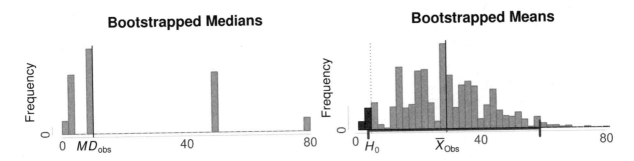

FIGURE 22.1. Bootstrap distributions. The right panel includes the bootstrap CI and *p* value (dark gray area).

Example 1d: *p* value for the mean. A one-tailed *p* value is determined in an intuitive way, as the proportion of bootstrapped statistics is more extreme than the value of the null hypothesis. A two-tail *p* value is easy to determine as well but would not make theoretical sense with the waiting time example. If H_0: *time* ≤ 5, the five stages are:

Stages 1 to 4: Proceed as in Example 1b.
Stage 5: Tally the number of $\overline{X}_b^*$ values equal or less the hypothesized value, expressed as

$$\#\{\overline{X}_b^* \le time_{\text{Null}}\}. \tag{4}$$

The *p* value is $1 + \#\{\overline{X}_b^* \le time_{\text{Null}}\} / (B+1)$.

Notice that the choice of plug-in statistic in Stage 2 is unrelated to the choice of statistic that summarizes the bootstrap distribution in stage 5. A standard deviation can be calculated on the *B* statistics regardless of plug-in equation used in Stage 2 (e.g., the median or mean). Similarly in Stage 5, the distribution of *B* means can be summarized in a variety of ways (e.g., standard error, CI, or *p*).

The code accompanying the chapter replicates the steps in our examples, including plotting simplified versions of the figures. These examples are intended to supplement the knowledge of novice bootstrappers (with limited exposure to R) and to provide a template for more complicated bootstraps that can arise in applied research. Software is further discussed at the end of the chapter.

Terminology

Before we move to slightly more complicated examples, we summarize the entities and notation. Typically a researcher draws a sample *X* to gain insight into its population distribution of single scores, *F* (this *F* is unrelated to the analysis of variance [ANOVA] *F* distribution). If we are interested in the mean of the population, μ, the appropriate plug-in static is the mean of the sample, $\overline{X}$. An inferential procedure mimics *F* with an empirical distribution, $\hat{F}$, to assess the accuracy of $\overline{X}$ (or any other plug-in statistic). Examples 1b to 1d calculate three common expressions of the uncertainty in the estimate of μ: the standard error, CI, and *p* value.

The empirical distribution, $\hat{F}$, should not be confused with the bootstrap distribution, which is a type of empirical *sampling* distribution. For instance, in Example 1a, $\hat{F}$ is a distribution of *N* single *observations*, whereas the bootstrap distribution is a collection of *B statistics* (that were each calculated from a bootstrap sample of *N* scores randomly drawn from the sampling frame). The distinction between these different types of distributions is explained in detail in Rodgers (1999).

The sampling frame is the mechanism behind $\hat{F}$, because it is the pool of single scores from which the bootstrap samples are drawn. The previous examples have used a sampling frame that was built directly from the observed sample. We will show three other types of bootstraps that are only indirect expressions of the sample. In the second half of the chapter, we discuss Monte Carlo methods, which are simulations in which $\hat{F}$ is entirely unconnected to an observed sample.

So far, the sampling frames produced empirical distributions that represent an observed population. We start using the notation $\hat{F}_{\text{Obs}}$ to distinguish it from an empirical distribution representing a null hypothesis, $\hat{F}_{\text{Null}}$. Examples 2a and 2b focus on this difference.

Bootstrapping With Novel Designs

The mean is a well-known statistic with an accessible theoretical sampling distribution; yet the bootstrap can help when the central limit theorem assumptions are not justifiable. The median is well known, but it does not have a good theoretical sampling distribution; the bootstrap can help by providing an accessible empirical sampling distribution.

In some scenarios, an established sampling distribution exists but does not fit the profile of an experimental design. For instance, the longitudinal, nested factorial design of Smith and Kimball (2010, Experiment 1) benefited from the flexibility of a bootstrap in two ways. First, a subject's final outcome was conditioned on their initial response in a way that prevented the ANOVA sampling distribution from representing it appropriately. Second, there was substantial heterogeneity in the variability, making it difficult to model appropriately. After the sampling frame was customized to fit the researchers' specific contrasts, a bootstrap was able to test hypotheses with 110 subjects that a parametric generalized linear model or multilevel model could not.

The bootstrap's flexibility perhaps is demonstrated best when it provides a sampling distribution for a *new statistic* that is created for a specific design protocol. In fact, "subject to mild conditions" the selected bootstrapped statistic

> can be the output of an algorithm of almost arbitrary complexity, shattering the naive notion that a parameter is a Greek letter appearing in a probability distribution and showing the possibilities for uncertainty analysis for the complex procedures now in daily use, but at the frontiers of the imagination a quarter of a century ago. (Davison, Hinkley, & Young, 2003, p. 142)

It is difficult to give concise examples of this flexibility, because several paragraphs would be needed just to describe a novel design; advice and examples are found in Boos (2003) and Davison and Hinkley (1997).

To provide an approximation, and to stimulate the reader to think deeper about such a constructed statistic, consider the following setting. Tukey's (1977) H-spread was designed to measure the distance across the middle half of a distribution (often referred to as the interquartile range). Suppose a theory implies interest in another distance, the distance across the middle 20% of the distribution (a range-type measure even less influenced by extreme scores than the H-spread). This statistic is sensible and interesting, but in this case, the statistical community has no background or statistical theory to help the applied researcher. But the bootstrap is every bit as facile and useful in this previously undefined setting as it is in applications involving other well-known statistics like the mean, median, or H-spread.

Bootstrapping Multivariate Observations

When two scores are collected from a subject, our definition of an observation is expanded to a bivariate point, $u_i = (x_i, y_i)$.

Example 2a: $\hat{F}_{Obs}$ for a correlation. Diaconis and Efron (1983) bootstrapped a correlation by using the observed sample as the sampling frame. In Example 1, N univariate points were drawn from a sampling frame of N univariate points. Here, N bivariate points are drawn from a sampling frame of N bivariate points.

Stage 1: Collect the sample and calculate r_{obs} from the N data points (pairs of X, Y values).

Stage 2: Prepare the sampling frame. To produce $\hat{F}_{Obs}$ in this case, use the observed sample.

Stage 3: Randomly draw N pairs of scores with replacement while keeping the pairs intact. For instance, if x_3 is selected, the accompanying value must be y_3 (i.e., the x and y scores for the third subject). Repeat this stage to form B bootstrap samples.

Stage 4: Calculate r^*_{Obs} for each bootstrap sample drawn in stage 3.

Stage 5: Calculate the CI $[r^*_{(250)}, r^*_{(9750)}]$ with $B = 9,999$. If a hypothesis test is desired, the null hypothesis can be rejected if ρ_{null} falls outside of the CI. As before, the standard error is the standard deviation of the B statistics in the bootstrap distribution.

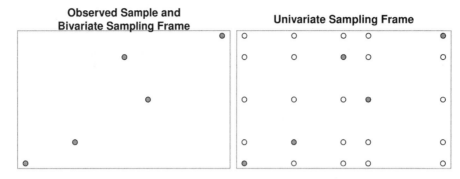

FIGURE 22.2. Scatter plots of a bivariate sampling frame based on $\hat{F}_{\mathrm{Obs}}$ (left) and a univariate sampling frame based on $\hat{F}_{\mathrm{Null}}$ (right).

Example 2b: $\hat{F}_{\mathrm{Null}}$ for a correlation. As early as 1935, Fisher (1970) developed a resampling method, called the *permutation test* or the *randomization test*. It is very similar to the bootstrap, except that it samples from the sampling frame without replacement.[6] Fisher did not intend to estimate the standard error but rather to calculate the *p* value of a null hypothesis, which is achieved by constructing a sampling frame that represents the null hypothesis.

In the case of a bivariate correlation, suppose the null hypothesis states that *X* and *Y* are linearly independent in the population. An interesting special case of linear independence (Rodgers, Nicewander, & Toothaker, 1984) that is often tested is $\rho_{\mathrm{Null}} = 0$. One approach is to conceptualize this as "every value of *X* has an equal chance of being associated with any value of *Y*." To reflect $\hat{F}_{\mathrm{Null}}$, the sampling frame enumerates all possible *X* and *Y* pairs—creating a sampling frame with N^2 bivariate points (see Lee & Rodgers, 1998). Figure 22.2 portrays the two different sampling approaches.

This procedure for bootstrapping $\hat{F}_{\mathrm{Null}}$ resembles Example 2a, with three exceptions. First, the sampling frame has N^2 points instead of *N*. Second, each of these points has a $1/N^2$ probably of being selected on each draw, instead of $1/N$. Finally, a hypothesis is tested by comparing r_{Obs} with the CI, instead of comparing ρ_{Null} with the CI.

Stage 1: Collect the sample and calculate r_{Obs} from the *N* data points (pairs of *X*, *Y* values).

Stage 2: Prepare the univariate sampling frame by combining every *x* with every *y* value.

Stage 3: Randomly draw *N* pairs of scores with replacement from the N^2 possible points in the sampling frame. Repeat this stage to form *B* = 9,999 bootstrap samples.

Stage 4: Calculate r^{*}_{Obs} for each bootstrap sample drawn in stage 3.

Stage 5: Calculate the CI $[r^{*}_{(250)}, r^{*}_{(9750)}]$. If a hypothesis test is desired, the null hypothesis can be rejected if r_{Obs} falls outside of the CI. The standard error is again the standard deviation of the bootstrap distribution.

This CI (derived from $\hat{F}_{\mathrm{Null}}$) represents the variability around ρ_{Null}, whereas the previous CI (derived from $\hat{F}_{\mathrm{Obs}}$) represents the variability around r_{Obs}. The two contrasting *p*-value equations for H_0: $\rho > \rho_{\mathrm{Null}}$ are $p_{\hat{F}_{\mathrm{Obs}}} = \dfrac{1 + \#\{r^{*}_{b} < \rho_{\mathrm{Null}}\}}{B+1}$ and $p_{\hat{F}_{\mathrm{Null}}} = \dfrac{1 + \#\{r^{*}_{b} > r_{\mathrm{Obs}}\}}{B+1}$. Notice that the value of ρ_{Null} is not present in the latter *p*-value equation because it is reflected within the sampling frame, which is constrained by its construction to have a correlation of zero. For testing hypotheses where ρ is nonzero, see Beasley et al. (2007).

Example 3a: Parametric bootstrap. The *parametric bootstrap* is similar to the nonparametric bootstrap in previous examples, except that $\hat{F}_{\mathrm{Obs}}$ and its sampling frame have distributional assumptions. In a correlational setting, an analyst might be able to assume the variables approximately follow a bivariate normal distribution with a linear relationship of r_{Obs} (Efron & Tibshirani, 1993, Section 6.5). In this case, scores in the sampling frame do not contain any observed scores. The sample influences the sampling

---

[6] "[The bootstrap] was designed to extend the virtues of permutation testing" (Efron & Tibshirani, 1993, p. 218).

frame only thorough r_{Obs}. For a given bootstrap sample, the N bivariate points are generated as follows:

Stage 1: Collect the sample and calculate r_{Obs} from the N data points (pairs of X, Y values).

Stage 2: State the parametric form of the estimated population. A linear, normal distribution is

$$\begin{pmatrix} X \\ Y \end{pmatrix} \sim N\left(\begin{pmatrix} \bar{X} \\ \bar{Y} \end{pmatrix}, \begin{pmatrix} \sigma_X^2 & \sigma_{XY} \\ \sigma_{XY} & \sigma_Y^2 \end{pmatrix} \right). \quad (5)$$

Stage 3: Randomly draw N bivariate points. The random number generator produces a unique point every draw. Repeat to form B bootstrap samples.

Stage 4: Calculate r_{Obs}^* for each bootstrap sample drawn in stage 3.

Stage 5: If desired, calculate the CI and p value as in Example 2a (and not like Example 2b).

Although $\hat{F}_{Obs}$ is now parametric, the bootstrap distribution itself is still considered nonparametric. The shape of the collection of r_{Obs}^* values has no equation or restrictions. The parametric bootstrap can be a good tool when the population's characteristics can be reasonably assumed, but the statistic's characteristics are not well known. This occurs with statistics like the median (that lack a closed-form sampling distribution) or for novel statistics that are tailored to a specific experimental protocol (e.g., Boos, 2003).

Example 3b: Semiparametric bootstrap. A *semiparametric* bootstrap draws observations from an $\hat{F}$ that is constructed from some parametric and some nonparametric assumptions. In a multiple regression setting, one could assume F has a linear relationship and the residuals are exchangeable but not assume the residuals are normally distributed. In this model, the ith subject's predicted score is $y_i = b_0 + b_1 x_{1,i} + b_2 x_{2,i} + e_i$, and e_i is their residual.

Stage 1: Collect the sample and calculate the sample coefficients (b_0, b_1, b_2) that estimate the population parameters $(\beta_0, \beta_1, \beta_2)$.

Stage 2: The sampling frame is formed from the N residuals $(e_1, \ldots, e_N)$.

Stage 3a: Randomly draw N residuals with replacement $(e_1^*, e_2^*, \ldots, e_N^*)$.

Stage 3b: If the independent variables (the Xs) are considered fixed, each bootstrap sample is

$$\begin{aligned} y_1^* &= b_0 + b_1 x_{1,1} + b_2 x_{2,1} + e_1^* = \hat{y}_1 + e_1^* \\ y_2^* &= b_0 + b_1 x_{1,2} + b_2 x_{2,2} + e_2^* = \hat{y}_2 + e_2^* \\ &\ldots \\ y_N^* &= b_0 + b_1 x_{1,N} + b_2 x_{2,N} + e_N^* = \hat{y}_N + e_N^*. \end{aligned} \quad (6)$$

This creates a bootstrap sample of N values: $(y_1^*, y_2^*, \ldots, y_N^*)$. Repeat this stage to form B bootstrap samples.

Stage 4: Calculate $b_0^*, b_1^*,$ and b_2^* with the same three-parameter linear model for each bootstrap sample created in Stage 3.

Stage 5: Calculate the desired statistics (similar to Example 2a) on the trivariate bootstrap distribution of (b_0^*, b_1^*, b_2^*).

The x values are considered fixed in this specific example, so they are not drawn randomly in stage 3b. Bootstrap distributions of other plug-in statistics such as R^2 may better address the specific research question (e.g., Manly, 2007, Chapter 7). The linear model does not necessarily have to minimize squared error. It could minimize the median of absolute values of deviations. Semiparametric bootstraps can provide a foundation for many generalized linear models (Davison & Hinkley, 1997, Section 7.2) and exploratory approaches, like loess curves and cubic splines (Hastie, Tibshirani, & Friedman, 2009).

If additional assumptions are justifiable, a semiparametric bootstrap can model dependencies more naturally than a nonparametric bootstrap. Drawing residuals as if they were interchangeable requires the assumption of homogenous variance (drawing observed samples, as described in Examples 2a and 2b, does not). Adjustments such as standardizing the residuals may improve the robustness of semiparametric approaches (for this and other techniques, see Davison & Hinkley, 1997, Sections 3.3, 6.2–6.3).

Bootstrapping data with dependencies. Bootstrapping is reasonably straightforward when the data are independently and identically distributed. However, psychological designs frequently model dependency among the observations (e.g., time-series), variables (e.g., multiple regression, repeated measures designs), or sampling levels (e.g., multilevel models). Sometimes a nonparametric bootstrap may not be able to accommodate these designs because it is difficult to incorporate the appropriate dependency into the sampling frame and also avoid distributional assumptions; instead parametric and semiparametric bootstraps can be used. For more strategies and applications, see Davison and Hinkley (1997) and Beasley and Rodgers (2009). Lahiri (2003) is a mathematically oriented book dedicated to dependent data.

Pragmatic Bootstrapping Issues

A statistical analysis can accommodate both bootstrap and parametric procedures. A researcher may believe a χ^2 distribution is appropriate for the fit statistic for testing a structural equation model (SEM), while also believing the CIs around the means and covariances are asymmetric. In this case, a parametric fit statistic can be complemented by bootstrapped standard errors. If a parametric distribution is problematic, the Bollen-Stine (Bollen & Stine, 1992) bootstrap distribution could be used instead (Enders, 2010, Section 5.11 & 5.15). Another illustration of a heterogeneous strategy is using parametric standard error of the mean and a bootstrapped H-spread. In short, adopting the bootstrap can be a gradual transition.

Confidence interval adjustments. The CI calculated in Example 2 is commonly called the percentile CI. Its simple definition is that the percentile of the bootstrap distribution maps directly to the percentile of the inferred population. For instance, the 250th smallest r^* (out of $B = 9,999$) estimates the population's 2.5% percentile, assuming the null hypothesis is true. However, this effortless relationship can produce biased estimates in common conditions and several CI adjustments have been developed to have less bias and greater efficiency.

At least eight CI adjustments have been proposed (many authors frequently use ambiguous or conflicting names; surveyed in Beasley & Rodgers, 2009, pp. 372–375). We prefer the BC*a* (which

stands for "bias-corrected and accelerated") adjustment because it has a favorable combination of efficiency, robustness, and wide applicability. It attempts to correct for bias in the bootstrap distribution and for heterogeneous variability in the plug-in statistic (Efron & Tibshirani, 1993, Chapter 14).

Bootstrap sample size. Nonparametric bootstraps are randomly drawn from the empirical sampling frame because complete enumeration of all possible bootstrap samples is rarely practical.[7] This introduces simulation error (which can be thought of a type of sampling error from $\hat{F}$) and fortunately increasing B to a reasonable number makes this error negligible. All the chapter's bootstrap examples complete in less than 5 sec, even when $N = 500$.

We recommend that at least 10^3 and 10^4 replications be run for standard errors and 95% CIs, respectively. Additional discussion and references are found in Beasley and Rodgers (2009, pp. 378–379), but reading this takes longer than completing $B = 99,999$. It may seem strange that our suggested B values have been chosen so that $(B + 1)\alpha$ is an integer (e.g., 9,999 instead of the more natural 10,000). Boos (2003) explained the "99 Rule" and how it slightly improves CI accuracy.

Additional bootstrap applications. Most psychological research questions and designs are more complex than the chapter's examples, but the principles remain the same. Examples and references to sophisticated designs and plug-in statistics are found in Beasley and Rodgers (2009, pp. 375–378). These include designs like time-series, stratified samples, circular variables, and models like generalized linear models, multilevel linear models, survival models, Bayesian analysis, mediation models, and SEM. The resampling procedures that influenced the development of the bootstrap are also discussed, including the permutation test and jackknife (also see Rodgers, 1999).

Limitations. Two commonly encountered limitations of parametric procedures that apply to the

---

[7]In Example 1, a small-data example, complete enumeration requires $5^5 = 3,125$ bootstrap samples, which actually requires less work than the suggested $B = 9,999$. However, this is rarely the case, because sample size is usually larger than $N = 5$; if one more score had been collected, complete enumeration requires $B = 6^6 = 46,656$. Even a moderate size of $N = 30$ requires $B \approx 10^{44}$. This number can be reduced by accounting for and reweighting redundant samples (e.g., the sample {11, 11, 4} produces the same statistic as {4, 11, 11}), but programming these shortcuts would take much longer than running a large B, and the sample still may not be small enough to be practical.

bootstrap and are worth stating here. First, inferences can be misleading when dependencies in the data are not appropriately modeled. Second, a flawed sampling process can produce problematic inferences (although the bootstrap may be less susceptible to this problem than traditional parametric procedures).[8]

The bootstrap does have problems if the plug-in statistic estimates a boundary, or a value close to a boundary, such as a minimum reaction time (Andrews, 2000). In this case, the estimate will be biased upward because the bootstrapped statistic of reaction time cannot be negative. Notice that it is acceptable to estimate a quantity near the boundary of a bootstrap distribution (such as the 2.5th percentile in Stage 5) but not near the boundary of the population distribution (Stage 4). Andrews (2000, Section 2) and LePage and Billiard (1992) discussed other potential concerns that are less likely to affect psychologists.

Beran (2003) wrote,

> Success of the bootstrap, in the sense of doing what is expected under a probability model for data, is not universal. Modifications to Efron's (1979) definition of the bootstrap are needed to make the idea work for estimators that are not classically regular. (p. 176)

When a novel plug-in statistic is developed (either bootstrap or parametric), good inferential performance is not assured. We advise that the new statistic be studied with a small simulation to assess if it has acceptable Type I error and adequate power, for the observed N. This proactive analysis (Steiger, 2007) should include several likely population values and nonnormal distributions. Many of the same tools and skills used to bootstrap can be applied to the proactive analysis.

We occasionally are asked whether the validity of bootstrap inferences suffers with small sample sizes. We feel that if an outlier (or otherwise unrepresentative sample) can mislead a bootstrap

distribution, then it is likely to be even more disruptive to a parametric sampling distribution. For instance, parametric inferences were more susceptible than bootstrap inferences when a bivariate correlation was calculated from a sample of five observations (Beasley et al., 2007). With a multivariate normal population, the procedures had comparable Type I error, whereas the parametric had slightly better power than the bootstrap. However, when the assumptions were violated by using skewed populations, the parametric procedure had liberal Type I error (reaching 0.15), whereas the bootstrap did not. Summarizing across all simulated values of N: The parametric procedure benefited when its assumptions were met, but could be unreliable when they were not. Of course it is irresponsible to claim this pattern will hold for all statistics and population distributions, which is another reason to perform a proactive analysis before using a novel plug-in statistic.

Software. Software for parametric procedures is much more available and user friendly than for the equivalent bootstraps. The flexibility that empowers the bootstrap also prevents automation. Eight years later, Fan's (2003) assessment of available bootstrapping software still applies. When bootstrapping a statistic, it is likely that writing code will be necessary.

R and S-PLUS have the most complete support for two reasons. First, these languages (which are almost exchangeable) have many concise routines useful to bootstrapping. For instance, the line "sample(x=obs, size=15, replace=TRUE)" randomly draws $N = 15$ scores from a vector called "obs." Second, most developments and publications involving applied bootstrapping have come from statisticians (and especially biostatisticians) who publish their examples in this language. Examples and documentation also can be found in Stata and SAS.[9] The SEM programs EQS and Mplus provide bootstrapping for better fit statistics and for more robust CIs (Enders, 2010, Table 11.1).

Two of the most popular bootstrap books use R and S-PLUS exclusively (Davison & Hinkley, 1997;

---

[8]With respect to the correlation, the bootstrap outperformed parametric procedures in simulations of restricted range (Chan & Chan, 2004; Mendoza, Hart, & Powell, 1991), nonnormal correlated populations (Beasley et al., 2007), and composite populations (Lee & Rodgers, 1998).

[9]Good starting points are http://www.stata.com/help.cgi?bootstrap, Poi (2004), and http://support.sas.com/kb/24/982.html.

Efron & Tibshirani, 1993).[10] They accommodate some common designs with less than 10 lines of code from the practitioner. The user defines their specific plug-in statistic, and then passes this definition to a reusable base routine provided by the package.

It can be tricky to define this specialized function, however, even for common analyses such as those that (a) incorporate multiple groups, (b) draw from $\hat{F}_{\text{Null}}$, or (c) use sampling frames that do not have exactly N points. If the base routine has trouble accommodating the plug-in function, we suggest that users create their own routine by starting with the code for a routine (like bcanon) in the bootstrap package and modifying it to fit the current design.[11]

The defined plug-in statistic needs to detect and react to atypical samples. In Example 2a, it is likely that one of the 9,999 bootstrap samples will have no variation, so that r^*_{Obs} is undefined. If unanticipated, this will either halt the program's execution or insert an undefined value into the bootstrap distribution (depending on the statistical software).

If the software supports a "Try-Catch" block, it can be used to recover from this event. One implementation of Example 2a catches the undefined statistic and forces another bootstrap sample to be drawn and calculated. Another implementation simply replaces the undefined values with zeros (which is much faster than having the computer construct a Try-Catch block). Even if this behavior is not ideal theoretically, it will happen too infrequently to have any noticeable effect.[12] If the software language does not provide error handling (and zero is not an appropriate substitute value for the statistic), the custom code should anticipate and test for illegal conditions.

Despite the additional issues to consider, bootstrapping can be valuable to a practitioner when it holds a statistical advantage. The bootstrap is a good candidate when the desired statistic lacks a closed-form standard error equation, when necessary parametric assumptions are not met, or especially when small sample sizes are combined with the previous restrictions.

BROADER SIMULATION METHODS

When simulation uses repeated random sampling to build a distribution, it is frequently called a *Monte Carlo method*. The bootstrap is a specific type of Monte Carlo simulation. It can create a distribution of statistics that lacks an equation for the probability density function (pdf) and the cumulative distribution function (cdf; i.e., the integral of the pdf). Thus, in the bootstrap, a collection of B points are simulated and substituted for the desired pdf or cdf.

In most Monte Carlo simulations, the distribution of the relevant statistic(s) has a tractable pdf but an intractable cdf. In other words, equations are available to calculate the probability for a single parameter value (e.g., $p(\theta = 2)$) but not for a range of parameter values (e.g., $p(0 \leq \theta \leq 2)$ or $p(\theta \leq 1.7)$); the standard error and other moments typically are not available either. Like the bootstrap, the general Monte Carlo method builds a collection of B points as a substitute for the desired distribution. Simulation literature commonly calls this the *target distribution, f*.[13]

The following simulation techniques are general and can evaluate many types of distributions, although we will discuss them in the context of the posterior distribution. A Bayesian posterior distribution is proportional to the product of the prior and likelihood distributions (as explained in Chapter 24 of this volume). Many posterior distributions have an equation for the pdf, but not for the cdf or standard error, and so simulation methods are an attractive tool.

Before the 1990s, most Bayesian analysts had to choose their prior and likelihood distributions carefully, so that the posterior's cdf had a closed-form

---

[10]Their routines are included in the "bootstrap" and "boot" packages. After loading the package, documentation appears after typing "?bootstrap" or "?boot." Both packages have good help files, with "boot" being slightly more thorough. Packages are discussed in "An Introduction to R," which is available on the help menu of R.

[11]In R, a routine's underlying code is presented when its name is entered by itself (e.g., "bcanon" when Efron & Tibshirani's, 1993, "bootstrap" package has been installed and loaded). Saving the code in a script allows it to be modified, executed, and saved.

[12]When $N = 5$ in Example 2a, roughly $5^{-4} = 0.16\%$ of bootstrap statistics will be undefined. When $N = 10$, this proportion drops to 10^{-9}. We believe this source of error is overwhelmed by sampling error and can be ignored.

[13]The target distribution, f, should not be confused with the bootstrap literature's F (or $\hat{F}$). F is the theoretical population distribution of single observations, whereas f is the desired distribution of statistics. If the simulation notation were applied to the bootstrap, f would be the bootstrap distribution.

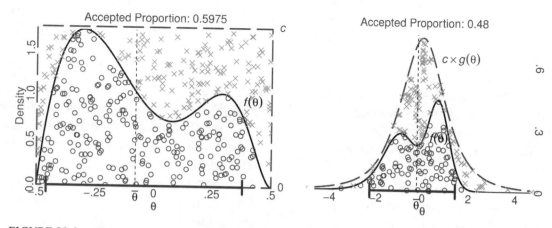

FIGURE 22.3. Rejection sampling of a bounded parameter (a) and unbounded parameter (b). The target distribution is solid, whereas the candidate distribution is dashed. A dark gray circle indicates an accepted candidate, whereas a light gray x is a rejected candidate.

equation.[14] This was not a weakness of Bayesian theory but rather a limitation of available Bayesian methods. This restriction was a common inconvenience for single-parameter models, but it made the use of many multiparameter models completely intractable (especially when the posterior distribution included parameters from different families of distributions). With the development of simulation, Bayesian methods are now arguably more flexible than frequentist (i.e., standard parametric) methods.

General Simulation

Simulation is unnecessary when the posterior describes a small number of parameters. A distribution can be systematically partitioned into small areas, which are calculated separately before being recombined. This deterministic technique, called *numerical integration*, can be a rectangular approximation used to estimate the area under a curve and is taught to all calculus students before the more elegant *analytical integration*. Analytical integration is not possible with most posterior distributions used in research, however, and even numerical integration is not practical when the posterior has many parameters. A target distribution has one dimension for every parameter; it is common for f to have too many dimensions to integrate deterministically.

When analytical and numerical integration are not feasible, simulation can be the next best method. As Monahan (2001) said, "Monte Carlo should be

viewed as just another way to compute an integral; numerical integration should be viewed as just another way to sample points in a space" (p. 235). Although our simple simulation examples include only one or two parameters, simulation's real benefit is evident in high-dimensional problems.

Example 4a: Rejection sampling with bounded support. *Rejection sampling* is a simple simulation technique in which points are generated and then accepted or rejected into the final collection of points (it is sometimes called *acceptance–rejection sampling*). To focus on rejection sampling, we will assume that the sample has been collected, and the prior and likelihood distributions have been defined so that the posterior's pdf can be found. Thus the posterior pdf is the target distribution, f.

Suppose the researcher has found f for a parameter, θ, that ranges between $-.5$ and $+.5$. The height of f (the bimodal solid line in Figure 22.3, left panel) can be found directly, but not the area underneath it (say from $\theta = 0$ to $\theta = .2$). To find this area and other quantities, five stages are needed:

Stage 1: Specify and graph f (the curved solid line in Figure 22.3, left panel).
Stage 2a: Determine the *candidate bounds*, represented by the endpoints of the horizontal axis in Figure 22.3, left panel. It should cover the minimum and maximum values of the target parameter (which is $[-.5, .5]$).

[14]One common conjugate relationship is a Gaussian prior and a Gaussian likelihood, resulting in a Gaussian posterior. Another common relationship is a beta prior and a binomial likelihood, resulting in a beta posterior.

Stage 2b: Determine the *density bounds*, [0, c]. It should start at zero and extend slightly beyond the tallest point f. The height is called the *scaling constant*, c.

Stage 2c: Plot the box for the candidates and the densities. Stage 2a determines the horizontal coordinates of the box, and stage 2b determines the vertical coordinates. It should completely envelope f.

Stage 3a: Draw a random uniformly distributed variate, x_b, from the candidate bounds [−.5, .5] (i.e., the width of the dashed box). Repeat this B times to generate $x_1, x_2, \ldots, x_b, \ldots, x_B$.

Stage 3b: For every candidate, draw a uniformly distributed variate, y_b, from the density bounds [0, c] (i.e., the height of the dashed box).

Stage 4: For every candidate, find the corresponding height of the target pdf, $f(x_b)$. Accept the candidate if $f(x_b) \geq y_b$. Accepted candidates are stored in a collection of target points. Plot each (x_b, y_b) point; in Figure 22.3, left panel, an accepted point is a dark gray circle, whereas a rejection is a light gray x.

Stage 5: Calculate the summary statistics of the distribution. Like the bootstrap, the inferences are estimated by calculating statistics on the distribution of accepted candidates. For instance, the estimated mean of the posterior is simply the mean of the accepted candidates. Similarly, the 95% Bayesian CI is marked by the .025 and .975 quantiles of the accepted candidates.

After the candidate and density bounds are established in stage 2, a pair of random numbers is drawn for every candidate in stage 3. The first variate is a parameter value (i.e., the point's horizontal position). The second variate is a density value (i.e., the vertical position). It is important that these variates can cover the range of both dimensions.

The target distribution is taller at $\theta = −.3$ than at $\theta = .1$, indicating that −.3 is more likely. Therefore in stage 4, we want more of the accepted candidates to be in the neighborhood of −.3 than in the neighborhood of .1. The height of f at $\theta = −.3$ is roughly 1.7 and c (the height of the dashed box) is 1.75. As a result, a candidate of $\theta = −.3$ has a 97% (= 1.7/1.75) chance of being accepted. For comparison, candidates in the neighborhood of $\theta = .1$ will be accepted 41% (= .72/1.75) of the time. When enough candidates are evaluated, the collection of accepted candidates will have more than twice as many values near −.3 than near .1. This allows the summary statistics calculated in Stage 5 to assess the properties of the posterior distribution.

The example's f was defined to be a proper probability distribution[15] (i.e., the total area under the curve, its integral, equals 1), which allows us to verify that the proportion of accepted candidates is approximately correct. The area of the box is 1.75 (= (.5 − −.5) × (1.75 − 0)) and the area under the target distribution is 1; 57.1% (= 1/1.75) of candidates should be accepted. In this example 57.8% were accepted, which will vary slightly between simulation runs.

Example 4b: Rejection sampling with unbounded support. The parameter in Example 4a was bound by [−.5, .5], which permitted a convenient box to be drawn around f. Two primary changes are necessary when θ is unbounded. First, an unbounded *candidate distribution*, g, is needed. In the previous example, the candidate distribution was the uniform distribution, U(−.5, .5), but now g should be chosen more carefully. Second, the density variate drawn in stage 3b will depend on the candidate drawn in stage 3a. It will no longer be fixed at U(0, c). The range of the uniform distribution will differ for each candidate. For instance, sometimes it is U(0, .35), and sometimes U(0, 1.3).

Stage 1: Specify and graph the target distribution, f (the solid bimodal line in Figure 22.3, right panel). Because f extends (−∞,∞), decide on reasonable bounds for the graph. The target's tails should practically be zero at the graph's boundaries.

Stage 2a: Choose an appropriate g. When f covers (−∞,∞), g also should be unbounded.

Stage 2b: Choose the density bounds. The scaling constant, c, should be defined $f(\theta) \leq c \times g(\theta)$, at all points (i.e., the solid line never exceeds the dashed line).

---

[15]Rejection sampling can estimate improper probability distributions whose total area is not 1. The total area underneath does not matter, as long as the heights along f are correctly proportioned. This is useful in Bayesian statistics, in which the posterior is known only up to a proportional constant.

Stage 2c: Plot the scaled candidate distribution, $c \times g(\theta)$. Make adjustments in Stages 2a to 2b until the candidate envelopes the target completely. In Figure 22.3, right panel, we ultimately settled on $g(\theta) = t_{df=3}(\theta)$ with $c = 2$.

Stage 3a: Draw random variate x_b from g. Repeat this B times.

Stage 3b: For every candidate, find the corresponding height of the dashed line (i.e., $c \times g(x_b)$). Draw the density variate y_b from $U(0, c \times g(x_b))$.

Stage 4: For every candidate, find $f(x_b)$. Accept and store the candidate if $f(x_b) \geq y_b$.

Stage 5: Calculate the desired summary statistics of the distribution as in Example 4a.

In Example 4a, the only explicit adjustment in Stages 2a to 2c was the c value because the candidate distribution already covered the range of the θ parameter. In this example, however, the analyst determines c and the family of the candidate distribution (along with distribution parameters like df). In practice, these are decided together with trial and error.[16]

The choice of candidate distribution has three requirements. First, after it is multiplied by c, it must be equal to or greater than the target distribution for all values in the target. For this reason, a heavy tailed distribution is a good initial try (like a t with few degrees of freedom). Second, the target distribution should have a quick and accessible random number generator. Third, the height of the target distribution should be easily calculated. Most statistical software provides a function for producing random variates from a t distribution and calculating its pdf.

Markov Chain Monte Carlo

An MCMC simulation introduces dependencies between the B statistics. The theoretical justification and foundations of MCMC are covered in Robert and Casella (2004) and Gamerman and Lopes (2006). Only a few details differ between rejection sampling and the simplest MCMC.

Example 5a: Independent Metropolis-Hastings.

Rejection sampling candidates are generated independently—for example, the 53rd candidate has no effect on the value or the rejection chances of the 54th candidate. This differs from the independent Metropolis-Hastings (IMH) sampler. On the bth step, there is a competition between the incumbent, z_b, and the candidate, x_b. The accepted candidate becomes the incumbent for the subsequent step, z_{b+1}. The sequence of z_b values is called a *chain*.

This example reuses f and g from Example 4b. The heights of these two distributions are $f(x_b)$ and $g(x_b)$ at point x_b.

Stage 1: Specify f.

Stage 2: Choose g. From g, draw the incumbent for the chain's first step, z_1.

Stage 3a: Draw the candidate x_b from g.

Stage 3b: Calculate a_b, which affects the candidate's chances of acceptance:

$$a_b = \frac{g(z_b)}{f(z_b)} \times \frac{f(x_b)}{g(x_b)}. \tag{7}$$

This is the ratio of the incumbent at the candidate and target distribution, multiplied by the ratio of the new candidate at the target and candidate distribution.

Stage 4: If $a_b \geq 1$, the new candidate wins and becomes the incumbent for the next step (so $z_{b+1} = x_b$). If $a_b < 1$, there is a runoff election in which the new candidate's probability of winning is a_b. Draw y_b from $U(0, 1)$. The new candidate wins if $a_b > y_b$; otherwise the incumbent is reelected and survives another step (so $z_{b+1} = z_b$).

Repeat *Stages 3a, 3b,* and *4* for $b = 1, 2, \ldots, B$ *steps.*

Stage 5: Calculate any summary statistics on the B incumbents, as in Example 4a.

As seen in the upper left panel of Figure 22.4, the candidate does not have to envelope the target distribution in an IMH. The histogram of the B accepted points matches the theoretical target distribution nicely. Compared with rejection sampling, it is less important to graph f and g because c does not exist. However, g is still required to support all possible

---

[16]Albert (2009, p. 99) provided an automatic way to find the scaling constant with a multivariate target distribution (although the candidate distribution and its parameter are still decided by a human). This approach improves efficiency because as c grows, more candidates are rejected and the simulation becomes less efficient. It also is useful with multivariate distributions where graphically determining c is difficult.

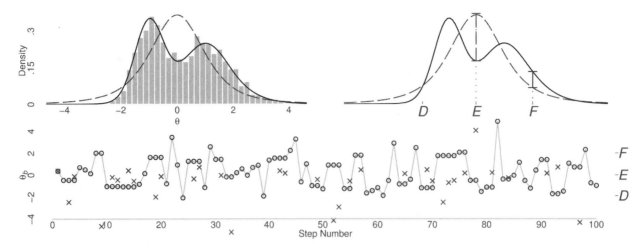

FIGURE 22.4. The target (f; solid) and candidate (g; dashed) distributions of an IMH (top left). A histogram of the accepted candidates closely matches the target distribution (top right). In the bottom panel, the chain's history is overlaid with victorious candidates (circles) and rejected new candidates (xs).

values of f. For instance if f supports $(-\infty, \infty)$, g cannot be $\chi^2_{(df=10)}$, which supports only $(0, \infty)$.

The top right panel identifies three points (D, E, F) to illustrate the logic of jumping. Assume the incumbent is D and the candidate is E at step 70. The first ratio in a_{70} (i.e., $g(z_{70})/f(z_{70})$) equals 1 because the target and candidate distribution are equal at the incumbent's position. Point E is at the mode of g incidentally, so it is the most likely position for a candidate. However, $g(E)$ would overestimate $f(E)$ by a factor of 2 if all candidates at E were accepted; to account for the disparity between the distributions, the second ratio in a_{70} (i.e., $f(x_{70})/g(x_{70})$) is roughly .5—indicating that half of the candidates are accepted.

Assume the candidate E was rejected at Step 70, and F is the new candidate for Step 71. The value x_{71} is guaranteed victory because the first ratio in a_{71} is one and the second ratio is greater than one. The MCMC's first 100 steps are shown in the bottom panel of Figure 22.4. Flat chain links indicate the incumbent was reelected. Notice there are many longtime incumbents with values around point F (e.g., see the flat sequence for Steps 71–76). Furthermore, there are many candidates around point E but few victories (e.g., see the xs for Steps 11–17 and 71–76).

If f and g are equal at both x_b and z_b, then a_b equals 1 and a jump is guaranteed. If f and g are always equal, every jump is guaranteed. We later discuss the Gibbs sampler, which exploits this

property in a multivariate context. In a univariate context, it would be better to simply draw x_b from f (instead of g) and always accept it. However, if it is possible to simulate directly from the univariate f, it is very likely that f has a tractable equations for its cdf and standard error—so simulation is unnecessary.

The IMH is called *independent* because the candidate distribution never changes, and thus g is independent of z_b. The IMH may be practical when f is tight and has well-defined boundaries. However, when f is complex and highly dimensional, capturing "the main features of the target distribution is most often impossible" (Robert & Casella, 2004, p. 284). An MCMC can cover a multivariate space better if the candidate distribution is able to wander, which is a feature of the next sampler.

Example 5b: Metropolis-Hastings. In a Metropolis-Hastings (MH) sampler, the incumbent influences g. In Example 5a, g was unaffected by the previous step and remained centered on $\theta = 0$; g could be expressed $g_0(x_b) = t(x_b|df = 3, mean = 0)$. The MH adds a location parameter to g: $g_z(x) = g(x_b|z_b) = t(x_b|df = 3, mean = z_b)$ and $g_x(z_b) = g(z_b|x_b) = t(z_b|df = 3, mean = x_b)$. Only two procedural changes are necessary. In Stage 3a, x_b is drawn from g_{zb}, which is centered around z_b. In Stage 3b, the acceptance variable is

$$a_b = \frac{g(z_b \mid x_b)}{f(z_b)} \times \frac{f(x_b)}{g(x_b \mid z_b)}. \tag{8}$$

We revisit the scenario depicted Figure 22.4, upper right panel. When D is the incumbent at Steps 70 and 71, the candidates are generated from a t_3 distribution centered around D. When point F wins Step 71, g_z will shift right, and the next candidate will be drawn from a t_3 distribution centered around point F. The target distribution never moves. The candidate distribution jumps around for each x_b and z_b as it tries to recover a chain of points that are representative of the target.

Inferences are calculated directly from the chain's B points. For instance, a multilevel model uses no explicit formula for the shrinkage from a level-one parameter toward a level-two parameter (e.g., Gelman & Hill, 2007, Equation 12.1) when estimated with an MCMC. The challenging aspect of an MCMC is getting the chain to represent f. Like a bootstrap, the equations for the estimates are simply summary statistics.

The MH is the oldest and most general and flexible of the MCMC samplers. A seminal article by Metropolis and Ulam (1949) established the term *Monte Carlo method*. Newer MCMC samplers can be more efficient, but more knowledge of the target distribution is required.

Example 6: Gibbs sample. The Gibbs sampler has two important differences from the MH. The basic MH changes every dimension at once, whereas Gibbs divides the problem into substeps and jumps in only one direction at a time. Every dimension has its own candidate distribution, which leads to the second difference between Gibbs and the MH—every candidate is accepted. The candidate and target distributions are identical, which permits direct simulation from f. When direct simulation is possible from conditional distributions, Gibbs *can* be more efficient than the MH. If f has four parameters $x = (x^{(1)}, x^{(2)}, x^{(3)}, x^{(4)})$, the Gibbs involves four substeps in every step:

Stage 1: Determine that the joint distribution of f exists (but it does not actually need to be specified).

Stage 2: Choose starting values for each parameter $(x_1^{(1)}, x_1^{(2)}, x_1^{(3)}, x_1^{(4)})$

Stage 3: In each substep, draw a variables' candidate while fixing the other three variables:

$$
\begin{aligned}
x_b^{(1)} &\sim f_1(x^{(1)} \mid \quad\quad x_{b-1}^{(2)}, x_{b-1}^{(3)}, x_{b-1}^{(4)}) \\
x_b^{(2)} &\sim f_2(x^{(2)} \mid x_b^{(1)} \quad\quad, x_{b-1}^{(3)}, x_{b-1}^{(4)}) \\
x_b^{(3)} &\sim f_3(x^{(3)} \mid x_b^{(1)}, x_b^{(2)} \quad\quad, x_{b-1}^{(4)}) \\
x_b^{(4)} &\sim f_4(x^{(4)} \mid x_b^{(1)}, x_b^{(2)}, x_b^{(3)} \quad\quad).
\end{aligned}
\tag{9}
$$

Stage 4: Automatically accept the multivariate candidate, $z_b = x_b = (x_b^{(1)}, x_b^{(2)}, x_b^{(3)}, x_b^{(4)})$.

Repeat *Stages 3* and *4 for b = 2, 3, . . .,B steps.*

Stage 5: Calculate any summary statistics as in Example 4a.

Stage 3 exhibits a leapfrog pattern. Variables jump one at a time, and then they stay still in the updated position until the others complete their turn. The jump for the first variable in line, $x_b^{(1)}$, relies on the values from the previous step $(x_{b-1}^{(2)}, x_{b-1}^{(3)}, x_{b-1}^{(4)})$. The jump for the second variable, $x_b^{(2)}$, relies on the current step's value for $x^{(1)}$ but on the previous step's value for $x^{(3)}$ and $x^{(4)}$ because they have not been updated yet. This sequence continues until the last variable is updated entirely from values from the bth step.

Examples 5 and 6 have used a single chain. A recommended practice is to run at least four independent chains (e.g., Robert & Casella, 2004, Chapter 12). The algorithms are modified by running Stages 2 through 4 once for each chain. It is important that chains' positions do not affect each other. However, the summary statistics in Stage 5 combine the chains and treat their points as one large sample.

Metropolis within Gibbs. The Gibbs advantage can be exploited even when it is not possible to simulate directly from the joint f. Suppose f_1, f_2, and f_3 could produce their respective candidates, but f_4 could not. This last substep could use an MH to draw $x^{(4)}$, while $x^{(1)}, x^{(2)}$, and $x^{(3)}$ are temporarily fixed. In fact, each substep could be replaced by a different MH. Consider a typical growth model in which each subject has three parameters; a study with 100 subjects has a target distribution with more than 300 dimensions. Robert and Casella (2010) explained the advantage:

It is most often the case that designing . . . a Metropolis Hastings algorithm on a large-dimensional target is challenging or even impossible. The fundamental gain in using a Gibbs-like structure is that it breaks down a complex model into a large number of smaller and simpler targets, where local MH algorithms can be designed at little expense. (p. 230)

Pragmatic MCMC Issues

Expectations for learning the MCMC method are different than those for the bootstrap and rejection sampling. For a student or researcher with a solid graduate-level statistics background (say, two or more rigorous statistics courses), we believe 1 or 2 days is a reasonable amount of time to understand the basics of bootstrap theory, program some necessary routines, and competently interpret the results for a two-factor experiment. However, learning MCMC takes more investment. Not only are the techniques more complicated—both conceptually and mathematically—but also they are usually applied to more complex experimental designs. But their power and flexibility should be obvious. With some (worthwhile) effort, readers can appreciate the capabilities of MCMC and understand applied articles containing an MCMC analysis.

Convergence and mixing.   The MH and Gibbs are defined so that f is guaranteed to be recovered after an infinite number of steps. Most applications require fewer steps, but deciding how many are needed is somewhat subjective.

There are two milestones for an MCMC. The chains' starting values (specified in Stage 2) are not necessarily on f, especially when f has many dimensions. It is recommended to run a chain for several hundred (or several thousand) steps during a *burn-in* period; these initial points are unlikely to represent f, so they are discarded and not considered by the Stage 5 statistics. Several indicators can assess different aspects of convergence, and the popular indicators are explained in MCMC and contemporary Bayesian books (e.g., Carlin & Louis, 2009; Robert & Casella, 2004).

After the burn-in milestone is passed, the next decision is how many steps are needed to adequately represent f. The primary concern is how well the chains continue to mix with each other and how quickly they cover f. Weak mixing can occur when successive points in a chain are strongly correlated or when a chain gets stuck in an isolated region of f, like a local maximum. One general strategy is to specify an equivalent model in which the parameters are "as independent as possible" (Robert & Casella, 2004, p. 396; for many specific strategies, see Gelman & Hill, 2007, especially Chapter 19).

Failing to converge is rarely a concern for a (properly specified) model that covers a few dimensions, because current computers are powerful enough to generate a chain long enough to cover f decisively. But their current brute-force nature is not ensured to be adequate for a target distribution with hundreds of dimensions (which occurs even for modest multilevel models, because each subject has multiple individual parameters).

MCMC software and resources.   After running a bootstrap for 30 s, simulation error is usually negligible (and 1 s is adequate for most one-dimensional distributions). The duration of a nontrivial MCMC is much longer. Compared with bootstrapping, each simulation replication is less efficient and most MCMC models are much more complex. Many problems require 5 min of computer time to get a rough estimate and 1 hour or more before simulation error is negligible. To reduce development time, we agree with Gelman and Hill (2007, p. 345) that similar models should be run initially with non-Bayesian software that uses maximum likelihood (ML).[17]

Various MCMC software offers different trade-offs of speed and ease of use. Most researchers new to MCMC begin with BUGS (Bayesian inference Using Gibbs Sampling). The software decides many of the technical details. For instance, the user does not need to determine the posterior distribution—only the prior and likelihood equations that ultimately define it.

---

[17]Although MCMC is less computationally efficient, it has at least three benefits over typical ML approaches. First, ML cannot incorporate prior information. Second, ML approaches fix the estimates of variance parameters instead of allowing their uncertainty to inform lower level parameter estimates appropriately (Gelman & Hill, 2007, p. 345). Third, ML finds only the mode of the likelihood distribution, whereas MCMC can capture many features of the target distribution, like its mean, modes, and quantiles (Robert & Casella, 2004, Section 9.4).

Also, BUGS tries to choose the most efficient sampler.[18] Almost all contemporary Bayesian books use BUGS (and R) for their computational examples. Its syntax is remarkably flexible, and it even can address frequentist models that may be impossible to run in frequentist software. BUGS has notable weaknesses, however, which their developers recently discussed (see Lunn, Spiegelhalter, Thomas, & Best, 2009, and their subsequent discussion).

Because BUGS is general, its performance is much slower than samplers that are written for a specific model, like the code in Examples 5 and 6. When writing a specific sampler, R has many functions that make MCMC code more manageable (e.g., Gelman & Hill, 2007, Section 18.4). The R packages MCMCpack and Umacs occupy a middle ground—many common MCMC details are handled automatically, but the exact samplers are still specified by the user (e.g., Gelman & Hill, 2007, Section 18.6).

The landscape of MCMC software is much more diverse since 2008. For the previous 10 years, the overwhelming choice has been a version of BUGS supported on Microsoft Windows (WinBUGS). In July 2009, their developers announced that "all future development work will be focused" on their open-source version called OpenBUGS, whereas WinBUGS "will remain available but not further developed" (OpenBUGS, 2009). Their syntax is almost identical, and both support Windows, so the transition should be smooth for users. The syntax was adopted by JAGS (Plummer, 2010), which is being developed independently of BUGS; JAGS may be more efficient for some types of hierarchical models.

These three programs easily interface with R (with packages like BRugs, R2WinBUGS, and rjags). Thus, a researcher can use R to (a) manipulate the data set, (b) estimate the model in BUGS or JAGS, and (c) diagnose convergence and view the model results. This workflow is demonstrated in most recent applied Bayesian books (e.g., Albert, 2009; Carlin & Louis, 2009; Gelman & Hill, 2007; Gill, 2008). In the past 2 years, SAS and Mplus have released MCMC routines, although we expect most books will continue to target the BUGS syntax.

Regardless of the software, we recommend starting with the simplest possible model (e.g., the sample's grand mean) and incrementally adding complexity (e.g., group- and subject-level covariates). Although this appears pedantic and tedious, any syntax and logic errors are more obvious when only one feature has changed. Common accidents like misspelling a variable or creating an unidentified model cause are easier to detect, and the overall process is less tedious.

Furthermore, an incremental approach naturally produces a sequence of nested models that can be statistically compared with one another (see Rodgers, 2010, for a modeling rationale). The complexity of the specified model should be given careful thought. As Fisher (1970) wrote,

> No human mind is capable of grasping in its entirety the meaning of any considerable quantity of numerical data.. . . The number of independent facts supplied by the data is usually far greater than the number of facts sought, and in consequence much of the information supplied by any body of actual data is irrelevant. It is the object of the statistical processes employed in the reduction of data to exclude this irrelevant information, and to isolate the whole of the relevant information contained in the data. (p. 6)

CONCLUSION

Simulation methods like MCMC and the bootstrap are tools that allow an applied researcher to approach questions that cannot be addressed with conventional analytic methods. The statistical tools required of well-trained behavioral science researchers now include traditional approaches such as ANOVA and categorical data analysis, along with more recently developed strategies for multilevel latent variable models and missing data. Simulation methods support the feasibility of these approaches. They provide access to many (underlying) distributions that were previously intractable, which permits statisticians to specify models that are more appropriate to their research goals.

---

[18] WinBUGS 1.4.3 prefers the Gibbs sampler, which is possible when the variable's conditional distribution is a conjugate form. If Gibbs is not available, WinBUGS evaluates other samplers (that we have not discussed), in descending order of expected efficiency (and ascending order of generality). It may eventually resort to the MH (Carlin & Louis, 2009, Chapter 3).

References

Albert, J. (2009). *Bayesian computation with* R (2nd ed.). New York, NY: Springer. doi:10.1007/978-0-387-92298-0

Andrews, D. W. K. (2000). Inconsistency of the bootstrap when a parameter is on the boundary of the parameter space. *Econometrica, 68,* 399–405. doi:10.1111/1468-0262.00114

Beasley, W. H., DeShea, L., Toothaker, L. E., Mendoza, J. L., Bard, D. E., & Rodgers, J. L. (2007). Bootstrapping to test for nonzero population correlation coefficients using univariate sampling. *Psychological Methods, 12,* 414–433. doi:10.1037/1082-989X.12.4.414

Beasley, W. H., & Rodgers, J. L. (2009). Resampling methods. In R. E. Millsap & A. Maydeu-Olivares (Eds.), *Quantitative methods in psychology* (pp. 362–386). Thousand Oaks, CA: Sage.

Beran, R. (2003). The impact of the bootstrap on statistical algorithms and theory. *Statistical Science, 18,* 175–184. doi:10.1214/ss/1063994972

Bollen, K. A., & Stine, R. A. (1992). Bootstrapping goodness-of-fit measures in structural equation models. *Sociological Methods and Research, 21,* 205–229. doi:10.1177/0049124192021002004

Boos, D. D. (2003). Introduction to the bootstrap world. *Statistical Science, 18,* 168–174. doi:10.1214/ss/1063994971

Carlin, B. P., & Louis, T. A. (2009). *Bayesian methods for data analysis* (3rd ed.). Boca Raton, FL: Chapman & Hall/CRC.

Chan, W., & Chan, D. W. L. (2004). Bootstrap standard error and confidence intervals for the correlation corrected for range restriction: A simulation study. *Psychological Methods, 9,* 369–385. doi:10.1037/1082-989X.9.3.369

Davison, A. C., & Hinkley, D. V. (1997). *Bootstrap methods and their application.* Cambridge, England: Cambridge University Press.

Davison, A. C., Hinkley, D. V., & Young, G. A. (2003). Recent development in bootstrap methodology. *Statistical Science, 18,* 141–157. doi:10.1214/ss/1063994969

Diaconis, P., & Efron, B. (1983, May). Computer-intensive methods in statistics. *Scientific American, 248,* 116–130. doi:10.1038/scientificamerican0583-116

Efron, B. (1979). Bootstrap methods: Another look at the jackknife. *Annals of Statistics, 7,* 1–26.

Efron, B., & Tibshirani, R. J. (1993). *An introduction to the bootstrap.* Boca Raton, FL: Chapman & Hall/CRC.

Enders, C. K. (2010). *Applied missing data analysis.* New York, NY: Guilford Press.

Fan, X. (2003). Using commonly available software for bootstrapping in both substantive and measurement analyses. *Educational and Psychological Measurement, 63,* 24–50. doi:10.1177/0013164402239315

Fisher, R. A. (1970). *Statistical methods for research workers* (14th ed.). New York, NY: Hafner.

Gamerman, D., & Lopes, H. F. (2006). *Markov chain Monte Carlo.* Boca Raton, FL: Chapman & Hall/CRC.

Gelman, A., & Hill, J. (2007). *Data analysis using regression and multilevel/hierarchical models.* New York, NY: Cambridge University Press.

Gill, J. (2008). *Bayesian methods* (2nd ed.). Boca Raton, FL: Chapman & Hall.

Hastie, T., Tibshirani, R., & Friedman, J. (2009). *The elements of statistical learning: Data mining, inference, and prediction* (2nd ed.). New York, NY: Springer.

Lahiri, S. N. (2003). *Resampling methods for dependent data.* New York, NY: Springer.

Lee, W., & Rodgers, J. L. (1998). Bootstrapping correlation coefficients using univariate and bivariate sampling. *Psychological Methods, 3,* 91–103. doi:10.1037/1082-989X.3.1.91

LePage, R., & Billiard, L. (Eds.). (1992). *Exploring the limits of bootstrap.* New York, NY: Wiley.

Lunn, D., Spiegelhalter, D., Thomas, A., & Best, N. (2009). The BUGS project: Evolution, critique and future directions. *Statistics in Medicine, 28,* 3049–3067. doi:10.1002/sim.3680

Manly, B. (2007). *Randomization, bootstrap and Monte Carlo methods in biology* (3rd ed.). Boca Raton, FL: Chapman & Hall.

Mendoza, J. L., Hart, D. E., & Powell, A. (1991). A bootstrap confidence interval based on a correlation corrected for range restriction. *Multivariate Behavioral Research, 26,* 255–269. doi:10.1207/s15327906mbr2602_4

Metropolis, N., & Ulam, S. (1949). The Monte Carlo method. *Journal of the American Statistical Association, 44,* 335–341. doi:10.2307/2280232

Monahan, J. F. (2001). *Numerical methods of statistics.* New York, NY: Cambridge University Press.

OpenBUGS. (2009, Jul 21). FrontPage—OpenBUGS [Wiki]. Retrieved from http://www.openbugs.info

Plummer, M. (2010). *JAGS Version 2.0.0 user manual.* Retrieved from http://iweb.dl.sourceforge.net/project/mcmc-jags/Manuals/2.0/jags_user_manual.pdf

Poi, B. P. (2004). From the help desk: Some bootstrapping techniques. *Stata Journal, 4,* 312–328.

Robert, C. P., & Casella, G. (2004). *Monte Carlo statistical methods.* New York, NY: Springer.

Robert, C. P., & Casella, G. (2010). *Introducing Monte Carlo methods with R*. New York, NY: Springer. doi:10.1007/978-1-4419-1576-4

Rodgers, J. L. (1999). The bootstrap, the jackknife, and the randomization test: A sampling taxonomy. *Multivariate Behavioral Research, 34*, 441–456. doi:10.1207/S15327906MBR3404_2

Rodgers, J. L. (2010). The epistemology of mathematical and statistical modeling: A quiet methodological revolution. *American Psychologist, 65*, 1–12. doi:10.1037/a0018326

Rodgers, J. L., Nicewander, W. A., & Toothaker, L. (1984). Linearly independent, uncorrelated, and orthogonal variables. *American Statistician, 38*, 133–134. doi:10.2307/2683250

Smith, T. A., & Kimball, D. R. (2010). Learning from feedback: Spacing and the delay-retention effect. *Journal of Experimental Psychology: Learning, Memory, and Cognition, 36*, 80–95. doi:10.1037/a0017407

Steiger, J. H. (2007, August). *Statistical games we all should play*. Paper presented at the 115th Annual Convention of the American Psychological Association, San Francisco, CA.

Tukey, J. W. (1977). *Exploratory data analysis*. Reading, MA: Addison-Wesley.

CHAPTER 23

DESIGNING SIMULATION STUDIES

Xitao Fan

This chapter provides a practical guide for designing Monte Carlo simulation studies. Simulation studies are often needed to provide empirical solutions to some problems in quantitative analysis. In this chapter, some quantitative techniques are used in the discussion, but the quantitative techniques themselves are not the focus of the chapter. The intended audience of the chapter includes the quantitative researchers from psychology and other social and behavioral sciences (e.g., education, sociology).

WHAT IS A SIMULATION STUDY?

As defined in *Merriam-Webster's Online Dictionary* (2010), *Monte Carlo* relates to or involves

> the use of random sampling techniques and often the use of computer simulation to obtain approximate solutions to mathematical or physical problems especially in terms of a range of values each of which has a calculated probability of being the solution.

Monte Carlo simulation may offer an empirical alternative to a theoretical approach (i.e., a solution based on statistical or mathematical theory), especially in situations in which the theoretical approach can be difficult to implement or even unavailable.

The Monte Carlo simulation approach in quantitative analysis is increasingly possible and more popular because of the technological advances in computing technology, as Monte Carlo simulation is typically computing intensive. Monte Carlo studies simulate sampling from a defined statistical population, generally for the purpose of estimating the sampling distribution of a statistic of interest. As I illustrate, this approach can be applied to a variety of situations in different disciplines.

Situations in Which Simulation Is Useful

Situations in which a simulation study can be useful include, but are not limited to, assessing the consequences of assumption violations, understanding a sample statistic that has unknown distribution characteristics, evaluating the performance of a technique when statistical theory is weak or even nonexistent, and understanding the statistical power of a technique under some specified data conditions (Fan, Felsovalyi, Sivo, & Keenan, 2002).

Consequences of assumption violations.

Statistical techniques are classified into two broad categories: parametric and nonparametric. Parametric statistical methods, including many widely used techniques, have theoretical assumptions about data distributions. Although statistical theories are usually efficient, the validity of statistical results is contingent on some theoretical assumptions. When the assumptions are violated to some degree, the validity of the analysis results may be in question. Statistical theory stipulates what the condition should be, but statistical theory does not typically provide clear indications about what the reality would be if the conditions are not satisfied in the data. As a result, statistical theory does not inform us about the seriousness of the consequences when

DOI: 10.1037/13620-023
APA Handbook of Research Methods in Psychology: Vol. 2. Research Designs, H. Cooper (Editor-in-Chief)

some assumptions are violated. In this situation, simulation becomes a viable empirical approach to understand these issues.

Understanding a sample statistic that has no theoretical distribution. In some situations, because of the complexity of a particular statistic, a theoretical sampling distribution of the statistic may not be available (e.g., canonical function and structure coefficients, factor pattern coefficients in exploratory factor analysis, and so on). In such a situation, simulation can inform us about the distribution characteristics of the sample statistic for the specified data conditions.

Other situations. There are many other situations in which simulation is useful or even necessary. For example, in exploratory factor analysis, one prominent issue is to retain statistically meaningful factors. For this purpose, competing approaches are available: eigenvalue greater than 1, scree plot, parallel analysis, and so on. If we are interested in understanding how these approaches would perform under different data conditions, a simulation study would be necessary. As another example, growth mixture modeling (GMM) has shown increased popularity for longitudinal data modeling in psychological research to explore the possibility that unobserved subpopulations may have different longitudinal growth trajectories. How well do the different enumeration indexes in GMM perform in identifying the correct number of latent heterogeneous subpopulations in a data sample? How is the performance of GMM influenced by different data conditions (e.g., sample size, degree of separation among the sub-populations)? This and similar issues typically do not have theoretical or analytical solutions; instead, simulation is often useful and necessary to obtain empirical answers to these questions.

BASIC STEPS IN A SIMULATION STUDY

Simulation studies are designed for different purposes, and not surprisingly, they may be very different. Some basic steps, however, are common for most simulation studies, and here is a quick summary of these steps.

Asking Questions Suitable for a Simulation Study

This may appear to be too obvious to warrant discussion, but this initial step is often important enough to shape the simulation study you are planning. Unless you ask the right question(s), it may not be possible or necessary to do a simulation study in the first place. As discussed in the introduction, simulation is usually concerned with the empirical sampling distribution characteristics of a statistic of interest, especially in cases in which statistical theory is weak, for example, canonical–discriminant function and structure coefficients (Thompson, 1991), or some important assumptions underlying the statistical theory are not viable and are violated to varying degrees (e.g., Type I error control of an independent-sample *t* test when the assumption of equal population variances is violated). In a more general sense, simulation is suitable for questions to which there are either no, or no trustworthy, analytical and theoretical solutions.

Simulation Study Design

Once the question(s) for a simulation study are identified (e.g., how well does independent-sample *t* test control Type I error when the assumption of equal population variances is violated?), a simulation study needs to be carefully designed to provide answers to those question(s). In a simulation design, the major factors that may potentially affect the outcome of interest should be included and manipulated. For example, in the context of an independent-sample *t* test when the equal population variance assumption is violated, it would be obvious that the design needs to include both equal and unequal population variances. In addition, the degree of unequal variances also needs to be varied. A reasonable design should include a range of unequal variance conditions ranging from minor (e.g., two-population variance ratio of 2:1) to more severe levels (e.g., two-population variance ratio of 8:1), with several intermediate levels. In addition, group sample size may also be considered in this design, both in terms of equal–unequal samples sizes of the two groups, and in terms of how the two groups with unequal sample sizes are paired with larger–smaller variance conditions. Furthermore, the total sample size is another factor that can be

| | | **TABLE 23.1** | | |

Schematic Design Representation of Independent
t-Test Simulation

| N | Two-group variance ratio | Two group sample size ratio | | |
		Equal	Unequal (1)[a] 0.7:0.3	Unequal (2)[b] 0.3:0.7
30	1:1	1,000[c]	1,000	1,000
	2:1	1,000	1,000	1,000
	4:1	1,000	1,000	1,000
	8:1	1,000	1,000	1,000
60	1:1	1,000	1,000	1,000
	2:1	1,000	1,000	1,000
	4:1	1,000	1,000	1,000
	8:1	1,000	1,000	1,000
120	1:1	1,000	1,000	1,000
	2:1	1,000	1,000	1,000
	4:1	1,000	1,000	1,000
	8:1	1,000	1,000	1,000

[a]The larger sample size group has larger population variance. [b]The larger sample size group has smaller population variance. [c]Number of replications in each cell condition.

manipulated. Assuming that these are the only three factors to be considered for a simulation, and the three factors are fully crossed, we may have the schematic representation of the design in Table 23.1.

The design for this seemingly simple problem (i.e., Type I error control of independent-sample *t* test with violation of equal population variance assumption) could be more complex if we are willing to consider either more levels of each manipulated factor (e.g., other unequal sample size variations in addition to 0.7:0.3 ratio) or if we are to expand the design to cover additional factors such as data normality conditions (e.g., normally distributed data condition, mildly to severely nonnormal data conditions). All of these potential factors, and their levels of variation to be included in the design, require careful considerations as guided by the literature, by practical constraints (e.g., scope of the simulation project), and by some other considerations specific to a researcher (e.g., desired degree of generalizability of the findings).

Data Generation

Once the design issues in a simulation study are settled, the next step is to generate sample data to which a statistical technique of interest (e.g., independent-sample *t* test) will be applied. Data generation is the most important step in any simulation study, as the validity of simulation findings hinge upon the validity of the data-generation process implemented in a simulation. In this sense, the importance of data generation in a simulation study can never be overemphasized. Depending on the complexity of a simulation study, the data-generation process may involve some or all following steps.

Generation of univariate sample data. Initially, sample data are generated on a univariate basis, even though multiple variables may be involved in a simulation. Univariate sample data generation can be accomplished through the use of an appropriate random number generator (for a normally distributed variable, for a uniformly distributed variable, and so on) usually available in any statistical software packages. Once the univariate random variables are generated for specified sample size conditions, some transformation(s) may follow so that the sample data will reflect the targeted data distribution shapes specified in a simulation study.

Transformation of univariate sample data. In most situations, univariate sample data need to be transformed to reflect the variables' population characteristics as specified in a simulation design. There are two major types of transformation. The first is linear transformation, in which the univariate sample data reflect the first two moments (population means and standard deviations of the variables) as specified in a design. This transformation is straightforward. For a sample of a random normal univariate X_i, the transformed variable will be as follows:

$$X_{i_{new}} = X_i \sigma_{population} + \mu_{population}, \qquad (1)$$

where $\sigma_{population}$ and $\mu_{population}$ are the specified population standard deviation and mean, respectively, for the variable.[1]

[1]This transformation step may not be obvious because in most statistical programs (e.g., R), the desired population mean and standard deviation can be directly specified in the data generation process. Behind the scenes, however, there are two steps: (a) generation of standard random normal variate and (b) transformation of this standard normal variate to the targeted population mean and standard deviation.

The second type of transformation involves nonlinear transformation in which the sample data reflect the third and fourth moments (i.e., skewness and kurtosis) of the population data as specified in a simulation design. This transformation is necessary if issues related to data nonnormality are of interest in a simulation study. This transformation is more complicated, and it will be discussed later.

Transformation to multivariate sample data.
Linear and nonlinear transformations involve univariate sample data. In many situations, multiple variables are involved in statistical analyses, and these multiple variables have specified intervariable correlation pattern. Procedures are needed to transform the sample data of independent variables to sample data of correlated variables that reflect the specified population correlation pattern. Procedures for implementing this transformation are discussed later.

Accumulation of the Statistic(s) of Interest
Most simulation studies in psychology and other related disciplines focus on the performance characteristics of some type(s) of statistical techniques. Once a data sample is generated on the basis of the specified population parameters and other considerations (e.g., sample size) in a simulation design, the statistical technique of interest is applied to the data sample for analysis, and the statistic(s) of interest will be computed from the data sample. The statistic of interest *from each random sample* is obtained, and this statistic of interest needs to be accumulated across the random samples that are repeatedly generated under the specified conditions (e.g., 1,000 random samples under each cell condition in Table 23.1). This process continues until the statistic of interest is obtained and accumulated across all random samples under all design conditions. For the illustrative design in Table 23.1, from each random sample, the statistic of interest is whether the t statistic has reached the statistical significance level of our definition (e.g., $\alpha = 0.05$). This is a dichotomous outcome, with $p < \alpha$ representing a Type I error under the *true* null hypothesis condition from which the sample data were generated,

and $p \geq \alpha$ representing a correct decision. From Table 23.1, there are 36 unique cell conditions with 1,000 replications in each, and the total number of accumulated statistic of interest will be 36,000 t-test outcomes (e.g., 1 for Type I error, and 0 for correct decision), with each outcome associated with the three other variables designating the three design conditions (total sample size, variance ratio, and group-size ratio).

Analysis of the Accumulated Statistic(s) of Interest
Once the statistic of interest from all the samples under all design conditions has been accumulated, the simulation process is complete. Depending on the nature of the question(s) in a simulation study, the follow-up data analyses may be simple or complicated. For the simulation represented in Table 23.1, data analysis can be simple descriptive analysis, which involves tabulation of the Type I error rate under each unique cell condition. Alternatively, a more sophisticated analysis approach could also be considered, such as using logistic regression analysis to model the dichotomous outcome (Type I error or not) to examine how and to what extent different design conditions could predict the occurrence of Type I error.

Drawing Conclusions
Ultimately, we conduct a simulation study to answer questions about certain statistical analysis outcomes and about what conditions may affect such outcomes. The simulation design and analyses of simulation results described thus far should be conducive to providing answers to the question(s) that motivated the simulation study in the first place. The validity of the conclusions drawn from a simulation study largely hinges on the simulation design (relevant design conditions included, appropriate levels of each design condition implemented, and so on) and the validity of the data-generation process. For the hypothetical simulation design in Table 23.1, we can draw some tentative conclusions about how unequal group variances may affect the Type I error rate of an independent sample t test, and how such an impact may be moderated by other conditions, such as how group sample size condition is paired

with unequal variance condition (e.g., the Type I error rate may be more severe when the smaller group has larger variance).

Our conclusions, however, must be limited to the design conditions implemented in the simulation design; extrapolation beyond these conditions and their levels should be avoided. To increase the generalizability of simulation study findings, not only the relevant conditions should be included, but the levels of each condition also should be carefully considered to cover a meaningful range of levels, including extreme levels when possible. Not having sufficient levels of a design condition limits the generalizability of simulation findings.

DATA GENERATION IN A SIMULATION STUDY

Common Random Number Generators

There are different random number generators[2] corresponding to different probability density functions—for example, binomial distribution, Cauchy distribution, exponential distribution, gamma distribution, Poisson distribution, normal distribution, uniform distribution, and so on. In simulation studies in psychology and related disciplines, the most commonly used random number generators are probably those for the normal, uniform, and binomial distributions. These random number generators are available in widely used general statistical software packages, such as SAS, SPSS, or R. For sample data generation, appropriate random number generators will be used, as dictated by the specific requirements of a simulation study.

Simulating Univariate Sample Data

Most Monte Carlo studies involve multiple variables. However, the ability to generate sample data of a single variable is the foundation for data generation involving multiple variables. Simulating sample data from a standard normal distribution is straightforward, whereas simulating sample data for a population with specified degree of nonnormality is more challenging. Because many analytical techniques assume data normality, the impact of data normality

assumption violation on the validity of statistical results often becomes an area of focus for empirical investigations. Consequently, data nonnormality is often one important area of research interest in Monte Carlo simulation studies.

Normally Distributed Sample Data With Specified First Two Moments

All statistical software packages have a normal variate generator to generate data samples from a normally distributed statistical population with a mean of zero and standard deviation of one [i.e., z scores $\sim N(0, 1)$]. Through a simple linear transformation, these sample z scores can then be transformed to a variable with specified first two moments (i.e., mean and standard deviation) of a population distribution. Linear transformation only changes the first two moments (i.e., mean and variance) of a distribution but *not* the shape of the distribution as defined by the third and fourth statistical moments (i.e., skewness and kurtosis). The linear transformation takes the following form:

$$X' = \mu_{x'} + z(\sigma_{x'}), \qquad (2)$$

where

X' is the transformed variable;

$\mu_{x'}$ is the desired population mean of the transformed variable;

z is the z score values generated through a random normal variate generator; and

$\sigma_{x'}$ is the desired population standard deviation of the transformed variable.

In many statistical software packages, this transformation is an automated process, and the user only needs to specify the values of $\mu_{x'}$ and $\sigma_{x'}$ when using the random normal variate generator.

Sample Data Generation From a Nonnormal Distribution

Although it is relatively easy to generate sample data from a normal distribution, it is considerably more complicated to generate data from a nonnormal distribution. Different algorithms, for example, the generalized lambda distribution (GLD) approach by

---

[2]As discussed in Fan et al. (2002), all random number generators are based on uniform distribution, and other distributions can be obtained from a uniform distribution through some transformation process. See Chapter 3 in Fan et al. for details.

Ramberg and Schmeiser (1974) and the power transformation approach by Fleishman (1978), have been developed to simulate nonnormality distribution conditions (Burr, 1973; Fleishman, 1978; Johnson, 1949, 1965; Johnson & Kitchen, 1971; Pearson & Hartley, 1972; Ramberg & Schmeiser, 1974; Ramberg, Dudewicz, Tadikamalla, & Mykytka, 1979; Schmeiser & Deutch, 1977). Of the competing approaches, the most widely known and widely used procedure for simulating sample data from nonnormal distributions is probably the Fleishman's power transformation approach, as described in the next section.

Fleishman's power transformation method.
Fleishman (1978) introduced a method for generating sample data from a population with desired degrees of skewness and kurtosis. This method uses polynomial transformation to transform a normally distributed variable to a variable with specified degrees of skewness and kurtosis. The polynomial transformation takes the following form:

$$Y = a + bZ + cZ^2 + dZ^3, \tag{3}$$

where

Y is the transformed nonnormal variable with specified population skewness and kurtosis;

Z is unit normal variate, that is, normally distributed variable with population mean of zero and variance of one; and

a, b, c, d are coefficients needed for transforming the unit normal variate to a nonnormal variable with specified degrees of population skewness and kurtosis. Of the four coefficients, $a = -c$.

The coefficients (a, b, c, d) needed for the transformation are tabulated in Fleishman (1978) for selected combinations of skewness and kurtosis values. Table 23.2 presents a small example set of Fleishman power transformation coefficients for skewness of .75 and for kurtosis ranging from −.20 to +3.20. The Fleishman method for generating sample data from nonnormal distributions is easy to implement in simulation because the coefficients needed for the nonnormal transformation are

TABLE 23.2

Coefficients for Selected Nonnormality Conditions

Skew[a]	Kurtosis	b	c	d
.75	−0.20	1.173302916	.207562460	−.079058576
.75	0.00	1.112514484	.173629896	−.050334372
.75	0.40	1.033355486	.141435163	−.018192493
.75	0.80	0.978350485	.124833577	.001976943
.75	1.20	0.935785930	.114293870	.016737509
.75	1.60	0.900640275	.106782526	.028475848
.75	2.00	0.870410983	.101038303	.038291124
.75	2.40	0.843688891	.096435287	.046773413
.75	2.80	0.819604207	.092622898	.054275030
.75	3.20	0.797581770	.089386978	.061023176

Note. Coefficient $a = -c$. Adapted from *SAS for Monte Carlo Studies: A Guide for Quantitative Researchers* (p. 67), by X. Fan, A. Felsovalyi, S. A. Sivo, and S. Keenan, 2002, Cary, NC: SAS Institute. Copyright 2002, SAS Institute Inc., Cary, NC, USA. All Rights Reserved. Reproduced with permission of SAS Institute Inc., Cary, NC.

[a]For negative skewness, reverse the signs of coefficient c and coefficient a.

tabulated in his 1978 article for many selected combinations of skewness and kurtosis. If non-normality conditions other than those tabulated in Fleishman (1978) are needed, Fan et al. (2002, Chapter 4) provided SAS codes for generating these coefficients once the targeted skewness and kurtosis are specified.

Because positive and negative skewness can be considered symmetrical, the tabulated transformation coefficients in Fleishman (1978) did not list negative skewness conditions. But the coefficients for negative skewness conditions can be obtained simply by reversing the signs of c and a.

The Fleishman (1978) method, similar to other approaches such as the GLD method (Ramberg & Schmeiser, 1974), does not cover the entire space of possible combinations of skewness and kurtosis. In other words, this approach cannot generate nonnormal data for certain skewness and kurtosis conditions (Fleishman, 1978; Tadikamalla, 1980). The comparative study by Tadikamalla (1980) indicated that the GLD approach by Ramberg and Schmeiser (1974) and the power transformation approach by Fleishman cover approximately the same parameter space of nonnormality as defined by skewness and kurtosis, but the Fleishman method is more efficient. Readers interested in this limitation may consult these references about the approximate parameter space (nonnormality conditions as defined by skewness and kurtosis) for which the method can generate nonnormal data. Other methods exist for the same purpose, such as those discussed in Burr (1973), Johnson (1949, 1965), and Schmeiser and Deutch (1977). Despite the limitation that the Fleishman method cannot cover some non-normality conditions, the Fleishman method is easier to use compared with other methods when *multivariate* nonnormal data conditions are desired in Monte Carlo simulation, as is discussed in the next section.

Simulating Multivariate Sample Data

In most Monte Carlo simulation studies, it is typical to involve multiple variables. For example, in any regression analysis, there must be two correlated variables at a minimum: the dependent variable (Y) and one predictor (X). The same is true for many other univariate statistical techniques (i.e., with only one dependent variable). Any multivariate statistical technique (i.e., more than one dependent variable in the same analysis), by definition, must have multiple variables in the system. In these simulation situations, the researcher not only has to control the univariate distributional characteristics as discussed but also must control the population intervariable relationship pattern. The degree of complexity in generating multiple variables with a specified intervariable relationship pattern largely depends on whether the individual variables involved are normally distributed. This discussion is divided into two sections: The first section covers normally distributed variables, and the second section covers nonnormal variables.

Sample Data From a Multivariate Normal Distribution

When all variables are normally distributed, it is relatively straightforward to impose a specified population intercorrelation pattern on the sample data of multiple variables. Kaiser and Dickman (1962) presented a matrix decomposition procedure that

imposes a specified correlation matrix on a set of otherwise-uncorrelated random normal variables. Given a specified population intercorrelation matrix R, the basic matrix decomposition procedure takes the following form (Kaiser & Dickman, 1962):

$$Z_{(k \times k)} = F_{(kk)} \times X_{(k \times N)}, \tag{4}$$

where

k is the number of variables involved;

N is the number of observations in a sample (sample size N);

X is a $k \times N$ data matrix, with N observations, each with k uncorrelated random normal variables (mean of 0 and standard deviation of 1);

F is a $k \times k$ matrix containing principal component factor pattern coefficients obtained by applying principal component factorization to the given population intercorrelation matrix R;

Z is the resultant $k \times N$ sample data matrix (N observations on k variables), as if sampled from a population with the given population intercorrelation matrix R; and

$k \times N$ are matrix dimensions (k rows and N columns).

Procedurally, to generate sample data of k variables with the desired population intercorrelation pattern as specified in R, take the following steps:

1. For a specified population intercorrelation matrix R, conduct a factor analysis using a principal component as the factor extraction method (the default option in statistical software packages, such as SAS or SPSS), requesting the option to keep the same number of factors as the number of variables in the specified population correlation matrix R, and obtain the matrix of factor pattern coefficients F.

2. Generate k uncorrelated random normal variables ($\mu = 0$, $\sigma = 1$), each with N observations. The dimension of this matrix was originally $N \times k$. It is then transposed to a $k \times N$ dimensions matrix X, that is, the matrix has k rows representing k variables, and N columns representing N observations.

3. Premultiply the uncorrelated sample data matrix X with the factor pattern matrix F. The resultant

Z matrix ($k \times N$) contains N observations on k correlated variables, as if the N observations were sampled from a population with a population intercorrelation pattern represented by R. This correlated data matrix is then transposed back to an $N \times k$ dimension sample data matrix for later statistical analysis in the simulation loop.

When individual variables are univariate normal, the multivariate data generated through this matrix decomposition procedure are multivariate normal (Vale & Maurelli, 1983). The procedural steps can be implemented in statistical software packages that have matrix computation capabilities (e.g., SAS and SPSS). Fan et al. (2002, Chapter 4) provided SAS illustrative examples for these procedural steps.

Sample Data From Multivariate Nonnormal Distribution

Although it is relatively straightforward to simulate sample data from a multivariate normal distribution with a desired population intervariable correlation pattern, it is considerably more difficult to simulate sample data from a multivariate nonnormal distribution. The following provides a brief discussion on the relevant issues and procedures for accomplishing this goal.

Interaction between nonnormality and intervariable correlations.   As discussed in previous sections, simulating sample data from a univariate nonnormal distribution can be accomplished through several procedures, and Fleishman's (1978) power transformation method was one of them. As pointed out, for univariate nonnormal variables, Fleishman's method has some limitation because it does not cover the entire space nonnormality as defined by all possible combinations of skewness and kurtosis. Fleishman's method, however, does offer "an advantage over the other procedures in that it can easily be extended to generate multivariate random numbers with specified inter-correlations and univariate means, variances, skews, and kurtoses" (Vale & Maurelli, 1983, p. 465). In other words, to simulate sample data from a *multivariate* nonnormal distribution with specified population univariate skewness and kurtosis, and specified population intervariable correlation pattern among the

variables, Fleishman's approach is the method of choice.

To generate multivariate nonnormal data, Vale and Maurelli (1983) showed that the application of a matrix decomposition procedure for controlling the intervariable correlations among the variables is not as straightforward as had been demonstrated. On the surface, the goal of simulating multivariate nonnormal data can be accomplished by (a) generating multivariate normal data with specified intervariable correlations through the matrix decomposition procedure, and (b) transforming each variable to the desired distributional shapes with specified univariate skewness and kurtosis. Unfortunately, the two processes interact, and the resultant multivariate nonnormal data will have an intervariable correlation pattern that differs from that specified in the matrix decomposition procedure.

Intermediate correlations.   Because data nonnormality and intervariable correlations interact, and such interaction causes sample data to deviate from the specified population intervariable correlation pattern, this interaction must be taken into account in the process of generating sample data from multivariate nonnormal distributions. Vale and Maurelli (1983) presented a procedure of decomposing an *intermediate* intervariable correlation matrix to counteract the effect of non-normality on the intervariable correlations.

The intermediate correlation procedure by Vale and Maurelli (1983) demonstrated that, for multiple correlated variables, simple implementation of matrix decomposition procedures does not work as expected when the variables are not normally distributed. To counteract the effect of nonnormal conditions on the intervariable correlations in the process of data generation, intervariable correlations that are different from those specified as population intervariable correlations must be derived and used in the matrix decomposition procedure. These derived correlations are called *intermediate correlations*, and the derivation of these intermediate correlations is based on the specified population intervariable correlation pattern to be modeled and on the specified univariate non-normality conditions as defined by the univariate skewness and kurtosis.

Derivation of intermediate correlations.

Derivation of all *pairwise* intermediate correlations is essential for simulating nonnormal data conditions. The derivation process takes into account both the originally specified population correlation between two variables and the population nonnormality conditions of the two variable as defined by univariate skewness and kurtosis. It is here that the Fleishman (1978) power transformation method is the method of choice, as the coefficients in Fleishman's power transformation can readily be used to derive the needed intermediate correlation coefficients. As Vale and Maurelli (1983) discussed, it is not obvious that other nonnormality transformation procedures (e.g., GLD approach; Ramberg & Schmeiser, 1974) can have the same direct extension to multivariate nonnormality data situations.

As discussed, any two normal variates Z_1 and Z_2, can be transformed through Fleishman's (1978) power transformation method into two nonnormal variables X_1 and X_2, each with its own known skewness and kurtosis:

$$X_1 = a_1 + b_1 Z_1 + c_1 Z_1^2 + d_1 Z_1^3 \text{ and}$$
$$X_2 = a_2 + b_2 Z_2 + c_2 Z_2^2 + d_2 Z_2^3. \tag{5}$$

Once the degrees of skewness and kurtosis are specified, the coefficients (a_i, b_i, c_i, and d_i, for $i = 1, 2$) are known (e.g., by consulting Fleishman's table in the original article or by using the SAS program codes provided in Fan et al., 2002, Chapter 4). The targeted population correlation between the two nonnormal variables X_1 and X_2 can be specified as $R_{X_1 X_2}$. Vale and Maurelli (1983) demonstrated that the following relationship exists:

$$R_{X_1 X_2} = \rho(b_1 b_2 + 3 b_1 d_2 + 3 d_1 b_2 + 9 d_1 d_2)$$
$$+ \rho^2 (2 c_1 c_2) + \rho^3 (6 d_1 d_2), \tag{6}$$

where ρ is the intermediate correlation coefficient. Here, all elements are known except the intermediate correlation coefficient ρ. The bivariate intermediate correlation coefficient ρ must be solved for all possible pairs of the variables involved. These intermediate correlation coefficients are then assembled into an intermediate correlation matrix, which is then factor analyzed to obtain the factor pattern matrix needed to transform uncorrelated variables into correlated ones (i.e., matrix decomposition procedure by Kaiser & Dickman, 1962).

There is no direct algebraic solution to solve the polynomial function for ρ; as a result, an iterative estimation approach is needed to arrive at an estimated solution. As an illustrative example, we have a three-variable situation with the specified univariate skewness and kurtosis conditions and the specified population intervariable correlation pattern, as shown in Table 23.3.

Appendix 23.1 provides SAS program codes (Fan et al., 2002, Chapter 4) using the Newton-Raphson method to solve for the intermediate correlation ρ between X_1 and X_2. Using this SAS program, all three pairwise intermediate correlation coefficients could be solved. After solving for each pairwise intermediate correlation coefficient among the three variables and assembling the resultant three intermediate correlation coefficients, we have the intermediate correlation matrix as shown in Exhibit 23.1.

This intermediate intervariable correlation matrix is then factor analyzed (decomposed). The resultant factor pattern matrix is then used in the matrix decomposition procedure to impose the specified population intervariable correlation pattern on a set of nonnormal variables. The result is a correlated multivariate nonnormal sample data that has the population intervariable correlation pattern as originally specified.

Checking the Validity of Data-Generation Procedures

Data generation is probably the most important component of a simulation experiment, as the validity of the results from a Monte Carlo simulation experiment hinges on the validity of the sample data-generation process. Because of this, it is important to empirically verify the data generation procedures first before implementing the simulation experiment. This can be done by generating sample data for some limited conditions and comparing sample data characteristics against the targeted population parameters.

As an example of data simulation verification, assuming that a planned Monte Carlo simulation experiment would involve three multivariate nonnormal variables shown in Table 23.3. Using the

TABLE 23.3

Three Nonnormal Variables for Simulation

	Targeted population parameters						
	M	*SD*	Skew	Kurtosis	Correlation matrix		
X₁	100	15	.75	0.80	1.00		
X₂	50	10	–.75	0.80	0.70	1.00	
X₃	0	1	.75	2.40	0.20	0.40	1.00
	Fleishman coefficients for the three variables						
	a	*b*	*c*	*d*			
X₁	–.124833577	.978350485	.124833577	.001976943			
X₂	.124833577	.978350485	–.124833577	.001976943			
X₃	–.096435287	.843688891	.096435287	.046773413			

Note. Adapted from *SAS for Monte Carlo Studies: A Guide for Quantitative Researchers* (p. 84), by X. Fan, A. Felsovalyi, S. A. Sivo, and S. Keenan, 2002, Cary, NC: SAS Institute. Copyright 2002, SAS Institute Inc., Cary, NC, USA. All rights reserved. Reproduced with permission of SAS Institute Inc., Cary, NC.

Exhibit 23.1.
Intermediate Correlation Matrix for Table 23.3
Data Conditions

X₁	1.0000		
X₂	0.7402	1.0000	
X₃	0.2054	0.4173	1.0000

Fleishman coefficients for the targeted univariate non-normal conditions, and after obtaining all the "intermediate" correlation coefficients (see Appendix 23.1 and Exhibit 23.1), we may do a quick data-generation verification by generating a large sample of 1 million observations using the SAS program codes in Appendix 23.2.[3] For such a large sample, we expect that the sample statistics will be very close to the population parameters (e.g., mean, standard deviation, skewness, kurtosis, and intervariable correlation coefficients).

One execution of the SAS program in Appendix 23.2 provided the comparison between the population parameters and the sample statistics (in parentheses) shown in Table 23.4. The sample statistics (in parenthesis) are very close, if not identical, to the population parameters for all the parameters (mean, standard deviation, skewness, kurtosis, and the intervariable correlations). This information provides assurance that the data-generation procedures implemented indeed produced sample data as defined by the population parameters.

Although the results from the quick verification as shown in Table 23.5 are comforting, a more rigorous verification check would involve examining the *empirical* sampling distribution characteristics of the simulated data samples relative to the population parameters. For the purpose of examining the sampling distribution characteristics, we may select one or more sample size condition(s) (e.g., $N = 100$), generate repeated samples (e.g., 1,000 replications) under that sample size condition, and then examine the sampling distributions of various sample statistics of interest (e.g., sample mean, sample skewness, sample kurtosis) relative to the population parameters. This more rigorous verification process is especially important in situations in which the simulation procedures may be relatively new (e.g., involving some relatively new algorithms), thus uncertainty may exist about the simulation outcomes.

[3]Use of the SAS program is not required; such verification can be carried out in any other programs, such as R or SPSS.

TABLE 23.4

Comparison Between Population Parameters and Sample Statistics (in Parentheses) From a Large Sample ($N = 1,000,000$)

	M	*SD*	Skew	Kurtosis	Correlation matrix		
X_1	100 (99.99)	15 (14.99)	.75 (.75)	0.80 (0.80)	1.00		
X_2	50 (49.99)	10 (10.01)	−.75 (−.75)	0.80 (0.81)	0.70 (0.70)	1.00	
X_3	0 (−.00)	1 (1.00)	.75 (.76)	2.40 (2.42)	0.20 (0.20)	0.40 (0.40)	1.00

In a simulation experiment, depending on the mathematical–statistical software and the platform used, how the data-generation procedures are implemented may be very different. In some cases (e.g., SPSS, SAS), the researcher needs to implement and program all the components for data generation. In some others (e.g., Mplus), the software has built-in data-generation procedures, and the researcher may need to specify only the targeted population parameters of a model. In such a case, it is the researcher's responsibility to verify the validity of the data-generation procedures. Although not always possible, the researcher should understand the algorithms for data generation as implemented in the software.

OTHER CONSIDERATIONS

Design Factors and Manipulation Levels

In a typical simulation experiment, careful consideration should be given to the population conditions to be simulated. In general, population conditions should include the major factors relevant for the outcome of interest, and each factor should vary to cover a reasonable and realistic range of values to enhance the degree of generalizability of findings. If a relevant, or even important, factor is missing in the design, our understanding about the phenomenon would be limited, as we would know nothing about the influence or effect of that factor on the outcome of interest. For each factor to be manipulated in the simulation, an appropriate range of levels should be covered in the design to increase the generalizability of findings from the simulation experiment.

As an example, we may be interested in understanding both Type I error control and statistical

TABLE 23.5

Population Parameters for Two Groups for Selected Conditions

Group variance ratio	Group difference (*d*)	Group sample size ratio[a]	Population parameters Group 1 (μ_1, σ_1^2, n_1)	Group 2 (μ_2, σ_2^2, n_2)
1:1	.00	0.5:0.5	50, 100, 60	50, 100, 60
		0.7:0.3	50, 100, 84	50, 100, 36
	.50	0.5:0.5	50, 100, 60	45, 100, 60
		0.7:0.3	50, 100, 84	45, 100, 36
2:1	.00	0.5:0.5	50, 100, 60	50, 50, 60
		0.7:0.3	50, 100, 84	50, 50, 36
	.50	0.5:0.5	50, 100, 60	45.67, 50, 60
		0.7:0.3	50, 100, 84	45.39, 50, 36

[a]This illustrative example only includes the condition of larger group with larger variance.

power of independent *t* test under conditions of (a) equal versus nonequal group variances, and (b) data normality versus nonnormality conditions. A cursory planning for this simulation experiment could lead us to five dimensions that can be manipulated: equal versus unequal group variances, data normality versus non-normality conditions, group difference on the outcome variable (as defined by effect size), total sample size (two groups combined), and equal versus unequal group sample sizes. These factors are included in the design for manipulation because we believe that each factor could have potential effect on the outcome of interest (i.e., Type I error control, or statistical power). Such a belief could be based on theoretical considerations (statistical power is related to sample size; violation of data normality assumption may affect the performance of *t* test, etc.) or based on some previous findings in the field (e.g., consequence of the violation of equal variance assumption is related to unequal sample sizes of two groups; Glass, Peckham, & Sanders, 1972). In other words, there should be a reasonable rationale about why a factor is included in a simulation experiment.

Once the factors to be manipulated in a simulation experiment are determined, the levels for each factor should be carefully considered. The primary consideration is that each factor should cover a reasonable and realistic range of levels so that the findings from the study will have a reasonable degree of generalizability. Although it is generally true that a wider range of a factor, and more levels within the range, would lead to better generalizability, a researcher needs to strike a balance between the desire to achieve better generalizability and the scope and manageability of a simulation experiment. For our hypothetical example concerning an independent group's *t* test, some deliberation about the levels of the multiple factors could lead to the following tentative decisions about the levels on each of the five factors:

1. For equality and nonequality of group variances, the group variance ratios could be
   1:1
   2:1
   4:1
   8:1
2. For data normality,
   normality (i.e., skew = 0, kurtosis = 0)
   slight nonnormality (e.g., skew = |1|, kurtosis = |1|)
   severe nonnormality (e.g., skew > |2|, kurtosis > |3|)
3. For group difference on the dependent variable to be tested (defined as standardized mean difference of *d*),
   $d = 0.0$ (no difference; for Type I error control)
   $d = 0.2$ (small effect size)
   $d = 0.5$ (medium effect size)
   $d = 0.8$ (large effect size)
4. For total sample size *N* (two groups combined),
   $N = 30$
   $N = 60$
   $N = 120$
   $N = 240$
5. For equal versus unequal group sample sizes (group sample size ratio for a given total *N*):
   equal ratio: 0.5:0.5
   #1 unequal ratio: 0.7:0.3 (larger group has larger population variance)
   #2 unequal ratio: 0.3:0.7 (smaller group has larger population variance)

For each manipulated factor, the levels implemented in a simulation experiment should be carefully considered such that the levels are reasonable. For some factors, the choice of the levels may be well-grounded in theory or in research practice. For example, for number 3 (group difference on the dependent variable to be tested), the four levels represent no difference, differences of small effect ($d = 0.20$), of medium effect ($d = 0.50$), and of large effect ($d = 0.80$), respectively, and these are widely used benchmarks in social science research (Cohen, 1988). On the other hand, for some factors, there may be some uncertainty and ambiguity with regard to the levels to be implemented. For example, for the data normality dimension (No. 2), the operationalization of *slight* and *severe* nonnormality levels are more subjective. In a real simulation experiment, the researcher may need a literature review concerning how, and to what extent, nonnormality conditions could be operationalized in a similar situation, and then make informed decisions about the levels of nonnormality (as defined by skewness and kurtosis) to be implemented in the experiment. In short, to the fullest extent possible, the selected levels of a factor in a simulation design should be grounded either in theory or in practice.

From Simulation Design to Population Data Parameters

Once simulation design issues are settled, the design (i.e., factors, and levels within each factor) need to be translated into population data parameters that statistically conform to the design conditions, so that it is possible to simulate data of random samples under the specified design conditions. Depending on the complexity of the design, the statistical technique, and some other considerations (e.g., software used for simulation), specification of population data parameters for simulation implementation may or may not be a straightforward process. In this section, two hypothetical simulation situations are discussed as illustrations of this process.

For the independent group's *t*-test simulation example described in the previous section, for the sake of simplicity, assume that we only consider normal data and total *N* of 120 (i.e., combined total sample size of 120). Furthermore, we only consider some selected conditions of group variance ratio (1:1 and 2:1), group difference on the dependent variable to be tested ($d = 0.00$ and $d = 0.50$), and group sample size ratio (for unequal group sample sizes, only the situation of larger group with larger variance). For these design conditions, the population parameters, that is, μ and σ^2 for the dependent variable, and the group sample sizes are shown in Table 23.5. In this example, Group 1 is specified to have population parameters of $\mu_1 = 50$ and $\sigma_1^2 = 100$. Once Group 1's parameters are known, and Group 2's population parameters are worked out for the selected design conditions in the table. The specification of Group 2's parameters is based on the following simple algorithms:

$$d = \frac{\mu_1 - \mu_2}{\sigma_{pooled}}, \tag{7}$$

where

$$\sigma_{pooled} = \sqrt{\frac{(n_1 - 1)\sigma_1^2 + (n_2 - 1)\sigma_2^2}{n_1 + n_2 - 1}}. \tag{8}$$

Once the design conditions are given, the only parameter that needs to be worked out is μ_2, whereas all others (μ_1, d, σ_{pooled}) are already known. The parameter μ_2 can be worked out as follows:

$$\mu_2 = \mu_1 - d * \sigma_{pooled}. \tag{9}$$

This example illustrates that it may take some work to translate the design conditions to population parameters to implement data simulation. Depending on the complexity of the design and some other factors (e.g., statistical techniques involved in the simulation experiment), this process could be considerably more complicated and time-consuming than illustrated here.

As a more complicated example, we are interested in assessing the potential adverse impact (e.g.,

biased estimates of growth model parameters) of misspecifying the residual structure in growth modeling analysis. In growth modeling analysis, it is common to assume that the residuals (ε_1 to ε_6) of the repeated measurements have homoscedastic ($var(\varepsilon_i) = var(\varepsilon_j)$) and uncorrelated ($Cov_{ij} = 0$) residuals, as shown in Figure 23.1a. However, the repeated measurements may have more complicated residual structure (e.g., Sivo, Fan, & Witta, 2005). More specifically, the residual structure may have heteroscedastic ($var(\varepsilon_i) \neq var(\varepsilon_j)$) and correlated ($Cov_{ij} \neq 0$) residuals, as shown in Figure 23.1b. What would the potential adverse impact be if the true residual structure as in Figure 23.1b was erroneously modeled as the simpler residual structure as in Figure 23.1a in growth modeling analysis? A simulation study may be designed to examine this issue (e.g., You, Fan, & Sivo, 2006).

Assuming that for one simulation condition, the growth model has the following model parameters:

1. Residual variances of the repeated measurements increase by an equal increment of 2.0, with the initial residual variance (of ε_1) being 20, and the largest (of ε_6) to smallest (of ε_1) ratio is 1.5:
   20 22 24 26 28 30
2. Correlation between adjacent residuals is 0.15: $r_{\varepsilon_i, \varepsilon_{i+1}} = 0.15$, and between nonadjacent residuals is 0.
3. Intercept is 50, with intercept variance of 100.
4. Slope is 2, with slope variance of 0.25.
5. Correlation between intercept and slope is 0.2.

From these model parameters, we have the following matrices (using Linear Structural Relations [LISREL] notation):

$$\Lambda_X = \begin{bmatrix} 1 & 0 \\ 1 & 1 \\ 1 & 2 \\ 1 & 3 \\ 1 & 4 \\ 1 & 5 \end{bmatrix}, \tag{10}$$

$$\Phi = \begin{bmatrix} 100 & 1.0 \\ 1.0 & .25 \end{bmatrix}, \tag{11}$$

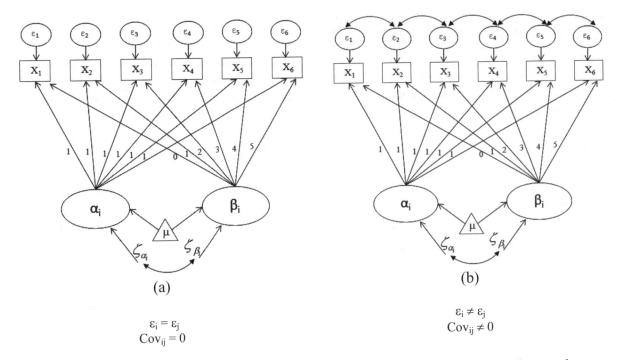

(a)

(b)

$$\varepsilon_i = \varepsilon_j$$
$$Cov_{ij} = 0$$

$$\varepsilon_i \neq \varepsilon_j$$
$$Cov_{ij} \neq 0$$

FIGURE 23.1. Linear growth models: homoscedastic and independent residuals (a); heteroscedastic and correlated residuals (b).

$$\Theta_\delta = \begin{bmatrix} 20 & 3.15 & 0 & 0 & 0 & 0 \\ 3.15 & 22 & 3.45 & 0 & 0 & 0 \\ 0 & 3.45 & 24 & 3.75 & 0 & 0 \\ 0 & 0 & 3.75 & 26 & 4.05 & 0 \\ 0 & 0 & 0 & 4.05 & 28 & 4.35 \\ 0 & 0 & 0 & 0 & 4.35 & 30 \end{bmatrix}, \text{ and} \tag{12}$$

$$k = \begin{bmatrix} 50 \\ 2 \end{bmatrix}, \tag{13}$$

where

Λ_X is the matrix for the intercept and slope coefficients;.

Φ contains the variances and the covariance for the intercept and slope;

Θ_δ is the variance/covariance matrix of the residuals; and

κ contains the intercept (initial level) and slope (growth rate) values.

In Φ and Θ_δ above, the off-diagonal elements are covariances. The relationship between covariance (COV_{ij}) and correlation (r_{ij}) is as follows:

$$r_{ij} = \frac{COV_{ij}}{\sigma_i \sigma_j}. \tag{14}$$

When the correlation (r_{ij}) and the variances of two variables $\left(\sigma_i^2, \sigma_j^2\right)$ are known, the standard deviations of the variables (σ_i, σ_j) are defined, and we can obtain the covariance between the two variables:

$$COV_{ij} = r_{ij}\sigma_i\sigma_j. \tag{15}$$

Once the four matrixes (Λ_X, Φ, Θ_δ, and κ) are defined for the specified condition of the growth model, the parameters (covariance matrix and mean vector) of the six repeated measurements (X_1–X_6) can be obtained:

$$COV_X = \Lambda_X \Phi \Lambda'_X + \Theta_\delta. \tag{16}$$

$$\mu_X = \Lambda_X \kappa. \tag{17}$$

For this particular simulation condition, the resultant population means, standard deviations, and correlation matrix of the six repeated measures are shown in Table 23.6. This represents only one condition of the simulation design; potentially, there are many other conditions that vary, for example, the correlation of adjacent residuals, the degree of heteroscedasticity of residual variances, and so on. For each unique combination defined by the design dimensions, such population parameters need to be

TABLE 23.6

Repeated-Measure Parameters for the Growth Model Condition

	X_1	X_2	X_3	X_4	X_5	X_6
μ	50	52	54	56	58	60
σ	10.9544	11.1467	11.3578	11.5866	11.8321	12.0933

Correlations

1.0000					
0.8529	1.0000				
0.8198	0.8447	1.0000			
0.8115	0.8110	0.8377	1.0000		
0.8023	0.8036	0.8036	0.8318	1.0000	
0.7925	0.7956	0.7972	0.7975	0.8270	1.0000

worked out so that random samples from the defined population can be simulated.

These two hypothetical examples show that translating simulation design conditions to data population parameters may involve a considerable amount of careful work.

Accumulation and Analysis of the Statistic(s) of Interest

By definition, a simulation experiment involves drawing many random samples from a defined population. From each sample randomly drawn from the defined population, some statistic(s) of interest need to be collected and stored for later analysis. Depending on the nature of the study, from each random sample, there may be only a very limited number of statistic(s) of interest, or there may be many statistics of interest. For the hypothetical example discussed previously for Type I error control and statistical power of independent *t* test, the statistic of interest may only be the statistical significance level of the *t* test from each random sample. For the growth modeling example, however, the purpose is to examine the potential adverse effect of misspecified residual structure on other model parameter estimates. In this situation, there may be many statistics of interest, such as the estimates of growth model intercept, slope, intercept and slope variance–covariance, model fit indexes, and so on.

The process of accumulation of the statistic(s) of interest over repeated random samples and across all

the design conditions can be straightforward or complicated, or anywhere in between, depending on many factors, such as the statistical software used, the analytical technique involved, and the statistic(s) of interest to be accumulated. In general, this is typically not an automated process by default; instead, it usually involves careful planning and execution, and it may involve some programming. Because various platforms exist to implement a simulation experiment, it is difficult to discuss a typical example. For the SAS environment, Fan et al. (2002) provided detailed simulation examples for this and other aspects of a simulation experiment; interested readers may consult this source for more details.

Once the statistic(s) of interest from all the random samples across all design conditions have been accumulated, the simulation process itself is complete. Depending on the nature of the research question(s) in a simulation study, follow-up data analysis may be simple or sophisticated. Considerations for follow-up data analysis are not different from many other data analysis situations. For the simulation represented in Table 23.1, data analysis can be simple descriptive analysis and involves tabulation of Type I error rate under each unique cell condition. A more sophisticated analysis approach could also be considered. For example, one may consider using logistic regression to model the dichotomous outcome (1 for Type I error or 0 for no Type I error in a sample) to assess how and to what extent different design conditions and their interactions have influenced the occurrence of Type I error.

For the illustrative growth modeling example discussed in the preceding paragraphs, in addition to descriptive results to be presented in tabular format, one may consider inferential analysis by obtaining bias estimates (bias = sample estimate–parameter) for different parameters (intercept, slope, intercept and slope variances, intercept and slope covariance, etc.), and then using a general linear model analysis to model the bias estimate as an outcome, with design dimensions, and their potential interactions, as independent variables (e.g., You et al., 2006).

Considerations for Presentation and Drawing Conclusions

A simulation experiment typically involves multiple factors in the simulation design, and each factor is manipulated to have a range of levels. As a result, the number of unique conditions can be quite large. This often poses challenges for presenting simulation findings. Commonly, findings are presented in simple tabular format, and the results are shown in table after table for all the conditions in the simulation design. But when a large number of tables are presented, the presentation and the subsequent discussion may easily become robotic and repetitive, and the presentation and discussion often lacks focus. As a result, the messages from the study are often muddied or buried in all these numbers and tables.

A better approach for presenting simulation findings is to focus on *representativeness* and *exceptions*. Representativeness means the general trends observed in the simulation results. Exceptions means those findings that are different from the general trends under certain and more limited conditions. It would be far more effective to present findings from some carefully selected conditions that illustrate the representativeness and exceptions and to discuss the extent to which the findings from other conditions are aligned with these two different observations.

Whenever possible, graphic representation, which is usually more concise and more condensed in terms of information content, should be used for presentation, as a good picture may be more effective than multiple tables. Graphic representation is effective both for showing observable trends and for illustrating exceptions in the simulation findings, as shown in Fan and Sivo (2007).

The validity and generalizability of the conclusions drawn from a simulation study depend on the adequacy and appropriateness of the simulation design (relevant design factors included, appropriate levels of each design factor implemented, etc.) and on the validity of the data-generation process (e.g., simulated sample data indeed reflect the intended population parameters as defined by the simulation design conditions). The conclusions must be limited to the conditions (i.e., design factors and the levels of the factors) as implemented in the simulation design; extrapolation beyond these conditions in the simulation design must be avoided. To increase the generalizability of simulation study findings, not only the relevant design factors should be included but also the levels of each design factor should be carefully planned to cover a meaningful range of levels, including extreme levels when possible. Failure to include a relevant factor (e.g., data nonnormality) in a simulation design excludes the possibility of drawing any conclusions about that factor. But for a factor included in the design, failure to implement a sufficient range of levels (e.g., for data nonnormality, only very minor nonnormality levels were implemented in the design) limits, sometimes severely, the generalizability of simulation findings.

APPENDIX 23.1: SAS CODES FOR DERIVING INTERMEDIATE CORRELATION BETWEEN X_1 AND X_2 IN TABLE 23.3

```
DATA D1;
  B1=.978350485; C1=-.124833577; D1=.001976943; * use
    Fleishman coefficients;
  B2=.978350485; C2=.124833577; D2=.001976943;
  TARGET=.70; * target population correlation;
  R=.5; * starting value for iteration;
DO I=1 TO 5;
  FUNCTION=(R**3*6*D1*D2+R**2*2*C1*C2+R*(B1*B2+3*
    B1*D2+3*D1*B2+9*D1*D2)-TARGET);
  DERIV=(3*R**2*6*D1*D2+2*R*2*C1*C2+(B1*B2+3*B1*D
    2+3*D1*B2+9*D1*D2));
  RATIO=FUNCTION/DERIV;
  R_TEMP = R - RATIO;
  IF ABS(R_TEMP - R)>.00001 THEN R = R_TEMP; OUTPUT;
END;
PROC PRINT; WHERE I=5; * print intermediate correlation r for
  the last iteration;
  VAR I RATIO R;
RUN;
```

Note. From *SAS for Monte Carlo Studies: A Guide for Quantitative Researchers* (p. 84), by X. Fan, A. Felsovalyi, S. A. Sivo, and S. Keenan, 2002, Cary, NC: SAS Institute. Copyright 2002, SAS Institute Inc., Cary, NC, USA. All Rights Reserved. Reproduced with permission of SAS Institute Inc., Cary, NC.

APPENDIX 23.2: SAS PROGRAM FOR DATA GENERATION VERIFICATION FOR TABLE 23.3 DATA CONDITIONS

```
DATA A (TYPE=CORR); _TYPE_='CORR'; INPUT X1-X3;
CARDS; * these are 'intermediate' correlation coefficients;
1.0000 . .
  .7402 1.0000 .
  .2054 .4173 1.0000
;
  * obtain factor pattern matrix for data generation;
PROC FACTOR N=3 OUTSTAT=FACOUT;
DATA PATTERN; SET FACOUT;
  IF _TYPE_='PATTERN';
  DROP _TYPE_ _NAME_;
RUN;
PROC IML;
  USE PATTERN; * read in the factor pattern as a matrix 'F';
  READ ALL VAR _NUM_ INTO F;
  F=F';
DATA=RANNOR(J(1000000,3,0)); *** generate data matrix
  (1000000×3);
DATA=DATA'; *** transpose data matrix (3×1000000);
Z = F*DATA; *** impose inter-correlations;
Z = Z'; *** transpose data matrix back (1000000×3);
  * Fleishman non-normality transformation;
X1 = -.124833577 + .978350485*Z[,1] + .124833577*Z[,1]##2
  + .001976943*Z[,1]##3;
X2 = .124833577 + .978350485*Z[,2] - .124833577*Z[,2]##2 +
  .001976943*Z[,2]##3;
X3 = -.096435287 + .843688891*Z[,3] + .096435287*Z[,3]##2
  + .046773413*Z[,3]##3;
X1=X1*15 + 100; * linear transformation for mean & std;
X2=X2*10 + 50;
X3=X3;
Z=X1||X2||X3;
CREATE A FROM Z [COLNAME={X1 X2 X3}]; * output a SAS
  working data 'A';
APPEND FROM Z;
  * obtaining descriptive stats for sample data;
PROC MEANS DATA=A N MEAN STD SKEWNESS KURTOSIS;
  VAR X1 X2 X3;
PROC CORR DATA=A NOSIMPLE NOPROB;
  VAR X1 X2 X3;
RUN; QUIT;
```

Note. Adapted from *SAS for Monte Carlo Studies: A Guide for Quantitative Researchers* (p. 86), by X. Fan, A. Felsovalyi, S. A. Sivo, and S. Keenan, 2002, Cary, NC: SAS Institute. Copyright 2002, SAS Institute Inc., Cary, NC, USA. All Rights Reserved. Reproduced with permission of SAS Institute Inc., Cary, NC.

References

Burr, I. W. (1973). Parameters for a general system for distributions to match a grid of α_3 and α_4. *Communications in Statistics, 2,* 1–21. doi:10.1080/03610927308827052

Cohen, J. (1988). *Statistical power analysis for the behavioral sciences* (2nd ed.). Hillsdale, NJ: Erlbaum.

Fan, X., Felsovalyi, A., Sivo, S. A., & Keenan, S. (2002). *SAS for Monte Carlo studies: A guide for quantitative researchers.* Cary, NC: SAS Institute.

Fan, X., & Sivo, S. (2007). Sensitivity of fit indices to model misspecification and model types. *Multivariate Behavioral Research, 42,* 509–529.

Fleishman, A. I. (1978). A method for simulating nonnormal distributions. *Psychometrika, 43,* 521–532. doi:10.1007/BF02293811

Glass, G. V., Peckham, P. D., & Sanders, J. R. (1972). Consequences of failure to meet assumptions underlying the fixed-effects analysis of variance and covariance. *Review of Educational Research, 42,* 237–288.

Johnson, N. L. (1949). Systems for frequency curves generated by methods of translation. *Biometrika, 36,* 149–176.

Johnson, N. L. (1965). Tables to facilitate fitting S_u frequency curves. *Biometrika, 52,* 547–558.

Johnson, N. L., & Kitchen, J. O. (1971). Tables to facilitate fitting S_B curves. *Biometrika, 58,* 223–226.

Kaiser, H. F., & Dickman, K. (1962). Sample and population score matrices and sample correlation matrices from an arbitrary population correlation matrix. *Psychometrika, 27,* 179–182. doi:10.1007/BF02289635

Merriam-Webster's online dictionary. (2010). Available at http://www.merriam-webster.com/dictionary/

Pearson, E. S., & Hartley, H. O. (Eds.). (1972). *Biometrika tables for statisticians* (Vol. 2). London, England: Cambridge University Press.

Ramberg, J. R., & Schmeiser, B. W. (1974). An approximate method for generating asymmetric random variables. *Communications of the Association for Computing Machinery, 17,* 78–82.

Ramberg, J. S., Dudewicz, E. J., Tadikamalla, P. R., & Mykytka, E. F. (1979). A probability distribution and its use in fitting data. *Technometrics, 21,* 201–214. doi:10.2307/1268517

Schmeiser, B. W., & Deutch, S. J. (1977). A versatile four parameter family of probability distributions suitable for simulation. *AIIE Transactions, 9,* 176–182. doi:10.1080/05695557708975140

Sivo, S., Fan, X., & Witta, L. (2005). The biasing effects of unmodeled ARMA time series processes on latent growth curve model estimates. *Structural Equation Modeling, 12,* 215–231. doi:10.1207/s15328007sem1202_2

Tadikamalla, P. R. (1980). On simulating nonnormal distributions. *Psychometrika, 45,* 273–279. doi:10.1007/BF02294081

Thompson, B. (1991). Invariance of multivariate results: A Monte Carlo study of canonical function and structure coefficients. *Journal of Experimental Education, 59,* 367–382.

Vale, C. D., & Maurelli, V. A. (1983). Simulating multivariate nonnormal distributions. *Psychometrika, 48,* 465–471. doi:10.1007/BF02293687

You, W., Fan, X., & Sivo, S. A. (2006, April). *Assessing the impact of failure to adequately model the residual structure in growth modeling.* Paper presented at the Annual Meeting of American Educational Research Association, San Francisco, CA.

CHAPTER 24

BAYESIAN MODELING FOR PSYCHOLOGISTS: AN APPLIED APPROACH

Fred M. Feinberg and Richard Gonzalez

Bayesian methods offer new insight into standard statistical models and provide novel solutions to problems common in psychological research, such as missing data. Appeals for Bayesian methods are often made from a dogmatic, theory-based standpoint concerning the philosophical underpinnings of statistical inference, the role of prior beliefs, claims about how one should update belief given new information, and foundational issues, such as the admissibility of a statistical decision. Although such a rhetorical approach is academically rigorous, it usually is not the kind of argument a practicing researcher wants to read about. Researchers care about analyzing their data in a rigorous manner that leads to clear, defensible conclusions. In this chapter, we address the reader who wants to learn something about what all the Bayesian fuss is about and whether the Bayesian approach offers useful tools to incorporate into one's data analytic toolbox. We hope this chapter prompts readers to learn more about what Bayesian statistical ideas have to offer in standard data analytic situations. Throughout the chapter, we highlight important details of the Bayesian approach; how it differs from the frequentist approach typically used in psychological research; and most important, where it offers advantages over the methods most commonly used by academic researchers in psychology and cognate disciplines.

SOME GENTLE PRELIMINARIES

Practicing research psychologists wish to understand and explain a variety of behaviors in humans and animals. Statistical methods and reasoning sharpen insight into experimental design and avoid the potential pitfalls of lay examination of data patterns. Deserving special mention is a point often missed in substantively focused studies: The purpose of statistical inference is to replace intuitions based on a mass of data with those achievable from examination of *parameters*. Except in nonparametric settings relatively rare in psychological and other social science research, understanding one's data relies critically on choosing an appropriate statistical model and both estimating and examining the distributions of its parameters. By this we mean the so-called *marginal distribution*—that is, everything we can say about a parameter once our data have been accounted for.

Too often, researchers shoehorn their hypotheses, which often concern individual-level behavior, into the straightjacket mandated by classical statistical methods. This approach typically requires large numbers of respondents for the central limit theorem to kick in, presumes equal variances in analysis of variance (ANOVA) designs, makes various untested assumptions about (lack of) correlation in errors and variables, requires balanced designs, and so on. Each of these requirements is necessary because the commonly used classical statistical tests do not achieve "nice" forms when their assumptions are violated. Imagine instead a world in which researchers can simply collect a data set and let the chosen statistical model summarize everything of interest it contains; the only assumptions one makes

We presented an earlier version of this chapter at a tutorial workshop on Bayesian techniques at the University of Michigan in March 2007. We thank the College of Literature, Science, and Arts and the Statistics Department of the University of Michigan for its financial support.

DOI: 10.1037/13620-024
APA Handbook of Research Methods in Psychology: Vol. 2. Research Designs, H. Cooper (Editor-in-Chief)

concern the underlying model generating the data and not aspects of the data set itself (e.g., balance, lack of error correlation, and so on); missing values do not mean throwing out a subject's data entirely; individuals can differ in their parameters; and covariates, like age and gender, can be used to describe how and why parameters differ across respondents.

Classical methods, such as nonparametric tests, can sometimes be used in the sorts of situations in which standard assumptions (like underlying normality) are known (or suspected) to be violated. But they typically come at a substantial cost in power: the ability to detect incorrect hypotheses. Bayesian statistical methods, however, provide a general framework that is adaptable to many different types of data, for the relatively modest—and steadily decreasing over time—price of additional computational effort. As we emphasize throughout this chapter, Bayesian methods dramatically expand a researcher's ability to work with real data sets and explain what they have to tell us. Bayesian methods do this by yielding marginal distributions for all parameters of interest, not merely summary measures like means and variances that are only asymptotically valid, and with many fewer presumptions about model forms and large-sample properties of estimators. It is for these reasons that we advocate their increased adoption by the psychological community. In this chapter, we take a first relatively nontechnical step in explaining how this might come about and what Bayesian methods might offer the practicing psychologist.

Many treatments of Bayesian statistics that have been written for (or by) psychologists have focused on the more philosophical issues. Some of these reviews have been made in the context of what is called the *null hypothesis debate*. Practicing research psychologists have become dissatisfied with conventional hypothesis testing and the mental gymnastics that one must undertake in most 1st-year psychology statistics courses to understand its underlying concepts. Examples include how one interprets the usual *p* value, as reflecting the probability of observing some sample statistic under the null hypothesis, or the classical interpretation of a confidence interval as the frequency of intervals that contain the true population parameter value. It is in this context that

Bayesian techniques are usually discussed as an alternative way of thinking about intervals, what a Bayesian calls *credible intervals*, and as a similarly different way to think about hypothesis testing, one that avoids many of the conceptual difficulties of the traditional *p* value. It has been argued that the Bayesian approach provides an alternative methodology and philosophical foundation for hypothesis testing (e.g., Jaynes, 1986).

A simple way of conceptualizing the distinction between the two approaches is about how one views uncertainty. A classical statistician views uncertainty as residing in the data one happens to observe: One needs to think about all the other observations that *could* have been made, under the hypothesized model, and base one's statistical test on the resulting distribution, which often achieves a "nice" form (e.g., one that can be looked up in a table). An example of this kind of logic is seen in the Fisherian interpretation of the *p* value (the probability of possible results that are "more extreme" than the observed result) and in some standard tests like the Fisher exact test for contingency tables, which uses the hypergeometric distribution to compute the probability of all contingency tables that are "more extreme" than the one that was actually observed.

The Bayesian approach places uncertainty not in the observations but rather in one's lack of knowledge. For a Bayesian, the observed data are not uncertain—you observed what you observed. But uncertainty has to be addressed somewhere in the analysis. A Bayesian places the uncertainty in our lack of knowledge about *parameters* and operationalizes that lack of knowledge in terms of a (joint) probability distribution over all unknown quantities, that is, parameters. Before any data are observed, the Bayesian summarizes everything known about the model's parameters in just such a distribution, called the *prior distribution*. This can include information from previously conducted studies, common-sense reasoning (e.g., gaining an inch in height will, all else equal, entail an upswing in weight), or even seemingly inviolable facts about parameters (e.g., variances cannot be negative). The prior distribution is then combined with (often called *updated by*) the likelihood, which is common from the usual frequentist analysis, to yield the *posterior* distribution. As we will see, literally everything researchers might wish to say about their data—estimation, testing, prediction, and so on—can be extracted, in a natural and direct way, from this posterior. In a sense, it replaces the entire canon of specialized test procedures so laboriously mastered in introductory statistics courses with one simple conceptual object.

In the next section, we refine and illustrate some of these issues, using elementary examples common to statistics texts of both the frequentist and Bayesian varieties. We also provide references to some presently available software and a few comprehensive, book-length treatments of Bayesian statistical methods. Throughout, we eschew formulas and other mainstays of *rigor* for a more user-oriented discussion, one especially geared to the practicing researcher in psychology.

THE NITTY-GRITTY OF THE BAYESIAN APPROACH

Estimating a Proportion

We begin with a relatively simple example, one common throughout statistical inference, in psychology and elsewhere: estimating the proportion of times a particular event occurs. To provide a specific context, consider a dependent variable that codes whether a couple has divorced within their first 20 years of marriage. The data set includes 10 couples, six of which were divorced within the 20-year window. Of course, any beginning student knows that this sample can be used to estimate the divorce rate: simply divide the number of divorces by the total number of couples, 6/10 = 0.6. But how do we know that is the best estimate of the true divorce rate in the population? How do we assess the uncertainty of this estimate?

To handle such questions within the classical framework, one reverts to the likelihood principle (i.e., "all the information in our sample is contained in the likelihood function"), makes an assumption about the independence of those 10 observations, and assumes the binomial model for the observed outcomes. To derive the usual maximum likelihood estimator for the proportion, we take the first derivative of the likelihood, set it to zero, and solve for

any unknown parameters, of which in our present example there is only one. Some of the computations in maximum likelihood estimation are simpler if one works with the logarithm of the likelihood—which, as a monotonic transformation, leaves the maximum intact—thus converting products to sums. In our exposition, we focus primarily on the likelihood itself because that is more convenient for Bayesian derivations, and point out when the log likelihood is used instead.

It is a common quip that the likelihood is the only thing about which both Bayesians and frequentists agree, and it is true that the likelihood plays a critical role in both accounts of statistical inference. In simple language, the likelihood function tells us how likely the parameters are to take one set of values, compared with any other. It is not a probability itself (indeed, it can even be greater than 1) but a *relative* statement, so that the likelihood ratio, a common concept in hypothesis testing, is a simple way to assess the comparative degree of appropriateness for any two given sets of parameters. In general, the likelihood is defined by

$$L(\theta \mid Y) = f(Y \mid \theta), \tag{1}$$

where Y represents the observations, θ represents the unknown parameters, and f is some probability density function. It is necessary to assume a distribution f, such as the binomial or normal (perhaps the two most common statistical models), to use maximum likelihood as the basis for parameter estimation. So, even within this classical approach, an important distributional assumption is made at the outset to estimate parameters of interest (e.g., a single population proportion in the binomial case, or the population mean and variance in the normal). It is therefore critical to conceptualize parameters as belonging to a specific model; it is the form of the model's likelihood function that allows the parameters to be estimated, regardless of whether the estimation is classical or Bayesian in nature.

To return to our sample problem, the likelihood for binomial data is given by

$$L(\pi \mid Y) = \binom{N}{Y} \pi^Y (1-\pi)^{N-Y}, \tag{2}$$

where π is the population proportion that is being estimated (in the binomial case, the unknown parameter θ is traditionally denoted as π). The number of trials (N) and the number of successes Y (which are the observations) are held fixed, and one searches for values of π that maximize the value of Equation 2. We say *values* because many likelihood functions can have multiple *local maxima*, only one of which is the true global maximum, that is, the single best choice of parameter(s). It is for this reason that maximum likelihood is conceptualized in terms of a search for unknown parameter(s), which in practice is a serious limitation for the classical approach, because multivariate optimization can be exceptionally computationally intensive.

Although the likelihood of Equation 2 may look just like an elementary statement about the probability of observing a particular set of data, in actuality, the inference is done in the other direction; that is, we infer parameter π given the data Y. In the classical estimation approach, the standard error of the parameter emerges by taking the expected value of the Hessian (the matrix of second derivatives) of the log likelihood. The logic justifying the use of the Hessian for this purpose involves imposing assumptions—most notably that the curvature of the log likelihood can be approximated by a multivariate Taylor series, up through its quadratic term. This is the underlying rationale for the typical approach taken by psychologists, computing a point estimate and constructing a confidence interval around that estimate. The classical approach focuses only on the maximum value of the likelihood (the point estimate) and approximates uncertainty (via the Hessian); all other details of parameter estimation are discarded in the classical approach. In this way, the classical statistician is forced to rely on a number of asymptotic (i.e., large sample) assumptions, without any practical way to verify them. It is only when these assumptions hold that the usual properties of estimators, like normality, can be shown to hold. When a problem comes along for which none of the typical distributions (z, t, F, chi-square, etc.) are provable asymptotic approximations, defensible inferences from the data become difficult, if not impossible. As we shall see, the Bayesian is not hampered by this restriction because Bayesian analysis

yields the *actual* distributions of any desired set of parameters (or functions of them) and rarely needs to call on the common distributions drilled into every beginning student of statistical inference.

The Bayesian approach also uses the likelihood (Equation 1 in general, or Equation 2 for our binomial example) but differs in how it is used. Although the classical statistician *maximizes* the likelihood by choosing the best parameter values θ, the Bayesian instead converts the problem into a statement about the (posterior) distribution θ. To keep notation simple and not have to keep track of different density functions, we use so-called bracket notation, which has become the standard way to represent useful properties and rigorous derivations in Bayesian analysis. As mentioned earlier, a key Bayesian property is that the posterior distribution is proportional to the product of the likelihood and prior distribution; this will be denoted as

$$[\theta|y] \propto [y|\theta][\theta]. \qquad (3)$$

The prior distribution $[\theta]$ reflects what we know (or do not know) about the parameters θ *before* consulting the data; the posterior distribution $[\theta|y]$ reflects what we know about the parameters θ *after* combining both the observed data and the information contained in the prior. Bayesians jump freely between talking about probabilities and talking about distributions when referring to priors and posteriors. We will also follow the convention of the field and speak only about proportionality ($\propto$) because this is all that is required for standard Bayesian inference techniques to be applied, a topic we return to later.

The change in reference turns out to be the key property of the Bayesian approach: Rather than work only with the likelihood $[y|\theta]$, as in the classical approach, Bayesians work with the posterior distribution $[\theta|y]$ (a quantity classical statisticians seek to make inferences about but that work in reverse direction with the likelihood). Under this approach, the posterior tells us literally everything we can know about the parameters θ once the data y are observed. The Bayesian merely has to *explore* the posterior and use it for inference. This is simple, at least in theory, but we need to explain what we mean by exploring the posterior.

We must also stress that it is not the case that Bayesians have the extra step of imposing a prior distribution whereas classical statisticians do not. There is a sense in which, when viewed through Bayesian eyes, classical statistics presumes that all values of a parameter are equally likely, what is called a *noninformative* prior in the Bayesian context. A Bayesian with a noninformative prior works with the same functional information as a classical statistician and has an analogous approach to such key issues as the interval constructed around a parameter estimate. The reason is that, with a suitably chosen noninformative prior, the Bayesian posterior is functionally the same as the classical likelihood. So, as long as the Bayesian acts on the posterior in the same way as the classical statistician (e.g., computes the maximum, also called the *mode*), then the two approaches yield identical results. Bayesians, however, provide a different, and some would say more nuanced, description of uncertainty and avoid some of the difficulties that plague classical analyses, such as problems with missing data and unbalanced designs in multilevel models.

The Bayesian framework also provides a language that is more natural to empirical researchers. For example, the Bayesian tradition does not promote the mind-twisting language of how to interpret a confidence interval (i.e., the percentage of such intervals that contain the true population value) and can more directly talk about an interval as representing a 95% degree of confidence (*credibility*) for the value of the unknown parameter. In our experience, students first encountering statistics are put off by counterfactual notions concerning what might happen if similar data were collected many times under identical circumstances. Rather, they ask conceptually direct questions about what can be said using *this* data set, as it is. Bayesian inference refers to the data one has, not the data one might obtain were the world to replay itself multiple times.

Conjugate Priors

One way to simplify calculating and sampling from the posterior—the main practical challenges in most Bayesian analyses—is by careful selection of the prior distribution. There are well-known prior-likelihood pairs, as on the right-hand side of Equation 3, that yield posteriors with the same *form* as the prior (i.e., the prior and posterior fall into the same distributional family, differing only in their parameters). For example, for binomial data, a beta prior distribution (i.e., beta-binomial pair) leads to a beta posterior distribution. Such *conjugate* priors make the overall Bayesian analysis easier to work with, both in terms of derivation and computation (see Box & Tiao, 1973/1992). For example, the beta distribution has two parameters, α and β, in its "functional" portion (i.e., leaving out constants that allow it to integrate to 1), $x^{\alpha-1}(1-x)^{\beta-1}$. Different values of α and β lead to different prior distributions over the unknown parameter π of the binomial distribution, making some values more likely than others *before recourse to the actual data*. For instance, the parameter pair $\alpha = 1$ and $\beta = 1$ produces a beta distribution that is uniform over [0,1], meaning that the prior presumes all values of the unknown binomial parameter π are equally likely; $\alpha = 2$ and $\beta = 2$ makes values of π near one half somewhat more likely; and $\alpha = 101$ and $\beta = 201$ makes values of π near one third quite a bit more likely (all these statements can be verified by simply graphing $x^{\alpha-1}(1-x)^{\beta-1}$ for the values in question). One then conducts an empirical study and observes Y successes out of N trials, such as in the example of six divorces in 10 couples (equivalently, six divorces and four nondivorces). The posterior distribution, when using a conjugate prior (i.e., the prior is beta and the likelihood is binomial), will also be a beta distribution, but the posterior parameters characterizing the posterior distribution are $\alpha + Y$ and $\beta + N - Y$, respectively. In other words, the posterior beta distribution has parameters that consist of both the prior parameter and the data (e.g., the first parameter of the posterior distribution is the sum of the prior parameter α and the observed number of divorces Y, and the second parameter is the sum of the prior parameter β and the number of nondivorces, $N - Y$). So, for our ongoing example, a uniform prior over the [0,1] interval (all proportions are equally likely), leads to a posterior that is a beta distribution with parameters 7 and 5 (i.e., $\alpha = \beta = 1$, $Y = 6$, $N = 10$). For reasons that can now be clearly seen, this process is often referred to as *updating* the prior, using the data to obtain the posterior from which all Bayesian inference follows.

The mode (i.e., the most likely value, where the density function reaches its largest value) of the beta distribution is $(\alpha - 1)/(\alpha + \beta - 2)$. So, the mode of the posterior for our ongoing divorce example using a uniform prior distribution is six tenths (i.e., the posterior has parameters $\alpha = 7$ and $\beta = 5$, so the mode is six tenths), the same value as the maximum likelihood estimator. Other summary measures of the posterior distribution are also possible. The mean of a beta distribution is $\alpha/(\alpha + \beta)$, so a Bayesian could take the estimate of the proportion to be $7/12 = 0.58$, rather than the classically derived maximum likelihood estimate of $6/10 = 0.60$ (see Figure 24.1). As the sample size gets larger, the impact of the particular choice of the prior becomes less influential. If we had 600 couples divorce out of 1,000, then the posterior mean would be $601/1002 = 0.5998$, which is very close to the maximum likelihood estimate of 0.60. The mode remains .6 for the uniform prior distribution.

We note that the classical and Bayesian estimates for the proportion coincide when the Bayesian uses a beta prior distribution with parameters α and β both very close to zero (note that α and β must be positive to give rise to a nondegenerate distribution; a so-called improper prior results if one literally sets both to zero because the functional part of the beta density, $x^{-1}(1-x)^{-1}$, does not have a finite integral over [0, 1]). Such an improper prior corresponds to a noninformative prior over the logit scale—that is, every value of the logit transform of π, or $log[\pi/(1 - \pi)]$, is equally likely—which can be used to provide a Bayesian justification for using logistic regression in the case of data that follow a binomial distribution.

The prior distribution has other effects on the analysis as well. For example, the prior can define the feasible search space while exploring the posterior distribution. Many statistical models impose restrictions on possible parameter values, such as that variances cannot be negative, which would seem to be an inviolable property that need not be specified, or even checked. Under classical estimation routines, however, negative variances can and do occur, especially in the case of mixture models, as users of programs that estimate such models soon discover. The prior distribution can address these issues by defining the effective feasible region for the unknown variance to be nonnegative (i.e., forcing the prior distribution to have mass only over nonnegative values). A recent example of using the prior to limit the search space of a parameter is the new Bayesian feature in the structural equation modeling program SPSS Amos. The user can specify priors that include, for instance, probability mass over the nonnegative real numbers, thus allowing one to place boundary conditions on the value of variances.

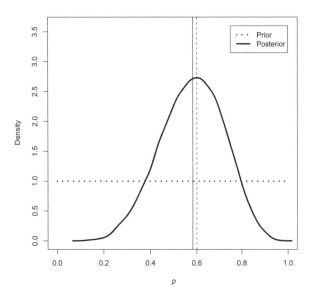

FIGURE 24.1. An example of six divorces out of 10 couples. The solid vertical line is the Bayesian estimate for the unknown proportion given a uniform prior (dotted horizontal line) and posterior distribution (thick solid curve). The theoretical posterior distribution is a beta; the thick solid curve is the estimated posterior distribution from MCMC sampling. The dashed vertical line is the maximum likelihood estimate (0.6).

The Whole Distribution and Nothing But the Whole Distribution

The previous subsection sells the Bayesian approach short. Comparing the Bayesian posterior mean to the parameter that emerges from the classical maximum likelihood framework is playing to the strength of the classical approach, which provides the estimate of the mean, and with a little more work and a few additional assumptions, a symmetric standard error (based again on asymptotic assumptions) emerges. The Bayesian approach has much more to offer, however. Instead of providing a point estimate and a standard error for a given parameter, the Bayesian approach provides its entire posterior distribution. This is available in the form of a sample *drawn* from the posterior, from which any quantity of interest can be computed. In some (all too rare) instances, as in the case of conjugate priors, closed-form solutions are possible, and so the entire posterior distribution takes a known form, and sample draws from the posterior are not needed. But, even when the posterior does not take such a known form—and this is the case in the vast majority of real-world applications—the researcher can, using the posterior, easily compute not only the mean but also the median, the mode, or any quantile one would like (such as the lower or upper 2.5%), even the entire shape of the distribution. Knowledge of the posterior distribution allows one to construct intervals for parameters of interest without making specific, potentially unfounded, assumptions, like symmetry (too often assumed, particularly so for bounded and skewed quantities like variances). Indeed, if the posterior distribution is asymmetric, one can easily construct an interval that accurately reflects this asymmetry.

Furthermore, when the unknown parameter θ is a vector, the posterior distribution becomes multidimensional. The classical approach to a parameter vector θ is to work with point estimates for each parameter separately, calculate a covariance matrix across parameters (via the Hessian), and rely on asymptotic results to make inferences. The Bayesian tackles the entire multivariate posterior distribution head on, however, by taking large samples from it directly. A few decades ago this was rather difficult to do for real-world data sets and models. Modern computers, along with some sampling techniques that emerged from statistical mechanics problems in physics (e.g., Gibbs sampling, simulated annealing), have revolutionized how an analyst can explore a posterior distribution. As mentioned, the solution turns out to be sampling: One takes a sample as large as one needs from the posterior distribution and uses that sample for inference and model comparison.

It is important to distinguish the Bayesian approach to sampling from the posterior from well-known *resampling* procedures, such as the bootstrap or the jacknife. The Bayesian approach produces samples of the unknown parameters, whereas other approaches to estimation or inference that make use of sampling involve sampling either the observations themselves or quantities from a model fitting procedure. For example, to bootstrap slopes in a regression equation, one can either create bootstrap samples of the original data set and compute regression parameters on each of those bootstrap samples (in which case there are as many regressions as bootstrap samples), or one can take bootstrap samples of the residuals after having fit a regression model to the original data (in which case only one regression is estimated). In neither case is the sampling done from the joint posterior distribution for all unknown model quantities, the cornerstone of Bayesian estimation.

Once the multivariate distribution of the parameter vector θ is in hand, one can use it in creative ways to solve some difficult problems. As mentioned, one can compute the mean or median of the posterior distribution. More interesting, one can compute *functions* of the unknown parameters. For example, one common test used in mediation analysis is the product of two unknown parameters: the slope of the predictor to the mediator and the slope of the mediator to the dependent variable (where the latter slope is computed in the context of a regression that also includes the predictor). The prospect of a well-behaved statistical test on the product of two regression slopes is nearly hopeless using frequentist techniques because it cannot be guaranteed to have a *standard* distribution. But the Bayesian perspective provides a well-behaved and reasonable solution. The analyst simply multiplies the samples of the two regression slopes (i.e., multiplies draws from the posterior distributions for both quantities) and instantly has a new posterior distribution for the product. One can then work with that posterior distribution in the usual way, such as compute the mean or median, or the 2.5% and 97.5% quantiles, to construct an interval that can be used to test the hypothesis that the population product is zero. One works with the posterior distribution directly without having to assume symmetry in the sampling distribution (as the classical approach requires, which is suspect in any case because the distribution of a product of random variables is not, in general, symmetric). Yuan and MacKinnon (2009) in fact provided an introductory account of how to implement this idea for testing mediation in normally distributed data.

It is relatively straightforward to extend this Bayesian approach to mediation to more complicated situations, such as when the mediator or the outcome (or both) involves binary data. In this setting, it is necessary to use a generalized linear model, such as logistic regression, for mediation, and the inference within the classical approach for products of parameters across two such general regressions becomes even more difficult. The Bayesian approach can easily handle mediation models in cases in which predictor, mediator, and outcome are on different scales (such as normally distributed, binary, ordinal, count, or survival data), and it can even be extended into new territories that have not been fully explored within the classical framework (such as a mixture model for mediation in which the analysis partitions the sample into different subgroups exhibiting different mediation patterns). So long as we can sample from the posterior, we can construct any interval or test of interest with little additional effort.

Another example that is relatively simple within the Bayesian approach is the statistical test for a random effect term. Many multilevel modeling programs provide a classical test for the variance for a random effect term against the null value of 0. Unfortunately, the classical test does not apply when testing a parameter at its boundary (i.e., variances are bounded below by 0). So, testing the variance against a null of 0 corresponds to a test that technically does not exist and erroneously produces significant results in all but very small samples. Thus, most tests for the variance of the random effect term that appear in popular programs are, if not overtly incorrect, potentially misleading. Some attempts have been made to address this issue using frequentist methods, but a Bayesian approach handles this problem directly, by yielding the posterior distribution of the variance term under a prior that is properly defined over the feasible range of the variance (a common one being a noninformative prior for the log of the variance). Bayesian testing procedures can compare measures of model fit for a model with a random effect to one without it, akin to the classical likelihood ratio test but valid for testing any set of candidate models against one another, not merely parametrically related (i.e., nested) ones.

Data, Parameters, and Missingness

The shorthand notation of θ to denote the unknown parameters masks the strength of the Bayesian approach. Any and all unknown quantities can be incorporated into the vector θ. For instance, missing data can be construed as unknown parameters and included in θ. The Bayesian practice of estimating the joint distribution enables one to properly capture the effect of missing data on the parameters of interest, such as a mean or regression slope; the overall uncertainty resulting from *all* unknown quantities are jointly modeled. Other unknowns that can enter the vector θ include terms representing random effects and those representing proportions or latent class indicators in mixture models. For each of these features of the Bayesian approach, the entire posterior distribution for all unknowns is estimated: We have not only the point estimate for the missing data but also their posterior distribution, and all other parameters are adjusted for the uncertainty because of the entire *pattern of missingness*. By comparison, the options built into frequentist statistical programs common in psychological analyses—casewise or listwise deletion, or the downright dangerous option to replace missing data by means—appear almost primitive.

Although this chapter lacks space for a full explication of these ideas, one of the major conceptual and computational advantages of the Bayesian approach is its recognition of just two kinds of quantities: Those you know (data) and those you do not know (parameters). Gone are the tedious distinctions between data types, latent variables, limited–censored–truncated, dependent versus independent, missing points or covariates, and the entire menagerie of specialized techniques one must master to deal with them. A Bayesian can simply treat anything not observed as a parameter in the model and, in a rigorous and natural way, numerically integrate over it. So, missing data includes not only literal morsels of unavailable information but also other unobservables such as latent variables or mixing parameters in a mixture model. Using a technique called *data augmentation* that fills in any missing values (which are treated as parameters) on each pass of the numerical simulator, dramatic simplifications in programming the likelihood are possible. As stated, a full description is well beyond the frame of this chapter. In our view, the ability of Bayesian analysis to seamlessly handle missing data is among its most powerful practical advantages, once researchers properly conceptualize the notion of missingness. We refer the interested reader to the classic texts by Little and Rubin (2002) and Gelman, Carlin, Stern, and Rubin (2004).

Techniques for Sampling From the Posterior Distribution

The idea of sampling from the posterior, and using the sample to compute summary measures such as expected value (means) and the distribution of parameters θ, is the modern contribution of the Bayesian framework. Bayesian computations were extremely difficult before this development of dedicated simulation techniques.

The key innovation in the Bayesian toolbox is the general technique of Markov chain Monte Carlo (MCMC) methods. The basic idea is to sample each unknown parameter in turn (including those that reflect missing data), sequentially cycling through each unknown many times, always conditional on the latest draws for all the others. Under fairly general conditions (which are both technical and satisfied in the vast majority of actual research settings), theorems show that the sampling will reach a *stationary distribution* for the parameters of interest. One of the complexities of Bayesian analysis is that one can only rarely sample from the desired posterior distribution immediately because this would require knowing approximately where it is largest. Instead, one can choose a start point at random, let the simulation go, and, usually within several thousand iterations, a stationary distribution is reached, after which everything produced by the simulator can be used for testing, inference, and forecasting.

Several diagnostic tests are available to identify when such a stationary distribution has been reached. Within the Bayesian framework, the stationary distributions are reached by sampling from the so-called conditional densities (i.e., probability densities for one or a set of parameters given specific values for all the others), but the researcher is interested in—and obtains—samples from the entire joint distribution for all unknown quantities (parameters). Samples from the stationary distribution then serve to estimate parameters and the uncertainty in each as well as assess model fit. The availability of the joint distribution allows for tests that are sometimes difficult, or practically impossible, within the standard framework. For example, if one wants to test the distribution of a product of two unknown parameters (a situation that arises in testing mediation models), it is straightforward to have the product distribution merely by multiplying the samples of the two unknown distributions (Yuan & MacKinnon, 2009). Additionally, it is trivial for the researcher to place a priori constraints on parameters, for example, specifying that the covariance matrix for random effects be diagonal or that specific parameters are uncorrelated. This can be done via the prior or within the sampling scheme, simply by setting any parameter or function of them to a specific value, like zero, and sampling for all the others conditional on the constraints. The analogous procedure in a frequentist analysis can be fantastically difficult, as such constraints can wreck asymptotic normality. But this poses no problems for Bayesians, who need not bother about asymptotics and presumptions of standard distributional forms.

Different methods lie within the MCMC family of algorithms, the dominant ones being Gibbs sampling and Metropolis-Hastings sampling. Loosely put, the former is used when conditional densities take "nice" forms (known distributions relatively easy to sample from), the latter when they do not. (For a good review of these methods, see Tanner 1996.) Bayesian algorithm design is complex and technical, so we cannot provide anything close to a complete description of the subject here. We can, however, readily convey the flavor of what is involved in a nontechnical way. The primary goal of Bayesian analysis is generating a sample from the posterior distribution. This means that the probability that a point (i.e., a set of parameter values) is in the sample is proportional to the height of the posterior distribution at that point. Or, more usefully, the ratio of the probability of any two points being in the sample is the ratio of the posteriors at those points. This is very close to the foundational insight of the dominant algorithm, Metropolis-Hastings, used in Bayesian analysis: If one is at a point that has already been accepted into the sample, one jumps to another point on the basis of whether its posterior is higher or lower. If it is higher, one jumps; if not, one jumps with probability related to the ratio of the posteriors. (There are some technicalities involving how one generates potential jumps as well, but this would take us far afield.)

This simple algorithm can, in principle, be used to navigate high-dimensional parameter spaces, that is, to estimate statistical models with dozens or even hundreds of parameters. In practice, there are many techniques used to make it efficient, like jumping along one dimension at a time, taking small steps (which make jumping more likely), and using special schemes to choose where to jump. If one can calculate closed-form expressions for particular densities (describing where to jump), it is possible to prove that one always jumps, eliminating a potentially long series of staying put.

When a large number, usually several tens of thousands, of such jumps have been made, one has that many drawn parameter values that can be used for inference. Unfortunately, these draws are often highly autocorrelated. In simple language, this means they do not jump around the distribution randomly, but rather move across it slowly, because where you jump *to* depends on where you jump *from*. In practice, one solves this problem via *thinning*, that is, by discarding all but every 10th, 20th, or 50th draw (the proportion is chosen by the researcher, using various assessment tools). Even with thinning, the researcher will typically have many thousands of points to use for inference, and this is nearly always sufficient to trace out a close approximation to the true marginal distribution of any subset of parameters of interest, even for missing values (which, as explained, are treated as parameters). And, if one does not have enough draws, it is simple to keep taking more, until one does.

Evaluating the Convergence of the Sampling Process

MCMC methods pose several practical questions that need to be addressed when analyzing data. What starting values should be used to initiate the sampling? How long should the cycle be (i.e., how long the burn-in period should be)? How much thinning should be done? Which algorithms will be efficient in terms of run time?

Rather than provide full answers to all these implementation issues, we will focus on one key aspect of the sampling process: the traceplot. This plot focuses on a single parameter and plots its drawn value against the iteration number. In the previously introduced case of the binomial proportion (of six divorces out of 10 couples), we use MCMC sampling to generate say 10,000 samples from a beta posterior (which arises from the conjugate beta prior and a binomial likelihood). Each of these samples represents a draw from the distribution. They can be plotted against iteration number and one can inspect whether there are systematic deviations or other obvious patterns. One looks for general stability in the traceplot, that is, for little evidence of systematic deviation (e.g., several hundred samples near $\pi = 1$, then several hundred near $\pi = 0$, both of which are endpoint values, indicating extreme deviations from a stable, interior solution). Figure 24.2 represents a well-behaved traceplot resulting from sampling from the posterior beta for our example of six divorces out of 10 couples. The sample was thinned by retaining only every 10th observation, hence 1,000 iterations are plotted out of 10,000 draws.

A more interesting example than estimating a simple proportion is using Bayesian methods to estimate the latent growth curve (we consider a real and more complex implementation of this at length at the conclusion of this chapter). This sort of model allows for two types of heterogeneity, for both slope and intercept (and higher order terms, too, given a sufficient number of time points per individual). Each subject is therefore allowed his or her own slope and intercept, but the regressions are estimated simultaneously both for efficiency and for proper modeling of the error term. The latent growth model can be estimated either in a multilevel

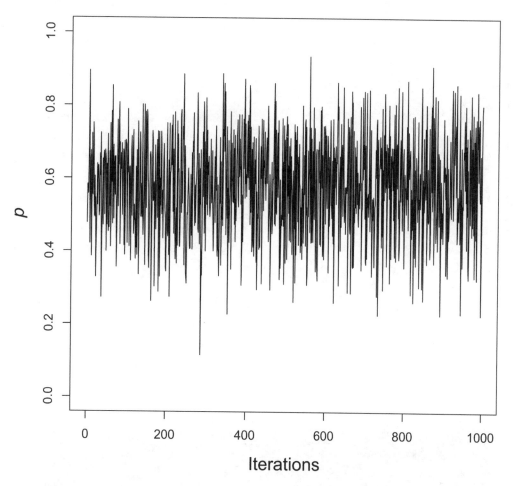

FIGURE 24.2. An example of a traceplot following the posterior density in Figure 24.1. The samples were thinned by 10. This example did not have a burn-in period because the sampling was done directly from the posterior beta with parameters 7 and 5, per the conjugate prior.

model using random terms for the slope and intercept (time points are nested within subject) or in a structural equations model using latent variables for slope and intercept (raw data are the indicators, paths are fixed to correspond to the unit vector for the intercept and the linear contrast for the slope). To illustrate, we borrowed a data set from one of our collaborators, involving four time points. We estimated a latent intercept and latent slope using the Bayesian estimation routine in Amos. The posterior distribution and the traceplot appear in Figure 24.3. We used the default in Amos of 500 iterations to burn-in, then estimated 200,000 samples, thinning by keeping every fourth, and resulting in 50,000 samples (the choice of thinning proportion is left to the researcher on the basis of the autocorrelation of the samples from the posterior; diagnostics appear in many programs to aid in this choice). The

estimate of the linear latent variable is 1.286 (this is the posterior mean); the 95% (credible) interval is (1.214, 1.356). The maximum likelihood estimate for this sample is 1.285 with a standard error of 0.036 (the estimate corresponds to the fixed effect term for the slope in the multilevel model). We do not present the complete output for the other parameters, such as the intercept and the random effect variances and covariances, but similar densities and traceplots are produced for every other parameter.

Model Comparison: Bayes Factors and Deviance Information Criterion

Among the many conceptual and pragmatic difficulties of the classical approach is model comparison. In some sense, determining which model best fits given data is among the key problems in all of

(a)

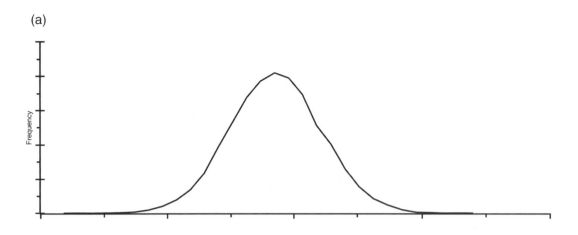

(b)

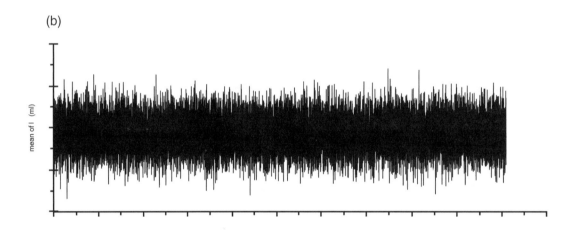

FIGURE 24.3. Example of a latent growth curve model. Results for the mean of the latent variable representing the linear term. The posterior density plot appears in panel (a); the traceplot appears in panel (b).

scientific inference. Although there are a number of specialized approaches to making this determination in classical statistics, they hold primarily for nested models. By contrast, Bayesian inference provides a general procedure for comparing *any* set of candidate models in terms of how well they are supported by the data: the Bayes factor.

Given two models, the Bayes factor quantifies how much more strongly the data favors one model over the other. Its calculation depends on one's ability to determine the so-called marginal likelihood for a model, which can be challenging in practical applications. Philosophically, the procedure is akin to the standard likelihood-ratio (LR) test in classical statistics, although the LR test depends on maximizing both model likelihoods, whereas the Bayes factor averages them over all parameters (via integrating over the prior distribution). Although it is not obvious, this one change pays great benefits: Not only can the Bayes factor compare any two candidate models but it also penalizes overparameterized models for needless complexity, unlike classical methods, which must attempt do so via various post hoc, synthetic measures such as the Akaike information criterion and the Bayesian information criterion, none of which is overtly preferred on theoretical grounds.

Because marginal likelihoods and Bayes factors can be difficult to calculate, Bayesian statisticians have sought other comparison metrics that are easily computed from standard simulation output (i.e., the draws themselves). Among the most promising of these is the deviance information criterion (DIC). DIC sums two terms, the first assessing model lack-of-fit and the second assessing model complexity (i.e., effective number of parameters). Large values of DIC therefore indicate high lack of fit, high complexity, or both, and are therefore a less desirable model. DIC is known to be valid only when the log-likelihood is itself approximately multivariate normal, and thus must be used with caution, although it is built into many Bayesian statistical programs, simplifying model comparison considerably.

Making Predictions

It is often argued, with some justification, that real-world users of statistics have little use for parameters in and of themselves. What real users care about is using a statistical model to run what-if analyses, that is, to make predictions. Predictions can address what will happen for those units (e.g., experimental subjects, longitudinal survey respondents, and so on) already in the data or new units, the likelihood of attrition or missingness, or even the future values of parameters themselves (e.g., Are the animals becoming less sensitive to stimuli over time?). In the classical, frequentist approach, this is done via prediction intervals, at least in the standard regression or general linear models framework. But this, again, is highly dependent on asymptotic normality (or other such distributional assumptions), which may not hold for a particular data set. A secondary issue is that predictions are often made from a frequentist model using point estimates for its parameters, even though those parameters may have a complex, and relatively loose (i.e., high variance), joint distribution of their own.

Once again, the Bayesian approach supplies a complete and conceptually appealing solution to prediction: A prediction is, like everything else, simply a distribution, one that we can calculate from

the posterior (not including the new observation about which we are trying to make predictions), and all available data. In simple terms, we integrate over the posterior of the parameters in the model. In symbols,

$$P\left(Y_{new} \mid Y\right) = \int P\left(Y_{new} \mid \theta\right) P\left(\theta \mid Y\right) d\theta. \qquad (4)$$

This tells us that, if we wish to know the distribution for a *new* observation, Y_{new}, we must consider all the data we already have, Y. And the way to incorporate this existing data is via the posterior probability of the parameters of the model, $P(\theta|Y)$. We simply average this (i.e., integrate) over the entire parameter space, θ. Once we have this *posterior predictive distribution*, $P(Y_{new}|Y)$, we can use it like any other distribution, to calculate means, modes, variance, quartiles, or more exotic functions. There is no guarantee that this predictive distribution will look like any of the standard distributions of elementary statistics. In fact, when this happens, it indicates that the prediction problem would have been difficult or impossible using frequentist tools alone. A simple lesson arising from this example is that the posterior distribution for the parameters, $P(\theta|Y)$, is a powerful object that can be used to readily obtain a great deal more information of use in practical statistical settings, especially so in forecasting.

Learning More About the Bayesian Approach

Many excellent textbooks provide detailed information about Bayesian inference. One of the classics is Box and Tiao (1973/1992), as much a research monograph as a textbook, which has made important contributions to several Bayesian problems. It provided much detail and explanation in deriving theoretical results in a Bayesian framework, although it did not cover modern MCMC-based approaches to Bayesian computation. Similarly, an early paper by Edwards, Lindman, and Savage (1963) made a strong case for use of Bayesian inference in psychological research.

Contemporary approaches to Bayesian estimation rely heavily on MCMC algorithms that sample the joint distribution of parameters. Such Monte Carlo techniques have been adapted to many novel model and data types, and there are excellent textbooks on the details of various Bayesian algorithms (e.g., Robert & Casella, 2004; Tanner, 1996) as well as general introductions (e.g., Congdon, 2003; Gelman et al., 2004; Gill, 2002).

Software

Although software to implement and conduct Bayesian analyses has come about only relatively recently, many choices are presently available. We recognize that software (and associated textbook) recommendations are always a moving target, so we restrict the discussion to current capabilities, with the caveat that these will certainly deepen over time. Among the most general frameworks is the Win-BUGS package (http://www.mrc-bsu.cam.ac.uk/bugs). A recent textbook teaches not only the program but also Bayesian statistics at an accessible level (Ntzoufras, 2009) and supplements two especially accessible, dedicated texts by Congdon (2003, 2007). The textbook by Gelman and Hill (2007) introduces Bayesian thinking and implementation of WinBUGS through the open-source statistics package R (http://www.r-project.org). Several SAS interfaces are available to work with WinBUGS (e.g., Smith & Richardson, 2007; Zhang, McArdle, Wang, & Hamagami, 2008), the multilevel program MLwiN has an interface to WinBUGS. A Microsoft Excel add-in, BugsXLA provides an interface to WinBUGS (http://www.axrf86.dsl.pipex.com/), and the structural equation modeling program Amos has introduced its own internal Bayesian estimation algorithm.

In addition, several books are tied to the statistical package R. These include Rossi, Allenby, and McCulloch (2005), which offers a specialized R package and several applications to marketing; the comprehensive regression textbook by Gelman and Hill (2007), which has several worked examples in R and also shows how to interface R with the dedicated Bayesian package WinBUGS; the introductory book by Gill (2002), which provides both R and WinBUGS code for standard statistical models; and the elementary book by Albert (2007), which does an exceptional job introducing theory and basic R code to implement Bayesian methods.

A welcome recent development is the inclusion of Bayesian tools in SAS, a venerable analysis platform for psychologists. By electing to include a "BAYES" statement, one can conduct Bayesian inference for a wide variety of standard specifications, most notably for generalized linear models, along with various common convergence diagnostics, like the Gelman-Rubin and Geweke. The recent addition of the MCMC procedure allows *user-specified* likelihoods and priors, with parameters that can enter the model in a linear or nonlinear functional manner. This addition literally opens the door for psychologists who wish to "go Bayesian," by allowing them to work within a software environment with which they are already comfortable.

TWO RICHER EXAMPLES ILLUSTRATING THE USEFULNESS OF THE BAYESIAN APPROACH

In this section we discuss two examples that we use to explore, at a deeper level, the concepts presented earlier in this chapter. The first is a general discussion of a canonical problem throughout the social sciences, and the second shows how a Bayesian approach can allow researchers to estimate a fairly complex model, for a real research problem, using modern-day software tools.

Multilevel Models: A Bayesian Take on a Classic Problem

We illustrate how Bayesian ideas can come into play when understanding multilevel or random effect models. Many areas of psychology have seen some form of multilevel or random effect (we will use the terms interchangeably) model come to the forefront in the past decade. Developmental psychologists use multilevel models to account for individual differences in growth-curve trajectories. Clinical psychologists use latent factors to model individual differences in scale response. Cognitive neuroscientists using functional magnetic resonance imaging in their research invoke a two-level model to account for both the intraindividual time course of the blood-oxygen-level dependence response and interindividual differences in parameters. These random effect and multilevel ideas are not new, having been developed actively since the 1940s, if not earlier. They appear in many of the early experimental design textbooks in chapters with such titles as "Random and Nested Effects" (e.g., Winer, 1971). An important special case of this framework is the well-known repeated measures analysis of variance, in which observations are nested within subject, each subject is assigned a parameter, and data are not treated as independent observations. The correlated structure of the repeated measures is modeled through random effect terms.

Among the major limitations of the early developments in random effect and multilevel modeling was that the problem was tractable (in closed form) only for balanced designs—that is, an equal number of subjects across conditions were needed to derive formulas—and for either linear or general linear models. The major advance in the past 20 years has been the development of specialized algorithms to handle the general problem of multilevel and random effect models for a rich variety of model and data types. The new algorithms can work with unequal number of subjects (e.g., not all classrooms have to contain the same number of pupils), missing data, and so-called latent variable formulations (e.g., random utility models) and can accommodate both predictors of the random effect terms and the use of the random effect terms to predict other parameters in the model.

An important issue in working with multilevel and random effect models is that to compute estimates and standard errors, it is necessary to average over the random effect terms. That is, to estimate parameters in the classic statistical framework, it is necessary to compute the likelihood of the data at each value of the hypothesis, weight the likelihood by a function of the value of the hypothesis, and sum the products over all possible hypotheses. Typical data sets involve multiple independent observations, so the overall likelihood is taken as the product of each observation's individual likelihood. The multiplication of likelihoods (one for each observation) is justified because of the independence assumption, just as we multiply the probability of independent coin tosses to compute the joint probability of outcomes over multiple independent coin tosses. In symbols, we denote the product over

multiple observations and use an integral to denote the average over the random effect term

$$\int \prod_i f(y_i \mid u) g(u) du, \tag{5}$$

where the product is taken over observations i, with likelihood $f(y_i|u)$ for a single observation, and distribution $g(u)$ over random effect u. This is a standard way to write the likelihood in the classical approach. One can then use well-known, specialized maximum likelihood techniques to estimate parameters and their standard errors directly from this likelihood (e.g., McCulloch & Searle, 2001), under suitable asymptotic assumptions.

The basic point we want to communicate is that the use of random effects involves some fairly complicated mathematical operations that do not lend themselves to easy descriptions. Expression 5 communicates the notion that there is a kind of averaging over the likelihood, where the likelihoods are weighted by the distribution $g(u)$ of the random effects. Expression 5 presents some difficult computational challenges, too. It is necessary to use specialized numerical algorithms to maximize this kind of likelihood, which contains an integral, and compute terms necessary in the classical framework, such as standard errors of the parameter estimates. There are several ways of performing a maximization over such an average, including quadrature methods and Laplace transforms, each with its pros and cons (e.g., McCulloch & Searle, 2001).

We use Expression 5 to make a simple point about the relation between Bayesian and classical methods. Expression 5 highlights a difficulty that has plagued statisticians for decades, spurring a cottage industry of ingenious computational techniques, all to more efficiently compute multilevel and random effect model parameters. Although frequentist statisticians have made great strides in surmounting the challenges that Expression 5 presents, it nonetheless entails a nasty integral, one that makes it impossible to write general, closed-form solutions, such as with unequal sample sizes or errors that are not normally distributed.

Bayesians looking at Expression 5 immediately spot a connection to a concept highly tractable within their framework. Expression 5 is proportional to the posterior distribution (e.g., Rossi & Allenby, 2003):

$$p(u \mid y) \propto \int \prod_i f(y_i \mid u) g(u) du. \qquad (6)$$

Although the classical statistician looks at the right-hand side of Equation 6 and frets about developing numerical procedures to maximize over a thorny integral, the Bayesian statistician instantly knows how to work with it, via well-established techniques for sampling from posterior distributions, such as MCMC. In addition, a set of useful tools for selecting a model, handling missing data, and assessing predictions comes along with the approach. There are a few drawbacks to the Bayesian approach. These include, for instance, having to write specialized code for specific problems (except for the simplest problems, one gives up the canned, off-the-shelf statistical package concept), work with new concepts that emerge from algorithms that use stochastic simulation, and choose a prior distribution. We do not view these as deal-breakers for using the Bayesian approach, as such issues also arise in a classical setting. For example, in a frequentist analysis, one assumes an underlying distribution and makes simplifying assumptions, such as equality of variances, to make a problem tractable; in a Bayesian setting, one selects a prior distribution. There are parallels in both cases, and in mathematical models one never completely gets away from assumptions. The key issue concerns which assumptions are more reasonable to make, which assumptions become irrelevant because of robustness issues, and which model makes difficult problems tractable.

We like this multilevel modeling example because it illustrates that there is a connection between the classical and Bayesian approaches in the case of random effect and multilevel models. The approaches turn out to be very similar: The classical statistician chooses to work with the right-hand side of Equation 6 and tackles the nasty integral directly, whereas the Bayesian chooses to work with the left-hand side, samples the posterior distribution to estimate parameters, and uses the posterior distribution to assess parametric uncertainty. They both work with the same idea; they just approach it using different methods, which we view as one of the major lessons of this chapter.

Research Example

To illustrate the power of Bayesian analysis, we present an example from recent work. We choose this example not only because it involves a data type—intent, measured on an ordinal scale—common in psychological research but also because all data and programs for analysis are freely available. The website http://cumulativetimedintent.com contains illustrative data in several formats, along with Bayesian and classical code in WinBUGS, MLwiN, and SAS, so the reader can verify directly what each approach, and program, offers in an applied context.

At the heart of the project was a need to better predict what people would purchase on the basis of their stated intentions. Studies relating intentions to behavior have been conducted for many years. The study we examine here (van Ittersum & Feinberg, 2010) introduced a new technique for eliciting individuals' intentions, by asking them to state their intent at multiple time periods on a probability scale. For example, "What is the likelihood (on an imposed 0%, 10%, 20%, . . . , 90%, 100% scale) you will have purchased this item 6 (and 12, 18, 24) months from now"? Each respondent's data looks like an increasing sequence of stated, scaled probabilities, over time. That is, can we merely *ask* people when they might purchase something and relate it, statistically, to whether and when they actually do?

In essence, this is a random effect model, but one not handled out of the box by classical estimation software. It is, however, especially amenable to Bayesian treatment. Of note for psychologists is that we can posit that each individual has some growth curve, which is taken to be linear in time (and perhaps other predictor variables as well). The key is how to relate these individual-level, latent growth curves to (a) the observable (stated probability on an ordinal scale), (b) covariates, and (c) one another. It turns out that each of these is natural in the Hierarchical Bayes approach, which is nothing more than a (nonlinear) hierarchical model, estimated using Bayesian techniques.

Suppose that the latent adoption *propensity* for subject i at time t is given by a simple linear expression,

$$Propensity_{it} = \beta_0 + \beta_1 t. \tag{7}$$

This specifies how the propensity changes over time for an individual but not how it varies *across* individuals. This is accomplished via a heterogeneity, or multilevel, model,

$$\beta_{1i} = \Delta z_i + u_i \tag{8}$$

$$u_i \sim N(0, \Omega_u). \tag{9}$$

This models slopes (β_{1i}) as a function of individual-level covariates (z_i) and coefficients (Δ). So-called unobserved heterogeneity, represented by u_i, is presumed normal, its degree measured by Ω_u. So far, this is exactly in keeping with standard practice in hierarchical linear models (HLM) and would in fact be equivalent to the standard formulation—which is amenable to frequentist analysis—except that we do not observe the propensity directly, but something related to it, with measurement error. Specifically, propensity, on an unbounded scale, must be functionally related to adoption probability on the unit scale. We choose a probit transform because of its conjugacy properties for Bayesian analysis:

$$\pi_{it} = \Phi(Propensity_{it}). \tag{10}$$

Because this resulting probability (π_{it}) is continuous, but our observable stated intent lies on a discrete scale, one more model stage is required. Given probability π_{it}, we can employ an especially parsimonious transformation, the *rank-ordered binomial*, to map from continuous latent, to discrete $(1, \ldots, K)$ observed, probabilities, which in this example has $K = 11$ (and values 0%, 10%, . . . , 100%):

$$p(Y_{it} = k) = \binom{K-1}{k-1} \pi_{it}^{k-1} (1 - \pi_{it})^{K-k}, k = 1, \ldots, K. \tag{11}$$

Conjoining all model stages yields the following hierarchical Bayes formulation:

Level I : $p(Y_{it} = k) = \binom{K-1}{k-1} \pi_{it}^{k-1} (1 - \pi_{it})^{K-k}, k = 1, \ldots, K$

$$Probit(\pi_{it}) = \beta_0 + \beta_1 t \tag{12}$$

Level II : $\beta_{1i} = \Delta z_i + u_i$

$$u_i \sim N(0, \Omega_u). \tag{13}$$

Whereas early Bayesian analyses would have required tedious specialized derivations and laborious programming, models like this one can be accommodated in dedicated software, with programs written in statistical language directly. Here, for illustration, we use MLwiN as a Bayesian computation platform (all code is posted at http://cumulativetimedintent.com). Coupled with noninformative priors, the resulting output includes samples from the posterior density for all model parameters. Automatically generated diagnostics help determine model convergence and provide plots of all marginal distributions, which do *not* have to be normal. Formal hypothesis testing proceeds off these density plots, without any distribution assumptions.

For example, we may wish to make inferences about parameters in both the Level II (heterogeneity, or dealing with the distribution of individual-level parameters) and Level I (dealing with individuals' parameters, or latent growth curves) models. Actual MLwiN output for this model, using real data, includes the following, which the program provides written in full statistical notation:

$probit(\pi_{it}) = -1.907(0.026)CONS + \beta_{1i} t$

$\beta_{1i} = 0.733(0.056) + u_{1i}$

$[u_{1i}] \sim N(0, \Omega_u): \Omega_u = [0.508(0.068)]$

PRIOR SPECIFICATIONS

$P(\beta_0) \propto 1$

$P(\beta_1) \propto 1$

$p\left(\dfrac{1}{\sigma_{u1}^2}\right) \sim Gamma(0.001, 0.001).$

All parts of the model are immediately recognizable as well as the estimated values of both the Level I and Level II parameters, with standard errors in parentheses. These are not merely point estimates in the usual sense, but the result of having taken 100,000 draws from the entire posterior distribution. The program automatically obtains the marginal distribution for each parameter of interest, and uses it to calculate the parameter's mean and variance, with the critical distinction that the variance is *not* merely an approximation from the Hessian (as in frequentist analyses) but rather comes from the entire marginal distribution directly.

The program also shows that it uses noninformative priors for the regression parameters (β_0 and β_1), and a mildly informative (i.e., very high variance) inverse gamma prior, a popular choice, for the variance (σ_{u1}^2).

We might interpret the model as follows. Each individual has a latent propensity to purchase (π_{it}), and the probit transform of that probability is linear in Time, with an intercept of −1.907 ($SE = 0.026$), and a coefficient (β_{1i}) with a mean of 0.733

($SE = 0.056$). However, there is some degree of *variation* in the value of this coefficient across respondents. The mean across respondents, as we have seen, is 0.733, but the variance is estimated to be 0.508 (standard error: 0.068). We would also wish to check that the traceplot for each of these parameters looked reasonable, meaning like a sequence of independent draws, with no patterns obvious to the eye. These appear in Figure 24.4, also as generated automatically in MLwiN, for the last 10,000 draws for each parameter (we have also included a kernel density for the variance and, as would be expected, it is not symmetric). Because we can access all these

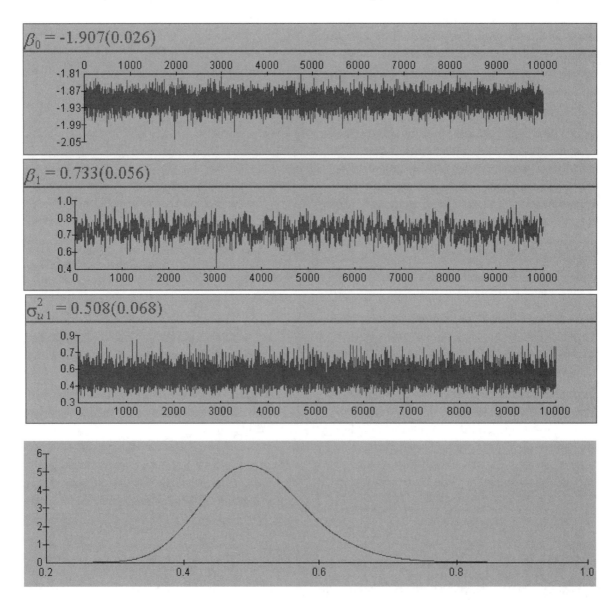

FIGURE 24.4. Traceplots for three parameters from a latent purchase intent model, with a kernel density for the variance, generated in MLwiN.

draws, and indeed have them for each of the respondent's individual slope coefficients (β_{1i}), we can calculate latent growth curves for each, error bars around them, and in fact *any* function of their parameters, all by operating on the posterior draws directly.

Although this model would not be impossible to estimate using classical techniques—indeed, one can program it using PROC NLMIXED in SAS, with some patience, by writing out the model likelihood directly—the Bayesian approach allows all parameters of interest to be calculated to any desired degree of accuracy. Moreover, we obtain a *distribution* for each of these parameters, and an arbitrarily large number of draws from each one. In practical terms, this means that the analyst is freed from making any assumptions about the asymptotic behavior of parameters and can perform on-the-fly postestimation tests on complex functions of the problem's parameters. This is completely beyond what frequentist techniques can offer, yet it is natural and straightforward using Bayesian estimation.

CONCLUSION

Some readers will get the sense that our views about Bayesian statistics are not entirely mainstream. Partisans will undoubtedly feel we did not portray their vantage point with sufficient detail. The classical statistician may take issue with superficial attention to the problem of defining one's prior. "Ambiguity over selecting a prior distribution is the Achilles' heel of the Bayesian approach," a classically inclined researcher may say. Bayesians may be incensed that we lump their elegant, comprehensive formalism with the classical approach by saying they both act the same when the Bayesian assumes a noninformative prior. "But you miss the important differences between how we interpret the results," will be shouted from the Bayesian rooftops. Let us be the first to acknowledge that some of the subtle details have been omitted. But that was completely intentional. We want to bring more researchers to the discussion, expose more people to the underpinnings of both classical and Bayesian approaches, and show researchers some new tools. We believe (and we have a pretty sharp prior on that belief) that the best way to accomplish this is by outlining the similarities of the approaches and the advantages each offers.

We hope this chapter has been a readable and accessible introduction to the basic notions of Bayesian statistics and that it provides a straightforward way to formulate some of the tools that the Bayesian tradition offers. In these relatively few pages we cannot cover all the ins and outs of conducting different types of Bayesian analyses—there are books that do that. If the reader's interest is piqued sufficiently to seek out some of the reference books and explore some of the software we mention, then this chapter has been successful.

Some areas of psychology have already started to apply modern Bayesian methods. For example, new models in item response theory have used Bayesian ideas to estimate multivariate, multilevel, second-order, item-response theory models (e.g., Duncan & MacEachern, 2008; Fox & Glas, 2001; Sheng & Wikle, 2008). We hope these and other examples will provide the inspiration to seek new ways to test your research ideas and that Bayesian methods provide some useful tools to carry out those tests.

References

Albert, J. (2007). *Bayesian computation with R*. New York, NY: Springer. doi:10.1007/978-0-387-71385-4

Box, G. E. P., & Tiao, G. C. (1992). *Bayesian inference in statistical analysis*. New York, NY: Wiley. (Original work published 1973)

Congdon, P. (2003). *Applied Bayesian modelling*. Chichester, England: Wiley. doi:10.1002/0470867159

Congdon, P. (2007). *Bayesian statistical modelling* (2nd ed.). Chichester, England: Wiley.

Duncan, K., & MacEachern, S. (2008). Nonparametric Bayesian modeling for item response. *Statistical Modelling, 8*, 41–66. doi:10.1177/1471082X0700800104

Edwards, W., Lindman, H., & Savage, L. (1963). Bayesian statistical inference for psychological research. *Psychological Review, 70*, 193–242. doi:10.1037/h0044139

Fox, J.-P., & Glas, C. (2001). Bayesian estimation of a multilevel IRT model using Gibbs sampling. *Psychometrika, 66*, 271–288. doi:10.1007/BF02294839

Gelman, A., Carlin, J. B., Stern, H. S., & Rubin, D. B. (2004). *Bayesian data analysis* (2nd ed.). Boca Raton, FL: Chapman & Hall.

Gelman, A., & Hill, J. (2007). *Data analysis using regression and multilevel/hierarchical models*. New York, NY: Cambridge University Press.

Gill, J. (2002). *Bayesian methods: A social and behavioral sciences approach*. Boca Raton, FL: Chapman & Hall.

Jaynes, E. (1986). Bayesian methods: General background. In J. H. Justice (Ed.), *Maximum entropy and Bayesian methods in applied statistics* (pp. 1–25). Cambridge, England: Cambridge University Press. doi:10.1017/CBO9780511569678.003

Little, R., & Rubin, D. (2002). *Statistical analysis with missing data* (2nd ed.). New York, NY: Wiley.

McCulloch, C. E., & Searle, S. R. (2001). *Generalized, linear, and mixed models*. New York, NY: Wiley.

Ntzoufras, I. (2009). *Bayesian modeling using WINBUGS*. Hoboken, NJ: Wiley. doi:10.1002/9780470434567

Robert, C., & Casella, G. (2004). *Monte Carlo statistical methods*. New York, NY: Springer.

Rossi, P. E., & Allenby, G. M. (2003). Bayesian statistics and marketing. *Marketing Science, 22*, 304–328. doi:10.1287/mksc.22.3.304.17739

Rossi, P. E., Allenby, G. M., & McCulloch, R. (2005). *Bayesian statistics and marketing*. Chichester, England: Wiley.

Sheng, Y., & Wikle, C. (2008). Bayesian multidimensional IRT models with a hierarchical structure. *Educational and Psychological Measurement, 68*, 413–430. doi:10.1177/0013164407308512

Smith, M. K., & Richardson, H. (2007). WinBUGSio: A SAS macro for the remote execution of WinBUGS. *Journal of Statistical Software, 23*, 1–10.

Tanner, M. A. (1996). *Tools for statistical inference: Methods for the exploration of posterior distributions and likelihood functions*. New York, NY: Springer.

van Ittersum, K., & Feinberg, F. M. (2010). Cumulative timed intent: A new predictive tool for technology adoption. *Journal of Marketing Research, 47*, 808–822.

Winer, B. J. (1971). *Statistical principles in experimental design* (2nd ed.). New York, NY: McGraw-Hill.

Yuan, Y., & MacKinnon, D. P. (2009). Bayesian mediation analysis. *Psychological Methods, 14*, 301–322. doi:10.1037/a0016972

Zhang, Z., McArdle, J., Wang, L., & Hamagami, F. (2008). A SAS interface for Bayesian analysis with WinBUGS. *Structural Equation Modeling, 15*, 705–728. doi:10.1080/10705510802339106

Part IV

DESIGNS INVOLVING EXPERIMENTAL MANIPULATIONS

Designs With Different Participant Assignment Mechanisms

CHAPTER 25

TYPES OF DESIGNS USING RANDOM ASSIGNMENT

Larry Christensen

Designs that use random assignment have generally been attributed to the British biometrician Ronald A. Fisher (1928). It is true that Fisher repeatedly stressed the need to randomly assign subjects to groups to validly apply the statistical technique of analysis of variance. Random assignment of subjects to groups, however, predated the development of the designs Fisher discussed.

Active experimentation and comparing the performance of experimental and control groups has been a tradition in psychological research from about the 1870s when researchers were conducting psychophysical studies (Dehue, 2001). Psychophysical researchers even constructed randomized orders to control for subject expectations of which stimuli would be presented next (Dehue, 1997). It was not until the 1920s, however, that random assignment of subjects to experiment and control conditions was proposed as a way to cancel out unwanted variation (Dehue, 2001). The emphasis that Fisher (1935) placed on the need for random assignment to validly apply his statistical technique and his elaboration of designs using random assignment provided a forceful argument and encouraged researchers to not only make use of the designs he elaborated on but also to use random assignment of subjects to treatment conditions.

The arguments made by Fisher (1935) and the credible evidence that these designs have produced are supported by the fact that such designs are considered to be the gold standard in the field of medicine for identifying causal relationships (Salmond, 2008) and that various government agencies have given priority to studies using such designs (Donaldson, 2009). This is because designs using random assignment have high internal validity, although they are not immune from all threats. These designs are presented in this chapter. Before presenting the randomized designs, I present two basic types of experimental designs because the characteristics of these two designs are components of the various designs that use random assignment.

BASIC EXPERIMENTAL RESEARCH DESIGNS

Research design refers to the outline, plan, or strategy that is used to seek an answer to a research question. Experimental designs are designs that represent the outline, plan, or strategy used to identify causal relationships. To accomplish this purpose and to be considered an experimental design, this plan or strategy must incorporate control over all components of the study, including the assignment of participants to groups, determination of who gets what treatment condition and in what order, and how much or what type of treatment each participant gets. In other words, the researcher must have control over all facets of the experiment to identify a causal relationship between the independent and dependent variables. Researchers use two basic types of designs when conducting experimental studies. They are typically referred to as between- and within-subjects designs.

DOI: 10.1037/13620-025
APA Handbook of Research Methods in Psychology: Vol. 2. Research Designs, H. Cooper (Editor-in-Chief)

Between-Subjects Design

The *between-subjects design* is an experimental research design that is characterized by the fact that each treatment condition is administered to a different group of subjects. For example, if a study was investigating the efficacy of three different drugs for treating depression, a different group of depressed individuals would receive each of the three drugs as illustrated in Figure 25.1. From Figure 25.1 you can see that the between-subjects design is comparing the effectiveness of three drugs, but the effectiveness of the drugs is made by comparing the effect each drug has on a different group of subjects. This hypothetical study is seeking to answer the question of which drug is most effective in treating depression *between* different groups of subjects. Hence the label *between-subjects design.*

Within-Subjects or Repeated-Measures Design

A *within-subjects design* is an experimental design in which each subject participates in every treatment condition as illustrated in Figure 25.2. All subjects are, therefore, repeatedly measured under all treatment conditions, which is why this design is also referred to as a *repeated-measures design.* From Figure 25.2 you can see that the within-subjects design is comparing the effectiveness of the three drugs by comparing the effect each drug has on the same group of subjects. The same group of subjects would first take Drug A, then Drug B, and then Drug C and the effect of each drug would be assessed at a predetermined time after consumption and before

Drug A	Drug B	Drug C
s_1	s_1	s_1
s_2	s_2	s_2
s_3	s_3	s_3
s_4	s_4	s_4
s_5	s_5	s_5
.	.	.
.	.	.
s_n	s_n	s_n

Same subjects in
all treatment
conditions

FIGURE 25.2.   Within-subjects design. Same subjects in all three drug conditions.

consuming the next drug. When using a within-subjects design the question being asked is, "Which drug is most effective *within* the same group of subjects"? Hence the label *within-subjects design.*

Advantages and Limitations of the Between- and Within-Subjects Designs

The between- and within-subjects designs represent the basic experimental designs used by researchers. Although they are both excellent designs, each has limitations and advantages. The between-subjects design has the advantages of being relatively easy to understand, being easy to design and analyze, and requiring the smallest number of statistical assumptions (Keppel & Wickens, 2004). The primary disadvantage of the between-subjects design is that each of the treatment conditions has different subjects. This one characteristic of the between-subjects design has two related implications. The first is that more subjects are needed when using this design versus the within-subjects design. The second is that there is more variability in the data because the between-subjects design does not allow the researcher to identify and control for the variability that exists between different subjects. This increased

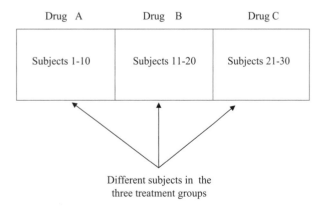

Different subjects in the
three treatment groups

FIGURE 25.1.   Illustration of a between-subjects design. Different subjects in each of the three drug conditions.

variability means that the between-subjects design is not as sensitive as the within-subjects design in terms of detecting a true treatment effect.

The within-subjects design has advantages over the between-subjects design in terms of creating equivalence of subjects in the various treatment groups, increasing the sensitivity of the study to detecting a treatment effect and in economy of subjects. The advantage in terms of economy of subjects is readily apparent because the number of subjects needed in a between-subjects design is equal to the number needed in one treatment condition times the number of treatment conditions. The number of subjects needed in a within-subjects study is equal to the number needed in one experimental treatment condition because all subjects participate in all treatment conditions. A study investigating the relative effectiveness of three drugs might require that each drug be administered to 20 subjects. If a between-subjects design were used, 60 subjects would be needed to complete the study. Only 20 subjects would be needed using a within-subjects design, however, because the same subjects would receive each of the three drugs.

When using a within-subjects design, there is no need to worry about equivalence of the subjects in the various treatment conditions because the same subjects are used in every treatment condition. Therefore, there is perfect matching of the subjects in all treatment conditions. In other words, the subjects serve as their own control because variables such as age, gender, prior experience, and motivation remain constant over the entire experiment.

The within-subjects design also has the advantage of being more sensitive to detecting a real treatment effect because subjects serve as their own control. When the same subjects participate in every treatment condition, there is less variability in the data from one treatment condition to the next because variation caused by individual differences between subjects is statistically isolated in the data analysis. This decreased variability has the effect of reducing the size of the error term in the statistical test, which increases the probability of a real treatment effect being detected. This increased sensitivity to detecting a real effect makes the within-subjects design a popular choice when it can be used effectively.

With all of these advantages, one might think that the within-subjects design is the experimental design of choice. However, the within-subjects design has some rather significant limitations. One limitation is that the statistical assumptions of this design are more complicated than the between-subjects design (Keppel & Wickens, 2004). From a design perspective, another limitation is perhaps more serious. The most serious limitation of the within-subjects design is that it is open to the confounding influence of a sequencing effect. A *sequencing* effect is an effect that occurs when the same subjects participate in more than one treatment condition. There are actually two different types of sequencing effects that can occur. An *order* sequencing effect arises from the order in which the treatment conditions are administered. As a subject participates in first one and then another treatment condition, they may experience increased fatigue, boredom, and familiarity with or practice with reacting to the independent variable or responding to the dependent variable. Any of these conditions could affect the subjects' responses to the dependent variable and confound the results of the study. It is important to remember that the changes in the subjects' responses caused by order sequencing effects are independent of the actual treatment condition or the sequence in which the treatment conditions are administered. Order effects occur in the same ordinal position regardless of the sequence in which the treatment conditions are administered.

The second type of sequencing effect is a carry-over effect. A *carry-over* effect occurs when the effect of one treatment does not dissipate before the presentation of the next treatment effect but rather carries over and influences the response to the next treatment condition. For example, a carry-over effect would exist if subjects were given Drug A and Drug A was still having an effect on the subjects when they were given Drug B. The measured effect of Drug B, therefore, would include the effect of Drug B plus the effect of Drug A that was carried over to the Drug B treatment condition.

There are experiments, such as learning, transfer of training, and forgetting experiments, in which carry-over and order effects are expected and desirable. In most studies, however, these sequencing effects are confounding variables that must be controlled. The most common way of controlling for sequencing effects is to incorporate some form of counterbalancing in the design of the study. Counterbalancing is an effective method of control when sequencing effects are linear. When nonlinear carryover effects occur, counterbalancing is not an effective method of control. For a more in-depth discussion of counterbalancing, see Christensen (2007).

BASIC RANDOMIZED DESIGN

The *basic randomized design* is a design in which a group of subjects are randomly assigned to either an experimental or control condition. The response of the subjects in these two conditions on the dependent variable is then compared to determine whether the treatment condition produced different results than existed in the control condition as illustrated in Figure 25.3. If a statistically significant difference does exist, then it is inferred that the treatment condition caused the difference. A randomized design is, therefore, a between-subjects design that incorporates random assignment of subjects to the various treatment conditions. Stotts, Schmitz, Rhoades, and Grabowski (2001) provided a good illustration of this design in their study investigating the use of a brief motivational interview to help patients complete a detoxification program and improve the outcome of a subsequent treatment program. Individuals who contacted the Treatment Research Clinic were randomly assigned to either receive or not receive the motivational interview before being admitted to the detoxification program. They were then assessed on outcome variables such as the percentage of participants who completed the detoxification program and percentage of participants who submitted cocaine-negative urine samples during the relapse prevention sessions.

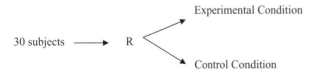

FIGURE 25.3. Structural representation of the basic randomized design. R indicates random assignment of subjects to treatment conditions.

It is the random assignment of subjects to the treatment conditions that makes this design so powerful because it is this component that provides maximum assurance of eliminating the effect of confounding extraneous variables. Random assignment of subjects to treatment conditions is such an important component because it is essential that the subjects in the experimental and control conditions be as similar as possible at the outset of the study to make a credible causal inference. The reason the control and experimental groups must be very similar at the outset of the experiment is because the control condition represents the effect that exists in the absence of the experimental treatment. Only by comparing the effect of the absence of the treatment (control condition) with the presence of the treatment (experimental condition) can an inference be made about the effect of the treatment condition.

For the control condition to function effectively as a contrasting condition, it must be as similar as possible to the experimental group on all variables that could affect the observed outcome. This means that you must identify the variables that need to be controlled and maximally ensure that the control and experimental group are as similar as possible on all of these variables. For example, if you were conducting a study testing the effect of a particular type of psychotherapy in treating depression, the experimental condition would involve the administration of the psychotherapeutic technique to depressed individuals and the control condition would involve an absence of the psychotherapeutic technique. However, many other variables other than the psychotherapeutic technique could affect the outcome of the experiment. Variables such as the time spent with a therapist, the attention provided by the therapist, the fact that the participants are paying for a service and may be given tasks to accomplish between therapy sessions, the severity of the depression experienced by the participants, whether they have experienced prior depressive episodes, whether they have previously been treated for depression and any other differences that may exist between the research participants age, gender, or family support could also affect the outcome of such a study. Such variables must be controlled.

The key issue is identification of what needs to be controlled. This is an important issue in all studies because it is impossible to identify all variables that could have an affect on the outcome of the experiment. There are many types of control groups that could be formed to account for many of the extraneous variables. Shadish et al. (2002) and Nock, Janis, and Wedig (2008) provided excellent discussions of control groups and various types of control groups that are appropriate to different experimental situations. Selection of the appropriate control group is essential for eliminating many of the threats to internal validity. Although an appropriately constructed control group is needed to control for many extraneous variables, there are many variables on which subjects differ such as age, gender, intelligence, and various personality characteristics that are not effectively controlled just by including a control group. Without controlling for such variables, a selection bias may exist in the study.

The most important method for controlling a selection bias is random assignment of subjects to the experimental and control groups because this is the only procedure that controls for both known and unknown sources of variation. The term *random* refers to the equiprobability of events. *Random assignment* refers to any procedure that assigns subjects to the comparison groups on the basis of chance. Random assignment, therefore, not only assigns the subjects to the various comparison groups by chance but all of the characteristics and variables associated with these subjects such as their age, level of motivation, and prior social experiences. This means that comparison groups that are created by means of random assignment will have the greatest probability of being similar to each other on both known and unknown sources of variation. The various comparison groups will, on average, be similar at the outset of the study, which means that any differences observed between the various groups at the end of the study are likely to be due to the treatment effect. A researcher can, therefore, draw a causal inference because the samples are "randomly similar to each other" (Shadish et al., 2002, p. 248) on all variables except the treatment condition.

One additional characteristics of the basic randomized design is that it does not include a pretest but rather relies on the random assignment of subjects to provide assurance that the experimental and control groups are similar. This is a reasonable assumption if the study includes a sufficiently large number of subjects. The absence of a pretest is also desirable if pretesting might sensitize the subjects to the experimental treatment condition because such sensitization could potentially alter the outcome.

Although the absence of a pretest is important in some studies, in others, the inclusion of a pretest is important. For example, attrition is a common occurrence in many field and therapy studies. *Attrition* occurs when subjects who are scheduled for participation in a study do not complete the study because they either fail to show up at the scheduled time and place or do not complete all phases of the study. Attrition is a problem because, it can compromise the benefit derived from random assignment. Random assignment creates similar groups of subjects at the outset of an experiment, and this similarity is assumed to carry over to the posttest. However, when attrition exists in a study the presumed equivalence probably does not carry over to posttesting because attrition cannot be assumed to be a random event. This means that attrition is differential or that the characteristics of the subjects that drop out from the various treatment groups are different. It is when differential attrition occurs that the benefit that is derived from random assignment is compromised and it can no longer be assumed that the subjects in the various treatment groups were similar at the outset of the experiment. The consequence of this is that there are nonrandom correlates of attrition that may influence the dependent variable and thereby contribute to any difference that may exist between the experimental and control conditions. In such situations, the ability to infer that the treatment condition produced the observed group differences at posttesting is compromised.

Obviously the best situation is to conduct an experiment in which attrition does not occur. In many studies, however, attrition is a fact of life. For example, in the beginning stages of a study investigating the influence of added sugar and caffeine on depression (Christensen & Burrows, 1990), attrition was such a dominant issue that the researchers had to request that subjects provide a $50 deposit to participate in the study. This dramatically reduced attrition. When attrition does occur, it is important to understand the extent to which it threatens the internal validity of the study. Shadish et al. (2002) discussed several methods for analyzing the effect of attrition. These methods make use of pretest scores, which is another reason why pretesting is important in some studies. If pretesting is part of the experimental design you plan to use, random assignment of subjects to the comparison groups is still essential to have the most robust experiment.

The advantage of this basic randomized design is the fact that it includes a control group and that subjects are randomly assigned to the comparison groups. These two factors provide maximum control of threats to the internal validity of the experiments. However, Bickman and Reich (2009) correctly pointed out that all threats to internal validity are not controlled in this design. It is also true that, although random assignment maximizes the probability of control of confounding extraneous variables, this assurance is not guaranteed. Even with random assignment of subjects, it is possible that the needed control of extraneous confounding variables has not been accomplished. This is particularly true when the number of subjects being randomly assigned is small. Additionally, this is not the most sensitive design for detecting the effect of the independent variable, which means that a larger number of subjects are required to obtain the needed sensitivity. In spite of this, randomized designs are generally thought of as providing more credible evidence of causal relationships than other designs because they reduce the likelihood of systematic bias. This is

why such designs are considered to be the gold standard to be used in treatment outcome research in fields such as medicine (Blair, 2004) and several U.S. federal agencies have decided that randomized control trials should be a factor to be considered in funding of research (Bickman & Reich, 2009). However, this opinion is not universally accepted (see Scriven, 2009).

The basic randomized design demonstrates its important characteristics for controlling threats to internal validity. I now discuss some of the extensions and variants of this basic design.

Multilevel Randomized Design

The simplest extension of the basic randomized design is a *multilevel randomized design* or a design that has more than two levels of the independent variable in which level refers to the number of different variations of the independent variable. There are many situations in which it would be appropriate to investigate a number of different levels of a single independent variable. Drug research is one area for which it would be advantageous to determine not only whether the drug produced a result different than a placebo (or different drug) condition but also whether differing amounts of the experimental drug produced different reactions. In such a case, subjects would be randomly assigned to as many groups as there were experimental drug and control conditions. If there were four drug groups in addition to the control condition, or five levels of variation of the drug, subjects would be randomly assigned to five groups as illustrated in Figure 25.4.

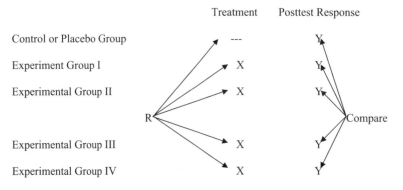

FIGURE 25.4. Multilevel randomized design with five levels of variation of the independent variable. R indicates that the subjects were randomly assigned to groups, X refers to the treatment condition, and Y refers to the posttest response.

A statistical test would then be used to determine whether any difference existed in the average responses of the subjects in the four groups.

This type of study is often called a *dose-response study* as it provides a response to different dosages of the drug. The advantage of such a study is that it provides a more fine-grained assessment of the effect of different drug dosages. It also allows one to detect effects that might be missed if only two dosages were tested because the different dosages might not produce significant differences.

An excellent example of the use of the multilevel randomized design is the National Institute of Mental Health Treatment of Depression Collaborative Program (Elkin, Parloff, Hadley, & Autry, 1985) investigating the relative efficacy of two forms of psychotherapy and pharmacotherapy in the treatment of depression. Two hundred thirty-nine outpatients diagnosed with a current episode of major depression were randomly assigned to receive interpersonal psychotherapy, cognitive–behavior therapy, pharmacotherapy (imipramine) plus clinical management, or a control that also included clinical management.

The multilevel randomized design is excellent for investigating the effect that exists from varying a number of different levels of one independent variable. The multilevel randomized design, however, provides only a one-dimensional view of behavior. In most psychology research, we are interested in the effect of several independent variables acting independently or in concert to provide a richer multidimensional view of behavior. Randomized designs that investigate the effect of two or more independent

variables, each of which has at least two levels of variation, are called *factorial designs*.

Factorial Designs

A *factorial design* is a design that investigates the independent and interactive effect of two or more independent variables on the dependent variable. In this design, the independent variables are referred to as *factors*. For example, assume you wanted to compare the effect of three different mood states (depressive, normal, and elated) and two different learning styles (visual and spatial) on recall of material studied for an hour. In this hypothetical study, there are two factors: mood state (or Factor A) and learning styles (or Factor B). The different variations of each factor are referred to as *levels* of the factor. Figure 25.5, which depicts this design, reveals that there are three different variations of the mood state factor so there are three levels of this factor, A_1, A_2, and A_3. There are two levels of the learning style factor because this factor includes two different learning styles: B_1 and B_2. Therefore, this design has six combinations of the two factors: A_1B_1, A_1B_2, A_2B_1, A_2B_2, A_3B_1, and A_3B_2. When a factorial design contains all possible combinations of the two factors, such as is the case with this design, it is referred to as a *completely crossed design*.

The description of a factorial design is often based on the number of factors included and the number of levels of each of the factors. In this example, there are two factors with three levels of one factor and two levels of the other factor so this design would be described as a 3×2 factorial design. If the design included a third factor with two levels of the

Mood State Factor

	Depressed	Normal	Elated
	(A_1)	(A_2)	(A_3)

Learning Style	Spatial (B_1)	A_1 B_1	A_2 B_1	A_3 B_1
Factor	Visual (B_2)	A_1 B_2	A_2 B_2	A_3 B_2

FIGURE 25.5. Illustration of a factorial design with three levels of one factor (mood state) and two levels of a second factor (learning style).

third factor, then the design would be described as a 3 × 2 × 2 factorial design.

Each one of the treatment combinations in a factorial design is referred to as a *cell*. Thus, in the design depicted in Figure 25.5, there are six cells. Subjects are randomly assigned to the various cells of a factorial design and each subject receives the combination of treatments corresponding to that cell. For example, subjects randomly assigned to the A_1B_2 cell would have a depressed mood state induced and would use a visual learning style, whereas a subject randomly assigned to the A_3B_1 cell would have an elated mood state induced and use a spatial learning style.

Factorial designs are frequently used in psychological research because they are rich in the information they provide. There are two types of information that are obtained from a factorial design: main effects and interaction effects. A *main effect* is the effect of one factor. All factorial designs contain more than one factor and the separate effect of each of these factors can be identified. This means that a factorial design contains within it a subset of single-factor effects. In the design depicted in Figure 25.5, there are two single-factor effects—the effect of the mood factor and the effect of the learning style factor. Each of these designs is referred to as a separate main effect, so there is a mood main effect and a learning

style main effect. The mood main effect tells us whether the different mood states produced different recall rates and the learning style factor tells us whether recall rates differ depending on whether one uses a visual or spatial learning style.

Although main effects provide information about specific factors, the information they provide refers to the average effect of each factor. It does not tell you whether the effect of one factor depends on the level of the other factor. This information could only be derived from an interaction effect. An *interaction* occurs when the effect of one factor varies over the levels of another factor. For example, an interaction would exist if the material studied using a visual learning strategy resulted in recall of 10% of the material when depressed, 20% when in a normal mood state, and 30% when elated; however, when using a spatial learning style, 30% of the material was recalled when depressed, 20% when in a normal mood state, and only 10% when elated. In this instance, the effect of mood state on percent of material recalled depended on whether one was using a visual or spatial learning strategy. Figure 25.6 presents a visual representation of this classic interaction effect and also reveals that the effect of mood state on recall of material studied depended on whether one used a visual or spatial learning strategy.

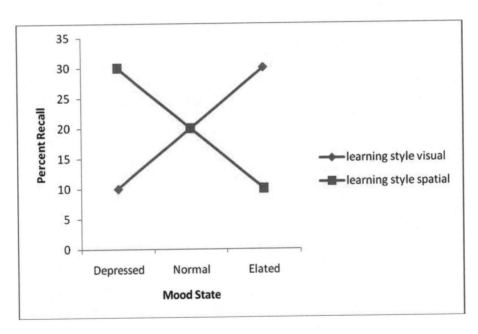

FIGURE 25.6.   Illustration of an interaction between mood and learning style.

This discussion of factorial designs has focused on a design with two factors. Mathematically and statistically there is no limit to the number of factors that can be included. Practically speaking there is a difficulty associated with increasing the number of factors. As the number of factors increases, the number of cells in the design increases, which means that more subjects are needed. A 3 × 2 factorial design has six cells; if 10 subjects were required per cell, 60 subjects would be needed. However, just adding a third factor with two levels makes it a 3 × 2 × 2 factorial design with 12 cells, so this design would require 120 subjects.

A second difficulty is that manipulating the combination of factors increases as more factors are included. It would be harder to simultaneously manipulate mood state, learning style, quality of tutoring, and anxiety level (a four-factor design) than it would be to manipulate only mood state and learning style. A final difficulty with factorial designs is that the interpretation of the interactions is more difficult as the number of factors increases. An interaction between the two factors of mood state and learning style would be easier to interpret than would an interaction between the three factors of mood state, learning style, and anxiety level.

In spite of these difficulties, factorial designs are popular and used frequently because of the advantages they afford when used properly. The first advantage is that the effect of more than one factor can be tested, which means that more than one hypothesis can be tested. In the multilevel randomized design, only one hypothesis can be tested. However, in a factorial design, you can test hypotheses relating to each main effect and each interaction effect.

A second advantage of factorial designs is that control of a potentially confounding variable can be created by building it into the design of the experiment. Whether an extraneous variable (such as intelligence level) should be included as a factor in the design of an experiment depends, in part, upon the number of factors already included and if there is an interest in the effect of different levels of the factor. If a design already included three factors, adding another factor may increase the complexity of the design to the point that it would be more appropriate to control for the potentially confounding variable in another way. If a decision is made that it would be appropriate to incorporate the potentially confounding variable into the design, then you have the advantage of controlling for the variable, removing variation that would otherwise be part of the estimate of error variance. This approach would give you information about the effect of this variable on the dependent variable.

The final advantage of factorial designs is that they enable the investigator to test for the interactive effect of the various factors. This is perhaps the most important advantage of factorial designs. Testing for interactive effects enables us to investigate the complexity of behavior because it enables us to see how the effect of one factor changes with the different levels of another factor. The importance of the presence of an interaction between the factors in a factorial design is apparent when you recognize that this means that the main effects alone do not fully describe the outcome of the experiment. In fact, the presence of interactions means that the main effects have little significance (Keppel & Wickens, 2004) and that attention should be focused on the interaction to understand the results of the study.

Although interactions are important because they reveal the complexity of behavior, they are often more difficult to detect than main effects (Shadish et al., 2002). This means that larger sample sizes (size to be determined by power analysis) might be necessary when interactions are the focus of attention. However, interactions often provide the richest and most valuable information, which is why this is the most important advantage of factorial designs.

MIXED DESIGNS

There are many times in psychological research when interest exists in one or more variables that fit into a randomized or between-subjects type of design and other variable(s) fit into a repeated-measure or within-subjects type of design. When this type of situation exists, a mixed design is needed because a *mixed design* combines the characteristics of a between-subjects design with the characteristics of a within-subjects design. The simplest form of a mixed design is one that includes one between-subjects factor and one within-subjects factor as illustrated in Figure 25.7.

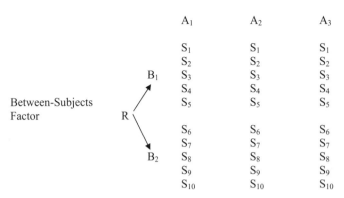

FIGURE 25.7.   Mixed design in which A represents the three levels of
the within-subjects or repeated-measures variable and B represents the
two levels of the between-subject variable. R indicates that the subjects
were randomly assigned to the two groups

From Figure 25.7 it can be seen that there are two factors, A and B, and that there are three levels of factor A and two levels of factor B. Figure 25.7 also reveals that subjects are randomly assigned to the two levels of factor B and that all subjects take each of the three levels of factor A. Therefore, factor B represents a between-subjects factor with random assignment of subjects and factor A represents a within-subjects or repeated-measures design.

Laney, Morris, Bernstein, Wakefield, and Loftus (2008) provided a good example of the use of a mixed design in their investigation of whether a false positive memory could be induced. This experiment randomly assigned subjects to a control or false memory group and then all subjects completed a food history inventory assessing the certainty of their memory of eating and liking certain foods the first time they ate them in childhood at two different time periods: before and after instilling a false memory in the false memory group of subjects. Therefore, this study used a mixed design because one factor (control vs. false memory) was tested using a between-subjects design and the other factor (time of assessment) was tested using a within-subjects or repeated-measures design.

A mixed models design is a popular design because it combines some of the advantages of both the between- and within-subjects factors. When using this design you can test for the main effect of both the between and within factors as well as the interaction between these factors. This design also has the advantage of needing fewer subjects than a factorial design because all subjects take all levels of the within factor. Therefore, the number of subjects needed is a multiple of the number of levels of the between factor. It also gives a more sensitive test of the within factor. The within factor, however, can only be included in this design when you are interested in testing for a potential change across levels of the within factor. When such change, or sequencing effect, is not of interest or would be considered to be a confounding variable, then the mixed design is not appropriate.

This discussion of the mixed design has focused on only one between and one within factor. This design can be extended to include more than one between or within factor. As with factorial designs, as many factors can be incorporated into the design as are considered necessary. These factors can be any combination of within and between factors. If a study was conducted using three factors, two of these factors could be within factors and one could be a between factor. Conversely, two could be between factors and one could be a within factor. The essential requirement for a mixed design is that it includes at least one within and at least one between factor.

NESTED DESIGNS

A *nested design* is a design in which each level of one factor appears at only a single level of another factor.

This unique characteristic of a nested design is illustrated in Figure 25.8. This figure, which depicts a two-factor design, reveals that there are subjects in cells $A_1B_1, A_1B_2, A_2B_3,$ and A_2B_4. There are no subjects in cells A_1B_3, A_1B_4, A_2B_1, or A_2B_2. Therefore, there are four cells with no subjects. This is as contrasted with a completely crossed-factorial design. Refer to the factorial design depicted in Figure 25.5. In this design, there are two factors, mood state (Factor A) and learning style (Factor B), and all combinations of the two factors are represented in the design. This is the essential difference between a factorial design and a nested design. In a factorial design, all combinations of levels of the factors are represented and tested. However, in a nested design, all combinations of the various factors are *not* represented. Instead, each level of one factor occurs at only one level of the other factor. One of the similarities between the two designs is that subjects are randomly assigned to cells, which is why both designs are designs with random assignment.

The fact that all combinations of factors in a nested design are not representing might seem strange and inappropriate. However, there are a variety of different types of studies in which it is necessary to use a nested type of design versus a completely crossed factorial design. The most typical situation in which nested designs are used is when it is necessary to administer one treatment to one entire site, such as school, clinic, community, or classroom, and another treatment to a different entire site. In other instances it may be necessary to have one treatment administered by some professionals and another treatment

administered by other professionals. Assigning entire sites to receive a specific treatment or assigning specific individuals to administer a particular treatment is done for a variety of reasons. In some situations it might be for the convenience of the investigator. For example, it might be easier to administer a specific treatment to an entire classroom instead of assigning some students in the classroom to receive one treatment and others to receive another treatment. In other instances it may be necessary to physically separate groups to prevent contamination or diffusion of treatments between groups (Shadish et al., 2002). Regardless of the reason for pairing specific sites or professionals with specific treatments, when this occurs, you have nested the sites or professionals with the treatment levels.

It is also important to remember that you need at least two levels of the nested factor at each level of the nesting factor to avoid confounding. For example, Figure 25.8 reveals that there are two levels of the nested Factor B at each level of the nesting Factor A.

To illustrate a nested design and its characteristics, I will focus on a slight modification of the study conducted by Samaan and Parker (1973). These investigators were interested in evaluating the relative effectiveness of two types of counseling, persuasive advice-giving and verbal reinforcement, on information-seeking behavior. Two counselors were trained to administer the persuasive advice-giving approach and two were trained to administer the verbal reinforcement approach. This study can be viewed as including two factors: type of counseling and the different counselors administering the different counseling types. Subjects were randomly assigned to receive either the persuasive advice-giving or the verbal reinforcement approach. However, different counselors administer each of these approaches. The subjects randomly assigned to receive the persuasive advice-giving are exposed to the counselors trained in this approach, and the subjects randomly assigned to the verbal reinforcement approach are exposed only to the counselors trained in this approach, as illustrated in Figure 25.9. Therefore, counselors are not combined with both levels of type of counseling. Rather two of the counselors exist at one level of type of counseling, and two exist at the other level of type of counseling. When the two

FIGURE 25.8. Illustration of a nested design where Factor B is nested in Factor A. Subjects are randomly assigned to four cells.

Larry Christensen

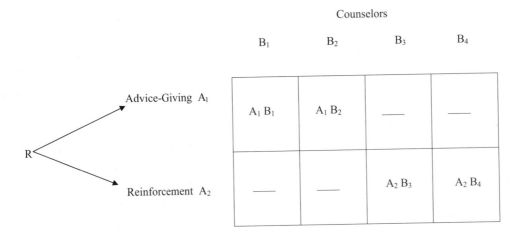

FIGURE 25.9. Nested design in which counselors are nested in type of counseling administered as illustrated by the fact that only two counselors deliver the advice-giving type of counseling and two counselors deliver the reinforcement type of counseling. The other cells are vacant.

factors are not crossed, one factor is said to be *nested* in the other factor. In this study, the counselors are nested in the type of counseling received because each counselor delivered only one type of counseling. Note that two counselors were nested within the nesting factor of type of counseling, which is necessary to avoid confounding. Nesting, therefore, has to do with how the various factors in the study are combined. If the factors are crossed, then a factorial design exists. If each level of one factor occurs only in combination with one level of another factor, however, that factor is said to be nested in the other factor. Hence the name, nested design.

The fact that the factors in a nested design are not crossed does have implications for the effects that can be tested. In a factorial design, all main effects and interaction effects can be tested. If a factorial design consisted of Factors A and B, then it would be appropriate to test for the main effect of Factor A, the main effect of Factor B, and the interaction between Factors A and B. With a nested design, however, all cells in the design are not represented and do not have subjects assigned to them. Therefore, all of the conventional tests that are conducted in a factorial design cannot be tested in a nested design. Before looking at what effects can be tested in a nested design, it is important to understand the distinction between random and fixed factors.

A *fixed factor* is a factor that has the levels specified by the experimenter. With a fixed factor, the experimenter chooses both the factor and the various levels of this factor that are to be investigated. For example, a researcher may choose to study the relative effectiveness of three types of therapy—pharmacotherapy, cognitive behavior therapy, and interpersonal therapy—in treating depression. In this study the researcher specified the type of factor that would be studied and specifically identified the three levels of that factor that would be investigated. Because the factor and the levels of the factor were selected by the researcher, there was no room for any variation so the factor is *fixed*.

This is as contrasted with a random factor. A *random factor* is one in which the levels are, strictly speaking, chosen by randomly sampling from a larger population. For example, if you were a superintendent of a school district, you might want to see what effect different teachers have on their students' reading achievement scores. It may not be feasible to include all teachers in the study, so you randomly select a few teachers from the district to participate in the study. In this case, you have randomly selected the teachers to participate in the study, so this factor of *teacher* would be considered a random factor. A similar situation may exist if you were investigating differences in classrooms, therapists, or drug dosages.

A truly random factor seldom if ever exists in studies (Keppel & Wickens, 2004). This is because the levels of the random factor more frequently

480

represent a convenience sample rather than a true random sample. Therapists chosen for a study will typically consist of those in a particular setting such as a counseling center, mental health center, or hospital. In spite of this, the nested factor is typically considered to be a random factor (Keppel & Wickens, 2004), although the levels of the nested factor may not and probably are not randomly selected from a defined population.

I now return to a consideration of the effects that can be tested in a nested design. Nested designs consist of at least one fixed factor and one random factor. The fixed factor is the nonnested factor. In the Samaan and Parker (1973) study, the fixed factor was the type of counseling given. Fixed factors can always be tested in a nested design assuming that you correctly select the appropriate error term. Selection of the appropriate error term for testing the various effects in a nested design is essential and the appropriate error terms in nested designs are not the same as in complete factorial or crossed-factorial design. This is because nested factors are almost always random, and this random variability must be accounted for in selecting the appropriate error term for testing various effects in this design. In this chapter, I do not elaborate on appropriate error terms for the various nested effect but only elaborate on the effects that can be tested.

Now consider the nested factor. In a nested design, it is not possible to test for the main effect of the nested factor. Look at Figure 25.8, and you can see why this is the case. From this figure you can see that there is one empty cell for each level of Factor B. There are empty cells for B_1 and B_2 at level A_2 and there are empty cells for B_3 and B_4 at level A_1. Therefore, any overall test of the main effect of Factor B would not be a test of whether any differences existed between the various levels of Factor B. This is because B_1 and B_2 would be affected by any effect exerted by level A_1, and B_3 and B_4 would be affected by any effect exerted by level A_2. This means that any overall test of the main effect of Factor B would include the main effect of Factor A as well as the influence of Factor B.

What then can be tested with regard to the nested factor? The typical effect tested is the effect of the nested factor within the factor in which it is nested. In Figure 25.8, Factor B is nested within Factor A so the effect tested would be the effect of B nested within A. If you conducted this test and a significant effect was found, this would mean that a difference existed in Factor B at level A_1 or at level A_2. Applying this to the Samaan and Parker (1973) study illustrated in Figure 25.9, this would indicate that a difference existed between the two counselors administering the persuasive advice-giving approach or the two counselors administering the reinforcement approach.

Now let us consider the interaction effect. In a completely crossed design it is possible to test the interaction between factors such as Factors A and B. However, such an interaction cannot be tested in a nested design. Just think about the meaning of an interaction and you can see why this is the case. Interaction means that the effect of one factor depends on the level of another factor being considered. If the Samaan and Parker (1973) study was a completely crossed design and an interaction effect was found, this would mean that the four counselors differed, but how they differed depended on whether they administered the persuasive advice-giving approach or the reinforcement approach. To get such an effect, it is necessary for each level of one factor to be represented in combination with each level of the other factor. In a nested design, this requirement does not exist. Figure 25.9 clearly reveals that the two levels of Factor A do not occur at all four levels of Factor B. Similarly, the four levels of Factor B do not occur at both levels of Factor A. Therefore, it is impossible to determine whether the effect of one factor depends on the level of the other factor being considered. In the Samaan and Parker (1973) study, it would be impossible to determine whether the four counselors obtained different results depending on whether they administered persuasive advice-giving or reinforcement because all four counselors did not administer both approaches.

The example I have used to illustrate a nested design involved only two factors with one fixed factor and one nested factor. You could also have a repeated-measures nested design or a mixed nested design. The defining characteristic would be that one of the factors would be a nested factor. Additionally, you could also have a nested design with more than two factors. For example, a three-factor design might contain two fixed factors and one nested factor. If you do construct a study using more than two factors or a repeated-measures or mixed nested design, there will be some limitations in the main and interaction effects that can be tested. In all nested designs, you cannot statistically test for the same effects that you can in a completely crossed design.

Nested designs are good designs that are frequently used to evaluate the effects of a social treatment. However, they do have limitations. Although crossed designs yield straightforward tests of main and interaction effects, nested designs do not. This feature of the design must be considered when contemplating the use of a nested design. Additionally, the measurement of effect size is more difficult in nested designs. If you do use a nested design and want to compute an effect size, consult Hedges (2009, Chapter 18). On the positive side, the use of a nested design can take care of a treatment diffusion effect that might exist in some research studies. In the final analysis, each researcher must weight the advantages and limitations of use of a nested design before selecting this design over a crossed factorial design.

CROSSOVER DESIGN

A *crossover design* is a within-subjects type of design in which subjects are randomly assigned to take different sequences of the levels of the factor being studied. Within-subjects designs, such as the crossover design, have the potentially confounding influence of order or carryover sequencing effects. This is why crossover designs include some form of

counterbalancing to balance out the effect of these sequencing effects. Only when these sequencing effects are balanced across the various levels of the factor being studied can the effect of that factor be measured.

Two-Treatment Condition Crossover Design

The simplest crossover design is one that consists of two levels of a factor or treatment condition. Subjects are randomly assigned to receive different sequences of these two levels or treatment conditions as illustrated in Figure 25.10. From this figure you can see that there are two sequences of the treatment conditions, treatment condition X followed by treatment condition Y, and treatment condition Y followed by treatment condition X. Subjects are randomly assigned to the two sequences and each randomly assigned group then takes their assigned sequence of the two treatment conditions.

Corr, Phillips, and Walker's (2004) study illustrates the use of the crossover design in their investigation of the effect of attending a day service on stroke victims ages 18 to 55. The day service provided these individuals the opportunity to participate in arts and crafts sessions, social events, outings, and some activities that gave them the opportunity to learn new skills. It was hypothesized that attending the day service would have an impact on the social functioning, leisure activities, quality of life, mood, valued roles, occupations, and self-concept of the stroke victims. To test the effect of the day service, 26 stroke victims were randomly assigned to one of two groups. One group attended the day service for 6 months and then did not attend for the next 6 months. The other group did not

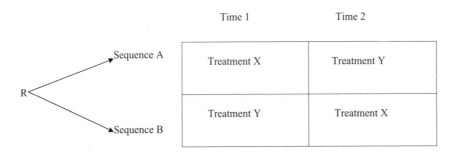

FIGURE 25.10. Illustration of a crossover design with two treatment condition. R represents random assignment of subjects to the two sequences.

attend for the first 6 months but attended for the second 6-month period. Therefore, each group received the treatment and control conditions but in a different sequence.

The primary advantage of this design is the increased power to detect a true treatment effect because the comparison between treatments is within-subjects. However, this advantage does come with the assumption that no carryover effect exists from one treatment condition to another. When it is reasonable to assume that subjects revert to their original state when a treatment is removed, the crossover design can be a good design to use. To try to minimize or ensure that no carryover effects occur, the carryover design frequently incorporates a rest or washout period interjected between the administration of the two treatments. When evidence exists that a rest or washout period does eliminate any carryover effects, as might exist in some medical and pharmaceutical studies (Jones & Kenward, 2003), this design is efficient and more powerful than a between-subjects design.

Even if it can be assumed that carry-over effects from one treatment condition to another have been eliminated by a rest or washout period, this does not eliminate the possibility that an order effect does not exist. This is why two groups of subjects are included in the two-treatment condition crossover design with each group receiving a different sequence of the two treatments. In other words, the treatment conditions are counterbalanced in this design. For example, in the Corr et al. (2004) study, one group of subjects received the day service treatment for 6 months and then the day service was eliminated for the next 6 months (treatment X and then Y), whereas the other group had to wait for 6 months before receiving the 6-month day service treatment (treatment Y and then X). The logic behind such counterbalancing is that any main effect of order is controlled, although not necessarily eliminated. Consequently, when order effects are controlled, there are no carryover effects, and there is no interaction between order and the treatment conditions (Kirk, 1995), this design provides for a good test of the treatment condition. When there is a risk that carryover effects have not been controlled or eliminated, you should consider changing the method of analysis to adjust for these contaminating effects (Cochran & Cox, 1992). Consult Hills and Armitage (1979) and Jones and Kenward (2003) for suggestions about to how to analyze the data in such cases. However, if you know beforehand that carry-over effects cannot be eliminated, especially nonlinear carry-over effects, it is probably best to use a between-subjects design (Maxwell & Delaney, 2000).

Before leaving this section on the two-treatment crossover design, I do want to mention that there are other sequences that could be used in addition to the AB and BA sequence. Jones and Kenward (2003) have elaborated in detail on two-treatment designs with more than two sequences or more than two time periods. A two-treatment design could, for example, include the following four sequences: AA, BB, AB, and BA, or it might include two sequences but three time periods producing the following sequences: ABB and BAA. Jones and Kenward pointed out that such designs have the advantage of obtaining estimators of carry-over effects or a treatment by time period interaction. If you use a crossover design and think you might have carry-over or a treatment by time period interaction and do not want to use a between-subjects design, consult Jones and Kenward.

Crossover Designs With More Than Two Treatments

Although many experiments focus on comparing the effect of two treatment conditions, the focus of other experiments is on comparing the effect of more than two treatment conditions. When a crossover design is used to compare more than two treatment conditions, some form of a Latin square design must be used. A *Latin square* is an $n \times n$ table filled with n different symbols in such a way that each symbol occurs exactly once in each row and exactly once in each column as shown in Figure 25.11. From this figure, you can see that each of the letters, A, B, and C, occur once in each row and column and that a Latin square really represents a form of counterbalancing. When using a crossover design, it is necessary to control for order and carry-over sequencing effect. The most effective way of controling for these effects is counterbalancing, which is why the Latin square is used when testing the effect of more than

A	B	C
B	C	A
C	A	B

FIGURE 25.11. Illustration of a Latin square.

two treatment conditions with a crossover design. Keppel and Wickens (2004) also pointed out that use of a counterbalanced design allows the variability caused by the sequencing effects to be extracted and eliminated from the error term, increasing the accuracy and power of the test of the treatment conditions. There are actually many different Latin squares that could be selected for use with crossover designs. The selection of a particular Latin square depends on factors such as the treatment comparisons that are of interest and their relative importance and the maximum number of subjects available for the study, and whether sequencing effects are present (Jones & Kenward, 2003). In most psychological studies using a within-subjects or repeated-measures type of design, it has to be assumed that some form of order or carry-over sequencing effect exists. The most efficient Latin square for controlling these sequencing effects is the balanced Latin square design. The term *balance* refers to a set of specific properties a Latin square design must have. The specific properties that must exist are (a) each treatment must occur once with each subject, (b) each treatment must occur the same number of times for each time period or trial, and (c) each treatment condition must precede and follow every other treatment an equal number of times. A Latin square created in this manner is said to be *diagram balanced* (Keppel & Wickens, 2004).

Williams (1949) has demonstrated that balance can be achieved using only one Latin square if an even number of levels of the factor exist and using two Latin squares if an odd number of levels of the factor exist. The advantage of using the Latin square designs suggested by Williams is that fewer subjects are needed for studies including more than three levels of the factor. Christensen (2007) and Keppel

and Wickens (2004) have provided excellent descriptions of the procedure to follow in constructing a balanced Latin square.

The use of a balanced Latin square design has the advantage of being very efficient in terms of number of subjects required because of the fewer number of counterbalanced sequences required. It is also the most efficient in terms of controlling for sequencing effects. The only sequencing effect that is not controlled is nonlinear carry-over effects. This is an important limitation. If nonlinear carry-over effects do exist, then you will get a biased measure of the effect of the factor being investigated. When nonlinear carry-over effects exist, Maxwell and Delaney (2000) have recommended switching to a between-subjects design. If this is not possible because of a restriction such as an insufficient number of subjects, consult Jones and Kenward (2003).

There are a couple other cautions that you need to remember if you are planning to use a Latin square with a crossover design. The first caution is that you must remember that a Latin square is a main effects design consisting of the three main effects of treatment, position (the time or trial in which the treatment was administered), and subjects. In a Latin square design, these three main effects are orthogonal, which means that they represent distinct and separate portions of variability that can be extracted to reduce the error term (Keppel & Wickens, 2004). The smaller error term results in a more powerful test, increasing the probability of detecting a significant treatment effect if one really exists. However, as Keppel and Wickens (2004), Kirk (1995), and others have pointed out, it is essential that the appropriate analysis is conducted. When analyzing a crossover design that uses a Latin square, consult these or other sources that directly focus on the appropriate method of analyzing such data.

The other significant point that must be remembered when using a crossover design with Latin square is that it is a model with no interactions. It is not an appropriate design to use in cases in which interactions are important to the researcher. The inability to obtain information about interactions may also be a problem when few subjects are available for study. With few subjects there may be an interaction between subjects and the position in which they receive the treatment. If few subjects are available for study, one or two subjects may skew the apparent treatment effect. For example, if only four subjects participated in a study with four levels of the treatment factor, and one of the four subjects showed a large order or carry-over effect, the results may indicate that the treatment condition administered last to this subject was most effective when it really only represented this subject's excessively large response to this treatment condition. This confounding effect exists primarily when few subjects participate. As additional subjects are added, such effects are reduced.

Keppel and Wickens (2004) have appropriately pointed out that such interactions confound the interpretation of the treatment factor because they increase the variability of this main effect. These authors recommend that when a large interaction is expected between subjects and the position in which the treatment factor is administered, an alternate design should be selected that allows for the measurement of this interaction.

DESIGNING RANDOMIZING STUDIES

Experimental studies make use of one of the randomized designs discussed in this chapter. However, conducting a good experimental study that provides the most credible evidence requires much more than just selecting and using a specific randomized design. Two important decisions that must be made, in addition to deciding on the most appropriate randomized control design for answering your research question, are the development of, or operationalization of the treatment condition, and identification of the control condition that will provide the needed control.

Constructing the Treatment Condition

When designing an experimental study, it is necessary to construct a treatment condition that produces the intended effect. The researcher is typically interested in the effect some conceptual variable has on individuals' responses. To investigate the effect of the conceptual variable, the researcher has to translate it into a set of concrete operations that capture that variable without influencing other factors. For example, assume that you wanted to investigate the

effect of depression on memory for recently learned material. This study would require you to develop a set of operations that would create a depressive mood state in individuals before having them learn a specific set of material.

To develop a depressive mood state in individuals, you could use the procedure developed by Velten (1968) that asks subjects to read and concentrate on 60 self-referent depressive statements. Using this procedure would give the researcher the desired control because the researcher would decide who received the induction of the depressive mood state, and all subjects selected to receive the induction would read and concentrate on the same 60 self-referent depressive statements. Although this procedure gives the researcher maximum control, there is also the question of the impact of this procedure. Specifically, does it create the same psychological process as some real-life events, such as losing a job or ending a marriage engagement. In other words, is the impact of the Velten procedure the same as that which would be created by some real-life event?

A tension that exists in some experiments is this conflict between achieving maximum control over extraneous variables while creating a set of operations that not only represents the conceptual variable being investigated but also has sufficient impact on the subjects to create the necessary psychological realism. We want to have maximum control over the treatment condition and the extraneous variables that could influence the outcome of the experiment. However, this can lead to the creation of a sterile experiment that has little impact on the subjects.

This tension between impact and control can be seen in the sometimes-competing goals of wanting to standardize the delivery of the treatment condition but also wanting to standardize the impact that the treatment condition has on all subjects. Standardizing the delivery of the treatment condition decreases the probability of confounding the extraneous variables influencing the treatment condition. Standardization of delivery may lead to the experimental treatment having a different impact on different individuals, however, and it is frequently more important to standardize the impact that the treatment condition has on the subjects (Wilson, Aronson, &

Carlsmith, 2010). Wilson et al. (2010) illustrated the importance of standardizing the impact of the treatment condition in an example of a drug study. In drug studies, the impact of the drug on all subjects should be the same. The most effective way to ensure that the impact is the same is to ensure that all subjects have the same concentration of the drug in their bloodstream. This means that a large person will take a larger dose of the drug than will a small person. Therefore, the amount of drug administered is not standardized, but the impact of the drug is.

So how can the tension between the need for experimental control and the need for achieving sufficient impact be resolved? Probably the best way to resolve this tension is through extensive pretesting in which the researcher continues to revise the treatment condition, pretesting its impact each time, until the researcher has created the desired psychological process. Using this repeated refinement process, the experimenter can arrive at the most appropriate balance between maintaining control over extraneous variables and achieving sufficient impact.

Constructing the Control Group

A *control group* is the group of subjects that either does not receive the treatment condition or receives some standard value. It is an essential component of any experiment because the control group represents the effect that exists in the absence of the treatment condition. In addition to representing the contrasting condition, the control group is essential to ruling out the effect of many of the threats to internal validity. However, it is not enough to merely construct a control group of randomly assigned individuals that does not receive the treatment condition or some standard treatment. To construct an appropriate experiment that adequately tests a treatment effect, it is essential to identify what needs to be controlled and then to provide the needed control.

Different experiments have different goals, and the type of control group that is constructed has a bearing on whether the goal of the experiment is achieved and the appropriate inferences that can be drawn from the experiment. Construction of the appropriate control group requires a clear identification of the research goal. For example, if the goal of the experiment is to determine whether a treatment

is effective, the appropriate control group would be a no-treatment control. From such a study, an inference could be made regarding the overall effectiveness of the treatment condition. If prior experimental results had already identified that the treatment (e.g., drug or psychosocial intervention) was effective, a study might have the goal of trying to identify the contribution of a specific part of the study to the overall treatment. For example, there is evidence (cited in Nock, Janis, & Wedig, 2008) demonstrating that the expectation of change and the hope for improvement can account for a significant portion of a clinical treatment effect. To determine whether the treatment is effective above and beyond the expectation of change and hope for improvement, the control group needs to include these two elements of an overall treatment condition. For such a study, a *wait-list* control group would probably be the most appropriate because the waited-list group would have the expectation of change and hope for improvement components. The participants in this control group would be told that they will receive the treatment but that they have to wait a set period of time before actually being administered the treatment. A control group fashioned in this way would have "mundane realism" (Wilson et al., 2010, p. 56) or would mirror real-world events because one frequently has to wait for treatment to be administered. The important point is that a decision has to be made regarding what needs to be controlled and then a control group needs to be formed that incorporates these controls. In many studies this goes beyond just randomly assigning subjects to a control group.

CONCLUSION

Research design refers to the strategy, outline, or plan that a researcher uses to answer a research question. There are two basic types of experimental research designs used by researchers: between-subjects and within-subjects designs. These two designs are distinguished by whether the various treatment conditions are administered to the same or different subjects. The basic randomized design is a between-subjects design in which the subjects have been randomly assigned to the various treatment conditions. It is the random assignment of subjects to the treatment conditions that allows this design to provide the most credible evidence about a causal relationship. This is because random assignment of subjects to treatment conditions provides the best assurance that confounding extraneous variables have not biased the results.

There are several extensions or variations of the basic randomized design. The simplest extension is the multilevel randomized design. This is a design that includes more than two levels of one independent variable and subjects are randomly assigned to the various levels of the independent variable. The basic randomized design can also be extended to include more than one independent variable. When more than one independent variable is included, the design is labeled a factorial design. In this design, subjects are randomly assigned to the various combinations of the factors and information is provided about the effect of each factor as well as the interaction between the various factors.

If a design includes one factor that is investigated using a between-subjects design and another factor is investigated using a within-subjects design, the design is labeled a *mixed design*. This is a popular type of design when sequencing effects that may exist in the within-subjects component do not represent a confounding factor. This is because this design is more efficient in terms of its use of subjects and provides a more sensitive test of the effect of the within-subjects factor.

There are also situations in which it is necessary to administer one treatment condition to all subjects in one site or situation and another treatment condition to all subjects in another site or situation. A nested design would be used in situations like this because each treatment condition would be nested in a specific site or situation. Although a nested design is appropriate to use in such situations, there are limitations to the information that can be obtained from this design.

A crossover design is a within-subjects design in which subjects are randomly assigned to take different sequences of the levels of the factor being studied. The simplest type of crossover design is the two-treatment condition crossover design. This design has two treatment levels and there are only two possible sequences of these two treatment levels. When there are more than two treatment conditions or more than two levels of a factor being investigated, it is necessary to incorporate some form of Latin square into the crossover design to control for sequencing effects. The most efficient Latin square for controlling sequencing effects is a balanced Latin square. However, including a Latin square with a crossover design allows you to test only for main effects. There are no interaction effects in this model.

Selection of the appropriate randomized design is essential when conducting an experimental study. However, designing an experimental study that produces the most credible evidence requires constructing an experimental treatment that has not only the desired impact but also the control over the influence of extraneous variables. Additionally, a control condition must be established to provide control of the variables that will allow the experiment to meet its stated goal.

References

Bickman, L., & Reich, S. M. (2009). Randomized controlled trials: A gold standard with feet of clay. In S. I. Donaldson, C. A. Christie, & M. M. Mark (Eds.), *What counts as credible evidence in applied research in evaluation practice?* (pp. 51–77). Los Angeles, CA: Sage.

Blair, E. (2004). Discussion: Gold is not always good enough: The shortcomings of randomization when evaluating interventions in small heterogeneous samples. *Journal of Clinical Epidemiology, 57,* 1219–1222. doi:10.1016/j.jclinepi.2004.06.003

Christensen, L. (2007). *Experimental methodology.* Boston, MA: Allyn & Bacon.

Christensen, L., & Burrows, R. (1990). Dietary treatment of depression. *Behavior Therapy, 21,* 183–194. doi:10.1016/S0005-7894(05)80276-X

Cochran, W. G., & Cox, G. M. (1992). *Experimental designs.* New York, NY: Wiley.

Corr, S., Phillips, C. J., & Walker, M. (2004). Evaluation of a pilot service designed to provide support following stroke: A randomized cross-over design study. *Clinical Rehabilitation, 18,* 69–75. doi:10.1191/0269215504cr703oa

Dehue, T. (1997). Deception, efficiency, and random groups. *Isis, 88,* 653–673. doi:10.1086/383850

Dehue, T. (2001). Establishing the experimenting society: The historical origin of social experimentation according to the randomized controlled design.

American Journal of Psychology, 114, 283–302. doi:10.2307/1423518

Donaldson, S. I. (2009). In search of the blueprint for an evidence-based Global society. In S. I. Donaldson, C. A. Christie, & M. M. Mark (Eds.), *What counts as credible evidence in applied research in evaluation practice?* (pp. 2–18). Los Angeles, CA: Sage.

Elkin, I., Parloff, M. B., Hadley, S. W., & Autry, J. H. (1985). NIMH Treatment of depression collaborative research program: Background and research plan. *Archives of General Psychiatry, 42,* 305–316.

Fisher, R. A. (1928). *Statistical methods for research workers.* Edinburgh, Scotland: Oliver & Boyd.

Fisher, R. A. (1935). *The design of experiments.* Oxford, England: Oliver & Boyd.

Hedges, L. V. (2009). Effect sizes in nested designs. In H. Cooper, L. V. Hedges, & J. C. Valentine (Eds.), *The handbook of research synthesis and meta-analysis* (2nd ed., pp. 337–356). New York, NY: Russell Sage.

Hills, M., & Armitage, P. (1979). The two-period cross-over clinical trial. *British Journal of Clinical Pharmacology, 8,* 7–20.

Jones, B., & Kenward, M. G. (2003). *Design and analysis of cross-over trials.* Boca Raton, FL: Chapman & Hall/CRC.

Keppel, G., & Wickens, T. D. (2004). *Design and analysis: A researcher's handbook.* Upper Saddle River, NJ: Pearson Prentice Hall.

Kirk, R. (1995). *Experimental design: Procedures for the behavioral sciences.* Boston, MA: Brooks/Cole.

Laney, C., Morris, E. K., Bernstein, D. M., Wakefield, B. M., & Loftus, E. L. (2008). Asparagus, a love story: Healthier eating could be just a false memory away. *Experimental Psychology, 55,* 291–300. doi:10.1027/1618-3169.55.5.291

Maxwell, S. E., & Delaney, H. D. (2000). *Designing experiments and analyzing data: A model comparison perspective.* Mahwah, NJ: Erlbaum.

Nock, M. K., Janis, I. B., & Wedig, M. M. (2008). Research designs. In A. M. Nezu & C. M. Nezu (Eds.), *Evidence-based outcome research: A practical guide to conducting randomized controlled trials for psychosocial interventions* (pp. 201–218). New York, NY: Oxford University Press.

Salmond, S. S. (2008). Randomized controlled trials: Methodological concepts and critique. *Orthopaedic Nursing, 27,* 116–124. doi:10.1097/01.NOR.0000315626.44137.94

Samaan, M. K., & Parker, C. A. (1973). Effects of behavioral (reinforcement) and advice-giving counseling on information-seeking behavior. *Journal of Counseling Psychology, 20,* 193–201. doi:10.1037/h0034575

Scriven, M. (2009). Demythologizing causation and evidence. In S. I. Donaldson, C. A. Christie, & M. M. Mark (Eds.), *What counts as credible evidence in applied research in evaluation practice?* (pp. 134–152). Los Angeles, CA: Sage.

Shadish, W. R., Cook, T. D., & Campbell, D. T. (2002). *Experimental and quasi-experimental designs for generalized causal inference.* Boston, MA: Houghton Mifflin.

Stotts, A. L., Schmitz, J. M., Rhoades, H. M., & Grabowski, J. (2001). Motivational interviewing with cocaine-dependent patients: A pilot study. *Journal of Consulting and Clinical Psychology, 69,* 858–862. doi:10.1037/0022-006X.69.5.858

Velten, E. (1968). A laboratory task for induction of mood states. *Behaviour Research and Therapy, 6,* 473–482. doi:10.1016/0005-7967(68)90028-4

Williams, E. J. (1949). Experimental designs balanced for the estimation of residual effects of treatments. *Australian Journal of Scientific Research, 2,* 149–168.

Wilson, T. D., Aronson, E., & Carlsmith, K. (2010). The art of laboratory experimentation. In S. T. Fiske, D. T. Gilbert, & G. Lindzey (Eds.), *Handbook of social psychology* (Vol. 1, pp. 51–81). Hoboken, NJ: Wiley.

CHAPTER 26

NONEQUIVALENT COMPARISON GROUP DESIGNS

Henry May

This chapter focuses on research designs in which the effects of a treatment or intervention are estimated by comparing outcomes of a treatment group and a comparison group but without the benefit of random assignment. In psychology and other social sciences, these designs often involve self-selection, in which the members of the treatment group are those who volunteered or otherwise sought to receive the treatment, whereas the comparison group members did not. Alternatively, assignment to the treatment group may be made through a subjective decision process. This is common in education research when an intervention targets schools or students and district or school staffs select whom to assign to the treatment. More generally, a nonequivalent comparison group design involves any comparison of treatment and control groups in which the treatment assignment mechanism cannot be modeled explicitly, and the treatment and comparison groups are likely to exhibit pretreatment differences on measured or unmeasured factors.

Given the probable and often obvious preexisting differences between the treatment and comparison groups in this design, it is normally imprudent to draw strong causal inferences about the effects of an intervention. The suitability of a nonequivalent group as a counterfactual (i.e., a group that tells you what would have happened to the treatment group in the absence of the treatment) is difficult to ensure and impossible to guarantee in a nonequivalent comparison group design. Therefore, much of the literature on this design revolves around the question of how to estimate the treatment's effect in the absence of random assignment. Nevertheless, because it is applicable in so many circumstances, the nonequivalent groups design is one of the most commonly implemented research designs in the social sciences (Campbell & Stanley, 1963; Shadish, Cook, & Campbell, 2002).

Much has been written about the nonequivalent comparison groups design, and the introduction to this chapter continues with a brief review of major contributions to that prior literature. The remainder of the chapter delves more deeply into key methodological issues and recent advances in analytical techniques. In the review of prior literature, readers will likely notice the ubiquitous contributions of Donald T. Campbell. His publications over several decades, along with those of his collaborators, created and refined the experimental–quasi-experimental paradigm and the framework of threats to internal and external validity that continues to guide the design of countless social science research projects.

The seminal text by Campbell and Stanley (1963) entitled *Experimental and Quasi-Experimental Designs for Research* defined the nonequivalent control group design as involving a comparison of treatment and comparison groups that were "as similar as availability permits, but yet not so similar that one can dispense with the pretest" (p. 47). They advocated strongly for the use of a pretest to (a) evaluate the similarity of the treatment and control groups prior to treatment and (b) statistically adjust for preexisting differences when estimating treatment impacts. In their discussion of the inferential

DOI: 10.1037/13620-026
APA Handbook of Research Methods in Psychology: Vol. 2. Research Designs, H. Cooper (Editor-in-Chief)

validity of the nonequivalent groups design, they pointed out that the use of a pretest in both groups allows a comparison of pre–post changes across the two groups, ostensibly removing preexisting differences from the comparison. This effectively mitigates many basic threats to internal validity (see the Key Threats to Internal Validity section) in that these threats must now operate on pre–post changes (i.e., not just the posttest), and they must operate differently for the treatment and control groups (i.e., they must interact with selection).

Although Campbell and Stanley (1963) used the term *control group* in their label for this design, others prefer the term *comparison group* to better differentiate this design from a randomized experiment and to place clear emphasis on the nonequivalence of the comparison group. Following that logic, this chapter will hereafter refer to the nontreatment group in this design as the *comparison* group.

In their 1963 text, Campbell and Stanley also introduced a simple and intuitive notation for describing this and other research designs in terms of group equivalence and timing of observations and treatments. Their notation for the nonequivalent control group design is as follows:

$$
\begin{array}{ccc}
O & X & O \\
\hline
O & & O
\end{array} \tag{1}
$$

The horizontal line in this notation differentiates the treatment and control groups, whereas the use of a dashed line signifies that the two groups are not equivalent. Outcomes are assessed (with each instance denoted by O) for both groups before and then again after the introduction of the treatment (X) in one group. Campbell and Stanley pointed out that the assignment of the treatment to one group or the other is "assumed to be random and under the experimenter's control" (1963, p. 47).[1] However, given the prevalence of volunteering and subjective allocation of the treatment in applied settings, this assumption is probably violated in most studies using the nonequivalent comparison group design. Fortunately, violations of this assumption have few practical implications for analysis or interpretation

of results—even with random assignment at the group level, the groups are still nonequivalent. The presence of volunteering or subjective allocation may make the nonequivalence overt (making specific threats to validity easier to identify), but group-level random assignment with only two groups does little to address either overt or hidden selection bias. Such a scenario would not improve validity unless the study can be repeated numerous times, which would be analogous to a cluster randomized experiment (see Boruch et al., 2004) using randomization within matched pairs of groups.

There exist numerous statistical methods to address group nonequivalence, and a thorough discussion of classical analytic issues was written by Reichardt (1979), which appeared as a chapter in the book edited by Cook and Campbell entitled *Quasi-Experimentation: Design and Analysis Issues for Field Settings*. Reichardt's chapter substantiated the need for a pretest in this design, and it reviewed a number of alternative methods for analyzing the pre–post data from a nonequivalent groups design. Unfortunately, the choice of preferred statistical model for producing unbiased effect estimates is not simple, and it is not consistent across applications of the nonequivalent groups design. Although the present chapter reviews the key methodological considerations raised by Reichardt (see the section Classical Statistical Adjustments), the reader is directed to Reichardt's chapter for a more detailed discussion of the issues involved in producing unbiased effect estimates using classical statistical models.

More recently, Shadish et al. (2002) built on these two prior works by reframing the discussion around a comprehensive theory of generalized causal inference. Their discussion of the nonequivalent comparison group design (Shadish et al., 2002, pp. 136–153) largely parallels that from Cook and Campbell (1979, pp. 103–133); however, this more recent work includes design enhancements that improve validity by combining multiple comparison groups with treatment replications or nonequivalent dependent variables (Shadish et al., 2002, pp. 153–161). The relevant chapter in their book also included an appendix that briefly reviewed

[1]Random assignment of two existing groups is different from random assignment of participants. For example, an experimenter might be able to assign a reading treatment randomly to one of two classrooms but not have control of which students were in each class.

recent advances in statistical approaches to dealing with selection bias, including propensity score modeling (see Volume 1, Chapter 2, this handbook), control function and instrumental variables analyses, and latent variable–structural equation modeling (see Chapter 19 of this volume).

To best reflect the continuous improvements in methodological theory, this chapter includes a concise discussion of key issues and perspectives from these prior works, followed by a more comprehensive discussion of recent advances in statistical and econometric methods that are directly applicable to the nonequivalent comparison groups design. Because this chapter provides a relatively nontechnical and broad discussion of theories and methodologies related to the nonequivalent groups design, the essential elements of each topic are presented in nontechnical language and are supported by references to more technical publications. The interested reader is directed to these references for more detail on the theory behind and procedures for each method.

The structure of the remainder of this chapter includes three main sections. The first section describes an illustrative example of a nonequivalent comparison group design, which will then be used as a foundation for discussing the methods and issues raised in subsequent sections. The second section includes a review of key threats to internal validity of the nonequivalent groups design, leaning heavily on the prior work of Campbell and colleagues. The third section focuses on the use of baseline measures to address selection issues and is divided into three parts: classical statistical adjustments (e.g., analysis of covariance [ANCOVA]), statistical models for controlling observable bias (e.g., regression, stratification, matching), and econometric techniques for controlling unobservable bias (e.g., instrumental variables analysis). Finally, the fourth section focuses on design enhancements, including extensions to the simple two-group pre–post design, cohort comparison groups, moderation–mediation analysis, and sensitivity analysis.

AN ILLUSTRATIVE EXAMPLE

A classic question in the clinical psychology literature has focused on the relative value of medication for patients participating in psychotherapy for depression. The basic question is, when a patient receives effective psychotherapy, is there any added benefit achieved (or harm inflicted) by augmenting the therapy with an antidepressant medication? Perhaps the medication improves the efficacy of the psychotherapy. Or, perhaps the medication does not improve the efficacy of the psychotherapy but increases the risk of suicide. Unfortunately, the truth is not easily ascertained without random assignment because myriad selection mechanisms are at work that determine who does or does not receive antidepressant medication. For example, the selection process may look something like the following. First, individuals suffering from clinical depression must be referred to or otherwise seek psychotherapeutic treatment. Of those seeking treatment, some will visit a psychologist and others will visit a psychiatrist, depending on a number of factors, including the relative availability of these two types of practitioners, relative costs, and personal preferences and beliefs. Of those who visit a psychologist, only a portion will visit a psychologist able to prescribe antidepressant medications, a possibility that currently exists in only a select number of states. Alternatively, patients enrolled in health management organization plans may receive a prescription for an antidepressant from their primary care physician along with a referral to a psychologist for psychotherapy, or they may receive only the referral for psychotherapy. The act of prescribing a medication will depend on a number of factors, including medical history, the time frame and severity of the depression, and the relative liberality with which the psychiatrist, psychologist, or physician issues such prescriptions. But this complicated process likely represents only a fraction of the mechanisms that determine whether a psychotherapy patient also receives an antidepressant medication. So we are left with a situation in which a simple comparison of patients receiving only psychotherapy to patients receiving psychotherapy plus medication is somewhat like comparing apples and oranges. Yes, the two groups are similar in many ways, but they are also different in many important ways that could exert significant influence on their outcomes.

In the simplest nonequivalent comparison group design, we would capture preexisting differences in outcomes between the psychotherapy and psychotherapy plus medication groups by collecting pretest data on the severity of depression (i.e., using a reliable and valid standardized measure) before the initiation of any treatment. Then at some point after the treatment begins (e.g., 12 weeks later), we would collect posttest data on the severity of depression. The basic idea is that by measuring preexisting differences in depression, one can adjust impact estimates accordingly. Of course, this is a simplistic approach to dealing with selection bias, and there are many reasons to believe that simply measuring preexisting differences in the severity of depression will fail to account for all of the important factors that influence differences in outcomes. For example, there may be no detectable differences in severity of depression between patients who visit a psychiatrist and those who visit a psychologist, but the treatment they receive (independent of the medication) may end up looking very different. In the sections that follow, key issues and analytic methods relevant to the nonequivalent groups design will be discussed, with illustrations intertwined throughout that tie back to this hypothetical study of the efficacy of antidepressant medication.

KEY THREATS TO INTERNAL VALIDITY

The nonequivalent comparison group design deals effectively with many basic threats to internal validity as long as a pretest is employed for both groups. It accomplishes this by focusing the impact analysis not on simple posttest differences between the treatment and comparison groups but on differences between the groups in their pre–post changes. The issue of selection as a main effect is addressed to the extent that pretreatment differences between the two groups are captured by the pretest, and these preexisting differences are subsequently factored out when calculating posttest impact estimates. In other words, any posttreatment differences attributable to the main effect of selection are subtracted (or statistically adjusted) from the final impact estimate under the assumption that pretreatment differences would persist in the posttest measure. For selection

bias to persist, the key issues of history, maturation, testing, instrumentation, regression to the mean, and mortality (now called attrition) must interact with selection to explain away differences in pre–post changes (Campbell & Stanley, 1963, p. 48). For example, maturation is an issue whenever natural improvement would occur even without a treatment. In a simple pre–post study without a comparison group, a main effect of maturation could explain completely a simple pre–post change (i.e., subjects were already improving without the treatment). In a study that includes a comparison group but no pretest, a main effect of selection could explain a difference in posttest scores between treatment and comparison groups (i.e., subjects in the two groups would have had different outcomes even without the treatment). With the inclusion of both a pretest and comparison group in a nonequivalent comparison group design, however, any main effect of maturation will be evident in the pre–post change of the comparison group as well and can be adjusted out of the impact estimate. For example, in our hypothetical study of antidepressants, all patients may be expected to improve because they are all participating in psychotherapy, and this general improvement (i.e., maturation) that happens regardless of whether one receives an antidepressant would be evident in the pre–post changes in the comparison group and could be adjusted out when calculating the impact of the antidepressants on the treatment group. On the other hand, if the rates of improvement without the treatment are different for the treatment and comparison groups (i.e., the maturation effect interacts with selection), it is impossible to determine whether differences in pre–post changes across the two groups are attributable to the treatment or to preexisting differences in maturation rates. For example, if those patients receiving antidepressants were already improving at a faster (or slower) rate than the comparison group, their average pre–post change would be larger (or smaller) even without the antidepressants. In general, we need to be concerned whether one group experiences improvement in their depression that was unrelated to whether they received a drug and instead attributable to other preexisting differences between the groups. Alternatively, if we can assume that the average rates of change (or lack thereof) without the treatment would be similar for subjects in the treatment and comparison groups, then differences in the pre–post changes of the two groups are more directly attributable to the effect of the treatment.

The logic of this approach is similar to that of difference-in-differences models from the econometric literature (Greene, 1993). This model, also known as a *change score* analysis or a *fixed-effects model* with two time points, is said to control for all time-invariant confounds. In other words, confounding factors will introduce bias only to the extent that they influence pre–post changes differentially between treatment and comparison groups. If the factors differentiating the groups are consistent over time and are unrelated to differences in pre–post change (i.e., they do not interact with time), then the difference-in-differences model will produce unbiased estimates of the treatment effect.

Beyond maturation-selection interactions, numerous other selection interactions may threaten the validity of inferences from the nonequivalent comparison group design. A history-selection interaction would occur whenever an event occurs between the pretest and posttest for one group but not the other (or more or less for one group). In essence, this "intrasession history" (Campbell & Stanley, 1963, p. 14) acts as an additional treatment, whose effects cannot be distinguished from the effects of the treatment of interest. For example, perhaps those patients seeing a psychiatrist are more likely to receive medication but also tend to have shorter psychotherapy sessions. If the antidepressants had a positive effect, it could be hidden by the diminished effect of less-intensive psychotherapy. Alternatively, if the antidepressants had no effect, the diminished effect of less intensive psychotherapy could even make the drugs appear harmful.

A testing-selection interaction would occur whenever repeated testing bias affects the two groups differently. In general, members of the comparison group receiving no treatment may become more fatigued by repeated testing, causing their posttest performance to worsen and resulting in a positive bias in the impact estimate. An instrumentation-selection interaction would occur whenever

the accuracy of measurement improved or degraded differently for the two groups. For example, observers may become bored when rating the comparison group given an absence of desired outcomes, resulting in a positive bias in the impact estimate. An attrition-selection interaction would occur whenever the treatment and comparison groups exhibited differential rates of loss of participants. In our hypothetical antidepressant study, if the drugs were beneficial and those not receiving them were more likely to discontinue treatment (thus missing the posttest), the treatment effect would be underestimated. This is because the outcomes for the psychotherapy-only group could have been biased upward (i.e., less severe depression on average) given that more patients with severe depression and less effective treatment would discontinue treatment and miss the posttest. Finally, a regression-selection interaction would occur whenever one group was selected from a more extreme position in a distribution of prior outcomes. In this case, posttest outcomes for the more extreme group would be expected to exhibit greater regression to the mean, resulting in either a positive or negative bias in the impact estimate. This is especially plausible in our hypothetical study of antidepressants given that drugs are most likely to be prescribed to those patients with the most severe pretreatment depression symptoms.

As Campbell and Stanley (1963) pointed out, regression-selection interactions are problematic in studies in which individuals self-select into a treatment, and attempts to create a comparison group by matching those who self-select into a treatment with those who did not is likely to introduce substantial regression-selection interaction bias (p. 49). This is because the members of the comparison group would likely represent an extreme group relative to the population of potential controls. In other words, of those who did not seek out the treatment, those selected for inclusion in the comparison group are likely to be quite unusual relative to the rest of that group. On the other hand, those who self-selected into the treatment group are probably not unusual relative to the population of potential treatment recipients. Thus, because the members of the comparison group are more extreme relative to the population from which they were drawn, the comparison group would be expected to exhibit greater regression to the mean.

Although the nonequivalent group design with a pretest of treatment and comparison groups does much to address threats to internal validity, there is no guarantee that selection interactions will be sufficiently controlled. In fact, for most studies utilizing this design, it is relatively easy to imagine a selection issue that weakens the credibility of causal inferences from those studies. There are a number of design and analytic steps that one can take to strengthen the validity of a nonequivalent groups comparison. However, without the benefit of random assignment, this can prove to be a complicated and often impossible task.

STATISTICAL AND ECONOMETRIC METHODS TO ADDRESS SELECTION ISSUES

The use of a pretest measure is a key component in addressing selection bias in the nonequivalent comparison group design. Unfortunately, the most effective analytic methods for dealing with selection bias are not necessarily consistent from one study to the next. This section provides a description of the rationale and assumptions underlying three classes of techniques for dealing with selection bias in nonequivalent group comparisons. The first approach relies on classical statistical analyses intended to adjust posttest outcomes for differences in pretest measure. The second approach attempts to explicitly control for factors confounded with treatment assignment and the outcome. Finally, the third approach attempts to deal directly with omitted variable bias (i.e., the bias attributable to unmeasured confounds not included in the model) by isolating the difference in the outcome that is unconfounded with other factors and thus is attributable solely to the impact of the treatment.

Classical Statistical Adjustments

For decades, the most common statistical analysis performed in conjunction with the nonequivalent

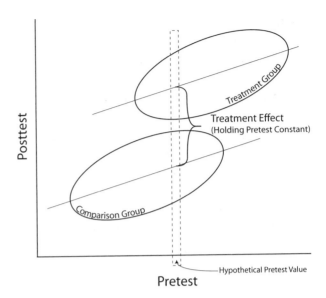

FIGURE 26.1. The logic of analysis of covariance in estimating treatment effects in a nonequivalent comparison group design.

comparison group design has been ANCOVA. The theory behind this method is that by including the pretest measure as a covariate in the model, the estimated impact of the treatment equals the difference between the treatment and comparison groups, after holding pretest scores constant. In other words, the ANCOVA seeks to estimate the expected difference in posttest scores between subjects who started with the same pretest score. In our hypothetical study of antidepressants, this is analogous to comparing the severity of depression at posttest for patients receiving or not receiving antidepressants who had identical severity of depression before treatment.

In an ANCOVA model, the relationship between pretest and posttest scores is captured in a regression equation, and the difference in intercepts between the regression lines for the treatment and comparison groups serves as the estimate of the treatment effect.[2] Figure 26.1 depicts this relationship using ovals to approximate the location of data points for the treatment and comparison groups, solid lines to depict the regression lines, and a dashed box to illustrate the idea of holding the pretest constant when estimating the posttest difference.

---

[2]The standard ANCOVA model assumes parallel pretest–posttest slopes in the treatment and comparison groups. This is referred to as the *homogeneity of regression assumption* (Wildt & Ahtola, 1978). This assumption can be relaxed by including an interaction between the pretest variable and the treatment indicator, although doing so makes interpretation of results in nonequivalent comparison designs very problematic (Reichardt, 1979, p. 170).

Unfortunately, although the ANCOVA approach may be intuitively appealing, it has a number of significant shortcomings. All of these shortcomings can cause the model to adjust inappropriately, either too much or too little, for preexisting differences between the groups. This leads to bias in the treatment effect, and this bias may be either positive or negative.

One likely source of bias is unreliability in the pretest measure, which is certain to occur in our study of antidepressants given that severity of depression cannot be measured with perfect reliability. Because the pretest–posttest relationship is estimated using a regression equation, the slope of that equation is subject to bias associated with measurement error in the pretest scores. It is well known that measurement error in an independent variable in a regression model will result in attenuation of the slope estimate toward zero proportionate to the unreliability in that predictor variable—the estimated slope will equal the true slope multiplied by the reliability of the predictor (i.e., $\beta_{Obtained} = \beta_{True} \times \rho_{xx}$). When unreliability attenuates the pretest slope in an ANCOVA model used to estimate impacts for a nonequivalent groups design, the estimate of the treatment effect will be biased whenever there are differences in the mean pretest scores of the treatment and comparison groups. Figure 26.2 presents a case in which the treatment and comparison groups are sampled from different ends of the same population and the effect of the treatment is zero. The attenuation in the pre–post regression slope is evident in the slope of the dashed lines, which is less steep than the slope for the full population (i.e., the solid line). This attenuation results in separation of the intercepts for the two groups, thus giving the illusion of a treatment effect. As demonstrated by Reichardt (1979, p. 163), as unreliability in the pretest increases, the degree of adjustment induced by the ANCOVA decreases, resulting in a failure to remove all of the preexisting differences from the impact estimate. Therefore, when measurement error exists in the pretest, a preexisting difference favoring the treatment group would result in a positively biased impact estimate, whereas a preexisting difference favoring the comparison group would result in a negatively biased impact estimate. If there is no pretest difference between treatment and comparison groups (e.g., as in a randomized experiment), then the attenuation in slope would cause both regression lines to pivot on the same fulcrum (i.e., the overall mean). Thus, no difference in intercepts would result from pretest unreliability if there were no preexisting difference on the pretest.

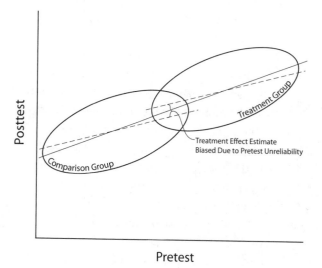

FIGURE 26.2. Measurement bias in the regression slope under an analysis of covariance model of treatment impact in a nonequivalent comparison group design.

Naturally, one might conclude that the bias in the ANCOVA's pre–post slope could be easily removed by dividing the estimated slope by the reliability of the pretest measure. In practice, the procedure for adjusting ANCOVA for unreliability in the pretest is slightly different but also simple. Consider that the regression slope coefficient represents the expected change in Y (i.e., the dependent variable) for each one-unit change in X (i.e., the independent variable). Because the biased regression coefficient in an ANCOVA is underestimated to a degree equal to the reliability in the pretest measure (i.e., r_{xx}), one way to increase the size of the slope coefficient by that exact amount is to change the scale of the X variable by that same amount. This is accomplished by rescaling the pretest scores by the reliability coefficient using the formula

$$X_{adj} = \overline{X}_j + \rho_{xx}\left(X_{ij} - \overline{X}_j\right), \qquad (2)$$

where $\overline{X}_j$ is the mean score for group j (e.g., treatment or comparison group), X_{ij} is the unadjusted pretest score for subject i in group j, and ρ_{xx} is the reliability of the pretest measure. This adjustment must be calculated separately for each group in the ANCOVA in order to shift the slopes but not the intercepts. Essentially, the adjustment shrinks the pretest scores toward their respective group means by an amount proportionate to the amount of unreliability in the pretest measure. This effectively changes the scale of the pretest measure in the ANCOVA so that what had originally been a one-unit change in the X variable is now only a ρ_{xx}-unit change in the X_{adj} variable. This translates to an increase in the slope coefficient equal to $1/\rho_{XX}$. Porter (1967) and Porter and Chibucos (1974) referred to this technique as the *estimated true scores adjustment* to ANCOVA.

Because the problem of unreliability and attenuation of the pretest slope is an artifact of regression analysis, another way to avoid this problem (but perhaps create other problems) is to forgo the regression aspect of covariance adjustment and analyze simple pre–post change scores instead. This is the approach taken by the difference-in-differences analysis mentioned earlier that is popular in econometric literature (Greene, 1993). When the data contain only two time points (i.e., pretest and posttest), the results are the same whether group differences in change scores are estimated after subtracting each subject's pretest score from their posttest score or, alternatively, fixed-effects (i.e., dummy variables) for subjects are included in a model that includes both pretest and posttest scores in the dependent variable (i.e., with two records, pretest and posttest, in the data set for each subject). Furthermore, the realized model is also equivalent to an ANCOVA model when the pretest slope has been fixed at a value of one. The implication of this is that a model analyzing change scores assumes that the pretest difference between treatment and comparison groups would persist in identical direction and magnitude in the absence of a treatment effect (e.g., a 10-point difference in the pretest would result in exactly a 10-point difference in the posttest). In our hypothetical study of antidepressants, this implies that the mean difference in depression scores between those receiving and not receiving medication would be identical in the pretest and posttest, if the medication had no effect. This requires that depression be measured on a perfectly interval scale (so that a difference of X has the same

interpretation at any point on the scale) and that the effect of psychotherapy alone is identical regardless of the pretest depression score (e.g., every patient's depression score is expected to drop by 20 points, regardless of where they started). In our example, these assumptions are difficult to justify.

Figure 26.3 illustrates the parallel trends assumption in change score and difference-in-difference models. The dotted lines and italicized labels represent the unobserved potential outcomes (e.g., the posttest outcome for the treatment group, had the treatment not been delivered).

Unfortunately, this assumption of parallel trends in potential outcomes is often violated in social science research. Factors that deflate the transfer of pretest differences to posttest scores include pre–post construct shift and construct nonequivalence. These terms refer to situations in which the meaning of what is measured changes slightly (i.e., a shift) or completely (i.e., nonequivalence) from pretest to posttest. For example, if identical or equated measures of depression severity are not used at pretest and posttest, then posttest differences cannot be expected to equal pretest differences.

Factors that can inflate or deflate the transfer of pretest differences to posttest scores include changes in measurement scale and pre–post changes in score variance (e.g., posttest scores may be more variable than pretest scores). Furthermore, the assumption

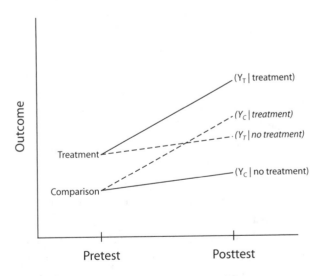

FIGURE 26.3. The parallel trends assumption of change score and fixed-effects analysis of treatment impacts in a nonequivalent comparison group design.

that the pre–post change for the comparison group serves as a good counterfactual for the treatment group can also be violated by any of the selection interactions mentioned thus far. These selection-interaction validity threats affect both change score and ANCOVA analyses.

Simply put, both ANCOVA and change score models have substantial potential for bias when estimating treatment effects in conjunction with a nonequivalent comparison group design. The choice between these two approaches has long been a topic of discussion, and although the problem has largely been solved, the news is not good. Although there are clear circumstances under which the ANCOVA works best and there are other circumstances under which the change score analysis works best, these circumstances are restrictive. Unfortunately, most circumstances involving a nonequivalent comparison group design in reality will induce bias in both analyses, and the two methods will often yield different results. The difference in results produced by these two analyses was originally presented as Lord's paradox (Lord, 1967). It is a paradox in that it is perplexing that the two methods so often produce different results despite the fact that they are intended to answer the same research question (i.e., "What is the treatment effect?"). Holland and Rubin (1983) were the first to solve Lord's paradox by evaluating the problem in the context of Rubin's potential outcomes framework for causal inference (Holland, 1986; Rubin, 1974). Their key revelation was that the decision to use ANCOVA versus change score analysis was driven by untestable assumptions about the potential outcomes for the two groups. In the context of a nonequivalent groups design, the implicit assumptions are whether the posttest scores for the treatment group, had the treatment not been delivered, are better approximated by adding the average change for the comparison group to the pretest scores of the treatment group (Option A), or using a within-group regression model to predict posttest outcomes for the treatment group (Option B). Option A leads to change score analysis, whereas Option B leads to ANCOVA. These assumptions are entirely untestable without additional data (e.g., multiple pretests), and the choice between these two analytical alternatives is not necessarily obvious.

Fortunately, choosing between ANCOVA and change score analysis becomes a little less perplexing when one realizes that the two approaches target different analytical questions (Hand, 1994; Wainer, 1991; Wright, 2005). The change score analysis simply seeks to determine whether, on average, one group experienced a larger pretest–posttest difference. Contrast this with the ANCOVA, which seeks to determine whether the posttest scores of subjects from the treatment group were, on average, higher or lower than those of comparison group subjects who had equivalent pretest scores. This logic also helps us understand when one approach may be more appropriate than the other. For example, whenever it is unreasonable to calculate a change score by subtracting the pretest from the posttest score (e.g., when the pretest and posttest are not on the same scale), the change score analysis can be eliminated as a viable option. On the other hand, the change score analysis may be less biased than the ANCOVA whenever it is reasonable to expect that in the absence of the treatment, the posttest scores will approximately equal the pretest scores. In the case of our hypothetical study of antidepressants, every patient's depression score is expected to change given that they are receiving psychotherapy, and there is no reason to believe that psychotherapy will yield the same degree of change for every value of the pretest measure, so ANCOVA is likely the better approach. However, ANCOVA is still not guaranteed to produce unbiased estimates in our case. Although being specific about the analytic questions and assumptions may help a researcher decide between ANCOVA and change score analysis in a nonequivalent groups study, the fact that the assumptions behind the choice are untestable suggests that the estimated treatment effect will not necessarily be unbiased.

To reach a higher level of certainty, one must go beyond the specificity of analytic questions and focus also on the ability of the analytic model to properly account for the treatment assignment mechanism. Maris (1998) used Rubin's causal model to present a mathematical explanation of the differences between ANCOVA and change score analyses and to show how their ability to produce unbiased treatment effects is related to the treatment assignment mechanism. Using empirical simulation, Wright (2005) verified and further illustrated Maris's results, which are as follows. Both ANCOVA and change score analysis produce unbiased results when assignment to treatment is random (i.e., as in a randomized experiment). When the pretest is used to assign subjects to the treatment, either using a cutoff (i.e., as in a regression discontinuity design; see Chapter 27 of this volume) or using blocked random assignment (i.e., all subjects with the same pretest score have the same probability of assignment to treatment), then ANCOVA is unbiased whereas change score analysis is biased. When the probability of assignment to treatment is correlated with the pretest, but the pretest does not precisely determine assignment probability (i.e., all subjects with the same pretest score do not have an identical probability of assignment to treatment), then ANCOVA is always biased and change score analysis will be unbiased only if the pre–post trends are independent of the groups.[3] Lastly, when treatment assignment is correlated with (but not determined by) the pretest and also with errors of measurement contained in the pretest (or other factors exhibiting the same measurement biases as the pretest), then both ANCOVA and change score analyses are biased. Unfortunately, this last case is most likely applicable to our example study of antidepressants, so we may be better served by seeking out other ways to address selection bias.

Matching to Address Overt Bias

An alternative to model-based adjustments for pretest differences involves the use of blocking or matching on pretreatment covariates. The logic here is that posttest comparisons are restricted to those subjects in the treatment and comparison groups that had similar pretreatment characteristics. This approach is similar to that of ANCOVA; however, blocking or matching does not usually rely on a linear regression to model equivalence.

In the simplest case of blocking, subjects in the treatment and comparison groups might be grouped into blocks on the basis of similar scores on the pretest. For example, in our hypothetical study of antidepressants, we might group patients with similar pretest depression scores into homogeneous blocks. As the number of blocks increases, the reduction of selection bias approaches that of the ANCOVA model after relaxing the assumptions of linearity or homogeneity of regression. Cochran (1968) demonstrated that the vast majority of selection bias associated with a covariate can be removed using as few as five blocks.

An alternative to blocking involves pair matching or caliper matching (Cochran & Rubin, 1973). Instead of categorizing subjects into broad groups, each subject in the treatment group is either matched to a subject from the comparison group with the same pretest score (i.e., pair matching) or is matched to a subject from the comparison group who has a pretest score that is close to the treatment subject's pretest score (i.e., caliper matching). Cochran and Rubin (1973) showed that the vast majority of selection bias associated with a pretest difference can be removed using a caliper as large as one half of a standard deviation.

Unfortunately, blocking and matching on the pretest is subject to the same sources of bias that threaten ANCOVA analyses, including measurement bias and selection interactions (Maris, 1998; Reichardt, 1979). Furthermore, because the pretest blocking or matching approaches can never perform better than an ANCOVA that appropriately models nonlinear and nonparallel regression trends, the value of blocking or matching on the pretest is limited.

One area in which matching holds greater promise is in multivariate matching using multiple pretreatment variables. For our hypothetical study of antidepressants, we could imagine measuring and then matching patients on initial severity of depression, age, gender, race, income, type of insurance, place of residence (e.g., city vs. suburbs), and various other factors related to the outcome. Rosenbaum (2002, 2010) presented several methods for matching on multiple covariates. Each of these methods relies on a distance matrix to evaluate the relative proximity of treatment and comparison

---

[3]This is analogous to the *parallel trends assumption* (see Figure 26.3), which implies that the comparison group trend can be used to estimate the change for the treatment group in the absence of the treatment, and the treatment group trend can be used to estimate the change for the comparison group if they had received the treatment.

group members on the multiple covariates. These matching methods can be distinguished on the basis of the method of linking treatment and comparison subjects and the number of treatment or comparison subjects that may be linked. Methods include caliper matching, greedy matching, and optimal matching. Multivariate caliper matching links subjects that have proximal values on all covariates. Greedy matching links subjects to the nearest neighbor matches and moves sequentially through the data set. Greedy matching is so named because once a match is made, it is not broken, even if a chosen match would be better matched to another subject farther down in the data set. In our hypothetical study of antidepressants, a greedy matching algorithm might match a subject in the treatment group to a control with a similar pretest score, despite the fact that that pretest score for that particular control was even closer to the pretest score for another treatment group member farther down in the data set. Alternatively, optimal matching links subjects in such a way that the total distance between matches is minimized. In other words, matches can be rearranged during the matching process so that the end result produces the closest matched set possible.

The different approaches to the number of links made in multivariate matching include pair matching, multiple control matching, and full matching. Pair matching links each treatment group member to one comparison group member, whereas multiple control matching links each treatment group member to at least one comparison group member. For example, each patient taking antidepressants may be matched to one comparison patient (with pair matching) or to two or more comparison patients (with multiple matching) who were not taking antidepressants but who were similar in other respects. Lastly, full matching links each treatment group member to at least one comparison group member and also allows each comparison group member to be matched to multiple treatment group members, although each subject appears in only one matched group. For example, patients taking antidepressants who are similar on other characteristics may be matched to the same comparison patients, thus producing a group that is consistent on measured

covariates but varied in terms of antidepressant treatment.

The objective of any matching method is to create blocks or strata that include at least one member of the treatment group and at least one member of the comparison group where the members in any given group are similar on all observed covariates. Among these matching methods, the most effective approach for balancing preexisting differences is optimal full matching, although matching using the propensity score (see following four paragraphs) may provide even better covariate balance (Gu & Rosenbaum, 1993).

Recall from the previous section that the solution to Lord's paradox requires an understanding of the relationship between the pretest and the treatment assignment mechanism. To ensure unbiased estimation of the treatment effect, comparisons of outcomes should be restricted to only those subjects with equal probability of assignment to the treatment. In other words, unbiased estimation of the treatment effect can be ensured only when the use of covariates in the analytical model serves to create a blocked random assignment design. Extending this logic, Rosenbaum and Rubin (1983) defined the *propensity score* as the probability that an individual is or was assigned to the treatment group. When an analysis compares outcomes for subjects with identical propensity scores, it mimics a blocked random assignment design, and the estimate of the effect of the treatment is unbiased.

In randomized experiments, the values of the individual propensity scores are known. If simple random assignment is used, then the propensity scores equal .5 if half of the study sample is assigned to the treatment. If blocked random assignment is used, then the propensity scores in each block are equal to the proportion of subjects that were assigned to the treatment from that block. In nonrandomized studies, the propensity scores are unknown, but they may be estimated using observed covariates. This is typically accomplished by building a logistic regression model predicting treatment assignment (i.e., $Y_i = 1$ if treated; $Y_i = 0$ if untreated) on the basis of observed pretreatment covariates. In our study of antidepressants, we could imagine using all of the covariates and matching factors previously mentioned as predictors of whether a patient receives antidepressant medication. The predicted probabilities from this model can serve as estimates of the individual propensity scores in an observational study. In general, the propensity score model includes all available covariates and may also include interactions and nonlinear terms. Because the objective is to maximize the precision and accuracy of the estimated propensity scores, it is advisable to include all available covariates, even if they do not meet the traditional criteria for statistical significance (Rosenbaum, 2002, 2010; Rubin, 1997; Rubin & Thomas, 1996).[4] The objective is to build a propensity score model that includes all relevant confounds such that the assignment to treatment is independent, conditional on the propensity score, of the potential outcomes. In other words, the objective is to remove all confounding between treatment assignment and any covariates related to the outcome.

Once the propensity score is estimated, it is common practice to estimate treatment–comparison group differences after implementing paired, multiple, or full matching using the propensity score as a single matching variable (see Rosenbaum, 2010). Alternatively, propensity score stratification may be used to group subjects by their propensity scores, much like blocking on the pretest. And, similar to blocking on the pretest, Rosenbaum and Rubin (1984) also cited Cochran (1968) in support of their recommendation for five strata when using propensity score stratification. Furthermore, Rubin (2004) recommended including covariates in the statistical model of program impacts, even after matching on the propensity score. Lastly, the propensity score may also be used as a covariate in an ANCOVA, although this approach imposes the assumption of a linear relationship between the propensity score and the outcome.[5]

Although the propensity score may be intuitively appealing, perhaps even ingenious, as a method for improving causal inference in nonexperimental studies, it has a number of important limitations. For example, as the number of relevant covariates increases, and the predictive power of the model improves, there is increased separation in estimated propensity scores between the treatment and comparison groups. This suggests that as the propensity score model improves in precision, the overlap in estimated propensity scores between the treatment and comparison groups diminishes, and the availability of suitable propensity score matches decreases. In other words, a propensity score model with very high predictive power may confirm that the treatment and comparison groups are, in fact, incomparable. Imagine if the logistic regression model predicting which patients do and do not receive antidepressant medication has such high predictive power that the estimated propensity scores for nearly all of those receiving medication were close to 1 and for nearly all of those not receiving medication were close to zero. This would suggest that (a) we could predict quite well (albeit not perfectly) who did and did not receive medication, and (b) the differences in the propensities of these two groups were so large that they are simply incomparable.

Even when there is substantial overlap in the distributions of propensity scores, there is no guarantee that stratification or matching will produce balance on all of the observed covariates. Even though the propensity score is remarkably effective when used as a single matching variable, it is imperative that covariate balance be evaluated by testing for treatment–control differences within strata or by comparing absolute differences in covariates within pairs or strata (see Rosenbaum, 2010, pp. 187–190). Shadish et al. (2002) pointed out that the propensity score model requires large samples (e.g., hundreds, if not thousands, of subjects in each group), lack of overlap in the distribution of propensity scores can limit analytic sample size and generalizability of results, the likelihood of missing data across many covariates complicates the estimation of propensity

---

[4]It is important that none of the predictors included in the propensity score model are caused by the treatment or the outcome. This suggests that mediators and other intermediate outcomes should be excluded from the propensity score model. The best way to ensure exclusion of intermediate and secondary outcomes may be to use only pretreatment variables, measured before the intervention, as predictors in the propensity score model.

[5]A curvilinear relationship may also be modeled by including a quadratic term for the propensity score. However, stratification is better able to handle many forms of nonlinearity in the relationship between the propensity score and the outcome.

scores, and the ability of the propensity score approach to produce unbiased estimates is dependent on the availability of all relevant confounding variables (i.e., those covariates related to treatment assignment and potential outcomes). This last point is crucial. If any unmeasured covariates exist that are related to both treatment assignment and the outcome after controlling for other observed covariates, the impact estimate will still be biased even after conditioning on the propensity score. In our hypothetical study of antidepressants, the sheer number of factors that are related to depression outcomes and that also influence whether a patient receives an antidepressant is so large that a propensity score model is unlikely to account for all aspects of selection bias—can we really expect to measure everything that determines whether a patient receives antidepressants and is also related to posttreatment outcomes?

Using Instrumental Variables to Address Hidden Bias

The problem of potential hidden bias plagues the nonequivalent comparison group design. In any such study, the validity of the conclusions may be questioned because there may be an uncontrolled confound that explains away the relationship between the treatment and the outcome. In most nonequivalent group designs, it is not hard to conjecture about specific unmeasured confounds that might exist, and the methods discussed up to this point can only hope to control those confounds that were actually measured. What is needed is a method that can control for both observed bias and also hidden bias associated with unobserved confounds. Recall that for the difference-in-differences model, it was argued that analysis of change scores removes the selection bias attributable to any time-invariant confounding variable. In that case, the effects of these variables might be controlled, even without explicitly measuring them. The econometric instrumental variables (IV) technique promises to do the same thing in the analysis of treatment effects in a nonequivalent groups design. Unfortunately, the literature on IV is highly technical and relies on

notation and vocabulary that, until recently, was inaccessible to noneconomists. The purpose of the following section is to provide a brief, minimally technical description of the theory and assumptions behind IV and describe common methods for producing IV-adjusted impact estimates.

To understand the IV technique, one must focus on one crucial, but often ignored, assumption underlying unbiased estimation in statistical modeling. That crucial assumption is that the predictor variables in a model must be uncorrelated with the model error term. In this case, the error term does not refer to model residuals. Although residuals are estimates of the errors, they will be biased estimates of the errors if the model itself is biased. To illustrate this, consider a simple regression model of a treatment impact:

$$Y_i = \beta_0 + \beta_1 T + \varepsilon_i, \tag{3}$$

in which Y_i is the outcome for individual i, β_0 is the model intercept representing the mean outcome under the control condition, β_1 is the effect of treatment T (coded one for the treatment group and zero for the comparison group), and ε_i is the variability in the outcome for individual i that is attributable to random error and any other unmeasured covariates. Because ε_i includes the influence of all unmeasured covariates, we could imagine separating ε_i into two parts. The first part, ξ_i, represents random error that is uncorrelated with anything. The second part, π, is a set (i.e., a vector) of regression slopes, which is multiplied by a set of relevant covariates X_i measured on each individual i. After substitution, our regression model looks like this:

$$Y_i = \beta_0 + \beta_1 T + (\pi X_i + \xi_i), \tag{4}$$

and the problem should start to become clear. If we were to actually measure all of the X variables and include them as controls in this model, the original estimate of the effect of T would change if T is correlated with any of the X variables. That is the nature of control variables and confounding in statistical models.[6] If the X variables are unmeasured, then the parameter estimate for T remains unadjusted (i.e., biased). Furthermore, because the T variable is

---

[6]For more information on control variables, confounding, and unbiased parameter estimation in linear statistical models, see Neter, Kutner, Nachtsheim, and Wasserman (1996).

correlated with at least one of the X variables, and the effects of the unmeasured X variables are subsumed in the error term, then T is correlated with the error term. This is a very bad situation if the objective is to estimate the causal effect of T on Y. If we estimate a naive model that does not include all of the relevant X variables as controls, then the part of the error term that is correlated with T is included in our estimate of the impact β. In other words, the naïve model does a bad job of properly attributing variation in the outcome to T versus the error term, and part of what should be attributed to unmeasured covariates and included in the error is attributed to the treatment.

IV techniques offer an opportunity to get around this problem under certain circumstances. For those readers already familiar with mediation analysis (Baron & Kenny, 1986), the logic of IV may sound somewhat familiar. In fact, IV analysis can be thought of as somewhat like a backward mediation analysis. First, the researcher must identify an *instrument*, which is a measureable variable that is (a) correlated with the treatment variable (i.e., it predicts treatment assignment); (b) through its correlation with the treatment, also correlated with the outcome; and (c) uncorrelated with any other covariate related to the outcome. In other words, a valid instrument has a significant relationship with the outcome variable but only as a result of its correlation with treatment assignment.[7] From a mediation perspective (i.e., in which the effect of one variable happens indirectly through its effect on an intermediate outcome), the effect of the instrument is mediated by the treatment; however, unlike in mediation analysis, we do not care about the direct or indirect effects of the instrument. We simply want to use the instrument to remove the influence of selection bias and adjust the estimated treatment effect to produce an unbiased causal effect.

The logic of how an IV analysis produces an unbiased estimate is shown in Figure 26.4. Here the causal effect on the outcome Y of the treatment T is equal to β. An additional covariate X is also related to the outcome, with a regression slope equal to π. The correlation between T and X is equal to ρ. If we were to estimate a naïve model with only T predicting Y, then our estimate of the slope for T would actually equal $\beta + \pi\rho$, which is clearly biased unless either ρ or π equal zero.[8] Unfortunately, we cannot use this formula to adjust our estimate of β because neither ρ nor π can be estimated since X has not been measured. However, if the relationship between the IV and Y occurs only because of the relationship between the IV and the treatment, then we can estimate β using our knowledge of α and γ. This is because a simple linear regression predicting Y only on the basis of the IV will yield a slope estimate γ, which is equal to the direct effect of the IV on Y (which we assume is zero because the IV's relationship with Y happens exclusively through T) plus an amount equal to the product of α and γ (i.e., $\gamma = 0 + \alpha\beta$). This follows from the same formula used to show the bias in the naïve impact estimate. Thus, with a little algebra, we can calculate β directly as γ/α. This is the IV estimate of the impact of T on Y.

Estimation of the IV model is typically done through two-stage least squares, in which both the regression of T on the IV and the regression of Y on the IV are estimated in a simultaneous equations process. Using simultaneous equations ensures that the standard errors of the IV estimate are unbiased. Structural equation modeling and maximum likelihood techniques can also be used to estimate the simultaneous equations in an IV analysis. Unfortunately, because of the stringent requirements of the exclusion restriction, good instruments are often hard to find.[9] For example, a good instrument has a strong correlation with the treatment variable. If the

---

[7]This is referred to in the econometric literature as the *exclusion restriction* because the instrument can be excluded from the causal model if the X's are observed.

[8]Either π or ρ would be equal to zero only if X were uncorrelated with either Y or T, respectively. If that were true, then X would not be confounded with the effect of T, and we would be able to estimate the effect of T without any adjustment. Of course, having no confounding variables is only likely to happen in a randomized experiment.

[9]For more on the assumptions of IV and assessment of the IV assumptions, see the following: Angrist, Imbens, and Rubin (1996); Bound, Jaeger, and Baker (1995); Buse (1992); Staiger and Stock (1997).

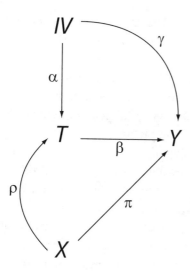

FIGURE 26.4. The logic of instrumental variables (IV) analysis and omitted variable bias in estimating the effect of a treatment (T) on an outcome (Y).

instrument has a low correlation with the treatment variable, then the denominator in the IV calculation is small, resulting in an unstable and usually biased estimate. This is referred to as having a *weak instrument* (Bound, Jaeger, & Baker, 1995). Even more common may be violations of the assumption that the instrument is uncorrelated with other confounding covariates. Angrist and Pischke (2009) pointed out that this assumption is analogous to saying that "the instrument is as good as randomly assigned" (p. 117). That means that the instrument is essentially random in relation to the unobserved covariates and potential outcomes while it is strongly correlated with treatment assignment. Obviously, finding such a variable may be impossible. Angrist and Krueger (2001) explained the problem of identifying good instruments and provided numerous examples. In general, the most promising instrumental variables are often those that are associated with a policy or circumstance that limits or enhances access to a treatment but that does so fairly arbitrarily (e.g., month of birth, policy differences across adjacent municipalities, and distance to a facility).

In our hypothetical study of antidepressants, there are at least a couple of candidates for use as an instrumental variable. First, consider the relative prevalence of psychiatrists or psychologists with prescribing privileges in a geographic area. If we first restrict our analyses to those patients who do not receive a prescription for an antidepressant from their primary care physician, then the likelihood of receiving an antidepressant is related to the likelihood of visiting or being referred to a practitioner with prescribing privileges and that is dependent on the availability of such practitioners in the area. Furthermore, it may be reasonable to expect that prescribing practitioners are relatively randomly distributed across geographic areas. Given this, we could calculate for each patient, the relative prevalence of practitioners with prescribing privileges within 10 miles of the patient's residence. We would then use simultaneous equations estimation to regress the depression posttest scores on the IV (to estimate γ) and also regress the treatment indicator (1 = antidepressant; 0 = no antidepressant) on the IV (to estimate α). Finally, β is calculated as γ/α.

As a potential IV, our measure of the prevalence of practitioners with prescribing privileges within 10 miles of the patient's residence is likely to meet the relevance assumption (i.e., it is related to the probability of receiving an antidepressant and hence is not a weak instrument); however, it is unlikely to meet the exclusion assumption. That is, the correlation between the number of prescribing practitioners near a patient's residence and that patient's depression posttest scores is unlikely to be solely attributable to whether that patient received a prescription for an antidepressant. For example, if practitioners with prescribing privileges are less likely to open offices in impoverished areas (because of crime, uninsured residents, and so on) and poverty is correlated with severity of depression, then the relationship between our IV and depression posttest scores may be attributable to an unmeasured confound (i.e., poverty), thus violating the exclusion restriction.

Another potential IV is whether different insurance carriers have different policies regarding their coverage for antidepressant medications. If some patients are forced to pay higher copayments for their antidepressants, they may be less likely to take the medication. Therefore, this potential IV is related to the probability of taking an antidepressant, but it may be otherwise uncorrelated with posttest depression scores. In other words, the relationship between the amount of the copayment and posttest depression scores is due solely to whether the patient fills the prescription. Of course, one could imagine violations of the exclusion restriction if the size of copayments was related to other confounding variables like income or age.

OTHER DESIGN ENHANCEMENTS TO ADDRESS SELECTION BIAS

This section briefly reviews a few additional design enhancements that are especially promising for improving the validity of nonexperimental comparison group designs. These enhancements are designed to do one of three things. First, they may address directly specific threats to internal validity, such as a probable selection-maturation interaction. Second, they may improve internal validity by explicitly testing a series of hypothesized causal relationships, thereby evaluating not just the overall impact of a program but its entire theory of action. Third, they may seek to quantify the potential for selection bias to establish a plausible range for the impact of a treatment.

Using Multiple Pretests

Recall that a key assumption in the analysis of pretest–posttest data from a nonequivalent groups design is that the pre–post trend for the comparison group (represented either with a simple change score or a pre–post regression model) represents what would have happened in the treatment group if the intervention had not been delivered (i.e., the counterfactual). In the case of a change score model, this implies that the pre–post difference for the comparison group can simply be added to the pretest for the treatment group to produce the expected outcome for the treatment group under the counterfactual. In the case of an ANCOVA model, this implies that the pooled within-groups pre–post regression can be used to extrapolate the expected posttest scores, given the observed pretest score, for the treatment group under the counterfactual.

With only two waves of data (i.e., the pretest and the posttest), these assumptions are untestable. If an additional pretest were available, with the time difference between the two pretests being similar to the time difference between the last pretest and the posttest, then one could explicitly test these

assumptions. The objective is to demonstrate that there is no difference in the pretest-one to pretest-two trend between the treatment and comparison groups. This helps to confirm that there is no selection–maturation interaction and that the two groups were experiencing similar trends before the introduction of the intervention.

In our hypothetical antidepressant study, multiple pretests would only be feasible if the antidepressants were not prescribed for several weeks after psychotherapy began. If that were the case, we could estimate the pretest-one to pretest-two change in depression scores to check for differences in trends before the start of antidepressant therapy in a subset of patients.

The statistical model used to test for differences in pretest trends could take several forms. The simplest approach is to estimate separate models for pretest trends and pre–post trends. The first model would use the second pretest as the outcome and the first pretest as a baseline in a change score model or as a covariate in an ANCOVA. A finding of no significant difference between treatment and comparison groups would support a conclusion of no difference in pretest trends. Once this is confirmed, a second model would be estimated to calculate treatment impact on posttest scores. An alternative to running separate models would be to extend the impact model to include repeated measures (including appropriate terms for autocorrelation of errors to model correlations in repeated measures over time) and to test simultaneously for differences in pretest-one to pretest-two trends as well as differences in pretest-two to posttest trends between the treatment and comparison group.

Even when using multiple pretests confirms a selection-maturation interaction through differential pretest trends, it may be that the pretreatment difference in trends does not explain completely the observed posttest difference between treatment and comparison groups. If the trend in the comparison group remains consistent over time, then the treatment estimate may be parameterized as the difference between treatment and comparison groups in pretest–posttest trends above and beyond the difference in trends that existed before the introduction of the treatment. This situation is far less desirable than having confirmed similar pretest trends, but it does help to remove at least some of the bias attributable to a selection-maturation interaction. More specifically, for selection-maturation to persist as a threat to validity, it must take the form of a three-way interaction between selection, maturation, and time. That is, the difference in maturation rates would need to be changing over time to explain away a treatment effect manifested as differences in changes in trends between the treatment and comparison groups.

Cohort Comparisons

Another design enhancement that can improve the internal validity of the nonequivalent comparison group design involves the use of one or more untreated cohorts as a comparison group. This is often possible when treatments are delivered to eligible persons on the basis of age (e.g., education interventions, health interventions, interventions related to age-based policies such as drinking or voting). The basic idea is that when an intervention is implemented or discontinued, adjacent cohorts differ in their access to the intervention—one cohort gets access whereas the prior cohort did not or vice versa.

There are multiple advantages to the cohort comparison approach. First, the treatment and comparison cohorts may be more likely to be similar on measured and unmeasured covariates. Second, the cohort comparison group design does not prevent the delivery of the treatment to any eligible participant (i.e., the treatment can be delivered to everybody). Third, when the treatment is not delivered to everyone but delivery is restricted to only those in certain cohorts (e.g., subjects in eligible cohorts self-select into the treatment), then cohort membership may be useful as an instrumental variable. Assuming the cohorts are similar on measured and unmeasured covariates, the subjects can be thought of as randomly assigned to cohorts (i.e., the instrument is uncorrelated with covariates), but cohort membership is highly correlated with participation in the treatment because only certain cohorts get access to the treatment (i.e., cohort membership is a strong instrument). In this case, using cohort membership as an instrument for the effect of the treatment has a good chance of producing a valid causal impact estimate.

In our hypothetical study of antidepressants, we could imagine a cohort comparison in a state that is about to enact new legislation allowing psychologists to prescribe antidepressants and other psychotropic medications. By comparing the outcomes of patients from cohorts receiving treatment just before and after enactment of this legislation, we can estimate an unbiased treatment effect as the differences in posttest depression scores so long as the patients in these two cohorts are comparable in all other respects. One clear example of how this assumption might be violated is if the enactment of the legislation coincided with an economic downturn or recovery. In that case, it would be impossible to distinguish the effects of the policy from the effects of changes in the economic situation.

Causal Modeling, Moderation, and Mediation Analyses

Cochran (1965) reflected on advice given by Sir Ronald Fisher regarding causal inference in observational studies, "make your theories elaborate" (p. 252). By this, Fisher meant that one should conceptualize and design a study in such a way that the hypothesized effects of an intervention could be tested on multiple outcomes and under multiple scenarios to establish consistent trends in results that support (or disconfirm) the theory of action behind an intervention. The logic of this perspective is evident in the literature on causal path modeling (Asher, 1983) and mediation and moderation analyses (Baron & Kenny, 1986). In causal path modeling of data from a nonequivalent comparison group design, a series of structural equations are used to estimate simultaneous relationships between treatment conditions and characteristics (e.g., dosage), covariates, intermediate outcomes, and final outcomes. The intent of this approach is to establish evidence of a causal chain that begins with the treatment. In our hypothetical study of antidepressants, we might include multiple outcomes in addition to posttreatment depression scores that are related to depression, such as motivation, concentration, sleep patterns (e.g., insomnia, hypersomnia), libido, appetite, and suicidal thoughts or actions. By exploring the relationships between antidepressant treatment and changes in these outcomes, we may better understand the mechanisms by which the drugs achieve their effects, if there are any.

Similarly, mediation and moderation analyses also use structural models to examine effects of interventions. One intent is to identify mediator variables, which are essentially intermediate outcomes on the causal pathway between the intervention and the outcome. In a mediation analysis, one is able to explore the degree to which the effect of an intervention on an outcome may follow directly from the effect of the intervention on one or more intermediate outcomes. A second intent is to identify moderator variables, which interact with the treatment to produce differential effects depending on the level of the moderator variable. For example, one might use moderation analysis to identify those factors that support or impede the impacts of an intervention. In the case of our antidepressant study, moderation analysis can be used to test for different levels of effectiveness of the drugs across subgroups of patients.

Although a well-designed path analysis or structural model for mediation or moderation may substantiate a theory of action behind an intervention, the model alone does little to address threats to internal validity. This is because these models typically operate in ways similar to that of simple ANCOVA or change score analyses. Thus, the same issues and threats to validity persist. The use of causal path analysis and mediation or moderation analyses should not be considered sufficient for valid causal inference. When these models are used, it is advisable to combine them with other techniques for addressing overt or hidden bias, such as propensity score matching and instrumental variables analysis.

Sensitivity Analysis

In a nonequivalent comparison group design, regardless of the steps taken to address threats to validity, there is always the possibility of an unmeasured confound that might explain any treatment effect. Even though the existence of potential unmeasured confounds cannot be debated, it is important to recognize that all confounds are not equal. Although every

confound, if controlled, might change the results of an impact analysis in a nonequivalent groups study, minor confounds would change the results only slightly, whereas major confounds can change results in dramatic ways. Rosenbaum (2002, 2010) advocated that sensitivity analyses be conducted in any observational study to determine the magnitude of uncontrolled selection bias that would need to exist to substantially reduce or render insignificant the estimate of impact.

The logic of such a sensitivity analysis begins with the notion that comparisons in a properly designed nonequivalent groups design have been appropriately matched, blocked, or modeled so that the treatment effect estimate is based on comparisons of subjects who have equal propensity scores. Under this assumption, it is helpful to think of the magnitude of selection bias in terms of the relative difference in propensity scores if the *matched* subjects did not in fact have equal probabilities of assignment to treatment. For example, two subjects with estimated propensity scores of .70 may actually have true propensity scores of .90 and .60, with the failure of the propensity score model to capture this difference because a key covariate was unobserved. In this situation, the actual propensity scores of .90 and .60, when converted to an odds ratio (i.e., $[.90/(1 - .90)]/[.60/(1 - .60)] = 6$), suggest that one subject is actually 6 times more likely to have experienced the treatment than his or her matched counterpart. This is a large potential bias.

A sensitivity analysis for a nonequivalent groups design reveals the magnitude of hidden bias (i.e., the odds ratio of propensity scores) required to reduce or eliminate the estimated effect of the treatment. If a sensitivity analysis yielded a figure of 6 as in the example, then one would conclude that to dismiss the estimate of treatment effect as being caused by selection bias, one or more unmeasured confounds would need to exist that would make the subjects in the treatment group at least 6 times more likely to experience the treatment than those in the comparison group. Given that odds ratios of 6 are quite uncommon in social science research, it is reasonable to conclude that the unobserved selection bias would need to be gigantic in order to dismiss the estimated treatment effect. The calculations behind sensitivity analyses are detailed in Rosenbaum (2002, Chapter 4); however, these calculations are applicable only to nonparametric analyses (i.e., McNemar's test, Wilcoxon's signed rank test, Hodges-Lehmann point estimate).

In our hypothetical study of antidepressants, it is reasonable to expect that the best predictor of prescription of antidepressants is the pretreatment severity of depression. Imagine then that the odds ratio for a one–standard deviation increase in depression severity is 3, suggesting that the likelihood of receiving an antidepressant triples with each standard deviation increase in pretreatment depression severity. Following that, if a sensitivity analysis revealed that an unmeasured confound would need to produce differences in propensity scores analogous to an odds ratio of 6, then that confound would need to have a predictive effect on the receipt of an antidepressant that was twice as large as the pretreatment severity of depression. Such a confound is unlikely to exist, thus bolstering the confidence with which results from this nonequivalent comparison group design can be interpreted.

CONCLUSION

Light, Singer, and Willett (1990) claimed, "You can't fix by analysis what you bungled by design" (p. v). Although that statement is generally true regarding nonequivalent comparison group designs, there are clearly a number of rather powerful tools that can enhance the validity of inferences from this design. Through explicit controls for measured confounds, enhancements to address validity threats, instrumental variables to remove hidden bias, and elaborate theories to test hypotheses, there is the potential for nonexperimental designs to provide useful information about the effects of interventions. In some cases, the accuracy of that information may rival that from a randomized experiment. Yet, even when the potential for selection bias persists, we can use sensitivity analysis to evaluate the robustness of the findings against likely or hypothetical confounding factors.

The recommendations that follow from this discussion of methods are similar to those proposed by Rubin (2004). First, a researcher should implement as many design enhancements as possible to address

probable threats to valid inference. Second, the researcher should collect both pre- and posttreatment data on as many relevant covariates, treatment indicators, intermediate outcomes, and final outcomes as feasible. Third, the researcher should use propensity score methods, matching, or blocking to account for major differences between treatment and comparison groups and remove most observable selection bias. Fourth, the researcher should use covariance analysis, regression modeling, and instrumental variables analysis (when feasible) to increase precision and provide additional control of observed and perhaps unobserved covariates not yet completely balanced. Lastly, the researcher should conduct sensitivity analyses to determine the extent to which unmeasured confounds may create selection biases large enough to substantially alter the impact estimates.

Although nonequivalent comparison group studies are quite susceptible to bias, the ability to extract useful information is especially important because many interventions are not amenable to study through an experimental design or a well-controlled quasi-experiment. In these cases, we are often forced to simply compare those who received the treatment with those who did not. Thankfully, we have several methods at our disposal that can help avoid apples to oranges comparisons and perhaps even turn lemons into lemonade.

References

Angrist, J. D., Imbens, G. W., & Rubin, D. B. (1996). Identification of causal effects using instrumental variables. *Journal of the American Statistical Association, 91*, 444–455. doi:10.2307/2291629

Angrist, J., & Krueger, A. B. (2001). Instrumental variables and the search for identification: From supply and demand to natural experiments. *Journal of Economic Perspectives, 15*, 69–85. doi:10.1257/jep.15.4.69

Angrist, J., & Pischke, S. (2009). *Mostly harmless econometrics: An empiricists' companion.* Princeton, NJ: Princeton University Press.

Asher, H. (1983). *Causal modeling.* Beverly Hills, CA: Sage.

Baron, R. M., & Kenny, D. A. (1986). The moderator–mediator variable distinction in social psychological research: Conceptual, strategic, and statistical considerations. *Journal of Personality and Social*

Psychology, 51, 1173–1182. doi:10.1037/0022-3514.51.6.1173

Boruch, R. F., May, H., Lavenberg, J., Turner, H. M., Petrosino, A., De Moya, D., . . . Foley, E. (2004). Estimating the effects of interventions that are deployed in many places: Place randomized trials. *American Behavioral Scientist, 47*, 608–633. doi:10.1177/0002764203259291

Bound, J., Jaeger, D. A., & Baker, R. M. (1995). Problems with instrumental variables estimation when the correlation between the instruments and the endogenous explanatory variables is weak. *Journal of the American Statistical Association, 90*, 443–450. doi:10.2307/2291055

Buse, A. (1992). The bias of instrumental variable estimators. *Econometrica, 60*, 173–180. doi:10.2307/2951682

Campbell, D. T., & Stanley, J. C. (1963). *Experimental and quasi-experimental designs for research.* Boston, MA: Houghton Mifflin.

Cochran, W. G. (1965). The planning of observational studies of human populations (with discussion). *Journal of the Royal Statistical Society, Series A (General), 128*, 234–266. doi:10.2307/2344179

Cochran, W. G. (1968). The effectiveness of adjustment by subclassification in removing bias in observational studies. *Biometrics, 24*, 295–313. doi:10.2307/2528036

Cochran, W. G., & Rubin, D. B. (1973). Controlling bias in observational studies: A review. *Sankhya: The Indian Journal of Statistics, Series A, 35*, 417–446.

Cook, T. D., & Campbell, D. T. (1979). *Quasi-experimentation: Design and analysis issues for field settings.* Chicago, IL: Rand McNally.

Greene, W. H. (1993). *Econometric analysis* (2nd ed.). New York, NY: Macmillan.

Gu, X. S., & Rosenbaum, P. R. (1993). Comparison of multivariate matching methods: structures, distances, and algorithms. *Journal of Computational and Graphical Statistics, 2*, 405–420. doi:10.2307/1390693

Hand, D. J. (1994). Deconstructing statistical questions. *Journal of the Royal Statistical Society: A, 157*, 317–356.

Holland, P. W. (1986). Statistics and causal inference. *Journal of the American Statistical Association, 81*, 945–970. doi:10.2307/2289064

Holland, P. W., & Rubin, D. B. (1983). On Lord's paradox. In H. Wainer & S. Messick (Eds.), *Principles of modern psychological measurement* (pp. 3–35). Hillsdale, NJ: Erlbaum.

Light, R. J., Singer, J. D., & Willett, J. B. (1990). *By design: Planning research on higher education.* Cambridge, MA: Harvard University Press.

Lord, F. M. (1967). A paradox in the interpretation of group comparisons. *Psychological Bulletin, 68*, 304–305. doi:10.1037/h0025105

Maris, E. (1998). Covariance adjustment versus gain scores—Revisited. *Psychological Methods, 3*, 309–327. doi:10.1037/1082-989X.3.3.309

Neter, J., Kutner, M. H., Nachtsheim, C. J., & Wasserman, W. (1996). *Applied linear statistical models* (4th ed.). New York, NY: McGraw-Hill.

Porter, A. C. (1967). *The effects of using fallible variables in the analysis of covariance.* (Unpublished doctoral dissertation). University of Wisconsin, Madison.

Porter, A. C., & Chibucos, T. R. (1974). Selecting analysis strategies. In G. Borich (Ed.), *Evaluating educational programs and products* (pp. 415–464). Englewood Cliffs, NJ: Educational Technology Press.

Reichardt, C. S. (1979). The statistical analysis of data from nonequivalent group designs. In T. D. Cook & D. T. Campbell (Eds.), *Quasi-experimentation: Design and analysis issues for field settings* (pp. 147–205). Chicago, IL: Rand McNally.

Rosenbaum, P. R. (2002). *Observational studies.* New York, NY: Springer-Verlag.

Rosenbaum, P. R. (2010). *Design of observational studies.* New York, NY: Springer-Verlag.

Rosenbaum, P., & Rubin, D. B. (1983). The central role of the propensity score in observational studies for causal effects. *Biometrika, 70*, 41–55. doi:10.1093/biomet/70.1.41

Rosenbaum, P. R., & Rubin, D. B. (1984). Reducing bias in observational studies using subclassification on the propensity score. *Journal of the American Statistical Association, 79*, 516–524. doi:10.2307/2288398

Rubin, D. B. (1974). Estimating causal effects of treatments in randomized and non-randomized studies. *Journal of Educational Psychology, 66*, 688–701. doi:10.1037/h0037350

Rubin, D. B. (1997). Estimating causal effects from large data sets using propensity scores. *Annals of Internal Medicine, 127*, 757–763.

Rubin, D. B. (2004). Teaching statistical inference for causal effects in experiments and observational studies. *Journal of Educational and Behavioral Statistics, 29*, 103–116. doi:10.3102/10769986029001103

Rubin, D. B., & Thomas, N. (1996). Matching using estimated propensity scores: Relating theory to practice. *Biometrics, 52*, 249–264. doi:10.2307/2533160

Shadish, W. R., Cook, T. D., & Campbell, D. T. (2002). *Experimental and quasi-experimental designs for generalized causal inference*. Boston, MA: Houghton Mifflin.

Staiger, D., & Stock, J. H. (1997). Instrumental variables regression with weak instruments. *Econometrica, 65*, 557–586. doi:10.2307/2171753

Wainer, H. (1991). Adjusting for differential base rates: Lord's paradox again. *Psychological Bulletin, 109*, 147–151. doi:10.1037/0033-2909.109.1.147

Wildt, A. R., & Ahtola, O. T. (1978). *Analysis of covariance*. Newbury Park, CA: Sage.

Wright, D. B. (2006). Comparing groups in a before–after design: When *t* test and ANCOVA produce different results. *British Journal of Educational Psychology, 76*, 663–675. doi:10.1348/000709905X52210

CHAPTER 27

REGRESSION-DISCONTINUITY DESIGNS

Charles S. Reichardt and Gary T. Henry

Regression-discontinuity (RD) designs are used to estimate the effects of treatments, programs, or interventions. The distinguishing feature of an RD design is that participants are assigned to treatment conditions on the basis of their scores on a quantitative variable. Participants with scores below a specified cutoff value on the quantitative variable are assigned to one treatment condition, whereas participants with scores above the cutoff value are assigned to no treatment or an alternative treatment. Effects of the treatments are evidenced by a discontinuity (at the cutoff score) in the relationship between the quantitative assignment variable and an outcome variable.

RD designs tend to produce more credible estimates of effects than most other quasi-experimental, nonexperimental, or observational studies. RD designs tend to produce less credible estimates of treatment effects than randomized experiments, but RD designs can sometimes be implemented in situations in which randomized experiments are not acceptable. This chapter describes the logic of the RD design as well as the design's strengths and weaknesses compared with both randomized experiments and other quasi-experiments.

THE LOGIC OF THE RD DESIGN

The prototypical RD design compares the effects of two treatments that are assigned to different groups of individuals. The two treatments could be a novel intervention and a standard intervention. Or one of the treatments could consist of a *control* condition

for which no treatment is provided above and beyond what the individuals seek out on their own. For simplicity, but without loss of generality, we shall refer to one of the treatments as the *experimental treatment* and the other treatment as the *comparison treatment*.

Which of the two treatments is assigned to an individual is determined by a cutoff score on a measured variable, called the *quantitative assignment variable* (QAV), on which each individual is assessed. Those individuals with a QAV score above the cutoff are assigned to one of the two treatment conditions, whereas individuals with a QAV score below the cutoff score are assigned to the other condition. Following the assignment of individuals to conditions, the two treatments are implemented and, after the treatments have had a chance to have their effects, the individuals in both groups are assessed on an outcome variable.

Any quantitative measure can be used as the QAV in an RD design. If the experimental treatment is intended to address a problem or deficit, the QAV could be a measure of the participants' need for the ameliorative intervention or their risk of negative outcomes in the absence of such an intervention, with the treatment given to those who reveal the greatest need on the QAV. For example, Trochim (1984) reported a series of RD designs in which tests of basic academic skills were used as the QAVs to assign low-performing children to compensatory education programs. Similarly, Jacob and Lefgren (2004) created an RD design based on the Chicago Public School's policy of assigning students to

DOI: 10.1037/13620-027

APA Handbook of Research Methods in Psychology: Vol. 2. Research Designs, H. Cooper (Editor-in-Chief)

summer remediation and retention in grade on the basis of low scores on an end-of-year test of academic ability. Buddelmeyer and Skoufias (2004) reported an RD design in Mexico used to assess the effects of a contingent cash benefit for which eligibility for the program was determined by a low score on the QAV of income.

Alternatively, the experimental treatment could be a reward (such as a scholarship), the QAV could be a measure of merit, and the treatment could be given to those who exhibit the greatest merit on the QAV. For example, the RD design was first introduced by Thistlewaite and Campbell (1960) who used it to assess the effects of receiving a certificate of merit, which was awarded on the basis of superior performance on a Scholarship Qualifying Test. Seaver and Quarton (1976) assessed the effects of making the dean's list on subsequent academic performance, where the QAV for making the dean's list was the grade point average from the prior academic term. And more recently, van der Klaauw (2002) assessed the impact of financial aid offers on college enrollment, where financial aid was awarded on the basis of a QAV of academic ability.

In addition to measures of need or merit, other types of QAVs could be used to determine eligibility for a treatment or admission to a program in an RD design. For example, a treatment allocated on the basis of first-come, first-served could be assessed in an RD design using either time of arrival or time of application for the treatment as the QAV. If different treatments are made available to people residing in different geographic regions that have sharp boundaries, the physical distance from the boundary could be used as the QAV in an RD design. DiNardo and Lee (2004) assessed the effects of unionization using the vote counts in favor of unionization in individual companies as the QAV, where a majority vote in favor of unionization was the cutoff score. Cahan and Davis (1987) estimated the effects of the first year of school using age as the QAV and the minimum age required to enroll a child in school as the cutoff score. Outcomes were assessed at the end of the academic year by comparing children who had been old enough to enter first grade the year before with children who had not been old enough to enter first grade the year before (also see Gormley &

Gayer, 2005, Gormley, Gayer, Phillips, & Dawson, 2005; Gormley, Phillips & Gayer, 2008; Wong, Cook, Barnett, & Jung, 2008).

Statistical precision and power increase as the correlation between QAV and the outcome measure increases. So using a QAV that is operationally identical to the outcome measure is often advantageous because it maximizes the correlation between the two. An example of operationally identical measures would be a pretest measure of cognitive ability being used to assign students to a remedial education program and a posttest measure of the same test being used as the outcome assessment. But the logic of the RD design holds regardless of the correlation between the QAV and the outcome measure. The RD design will still work, for example, even if the QAV is completely uncorrelated with the outcome measure, in which case the design takes on many of the properties of a randomized experiment.

The QAV could be derived from subjective judgments as long as those judgments are given numerical values so individuals can be ordered and a cutoff value specified. If desired, the QAV could be a composite of several separate measures for which each measure is differentially weighted. For example, Henry, Fortner, and Thompson (2010) created an RD design for which the lowest scoring school districts were assigned to treatment using an index of education advantage composed of four separate variables: teacher stability, teacher experience, children not living in poverty, and students meeting state proficiency standards. All that is required is that the separate measurements be combined quantitatively into a single index, which is used as the QAV. Neither the QAV nor any of the separate measures used in its composition need be free of measurement error. The only requirement is that the QAV be used to assign participants to treatment conditions according to a cutoff value.

It may be more difficult to select an appropriate cutoff score when, as sometimes occurs, participants "trickle" into a study rather than being assigned to treatment conditions all at one time. With trickle processing, it may be necessary to alter the cutoff score as the study progresses because the flow of participants and their QAV scores are not as anticipated with, for example, either too few or too many being eligible to receive the experimental treatment. In this case, different groups of participants could be assigned to conditions using different cutoff scores for which each group is conceptualized as a separate RD design. The data from these multiple designs could be analyzed either separately or as a single large sample if the QAV scores in each separate group are standardized so the different cutoff scores are aligned at the same location on the standardized QAV scale.

Patterns of Treatment Effects

An effect of the experimental condition is evidenced in an RD design by a discontinuity in the relationship between the QAV and the outcome variable that occurs at the cutoff score on the QAV. The presence of a discontinuity is assessed by comparing regression lines in the two treatment groups, in a way that is best explained pictorially. Figures 27.1, 27.2, and 27.3 present three outcomes for an RD

design. Each of the figures displays scatterplots of the scores of the individuals in the treatment and comparison conditions. In each figure, scores on the QAV are plotted along the horizontal axis and scores on the outcome variable are plotted along the vertical axis. The cutoff score falls at the value of 30 on the QAV and is represented in the figures by a vertical line at the score of 30 on the horizontal axis. Individuals with a score on the QAV below 30 were assigned to the experimental condition, and their scores in the figures are denoted by squares. Individuals with a QAV score at or above 30 were assigned to the comparison condition, and their scores in the figures are denoted by circles. The sloped lines in the figures are the regression lines that pass through the scatter of the data points in the experimental and comparison conditions.

In Figure 27.1, the experimental treatment has no effect compared with the comparison treatment because the regressions in the two conditions fall on the same line. In Figure 27.2, the experimental

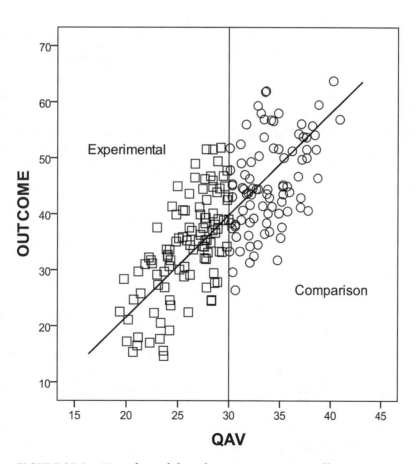

FIGURE 27.1.   Hypothetical data showing no treatment effect.

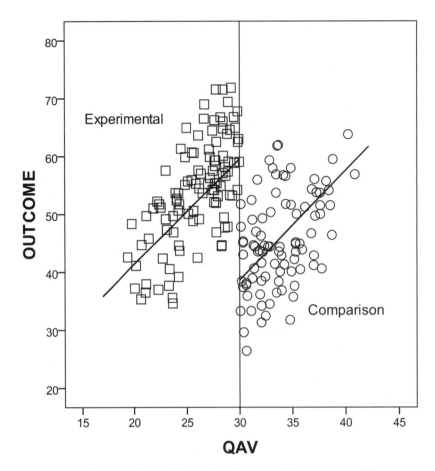

FIGURE 27.2.   Hypothetical data showing a positive treatment effect.

treatment has a positive effect compared with the comparison treatment because the regression line in the experimental group is displaced upwardly (positively) compared with the regression line in the comparison group. In other words, the presence of a break or discontinuity between the regression lines in the experimental and comparison conditions at the cutoff score reveals the presence of a treatment effect. Absence of a discontinuity indicates the lack of a treatment effect at the cutoff score.

Figure 27.3 depicts yet another potential outcome of an RD design. As in Figure 27.2, the regression line from the experimental group in Figure 27.3 is displaced vertically compared with the regression line for the comparison group, which reveals that the experimental condition has a positive effect compared with the comparison condition. But unlike in Figure 27.2, the regression lines in the two groups in Figure 27.3 are not parallel, which reveals the experimental treatment has a different effect for individuals with different QAV scores. That is, the

degree of vertical displacement between the two regression lines in Figure 27.3 depends on the score on the QAV. Were the regression line from the comparison group to be extrapolated to the left of the cutoff score, the vertical discrepancy between the regression line from the experimental group and the extrapolated regression line from the comparison group would be larger for individuals with lower QAV scores. This means an interaction between the treatment and the QAV is present. A discontinuity or break in the regression lines at the cutoff point, as illustrated in both Figures 27.2 and 27.3, is called an effect of a *change in level*, whereas nonparallel regression lines, as illustrated in Figure 27.3, are called an effect of a *change in slope*.

The Statistical Analysis of Data From RD Designs

The analysis of covariance (ANCOVA) model (which is a special case of multiple regression) is the classic method for analyzing data from an RD design. We

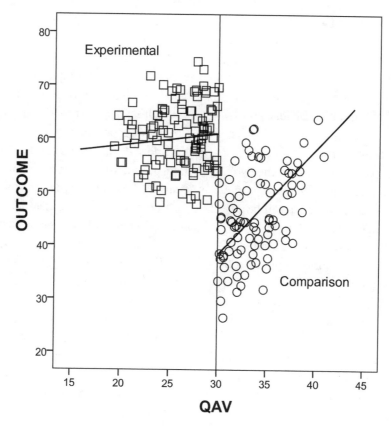

FIGURE 27.3.   Hypothetical data showing a treatment effect that produces a change in level and a change in slope.

introduce the ANCOVA model in its simplest form and then describe a variety of embellishments that can be added to the elementary model.

Change in level.   The simplest ANCOVA model for the analysis of data from an RD design is

$$Y = a + B_t\,T + B_x\,(X - X') + E. \qquad (1)$$

The model contains three observed variables: Y, T, and X. The Y variable is the individuals' scores on the outcome measure, T is a dummy variable representing assignment either to the treatment condition ($T = 1$) or to the comparison condition ($T = 0$), X is the individuals' scores on the QAV, and X' is the value of the cutoff score on the QAV. In Figures 27.1, 27.2, and 27.3, the cutoff score is 30, so X' equals 30. The notation $(X - X')$ means that the value of X' is subtracted from all the QAV scores before these scores are entered into the model as an independent variable. The model could be fit using either an ANCOVA option in a statistical package or a multiple regression option where Y is regressed onto T and $X - X'$.

The model in Equation 1 specifies that the regression of Y onto $X - X'$ (which represents the QAV scores) is a straight line that has the same slope in the two treatment groups. If the experimental treatment has an effect, it does nothing more than displace the regression line in the experimental group upward or downward compared with the regression line in the comparison group. This means the treatment effect is constant across the QAV. The value of B_t is the size of the vertical displacement of the regression line in the experimental group compared with the comparison condition. The value of B_x is the slope of the two parallel regression lines. This model would well fit the data in Figures 27.1 and 27.2, where the regression surfaces in the two groups are straight lines and parallel, and the treatment has either no effect or a constant effect across the values of the QAV. The value of the a parameter in Equation 1 is the intercept of the regression slope in the comparison condition and is usually of little interest in the analysis. The E variable in the model is the disturbance or error term, which

515

represents all the factors not included in the regression that influence an individual's score on *Y* and allows the individual data points, such as in Figures 27.1 and 27.2, to scatter around the regression lines.

The precision of the estimate of the treatment effect (and the power of the statistical analysis to detect a treatment effect) in Equation 1 will generally be greatest when the cutoff score is specified so that equal numbers of participants are in the two treatment groups. But the design can still be implemented if circumstances demand the cutoff be an extreme, rather than middle, score along the QAV. In any case, if an extreme cutoff score is used, data from one of the treatment conditions should not be omitted to make the sample sizes equal. More data are better than fewer data, even if it means the treatment groups will be unequal in size.

Treatment effect interactions. A slightly more complex model is required to fit the data in Figure 27.3, in which the treatment effect alters the level as well as the slope of the regression line in the experimental group. The more complex model is as follows:

$$Y = a + B_t\, T + B_x\, (X - X') + B_{tx}\, T(X - X') + E. \quad (2)$$

The notation $T(X - X')$ means a variable is created that is the product of the dummy variable *T* and the $(X - X')$ variable. In this model, the value of B_t is the size of the vertical displacement of the regression lines at the cutoff score. If the regression lines are not parallel, as in Figure 27.3, the size of the vertical displacement between the two regression lines depends on where the displacement is measured along the QAV. In Figure 27.3, for example, the displacement is greater for smaller values of the QAV than for larger values. By including the QAV scores scaled as $(X - X')$ in Equation 2, the model estimates the vertical displacement at the cutoff score on the QAV. If the value of X' is not subtracted from the value of *X*, the vertical displacement between the regression lines will be estimated at the point at which the QAV equals zero, which is likely to be uninformative or even misleading. To estimate the vertical displacement at a different value along the QAV, such as at QAV = X'', create the new variable $X - X''$ and enter that variable in place of the $X - X'$ variable in the two places it appears in Equation 2.

The value of B_x in Equation 2 is the slope of the regression line in the comparison group. The value of B_{tx} is the difference between the slopes in the experimental and comparison groups, and it represents the effect of a treatment interaction. A positive value of B_{tx} means the slope in the experimental group is steeper than in the comparison condition. For more details on fitting the statistical model and interpreting the results in the presence of an interaction, see Reichardt, Trochim, and Cappelleri (1995).

In the presence of a treatment effect interaction, methodologists often suggest placing more emphasis on the estimate of the vertical displacement at the cutoff score on the QAV than on the estimate of the vertical displacement at any other point along the QAV. This is because estimating the vertical displacement at the cutoff score requires minimal extrapolation of the regression lines in the two groups. To estimate the vertical displacement of the regression lines at any other point along the QAV would require extrapolation of the regression line from one of the treatment groups into a region where there are no data from that group. For example, to estimate the vertical displacement for a value of the QAV less than X' in Figure 27.3, the regression line for the comparison group would have to be extrapolated to the left of the cutoff point where there are no individuals from the comparison group. Estimates of treatment effects on the basis of such extrapolations tend to be both less powerful and less credible than estimates of effects at the cutoff score. On the other hand, in some instances, the experimental group might be composed only of individuals who fall at one of the extreme ends of the distribution of QAV scores, so little or no variation among the QAV scores occurs in that group. In that case, the estimate of the regression slope in the experimental group may be unstable, which could make an estimate of the vertical displacement of the regression lines at the cutoff point imprecise. Under these conditions, a more precise estimate of the vertical displacement might be obtained by replacing X' in Equation 2 with the mean of the QAV in the experimental group. With that change, the model would estimate the average effect of the treatment for the individuals in the experimental group rather than the effect of the treatment for individuals at the cutoff score.

If the regression lines in the treatment groups are parallel, fitting Equation 2, which includes the $T(X - X')$ interaction term, rather than Equation 1, can reduce the power of the analysis. But fitting Equation 1 rather than Equation 2, when the regression lines are not parallel, can bias the estimate of the treatment effect. Researchers often drop the interaction term if it is not statistically significant so as not to suffer a loss in power, but we recommend caution in dropping the term *if* doing so substantially alters the size of the estimate of the treatment effect, for fear a bias might be introduced.

Curvilinearity. To obtain an estimate of the treatment effect unbiased by selection, the relationship between the QAV and the outcome must be modeled correctly. The models in Equations 1 and 2 fit a straight regression line to the data in each treatment group. However, the regression surfaces might be curvilinear rather than linear. Figure 27.4 illustrates how fitting straight lines in the presence of curvilinearity could bias the estimate of the treatment effect. To make the illustration as simple as possible, the scatter in the data has been removed, so the data points all fall directly on top of the regression lines. As Figure 27.4 shows, the regression surface is curvilinear with no discontinuity at the cutoff score of 40 on the QAV. A model that fits the proper curvilinear regression surfaces would correctly estimate the treatment effect to be zero. But if straight lines were fit to the data, as shown in Figure 27.4, a discontinuity at the cutoff would be found along with a treatment effect interaction. In other words, an improper analysis that fit straight, rather than curved, regression lines would produce both a discontinuity and a treatment effect interaction when, in fact, neither of these effects is present.

To avoid such biases in the estimates of a treatment effect, curvilinearity in the regression surfaces must be modeled correctly. One approach to modeling

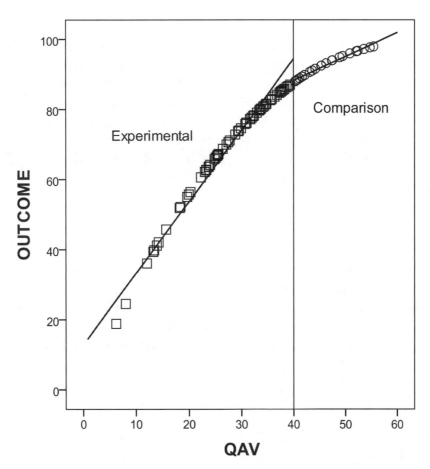

FIGURE 27.4.   Bias resulting from fitting straight lines to a curvilinear relationship.

curvilinearity is to apply a nonlinear transformation to the scores on either the QAV or the outcome variable to turn a curvilinear relationship between the untransformed scores into a linear relationship between the transformed scores (Draper & Smith, 1998). The alternative, and more common, approach is to model curvilinearity by adding polynomial terms to the ANCOVA equation. For example, the following model adds a quadratic term:

$$Y = a + B_t T + B_x (X - X') + B_{tx} T(X - X') + B_{x2} (X - X')^2 + E. \qquad (3)$$

Equation 3 is the same as Equation 2 except the quadratic term $B_{x2} (X - X')^2$ has been added. This term allows the regression surfaces in the two groups to take on a quadratic curvature. Equation 4 adds an interaction term to allow the quadratic curvature in the regression surfaces to differ across the treatment groups, which would be evidence of a treatment effect interaction:

$$Y = a + B_t T + B_x (X - X') + B_{tx} T(X - X') + B_{x2} (X - X')^2 + B_{tx2} T(X - X')^2 + E. \qquad (4)$$

Higher order polynomial terms with or without interaction terms could be added as well. For example, both a cubic term $B_{x3} (X - X')^3$ and a cubic interaction term $B_{tx3} T (X - X')^3$ could be added to allow the regression surface to take on a cubic curvature and to allow for a treatment effect interaction in the shape of the cubic curvature. All polynomial terms are entered with the QAV variable scaled as $(X - X')$. Norming the X variable in this fashion means any change in level caused by the treatment effect is estimated at the cutoff score. To estimate the change in level at an alternative location along the QAV variable (say at X'' rather than X'), the value of X' should be replaced everywhere by X''.

In theory, any curvilinear shape can be fit perfectly if enough polynomial terms are added to the model. In practice, however, there are limits to the number of polynomial terms that can reasonably be added because of limits imposed by sample size and multicolinearity. Adding polynomial terms can increase the power of the statistical analysis to the extent they cause the fitted regression surface to more closely model the true regression surface. But adding polynomial terms also tends to reduce

statistical power because of multicolinearity and because the polynomial terms are correlated both among themselves and with treatment assignment. Underfitting the model by including too few polynomial terms can bias the estimates of treatment effects but overfitting can severely reduce statistical power. Hence, the researcher must walk the narrow line between under- and overfitting the statistical model. Prevailing practice and advice from methodologists seems to be to fit additional, higher order polynomials as long as each additional polynomial term is statistically significant.

Plotting the relationship between the QAV and outcome scores can help in modeling curvilinearity properly. Plot the data before analyses are conducted to diagnose the nature of any curvilinearity that exists and plot the residuals after analyses have been conducted to see whether the models have properly fit the curvilinearity that was present. Including both straight and best-fitting lines in the plots can help point out departures from linearity. Best-fitting lines can be plotted using locally weighted polynomial (loess) regression, which uses subsets of the data to plot the best-fitting regression line for each point along the independent variable. Alternatively other forms of smoothing, such as mean or median smoothing can be used to view the relationship between the QAV and outcomes variable. A general rule is that the degree of the polynomial function fit in Equation 4 should be the number of inflection points in the smoothed curve plus one.

Supplementary sources of data can sometimes also be used to diagnose curvilinearity. For example, if an operationally identical measure of the outcome variable was collected before the implementations of the treatments, the plot of this prior measure versus the QAV scores could be examined. Because treatment effects cannot be present in the pretest data, any lack of smoothness in the relationship between the QAV and the pretest scores is due to curvilinearity from one source or another. Assuming the true outcome scores would behave much the same as the operationally identical pretest scores, the same curvilinearity would be presumed to arise in the true outcome scores as well. Marcantonio and Cook (1994; also see Riecken et al., 1974) provided an example of this strategy in a study of the effects of Medicaid. In 1967, families with incomes less than $3,000 were eligible for Medicaid payments, and a plot of the outcome variable in 1967 versus income revealed a dramatic discontinuity. A plot of the outcome variable versus income in a year before the start of Medicaid revealed a straight-line relationship between the two with no discontinuity, thereby increasing one's confidence that the discontinuity discovered in the 1967 data was due to the effects of Medicaid and not improperly modeled curvilinearity. Alternatively, a researcher might obtain data on both the QAV and outcome scores from a comparable cohort of individuals, perhaps from a neighboring locale, where the experimental treatment was not available. Again, the pattern of curvilinearity that was or was not present in the auxiliary data would suggest the pattern of curvilinearity to suspect in the real data of interest.

Curvilinearity can arise because the true underlying relationship between two constructs is curvilinear or because anomalies of the measurement process introduce twists or turns into an observed relationship. For example, measurement inconsistencies because of floor and ceiling effects can make an otherwise linear relationship curvilinear. It pays to be sensitive to, and on the lookout for, data to confirm or disconfirm the existence of such measurement problems. For example, curvilinearity because of floor or ceiling effects is often evidenced by a buildup of scores at the high or low ends of univariate distributions of the QAV and outcome scores. If everything else is the same, the larger the treatment effect is the less plausibly it can be explained as being caused by bias introduced by curvilinearity.

Covariates.   Covariates measured before the administration of the treatment can be added to the statistical model to increase statistical power without biasing the treatment effect estimate (Imbens & Lemieux, 2008). Equation 5 adds the covariate Z to Equation 4:

$$Y = a + B_t T + B_x (X - X') + B_{tx} T(X - X')$$
$$+ B_{x2} (X - X')^2 + B_{tx2} T(X - X')^2 + B_z Z + E. \quad (5)$$

Interaction or polynomial terms for the covariate could also be added to model a treatment interaction

or a curvilinear relationship between the covariate and the outcome measure. The power of the statistical analysis is maximized when the covariate is highly related to the outcome variable but little related to both the QAV and the other independent variables in the model. In other words, power is greatest when covariates are added that predict the outcome above and beyond any of the other variables in the model. Adding covariates that do not well predict the outcome and are correlated with the other variables in the model could reduce, rather than increase, power because of multicolinearity.

Fitting models to the data.   Our presentation began with the simplest ANCOVA model and built up to more complex models. Underfitting the model by including too few terms can lead to bias, but overfitting by including too many terms can reduce the power of the analysis because of multicolinearity. Common practice is to include or exclude terms on the basis of their statistical significance. Because overfitted models may suffer from low power because of multicolinearity, we would caution against excluding terms solely because they are not statistically significant. It is important to use diagnostics such as the variance inflation factor (VIF) and to understand the effects of multicolinearity. Perhaps most important, researchers should attend to the size of the treatment effect estimates. The analyst can place the most confidence in the results if the treatment effect estimates vary little across different models as terms are added or omitted. If the sizes of the treatment effect estimates vary meaningfully as terms are dropped, even if the dropped terms are not statistically significant, it is possible that the term is not statistically significant because of its low power to detect its importance rather than because the term is not needed to model the data correctly.

In this vein, note how difficult it can be to distinguish between a model that fits a curvilinear relationship and a model that fits straight lines plus a treatment effect interaction. Such a difficulty would arise, for example, with the relatively subtle degree of curvilinearity that exists in Figure 27.4. If the data points in that figure scattered widely around the best-fitting line rather than falling directly on top of the line, both a curvilinear model and a linear model with an interaction would account for the data quite well if these two models were fit separately, therefore making it difficult to choose between them. In addition, it would be difficult to choose between the two model specifications if both curvilinear and linear interaction terms were included in the same model simultaneously because of the multicolinearity between these terms. Because of the difficulty of distinguishing between linear interactions and curvilinearity, some methodologists have suggested that an apparent interaction should not be taken as evidence of a treatment effect unless a discontinuity in level exists at the cutoff score. But such a restriction would not solve the problem of misinterpretation in Figure 27.4, in which curvilinearity, if improperly modeled, can masquerade as both a linear treatment interaction and a discontinuity in level.

Uncertainty about which model correctly fits the data will virtually always be present. In such cases, researchers should report results from a range of plausible models and draw conclusions on the basis of the range of treatment effect estimates thereby produced (Reichardt & Gollob, 1987). Sifting through models and reporting only the treatment effect estimates that are most desirable is not an appropriate analysis strategy. In addition to bracketing the size of the treatment effect by using a range of plausible models, analysts should also bracket the size of the treatment effect by repeating the statistical analyses using only the slices of data most proximate to the cutoff score (Imbens & Lemieux, 2008). For example, analyses could be repeated using data from only that half of the participants in each treatment condition whose scores on the QAV are closest to the cutoff score. Then the analysis could be repeated again using data from only that quarter of the participants in each treatment condition whose scores on the QAV are closest to the cutoff. The intuition for restricting the data to participants with QAV scores closest to the cutoff is that (a) these participants are most similar on other characteristics so the treatment effect estimates are less likely to be biased by confounding variables and (b) the treatment effect estimates are least likely to be sensitive to misspecification of the relationship between the

QAV and the outcome variable. Of course, the obvious disadvantage of reducing the sample size is a loss of power and reliability.

Discontinuities in the Absence of a Treatment Effect

The analysis of data from an RD design assumes the regression of the outcome variable on the QAV would be continuous (rather than discontinuous) at the cutoff score in the absence of a treatment effect. The results of the RD analysis would be biased if the regression surface would have been discontinuous at the cutoff point even in the absence of a treatment effect. It is difficult to test the assumption of no discontinuity in the absence of a treatment effect directly. But the assumption can be tested indirectly (Imbens & Lemieux, 2008). One approach is to look for discontinuities in the relationship between the outcome variable and the QAV at locations other than the cutoff score. A discontinuity at the cutoff point that is no greater than at other points on the QAV reduces the plausibility of a treatment effect at the cutoff point, if everything else is the same. Another approach, which is often referred to as a *falsification test*, is to look for discontinuities in the relationship at the cutoff value of the QAV and the outcome variables collected before the treatment was implemented. Because discontinuities in such relationships cannot be a result of the treatment, the presence of such discontinuities raises the suspicion that any discontinuity in the relationship between the QAV and the real outcome variable is also not due to the treatment.

A discontinuity in the absence of a treatment effect could be introduced if another treatment were implemented concurrently with the treatment under study (which is called a violation of the assumption of no hidden treatments; Rubin, 2005). For example, imagine estimating the effects of Medicaid payments that are made available to anyone with income below the poverty line when, at the same time as Medicaid is introduced, other transfer payments, such as food stamps, are also introduced using the same eligibility criteria of income below the poverty line. In that case, the RD design would estimate the joint effects of Medicaid and the other transfer payments rather than the effects of Medicaid alone. Researchers should explicitly consider the following three other potential sources of discontinuity.

No shows. If individuals eligible to participate in the study know their scores on the QAV and know the cutoff score required to place them into a desired treatment, those who fail to qualify for a desired experimental treatment may decide not to show up for the study. This can introduce a discontinuity between the regression lines in the treatment groups, which makes the experimental treatment look more effective than it really is because the most attentive individuals are removed from the less desirable treatment condition more than from the desirable condition. To avoid this bias, it is best to keep the cutoff score confidential or make it impossible to determine one's QAV score ahead of time.

Attrition. Participants sometimes drop out of research studies once they have begun or fail to complete the outcome measurements. Such participants produce *incomplete* or *missing* data. Estimates of the treatment effects in the RD design can be biased because of missing data, especially when data are missing because participants drop out differentially across the treatment conditions. The best strategy is to prevent attrition. The means of preventing attrition and coping with missing data are much the same in randomized experiments as in RD designs, and readers are advised to consult the literature in that area for advice (Schafer & Graham, 2002).

Misassignment to treatment conditions.
Participants sometimes "cross over" from one treatment condition to another to receive a treatment to which they should not have been assigned according to the cutoff rule in the RD design. For example, administrators or researchers might respond to pressure to admit participants into a desired treatment when their QAV scores fall just below the cutoff score needed to obtain that treatment because those participants are particularly deserving or demanding of the desired treatment. Alternatively, misassignment might arise when the cutoff score is known to the participants ahead of time, the values of the QAV scores are reported by the participants (rather than measured independently by the researchers), and

participants lie about, or otherwise manipulate, their QAV scores to push their score across the cutoff and thereby receive the treatment they most desire. (This provides another reason to keep the cutoff score hidden from the participants before the treatments are assigned.) Or individuals assigned to a less desirable treatment might arrange to receive the more desirable treatment from a source outside the study. Often participants with QAV scores nearest the cutoff are most likely to cross over, resulting in what has come to be known as a *fuzzy* assignment.

Treatment crossovers can bias the estimates of the treatment effect because the more motivated or desperate participants tend to cross over from one treatment to the other and are therefore underrepresented in one group and overrepresented in the other. Methods developed to address the problems introduced by treatment crossovers in randomized experiments are applicable to RD designs as well. If the true values of the QAVs are known, the simplest strategy is to analyze the data according to how participants should have been assigned to the treatment conditions, rather than according to the condition they actually received (Boruch, 1997). Such an analyze-as-assigned-rather-than-as-treated strategy will tend to produce an underestimate of the treatment effect and is called the intent-to-treat estimate. The intent-to-treat estimate may be conservative, but it is considered better than using an analyze-as-treated estimate, which is more likely to produce biases of unknown direction.

Methodologists have also suggested the following four additional strategies for coping with the effects of fuzzy assignment in the RD design. First, if misassignments appear to be restricted to a narrow range near the cutoff score, bias can be avoided by conducting the statistical analysis and omitting all the scores inside this range. Second, if misassignment would occur because researchers or administrators insist subjective criteria be used to determine treatment assignment, these subjective assessments can be quantified and made a part of the QAV. By making the subjective assessments that would be responsible for a misassignment part of the QAV, one presumably removes the incentive for researchers or administrators to misassign participants. Third, those individuals who are likely to be assigned to a given treatment even if their QAVs fall on the "wrong" side of the cutoff score can be omitted from the study. If this last strategy is used, individuals should be omitted from the study before examining their QAVs, otherwise there will be a tendency to drop participants differentially from the two groups, which could introduce a bias. That is, if QAVs are known, there will be a tendency to omit from the analysis only those with QAVs that fall on one side of the cutoff, namely, the side that failed to qualify for the most desirable treatment. Fourth, using the QAV as an identifying instrument in a two-stage least squares, instrumental variable analysis is also an available strategy but beyond the scope of the current chapter (Foster & McLanahan, 1996; van der Klaauw, 2002, 2008).

The distribution of QAV scores. If one of the treatment conditions is more appealing than the other, the three sources of bias (i.e., no shows, attrition, and crossovers) will tend to alter the distribution of scores on the QAV on one side of the cutoff score as compared with the other. That is, no-shows, attrition, and crossovers would be expected to produce either a localized bulge in the height of the distribution of the QAV scores on one side of the cutoff score or a localized dip in the height of the distribution on the other side, or both. Therefore, evidence of these three sources of bias can be obtained by plotting the frequency distribution of the QAV scores and looking for a discontinuity at the cutoff score. McCrary (2008) provided a test of the statistical significance of such a discontinuity in the QAV frequency distribution.

Elaborations of the Prototypical RD Design

The preceding sections have considered only the simplest RD design. The simple RD design, however, can be embellished in a variety of ways to better tailor the design to the demands of the research setting.

More than one cutoff score. The prototypical RD design compares two treatment conditions and assigns participants to those conditions using a single cutoff score on the QAV. In addition, an RD design could be used to compare two treatment

conditions using two cutoff scores in which case one of the treatment conditions is assigned to participants with scores in between the two cutoff scores and the other condition is assigned to participants with scores beyond either of the two cutoff scores. Alternatively, two cutoff scores could be used to compare three different treatment conditions. The statistical model for data from RD designs with more than one cutoff score would include additional dummy variables and interaction terms to estimate changes in level and slope at each cutoff score.

RD designs combined with randomized experiments. An RD design can be combined with a randomized experiment (Boruch, 1975; Shadish, Cook, & Campbell, 2002). When comparing two treatments, one combination of designs would use two cutoff scores to create two extreme groups of participants on the basis of their QAV scores. One of the extreme groups on the QAV measure would receive the comparison condition, the other extreme group would receive the experimental condition, and those in the middle (in between the two cutoff scores) would be randomly assigned to the treatment conditions. This design could satisfy a desire by administrators to assign most participants to treatments on the basis of need or merit, while acknowledging that, because measures of need or merit are fallible, it would be most equitable to give all the participants who fell within a middle range on the QAV an equal chance to receive the experimental treatment.

Another design option, using a single cutoff score, would be to assign individuals with QAV scores on one side of the cutoff to one of the treatment conditions and assign individuals with QAV scores on the other side of the cutoff score to one of the two treatment conditions at random. For example, everyone with scores at one end of the QAV could be given the experimental treatment, whereas those with scores on the other side of the cutoff could be assigned to the experimental and comparison conditions at random. Designs that combine randomized experiments with RD designs are likely to be more powerful and produce results that are more credible than those produced either by RD designs without random assignment or by random assignment without the additional data from the RD portion of a design for which individuals are not assigned to treatments at random.

Cluster designs.   Cluster RD designs are analogous to cluster randomized experiments in that groups or clusters of individuals, such as schools, classrooms, or clinics, are assigned to treatment conditions. In cluster RD designs, assignment to treatment conditions is based on a QAV measured at the cluster level so all individuals in a given cluster are assigned to the same treatment condition. For example, Henry et al. (2010) used a cluster design to assess the effects on student achievement of supplemental funding awarded to schools at the district level, where the QAV was a measure of district educational disadvantage. In cluster designs in which outcomes are measured at the individual level, but treatments are assigned at a higher level, multilevel models can maximize the power of the analysis to detect treatment effects. For example, Henry et al. used a multilevel model to assess the effect of supplemental funding at the district level on outcomes measured at the individual student level, controlling for the students' prior achievement as well as other individual, classroom, and school characteristics. However, Schochet (2008) has shown that the power of cluster designs is less than the power of noncluster designs and that power tends to increase as the number of clusters, rather than the number of participants within a cluster, increases.

RD Designs Employing Comparisons Across Settings, Outcome Variables, or Times

In classic RD designs, as described in the preceding sections, participants are measured and assigned to treatment conditions (either individually or in clusters) on the basis of a QAV. Because the treatment effect is estimated by drawing a comparison across participants, such designs are called RD designs comparing participants. Three other types of RD designs are also possible based on drawing comparisons across either settings, outcome variables, or times (Reichardt, 2006). Each of these three types of RD designs is described in the following paragraphs.

First, to determine whether adding traffic lights to highway intersections reduces traffic accidents,

imagine a design in which traffic lights are installed at intersections using a quantitative assignment rule based on the volume of traffic passing through the intersection during the previous month. In other words, imagine a design in which a representative set of intersections without traffic lights is selected, traffic lights are added to the intersections that had the heaviest traffic during the preceding month, and the number of traffic accidents at each intersection during the ensuing year is tallied. The effect of adding traffic lights is then estimated by regressing the number of accidents during the ensuing year onto the QAV of traffic volume at the intersections, and measuring the size of any discontinuity in the regression lines at the cutoff point that demarcates those intersections that received a traffic light and those that did not. That is, settings that receive a traffic light are compared with settings that do not receive a traffic light to determine how people behave differently in the different settings. Because the treatment effect is estimated by drawing a comparison across different settings, such a design is called an RD design comparing settings.

Second, consider a design in which letters of the alphabet are assigned to different treatment conditions using a quantitative assignment variable. For example, imagine assessing the effectiveness of a new educational television series designed to teach prereading skills. During the 1st year of production, the show is able to teach only half the letters of the alphabet, and the producers of the show want to teach the most important letters. The frequency with which each letter appears in the English language is measured, and this measure is used as the QAV. The 13 most frequently appearing letters are taught during the 1st year of the show. At the end of the 1st year, a group of children who have been viewers of the show are tested to assess their knowledge of all 26 letters. The effect of the show is estimated by regressing the scores on the outcome measures onto the QAV and looking for a discontinuity between the regression lines across the two groups of letters. Because the treatment effect is estimated by comparing performances across letters of the alphabet (where each letter is a different outcome variable), such a design is called an RD design comparing outcome variables.

Third, the *interrupted time-series* (ITS) design (see Chapter 32 of this volume) is an RD design in which different temporal occasions are assigned to different treatment conditions using time as the QAV (Marcantonio & Cook, 1994). Hence, an ITS design is called an RD design comparing times.

ITS designs and classic RD designs (i.e., RD designs comparing participants) are widely recognized in the literature on quasi-experimentation. The other two types of RD designs (i.e., RD designs comparing settings and RD designs comparing outcome variables) are not nearly as well known but could often be used to advantage. For example, the original evaluations of the effects of *Sesame Street* (Cook et al., 1975) employed a relatively weak nonequivalent group (NEG) design (see Chapter 26 of this volume) but could have used a more credible RD design comparing outcome variables as in the preceding example of an evaluation of an educational television show comparing letters of the alphabet.

RELATIVE STRENGTHS AND WEAKNESSES OF THE RD DESIGN

NEG designs tend to be easier to implement than RD designs. The reason is that NEG designs place no restrictions on how units are assigned to treatment conditions, whereas RD designs require that units (i.e., participants, times, settings, or outcome variables) be assigned according to a quantitative assignment rule. In addition, an RD design may have less statistical power than an NEG design. Because an RD design allows no overlap between the treatment groups on the QAV whereas the treatment groups in a NEG design could overlap substantially on covariates, the power of RD designs tends to be reduced by multicolinearity more than the power of NEG designs.

Estimates of effects from RD designs tend to be more credible than estimates from NEG designs, especially in light of recent evidence comparing estimates of effects from RD designs to those from randomized experiments and NEG designs (Cook, Shadish, & Wong, 2008). The nature of selection differences is known in RD designs because RD designs impose a quantitative assignment rule. In contrast, the nature of selection differences is usually unknown in NEG designs, so the specification and modeling of selection differences is more difficult and leads to less credible estimates (Reichardt, 1979).

In contrast, estimates of treatment effects derived from randomized experiments tend to be more credible than estimates from RD designs. The reason is twofold. First, the effects of selection differences must be modeled in RD designs by using the QAV as a covariate in a regression analysis. Using an improper model (such as fitting linear regression surfaces when the true regression shape is curvilinear) can bias the estimates of treatment effects. In randomized experiments, selection differences between groups are random, which can be modeled without using covariates to fit a regression surface, so there is less chance of error and bias. Second, estimating treatment effect interactions (in which case the effect of the treatment varies across QAV scores) in RD designs involves extrapolating the regression line from the comparison condition into a region on the QAV that contains no data from the comparison group and extrapolating the regression line from the experimental condition into a region on the QAV that contains no data from the experimental condition. In contrast, treatment effect interactions in randomized experiments can be estimated without extrapolating regression surfaces into regions that do not contain relevant data.

The results from RD designs are also less precise and powerful than from randomized experiments because the QAV and the treatment-assignment dummy variable are correlated in the RD design. In contrast, any covariates included in the analysis of data from a randomized experiment are uncorrelated with the treatment-assignment dummy variable and therefore cannot diminish precision and power because of multicolinearity. To obtain the same precision and power as in a randomized experiment, an RD design must have more than two times as many participants (Cappelleri, Darlington, & Trochim, 1994; Goldberger, 1972; Schochet, 2008). In addition, a larger sample size is needed in an RD design, as compared with a randomized experiment, to ensure that the regression surface between the QAV and outcome score is modeled correctly.

Randomized experiments can be more difficult to implement than RD designs. Whether for ethical or practical reasons, situations arise in which administrators and participants are more likely to resist the random assignment of a desirable treatment than assignment on the basis of a measure of need or merit. Under such circumstances, it can be easier for researchers to implement an RD design than a randomized experiment.

CONCLUSION

NEG designs are often easier to implement than RD designs and can have more power than RD designs. But RD designs tend to produce treatment effect estimates that are more credible than estimates from NEG designs. The credibility of the RD design derives from the fact that units (i.e., participants, settings, outcome variables, or times) are assigned to treatment conditions on the basis of a quantitative assignment rule. Knowing the quantitative rule by which units are assigned to treatments allows the researcher to model the effects of selection differences between the treatment groups with greater confidence than is possible in NEG designs in which the rule by which units are assigned to treatments is not explicit or quantitative.

Conversely, RD designs tend to produce less credible results than do randomized experiments. And randomized experiments are also more powerful. But RD designs can sometimes be implemented in cases in which randomized experiments cannot.

In spite of its potential advantages compared with NEG designs and randomized experiments, the RD design has been used relatively infrequently in psychological research in the past. The primary reason, we suspect, is that many psychological researchers are simply unaware of the design and its advantages. Because of its relative strengths, the RD design is receiving increased attention and emphasis from funding agencies, such as the Institute for Educational Science (Cook & Wong, in press). The design has also received a great deal of attention in the economics literature in recent years (Cook, 2008). We suspect the RD design is poised for a similar surge of interest among research psychologists, especially in applied areas of research in which randomized experiments are not always practical.

References

Boruch, R. F. (1975). Coupling randomized experiments and approximations to experiments in social program evaluation. *Sociological Methods and Research, 4*, 31–53. doi:10.1177/004912417500400103

Boruch, R. F. (1997). *Randomized experiments for planning and evaluation: A practical guide.* Thousand Oaks, CA: Sage.

Buddelmeyer, H., & Skoufias, E. (2004). *An evaluation of the performance of regression discontinuity design on PROGRESA.* Bonn, Germany: Institute for the Study of Labor.

Cahan, S., & Davis, D. (1987). A between-grade-levels approach to the investigation of the absolute effects of schooling on achievement. *American Educational Research Journal, 24*, 1–12.

Cappelleri, J. C., Darlington, R. B., & Trochim, W. M. K. (1994). Power analysis of cutoff-based randomized clinical trials. *Evaluation Review, 18*, 141–152. doi:10.1177/0193841X9401800202

Cook, T. D. (2008). Waiting for life to arrive: A history of the regression-discontinuity design in psychology, statistics, and econometrics. *Journal of Econometrics, 142*, 636–654. doi:10.1016/j.jeconom.2007.05.002

Cook, T. D., Appleton, H., Conner, R. F., Shaffer, A., Tamkin, G., & Weber, S. J. (1975). *"Sesame Street" revisited.* New York, NY: Russell Sage.

Cook, T. D., Shadish, W. R., & Wong, V. C. (2008). Three conditions under which experiments and observational studies produce comparable causal estimates: New findings from within-study comparisons. *Journal of Policy Analysis and Management, 27*, 724–750. doi:10.1002/pam.20375

Cook, T. D., & Wong, V. C. (in press). Empirical tests of the validity of the regression discontinuity design. *Annales d'Economie et de Statistique.*

DiNardo, J., & Lee, D. S. (2004). Economic impacts of new unionization on private sector employers: 1984-2001. *Quarterly Journal of Economics, 119*, 1383–1441. doi:10.1162/0033553042476189

Draper, N. R., & Smith, H. (1998). *Applied regression analysis* (3rd ed.). New York, NY: Wiley.

Foster, M. E., & McLanahan, S. (1996). An illustration of the use of instrumental variables: Do neighborhood conditions affect a young person's chance of finishing high school? *Psychological Methods, 1*, 249–260. doi:10.1037/1082-989X.1.3.249

Goldberger, A. S. (1972). *Selection bias in evaluating treatment effects: Some formal illustrations.* (Discussion Paper 123-72). Madison: University of Wisconsin, Institute for Research on Poverty.

Gormley, W. T., Jr., & Gayer, T. (2005). Promoting school readiness in Oklahoma: An evaluation of

Tulsa's pre-K program. *Journal of Human Resources, 40,* 533–558.

Gormley, W. T., Jr., Gayer, T., Phillips, D., & Dawson, B. (2005). The effects of universal pre-K on cognitive development. *Developmental Psychology, 41,* 872–884. doi:10.1037/0012-1649.41.6.872

Gormley, W. T., Jr., Phillips, D., & Gayer, T. (2008). Preschool programs can boost school readiness. *Science, 320,* 1723–1724. doi:10.1126/science.1156019

Henry, G. T., Fortner, C. K., & Thompson, C. L. (2010). Targeted funding for educationally disadvantaged students: A regression discontinuity estimate of the impact on high school student achievement. *Educational Evaluation and Policy Analysis, 32,* 183–204. doi:10.3102/0162373710370620

Imbens, G. W., & Lemieux, T. (2008). Regression discontinuity designs: A guide to practice. *Journal of Econometrics, 142,* 615–635. doi:10.1016/j.jeconom.2007.05.001

Jacob, B. A., & Lefgren, L. (2004). Remedial education and student achievement: A regression-discontinuity analysis. *Review of Economics and Statistics, 86,* 226–244. doi:10.1162/003465304323023778

Marcantonio, R. J., & Cook, T. D. (1994). Convincing quasi-experiments: The interrupted time series and regression-discontinuity designs. In J. S. Wholey, H. P. Hatry, & K. E. Newcomer (Eds.), *Handbook of practical program evaluation* (pp. 133–154). San Francisco, CA: Jossey-Bass.

McCrary, J. (2008). Manipulation of the running variable in the regression discontinuity design: A density test. *Journal of Econometrics, 142,* 698–714. doi:10.1016/j.jeconom.2007.05.005

Reichardt, C. S. (1979). The statistical analysis of data from nonequivalent group designs. In T. D. Cook & D. T. Campbell (Eds.), *Quasi-experimentation: Design and analysis issues for field settings* (pp. 147–205). Chicago, IL: Rand McNally.

Reichardt, C. S. (2006). The principle of parallelism in the design of studies to estimate treatment effects. *Psychological Methods, 11,* 1–18. doi:10.1037/1082-989X.11.1.1

Reichardt, C. S., & Gollob, H. F. (1987). Taking uncertainty into account when estimating effects. In M. M. Mark & R. L. Shotland (Eds.), *Multiple methods for program evaluation* (New Directions for Program Evaluation, No. 35, pp. 7–22). San Francisco, CA: Jossey-Bass.

Reichardt, C. S., Trochim, W. M. K., & Cappelleri, J. C. (1995). Reports of the death of regression-discontinuity

analysis are greatly exaggerated. *Evaluation Review, 19,* 39–63. doi:10.1177/0193841X9501900102

Riecken, H. W., Boruch, R. F., Campbell, D. T., Caplan, N., Glennan, T. K., Jr., Pratt, J. W., . . . Williams, W. (1974). *Social experimentation: A method for planning and evaluating social intervention.* New York, NY: Academic Press.

Rubin, D. B. (2005). Causal inference using potential outcomes: Design, modeling, decisions. *Journal of the American Statistical Association, 100,* 322–331. doi:10.1198/016214504000001880

Schafer, J. L., & Graham, J. W. (2002). Missing data: Our view of the state of the art. *Psychological Methods, 7,* 147–177. doi:10.1037/1082-989X.7.2.147

Schochet, P. Z. (2008). *Technical methods report: Statistical power for regression discontinuity designs in education evaluations.* Washington, DC: Institute for Education Sciences, National Center for Education Evaluation and Regional Assistance.

Seaver, W. B., & Quarton, R. J. (1976). Regression-discontinuity analysis of dean's list effects. *Journal of Educational Psychology, 66,* 459–465.

Shadish, W. R., Cook, T. D., & Campbell, D. T. (2002). *Experimental and quasi-experimental designs for generalized causal inference.* Boston, MA: Houghton Mifflin.

Thistlewaite, D. L., & Campbell, D. T. (1960). Regression-discontinuity analysis: An alternative to the ex-post-facto experiment. *Journal of Educational Psychology, 51,* 309–317. doi:10.1037/h0044319

Trochim, W. M. K. (1984). *Research designs for program evaluation: The regression-discontinuity approach.* Newbury Park, CA: Sage.

van der Klaauw, W. (2002). Estimating the effect of financial aid offers on college enrollment: A regression discontinuity approach. *International Economic Review, 43,* 1249–1287. doi:10.1111/1468-2354.t01-1-00055

van der Klaauw, W. (2008). Regression discontinuity analysis: A survey of recent developments in economics. *Labour, 22,* 219–245. doi:10.1111/j.1467-9914.2008.00419.x

Wong, V. C., Cook, T. D., Barnett, W. S., & Jung, K. (2008). An effectiveness-based evaluation of five state pre-kindergarten programs. *Journal of Policy Analysis and Management, 27,* 122–154. doi:10.1002/pam.20310

Experimental Manipulations in Applied Settings

Chapter 28

TREATMENT VALIDITY FOR INTERVENTION STUDIES

Dianne L. Chambless and Steven D. Hollon

That psychologists conduct sound research is important whatever their research areas, but it is especially important when the results of this research have a substantial impact on people's lives. This is the case for intervention research, the findings of which may influence the type of treatments people receive. Sound intervention research is critical for determining what treatments are beneficial and what treatments are ineffective or even harmful. Moreover, intervention research is typically very expensive to conduct, with a single project often taking 5 to 7 years to complete and costing well over $1 million. This means that relatively little psychosocial intervention research is conducted, making the validity of each trial that much more important.

Intervention research is challenging, and during such a study (often called a *trial*), investigators will be faced with many uncontrollable events they could not have foreseen. Common problems in treatment research are predictable, however, and many potential difficulties in interpretation of findings can be avoided with proper attention to design before the trial begins. In this chapter we will review the most common design questions in intervention research and will specify the basic elements we believe must be present to permit researchers to draw valid conclusions from their data.

ASSESSMENT

Assessment is something of a stepchild for intervention researchers. Researchers often pay inadequate attention to whether the assessment measures they select reliably and validly assess the constructs they wish to measure. There is an unfortunate tendency to choose measures simply because they are in widespread use or because the names of the measures suggest that they represent the constructs of interest. Without valid and appropriate measurement, the results of a study are severely compromised if not meaningless, and time spent up front on selection of appropriate measures will pay off in the end. This is not a task to pass off to an inexperienced research assistant.

Several types of assessment are important: First, how will the investigator determine that the participants represent the types of people to whom this research is supposed to generalize (a critical aspect of the external validity of the study)? In prevention research, the potential participant pool may be everyone who was exposed to some stressor such as a hurricane or all couples attending a given church who are engaged to be married. In such cases, the definition of the sampling frame may be relatively straightforward, although in cases of exposure to stressors, the researcher will want to carefully assess the degree of exposure. In psychotherapy research, it is common, although not mandatory, for the participant pool to be defined in terms of the primary diagnosis conferred, with predefined exclusions of those who have other conditions that might render the proposed treatment inappropriate. For example, investigators typically exclude patients with a history of psychosis from trials of

Preparation of this chapter was supported in part by National Institute of Mental Health Grant K02 MH01697 awarded to Steven D. Hollon.

DOI: 10.1037/13620-028
APA Handbook of Research Methods in Psychology: Vol. 2. Research Designs, H. Cooper (Editor-in-Chief)

nonpsychotic disorders. In such research, the researcher needs to convince readers that the diagnoses were reliably and validly made. For studies of psychiatric disorders, this generally means that structured diagnostic interviews were used and that the researcher demonstrated satisfactory interrater reliability for diagnoses by having a randomly selected sample of diagnostic interviews repeated or rated by a second diagnostician who is not informed of the first diagnostician's decisions. Alternatively, participants may be selected on the basis of their scores on self-report measures. For example, couples may be selected for marital therapy on the basis of their stated desire for couples therapy and their falling below some threshold of marital satisfaction on a psychometrically sound inventory. In a research report, investigators are encouraged to clearly report the reasons that potential participants were excluded from the study, decided against participation, or later dropped out, along with numbers for those categories of people, perhaps using a chart advocated by the CONSORT guidelines to standardize the report (Altman et al, 2001). Figure 28.1, taken from Striegel-Moore et al.'s (2010) study on guided self-help for recurrent binge eating, provides an example of a CONSORT chart.

Second, how will the investigator know whether the intervention had the desired effect? Here is it crucial to select reliable and valid outcome measures appropriate to the sample being studied. Because each method of measurement captures only a piece of the latent variable the researcher wants to assess, it is preferable to use multiple methods of assessment, including, for example, self-report, interviewer, and observational or behavioral measures. In research on children, it is desirable to obtain ratings from parents and teachers as well as from the children themselves (Kazdin, 2003; Kraemer et al., 2003). When researchers use interviewer and observational measures, they must demonstrate adequate interrater reliability for all occasions of assessment (e.g., pretest, posttest, follow-up). If, as is usually the case, it is too expensive to have reliability ratings for every participant assessed, investigators should randomly sample from all occasions of assessment for reliability ratings and report these findings using

measures of reliability appropriate for the level of measurement (e.g., Cohen, 1960; Shrout & Fleiss, 1979).

Third, how will the investigators know whether the intervention works for the reasons that they propose? Reliable and valid measurement is required to test such process or mediational questions (Baron & Kenny, 1986). For example, if the researcher proposes that psychotherapy works because the client forms a close working alliance with the therapist (e.g., Bordin, 1979), a good measure of the working alliance must be included.

Careful determination of all of the constructs that need to be assessed in the study and selection of appropriate means of measurement are critical to the ultimate success of the trial. Attention to the validity of assessment speaks to the construct validity of the research, a topic we will develop further in a later section.

SELECTION OF THE RESEARCH DESIGN

Randomization

Single-case and quasi-experimental designs will be covered in other chapters. Here we concentrate on the randomized controlled trial (RCT), which permits the strongest inferences of causality, that is, allows the investigator to say with the most confidence that any changes observed are due to the intervention (Shadish, Cook, & Campbell, 2002). In such a design, each individual participant is assigned at random to an intervention condition; alternatively, randomization occurs at some group level. For example, classrooms of children may be assigned at random to a prevention program or alternative condition, or wards of a hospital may be assigned at random to an experimental procedure, whereas other wards serve as a waiting list control condition. This approach to assignment is sometimes called *cluster randomized assignment* (see Campbell, Elbourne, & Altman, 2004, for a discussion of methodological issues in such studies). Randomization is the best method for guarding against *selection* effects (Shadish et al., 2002), the presence of systematic differences between groups that imperil the investigator's ability to draw the conclusion that the intervention rather than preexisting

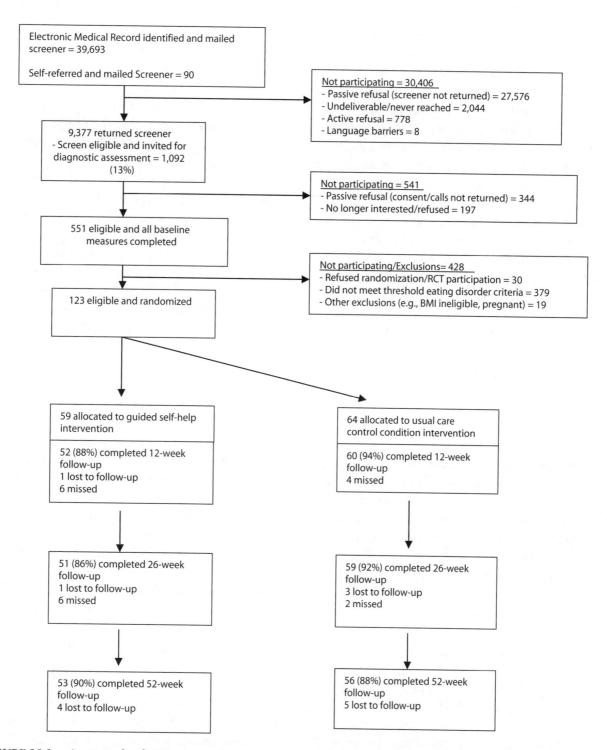

FIGURE 28.1. An example of a CONSORT flowchart. RCT = randomized controlled trial. From "Cognitive Behavioral Guided Self-Help for the Treatment of Recurrent Binge Eating," by R. H. Striegel-Moore, G. T. Wilson, L. DeBar, N. Perrin, F. Lynch, F. Rosselli, and H. C. Kraemer, 2010, *Journal of Consulting and Clinical Psychology, 78*, p. 314. Copyright 2010 by the American Psychological Association.

differences between groups led to the observed difference in outcome.

When very large numbers of participants are involved, the experimenter can be relatively

confident that randomization will ensure that treatment conditions will not differ on important variables other than receipt of the intended intervention. However, intervention trials are often not so large, and fairly frequently treatment groups will be found to differ significantly on one or more variables before treatment. For this reason, investigators would do well to consider in advance the presence of other variables that might be related to outcome and on which participants might differ. For example, suppose the investigator believes that patients with borderline personality disorder are likely to do worse in treatment for major depressive disorder than patients without such personality pathology. In this case the investigator might block or stratify the patients on presence or absence of borderline personality disorder before randomization and then conduct randomization within blocks. Such a practice makes it more likely that each treatment condition will have roughly equal numbers of patients with this personality disorder, particularly if the researcher uses procedures to foster balance across conditions or blocks within conditions, among the most common of which is *urn randomization* (Wei & Lachin, 1988). In urn randomization, the probability that subsequent patients will be assigned to a specific treatment condition is adjusted on an ongoing basis to reflect the number and type of patients previously assigned to that condition. Urn randomization is used to decrease the likelihood that randomization will fail (distribute uneven numbers or types of patients across the treatment conditions) simply on the basis of chance. Knowledge of the literature on factors associated with treatment outcome will guide the investigator in the selection of the most important blocking variables, in that it is not possible to stratify on numerous factors.

In implementing randomization the researcher needs to separate knowledge of eligibility from knowledge of the randomization sequence. Randomization should occur only after it has been determined that a patient meets eligibility criteria. Otherwise the investigator risks having unintentional biases creep in. For example, suppose the investigator is handling random assignment and knows that the next patient in the randomization sequence will be assigned to his or her favored treatment. When that patient proves to be a difficult case the investigator suspects will not do well, he or she might unintentionally find a reason this patient is not eligible for the study. Procedures should be in

place to prevent such temptation, for example, by having someone not involved in eligibility determination (e.g., the project data manager) maintain the randomization sequence in secret, providing the patient's treatment condition assignment only once a firm decision has been made regarding eligibility, and the patient's status on any blocking variables is known (Efron, 1971).

The Comparison Group

Selection of the appropriate comparison group should be determined by the research question. Do we simply want to know whether a treatment is beneficial? If so, the control condition for the RCT can be a waiting list control group that accounts for potential confounding variables, such as the effects of the assessment procedures and the passage of time, during which the problem might run its course or be affected by healing agents in the patient's natural environment. Such a design tells us whether our treatment is *efficacious*, that is, better than no treatment. We might be dissatisfied with this information and want to know whether our treatment works better than some placebo or basic treatment. If it does, then we might call the treatment *efficacious and specific* (Chambless & Hollon, 1998). The design testing specificity allows the investigator to control for additional variables, such as hope and expectancy of change, a caring relationship with a professional, and education about one's disorder.

Why do we care whether a treatment is specific? Is it not enough to know that it works? From a practical standpoint, we care because interventions are often costly and require extensive training and supervision of the interventionists. If patients benefit as much from regular meetings with a caring counselor as from a more elaborate and expensive intervention, then we have no need for a more complex intervention requiring extensive training. From a theoretical standpoint, we care because we wish to understand why change occurs, and we base our interventions on hypotheses about the critical changes processes. If our treatment fares no better than a basic control treatment, we need to question our beliefs about the necessary ingredients for change. Thus, tests of specificity speak to the issue of construct validity.

Finally, the investigator might wish to know which of two or more rival interventions is superior in the treatment or prevention of a given disorder. This is yet another form of the specificity question, and the most ambitious type of trial to mount because it requires large numbers of participants (see discussion on power in the section Appropriate Statistical Analysis). Such trials might involve the comparison of different schools of psychotherapy or of psychotherapy versus pharmacotherapy (Hollon, 1996; Mohr et al., 2009).

Special concerns arise when the comparison condition the investigator selects is treatment as usual (TAU; Mohr et al., 2009; Nathan, Stuart, & Dolan, 2000). Such designs are especially common in effectiveness studies, in which investigators transport research clinic-tested treatments to clinical settings in the community. In such a design, the investigator does not dictate the contents of the comparison condition but relies on ordinary clinical care at the agency where the research is conducted or refers the participants randomized to TAU to community resources. Such studies have substantial external validity, in that they tell us whether the treatment in question is superior to what patients would otherwise have gotten, and they avoid the ethical problem of withholding treatment from someone who seeks it. However, internal validity problems can make their results hard to interpret: In many cases, the TAU group receives very little intervention, and any superiority of the new treatment may be due simply to the fact that the participants in that condition actually got treatment. In addition, the therapists in the new treatment may receive special training and supervision, creating the sort of excitement that can lead to a Hawthorne effect (i.e., improvement from the mere fact of being studied vs. improvement for the hypothesized reasons; Shadish et al., 2002). In other cases, there are problems in generalization of the results because the investigator fails to determine what sort of treatment the participants in the TAU condition received. Lacking this knowledge, how can we guess whether because the new treatment was superior to TAU in Clinic A it would be similarly superior in Clinic B where services are better than those of Clinic A? Only if the investigator has the resources to study TAU in a large

number of clinics that represent adequately the range of services in the community, does it becomes possible to conclude that on average the new treatment is better than typical practice.

Design issues for the investigator do not end with selection of the proper control group for the research question. To what degree should the investigator favor realistic conditions in the research versus tight control of factors such as amount of time in therapy? For example, patients in the community receiving psychotherapy for their depression generally meet with their therapists for 45 to 50 min at least once weekly. If they are in pharmacotherapy, however, after initial sessions they would rarely see their physician for more than 15-min sessions. Should the investigator constrain both treatment interventions to 45- to 50-min sessions even though this would not mimic real-world conditions and would be expensive in terms of the increase in physicians' time in the study? We have seen a change in this choice over our decades in the intervention field, where earlier researchers and reviewers favored carefully equating treatments on amount of time but, more recently, delivery of the treatments permits differences in amount of time and attention consistent with the way treatments are delivered in the field. As such, the field has moved from a more rigid adherence to maintenance of internal validity (by equating all conditions tightly on time in treatment) to permitting more focus on external validity (matching more closely what happens in the clinic) (Nathan et al., 2000). There is no right answer to this dilemma. Rather, the investigator must carefully consider the match of the design with the question he or she is attempting to answer and clearly describe any limitations in the interpretation of findings that follow from this choice in the discussion section of any report of the trial.

When two or more psychotherapy conditions are compared, the investigator must decide whether therapists are to be crossed or nested within treatments. When therapists are crossed with treatment condition, each therapist delivers all treatment conditions. When therapists are nested within treatment, each therapist implements only one of the treatment conditions. In the crossed case, the investigator can be sure that, if two treatments are found to differ, it is not because particularly good therapists were more likely to be assigned to one treatment condition than another. However, the more the treatments are theoretically distinctive and require extensive training and commitment, the less likely it is that any one therapist can carry out two or more treatments with equal competence and commitment. For example, the committed cognitive therapist might not do a credible job of psychodynamic psychotherapy and might communicate to patients in psychodynamic therapy that they are receiving the less preferred treatment. The nested condition avoids this problem if the investigator recruits therapists who are equally skilled in and committed to their treatment approach for each condition—not an easy thing to do given the difficulty in assessing therapist competence reliably and validly (Waltz, Addis, Koerner, & Jacobson, 1993) and in finding skilled adherents of each treatment condition in many geographic areas. However, it leaves open the concern that the investigators may have unintentionally selected skilled therapists for their favored condition and less adequate ones for the other treatments.

ATTRITION

Attrition in intervention research is a common source of threats to both the internal and external validity of the findings. External validity is affected by a form of attrition that arises before potential participants ever begin the program. Who met criteria for entry to the study but chose not to participate? The larger the refusal rate, the less able we are to generalize the results of the study to the population of interest. The investigator can help the reader determine external validity in this sense by reporting how many suitable people were offered admission to the trial but refused and what reasons they gave for their rejection, perhaps using a flow chart such as that in Figure 28.1 to make attrition across the course of the trial easy to assess. Such a chart provides valuable information but does not reveal one important form of attrition: It is virtually impossible to determine how many potential participants learned of the procedures of the trial and decided against application for what might be important reasons that speak to a treatment's acceptability.

Once participants enter the study, the investigator faces the problem of maintaining their cooperation with the data-collection effort and retaining them in treatment. The longer the study, the more likely it is that participants will fail to continue with treatment, assessment, or both. Dropouts are a problem even in pretest–posttest designs, but attrition is especially problematic at follow-up when participants no longer have the incentive of receipt of the intervention to maintain their compliance with assessment procedures. The more people drop out of a research trial, the less representative the data are of the average person who enters treatment—a threat to external validity (Shadish et al., 2002).

Problems with attrition are even graver when attrition is differential (Shadish et al., 2002). Here internal validity is threatened. Differential attrition is obvious when dropout rates are higher in one intervention condition than another. It is more subtle, but equally dangerous, when different kinds of people drop out of one condition than another. Imagine two treatment conditions for which one condition is arduous but effective for those who stay the course, whereas the other condition is less demanding but also less effective. It is possible that for those people who complete treatment, the arduous treatment is more effective than the comparison condition, but that the less motivated people drop out of the demanding treatment. A comparison of treatment completers then yields findings that do not represent the results for the group of patients who started treatment: The investigators have lost the benefits of random assignment because there are now systematic differences between people in different treatment conditions (more motivated participants are in one condition than another), and internal validity is threatened. We address the problems of attrition further when we discuss statistical conclusion validity. For now, we note only that the reader of any report based on completer rather than intention-to-treat analyses (Hollis & Campbell, 1999) should be wary and that investigators should make every attempt to continue to collect data on people who drop out of treatment (Lavori, 1992), for example, by using financial incentives to keep participants involved.

MODERATION AND MEDIATION

Researchers are usually not content to know simply whether or not a treatment works. They also want to know whether it works especially well or especially poorly for one type of participant or another and how a treatment works when it works. The first question concerns moderation and the second mediation (Baron & Kenny, 1986).

Moderation

Many psychotherapists believe it is important to select a treatment that matches a client in some important regard, and the search for client characteristics that predict better outcomes for one treatment than for another has become something of a quest for the Holy Grail in psychotherapy research. This sort of moderation effect, represented in statistical tests as a disordinal interaction, is not often found and is replicated even less often, perhaps because sample sizes are generally inadequate to detect such effects reliably or because they are truly rare. The failure of Project MATCH (Project MATCH Research Group, 1997) represents a sad example: This very large, very expensive, and well-conducted study was explicitly designed to test patient-treatment matching hypotheses in a sample of more than 1,700 patients with alcoholism. On the whole, previous findings from the moderation literature with alcohol-abusing or -dependent patients failed to replicate.

A different sort of moderation is the ordinal interaction. In one sort of ordinal interaction, the investigator may identify patient characteristics that are associated with poor treatment outcome relative to a control condition. For example, Fournier et al. (2010) found that antidepressant medication was significantly better than placebo but only for patients with severe depression. In such a case, we can say that treatment is efficacious but only for certain kinds of clients. Researchers are often less excited about this sort of interaction, in that it does not tell us what treatment would be better, for example, for patients who had less severe depression.

When moderator variables are selected after the trial has been conducted (at which point the researcher has knowledge of the results) rather than a priori, the investigator needs to be especially cautious in interpreting the findings, which may capitalize on chance (Kraemer, Wilson, Fairburn, & Agras, 2002). Until replicated, the results should be seen as heuristic for future research rather than definitive. For example, in the Treatment of Depression Collaborative Research Program (TDCRP), Elkin et al. (1989) conducted post hoc moderation analyses and reported that for patients with severe depression, cognitive therapy was not as effective as antidepressant medication. This effect was widely cited, and Elkin et al.'s caution that the moderation results were exploratory was often forgotten. Yet when DeRubeis, Gelfand, Tang, and Simons (1999) conducted a mega-analysis or patient-level meta-analysis[1] of four trials comparing cognitive therapy and antidepressant medication for severe depression (including the TDCRP), they found no evidence of superiority for medication over cognitive therapy.

According to some experts (Kraemer et al., 2002), the investigator should consider as potential moderators only those variables that can be assessed before treatment. In our view, this approach is too restrictive and risks overlooking important findings. For example, Addis et al. (2006) randomly assigned therapists in a health maintenance organization to training in cognitive-behavior therapy for panic disorder or to a waiting list for training. Panic disorder patients who saw the specially trained therapists improved significantly more than patients who saw the waiting-list therapists, but only when patients received at least eight sessions of treatment. When patients received fewer than eight sessions, there were no differences between conditions—a moderation effect. Note that in this study Addis et al. did not experimentally assign patients to fewer or more than eight sessions. Accordingly, this part of the report is quasi-experimental in nature and does not have the force of an investigation in which patients were randomly assigned to briefer or longer treatment.

[1]In ordinary meta-analysis (Lipsey & Wilson, 2001), the researcher works with summary-level data (e.g., means, standard deviations, or effect sizes), whereas in mega-analysis or patient-level meta-analysis, the researcher works with the raw data from the original studies. As noted by Olkin (1995), this allows for more sophisticated analyses of the data in which the mega-analyst can examine hypotheses for which the original experiments did not provide analyses, such as the effects of individual patient characteristics and subgroup analyses.

Mediation

Analyses of mediation go deeper and test not whether patients have changed on clinical endpoints but what processes might account for that change. In essence, tests of mediation are tests of causal agency or proposed mechanisms. What components of the larger treatment package played a causal role in bringing about the change in outcomes observed, and what mechanisms in the patient played a causal role in transmitting the impact of treatment to the outcomes of interest? Such tests speak to the construct validity of the research. For example, it goes without saying that cognitive therapists believe that changing patients' maladaptive cognitions is the central curative process in psychotherapy. In treatment research, mediation is tested by determining whether changes in the outcome variable over time or differences in treatment efficacy between two treatment conditions (e.g., cognitive–behavior therapy vs. a placebo) can be statistically accounted for by changes in the mediator (e.g., cognitive change; Kraemer et al., 2002). For example, Smits, Rosenfield, McDonald, and Telch (2006) collected data across 15 exposure trials from patients in treatment for social phobia, assessing cognitive variables before each exposure trial and fear after each trial. The authors demonstrated that reductions in patients' predictions that they would look anxious, stupid, and so forth statistically accounted for reductions in fear across trials. A critical factor in the appropriate test of mediation is the researcher's ability to demonstrate that change in the mediator preceded change on the outcome variable. Otherwise, the mediator could just as easily have been caused by the outcome as the converse or be a time-varying third variable not causally related to the outcome at all. We will return to this point with a specific example in the Alliance section.

STATISTICAL CONCLUSION VALIDITY

Type I and II Errors

Perhaps because the opportunity to collect data in an intervention trial is precious, investigators tend to want to collect data on many variables, including outcome variables. This is understandable but runs the risk of Type I error. Investigators have been known to test 20 or more outcome variables, all with an alpha level of .05, and then interpret a smattering of significant effects as indicating they have demonstrated efficacy for the treatment tested. Worse yet, the investigator might report only those measures that yielded findings consistent with the hypothesis. After the fact, it is tempting to conclude that the measures yielding significant outcomes are the most valid measures.

Using a large number of outcomes and then adopting stringent Bonferroni-corrected alpha values is not a reasonable strategy for intervention research, in which each additional participant is costly and difficult to recruit (Nakagawa, 2004). The necessary sample sizes for testing large numbers of outcomes with experiment-wise corrections to p values are unlikely to be achieved. Rather, the investigator should select the best measure(s) as the primary measure(s) of outcome (a judicious number of other variables can still be tested as secondary outcomes) or seek to cut the number of outcome variables by reducing the data before hypothesis testing (Rosenthal & Rosnow, 2008), for example, by conducting a principal components analysis of the outcome variables and using the component scores rather than individual variables for hypothesis testing. Kraemer et al. (2003) have provided suggestions for combining data from multiple informants, the sort of data common in research with children.

The problem of Type II error also plagues intervention research. If a treatment is genuinely effective, most often it will be found to be statistically significantly different from a waiting-list condition. Comparisons with an active treatment are another matter, however, because effects sizes in this case are likely to be no more than medium. Psychotherapy research trials are typically underpowered to detect this sort of difference (Kazdin & Bass, 1989), and researchers and readers frequently make the mistake of concluding there is no difference between treatments when from the outset the sample size precluded differences of a medium size from being statistically significant. With increased awareness of this problem, researchers have banded together across centers to conduct multisite trials to obtain the sample sizes they need to test important questions of differential efficacy. This, of course, introduces another set of challenges in ensuring that methods are comparable across two or more sites (Kraemer, 2000).

Noninferiority and Equivalence Testing

Often in intervention research, the investigator's goal is not to test whether one intervention is better than another but rather to test whether some new intervention is as good as a well-established treatment. Perhaps this new intervention is briefer, less costly, or easier to implement than the standard treatment. A frequent mistake is for the researcher to conduct standard tests for statistically significant differences between interventions' impact, find none, and declare that the two procedures are comparable in their efficacy. This is not correct, however; they were just not statistically significantly different in this trial. To conduct a proper test of the investigator's hypothesis requires a test of noninferiority (the new intervention is no worse than the standard intervention) or of equivalence (the new intervention is neither worse than nor better than the standard intervention; Stegner, Bostrom, & Greenfield, 1996).

To conduct such tests, the investigators must identify in advance what effect they consider so small as to be clinically irrelevant (Piaggio, Elbourne, Altman, Pocock, & Evans, 2006). It is best if the field has some consensus on how small that difference should be and on what outcome variable it should be tested. The investigators then conduct statistical tests for equivalence or noninferiority (Stegner et al., 1996), depending on which fits best with their research question. These tests involve rejecting the null hypothesis that the two interventions are different in their efficacy rather than the usual null hypothesis of no difference. Equivalence and noninferiority trials have become common in biomedical research but not in psychological research, in part because the large sample sizes required for this approach are unlikely in psychotherapy research. Some large-scale intervention or prevention trials might have the requisite sample sizes. Because sloppy research can lead investigators to find no difference between treatments when such a difference does exist (error swamps the treatment

effect), equivalence and noninferiority trials must be exquisitely conducted with an eye to internal validity for the reader to have confidence in their conclusions.

Effect Size and Clinically Significant Change

A common error for researchers and research consumers is to state that the treatment effect was really big because the p value was very small. Despite decades of exhortations that psychologists should report and interpret the effect sizes derived from their findings (e.g., Wilkinson & Task Force on Statistical Inference, 1999), researchers and consumers of research still confuse the interpretation of a p value with the size of the effect. Because the p value is highly dependent on not only the size of the effect but also the sample size, we cannot determine how big the difference was between two intervention conditions by a report of the p value alone. To give the research consumer an idea of how big the difference is in a way that is not dependent on the scale of the particular outcome measure used, the researcher should report an effect size, which is commonly given in standard deviation units, although this varies with the type of statistical analysis (Cohen, 1988; Kraemer & Kupfer, 2006).

Even the effect size, however, can be hard to interpret, as changes will be bigger on measures that are more reliable (because the standard deviation will be smaller). Patients might change substantially according to average effect sizes on a very reliable measure but still be quite impaired. Accordingly, if the investigator wishes to report how many of the patients are doing well, it is best to incorporate an additional approach. These approaches might include reporting what percentage of patients in each group no longer meet diagnostic criteria for the primary diagnosis at the end of treatment or reporting what percentage of patients in each group meet criteria for clinically significant change (Jacobson & Truax, 1991). The calculation of clinically significant change, as formulated by Jacobson and Truax (1991), includes determining whether a given patient has changed to a statistically reliable degree, and whether she or he is more likely to fall in the distribution of the scores of a normal sample rather than a sample of people with the disorder under investigation.

Research groups in some areas have developed conventions for what they consider recovery in their field that are based on yet different criteria. For example, researchers in major depression have adopted a set of criteria for the definition of recovery from a major depressive episode (Frank et al., 1991). Whatever method researchers choose, they may then test whether the intervention groups differ on the percentage of patients recovered, although this test will generally be less powerful than tests of the continuous variables.

Once some metric of success has been established, the investigator may then report the results using an effect size from biomedical research that has become increasingly popular in psychiatric research, that is, *number needed to treat* (NNT). NNT is the number of patients one would have to treat with a given approach to achieve one more successful case than if an equal number of patients received the control or alternative intervention. The smaller the NNT, the larger the treatment effect size. For example, the results of meta-analysis of psychotherapy versus waiting-list control groups recast as NNT by Kraemer and Kupfer (2006) suggested that for every 3.1 patients who received psychotherapy rather than being on a waiting list, one more patient would improve. Kraemer and Kupfer (2006) described methods for converting continuous measures of outcome into NNT as well.

Appropriate Statistical Analysis

Standards for the statistical analysis of data from intervention research are ever higher, and readers of older research papers may find procedures that would lead a manuscript to be rejected for publication in the 21st century. Several common issues arise.

First, as noted, missing data are common in longitudinal research. Patients drop out of treatment, and participants fail to complete all assessment points. The investigator who conducts only *completer analyses* of people who provide all data and who complete treatment is analyzing data that are unrepresentative of the sample that was randomized to intervention conditions. Once awareness of this

problem developed, researchers began to use a procedure called *last observation carried forward* (LOCF) to cope with missing data (Shao & Zhong, 2003). For example, if the client drops out of treatment, refuses posttest assessment, or both, her or his pretest score (or most recent score available) is substituted for the missing datum at posttest. Although this may be a better approach than a completer analysis, it may underestimate treatment effects, in that people sometimes disappear from trials because they are doing well and feel no further need for assistance. (See Lavori, 1992, for a further critique of the LOCF approach.) Accordingly, the development of more sophisticated approaches to missing data has been a boon to intervention research. The approach variously called hierarchical linear modeling, random regression modeling, and multilevel modeling allows the investigator to model the trajectory across time on the outcome variable for each subject on the basis of however many data points that subject completed (Bryk & Raudenbush, 1987). The trajectories for the individual subjects then become the data for between-group analysis. If data are missing at random or missing completely at random, multilevel modeling approaches can cope well with less than complete data (Hedeker & Gibbons, 1997). To get the greatest benefit from this approach, the investigator would do well to collect outcome data at multiple points across the trial rather than just at pretest, posttest, and follow-up. Multiple data points not only provide greater statistical power (de Jong, Moerbeek, & van der Leeden, 2010) but also allow a better determination of the individual trajectories and is especially helpful in the case of dropout.

Multilevel modeling allows the investigator to address readily a second common statistical problem in intervention research, that of nesting. Usually a given therapist sees multiple patients in a trial, and to the degree that there are any differences across therapists in how effective they are, patients seen by a particular therapist share some variance in their outcomes that is due to the therapist. Other forms of nesting include the group in trials of group therapy, the classroom and the school in interventions conducted in education settings, and the site in multisite trials. When nesting is ignored in the analyses, Type

I error can increase dramatically (de Jong et al., 2010). Multilevel modeling allows the researcher to build such nesting into the statistical analysis. A particularly thorny issue in studies involving nesting is whether to treat therapists, for example, as fixed or random effects. To treat therapists as fixed effects in the analyses means that the investigator cannot generalize the results of the trial beyond these specific therapists—a point largely ignored in the treatment literature. If therapists are treated as a random effect, it is reasonable to generalize the results of the study to similar therapists with comparable training (Crits-Christoph, Tu, & Gallop, 2003). Because inclusion of therapists as a random effect diminishes statistical power, investigators are loath to do this (Crits-Christoph et al., 2003).

The third common problem we will mention arises when full randomization is not possible because the investigator is conducting quasi-experimental research or when the investigator randomizes intact groups (e.g., schools) to an intervention program. In such cases, it is likely that there will be pretreatment differences between intervention conditions. Given large enough sample sizes, the investigator can overcome the problems represented by the preintervention differences with propensity score analysis (Joffe & Rosenbaum, 1999). In this approach, logistic regression is used to predict treatment group assignment by all possible covariates to yield a predicted probability of being in one group versus the other. This resulting probability score can then be used as a single covariate in the analyses of outcome. Alternatively, the propensity score may be used to form a number of strata within which participants are fairly closely matched. In this case, the analyses are conducted within strata. The latter approach clearly requires a large sample to execute with adequate power. If the investigator has collected data on all the important covariates, then propensity score analysis is effective in diminishing selection effects (Shadish et al., 2002).

CONSTRUCT VALIDITY OF AN EXPERIMENT

Construct validity refers to the extent to which one can make inferences from the procedures of a study to the higher order constructs they were intended to represent (Shadish et al., 2002). With respect to randomized controlled trials, that means the extent to which the investigator has accurately identified the causally active components of the treatment manipulation. Most treatments consist of multiple components, some specified by theory and others common to the treatment enterprise. Construct validity asks whether we understand the causally active components of the intervention and the mechanisms through which they operate.

As previously described in the section on selection of control groups, different types of control groups allow for increasingly greater confidence that the theory as specified was adequately tested. For example, cognitive therapy is predicated on a theory that states that teaching patients to examine the accuracy of their beliefs should reduce distress. If we were to compare cognitive therapy to its absence we might very well produce an internally valid difference that could be attributed to the experimental manipulation (and thereby establish its efficacy), but it would not do much to convince a skeptic that it was the targeting of inaccurate beliefs that led to the subsequent reduction in distress. It could just as well have been the nonspecific aspects of the treatment package (expectation for change and personal contact with the therapist) that were responsible for the change observed. Construct validity would be enhanced if cognitive therapy were found to be superior to a nonspecific control that was equated for the mobilization of expectations and therapist contact. Construct validity would be enhanced even further if change in cognition was linked to subsequent change in distress in a manner suggestive of causal mediation. The issue then with respect to construct validity is whether the experiment conducted provides an adequate test of the underlying substantive theory. To do so it must implement the treatment in question in an adequate fashion and control for other alternative explanations not specified by theory.

Treatment Manuals

Treatment manuals represent an attempt to specify the underlying principles and specific behaviors that together constitute a treatment intervention.

Manuals differ in the extent to which they constrain the therapist's behavior: Some provide considerable latitude for the clinician to respond to the specific needs of the client as they unfold over time, whereas others go so far as to specify the actual dialogue that the therapist is supposed to follow across the course of treatment (Luborsky & DeRubeis, 1984). Treatment manuals serve a useful purpose in communicating what is done in a given intervention and facilitate dissemination to other researchers and therapists in other settings. They also reduce variability between therapists within a trial (Crits-Christoph et al., 1991), thereby enhancing the extent to which the essential aspects of a treatment are implemented (construct validity) and increasing the likelihood that treatment differences will be detected relative to controls (statistical conclusion validity).

Nonetheless, treatment manuals are neither necessary nor sufficient to ensure that an intervention has been adequately implemented in a given trial. In the classic Temple study, experienced psychoanalytic therapists operated without a formal treatment manual but were able to instantiate dynamic treatment in a representative fashion nonetheless, due no doubt to years of training and their experience in analysis (Sloane, Staples, Cristol, Yorkson, & Whipple, 1975). At the same time, despite training to a manual, the National Institute of Mental Health (NIMH) TDCRP found that therapists with prior experience with cognitive therapy got considerably better results than those who did not have prior experience (Jacobson & Hollon, 1996). To assure the research consumer that the treatment was faithfully and well conducted, additional steps are required of the investigator. We turn to those next.

Therapist Adherence

Adherence refers to the extent that the therapists implement the therapy as intended. A study would have little construct validity if therapist behavior bore no relationship to what was intended by theory. Adherence can be measured on the basis of therapist self-report or the completion of postsession checklists, but the preferred manner is by actual direct observation of the session itself, often in the form of ratings of audio or video tapes

(Chevron & Rounsaville, 1983). Such methods require observers trained to recognize the behaviors specified by theory but do not necessarily require that those observers be competent to implement the therapy themselves. For example, Hill, O'Grady, and Elkin (1992) found that cognitive therapy could readily be distinguished from interpersonal psychotherapy and each from the clinical management component of pharmacotherapy by nonprofessional raters listening to audiotapes from the TDCRP.

Therapist Training and Competence

Competence refers to the extent to which the therapists perform the intended therapy in a skillful fashion. Competence is related to adherence (you cannot perform a therapy well if you are not performing the therapy) but can be differentiated at least in theory: It is possible to implement the various components of a treatment in a highly recognizable manner that is neither skillful nor responsive to the needs of the patient at a given moment. To use an analogy, it is possible to play a musical piece in a manner that others could recognize without doing so in a manner that is pleasing to the ear. In the TDCRP, adherence unexpectedly functioned as a suppressor variable, the inclusion of which enhanced the relation between competence and outcome in cognitive therapy, suggesting that at least some of the therapists were adherent to the approach without being all that competent in its execution (Shaw et al., 1999). Like adherence, competence can be rated in a variety of ways but most often is rated by expert therapists working from tapes of actual sessions.

Therapist training is intended to enhance both adherence and especially competence. Just how much training is required and how best it is accomplished is a matter of some debate, but it seems fair to say that the strategies pursued should match the purposes of the study. In the typical efficacy trial, the goal is usually to determine whether a given treatment has a causal impact under ideal conditions. In such a trial, it seems reasonable to ask that the therapists be trained to the point at which they can implement the therapy in a manner specified by theory. In other types of trials, especially some types of effectiveness studies, the goal may be to see how much change can be produced by therapists trained to whatever level of competence is allowed given the pragmatic constraints in the natural environment. Either level of training is fine so long as it is clear what was going on, and causal inferences are drawn in an appropriate manner.

Training is often supplemented by subsequent supervision that may continue through the duration of the trial. Again, just how to supervise and how much supervision to provide should be determined by the questions being asked in the particular trial, and problems arise only when the inferences drawn do not match the implementation. For example, in the TDCRP, therapists with varying levels of prior experience with and commitment to cognitive therapy were provided with several days of training and intensive supervision while working with several practice cases each. Once the study proper started, supervision was cut back unless ratings on a competence measure dropped below a preset cutoff (Shaw, 1984). What the investigators found was that rated levels of competence dropped from the training phase into the study proper (Shaw et al., 1999) and that cognitive therapy was less efficacious than medications and no better than pill-placebo for patients with more severe depressions (Elkin et al., 1995). By way of contrast, in a subsequent trial DeRubeis et al. (2005) selected experienced cognitive therapists at one site and, at a second site, continued intensive training throughout the course of the study proper for the less experienced cognitive therapists at that site. The investigators found that cognitive therapy was as efficacious as medications and superior to pill-placebo in the treatment of patients with depressions of comparable severity. Although both trials were intended to speak to the efficacy of cognitive therapy as specified by theory, they differed considerably in the nature of the therapists who they selected and the quality and intensity of the training and supervision that they provided—differences that appear to be reflected in the outcomes that they generated.

Allegiance

Investigator allegiance is an important correlate of variance in outcomes across the treatment literature (Luborsky et al., 1999). Treatments usually do better in the hands of investigators who are invested in their outcomes, and comparisons between different treatments often rise and fall on the basis of who carries out the study. There are at least two possible interpretations. First, it may be that investigators with a vested interest cannot or will not conduct a fair trial and that bias (untended or otherwise) colors the results. Second, it could be that some investigators are simply more competent when it comes to implementing some treatments than others and that differential outcome across studies reflects differential competence of the investigators. For example, cognitive therapy was found to be superior to antidepressant medications in a study conducted at the site where the psychosocial treatment was first developed (Rush, Beck, Kovacs, & Hollon, 1977). However, pharmacotherapy was not adequately implemented: Dosages were marginal, and tapering was begun before the end of treatment. Subsequent studies that did a better job of implementation typically found cognitive therapy as efficacious as but not better than medication (e.g., Hollon et al., 1992).

Unintended bias can be addressed by adherence to principles of good research design (random assignment and blinded evaluators), but differential competence can be resolved only by including investigators in the research team who have expertise (and are invested) in each of the modalities tested. This is the principle of adversarial collaboration that has been described in the cognitive psychology literature to offset the operation of bias (Mellers, Hertwig, & Kahneman, 2001). It is important that this allegiance and expertise permeate all aspects of the study, starting with the investigator team and including the therapists who provide the actual interventions.

Expectancy

Patients enter treatment in the hope that it will make things better, and expectations of improvement have been shown to have a powerful effect on outcomes in their own right. Some treatments do a better job of mobilizing expectations for change than others, and differences in expectations can influence the comparisons between conditions. To the extent that the mobilization of expectations can be considered an inherent part of a given intervention, then expectancies pose no threat to the internal validity of the design: An effect is an effect and can be attributed to the intervention regardless of how it was produced.

Isolating the contribution of expectancy effects, however, can play a major role in determining whether a treatment works for the reasons specified by theory, a matter of construct validity. For example, it is routine to test new medications against a pharmacologically inert pill-placebo that controls for all the psychological aspects of medication-taking, including the expectation of change. Only if the novel medication exceeds that pill-placebo control in a beneficial fashion is it allowed to be marketed to patients. The pill-placebo control is presumed to generate similar expectations for relief to those generated by the actual medication (as well as other nonspecific benefits of contact with a treating professional), and any differences observed are presumed to be the consequence of the pharmacological properties of the medication. Similar steps are often taken in psychotherapy research to determine whether comparison conditions are equated for the expectations that they generate at the outset of treatment, and studies are sometimes criticized for including intent-to-fail controls if they cannot be shown to be equated for initial expectations (Baskin, Tierney, Minami, & Wampold, 2003). We suspect that expectancy differences may be one result of differences in allegiance to different treatments. That is, if investigators compare some alternative treatment to their preferred treatment, they may inadvertently do so in a way that communicates to patients and therapists which treatment is expected to be inferior (e.g., by their enthusiasm, the quality of the training materials, and supervision provided).

Alliance

Patients not only have expectations regarding treatment outcomes but also form relationships with their therapists. The quality of the working alliance represents one attempt to operationalize the quality of the therapeutic relationship, and the term is often used in a generic fashion to refer to the larger construct of relatedness between patient and therapist (Goldfried, 1980). It has long been noted that

various measures of alliance predict treatment outcome (Horvath & Symonds, 1991). What is not so clear, however, is whether the therapeutic alliance plays a causal role in producing those outcomes. In most instances, alliance is rated periodically across treatment and correlated with treatment outcome. This means that early change in symptoms could be driving the quality of the relationship rather than the other way around.

In a pair of studies, DeRubeis and colleagues tested this hypothesis by assessing symptom change both before and after therapy sessions that were rated both for techniques specific to cognitive therapy and for nonspecific quality of the therapeutic alliance (DeRubeis & Feeley, 1990; Feeley, DeRubeis, & Gelfand, 1999). They found that after they controlled for prior symptom change, adherence to cognitive therapy in early sessions predicted subsequent change in depression, whereas ratings of the therapeutic alliance did not. Moreover, rated quality of the therapeutic alliance improved over time as a consequence of prior symptom change. These findings suggest that for cognitive therapy (as practiced in their samples), adherence to the techniques specified by theory drove subsequent symptom change and that change in turn drove the rated quality of the therapeutic alliance. At the same time, other studies that have controlled for prior symptom change in a similar fashion have found that rated quality of the alliance does sometimes predict subsequent symptom change (Klein et al., 2003), although effect sizes are lower than in studies in which the temporal sequence problem was ignored. What seems likely is that the therapeutic alliance may be either a cause or a consequence of improvement in treatment and that it is important to control for the temporal relations between treatment process and symptom change whenever investigating such effects.

Exclusion of Medication or Medication Stability

One issue that is sometimes confronted in psychotherapy research is what to do about patients who enter a study already on medications. On the one hand, patients often are reluctant to give up medications that they are already on, and excluding those patients from the trial would reduce the external validity of the design. On the other hand, patients are taking medications precisely because they think they make a difference, and to the extent this is true, such effects can obscure (or facilitate) the effects of psychotherapy. This problem is especially common in the treatment of anxiety and panic disorder in which case patients often are quite unwilling to make any changes in long-standing medication patterns.

Some investigators resolve this dilemma by asking patients to discontinue any psychoactive medications before entering the trial (and losing at least some potential patients who refuse to do so), whereas others are willing to allow patients to remain on stable doses of existing medications. Either strategy represents a reasonable accommodation to the practical realities of conducting clinical trials with patients who can choose to not participate, and causal inferences can still be drawn so long as they are tempered by recognition of the possible influences of concurrent medication usage. In such situations, it is particularly important to monitor what medications patients are taking and to conduct secondary analyses that control for medication usage. Changes in medication usage that occur after randomization are particularly problematic because they could be a consequence of differential treatment. Early comparative trials often found that the beneficial effects of adding psychotherapy were obscured by the fact that medication doses typically were lower in combination treatment (Hollon & Beck, 1978).

Exclusion of Other Treatment

Similar issues are raised by allowing patients to pursue other psychosocial treatment during the course of the study proper. As was the case for off-protocol medication treatment, excluding patients who refuse to give up ongoing psychotherapy threatens the external validity of the design, whereas allowing such patients in the trial presents problems for construct validity (if comparable in nature across conditions) or internal validity (if differential across the conditions). Moreover, having patients in two different kinds of psychotherapies risks having them working at cross-purposes. What many investigators do is to ask that patients discontinue any outside psychotherapy directed at the disorder under study for the duration of the trial, but they often make exceptions for psychosocial interventions directed at other issues, such as marital or family therapy.

Adequacy of Dose of Treatment

The essence of construct validity is that the underlying constructs are tested in a manner specified by theory. That suggests that what constitutes an adequate dose of treatment is determined by the question being addressed. There is nothing inherent in any given dose of treatment, but the doses selected for testing ought to be consistent with what is specified by theory. For example, neither the early study that compared cognitive therapy to inadequate doses of medication treatment (Rush et al., 1977) nor the subsequent NIMH TDCRP that left the implementation of cognitive therapy in the hands of relatively inexperienced therapists (Elkin et al., 1989) provided an adequate basis for comparing the relative efficacy of the two modalities as each is ideally practiced. Meta-analytic reviews suggested that each is comparable to the other when optimally implemented (Cuijpers, van Stratten, van Oppen, & Andersson, 2008). However, those same meta-analytic reviews also showed an advantage for full-strength medication treatment over relatively abbreviated courses of psychotherapy in managed care settings. It seems fair to conclude from these reviews that medication treatment is superior to psychotherapy when the latter must be restricted in dosage because of pragmatic constraints so long as one does not conclude that that relative inferiority reflects anything other than those pragmatic constraints.

EXTERNAL VALIDITY

External validity refers to the extent that treatment outcomes observed in controlled trials can be generalized to populations and settings of interest (Shadish et al., 2002). Several aspects of generalizability need to be considered. including but not limited to variation across patients, therapists, and settings. External validity is closely related to the notion of clinical utility and sometimes is considered in conjunction with cost (American Psychological Association [APA], 2002).

Continuum of Efficacy-Effectiveness Research

It has become commonplace in recent years to differentiate between efficacy and effectiveness research (Nathan et al., 2000). According to this distinction, efficacy research is said to be conducted in highly controlled settings using carefully selected patients who are randomly assigned to treatment by highly trained therapists. Conversely, effectiveness research is thought to be conducted in real-world settings in which random assignment to differential treatment is not always feasible and in which presumably more complicated patients are treated by less experienced therapists working under pragmatic constraints imposed by their many clinical demands (Seligman, 1995). Although there is some truth to these perceptions, we think it is unwise to draw too sharp a distinction between efficacy and effectiveness research and prefer instead to think in terms of internal and external validity (Chambless & Hollon, 1998). Any given study can be evaluated with respect to how it scores on each dimension. The goal is to determine how well a given intervention works in the real-world settings in which it needs to be applied to wholly representative patients.

Treatment outcomes are largely a function of two sets of factors: patients and procedures. Patients' characteristics are fixed at the time they first present for treatment, but procedures (including therapist skills and setting considerations) can be changed if there is sufficient reason. That is why we think that it is especially important to conduct research on wholly representative patient samples. If a treatment does not work for the patients for whom it is intended, then there is little that can be done to improve the situation. There can be great value in first establishing that something works under ideal conditions even if it does not initially generalize well to real-world settings, however, because therapists can be better trained and contexts modified if there is sufficient reason to do so. That is why we emphasize internal validity over external validity and selecting representative patients (rather than therapists or settings) in early trials.

Generalizations

To clinical settings. It is important to know whether treatments that are efficacious in research settings generalize to the kinds of applied settings in which most patients are treated. Applied settings can vary with respect to the caseload expected, the length of treatment that is feasible, and the demands on clinician time (Weisz & Addis, 2006). For example, we were once informed by therapists who worked for a large managed care organization that they could see patients as often as they thought appropriate, just so long as they started six new patients a week. Although no constraint was placed on the number of sessions that could be offered to any given patient, the pressure to add so many new patients effectively limited the number of sessions that could be provided.

To patients in community settings. There is a widespread perception that patients treated in efficacy studies in research settings are necessarily less complicated or comorbid than patients found in community settings (Westen, Novonty, & Thompson-Brenner, 2004). Although this may have been the case in early analogue studies, there is no necessary reason why complex and comorbid patients must be excluded from controlled trials. For example, two thirds of a sample of patients selected on the basis of meeting criteria for major depressive disorder in a recent efficacy trial conducted in a research clinic met criteria for one or more additional Axis I disorders and half met criteria for one or more Axis II disorders (DeRubeis et al., 2005).

Conversely, when Stirman, DeRubeis, Crits-Christoph, and Brody (2003) matched information found in community outpatients' charts to the inclusion and exclusion criteria used in published trials, they found nearly 80% of the diagnosed patients in community settings would have qualified for inclusion in one or more RCTs. The major reason patients would have been excluded from RCTs was not that they were too complicated or comorbid. Rather, their conditions were not severe enough, in that many carried diagnoses of adjustment disorder. Such disorders are by definition transient and will likely never warrant the conduct of an RCT. It is likely that at least some of these patients would have met criteria for Axis I or Axis II disorders if diagnosed according to strict research criteria; clinicians in applied settings often give diagnoses of adjustment disorder to avoid stigma. If so, then an even larger proportion of the patients seen in applied settings would likely qualify for inclusion in one or more controlled clinical trials. Clearly, research needs to be done with the kinds of patients found in applied community settings, but it is not clear that they will prove to be all that different from patients found in clinical research sites.

To clinicians in community settings. Clinicians in community settings are likely to be less experienced with specific disorders and less highly trained than clinicians in research settings. It is an open question just how well these clinicians can implement the kinds of treatments developed in research settings and tested in efficacy studies. On the one hand, there is little evidence that experience or professional status necessarily guarantees superior performance (Jacobson & Christensen, 1996), but on the other, much of the variability in outcomes across different studies appears to be related to the competence with which the therapists can perform the given interventions (Jacobson & Hollon, 1996). It is likely that years of experience and professional status are not particularly good markers of competence with a particular approach.

It is not clear just how much training is required to allow community clinicians to perform with the same level of proficiency as research therapists or how feasible such training is to provide in community settings. What does appear to be clear is that the provision of treatment manuals and brief workshops are not sufficient to help community therapists reach a reasonable level of proficiency (Miller, Sorensen, Selzer, & Brigham, 2006). The same concerns apply to pharmacotherapy as practiced in the community; surveys suggest that typical practice often falls far short of what gets done in controlled trials in research settings (Trivedi et al., 2004).

To patients of diverse backgrounds. It is important to include a diverse array of patients with respect to race, ethnicity, and socioeconomic status (SES) in research trials to determine whether study findings generalize to such patients. Minority patients not only tend to be few in number in clinical trials (just because they are fewer in number) but also often are underrepresented because they are suspicious of the motives of clinical researchers (with considerable historical justification). Language can be a barrier for many ethnic patients, and low SES patients often face barriers to participation with respect to transportation and child care. It is often the case that special efforts have to be made to recruit and retain such patients in controlled trials (Miranda et al., 2003).

To other research settings. Treatments typically are developed by a single individual or group and tested in the sites at which they were first developed. This means that early studies typically are done by groups that are invested in the treatment they are testing. Replication is a key principle in science, and if a treatment is truly efficacious, then other investigators at other sites should be able to replicate the findings generated in those initial trials. Some shrinkage is to be expected, as it is unlikely that other groups will be as expert in a given modality as the people who developed it. Nonetheless, if a treatment is to have value in real-world applications, then it must perform well in the hands of other groups at other sites. At the same time, the principle of replication implies that those other groups put in a good faith effort to learn how to implement the treatment in a reasonable fashion. Replication means that we should be able to reproduce the earlier findings if we implement the same procedures: With respect to treatment trials, this means that we must implement the treatment in question with reasonable fidelity.

Feasibility

Feasibility refers to the ease with which treatment can be delivered to actual patients in the settings in which they are typically treated (APA, 2002). Feasibility incorporates such factors as acceptability, patients' willingness and ability to comply with the requirements of the intervention, ease of dissemination, and cost-effectiveness. We examine each set of issues in turn.

Acceptability and patient-preference designs. For a treatment to be applied in actual practice, it must be acceptable to potential patients and also to other relevant parties, including therapists and administrators. There are many reasons why individual patients may prefer not to receive particular treatments, and these preferences need to be respected (APA, Task Force on Evidence-Based Practice, 2006). At the same time, patients often have trouble accepting the very interventions that are most likely to be useful to them. For example, exposure therapy is the best established psychological treatment for obsessive–compulsive disorder, yet it is frightening to most patients because it calls for them to do exactly those things that they most fear. Similarly, patients often refuse to take monoamine oxidase inhibitors because of the dietary restrictions required to avoid the risk of hypertensive crisis, despite the fact that these medications often represent the best pharmacological option for patients who are refractory to easier to manage medications.

Therapists also may be reluctant to implement treatments that they find threatening or distasteful, and some go so far as to ignore empirically supported interventions in favor of more traditional approaches that they find more compelling or in which they are already trained. Administrators also may play a role. We recently encountered a situation in which the Office of Legal Affairs tried to prevent a therapist from conducting exposure therapy with a competitive swimmer who had developed a morbid fear of drowning because it wanted to limit the legal exposure of the university in the unlikely event that the patient drowned during treatment.

Acceptability also plays a role in the decision to randomize. Given that patients differ in terms of how they are likely to change over time in the absence of treatment, we have argued in the section on Randomization that random assignment to intervention conditions is essential if any differences observed in outcomes are to be attributed to the experimental manipulation. Something like hormone replacement therapy provides a cautionary tale regarding what happens when we do not randomize and allow patients characteristics to determine treatment: Prognosis gets misconstrued as a treatment effect (Chlebowski et al., 2003; Manson et al., 2003).

That being said, no one likes to be randomized, and no one likes to randomize someone else to treatment. Prospective patients dislike the notion of leaving their fates to chance, and clinicians typically assume, rightly or wrongly, that they have the experience and expertise to select the best treatment for a given patient. Some have gone so far as to say that randomization may turn out to be worse than useless: Choice is itself curative, and patients may adhere better if they get the treatment they prefer (Seligman, 1995). A number of potential solutions have been proposed, from relying on retrospective surveys of patient satisfaction to the use of quasi-experimental designs that attempt to control for some of the threats to internal validity, to the use of benchmarking in which the results of open trials in applied settings are compared with those obtained in randomized controlled trials. Retrospective surveys are wholly uncontrolled and highly susceptible to the risk of confounding patient characteristics with treatment effects, quasi-experimental designs provide some protection against internal validity threats but that protection is only partial, and benchmarking is interpretatively ambiguous because any similarities or differences observed could be the product of differences in patients or procedures.

These concerns have led to an interest in the patient-preference design. Brewin and Bradley (1989) proposed a comprehensive cohort design that restricts randomization to only those patients who are willing to accept it; those who refuse are provided with the treatment they prefer. Others have proposed a two-stage randomization design in which patients are randomized to be (a) randomized to condition or (b) allowed to pick their treatment (Wennberg, Barry, Fowler, & Mulley, 1993). Neither approach is wholly satisfying because causal inferences can be drawn with any confidence only for patients who were randomized to the respective treatment conditions. The comprehensive cohort design does allow randomized patients to be benchmarked against those who refused and got their preferred treatment, and the two-stage randomized design does allow causal inferences to be drawn about the effects of patient choice. It remains unclear just how great a problem we are dealing with. A systematic meta-analytic review of patient-preference designs found that patient preferences led to substantial rates of refusal; prospective patients who are employed and well-educated are especially likely to refuse randomization (King et al., 2005). This suggests that patient preferences are a threat to the external validity of the typical RCT. At the same time, there was little evidence that patient preferences compromised the conclusions drawn from the studies: Differences in outcomes between randomized and preference groups typically were small (especially in larger studies) and when they were evident in smaller trials, were inconsistent in direction. The preference problem may not be as big as some believe.

The recent NIMH-funded Sequenced Treatment Alternatives to Relieve Depression (STAR*D) project used a particularly interesting strategy called equipoise stratified randomization in which patients or clinicians were allowed to rule out treatment strategies that they found unacceptable. Patients were subsequently randomized to the remaining options and only included in analyses that compared patients who accepted randomization to a given option (Lavori et al., 2001). For example, patients who showed a partial response to their initial medication could choose to not be switched, and patients who were unable to tolerate their initial medication could choose to not have their medication augmented. This approach appears to be the most compelling of the patient-preference strategies and has generated considerable enthusiasm in the field. Still, it is not without its problems. Rates of refusal were suspiciously high for some conditions (less than a third of the participants were willing to be randomized to cognitive therapy): Permitting patients to opt out of specific strategies might encourage greater rates of refusal than might otherwise have occurred. Moreover, treating clinicians often have even stronger preferences than their patients, which may inflate rates of refusal. Nonetheless, equipoise stratified randomization is an interesting approach that warrants further consideration.

Compliance by clients with treatment requirements. Even the most efficacious treatment will not work if the client does not implement the necessary steps. This issue is closely related to acceptability but is slightly more subtle. Patients may readily accept a treatment but not necessarily carry through with all the steps required to derive maximum benefit. For example, compliance with homework tends to predict subsequent improvement in cognitive therapy for depression (Burns & Spangler, 2000). Similarly, it would be inappropriate to say that a medication does not work if a patient does not take it. From a methodological standpoint, it is important to assess compliance so that accurate conclusions can be drawn with respect to treatment efficacy. For example, in a recent follow-up design, we monitored medication compliance in patients assigned to continuation treatment and conducted secondary analyses in which we censored patients who were less than fully compliant in the several weeks before a relapse (Hollon et al., 2005). Whereas the primary analysis that left such relapses uncensored provided the best estimate of how patients actually did on continuation medication, the secondary analyses provided an estimate of how those patients would have done if they all had been compliant.

Ease of dissemination. Some treatments are easier to learn than others and therefore easier to disseminate. Classical psychoanalysis required a training analysis of many years' duration, and even those aiming to practice psychoanalytically oriented psychotherapy were encouraged to pursue personal therapy as part of the training process. It is likely that such requirements contributed to the gradual decline in the number of such practitioners across recent decades (Norcross, Karpiak, & Santoro, 2005). No intervention has grown so rapidly over that same period as cognitive–behavioral therapy, whereas the number of practitioners professing an allegiance to more purely behavioral therapies has stayed relatively constant over that same interval. That may be subject to change in years to come as the so-called third-wave behavioral approaches gain greater credibility in the treatment community, fueled in part by the perception that it is easier to learn to do simple behavioral interventions than to also learn more complicated cognitive strategies. From a methodological perspective, it is important to report just what was required to implement the treatment(s) in a given study, including who the therapists were, how they were selected, how much training was required, and what kind of supervision was provided.

Cost-effectiveness.   Consideration of the costs of treatment should be conceptually distinct from the scientific evidence for its effectiveness, but costs need to be considered nonetheless (APA, 2002). Costs include the expense to the patient and the health care professional as well as the cost of any technology or equipment involved in the intervention. Clearly, those interventions that produce the same outcome at a lower cost than others are to be preferred. It becomes more difficult to decide on the appropriate course of action when the most expensive treatments are also the most efficacious. Health care economists have developed ways to quantify the costs of leaving problems unresolved (e.g., how much is a depression-free day worth?), and it is often possible to evaluate the relative costs of an intervention against the value it provides. Conducting a sophisticated cost-effectiveness analysis requires collecting information not just on the direct costs of treatment but also on the indirect costs incurred, such as time lost from work and child care and transportation expenses. Moreover, given that costs are often not normally distributed (a single hospitalization can be extremely expensive), the sample sizes required to conduct a sophisticated cost–benefit analysis are often exponentially larger than those required to detect a treatment effect. Nonetheless, information regarding the differential costs and benefits of different treatments can be valuable in evaluating the relative merits of different treatments.

Relative cost-effectiveness also can be influenced by the health care system in which it is embedded. In the United States, health care organizations often have little incentive to provide preventive interventions even when they are cost-effective over the long run because job change happens with sufficient frequency that third-party payers rarely profit from the long-term benefits of preventive care (Stricker et al., 1999). Conversely, in Great Britain, with its single-payer system, the National Health Service has invested £130 million to train therapists to provide

the cognitive and behavioral interventions shown to have enduring effects that make them more cost-effective than long-term medication treatment (Clark et al., 2009). This means that cost-effectiveness is not absolute and must be considered in the context of the larger economic system in which it is embedded.

CONCLUSION

Methodology for intervention research necessarily cuts across many of the topics of other chapters in these volumes, and we have only touched on complex issues that deserve prolonged discussion. We refer the reader to other chapters in these volumes for additional information and also to excellent texts such as Shadish et al. (2002) and Kazdin (2003) on research design and MacKinnon (2008) on mediation. In addition, we believe the reviewer will find it useful to refer to the CONSORT statements on non-inferiority and equivalence trials (Piaggio et al., 2006) and randomized controlled trials (Altman et al., 2001; Boutron, Moher, Altman, Schulz, & Ravaud, 2008), the TREND statement on quasi-experiments (Des Jarlais, Lyles, & Crepaz, 2004), and the APA's paper on journal article reporting standards (APA, Publications and Communications Board Working Group on Journal Article Reporting Standards, 2008). Although these statements are designed to encourage uniform reporting of critical design features, being reminded of what these features are when planning the research rather than after the fact facilitates the conduct of sound research.

References

Addis, M. E., Hatgis, C., Cardemil, E., Jacob, K., Krasnow, A. D., & Mansfield, A. (2006). Effectiveness of cognitive–behavioral treatment for panic disorder versus treatment as usual in a managed care setting: 2-year follow-up. *Journal of Consulting and Clinical Psychology, 74,* 377–385. doi:10.1037/0022-006-X.74.2.377

Altman, D. G., Schulz, K. F., Moher, D., Egger, M., Davidoff, F., Elbourne, D., ... Lang, T. (2001). The Revised CONSORT Statement for reporting randomized trials: Explanation and elaboration. *Annals of Internal Medicine, 134,* 663–694.

American Psychological Association. (2002). Criteria for evaluating treatment guidelines. *American Psychologist, 57,* 1052–1059. doi:10.1037/0003-066-X.57.12.1052

American Psychological Association, Publications and Communications Board Working Group on Journal Article Reporting Standards. (2008). Reporting standards for research in psychology: Why do we need them? What might they be? *American Psychologist, 63,* 839–851. doi:10.1037/0003-066X.63.9.839

American Psychological Association, Task Force on Evidence-Based Practice. (2006). Evidence-based practice in psychology. *American Psychologist, 61,* 271–285. doi:10.1037/0003-066X.61.4.271

Baron, R. M., & Kenny, D. A. (1986). The moderator/mediator variable distinction in social psychological research: Conceptual, strategic, and statistical considerations. *Journal of Personality and Social Psychology, 51,* 1173–1182. doi:10.1037/0022-3514.51.6.1173

Baskin, T. W., Tierney, S. C., Minami, T., & Wampold, B. E. (2003). Establishing specificity in psychotherapy: A meta-analysis of structural equivalence of placebo controls. *Journal of Consulting and Clinical Psychology, 71,* 973–979. doi:10.1037/0022-006X.71.6.973

Bordin, E. S. (1979). The generalizability of the psychoanalytic concept of the working alliance. *Psychotherapy: Theory, Research, and Practice, 16,* 252–260. doi:10.1037/h0085885

Boutron, I., Moher, D., Altman, D. G., Schulz, K. F., & Ravaud, P. (2008). Extending the CONSORT Statement to randomized trials of nonpharmacologic treatment: Explanation and elaboration. *Annals of Internal Medicine, 148,* 295–309.

Brewin, C. R., & Bradley, C. (1989). Patient preferences and randomised clinical trials. *British Medical Journal, 299,* 313–315. doi:10.1136/bmj.299.6694.313

Bryk, A. S., & Raudenbush, S. W. (1987). Application of hierarchical linear models to assessing change. *Psychological Bulletin, 101,* 147–158. doi:10.1037/0033-2909.101.1.147

Burns, D. D., & Spangler, D. L. (2000). Does psychotherapy homework lead to improvements in depression in cognitive-behavioral therapy or does improvement lead to increased homework compliance? *Journal of Consulting and Clinical Psychology, 68,* 46–56. doi:10.1037/0022-006X.68.1.46

Campbell, M. K., Elbourne, D. R., & Altman, D. G. (2004). CONSORT Statement: Extension to cluster randomised trials. *BMJ (Clinical Research Ed.), 328,* 702–708. doi:10.1136/bmj.328.7441.702

Chambless, D. L., & Hollon, S. D. (1998). Defining empirically supported therapies. *Journal of Consulting and Clinical Psychology, 66,* 7–18. doi:10.1037/0022-006X.66.1.7

Chevron, E. S., & Rounsaville, B. J. (1983). Evaluating the clinical skills of psychotherapists: A comparison of techniques. *Archives of General Psychiatry, 40,* 1129–1132.

Chlebowski, R. T., Hendrix, S. L., Langer, R. D., Stefanick, M. L., Gass, M., Lane, D., . . . McTiernan, A. (2003). Influence of estrogen plus progestin on breast cancer and mammography in healthy postmenopausal women. *JAMA, 289,* 3243–3253. doi:10.1001/jama.289.24.3243

Clark, D. M., Layard, R., Smithies, R., Richards, D. A., Suckling, R., & Wright, B. (2009). Improving access to psychological therapy: Initial evaluation of two UK demonstration sites. *Behaviour Research and Therapy, 47,* 910–920. doi:10.1016/j.brat.2009.07.010

Cohen, J. (1960). A coefficient of agreement for nominal scales. *Educational and Psychological Measurement, 20,* 37–46. doi:10.1177/001316446002000104

Cohen, J. (1988). *Statistical power analysis for the behavioral sciences* (2nd ed.). Hillsdale, NJ: Erlbaum.

Crits-Christoph, P., Baranackie, K., Kurcias, J. S., Beck, A. T., Carroll, K., Perry, K., . . . Zitrin, C. (1991). Meta-analysis of therapist effects in psychotherapy outcome studies. *Psychotherapy Research, 1,* 81–91. doi:10.1080/10503309112331335511

Crits-Christoph, P., Tu, X., & Gallop, R. (2003). Therapists as fixed versus random effects—some statistical and conceptual issues: A comment on Siemer and Joormann (2003). *Psychological Methods, 8,* 518–523. doi:10.1037/1082-989X.8.4.518

Cuijpers, P., van Stratten, A., van Oppen, P., & Andersson, A. (2008). Are psychological and pharmacological interventions equally effective in the treatment of adult depressive disorders? A meta-analysis of comparative studies. *Journal of Clinical Psychiatry, 69,* 1675–1685. doi:10.4088/JCP.v69n1102

de Jong, K., Moerbeek, M., & van der Leeden, R. (2010). A prior power analysis in longitudinal three-level multilevel models: An example with therapist effects. *Psychotherapy Research, 20,* 273–284. doi:10.1080/10503300903376320

DeRubeis, R. J., & Feeley, M. (1990). Determinants of change in cognitive therapy for depression. *Cognitive Therapy and Research, 14,* 469–482. doi:10.1007/BF01172968

DeRubeis, R. J., Gelfand, L. A., Tang, T. Z., & Simons, A. D. (1999). Medications versus cognitive behavior therapy for severely depressed outpatients: Mega-analysis of four randomized comparisons. *American Journal of Psychiatry, 156,* 1007–1013.

DeRubeis, R. J., Hollon, S. D., Amsterdam, J. D., Shelton, R. C., Young, P. R., Salomon, R. M., . . . Gallop, R. (2005). Cognitive therapy vs. medications in the treatment of moderate to severe depression. *Archives of General Psychiatry, 62*, 409–416. doi:10.1001/archpsyc.62.4.409

Des Jarlais, D. C., Lyles, C., & Crepaz, N. (2004). Improving the reporting quality of nonrandomized evaluations of behavioral and public health interventions: The TREND Statement. *American Journal of Public Health, 94*, 361–366. doi:10.2105/AJPH.94.3.361

Efron, B. (1971). Forcing a sequential experiment to be balanced. *Biometrika, 58*, 403–417. doi:10.1093/biomet/58.3.403

Elkin, I., Gibbons, R. D., Shea, M. T., Sotsky, S. M., Watkins, J. T., Pilkonis, P. A., & Hedeker, D. (1995). Initial severity and differential treatment outcome in the National Institute of Mental Health Treatment of Depression Collaborative Research Program. *Journal of Consulting and Clinical Psychology, 63*, 841–847. doi:10.1037/0022-006-X.63.5.841

Elkin, I., Shea, M. T., Watkins, J. T., Imber, S. D., Sotsky, S. M., Collins, J. F., . . . Parloff, M. B. (1989). National Institute of Mental Health Treatment of Depression Collaborative Research Program: General effectiveness of treatments. *Archives of General Psychiatry, 46*, 971–982.

Feeley, M., DeRubeis, R. J., & Gelfand, L. A. (1999). The temporal relation of adherence and alliance to symptom change in cognitive therapy for depression. *Journal of Consulting and Clinical Psychology, 67*, 578–582. doi:10.1037/0022-006X.67.4.578

Fournier, J. C., DeRubeis, R. J., Hollon, S. D., Dimidjian, S., Amsterdam, J. D., Shelton, R. C., & Fawcett, J. (2010). Antidepressant drug effects and depression severity: A patient-level meta-analysis. *JAMA, 303*, 47–53. doi:10.1001/jama.2009.1943

Frank, E., Prien, R. F., Jarrett, R. B., Keller, M. B., Kupfer, D. J., Lavori, P. W., . . . Weissman, M. M. (1991). Conceptualization and rationale for consensus definitions of terms in major depressive disorder: Remission, recovery, relapse, and recurrence. *Archives of General Psychiatry, 48*, 851–855.

Goldfried, M. R. (1980). Toward the delineation of therapeutic change principles. *American Psychologist, 35*, 991–999. doi:10.1037/0003-066X.35.11.991

Hedeker, D., & Gibbons, R. D. (1997). Application of random-effects pattern-mixture models for missing data in longitudinal studies. *Psychological Methods, 2*, 64–78. doi:10.1037/1082-989X.2.1.64

Hill, C. E., O'Grady, K. E., & Elkin, I. (1992). Applying the Collaborative Study Psychotherapy Rating Scale to rate therapist adherence in cognitive-behavior therapy, interpersonal therapy, and clinical management. *Journal of Consulting and Clinical Psychology, 60*, 73–79. doi:10.1037/0022-006-X.60.1.73

Hollis, S., & Campbell, F. (1999). What is meant by intention to treat analysis? Survey of published randomised controlled trials. *BMJ (Clinical Research Ed.), 319*, 670–674.

Hollon, S. D. (1996). The efficacy and effectiveness of psychotherapy relative to medications. *American Psychologist, 51*, 1025–1030. doi:10.1037/0003-066-X.51.10.1025

Hollon, S. D., & Beck, A. T. (1978). Psychotherapy and drug therapy: Comparisons and combinations. In S. L. Garfield & A. E. Bergin (Eds.), *Handbook of psychotherapy and behavior change: An empirical analysis* (2nd ed., pp. 437–490). New York, NY: Wiley.

Hollon, S. D., DeRubeis, R. J., Evans, M. D., Wiemer, M. J., Garvey, M. J., Grove, W. M., & Tuason, V. B. (1992). Cognitive therapy, pharmacotherapy and combined cognitive-pharmacotherapy in the treatment of depression. *Archives of General Psychiatry, 49*, 774–781.

Hollon, S. D., DeRubeis, R. J., Shelton, R. C., Amsterdam, J. D., Salomon, R. M., O'Reardon, J. P., . . . Gallop, R. (2005). Prevention of relapse following cognitive therapy versus medications in moderate to severe depression. *Archives of General Psychiatry, 62*, 417–422. doi:10.1001/archpsyc.62.4.417

Horvath, A. O., & Symonds, B. D. (1991). Relation between working alliance and outcome in psychotherapy: A meta-analysis. *Journal of Counseling Psychology, 38*, 139–149.

Jacobson, N. S., & Christensen, A. (1996). Studying the effectiveness of psychotherapy: How well can clinical trials do the job? *American Psychologist, 51*, 1031–1039. doi:10.1037/0003-066X.51.10.1031

Jacobson, N. S., & Hollon, S. D. (1996). Cognitive behavior therapy vs. pharmacotherapy: Now that the jury's returned its verdict, it's time to present the rest of the evidence. *Journal of Consulting and Clinical Psychology, 64*, 74–80. doi:10.1037/0022-006X.64.1.74

Jacobson, N. S., & Truax, P. (1991). Clinical significance: A statistical approach to defining meaningful change in psychotherapy research. *Journal of Consulting and Clinical Psychology, 59*, 12–19. doi:10.1037/0022-006X.59.1.12

Joffe, M. M., & Rosenbaum, P. R. (1999). Propensity scores. *American Journal of Epidemiology, 150*, 327–333.

Kazdin, A. E. (2003). *Research design in clinical psychology* (4th ed.). Boston, MA: Allyn & Bacon.

Kazdin, A. E., & Bass, D. (1989). Power to detect differences between alternative treatments in comparative psychotherapy outcome research. *Journal of Consulting and Clinical Psychology, 57*, 138–147. doi:10.1037/0022-006X.57.1.138

King, M., Nazareth, I., Lampe, F., Bower, P., Chandler, M., Morou, M., . . . Lai, R. (2005). Impact of participant and physician intervention preferences on randomized trials: A systematic review. *JAMA, 293*, 1089–1099. doi:10.1001/jama.293.9.1089

Klein, D. N., Schwartz, J. E., Santiago, N. J., Vivian, D., Vocisano, C., Castonguay, L. G., . . . Keller, M. B. (2003). Therapeutic alliance in depression treatment: Controlling for prior change and patient characteristics. *Journal of Consulting and Clinical Psychology, 71*, 997–1006. doi:10.1037/0022-006X.71.6.997

Kraemer, H. C. (2000). Pitfalls of multisite randomized clinical trials of efficacy and effectiveness. *Schizophrenia Bulletin, 26*, 533–541.

Kraemer, H. C., & Kupfer, D. J. (2006). Size of treatment effects and their importance to clinical research and practice. *Biological Psychiatry, 59*, 990–996. doi:10.1016/j.biopsych.2005.09.014

Kraemer, H. C., Measelle, J. R., Ablow, J. C., Essex, M. J., Boyce, W. T., & Kupfer, D. J. (2003). A new approach to integrating data from multiple informants in psychiatric assessment and research: Mixing and matching contexts and perspectives. *American Journal of Psychiatry, 160*, 1566–1577. doi:10.1176/appi.ajp.160.9.1566

Kraemer, H. C., Wilson, G. T., Fairburn, C. G., & Agras, W. S. (2002). Mediators and moderators of treatment effects in randomized clinical trials. *Archives of General Psychiatry, 59*, 877–883. doi:10.1001/archpsyc.59.10.877

Lavori, P. W. (1992). Clinical trials in psychiatry: Should protocol deviation censor patient data? *Neuropsychopharmacology, 6*, 39–48.

Lavori, P. W., Rush, A. J., Wisniewski, S. R., Alpert, J., Fava, M., Kupfer, D. J., . . . Trivedi, M. (2001). Strengthening clinical effectiveness trials: Equipoise-stratified randomization. *Biological Psychiatry, 50*, 792–801. doi:10.1016/S0006-3223(01)01223-9

Lipsey, M. W., & Wilson, D. B. (2001). *Practical meta-analysis.* Thousand Oaks, CA: Sage.

Luborsky, L., & DeRubeis, R. J. (1984). The use of psychotherapy treatment manuals: A small revolution in psychotherapy research style. *Clinical Psychology Review, 4*, 5–14. doi:10.1016/0272-7358(84)90034-5

Luborsky, L., Diguer, L., Seligman, D. A., Rosenthal, R., Krause, E. D., Johnson, S., . . . Schweizer, E. (1999). The researcher's own therapy allegiances: A "wild card" in comparisons of treatment efficacy. *Clinical Psychology: Science and Practice, 6*, 95–106. doi:10.1093/clipsy/6.1.95

MacKinnon, D. P. (2008). *Introduction to statistical mediation analysis.* New York, NY: Erlbaum.

Manson, J. E., Hsia, J., Johnson, K. C., Rossouw, J. E., Assaf, A. R., Lasser, N. L., . . . Cushman, M. (2003). Estrogen plus progestin and the risk of coronary heart disease. *New England Journal of Medicine, 349*, 523–534. doi:10.1056/NEJMoa030808

Mellers, B., Hertwig, R., & Kahneman, D. (2001). Do frequency representations eliminate conjunction effects: An exercise in adversarial collaboration. *Psychological Science, 12*, 269–275. doi:10.1111/1467-9280.00350

Miller, W. R., Sorensen, J. L., Selzer, J. A., & Brigham, G. S. (2006). Disseminating evidence-based practices in substance abuse treatment: A review with suggestions. *Journal of Substance Abuse Treatment, 31*, 25–39. doi:10.1016/j.jsat.2006.03.005

Miranda, J., Chung, J. Y., Green, B. L., Krupnick, J., Siddique, J., Revicki, D. A., & Belin, T. (2003). Treating depression in predominantly low-income young minority women. A randomized controlled trial. *JAMA, 290*, 57–65. doi:10.1001/jama.290.1.57

Mohr, D. C., Spring, B., Freedland, K. E., Beckner, V., Arean, P., Hollon, S. D., . . . Kaplan, R. (2009). The selection and design of control conditions for randomized controlled trials of psychological interventions. *Psychotherapy and Psychosomatics, 78*, 275–284. doi:10.1159/000228248

Nakagawa, S. (2004). A farewell to Bonferroni: The problems of low statistical power and publication bias. *Behavioral Ecology, 15*, 1044–1045. doi:10.1093/beheco/arh107

Nathan, P. E., Stuart, S. P., & Dolan, S. L. (2000). Research on psychotherapy efficacy and effectiveness: Between Scylla and Charybdis? *Psychological Bulletin, 126*, 964–981. doi:10.1037/0033-2909.126.6.964

Norcross, J. C., Karpiak, C. P., & Santoro, S. O. (2005). Clinical psychologists across the years: The Division of Clinical Psychology from 1960 to 2003. *Journal of Clinical Psychology, 61*, 1467–1483. doi:10.1002/jclp.20135

Olkin, I. (1995). Meta-analysis: Reconciling the results of independent studies. *Statistics in Medicine, 14*, 457–472. doi:10.1002/sim.4780140507

Piaggio, G., Elbourne, D. R., Altman, D. G., Pocock, S. J., & Evans, S. J. W. (2006). Reporting of noninferiority and equivalence randomized trials: An extension of the CONSORT Statement. *JAMA, 295*, 1152–1160. doi:10.1001/jama.295.10.1152

Project MATCH Research Group. (1997). Matching alcoholism treatments to client heterogeneity: Project MATCH posttreatment drinking outcomes. *Journal of Studies on Alcohol, 58*, 7–29.

Rosenthal, R., & Rosnow, R. L. (2008). *Essentials of behavioral research: Methods and data analysis* (3rd ed.). New York, NY: McGraw-Hill.

Rush, A. J., Beck, A. T., Kovacs, M., & Hollon, S. D. (1977). Comparative efficacy of cognitive therapy and pharmacotherapy in the treatment of depressed outpatients. *Cognitive Therapy and Research, 1,* 17–37. doi:10.1007/BF01173502

Seligman, M. E. P. (1995). The effectiveness of psychotherapy: The *Consumer Reports* study. *American Psychologist, 50,* 965–974. doi:10.1037/0003-066X.50.12.965

Shadish, W. R., Cook, T. D., & Campbell, D. T. (2002). *Experimental and quasi-experimental designs for generalized causal inference.* Boston, MA: Houghton-Mifflin.

Shao, J., & Zhong, B. (2003). Last observation carry-forward and last observation analysis. *Statistics in Medicine, 22,* 2429–2441. doi:10.1002/sim.1519

Shaw, B. F. (1984). Specification of the training and evaluation of cognitive therapists for outcome studies. In J. Williams & R. Spitzer (Eds.), *Psychotherapy research: Where are we and where should we go?* (pp. 173–188). New York, NY: Guilford Press.

Shaw, B. F., Elkin, I., Yamaguchi, J., Olmsted, M., Vallis, T. M., Dobson, K. S., ... Imber, S. D. (1999). Therapist competence ratings in relation to clinical outcome in cognitive therapy for depression. *Journal of Consulting and Clinical Psychology, 67,* 837–846. doi:10.1037/0022-006X.67.6.837

Shrout, P. E., & Fleiss, J. L. (1979). Intraclass correlations: Uses in assessing rater reliability. *Psychological Bulletin, 86,* 420–428. doi:10.1037/0033-2909.86.2.420

Sloane, R. B., Staples, F. R., Cristol, A. H., Yorkson, N. J., & Whipple, K. (1975). *Psychotherapy versus behavior therapy.* Cambridge, MA: Harvard University Press.

Smits, J. A. J., Rosenfield, D., McDonald, R., & Telch, M. J. (2006). Cognitive mechanisms of social anxiety reduction: An examination of specificity and temporality. *Journal of Consulting and Clinical Psychology, 74,* 1203–1212. doi:10.1037/0022-006X.74.6.1203

Stegner, B. L., Bostrom, A. G., & Greenfield, T. K. (1996). Equivalence testing for use in psychosocial and services research: An introduction with examples. *Evaluation and Program Planning, 19,* 193–198. doi:10.1016/0149-7189(96)00011-0

Stirman, S. W., DeRubeis, R. J., Crits-Christoph, P., & Brody, P. E. (2003). Are samples in randomized controlled trials of psychotherapy representative of community patients? A new methodology and initial findings. *Journal of Consulting and Clinical Psychology, 71,* 963–972. doi:10.1037/0022-006X.71.6.963

Stricker, G., Abrahamson, D. J., Bologna, N. C., Hollon, S. D., Robinson, E. A., & Reed, G. M. (1999). Treatment guidelines: The good, the bad, and the ugly. *Psychotherapy: Theory, Research, Practice, Training, 36,* 69–79. doi:10.1037/h0087755

Striegel-Moore, R. H., Wilson, G. T., DeBar, L., Perrin, N., Lynch, F., Rosselli, F., & Kraemer, H. C. (2010). Cognitive behavioral guided self-help for the treatment of recurrent binge eating. *Journal of Consulting and Clinical Psychology, 78,* 312–321. doi:10.1037/a0018915

Trivedi, M. H., Rush, A. J., Crismon, M. L., Kashner, T. M., Toprac, M. G., Carmody, T. J., ... Shon, S. P. (2004). Clinical results for patients with major depressive disorder in the Texas Medication Algorithm Project. *Archives of General Psychiatry, 61,* 669–680. doi:10.1001/archpsyc.61.7.669

Waltz, J., Addis, M. E., Koerner, K., & Jacobson, N. S. (1993). Testing the integrity of a psychotherapy protocol: Assessment of adherence and competence. *Journal of Consulting and Clinical Psychology, 61,* 620–630. doi:10.1037/0022-006X.61.4.620

Wei, L. J., & Lachin, J. M. (1988). Properties of the urn randomization in clinical trials. *Controlled Clinical Trials, 9,* 345–364. doi:10.1016/0197-2456(88)90048-7

Weisz, J. R., & Addis, M. E. (2006). The research–practice tango and other choreographic challenges: Using and testing evidence-based psychotherapies in clinical care settings. In C. D. Goodheart, A. E. Kazdin, & R. J. Sternberg (Eds.), *Evidence-based psychotherapy: Where practice and research meet* (pp. 179–206). Washington, DC: American Psychological Association. doi:10.1037/11423-008

Wennberg, J. E., Barry, M. J., Fowler, F. J., & Mulley, A. (1993). Outcomes research, PORTs, and health care reform. *Annals of the New York Academy of Sciences, 703,* 52–62. doi:10.1111/j.1749-6632.1993.tb26335.x

Westen, D., Novonty, C. M., & Thompson-Brenner, H. (2004). Empirical status of empirically supported psychotherapies: Assumptions, findings, and reporting in controlled clinical trials. *Psychological Bulletin, 130,* 631–663. doi:10.1037/0033-2909.130.4.631

Wilkinson, L., & Task Force on Statistical Inference. (1999). Statistical methods in psychology journals: Guidelines and explanations. *American Psychologist, 54,* 594–604. doi:10.1037/0003-066X.54.8.594

CHAPTER 29

TRANSLATIONAL RESEARCH

Michael T. Bardo and Mary Ann Pentz

Translational research generally refers to the advancement of basic science research findings into application and everyday practice. Although many different specific definitions have been proposed, translational research is envisioned to be on a continuum and can be categorized into at least two broad categories, that is, Type I and Type II (Sussman, Valente, Rohrbach, Skara, & Pentz, 2010). Type I translational research begins at the point at which application to a specific problem is the goal. It involves moving basic science into proof-of-concept and theory testing studies, including efficacy trials in which a specific treatment is evaluated in a relatively small sample of volunteers or clients and patients under controlled conditions. In contrast, Type II translational research refers to the movement of treatments from controlled efficacy trials into effectiveness trials as well as the dissemination of the treatment into everyday practice. In contrast to efficacy trials, effectiveness trials occur in a broad real-world context, such as in clinics, schools, or communities, under less controlled conditions. Type II translational research also involves evaluating education and training on new treatments, conducting economic analyses (e.g., cost-effectiveness), and evaluating policy decisions.

Type I and Type II translational research are broad categories used by the National Institutes of Health (NIH). Researchers and policymakers have suggested that Type II research is too broad, however, because it encompasses effectiveness,

implementation, dissemination, and policy research, and it does not adequately address translation of evidence-based treatments from one outcome to another. An alternative is to categorize translational research into four types (T1–T4; Khoury et al., 2007). Using these more narrow categories, T1 includes basic science, etiology, and epidemiological research that leads to small-scale efficacy trials, and thus it is essentially the same as Type I translational research. T2 includes both effectiveness and replication trials that test the treatment under less rigorous observational conditions than in T1 as well as guideline development. T3 includes both implementation and dissemination research, which is expected to yield evidence-based treatments that are sufficiently robust to be transportable to a variety of settings, populations, and real-life conditions, thus culminating in the production of evidence-based standards for practice. T4 includes broad public health impact studies, cost–benefit and comparative effectiveness research, and policy change and impact studies. T4 would be expected to yield information on shifts in population health after large-scale dissemination of evidence-based treatments and policies. Table 29.1 summarizes some of the research methods that are appropriate for the broad categories of Type I and II translational research as well as the more narrowly reformulated T1–T4 categories. For the purpose of this chapter, we will primarily use the broad categories defined by Type I and II research.

The authors thank Emily Denehy for assistance in preparing this chapter. Supported by National Institutes of Health Grants P50 DA05312 and R01 HD052107.

DOI: 10.1037/13620-029
APA Handbook of Research Methods in Psychology: Vol. 2. Research Designs, H. Cooper (Editor-in-Chief)

TABLE 29.1

Sample Research Methods for Translational Research Relevant to Psychologists

Category	Stage	Design	Measures	Outcomes
Type I basic research (T1)	Proof-of-concept Theory testing Etiology	Small sample Random control Longitudinal	Biological Behavioral Questionnaires	Behavior change
Type I to II crossover	Replication Extension	RCT Partial factorial	Survey	Behavior change Relative behavior change
Type II: Program diffusion (T2)	Adoption Implementation Dissemination Sustainability	RCT Sequential RCT		
Type II: Program to practice (T3)	Standards development Guideline training Distribution	RCT Quasi-experimental Comparative effectiveness	Survey Clinic records, time, cost, uptake	Relative balance of costs, health outcomes, practitioner use
Type II: Practice to policy (T4)	Consensus Legislation Funding	Time series Quasi-experimental Single group	Voting records Set aside Funding	Policy awareness, support, compliance
Translation across health behaviors	Treatment Development/adaptation Mediator identification	Formative Qualitative Small quasi-experimental Pilot RCT	Survey	Mediator change Multiple health behavior change

Note. RCT = randomized controlled trial.

GENERAL FEATURES OF TRANSLATIONAL RESEARCH

Across both Type I and II research, several key features or general guidelines define successful translational research. First, by definition, translational research needs to be *interdisciplinary* because it is highly unlikely that any one researcher would have the skill set needed at each step of the translational continuum. Interdisciplinary research is often facilitated by infrastructural connections (e.g., a common building, an organizational structure with identified leadership) built around a broad theme, such as cancer, emotion, or gender issues. Areas of interdisciplinary research may also generate new subdisciplines, such as bioengineering or molecular psychiatry. In the field of psychology specifically, cross-connections among clinical and experimental areas have yielded such new areas as health psychology, psychoneuroimmunology, and social neuroscience. These blended fields are likely to become self-sustaining because new graduate training programs have developed within many of these interdisciplines.

Second, translational research needs to define a *unifying goal* around which the interdisciplinary team is focused. This requires a leadership that has a vision of the entire process, from basic science to real-world application. Although statistical and methodological commonalities may exist across different disciplines, these commonalities alone are insufficient to organize a translational group of investigators. Instead, the goal should be conceptual or mechanistic in nature. For example, one may have a goal to reduce childhood maltreatment to prevent later depression. Maltreatment and depression can be studied on multiple levels, including biomedical, psychological, and social or cultural levels, and mediational variables can be tested at each of these levels. For example, the relation between childhood maltreatment and depression may be mediated by biological factors (e.g., gene expression and deoxyribonucleic acid methylation), psychological factors (e.g., self-esteem), and sociological factors (e.g., poverty). Understanding the relation of variables emanating from the unifying goal can be used to generate novel ideas about potential interventions and social policies as well as developing new assessment protocols.

Third, successful translational research should provide a *feedback loop* between basic research and real-world application (Figure 29.1). Although translational research is most often thought of as moving from basic science to application, the reverse is also true because basic scientists need to be informed about what succeeds and fails in the real world. Ginexi and Hilton (2006) have discussed

this issue in relation to the development and implementation of drug abuse prevention programs. Even when science accumulates, ineffective practices may survive because of buy-in by stakeholders expecting success or because societal pressures force practitioners to be optimistic when taking positive action. This may be especially true for ineffective practices that are inexpensive. For example, the Drug Abuse Resistance Education (DARE) program, which is a school-based program intervention delivered by police officers to reduce drug use and violence, has been shown repeatedly to have no lasting effects (Clayton, Cattarello, & Johnstone, 1996; Lynam et al., 1999; West & O'Neal, 2004). DARE continues to be used across much of the United States,

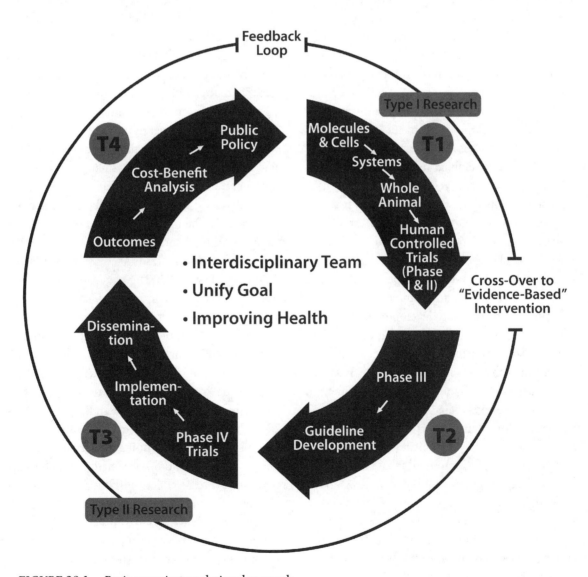

FIGURE 29.1.   Basic steps in translational research.

however, likely because it is relatively inexpensive and it is viewed favorably by parents and teachers. When an ineffective program is widely adopted and accepted, researchers are challenged to design a competing inexpensive, evidence-based program that would receive buy-in similar to the widely adopted program Such a goal exemplifies the circular feedback loop in translational research.

TYPE I TRANSLATIONAL RESEARCH

Because the conceptual framework that describes translational research emanated from NIH and is dominated by biomedical researchers, it is not surprising that the initial step of Type I translational research typically starts with molecular or cellular mechanisms. This can include working with small molecules, genetic material, or specialized cell lines. In the second step, organ systems or laboratory animals are often used. Finally, in the third step, human test trials are performed to determine safety and efficacy of the new treatment. Although these three steps are often used in developing new medical treatments, not all three of these steps are necessary for other types of research more familiar to psychologists. For example, a potential new psychosocial intervention, such as a new treatment for dyslexia or a new psychotherapeutic approach, may skip the cell- and animal-based steps of Type I research and simply begin with epidemiological and etiological studies.

To illustrate the basic steps of Type I translational research, we can use an example from research aimed at medication development (Day, Rutkowski, & Feuerstein, 2009; Lerman et al., 2007). Consider, for example, the practice of treating depression with a new medication. Type I translational research involves the synthesis of a library of chemical compounds that are screened for their in vitro efficacy for interacting with some selected depression-relevant neurobiological target (e.g., serotonin transporter). Compounds that "hit" the target are subsequently evaluated in vivo using an animal model of depression (e.g., learned helplessness). The most promising hits are then tested for toxicity and pharmacokinetics in at least two different animal species in preparation for filing an investigational new drug application to the Food and Drug Administration (FDA). The first stage of testing of an antidepressant drug in human subjects is referred to as a Phase I clinical trial, in which the safety of the drug is established in healthy volunteers in an in-patient setting. This is followed by a small-scale efficacy study to demonstrate antidepressant activity at safe doses (Phase II trial).

Type I translational research in the drug abuse field has benefited greatly from laboratory animal models and human neuroimaging technologies (Gual, 2008). As for the use of laboratory animals, a major advantage is being able to conduct experimental work under conditions that offer exquisite control over many extraneous variables. Thus, hypotheses can be tested with a relatively few number of subjects. In addition, use of laboratory animals allows for the use of modern neuroscience techniques that are often not possible to use in humans. Although laboratory animal models are not essential for conducting Type I translational research, many fields have benefited from preclinical research using nonhuman animals. For example, laboratory animal research is integral for developing medications to treat drug abuse (Haney & Spealman, 2008; Kreek, Zhou, Butelman, & Levran, 2009; Lerman et al., 2007). Great strides have also been achieved using genetically engineered rodents to understand the role of leptin and other neurohormones in eating disorders (Klein & Walsh, 2005) and in understanding traits such as impulsivity (Potenza & Taylor, 2009). Such disorders as anorexia nervosa, attention-deficit/hyperactivity disorder (ADHD), social anxiety, panic, and depression have also been modeled in laboratory animals (Cuthbert, 2002; Klein & Walsh, 2005; Lapiz-Bluhm et al., 2008; Porsolt, Brossard, Hautbois, & Roux, 2001; Roth, 2008; Vendruscolo, Izidio, & Takahashi, 2010). Koob, Kenneth Lloyd, and Mason (2009) have argued that because no animal model captures all aspects of a human disorder, a reverse validity approach should be tested in which treatments shown to be effective in humans are used to validate and refine the animal models. The aim is to have better consilience across preclinical and clinical findings to increase our understanding of various health risks, as has been suggested for alcohol dependence (Crabbe, Bell, & Ehlers, 2010).

Neuroimaging technologies can be used to determine whether the results obtained with laboratory animals generalize to humans. This point is illustrated by Type I translational research on drug abuse prevention that has focused on the trait of *sensation seeking* (Zuckerman, 1988). On the basis of rat and human studies, high sensation seekers have been shown to be more sensitive to the rewarding effects of drugs compared with low sensation seekers (Cain, Saucier, & Bardo, 2005; Stoops et al., 2007). Human high sensation seekers also show greater functional magnetic resonance imaging activation in reward-relevant brain regions and blunted activation in self-regulatory brain regions in response to emotionally arousing visual stimuli (Joseph, Liu, Jiang, Lynam, & Kelly, 2009). Jiang et al. (2009) also found that high sensation seekers have reduced ventral prefrontal responses to new stimuli compared with low sensation seekers using cortical evoked potentials, suggesting that high sensation seekers have a delay in activation of inhibitory prefrontal cortex. These formative results illustrate how neuroimaging techniques may be used to identify preexisting differences in brain function associated with sensation-seeking status. Moreover, these basic research findings may have important implications for the design of antidrug mass media messages because these messages are often tailored to appeal to high sensation seekers (Palmgreen, Donohew, Lorch, Hoyle, & Stephenson, 2001; Palmgreen, Lorch, Stephenson, Hoyle, & Donohew, 2007). In particular, neuroimaging technologies may prove to be useful for screening various intervention stimulus materials before the design and implementation of an expensive full-scale efficacy trial.

Cross-species generalizations are always open to criticism given species-typical differences in physiology and behavior. Among mammals, despite the remarkable consistency in drug actions from rodents to humans (e.g., pain relief, reward, antidepressant, and anxiolytic effects), there are many examples of failed pharmacotherapies that initially looked promising on the basis of research conducted in laboratory animals. One example is the use of opiate antagonists to treat heroin dependence. Although naltrexone blocks opiate self-administration in rats

and rhesus monkeys (Ettenberg, Pettit, Bloom, & Koob, 1982; Rowlett, Wilcox, & Woolverton, 1998), clinical trials revealed that opiate antagonists are not widely effective in humans because of poor patient compliance (Capone et al., 1986).

There are also advantages and limitations in Type I translational experimental research involving human subjects. Similar to animal research, control over extraneous variables allows for studying underlying mechanisms with a relatively few number of subjects. In addition, controlled human studies allow for the so-called proof-of-concept demonstration. When introduction of a treatment, program, or product into the real world is the goal, it is advisable to test it in the laboratory first. Randomized clinical trials (RCTs) are expensive, so a small-scale proof-of-concept study is useful for identifying promising treatments.

TYPE I TO TYPE II CROSSOVER

Once Type I translational research yields a potential treatment on the basis of small-scale efficacy trials, the findings are typically subject to review to determine whether it is eligible for evidence-based status—that is, it has shown significant effects on changing the behavior that was the target of treatment, as is the case for reduction of drug use prevalence rates in an adolescent population (August et al., 2004). The criteria used to determine evidence-based status differ slightly according to the group conducting the review—for example, Cochrane Reviews of randomized controlled trials, the Center for Substance Abuse Prevention's National Registry of Effective Programs, Blueprints for violence prevention, the Center for Disease Control's registry of model education programs, the American Psychological Association's Division 12 Task Force on Empirically Supported Treatments, and the National Institute for Health and Clinical Excellence, or NICE, in the United Kingdom (see Brown, Berndt, Brinales, Zong, & Bhagwat, 2000; Center for Substance Abuse Prevention, 2002; Chambless & Ollendick, 2001; Littlejohns, 2009). Overall, however, these groups have the following criteria in common: (a) use of a strong, defensible research design (either quasi-experimental or experimental); (b) a longitudinal measurement design, with significant effects; (c) use of standardized protocol materials; (d) monitoring and reporting of quality of implementation; and (e) evidence of replication to more than one study, group of researchers, or sites (D. S. Elliot, 1997; Flay et al., 2005; Pentz, 2003).

In the areas of drug abuse and violence prevention, Type I translational research has produced a substantial number of evidence-based programs (Center for Substance Abuse Prevention, 2002; D. S. Elliot, 1997). Studies in this area represent a progression from laboratory animal and human etiological research on brain-behavior relationships, to epidemiological research on sensation-seeking, peer pressure, and perceived social norms as risk factors for drug use experimentation, to early prevention studies focused on knowledge change, to later efficacy trials focused on counteracting social behavioral risk factors for drug use (Pentz, Jasuja, Rohrbach, Sussman, & Bardo, 2006). These later efficacy trials have yielded more than 100 evidence-based drug abuse– and violence-prevention programs, many of them school based and focused on early adolescent populations (see D. S. Elliot, 1997). Others have extended Type I research that was conducted originally on a school program to include multiple, additional program components such as mass media, community organization, and parent program components (Pentz, 2003, 2004b). This type of extension may be considered a crossover of Type I to Type II research if the addition of multiple components constitutes a *new* feature to be tested in an efficacy or effectiveness trial (Pentz et al., 2006). Similarly, replication of a program to a different type of setting or population than was tested in the original efficacy trial can also represent Type I to Type II crossover if the differences constitute a new researchable question, for example, replication of a program with a population-based sample to a high-risk sample of youth (August et al., 2004; Pentz, 2007).

Once a treatment, program, or product has achieved evidence-based status as a Type I study, it may progress to Type II studies, which typically involves having the resources and time to negotiate commitments from multiple sites. Progression to Type II studies may depend on several practical factors, including but not limited to public demand for

a treatment or political pressure to demonstrate that an evidence-based treatment has utility in the real world (Pentz, Mares, Schinke, & Rohrbach, 2004). Overall, whether it culminates in an evidence-based psychosocial intervention, disease-risk screening protocol, or pharmaceutical treatment, the progression of Type I to Type II translational research is designed to address whether an evidence-based treatment evaluated previously under conditions of high levels of monitoring, resources, and support can be translated effectively to real-world conditions and still yield effects on a target health outcome such as drug use (Flay et al., 2005).

TYPE II TRANSLATIONAL RESEARCH

Although Type I translational research is sometimes referred to as *bench to bedside*, Type II research can be referred to as *bedside to community*. As discussed, Type II translational research consists of effectiveness trials under real-world conditions (T2), implementation and dissemination research (T3), and outcomes research (T4). On the basis of the outcome findings and cost–benefit analyses, Type II research then forms a feedback loop to inform subsequent Type I translational research to conduct further basic research (see Figure 29.1).

To illustrate the basic features of Type II translational research, the example introduced about developing a new antidepressant medication can be continued. In that example, Type I translational research ended with a small-scale efficacy trial (Phase II clinical trial). The broad goal of Type II research would be to disseminate the antidepressant to local pharmacies and monitor the overall health impact in the affected patient population. This would begin with a Phase III clinical trial in which the drug is evaluated in a large number of patients across multiple sites using a randomized controlled experimental design. Although this step is still a controlled trial, if the drug is found to be efficacious, it can be categorized as Type II translational research because the drug can be disseminated to market under FDA guidelines. This is followed by a Phase IV trial, also known as *postmarketing surveillance*, to monitor any potential for long-term harmful effects. On the basis of Phase IV information, a drug can be removed from practice (e.g., the nonsteroidal anti-inflammatory drug rofecoxib, marketed as Vioxx for arthritis treatment, was withdrawn because of increased risk for heart attack) or can receive modified label precautions (e.g., hormone replacement therapy in postmenopausal women was relabeled because of increased risk for breast cancer and cardiovascular disease).

Similarly, in the case of psychological research, in which case the treatment may be a psychosocial intervention, Type II translational research involves dissemination of evidence-based practices to the real world (August et al., 2004; Best, Stokols, et al., 2003a). Type II research includes the dissemination of small-scale interventions to broader settings, such as whole communities as well as the study of factors that promote or impede dissemination. Although RCT designs can still be applied, smaller scale comparative effectiveness studies might be more efficient, with the evidence-based intervention evaluated in community or public health settings against *standard* practice in those settings. In this type of translational research, clinic records of practitioner compliance with guidelines and numbers of clients served are measures of translation, and outcomes include relative cost and observable changes in health outcomes (Glasgow, 2010).

Type II translational research also includes the movement of research findings from practice to policy (Oesterle, Hawkins, Fagan, Abbott, & Catalano, 2010; Pentz, Mares, et al., 2004). RCTs on policy may not be realistic because of the lack of experimental control over policy dissemination and size of settings covered by a policy, for example, whole states. Limited time-series and single-group designs may be useful for starting a study when a policy change aimed at deterrence (e.g., alcohol control) is about to take effect (DeJong & Hingson, 1998). Voting records of policy change may be used to mark the baseline time period, and population surveys and population health records might be used to identify potential mediators of policy effectiveness (e.g., public support of the policy) as well as the impact of the policy on public health outcomes over time.

In the drug abuse–prevention field, research has been guided by several models and theories, including the Center for Substance Abuse Prevention's

logic model (Center for Substance Abuse Prevention, 2002), Glasgow's Reach, Effectiveness–Adoption, Implementation, and Maintenance (RE-AIM) model (Glasgow & Emmons, 2007), Wandersman and colleagues' interactive systems model (Wandersman et al., 2008), and diffusion of innovation theory (Rogers, 1995). Similarly, the treatment field has been guided by Rogers's diffusion of innovation theory (Sanson-Fisher, 2004).

Rogers's (1995) diffusion of innovation theory postulates four stages of diffusion that are applicable to Type II translational research: *adoption, implementation, dissemination,* and *sustainability. Adoption* research refers to the study of factors that facilitate uptake of an evidence-based treatment. Rogers (1995) proposed five factors that facilitate adoption: (a) *trialability*, or the opportunity to try out the treatment on a small scale without committing permanent resources or disseminating widely; (b) *observability*, or indicators of effectiveness that can be easily observed by either consumers or implementers; (c) *relative advantage*, or the perceived benefit of choosing the new treatment over existing treatments; (d) *low complexity*, or user-friendliness of the treatment; and (e) *compatibility*, or fit of the new treatment with existing organizational standards and values. Several Type II studies have evaluated one or more of these adoption factors, yielding mixed results (Mihalic & Irwin, 2003; Pentz, Jasuja, Li, McClure, & Chou, 2003). Of these factors, observability, relative advantage, and low complexity tend to show the most consistent positive effects on adoption (Pentz, Chou, et al., 2004; Pentz et al., 2003). Other factors that appear to improve adoption include the provision of *pretraining* to familiarize potential adopters with treatment features, the use of snowball sampling and network analyses to identify key stakeholders to promote the treatment, and positive local media coverage (Pentz, 2007; Valente, Chou, & Pentz, 2007).

Implementation refers to the quality or fidelity of delivery. Various studies suggest that quality of implementation may consist of at least three factors: (a) adherence to standards, (b) amount of treatment delivered, and (c) adaptation for the purpose of improving ease of implementation as well as audience and consumer acceptance (referred to as *reinvention* in Rogers's early theoretical work; Pentz, 2003; Rogers, 1995). Adherence and amount of treatment delivered have been associated with greater magnitude of effects on behavior (Pentz, 2003). The impact of adaptation is less clear because the definition of adaptation has varied widely across Type II studies, including (a) cultural and language adaptation; (b) adaptation of protocols, timing, and types of implementers to different settings; (c) adaptation to different populations, including different age and risk groups; and (d) adaptation that represents either extension of a treatment to increase effects or replication to examine effectiveness under uncontrollable conditions that differed from the original Type I testing conditions (Best, Stokos, et al., 2003a; Collins, Murphy, & Bierman, 2004; Guerra & Knox, 2008; Pentz, 2007; Solomon, Card, & Malow, 2006; Sussman et al., 2006).

Two examples illustrate the challenges of conducting Type II translational research on adaptation. One is cultural adaptation (Guerra & Knox, 2008). There is some disagreement in the field of drug abuse prevention about whether a universal intervention program is appropriate for use with most racial and ethnic groups (Mihalic & Irwin, 2003). Some have argued that new or specifically tailored interventions need to be developed to reach ethnic groups that were not the initial focus of the program (Castro, Barrera, & Martinez, 2004). Research suggests that in most cases, universal interventions can be self-adapted or adapted by developers with few changes in language and context (Pentz et al., 2006; Sussman et al., 2006). However, additional research suggests that special culturally tailored interventions may fare better if adolescents depend on their own cultural group as peer leaders for behavior (Valente, Fujimoto, Chou, & Spruijt-Metz, 2009). A second example is replication because of uncontrollable conditions or historical events. In one drug abuse–prevention study, two communities in a large dissemination trial closed factories that had served as the major source of employment during an economic downturn (Pentz et al., 2003). The change resulted in loss and turnover of site facilitators and community leaders involved in the trial, and subsequently, required an adaptation to community leader training and replacement protocols.

Dissemination may constitute two distinct types. One is dissemination of a treatment to a greater number of *receivers* within the same sites and populations. For example, dissemination of a drug abuse–prevention program may occur after an individual teacher has tried the program with one classroom in one school and other teachers, the principal, and perhaps the school superintendent determine that the program has merit, and thus they decide to use the program in additional classrooms with additional teachers in the same school. This type of dissemination might be considered internal to a system and can occur without the program having been sustained in the original classroom for a long period of time. For example, a school program had a spontaneous 28% rate of dissemination that occurred as part of a large dissemination trial (Pentz et al., 2003). The spontaneous dissemination consisted of teachers naturalistically sharing the program, materials, and training methods with other teachers in the same school, without any research support or prompting. Another type of dissemination is called *outward* or *external* dissemination (Pentz, 2007). This type of dissemination typically takes place in settings in which organizations and individuals are not the initial adopters or implementers. External dissemination may require that sustainability is already achieved in the original site so that it can serve as a model for other potential sites. Delivery systems for drug abuse–prevention programs have included community coalitions, agricultural extension universities systems, and state-to-community training in prevention operations (Pentz, 2007).

Sustainability is the fourth stage of diffusion and, in our ongoing example from the drug abuse–prevention field, refers to research on whether an evidence-based prevention program is sustained after initial implementation, without researcher or developer support. Thus far, results of prevention dissemination trials suggest that the following factors predict sustainability of evidence-based prevention programs and prevention delivery systems: (a) ability of the prevention adopter organization to secure external funding after a research study has ended; (b) inclusion of regular training and retraining of community leaders and program implementers; (c) involvement of school administrators in the adopter organization; (d) efficient planning and communication among organization members; (e) resource sharing among community organizations for prevention activities; and (f) identification of an internal structure for conducting prevention training, for example, committees or work groups (Best, Moor, et al., 2003).

Similar to diffusion of innovation theory, the RE-AIM model addresses stages of diffusion (Table 29.2), but the broad dissemination of a treatment to different populations is more prominent (Glasgow & Emmons, 2007; Jilcott, Ammerman, Sommers, & Glasgow, 2007). In the RE-AIM model, reach encompasses both the broad dissemination to the general population and ensuring that the population that might benefit most from the intervention is actually receiving the intervention. Considered together, diffusion of innovation theory and RE-AIM are both useful for generating testable hypotheses for Type II translational research. Diffusion of innovation theory provides specific variables as predictors and outcomes of each of the four stages of diffusion, particularly for the adoption stage (Pentz, 2007). The RE-AIM model has been used to evaluate the dissemination of evidence-based prevention and clinical practices as well as the dissemination of prevention policies (Glasgow & Emmons, 2007).

Composite scores that represent each stage of the RE-AIM model have been developed, with the aim of generating an overall weighted score for an evidence-based intervention to determine its overall public health effectiveness compared with standard practice guidelines (Jilcott et al., 2007). This type of scoring in the RE-AIM model is not yet operationalized from diffusion of innovation theory. Thus, RE-AIM has the advantage of being useful in comparative effectiveness research (Pentz, 1998), an area that is gaining ground at NIH, for example, at the Agency for Research on Health Care and Quality (http://effectivehealthcare.ahrq.gov).

TRANSLATION ACROSS MULTIPLE BEHAVIORS

In addition to reframing translational research into two broad categories (Type I and II) or four narrow categories (T1–T4), another type to consider is translation of a treatment across multiple behaviors (D. L. Elliot et al., 2004; Werch, Moore, DiClemente, Bledsoe, & Jobli, 2005; also see bottom row of Table 29.1). This type of translation adapts the same treatment to target two or more behaviors or comorbidities. For example, the monoamine reuptake inhibitor bupropion initially was developed to treat depression,

---

TABLE 29.2

Comparison of Diffusion of Innovation and RE-AIM

Parameter	Diffusion of innovation	RE-AIM
Stage	Preadoption training[a] Evidence-based intervention[a] Adoption Implementation Dissemination	Reach Effectiveness Adoption Implementation Assumed from reach[a]
Measures	Adoption (trialability, observability, relative advantage, low complexity, compatibility) Implementation (adherence, quality, amount) Sustainability (percent of sites or implementers still implementing × length of time) Dissemination (percent increase in external sites using)	Reach × Effectiveness (individual impact) Adoption × Implementation × n of settings × average individuals served per setting

Note. For further details of RE-AIM model, see Dzewaltowski, Glasgow, Klesges, Estabrooks, and Brock (2004); Glasgow, Vogt, and Boles (1999); and King, Glasgow, and Leeman-Castillo (2010). RE-AIM = Reach, Effectiveness–Adoption, Implementation, and Maintenance model.
[a] Not included in the original model.

but later evidence indicated that it also had efficacy as a tobacco smoking pharmacotherapy (Paterson, 2009). Similarly, the opioid antagonist naltrexone initially was developed to treat heroin dependence but also is now used to treat alcohol dependence (Johnson, 2010). For this type of translation, it is useful to know whether there is a causal relation between two different health risks (e.g., obesity and diabetes) or whether the two different health risks are accounted for by some common influence (e.g., sensation seeking as a risk factor for both HIV infection and drug use). In the first example, diabetes might be reduced by targeting obesity, whereas in the second example, both HIV infection and drug use might be reduced by targeting high sensation seekers.

Translation across multiple risk behaviors also is applicable to psychosocial interventions in the prevention field. For example, evidence-based drug abuse– and violence-prevention programs have been adapted recently to an obesity prevention program (Pentz, 2009; N. R. Riggs, Sakuma, & Pentz, 2007). For this translation, *proof of concept* was established first by evaluating common links in developmental stage, risk factors, and mediators for drug use and obesity (Pentz, 2004a, 2009). Etiological and epidemiological studies then verified that these links exist, after which steps were taken to develop a new program on the basis of core elements and theory from the original evidence-based programs that addressed the risk factors and mediators common to both drug use and obesity. This was followed by formative evaluation of content, sequencing, delivery, and mapping prevention concepts to a theoretical model (Pentz, 2004b; Sussman, 2001). An efficacy study then assessed changes in both hypothesized mediators and target health behaviors, for example, physical activity and eating behavior (Pentz, 2004a). Although all of these steps may be considered Type I research, they also could be considered a special case of Type I to II crossover.

In this example, four steps were used to establish proof of concept. First, the developmental stage for drug use and obesity risk behaviors was found to coincide, with both starting to escalate between late childhood and early adolescence (Golub et al., 2008); the neurobiological mechanisms underlying drug use and food intake use also were found to overlap (Chambers, Taylor, & Potenza, 2003; Volkow & Wise, 2005). Second, drug use and obesity were shown to share common risk factors, particularly high sensation seeking, peer pressure, and poor impulse control (Donovan, Jessor, & Costa, 1993; Jasuja, Chou, Riggs, & Pentz, 2008; Pentz et al., 2006); ready access to drugs and inexpensive processed snack foods are also common risk factors (Pentz, 2009). Third, common mediators then were harnessed as skills to promote in a prevention program, primarily centered around executive cognitive functioning, social competence, emotional regulation, and impulse control (Davis, Levitan, Muglia, Bewell, & Kennedy, 2004; Nguyen-Michel, Unger, & Spruijt-Metz, 2007; N. Riggs, Chou, Spruijt-Metz, & Pentz, 2010; N. R. Riggs, Greenberg, Kusche, & Pentz, 2006). Fourth, common instructional methods captured by social learning and cognitive theories were used for both drug use and obesity prevention (N. R. Riggs et al., 2007); in addition, peer leader role models were used to facilitate program implementation on the basis of emerging research on social network analysis (Valente et al., 2009). Sequencing, delivery, and program length then were determined through a series of formative evaluation studies, with consideration of developmental stage (late childhood to early adolescence), setting (school), and practicality (lessons needed to fit within school educational constraints; Pentz, 2009). The final program reflected these findings (N. R. Riggs et al., 2007).

BENEFITS AND BARRIERS

Perhaps the most important benefit of translational research is that it promotes directly the creation and dissemination of new treatments, assessments, and services that improve physical and mental health. The NIH has provided a major impetus for translational research through the Roadmap Initiative (http://nihroadmap.nih.gov). The initiative seeks to accelerate translational research across various behaviorally relevant health areas, including aging, neurological diseases, addictions, and mental health. The National Institute of Mental Health in particular is now invested in forging new translational connections across behavioral and systems-level neuroscience domains, including child development, temperament, emotion, motivation, attention, social processes, and genetics (Cuthbert, 2002). As part of this large effort, translational research has come to permeate all subdisciplines within psychology.

On the basis of the NIH Roadmap for translational research, a strong case can be made for psychology being an integral component of the health mission (Carr, 2008). Although it is recognized widely that many diseases are caused or exacerbated by unhealthy behaviors, the biomedical fields still tend to relegate the role of psychology to specific physician–patient interactions and patient behaviors. Setting aside the issue of drug prescription privileges for clinical psychologists, there is a general need for doctoral psychology programs to integrate knowledge from the neurosciences into the field to enhance the role of psychology in health care driven by translational principles. Consistent with this push, new types of training programs are emerging, such as *health psychology* and *biobehavioral health*. Given the continuing emphasis on translational research, this wave will not crest anytime soon.

Despite the push for translational research in psychology and related disciplines, there are hurdles to overcome to achieve success. Perhaps the biggest hurdle rests in the bias toward independent thinking and productivity in academics. Because of tenure and promotion decisions, a premium is often placed on independent achievements, thus opposing the team-oriented approach necessary to conduct translational research. This hurdle may become amplified because translational research emphasizes bottom-line products, which may involve patent and copyright profits, rather than theoretical advancements. In addition, younger investigators who are rushed into producing empirically based publications to build a dossier worthy of tenure may find that translational research moves too slowly and depends on too many collaborators. As has been mentioned (Nunes, Carroll, & Bickel, 2002), a parochialism among basic and applied researchers extends to professional journals that have a narrow focus. Strong leadership and steady extramural funding are the main antidotes for breaking down these barriers to successful translational research.

Perhaps the most serious impediment to translational research rests in the high cost that typically accompanies a large team-oriented strategy. Although this may be a barrier in the initial stages, the benefits achieved may be transportable to various psychosocial and health problems. In the example illustrated earlier in this chapter, a drug abuse–prevention intervention has been translated into a new obesity prevention intervention (Pentz, 2009; N. R. Riggs et al., 2007). By translating a program across multiple health risk behaviors, the overall cost should be reduced in the long run.

FUTURE DIRECTIONS

Pervasive gaps between basic and applied research continue to hamper effective translational research. Although some specialized fields of research have provided multiple examples of successful translational research (e.g., drug discovery, drug abuse prevention interventions), many areas lag in providing examples that illustrate all of the stages of translational research (see Figure 29.1). In some cases, there is almost a total lack of translational research. For example, although the diagnosis of autism spectrum disorders in children is increasing, only recently have advocacy groups pointed out the need for translational research to address this challenge (Msall, 2009).

There are also gaps in translational research that exist almost completely within the discipline of psychology. For example, as discussed by Tashiro and Mortensen (2006), basic research in social psychology is replete with causal mechanisms that are potentially applicable to clinical psychology. Social psychology has uncovered theoretical information from controlled laboratory studies about clinically relevant constructs, such as self-efficacy, self-esteem, and emotional regulation. However, many experimental social psychologists tend to study these constructs as moment-to-moment variables that are subject to change with a brief manipulation, whereas clinical psychologists are more interested in studying the long-lasting therapeutic changes in these constructs. This parallel but often disconnected work provides an example that is ripe for a more translational perspective. As a case in point, Wiers, Rinck, Kordts, Houben, and Strack (2010) used an implicit training procedure to have participants react automatically to either avoid or approach alcohol stimuli. When subsequently tested for their alcohol drinking behavior, participants trained to avoid alcohol stimuli reduced their drinking, indicating that implicit training can enable participants to gain control over long-term clinically relevant behaviors.

Another direction for potential growth is found in the development of more treatments that yield multiple behavior changes. For example, a program that simultaneously addresses subjective well-being, social competence, physical activity, healthy eating, and drug abuse prevention might facilitate wide-ranging adoption by schools. If the program results in healthy lifestyle change, it conceivably could impart a large social and economic impact on health as well. Similarly, such a strategy is also applicable to a range of other health outcomes, such as the development of medications that target both cholesterol and blood pressure or the implementation of physical exercise programs that target depression, cardiovascular disease, and bone health.

Finally, another shortcoming in translational research involves problems related to our ability to identify what represents effective practice in the real world. This question has important implications for whether fidelity of implementation of evidence-based treatments can be maintained over a long period of time. In particular, little is known about the extent to which researchers and practitioners who market psychosocial treatments are following evidence-based standards. There is also a lack of consensus in the field about what constitutes core elements of evidence-based interventions (Mihalic & Irwin, 2003). Furthermore, treatments tested on an initial population may need to be periodically reexamined for their continued relevance in the face of population shifts because of cohort effects, changes in secular trends, and changing contexts for health behavior. Such information can provide feedback to basic researchers interested in modifying or replacing the treatment to produce lasting improvement in physical and mental health.

References

August, G. J., Winters, K. C., Realmuto, G. M., Tarter, R., Perry, C., & Hektner, J. M. (2004). Moving evidence-based drug abuse prevention programs from basic science to practice: Bridging the efficacy-effectiveness interface. *Substance Use and Misuse, 39,* 2017–2053. doi:10.1081/JA-200033240

Best, A., Moor, G., Holmes, B., Clark, P. I., Bruce, T., Leischow, S., . . . Krajnak, J. (2003). Health promotion dissemination and systems thinking: Towards an integrative model. *American Journal of Health Behavior, 27,* S206–S216.

Best, A., Stokols, D., Green, L. W., Leischow, S., Holmes, B., & Buchholz, K. (2003). An integrative framework for community partnering to translate theory into effective health promotion strategy. *American Journal of Health Promotion, 18,* 168–176.

Brown, C. H., Berndt, D., Brinales, J. M., Zong, X., & Bhagwat, D. (2000). Evaluating the evidence of effectiveness for preventive interventions: Using a registry system to influence policy through science. *Addictive Behaviors, 25,* 955–964. doi:10.1016/S0306-4603(00)00131-3

Cain, M. E., Saucier, D. A., & Bardo, M. T. (2005). Novelty seeking and drug use: Contribution of an animal model. *Experimental and Clinical Psychopharmacology, 13,* 367–375. doi:10.1037/1064-1297.13.4.367

Capone, T., Brahen, L., Condren, R., Kordal, N., Melchionda, R., & Peterson, M. (1986). Retention and outcome in a narcotic antagonist treatment program. *Journal of Clinical Psychology, 42,* 825–833. doi:10.1002/1097-4679(198609)42:5<825::AID-JCLP2270420526>3.0.CO;2-B

Carr, J. E. (2008). Advancing psychology as a bio-behavioral science. *Journal of Clinical Psychology in Medical Settings, 15,* 40–44. doi:10.1007/s10880-008-9093-z

Castro, F. G., Barrera, M., Jr., & Martinez, C. R., Jr. (2004). The cultural adaptation of prevention interventions: Resolving tensions between fidelity and fit. *Prevention Science, 5,* 41–45. doi:10.1023/B:PREV.0000013980.12412.cd

Center for Substance Abuse Prevention. (2002). *SAMHSA model programs: Effective substance abuse and mental health programs for every community.* Retrieved from http://nrepp.samhsa.gov

Chambers, R. A., Taylor, J. R., & Potenza, M. N. (2003). Developmental neurocircuitry of motivation in adolescence: A critical period of addiction vulnerability. *American Journal of Psychiatry, 160,* 1041–1052. doi:10.1176/appi.ajp.160.6.1041

Chambless, D. L., & Ollendick, T. H. (2001). Empirically supported psychological interventions: Controversies and evidence. *Annual Review of Psychology, 52,* 685–716. doi:10.1146/annurev.psych.52.1.685

Clayton, R. R., Cattarello, A. M., & Johnstone, B. M. (1996). The effectiveness of Drug Abuse Resistance Education (Project DARE): 5-year follow-up results.

Preventive Medicine, 25, 307–318. doi:10.1006/pmed.1996.0061

Collins, L. M., Murphy, S. A., & Bierman, K. L. (2004). A conceptual framework for adaptive preventive interventions. *Prevention Science, 5*, 185–196. doi:10.1023/B:PREV.0000037641.26017.00

Crabbe, J. C., Bell, R. L., & Ehlers, C. L. (2010). Human and laboratory rodent low response to alcohol: Is better consilience possible? *Addiction Biology, 15*, 125–144. doi:10.1111/j.1369-1600.2009.00191.x

Cuthbert, B. N. (2002). Social anxiety disorder: Trends and translational research. *Biological Psychiatry, 51*, 4–10. doi:10.1016/S0006-3223(01)01326-9

Davis, C., Levitan, R. D., Muglia, P., Bewell, C., & Kennedy, J. L. (2004). Decision-making deficits and overeating: A risk model for obesity. *Obesity Research, 12*, 929–935. doi:10.1038/oby.2004.113

Day, M., Rutkowski, J. L., & Feuerstein, G. Z. (2009). Translational medicine—a paradigm shift in modern drug discovery and development: The role of biomarkers. *Advances in Experimental Medicine and Biology, 655*, 1–12. doi:10.1007/978-1-4419-1132-2_1

DeJong, W., & Hingson, R. (1998). Strategies to reduce driving under the influence of alcohol. *Annual Review of Public Health, 19*, 359–378. doi:10.1146/annurev.publhealth.19.1.359

Donovan, J. E., Jessor, R., & Costa, F. M. (1993). Structure of health-enhancing behavior in adolescence: A latent-variable approach. *Journal of Health and Social Behavior, 34*, 346–362. doi:10.2307/2137372

Dzewaltowski, D. A., Glasgow, R. E., Klesges, L. M., Estabrooks, P. A., & Brock, E. (2004). RE-AIM: Evidence-based standards and a Web resource to improve translation of research into practice. *Annals of Behavioral Medicine, 28*, 75–80. doi:10.1207/s15324796abm2802_1

Elliot, D. L., Goldberg, L., Moe, E. L., Defrancesco, C. A., Durham, M. B., & Hix-Small, H. (2004). Preventing substance use and disordered eating: Initial outcomes of the ATHENA (athletes targeting healthy exercise and nutrition alternatives) program. *Archives of Pediatrics and Adolescent Medicine, 158*, 1043–1049. doi:10.1001/archpedi.158.11.1043

Elliot, D. S. (Ed.). (1997). *Blueprints for violence prevention.* Boulder: Center for the Study and Prevention of Violence, University of Colorado.

Ettenberg, A., Pettit, H. O., Bloom, F. E., & Koob, G. F. (1982). Heroin and cocaine intravenous self-administration in rats: Mediation by separate neural systems. *Psychopharmacology, 78*, 204–209. doi:10.1007/BF00428151

Flay, B. R., Biglan, A., Boruch, R. F., Castro, F. G., Gottfredson, D., Kellam, S., . . . Ji, P. (2005). Standards of evidence: Criteria for efficacy, effectiveness, and dissemination. *Prevention Science, 6*, 151–175. doi:10.1007/s11121-005-5553-y

Ginexi, E. M., & Hilton, T. F. (2006). What's next for translation research? *Evaluation and the Health Professions, 29*, 334–347. doi:10.1177/0163278706290409

Glasgow, R. E. (2010, May). *Translation research: Design and methodology considerations.* Seminar presented at the Society for Behavioral Medicine Conference, Seattle, WA.

Glasgow, R. E., & Emmons, K. M. (2007). How can we increase translation of research into practice? Types of evidence needed. *Annual Review of Public Health, 28*, 413–433. doi:10.1146/annurev.publhealth.28.021406.144145

Glasgow, R. E., Vogt, T. M., & Boles, S. M. (1999). Evaluating the public health impact of health promotion interventions: The RE-AIM framework. *American Journal of Public Health, 89*, 1322–1327. doi:10.2105/AJPH.89.9.1322

Golub, M. S., Collman, G. W., Foster, P. M., Kimmel, C. A., Rajpert-De Meyts, E., Reiter, E. O., . . . Toppari, J. (2008). Public health implications of altered puberty timing. *Pediatrics, 121*, S218–S230. doi:10.1542/peds.2007-1813G

Gual, A. (2008). Translational research: A necessary and difficult step forward in the addictions field. *Addiction, 103*, 1065–1066, discussion 1067–1068. doi:10.1111/j.1360-0443.2008.02205.x

Guerra, N. G., & Knox, L. (2008). How culture impacts the dissemination and implementation of innovation: A case study of the Families and Schools Together program (FAST) for preventing violence with immigrant Latino youth. *American Journal of Community Psychology, 41*, 304–313. doi:10.1007/s10464-008-9161-4

Haney, M., & Spealman, R. (2008). Controversies in translational research: Drug self-administration. *Psychopharmacology, 199*, 403–419. doi:10.1007/s00213-008-1079-x

Jasuja, G. K., Chou, C. P., Riggs, N. R., & Pentz, M. A. (2008). Early cigarette use and psychological distress as predictors of obesity risk in adulthood. *Nicotine and Tobacco Research, 10*, 325–335. doi:10.1080/14622200701825064

Jiang, Y., Lianekhammy, J., Lawson, A., Guo, C., Lynam, D., Joseph, J. E., . . . Kelly, T. H. (2009). Brain responses to repeated visual experience among low and high sensation seekers: Role of boredom susceptibility. *Psychiatry Research: Neuroimaging, 173*, 100–106. doi:10.1016/j.pscychresns.2008.09.012

Jilcott, S., Ammerman, A., Sommers, J., & Glasgow, R. E. (2007). Applying the RE-AIM framework to assess the public health impact of policy change. *Annals*

of Behavioral Medicine, 34, 105–114. doi:10.1007/
BF02872666

Johnson, B. A. (2010). Medication treatment of different
types of alcoholism. *American Journal of Psychiatry,*
167, 630–639. doi:10.1176/appi.ajp.2010.08101500

Joseph, J. E., Liu, X., Jiang, Y., Lynam, D., & Kelly, T. H.
(2009). Neural correlates of emotional reactivity
in sensation seeking. *Psychological Science, 20,*
215–223. doi:10.1111/j.1467-9280.2009.02283.x

Khoury, M. J., Gwinn, M., Yoon, P. W., Dowling, N.,
Moore, C. A., & Bradley, L. (2007). The continuum
of translation research in genomic medicine: How
can we accelerate the appropriate integration of
human genome discoveries into health care and disease prevention? *Genetics in Medicine, 9,* 665–674.
doi:10.1097/GIM.0b013e31815699d0

King, D. K., Glasgow, R. E., & Leeman-Castillo, B. A.
(2010). Reaiming RE-AIM: Using the model to plan,
implement, and evaluate the effects of environmental
change approaches to enhancing population health.
American Journal of Public Health, 100, 2076–2084.
doi:10.2105/AJPH.2009.190959

Klein, D. A., & Walsh, B. T. (2005). Translational
approaches to understanding anorexia nervosa.
International Journal of Eating Disorders, 37, S10–S14.
doi:10.1002/eat.20108

Koob, G. F., Kenneth Lloyd, G., & Mason, B. J. (2009).
Development of pharmacotherapies for drug addic-
tion: A Rosetta stone approach. *Nature Reviews. Drug*
Discovery, 8, 500–515. doi:10.1038/nrd2828

Kreek, M. J., Zhou, Y., Butelman, E. R., & Levran,
O. (2009). Opiate and cocaine addiction: From
bench to clinic and back to the bench. *Current*
Opinion in Pharmacology, 9, 74–80. doi:10.1016/j.
coph.2008.12.016

Lapiz-Bluhm, M. D., Bondi, C. O., Doyen, J., Rodriguez,
G. A., Bedard-Arana, T., & Morilak, D. A. (2008).
Behavioural assays to model cognitive and affective
dimensions of depression and anxiety in rats. *Journal*
of Neuroendocrinology, 20, 1115–1137. doi:10.1111/
j.1365-2826.2008.01772.x

Lerman, C., LeSage, M. G., Perkins, K. A., O'Malley, S.
S., Siegel, S. J., Benowitz, N. L., & Corrigall, W. A.
(2007). Translational research in medication development for nicotine dependence. *Nature Reviews:*
Drug Discovery, 6, 746–762. doi:10.1038/nrd2361

Littlejohns, P. (2009). NICE at 10 years: New challenges ahead. *Expert Review of Pharmacoeconomics*
and Outcomes Research, 9, 151–156. doi:10.1586/
erp.09.13

Lynam, D. R., Milich, R., Zimmerman, R., Novak, S. P.,
Logan, T. K., Martin, C., . . . Clayton, R. (1999).
Project DARE: No effects at 10-year follow-up.
Journal of Consulting and Clinical Psychology, 67,
590–593. doi:10.1037/0022-006X.67.4.590

Mihalic, S. F., & Irwin, K. (2003). Blueprints for violence
prevention: From research to real-world settings—
Factors influencing the successful replication of
model programs. *Youth Violence and Juvenile Justice,*
1, 307–329. doi:10.1177/1541204003255841

Msall, M. E. (2009). Establishing a translational science
for autistic spectrum disorders for children and
their families: Optimizing function, participation,
and well-being. *Journal of Pediatrics, 154,* 319–321.
doi:10.1016/j.jpeds.2008.10.039

Nguyen-Michel, S. T., Unger, J. B., & Spruijt-Metz, D.
(2007). Dietary correlates of emotional eating in
adolescence. *Appetite, 49,* 494–499. doi:10.1016/
j.appet.2007.03.005

Nunes, E. V., Carroll, K. M., & Bickel, W. K. (2002).
Clinical and translational research: Introduction
to the special issue. *Experimental and Clinical*
Psychopharmacology, 10, 155–158. doi:10.1037/
1064-1297.10.3.155

Oesterle, S., Hawkins, J. D., Fagan, A. A., Abbott, R. D.,
& Catalano, R. F. (2010). Testing the universality of
the Effects of the Communities That Care Prevention
System for preventing adolescent drug use and
delinquency. *Prevention Science, 11,* 411–423.
doi:10.1007/s11121-010-0178-1

Palmgreen, P., Donohew, L., Lorch, E. P., Hoyle, R. H., &
Stephenson, M. T. (2001). Television campaigns and
adolescent marijuana use: Tests of sensation seeking targeting. *American Journal of Public Health, 91,*
292–296. doi:10.2105/AJPH.91.2.292

Palmgreen, P., Lorch, E. P., Stephenson, M. T., Hoyle, R.
H., & Donohew, L. (2007). Effects of the Office of
National Drug Control Policy's Marijuana Initiative
Campaign on high-sensation-seeking adolescents.
American Journal of Public Health, 97, 1644–1649.
doi:10.2105/AJPH.2005.072843

Paterson, N. E. (2009). Behavioural and pharmacological mechanisms of bupropion's anti-smoking effects:
Recent preclinical and clinical insights. *European*
Journal of Pharmacology, 603, 1–11. doi:10.1016/j.
ejphar.2008.12.009

Pentz, M. A. (1998). Cost, benefits and cost-effectiveness
of comprehensive drug abuse prevention. *NIDA*
Research Monograph, 176, 111–129.

Pentz, M. A. (2003). Evidence-based prevention:
Characteristics, impact, and future direction. *Journal*
of Psychoactive Drugs, 35(Suppl. 1), 143–152.

Pentz, M. A. (2004a). *Applying theory and methods of*
community-based drug abuse prevention to pediatric
obesity prevention. Retrieved from http://www.niddk.
nih.gov/fund/other/management_pediatric_obesity/
SUMMARY_REPORT.pdf

Pentz, M. A. (2004b). Form follows function: Designs
for prevention effectiveness and diffusion research.

Prevention Science, 5, 23–29. doi:10.1023/B:PREV. 0000013978.00943.30

Pentz, M. A. (2007). Disseminating effective approaches to drug abuse prevention. In M. K. Welch-Ross & L. G. Fasig (Eds.), *Handbook on communicating and disseminating behavioral science* (pp. 341–364). Thousand Oaks, CA: Sage.

Pentz, M. A. (2009). Understanding and preventing risks for obesity. In R. DiClemente, R. Crosby, & J. Santelli (Eds.), *Adolescent health: Understanding and preventing risk* (pp. 147–164). Hoboken, NJ: Wiley.

Pentz, M. A., Chou, C. P., McClure, M., Bernstein, K., Mann, D., & Ross, L. (2004). *Adoption and early implementation of STEP.* Washington, DC: Society for Prevention Research.

Pentz, M. A., Jasuja, G. K., Li, C., McClure, M., & Chou, C. P. (2003). *Predictors of diffusion of evidence-based prevention programs: Early results of the STEP Trial.* Washington, DC: Society for Prevention Research.

Pentz, M. A., Jasuja, G. K., Rohrbach, L. A., Sussman, S., & Bardo, M. T. (2006). Translation in tobacco and drug abuse prevention research. *Evaluation and the Health Professions, 29,* 246–271. doi:10.1177/0163278706287347

Pentz, M. A., Mares, D., Schinke, S., & Rohrbach, L. A. (2004). Political science, public policy, and drug use prevention. *Substance Use and Misuse, 39,* 1821–1865. doi:10.1081/JA-200033226

Porsolt, R. D., Brossard, G., Hautbois, C., & Roux, S. (2001). Rodent models of depression: Forced swimming and tail suspension behavioral despair tests in rats and mice. *Current Protocols in Neuroscience, 14,* 8.10A.1–8.10A. doi:10.10.1002/0471142301.ns0810as14

Potenza, M. N., & Taylor, J. R. (2009). Found in translation: Understanding impulsivity and related constructs through integrative preclinical and clinical research. *Biological Psychiatry, 66,* 714–716. doi:10.1016/j.biopsych.2009.08.004

Riggs, N., Chou, C. P., Spruijt-Metz, D., & Pentz, M. A. (2010). Executive cognitive function as a correlate and predictor of child food intake and physical activity. *Child Neuropsychology, 16,* 279–292. doi:10.1080/09297041003601488

Riggs, N. R., Greenberg, M. T., Kusche, C. A., & Pentz, M. A. (2006). The mediational role of neurocognition in the behavioral outcomes of a social-emotional prevention program in elementary school students: Effects of the PATHS Curriculum. *Prevention Science, 7,* 91–102. doi:10.1007/s11121-005-0022-1

Riggs, N. R., Sakuma, K. L., & Pentz, M. A. (2007). Preventing risk for obesity by promoting self-regulation and decision-making skills: Pilot results from the PATHWAYS to health program

(PATHWAYS). *Evaluation Review, 31,* 287–310. doi:10.1177/0193841X06297243

Rogers, E. M. (1995). Elements of diffusion. In E. M. Rogers (Ed.), *Diffusion of innovations* (4th ed., pp. 1–38). New York, NY: Free Press.

Roth, W. T. (2008). Translational research for panic disorder. *American Journal of Psychiatry, 165,* 796–798. doi:10.1176/appi.ajp.2008.08040533

Rowlett, J. K., Wilcox, K. M., & Woolverton, W. L. (1998). Self-administration of cocaine-heroin combinations by rhesus monkeys: Antagonism by naltrexone. *Journal of Pharmacology and Experimental Therapeutics, 286,* 61–69.

Sanson-Fisher, R. W. (2004). Diffusion of innovation theory for clinical change. *Medical Journal of Australia, 180(Suppl. 6),* S55–S56.

Solomon, J., Card, J. J., & Malow, R. M. (2006). Adapting efficacious interventions: Advancing translational research in HIV prevention. *Evaluation and the Health Professions, 29,* 162–194. doi:10.1177/0163278 706287344

Stoops, W. W., Lile, J. A., Robbins, C. G., Martin, C. A., Rush, C. R., & Kelly, T. H. (2007). The reinforcing, subject-rated, performance, and cardiovascular effects of d-amphetamine: Influence of sensation-seeking status. *Addictive Behaviors, 32,* 1177–1188. doi:10.1016/j.addbeh.2006.08.006

Sussman, S. (2001). *Handbook of program development for behavior research and practice.* Thousand Oaks, CA: Sage.

Sussman, S., Valente, T. W., Rohrbach, L. A., Skara, S., & Pentz, M. A. (2010). Translation in the health professions: Converting science into action. *Evaluation and the Health Professions, 33,* 7–11. doi:10.1177/016327 8705284441

Tashiro, T., & Mortensen, L. (2006). Translational research: How social psychology can improve psychotherapy. *American Psychologist, 61,* 959–966. doi:10.1037/0003-066X.61.9.959

Valente, T. W., Chou, C. P., & Pentz, M. A. (2007). Community coalitions as a system: Effects of network change on adoption of evidence-based substance abuse prevention. *American Journal of Public Health, 97,* 880–886. doi:10.2105/AJPH.2005.063644

Valente, T. W., Fujimoto, K., Chou, C. P., & Spruijt-Metz, D. (2009). Adolescent affiliations and adiposity: A social network analysis of friendships and obesity. *Journal of Adolescent Health, 45,* 202–204. doi:10.1016/j.jadohealth.2009.01.007

Vendruscolo, L. F., Izidio, G. S., & Takahashi, R. N. (2010). Drug reinforcement in a rat model of attention deficit/hyperactivity disorder—the Spontaneously Hypertensive Rat (SHR). *Current*

Drug Abuse Reviews, 2, 177–183. doi:10.2174/1874473710902020177

Volkow, N. D., & Wise, R. A. (2005). How can drug addiction help us understand obesity? *Nature Neuroscience, 8,* 555–560. doi:10.1038/nn1452

Wandersman, A., Duffy, J., Flaspohler, P., Noonan, R., Lubell, K., Stillman, L., . . . Saul, J. (2008). Bridging the gap between prevention research and practice: The interactive systems framework for dissemination and implementation. *American Journal of Community Psychology, 41,* 171–181. doi:10.1007/s10464-008-9174-z

Werch, C. C., Moore, M. J., DiClemente, C. C., Bledsoe, R., & Jobli, E. (2005). A multihealth behavior intervention integrating physical activity and substance use prevention for adolescents. *Prevention Science, 6,* 213–226. doi:10.1007/s11121-005-0012-3

West, S. L., & O'Neal, K. K. (2004). Project DARE outcome effectiveness revisited. *American Journal of Public Health, 94,* 1027–1029.

Wiers, R. W., Rinck, M., Kordts, R., Houben, K., & Strack, F. (2010). Retraining automatic action-tendencies to approach alcohol in hazardous drinkers. *Addiction, 105,* 279–287. doi:10.1111/j.1360-0443.2009.02775.x

Zuckerman, M. (1988). Sensation seeking and behavior disorders. *Archives of General Psychiatry, 45,* 502–503.

CHAPTER 30

PROGRAM EVALUATION: OUTCOMES AND COSTS OF PUTTING PSYCHOLOGY TO WORK

Brian T. Yates

Program evaluation uses experimental and quasi-experimental designs, case studies, and diverse other methodologies to ask how well psychological and other interventions developed in more controlled settings work in the real worlds of schools, clinics, offices, factories, farms, streets, and battlefields (cf. Guttentag & Struening, 1975; Mertens, 2005; Posavac & Carey, 2003; Scriven, 1991; Silverman, 2004). Program evaluations now decide which programs are given the moniker of *evidence-based practice*, which often determines whether the program is publicly fundable or not. In education, the What Works Clearinghouse (see http://www.ies.ed.gov/ncee/wwc) conducts several hundred meta-analytic reviews each year of research studies and program evaluations to examine what works in education according to program evaluations. For substance abuse and mental health services, there is a searchable database of the National Registry of Evidence-Based Programs and Practices (see http://www.repp.samhsa.gov).

Summative evaluation asks whether a program worked and, increasingly, what the program cost. Not all programs that work may be judged worth their cost. *Formative* evaluation seeks to improve programs by understanding why a program works well or poorly or not at all, or actually harms rather than helps. For this purpose, formative evaluation discovers which activities of the program actually changed the psychological processes that were supposed to lead to the desired outcomes and increasingly considers the costs of those activities as well (Yates, 1980, 1996). Outcomes evaluated in summative or formative evaluation can be as diverse as

reduced depression, improved negotiation skills, enhanced athletic performance, or cessation of drug abuse. Outcomes can encompass results that matter to funders, such as increased days of employment, reduced HIV transmission, and human services no longer needed. Even the monetary value of those outcomes is considered, such as income received and heath care and criminal justice costs avoided. In addition, program evaluation increasingly includes descriptions and analyses of the *resources consumed* by program operations: the types, amounts, and monetary values of psychologists' time, clients' time, office space, and other resources that make the program possible. Some evaluations contrast program costs to program outcomes with cost-effectiveness, cost-benefit, and cost-utility analyses. Some state governments use program evaluations to develop cost-benefit findings, which are used to recommend which programs should receive state funding and which should not (e.g., Aos, Lieb, Mayfield, Miller, & Pennucci, 2004).

Obviously, program evaluation is powerful—perhaps the most powerful short-term application of psychological and other research methodologies to date. Learning more about it is essential for psychologists, whether scientists, scientist-practitioners, or practitioners. We need to understand it to evaluate our own and other programs, to contribute positively to evaluations performed on our programs by others, and to recognize and prevent its possible misuse. To aid in this effort, this chapter begins with a comprehensive model of program evaluation, uses examples to explain how to resolve measurement

DOI: 10.1037/13620-030
APA Handbook of Research Methods in Psychology: Vol. 2. Research Designs, H. Cooper (Editor-in-Chief)

and design issues for each part of the model, and ends by describing current issues facing program evaluation and program evaluators.

A COMPREHENSIVE MODEL OF PROGRAM EVALUATION

It is natural to ask questions about goods and services, and even to judge them for their value or worth to oneself if not to society. When many individuals ask these questions and decide to purchase or not purchase goods and services for themselves in a free and open marketplace, very often only the most effective, cost-effective, and cost-beneficial alternatives survive the competition and flourish. However, when a relatively few government officials make decisions to acquire goods or services that are not widely available in the private marketplace, or when government decision makers are relatively uninformed about the value of the things or services being considered for purchase, economic forces of competition in quality, price, and supply are impeded and do not foster value.

In these contexts and others, program evaluation can step in to provide to potential purchasers, funders, clients, and other interested parties the information necessary for market forces to work again. This feedback can be about the quality of materials offered; the strength, durability, and reliability of outcomes of services; and the costs of those endeavors. Moreover, program evaluation can provide feedback on the many types of outcomes and the diverse costs that may be experienced in the long as well as the short run. This information can reduce the likelihood of decisions that minimize immediate costs to some interest groups while resulting in large future costs to the public. Program evaluation also can provide information on the outcomes and costs experienced at a particular moment in time by different groups of people, from those receiving the materials or services to those in communities near and far from the recipients. Typically, the marketplace does not provide feedback that is this all-encompassing, temporally comprehensive, or inclusive. Evaluation can provide this feedback not only to funders of programs but also to providers of programs and to clients and communities served by those programs.

This view of the purpose of program evaluation is compatible with a variety of mission statements made for program evaluation in past decades, including the following: "The proper mission of evaluation is not to eliminate the fallibility of authority or to bolster its credibility. Rather, its mission is to facilitate a democratic, pluralistic process by enlightening all the participants" (Cronbach et al., 1980, p. 1). Additionally, Guba and Lincoln (1989) wrote,

> Evaluation is an investment in people and in progress. . . . we do not treat evaluation as a *scientific* process, because it is our conviction that to approach evaluation scientifically is to miss completely its fundamentally social, political, and value-oriented character. (cover page, p. 7)

Program evaluation asks, and attempts to answer, questions such as, "Are our children being educated?" "Is treatment offered at that clinic effective?" "Is it worth the time and money?" and "What programs work to build safer communities, and how much do they cost?" In addition, because program evaluation is not necessarily limited to publicly funded human services, it also may ask, "How can we run our business better and greener?" "How can we make our farms more productive?" Program evaluation also can be applied to government efforts beyond social services, even addressing questions such as, "How should, or can, we win this war?" All of these questions are important to diverse entities for many reasons. Program evaluators answer them, or try to. How these questions are asked, and challenges in hearing and understanding the answers, are the topics of this chapter.

Outcomes

A *program* is an organized effort by one or more persons to maintain or change the nature of people, communities, or environments. Programs reliably consume *resources*, such as time, space, and energy, to conduct specific *activities* that psychological and other theories suggest for inducing changes in biological, psychological, and social *processes* that result in the *outcomes* of the program. Some outcomes are intended, such as improved knowledge.

Other results of programs are unintended, such as acquisition of skills to manipulate peers, negative attitudes toward formal education, and development of creative genius (cf. Morell, 2010). Unintended effects of some programs have exacerbated rather than remediated the problem being addressed, including increasing rather than decreasing willingness to use and actual use of alcohol, tobacco, and other drugs by children (cf. Yates, 2002). There can be short- and long-term outcomes, such as improved performance on a mathematics section of a test at the end of the year, or better performance in an algebra class several years later. Outcomes also can be monetary, such as higher earnings during the decade following college graduation or a reduction in future spending for health care services.

Descriptive statistics.   Program evaluation often begins by describing whether the program did what it said it would do. For example, asking such questions as, "Did teachers introduce and provide guidance in the prescribed exercises for enhanced mathematics performance?" "Were the 50 motorcycle awareness billboards placed in commonly traveled venues in the target counties for 30 to 45 days each?" "Were sessions attended by clients?" and "Did captains provide peer support program referrals for soldiers exhibiting three or more signs of post-traumatic stress disorder during the 4 weeks following ignition of an improvised explosive device or other unexpected potentially fatal explosion in their immediate vicinity?" These questions of simple adherence of actual program operations to planned program activities are the essence of some program evaluations. Programs with high adherence or high *fidelity* to planned activities typically are evaluated positively. These evaluations assume, however, that if program activities are performed faithfully they will almost inevitably lead to desired program outcomes. This, of course, is not always the case in settings such as schools or communities, or in the contexts for such important and complex behaviors as health or education. In fact, it is not often the case.

Programs can insist that they should not be evaluated negatively if the prescribed activities were implemented but the desired outcomes failed to occur. This can be seen as self-serving. Because

there is little agreement on the best way to teach complex skills or prevent or remediate most problems, program evaluations usually move beyond an assessment of adherence to planned program activities to an assessment of whether the desired outcomes of the program occurred. Those outcomes were what was desired by program funders, after all: the means to achieve those outcomes are often left to programs to devise and implement as long as ethical and moral boundaries are not crossed and as long as budget constraints are not exceeded. This description usually is both quantitative and qualitative, using numbers including statistics and using words to represent subjective judgments.

For example, in an evaluation of a fourth-grade classroom, average reading levels might be measured with a standardized test. Additional statistics would be generated to describe reading outcomes more completely, such as minimum and maximum performance on the reading exam and the reading level attained by a certain percentile of the class. These and other numbers could be generated not just for the variable "reading level," but other characteristics of reading ability such as text-reading fluency and comprehension. Other measures of outcomes could be included as well, ranging from the number of books read in the year to time spent reading nonsocial media online as well as in print and even positive self-regard as a literate person. In addition, teachers might note that the student reads well, "especially when integrating multiple plot lines into a cohesive story," or that the reader "can and often does relate the story being told to his own life, finding guidance from the readings."

Groupings by demographic variables.   Many programs focus on changing the behavioral, cognitive, emotional (affective), or biological processes of *clients,* who can be individuals, families, organizations, businesses, or military units. Outcomes should be particularly evident for and to clients. Outcomes also can be described for different types of clients, that is, outcomes can be summarized with numbers or words for groupings of clients, such as those of different genders, ethnicities, ages, or socioeconomic classes, or those with different mental and physical challenges. Statistical techniques such as *t* tests and analysis of variance can tell evaluators whether the outcomes of a program were better for one group of clients than another. For example, reading scores between the start of ninth and 10th grades can be compared statistically for girls and boys, or students of different ethnicities, to show whether apparent small differences in scores are statistically significant. Moreover, change in reading scores for different types of students can be compared statistically to decide whether one type of student improved more than another. Sophisticated statistical analyses, such as analysis of covariance, can adjust for differences that existed between the groups of clients so that the evaluation can answer questions like, "Was the difference in reading levels found after fourth grade only caused by differences that existed between the groups of clients before fourth grade, or did the groups become more similar (or more different) in reading skills?"

Levels of specificity.   Outcomes also can be measured at one level of specificity, such as the individual student, and aggregated to represent outcomes for groupings of clients, such as "reading test scores of students in Mr. Crosstree's ninth-grade reading class in June 2013," "ninth-grade students in public schools in Washington, DC in June 2013," or "ninth-grade students in public schools in the United States of America in June 2013." Levels of specificity can be understood as a particular type of grouping: one that includes different areas of a hierarchy of organization by geographic location (as in the examples in the preceding sentence), or by type of outcome (e.g., two particular reading skills such as increased vocabulary and text comprehension, versus reading skills in general), or over time (e.g., between ninth and 10th grade, for high school, or for one's entire education or lifetime).

Impacts on other programs.   A type of outcome that is increasingly common in program evaluation is the effect that one program may have on other programs. Given the expense of social entitlements such as health care as well as the expense of criminal justice services, and the decreasing amount of funds available for entitlements, decision makers often ask whether those expenses can be reduced. Some programs assert that they can reduce other programs'

expenses. For example, substance abuse prevention and treatment programs have been found to reduce subsequent use of health care expenses as well as criminal justice services by persons who participate in these programs (e.g., Aos et al., 2004). Advocates for some programs have essentially told funders of social services that "you're going to pay more later if you don't pay some now" for the relatively inexpensive treatment and prevention programs being advocated. Foreign aid, too, has been justified by some as a type of program that not only does immediate good in needy parts of the world but also may help avoid social and political unrest that would require far more expensive humanitarian aid and possible military responses in the future (e.g., Collier, 2007; see also Clements, Chianca, & Sasaki, 2008). The challenge for the program evaluator is how to measure these impacts in a meaningful manner that can be replicated by others, including critics of the program.

Time of measurement.   Implicit in a description of the outcomes of a program is the notion that something important has changed and, more specifically, that something important has improved and has continued to be so. If a particular education regimen is meant to improve reading, reading can be measured before and after the program has been implemented. Measures of reading then can be examined to see whether reading has changed and, hopefully, improved. Some programs are expected to have outcomes that endure long after the program has been completed, such as education (e.g., reading skills are expected to be retained). Some health promotion programs are acknowledged to succeed in relapse prevention for limited periods of time (e.g., 6, 12, or 36 months) and only for some clients. Obesity treatment, smoking cessation treatment, and substance abuse treatment are programs whose immediate posttreatment outcomes may be quite positive but whose long-term success is crucial to measure as well. For such programs, *relapse* or *survival rates* can be calculated, as in "80% of patients completing the program continued to exhibit the desired outcomes for at least 2 years." Statistical *survival analyses* can distinguish whether the relapse rate for a program was less severe for clients completing the program relative to what would be expected without the program or in a different program.

Intent-to-treat versus as-treated. Perhaps the reader noticed the phrase "completing the program" in the preceding paragraph and became somewhat skeptical about the program outcome statistic of 80%. An important distinction is made in program evaluation between outcomes for clients completing a program and outcomes for clients who began but did not complete it. Outcomes for *as-treated* (AT) clients typically are better than outcomes for *intent-to-treat* (ITT) clients because those who begin treatment or another program but do not show early signs of benefiting from the program often drop out of treatment. Some programs, including most substance abuse treatments, intentionally expel clients who show poor preliminary outcomes—for example, those who relapse early and often. The same can be said of some education institutions, although many of these have policies that officially retain students with poor outcomes while placing them in the socially embarrassing and dropout-inducing position of repeating the program—for example, repeating ninth grade.

There also is value in knowing the outcomes of a program for clients who do manage to complete it. Acknowledging this, program evaluations now typically report separately the AT and ITT outcome statistics. The number of clients in each analysis often is important to note as well. For instance, a program that is 80% successful in cessation of gang activity 2 years later for the 20 communities that completed the program may be only 20% successful for the 100 communities that began the program.

Measures. Program operators' judgments of clients' performance can be used as a measure of outcomes, as can clients' own reports of their performance. Both can provide unique information on program outcomes, but both can be biased in favor of, or occasionally against, finding the outcomes desired by the program operator or the client. To reduce these biases, standardized measures have been developed to measure outcomes. Although standardized measures also can perpetuate biases for or against a program, and for or against some types of clients, their availability, economy, and acceptability to many funders of evaluations make them appealing to many evaluators. Some standardized measures directly assess client performance, such as reading ability or verbal aptitude. Others are completed by a third party who may have a history of interacting with the client or by a person interacting with the client for the first time and in a professional capacity. These assessments can be evaluated, too (Yates & Taub, 2003).

Outcomes rarely are sufficient for a program evaluation. Not only are outcomes of most programs not as beneficial as desired by most clients and most program providers, but just knowing the outcome of a program often is insufficient for either a summative or formative program evaluation. Many questions can be asked about programs and their costs. When outcomes are good or similar to those desired, advocates for the program (typically including but not limited to the program providers) wish to conclude that the program was responsible for some or all of the positive outcomes. Experience has shown that this may not be the case, however. Whether spontaneous remission of cancer, smoking cessation maintained without professional intervention, or acquisition of basic social or language skills without formal education in those skills, it often seems that programs may well not be responsible for *all* of the positive outcomes experienced by clients.

Furthermore, it certainly is common to ascribe the cause of any *negative* outcomes to either poor compliance with program edicts (e.g., not complying with highly aversive chemotherapy), low participation in program activities (such as missing classes or group meetings), iatrogenic external factors (e.g., smoking advertisements in subways, peer pressure), problems the client had before engagement in the program (e.g., poor attention skills or other learning disabilities, inadequate social skills, hyperactivity, a history of substance abuse), or cultural offensiveness of some program activities. Perhaps not *whether* but *how much* these or other factors, or even the program, were responsible for program failures is an important area of investigation for program evaluators. Understanding the causes of program failures, even more than program successes, can help programs improve.

The following types of program evaluation describe different ways of revealing the layers of a program and its many operations, effects, and costs. Most evaluations focus on a subset of all possible program operations, effects, final results, and costs. The more formative, potentially constructive evaluations generally include more information about what acts are performed by providers, clients, and others during the program, attempting to describe causal linkages between resources consumed, the activities performed, processes engaged, and outcomes achieved. The first type of program evaluation examines possible linkages between the activities and the outcomes of a program.

Activity–Outcome Evaluation

Logic models. In addition to "What are the outcomes of the program?", many program evaluations ask, "Did the program cause those outcomes?" Once it is acknowledged that the measurable behaviors, cognitions, and affects of clients probably have a variety of causes and that the program may be only one of these, a set of possible *causes* of outcomes is hypothesized. These can be listed and graphically tied to specific activities in the programs that are supposed to cause those outcomes. Program evaluators call this a *logic model*. The left side of Figure 30.1 lists activities for three types of programs: education, health, and military. The right side of Figure 30.1 lists some of the outcomes commonly hoped for in these programs.

For education, reading skills are the focus of the program evaluation depicted. More specific measures of reading skills that occur sooner than the goal of being able to read at a 12th-grade level are detailed, including vocabulary, comprehension of text, and generation of text, that is, writing. These outcomes are described in the simple logic model in Figure 30.1 as being caused by the program activities of parents reading books to their children at home, classroom instruction in sentence diagramming, and self-paced readings and quizzes.

For health care, the logic model in the middle panel of Figure 30.1 depicts the outcome of improved longevity measured as years lived and quality of those years. In addition to those more global or *macro level* outcomes, more specific *meso level* measures of health that are closer or more *proximal* to the program activities are approximation to

cardiovascular sufficiency, increased pulmonary capacity, and improved balance in the patients' immune systems. These health outcomes can be described as caused by a wide range of prevention and treatment program activities, ranging from use of smartphone-based interventions for improving nutritional balance to enhanced regular aerobic exercise and improved relationships for better social support.

For the military program, the macrolevel outcome of *readiness* is operationalized as having adequate resources for both defense and offense, and having concrete, specific plans in place for the use of those resources in response to existing and new challenges. These more specific outcomes are described by the logic model in the bottom panel of Figure 30.1 as being associated with the more specific program activities of procurement of necessary defense and offense materiel and personnel, and training of personnel in use of that materiel in situations that progressively approximate battlefield sites. This training could involve systematically escalating exposure to unpredictable threat potential such as increasingly aggressive provocations by battlefield residents.

Activity–outcome evaluation planning. It is tempting to connect the more specific outcomes listed in the right column of Figure 30.1 to one or more specific activities listed in the left column of Figure 30.1. Drawing connections thought to exist between an activity and an outcome would be a program evaluator's way of graphically expressing a *hypothesis* regarding the program. Experts could be consulted to see whether they thought the hypothesized connections existed, and theories could be consulted as well. Program evaluators also recognize that experts have their own biases toward and against specific activity–outcome connections, and frequently seek to test the hypothesized activity–outcome linkages by measuring the outcomes, the activities, and relationships between the two in empirical tests of activity–outcome hypotheses.

If data already were available on the outcomes of a program and its activities, a variety of statistical analyses could test the existence, direction, and strength of these activity–outcome relationships,

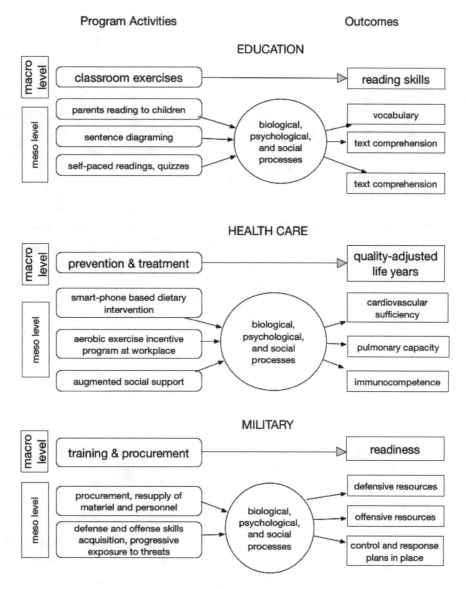

FIGURE 30.1.   Activity–outcome logic models at macro and meso levels of specificity for evaluation of educational, health, and military programs.

including simple correlations, multiple regressions, and structural equation modeling for path analyses that focused on the degree to which clients participated in the program and its specific activities, and the degree to which clients experienced the expected outcomes (cf. Yates, 1980, 1996). There should be a dose–response relationship between the types, intensities, and durations of activities actually conducted and engaged in by clients and the desired outcomes. In this way, greater fidelity to program activities planned should be associated with greater achievement of program outcomes. Also, it would be surprising but possibly illuminating if poor fidelity to activity plans nevertheless was followed by wonderful outcomes. That would call into question the hypothesized activity–outcome relationships.

Most readers will recognize, however, that even a strong correlation does not mean that a causal relationship exists between program activities and program outcomes. Simpler analyses of relationships between participation in an activity and outcomes even could find that more participation was related to *poorer* outcomes, perhaps because clients or communities that were in worse shape before participating in the program were offered more activities in hopes of helping them but that those initially worse-off clients or communities did not improve as much as those who began program participation with less severe problems.

Why not use classic research design in program evaluation: A randomized clinical trial? Many readers probably have recognized that the evaluation problems described thus far and many others could be eliminated if clients eligible for a program simply were assigned by a random lottery either to the program or to wait until the evaluation was completed. The latter, *wait-list condition* often is called a *control group* or, in more contemporary terminology, a *counterfactual*. Outcomes would be measured for both clients in and waiting for the program, perhaps before, during, and a few times after the program. These measures then would be compared at each point in time for clients in and not in the program in comprehensive statistical analyses, such as multivariate analyses of variance, developed over many decades for just such tests of program effectiveness. If a sufficient number of clients were randomized to each of the two groups, all characteristics that could otherwise explain differences in outcomes should be distributed similarly among clients in the program or control conditions. No statistically significant differences should exist on outcome measures at the start of the program, and significant differences on the same measures should be found between clients in the program and control conditions after completion of the program. Also, as much as possible, those involved in the evaluation would be unaware of which individuals were receiving program services and which were in the control condition.

"We would if we could but we can't" is the answer that many evaluators will give to the question, "Why don't you just do a real experiment for your evaluation?" For a true clinical trial that avoids confusing program outcomes with what are essentially placebo effects resulting from expectations of program success and little else, procedures are used that keep both the client and the provider unaware of whether the program being evaluated is the *real* program or just a placebo. These procedures often are difficult or impossible to use in many human

service programs. Hopefully, program providers know whether they are providing the program. Also, although it is possible to lie to clients and tell them they are in a program when they actually are in a control condition, many program providers and evaluators view this as unethical and unrealistic.

Furthermore, most clients refuse to wait to participate in a program, and many client advocates view participation in publicly funded health and other human services as their *entitlement*, that is, their right as a citizen or resident. Arguments that the program may not help, or may even hurt, rarely succeed in dissuading clients from seeking program services. And, even when clients or their advocates agree to random assignment to the program or waiting list, frequent sabotage occurs: Advocates, clients, program providers, and evaluation staff sympathetic to client needs may surreptitiously ensure that the more desperate, needy clients are enrolled in the program *even if those clients drew assignment to a waiting list control condition*. This can reduce the validity of program evaluation. If more needy clients show poorer outcomes because of poorer potential, even the measured magnitude of program outcomes, not to mention future program funding, may be diminished.

In addition, many programs are so broad in scope that random assignment is not feasible, at least in a nontotalitarian political context. Consider the evaluation built into a multicommunity study of the effectiveness of alternative health promotion programs. The Stanford Three Community Study (Meyer, Maccoby, & Farquhar, 1980) evaluated effects of a mass media program to increase individuals' awareness of risk factors and risky behaviors for coronary heart disease (CHD) as well as positive change in individuals' CHD-related behaviors. This program was compared with both a no-program control condition and a third condition that added to the media program a face-to-face program for residents with high CHD risk. The three conditions were implemented in three similar cities. Although heralded at the time as an experimental study, it was not completely experimental in that it did not randomly assign persons to live in the different cities. Despite this, useful evaluation findings were generated (Leventhal, Safer, Cleary, & Guttman, 1980). It was particularly important that a control condition was included because some behavioral and biological risk factors *increased* in that condition. Although they only sometimes decreased in the media condition, they consistently decreased in the media plus face-to-face conditions. It could be argued that the media plus face-to-face program was actually more effective than simple pre–post change measures for the city suggested because, without a program, the risk factors would have increased.

Some might say that evaluation of the outcomes of such a program should not be done because it cannot be done well, that is, using a truly randomized design. The role of evaluation, then, would be limited to basic and applied settings that, at most, presented simplified *analogues* of communities such as those in which the health programs were implemented. Although that role is more comfortable to some, the not-so-occasional failure in the real world of programs shown to be markedly effective in more carefully controlled analogue settings suggests that evaluation is needed in final real-world implementations (cf. Kazdin, 2003). These evaluations can provide feedback to theories not only on what should work but also what *does* work and why. If a program does not work, that feedback can be even more important, but only if measures have been taken that can verify each major step in the logic model that is supposed to capture the essential activities, processes, and outcomes of the program.

Natural experimentation. A natural approach to resolving this problem is to simply observe, rather than manipulate, the operation of the program and the engagement or nonengagement of clients. A dose–response relationship often is desired: The more a client participates in a program, the better the outcomes should be. If the client of the program is a community rather than a person, then communities in which the program is more completely implemented ideally should experience better outcomes. Sometimes the expected dose–response relationship is found, as Howard, Kopta, Krause, and Orlinsky (1986) discovered, in evaluations of therapy outcome. Sometimes, however, hypothesized dose–response relationships may not be found. The reverse may be concluded

if clients with greater needs at the start of program participation are encouraged to participate more than less needy clients and if greater initial severity of client problems limits program effectiveness. Because the determinants of opportunities to participate in programs may be related to preexisting factors that may also affect program results, conclusions of natural experiments are always somewhat suspect.

Treatment-as-usual comparison. A more satisfactory, if still not entirely acceptable, alternative is to compare new programs to treatment as usual (TAU). In some cases, TAU would be an existing program; in others, it would be no program. If the new program had substantially better outcomes than the alternative, it is judged positively. If not, TAU continues. This approach to evaluation entrenches the status quo. It also does not satisfy persons who feel that they or their advocatee are entitled to participate in the program. Moreover, relative to evaluations comparing outcome measures for clients who do or do not participate in a program, profoundly larger samples of clients need to be recruited (and notably larger budgets for the evaluation need to be obtained) to test whether a significant difference exists between TAU and an innovative program (which each can be assumed to have some impact in similar, positive directions). A methodology called *power analysis* (see Volume 1, Chapter 11, this handbook) shows exactly how many clients are needed in program comparisons, depending on the anticipated size of the program effect.

Hybrid designs for program evaluation. A hybrid approach to coping with problems of random assignment to a program or control condition is to invite potential clients to either TAU, the new program, or no program at all. Outcome measures would be taken on all clients, including those in the "no program at all" or "other counterfactual condition." At the end of the evaluation, clients in all conditions would be invited to receive whichever program produced the best outcomes. This strategy mitigates a number of potential concerns, but it is less appropriate for potentially life-saving or life-sustaining programs, such as chemotherapy adherence regimens and drug abuse treatments.

Yet another method is to simply offer the new program as an alternative and then adjust statistically for whatever differences are found between clients who do and do not participate in the program. The differences of particular focus in this approach usually are those demographic characteristics, severity of problem preprogram, and number of previous attempts to remedy the problem. How those potentially *confounding* variables are related to outcomes often can be characterized mathematically, and outcomes then can be adjusted for any differences between clients on those variables. Hopefully, what remains after these *propensity score adjustment* analyses are the differences in outcomes that would have been found if clients who did and did not participate in the program were similar on all possibly confounding characteristics. Sometimes this method of adjustment works and sometimes it is overwhelmed by the complexity of relationships between confounding variables and outcomes (see Graham, 2010; Schneeweiss et al., 2010). Often, postadjustment differences between conditions before treatment are judged for their size (often their *effect size*).

Yet more alternatives: Sort-of experimental approaches. Often going by the elegant term quasi-experimental designs (QEDs; Shadish, Cook, & Campbell, 2002), this family of alternatives to randomized trial designs is frequently more feasible, often more ethical, and occasionally even more acceptable than experimental evaluation designs that randomize clients to program or waiting list conditions. Program evaluations often are funded for and focused on one program, not one program versus competitors. In situations in which a single program is being evaluated, and especially when it cannot be compared with another program or a counterfactual, QEDs are opportunistic: They can be used only in certain contexts. For example, if a long stream of measurements exists from the time before the program is implemented, and if similar measurements can be taken during and after the program is implemented, *and* if the direction or trend of the preprogram measures is simple and clear, effects of the program can be detected in a change in the direction of the measures.

For instance, if motorcycle fatalities have increased steadily over the past 24 months (after adjustment for seasonal variation in the number of motorcycles on the roadways), and a motorcycle awareness program is instituted for drivers of cars, a change in slope or intercept of the motorcycle fatalities trend line beyond the variability expected by chance could show the program's outcome. In other words, the implementation of the program should create a *discontinuity* in the pattern of fatalities over time (and over seasons). Because statistical regression often is involved in quantitatively characterizing or *modeling* the trend over time, this is called *regression discontinuity* QED (see Chapter 27 of this volume). This QED does not provide a viable evaluation, however, if measures of outcome are not available for a number of points before as well as following initiation of the program or if the outcome measure itself changes after program implementation. Readers might wonder how a measure itself could change, but this can happen in program evaluation when persons compiling motorcycle fatality data become aware of how their employment status may change if the motorcycle fatality reduction program does not have the desired outcomes. Similar QEDs also can be used to examine effects of policy changes on health. For example, Stolzenberg and D'Alessio (2003) found little effect of the repeal of a motorcycle helmet use law on injuries or fatalities.

A rich variety of similar, ingenious research designs are detailed in the chapter on QEDs in this handbook (see Chapter 26 of this volume) and time-series designs (see Chapter 32 of this volume). Often these designs can be readily adapted to entire programs, too, by simply changing the level of specificity. Some QEDs compare outcome measures that are hypothesized to change as a result of specific operations in the program against outcome measures that are not supposed to change as a direct result of those program operations. For instance, if a reading comprehension enhancement program is implemented in a school, measures of reading comprehension should change but performance in mathematics might not. Essentially, one outcome measure serves as a "control" for the other targeted outcome. If both reading and math scores improved similarly, the program evaluation is inconclusive. Perhaps the reading comprehension program had more comprehensive effects than originally assumed. More likely, social pressure or teachers' increased expectations for student performance were responsible for the improvement, rather than the program.

Other versions of QEDs focus the same basic program first on one outcome measure, then on another, and hypothesize that the outcome measures should change only when the program is focused on the specific outcome. In one version of what are termed *multiple baseline designs*, Lombard, Neubauer, Canfield, and Winett (1991) first measured sunscreen use by children, adults, and lifeguards at two community pools; then introduced at one pool a variety of social psychological interventions to increase sunscreen use; and later tried the same interventions at a different pool. Sunscreen use increased in response to interventions at the first pool in particular, and more for some groups of participants than others. Yet another version of the multiphase QED measures outcomes before, during, and after the program, often reinstituting the program in the end. With A assigned to the baseline phase and B assigned to a program implementation phase, this would be called an *ABAB design*.

Evaluation findings modify logic models. In terms of logic models guiding a program evaluation, the result of these research designs and analyses could include erasure of some hypothesized connections between activities and outcomes and the creation or strengthening of other hypothesized connections. The simplified, empirically validated logic models then could provide guidance for future attempts to achieve similar outcomes in replications of the programs. Activities that were not found to contribute to outcomes could be dropped from future programs.

It is possible that specific program activities lead to specific outcomes only for some groupings of clients. For example, some types of psychological intervention may lead to reduced problem behaviors only for clients who are cognitively capable of comprehending critical concepts of the intervention or who have the self-management skills to implement the interventions in their daily lives. Whatever the reason, analyses of activity–outcome relationships in programs often consider how client gender, age, and ethnicity may moderate achievement of program

outcomes and then report these findings along with the more global failure or success to achieve outcomes by clients overall.

Activity–Process–Outcome Evaluations

Few program operators, and fewer individuals providing or receiving services within a program, would assert that the procedures of the program and the activities in which clients engage directly cause outcomes. Asking students to compete in generating as many words as possible in 60 s to fill in a blank in a sentence does not itself build vocabulary. Asking a client to talk about his or her problem, and listening to it, does not directly solve emotional problems. Even offering clean hypodermic needles in exchange for used ones does not by itself reduce transmission of HIV. And showing one's children how to balance income and spending does not by itself cause them to treat their money with greater care.

Instead, a variety of biological, psychological, and social (in a word, *biopsychosocial*) processes largely unseen and perhaps unseeable may mediate the relationship between program activities and the most immediate outcomes. Isolation of these processes is a task for which psychologists and psychological theories are uniquely suited. For example, students' embarrassment at not being able to generate more than a few words to fill in blanks in seemingly simple sentences might be said to moderate their interest in, search for, and retention of synonyms. When clients attempt to put their problems into words to communicate with a therapist, they may become aware of a number of things, including possible biases in the way they present themselves to others, possibly fostering personal growth and more mature social interactions in the future. Offering clean needles to addicts may result in reduced HIV rates in the community via a number of causal pathways, including increased awareness of the dangers of using needles already used by others. Similar activity–process–outcome relationships could be diagrammed, and tested empirically, for the education, health care, and military programs for which activity–outcome relationships were logic-modeled in Figure 30.1.

When the malleable biopsychosocial processes that likely determine outcomes are identified by theoretical research in a field, a program developer then is able to find activities that can affect the processes critical to achieving the desired outcomes. Indeed, a program evaluator's conceptualization of the worth of many theories is that they can explain why different interventions result in particular outcomes in clinical, business, health, and military settings. Thus, the value of theories of social, health, and community psychology for program evaluators may lie in specifying which social and community processes are responsible for outcomes, such as theft and assault. The importance of theories of neuropsychology is, for program evaluators, their ability to isolate the key neurological processes that need to be changed to achieve the desired outcomes. If, for example, certain neurotransmitters and reuptake inhibitors need to be modified to allow cognitive–behavioral treatments for substance abuse to succeed, perhaps program success can be better evaluated, understood, and achieved.

By including measures of the principal processes hypothesized to determine program outcomes as well as measures of program activities and outcomes, program evaluation may be able to identify causes of program failures as well as program successes. For example, Kissel (1997) showed that a program intended to prevent drug abuse in fourth graders by using activities designed to increase social responsibility and other processes actually *decreased* participants' social responsibility (especially girls' social responsibility). Kissel found that the drug prevention program actually increased willingness to use drugs as well as use of gateway drugs (cf. Yates, 2002). Fortunately, perhaps, children in the various conditions eventually were indistinguishable in terms of measured willingness to use drugs and actual use of gateway drugs.

Cost–Activity–Process–Outcome Evaluations

Costs are important to those who decide to fund programs. When broadly defined as resources rather than money (Yates, 1980, 1994), costs are important to clients and communities, too. Even when the desired outcomes occur, and are conclusively demonstrated to be the result of the biopsychosocial processes evoked by the activities verified as being performed by the program and its participants, a program still may not be funded or continued because of the resources it requires. Funders, providers, individuals receiving services, or community members may prefer an alternative program if that alternative achieves similar outcomes with fewer of whatever resources are most scarce. Usually the scarcest resource is money, but sometimes it also is the time of clients as well as program providers, affordable transportation, reliable communications, safe space, or tolerance for having homeless families, former felons, or former substance abusers living in the community. Sometimes the alternative to an innovative program is no program at all, and sometimes this null program is preferred precisely because it does not appear to cost anything. Even positive evaluations of programs have resulted in no program being implemented because the program would exceed perceived constraints on available funds (e.g., "nice pilot study, but we just can't afford that new program") or because of who would be tolerated in the community (e.g., "we just don't want any drug abusers coming into our neighborhood, even if they are in treatment and do get better and eventually go to the health clinic less; while in treatment they'll attract drug dealers, who will then attract more drug abusers").

Often going by the amorphous and ambiguous term *cost study*, an increasing number of program evaluations include measures of costs and well as outcomes. Some cost-inclusive evaluations even measure budget limits and constraints on other resources, such as the amount of volunteered time and donated space available in a community (Yates, 1980, 2010).

Cost analysis.   By themselves, cost studies can be just that: evaluations that measure the value of the resources consumed by the operation of a program. These can be complex evaluations. Accounting records can be analyzed to describe the amount of money spent to procure each major resource, such as dollars paid for staff salaries and benefits, or for lease of program facilities. Total dollar amounts, however, describe the amounts and types of resources used in a program about as well as kilograms describe the amounts and types of vegetables sold in a grocery store: maybe globally, but not at a level of specificity that allows replication of the program. For a cost evaluation of most programs, accounting records need to be augmented by surveys of providers, clients, and community members to include quantitative measures of the amount of resources used by the program that do not appear on accounting records. These include volunteered time and volunteered overtime from program staff, space donated by community or government organizations, payroll and other services provided by organizations within which a program may be affiliated, and equipment and materials donated by persons seeking tax deductions.

A variety of procedures are available for measuring the amount and monetary value of these resources (cf. Yates, 1999), including structured interviews (e.g., French, Salome, & Carney, 2002). Placing a dollar or euro or yen sign in front of a number does not guarantee its reliability or validity. As with any other measure of any other variable, reliability and validity of cost assessments are of concern and need to be (and can be) measured and researched. Because programs often find continued operation difficult without having clients appear at their doors on a regular basis, some cost-inclusive evaluations measure the amount of client time spent engaged in activities related to the program as well as client time spent in sessions and other structured program activities. Time and money spent getting to and from the program can be substantial in urban and especially in rural environments; not including client transportation time in an evaluation could lead to erroneous conclusions, for example, that an outpatient program would be less expensive than an inpatient program. Less expensive *for whom* is an important question.

Cost–benefit analysis. Often, a cost evaluation will include measures of outcomes as well as measures of the resources used to produce those outcomes. In a cost–*benefit* analysis (CBA), outcomes that are monetary (such as increased client income following program participation) are compared with the value of resources used by the program, that is, the program costs. Because outcomes and costs are measured in the same units in CBA (usually

monetary ones), one can calculate ratios of outcomes divided by costs as well as net benefits. These are intuitively understandable and seem to be obvious decision aids. Decisions about program funding seem easier when one can see whether a program is "worth it" if its outcomes exceed its costs, that is, if the outcomes-to-cost ratio exceeds one or if outcomes minus costs exceed zero. Nevertheless, these ratios and the findings and funding decisions made with them can be no better than the benefit and cost data on which they are based. Focusing on the monetary outcomes also may bias funding decisions against programs whose primary outcomes are neither monetary nor readily monetizable, for example, enhanced well-being, quality of life, enlightenment, and satisfaction.

Cost-effectiveness analysis In a cost-*effectiveness* analysis (CEA), the types and values of resources consumed by the program (its costs) are compared with the *non*monetary outcomes of that program. As an alternative to CBA, CEA is often preferred by human service providers and human service evaluators because it seems less myopically focused on the pecuniary. Because costs and outcomes are measured in different units in CEA, however, decision makers sometimes are stymied by such evaluation findings as "$10,225 of personnel time, space, equipment, and materials were required, on average, to move clients from clinical to nonclinical scores on the Beck Depression Inventory." Although this figure certainly can be meaningful to persons caring for those with depression, many potential funders find it difficult to judge whether that program is better or worse than a program using different amounts to achieve different outcomes, for example, "$7,890 was spent, on the average, to increase vocabulary 10% in fourth graders who began the year reading at a third-grade level." The limited application of CEA to comparisons of programs that have similar outcomes (and to waiting list and similar control conditions for which similar outcomes can be measured) has increased the popularity of a third approach to including costs in evaluation.

Cost-utility analysis. What if outcomes of diverse programs in education, health, mental health, business, and even some military venues could be translated into the same units? Then programs in these different areas could be compared in terms of their outcomes and their costs and cost-effectiveness. Although economists have searched for measures that could be applied with reliability to diverse programs, such as clients' willingness to pay for services, the face validity of such measures diminishes when one realizes that many choices made by people in the marketplace of goods and services are not always rational and perhaps need not be (Kahneman, 2003). *Years of life* is an appealing measure of program outcome, especially to those of us who may have fewer years left to live than we already have lived, but the *quality* of those years seems as important as its quantity. By surveying persons who do and do not have different disabilities, two outcome measures common to most programs one could evaluate have been developed: *quality-adjusted life years* (QALYs) and *disability-adjusted life years* (DALYs). Incorporating these into CEA results in measures of cost per QALY and cost per DALY, both forms of what is now termed *cost-utility analysis* (CUA). Presenting the best of CEA and CBA, CUA promises a universal metric for decision makers who include costs in their evaluations as well as outcomes. More seasoned cost-inclusive evaluators recognize, however, that simple ratios of cost to QALY or cost to DALY can obscure important relationships between those indexes and other program characteristics, including program size. There may be, for example, economies of scale in program operations, such that cost to QALY varies according to program size as much or more so than the specific activities of the program.

Cost-activity-outcome analysis. Including the specific activities of a program in its evaluation, along with its costs and outcomes, is done in some CEAs and CBAs that focus on understanding and improving programs. It often is hoped that for programs not generating desired outcomes, using existing program resources to support different activities might allow the same program to improve. Some programs use activities corresponding to particular theories or models of the condition they are trying to address. For example, a program for consumers of mental health services might posit that providing

opportunities to receive support from other consumers of similar services could improve outcomes compared with a program providing only traditional therapies. Different models of doing this have, in fact, been compared in a variety of multisite evaluations. Outcomes and costs differed between sites using different models of how to provide support to consumers from consumers, but the manner in which the models were delivered (i.e., the *delivery system*) seemed to determine costs more than the particular model being applied. Programs that could adjust staff, space, and other resources in response to changes in demand for services were the least costly and, coincidentally perhaps, were the most effective (cf. Yates, 2010).

Cost-activity-process-outcome analysis. To truly understand a program, however, means understanding the psychological as well as the economic and other *mechanics* of the program. Linkages between outcomes and activities of programs are, as noted, likely mediated by psychological processes. Including these processes in a comprehensive evaluation of a program can improve understanding of why programs sometimes do not generate the outcomes intended. Considering costs can assist in this form of formative evaluation. In the substance abuse–prevention program evaluation already detailed, the iatrogenic component identified in the evaluation was small student groups (Kissel, 1997). These groups were offered despite the possibility, now increased in likelihood in retrospect, that increasing social interaction between students who were considered at risk for substance abuse might not generate the outcomes desired. Why were these groups included among program activities? One factor could have been their *cost*. Among the activities formally recognized in the program plan, small student groups were the least costly component in terms of staff, space, and other resources. For programs that include activities with varying impacts on processes that are linked to the goal outcomes, and that consume different amounts of resources such as staff and client time and space, linear programming and other forms of *operations research* can incorporate findings from evaluations of costs, activities, processes, and outcomes to decide which activities to use and how much in a program (Yates, 1980, 1996).

CRITICAL ISSUES IN PROGRAM EVALUATION

Effects of Interest Group Perspectives on Program Evaluation

Program evaluation usually is very *participatory*: The opinions of those persons, communities, government agencies, corporations, and military units instigating, participating in, and affected by program evaluations can and often do affect everything about an evaluation. The influence of these stakeholders ranges from selection of measures through the evaluation research design proposed, the design actually implemented, whether the measures proposed are actually used, and the analyses planned and conducted to the results found, reported, and used, ignored, or transformed into somewhat or entirely different findings.

Evaluators are not the only ones in charge. Researchers accustomed to settings in which only one interest group is empowered, that is, the researchers themselves, may be surprised when they venture into the world of program evaluation: They are not the only ones in charge, even of the evaluation. In program evaluation, the persons leading the evaluation may come from a research community, but they now are engaged in a different community. Their opinions matter, often, but they no longer have final say in any matter. Program evaluators are recognized as having great knowledge and often wisdom about how to do some forms of evaluation. Nonetheless, evaluations that can affect whether a program is initiated, funded, continued, grown, or terminated necessarily get the attention and involvement of those who operate the program, those who are served by it, those who fund it, and those who can be affected by it and by changes in its operations. In such a potentially volatile context, program evaluators may experience not only resistance to evaluation but also subterfuge and even litigation. Program evaluation is not for the faint of heart. Little worth doing is easy; program evaluation is no exception.

Cultures and measures. Training in cultural competency is increasingly necessary for evaluators to be effective (see Orlandi, Weston, & Epstein, 1992). In some evaluations, relatively minor steps can satisfy demands of competing interest groups. Diverse viewpoints on what program outcomes are or should be might be represented adequately by including measures favored by each stakeholder group. This strategy works well only if the evaluation budget allows it and if those responding to the measures have sufficient time. More challenges emerge if some interest groups wish certain measures to *not* be used, and if those are precisely the measures that other interest groups advocate. This is often the case with outcomes that are viewed as biased against the culture or norms of some interest groups. In addition, some outcome measures may be agreed on by several stakeholder groupings, but goals for movement on those measures can be in direct opposition. For example, in evaluating monetary outcomes of adding consumer-operated mental health services to traditional mental health services, I found that several programs hoped that the use of health services by consumers would increase permanently, whereas others hoped that the use of health services would decrease after a transient increase.

Some stakeholders also advocate that certain evaluation designs be used and that others be avoided. Some evaluators posit that classic experimental designs favor theories and approaches to social change that evolved in concert with those designs. For example, Guba and Lincoln (1989) asserted that the rigors and measures associated with randomized clinical trials favor traditional interventions developed by established behavioral and medical scientists (see also Seigart & Brisolara, 2002). Case studies and qualitative as opposed to quantitative analyses may, it has been argued, be more likely to lend support to certain alternative programs (cf. Guba & Lincoln, 1989). Some client groups, including African Americans and Native Americans, have long, terrible histories of being abused by researchers (cf. Kazdin, 2003). This has led to strong resistance to any evaluation that seems akin to research (as much evaluation does). These and other client interest groups often and rightly request special assurances and internal controls in the evaluation, or they may decide that the effort and risks of participating in evaluations simply are not worth, for them, the sometimes questionable results of evaluation. Cultural differences can be so large that outcomes may be defined less by empirical evidence collected by the evaluator on standardized measures from the research literature than by information sifted by clients through belief- and trust-based *indigenous frameworks* developed by their communities (see LaFrance, 2004). Differences of culture, and of school of thought within cultures, also can determine what biopsychosocial processes are posited, measured, and avoided as well as what activities are or are not acknowledged as being part of the program. Consider, for example, how behavioral versus psychoanalytic theories might explain effects of pregnancy prevention education, or how different communities might or might not allow the full range of their religion-based program activities to be measured. Ideally there would be no problems with resistance to measurement and evaluation of any costs, activities, processes, or outcomes, but in evaluation practice there often are.

Stakeholders, costs, and monetary outcome measures.

In some evaluations, too, inclusion of program costs as well as monetary outcomes is anathema to some stakeholders. Many researchers do not want to involve costs in considerations of whether a type of program should be listed in rosters of evidence-based programs. Often it is felt that the effectiveness of a program should be demonstrated first and that inexpensive means of delivering the effective interventions can be developed later once the interventions are listed officially as evidence-based practices. Some providers and clients also wish to avoid the inclusion of program costs in program evaluations, fearing that if the cost figures coming out of the evaluation are too high, then even a program shown to be effective will not be funded. Monetary outcomes generate similar negative feelings in a variety of interest groups, even though employment and the income that results from it can be strong arguments in favor of funding. In these and similar situations, evaluators need to communicate clearly with all interest groups to keep them informed about the likely ramifications of excluding certain measures and evaluation designs.

Summative Versus Formative Evaluation

Formative evaluation not only is a long-recognized type of evaluation, as noted at the start of this chapter, but also is a potential antidote for the conceptualizations of evaluation that generate fear, resistance, and often failure of an evaluation. Formative evaluation can inform and even advocate for those who provide and receive services from the program, empowering those who usually are the subjects *of* evaluation, rather than just illuminating awareness of program activities and outcomes for funders.

To understand a program frequently requires more information and time than is necessary to judge a program, making formative evaluation more demanding on clients, program operations, and communities affected by the program. The more costly nature of formative evaluation makes it less popular with some funders and evaluators, but ultimately it may more useful to all concerned. In contrast, program evaluation often is assumed to be summative by those unfamiliar with the field and by those who have much to lose in an evaluation. Telling stakeholders that you are "here to help" at the start of an evaluation can, dishearteningly, communicate something entirely different than what was intended. Often, some stakeholders fear that the evaluation will show that the program is not working or is not affordable. Sometimes these fears are unrealistic; other times they are not. No matter how formative the evaluator says the evaluation will be, others involved in the evaluation realize that evaluation findings are not the property of the evaluator but of the evaluation funders and then, once they are presented and published, of the professional and lay public. Funders often make it clear the programs that do not work should not receive funding. The suggestion that providers surely would not wish to participate in a program that was not working, or that was unduly expensive, sometimes falls on the ears of providers more concerned with maintaining their employment.

Meta-Evaluation

Does evaluation work? Is evaluation worth it? These questions, identified as forms of *meta-evaluation* by Scriven (1969; see also Cooksy & Caracelli, 2005; Stufflebeam, 2001), are so rarely asked by evaluators as to suggest minor hypocrisy. Understandably, like most professionals, evaluators have to have faith in their efforts to pursue them despite the many challenges they face, some of which are introduced in this chapter. And, evaluating evaluation is something that happens all the time during any evaluation. Some stakeholder somewhere is almost always asking, "Is this evaluation worth it?" Sometimes that question occurs to evaluators as well.

Rigorous studies of the outcomes of evaluation are lacking. The random assignment of programs to evaluation and nonevaluation (or waiting-for-evaluation) control conditions seem absent in the literature. Formal analyses of the potential, but by no means guaranteed, cost-effectiveness, cost-benefit, and cost-utility of evaluation are unknown. Arguments readily can be made that without evaluation, programs and treatments and prevention efforts might be funded and operated that had either no perceivable outcomes (other than increased income for program providers) or iatrogenic outcomes for clients or communities or others. Certainly such results have been found for well-meant efforts in treatment and prevention (e.g., Yates, 2002). If evaluation had been conducted earlier, or even built into the programs from the beginning, perhaps the damage to clients could have been avoided and the funds used for better purposes. That, however, cannot be said with certainty. This is just one of many areas in which program evaluation can be expected to venture into its promising future.

References

Aos, S., Lieb, R., Mayfield, J., Miller, M., & Pennucci, A. (2004). *Benefits and costs of prevention and early intervention programs for youth* (Report to the Washington State Legislature). Olympia, WA: Washington State Institute for Public Policy. Retrieved from http://www.wsipp.wa.gov

Clements, P., Chianca, T., & Sasaki, R. (2008). Reducing world poverty by improving evaluation of development aid. *American Journal of Evaluation, 29,* 195–214. doi:10.1177/1098214008318657

Collier, P. (2007). *The bottom billion: Why the poorest countries are failing and what can be done about it.* Oxford, England: Oxford University Press.

Cooksy, L. J., & Caracelli, V. J. (2005). Quality, context, and use: Issues in achieving the goals of metaevaluation. *American Journal of Evaluation, 26,* 31–42. doi:10.1177/1098214004273252

Cronbach, L. J., Ambron, S. R., Dornbush, S. M., Hess, R. D., Hornik, R. C., Phillips, D. C., . . . Weiner, S. S. (1980). *Toward reform of program evaluation.* San Francisco, CA: Jossey-Bass.

French, M. T., Salome, H. J., & Carney, M. (2002). Using the DATCAP and ASI to estimate the costs and benefits of residential addiction treatment in the State of Washington. *Social Science and Medicine, 55,* 2267–2282. doi:10.1016/S0277-9536(02)00060-6

Graham, S. E. (2010). Using propensity scores to reduce selection bias in mathematics education research. *Journal for Research in Mathematics Education, 41,* 147–168.

Guba, E. G., & Lincoln, Y. S. (1989). *Fourth generation evaluation.* Newbury Park, CA: Sage.

Guttentag, M., & Struening, E. L. (1975). *Handbook of evaluation research* (Vols. 1–2). Beverly Hills, CA: Sage.

Howard, K. I., Kopta, S. M., Krause, M. S., & Orlinsky, D. E. (1986). The dose–effect relationship in psychotherapy. *American Psychologist, 41,* 159–164. doi:10.1037/0003-066X.41.2.159

Kahneman, D. (2003). Maps of bounded rationality: Psychology for behavioral economics. *American Economic Review, 93,* 1449–1475. doi:10.1257/000282803322655392

Kazdin, A. E. (2003). *Research design in clinical psychology* (4th ed.). Boston, MA: Allyn & Bacon.

Kissel, A. V. (1997). *What costs, procedures, and processes are critical to preventing youth substance abuse?* (Masters thesis 8059.) American University, Washington, DC. Available from University Microfilms, Inc. (Order No. 13-88995)

LaFrance, J. (2004). Culturally competent evaluation in Indian Country. *New Directions for Evaluation, 102,* 39–50. doi:10.1002/ev.114

Leventhal, H., Safer, M. A., Cleary, P. D., & Guttman, M. (1980). Cardiovascular risk modification by community-based programs for lifestyle change: Comments on the Stanford study. *Journal of Consulting and Clinical Psychology, 48,* 150–158. doi:10.1037/0022-006X.48.2.150

Lombard, D., Neubauer, T. E., Canfield, D., & Winett, R. A. (1991). Behavioral community intervention to reduce the risk of sun cancer. *Journal of Applied Behavior Analysis, 24,* 677–686. doi:10.1901/jaba.1991.24-677

Mertens, D. M. (2005). *Research and evaluation in education and psychology: Integrating diversity with quantitative, qualitative, and mixed methods.* Thousand Oaks, CA: Sage.

Meyer, A. J., Maccoby, N., & Farquhar, J. W. (1980). Reply to Kasl and Levental et al. *Journal of Consulting and Clinical Psychology, 48,* 159–163. doi:10.1037/0022-006X.48.2.159

Morell, J. A. (Ed.). (2010). *Evaluation in the face of uncertainty.* New York, NY: Guilford Press.

Orlandi, M. A., Weston, R., & Epstein, L. G. (1992). *Cultural competence for evaluators.* Rockville, MD: Office for Substance Abuse Prevention.

Posavac, E. J., & Carey, R. G. (2003). *Program evaluation: Methods and case studies* (6th ed.). Upper Saddle River, NJ: Prentice Hall.

Scriven, M. (1969). An introduction to meta-evaluation. *Educational Products Report, 2,* 36–38.

Scriven, M. (1991). *Evaluation thesaurus.* Newbury Park, CA: Sage.

Schneeweiss, S., Patrick, A. R., Solomon, D. H., Mehta, J., Dormuth, C., Miller, M., . . . Wang, P. S. (2010). Variation in the risk of suicide attempts and completed suicides by antidepressant agent in adults: A propensity score–adjusted analysis of 9 years' data. *Archives of General Psychiatry, 67,* 497–506. doi:10.1001/archgenpsychiatry.2010.39

Seigart, D., & Brisolara, S. (2002). Feminist evaluation. *New Directions for Evaluation, 96*(Winter), 1–2.

Shadish, W. R., Cook, T. D., & Campbell, D. T. (2002). *Experimental and quasi-experimental designs for generalized causal inference.* Boston, MA: Houghton Mifflin.

Silverman, D. (Ed.). (2004). *Qualitative research: Theory, method and practice* (2nd ed.). London, England: Sage.

Stolzenberg, L., & D'Alessio, S. J. (2003). "Born to be wild": The effect of the repeal of Florida's mandatory motorcycle helmet-use law on serious injury and fatality rates. *Evaluation Review, 27,* 131–150. doi:10.1177/0193841X02250524

Stufflebeam, D. L. (2001). The metaevaluation imperative. *American Journal of Evaluation, 22,* 183–209.

Yates, B. T. (1980). *Improving effectiveness and reducing costs in mental health.* Springfield, IL: Charles C Thomas.

Yates, B. T. (1994). Toward the incorporation of costs, cost-effectiveness analysis, and cost-benefit analysis into clinical research. *Journal of Consulting and Clinical Psychology, 62,* 729–736. doi:10.1037/0022-006X.62.4.729

Yates, B. T. (1996). *Analyzing costs, procedures, processes, and outcomes in human services.* Thousand Oaks, CA: Sage.

Yates, B. T. (1999). *Measuring and improving cost, cost-effectiveness, and cost-benefit for substance abuse treatment programs.* Bethesda, MD: National Institute on Drug Abuse.

Yates, B. T. (2002). Roles for psychological procedures, and psychological processes, in cost-offset research: Cost–procedure–process– outcome analysis. In N. A. Cummings, W. T. O'Donohue, & K. E. Ferguson (Eds.), *The impact of medical cost offset on practice and research: Making it work for you* (pp. 91–123). Reno, NV: Context Press.

Yates, B. T. (2010). Evaluating costs and benefits of consumer-operated services: Unexpected resistance, unanticipated insights, and deja vu all over again. In J. A. Morell (Ed.), *Evaluation in the face of uncertainty* (pp. 224–230). New York, NY: Guilford Press.

Yates, B. T., & Taub, J. (2003). Assessing the costs, benefits, cost-effectiveness, and cost-benefit of psychological assessment: We should, we can, and here's how. *Psychological Assessment, 15,* 478–495. doi:10.1037/1040-3590.15.4.478

PART V

QUANTITATIVE RESEARCH DESIGNS INVOLVING SINGLE PARTICIPANTS OR UNITS

CHAPTER 31

SINGLE-CASE EXPERIMENTAL DESIGNS

Shireen L. Rizvi and Suzannah J. Ferraioli

Psychology is the scientific study of the mind and behavior. The history of the field is rich with documented phenomena based on the experience of one person (e.g., "Little Albert," Phinneas Gage, "Anna O."). Often, these case examples led to the further development or widely practiced subfields of study, such as behavioral approaches to psychotherapy or neuropsychology. Despite this emphasis on individual behavior, in recent years, psychological research, especially in the area of treatment evaluation, has tended to emphasize large-scale group comparison approaches and deemphasized the study of the single participant or unit. In this chapter, we seek to introduce the reader to single-case experimental designs (SCEDs) as not only a viable alternative to the group comparison approach but also as a more appropriate approach in certain circumstances.

SCEDs are used to empirically examine the effects of an intervention, or other controlled action, on a behavior of interest in one or multiple participants. They are controlled experiments from which valid causal inferences may be drawn. The effects of the intervention are examined by comparing the presence, absence, or rate of behavior during the intervention phase to a period of time when the intervention was absent. In SCED research, there is a heavy reliance on repeated observations over time. These observations begin before the intervention is applied, to establish a baseline period, and then continue through the intervention phase. There are many types of single-case designs, which are examined in detail later in this review. Although the various methods have their own strengths and weaknesses, each provides a strategy for evaluating an intervention with rigor and with attention to both internal and external validity concerns.

In this chapter, we first provide a detailed description of the key components of SCED, which includes a comparison of these components in SCED to the more widely used group comparison approach. Then, a description of the most common SCED methodologies is described. These designs include AB (in which A designates a baseline or *no-treatment* phase and B designates a *treatment* phase), ABA, ABAB, multiple baseline (across subjects, behaviors, and settings), changing criterion, and alternating treatments. We finish by discussing data analysis procedures for SCEDs.

IMPORTANT DESIGN FEATURES IN SCED AND COMPARISON WITH GROUP DESIGN

Research in psychology has historically stressed the importance of both a *nomothetic* (relevance to a group) and an *idiographic* (relevance to the individual) approach. This is perhaps less true in the realm of treatment evaluation, an area of study in which group comparisons are considered the gold standard and, with some notable exceptions, are the most common research design in psychotherapy evaluation. With an increasing emphasis placed on defining empirically supported treatments for psychological disorders, operational definitions of sound experimental design are especially relevant. To this end, the Task Force on Promotion and Dissemination of Psychological Procedures (1995) discussed both

DOI: 10.1037/13620-031
APA Handbook of Research Methods in Psychology: Vol. 2. Research Designs, H. Cooper (Editor-in-Chief)

group design and SCED as appropriate strategies for evaluating treatment efficacy. In this section, the characteristics of SCED are described and then compared with their representation in group design.

Experimental Control

In treatment research, experimental control is achieved by comparing a particular intervention either with a control group or with an alternative treatment approach. It is a common misconception that SCED is synonymous with *case study*, a clinical description of an individual's psychopathology and progression through treatment (Eisenhardt, 1989; Hilliard, 1993; Horner et al., 2005). Case studies are retrospective, nonsystematic accounts of treatment response and are not included as empirical evidence when evaluating treatment efficacy, in part because of the lack of experimental control. In contrast, SCED includes a systematic comparison in that the individual participant serves as his own control. Potential treatment effects are then analyzed by comparing the individual at various points throughout the experimental design using visual (or graphic) analysis. However, with the growing desire to operationalize and document evidence-based practices in the fields of education and special education, more emphasis is being placed on statistical models of analysis to fulfill the requirements of various groups (e.g., the What Works Clearinghouse of the Department of Education). More details on the variations of experimental control in SCED are included in the descriptions of the various design options.

Unlike in SCED, in group design, the behavior of individuals (e.g., number of behaviors per day, ratings on a self-report measure, symptom scores on a diagnostic measure) is averaged with other members of that group and then compared with another (or multiple other) conditions. It would be impossible to meaningfully examine the individual response of the sometimes hundreds of participants enrolled in the study. Instead, the mean rating scores are calculated for each treatment condition and then compared statistically. Through these approaches, variability among group members is thus reduced and conclusions are drawn on the basis of the overall (average) performance of each condition. Statistical analysis is used to objectively determine whether

any differences between groups are based on chance (the *null hypothesis*) or whether existing variability is greater than can be accounted for by chance and is therefore likely representative of a treatment effect (the *alternative hypothesis*). Group designs may include comparisons of a treatment to a control group (i.e., wait-list, no-treatment, or placebo group), comparisons between treatments, or multiple evaluations of one group throughout a treatment (*repeated-measures design*). An important refinement of group design is the *randomized controlled trial* (RCT), a group comparison in which a large number of participants are randomly assigned to treatment conditions (see Chapter 25 of this volume). An RCT, however, is not the only methodology that has sufficient validity to draw robust conclusions regarding treatment efficacy. SCEDs may also compare the presence of an intervention to its absence or withdrawal and compare treatment variations. Although RCTs are heralded as the gold standard of empirical psychological research, they also have some limitations. Although experimental control may be increased with such an approach compared with uncontrolled methods, issues such as variability must be attended to and addressed in a meaningful way so as not to draw inaccurate conclusions about individuals who comprise the broader group.

Variability

Whether it is descriptive, correlational, or applied in nature, research on human subjects consistently documents behavioral variation. Sources of discrepancy can include individual variation as well as variability introduced by external confounds (e.g., maturation, participant characteristics, situational differences). Group design relies on the aggregation of outcomes in large samples to minimize intersubject variability, or variation in response between groups of individuals. Large-group comparisons capitalize on the fact that as sample size increases, the collective performance regresses toward the mean. Although statistically this trend contributes to establishing significant and powerful findings, it can often mask differential treatment response (also see Volume 1, Introduction, this handbook). For example, a study evaluating the effects of a new drug may find a statistically significant treatment effect for those receiving medication compared with a control group. However, this could reflect very large gains for some participants and little or no gains for other participants (or even possibly worsening). Investigations of the *clinical heterogeneity* of the population have suggested the importance of considering individual patient characteristics when evaluating treatment efficacy (Mattocks & Horowitz, 2000). Indeed, results from group comparison designs can only inform us as to the average response to an intervention, even though it is possible that no individual in the study achieved that exact response. Variability between and within participants is usually not discussed.

In applied research, the focus of treatment effects on one participant introduces the issue of intrasubject variability, or the inherent fluctuations in an individual's behavior. SCED strategically diminishes potential external confounds through its various design options; therefore, from an SCED perspective, variability provides valuable information, and it is often highlighted and embraced as important data to understand. Variable data trends frequently guide experimental design and inform treatment decisions. For example, situations in which a participant demonstrates sporadic responding indicates a need to examine the whole or components of a treatment and make changes accordingly. In an analysis of treatment options for *vocal stereotypy* (repetitive, nonfunctional use of words and sounds) in a child with autism, variable data were documented both in the baseline phase and the first treatment condition (Taylor, Hoch, & Weissman, 2005). The investigators moved from a scheduled reinforcement intervention to a differential reinforcement approach, and a dramatic decrease both in the presence and variability of vocal stereotypy occurred in the second and third treatment conditions. Of course, behavioral fluctuation can also signify treatment inefficacy or a weak intervention if it persists across multiple conditions or time points. Thus, these data are also critical in that they prevent the continuation of an unsuccessful approach and encourage the empirical evaluation of potential alternatives.

Variability is an important construct in SCED research. In contrast to group designs in which participants' scores over as few as one assessment point are averaged and compared, SCED requires a careful attention to repeated assessment. Variability is examined and used to determine the effectiveness of a particular intervention.

Continuous Assessment

As alluded to previously, one of the hallmarks of SCED is the use of continuous assessment throughout the evaluation process. Because these approaches use repeated data of one individual, it is not appropriate to use traditional statistical analyses to compare behavior from two points in time (i.e., pre- and post-treatment). In an evaluation of one individual, limits to statistical power interfere with the ability to garner meaningful statistical results from a small number of assessment points. SCED may provide a useful alternative when it is impractical to collect enough data to statistically detect treatment effects. Here, data are collected at systematic intervals throughout baseline, treatment, and possibly post-treatment phases. Continuous assessment is central to SCED in part because of its reliance on visual analysis to determine effects. Multiple data points increase the likelihood that patterns will emerge from the data and that these trends will be observable and reliable. Variability in the data can also become apparent (or be minimized) with continuous assessment as compared with limited behavioral sampling.

The use of continuous assessment also allows for another unique feature of SCED: the possibility of evaluating rapidly changing designs. In a group approach, the treatment design is specified before implementation and outcome data rely merely on pretest and posttest sampling. Alternatively, repeated sampling throughout SCED provides ongoing information on the effects of an intervention as it progresses, and changes to the design can be implemented as the individual's behavior improves, worsens, or remains stable. This degree of manipulation may enhance treatment efficiency, such as in the case of using stimulus fading to decrease fluid refusal in a 6-year-old boy diagnosed with a pervasive developmental disorder and failure to thrive (Patel, Piazza, Kelly, Ochsner, & Santana, 2001). The investigators combined high-calorie nonpreferred fluids (i.e., Carnation Instant Breakfast) with preferred fluids (i.e., water) at an increasing ratio as the child increased his fluid acceptance. Session-by-session data provided ongoing information regarding the child's liquid refusal. By allowing the intervention to flexibly adapt to the participant's performance, the investigators efficiently exacted behavior change within 8 days. This example highlights the ability to tightly control the relationship between intervention and outcome, a dimension that critically relates to the establishment of internal validity and ethical considerations in treatment research.

Behavioral assessment itself differs greatly from the outcome data that are classic of group designs, which are usually characterized by self-report measures, performance on semi- or standardized tests, scores on diagnostic measures, or some combination of these. Again, these types of measures rely on minimizing individual variability by placing a participant along a continuum (e.g., a score on a broad measure of behavior, level of symptom severity) or into a discrete category (e.g., a relative score, a diagnostic label, clinically versus nonclinically symptomatic) that is then averaged with the rest of the group and compared with alternative conditions (Fava, Rafanelli, Grandi, Conti, & Belluardo, 1998; Sensky et al., 2000; Woody, McLean, Taylor, & Koch, 1999). By contrast, the outcome data of SCED are often characterized by ongoing observation of one or more specific aspect of an individual's behavior in his typical environment. This approach is advantageous in that it allows for a naturalistic measure of treatment effects that arguably contributes to the clinical significance of the intervention. To highlight this point, consider the research on teaching social skills to children with autism spectrum disorders. Rather than rely on standardized interviews and rating scales of socialization, investigators commonly delineate socially relevant dependent variables, such as frequency of appropriate social skills with peers (Laushey & Heflin, 2000), frequency of social initiations (Lee, Odom, & Loftin, 2007), and responses to peer initiations (Owen-DeSchryver, Carr, Cale, & Blakeley-Smith, 2008). The paramount importance of the individual in SCED demands that treatment effects are relevant to a participant's functioning outside a laboratory setting and that benefits in the natural environment are supported by data.

Interobserver Agreement

Experimentally sound methodology in SCED requires careful selection of target behaviors, specifically those that are *observable, measurable, and definable* (Cooper, Heron, & Heward, 2007); these are discussed in more detail later. An o*perational definition* encompasses the minimum characteristics of a behavior required to render its measurement reliable across observers; these traditionally include elements such as topography, rate or frequency, duration, and examples of occurrence and nonoccurrence. A discrete definition of behavior contributes to the internal validity of a treatment and is central to establishing interobserver agreement (IOA), or reliability.

IOA is the extent to which independent observers document the same behavior and are consistent in their recording of that behavior (Cooper et al., 2007; Kazdin, 2010). Achieving IOA is essential for capturing the true nature of an individual's behavior, confirming an adequate operational definition, and reducing potential observer bias. In the field of applied behavior analysis, adequate IOA is most often defined as 80% agreement established across at least 25% to 33% of sessions (Kennedy, 2005). The various approaches to choosing a data-collection method and calculating IOA are beyond the scope of this chapter (for a comprehensive review of these procedures, see Kazdin, 1982; Viera & Garrett, 2005; Watkins & Pacheco, 2000).

Internal Validity

Experimental design ultimately aims to establish a proposed model (in applied research, the intervention) as contributing uniquely to changes in outcome, above and beyond other potential sources of variability. This lofty goal is theoretically impossible to attain, but research rightly prioritizes demonstrating adequate internal validity through various design options. Prospective threats to internal validity provide a framework for examining these issues, and have been excellently delineated by Kazdin (1980, 1982). Environmental and temporal threats can be especially relevant to SCED and include confounds of *history* and *maturation*. The former refers to extraneous events that occur concomitantly with, but are not directly related to, the intervention.

Examples may include a change at home, physical injury, administration of a new medication, or obtaining a windfall. Maturation describes an individual's natural tendency to change over time. In younger individuals, this may involve becoming smarter, hitting developmental milestones, or getting stronger; adult participants may start to feel older, slower, more or less restless, or bored. History and maturation are controlled directly through the focus on the individual and through experimental design in SCED, and both will be discussed in depth later in the chapter.

Intervention-related confounds include issues of *testing, instrumentation,* and *diffusion of treatment.* The use of continuous assessment may exact some systematic change as a result of repeated testing. Practice effects are well documented in research that utilizes standardized and performance-based outcome measures, such as verbal and motor tasks (Petersen, van Mier, Fiez, & Raichle, 1998), cognitive tests (Collie, Maruff, Darby, & McStephen, 2003), and achievement tests (Kulik, Kulik, & Bangert, 1984). These types of assessments are less relevant in SCED, however, because they are generally not conducive to repeated measurement and are broader behavioral targets than are traditionally used. Research suggests that designs utilizing rigorous methodology are less susceptible to testing confounds (Donovan & Radosevich, 1999). Baseline logic also counteracts this particular concern because it is necessary to establish a stable baseline before applying treatment. Experimentally sound SCED includes a baseline phase with repeated assessment, and performance must hold up against potential testing effects before a new phase is initiated. Extended baselines are therefore best practice when testing concerns are raised. Instrumentation issues refer to deviations in the assessment technique throughout the experimental design. The use of human observers to code behavior data reliably introduces possible bias and deviation in scoring over time. Thus, periodic and acceptable IOA checks are used to protect against the threat of instrumentation confounds.

Diffusion of treatment occurs when the effects of an intervention presented to one group (or individual) are inadvertently provided to another group (or individual) who is intended to be in a no-treatment or alternative treatment phase. Instances in which the same interventionist is responsible for manifold treatments or multiple phases of treatment might indicate a diffusion of treatment concern. For example, a teacher running a new reinforcement schedule with one child in her classroom may be likely to unintentionally reinforce other students in the classroom more frequently as well. In these cases, it is important to evaluate baselines and reversal phases to assess for spontaneous therapeutic trends in behavior that do not occur concomitantly with the application of treatment.

External Validity

Once the efficacy of an intervention has been established, it becomes necessary to demonstrate the external validity or generality of the approach. Group work generally focuses on *generalizability across subjects* in an attempt to indicate that effective treatments for a particular sample can also benefit members of the general population. SCED are often erroneously criticized as having low external validity, especially as related to limited sample size (Birnbrauer, 1981). Ostensibly, a treatment established by a large number of participants is statistically more likely to generalize to a population than an approach validated in one individual, particularly when acceptable effect sizes have been established. Group designs are therefore well suited to accurately predicting average performance in new subjects. However, any treatment sample will be composed of responders and nonresponders, and in the absence of moderator analyses, there is no reliable way to determine how that treatment will apply to a specific individual. Although information on general responsiveness is certainly a critical component of empirically validating new treatments, when the goal is to provide treatment in a clinical context, the flexibility and individualization for the client of interest intrinsic to SCED provide an alternative aspect of external validity (Goldfried & Wolfe, 1998). Although interventions will not be adapted in the same way for each subsequent client, the treatment should be similarly flexible to meet those persons' needs.

Additional types of external validity are highlighted in SCED that are less emphasized in other research methodologies. Of particular note are generality across settings, generality across behavior, and generality across time. *Generality across settings* is concerned with the extent to which behavior change persists outside of the treatment context, such as in novel environments, with novel people, and with untargeted materials. *Generality across behavior* describes the extent to which the treatment exacts change in behavior not specifically targeted by the original intervention. For example, parents who provide teenagers with reinforcement for completing homework may also find their children more likely to fulfill their chores. Improvements in behavior are only clinically relevant if they prove robust after the discontinuation of treatment. Maintenance of treatment effects, or *generality over time*, occurs when these benefits persist after treatment components are no longer in place. Longitudinal follow-up assessments are important tools for establishing behavior maintenance as well as other types of generalization effects.

These collective domains of external validity are often included in the research design, such as in the case of multiple baseline across settings designs. Although the primary concern is whether treatment benefits will extend beyond the immediate environment, generalization can be an important part of establishing internal validity as well. To support the supposition that the intervention is uniquely responsible for behavior change whereas external factors remain stable, data trends must be distinctively associated with treatment-related changes. Therefore, during the experimental design, spontaneous generalization can actually weaken the strength of a treatment. For this reason, researchers aim to establish external validity following the completion of an effective treatment, and individual design approaches signal when generalization occurs naturally.

Ethical Considerations

Researchers in applied settings must place considerable emphasis on the ethical implications of empirical procedures. Ethical issues also extend to experimental design, and intrinsic flaws in research methods can limit the justification for employing certain techniques. Perhaps the most commonly raised issue in treatment evaluation research is whether withholding or delaying treatment to

certain groups or persons is ethically justified. The use of wait-list control, placebo, and no-treatment comparison groups has drawn substantial criticism throughout the history of group research (Beecher, 1966). Although these concerns are also valid in the context of SCED, the inherent qualities in these designs tend to safeguard against them. Because the individual often acts as his own comparison, treatment is not withheld completely, and the participant generally receives the intervention after a relatively short baseline. In the case of multiple baseline designs (MBDs), participants in the second, third, or fourth tiers do experience a delay in treatment, but it is usually shorter than that of a wait-list control group.

Certainly, SCED raises its own unique ethical concerns, the most significant of which is the withdrawal of a potentially effective treatment within a reversal, multiple treatments, or changing criterion design (CCD). For example, if self-injurious behavior is the target behavior, withdrawing a seemingly effective intervention to determine whether self-injurious behavior reappears in an ABAB design would be an obviously unethical approach (Rizvi & Nock, 2008). A sufficiently stable baseline must also be present to show convincing treatment effects, which may necessitate a prolonged baseline period without intervening. In these types of situations, the ethics of participant treatment conflicts with the ethics of establishing internal validity and ensuring that the intervention is directly responsible for behavior change. Ensuring this functional relationship can also be considered an ethical obligation in that empirically demonstrating the effectiveness of an intervention prevents the use and dissemination of potential ineffective treatments. This same argument has been used to uphold the use of comparison conditions in group design, and researchers utilizing SCED and group approaches alike must assess the relative merits of each argument to ethically guide their methodological decision making.

SCED METHODOLOGY AND TYPES OF DESIGNS

Common Elements Across All Designs

Before describing the different types of SCEDs that have varying degrees of complexity, it is useful to expand on some of their common features. These features have been outlined more extensively in other writings; interested readers are referred to Barlow, Nock, and Hersen (2009) and Kazdin (2010) for more thorough resources on this topic.

In general, there is standard nomenclature for components of the SCED methodology. A indicates a baseline or no-treatment phase and B indicates a treatment phase. These two components can be combined in multiple ways to illustrate a treatment effect (or lack thereof). For the effects of the intervention to be most clear, it needs to be demonstrated that a target behavior (outcome variable) changes only when the intervention is applied. Without a baseline, it is impossible to determine whether the intervention had a true effect in contrast to whether any changes were attributable to nontreatment factors. The baseline period therefore serves both a descriptive function (i.e., it helps determine the extent of the problem in the participant) as well as a predictive function.

Baseline phases of SCED provide the basis for prediction or the assumption that under the same conditions (i.e., contingencies, setting, time) the behavior will remain the same. That is, in the absence of intervention, prediction suggests that future data can be accurately extrapolated from existing baseline data. Hypotheses generated from prediction are then tested with the application of the intervention. In other words, the question of interest is whether the behavior during the intervention phase differs from what one would predict on the basis of the baseline data.

In terms of features of the baseline period, it is highly desirable to establish what is called a *stable baseline* such that the target behavior is relatively stable during the A phase. The predictive nature of the baseline period makes stability an important feature—if the behavior shows a lot of variability or change in the time before the intervention is applied, it is very difficult to draw valid conclusions about the effects of the intervention. As a case in point, Rizvi and Linehan (2005) attempted to examine the effects of a targeted behavioral intervention to reduce shame in suicidal individuals with borderline personality disorder using a multiple baseline across subject design. Upon attempting to establish

a stable baseline, however, the researchers discovered that the adage of individuals with borderline personality disorder being "stably unstable" (Schmideberg, 1959, as cited in Paris, 2002, p. 315) was applicable. The lack of a stable baseline tempered the conclusions that could be drawn about the effects of the behavioral intervention at reducing shame. Kazdin (2001) described a stable rate of behavior as one in which there is little variability as well as a lack of trend (or slope). Although baselines that are not stable can still be used to demonstrate effects, conclusions drawn from such a study must be more tentative and usually require replication to substantiate claims of effectiveness (see Barlow et al., 2009, for more information about what to do with different baseline patterns).

Another common feature across all designs is the identification of a specific target behavior that is concrete, observable, and measurable. A target behavior could be a score on an assessment measure (questionnaire or interview), physiological measure such as heart rate or galvanic skin response, or a direct observation. The key is that it is operationally defined. The target behavior ideally should be carefully and consistently described, quantifiable, and publicly accessible. Hawkins and Dobes (1975) specified three criteria for a target behavior: objectivity, clarity, and completeness. *Objectivity* is defined as observable characteristics of the behavior of interest or environmental events. *Clarity* refers to the notion that the definition of the behavior be so precise and interpretable that any observer could note its presence (or absence). Finally, the requirement of *completeness* refers to the establishment of boundary conditions such that it is possible to easily determine which responses are included and excluded. For example, it may be specified that a tantrum occurs when a child vocalizes above speaking level, throws items, and stamps his feet, but not when throwing occurs independently of the other two behaviors.

As discussed, continuous and frequent measurement is another hallmark feature of SCED. The same reliable and valid measurement is applied continuously and regularly so that changes over time can be assessed and interpreted. Assessments can occur within the same hour, day, or week. Measurements do not need to occur at equal time intervals, but consistency of measurement often aids in interpretation. Rarely does more than a week transpire between assessments in SCED. If too much time elapses between measurement periods, important data may be lost and it would be difficult to make conclusions regarding the strength of the intervention. The appropriate length of time between assessments will depend on the behavior of interest. Indeed, sometimes having too *short* a time period between assessments could be problematic, as in the case of shame and borderline personality disorder discussed earlier (Rizvi & Linehan, 2005). That is, often more time is needed to reduce variability in responding and to allow a more accurate treatment effect to appear.

Finally, across all SCEDs, it is important that the methodology include the systematic application of the intervention at its designated time and only then. That is, once the baseline period has been established, the intervention should be applied in a consistent and conscientious matter. The key is that the researcher ideally creates a design such that the only difference between the baseline phase and the intervention phase is the intervention. Although extraneous factors can never be ruled out completely, this careful attention to timing and application can reduce the likelihood of carryover effects or other threats to internal validity.

Basic AB Design

The AB design is the simplest of all SCED methodologies. It is also the weakest in terms of validity and is rarely used to demonstrate intervention effects. However, it will be briefly described here because it forms the basis for most other designs. Although it does not have the same degree of experimental rigor as other SCEDs, the AB design is still different than a case study approach in several ways. First, attention is paid to determining a priori an operationally defined behavior, which is monitored for a period of time without intervention to establish the baseline A phase. Second, the intervention B phase is systematically introduced and monitoring continues. Because the implementation of phase changes is dependent on performance, the experimenter can control when the application of treatment occurs. Any changes in

the target behavior from A to B are attributed to the intervention.

There are problems with using this methodology to determine a cause and effect relationship between the intervention and the behavior change. Campbell and Stanley (1966) have classified this as a "quasi-experimental design" primarily because, in the absence of more rigorous control, it is not possible to rule out other factors that might have caused the change. Because there is only one participant or unit in an AB design, threats to internal validity, such as history and maturation may have been responsible for the change in the dependent variable. Despite this limitation, AB designs are often useful in settings in which other types of experimental methodologies are not feasible. For example, in clinical private practice settings, psychologists could use AB designs to demonstrate that their treatment strategies are likely effective for a number of clinically relevant behaviors (Barlow et al., 2009).

As an illustration, a clinician treating a man with severe depression may first have several sessions during which she conducts a thorough assessment and evaluates symptoms. In the first session, she learns that the man spends the majority of time physically in bed, either sleeping or watching television. She asks that he monitor how many hours a day he remains in bed each day between sessions and continues this throughout the assessment period. The clinician then decides, on the basis of her orientation and research evidence, to apply behavioral activation therapy (Martell, Dimidjian, & Herman-Dunn, 2010) starting in the 5th week of treatment and immediately targets hours spent in bed. The client continues to monitor the number of hours in bed, this time as a means of noting treatment response. Hypothetical data for this scenario are displayed in Figure 31.1. The figure demonstrates how one would indicate an AB design with a vertical line to indicate a change in phases from A (baseline/assessment) to B (treatment). More information about how to interpret this information is found in the Data Analysis section.

Many other factors could be responsible for the change in the client's behavior from A to B, besides the therapist's behavioral activation intervention. Having just one participant in a single AB design

Behavior

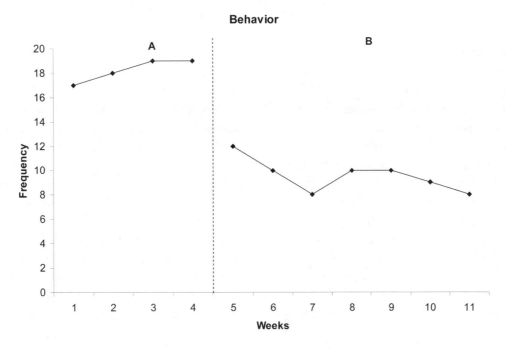

FIGURE 31.1.   A representative AB design.

does not rule out many threats to internal validity. The attention paid to deliberate application of an intervention, after establishing a stable baseline period, and continued monitoring of the target variable are key components of SCED. Furthermore, there is no way to rule out possible social desirability effects or other phenomena related to asking a person to record his or her own behavior. Although these issues are important to consider and may limit the validity of the findings, they have more to do with measurement error than with the choice of design. Adding further elements to the traditional AB design increases the likelihood of being able to make causal interpretations, such as in the designs that follow.

Withdrawal or Reversal Designs: ABA and ABAB

ABA design, a type of methodology also referred to as *withdrawal* or *reversal* design, allows for more definitive conclusions about the effects of the intervention and is preferable, though not always feasible, to AB designs. In an ABA design, the baseline phase A is followed by an intervention phase B and effects of the intervention are monitored. Following this standard protocol, the intervention is removed and monitoring continues in the subsequent,

second, A phase. If the intervention led to improvement in the target behavior during the B phase and then the target behavior reverts to its original baseline levels after it is withdrawn, the researcher can conclude with a reasonable amount of certainty that the intervention, and not other extraneous variables, were responsible for the shifts.

The ABAB design is yet more rigorous than the ABA design and has the added advantage that it ends with the participant on a B phase of the study; thus, hopefully, leaving him or her with the full benefits of the intervention. In this four-phase methodology, the power of the intervention is further strengthened if the effects on the target behavior are notable in both B phases. For example, a relatively simple study was conducted by Martinez and Wong (2009) to examine the effects of reminders (*prompts*) on attendance at groups for Spanish-speaking women who were living in transitional housing because of domestic violence. In this study, the group was the individual unit. During the baseline phase, attendance at group (defined as the number of women attending the weekly group meeting) was observed. The first intervention phase began at Week 3. In this phase, clients received written reminders on their door the morning of the group as well as a telephone call. After 3 weeks of intervention, the prompts were removed (not given) for 2 weeks, and attendance rates were observed. Finally, in the fourth phase, prompts were reinstated. Figure 31.2 clearly demonstrates that there was a relationship between reminders and attendance at the groups.

Although withdrawal or reversal designs are advantageous regarding experimental rigor and direct verification, they can prove impractical or undesirable in certain circumstances (Cooper et al., 2007). Ethical implications of withdrawing an effective intervention are a concern when the targeted behavior is dangerous to the individual or others (e.g., self-injury, aggression, substance abuse; Rizvi & Nock, 2008). Other behaviors, such as acquiring language or a vocational skill, are not conducive to a withdrawal phase because they are unlikely to reverse or be *unlearned*. This instance speaks to the problem of carryover effects, which is the primary obstacle to using reversal designs in some circumstances. If the effects of B are likely to carry over into the next A phase, then the behavior might not revert to baseline levels and it would be more difficult to interpret any changes in the behavior to the intervention. To alleviate these concerns, the MBD was first introduced as an alternative to the reversal (Baer, Wolf, & Risley, 1968) and is now the most widely used design in the field of applied behavior analysis.

Multiple Baseline Design

MBD establishes concurrent baselines and then implements an intervention at staggered points in time across two or more dimensions of the design. These dimensions include the three subcategories of MBD: multiple baseline across behaviors, multiple baseline across settings, and multiple baseline across subjects. In each of these variations, baseline data are collected initially on the target behavior across each dimension, or tier, of the design. When stable baselines have been established, the intervention is applied to the first tier while the other tiers remain in the baseline phase. Decisions regarding when to implement treatment in the second tier vary; some methodologies require therapeutic data trends whereas others rely on a prespecified period of time or number of sessions. The appropriate approach varies as a function of the research question and the independent and dependent variables, but when used once, it should be applied consistently to subsequent tiers. During the application of treatment in the second tier, subsequent tiers remain in baseline while previous tiers remain in treatment. This time-lapsed provision of the intervention is what gives MBD its staggered baselines.

Multiple baseline across behaviors involves choosing two or more behaviors to target with a single intervention in a single participant. Each behavior is

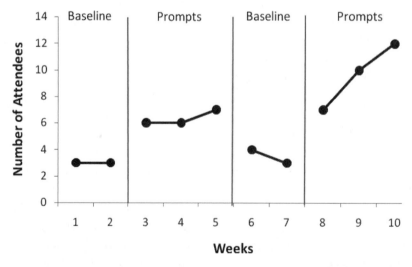

FIGURE 31.2. Example of an ABAB, or reversal, design. From "Using Prompts to Increase Attendance at Groups for Survivors of Domestic Violence," by K. K. Martinez and S. E. Wong, 2009, *Research on Social Work Practice, 19,* p. 462. Copyright 2009 by Sage Publications. Reprinted with permission.

baselined at the same time, and treatment is sequentially staggered across them. Ideally, the chosen behaviors are independent of each other while remaining relevant to the intervention, as illustrated by a study on posture performance by Gravina, Austin, Schoedtder, and Loewy (2008). Self-monitoring techniques (the intervention) were taught to employees performing assembly and computer tasks and were successively applied to various posture behaviors (i.e., back, shoulder, head, leg, arm, and wrist position). The results for Participant 3 are shown in Figure 31.3; these data illustrate increases in *safe* posture across three behaviors (head posture during assembly, shoulder posture during assembly, and head posture during typing) that occur concomitantly with the application of the intervention.

Multiple baseline across settings provides one treatment to a single individual across two or more settings, situations, or time periods. Various dimensions may include time of day (e.g., morning, afternoon, evening), locations (e.g., school, home, community), or interventionists (e.g., parent, teacher, unfamiliar adult). For example, a multiple baseline across settings design was used to evaluate the effects of parent-implemented differential reinforcement on food selectivity (Najdowski, Wallace, Doney, & Ghezzi, 2003). The reinforcement schedule was applied first at home while assessment in an alternative setting (i.e., restaurant) remained in baseline. The intervention was then incrementally applied (i.e., reinforcement providing for an increasing number of bites) in both the home and the restaurant in a staggered fashion. By intervening first at home and then in the community, the parents increased food acceptance in naturalistic and socially significant environments (see Figure 31.4).

Multiple baseline across participants may be the most commonly used variation of the MBD; here, a single intervention targets the same behavior(s) in two or more individuals. Participant baseline data are collected at the same time and treatment is then sequentially applied to each subject. It is recommended that participants share similar characteristics or a treatment environment to reduce the potential influence of extraneous factors. In a study by Chorpita and colleagues, a multiple baseline across participants design was employed to evaluate

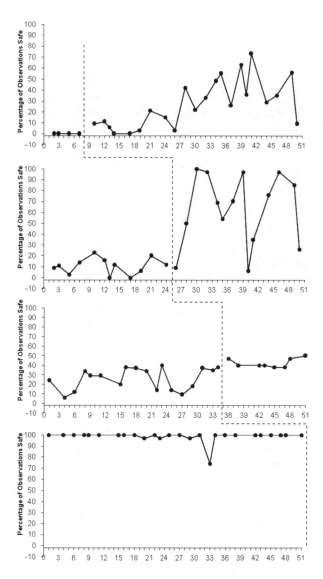

FIGURE 31.3.   Example of multiple baseline design. From "The Effects of Self-Monitoring on Safe Posture Performance," by N. Gravina, J. Austin, L. Schoedtder, and S. Loewy, 2008, *Journal of Organizational Behavior Management, 28,* p. 248. Copyright 2008 by Taylor & Francis. Reprinted with permission.

the initial efficacy of modular cognitive behavioral therapy to treat anxiety in seven Asian and Pacific Islander students ages 7 to 13 (Chorpita, Taylor, Francis, Moffitt, & Austin, 2004). Baselines were staggered according to a fixed-time schedule (i.e., 1.5 or 3 weeks) and stability of the data. Figure 31.5 illustrates decreases in the participants' fear ratings occurring uniquely with the presentation of treatment. These effects are apparent in the changes in behavior trends (i.e., slopes of the data) and the overall decrease in the dependent variable. At times

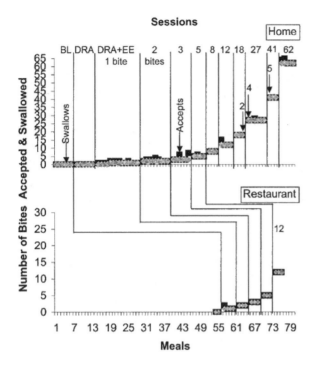

FIGURE 31.4.   Example of multiple baseline design across settings. From "Parental Assessment and Treatment of Food Selectivity in Natural Settings," by A. C. Najdowski, M. D. Wallace, J. K. Doney, and P. M. Ghezzi, 2003, *Journal of Applied Behavior Analysis, 36*, p. 385. Copyright 2003 by the Society for the Experimental Analysis of Behavior, Inc. Reprinted with permission.

these changes occurred immediately following treatment (i.e., Child 1, 2, 3, 6, and 7); for other participants (i.e., Child 4 and 5), a delayed intervention effect was observed.

MBD is not mutually exclusive to other design options, and in many situations the use of a combination design is warranted by the research question or treatment progression. Additional components can be added to an intervention, such as reversals or multiple treatment packages, as long as they are also staggered to create the multiple baseline effect. Combination designs are useful when treatment is not progressing in the first intervention phase or when the unique contribution of treatment components is being evaluated (i.e., component analysis). The inclusion of aspects of a peer-mediated social skills intervention for children with autism was assessed by combining a multiple baseline and a multiple treatment design (Odom, Hoyson, Jamieson, & Strain, 1985). An MBD was initially

used to demonstrate the efficacy of the treatment package as a whole across three settings. Following adequate representation of treatment effects in all tiers, the investigators sequentially removed specific elements of treatment to establish whether they were critical to the success of the intervention. In this case, the data indicated that reinforcement did not contribute to efficacy, whereas provision of teacher prompts appeared to functionally relate to the dependent variable (see Figure 31.6).

Two tiers are required to conduct an MBD, but the use of three or more tiers is considered best practice because it contributes to elements of internal validity. Treatment effects suggested across multiple dimensions provide more opportunities for verification and replication. It may also be in the best interest of the investigator to use three or more tiers to protect against potential two-tier situations in which positive effects are demonstrated in one, but not both, of the conditions. A functional relationship cannot be determined by these data unless they are replicated in additional participants, settings, or behaviors. Replication is demonstrated through observation of a similar change in behavior following the application of treatment in Tier 2 as was seen in Tier 1. Each subsequent tier provides an additional opportunity for replication, highlighting another way in which using more than two tiers can contribute to the internal validity of a treatment.

A few limitations of MBD must be noted. First, MBD relies heavily on independence of baselines (i.e., baselines that are not affected by the presence of treatment in another tier), which cannot always be established. In many cases, interventions implemented for one behavior, individual, or setting may affect subsequent tiers simultaneously, even though they are not directly targeted. These cases of interdependent baselines detract from the capacity to draw convincing conclusions regarding the relationship between the independent and dependent variables. For example, spontaneous generalization of imitation was observed in a multiple baseline across behaviors design for children with autism receiving a social milieu intervention (Stephens, 2008). The provision of treatment to the first targeted behavior (rubbing arm) resulted in increased performance in untrained imitative behaviors (point to ear, hug

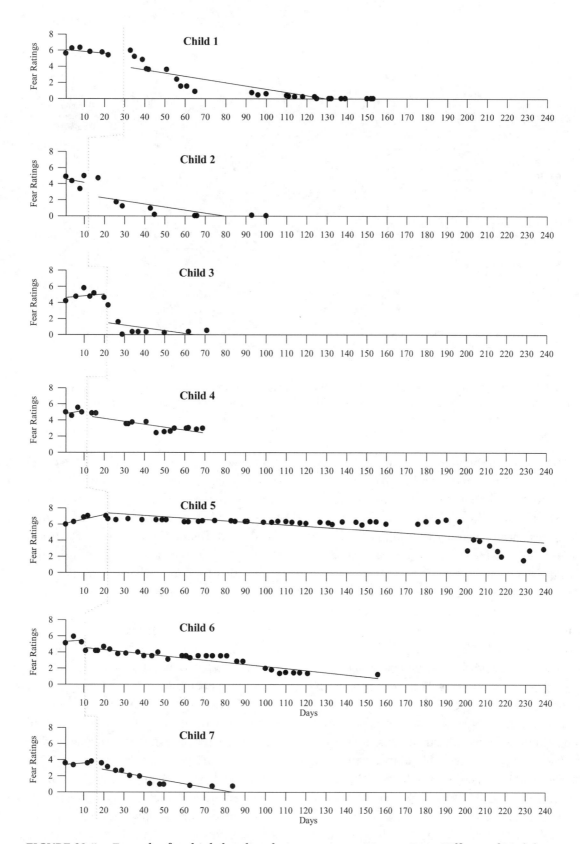

FIGURE 31.5. Example of multiple baseline design across participants. From "Efficacy of Modular Cognitive Behavior Therapy for Childhood Anxiety Disorders," by B. F. Chorpita, A. A. Taylor, S. E. Francis, C. Moffitt, and A. A. Austin, 2004, *Behavior Therapy, 35*, p. 276. Copyright 2004 by Elsevier. Reprinted with permission.

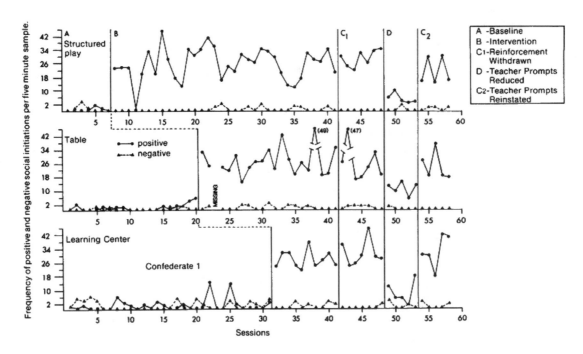

FIGURE 31.6.   Example of multiple baseline design with component analysis. From "Increasing Handicapped Preschoolers' Peer Social Interactions: Cross-Setting and Component Analysis," by S. L. Odom, M. Hoyson, B. Jamieson, and P. S. Strain, 1985, *Journal of Applied Behavior Analysis, 18,* p. 8. Copyright 2003 by the Society for the Experimental Analysis of Behavior, Inc. Reprinted with permission.

self). Inconsistent responding across tiers can also detract from our interpretation of the data. Variable data observed in a design utilizing relatively few (i.e., 2 or 3) tiers profoundly affect internal validity, whereas inconsistent data across multiple tiers limits external validity or the ability to generalize effects to new dimensions.

Another possible limitation of MBD is that sometimes it is difficult to establish a stable baseline, depending on the variable of interest or the population being studied. In these cases, it may be useful to run an extended baseline until the data stabilize or a trend becomes apparent. The use of prolonged baselines raises both ethical and methodological concerns, however. Ethical arguments favor MBD for not withdrawing effective treatment, but staggered baselines effectively withhold treatment for a finite period of time. Again, the ethics of a limited baseline phase must be weighed against the desire to demonstrate empirically that an intervention is responsible for behavior change, and the ethics of implementing an ineffective treatment should be questioned. Methodologically, protracted baselines may invite design flaws such as interdependence,

spontaneous generalization, and effects of repeated testing. These concerns can be partially addressed by carefully monitoring behavior and intervening as soon as stable baselines are achieved. A variation of the MBD, the *multiple probe design* (Horner & Baer, 1978), proactively moderates these issues through systematic yet limited behavioral assessment as opposed to continuous assessment.

Changing Criterion Design

The CCD (Hartmann & Hall, 1976) is distinguished from other approaches in that it does not require the withdrawal of an intervention, an extended baseline, or treatment implementation across multiple behaviors or participants. Instead, it relies on continual, incremental changes in criteria that are matched to the individual's performance in treatment. CCD begins with a baseline phase, which is followed by implementation of treatment. This treatment phase is then divided into subphases, each of which is defined by the criterion rate for the target behavior. Once responding becomes stable in a subphase, an incremental shift in criteria occurs and another subphase is implemented. Baseline serves as a control and allows for *predictions* of behavior, as does each subphase; behavior is expected to remain stable without a criterion shift. Subphases provide opportunities for both *verification* and *replication*. Verification occurs each time the criterion is continued and no change in responding is observed, whereas criterion shifts that are accompanied by behavior change illustrate replication. Criterion reversals can also be incorporated to provide additional evidence for verification. Following a therapeutic trend in behavior, a countertherapeutic criterion shift may be implemented to evaluate whether performance will also reverse. Direct verification is evident when countertherapeutic criterion shifts result in a worsening of outcome.

CCD is often associated with health-related outcomes and, like other designs, can be used to increase or decrease a target behavior. Foxx and Rubinoff (1979) used a CCD to evaluate the efficacy of a monetary reinforcement with response cost procedure in reducing caffeine intake in three adults. The data from Participant 1 are shown in Figure 31.7. This study implemented four treatment phases, or subphases, each incrementally decreasing the crite-

rion below which participants were required to maintain their caffeine intake. When stable responding was achieved in one subphase, the criterion was lowered, and the participant limited caffeine consumption to the new rate to earn a monetary reward.

Alternatively, de Luca and Holborn (1992) used a reinforcement procedure to increase exercise in obese and nonobese boys via CCD. Baseline data were collected on the mean number of revolutions per minute on a stationary bicycle, and treatment was provided in five subphases. As performance stabilized above the criterion line, small increases in the revolutions per minute were introduced. The authors included a brief reversal during the fourth subphase, in which the intervention was withdrawn and the dependent variable decreased. However, a subsequent return to the contingency of the third subphase increased outcome to prereversal levels (see Figure 31.8).

Characteristics of the subphases must be carefully considered when utilizing CCD. First, the length of each subphase must provide adequate opportunity for responding rates to stabilize. Second, the minimum of two criterion shifts generally does not

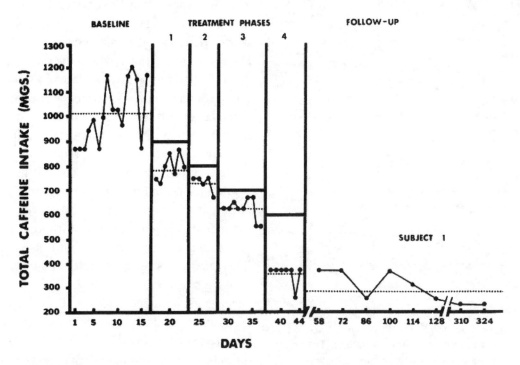

FIGURE 31.7. Example of decreasing behavior with a changing criterion design. MGS. = milligrams. From "Behavioral Treatment of Caffeinism: Reducing Excessive Coffee Drinking," by R. M. Foxx and A. Rubinoff, 1979, *Journal of Applied Behavior Analysis, 12*, p. 339. Copyright 1979 by the Society for the Experimental Analysis of Behavior, Inc. Reprinted with permission.

provide acceptable opportunities for verification and replication. Similarly to the tiers in a MBD, the number of subphases in CCD should sufficiently illustrate the functional relationship between treatment and outcome to enhance internal validity. However, a large number of shifts allows more room for ambiguity as the intervention progresses (as a function of natural variability), and some experimental control may therefore be sacrificed. Third, there are no clear decisional guidelines regarding the magnitude of each criterion shift. In general, performance should guide how large a criterion change should be used.

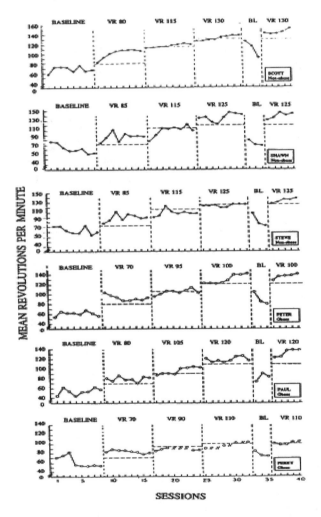

FIGURE 31.8. Example of increasing behavior with a changing criterion design. From "Effects of a Variable-Ratio Reinforcement Schedule With Changing Criteria on Exercise in Obese and Nonobese Boys," by R. V. de Luca and S. W. Holborn, 1992, *Journal of Applied Behavior Analysis, 25,* p. 674. Copyright 1992 by the Society for the Experimental Analysis of Behavior, Inc. Reprinted with permission.

For example, significant, stable jumps in the level of the target behavior may indicate a larger shift in criterion than smaller or variable increases. Best practice suggests using gradual changes to maximize the participant's likelihood of meeting the new criterion.

When determining the appropriateness of CCD there are several limitations to consider. Close correspondence between each subphase and behavior change is essential for establishing the efficacy of the intervention, and target behaviors that may show a treatment delay are not best served by this design. It can be difficult to determine whether correspondence is close enough to infer a functional relationship in the absence of guidelines. If there is doubt, a criterion reversal or treatment reversal phase can add to the experimental rigor of the design. Conversely, rapid behavior change may also interfere with the ability to evaluate treatment effects within CCD; behavior that is likely to be quickly or categorically acquired (e.g., skill acquisition) is better served by a multiple baseline or multiple treatments design.

Alternating Treatments Design

The final type of design to be described is the *alternating treatments* design (ATD), which is primarily used to determine the differential effects of two or more types of treatment within the same individual. An ATD then can be used in place of a standard group comparison design, which would involve a much larger number of participants and resources. In an ATD, two or more treatments (conditions, interventions) are applied in a random order each session with a participant. The target behavior is continuously monitored and any differential effects of the alternating treatments are observed. An ATD can include a baseline period for its predictive function against two or more interventions, but a baseline period is not required in this design.

As in reversal designs, the possibility of carryover effects must be attended to in ATD methodology. In ATD, there is the added possibility of order effects if the alternating treatments are applied in the same order (e.g., Intervention A always precedes Intervention B). If Intervention A is applied in Session 1, but its effects continue into Session 2 when Intervention B is applied, it is difficult to determine whether results from Session 2 are due to Intervention A, Intervention B, or both. This effect is also known as *multiple-treatment interference*. A means of reducing the possibility of interference is to counterbalance the application of the different interventions. Without counterbalancing, the conclusions that can be drawn about the effects of different treatments are limited.

In contrast to every other design described thus far, data for ATD are plotted on two or more lines, with each line representing a different treatment. This structure helps the researcher delineate the differential effects of each treatment. For example, Figure 31.9 details hypothetical data for an ATD with two treatment conditions. In this hypothetical example, assuming that a higher score on the target variable is preferable, one can clearly note the advantage of Treatment A to Treatment B. Furthermore, the seemingly random order of the application of the two interventions reduces the likelihood that the effects are due to ordering or carryover.

There are a few advantages to ATD compared with other SCED methodologies that may make it an appealing option for clinical researchers. For one, it is possible using this design to compare treatment to no-treatment conditions in a rapid manner.

Depending on the nature of the target variable, if there are multiple treatment or training sessions in the same day, or the same week, an ATD can be executed very quickly. A second advantage is that when two or more interventions are compared, it does not involve a withdrawal of treatment and it does not require a baseline phase. Taken together, these advantages mean that it is often faster to execute an ATD and gather a useful amount of data than with other designs. In addition, ATDs are considered even more flexible than other SCED methodologies (Barlow et al., 2009), in that one can begin with active treatment immediately, which is far preferable in most clinical settings and alleviates any ethical concerns about no treatment phases.

DATA ANALYSIS AND SIGNIFICANCE IN SCED

The standard method for evaluating the effects in SCED is visual inspection or graphic analysis. Essentially, this method refers to careful inspection of the plots of data points over time with a clear indication (usually by way of a vertical line) of shifts in phases. The figures interspersed throughout this chapter have demonstrated many different

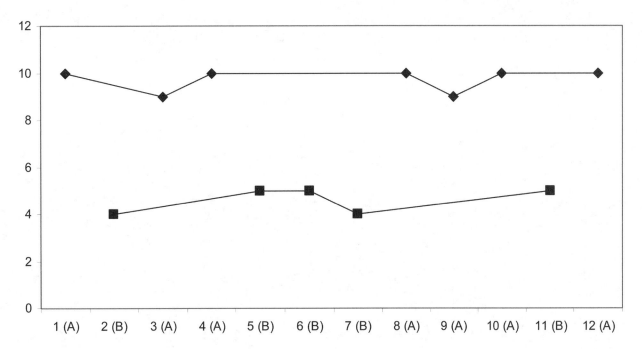

FIGURE 31.9. A representative alternating treatments design.

ways to graph data on the basis of design type. More sophisticated analytic procedures for examining SCED data and time-series designs have been developed (for details on this topic, see Chapter 32 of this volume; see also van den Noortgate & Onghena, 2007). In this section, we focus on the use of visual inspection and also address issues of significance more broadly.

Visual inspection is central to determining the extent of treatment effects, or how much change is observed as a result of the intervention. Data can be examined across several important dimensions. A change in *level* denotes the magnitude of the shift between conditions and signals the immediacy of behavioral response. Changes in level, as seen in Figure 31.10, are determined across phase change lines, between the last data points in one condition and the first data points in the next condition.

Changes in *means* are also assessed across phases and account for shifts in the average rate of performance as conditions are altered. Both level and means provide information on the magnitude of behavior change as treatment is applied, withdrawn, or modified (see Figure 31.11).

Trend refers to the slope of the behavior or the rate of change between phases. Positive slopes indicate increasing trends, negative slopes indicate decreasing trends, and horizontal slopes indicate no trend (see Figure 31.12). Applied research distinguishes between *therapeutic* (in the direction of the desired behavior change) and *countertherapeutic* (in the opposite direction from the desired behavior change) trends. Changes in trend can be especially important when evaluating treatments that may evoke delayed treatment effects.

The *latency* of change refers to the time differential between the phase shift and the response. Large shifts in level denote short latencies, whereas a change in trend may occur with longer latencies. Although brief latencies more strongly demonstrate a tight, functional relationship, delayed treatment effects may have clinical relevance (see Figure 31.13).

Currently, there are no concrete guidelines for visual inspection and determining what constitutes significant change. Researchers rely on consistent patterns and obvious changes in means, level, and trend to document treatment effects. Although these methods are less reliable than statistical analyses,

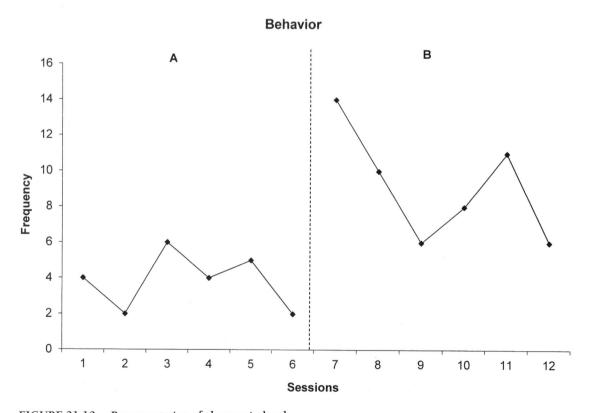

FIGURE 31.10. Representation of changes in level.

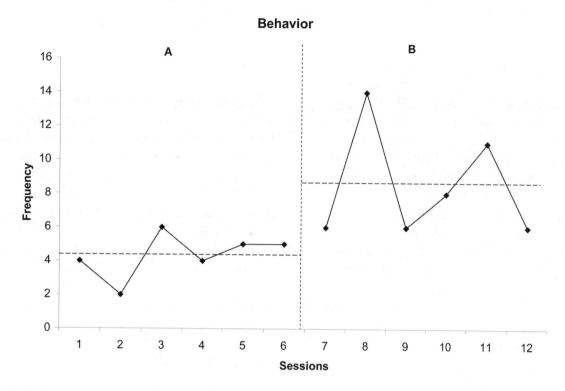

FIGURE 31.11.   Representation of changes in means.

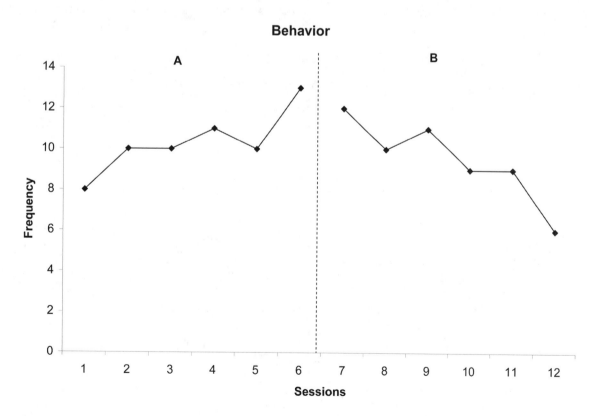

FIGURE 31.12.   Representation of changes in trend.

they are generally considered more conservative because larger changes in behavior are required to constitute a significant effect. Statistical comparisons of means often pick up on very small differences between conditions that may not be observable in an individual's day-to-day life; when visual inspection indicates a treatment effect, it is much more likely to have resulted in applied, observable behavior change (Parsonson & Baer, 1986). Variability in the data can especially detract from the ability to draw conclusions in the data. Small changes in behavior are much more reliably observed when data are stable within conditions. Significant variability requires large changes in behavior for these shifts to be apparent. Again, this can be conceptualized as a more conservative data analysis strategy; when behavior change is observed despite considerable variability, the treatment effects are more convincing.

There has been a recent effort to respond to criticisms regarding the subjective nature of visual inspection and to create more specific guidelines regarding what additional elements of methodology and data in SCED must be present to classify a treatment as evidence based. Formal criteria have been proposed in the areas of autism (Reichow, Volkmar, & Cicchetti, 2008) and special education

(Horner et al., 2005), and more general best practice recommendations are available in the fields of special education (Odom et al., 2005) and school psychology (Stoiber & Kratochwill, 2000). As an example of visual analysis criteria, Reichow et al. (2008) have suggested that 100% of the graphs presented contain less than 25% overlap of data points between adjacent conditions, in addition to a large shift in either the level or trend that coincides with the implementation or removal of the independent variable. These types of criteria operationalize behavior change and lead to interpretations that are more reliable among consumers of research. Additional methodological criteria that have been suggested include specifying the number of treatment effect demonstrations, the need for replication by multiple researchers, and the use of secondary quality indicators, such as treatment fidelity checks, social validity measures, and generalization assessments.

It may also be important to determine whether the results of the SCED also have *clinical significance*. Establishing experimental significance provides empirical support for treatment efficacy, but it lacks indicators of whether the effects of the intervention are important, relevant, or impactful for an individual's

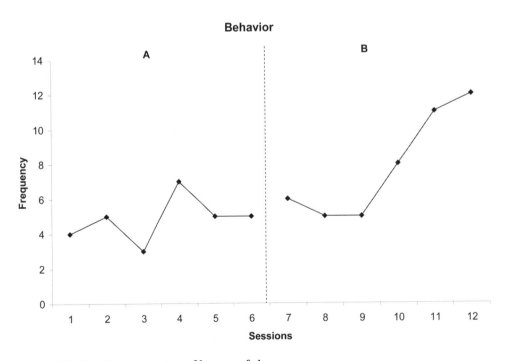

FIGURE 31.13. Representation of latency of change.

life. Measures of clinical significance aim to bridge this gap by supplementing efficiency data with evidence supporting the applied importance of the treatment approach. In many ways, the nature and choice of a continuous assessment measure can contribute to the clinical validity of an intervention. In the example of a social skills intervention for children with autism, outcome data were collected on duration and frequency of social interactions with peers in the students' classroom (Odom et al., 1985). Improvements in these behaviors are likely to be impactful to the participants in the real world and to exemplify the concept of *social validity*. There are several ways to enhance and measure the social validity of an intervention. Treatments that can be applied in naturalistic settings (e.g., school, home, community, work) are more likely to generalize and persist following their completion (Nordquist & Wahler, 1973). Likewise, dependent variables that can be measured in naturalistic settings will be relevant to the individual outside of the treatment setting.

Incorporating social validation measures into research is considered best practice in applied research and is generally unique to SCED. *Social comparison* and *subjective evaluation* indexes are used to establish clinical significance. Social comparison involves comparing participant performance before and after treatment against individuals with typical behavior. Examples include comparing the social skills of a student with autism against those of a typically developing student or the mood score of an individual with depression against the score of a nonclinical person. Subjective evaluation occurs when an expert in the behavior of interest judges the participant's change in behavior. For example, a parent who interacts with her child every day may notice a greater decrease in her son's tantrums than a neighbor who sees him once a week. Social validity measures are not absolutely reliable and may be subject to inherent flaws. It is often difficult to determine a purely "typical" group for social comparison, and subjective evaluation can be susceptible to the bias of the rater. Clinical significance should not be the only criterion by which to establish efficacy, but with experimentally significant data, this additional dimension can greatly contribute to the usefulness of a treatment approach.

CONCLUSION

In this chapter, we have sought to provide an introduction to SCEDs and to stimulate more enthusiasm in using such designs in psychological research. Although group comparison designs have their advantages, it is important to recognize that many of the same questions can be answered with sufficient rigor and validity with far fewer participants and lower cost in single-case designs. A number of different types of designs exist that can be used to study a wide variety of behavioral problems. These include AB, withdrawal or reversal, multiple baseline, changing criterion, and alternating treatments designs. There are also sufficient data analytic techniques to be able to make decisions about statistical and clinical significance. Together, these features suggest that SCEDs offer a great deal of flexibility to the researcher without losing any experimental rigor.

References

Baer, D. M., Wolf, M. M., & Risley, T. R. (1968). Some current dimensions of applied behavior analysis. *Journal of Applied Behavior Analysis, 1*, 91–97. doi:10.1901/jaba.1968.1-91

Barlow, D. H., Nock, M. K., & Hersen, M. (2009). *Single case experimental designs*. Boston, MA: Pearson Education.

Beecher, H. K. (1966). Ethics and clinical research. *New England Journal of Medicine, 274*, 1354–1360. doi:10.1056/NEJM196606162742405

Birnbrauer, J. S. (1981). External validity and experimental investigation of individual behaviour. *Analysis and Intervention in Developmental Disabilities, 1*, 117–132. doi:10.1016/0270-4684(81)90026-4

Campbell, D. T., & Stanley, J. C. (1966). *Experimental and quasi-experimental designs for research*. Chicago, IL: Rand McNally.

Chorpita, B. F., Taylor, A. A., Francis, S. E., Moffitt, C., & Austin, A. A. (2004). Efficacy of modular cognitive behavior therapy for childhood anxiety disorders. *Behavior Therapy, 35*, 263–287. doi:10.1016/S0005-7894(04)80039-X

Collie, A., Maruff, P., Darby, D. G., & McStephen, M. (2003). The effects of practice on the cognitive test performance of neurologically normal individuals assessed at brief test-retest intervals. *Journal of the International Neuropsychological Society, 9*, 419–428. doi:10.1017/S1355617703930074

Cooper, J. O., Heron, T. E., & Heward, W. L. (2007). *Applied behavior analysis*. Upper Saddle River, NJ: Pearson Prentice Hall.

de Luca, R. V., & Holborn, S. W. (1992). Effects of a variable-ratio reinforcement schedule with changing criteria on exercise in obese and nonobese boys. *Journal of Applied Behavior Analysis, 25,* 671–679. doi:10.1901/jaba.1992.25-671

Donovan, J. J., & Radosevich, D. J. (1999). A meta-analytic review of the distribution of practice effects: Now you see it, now you don't. *Journal of Applied Psychology, 84,* 795–805. doi:10.1037/0021-9010.84.5.795

Eisenhardt, K. M. (1989). Building theories from case study research. *Academy of Management Review, 14,* 532–550.

Fava, G. A., Rafanelli, C., Grandi, S., Conti, S., & Belluardo, P. (1998). Prevention of recurrent depression with cognitive behavioral therapy. *Archives of General Psychiatry, 55,* 816–820. doi:10.1001/archpsyc.55.9.816

Foxx, R. M., & Rubinoff, A. (1979). Behavioral treatment of caffeinism: Reducing excessive coffee drinking. *Journal of Applied Behavior Analysis, 12,* 335–344. doi:10.1901/jaba.1979.12-335

Goldfried, M. R., & Wolfe, B. E. (1998). Toward a more clinically valid approach to therapy research. *Journal of Consulting and Clinical Psychology, 66,* 143–150. doi:10.1037/0022-006X.66.1.143

Gravina, N., Austin, J., Schoedtder, L., & Loewy, S. (2008). The effects of self monitoring on safe posture performance. *Journal of Organizational Behavior Management, 28,* 238–259. doi:10.1080/01608060802454825

Hartmann, D. P., & Hall, R. V. (1976). The changing criterion design. *Journal of Applied Behavior Analysis, 9,* 527–532. doi:10.1901/jaba.1976.9-527

Hawkins, R. P., & Dobes, R. W. (1975). Behavioral definitions in applied behavioral analysis: Explicit or implicit. In B. C. Etzel, J. M. LeBlanc, & D. M. Baer (Eds.), *New developments in behavioral research: Theory, methods, and applications* (pp. 167–188). Hillsdale, NJ: Erlbaum.

Hilliard, R. B. (1993). Single-case methodology in psychotherapy process and outcome research. *Journal of Consulting and Clinical Psychology, 61,* 373–380. doi:10.1037/0022-006X.61.3.373

Horner, R. D., & Baer, D. M. (1978). Multiple-probe technique: A variation of the multiple baseline. *Journal of Applied Behavior Analysis, 11,* 189–196. doi:10.1901/jaba.1978.11-189

Horner, R. H., Carr, E. G., Halle, J., McGee, G., Odom, S., & Wolery, M. (2005). The use of single-subject research to identify evidence-based practice in special education. *Exceptional Children, 71,* 165–179.

Kazdin, A. E. (1980). *Research designs in clinical psychology.* New York, NY: Harper & Row.

Kazdin, A. E. (1982). *Single-case research designs: Methods for clinical and applied settings.* New York, NY: Oxford University Press.

Kazdin, A. E. (2001). *Behavior modification in applied settings* (6th ed.). Belmont, CA: Wadsworth.

Kazdin, A. E. (2010). *Single-case research designs: Methods for clinical and applied settings* (2nd ed.). New York, NY: Oxford University Press.

Kennedy, C. H. (2005). *Single-case designs for educational research.* Boston MA: Allyn & Bacon.

Kulik, J. A., Kulik, C. C., & Bangert, R. L. (1984). Effects of practice on aptitude and achievement test scores. *American Educational Research Journal, 21,* 435–447.

Laushey, K. M., & Heflin, L. J. (2000). Enhancing social skills of kindergarten children with autism through the training of multiple peers as tutors. *Journal of Autism and Developmental Disorders, 30,* 183–193. doi:10.1023/A:1005558101038

Lee, S., Odom, S. L., & Loftin, R. (2007). Social engagement with peers and stereotypic behavior of children with autism. *Journal of Positive Behavior Interventions, 9,* 67–79. doi:10.1177/10983007070090020401

Martell, C. R., Dimidjian, S., & Herman-Dunn, R. (2010). *Behavioral activation for depression: A clinician's guide.* New York, NY: Guilford Press.

Martinez, K. K., & Wong, S. E. (2009). Using prompts to increase attendance at groups for survivors of domestic violence. *Research on Social Work Practice, 19,* 460–463. doi:10.1177/1049731508329384

Mattocks, K. M., & Horowitz, R. I. (2000). Placebos, active control groups, and the unpredictability paradox. *Biological Psychiatry, 47,* 693–698. doi:10.1016/S0006-3223(00)00839-8

Najdowski, A. C., Wallace, M. D., Doney, J. K., & Ghezzi, P. M. (2003). Parental assessment and treatment of food selectivity in natural settings. *Journal of Applied Behavior Analysis, 36,* 383–386. doi:10.1901/jaba.2003.36-383

Nordquist, V. M., & Wahler, R. G. (1973). Naturalistic treatment of an autistic child. *Journal of Applied Behavior Analysis, 6,* 79–87. doi:10.1901/jaba.1973.6-79

Odom, S. L., Brantlinger, E., Gersten, R., Horner, R. H., Thompson, B., & Harris, K. R. (2005). Research in special education: Scientific methods and evidence-based practices. *Exceptional Children, 71,* 137–148.

Odom, S. L., Hoyson, M., Jamieson, B., & Strain, P. S. (1985). Increasing handicapped preschoolers' peer social interactions: Cross-setting and component analysis. *Journal of Applied Behavior Analysis, 18,* 3–16. doi:10.1901/jaba.1985.18-3

Owen-DeSchryver, J. S., Carr, E. G., Cale, S. I., & Blakeley-Smith, A. (2008). Promoting social interactions between students with autism spectrum disorders and their peers in inclusive school settings.

Focus on Autism and Other Developmental Disabilities, 23, 15–28. doi:10.1177/1088357608314370

Paris, J. (2002). Implications of long-term outcome research for the management of patients with borderline personality disorder. *Harvard Review of Psychiatry*, 10, 315–323. doi:10.1080/10673220216229

Parsonson, B. S., & Baer, D. M. (1986). The graphic analysis of data. In A. Poling & R. W. Fuqua (Eds.), *Research methods in applied behavior analysis: Issues and advances* (pp. 157–186). New York, NY: Plenum Press.

Patel, M. R., Piazza, C. C., Kelly, M. L., Ochsner, C. A., & Santana, C. M. (2001). Using a fading procedure to increase fluid consumption in a child with feeding problems. *Journal of Applied Behavior Analysis*, 34, 357–360. doi:10.1901/jaba.2001.34-357

Petersen, S. E., van Mier, H., Fiez, J. A., & Raichle, M. E. (1998). The effects of practice on the functional anatomy of task performance. *Proceedings of the National Academy of Sciences of the United States of America*, 95, 853–860. doi:10.1073/pnas.95.3.853

Reichow, B., Volkmar, F. R., & Cicchetti, D. V. (2008). Development of the evaluative method for evaluating and determining evidence-based practices in autism. *Journal of Autism and Developmental Disorders*, 38, 1311–1319. doi:10.1007/s10803-007-0517-7

Rizvi, S. L., & Linehan, M. M. (2005). The treatment of maladaptive shame in borderline personality disorder: A pilot study of "Opposite Action." *Cognitive and Behavioral Practice*, 12, 437–447. doi:10.1016/S1077-7229(05)80071-9

Rizvi, S. L., & Nock, M. K. (2008). Single-case experimental designs for the evaluation of treatments for self-injurious and suicidal behaviors. *Suicide and Life-Threatening Behavior*, 38, 498–510. doi:10.1521/suli.2008.38.5.498

Sensky, T., Turkington, D., Kingdon, D., Scott, J. S., Scott, J., Siddle, R., . . . Barnes, R. E. (2000). A randomized controlled trial of cognitive-behavior therapy for persistent symptoms in schizophrenia resistant to medication. *Archives of General Psychiatry*, 57, 165–172. doi:10.1001/archpsyc.57.2.165

Stephens, C. E. (2008). Spontaneous imitation by children with autism during a repetitive musical play routine. *Autism*, 12, 645–671. doi:10.1177/1362361308097117

Stoiber, K. C., & Kratochwill, T. R. (2000). Empirically supported interventions and school psychology: Rationale and methodological issues—Part I. *School Psychology Quarterly*, 15, 75–105. doi:10.1037/h0088780

Task Force on Promotion and Dissemination of Psychological Procedures. (1995). Training in and dissemination of empirically-validated psychological treatments: Report and recommendations. *Clinical Psychologist*, 48, 3–23.

Taylor, B. A., Hoch, H., & Weissman, M. (2005). The analysis and treatment of vocal stereotypy in a child with autism. *Behavioral Interventions*, 20, 239–253. doi:10.1002/bin.200

van den Noortgate, W., & Onghena, P. (2007). The aggregation of single-case results using hierarchical linear modeling. *Behavior Analyst Today*, 8, 52–75.

Viera, A. J., & Garrett, J. M. (2005). Understanding interobserver agreement: The kappa statistic. *Family Medicine*, 37, 360–363.

Watkins, M. W., & Pacheco, M. (2000). Interobserver agreement in behavioral research: Importance and calculation. *Journal of Behavioral Education*, 10, 205–212. doi:10.1023/A:1012295615144

Woody, S., McLean, P. D., Taylor, S., & Koch, W. J. (1999). Treatment of major depression in the context of panic disorder. *Journal of Affective Disorders*, 53, 163–174. doi:10.1016/S0165-0327(98)00117-7

CHAPTER 32

TIME-SERIES DESIGNS

Richard McCleary and David McDowall

Time-series designs are distinguished from other designs by the properties of time-series data and by the necessary reliance on a statistical model to control threats to validity. In the long run, a time-series is a realization of a latent causal process. Representing the complete time-series as

$$\ldots, Y_{-2}, Y_{-1}, Y_0, \{Y_1, \ldots, Y_N\}, Y_{N+1}, Y_{N+2}, \ldots, \quad (1)$$

the observed series $\{Y_1, \ldots, Y_N\}$ is a probability sample of the complete realization. The probability sampling weights for $\{Y_1, \ldots, Y_N\}$ are specified in a statistical model, which, for present purposes, is written in a general linear form as

$$Y_t = f(a_t) + g(X_t). \quad (2)$$

The a_t term of this model is the tth observation of a strictly exogenous innovation series with the white noise property,

$$a_t \sim iid\ N(0,\sigma^2). \quad (3)$$

The X_t term is the tth observation of a causal time-series. Although X_t is ordinarily a binary variable coded for the presence or absence of an intervention, it can also be a purely stochastic series. In either case, the model is constructed by a set of rules that allow for the solution,

$$a_t = f^{-1}[Y_t - g(X_t)]. \quad (4)$$

Because a_t has white noise properties, the solved model satisfies the assumptions of all common tests of statistical significance.

THREE DESIGN CATEGORIES

We elaborate on the specific forms of the general model and on the set of rules for building models at a later point. For present purposes, the general model allows three design variations: (a) descriptive time-series designs, (b) correlational time-series designs, and (c) experimental or quasi-experimental time-series designs.

Descriptive Designs

The earliest time-series designs used observed cycles or trends in a series to infer the nature of a latent causal mechanism. Historical examples include Wolf's (1848; Yule, 1927) investigation of sunspot activity and Elton's (1924; Elton & Nicholson, 1942) investigation of lynx populations. In both cases, time-series analyses revealed cycles or trends that corroborated substantive interpretations of the phenomenon.

Kroeber's (1919; Richardson & Kroeber, 1940) analyses of cultural change illustrate the poor fit of descriptive time-series designs to many social and behavioral phenomena. Kroeber (1944) hypothesized that women's fashions change in response to political and economic variables. During stable periods of peace and prosperity, fashions changed slowly; during wars, revolutions, and depressions, fashions changed rapidly. Because political and economic cataclysms were thought to recur in long historical cycles, Kroeber tested his hypothesis by searching for the same cycles in women's fashions.

Figure 32.1 plots one of Richardson and Kroeber's (1940) annual fashion time series. Although

DOI: 10.1037/13620-032
APA Handbook of Research Methods in Psychology: Vol. 2. Research Designs, H. Cooper (Editor-in-Chief)

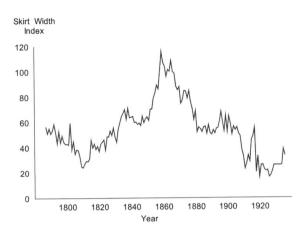

FIGURE 32.1.   Annual skirt widths, 1787 to 1936.

Kroeber believed that the long cycles in this series corroborated his cultural unsettlement theory, wholly random processes can generate identical patterns. Whereas most time-series designs treat $f(a_t)$ as a *nuisance* function whose sole purpose is to control the threats to statistical conclusion validity posed by cycles and trends, the descriptive time-series design infers substantive explanations from $f(a_t)$. Although the statistical models and methods developed for the analysis of descriptive designs are applied for exploratory purposes (see Mills, 1991), they are currently not widely used for null hypothesis tests.

Correlational Designs

A second type of time-series design attempts to infer a causal relationship between two series from their covariance. Historical examples include Chree's (1913) analyses of the temporal correlation between sunspot activity and terrestrial magnetism and Beveridge's (1922) analyses of the temporal correlation between rainfall and wheat prices. The validity of correlational inferences rests heavily on theory. When theory can specify a single causal effect operating at discrete lags, as in these natural science examples, correlational designs support unambiguous causal interpretations. Lacking theoretical specification, however, correlational designs do not allow strong causal inferences.

Analyses of the temporal correlation between lynchings and cotton prices by Hovland and Sears (1940) illustrate the inferential problem. To test the frustration-aggression hypothesis of Dollard et al. (1939), Hovland and Sears estimated a Pearson product–moment correlation coefficient from the annual time-series plotted in Figure 32.2. Assuming that the correlation would be zero in the absence of a causal relationship, Hovland and Sears interpreted the statistically significant estimate as corroborating evidence. Because of common stochastic time-series properties, however, especially trend, causally independent series will be correlated. Controlling for trend, Hepworth and West (1988) reported a small, significant correlation between the series but warned against causal interpretations. The correlation is an artifact of the war years 1914 to 1918, when the demand for cotton and the civilian population moved in opposite directions (McCleary, 2000). If the war years are excluded, the correlation is not statistically significant.

Where theory supports strong specification, correlational time-series designs continue to be used.

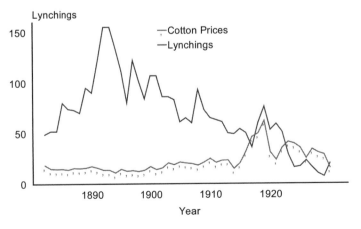

FIGURE 32.2.   Annual cotton prices and lynchings, 1886 to 1930.

Other than limited areas in economics and psychology, however, social theories will not support the required specification. Even in these areas, causal inferences require the narrow definition of Granger causality (Granger, 1969) to rule out plausible alternative interpretations.

Quasi-Experimental Designs

The third type of time-series design infers the latent causal effect of a temporally discrete intervention or treatment from discontinuities or interruptions in a time series. Campbell and Stanley (1963, pp. 37–43) called this design the "time-series experiment," and its use is currently the major application of time-series data for causal inference. Historical examples of the general approach include investigations of workplace interventions on health and productivity by the British Industrial Fatigue Research Board (Florence, 1923) and by the Hawthorne experiments (Roethlisberger & Dickson, 1939). Fisher's (1921) analyses of agricultural interventions on crop yields also relied on variants of the time-series quasi-experiment.

In the simplest case of the design, a discrete intervention breaks a time-series into pre- and post-intervention segments of N_{pre} and N_{post} observations. For pre- and postintervention means, μ_{pre} and μ_{post}, analysis of the quasi-experiment tests the null hypothesis

$$H_0: \omega = 0, \text{ where } \omega = \mu_{post} - \mu_{pre}; H_A: \omega \neq 0. \quad (5)$$

Rejecting H_0, H_A attributes ω to the intervention. In practice, however, treatment effects are almost always more complex than the simple change in level implied by this null hypothesis.

Figure 32.3 illustrates a typical example of the time-series quasi-experimental design. The data are 50 daily self-injurious behavior counts for an institutionalized patient (McCleary, Touchette, Taylor, & Barron, 1999). Beginning on the 26th day, the patient is treated with Naltrexone, an opiate-blocker. The plotted time series leaves the visual impression that the opiate-blocker has reduced the incidence of self-injurious behavior. Indeed, the difference in means for the 25 pre- and 25 postintervention days amounts to a 42% reduction. The value of $F = 32.56$ associated with this difference occurs

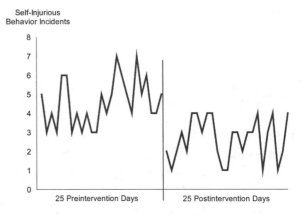

FIGURE 32.3. Self-injurious behavior incidents for a single institutionalized patient before and after an opiate-blocker regimen.

by chance with $p < .0001$, and the null hypothesis can be rejected in favor of the alternative: The medication is an effective treatment for self-injurious behavior.

This conclusion ignores a serious threat to validity. Whereas the null hypothesis test assumes that the daily counts are independent, in fact, the count on any given day is predictable from the count on the preceding day. The visual evidence of Figure 32.3 leaves the unambiguous impression that the opiate-blocker reduced the rate of self-injurious behavior for this patient. Visual evidence can be deceiving, of course, and that is why statistical hypothesis tests are conducted. Because of the day-to-day dependence of these data, however, the value of $F = 32.56$ cannot be interpreted.

More generally, time-series experiments and quasi-experiments present many challenges to valid inferences about causal effects. A solid rationale for the design is mostly due to the work of Donald T. Campbell and his collaborators (Campbell & Stanley, 1963; Cook & Campbell, 1979; Shadish, Cook, & Campbell, 2002). Campbell and associates extensively considered threats to the design's validity and proposed ways to address them when they were plausible. A general conclusion from Campbell's work is that experimental and quasi-experimental time-series designs face fewer threats to validity than do most other nonexperimental designs. This conclusion is largely responsible for the current popularity of time-series research.

FOUR TYPES OF VALIDITY

Campbell and Stanley (1963; Campbell, 1963) divided the empirical threats to valid inference into two categories. Threats to internal validity addressed the question, "Did in fact the experimental treatments make a difference in this specific experimental instance?" Threats to external validity addressed the question, "To what populations, settings, treatment variables, and measurement variables can this effect be generalized?"

Recognizing the incompleteness of the dichotomy, Cook and Campbell (1979) added two additional categories. Threats to statistical conclusion validity addressed questions of confidence and power that had previously been included implicitly as threats to internal validity. Threats to construct validity addressed questions of confounding that had previously been included implicitly as threats to external validity. Shadish et al. (2002) used the same four categories but expanded the list of threats to valid inference in each category.

Table 32.1 lists the threats to validity that are relevant to time-series studies. Time-series designs differ from other approaches in that common threats to validity are controlled by a statistical model. This applies not only to quasi-experimental designs but also to designs that would be considered *true experiments*. When a treatment or intervention can be manipulated experimentally, presumably to control threats to internal validity, the manipulation raises threats to construct and external validity that can be controlled by the statistical model.

Trade-offs among the four validities are implicit in our tradition. The salient flaw in the Campbell and Stanley (1963) two-category system was that all eight threats to internal validity and all four threats to external validity could be controlled by design. Campbell and his colleagues proposed the four-validity system in large part to correct this misconception. The trade-off among validities is a crucial consideration for time-series studies. Although threats to internal validity can be controlled, in principle, by experimental manipulation of the treatment, in practice, experimental manipulation raises near-fatal threats to construct and external validity. Accordingly, we analyze time-series experiments as if they were quasi-experiments.

Statistical Conclusion Validity

Shadish et al. (2002) identified nine threats to statistical conclusion validity or "reasons why researchers may be wrong in drawing valid inferences about the existence and size of covariation between two variables" (p. 45). Although the consequences of any particular threat will vary across settings, the threats to statistical conclusion validity fall neatly into categories involving misstatements of the Type I and Type II error rates.[1]

Type I errors (also known as α-errors or *false-positive* errors) occur when a true H_0 is mistakenly rejected; that is, when the intervention has no effect but the test statistic suggests otherwise. Under a convention established by Fisher (1925), the Type I error rate is fixed at $\alpha \leq 0.05$, corresponding to a confidence level of at least 0.95 (or 95% confidence).

Type II errors (also known as β-errors or *false-negative* errors) occur when a false H_0 is mistakenly accepted; that is, when the intervention has an effect but the test statistic suggests otherwise. Following Neyman and Pearson (1928), the conventional Type II error rate is fixed at $\beta \leq 0.2$, corresponding to statistical power level of at least 0.8 (or 80% statistical power). Whereas the Type I error rate is set a priori,

---

TABLE 32.1

Four Types of Validity From Shadish, Cook, and Campbell (2002)

Type of validity	Threat to validity
Statistical conclusion validity	Low statistical power
	Violated assumptions of the test
Internal validity	History
	Maturation
	Regression artifacts
	Instrumentation
Construct validity	Reactivity
	Novelty and disruption
External validity	Interaction over treatment variations
	Interaction with settings

---

[1]The most comprehensive authority on this topic is Kendall and Stuart (1979, Chapter 22). Cohen (1988) and Lipsey (1990) provided more accessible treatments of the topic.

the Type II error rate is conditioned on the Type I error rate and a likely effect size.[2]

For both Type I and Type II errors, uncontrolled threats to statistical conclusion validity distort the nominal values of α and β, leading to invalid inferences. The threats are controlled by a statistical model. The most widely used models for that purpose are the AutoRegressive Integrated Moving Average (ARIMA) models of Box and Jenkins (1970). Under H_0, an ARIMA model is written as

$$\varphi(B)Z_t = \theta(B)a_t \, Zt = Y_t - \mu_Y, \tag{6}$$

where Z_t and a_t are the tth observations of a stationary time-series and an *iid* $N(0,\sigma^2)$ error series respectively; and where $\varphi(B)$ and $\theta(B)$ are polynomial lag operators. If the parameters of $\varphi(B)$ and $\theta(B)$ are appropriately constrained, the ARIMA model can be solved for a_t:

$$\theta(B)^{-1}\varphi(B)Z_t = a_t. \tag{7}$$

To test H_0, the intervention is represented by a step function (or dummy variable) defined such that

$$X_t = 0 \text{ for } t \le N_{pre}; \, X_t = 1 \text{ thereafter.} \tag{8}$$

A *transfer* function of X_t is then added to the right-hand side of the ARIMA model:

$$\theta(B)^{-1}\varphi(B)Z_t = a_t + \delta(B)\omega X_t, \tag{9}$$

where $\delta(B)$ is a polynomial lag operator and ω is the effect of X_t on Z_t. Because a_t is an *iid* $N(0,\sigma^2)$ error term, the null hypothesis

$$H_0: \omega = 0 \tag{10}$$

can be tested with ordinary test statistics, such as t or F, effectively controlling all Type I threats to statistical conclusion validity.

Because the $\varphi(B)$ and $\theta(B)$ lag operators serve the sole purpose of transforming Z_t into the underlying a_t error, ARIMA models are not unique. Methods for building a parsimonious, statistically adequate ARIMA model have been described in Glass, Willson, and Gottman (1975); McCleary and Hay (1980); and especially McDowall, McCleary, Meidinger, and Hay (1980). The $\varphi(B)$ and $\theta(B)$ lag operators can be used for descriptive purposes, but with respect to H_0, they are *nuisance* parameters. The transfer function of X_t, in contrast, is a theoretical construct, specified on purely theoretical grounds. We return to this topic when the threats to construct validity are considered.

Although the Type II threats to statistical conclusion validity are straightforward, they are poorly understood and often ignored. The failure to reject H_0 does not imply that H_0 is true. The decision to accept H_0 as true requires, first, a consensus decision on the *likely* effect size (or value of ω); and, second, a demonstration that the time-series quasi-experiment was designed to yield a Type II error rate of $\beta \le 0.2$ for the likely effect size. In sum, the decision to accept H_0 as true requires the research begin with an analysis of statistical power.

Of the several factors that determine statistical power of a time-series design, the likely effect size is the most important. Small effects are difficult to detect even under the best circumstances. In addition to the likely size of the effect, the statistical power of a time-series quasi-experiment is a function of the series length, balance, and to a lesser extent, the quality of the ARIMA model. Because maximum likelihood estimates rely on large sample properties, analyses of short time series will often fail to achieve the nominal level of power. Most authorities recommend $N_{pre} + N_{post} > 50$ as the minimum length for a time series. Statistical power increases proportional to the square root of series length. But for a given length, power is highest when the design is balanced such that $N_{pre} = N_{post}$.

Even when the series is long and the design is balanced, the statistical power of a time-series quasi-experiment can be affected adversely by a poor-fitting ARIMA model. In addition to the purpose of transforming Z_t into a_t, the ARIMA model decomposes the time-series variance into stochastic and deterministic components, $f(a_t)$ and $g(X_t)$. To ensure an optimal decomposition, the ARIMA model used to test H_0 should have the lowest residual variance among the several statistically adequate models.

---

[2]Cohen (1988, pp. 3–4) and Lipsey (1990, pp. 38–40) set the conventional Type I and Type II error rates at $\alpha = .05$ and $\beta = .2$, respectively. If the Type I error rate is set lower, say, $\alpha = .01$, the Type II error rate is set at $\beta = .04$ to maintain a 4:1 ratio of Type II to Type I errors. The 4:1 convention dates back at least to Neyman and Pearson (1928) and reflects the view that science should be conservative.

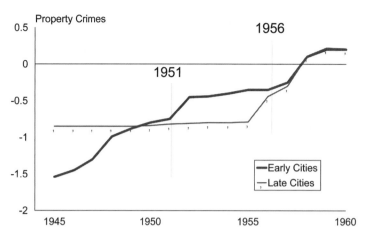

FIGURE 32.4.   Annual property crimes for cities with commercial television broadcast service in 1951 and for cities with television in 1955.

Internal Validity

Under some circumstances, all nine of the threats to internal validity identified by Shadish et al. (2002, p. 55) might apply to the time-series quasi-experiment. Typically, however, only four threats are plausible enough to pose serious difficulties. *History* and *maturation*, which arise from the use of multiple temporal observations, can threaten virtually any application of the design. *Instrumentation* and *regression* can also be problems, but only for interventions that involve advanced planning. For unplanned interventions—what Campbell (1963, pp. 229–230) called "natural experiments"—these threats are much less realistic.

The largest, most obvious, and most frequent threats to internal validity involve the operation of history. Historical threats come from changes in a time series that occur coincidently with an intervention but are due to other causes. A standard design-based approach to making these threats less plausible is to analyze one or more comparison series. The comparisons can take many forms, and a careful choice can substantially narrow the scope within which history can operate. An analysis might consider no-treatment control series that the intervention should not have influenced, for example, or study multiple periods during which the intervention was and was not in operation. A consistent pattern of results across different variables or time periods reduces the plausibility of historical threats and helps support the existence of an intervention impact.

An illustration of the effective use of comparison series comes from Hennigan et al. (1982), who studied changes in property crime following the introduction of commercial television. In 34 *early* cities, broadcasting began in 1950, whereas in 34 *late* cities, television was not available until 1954. The time series in Figure 32.4 show the annual log-transformed levels of property crimes for both groups of cities.

History is a plausible threat to inferences about the effects of television when studying the early or late cities alone. Other variables also changed during the years in which each group adopted television, and many of these might explain a change in crime. The Korean War was under way in 1951, for example, and an economic recession began in 1955. More generally, criminological theories suggest multiple factors that might influence property crimes and that could have changed around the time that broadcasting began in either of the groups.

Considering both time series together makes the changes in crime much more difficult to dismiss as artifacts of history. To be plausible, a historical explanation would have to account for increases that occurred at two different time points but affected only one group of cities at each. Although not impossible, constructing such an explanation would be a difficult enterprise.

In contrast to history, methods for addressing the other three threats to internal validity do not heavily rely on design variations. Maturation, which like history is plausible in all applications of the

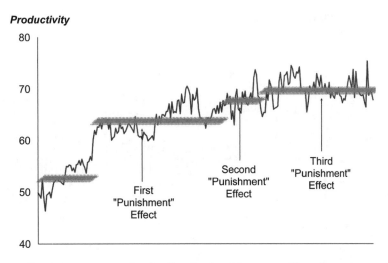

FIGURE 32.5. Weekly productivity measures for the first bank wiring room (Hawthorne) experiment. Estimated interventions are plotted against the series.

time-series quasi-experiment, requires a statistical modeling approach. Maturation threats appear as trends in the data and are due to developmental processes that are independent of the intervention. Time-series data often display such trends, and trending patterns are especially common in the long series that are most desirable for analysis. Maturational trends are a problem for inference because they can easily produce false evidence of an intervention effect.

Figure 32.5 illustrates one of the best-known examples of the maturation threat, the so-called Hawthorne effect. The data consist of weekly productivity levels for a group of five machine operators in the bank wiring room of the Western Electric Company's Hawthorne Works. Researchers manipulated daily rest breaks during the study period and claimed after a visual inspection of the series that the breaks helped increase productivity. Questioning this conclusion, Franke and Kaul (1978) argued that any productivity increases were instead due solely to fear generated by the imposition of three "punishment" regimes. Their statistical analysis, which included interventions at the beginning of each regime, supported this hypothesis.

Maturation provides an explanation that challenges the interpretations of both Franke and Kaul (1978) and the original researchers. Figure 32.5 shows the presence of a systematic trend in produc-

tivity that could easily have resulted from increases in worker experience. The trend closely follows the patterns that each set of researchers observed, and this makes maturation a plausible alternative explanation of their findings. A reanalysis that controlled for the trend in fact found a small effect of the rest breaks and no effect at all for the punishment regimes (McCleary, 2000).

Unlike other threats to internal validity, which are ordinarily handled by design, maturation threats are controlled by the statistical model. Under H_0, the causal effect of X_t vanishes, leaving a simple model that represents the time series as a weighted sum of past and present white noise innovations:

$$Z_t = \varphi(B)^{-1}\theta(B)\,a_t. \qquad (11)$$

Proper solutions of this model are guaranteed by constraining the parameters of $\varphi(B)$ and $\theta(B)$ to the bounds of stationarity-invertibility.[3]

This assumes a *stationary* time series, however, and this assumption is unwarranted in many instances. Kroeber's fashion time series (Figure 32.1), for example, shows the drifting pattern characteristic of a nonstationary random walk process. Segments of Kroeber's series are indistinguishable from the steady secular trend that poses the maturation threat in the Hawthorne experiment (Figure 32.5).

Although nonstationary time series are commonly encountered in the social sciences, most are

[3]Although the bounds of stationarity and invertibility are identical, they are distinct properties of a time series. See Box and Jenkins (1970, pp. 53–54). All modern time-series software packages report parameter estimates that are constrained to the stationarity–invertibility bounds.

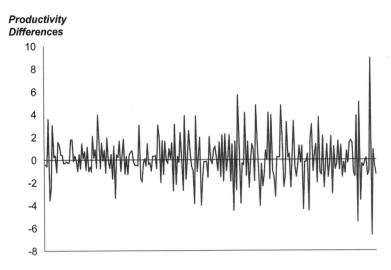

FIGURE 32.6. Weekly productivity measures from Figure 32.5, differenced.

stationary in first-differences. Using ∇ to represent the differencing operation

$$\nabla Y_t = Y_t - Y_{t-1}, \qquad (12)$$

a nonstationary time series can be modeled as

$$\nabla Y_t = \varphi(B)^{-1}\theta(B)\, a_t \qquad (13)$$

or

$$Y_t = \nabla^{-1}\varphi(B)^{-1}\theta(B)\, a_t. \qquad (14)$$

Figure 32.6 plots the first-differences of the Hawthorne experiment time series. The differenced series fluctuates around a constant level, and maturation is no longer a plausible threat to internal validity.[4]

In addition to controlling maturation threats, differencing removes the confounding effects of cross-sectional *fixed* causes of Y_t. To illustrate, suppose that Y_t is the U.S. unemployment rate and that W represents the causes of Y_t that vary cross-sectionally but that are constant over short periods of time. When consecutive observations are differenced,

$$Y_t - Y_{t-1} = f(a_t) - f(a_{t-1}) + W - W \qquad (15)$$

$$\nabla Y_t = f(a_t) - f(a_{t-1}), \qquad (16)$$

the confounding effects of W vanish from the model. This property of the difference equation model is the

motivation for the use of fixed-effects panel models in economics (Greene, 2000).

Like the maturation threat to internal validity, the regression threat is controlled by the statistical model. Whereas the maturation threat is plausible in both time-series experiments and quasi-experiments, however, the regression threat is plausible only in quasi-experiments involving planned interventions. The regression threat arises whenever the intervention is a reaction to an unusually high or low level of the time series. Regardless of the intervention's effects, regression to the mean is likely to produce an increase or decrease in the series level.

In one of the earliest formal applications of the time-series quasi-experiment, Campbell and Ross (1968) studied the impact on highway fatalities of a 1955 speeding crackdown in Connecticut. Traffic deaths dropped significantly after the crackdown began, but Campbell and Ross showed that the decrease was largely attributable to a regression artifact. Fatalities were unusually high in 1955, and the crackdown was a response intended to reduce them. A drop was then predictable as deaths regressed back toward their historically average levels.

Regression becomes a less plausible threat to internal validity as the length of a time series increases. Introducing the intervention at an unusually high (or low) point in the series will create a transient bias in estimates of the pre- and

---

[4]The mean of the first-differenced time series is interpreted as the secular trend of Y_t.

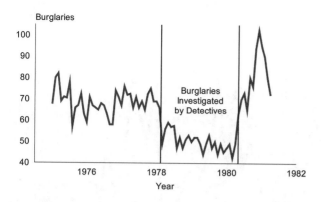

FIGURE 32.7. Monthly burglaries for Tucson, 1975 to 1981. During a 24-month period, burglaries are assigned to detectives for investigation.

postintervention means. As the pre- and postintervention series grow longer, the bias becomes proportionately smaller, and eventually it reaches zero. The recommendation to use a total series length of 50 or more observations for the time-series quasi-experiment is in part intended to reduce the plausibility of regression threats (McCleary & Hay, 1980; McDowall et al., 1980).

Instrumentation is also a plausible threat to planned interventions because new methods for measuring the outcome variable often accompany the introduction of other changes. Figure 32.7 (from McCleary, Nienstedt, & Erven, 1982) presents a monthly plot of Tucson burglary counts. For 2 years beginning in 1979, detectives replaced uniformed officers in performing burglary investigations. In 1981, the investigative responsibility was returned to the uniformed officers. Consistent with the notion that detectives are more proficient in pre-

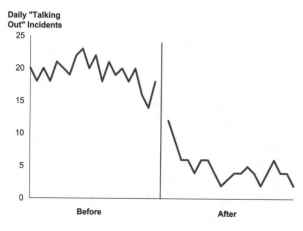

FIGURE 32.8. Daily disruptions caused by talking out before and after a behavioral intervention.

venting burglaries, the counts were lower when they handled the cases.

Although the switching intervention feature of the design effectively rules out history, all other internal validity threats are still plausible. Additional analysis showed that detectives and uniformed officers did not keep records in the same way, and this difference reduced the number of burglaries that the detectives recorded. Allowing for the influence of the instrumentation change, burglary counts did not vary significantly with the type of officer responsible for the investigations.

Construct Validity

Shadish et al. (2002) identified 14 "reasons why inferences about the constructs that characterize study operations may be incorrect" (p 73). One of the 14 threats to construct validity, *novelty and disruption,* is relevant to experimental and quasi-experimental time-series designs. Regardless of whether an intervention has its intended effect, the time series is likely to react to the novelty or disruption associated with it. If the general form of the artifact is known, it can be incorporated into the statistical model.

Figure 32.8 illustrates one aspect of this threat to construct validity. Hall et al. (1971) counted the number of talking out disruptions in a classroom for 20 consecutive days. When a behavioral intervention is implemented on the 21st day, the time series changes gradually, falling to a lower daily level of disruption. If the gradual nature of the response is not taken into account, the effectiveness of the intervention is underestimated. Because gradual responses to interventions are a common feature of behavioral research, the uncontrolled threat to construct validity can have serious consequences.

Figure 32.9 illustrates the complementary aspect of this threat to construct validity. Similar to Figure 32.3, these data are daily counts of self-injurious behavior incidents but for a different patient (McCleary et al., 1999). Instead of receiving an opiate-blocker, beginning on the 26th day, this patient received a placebo. The level of the time series dropped immediately but then, within a few days, returned to its preintervention level. Placebo effects of this sort are common in time-series experiments. Given a well-behaved time-series process and a

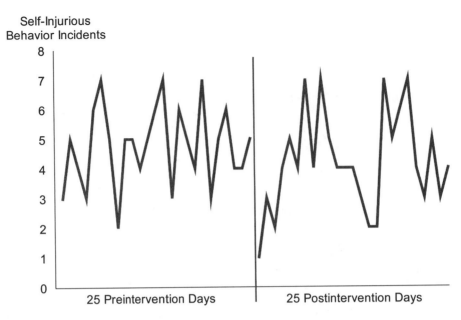

FIGURE 32.9. Self-injurious behavior incidents for a single institutionalized patient before and after a placebo regimen.

sufficient number of postintervention observations, the threat to construct validity may be ignored. Under more realistic circumstances, however, the placebo effect must be incorporated into the analytical model.

Campbell and Stanley (1963, p. 43) recognized the threat to validity posed by a dynamic response to an intervention; still, their external validity assessment of the time-series quasi-experiment seemed to leave the issue open. Addressing the same threat from a modeling perspective, Box and Jenkins (1970; Box & Tiao, 1975) proposed a lagged polynomial parameterization of $h(X_t)$ that allows for hypothesis testing. The polynomial lag makes the ARIMA model inherently nonlinear, complicating the interpretation of analytic results. The polynomial lag provides a straightforward method of controlling novelty and disruption threats to construct validity, however, and has become widely accepted in the social sciences.

Figure 32.10 shows four variations of the same general polynomial lag model. The model variations in the top row depict *permanent* responses to the intervention. The series may respond to the intervention *instantaneously* or *gradually* but, in either case, the response is permanent. A *gradual, permanent* response model seems to capture the effect of the behavioral intervention on the daily time series of disruptive talking out incidents (Figure 32.8).

The model variations in the bottom row of Figure 32.10 depict *temporary* responses to the intervention. Both responses model placebo artifacts, spiking at the onset of the intervention but then decaying over time to reveal the long-run effect of the intervention or treatment. The *gradual, temporary* response model seems to capture the effect of a placebo intervention on the daily time series of self-injurious behavior (Figure 32.9).

Permanent and temporary responses can be combined in a model. Figure 32.11 shows a time series of divorce rates for Australia before and after the 1975 Family Law Act, which allowed for no-fault divorce. Opponents of the act argued that its no-fault provisions would lead to an increase in divorces. An evaluation of the act by the Australian government found that although divorces did rise following the act, the divorce rate fell back to its pre-1975 level after 3 years. The fact that post-1975 divorce rates were higher was attributed to secular trend.

Reanalyzing these data, McCleary and Riggs (1982) hypothesized a complex response to the act, realized as the sum of a permanent and a temporary increase in divorce. The temporary spike in divorces decayed rapidly in the years immediately following 1975. Divorces never returned to their pre-1975 rates, however, and instead stabilized at a new higher level.

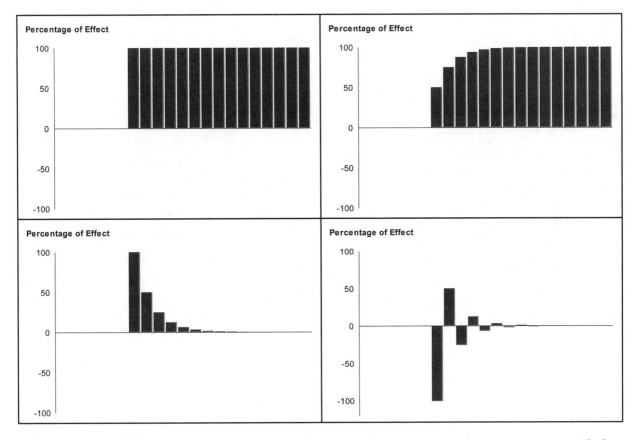

FIGURE 32.10. Model responses to an intervention. The top row illustrates permanent response patterns. The bottom row illustrates temporary response patterns.

Whether or not they have permanent effects, new laws often have temporary effects that are well modeled as decaying spikes. Failure to allow for these temporary effects can lead to invalid inferences. At the individual level, placebo artifacts pose an analogous threat to construct validity. Although these threats are easily controlled with an explicit complex response model, by allowing the possibility of several responses, the model raises a potential threat to statistical conclusion validity: *fishing*. To control the fishing threat, the complex response model must be fully specified before any hypothesis test.

Finally, we return to the trade-off implicit in the four-validity system. In principle, all nine threats to internal validity can be controlled by manipulating the intervention or treatment experimentally. Internal validity is bought at the expense of construct validity, however, which may be more threatening in single-subject designs. Although the opiate-blocker regimen appears to reduce self-injurious behavior, implementation of the regimen provokes a week-long reaction to the novelty and disruption. Because none of the common threats to internal validity seem plausible, trading construct for internal validity may be unwarranted.

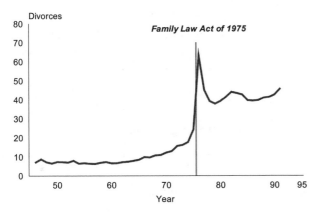

FIGURE 32.11. Australian divorces before and after the 1975 Family Law Act.

External Validity

A time-series quasi-experiment typically considers an intervention's influence on only one series, and this makes it highly vulnerable to external validity threats. External validity considers whether findings hold "over variations in persons, settings, treatments, and outcomes" (Shadish et al., 2002, p. 83), and threats to it are always plausible when analyzing a single series. Ruling out external validity threats necessarily requires replicating the quasi-experiment over a diverse set of conditions.

The evaluation research literature shows many cases in which effect estimates exist to support every possible conclusion about a program's impact. Evaluations of gun control policies, for example, include numerous instances of positive, negative, and null effect estimates (Reiss & Roth, 1993, pp. 255–287). In these situations, the variance of the effects across replications can be more informative than is a single-point estimate of the average effect.

If several quasi-experimental replications exist, they allow external validity to be assessed in one of two ways. First, the set of individual time series can be assembled to form a single vector series, $\mathbf{Y}_t$:

$$\mathbf{Y}_t' = \{Y_{1,t}, Y_{2,t}, \ldots, Y_{k,t}\}. \tag{17}$$

A statistical analysis can then take advantage of the variation in the replications to obtain estimates of both the average impact and its expected variability (e.g., McGaw & McCleary, 1985). Second, an analysis can decompose the set of individual impact estimates,

$$\omega' = \{\omega_1, \omega_2, \ldots, \omega_k\}, \tag{18}$$

into components associated with various external validity threats.

The second approach is a restricted case of the first, and in theory, it is less desirable. Still, the first and more general model makes highly demanding assumptions, and time-series often do not conform to them. Because the second approach places fewer requirements on the data, it is therefore generally more practical to apply. Statistical models for the second approach come from meta-analysis and divide the effect variance into components caused by the setting, intervention, and other potential threats to external validity. McDowall, Loftin, and Wiersema (1992) used this approach to estimate the overall impact and variability of sentencing laws,

and McCleary (2000) used it to combine estimates from the Hawthorne experiments.

DYNAMIC INTERVENTION ANALYSES

A salient advantage of time-series designs over other before–after designs is the capability of modeling *dynamic* responses to the intervention. Proper specification of a dynamic response model, such as those shown in Figure 32.10, requires a parsimonious theory of the response. One theory that has proved useful in psychological research restricts the response to one of four types defined by dichotomizing *onset* and *duration*. The response may be *abrupt* or *gradual* in onset and *permanent* or *temporary* in duration. Although general transfer function specifications (Box & Jenkins, 1970; Box & Tiao, 1975) allow a wider range of responses, the four-type theory is more realistic for psychological interventions and more appropriate for testing intervention null hypotheses.

The talking out intervention plotted in Figure 32.8 is a typical *gradual, permanent* response to an intervention. Though implemented on the 21st day, the full effect of the intervention is not realized immediately but, rather, accumulates gradually over several days. If a time-series model is written as the sum of stochastic and intervention components,

$$Y_t = f(a_t) + g(X_t). \tag{19}$$

The stochastic component plays no meaningful role in our explication of the intervention analysis. Procedures for building statistically adequate ARIMA models of $f(a_t)$ are described elsewhere (McCleary & Hay, 1980) but are of little interest here. Subtracting the stochastic component from the series

$$Z_t = Y_t - f(a_t) = g(X_t) \tag{20}$$

leaves the dynamic intervention component:

$$Z_t = g(X_t). \tag{21}$$

The simplest dynamic model of a gradual, permanent response to X_t is

$$g(X_t) = X_t \omega \, (1 - \delta B)^{-1}, \tag{22}$$

TABLE 32.2

Parameter Estimates for Dynamic Intervention Models

Gradual response, permanent change	Abrupt response, temporary change
$g(X_t) = X_t\omega\,(1 - \delta B)^{-1}$	$g(X_t) = (1 - B)X_t\omega\,(1 - \delta B)^{-1}$
Talking out (Figure 32.8)	Self-injurious behavior (Figure 32.9)
$\omega = -6.79$ $\quad t(\omega) = -6.81$	$\omega = -3.65$ $\quad t(\omega) = -3.04$
$\delta = 0.56$ $\quad t(\delta) = 8.48$	$\delta = 0.57$ $\quad t(\delta) = 3.02$

---

where B is a backward lag operator defined such that

$$B^k X_t = X_{t-k} \text{ for any integer } k. \tag{23}$$

A Taylor series expansion of the right-hand side yields the more useful series identity:

$$Z_t = X_t\omega\,(1 + \delta B + \delta^2 B^2 + \delta^3 B^3 + \ldots) \tag{24}$$

$$= X_t\omega + \delta X_{t-1}\omega + \delta^2 X_{t-2}\omega + \delta^3 X_{t-3}\omega + \ldots \tag{25}$$

X_t is defined as a binary variable such that

$$X_t = 0 \text{ for preintervention days}$$
$$t = 1, \ldots, 20 \tag{26}$$

$$X_t = 1 \text{ for postintervention days}$$
$$t = 21, \ldots, 40. \tag{27}$$

Before the intervention, $X_{t \le 20} = 0$, so

$$Z_{t \le 20} = 0. \tag{28}$$

Thereafter, $X_{t > 20} = 1$. On the jth postintervention day,

$$Z_{20+j} = \omega + \delta\omega + \delta^2\omega + \ldots + \delta^{j-1}\omega. \tag{29}$$

Because δ is a fraction, δ^{j-1} is a very small number.

Parameter estimates for the talking out time-series are reported in the left-hand panel of Table 32.2.[5] Substituting the estimates of ω and δ into the series identity,

$$Z_{21} = -6.79(1) = -6.79 \tag{30}$$
$$Z_{22} = -6.79(1 + .56) = -10.59 \tag{31}$$
$$Z_{23} = -6.79(1 + .56 + .31) = -12.72 \tag{32}$$
$$Z_{24} = -6.79(1 + .56 + .31 + .18) = -13.91 \tag{33}$$
$$Z_{25} = -6.79(1 + .56 + .31 + .18 + .10) = -14.58. \tag{34}$$

Daily changes in talking out continue throughout the postintervention segment, but reductions

become smaller and smaller. Eventually, the effect will converge on

$$-6.79 / (1 - .56) = -15.43, \tag{35}$$

but by the end of the fifth postintervention day, 95% of this effect has been realized.

The self-injurious behavior time series in Figure 32.9 presents a typical *abrupt, temporary* response to an intervention that, in this case, is a placebo. On the first postintervention day, this patient's rate of self-injurious behavior drops abruptly but, in subsequent days, returns to its preintervention level. The simplest dynamic model of an abrupt, temporary effect is

$$Z_t = \nabla X_t\omega\,(1 - \delta B)^{-1}. \tag{36}$$

This model has the series identity:

$$Z_t = \nabla X_t\omega + \delta\,\nabla X_{t-1}\omega + \delta^2\,\nabla X_{t-2}\omega + \delta^3\,\nabla X_{t-3}\omega + \ldots \tag{37}$$

Whereas X_t remains on throughout the postintervention period, the first difference of X_t, ∇X_t, turns on in the first postintervention day and then turns off again:

$$\nabla X_t = 0 \text{ for days } t = 1, \ldots, 25 \tag{38}$$

$$\nabla X_t = 1 \text{ for } t = 26 \tag{39}$$

$$\nabla X_t = 0 \text{ for days } t = 27, \ldots, 50. \tag{40}$$

Before the intervention, $\nabla X_{t \le 25} = 0$ and

$$Z_{t \le 25} = 0. \tag{41}$$

On the first day of the intervention, $\nabla X_{26} = 1$, so

$$Z_{26} = \omega. \tag{42}$$

But thereafter, $\nabla X_{t > 26} = 0$ again, and

$$Z_{26+j} = \delta^{j-1}\omega. \tag{43}$$

---

[5]Parameters estimated with the SCA Statistical System (Liu, 1999).

Again, as $\omega\delta^{j-1}$ approaches 0, the placebo effect decays.

Parameter estimates for the placebo self-injurious behavior time series are reported in the right-hand column of Table 32.2. Substituting the estimates of ω and δ into the series identity,

$$Z_{26} = -3.04, \tag{44}$$

$$Z_{27} = -3.04\,(.57) = -1.73, \tag{45}$$

$$Z_{28} = -3.04\,(.57)^2 = -0.99, \tag{46}$$

$$Z_{29} = -3.04\,(.57)^3 = -0.56, \text{ and} \tag{47}$$

$$Z_{30} = -3.04\,(.57)^4 = -0.32. \tag{48}$$

By end of the fifth postintervention day, 90% of the placebo effect has dissipated.

In either of these two dynamic models, the parameter δ determines the rate of postintervention change in the time series. Intervention null hypotheses can be devised around the value of δ to test properties of the response.

CONCLUSION

Time-series data and time-series designs have a long history in psychological research. Of the many uses of time-series data, causal inferences from experiments and quasi-experiments are currently their widest application. Given a reasonably long time series, balanced data, and an adequate ARIMA model, the time-series quasi-experiment is among the most useful and valid quasi-experimental designs.

The advantages of the time-series quasi-experiment are especially apparent in the absence of naturally defined control groups. To emphasize this property, Campbell and Stanley (1963) cited the hypothetical example of a chemist who, dipping an iron bar into nitric acid, attributes the bar's loss of weight to the acid bath: "There may well have been 'control groups' of iron bars remaining on the shelf that lost no weight but the measurement and reporting of these weights would typically not be thought necessary or relevant" (p. 37).

The design is also vulnerable to multiple threats to validity, of course, and one would normally not use it in situations in which randomized controlled trials are possible. These cases aside, the time-series

quasi-experiment is a feasible and relatively strong design across a wide range of circumstances.

References

Beveridge, W. H. (1922). Wheat prices and rainfall in western Europe. *Journal of the Royal Statistical Society, 85,* 412–475. doi:10.2307/2341183

Box, G. E. P., & Jenkins, G. M. (1970). *Time series analysis: Forecasting and control.* San Francisco, CA: Holden-Day.

Box, G. E. P., & Tiao, G. C. (1975). Intervention analysis with applications to economic and environmental problems. *Journal of the American Statistical Association, 70,* 70–79. doi:10.2307/2285379

Campbell, D. T. (1963). From description to experimentation: Interpreting trends as quasi-experiments. In C. W. Harris (Ed.), *Problems in measuring change* (pp. 212–243). Madison: University of Wisconsin Press.

Campbell, D. T., & Ross, H. L. (1968). The Connecticut crackdown on speeding: Time series data in quasi-experimental analysis. *Law and Society Review, 3,* 33–53. doi:10.2307/3052794

Campbell, D. T., & Stanley, J. C. (1963). Experimental and quasi-experimental designs for research. Chicago, IL: Rand-McNally.

Chree, C. (1913). Some phenomena of sunspots and of terrestrial magnetism at Kew Observatory. *Philosophical Transactions of the Royal Society of London, Series A, 212,* 75–116. doi:10.1098/rsta.1913.0003

Cohen, J. (1988). *Statistical power analysis for the behavioral sciences* (2nd ed.). Englewood Cliffs, NJ: Erlbaum.

Cook, T. D., & Campbell, D. T. (1979). *Quasi-experimentation: Design and analysis issues for field settings.* Boston, MA: Houghton-Mifflin.

Dollard, J., Doob, L. W., Miller, N. E., Mowrer, O. H., & Sears, R. R. (1939). *Frustration and aggression.* New Haven, CT: Yale University Press.

Elton, C. S. (1924). Fluctuations in the numbers of animals: Their causes and effects. *Journal of Experimental Biology, 2,* 119–163.

Elton, C., & Nicholson, M. (1942). The ten-year cycle in numbers of the lynx in Canada. *Journal of Animal Ecology, 11,* 215–244. doi:10.2307/1358

Fisher, R. A. (1921). Studies in crop variation: An examination of the yield of dressed grain from Broadbalk. *Journal of Agricultural Science, 11,* 107–135. doi:10.1017/S0021859600003750

Fisher, R. A. (1925). *Statistical methods for research workers.* London, England: Oliver & Boyd.

Florence, P. S. (1923). Recent researches in industrial fatigue. *Economic Journal, 33*, 185–197. doi:10.2307/2222844

Franke, H. F., & Kaul, J. D. (1978). The Hawthorne experiments: First statistical interpretation. *American Sociological Review, 43*, 623–643. doi:10.2307/2094540

Glass, G. V., Willson, V. L., & Gottman, J. M. (1975). *Design and analysis of time series experiments*. Boulder: Colorado Associated University Press.

Granger, C. W. J. (1969). Investigating causal relationships by econometric models and cross-spectral methods. *Econometrica, 37*, 424–438. doi:10.2307/1912791

Greene, W. H. (2000). *Econometric analysis* (4th ed.). Englewood Cliffs, NJ: Prentice-Hall.

Hall, R. V., Fox, R., Willard, D., Goldsmith, L., Emerson, M., Owen, M., . . . Porcia, E. (1971). The teacher as observer and experimenter in the modification of disputing and talking-out behaviors. *Journal of Applied Behavior Analysis, 4*, 141–149. doi:10.1901/jaba.1971.4-141

Hennigan, K. M., Del Rosario, M. L., Heath, L., Cook, T. D., Wharton, J. D., & Calder, B. J. (1982). Impact of the introduction of television on crime in the United States: Empirical findings and theoretical implications. *Journal of Personality and Social Psychology, 42*, 461–477. doi:10.1037/0022-3514.42.3.461

Hepworth, J. T., & West, S. G. (1988). Lynchings and the economy: A time-series reanalysis of Hovland and Sears. *Journal of Personality and Social Psychology, 55*, 239–247. doi:10.1037/0022-3514.55.2.239

Hovland, C. I., & Sears, R. R. (1940). Minor studies of aggression IV. Correlation of lynchings with economic indices. *Journal of Psychology, 9*, 301–310. doi:10.1080/00223980.1940.9917696

Kendall, M., & Stuart, A. (1979). *The advanced theory of statistics* (4th ed., Vol. 2). London, England: Charles Griffin.

Kroeber, A. L. (1919). On the principle of order in civilization as exemplified by changes of fashion. *American Anthropologist, 21*, 235–263. doi:10.1525/aa.1919.21.3.02a00010

Kroeber, A. L. (1944). *Configurations of cultural growth*. Berkeley: University of California Press.

Lipsey, M. (1990). *Design sensitivity: Statistical power for experimental research*. Thousand Oaks, CA: Sage.

Liu, L.-M. (1999). *Forecasting and time series analysis using the SCA statistical system*. Villa Park, IL: Scientific Computing Associates.

McCleary, R. (2000). Evolution of the time series experiment. In L. Bickman (Ed.), *Research design: Donald Campbell's legacy* (pp. 215–234). Thousand Oaks, CA: Sage.

McCleary, R., & Hay, R. A., Jr. (1980). *Applied time series analysis for the social sciences*. Beverly Hills, CA: Sage.

McCleary, R., Nienstedt, B. C., & Erven, J. M. (1982). Uniform crime reports and organizational outcomes: Three time series quasi-experiments. *Social Problems, 29*, 361–372. doi:10.1525/sp.1982.29.4.03a00030

McCleary, R., & Riggs, J. E. (1982). The 1975 Australian Family Law Act: A model for assessing legal impacts. *New Directions for Program Evaluation, 16*, 7–18.

McCleary, R., Touchette, P., Taylor, D. V., & Barron, J. L. (1999, March). *Contagious models for self-injurious behavior*. Poster presentation, 32nd Annual Gatlinburg Conference on Research and Theory in Mental Retardation, Charleston, SC.

McDowall, D., Loftin, C., & Wiersema, B. (1992). A comparative study of the preventive effects of mandatory sentencing laws for gun crimes. *Journal of Criminal Law and Criminology, 83*, 378–394. doi:10.2307/1143862

McDowall, D., McCleary, R., Meidinger, E. E., & Hay, R. A., Jr. (1980). *Interrupted time series analysis*. Beverly Hills, CA: Sage.

McGaw, D. B., & McCleary, R. (1985). PAC spending, electioneering, and lobbying: A vector ARIMA time series analysis. *Polity, 17*, 574–585. doi:10.2307/3234659

Mills, T. C. (1991). *Time series techniques for economists*. New York, NY: Cambridge University Press.

Neyman, J., & Pearson, E. S. (1928). On the use and interpretation of certain test criteria for purposes of statistical inference. *Biometrika, 20A*, 175–240.

Reiss, A. J., & Roth, J. A. (1993). *Understanding and preventing violence*. Washington, DC: National Academies Press.

Richardson, J., & Kroeber, A. L. (1940). Three centuries of women's dress fashions: A quantitative analysis. *Anthropological Records, 5*, 111–153.

Roethlisberger, F., & Dickson, W. J. (1939). *Management and the worker*. Cambridge, MA: Harvard University Press.

Shadish, W. R., Cook, T. D., & Campbell, D. T. (2002). *Experimental and quasi-experimental designs for generalized causal inference*. New York, NY: Houghton Mifflin.

Wolf, J. R. (1848). Nachrichten über die Sternwarte in Bern [News from the observatory in Berne]. *Mittheilungen der naturforschenden gesellschaft in Bern, Nr. 114–115*. ETH–Bibliothek Zürich, Rar 4201. doi:10.3931/e-rara-2007

Yule, G. U. (1927). On a method of investigating periodicities in in disturbed series with special reference to Wolfer's sunspot numbers. *Philosophical Transactions of the Royal Society of London, Series A, 226*, 267–298.

PART VI

DESIGNS IN NEUROPSYCHOLOGY AND BIOLOGICAL PSYCHOLOGY

SECTION 1

Neuropsychology

CHAPTER 33

CASE STUDIES IN NEUROPSYCHOLOGY

Randi C. Martin and Corinne Allen

The case study approach has a long history in the study of cognitive processes and their localization in the brain. A well-known example is Paul Broca's research on his patient Tan, nicknamed because of his inability to say anything but the word *tan* (Broca, 1861). A postmortem autopsy in the mid-1800s indicated that Broca's patient had damage to a region of the left frontal lobe, which Broca concluded was responsible for speech production. Although certainly not the earliest study of a patient with selective behavioral deficits, it is one of the most influential. To this day, researchers refer to this left frontal area as "Broca's area." This chapter discusses how to investigate an individual patient with a behavioral deficit and how that deficit can be informative about normal cognition and brain localization.

OBJECTIVES AND RELATION TO THE INFORMATION-PROCESSING APPROACH

There are two main objectives to cognitive neuropsychological research (McCloskey, 2001; Miceli, 2000). The first objective is to gain insight into the functional organization of cognitive processes and the second is to determine the neural bases of these processes. Meeting the first objective involves understanding the cognitive breakdowns that result from brain damage and determining the implications of these deficits for models of the intact cognitive system. The information-processing approach to cognition serves as a foundation for cognitive neuropsychological research, as it does in cognitive psychology in general. The approach views cognitive

processing from a computational point of view, such that several modules—or components—function together to contribute to a specific cognitive domain such as word retrieval (Fodor, 1983). Often, a given cognitive domain is visually represented by a model using a box-and-arrow diagram or connectionist network, with the model used to guide testing. As an example, Figure 33.1a shows a box-and-arrow representation of the cognitive architecture assumed to underlie picture naming and Figure 33.1b shows a connectionist architecture (based on Dell & O'Seaghdha, 1992; Dell, Schwartz, N. Martin, Saffran, & Gagnon, 1997; N. Martin & Saffran, 1992; R. C. Martin, Lesch, & Bartha, 1999). In Figure 33.1a, the boxes correspond to individual components that contribute to the system as a whole, such that separate boxes represent separate processing modules. For example, in picture naming, an analysis of the picture leads to a visual representation of the features of the object that is used to access a semantic representation. The semantic representation is used to access a lexical representation, and the lexical representation is used to access a phonological representation of the depicted object's name. The phonological representation is then used to guide articulation. Figure 33.1b is similar, but depicts more specifically how the activation of semantic features leads to the activation of not only the target lexical representation but also the lexical representations of words that are both semantically and phonologically related to the target. That is, semantic features connect to all of the lexical representations to which they apply. Thus, activation of the semantic features

DOI: 10.1037/13620-033
APA Handbook of Research Methods in Psychology: Vol. 2. Research Designs, H. Cooper (Editor-in-Chief)

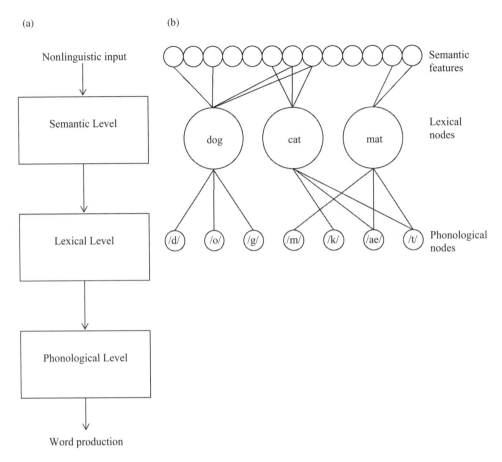

(a)

Nonlinguistic input

Semantic Level

Lexical Level

Phonological Level

Word production

(b)

Semantic features

dog   cat   mat — Lexical nodes

/d/ /o/ /g/ /m/ /k/ /ae/ /t/ — Phonological nodes

FIGURE 33.1. Examples of the visually represented cognitive architecture assumed to underlie picture naming: a box-and-arrow representation (a) and a connectionist architecture (b).

for *cat* leads to some activation of *dog, lion, tiger,* and other concepts that are similar to *cat.* Activation of the lexical representation for *cat* leads to activation of the phonemes /k/, /ae/, and /t/. In Dell et al.'s (1997) model, activation feeds back from subsequent levels to prior levels. Feedback from the phonological to the lexical level results in the activation of lexical representations for words sharing phonemes with the target (e.g., representations for *cat, mat,* and *cap* would also become activated).

A complex cognitive system such as that involved in picture naming, then, is represented by a theoretical cognitive architecture that describes the stages of information processing. A disruption of any representation or any connections among them should lead to deficits—for example, a disruption in semantic representations per se or a disruption in accessing phonological representations from lexical representations should lead to a deficit in picture naming. One

can use the model to determine the component or components that have been affected. For example, if a patient has disrupted semantic representations, then one should see a deficit in picture naming and also in semantic tasks involving words or pictures, for instance, in choosing a picture to match a spoken word. If the patient has a deficit in phonological retrieval, but not in semantics, then performance on comprehension tasks should be preserved. Also, the nature of the errors should differ for the two types of patients. That is, one might see primarily semantically related errors (e.g., producing *apple* for a picture of a banana) in patients with semantic disruptions but primarily phonological errors (e.g., producing *banner* for a picture of a banana) or a circumlocution (e.g., "it's a kind of fruit . . . monkeys like it") for a patient with difficulty in phonological retrieval.

Not only can models be used in the interpretation of deficits, but patient data can be used to test the assumptions of a model. If findings contradict assumptions of the model, then the researcher can propose changes in the model to accommodate the findings. For example, patient error data can be examined to determine whether the assumption of feedback between levels in the connectionist naming model (Foygel & Dell, 2000) is warranted. On the basis of an analysis of patient errors, Rapp and Goldrick (2000) concluded that a model with feedback from the phonological to the lexical level but not with feedback from the lexical to the semantic level best accommodated the data. Although much has been learned about the architectures proposed in Figures 33.1a and 33.1b through the study of normal populations, much has been learned as well by studying patients who have disrupted naming (e.g., Foygel & Dell, 2000; Rapp & Goldrick, 2000; Ruml, Caramazza, Shelton, & Chialant, 2000; Schwartz, Dell, Martin, Gahl, & Sobel, 2006). As stated by McCloskey (2001), "Complex systems often reveal their inner workings more clearly when they are malfunctioning, than when they are running smoothly" (p. 594). These architectural theories also have implications for clinical interventions. For instance, one might develop different remediation programs for word retrieval depending on whether the patient's deficit is at a phonological or semantic level (e.g., Drew & Thomson, 1999; Raymer, Thompson, Jacobs, & Le Grand, 1993; Wambaugh et al., 2001).

The second cognitive neuropsychological objective is to identify brain–behavior relations—anatomically localizing individual components of a cognitive architecture and the connections that link regions. In meeting the second goal, the assumption is that the cognitive components in models such as those in Figure 33.1 are localized to specific brain regions. All components need not be anatomically localized to a single area but rather can span a large network of areas through distant connections. With lesions, for example, researchers can determine what regions of the brain are necessary for which aspect of task performance, leading to inferences about the neural substrates of cognition. As a concrete example, neuropsychological research played a large role in specifying the theory of visual processing that proposes two streams—a what and a where stream. According to Mishkin, Ungerleider, and Macko

(1983), the ventral, inferior temporal stream is involved in object identification (*what*), whereas the more dorsal, parietal stream is involved in spatial perception (*where*). The original what–where distinction has been revised into a what–how distinction, which better classifies the dorsal pathway's involvement in spatial perception and visuomotor guidance (Goodale & Milner, 1992). Neuropsychological data from case studies were instrumental in establishing this pathway distinction in the human visual system (e.g., Newcombe, Ratcliff & Damasio, 1987; Perenin & Vighetto, 1988), with research on the topic demonstrating a dissociation between patients who showed visual object agnosia, which consists of an inability to recognize visually presented objects (*what*), and those who showed optic ataxia, which involves an inability to reach toward objects and correctly orient one's hand during the reach (*how*). Critically, these patients are differentiated on their behavioral deficits and also on the location of their brain damage. Visual object agnosia tends to be associated with temporal lobe damage, whereas optic ataxia is associated with parietal lobe damage. These neuropsychological data have played a role in characterizing both the function of the dorsal and ventral streams as well as their anatomical basis in humans.

ASSUMPTIONS IN THE COGNITIVE NEUROPSYCHOLOGICAL APPROACH

The two neuropsychological objectives have some basic underlying assumptions, which are critical to understanding how individual patient deficits can inform models of normal cognitive processing. These assumptions have been discussed extensively elsewhere and will only be briefly summarized here (e.g., Caramazza, 1986; Coltheart, 2001; see also Shallice, 1988). First, the *modularity* assumption suggests that cognition can be decomposed into functional and anatomical modules, as described. The use of the term *modular* would seem to imply an architecture like that shown in Figure 33.1a rather than that shown in Figure 33.1b. Even the model in Figure 33.1b is quasi-modular, however, given that distinct types of representations occur at different levels, even though there is spreading activation between levels (see Dell & O'Seaghdha, 1992, for discussion).

In the model in Figure 33.1a, a single lexical representation is selected on the basis of the activated semantic information and then this lexical representation is used to access a phonological representation (e.g., Levelt et al., 1991; Roelofs, 1992). On the other hand, in Figure 33.1b, the semantic representation activates several lexical representations that share semantic features with the target. These activated, nontarget representations send some degree of activation to phonological representations that are related to the target. The result of the continued influence of semantic information from nontargets on the activation of phonological representations leads to greater activation at the phonological level for word forms that share both phonological and semantic information with the target (leading to the production of so-called mixed errors—e.g., saying, "rat" for "cat"). Thus, in a model with cascaded activation, the predicted pattern of errors may not be as tidy as in a discrete system with only one input and output for each processing level. However, even for models making the assumption of cascaded processing, like that in Figure 33.1b, different relative proportions of different types of errors can be predicted on the basis of on where the disruption in the model occurs (Dell et al., 1997; Foygel & Dell, 2000; Rapp & Goldrick, 2000). Thus, even though the models in Figures 33.1a and 33.1b differ in some ways, they both assume functional models that can be selectively affected by brain damage.

Anatomical modularity assumes that functional modules, or component processes, are localized to specific regions of the brain. That is, it is possible that localized damage could impair a single, specific component of word production (e.g., the region representing semantic information is different from that representing phonological information). In fact, evidence suggests that semantic representations are stored in middle and inferior temporal regions, whereas phonological representations are stored in the left superior temporal region (e.g., Hickok & Poeppel, 2007). If there were no functional or anatomical modularity, we would expect even localized damage to produce widespread cognitive effects. Most of the time, however, this is not the case: Damage from lesions, for example, produces deficits to specific aspects of a single cognitive system.

The second assumption—the *uniformity* assumption—maintains that a specific cognitive architecture is the same across people with similar developmental backgrounds. This assumption does not maintain that individuals are exactly the same, as there are obvious differences in background knowledge, intelligence, and so on (Miceli, 2000). Uniformity assumes that information-processing components are the same from person to person and that these components function in the same way across individuals. The uniformity assumption allows researchers to develop cognitive theories without having to hypothesize specific architectures for every individual. In practice, this assumption is supported by the fact that specific deficits can be, and have been, replicated across individuals. Because architectures are hypothesized to be uniform across people, researchers can develop generalized cognitive theories.

The third and final assumption that is critical to neuropsychological research is *subtractivity*. This assumption asserts that neural dysfunction impairs or removes a component's functional role in the overall cognitive architecture, rather than adding new components. Brain damage results in a breakdown of the cognitive process by affecting at least one of the architecture's components, while leaving the remaining components intact. These intact components function normally, allowing researchers to make inferences about the function of individual modules on the basis of patterns of both spared and impaired behavior. Although cognitive deficits might cause a patient to perform a task differently, because of strategy changes, the subtractivity assumption still holds—the patient's strategy is likely to be one that could also be used by neurally intact individuals (Vallar, 2000). For example, a patient with a deficit in holding onto phonological information in short-term memory (STM) might try to perform a digit span task by retaining the visual appearance of numbers rather than their names. Normal subjects could show the same pattern under conditions in which phonological storage is disrupted by a secondary task, such as the articulation of irrelevant speech. The subtractivity assumption plays a large role in allowing researchers to use neuropsychological data to develop and test cognitive theories describing the organization of normal, undamaged cognitive architectures. (For further discussion on the plausibility of these assumptions, see Vallar, 2000.)

The subtractivity assumption applies to cognitive modules, but it does not apply to localization. That is, damage to a portion of the brain used to support a particular cognitive function might result in nearby brain areas (or homologous regions in the contralateral hemisphere) taking over this function (though perhaps with less efficiency; e.g., Cramer & Bastings, 2000; Thulborn, Carpenter, & Just, 1999). The important point here is that the brain does not invent any new cognitive components as a result of brain damage, even though the localization of a particular function may change as a result of recovery from brain damage. If new functions were developed as a result of brain damage, then it would be impossible to use the findings from patients to draw conclusions about the operation of the normal cognitive system. Given the progress in learning about cognitive function through patient studies, the assumption that no new components are created seems justified.

METHODS OF TESTING IN THE CASE STUDY APPROACH

The single-case approach to cognitive neuropsychology can be applied to either acquired or developmental deficits. Acquired deficits are the result of cerebrovascular accidents (e.g., stroke), neurological disease (e.g., Parkinson's disease, Alzheimer's disease), traumatic brain injury (e.g., head trauma in car accident), and brain tumors. Developmental disorders are present from childhood and are not linked to the onset of a brain abnormality because of disease or injury. For example, children who have been given appropriate reading instruction but continue to have reading and spelling difficulties may be classified with developmental dyslexia, and typically, no lesion is evident in these children's brains. (This is not to say that there are no brain abnormalities present in these children. However, the deficits may be subtle, such as reduced density in white matter tracts connecting particular brain regions, and as yet uncovered.)

Preliminary Standardized Testing

Single-case studies typically utilize a combination of standardized neuropsychological testing and cognitive–experimental testing. Patients may first be given basic test batteries to screen their abilities and to determine in which domain their particular deficit lies (McCloskey, 2001). Standardized test batteries such as the Western Aphasia Battery (Kertesz, 1982) may be used, which has some advantage in that administration and scoring techniques are uniform across patients and testing sessions, allowing a comparison of results across research labs or clinical settings. The results of standardized instruments give researchers a general look at the patient's impaired and preserved abilities. Although these instruments have a good sensitivity for disorder detection, they are not good at specifying the specific cognitive modules that have been affected (Alexander, 2000). For example, suppose that a test battery reveals that a patient has agrammatic speech (i.e., speech characterized by simplified grammatical structure and the omission of inflections and function words, such as prepositions and determiners). Such a finding would not indicate the source of the deficit, as it might result from any of the following: (a) difficulty accessing words or morphemes with little semantic representation (as for inflections or function words), (b) difficulty retrieving syntactic frames for production, or (c) difficulty producing phonological information for unstressed words or morphemes (which would include some inflections and function words). It is the job of the cognitive neuropsychologist to investigate these possibilities.

Testing in Specific Cognitive Domains

Following broad deficit classification, researchers investigate impaired and preserved behavior more specifically. This is typically done by assessing patients on a variety of tasks using testing methods from cognitive–experimental psychology. In our lab, for example, we are interested in the role of STM and executive function in language processing (e.g., Hamilton & Martin, 2007; R. C. Martin & Allen, 2008; R. C. Martin & He, 2004). Thus, we have a set of tasks assessing of a wide range of language and STM abilities, including (but not limited to) measures of input and output phonology (i.e., the phonology involved in perception and production), picture naming, semantic knowledge, vocabulary, single-word and sentence comprehension, sentence production, and executive function. For each cognitive function of interest, several measures are usually obtained to ensure confidence that the patient shows impairment on the underlying component. That is, poor performance on any one task might be due to extraneous factors such as distraction or fatigue, or to specific features of the task that are unrelated to the construct of interest. For example, a patient might do poorly on an STM task involving repetition of a word list because of difficulties in speech output rather than because of an STM deficit. Thus, one should also test the patient on STM tasks that do not involve output—such as on a recognition probe task (i.e., judging whether a probe word was in a preceding list). Consistently poor performance on STM tasks irrespective of output modality provides converging evidence for a deficit in the cognitive construct of interest. Accordingly, the results of such tasks provide a more detailed insight into the nature of the patient's abilities, well beyond the information gained from standardized test batteries. And, as noted, it is important to characterize the patient's preserved abilities as well as the areas of deficit to establish how disruption to the cognitive system gives rise to the observed symptoms. As one aspect of determining preserved abilities, it is essential to rule out the possibility that patient deficits are caused by peripheral dysfunctions (Heaton & Marcotte, 2000)—for example, one would not want to incorrectly attribute poor language production to a deficit in central aspects, such as lexical selection or syntactic formulation, when it actually results from a speech–motor impairment. Thus, assessments of peripheral motor abilities and visual and auditory acuity are important components of the testing protocol.

Precise Theory-Based Testing

Given initial findings about the source of a patient's deficit, researchers further assess patient abilities using tasks that help to decide among competing cognitive theories. The tasks to include, stimuli to include in tasks, and the scoring methodologies are all decisions that should be guided by relevant

theory. Theoretical guidance does more than just support Hypothesis A—it also strengthens Hypothesis A by refuting Hypothesis B. Given that patients often have impairments to multiple cognitive components, utilization of a theoretical framework helps to determine which aspects of performance are relevant to the process of interest (Miceli, 2000, p. 370). For example, suppose that we are interested in sentence comprehension and how an aphasic patient's comprehension difficulties increase as the syntactic complexity of sentences increases. Many hypotheses have been proposed regarding the source of such sentence comprehension deficits for patients showing good single-word comprehension (for reviews, see R. C. Martin, 2001; R. C. Martin, Vuong, & Crowther, 2007), ranging from deficits in comprehending function words and inflections, to disruption of specific linguistic rules that are needed to understand certain complex constructions, to STM deficits, to difficulty resolving interference from competing syntactic and semantic analyses. For our patient of interest, we might find that he or she, like many aphasic patients, has a reduced word span (e.g., two items compared with a typical span of five or six items for healthy controls). The reduced span would be consistent with the notion that an STM deficit was a source of comprehension difficulty, as complex constructions would typically be long and involve integrating information across some distance in the sentence (e.g., linking *boy* as the object of *carried* and the subject of *had* in "The boy that the girl carried had red hair"). On the other hand, it is possible that the span deficit and comprehension deficit derive from different sources. Let us suppose that we wished to decide between the reduced span and interference hypotheses regarding the source of the sentence comprehension deficit. We might present sentences in which the distance between words that have to be integrated is varied and in which interference from semantic and syntactic features of intervening material is also varied. For example, we might assess reaction time and accuracy in answering comprehension questions, such as, "Did the woman complain?" following simple sentences with high or low interference from intervening material. In the high-interference condition, the sentence contains other intervening nouns that are plausible subjects of *complain*.

> Base sentence:
> 1. The woman complained to the manager.
>
> Increasing distance, low interference:
> 2. The woman near the third aisle complained to the manager.
> 3. The woman near the third aisle of the grocery department complained to the manager.
>
> Increasing distance, high interference:
> 4. The woman near the older clerk complained to the manager.
> 5. The woman near the youngest son of the older clerk complained to the manager.

If distance is the critical factor, then increasing distance should disproportionately impair the patients' performance relative to controls for both the low-interference and high-interference conditions. In contrast, if only interference is important, then distance may have no effect at all in the low-interference condition. An effect of distance only in the high-interference condition would imply that it is the amount of interference and not distance that is critical. Preliminary data from our lab indicated that for some patients, interference and not distance is critical (R. C. Martin, 2009). Even if distance were the important factor in both the low- and high-interference conditions, it might still be possible that STM as tapped by span tasks was not the same as the STM tapped by sentence comprehension (see Caplan & Waters, 1995, 1999); that is, there may be working memory resources that are specialized for sentence processing. One would need to show that all patients with similar span deficits showed similar effects of distance; however, considerable existing data suggest that this is not the case (Caplan & Waters, 1999; R. C. Martin & He, 2004). That is, patients with very reduced span have good comprehension of a variety of sentence types with long distance dependencies. Thus, these data suggest that the working memory resources that are involved in sentence processing diverge from those that are involved in typical span tasks.

Multiple Single-Patient Approach

Although this chapter discusses the single–case study approach in neuropsychological research, research along these lines is not limited to single patients insofar as researchers can bring together the results from several single case studies to speak to the same cognitive process. If, for example, a researcher has two patients with STM deficits, each patient's abilities can be thoroughly assessed, with patients then being compared to determine how they are the same and how they differ. The ways in which their deficits diverge can provide details about the architecture of STM. For example, Martin and colleagues (e.g., R. C. Martin & He, 2004; R. C. Martin, Shelton, & Yaffee, 1994) have suggested that two types of STM deficits can be identified in patients with aphasia: Some patients have a deficit in maintaining phonological information, whereas other patients have a deficit in maintaining lexical–semantic information. The two patient types differ in terms of the influence of phonological and semantic factors on their STM pattern. These distinct patterns across different patients have provided evidence for a multiple capacity view of STM. This sort of multipatient comparison is known as the *multiple single-patient approach* (McCloskey, 2001) in cognitive neuropsychological research.

PATTERNS OF DEFICITS IN PATIENT DATA

Traditionally, there are thought to be three main data patterns that emerge from the single–case study and multiple single-patient approaches: associations, dissociations, and double dissociations.

Associations

Associations involve the co-occurrence of two or more deficits. For example, a patient with intact visual processing may demonstrate a deficit in object recognition that affects the recognition of objects and faces. In this case, a deficit in object recognition co-occurs with a deficit in face recognition, such that performance on each behavior is poor. Associations between behaviors may lead to the conclusion that a single cognitive module controls both object and face recognition, and disruption to this module results in a functional syndrome (or collection of symptoms; Vallar, 2000). If it does, then the association has theoretical implications.

Although a single cognitive architecture for all object processing is one interpretation, it is possible that the face–object association is caused by damage to two separate functional modules, one responsible for object recognition and another for face recognition. These modules may be localized in neurally proximal regions, which results in the frequent co-occurrence of object and face recognition deficits. In this case, the association has little implication for models of cognition.

Single Dissociation

In contrast to an association, a *dissociation* occurs when one cognitive process is selectively impaired whereas another is spared. In a single dissociation, a patient demonstrates impaired performance on task A, which is thought to tap one cognitive module, coupled with intact performance on task B, which is thought to tap a different cognitive module. The dissociation provides evidence that the cognitive modules are distinct. For example, the assumption that the same recognition module controls object and face recognition would be inconsistent with a patient who demonstrates a pattern of normal object recognition but impaired face recognition. In fact, this selective deficit in face recognition has been reported and is known as prosopagnosia (see Shallice, 1988, for discussion).

Although it is possible that the single dissociation occurs because of separate processing modules, differential difficulty could instead be the source— that is, Task A may simply be more difficult than Task B. For example, a dissociation between face and object recognition may occur because of separate processing modules, or because the complexity of facial stimuli and the overall similarity of faces may make face recognition a more difficult task than object recognition. If this possibility were in fact true, both object and face recognition processes would be impaired by more severe damage to the recognition module. Although the complexity argu-

ment could be raised for any single dissociation, McCloskey (2001) maintained that this is often an implausible argument against separate modules, as neuropsychological work can involve in-depth assessment that rules out such claims. For instance, one can vary the difficulty of the discriminations required for face and object recognition to determine whether the dissociation still holds.

Double Dissociation

A third data pattern resulting from neuropsychological case studies is the *double dissociation*. A double dissociation is essentially two dissociations in opposite directions. A double dissociation occurs when Patient 1 demonstrates impaired performance on Task A but intact performance on Task B, whereas Patient 2 demonstrates the opposite pattern—intact performance on Task A but impaired performance on Task B. To continue with the object recognition example, double dissociations have been found between deficits in object and face processing, known as *visual–object agnosia* and *prosopagnosia*, respectively (see Shallice, 1988). Importantly, double dissociations rule out the possibility that the same module controls these two processes, but they dissociate because of differences in processing requirements. Instead, the fact that both recognition processes can be selectively damaged suggests that object and face recognition involve functionally and anatomically separate cognitive modules (cf. Grill-Spector, Kourtzi, & Kanwisher, 2001; Kanwisher, 2000; but see Gauthier, Skudlarski, Gore, & Anderson, 2000; Gauthier & Tarr, 1997, for an opposing view).[1]

Although the existence of double dissociations provides strong evidence for separate cognitive modules, in some domains, it will not be possible to observe a double dissociation because one side of the dissociation is not a theoretical possibility. For instance, in the experiment on sentence comprehension that contrasted distance and interference, one

---

[1]As a note of caution, Coltheart (2001) has pointed out that researchers should be aware of the implications of the word *separate* when assuming that processes utilize separate processing modules. That is, although a double dissociation allows researchers to conclude that two cognitive systems involve separate processes, we must clarify what is meant by *separate*. Specifically, double dissociations allow researchers to infer that the two processing systems are not identical. Coltheart pointed out, however, that these processes are not likely to be completely separate because they may still involve some overlapping processing components. For example, it is not unreasonable to assume that object and face recognition involve overlapping visual perception processes, even if the recognition processes are not identical. As such, double dissociations do not allow for the conclusion that two domains involve completely separate cognitive modules per se but rather that at least one module is unique to the individual processes.

might observe patients who were affected by interference but not distance and fail to find patients who show the reverse. This could arise because distance per se is not a critical factor in determining sentence comprehension for anyone—whether for healthy individuals or brain damaged patients (see McElree, Foraker, & Dyer, 2003). Likewise, in the domain of picture naming, one can find patients with preserved semantic knowledge, as evidenced by performance on comprehension tests, who show impaired picture naming; however, one cannot find the reverse—impaired comprehension and preserved naming—as naming appears to be dependent on access to a semantic representation. Thus, double dissociations cannot be taken as the gold standard in all domains for establishing the existence of a cognitive component or set of components in a particular model. Different approaches can be taken to provide solid supporting evidence for the existence of separate modules. For instance, one can make parametric variations in demands on a hypothesized component and show that the patients' performance varies in line with these demands for one component but not for another (as was described in the example manipulating distance and interference in sentence comprehension). Showing that a patient's performance is affected by the degree of interference and unaffected by distance (even with extreme manipulations) argues against a claim that resolving interference is just more demanding of cognitive resources than is the effect of distance.

Moreover, simply demonstrating a dissociation or double dissociation does not reveal the inner workings of the hypothesized module. To do so, one can look at detailed patterns of performance, such as the frequency of different types of errors, in establishing more precisely the nature of the processing in the hypothesized model. For instance, the cascaded model of picture naming (Figure 33.1b) predicts that mixed errors (i.e., the production of errors that are both semantically and phonologically related to the target) should be greater than chance level. That is, if semantic relatedness did not affect phonological errors in naming, then the production of phonologically related words that were also semantically related (saying "rat" for "cat") should be because of chance. If semantic relatedness does affect the production of phonologically related

errors, then mixed errors should occur at a higher than chance level. If the mixed errors do occur as predicted, then this would support the theoretical inference that activation of semantically related lexical representations persists and influences phonological retrieval.

IDENTIFYING BEHAVIORAL DEFICITS

One issue that has not yet been discussed concerns how a patient's performance is characterized as impaired, as opposed to preserved. In other words, what is a deficit, and how is a deficit defined? In much neuropsychological work, the standard against which patient performance is assessed is the performance of neurologically intact controls matched on various demographic factors. Some cutoff point is used—such as the patient being outside the range of control performance, or less restrictively, scoring, for example, at the fifth percentile or below on a set of measures designed to assess a particular cognitive function. Standardized assessments tend to include norms from large samples of subjects across various age groups. Using these norms, cutoff points are established to determine what maximum score is needed for performance to be classified as unimpaired. Unfortunately, in the laboratory setting, it is not always possible to collect healthy control data on very large groups of subjects across many tasks. Instead, nonstandardized tasks require researchers to collect measures from demographically matched control groups. The performance of healthy, matched controls is used as a reference, from which deviation is measured. Crawford and Howell (1998) have advocated a modified *t* test as appropriate for testing whether single cases differ from a control group, thus making it appropriate for neuropsychological research (see Crawford & Howell, 1998, for more details). Many times, it is also advisable to use proportional or log-transformed data when using reaction time measures (Verhaeghen & De Meersman, 1998). That is, a standard finding in studies of healthy adults is that those individuals with slower reaction times tend to show larger effects (e.g., they show bigger effects of word frequency on picture naming latencies). This pattern can be explained by assuming that for those with longer overall latencies, all cognitive processes have been slowed. Consequently, if a patient showed a large reaction time effect, this may reflect an overall slowing of all cognitive processes for the patient, instead of a disruption in a specific component. If the patient's reaction time effect remains outside of the control range after a log transformation of reaction times in each condition, this provides more solid evidence that a specific component has been disrupted.

NEUROANATOMICAL LOCALIZATION

Given that a brain lesion for an individual patient with a persisting cognitive deficit is typically large and affects several different cognitive modules, it is often impossible to draw strong conclusions about neuranatomical localization from an individual case. The multiple single-case approach is called for, in which a large number of individual cases have been studied so that one has a good grasp of the cognitive components affected in each case. Then, techniques involving lesion overlap or voxel-based lesion symptom mapping can be used to determine the likely area underlying a particular component (e.g., Bates et al., 2003; Damasio, 2000). For the use of either technique, it is important to include patients who do *not* have a deficit to the cognitive component of interest as well as those who do. Otherwise, one may conclude that a specific region is involved in a given cognitive function, but this region is one that is typically damaged in all patients with a particular etiology (e.g., middle cerebral artery infarction) and is not specific to the component of interest (Hillis et al., 2004).

SINGLE CASE VERSUS GROUP STUDIES

This chapter has focused on the single–case study approach to cognitive neuropsychological research; however, an alternative is the group-study approach (Chapter 34 of this volume). Some researchers have taken extreme views, arguing for one approach to the exclusion of the other (for two opposing arguments, see Caramazza, 1986, and Caramazza & McCloskey, 1988, vs. Robertson, Knight, Rafal, & Shimamura, 1993). Both approaches have a similar

goal, which is to study patients with cognitive impairments in order to make inferences about cognitive architecture and its underlying neural substrate. As described, the single–case study approach involves an in-depth examination of a patient's abilities. The single–case study approach allows researchers to show that patient impairments rarely result from damage to a single component but instead result from a combination of several damaged components. Studying the specific deficits on a large variety of theoretically motivated tasks can eventually lead to hypotheses about the function of underlying damaged component(s).

The group approach assesses a collection of impaired individuals on various tasks of interest. Such patients are often grouped according to some criterion, such as clinical classification (e.g., Broca's vs. Wernicke's aphasia), symptom presence (reduced use of grammatical markers), neurological criteria (frontal vs. posterior brain damage), performance on experimental tasks (inability to comprehend syntactically complex sentences), or some combination of these criteria. Grouping along one criterion assumes that patients have homogenous damage to the same cognitive components (Miceli, 2000), but in fact these groupings do not guarantee that this is the case. For example, suppose that you are interested in understanding the source of agrammatic speech. Although such speech is frequently observed in patients who are classified as Broca's aphasics, this is not always the case. Thus, choosing a group of patients who are Broca's aphasics as assessed by performance on a standardized battery will not guarantee that the patients have the behavioral deficit of interest. Moreover, even if a patient group is selected on the basis of having agrammatic speech, this will not guarantee that all have agrammatic speech for the same reason. As discussed, there are different possible sources for this speech production pattern. Additionally, it is unlikely that the differential source of impairment will be discovered when patient performance is averaged across individuals, as specific impairments may be wiped out in averages, concealing this potentially informative information. Lastly, grouping patients by lesion location only ensures that you are investigating patients with damage to similar brain regions—it does not control for the similarity of symptoms. Thus, no matter how grouping is done, it is unlikely that group studies will be composed of patients with identical spared and impaired cognitive components. Although it has often been argued that large samples are representative of the normal population, this is not necessarily the case in patient group studies. In fact, Caramazza (1986) has argued that you can only appropriately group patients together after each has received extensive testing to determine the exact nature of their deficit in terms of the underlying cognitive architecture, at which point you will have completed several single case studies and grouping seems redundant. Thus, patient selection issues in group studies are difficult to overcome.

Although there are clearly limitations to group studies, they are not without their benefits (for further discussion, see Chapter 34 of this volume). Group studies are particularly beneficial when studying a domain in which cognitive theory is not well developed and associated cognitive impairments are not yet known or understood (Caramazza & Coltheart, 2006; Coltheart, 2001). In this context, group studies allow for a preliminary understanding of patient deficits and the development of theoretically motivated modular components. Additionally, group studies may be beneficial when attempting to provide evidence for associations of function. They allow the use of statistical approaches, such as correlational measures and analyses of covariance, to control for nonrelevant factors.

The single–case study approach is not without its criticisms. Given "each patient may be as unique as a snowflake" (Buxbaum, 2006, p. 194), how can you replicate a finding in another patient? A related problem is that particular deficits may be exceedingly rare. As Coltheart (2001) argued, however, rarity does not make the patient findings any less applicable to cognitive theorizing. Assuming that the data have been collected in a thorough, well-controlled, and theoretically motivated fashion and that alternative theoretical explanations have been ruled out, then the findings would still be considered valid. However, researchers are likely to be more confident about the conclusions drawn from the case if replication does occur. If only one

case is ever reported, one might conclude that the individual had some unusual brain organization or that chance factors led to the particular constellation of impaired and spared function observed for that patient. What is often true, however, is that once the findings for an individual patient have been published, other labs around the world start looking for similar patients, and additional cases are uncovered. Thus, replication occurs over time. Additionally, between-patient replication is possible using patients with similar impairments—although the impairments of these additional patients may not have exactly the same character, they serve as a source of converging evidence that provides support for or challenges the same theories. Miceli (2000) pointed out that replication can occur at two levels. It is much less difficult to get replication at the general level, such as finding a patient with a particular deficit. For example, many patients have demonstrated deficits in phonological STM (e.g., R. C. Martin et al., 1994; Vallar & Papagno, 2002). This pattern of general replication, however, does not guarantee detailed replication. That is, the fact that these patients exhibit a similar behavioral pattern of phonological STM deficits does not guarantee that they will all show similar impairments across other cognitive tasks, such as sentence comprehension and word repetition. In contrast to general replication, this sort of detailed replication requires that patients exhibit the same patterns of behavior across all domains.

Although it might be difficult to find another patient to provide detailed replication of a previous finding, converging evidence also plays a strong role in supporting the implications for cognitive theories that are drawn from individual cases. That is, the findings from an individual case can lead to the proposal or revision of a cognitive model. The proposed model will lead to predictions that either are or are not borne out by further patients, whether or not they provide an exact replication of a previous case. That is, the findings from one patient may lead to modification of a theory, which may then predict the existence of another data pattern in a different type of patient—which might then be looked for and reported. In addition, inferences to cognitive theory are not limited to neuropsychological data;

researchers can find support through other methods in cognitive psychology. That is, support for a given hypothesis or a specific theoretical breakdown of cognitive components should also include behavioral research or neuroimaging findings with neurally intact individuals and computational modeling to accommodate findings from brain damaged and healthy individuals.

CONCLUSION

The case study approach in cognitive neuropsychology aims to use the data from patients with brain damage to inform theories of normal cognition. In this approach, a detailed assessment of the patient's performance is obtained to determine the areas of impaired and spared functioning. Multiple measures are obtained for each hypothesized component to provide converging evidence that the component is spared or impaired. Theory within a domain is used to guide the use and development of behavioral tests. The findings may provide support for one theory over others or challenge all existing theories. Additionally, the case study approach is often used in comparing multiple cases in which different patients show a disruption of different components of a cognitive process. Lastly, the case study approach avoids problems associated with a lack of homogeneity across patients when they are grouped on the basis of a clinical syndrome, lesion localization, or other dimension. A group study approach may be preferred, however, when investigating a new domain in which there is little theoretical guidance, when patients with pure deficits are exceedingly rare, or when a correlational approach may be advantageous.

References

Alexander, M. P. (2000). The clinical evaluation of mental status. In F. Boller & J. Grafman (Eds.), *Handbook of neuropsychology* (Vol. 1, pp. 3–25). Oxford, England: Elsevier.

Bates, E., Wilson, S. M., Saygin, A. P., Dick, F., Sereno, M. I., Knight, R. T., & Dronkers, N. F. (2003). Voxel-based lesion-symptom mapping. *Nature Neuroscience, 6*, 448–450.

Broca, P. (1861). Perte de la parole, ramollissement chronique et destruction partielle du lobe antérieur gauche du cerveau [Loss of speech, chronic softening and partial destruction of the left anterior lobe of the brain]. *Bulletin de la Société Anthropologique, 2*, 235–238.

Buxbaum, L. J. (2006). On the right (and left) track: Twenty years of progress in studying hemispatial neglect. *Cognitive Neuropsychology, 23*, 184–201. doi:10.1080/02643290500202698

Caplan, D., & Waters, G. S. (1995). Aphasic disorders of syntactic comprehension and working memory capacity. *Cognitive Neuropsychology, 12*, 637–649. doi:10.1080/02643299508252011

Caplan, D., & Waters, G. S. (1999). Verbal working memory and sentence comprehension. *Behavioral and Brain Sciences, 22*, 95–126. doi:10.1017/S0140525X99001788

Caramazza, A. (1986). On drawing inferences about the structure of normal cognitive systems from the analysis of patterns of impaired performance: The case for single-patient studies. *Brain and Cognition, 5*, 41–66. doi:10.1016/0278-2626(86)90061-8

Caramazza, A., & Coltheart, M. (2006). Cognitive Neuropsychology twenty years on. *Cognitive Neuropsychology, 23*, 3–12. doi:10.1080/02643290500443250

Caramazza, A., & McCloskey, M. (1988). The case for single-patient studies. *Cognitive Neuropsychology, 5*, 517–527. doi:10.1080/02643298808253271

Coltheart, M. (2001). Assumptions and methods in Cognitive Neuropsychology. In B. Rapp (Ed.), *The handbook of cognitive neuropsychology: What deficits reveal about the human mind* (pp. 3–21). Philadelphia, PA: Psychology Press.

Cramer, S. C., & Bastings, E. P. (2000). Mapping clinically relevant plasticity after stroke. *Neuropharmacology, 39*, 842–851. doi:10.1016/S0028-3908(99)00258-0

Crawford, J. R., & Howell, D. C. (1998). Comparing an individual's test score against norms derived from small samples. *Clinical Neuropsychologist, 12*, 482–486.

Damasio, H. (2000). The lesion method in cognitive neuroscience. In F. Boller & J. Grafman (Eds.), *Handbook of neuropsychology* (Vol. 1, pp. 77–102). Oxford, England: Elsevier.

Dell, G. S., & O'Seaghdha, P. G. (1992). Stages of lexical access in speech production. *Cognition, 42*, 287–314. doi:10.1016/0010-0277(92)90046-K

Dell, G. S., Schwartz, M. F., Martin, N., Saffran, E. M., & Gagnon, D. A. (1997). Lexical access in aphasic and nonaphasic speakers. *Psychological Review, 104*, 801–838. doi:10.1037/0033-295X.104.4.801

Drew, R. L., & Thomson, C. K. (1999). Model-based semantic treatment for naming deficits in aphasia. *Journal of Speech, Language, and Hearing Research, 42*, 972–989.

Fodor, J. A. (1983). *The modularity of mind*. Cambridge, MA: MIT Press.

Foygel, D., & Dell, G. S. (2000). Models of impaired lexical access in speech production. *Psychological Review, 42*, 182–216.

Gauthier, I., Skudlarski, P., Gore, J. C., & Anderson, A. W. (2000). Expertise for cars and birds recruits brain areas involved in face recognition. *Nature Neuroscience, 3*, 191–197. doi:10.1038/72140

Gauthier, I., & Tarr, M. J. (1997). Becoming a "Greeble" expert: Exploring mechanisms for face recognition. *Vision Research, 37*, 1673–1682. doi:10.1016/S0042-6989(96)00286-6

Goodale, M. A., & Milner, A. D. (1992). Separate visual pathways for perception and action. *Trends in Neurosciences, 15*, 20–25. doi:10.1016/0166-2236(92)90344-8

Grill-Spector, K., Kourtzi, Z., & Kanwisher, N. (2001). The lateral occipital complex and its role in object recognition. *Vision Research, 41*, 1409–1422. doi:10.1016/S0042-6989(01)00073-6

Hamilton, A. C., & Martin, R. C. (2007). Proactive interference in a semantic short-term memory deficit: Role of semantic and phonological relatedness. *Cortex, 43*, 112–123. doi:10.1016/S0010-9452(08)70449-0

Heaton, R. K., & Marcotte, T. D. (2000). Clinical neuropsychological tests and assessment techniques. In F. Boller & J. Grafman (Eds.), *Handbook of neuropsychology* (Vol. 1, pp. 27–52). Oxford, England: Elsevier.

Hickok, G., & Poeppel, D. (2007). The cortical organization of speech processing. *Nature Reviews Neuroscience, 8*, 393–402. doi:10.1038/nrn2113

Hillis, A. E., Work, M., Barker, P. B., Jacobs, M. A., Breese, E. L., & Maurer, K. (2004). Re-examining the brain regions crucial for orchestrating speech articulation. *Brain: A Journal of Neurology, 127*, 1479–1487. doi:10.1093/brain/awh172

Kanwisher, N. (2000). Domain specificity in face perception. *Nature Neuroscience, 3*, 759–763. doi:10.1038/77664

Kertesz, A. (1982). *Western aphasia battery*. New York, NY: Grune Stattron.

Levelt, W. J. M., Schriefers, H., Vorberg, D., Meyer, A. S., Pechmann, T., & Havinga, J. (1991). The time course of lexical access in speech production: A study of picture naming. *Psychological Review, 98*, 122–142. doi:10.1037/0033-295X.98.1.122

Martin, N., & Saffran, E. M. (1992). A computational account of deep dysphasia: Evidence from a single case study. *Brain and Language, 43*, 240–274. doi:10.1016/0093-934X(92)90130-7

Martin, R. C. (2001). Sentence comprehension deficits. In B. Rapp (Ed.), *Handbook of cognitive neuropsychology* (pp. 349–374). Philadelphia, PA: Psychology Press.

Martin, R. C. (2009, May). *Language processing and working memory: Evidence from neuropsychology*. Paper presented at the 21st Annual Meeting of the Association for Psychological Science, San Francisco, CA.

Martin, R. C., & Allen, C. M. (2008). A disorder of executive function and its role in language processing. *Seminars in Speech and Language, 29*, 201–210. doi:10.1055/s-0028-1082884

Martin, R. C., & He, T. (2004). Semantic short-term memory and its role in sentence processing: A replication. *Brain and Language, 89*, 76–82. doi:10.1016/S0093-934X(03)00300-6

Martin, R. C., Lesch, M. F., & Bartha, M. C. (1999). Independence of input and output phonology in word processing and short-term memory. *Journal of Memory and Language, 41*, 3–29. doi:10.1006/jmla.1999.2637

Martin, R. C., Shelton, J. R., & Yaffee, L. S. (1994). Language processing and working memory: Neuropsychological evidence for separate phonological and semantic capacities. *Journal of Memory and Language, 33*, 83–111. doi:10.1006/jmla.1994.1005

Martin, R. C., Vuong, L. C., & Crowther, J. E. (2007). Sentence-level deficits in aphasia. In M. G. Gaskell (Ed.), *The Oxford handbook of psycholinguistics* (pp. 425–439). Oxford, England: Oxford University Press.

McCloskey, M. (2001). The future of Cognitive Neuropsychology. In B. Rapp (Ed.), *The handbook of cognitive neuropsychology: What deficits reveal about the human mind* (pp. 593–610). Philadelphia, PA: Psychology Press.

McElree, B., Foraker, S., & Dyer, L. (2003). Memory structures that subserve sentence comprehension. *Journal of Memory and Language, 48*, 67–91. doi:10.1016/S0749-596X(02)00515-6

Miceli, G. (2000). The role of cognitive theory in neuropsychological research. In F. Boller & J. Grafman (Eds.), *Handbook of neuropsychology* (Vol. 1, pp. 367–389). Oxford, England: Elsevier.

Mishkin, M., Ungerleider, L. G., & Macko, K. A. (1983). Object vision and spatial vision: two cortical pathways. *Trends in Neurosciences, 6*, 414–417. doi:10.1016/0166-2236(83)90190-X

Newcombe, F., Ratcliff, G., & Damasio, H. (1987). Dissociable visual and spatial impairments following right posterior cerebral lesions: Clinical, neuropsychological and anatomical evidence. *Neuropsychologia, 25*, 149–161. doi:10.1016/0028-3932(87)90127-8

Perenin, M. T., & Vighetto, A. (1988). Optic ataxia: A specific disruption in visuomotor mechanisms. *Brain:*

A Journal of Neurology, 111, 643–674. doi:10.1093/brain/111.3.643

Rapp, B., & Goldrick, M. (2000). Discreteness and interactivity in spoken word production. *Psychological Review, 107*, 460–499. doi:10.1037/0033-295X.107.3.460

Raymer, A. M., Thompson, C. K., Jacobs, B., & Le Grand, H. R. (1993). Phonological treatment of naming deficits in aphasia: Model-based generalization analysis. *Aphasiology, 7*, 27–53. doi:10.1080/02687039308249498

Robertson, L. C., Knight, R. T., Rafal, R., & Shimamura, A. P. (1993). Cognitive neuropsychology is more than just single-case studies. *Journal of Experimental Psychology: Learning, Memory, and Cognition, 19*, 710–717. doi:10.1037/0278-7393.19.3.710

Roelofs, A. (1992). A spreading-activation theory of lemma retrieval in speaking. *Cognition, 42*, 107–142. doi:10.1016/0010-0277(92)90041-F

Ruml, W., Caramazza, A., Shelton, J. R., & Chialant, D. (2000). Testing assumptions in computational theories of aphasia. *Journal of Memory and Language, 43*, 217–248. doi:10.1006/jmla.2000.2730

Schwartz, M. F., Dell, G. S., Martin, N., Gahl, S., & Sobel, P. (2006). A case-series test of the interactive two-step model of lexical-access: Evidence from picture naming. *Journal of Memory and Language, 54*, 228–264. doi:10.1016/j.jml.2005.10.001

Shallice, T. (1988). *From neuropsychology to mental structure*. New York, NY: Cambridge University Press. doi:10.1017/CBO9780511526817

Thulborn, K. R., Carpenter, P. A., & Just, M. A. (1999). Plasticity of language-related brain function during recovery from stroke. *Stroke, 30*, 749–754.

Vallar, G. (2000). The methodological foundations of human neuropsychology: Studies in brain-damaged patients. In F. Boller & J. Grafman (Eds.), *Handbook of neuropsychology* (Vol. 1, pp. 305–344). Oxford, England: Elsevier.

Vallar, G., & Papagno, C. (2002). Neuropsychological impairments of verbal short-term memory. In A. D. Baddeley, M. D. Kopelman, & B. A. Wilson (Eds.), *Handbook of memory disorders* (pp. 249–270). Chichester, England: Wiley.

Verhaeghen, P., & De Meersman, L. (1998). Aging and the Stroop effect: A meta-analysis. *Psychology and Aging, 13*, 120–126. doi:10.1037/0882-7974.13.1.120

Wambaugh, J. L., Linebaugh, C. W., Doyle, P. J., Martinez, A. L., Kalinyak-Fliszar, M., & Spencer, K. A. (2001). Effects of cueing treatments on lexical retrieval in aphasic speakers with different levels of deficit. *Aphasiology, 15*, 933–950. doi:10.1080/02687040143000302

CHAPTER 34

GROUP STUDIES IN EXPERIMENTAL NEUROPSYCHOLOGY

Lesley K. Fellows

WHY NEUROPSYCHOLOGY?

A fundamental assumption of neuropsychology, and of cognitive neuroscience more generally, is that behavior has a biological basis—that it results from processes that are executed in the nervous system. Following from this assumption, emotions, thoughts, percepts, and actions can be understood in neurobiological terms. This premise was advanced by the philosophers of ancient Greece, supported, in part, by observations of patients with brain injury (Gross, 1995). The fact that damage to the brain could lead to paralysis, disorders of sensation, or even disruptions of consciousness suggested that this organ was *the seat* of such abilities, although the broad claim that brain function underlies behavior was not without controversy over the centuries that followed (Crivellato & Ribatti, 2007).

The 19th century saw, on the one hand, major developments in understanding the anatomy and physiology of the brain and, on the other, more systematic descriptions of behavioral changes resulting from neurological diseases. These advances laid the groundwork for current thinking about the brain. Here again, clinical observations provided an important impetus, as did analyses of individual differences in normal behavior: Neurologists such as Paul Broca and Carl Wernicke reported that focal brain injury to specific areas within the left hemisphere disrupted particular aspects of language (Feinberg & Farah, 2006). Their thinking was influenced, in part, by Franz-Joseph Gall and others who developed the concept of phrenology in about the same period. Phrenology was based on observations of specific

individual differences in skull shape (explicitly thought to be a proxy for underlying brain structure) in relation to individual differences in behavior. Complex traits like *benevolence* and *wit* were thus related to particular parts of the brain. Although the methods are clearly flawed to the eye of the modern reader, the underlying concept of localization, that brain structure and function are related, had a major impact on the development of clinical neurology and of experimental neuropsychology.

The work of Broca, Wernicke, and other 19th- and early 20th-century neurologists illustrated how observation in clinical populations can (a) provide insights into how a complex behavior (like language) can be segmented into simpler components (e.g., production and comprehension) and (b) how such components can be related to specific regions of the brain. Both defining the components of behavior and relating these components to the brain can be done on the basis of a single, carefully studied case (see Chapter 33 of this volume). However, the limitations of clinical observations in humans were also apparent in these early days. Clinicians were (and are) acutely aware of wide variability in the clinical presentation of a particular pathological condition, determined both by differences in premorbid individual characteristics (e.g., age, education, or health status) and differences in the specific details of the pathological process. Case series and group studies provide an important means of determining the generalizability of inferences that can be drawn from individual observations.

DOI: 10.1037/13620-034
APA Handbook of Research Methods in Psychology: Vol. 2. Research Designs, H. Cooper (Editor-in-Chief)

Gordon Holmes, a British neurologist whose work on the effects of penetrating brain injury in World War I soldiers helped to establish the retinotopic organization of primary visual cortex, poetically captured the limitations of clinical observation in a lecture delivered in 1944:

> My own work on the visual cortex has been limited to observation in man.... This has required the collection of a large number of observations, for while the physiologist can rely on experiments when he can select and control, ... the clinician must depend on the analysis of observations which are rarely so simple or clear cut.... The physiologist may be compared with the builder in ... hewn stones which can easily be fitted together, the physician resembles the mason who has to use irregular rubble and therefore requires more time and labour to attain his end. But in some branches of neurology, the "rubble" collected and put together by the clinician is essential. (Holmes, 1944/1979, pp. 440–441)

Holmes underlined two key points: (a) that the limitations inherent to studying the effects of brain injury in humans can be minimized by gathering data from many subjects and by interpreting these data in the context of converging evidence from other methods and (b) that the limitations are offset by the fact that these observations provide crucial insights that may not be acquired in any other way. As this chapter will describe, there have been many logistical, technical, and analytic advances in human lesion studies over the past century. However, Holmes's comments on the core advantages and limitations remain as pertinent as ever.

INFERENTIAL STRENGTHS OF LESION STUDIES

Research on effects of brain injury on behavior addresses two main issues: First, it can establish that a particular region of the brain is necessary for the expression of a particular behavior, in turn, supporting the inference that it is critical for a particular

cognitive process (Fellows et al., 2005; Rorden & Karnath, 2004). In principle, this is a powerful form of evidence because it addresses causality. Although cognitive neuroscience now has many other methods available to investigate brain–behavior relations, most provide correlational data. Standard functional neuroimaging methods, for example, reveal brain regions in which blood-oxygen-level dependent (commonly referred to as BOLD) signal (itself a correlate of neural activity) is correlated with a behavioral process of interest. These findings can be informative, but alone they are insufficient to establish that the brain regions so identified are in fact necessary for the behavior in question (Fellows et al., 2005; Rorden & Karnath, 2004).

These inferential considerations are particularly relevant in the study of complex behaviors, and in new areas of enquiry. Consider risky decision making as an example. Imagine yourself at the blackjack table, deciding how much to stake on the next card. Several correlated processes are likely under way in your brain. You may be calculating the odds of winning, integrating your recent history of wins and losses, and weighing these factors to reach a decision. You may be imagining how you would spend your winnings, or how you would explain a loss to your spouse. It is likely that you are experiencing substantial changes in arousal and autonomic tone: A pounding heart and sweaty palms often accompany a risky choice. Whether all of these putative processes are distinct, important to the decision, or simply correlated epiphenomena are empirical questions. Interpreting functional magnetic resonance imaging (fMRI) activations in this situation is not easy—for example, is a given area more active because it is critically involved in risky decision making or is it important in central autonomic control, mediating the changes in sympathetic nervous system outflow that result in the pounding heart? Although careful design can help to minimize these uncertainties of interpretation, the nature of correlational evidence means that they can never be eliminated entirely. Converging evidence from loss-of-function methods, such as lesion studies, can help test necessity claims. If we take a hypothetical "risky decision" brain area as an example, a study of patients with damage to that area could directly test whether it was critical for the decision, for the autonomic changes that accompany that decision, or for both. Such an experiment would shed light both on the critical components of decision making (do autonomic changes influence choice?) and on the brain substrates of the critical processes (e.g., Critchley et al., 2003).

More profoundly, the study of patients can provide biological constraints to psychological theory. The usual form this has taken is that of dissociation of cognitive processes. Two putative psychological constructs may be considered distinct if brain injury disrupts one and not the other—establishing what is termed a *function dissociation*. As will be described, experiments of this kind have been influential, but how these are best designed and interpreted is not without controversy.

WHAT DO GROUP STUDIES ADD TO THE ANALYSIS OF SINGLE CASES?

Group studies address two potential problems of interpretation that plague single cases: One is that observed deficits in a single patient may be due to premorbid differences in function—normal individual differences may thus be misattributed to the lesion. This may be implausible for some deficits: Common sense dictates that major hemiparesis or visual field defects are outside the range of normal variation and can generally be safely linked to the brain injury. But other aspects of behavior, such as executive functions, emotional, or social processes, may differ substantially across healthy individuals, making it more likely that such a difference will be found by chance in a brain-injured patient. Idiosyncrasies in brain organization, in structure–function mapping, or in recovery from brain injury can also contribute to exceptional performance in a single case.

Even if we can safely assume that the patient's brain, function, and brain–function relations were representative before the injury, a second source of variability would make group studies important. For obvious reasons, brain lesions in human subjects are not under experimental control. As a result, there is substantial inherent variability in the extent and causes of brain injury. Group studies help to

exclude potential lesion-related confounds that might explain the observations in a single case; for example, they can establish that it is the site of damage, rather than its etiology, that underlies the behavior change.

Another common and related problem that can be addressed by group studies is that lesions are often more extensive, or less precisely located, than is ideal for testing a given structure–function hypothesis. If the function is disrupted but the lesion is large, the conclusions cannot be specific. If a group of patients with lesions varying in extent but overlapping in some smaller area are found to have a common impairment in function, one can infer that the function likely relies on the region of overlap that is common across patients. Recent methods have built on this logic to allow statistical tests of structure–function relations at the voxel level and will be discussed in more detail later in this chapter. Thus, lesion extent can limit structure–function mapping in single case studies but can at least be addressed, and maybe turned to advantage, in group studies.

Group studies in neuropsychology are strictly observational rather than experimental. Like case-control studies in epidemiology, they are vulnerable to confounds and biases, but they can nevertheless offer important insights. These biases are predictable and generally can be avoided with careful design or addressed with appropriate analyses. The observational nature of this approach to lesion–function mapping means that there is no imposed directionality: Studies may begin from either lesion or function. These two perspectives are discussed in turn.

DESIGNS DRIVEN BY BEHAVIOR

A major challenge in both psychology and cognitive neuroscience is to define the architecture of behavior. One way or another, the complexity of behavior needs to be parsed into analyzable constituents, whether these are conceptualized as modules, processes, or interacting networks (Dunn & Kirsner, 2003). The challenge is to identify the appropriate constituent parts and then to understand how they interact from both a psychological and a neural point of view.

Arguably, this enterprise has been most successful when it has been closely linked to neurobiology. For example, we now have a detailed understanding of visual processing that begins from response properties of single neurons in the retina, moves to how these are combined in the initial stages of cortical visual processing, and continues from there to the computations that support object or face recognition (Farah, 2004; Van Essen, Felleman, DeYoe, Olavarria, & Knierim, 1990). This enterprise obviously requires data gathered with a variety of methods. Studies in patients with brain injury can provide important insights into the biologically relevant lines of cleavage for a given (complex) behavior, by helping to identify associations and dissociations between putative component processes.

When behavior is treated as the independent variable, patients are selected on the basis of the presence of some behavioral manifestation—either a clinical syndrome or performance on a particular task. Additional behavioral measures aiming to isolate putative component processes are then administered to determine whether these processes are, in fact, distinct (i.e., dissociable). A single dissociation refers to a situation in which subjects are impaired on a task that presumably assesses a particular ability but are unimpaired on another task that assesses a separate ability. Single dissociations are evidence in favor of a hypothesis that the tasks measure distinct component processes (Damasio & Damasio, 1989; Shallice, 1988). However, there are practical issues that make alternative explanations for such patterns quite likely: As one example, dissociations assume that the tasks being used are approximately equally difficult. An easy task and a hard task tapping the same component process would show apparent dissociation because at least some patients would fail the hard task but pass the easy task (Shallice, 1988).

This potential explanation is less likely if a double dissociation can be demonstrated: Here, one set of patients fails Task A but does well on Task B, whereas another set shows the opposite pattern. The explanatory power and experimental elegance of double dissociation has been a touchstone since the early days of experimental neuropsychology (Teuber, 1955).

How Do You Know a Dissociation When You See One?

The logic of dissociation is clear in principle but can be challenging to operationalize in practice. (See Dunn & Kirsner, 2003, for a more detailed analysis of these challenges.) How intact must a group be in Task A? How impaired in Task B? What is the likelihood of such dissociations occurring by chance, in a given population, and for any given pair of tasks? One common approach is to test for a crossover interaction in the performance of two tasks, across two groups, but other patterns may be as or more important, depending on the relations between the tasks and on the relations between a given cognitive process and performance on the task that is meant to measure it (Bates, Appelbaum, Salcedo, Saygin, & Pizzamiglio, 2003; Dunn & Kirsner, 2003; Shallice, 1988).

Conceptual Precision

An important first step in any experiment of this sort is to start from a position of conceptual clarity: A model of the component processes of interest that is well-justified will dictate the appropriate analyses. A priori hypotheses might come from existing experimental work in humans using lesion or other methods, from animal studies, from computational models, or from combinations of these sources.

Measurement Reliability

Once processes of interest are identified, tasks are needed to measure the relevant behavior as specifically as possible. Ideally, such measures will have good psychometric properties: no ceiling or floor performance, good test–retest reliability, and performance that is minimally influenced by demographic or education factors (Laws, 2005). Brain-injured patients are typically older and less educated, on average, than the convenience samples of healthy undergraduates often used in the development of new measures. Because the time and energy of these patients are limited, it is wise to pilot new tasks in healthy subjects who are otherwise demographically similar to the target patient population. That said, the appropriate reference population for the actual experiment may not be healthy subjects. Depending on the hypothesis, patients with brain injury may provide more relevant comparison data, and such comparisons may be less affected by the ceiling effects that can be a problem in healthy reference groups.

Measurement variation, that is, the extent to which task performance will vary if the same subject is tested repeatedly, is a source of noise that in principle is under the experimenter's control. It may have important influences on the analysis and should be minimized to the extent possible (Bates, Appelbaum, et al., 2003). In addition to piloting in demographically relevant healthy populations, attention needs to be given to particular challenges that may arise in patient populations. Depending on the patient population of interest, relevant issues might include (a) difficulty understanding instructions, (b) difficulty with motor or perceptual aspects of the tasks that are related to the lesion but not of interest (e.g., because of weakness interfering with responding, or disruption of primary sensory processing), and (c) nonspecific changes in arousal or attention related to the injury or to psychoactive medications (e.g., anticonvulsants) that may be more commonly taken by those in the target group than in the reference group. Some of these issues can be addressed in the experiment. For example, patients may need simplified instructions, additional practice, or modifications of how stimuli are presented or responses collected. These problems also apply to single case studies, but their solutions may be different in group studies. In single cases, there may be more flexibility in optimizing the details of the task to accommodate patient-specific factors. In groups, there is a trade-off between using a consistent measure across all participants (and so allowing the results to be easily pooled) and adapting the task to individual restrictions.

Interindividual Variability

A second source of variability relates not to the measurement tools but rather to the individuals being measured. Individual differences in group lesion studies can be conceptualized as arising from three potential sources, and these differences can be of no interest or of major interest. The first source is individual differences of the same sort that one finds in

healthy populations. People differ in their cognitive capacities. This may be particularly true for certain cognitive capacities. This variation is generally only a nuisance in lesion studies, increasing the variance across both experimental and reference groups. It can become a confound, however, if such individual differences are not randomly distributed across groups. This can be due to sampling error, systematic sampling bias, or nonindependence of lesion-related variables. The simplest form of sampling error is that, by chance, more subjects from one end of the normal range are present in one group than another. This risk is minimized by increasing the sample size (indeed, avoiding this risk is an important motivation of group versus single case studies), but patient studies have practical limits on sample size that make this a challenge.

Sampling bias may occur for other reasons. For example, some normal individual difference may also make it more likely that an individual would suffer a particular neurological injury. This problem is illustrated, for example, in studying the links between impulsivity and the frontal lobes: If patients who have suffered frontal lobe damage from traumatic brain injury are found to be more impulsive, does this establish that the frontal lobes are important in impulse control? Or do impulsive people get into situations in which they suffer such injuries more often than the less impulsive, so that this normal individual difference ends up overrepresented in the patient group?

A second source of individual variability relates to inevitable variation in the nature and extent of brain injury within a group. Furthermore, variation in lesion location is not the only lesion-related determinant of this kind of variability: Factors such as comorbidity and medication use may differ systematically with lesion etiology or location and so be another source of bias.

Do Lesion Data Matter in Behavior-Driven Designs?

One can test the hypothesis that two processes are functionally dissociable in a patient population without ever considering the details of their lesions. In principle, dissociation, particularly double dissociation, addresses the issue. In practice, however, there are many nuances in determining what the thresholds might be for establishing dissociations, including the need to consider departures from correlations across tasks as well as (or instead of) absolute performance in each of two tasks. Even if the experimental goal is purely to understand the architecture of cognitive processes, rather than their relation to the brain, lesion analysis can provide external validation of claims of dissociation. Consistent lesion location–function mapping bolsters the argument that what impaired (or unimpaired) patients have in common is disruption of a specific system, rather than some demographic or task-related confound (Robertson, Knight, Rafal, & Shimamura, 1993).

LESION-DRIVEN DESIGNS

It is equally possible to study structure–function relations in the human brain with the brain injury treated as the independent variable. Rather than aiming to discern how behavior can be dissected, the starting point is to determine the cognitive processes for which a given brain region is necessary. Of course, these two aims converge on the same central questions.

Characterizing Lesions

In the early days of neuropsychology, lesion characterization was based on neurosurgical sketches, plain X-rays of the skull, or the results of autopsies. Computerized tomography (CT) and, more recently, structural magnetic resonance imaging (MRI), have dramatically improved the quality of anatomical data.

The first step in characterizing lesions is thus to acquire either MRI or CT images of each patient's brain. MRI is preferred because it offers better resolution, and in many cases better sensitivity, than CT, and it avoids exposing the participant to ionizing radiation. However, MRI may be contraindicated in patients with pacemakers or surgical clips, for example, or not tolerated because of claustrophobia. Ideally, high-resolution imaging should be acquired in the whole patient sample using standard parameters and equipment, as close to the time of behavioral testing as possible. That said, it may be much more practical to use the most recently available clinical imaging. This is less resource intensive, minimizes patient inconvenience, and often provides lesion data that are of more than adequate resolution for testing a given hypothesis. Regardless of approach, the quality (and so anatomical precision) of the lesion characterization needs to be considered in the analysis.

The simplest way of presenting lesion data is to reproduce the imaging as-is for each patient. This works well for single cases but becomes awkward in group studies. Indeed, it is only appropriate to reproduce individual scans if the behavioral data are also presented for each individual, that is, in case series format. If behavioral data are presented as group means, imaging data also need to be presented in a form that allows insights into what is common in the group. This can be achieved simply—for example, by tabulating the number of subjects with damage to particular regions. However, modern imaging data are acquired in digital form, permitting group lesion data to be presented as brain images that are much more accessible, and also are more easily related to the wider literature, particularly fMRI studies.

Individual lesions first need to be represented in a common space. This can be achieved in two main ways: either by manually tracing the lesion onto some common template (Damasio & Damasio, 1989; Kimberg, Coslett, & Schwartz, 2007) or by manually or automatically defining the lesion on the individual patient's anatomical scan and then warping the brain (and the lesion) onto a standard template. The first method is labor intensive and requires substantial expertise. The second method relies on the same algorithms used to warp individual scans into common space for fMRI analysis in healthy subjects and can be more automatized. However, the anatomical distortions caused by the presence of a lesion lead to particular technical issues that need to be addressed thoughtfully if this approach is taken (Nachev, Coulthard, Jager, Kennard, & Husain, 2008; Rorden & Brett, 2000). Regardless of approach, defining the boundaries of lesions always involves some judgment and so is a potential source of error.

Registering individual lesions to a common template allows these data to be shown in aggregate—most commonly as overlap images (generated by representing the arithmetic sum of damage in each voxel, across the group), which show the degree to which damage affects common brain structures for a given group of patients (Frank, Damasio, & Grabowski, 1997; Makale et al., 2002; Rorden & Brett, 2000). Such images can also demonstrate the absence of common damage in two groups that are meant to be anatomically distinct. Digitized lesion data that are represented in a common space can be used in more complex computations, including statistical tests of structure–function relations (see the section Finer Grained Lesion–Symptom Mapping), and are more readily linked to other sources of data that are also expressed in common brain coordinates, notably fMRI studies.

REGION OF INTEREST DESIGNS

When there is an a priori hypothesis about the functional role of a particular brain region, region of interest (ROI) designs are appropriate. Here, participants are identified on the basis of the presence of damage affecting (or sometimes restricted to) some specified region of the brain. Behaviors of interest are measured with one or several tasks, and performance is compared with appropriate reference groups. If impairment is identified, it is evidence that the brain region plays a necessary role in task performance and, by extension, in the cognitive process of interest. The major advantage of this approach is its hypothesis-driven design and the statistical power that accompanies such designs. This power means that relatively small sample sizes may be adequate, particularly because effect sizes in lesion studies are often quite large. Such designs may have directional hypotheses, making one-tailed statistical tests appropriate.

There are several important design issues to consider in these focused studies. The first is the appropriate reference group. One common approach is to compare participants with damage to a particular region to a healthy group, matched on demographic characteristics. This provides some control over potential demographic confounds (although perhaps not as much as one might think, depending on the sample size and the variance in these demographic characteristics). However, one cannot unequivocally

conclude that the effects are due to damage in a particular region. They may relate to some effect of brain damage more generally, including effects of confounding factors that may be more common in those with brain injury than in those without. Furthermore, it may be difficult to avoid ceiling effects in a healthy control group. To address these problems, many studies include a comparison group with brain injury that spares the region of interest. If the aim is to exclude generic effects of brain damage (or confounds more likely to be present in ill than in healthy participants) in the interpretation of the findings, then any site of damage that spares the region in question is fine. This is something of a missed opportunity, however. If the lesioned comparison group is selected so that the lesions affect a second, specific brain region, then that group can serve double duty: both controlling for nonspecific effects of injury, and establishing that the other region is not necessary for the process in question. Such a targeted approach also assesses the possibility that the lesioned reference is impaired on some other task, providing insurance against the claim that the reference group is somehow less impaired for whatever reason. In the end, one is left with a focused double dissociation.

This elegant design is not easy to achieve and, when achieved, is still potentially susceptible to the problems described for functional dissociations. The main practical difficulty is in recruiting an appropriate lesioned comparison group, whether it involves patients with anatomically common or disparate lesions, matched to the experimental group on both clinical and demographic variables. Systematic recruitment methods, such as patient registries, can make this more feasible (Fellows, Stark, Berg, & Chatterjee, 2008).

If it is impossible to recruit a lesioned comparison group, then the next best approach is to thoroughly characterize the relation between demographic variables and task performance in a healthy reference group, in which adequate sample sizes are much more feasible, and then use that information to inform analyses of the patient data. For example, demographic characteristics that differ between patient groups can be shown not to substantially influence task performance in a large healthy reference group, or the influence can be characterized sufficiently to allow these contributions to be covaried out in the primary analysis. A common approach along these lines is to express performance of each lesioned participant as a percentile or z score on the basis of performance in a larger healthy reference sample (e.g., Gläscher et al., 2009; Tsuchida & Fellows, 2009). Although desirable, this may not always be feasible, depending on the reference data available for a given task.

It is important to consider what an ROI design does not do: It does not necessarily impose a true anatomic boundary. Also, it is obvious that nothing will be learned about the potential contributions of brain regions outside that boundary. Perhaps less obviously, there can be a risk of not detecting effects that are, in fact, related to damage within the boundary. This can happen if the region is much larger than the actually critical brain area; effects caused by damage in the smaller area are diluted by normal performance in those with damage affecting the larger, but not critical, area. The group as a whole will have variable performance, and the statistical analyses may fail to detect effects. Finally, effects that are detected with a given ROI may nevertheless have been better captured by a different anatomical boundary.

STATISTICS FOR ROI DESIGNS

When the data are considered as group means, the same statistical approaches used for comparing groups in any study are appropriate. ROI designs commonly are limited to small samples and may involve skewed behavioral data (either because of ceiling effects in the control group, or substantial variability in the patient group, or both). These issues obviously need to be taken into account when planning the analysis, if they cannot be avoided in the design. Sometimes group studies are better analyzed as a series of single cases. This approach may be suitable when the group of patients varies widely on relevant demographic or other variables, or indeed, in task performance. Sometimes this approach is taken post hoc, in which case, the results should be considered with particular caution, given the ease with which confounds other than lesion location may explain observed effects.

PITFALLS IN ROI DESIGNS

Recruitment Bias

The observational nature of human lesion studies, in general, requires particular care to minimize potential bias. When testing a structure–function hypothesis with an anatomical ROI design, efforts should be made to include all subjects with damage to the region in question. It is common to undertake what might be called a *hybrid* study—for example, including patients with both left hemisphere damage *and* aphasia and then asking a more specific question about language processes. This runs the risk of distorting the results. At the least, it may magnify apparent structure–function relations, by picking desired patients with both lesion and dysfunction. It may give spurious findings as well because subjects without impairment provide important constraints in lesion–function mapping (Rorden, Fridriksson, & Karnath, 2009). At the other end of the spectrum, patients may be excluded because they are too impaired to perform the experimental tasks. This is unavoidable but important to keep in mind. For example, it might be difficult to study the neural processes related to the control of behavior. If damage to some key structure resulted in severe agitation, such patients are unlikely to be approached (and if approached, to agree) to participate in cognitive neuroscience research. Similarly, severe aphasia often precludes informed consent, so such patients may be systematically excluded.

Control Groups

As in epidemiologic case-control studies, the reference group is important in lesion studies. In principle, those in the control group should differ from the patient group only in that they have not suffered a brain injury. Subjects drawn from the same population are optimal. Practically, this is often challenging to achieve, but it can be accomplished in several ways. If healthy subjects are needed, then individuals with similar demographic profiles should be recruited, perhaps even friends or family members of the patients. Patients with damage to other brain regions (but due to the same causes as damage in the group of interest) are often better choices because they are more likely to be matched on potentially confounding variables, such as medication usage, or nonspecific psychological effects of serious illness. However, depending on the size of the groups and the anatomical specificity of the hypotheses, it can be harder to match such subjects on demographic variables.

All Lesions Are Not Created Equal

Lesions do not occur at random. There are systematic biases in who suffers a brain injury, in the extent to which an injury that affects one part of the brain will be accompanied by damage to other parts of the brain, in the destructiveness of a given injury, and in the time course and mechanisms of recovery from that injury. For example, ischemic stroke damages parts of the brain that are supplied by particular blood vessels. These vascular territories mean that damage to one area, for example, inferior frontal lobe, will be more commonly associated with damage to another area in the same territory (e.g., insula, inferior parietal lobe). Conversely, such damage will almost never be associated with damage to the areas that are supplied by other blood vessels, such as the other hemisphere, the frontal pole, or the occipital lobe. Furthermore, some vascular territories are more commonly affected than others. Injury to the areas supplied by the middle cerebral artery, for example, will be overrepresented in a given series of unselected stroke patients. These regularities have implications for interpreting the results of lesion studies (Rorden & Karnath, 2004) and constrain the brain regions that can be readily studied by lesion methods.

Lesion etiology can also affect the accuracy of the lesion mapping, and the observable structure–function relations: Slow-growing tumors push normal brain tissue aside without necessarily disrupting function, which can lead to lesions that appear quite large but have much milder functional effects. Cortical resections in epilepsy have precise margins and spare the white matter—two advantages—but the cortex that is resected is often not normal and may have been abnormal for a long time.

Relatedly, the degree to which compensation can occur depends on the time course over which the brain disorder develops, its extent, and the time since injury. There is no doubt that the functional effects of stroke evolve over time (Fruhmann Berger, Johannsen, & Karnath, 2008). The effects of brain damage can be studied at any time point, but this is a highly relevant variable and must be considered in both study design and interpretation. The development of MRI sequences that can delineate ischemic brain tissue very shortly after the onset of acute stroke has provided the opportunity to do hyperacute lesion–function mapping (Marsh & Hillis, 2008; Newhart, Ken, Kleinman, Heidler-Gary, & Hillis, 2007). Such work can identify regions that are normally necessary for a given function. In contrast, studies examining chronic impairments after brain damage are perhaps better thought of as identifying regions that are necessary for the recovery of a given function: Deficits still present months or years after an injury are, by definition, resistant to compensatory mechanisms.

Finer Grained Lesion–Symptom Mapping

Regions of interest can, in principle, be any size. In practice, there is a lower limit of resolution imposed by the volume of brain tissue that is injured in individual subjects, the extent to which those volumes overlap in a given sample, or the resolution of the imaging methods that are used to characterize the injury. Lesion volume, rather than imaging resolution, is typically the limiting factor in the MRI era. The upper limit of resolution is determined by conceptual issues; determining that some function is related to the integrity of the whole brain, for example, is likely to be of limited interest. That said, many core concepts in neuropsychology began with regions of interest encompassing entire cerebral hemispheres, and defining such broad structure–function relations may still be important as cognitive neuroscience tackles new areas of study, such as in social or affective domains.

Converging evidence argues that structure–function relations are considerably more discrete than is captured by examining hemispheric, or even lobar, effects. There are practical limits to the regional specificity that can be attained in group studies with ROI designs. If the study is restricted to patients with damage to some specific and small brain area, an adequate sample is unlikely to be recruited in a reasonable time. An alternative is to enroll patients with variable damage to a relatively broad region—even one hemisphere or the whole brain—and then undertake analyses to establish which subregion contributes to the observed deficits in function.

There are three main approaches to analyzing data from patients who have variable damage in a large brain region. The one with the longest history involves a secondary analysis in a standard ROI study. Having established that some anatomically defined group is impaired and observing the usual variability in that impairment, one may ask whether there is an anatomical basis to that variability. That is, whether damage to a specific subregion is a main determinant of task performance. This can be addressed qualitatively by examining the pattern of lesions in the impaired and unimpaired subgroups, in essence, carrying out a behavior-driven analysis nested in the original ROI study. Lesion overlap methods are often used to this end: The lesion overlap image for impaired and unimpaired subgroups can be examined visually, or lesion extent can be subtracted across these groups to identify the potentially critical subregion (e.g., Milne & Grafman, 2001). Alternative but analogous methods include tabulating the presence or absence of injury to Brodmann areas and comparing the outcome in patients with and without behavioral impairment.

There are drawbacks to this approach. First, it is important to realize that it is usually undertaken post hoc. Any finding needs confirmation in a new experiment that is designed to test the specific ROI a priori. Selection bias and confounding factors can easily influence the results. Such subregion analyses usually involve very small sample sizes, and it can be impossible to properly account for other (e.g., demographic) contributors to observed effects. This approach is also prone to problems because of the nonindependence of damage (see the section All Lesions Are Not Created Equal). Results from such analyses should be treated with particular caution when the a priori, ROI-based analysis does not establish significant differences between groups. A multiple ROI approach can be applied a priori. Several studies have taken this approach (e.g., Picton et al., 2007; Stuss, Murphy, Binns, & Alexander, 2003). The main difficulty, beyond the perennial

limitations of sample size, is in determining how to appropriately correct for multiple comparisons.

Recently, statistical methods that were developed for fMRI have been adapted for examining structure–dysfunction relations at a voxel-by-voxel level. This is a natural extension of multi-ROI designs, with the (potential) advantage of principled control of multiple comparisons. Once lesions volumes are registered to a common template, univariate statistics can be applied to test whether the performance of patients with damage to a given voxel differs from performance of patients with damage that spares the voxel. This results in a statistical map showing the strength of association between damage and dysfunction in anatomical space.

This approach, commonly referred to as voxel-based lesion–symptom mapping (VLSM), does not require imposing potentially arbitrary (or somehow "wrong") ROI boundaries and allows task performance to be considered either as a dichotomous (intact–impaired) or continuous variable. The latter avoids having to impose a second, potentially arbitrary, boundary on the data. VLSM also has the potential to map networks, that is, to identify several regions that may contribute to task performance within a single experiment. Several variations of this method, using different statistical approaches, have been developed (see Bates, Wilson, et al., 2003; Chen, Hillis, Pawlak, & Herskovits, 2008; Kinkingnéhun et al., 2007; Rorden et al., 2009; Rorden & Karnath, 2004; Rorden, Karnath, & Bonilha, 2007; Solomon, Raymont, Braun, Butman, & Grafman, 2007).

These advantages come with trade-offs. As with fMRI analysis, this massively univariate approach requires conservative correction for multiple comparisons, which in turn demands a substantial sample size. The number of subjects is not the only consideration; lesion overlap and distribution are also important determinants of a study's power. Methods exist to estimate the anatomical extent of adequate power in a given sample, and this is an important adjunct in interpreting VLSM analyses (Kimberg et al., 2007; Rudrauf et al., 2008). Systematic approaches to patient recruitment are also critical in acquiring a suitable sample size, and in ensuring that the sample has been appropriately characterized (Fellows et al., 2008).

White Matter Damage and Disconnection Effects

With the exception of certain neurosurgical resections, lesions are rarely confined to a single structure and often disrupt the white matter leading into or away from a given gray matter region or fibers of passage (i.e., adjacent tracts that may have nothing to do with the damaged gray matter beyond physical proximity). This can pose challenges in interpreting lesion studies. Observed behavioral effects might be due to the white matter damage, which would be particularly misleading if it involves fibers of passage. Modern neuroimaging can assess the extent of white matter injury, either in standard structural scans, or by using tract-specific imaging such as diffusion tensor imaging. Furthermore, white matter atlases are becoming increasingly sophisticated. Thus, methods exist to address possible white matter contributions and are beginning to be applied to structure–function mapping (Catani, Jones, & ffytche, 2005; Karnath, Rorden, & Ticini, 2009; Philippi, Mehta, Grabowski, Adolphs, & Rudrauf, 2009; Rudrauf, Mehta, & Grabowski, 2008; Thiebaut de Schotten et al., 2008; Urbanski et al., 2008).

Developments in image analysis to study network properties of the brain, whether captured by structural or functional measures, may prove useful as adjuncts to the lesion approaches discussed so far (Dosenbach, Fair, Cohen, Schlaggar, & Petersen, 2008; He, Dagher, et al., 2009; He, Wang, et al., 2009). At the least, these techniques draw attention to network-oriented conceptual frameworks.

Clinical Conditions With Diffuse Damage

Brain–behavior relations can also be studied in clinical conditions that have multifocal or diffuse damage. Traumatic brain injury, multiple sclerosis, and degenerative dementias are examples. Imaging methods can quantify regional cortical and white matter changes, even when these are subtle or diffuse, and such changes can be correlated with behavior. Most of the pitfalls that have been discussed also apply to such studies. There are additional challenges in interpreting anatomical data when multiple areas are dysfunctional in a more or less correlated (and more or less detectable) way, and in interpreting behavioral data when multiple

cognitive functions that may be necessary for a given task are also degraded in more or less correlated ways.

CONCLUSION

Studies of disrupted function can provide important insights into the architecture of cognitive processes and can identify the brain substrates critical for these processes. Lesion studies in humans have particular inferential strengths, explaining their long and fruitful history in neuroscience and psychology, and recent advances in anatomical imaging and statistical analysis contribute to the continued relevance of such work (Catani & ffytche, 2010; Chatterjee, 2005). The ability to learn about brain function from the experience of people with brain injury has intrinsic worth beyond its inferential logic: Patients and families can provide rich descriptions of how brain damage has affected their lives, which can lead to unexpected insights beyond the laboratory context. Such anecdotal evidence can provide interesting starting points for hypothesis-driven experiments, the results of which may in turn be directly relevant to patient care. The observational nature of these studies requires thoughtful experimental design, and this chapter has aimed at providing an overview of the main factors to be considered in such designs.

References

Bates, E., Appelbaum, M., Salcedo, J., Saygin, A. P., & Pizzamiglio, L. (2003). Quantifying dissociations in neuropsychological research. *Journal of Clinical and Experimental Neuropsychology, 25,* 1128–1153. doi:10.1076/jcen.25.8.1128.16724

Bates, E., Wilson, S. M., Saygin, A. P., Dick, F., Sereno, M. I., Knight, R. T., & Dronkers, N. F. (2003). Voxel-based lesion-symptom mapping. *Nature Neuroscience, 6,* 448–450.

Catani, M., & ffytche, D. H. (2010). On "the study of the nervous system and behaviour." *Cortex, 46,* 106–109. doi:10.1016/j.cortex.2009.03.012

Catani, M., Jones, D. K., & ffytche, D. H. (2005). Perisylvian language networks of the human brain. *Annals of Neurology, 57,* 8–16. doi:10.1002/ana.20319

Chatterjee, A. (2005). A madness to the methods in cognitive neuroscience? *Journal of Cognitive*

Neuroscience, 17, 847–849. doi:10.1162/089892 9054021085

Chen, R., Hillis, A. E., Pawlak, M., & Herskovits, E. H. (2008). Voxelwise Bayesian lesion-deficit analysis. *NeuroImage, 40*, 1633–1642. doi:10.1016/j.neuroimage.2008.01.014

Critchley, H. D., Mathias, C. J., Josephs, O., O'Doherty, J., Zanini, S., Dewar, B. K., . . . Dolan, R. J. (2003). Human cingulate cortex and autonomic control: Converging neuroimaging and clinical evidence. *Brain: A Journal of Neurology, 126*, 2139–2152. doi:10.1093/brain/awg216

Crivellato, E., & Ribatti, D. (2007). Soul, mind, brain: Greek philosophy and the birth of neuroscience. *Brain Research Bulletin, 71*, 327–336. doi:10.1016/j.brainresbull.2006.09.020

Damasio, H., & Damasio, A. R. (1989). *Lesion analysis in neuropsychology*. New York, NY: Oxford University Press.

Dosenbach, N. U., Fair, D. A., Cohen, A. L., Schlaggar, B. L., & Petersen, S. E. (2008). A dual-networks architecture of top-down control. *Trends in Cognitive Sciences, 12*, 99–105. doi:10.1016/j.tics.2008.01.001

Dunn, J. C., & Kirsner, K. (2003). What can we infer from double dissociations? *Cortex, 39*, 1–7. doi:10.1016/S0010-9452(08)70070-4

Farah, M. J. (2004). *Visual agnosia* (2nd ed.). Cambridge, MA: MIT Press.

Feinberg, T. E., & Farah, M. (2006). A historical perspective on cognitive neuroscience. In T. E. Feinberg & M. Farah (Eds.), *Patient-based approaches to cognitive neuroscience* (pp. 3–20). Cambridge, MA: MIT Press.

Fellows, L. K., Heberlein, A. S., Morales, D. A., Shivde, G., Waller, S., & Wu, D. H. (2005). Method matters: An empirical study of impact in cognitive neuroscience. *Journal of Cognitive Neuroscience, 17*, 850–858. doi:10.1162/0898929054021139

Fellows, L. K., Stark, M., Berg, A., & Chatterjee, A. (2008). Establishing patient registries for cognitive neuroscience research: Advantages, challenges, and practical advice based on the experience at two centers. *Journal of Cognitive Neuroscience, 20*, 1107–1113. doi:10.1162/jocn.2008.20065

Frank, R. J., Damasio, H., & Grabowski, T. J. (1997). Brainvox: An interactive, multimodal visualization and analysis system for neuroanatomical imaging. *NeuroImage, 5*, 13–30. doi:10.1006/nimg.1996.0250

Fruhmann Berger, M., Johannsen, L., & Karnath, H. O. (2008). Time course of eye and head deviation in spatial neglect. *Neuropsychology, 22*, 697–702. doi:10.1037/a0013351

Gläscher, J., Tranel, D., Paul, L. K., Rudrauf, D., Rorden, C., Hornaday, A., . . . Adolphs, R. (2009). Lesion mapping of cognitive abilities linked to intelligence.

Neuron, 61, 681–691. doi:10.1016/j.neuron.2009.01.026

Gross, C. G. (1995). Aristotle on the brain. *Neuroscientist, 1*, 245–250. doi:10.1177/107385849500100408

He, Y., Dagher, A., Chen, Z., Charil, A., Zijdenbos, A., Worsley, K., & Evans, A. (2009). Impaired small-world efficiency in structural cortical networks in multiple sclerosis associated with white matter lesion load. *Brain: A Journal of Neurology, 132*, 3366–3379. doi:10.1093/brain/awp089

He, Y., Wang, J., Wang, L., Chen, Z. J., Yan, C., Yang, H., . . . Evans, A. (2009). Uncovering intrinsic modular organization of spontaneous brain activity in humans. *PLoS ONE, 4*(4), e5226. doi:10.1371/journal.pone.0005226

Holmes, G. (1979). The organization of the visual cortex in man. In C. G. Phillips (Ed.), *Selected papers of Gordon Holmes* (pp. 438–451). Oxford, England: Oxford University Press. (Original work published 1944)

Karnath, H. O., Rorden, C., & Ticini, L. F. (2009). Damage to white matter fiber tracts in acute spatial neglect. *Cerebral Cortex (New York, NY), 19*, 2331–2337. doi:10.1093/cercor/bhn250

Kimberg, D. Y., Coslett, H. B., & Schwartz, M. F. (2007). Power in voxel-based lesion-symptom mapping. *Journal of Cognitive Neuroscience, 19*, 1067–1080. doi:10.1162/jocn.2007.19.7.1067

Kinkingnéhun, S., Volle, E., Pelegrini-Issac, M., Golmard, J. L., Lehericy, S., du Boisgueheneuc, F., . . . Dubois, B. (2007). A novel approach to clinical-radiological correlations: Anatomo-Clinical Overlapping Maps (AnaCOM): Method and validation. *NeuroImage, 37*, 1237–1249. doi:10.1016/j.neuroimage.2007.06.027

Laws, K. R. (2005). "Illusions of normality": A methodological critique of category-specific naming. *Cortex, 41*, 842–851.

Makale, M., Solomon, J., Patronas, N. J., Danek, A., Butman, J. A., & Grafman, J. (2002). Quantification of brain lesions using interactive automated software. *Behavior Research Methods, Instruments, and Computers, 34*, 6–18. doi:10.3758/BF03195419

Marsh, E. B., & Hillis, A. E. (2008). Dissociation between egocentric and allocentric visuospatial and tactile neglect in acute stroke. *Cortex, 44*, 1215–1220. doi:10.1016/j.cortex.2006.02.002

Milne, E., & Grafman, J. (2001). Ventromedial prefrontal cortex lesions in humans eliminate implicit gender stereotyping. *Journal of Neuroscience, 21*(12), RC150.

Nachev, P., Coulthard, E., Jager, H. R., Kennard, C., & Husain, M. (2008). Enantiomorphic normalization of focally lesioned brains. *NeuroImage, 39*, 1215–1226. doi:10.1016/j.neuroimage.2007.10.002

Newhart, M., Ken, L., Kleinman, J. T., Heidler-Gary, J., & Hillis, A. E. (2007). Neural networks essential for naming and word comprehension. *Cognitive and Behavioral Neurology, 20,* 25–30. doi:10.1097/WNN.0b013e31802dc4a7

Philippi, C. L., Mehta, S., Grabowski, T., Adolphs, R., & Rudrauf, D. (2009). Damage to association fiber tracts impairs recognition of the facial expression of emotion. *Journal of Neuroscience, 29,* 15089–15099. doi:10.1523/JNEUROSCI.0796-09.2009

Picton, T. W., Stuss, D. T., Alexander, M. P., Shallice, T., Binns, M. A., & Gillingham, S. (2007). Effects of focal frontal lesions on response inhibition. *Cerebral Cortex (New York, NY), 17,* 826–838. doi:10.1093/cercor/bhk031

Robertson, L. C., Knight, R. T., Rafal, R., & Shimamura, A. P. (1993). Cognitive neuropsychology is more than single-case studies. *Journal of Experimental Psychology: Learning, Memory, and Cognition, 19,* 710–717. doi:10.1037/0278-7393.19.3.710

Rorden, C., & Brett, M. (2000). Stereotaxic display of brain lesions. *Behavioural Neurology, 12,* 191–200.

Rorden, C., Fridriksson, J., & Karnath, H. O. (2009). An evaluation of traditional and novel tools for lesion behavior mapping. *NeuroImage, 44,* 1355–1362. doi:10.1016/j.neuroimage.2008.09.031

Rorden, C., & Karnath, H. O. (2004). Using human brain lesions to infer function: A relic from a past era in the fMRI age? *Nature Reviews Neuroscience, 5,* 812–819. doi:10.1038/nrn1521

Rorden, C., Karnath, H. O., & Bonilha, L. (2007). Improving lesion-symptom mapping. *Journal of Cognitive Neuroscience, 19,* 1081–1088. doi:10.1162/jocn.2007.19.7.1081

Rudrauf, D., Mehta, S., Bruss, J., Tranel, D., Damasio, H., & Grabowski, T. J. (2008). Thresholding lesion overlap difference maps: Application to category-related naming and recognition deficits. *NeuroImage, 41,* 970–984. doi:10.1016/j.neuroimage.2007.12.033

Rudrauf, D., Mehta, S., & Grabowski, T. J. (2008). Disconnection's renaissance takes shape: Formal incorporation in group-level lesion studies. *Cortex, 44,* 1084–1096. doi:10.1016/j.cortex.2008.05.005

Shallice, T. (1988). *From neuropsychology to mental structure.* New York, NY: Cambridge University Press. doi:10.1017/CBO9780511526817

Solomon, J., Raymont, V., Braun, A., Butman, J. A., & Grafman, J. (2007). User-friendly software for the analysis of brain lesions (ABLe). *Computer Methods and Programs in Biomedicine, 86,* 245–254. doi:10.1016/j.cmpb.2007.02.006

Stuss, D. T., Murphy, K. J., Binns, M. A., & Alexander, M. P. (2003). Staying on the job: The frontal lobes control individual performance variability. *Brain: A Journal of Neurology, 126,* 2363–2380. doi:10.1093/brain/awg237

Teuber, H. L. (1955). Physiological psychology. *Annual Review of Psychology, 6,* 267–296. doi:10.1146/annurev.ps.06.020155.001411

Thiebaut de Schotten, M., Kinkingnéhun, S., Delmaire, C., Lehericy, S., Duffau, H., Thivard, L., . . . Bartolomeo, P. (2008). Visualization of disconnection syndromes in humans. *Cortex, 44,* 1097–1103. doi:10.1016/j.cortex.2008.02.003

Tsuchida, A., & Fellows, L. K. (2009). Lesion evidence that two distinct regions within prefrontal cortex are critical for n-back performance in humans. *Journal of Cognitive Neuroscience, 21,* 2263–2275. doi:10.1162/jocn.2008.21172

Urbanski, M., Thiebaut de Schotten, M., Rodrigo, S., Catani, M., Oppenheim, C., Touze, E., . . . Bartolomeo, P. (2008). Brain networks of spatial awareness: Evidence from diffusion tensor imaging tractography. *Journal of Neurology, Neurosurgery, and Psychiatry, 79,* 598–601. doi:10.1136/jnnp.2007.126276

Van Essen, D. C., Felleman, D. J., DeYoe, E. A., Olavarria, J., & Knierim, J. (1990). Modular and hierarchical organization of extrastriate visual cortex in the macaque monkey. *Cold Spring Harbor Symposia on Quantitative Biology, 55,* 679–696.

SECTION 2

Biological Psychology

CHAPTER 35

GENETIC METHODS IN PSYCHOLOGY

Karestan C. Koenen, Ananda B. Amstadter, and Nicole R. Nugent

The Genomic Era (Guttmacher & Collins, 2002, 2003; Varmus, 2002) was born on April 14, 2003, when the International Human Genome Sequencing Consortium, led in the United States by the National Human Genome Research Institute (NHGRI) and the Department of Energy, announced that the human genome had been sequenced. This momentous event occurred exactly 50 years after James Watson and Francis Crick (1953) published their seminal paper that described deoxyribonucleic acid's (DNA's) double helix. The Genomic Era has brought genetics into the mainstream of psychology research. The present chapter begins with a brief summary of the principles of Mendelian genetics and the limitations of this approach to most outcomes of interest in psychology. We then move on to discuss quantitative genetic designs, including family, twin, and adoption studies. We next describe molecular genetic study approaches. We end with a review of some of the most important design considerations for psychologists who are interested in conducting a genetically informative study.

MENDELIAN GENETICS

Genetic methodology has been heavily influenced by Mendelian rules of inheritance, in which a single gene exerts its effects on the *phenotype* in a *dominant* or *recessive* manner. Mendelian (Mendel, 1866) modes of transmission provided the early framework for molecular genetic research. Studying pea plants in his monastery, Mendel observed that the expression of offspring traits could be predicted on

the basis of parent traits. Offspring inherited a given trait from both parents, with observable offspring traits evidencing a pattern of dominance, in which only one trait was expressed even when the offspring had inherited two different traits. This was the basis of his first law, the law of segregation. Mendel also noted that multiple traits, such as plant height and pea shape, were inherited separately. Accordingly, his second law, the law of independent assortment, proposed that traits are inherited independent of one another. Such single-trait, dominance models of inheritance are the cornerstone of genetic history and have shaped genetic research designs as well as analytic strategies. Mendelian inheritance is consistent with qualitative differences—lending it to *case-control* studies in which frequencies of genes are compared in individuals who are *affected* (show the disease or disorder) versus *unaffected* (do not show the disease or disorder). However, many phenotypes in psychology are *complex* or quantitative and are likely influenced by multiple genes (i.e., *polygenic*), environmental factors, and even by interactions among genes as well as interactions between genes and environment. Accordingly, methodological approaches that assume single-gene Mendelian heritability patterns would fail to identify real genetic effects. Researchers interested in examining the influence of genes on psychological outcomes will need to carefully design studies that permit identification of these unique patterns of genetic transmission. Furthermore, in psychology, most behaviors and disorders are complex and, therefore, may represent a complicated interplay of

DOI: 10.1037/13620-035
APA Handbook of Research Methods in Psychology: Vol. 2. Research Designs, H. Cooper (Editor-in-Chief)

multiple genes (with possible differences in transmission across the involved genes) and environmental influences. Behavioral genetic science has become increasingly sophisticated in methods available to model (a) the complex transmission of genetic influences and (b) the interplay of genes and environment on outcomes.

QUANTITATIVE GENETIC DESIGNS

The section begins with a brief overview of the basics of quantitative genetic methodology, beginning with the three main quantitative genetic paradigms (e.g., family studies, twin studies, adoption studies), and then giving brief mention of other genetically informed designs (e.g., offspring of twins, twins reared apart). These paradigms help answer two basic questions: (a) Are there genetic influences on the phenotype (could be a behavior, a diagnosis, etc.), and (b) what are the respective contributions of genes and environment on a phenotype? By determining whether a phenotype is influenced by genes, quantitative genetic paradigms lay the foundation for other types of genetic investigations (e.g., molecular genetics). With the advent of advanced statistical modeling software such as Mplus and Mx (Muthén & Muthén, 2004; Neale, Boker, Xie, & Maes, 2002), quantitative genetic paradigms also can answer much more sophisticated questions in psychological research, including hypotheses about mediators and moderators of genetic influences on psychological phenotypes. The interested reader is referred to Kendler (1993), Kendler and Prescott (2006), and Neale and Cardon (1992) for a thorough description of behavioral genetic research methodology.

Family Studies

For a disorder to have a genetic component, it must be familial, that is, more common within families than across them. Specifically, if risk for a psychological disorder, such as schizophrenia, is in part influenced by genetic factors, biological relatives (family members) of individuals with the disorder (referred to as *probands* in genetic studies) should have a higher prevalence of schizophrenia than nonrelatives. Moreover, among biological relatives of individuals with schizophrenia, the prevalence of the disorder should be higher in first-degree relatives (parents, siblings) than second-degree relatives (aunts, uncles, grandparents, and so on). Evidence of familial aggregation exists for the majority of psychological disorders, suggesting that an underlying genetic component is responsible for at least some of the variance in the outcome (Kendler, 1993). Notably, the familial aggregation pattern includes both genetic and environmental influences as well as interactions between the two, complicating the interpretation of family study findings.

Twin Studies

The recognition that twins can inform our knowledge of human behavior dates back to the pioneering work of several great minds in the history of science, including Augustine of Hippo, Hippocrates, and Sir Francis Galton (Kendler & Prescott, 2006; Rende, Plomin, & Vandenberg, 1990); however, it was not until the 1920s that the differentiation of monozygotic (MZ) and dizygotic (DZ) twins was made. Modern twin studies compare concordance measures (such as odds ratios) in MZ pairs who are genetically identical versus DZ pairs who share half of their genetic makeup with their twin (Kendler & Prescott, 2006), and by doing so, twin studies disentangle the role of genetic and environmental factors in phenotype. The twin design produces calculations of the proportion of the variance in a trait or disorder explained by genetic factors; the resultant variance attributed to genetic factors is termed heritability.

Twin study methodology has two key assumptions, *random mating* and *equal environment* (Kendler & Prescott, 2006). These assumptions are the basis for the mathematical equations described in this chapter. The random mating assumption suggests that mating is not influenced by genetic background. If the parents of twins are genetically correlated, then DZ twins may share more than half of their genes with their twin pair, which would underestimate the degree to which genetics influence a phenotype. The equal-environment assumption is based on the premise that twin pairs (DZ and MZ) share 100% of the common environment. In other words, this assumption suggests that the shared environment would be the same for both types of twin pairs. Whereas violation of the random mating assumption may lead to an overestimation of the role of genetics in a phenotype, violation of the equal environment assumption may overestimate the contribution of genetic factors.

Basic twin models estimate the contribution of three factors: (a) additive genetic factors, A, which assume that the genetic architecture of a phenotype arises from multiple genetic loci; (b) shared environmental factors, C, which correspond to aspects of the twins' environment that are common to both twin pairs, such as socioeconomic status (SES), parental relationship, and so on; and (c) individual-specific environmental factors, E, which are aspects of the environment that are not shared between the twins, such as their individual social support, one twin who was in an accident, and so forth. Therefore, this basic model is often referred to as the *ACE model*. The statistical modeling assumes that MZ twins share 100% of their genes and 100% of the shared environment (and therefore the correlation between twins on a phenotype is $rMZ = A^2 + C^2$) and that DZ twins share approximately 50% of their genes and 100% of the shared environment ($rDZ = 1/2A^2 + C^2$; Kendler & Prescott, 2006). From these basic assumptions, the relative contribution of additive genetic factors A, shared environment C, and individual unique environment E can be calculated. The A factor estimate is derived from the equation $A^2 = rMZ - rDZ$, the C factor is calculated from the equation $C^2 = 2rDZ - rMZ$, and lastly, the E factor is derived from the equation $A^2 = 1 - rMZ$ (Kendler & Prescott, 2006; Plomin, DeFries, McClearn, & McGuffin, 2001). Two main types of correlations are used for twin studies in psychology. If a phenotype is continuous (e.g., score on a personality measure), a Pearson (product–moment) correlation is used. For categorical phenotypes, such as post-traumatic stress disorder (PTSD) diagnosis, the tetrachoric correlation, which assumes an underlying normal distribution of liability, is used to calculate heritability (Falconer, 1960).

Three general interpretations are possible from the basic ACE model (Kendler & Prescott, 2006). First, if MZ twins are significantly more similar on a characteristic than DZ twins, then this phenotype is interpreted as being genetically influenced. Second, if the correlation between twin pairs for a phenotype is the same in MZ and DZ twins, then the shared environment is contributing to the phenotype. Lastly, the unique environment is likely contributing to a phenotype if the intratwin correlation between MZ twins is large. Maximum likelihood estimation methods are now nearly universally employed in twin studies (typically utilizing a structural equation modeling program, such as Mx), affording the ability to compare models, to obtain confidence intervals of the parameters, to examine gene by environment correlations and gene by environment interactions, and to construct multivariate models (Neale et al., 2002; Neale & Cardon, 1992). A more detailed description of gene–environment interplay is provided in the molecular genetics section of this chapter.

Adoption Studies

Adoption studies test for an association between a phenotype in adoptees and the prevalence of that phenotype in their biological versus adoptive parents (Lemery & Goldsmith, 1999). The logic of this design is that adoptees share 50% of their genes with their biological parent and 0% of the shared environment; conversely, adoptees share 0% of their genes and 100% of the common environment with their adopted parents. If adoptees are more similar to their biological parents on a phenotype than they are to their adopted parents, then the assumption is that genetic factors are important to the phenotype. If there is a high degree of correspondence in an outcome between nonrelated family members of the adoptee, then it is assumed that the environment is a contributing factor to the phenotype. Conversely, if adoptees have a greater resemblance to their adopted parents on a phenotype than they do to their biological parents, then the environment is assumed to be a contributing factor. This type of design may be limited by a restricted range of family environments, leading to poor generalizability. This could be due to numerous factors, such as the uniqueness of the situation, the likelihood that adoptive parents create a good home environment, and that biological parents may have numerous comorbid conditions that are often not well characterized (Stoolmiller, 1999). Adoption studies are rarer than twin studies, mainly because of the increased difficulty in finding participants.

Other Behavioral Genetic Study Methodologies

Examination of parents, offspring, and even partners of twins can also provide information on the relative genetic and environmental contributions to a psychological phenotype (Nance & Corey, 1976). For example, if a twin (MZ or DZ) who is a parent has a psychological disorder, such as depression, the offspring of this twin would be at both genetic risk, because the genes could be transmitted to the offspring, and environmental risk, because being raised by a parent with depression is a risk factor for depression onset in offspring. If the co-twin does not have the phenotype, in our example depression, then the offspring of this co-twin would be at genetic risk but not environmental risk for developing depression. Another form of behavioral genetic methodology is the *separated twin design*. These studies compare MZ and DZ twins reared apart versus together; however, these situations are quite rare, and the family of origin is often unique, limiting generalizability. Many current genetically informed designs are combining behavioral genetic methods with molecular genetic (gene-finding) techniques; this combination has great potential to impact our knowledge about the etiologic roots of psychological disorders. However, quantitative studies are unable to inform our understanding of which genes may influence behavioral or psychological phenotypes.

Molecular Genetic Study Designs

It was the identification of the molecular structure of DNA that provided the foundation of our understanding of the functional elements of heritability (Watson & Crick, 1953). Watson and Crick (1953) proposed a double-stranded helical structure composed of pairings between thymine (T) and adenine (A) and between guanine (G) and cytosine (C). This pattern of double-stranded molecules explained two of the major genetic questions of the time: How is genetic information replicated and how is it translated into observable outcomes? The two strands "unzip" to replicate and to permit transcription of

DNA to messenger ribonucleic acid (RNA) and then to amino acids. Although a thorough review of molecular genetics is outside the scope of the present chapter, interested readers are directed to an excellent text on the topic (Strachan & Read, 2004) or to interactive websites (see Exhibit 35.1). Once the basic structure of DNA was understood, researchers began to characterize the translation of DNA to biological outcomes and, later, to observable phenotypes relevant to psychology.

The Human Genome Project (Lander et al., 2001; Venter et al., 2001; see also http://www.genome.gov/Education) is one of the most exciting scientific accomplishments of the past decade. The project, begun in 1990, was an international collaboration to characterize the location and function of 20,000 to 25,000 genes of the human genome. Emerging in part from the Human Genome Project, the International HapMap Project (see http://hapmap.ncbi.nlm.

Exhibit 35.1
Websites to Learn More

Educational Resources
The Gene Almanac: http://www.dnalc.org
Learn.Genetics: http://learn.genetics.utah.edu
Teach.Genetics: http://teach.genetics.utah.edu
National Human Genome Research Institute: http://www.genome.gov/Education
Neuroscience Gateway: http://www.brainatlas.org

Collaborative Genetic Research Efforts
1000 Genomes Project: http://www.1000genomes.org

Genetic Search Engines
Online Mendelian Inheritance in Man: http://www.ncbi.nlm.nih.gov/omim
Database of Single Nucleotide Polymorphisms (dbSNP): http://www.ncbi.nlm.nih.gov/projects/SNP
Ensembl genome browser: http://www.ensembl.org

Behavioral Genetic Organizations
Behavior Genetics Association: http://www.bga.org
Human Genome Organization: http://www.hugo-international.org
International Behavioral and Neural Genetics Society: http://www.ibngs.org
International Society for Twin Studies: http://www.ists.qimr.edu.au
International Society of Psychiatric Genetics: http://www.ispg.net

nih.gov) entailed an even more detailed mapping of genetic diversity in the human genome; the HapMap project was aimed at accelerating the identification of genes involved in human illness and disease. The ENCyclopedia Of DNA Elements (ENCODE) Project (see http://www.genome.gov/10005107) is a public research consortium initiated in 2003 involving (a) a pilot study aimed at assessing methods for analyzing the genome and (b) the development of technology for high throughput data on functional elements in the human genome.

Informed by the wealth of data afforded by these projects, *molecular genetic* studies in psychology have sought to identify variants in specific genes that increase the risk of having a given phenotype such as depression or schizophrenia. Although the precise definition of a gene has changed over time (Gerstein et al., 2007), for the present purposes, genes are considered to be functional units of DNA sequences. Research aimed at identifying genes that explain individual differences in risk for psychological disorders focuses on the tiny fraction of the DNA sequences that differs among individuals (possibly less than 1% of human DNA).

The majority of human genetic variation is composed of single nucleotide polymorphisms (SNPs, pronounced "snips"), which occur when a single nucleotide (A, T, C, or G) in the DNA sequence is altered, forming different alleles (the genetic term that refers to one of the various forms of a genetic locus). An example of a SNP is a change in the DNA sequence from CTT to CAT, with the alleles of this SNP being T and A. By definition, the frequency of SNPs must be at least 1%. For example, the apolipoprotein E (*ApoE*) gene is composed of two SNPs with each possible allele varying by a single nucleotide. Early in molecular genetic research, converging and consistent studies identified a robust effect of *ApoE* on risk for Alzheimer's (Farrer et al., 1997).

A second type of polymorphism is the variable number tandem repeat (VNTR) polymorphism (also referred to as microsatellite markers). Aptly named, VNTRs involve segments of repeated base pairs. For example, the STin2 VNTR is a 17-base pair VNTR located in intron 2 of the human serotonin transporter gene (*SLC6A4*). The two most common alleles are 10-repeat units (STin2.10) and 12-repeat

units (STin2.12). The STin2.12 allele, reported to enhance transcription of the serotonin transporter protein, is a likely risk factor for schizophrenia (Fan & Sklar, 2005).

Studies that identify a genetic marker that appears to predict a given phenotype cannot assume that the marker itself is the functional allele. This is because the marker may simply be in linkage disequilibrium to the functional allele. *Linkage disequilibrium* refers to the tendency for alleles that are in proximity on a chromosome to be inherited together. (Because of patterns of inheritance such as population stratification, linkage disequilibrium may also exist between markers on different chromosomes or regions.) Thus, an identified association between a phenotype and candidate gene may simply point to a region on the chromosome where the functional gene is located and does not necessarily mean that the candidate gene itself is responsible for the phenotype. Although it is easy to see how linkage disequilibrium might complicate genetic research, linkage disequilibrium has also been used as a tool for mapping complex disease loci through genomewide association studies (Ardlie, Kruglyak, & Seielstad, 2002; Reich et al., 2001). Linkage disequilibrium can be informed by characterization of *haplotype* blocks, or DNA sequences that are inherited together and that are separated by recombination sites (Daly, Rioux, Schaffner, Hudson, & Lander, 2001). One way to identify a putative causal locus is to assay a selective set of SNPs that span the entire gene. These SNPs can then be used to test possible associations of haplotype blocks on the phenotype of interest. The haplotypes that are estimated may be used in place of the specific genotypes in association analysis. Although selection of haplotype block definition has resulted in some differences when competing approaches are examined concurrently, most methods appear to capture the underlying genetic architecture (Zeggini et al., 2005). Researchers interested in identifying relevant SNPs can use the HapMap.

Population stratification occurs when a sample includes subpopulations characterized by little mating between them and, consequently, the subsamples show different allelic frequencies that are unrelated to the phenotype under investigation

(Freedman et al., 2004; Hutchison, Stallings, McGeary, & Bryan, 2004; Pritchard & Rosenberg, 1999). If there are differences between the subpopulations in prevalence or genetic mechanism of the phenotype, discovery of an allelic difference may be erroneously attributed to the phenotype. Population *admixture*, arising from mating between subpopulations, presents similar challenges as, again, linkage disequilibrium patterns that vary as a function of admixture may be misinterpreted as markers of the phenotype. One solution to this problem is to conduct within-family tests of association, such as the transmission disequilibrium test (Spielman & Ewens, 1996), but these tests require particular configurations of family data. An alternative is to use a design incorporating an unlinked genetic marker to detect and control for population stratification (Pritchard & Rosenberg, 1999; Pritchard, Stephens, Rosenberg, & Donnelly, 2000).

Linkage Studies

Linkage analysis applies phenotypic data from family members to identify the location of the disease gene relative to a genetic marker or DNA sequence that has a known chromosomal location. *Linkage* is said to occur when the disease gene and genetic marker cosegregate or tend to be inherited together. Rather than focusing on a single locus, many linkage analysis studies scan the whole genome using hundreds of markers to identify linkage. Typically, this would be represented by a *log of odds ratio* (LOD; parametric) score, which is a statistical estimate of whether two loci are likely to lie near each other on a chromosome and are therefore likely to be inherited together. An LOD score of 3 or more is generally taken to indicate linkage. Nonparametric methods have also been devised to examine linkage, including analysis packages such as SOLAR (http://solar.sfbrgenetics.org/download.html; Almasy & Blangero, 1998) and MERLIN (http://www.sph.umich.edu/csg/abecasis/Merlin/index.html; Abecasis, Cherny, Cookson, & Cardon, 2001). Most studies within psychology have identified relatively small gene effects, however, and attempts to replicate linkage findings have been particularly difficult in complex disorders, possibly because the small effects require extremely large samples to replicate.

Another potential explanation for replication difficulties is the likelihood that complex disorders may be the product of gene–gene interactions or gene–environment interactions. Accordingly, linkage investigations are challenged by balancing examination of both additive and epistatic (interactive) gene effects (Risch, 1990).

In spite of these challenges, linkage studies have provided a critical foundation for molecular genetic research. Linkage studies are particularly amenable to single-gene disorders. The marker for the single gene responsible for Huntington disease, for example, was identified using linkage analysis of five generations of a single family (Gusella et al., 1984). Additionally, one of the strengths of linkage analysis is the potential to identify genetic influences that might not have been predicted using existing research frameworks. For example, emerging from genetic linkage research, evidence was found for *chromosome 13 syndrome* (later referenced as *panic disorder* [PD] *syndrome*) involving PD as well as kidney or bladder problems, headaches, thyroid problems, or mitral valve prolapse (Hamilton et al., 2003; Weissman et al., 2000; Weissman et al., 2004). A recent investigation replicated and extended these findings, reporting that participants with PD or social anxiety disorder (as well as their first-degree relatives) were markedly more likely to report chromosome 13 syndrome medical concerns than comparison participants (Talati et al., 2008).

However, linkage studies of complex disorders that involve multiple genes exerting small effects require much larger samples and generally involve designs that include multiple families. Indeed, an analysis by Risch and Merikangas (1996) suggested that the number of families required to sufficiently power a linkage study of genes influencing common diseases was prohibitively large, leading them to recommend the use of population-based association studies for examinations of common diseases. Illustrated elegantly by Ardlie et al. (2002), linkage studies are perhaps best powered for studies of infrequent alleles with moderate to strong effects, whereas association studies are more appropriate as the frequency of the alleles increases and the effect size of the alleles decrease.

Association Studies

Candidate gene association studies are more targeted than linkage studies and use extant research (i.e., linkage studies or information about the putative function of a particular gene) to guide the selection of genes that are then tested for potential associations with the disorder. The association method detects genes with small effects on risk and has been, until recently, the method of choice for molecular genetic studies of complex common disorders (Risch & Merikangas, 1996). Disorders are referred to as *complex* when their etiology is thought to involve a combination of many genes and environmental factors, which is the case in all anxiety disorders. Association studies correlate a DNA marker's alleles with an outcome. Figure 35.1 presents an example of the case-control association design.

We examined whether *RGS2* (regulator of G-protein signaling 2) gene and generalized anxiety disorder (GAD) were associated in an epidemiologic sample of hurricane-exposed adults (Acierno et al., 2007; Koenen, Amstadter, et al., 2009). The figure

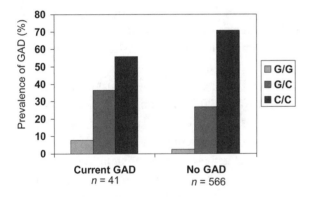

FIGURE 35.1.   The candidate gene study design is used to test for association between specific polymorphisms and a disorder or trait. This figure shows results from a study examining the association between variation in the *RGS2* (regulator of G-protein signaling 2) gene and generalized anxiety disorder (GAD) in an epidemiologic sample of hurricane-exposed adults (Acierno et al., 2007; Koenen, Amstadter, et al., 2009). The figure shows the prevalence of genotypes for rs4606, a single nucleotide polymorphism in *RGS2*, in individuals with current GAD versus individuals without current GAD. In this case, a single base has one of two alleles (e.g., G or C). Individuals have one of three genotypes: GG, GC, or CC. Individuals with GAD have a higher frequency of allele C ($p < .05$), suggesting that allele C confers increased risk of GAD.

shows the prevalence of genotypes for rs4606, a single nucleotide polymorphism in *RGS2*, in individuals with current GAD versus individuals without the disorder. The SNP that we examined, rs4606, is biallelic or has one of two alleles (e.g., G or C). Individuals have one of three genotypes: GG, GC, or CC. Individuals with GAD have a higher frequency of allele C ($p < .05$), suggesting that allele C confers increased risk of GAD. However, further studies are needed to determine whether this SNP is causally implicated in the etiology of the disorder (called the *causal variant*). Continued research to determine the actual causal variant is especially important in association studies, as the marker identified may simply be *near* the causal variant.

One major limitation of candidate genes association studies, particularly in studies using unrelated case-control samples, is the potential confound of population stratification. Haplotype relative risk (HRR) methods have been devised to control for population stratification (Falk & Rubinstein, 1987; Guo, Lunetta, DeStefano, & Cupples, 2009). The HRR was originally developed for family case-control investigations (also called *trios*), involving families recruited on the basis of offspring phenotype; in the HRR approach, parent haplotypes found in the probands were treated as cases, whereas parent haplotypes that were not found in probands were treated as controls, permitting comparisons of markers transmitted to probands versus those that were not transmitted. Recent research has expanded the HRR method to combine case-parent trios and unrelated case-controls using an expectation–maximization algorithm (Guo et al., 2009).

Theory-driven selection of candidate genes is both a strength and limitation of gene-association research. An exemplar for translational application, candidate genes in gene association studies are generally selected on the basis of converging research and theory spanning animal models, preclinical research, psychopharmacology, neurobiology, and linkage studies. In practice, this has led to considerable focus on a handful of genes implicated in serotonergic, dopaminergic, and stress response systems, with the same generalist genes evidencing associations with multiple disorders. As Plomin and Davis (2009) pointed out, "'generalist' genes may affect several disorders within major domains such as internalizing disorders" (p. 64). As reported in a systematic review of anxiety disorders, a remarkable number of genes have demonstrated replicated effects within and across anxiety disorder categories (Nugent, Fyer, Weissman, & Koenen, 2010). This is further supported by quantitative studies. For example, genetic influences on major depression account for the majority of the genetic variance in PTSD (Fu et al., 2007; Koenen et al., 2008). Moreover, many of the polymorphisms with replicated effects are putatively functional variants that influence neurobiologic systems that have been previously implicated in behavioral and psychiatric outcomes on the basis of a wealth of animal, preclinical, clinical, and pharmacological findings.

A note about methods for monitoring internal quality control is important. Most genotyping laboratories will conduct within- and cross-investigation assessments of quality control. Examples of this include use of multiple raters, inclusion of duplicates, and inclusion of both positive and negative controls. As yet another method for assessing quality control, researchers are also encouraged to test for *Hardy-Weinberg equilibrium*, which refers to the algebraically determinable genotype ratios expected in a randomly breeding population. This is represented as $(p + q)^2 = p^2 + 2pq + q^2$, such that p represents the frequency of one gene in a population and q is the frequency of its single allele, making p^2 the expected proportion of p homozygotes, q^2 the proportion of q homozygotes, and $2pq$ the proportion of expected heterozygotes. Accordingly, Hardy-Weinberg equilibrium has been used for genotyping quality control as well as fine mapping (Wittke-Thompson, Pluzhnikov, & Cox, 2005). Importantly, however, the Hardy-Weinberg principle assumes random mating across individuals. As noted, factors such as assortative mating bring this assumption into question.

Genomewide Association Studies (GWAS)

Technological advances in sequencing as well as evidence for a previously unrecognized role of noncoding regions of RNA have converged to support the feasibility and importance of GWAS as an emerging area of molecular genetic research. Furthering this effort, the 1000 Genomes Project is sequencing the genomes of 1,200 individuals (http://www.1000genomes.org). GWAS studies adopt an agnostic approach, testing possible associations across the entire genome rather than selecting only a few candidate genes. This exciting approach has the potential to identify important, previously unconsidered, genetic influences on health and psychology as well as to reinforce the relative importance of previously studied candidate genes. Already, GWAS studies point to the importance and prevalence of VNTRs (Estivill & Armengol, 2007). GWAS studies may also focus on genetic variants believed to be functional, increasing power by reducing the number of tests aimed at loci with little likelihood of an effect.

Gene–Environment Interplay

Perhaps the most exciting area of genetic research in psychology is the examination of gene–environment interplay. Gene–environment interaction (GxE) studies represent variations on traditional models (i.e., family, sibling, twin, adoption, and association studies) of measuring genetic and environmental influences on human behavior. Although research has explored the degree to which GxE interaction affects nearly all psychiatric outcomes (i.e., Rutter, Moffit, & Caspi, 2006; Wermter et al., 2010), it has been proposed that GxE interactions are specific to select psychiatric outcomes (Rutter, 2010). The interaction of genes and environment has often been framed in terms of a diathesis-stress model, in which psychiatric pathology is seen as the result of a genetic vulnerability (hence, risk-conferring genes) combined with environmental influences (Kidd, 1991). Recent GxE conceptualizations have proposed that certain genes may confer differential susceptibility or environmentally sensitive *plasticity* (Belsky et al., 2009; Belsky & Pluess, 2009; Fox, Hane, & Pine, 2007). Such a model explains why seemingly pathogenic genes might continue over generations of proliferation, and moreover, would even be relatively common, as these genes would be beneficial under specific environmental conditions. Although this may appear to be an insignificant distinction, it is linked to different patterns of data. For example, differential susceptibility would be associated with a crossover interaction in the presence of a continuum of positive and negative environments.

Indeed, researchers have suggested that differential responding to an environmental pathogen is perhaps one of the most important indicators of a GxE, in which the effects of environmental exposure are moderated by genotype (Moffitt, Caspi, & Rutter, 2005). Moffitt et al. (2005) outlined seven strategic steps for conducting molecular GxE research: (a) considering quantitative studies; (b) selecting the environmental factor; (c) carefully measuring the environmental risk; (d) selecting candidate genes; (e) testing for an interaction; (f) systematically testing whether the interaction holds when one gene, environment, or outcome variable is replaced with another gene, environment, or outcome variable; and (g) conducting replication and meta-analytic studies. Unfortunately, relatively few studies meet these stringent criteria. Although the most common interpretation of a GxE interaction is that the genotype modifies the relation between the environmental exposure and the phenotype (Caspi et al., 2003), it is also possible that the environment modifies the relation between the gene and the phenotype. Considering this alternative interpretation is important when designing a GxE study.

We examined a GxE interaction using the same genotype as shown in Figure 35.1, *RGS2* (regulator of G-protein signaling 2) and posthurricane PTSD symptoms in a sample of hurricane exposed-adults (Acierno et al., 2007; Amstadter et al., 2009). Notably, there was no main effect of genotype on posthurricane PTSD symptoms. As shown in Figure 35.2, however, the rs4606 polymorphism was related to posthurricane PTSD symptoms under conditions of high stressor exposure (high level of hurricane exposure, low social support). Similar to the GAD results shown in Figure 35.1, the C genotype was associated with increased PTSD symptoms under stress conditions.

Yet another type of gene–environment interplay is the extent to which individuals create and influence their own environments, referred to as *gene–environment correlation* (rGE; Plomin, DeFries, & Loehlin, 1977; Rutter, 2010). rGE refers to the passive, active, and reactive mechanisms whereby

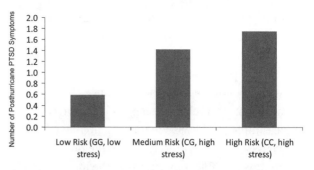

FIGURE 35.2.   A Gene × Environment interaction design examines variation in a specific gene (e.g., polymorphisms), features of the environment (e.g., stressor exposure), and a disorder or trait. This figure shows results from a study examining the same genotype as shown in Figure 35.1, *RGS2* (regulator of G-protein signaling 2) and posthurricane posttraumatic stress disorder (PTSD) symptoms from a sample of hurricane-exposed adults (Acierno et al., 2007; Amstadter et al., 2009). Notably, there was not a main effect for genotype on posthurricane PTSD symptoms. As shown in this figure, however, the rs4606 polymorphism was related to posthurricane PTSD symptoms under conditions of high stressor exposure (high level of hurricane exposure, low social support). Similar to the GAD results shown in Figure 35.1, the C genotype was associated with higher PTSD symptoms under stress conditions.

genetic factors influence the environment. A recent systematic review explored genetic influences on environmental measures, with heritability across environmental measures estimated to be 27% (Kendler & Baker, 2007). Importantly, weighted mean heritability was modest, including heritability of negative life events (39%) and selection into trauma (36%). Accordingly, one of the challenges of GxE research in psychological phenotypes is to distinguish between GxE and rGE effects.

DESIGN CONSIDERATIONS

Participants

Selection of participants in genetic research begins first with a decision between (a) one of the family-based designs (i.e., twin studies, sibling studies, trios, extended pedigrees, and so on) or (b) case-control designs, although certainly some studies have compromised by utilizing both family and case-control designs. Both designs, however, require researchers to operationalize "caseness" or to define *probands*.

Defining probands. As with other areas of psychology, the criteria for including probands is a balance between representativeness and purity of the phenotype. For example, PTSD is highly comorbid with both depression and substance abuse. Accordingly, researchers interested in a representative sample might wish to include anyone with PTSD, regardless of comorbidity, in the proband group. It is possible, however, that the inclusion of such comorbidity may alter the findings to be specific to the comorbid consideration. For example, comorbid PTSD and substance abuse was examined in a case-control investigation of combat veterans with and without PTSD; the analyses revealed a positive association between *DRD2A1* and PTSD only in the subset of PTSD cases who engaged in harmful drinking (Young et al., 2002). On the other hand, early approaches to linkage analyses involved selection of probands who evidenced the disorder (i.e., major depressive disorder) but who had no history of comorbidities (i.e., PTSD, anxiety disorders, substance abuse) *and* whose first-degree relatives were also comorbidity free. The limitation to this approach is the degree to which such families are representative of the phenotype and underlying genetic influences of interest.

The example of using probands with a given diagnosis introduces another shifting paradigm of genetic research. Historically, a majority of linkage and association studies have compared probands or cases who have the disorder with controls who do not have the disorder. This qualitative approach has been partly attributed to the legacy of the Mendelian focus on single-gene transmission of qualitative traits (Plomin, Haworth, & Davis, 2009). Biometricians have long argued for the genetic transmission of normally distributed quantitative traits, and echoing Fisherian resolution of quantitative–qualitative debates (Fisher, 1918), leaders in the field have interpreted GWAS findings to support the presence of quantitative traits (Plomin et al., 2009). Certainly qualitative approaches, comparing cases with either controls or *supernormal controls* (individuals completely free of any symptoms of psychopathology) provide important and valuable information in both molecular and quantitative research methods. However, if the disorder is interpreted to be a quantitative trait, then future research efforts that more accurately reflect the continuous phenotype score may be better powered to detect differences. As Plomin et al. (2001) argued, artificial dichotomization of continuous traits may result in inaccurate categorization of subthreshold individuals, adding measurement error to the analysis. Accordingly, researchers may wish to consider using continuous indexes of the phenotype (e.g., depression severity) and to sample participants who represent the entire continuum of symptom levels.

One often underrecognized consideration in participant selection in genetic paradigms is the developmental stage of participants. Most psychological constructs include a role for developmental processes. Disorder-specific variables such as age of onset, age-related gender differences in prevalence, and course of disorder all inform our understanding of the biological and environmental influences at play and need to be considered in the selection of participants. For example, prior research supports developmental changes in the environmental and genetic influences on substance use behaviors (e.g., see Derringer, Krueger, McGue, & Iacono, 2008; Kendler et al., 2008; Kendler & Myers, 2009). Given developmental differences across neurobiological development, social development, and cognitive development, humans may be more or less vulnerable to the effects of trauma at certain developmental stages, or the exact outcomes of trauma (e.g., depression versus PTSD) may differ partly as a function of age (e.g., multifinality). For example, converging evidence from developmental neuroscience and behavioral genetics suggests that adolescence and young adulthood may represent a "stress-sensitive developmental period" (Walker, Sabuwalla, & Huot, 2004, p. 807).

Developmental and age considerations partly overlap with considerations such as whether research is examining onset or course. When considering disorder etiology, it is useful to distinguish between risk factors for onset or development of the disorder and risk factors for course or chronicity of the disorder. Factors that influence who develops the disorder in the first place may differ from those that influence who recovers from the disorder once it develops. For example, members of disadvantaged ethnic groups are not at higher risk for the development of psychiatric disorders; however, if the disorder occurs, these disadvantaged individuals may display greater chronicity compared with nondisadvantaged individuals. Breslau, Kendler, Su, Gaxiola-Aguilar, and Kessler (2005) found that Hispanic individuals who developed a psychiatric disorder had symptoms that were more chronic than those of non-Hispanic Whites.

Comparison groups.   Selection of control groups is yet another tricky endeavor in genetic research. Some early genetic studies focused on control groups that were free of any symptomatology across all diagnoses (and even among first-degree relatives), leading researchers to criticize the use of supernormal controls (Kendler, 1990). Supernormal controls may come from families with lower rates of psychological concerns than average population levels, arguably increasing the potential for coaggregation of disorders in proband families. Given the importance of environmental influences across all psychological constructs, it is important for comparison participants to share important environmental influences with probands. Genetically informed studies in psychology are complicated by the practical reality that for many psychological phenotypes, such as substance use disorders, the phenotype is conditional on an environmental exposure. For example, if a family member did not meet criteria for nicotine dependence, it could be that they had not been exposed to nicotine and therefore never had been at risk for dependence. To classify this family member as nicotine-dependent negative may mask a genetic influence that was not expressed because of the lack of environmental exposure. This is also demonstrated in PTSD research; as exposure to trauma is a necessary condition of PTSD, control participants must have experienced some degree of trauma to permit comparisons between groups that did and did not develop PTSD. If trauma exposure is either unknown or inconsistent in controls, it is possible that some of the control participants might have developed PTSD in response to trauma. Careful consideration needs to be given to inclusion and exclusion criteria in genetic studies.

Other challenges.   Population stratification is not dissimilar from familiar confounds in psychology, such as SES. Nonetheless, it is an important consideration in genetic research and can be partly addressed through participant selection. For example, some researchers have focused on participants of homogeneous ancestry to minimize this concern. However, in areas with significant ancestral diversity, such as the United States, selecting participants of homogeneous ancestry is difficult; focusing on African Americans, for example, one study found that ancestry included Niger-Kordofanian, European, and other African populations with considerable admixture (Tishkoff et al., 2009). Indeed, many families may have passed along limited or incomplete ancestral information to their offspring, and research has shown that self-reported race differs from actual genetically determined ancestry (Yaeger et al., 2008).

Environmental Exposure

A review of nearly three dozen quantitative studies concluded that the genetic influences on anxiety and depression are largely the same, with nonshared environment determining the expression of the genetic vulnerability (Middeldorp, Cath, Van Dyck, & Boomsma, 2005). Selection and measurement of an environmental pathogen should involve careful consideration of biological plausibility, causal effects of the pathogen, age-specificity of risks, duration of risk exposure, and time since exposure (Moffitt et al., 2005). Environment may interact with genes by (a) *triggering* the expression of a genetic vulnerability, (b) *compensating* for a genetic predisposition, (c) *determining expression* of a genetic predisposition, and (d) *potentiating* a genetic predisposition (Shanahan & Hofer, 2005). Measurement of each of these environmental influences is tied to important differences in design. Early life stress, for example, may represent a trigger for genetic vulnerability to depression or anxiety, whereas the proximal process of parent–child relationship or the environmental context of neighborhood may be posited to compensate for or potentiate the effects of genes. Measures must be applied in a population with a sufficient range of exposure to the environmental pathogen because only a main effect of genotype will be identified if all (or nearly all) participants have experienced the environmental factor (Uher & McGuffin, 2010).

Measures of the environment can include both pathogenetic environmental influences (such as trauma) and buffering influences (such as social support). For example, Kilpatrick et al. (2007) found that the 5-HTTLPR *SLC6A4* genotype was associated with increased risk of PTSD only among adults with high stress exposure (low social support, high hurricane exposure). Using the same sample, county-level crime rate and percent unemployment modified the association between the 5-HTTLPR genotype and PTSD (Koenen, Aiello, et al., 2009). Kilpatrick et al.'s (2007) investigation also implemented a new approach to the collection of genetic samples.

Sample Collection Methods

The collection of a sufficient amount of high-quality genomic DNA is critical for any study aiming to examine the molecular genetic underpinnings of a phenotype. New advances in genomic DNA collection methods have increased ease of collection, lowered costs of collection, and made it more feasible for researchers to conduct genetically informed studies. The following section reviews the most frequently used DNA collection procedures.

Peripheral blood.   Collection of peripheral blood samples has been the historically employed means of obtaining DNA (Lench, Stanier, & Williamson, 1988). It consistently yields a high quantity of DNA with excellent purity (Lahiri & Schnabel, 1993), especially if the DNA is isolated shortly after the blood draw. A 10–20 ml blood draw (yielding approximately 30–60 µg of DNA per ml of whole blood) using an ethylenediaminetetraacetic acid (EDTA) or heparin tube is frequently employed. Use of these types of tubes is critical, as they contain an anticoagulant that will prevent clotting. DNA can be isolated from fresh blood or frozen blood (standard practice is to store the frozen samples at –70° Celsius; thawing and refreezing blood may degrade the DNA; Lahiri & Schnabel, 1993). Extraction of DNA from B-lymphocytes is another option, and cell lines can be produced from lymphocytes allowing

for an unlimited source of DNA, assuming the cell line is stable. For a thorough discussion of procedures and issues with DNA banking, see (Steinberg et al., 2002).

Buccal cells.   Given the invasiveness of obtaining a blood sample, researchers have been increasingly using buccal cell collection for DNA isolation (Feigelson et al., 2001). There are quite a few ways in which buccal cells can be collected, including but not limited to cytobrushes, cotton swabs, saliva collection, and mouthwash procedures (Le Marchand et al., 2001). Generally the collection methods from lowest to highest yield are cytobrushes/cotton swabs, mouthwash kits, and saliva collection kits (García-Closas et al., 2001; Rylander-Rudqvist, Hakansson, Tybring, & Wolk, 2006).

Our group used a mouthwash procedure to collect buccal cells in an epidemiologic sample of hurricane exposed adults (Kilpatrick et al., 2007; Koenen, Aiello, et al., 2009), and samples were sent through the mail. Participants were interviewed over the phone, and those who consented to participate in the genetic component of the study were mailed a mouthwash kit, detailed instructions, and a prepaid envelope to return their specimen to our laboratory. Participants were compensated for the sample. Comparisons of participants (42.2%) who did and did not return saliva samples found that there were no significant differences on any major variables (Galea, Acierno, Ruggiero, Resnick, & Kilpatrick, 2006), underscoring the viability of biologic data collection via U.S. mail for the purposes of genetic analyses. The saliva collection kits used in this study yielded approximately 10 to 30 µg of DNA from each sample, with a failure rate of about 3% (no higher than that found in studies in which samples were not mailed to the laboratory before DNA extraction).

To better understand the acceptability of submitting saliva samples for DNA extraction and analysis via the U.S. mail, we contacted (by phone) a randomly selected subset of adults from a recent post-disaster epidemiologic study. Respondents were told,

> We are thinking of doing a follow-up study to look at whether certain genes influence how people respond to stressful

life events. This would require you to spit in a test tube we would send you and then mail it back to the lab. We would pay people $50 to do this, and the results of the test would be strictly confidential. Would you be willing to consider participating in this follow-up study?

Of the 131 disaster-exposed adults, 75.6% (*n* = 99) said they would be willing to participate. In sum, these results as well as the results from our prior hurricane study underscore the feasibility of buccal cell collection for DNA isolation via U.S. mail.

Sample Collection Considerations

There are a few considerations to keep in mind when deciding on which type of sample to collect. The quantification of DNA, usually using spectrophotometric quantification methods, is used to determine the quantity and purity of DNA in a sample. Using a spectrophotometer will help to determine whether the DNA is contaminated by other molecules (e.g., proteins, hemoglobin) and will also produce an estimate of the amount of DNA in a sample. The quantity (and purity) of DNA yielded from different collection methods is one important consideration. Depending on study design (e.g., GWAS vs. candidate gene), a high yield may be required and would necessitate use of whole blood versus buccal cell collection, depending on the genetic platform to be used. Furthermore, for DNA banked samples, extraction from lymphocytes may need to be used to create cell lines. Additionally, the time that will lapse from sample collection to DNA isolation is an important consideration. The stability of DNA in frozen blood is higher than the stability of DNA in buccal cells; however, a recent study extracted DNA from cytobrushes that were stored at –80° C for approximately 7 years with good success (Woo et al., 2007).

Measuring Phenotypes

Although many different methodological paradigms are used to examine genetics in psychology, all methodologies share a vital condition: that the phenotype is accurate and valid.

Psychiatric diagnosis. The diagnostic category, no matter how specifically and carefully defined, may not be closely tied to a biologic mechanism and therefore not to a genetic mechanism (Meyer-Lindenberg & Weinberger, 2006). In short, there seems to be a shared lack of confidence among experts of the promise or utility of clinical psychiatric diagnoses as phenotypes in the gene-finding process (Insel & Lehner, 2007). Nevertheless, until other biomarkers or endophenotypes are available and are proven useful, gene-phenotype studies often need to rely on diagnostic categories.

Great care in the study design needs to be given to assessment methodology and consideration of multiple issues is necessary (e.g., psychometric properties of the instrument, training of staff who will administer the assessments and interviews, reliability checks of interviews to ensure that they were administered properly). When determining the phenotype of interest and the measures used to assess the phenotype, thought should be given to the planned statistical analyses (e.g., Will the phenotype be considered quantitative? Does the measure produce a continuous scale of severity or number of symptoms? Does the measure yield a dichotomous outcome—diagnosis present or absent?). Consideration of the degree of heterogeneity within diagnostic categories is also needed. Take, for example, schizophrenia; patients with very different symptom profiles can meet criteria for the disorder, resulting in great variability within the phenotype. Another consideration is the use of diagnostic endpoints that infer a threshold that may be artificial. Examination of continuous measures of quantitative traits (or the extremes of these trait distributions) may afford greater statistical power and may decrease the statistical error conferred by potential miscategorization of subthreshold individuals into either case or control status (Plomin et al., 2009).

Endophenotypes. *Endophenotypes* are defined as "measurable components unseen by the unaided eye along the pathway between disease and distal genotype" (Gottesman & Gould, 2003, p. 636). According to Gottesman and Gould (2003), the following conditions must be met to be considered a endophenotype: The endophenotype must be heritable, be related to the illness, be state independent, and cosegregate with the illness in families. Other authors have argued that endophenotypes must also have good psychometric properties, be stable over time, and show increased expression in unaffected relatives of probands (cited in Almasy & Blangero, 2001). The concept of the use of endophenotypes or intermediary phenotypes in psychology and psychiatry has gained popularity in recent years: "As genes do not encode for psychopathology, it is reasonable to expect that the association or penetrance of gene effects will be greater at the level of relatively more simple and biologically based phenotypes" (Meyer-Lindenberg & Weinberger, 2006, p. 818).

There have been numerous success stories of how endophenotypes have been used in psychology. Electrophysiological measures (e.g., electroencephalography, event-related potentials, event-related oscillation) have been used in the context of genetic studies of alcoholism, yielding replicated gene-endophenotype findings (for a review, see Porjesz et al., 2005). Neuropsychological endophenotypes have also been used in schizophrenia research, with replicated results suggesting that variation in *RELN* is related to verbal and visual working memory and to executive functioning (Wedenoja et al., 2008). With recent advances in imaging methodologies, mechanistic aspects of brain function are also beginning to yield feasible endophenotypes (Meyer-Lindenberg & Weinberger, 2006).

CONCLUSION

Given recent advances in quantitative and molecular genetic research techniques, genetically informed psychological research is highly feasible. The intersection of research methodologies used in psychology with those used in genetics is an exciting area of growth in the field. The formation of transdisciplinary research teams to conduct genetically informed psychological studies has the potential to inform the field's knowledge of the complex nature of many phenotypes of interest. Quantitative studies can help to disentangle the influences of genes and environment, informing some of the most central questions in psychology such as why some people develop symptomatology and what factors can prevent or ameliorate such symptoms. Molecular

genetic research techniques have the potential to identify the chromosomal regions of interest for various phenotypes. As molecular studies increasingly refine investigations to the true putatively functional genotypes, resultant understanding regarding the neurobiological effects of these variants can inform both theory and treatment. Of great relevance to the field of psychology is the GxE design, which will help researchers gain an understanding of the complex relationships between genetic variants and environmental factors. Although the field of genetically informed psychological studies is in its infancy, the field is at an exciting time in its development trajectory with great promise to uncover findings that will lead to improving the understanding of, and treatment of, various psychological conditions.

References

Abecasis, G. R., Cherny, S. S., Cookson, W. O., & Cardon, L. R. (2001). Merlin—Rapid analysis of dense genetic maps using sparse gene flow trees. *Nature Genetics, 30*, 97–101. doi:10.1038/ng786

Acierno, R., Ruggiero, K. J., Galea, S., Resnick, H. S., Koenen, K., Roitzsch, J., . . . Kilpatrick, D. G. (2007). Psychological sequelae resulting from the 2004 Florida hurricanes: Implications for post-disaster intervention. *American Journal of Public Health, 97*(Suppl. 1), S103–S108. doi:10.2105/AJPH.2006.087007

Almasy, L., & Blangero, J. (1998). Multipoint quantitative-trait linkage analysis in general pedigrees. *American Journal of Human Genetics, 62*, 1198–1211. doi:10.1086/301844

Almasy, L., & Blangero, J. (2001). Endophenotypes as quantitative risk factors for psychiatric disease: Rationale and study design. *American Journal of Medical Genetics, 105*, 42–44.

Amstadter, A. B., Koenen, K. C., Ruggiero, K. J., Acierno, R., Galea, S., Kilpatrick, D. G., & Gelernter, J. (2009). Variant in RGS2 moderates posttraumatic stress symptoms following potentially traumatic event exposure. *Journal of Anxiety Disorders, 23*, 369–373. doi:10.1016/j.janxdis.2008.12.005

Ardlie, K. G., Kruglyak, L., & Seielstad, M. (2002). Patterns of linkage disequilibrium in the human genome. *Nature Reviews: Genetics, 3*, 299–309. doi:10.1038/nrg777

Belsky, J., Jonassaint, C., Pluess, M., Stanton, M., Brummett, B., & Williams, R. (2009). Vulnerability genes or plasticity genes? *Molecular Psychiatry, 14*, 746–754. doi:10.1038/mp.2009.44

Belsky, J., & Pluess, M. (2009). Beyond diathesis stress: Differential susceptibility to environmental influences. *Psychological Bulletin, 135,* 885–908. doi:10.1037/a0017376

Breslau, J., Kendler, K. S., Su, M., Gaxiola-Aguilar, S., & Kessler, R. C. (2005). Lifetime risk and persistence of psychiatric disorders across ethnic groups in the United States. *Psychological Medicine, 35,* 317–327. doi:10.1017/S0033291704003514

Caspi, A., Sugden, K., Moffitt, T. E., Taylor, A., Craig, I., Harrington, H., . . . Poulton, R. (2003). Influence of life stress on depression: Moderation by a polymorphism in the 5-HTT gene. *Science, 301,* 386–389. doi:10.1126/science.1083968

Daly, M. J., Rioux, J. D., Schaffner, S. F., Hudson, T. J., & Lander, E. S. (2001). High-resolution haplotype structure in the human genome. *Nature Genetics, 29,* 229–232. doi:10.1038/ng1001-229

Derringer, J., Krueger, R. F., McGue, M., & Iacono, W. G. (2008). Genetic and environmental contributions to the diversity of substances used in adolescent twins: A longitudinal study of age and sex effects. *Addiction, 103,* 1744–1751. doi:10.1111/j.1360-0443.2008.02305.x

Estivill, X., & Armengol, L. S. (2007). Copy number variants and common disorders: Filling the gaps and exploring complexity in genome-wide association studies. *PLOS Genetics, 3*(10), e190. doi:10.1371/journal.pgen.0030190

Falconer, D. S. (1960). *Introduction to quantitative genetics.* Edinburgh, Scotland: Oliver & Boyd.

Falk, C. T., & Rubinstein, P. (1987). Haplotype relative risks: An easy reliable way to construct a proper control sample for risk calculations. *Annals of Human Genetics, 51,* 227–233. doi:10.1111/j.1469-1809.1987.tb00875.x

Fan, J. B., & Sklar, P. (2005). Meta-analysis reveals association between serotonin transporter gene STin2 VNTR polymorphism and schizophrenia. *Molecular Psychiatry, 10,* 928–938. doi:10.1038/sj.mp.4001690

Farrer, L. A., Cupples, L. A., Haines, J. L., Hyman, B., Kukull, W. A., Mayeux, R., . . . van Duijn, C. M. (1997). Effects of age, sex, and ethnicity on the association between apolipoprotein E genotype and Alzheimer disease: A meta-analysis. *JAMA, 278,* 1349–1356. doi:10.1001/jama.278.16.1349

Feigelson, H. S., Rodriguez, C., Robertson, A. S., Jacobs, E. J., Calle, E. E., Reid, Y. A., & Thun, M. J. (2001). Determinants of DNA yield and quality from buccal cell samples collected via mouthwash. *Cancer Epidemiology, Biomarkers, and Prevention, 10,* 1005–1008.

Fisher, R. A. (1918). The correlation between relatives on the supposition of Mendelian inheritance. *Transactions of the Royal Society of Edinburgh, 52,* 399–433.

Fox, N. A., Hane, A. A., & Pine, D. S. (2007). Plasticity for affective neurocircuitry: How the environment affects gene expression. *Current Directions in Psychological Science, 16,* 1–5. doi:10.1111/j.1467-8721.2007.00464.x

Freedman, M. L., Reich, D., Penney, K. L., McDonald, G. J., Mignault, A. A., Patterson, N., . . . Altshuler, D. (2004). Assessing the impact of population stratification on genetic association studies. *Nature Genetics, 36,* 388–393. doi:10.1038/ng1333

Fu, Q., Koenen, K. C., Miller, M. W., Heath, A. C., Bucholz, K. K., Lyons, M. J., . . . Tsuang, M. T. (2007). Differential etiology of posttraumatic stress disorder with conduct disorder and major depression in male veterans. *Biological Psychiatry, 62,* 1088–1094. doi:10.1016/j.biopsych.2007.04.036

Galea, S., Acierno, R., Ruggiero, K. J., Resnick, H. S., & Kilpatrick, D. G. (2006). Social context and the psychobiology of trauma. *Annals of the New York Academy of Sciences, 1071,* 231–241. doi:10.1196/annals.1364.018

García-Closas, M., Egan, K. M., Abruzzo, J., Newcomb, P. A., Titus-Ernstoff, L., Franklin, T., . . . Rothman, N. (2001). Collection of genomic DNA from adults in epidemiological studies by buccal cytobrush and mouthwash. *Cancer Epidemiology, Biomarkers, and Prevention, 10,* 687–696.

Gerstein, M. B., Bruce, C., Rozowsky, J. S., Zheng, D., Du, J., Korbel, J. O., . . . Snyder, M. (2007). What is a gene, post-ENCODE? History and updated definition. *Genome Research, 17,* 669–681. doi:10.1101/gr.6339607

Gottesman, I. I., & Gould, T. D. (2003). The endophenotype concept in psychiatry: Etymology and strategic intentions. *American Journal of Psychiatry, 160,* 636–645. doi:10.1176/appi.ajp.160.4.636

Guo, C.-Y., Lunetta, K. L., DeStefano, A. L., & Cupples, L. A. (2009). Combined haplotype relative risk (CHRR): A general and simple genetic association test that combines trios and unrelated case-controls. *Genetic Epidemiology, 33,* 54–62. doi:10.1002/gepi.20356

Gusella, J. F., Tanzi, R., Anderson, M., Hobbs, W., Gibbons, K., Raschtchian, R., . . . Conneally, P. M. (1984). DNA markers for nervous system diseases. *Science, 225,* 1320–1326. doi:10.1126/science.6089346

Guttmacher, A. E., & Collins, F. S. (2002). Genomic medicine—A primer. *New England Journal of Medicine, 347,* 1512–1520. doi:10.1056/NEJMra012240

Guttmacher, A. E., & Collins, F. S. (2003). Welcome to the genomic era. *New England Journal of Medicine, 349,* 996–998. doi:10.1056/NEJMe038132

Hamilton, S. P., Fyer, A., Durner, M., Heiman, G., Baisre de Leon, A., Hodge, S., . . . Weissman, M. M. (2003).

Further genetic evidence for a panic disorder syndrome mapping to chromosome 13q. *Proceedings of the National Academy of Sciences of the United States of America, 100*, 2550–2555. doi:10.1073/pnas.0335669100

Hutchison, K. E., Stallings, M., McGeary, J., & Bryan, A. (2004). Population stratification in the Candidate Gene Study: Fatal threat or red herring? *Psychological Bulletin, 130*, 66–79. doi:10.1037/0033-2909.130.1.66

Insel, T. R., & Lehner, T. (2007). A new area in psychiatric genetics? *Biological Psychiatry, 61*, 1017–1018. doi:10.1016/j.biopsych.2007.01.016

Kendler, K. S. (1990). The super-normal control group in psychiatric genetics. Possible artifactual evidence for coaggregation. *Psychiatric Genetics, 1*, 45.

Kendler, K. S. (1993). Twin studies of psychiatric illness: Current status and future directions. *Archives of General Psychiatry, 50*, 905–915.

Kendler, K. S., & Baker, J. S. (2007). Genetic influences on measures of the environment: A systematic review. *Psychological Medicine, 37*, 615–626. doi:10.1017/S0033291706009524

Kendler, K. S., Gardner, C. O., Annas, P., Neale, M. C., Eaves, L. J., & Lichtenstein, P. (2008). A longitudinal twin study of fears from middle childhood to early adulthood: Evidence for a developmentally dynamic genome. *Archives of General Psychiatry, 65*, 421–429. doi:10.1001/archpsyc.65.4.421

Kendler, K. S., & Myers, J. (2009). A developmental twin study of church attendance and alcohol and nicotine consumption: A model for analyzing the changing impact of genes and environment. *American Journal of Psychiatry, 166*, 1150–1155. doi:10.1176/appi.ajp.2009.09020182

Kendler, K. S., & Prescott, C. A. (2006). *Genes, environment, and psychopathology: Understanding the causes of psychiatric and substance use disorders.* New York, NY: Guilford Press.

Kidd, K. K. (1991). Trials and tribulations in the search for the gene causing neuropsychiatric disorders. *Biodemography and Social Biology, 38*, 163–178.

Kilpatrick, D. G., Koenen, K. C., Ruggiero, K. J., Acierno, R., Galea, S., Resnick, H. S., . . . Gelernter, J. (2007). The serotonin transporter genotype and social support and moderation of posttraumatic stress disorder and depression in hurricane-exposed adults. *American Journal of Psychiatry, 164*, 1693–1699. doi:10.1176/appi.ajp.2007.06122007

Koenen, K. C., Aiello, A., Bakshis, E., Amstadter, A. B., Ruggiero, K. J., Acierno, R., . . . Galea, S. (2009). Modification of the association between serotonin transporter genotype and risk of posttraumatic stress disorder in adults by county-level social environment. *American Journal of Epidemiology, 169*, 704–711. doi:10.1093/aje/kwn397

Koenen, K. C., Amstadter, A. B., Ruggiero, K. J., Acierno, R., Galea, S., Kilpatrick, D. G., & Gelernter, J. (2009). RGS2 and generalized anxiety disorder in an epidemiologic sample of hurricane-exposed adults. *Depression and Anxiety, 26*, 309–315. doi:10.1002/da.20528

Koenen, K. C., Fu, Q. J., Ertel, K., Lyons, M. J., Eisen, S. A., True, W. R., . . . Tsuang, M. T. (2008). Common genetic liability to major depression and posttraumatic stress disorder in men. *Journal of Affective Disorders, 105*, 109–115. doi:10.1016/j.jad.2007.04.021

Lahiri, D. K., & Schnabel, B. (1993). DNA isolation by a rapid method from human blood samples: Effects of MgCl2, EDTA, storage time, and temperature on DNA yield and quality. *Biochemical Genetics, 31*, 321–328. doi:10.1007/BF00553174

Lander, E. S., Linton, L. M., Birren, B., Nusbaum, C., Zody, M. C., Baldwin, J., . . . International Human Genome Sequencing Consortium. (2001). Initial sequencing and analysis of the human genome. *Nature, 409*, 860–921. doi:10.1038/35057062

Le Marchand, L., Lum-Jones, A., Saltzman, B., Visaya, V., Nomura, A. M. Y., & Kolonel, L. N. (2001). Feasibility of collecting buccal cell DNA by mail in a cohort study. *Cancer Epidemiology, Biomarkers, and Prevention, 10*, 701–703.

Lemery, K. S., & Goldsmith, H. H. (1999). Genetically informative designs for the study of behavior development. *International Journal of Behavioral Development, 23*, 293–317. doi:10.1080/016502599383838

Lench, N., Stanier, P., & Williamson, R. (1988). Simple non-invasive method to obtain DNA for gene analysis. *Lancet, 331*, 1356–1358. doi:10.1016/S0140-6736(88)92178-2

Mendel, G. J. (1866). Versuche ueber Pflanzenhybriden [Experiments in plant hybrids]. *Verhandlungen des Naturfurschunden Vereines in Bruenn, 4*, 3–47.

Meyer-Lindenberg, A., & Weinberger, D. R. (2006). Interpediate phenotypes and genetic mechanisms of psychiatric disorders. *Nature Neuroscience, 7*, 818–827. doi:10.1038/nrn1993

Middeldorp, C. M., Cath, D. C., Van Dyck, R., & Boomsma, D. I. (2005). The co-morbidity of anxiety and depression in the perspective of genetic epidemiology: A review of twin and family studies. *Psychological Medicine, 35*, 611–624. doi:10.1017/S003329170400412X

Moffitt, T. E., Caspi, A., & Rutter, M. (2005). Strategy for investigating interactions between measured genes and measured environments. *Archives of General Psychiatry, 62*, 473–481. doi:10.1001/archpsyc.62.5.473

Muthén, L. K., & Muthén, B. O. (2004). Mplus Version 3.11 [Computer software]. Los Angeles, CA: Authors.

Nance, W. E., & Corey, L. A. (1976). Genetic models for the analysis of data from the families of identical twins. *Genetics, 83,* 811–826.

Neale, M. C., Boker, S. M., Xie, G., & Maes, H. (2002). *Mx: Statistical modeling* (6th ed.). Richmond: Virginia Institute for Psychiatric and Behavioral Genetics, Virginia Commonwealth University.

Neale, M. C., & Cardon, L. R. (1992). *Methodology for genetic studies of twins and families.* Dordrecht, the Netherlands: Kluwer.

Nugent, N. R., Fyer, A., Weissman, M. M., & Koenen, K. C. (2010). Genetics of anxiety disorders. In H. B. Simpson, Y. Neria, R. Lewis-Fernandez, & F. Schneier (Eds.), *Anxiety disorders: Theory, research, and clinical perspectives* (pp. 139–155). New York, NY: Cambridge University Press.

Plomin, R., & Davis, O. S. P. (2009). The future of genetics in psychology and psychiatry: Microarrays, genome-wide association, and non-coding RNA. *Journal of Child Psychology and Psychiatry, 50,* 63–71. doi:10.1111/j.1469-7610.2008.01978.x

Plomin, R., DeFries, J. C., & Loehlin, J. C. (1977). Genotype–environment interaction and correlation in the analysis of human behavior. *Psychological Bulletin, 84,* 309–322. doi:10.1037/0033-2909.84.2.309

Plomin, R., DeFries, J. C., McClearn, G. E., & McGuffin, P. (2001). *Behavioral genetics.* New York, NY: Worth.

Plomin, R., Haworth, C. M. A., & Davis, O. S. P. (2009). Common disorders are quantitative traits. *Nature Reviews: Genetics, 10,* 872–878. doi:10.1038/nrg2670

Porjesz, B., Rangaswamy, M., Kamarajan, C., Jones, K. A., Padmanabhapillai, A., & Begleiter, H. (2005). The utility of neurophysiological markers in the study of alcoholism. *Clinical Neurophysiology, 116,* 993–1018. doi:10.1016/j.clinph.2004.12.016

Pritchard, J. K., & Rosenberg, N. A. (1999). Use of unlinked genetic markers to detect population stratification in association studies. *American Journal of Human Genetics, 65,* 220–228. doi:10.1086/302449

Pritchard, J. K., Stephens, M., Rosenberg, N. A., & Donnelly, P. (2000). Association mapping in structured populations. *American Journal of Human Genetics, 67,* 170–181. doi:10.1086/302959

Reich, D. E., Cargill, M., Bolk, S., Ireland, J., Sabeti, P. C., Richter, D. J., . . . Lander, E. S. (2001). Linkage disequilibrium in the human genome. *Nature, 411,* 199–204. doi:10.1038/35075590

Rende, R. D., Plomin, R., & Vandenberg, S. G. (1990). Who discovered the twin method? *Behavior Genetics, 20,* 277–285. doi:10.1007/BF01067795

Risch, N. (1990). Linkage strategies for genetically complex traits. I. Multilocus models. *American Journal of Human Genetics, 46,* 222–228.

Risch, N., & Merikangas, K. (1996). The future of genetic studies of complex human diseases. *Science, 273,* 1516–1517. doi:10.1126/science.273.5281.1516

Rutter, M. (2010). Gene–environment interplay. *Depression and Anxiety, 27,* 1–4. doi:10.1002/da.20641

Rutter, M., Moffit, T. E., & Caspi, A. (2006). Gene–environment interplay and psychopathology: Multiple varieties but real effects. *Journal of Child Psychology and Psychiatry, 47,* 226–261. doi:10.1111/j.1469-7610.2005.01557.x

Rylander-Rudqvist, T., Hakansson, N., Tybring, G., & Wolk, A. (2006). Quality and quantity of saliva DNA obtained from the self-administered Oragene method—A pilot study on the cohort of Swedish men. *Cancer Epidemiology, Biomarkers, and Prevention, 15,* 1742–1745. doi:10.1158/1055-9965.EPI-05-0706

Shanahan, M. J., & Hofer, S. M. (2005). Social context in gene-environment interactions: Retrospect and prospect. *Journal of Gerontology: Psychological Sciences, 60B,* 65–76. doi:10.1093/geronb/60.Special_Issue_1.65

Spielman, R. S., & Ewens, W. J. (1996). The TDT and other family-based tests for linkage disequilibrium and association. *American Journal of Human Genetics, 59,* 983–989.

Steinberg, K., Beck, J., Nickeron, D., García-Closas, M., Gallagher, M., Caggana, M., . . . Sampson, E. (2002). DNA banking for epidemiologic studies: A review of current practices. *Epidemiology, 13,* 246–254. doi:10.1097/00001648-200205000-00003

Stoolmiller, M. (1999). Implications of the restricted range of family environments for estimates of heritability and nonshared environment in behavior-genetic adoption studies. *Psychological Bulletin, 125,* 392–409. doi:10.1037/0033-2909.125.4.392

Strachan, T., & Read, A. P. (2004). *Human molecular genetics.* New York, NY: Garland.

Talati, A., Ponniah, K., Strug, L., Hodge, S., Fyer, A., & Weissman, M. M. (2008). Panic disorder, social anxiety disorder, and a possible medical syndrome previously linked to chromosome 13. *Biological Psychiatry, 63,* 594–601. doi:10.1016/j.biopsych.2007.07.021

Tishkoff, S. A., Reed, F. A., Friedlaender, F. R., Ehret, C., Ranciaro, A., Froment, A., . . . Williams, S. M. (2009). The genetic structure and history of Africans and African Americans. *Science, 324,* 1035–1044. doi:10.1126/science.1172257

Uher, R., & McGuffin, P. (2010). The moderation by the serotonin transporter gene of environmental adversity in the etiology of depression: 2009 update. *Molecular Psychiatry, 15,* 18–22. doi:10.1038/mp.2009.123

Varmus, H. (2002). Getting ready for gene-based medicine. *New England Journal of Medicine, 347,* 1526–1527. doi:10.1056/NEJMe020119

Venter, J. C., Adams, M. D., Myers, E. W., Li, P. W., Mural, R. J., Sutton, G. G., . . . Zhu, X. (2001). The sequence of the human genome. *Science, 291(5507)*, 1304–1351. doi:10.1126/science.1058040

Walker, E. F., Sabuwalla, Z., & Huot, R. (2004). Pubertal neuromaturation, stress sensitivity, and psychopathology. *Development and Psychopathology, 16*, 807–824. doi:10.1017/S0954579404040027

Watson, J. D., & Crick, F. H. C. (1953). Molecular structure of nucleic acids. *Nature, 171*, 737–738. doi:10.1038/171737a0

Wedenoja, J., Loukola, A., Tuulio-Henriksson, A., Paunio, T., Ekelund, J., Silander, K., . . . Peltonen, L. (2008). Replication of linkage on chromosome 7q22 and association of the regional Reelin gene with working memory in schizophrenia families: Association of Reelin with working memory. *Molecular Psychiatry, 13*, 673–684. doi:10.1038/sj.mp.4002047

Weissman, M. M., Fyer, A., Haghighi, F., Heiman, G., Deng, Z., Hen, D., . . . Knowles, J. A. (2000). Potential panic disorder syndrome: Clinical and genetic linkage evidence. *American Journal of Medical Genetics, 96*(1), 24–35. doi:10.1002/(SICI)1096-8628(20000207)96:1<24::AID-AJMG7>3.0.CO;2-E

Weissman, M. M., Gross, R., Fyer, A., Heiman, G. A., Gameroff, M. J., Hodge, S. E., . . . Wickramaratne, P. J. (2004). Interstitial cystitis and panic disorder: A potential genetic syndrome. *Archives of General Psychiatry, 61*, 273–279. doi:10.1001/archpsyc.61.3.273

Wermter, A.-K., Laucht, M., Schimmelmann, B., Banaschweski, T., Sonuga-Barke, E., Rietschel, M., & Becker, K. (2010). From nature versus nurture, via nature and nurture, to Gene × Environment interaction in mental disorders. *European Child and Adolescent Psychiatry, 19*, 199–210. doi:10.1007/s00787-009-0082-z

Wittke-Thompson, J. K., Pluzhnikov, A., & Cox, N. J. (2005). Rational inferences about departures from Hardy-Weinberg equilibrium. *American Journal of Human Genetics, 76*, 967–986. doi:10.1086/430507

Woo, J. G., Sun, G., Haverbusch, M., Indugula, S., Martin, L. J., Broderick, J. P., . . . Woo, D. (2007). Quality assessment of buccal versus blood genomic DNA using the Affymetrix 500 K GeneChip. *BMC Genetics, 8*, 79. doi:10.1186/1471-2156-8-79

Yaeger, R., Avila-Bront, A., Abdul, K., Nolan, P., Grann, V., Birchette, M., . . . Joe, A. K. (2008). Comparing genetic ancestry and self-described race in African Americans born in the United States and in Africa. *Cancer Epidemiology, Biomarkers, and Prevention, 17*, 1329–1338. doi:10.1158/1055-9965.EPI-07-2505

Young, R. M., Lawford, B. R., Noble, E. P., Kanin, B., Wilkie, A., Ritchie, T., . . . Shadforth, S. (2002). Harmful drinking in military veterans with posttraumatic stress disorder: Association with the D2 dopamine receptor A1 allele. *Alcohol and Alcoholism, 37*, 451–456. doi:10.1093/alcalc/37.5.451

Zeggini, E., Barton, A., Eyre, S., Ward, D., Ollier, W., Worthington, J., & John, S. (2005). Characterisation of the genomic architecture of human chromosome 17q and evaluation of different methods for haplotype block definition. *BMC Genetics, 6*, 21. doi:10.1186/1471-2156-6-21

CHAPTER 36

GENETIC EPIDEMIOLOGY

Lannie Ligthart and Dorret I. Boomsma

Individual differences in psychological or behavioral traits can be explained by a combination of genetic and environmental differences between individuals. When a trait is said to be highly genetic, this means that a large proportion of the variance in the trait is explained by genetic factors, that is, the effect of one or more genes that each have their influence on the expression of the trait. Environmental factors can range from intrauterine environment to the influence of the family environment, life events, friends and many other unidentified nongenetic factors. In this chapter we provide an overview of methods used to model the contribution of genes and environment to variance in a trait or a set of traits, and to localize and identify the regions of the genome that may be involved. The area of research that focuses on quantifying genetic effects is called *behavior genetics* or *genetic epidemiology*. Genes can be localized and identified with *genetic linkage* and *association* methods. Finally, we discuss factors that influence the expression of genes (such as *epigenetic* modification) and methods to study how gene expression is regulated and how genes interact.

Genetic information is encoded in deoxiribonucleic acid (DNA) molecules. The DNA code contains the units of genetic information we call *genes*. There is no real agreement on what exactly defines a gene; the definition has evolved along with the advances in science. Commonly used definitions of a gene include "a unit of inheritance" or "a packet of genetic information that encodes a protein or ribonucleic acid (RNA)." The estimated number of genes in the human genome is also a subject of debate. Not too long ago it was predicted that the human genome contained around 100,000 to 150,000 genes (e.g., Liang et al., 2000). However, more recent estimates have gone down to 20,000 to 25,000 (International Human Genome Sequencing Consortium, 2004).

In humans, the DNA molecules are organized in 2 by 23 *chromosomes*: 22 pairs of *autosomes* and one pair of *sex chromosomes*. The genetic sequence as a whole is called the *genome*, and a location in the genome that for instance contains a gene or a genetic marker is referred to as a *locus*. A *quantitative trait locus* (QTL) is a locus that harbors a gene influencing a quantitative trait, that is, a trait that varies on a quantitative scale, or the liability to a complex disorder, when the assessment of the trait is on an interval or ordinal scale.

The nuclei of nearly all human cells contain two versions of each chromosome and therefore of each gene. The two corresponding chromosomes are called *homologous* chromosomes. One is received from the mother, the other from the father. In addition, a small amount of DNA is contained in the (maternally inherited) *mitochondria*. Although most of the human DNA sequence is identical in all individuals, at some loci different versions of the sequence occur. These variants are called *alleles*.

This work was supported by Netherlands Organization for Scientific Research Grants NWO 575-25-006 (Database Twin Register), NWO-MW 904-61-193 (Resolving Cause and Effect in the Association Between Regular Exercise and Psychological Well-Being), NWO/SPI 56-464-14192 (Spinozapremie), and NWO 480-04-004 (Twin-Family Database for Behavior Genetics and Genomics Studies); the Borderline Personality Disorder Research Foundation; the Centre for Neurogenetics/Cognition Research; and the Center for Medical Systems Biology.

DOI: 10.1037/13620-036
APA Handbook of Research Methods in Psychology: Vol. 2. Research Designs, H. Cooper (Editor-in-Chief)

The word *allele* can refer to a gene variant and also to versions of a genetic marker or any other fragment of DNA sequence. Individuals who carry the same allele at both homologous chromosomes are called *homozygous*. Individuals with two different alleles are *heterozygous*. The two alleles together, either at one or at multiple loci, make up a person's *genotype*. The term *haplotype* indicates a combination of alleles at multiple loci that an individual receives from one parent (Ott, 1999). It usually refers to a combination of alleles transmitted close together on the same chromosome. Finally, the observed characteristics of an individual are called *phenotypes*.

Alleles affecting quantitative traits can exert their effect in various ways. When the alleles act independently, the effects simply add up, in which case we speak of *additive* genetic effects. When the effect of one allele depends on the effect of another, that is, there is an interaction between them, they are referred to as *nonadditive* effects. There are several forms of nonadditivity. Interactions between two alleles at the same locus are referred to as *dominance*. When the interaction is between alleles at two different loci, it is referred to as *epistasis*. An excellent online tutorial by Shaun Purcell that addresses additivity and dominance can be found on the web (http://pngu.mgh.harvard.edu/~purcell/bgim/index2.html#sgene).

In this chapter we provide an overview of genetic epidemiological methods and developments, in three parts. The first part describes the estimation of heritability as well as more advanced modeling based on twin methodology. In Part II, methodology used to localize and identify genes will be discussed. Finally, in Part III, we focus on the gene expression and epigenetic modification of the DNA.

PART I: ESTIMATING HERITABILITY

It is often observed that human traits run in families. This is not only the case for diseases or physical appearance but also can apply to personality and behavior. The mere fact that a trait is familial, however, does not tell us whether the trait is heritable because familial resemblance can also be the result of the influence of a shared family environment.

One method to investigate genetic influences is by studying adopted children and their biological and adoptive parents. Similarities between adopted children and their biological parents reflect genetic influences, whereas similarities between adopted children and their adoptive parents reflect the effects of the family environment. However, there are some disadvantages to adoption studies: Adoptions are relatively rare, and adoptive children and parents cannot be assumed to be representative of the general population (Martin, Boomsma, & Machin, 1997; Plomin, DeFries, McClearn, & McGuffin, 2008).

The Classical Twin Model

For the reasons described, many studies use data from twins and their families. In twin studies, the resemblance between monozygotic (MZ) and dizygotic (DZ) twins is compared to estimate the contribution of genes, shared environment, and nonshared environment to the variance in a trait. This is based on the fact that MZ twins share 100% of their segregating genes, whereas DZ twins share on average 50%. Note that this percentage refers to the portion of the genome in which variation occurs, because more than 99% of the genome is identical between humans; this part is therefore entirely shared in both MZ and DZ twins. In contrast, both MZ and DZ twins share the home environment. This means that differences between MZ twins must be due to nonshared environmental influences, whereas the extent to which MZ twins are more similar than DZ twins reflects the influence of genetic factors. Using these principles, the variance in a trait can be decomposed into variance explained by additive genetic factors (A), common or shared environment (C), and nonshared environment or measurement error (E). In the absence of dominance or epistasis, the percentage of variance in a trait that is explained by additive genetic factors equals the heritability of the trait, which can be estimated by taking twice the difference between the MZ and DZ twin correlation: $h^2 = 2(rMZ - rDZ)$.

When $rMZ > 2rDZ$, there is evidence for a contribution of nonadditive genetic influences, also referred to as genetic dominance (D), which also includes effects of epistasis. In this case, the percentage of variance explained by A and D together is referred to as the *broad-sense heritability*; A alone is called the *narrow-sense heritability*.

The contribution of A, C, D, and E to the trait variance can be estimated on the basis of biometrical genetic theory. Discussing the biometrical model in detail is beyond the scope of this chapter, but it is the basis of a few important principles on which twin models are based (for a detailed introduction, see Falconer & Mackay, 1996).

As explained, the total phenotypic variance of a trait (P) can be decomposed into components explained by A, C, D, and E: $V_P = V_A + V_D + V_C + V_E$. We here assume that there is no interaction or correlation between genetic and environmental factors (the covariance between A and D is zero by definition).

The covariance between MZ twins is expressed as follows: $cov(MZ) = V_A + V_D + V_C$. Because V_E is by definition nonshared variance, it cannot contribute to covariance of family members. V_C is, by definition, shared, and the genetic variance is also entirely shared because MZ twins are genetically identical. The expectation for the DZ twin covariance is expressed as follows: $cov(DZ) = \frac{1}{2}V_A + \frac{1}{4}V_D + V_C$. On average one half of the additive genetic variance is shared between DZ twins (and between nontwin siblings). To share nonadditive variance, two relatives have to share both alleles of a gene, an event that occurs with a probability of 25% in DZ twins (or full siblings). Figure 36.1 shows a graphic representation of the model that arises from these principles.

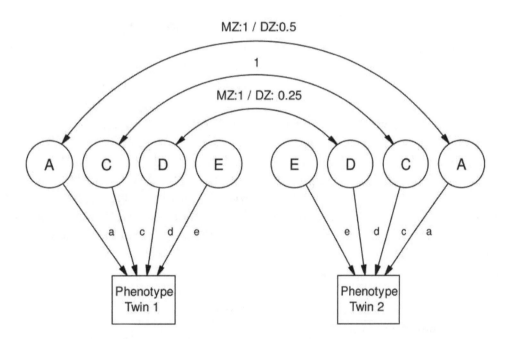

FIGURE 36.1.   Univariate twin model. Path diagram showing the A, C, D, and E factors for a twin pair, and the correlations between each of the factors for MZ and DZ twins. Following the tracing rules of path analysis (Wright, 1934), the phenotypic variance explained by each component is calculated as the squared path coefficient: The genetic variance for an individual is calculated as a^2, the shared environmental variance equals c^2, and so on. The total variance is derived by summing the variance explained by the individual components: $a^2 + c^2 + d^2 + e^2$. The covariance between twins is calculated by tracing the path from twin 1, through the double-headed arrow, to twin 2. For instance, the genetic covariance between MZ twins equals $a \times 1 \times a = a^2$, whereas for DZ twins it equals $a \times .5 \times a = .5a^2$. The total covariance is calculated by adding up all paths contributing to the covariance (i.e., all paths that connect the two twins), which is $a^2 + c^2 + d^2$ for an MZ pair and $.5a^2 + c^2 + .25d^2$ for a DZ pair. When only data from twins reared together are available, it is not possible to estimate C and D at the same time because there is not enough information; an ACDE model is not identified. Therefore, the twin correlations are used to decide whether an ACE or an ADE model is more plausible.

Structural Equation Modeling

To estimate the contribution of all genetic and environmental factors to a trait and assess their significance, models can be evaluated and compared using *structural equation modeling* (SEM). The parameters of a model (which include means, variances, and covariances) can be estimated using an optimization approach such as maximum likelihood estimation. The relative goodness-of-fit of different models can be assessed by calculating minus twice the log-likelihood (–2LL) of the data given the model and comparing these values between models. By dropping or equating parameters, the fit of different models can be compared with a likelihood ratio test. Genetic SEM usually involves a multiple group design in which data from, for example, MZ and DZ twins are analyzed simultaneously and parameters (a, c, d, and e in Figure 36.1) are constrained to be equal across groups to ensure identification of the model. Usually, a fully saturated model that includes estimates for all parameters is tested first. Then the significance of parameters can be tested by constraining them to be zero. For instance, it can be tested whether the C factor has an effect on the variance of the trait, by fixing the c path coefficient at zero and then comparing the original model with the constrained model. When dropping or equating parameters does not result in a significant deterioration of the model fit, this indicates the more parsimonious model fits the data as well as the more complex model. The best model is the most parsimonious model that still provides a good explanation of the observed data. Significance is determined on the basis of the difference in –2LL between two models, which is asymptotically distributed as χ^2. The degrees of freedom of the test are equal to the difference in the number of parameters. For very large samples, alternative fit indexes have been proposed, such as the root-mean-square error of approximation (RMSEA; Browne & Cudeck, 1993), the Bayesian information criterion (BIC; Schwarz, 1978), and the Akaike information criterion (AIC; Akaike, 1987).

Twin Models and Categorical Data

In the case of a continuous variable, the trait is assumed to be normally distributed (which is indeed expected for traits that are affected by many genes; Fischer, 1918). Noncontinuous phenotypes (e.g., presence or absence of a disorder, or categories representing levels of severity of a phenotype) are not normally distributed and cannot be analyzed the same way. However, they may reflect a categorization of an underlying normally distributed trait. In this situation, a liability threshold model (Falconer, 1965) is often used. A threshold model assumes that the categories of a variable reflect an imprecise measurement of an underlying normal distribution of liability with a mean of 0 and a variance of 1. One or more thresholds (expressed as z scores) divide this distribution into discrete classes (e.g., affected versus unaffected for a disease phenotype, or no symptoms–mild–moderate–severe for a trait measured on a continuous scale, such as a neuroticism or depression score). The area under the curve between two thresholds represents the proportion of cases within a category (Figure 36.2). The resemblance of relatives (e.g., twins) is expressed as tetrachoric or polychoric correlations, which represent the correlation of relatives on the liability dimension.

Extensions of the Classical Twin Model

The classical twin design can be extended to also include data from siblings, parents, and spouses. The genetic similarity between nontwin sibling pairs is the same as the resemblance between DZ twins, that is, on average 50% of the segregating genes. Adding data from one or more nontwin siblings to the model (often referred to as an *extended twin design*) results in a substantial increase in power to detect genetic and shared environmental effects (e.g., Posthuma & Boomsma, 2000).

The similarity between parents and children is 50% for additive genetic effects but 0% for dominance; because dominance reflects an interaction between two alleles at the same locus, to share these effects two individuals have to share both alleles. By definition, however, parents transmit only one allele to their children (Falconer & Mackay, 1996).

Data from parents and spouses can be used to account for the effects of parental influence (i.e., cultural transmission) and assortative mating (i.e., phenotypic correlations between spouses) (Fulker,

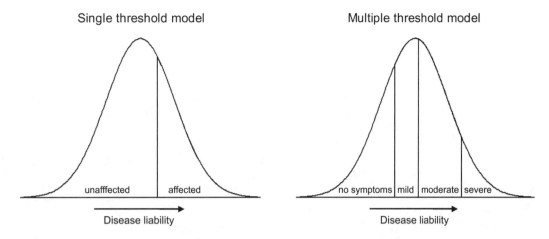

Single threshold model

Multiple threshold model

unafffected | affected

Disease liability

no symptoms | mild | moderate | severe

Disease liability

FIGURE 36.2.   Threshold models. In both cases a normal distribution of liability underlies the observed phenotypes, which have been categorized into discrete classes. Single threshold model: This represents a disease phenotype with affected and unaffected individuals. Multiple threshold model: In this case an ordinal variable with categories corresponding to different levels of severity, in this case ranging from no symptoms, via mild and moderate, to a severe phenotype.

1982). An example of this method can be found in Distel et al. (2009), who investigated whether cultural transmission from parents to offspring had an effect on borderline personality features. They found that cultural transmission did not play a role; however, there was some evidence for assortative mating, although this explained only a small amount of the variance in the trait.

Multivariate Models

A useful extension of the models described thus far is to analyze multiple traits simultaneously. Bivariate or multivariate models can be used to quantify the genetic and environmental overlap in correlated traits and to explore the etiology of the association (or *comorbidity*) between traits. For example, it is possible to test whether the same genes affect different correlated traits, or whether a similar environment is responsible for the correlation.

In addition to the MZ and DZ twin correlations, a multivariate model also includes the phenotypic correlation between traits (within a person), and the *cross-twin cross-trait correlation* (the correlation between Trait 1 in Twin 1 and Trait 2 in Twin 2). The function of the cross-twin cross-trait correlations is similar to that of the regular twin correlations in a univariate model: If the cross-twin cross-trait correlation is higher in MZ than in DZ twins, this indicates that the two traits share a genetic component, in other words, there is a

genetic correlation between them. Shared and nonshared environmental correlations are calculated similarly. Figure 36.3 shows an example of a bivariate ACE model. The cross-twin cross-trait correlations are modeled by adding the cross-paths a_{21}, c_{21}, and e_{21}. If the a_{21} path is significant, this implies that a genetic correlation is present, and similarly, significance of c_{21} and e_{21} indicates shared and nonshared environmental correlations, respectively. For instance, following the tracing rules of path analysis (Wright, 1934), the genetic covariance between Phenotype 1 in Twin 1 and Phenotype 2 in Twin 2 in DZ twins is given by $a_{11} \times 0.5 \times a_{21}$.

An example of a bivariate twin analysis is described in Ligthart, Nyholt, Penninx, and Boomsma (2010). In this analysis, the relationship between migraine and depression was investigated, to test the hypothesis that the often-reported comorbidity of these disorders is due to a shared underlying genetic factor. The phenotypic correlation between the two traits was estimated at .28. Most of the shared variance was explained by genetic factors (55%), the remaining variance was due to nonshared environment. There was a significant genetic correlation between the traits ($r = .30$). Thus, it can be concluded that migraine and depression are in part influenced by the same genetic and nonshared environmental factors but that the proportion of variance explained by this relationship is modest.

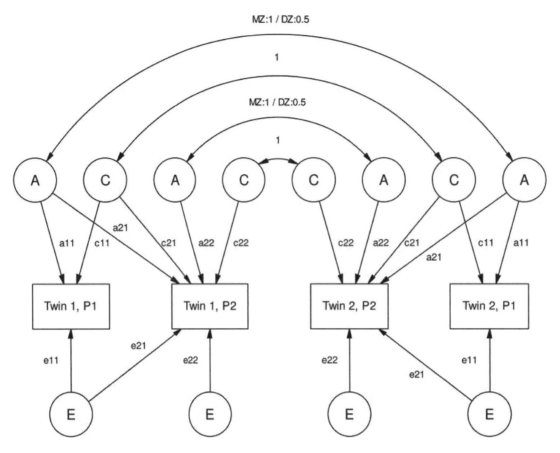

FIGURE 36.3.   Example of a bivariate twin model. A bivariate ACE model, with two twins and two phenotypes (P1 and P2).

Another application is the extension to longitudinal models. By measuring correlations between repeated measures at different time points, it can be determined whether stability over time is due to genetic or environmental factors. An example can be found in Bartels et al. (2004), who investigated the contribution of genes and environment to stability in internalizing and externalizing problem behavior in children ages 3 to 12 years old. They found that genetic factors were responsible for both stability and change over time, whereas a common set of shared environmental factors mostly accounted for stability in problem behavior across different ages. Nonshared environment played only a modest role in explaining stability or change in problem behaviour.

Sex × Genotype and Age × Genotype Interaction

The influence of genetic and environmental factors may differ for males and females. Therefore it may be useful to first test a full model in which all parameter estimates are different for the two sexes, and then test whether the estimates for males and females can be constrained to be equal. In many situations, means or thresholds have to be modeled separately for males and females, for instance, because a trait (e.g., migraine or depression) is more prevalent in women. Apart from that, several different hypotheses can be tested:

1. The variance components (i.e., V_A, V_D, V_C, and V_E) are the same for males and females.
2. The variance components are proportionally the same in males and females, but in one sex, the total trait variance is larger. A way to model this is by constraining all variance components in one sex to be a scalar multiple of the variance components in the other sex.
3. The variance components differ, for instance when a trait is more heritable in one sex than in

the other. In this case, the variance components have to be estimated separately for men and women. A difference in heritability may arise for different reasons: The genetic variance can be the same in the two sexes, but the environmental variance could be larger in men than in women. Because heritability is expressed as a ratio (genetic variance over total variance) this would lead to a lower heritability estimate in men.

To test which of these models fits the data best, one starts with a full model in which all parameters are estimated separately for males and females. Then, by constraining the parameters step by step, it is tested whether parameter estimates differ significantly between men and women. This same method can be applied when data are available for different age-groups (e.g., adolescents versus adults) to test whether estimates of heritability differ depending on age. The actual implementation of the model depends on whether data have been collected in a cross-sectional design in subjects of different ages, or in a longitudinal study in which the same subjects are measured repeatedly across time. A more detailed discussion of these models can be found in, for example, Neale and Cardon (1992) or in the special issue of the journal *Behavior Genetics* that was published in 1989 (Martin, Boomsma, & Neale, 1989).

Finally, when data from DZ opposite-sex (DOS) twins are available, it is possible, in addition to quantitative differences, to also test whether qualitative sex differences are present (i.e., whether different genes affect the trait in males and females). This is tested by estimating the correlation between the latent genetic factors in DOS twins, while this correlation remains fixed at .5 in the same-sex pairs. If the correlation in DOS twins is significantly lower than .5, this is an indication that the genetic factors affecting males and females are (partly) different. It is also possible that different environmental factors influence a trait in men and women. In this case, the correlation between the C factors (see Figure 36.1) would be estimated in DOS twin pairs (or in opposite-sex siblings). It is not possible to estimate the correlations for genetic and shared environmental factors simultaneously using a classical twin

design, as there is only one data point available that is informative for this test.

Genotype × Environment Interaction

The expression of genes may also depend on environmental factors—sometimes referred to as moderators. For example, the expression of the genotype may be more clearly seen in a permissive environment. An interesting case of gene–environment interaction (GxE) was found in a study by Boomsma, de Geus, van Baal, and Koopmans (1999), who observed that a religious upbringing reduced the influence of genetic factors on *disinhibition*, one of the dimensions of the sensation seeking scales. In a study of female twins, Heath, Eaves, and Martin (1998) found that being in a marriage-like relationship served as a protective factor by reducing the impact of a genetic liability to depression.

A commonly used method to test for the presence of GxE is to include a moderator (the environmental variable) in the model that affects the path coefficients that represent the genetic and environmental variance of the trait of interest. In this approach, the moderator variable can be discrete (e.g., sex) or continuous (e.g., age). If GxE is present but not modeled, this can result in biased parameter estimates. Interaction between A and C will present as A, whereas interaction between A and E will present as E (Purcell, 2002).

When it is known which genes influence a particular phenotype it is also possible to test for interaction of the environment with a specific gene variant. In a famous study, Caspi et al. (2003) investigated the association between the serotonin transporter gene and depression in individuals who had experienced stressful life events and individuals who had not. It was found that stressful life events were associated with depression but only in individuals who carried at least one copy of the short allele of the serotonin transporter gene. The strongest effect was observed in individuals who carried two copies of the short allele, and the effect was nonsignificant in carriers of two long alleles. As spectacular as these results were, it now is thought they may have been chance findings because few studies have succeeded in reproducing them. A large meta-analysis of the many replication studies failed to show significant evidence of either a main effect of the serotonin transporter gene or an interaction between this gene and stressful life events (Risch et al., 2009). Influential examples of GxE research can be found in Moffitt, Caspi, and Rutter (2005) and Munafò, Durrant, Lewis, and Flint (2009).

PART II: GENE-FINDING

Once it has been established that a trait is heritable, the next step is to find the genes involved. The two primary statistical methods for gene-finding are *linkage* and *association*. Unlike the methods described in the section Part I: Estimating Heritability, linkage and association require the collection of DNA samples and the measurement of genotypes.

Linkage analysis is a method that localizes regions possibly influencing the trait of interest by using pedigree information. In short, the objective is to determine whether relatives who are phenotypically similar are also genotypically similar in a particular region of the genome. If this is the case, this region may harbor a gene involved in the trait of interest. Linkage is based on the principle that two loci that are physically close together (e.g., an observed fragment of DNA and an unobserved disease locus) are more likely to be coinherited. How this works will be discussed in more detail in the section Parametric Linkage. Because the information in a linkage study comes from the pedigree structure, it is necessary to collect family data.

Association analysis can go one step further: not only can the location of the involved regions be determined but also which genetic variant (allele) is associated with the phenotype. In other words: Do individuals with a certain phenotype have a different frequency of allele X than individuals who do not have this phenotype? This can be tested with a straightforward chi-square or regression test. Association studies have a higher resolution than linkage studies and have often been used to follow up promising linkage results. As we will see, using family data has certain advantages; however, association studies can also be performed using data from unrelated individuals. An introduction to linkage and association studies can be found in Balding (2006), Nyholt (2008), and Vink and Boomsma (2002).

Markers

Because—due to technical and financial limitations—it is currently not feasible to characterize the entire human DNA sequence in large numbers of individuals, gene-finding studies rely on markers. Markers are genetic variants (also called *polymorphisms*) with a known location that can be used as indicators of the approximate location of the real, usually unmeasured locus of interest. When we say an individual is genotyped for a linkage or association study, this means their DNA is characterized at a selected number of marker loci, either in a specific region (in candidate gene studies) or throughout the genome (in genome-wide studies).

Several types of markers are used in gene-finding studies. *Single nucleotide polymorphisms* (SNPs) are single base pairs with two variants (e.g., some individuals have an A, others have a C). Theoretically (if single base pair mutations have occurred multiple times at the same locus) there can be four variants (A, C, T, and G), but for practical reasons only SNPs with two variants are selected for gene-finding studies. *Microsattellites* are sequence-length polymorphisms that consist of a varying number of repeats of a short (usually 1–4 bp) sequence of DNA, for example, CACACACACACACA. A third and more recently recognized type of polymorphism is the *copy number variant* (CNV). CNVs are DNA fragments ranging from kilobases (Kb) to even megabases (Mb) in size, of which different numbers of copies are present in different individuals. Interestingly, the presence of discordance in CNVs has been demonstrated within MZ twin pairs (Bruder et al., 2008). This implies that the assumption that MZ twins are genetically identical is not always entirely correct. We currently are at the beginning of an exciting new line of research studying genetic dissimilarities within MZ twins pairs. How the study of genetic differences in discordant MZ twin pairs may be used as an effective gene-finding strategy is discussed by Zwijnenburg, Meijers-Heijboer, and Boomsma (2010).

Parametric Linkage

Broadly speaking, two types of linkage analysis can be distinguished: parametric and nonparametric linkage. Parametric (or model-based) linkage requires the specification of a genetic model, that is, allele frequencies and penetrances (three parameters specifying the probability that an individual expresses the phenotype given zero, one, or two copies of the risk allele). Genotype and phenotype data from multiple generations are required to perform this type of analysis.

An important concept in parametric linkage analysis is the *recombination fraction*. Recombination occurs when during meiosis the maternal and paternal chromosome cross over, break, and rejoin, resulting in gametes with chromosomes that are a combination of the maternal and paternal chromosome.

The recombination fraction, used in linkage analysis, is the probability that the alleles at two loci are recombinant (i.e., an odd number of recombination events has occurred between them). This depends on the distance between the loci. When two loci are located on different chromosomes, or on the same chromosome but far apart, the probability of the individual being a recombinant is around 50%, that is, the recombination fraction (θ) is .5. The smaller the distance between the two loci, the lower the probability of a recombination event between them, and the lower θ will be, with $\theta = 0$ indicating perfect linkage.

To test for linkage, a genetic model is assumed, and the likelihood of the observed pedigree data under the alternative hypothesis of linkage ($\theta < .5$) is compared with the likelihood under the null hypothesis of no linkage ($\theta = .5$) between the measured marker locus and the hypothetical trait locus. The result of this test is expressed as the logarithm of odds (LOD), called the *LOD score*. The higher the LOD score, the stronger the evidence for linkage. A detailed discussion of parametric linkage methods can be found in Ott (1999).

Parametric linkage is most suited for traits that are influenced by a single gene and follow a relatively simple pattern of inheritance because in this situation it is relatively easy to specify a genetic model. A good example of a successful parametric linkage study is described by Joutel et al. (1993), who used data from two large multigenerational families to map the first locus for familial hemiplegic migraine (the FHM1 locus) to chromosome 19. A few years later, Ophoff et al. (1996) identified several mutations in a gene in this area (CACNA1A),

which caused the FHM phenotype. For many behavioral and psychological traits, however, specifying the correct genetic model is not straightforward.

Nonparametric (Model-Free) Linkage

Most behavioral and psychological phenotypes are complex, that is, they are influenced by many genes that each have a small effect. In this case it is difficult to specify a genetic model. Therefore, complex traits are usually analyzed using nonparametric (also called model-free) linkage techniques. The nonparametric approach does not require the specification of a genetic model. In short, in nonparametric linkage, it is tested whether relatives with similar phenotypes also have similar genotypes. Genotypic similarity is expressed in a measure called *identity by descent* (IBD). Two alleles are said to be IBD if they not only have the same DNA sequence (referred to as *identity by state*, or IBS) but also were inherited from the same ancestor. Because there are two alleles for each locus, a pair of individuals can share zero, one, or two alleles IBD. The expected probabilities for these values are 25%, 50%, and 25%, respectively (see Figure 36.4).

To test for linkage, the IBD values for all pairs of related individuals in the sample are estimated. For IBD estimation, the availability of parental genotypes greatly increases the accuracy of the estimates. For this reason, parental genotype data are used in linkage analysis, even when the actual LOD scores are based on data from siblings only.

Several algorithms have been developed to estimate IBD values. The Elston-Stewart algorithm (Elston & Stewart, 1971) is suited for analysis of very large pedigrees, but only for a limited number of markers at a time, because the complexity of the calculations increases exponentially with the number of markers. The Lander-Green algorithm (Lander & Green, 1987) is better suited to handle the large numbers of markers included in most modern linkage studies but is limited to smaller pedigrees. A useful discussion of IBD estimation can be found in Ferreira (2004).

Haseman-Elston Regression

One of the first nonparametric linkage methods based on IBD estimation was introduced by

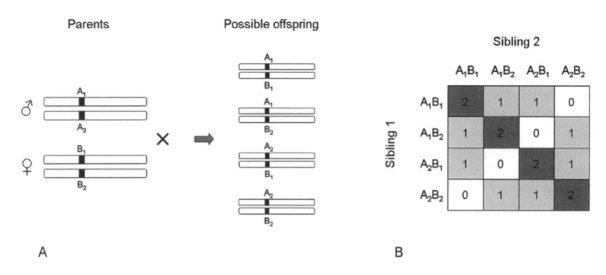

FIGURE 36.4.   Possible allele combinations and identity by descent (IBD). All possible genotypes for the offspring of two parents with genotypes A_1A_2 and B_1B_2 (A). There are four possible genotypes for the offspring which all occur with equal probability of 25%. The IBD value for all possible sibling pairs resulting from the mating depicted in Figure 36.4a (B). An IBD value of 0 or 2 occurs in four out of 16 possibilities. Thus the probabilities are 25%, 50%, and 25% for IBD 0, 1, and 2, respectively. In this example, where both parents are heterozygotes, the IBD values of the offspring can easily be determined. In many situations, however, there is insufficient information to know the IBD status with certainty. In this case, IBD probabilities have to be estimated.

Haseman and Elston (1972). This method is now known as Haseman-Elston (HE) regression. The idea was to take the squared difference in trait values for each sibling pair and regress it on the estimated IBD values at a given marker locus. There is evidence for linkage when high IBD values are associated with strong phenotypic similarity (i.e., small squared trait differences). Thus, a significant negative regression slope indicates the presence of linkage. A drawback of HE regression is that fairly large samples are needed for sufficient statistical power to detect linkage. One method to increase power is by selecting only the most extreme cases from a population (Carey & Williamson, 1991; Dolan & Boomsma, 1998). This is possible because HE regression has the advantage that it does not rely on assumptions about the trait distribution.

Several extensions to HE regression have been proposed through the years, which improve power by using not only the squared trait differences but also the squared trait sum (e.g., Sham, Purcell, Cherny, & Abecasis, 2002).

Variance Components Linkage

A nonparametric linkage method developed in the 1990s is based on variance components (VC; e.g.,

Almasy & Blangero, 1998; Amos, 1994). VC linkage is based on an approach similar to that described in the section about heritability estimation. In addition to the genetic and environmental components A, C, D, and E, we can model the effect of a specific QTL (Q), using IBD estimations. Figure 36.5 shows a model that incorporates A (background genetic effects), Q (QTL effect), and E (environment). The correlation between the QTL factors of DZ twins and siblings equals the estimated proportion of alleles IBD, which is referred to as $\hat{\pi}$ (called "pi-hat").

To test whether there is significant linkage at a certain locus, the path coefficients for the Q-factor (q) are constrained to be zero. A significant deterioration of the model fit is taken as evidence for linkage. This procedure is repeated for all loci and significance levels should be adjusted accordingly. The advantage of VC linkage is that, unlike HE regression, it can be used with any type of pedigree, and it is generally more powerful. An important disadvantage, however, is its reliance on the assumption of normality of the trait distribution. Hence, the analysis of data from selected samples with variance components linkage is more involved than when HE regression is used.

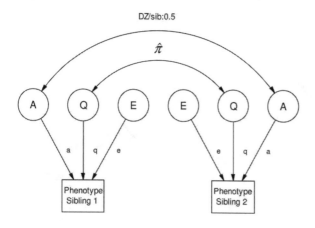

FIGURE 36.5. AQE model to test for linkage using a variance components approach. The correlation between the quantitative trait locus (QTL) effects for Sibling 1 and Sibling 2 equals $\hat{\pi}$ (= identity by descent/2), whereas the correlation between the background genetic factors of siblings or DZ twins is .5. If the mode of inheritance of the trait is largely unknown, the remaining familial variance that cannot be attributed to Q can also be modeled as simply *familial*. If data on MZ twins are also available, the familial variance can be decomposed into A and C. MZ twins do not contribute any information to detect linkage (as they are perfectly correlated for all QTLs).

The Affected Sib Pair Method

For disease phenotypes (i.e., affected vs. unaffected) a commonly used linkage method is the *affected sib-pair* (ASP) test (see, e.g., Nyholt, 2008). In an ASP design, it is tested whether sibling pairs who are both affected for a disorder share more alleles IBD than expected in the absence of linkage (in which case the distribution should be roughly one quarter, one half, and one quarter for IBD values of 0, 1, and 2, respectively).

An example of a study in which the ASP approach was used is a recent linkage study of major depressive disorder (MDD). This study included 133 Australian and Dutch families with a total number of 278 affected siblings. Suggestive evidence for linkage was found in regions of chromosomes 2, 8, and 17 (Middeldorp et al., 2009).

The Multiple Testing Problem (1)

At present, linkage is usually performed genome-wide, in an exploratory fashion. Because in a genomewide linkage study several hundred markers are tested simultaneously, a multiple testing burden

is inevitable. Therefore, stringent significance thresholds have to be applied. On the basis of a simulation study, Lander and Kruglyak (1995) proposed using an LOD score of 3.6 to indicate significant linkage, which corresponds to a *p* value of 2×10^{-5} and should be roughly equivalent to a genomewide significance level of 5%. This has become a widely used threshold to define significance in linkage studies. Alternatively, permutation or simulation approaches using the observed data can be used to determine empirical *p* values (see, e.g., Jung, Weeks, & Feingold, 2006; Sawcer et al., 1997; Wan, Cohen, & Guerra, 1997). This has the advantage that no assumptions need to be made about the null distribution of the linkage statistic.

Association

An association study tests whether a particular allele or genotype is more prevalent in individuals with a certain phenotype. For instance, do individuals with allele C at a given SNP have a higher depression score than individuals with allele A?

Association analysis can be performed in unrelated individuals or in family-based samples. Studies in unrelated samples are often set up as case-control studies: allele or genotype frequencies are compared between a selection of cases and a group of matched controls. Considerations in the design of genetic case-control studies have been discussed in more detail by Sullivan, Eaves, Kendler, and Neale (2001). It is also possible to test for association with a continuous phenotype: In this case, mean trait values are compared between individuals with different genotypes. The advantage of case-control association studies is the relative ease of collecting samples and the straightforward statistical tests that can be used. The disadvantage, however, is that the presence of an underlying population substructure can lead to spurious results, a phenomenon referred to as *population stratification*. This phenomenon was illustrated in a famous paper by Hamer and Sirota (2000). The paper described a hypothetical study in a student population consisting of Caucasian and Asian subjects, in which a gene was identified for eating with chopsticks. This is not a true association, however, but rather the result of the fact that for all sorts of reasons, allele frequencies can differ

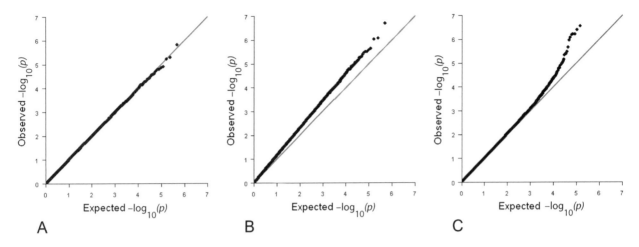

FIGURE 36.6.   Examples of Q-Q plots. The expected distribution of *p* values (*x*-axis) is plotted against the observed distribution (*y*-axis). For convenience, *p* values in a genomewide study are often shown on a logarithmic scale, that is, $-\log_{10}(p)$. The observations closely follow the expected distribution (shown in gray), indicating there is probably no association and no inflation of the distribution either (A). Inflation across the whole distribution, which may indicate population stratification (B). An excess of small *p* values in the tail of the distribution, possibly indicating some true associations (C).

between the two populations. The two populations happen to also differ in terms of eating with chopsticks, which is entirely culturally determined. From the association analysis, it falsely appears that the gene has something to do with the chopsticks.

One way to deal with stratification issues is by using a family-based association test, such as the haplotype relative risk (Falk & Rubinstein, 1987; Terwilliger & Ott, 1992) or the transmission disequilibrium test (Spielman, McGinnis, & Ewens, 1993), which use data from heterozygous parents and affected children to determine which parental alleles are transmitted to an affected child and which are not. Thus, the nontransmitted alleles serve as *internal* control genotypes, which eliminates the need for external controls and the risk of stratification issues. The disadvantage is that family-based samples are more difficult to collect because both parents have to be present (which can be particularly challenging for late-onset phenotypes such as Alzheimer's disease or aging).

An alternative approach, suitable for quantitative traits, was developed by Fulker, Cherny, Sham, and Hewitt (1999). With this method, which uses data from sibling pairs, the effects of genes on phenotypic means are partitioned into a between- and within-family component. A within-family association test is not affected by population stratification because

siblings within a family belong to the same stratum. Thus, it is tested whether the allele is associated with the phenotype in siblings within the same family, whether they are associated in siblings from different families, and whether the effect size of these tests is the same. If the gene effect is different between families than within families, there is evidence for population stratification. If, however, the within-family effect alone is significant, regardless of the between-family effect, this means there is still evidence for a true association effect that is not due to population substructure (Fulker et al., 1999). This method has been implemented in the QTDT program (Abecasis, Cardon, & Cookson, 2000).

In situations in which unrelated individuals are used for association analysis, other methods are available to assess and control for population stratification, such as calculating the *genomic inflation factor* and applying *genomic control* (discussed in the section Genomic Inflation).

Linkage Disequilibrium

An important concept in association studies is the phenomenon of *linkage disequilibrium* (LD). When two loci are in linkage *equilibrium*, the genotype at Locus 1 is independent of the genotype at Locus 2. This is usually the case when loci are on different chromosomes or far apart on the same chromosome.

However, if two loci are close together and over generations little recombination has taken place between them, then the genotype at Locus 1 may be associated with the genotype at Locus 2. Therefore, when an association is found, this can be due to either direct or indirect association. In the case of *direct association*, the association signal comes from the actual causal variant, in other words, the marker itself is the polymorphism that causes the variation in the phenotype. An association that arises because the marker is in LD with the causal variant is called *indirect association*.

Candidate Gene Studies Versus Genomewide Association

Until recently, association studies focused on smaller candidate regions. On the basis of existing knowledge (e.g., theories about biochemical pathways or evidence from linkage studies), candidate genes were identified and genotyping was restricted to the region of interest. Good examples are association studies of the serotonin receptor and transporter genes in both depression and migraine studies. Both conditions are often successfully treated with drugs that interact with the serotonergic system (SSRIs and triptans, respectively), suggesting a possible causal involvement of serotonin in the etiology of the disorders. In spite of the large number of studies conducted, it has proven difficult to unequivocally demonstrate a role of serotonin receptor or transporter genes in the pathogenesis of depression (Anguelova, Benkelfat, & Turecki, 2003; Risch et al., 2009). A similar conclusion can be drawn for migraine (Colson, Fernandez, Lea, & Griffiths, 2007). Although there is limited evidence for a possible role of certain serotonin-related genes in migraine and depression, the majority of candidate–gene association studies have returned negative results. This may be illustrative of the main weakness of the candidate gene approach: Usually our knowledge about the pathways involved is limited, making it difficult to determine which genes are good candidates.

Because of the availability of faster and cheaper genotyping techniques, it has become feasible to genotype enough markers (from 300,000 up to 1 million) to cover most of the common variation in the entire human genome, and perform genomewide association (GWA) studies (also referred to as GWAS). Several companies (e.g., Illumina, Affymetrix) produce predesigned SNP chips that include a selection of carefully chosen *tag SNPs*. Tag SNPs are selected on the basis of LD patterns, in such a way that a minimum number of SNPs captures a maximum amount of genetic variation in the population for which it is designed. In contrast with candidate gene studies, a GWA study is exploratory in nature; no prior hypothesis about the location of causative genes is necessary. Indeed, many of the associations identified through GWA studies to date were not previously regarded as candidates, demonstrating the use of exploratory gene-finding studies (Manolio & Collins, 2009).

The Multiple Testing Problem (2)

Because of the large numbers of markers used, the multiple testing burden in a GWA study is even larger than in a linkage study, which makes it crucially important to use appropriate significance thresholds. The exact multiple testing burden depends on the set of SNPs included in the study and on the population studied. For instance, African populations are known to have less LD and more SNPs, and therefore the multiple testing burden will be higher than in a European population. Several authors have proposed cutoff values for significance in GWA studies. Pe'er, Yelensky, Altshuler, and Daly (2008) recommended multiplying the nominal *p* value by the genomewide testing burden, which, according to their calculations, is roughly half a million tests when all common SNPs are tested in a European (HapMap CEU) population. To obtain a genomewide significance level of 5%, this means a nominal threshold of $p = 1 \times 10^{-7}$ should be used. Dudbridge and Gusnanto (2008) used a permutation approach to estimate the genomewide significance threshold in the U.K. Caucasian population. They estimated that genomewide significance at the 5% level corresponded to a nominal *p* value of 7.2×10^{-8}, and state that any *p* value below 5×10^{-8} can be considered "convincingly significant" (Dudbridge & Gusnanto, 2008, p. 233).

Even the use of strict significance thresholds has not been able to avoid the fact that many candidate–gene association studies have produced results that could not be replicated, possibly because many of them were false positive findings (Hirschhorn, Lohmueller, Byrne, & Hirschhorn, 2002). Because the credibility of a finding increases considerably when it is replicated in multiple independent samples, it is now a common requirement for GWA studies that results be replicated internally (i.e., in an independent sample described in the same study) to be published. Because replication studies typically involve a much smaller number of SNPs, the significance threshold required is commonly adjusted according to the number of SNPs tested. Given the small expected effect sizes of SNPs for complex traits, however, it is a challenge to distinguish real associations with a small effect size from false positives. Therefore, it is not trivial to decide which associations are most likely to be true and replicable.

Genomic Inflation

As mentioned, population substructure is a factor that can lead to spurious results in an association study. Therefore, in the design of a GWA study, it is important to carefully select the individuals to be genotyped to avoid problems related to stratification within the sample. Once the data have been collected, it is common practice to run some quality control checks to scan for potential problems. A good way to get a first impression of the results is by creating a *quantile–quantile plot* (Q-Q plot; see Figure 36.6). In a Q-Q plot, the quantiles of the expected distribution of $-\log 10(p)$ values are plotted against the quantiles of the observed distribution (McCarthy et al., 2008). Under the assumption of no true association signals, this should result in a straight diagonal line. An excess of small p values, resulting in a deviation in the tail of the distribution, may indicate true association signals. However, if the observed findings are inflated (i.e., show an excess of small p values) across the entire distribution, this may indicate population stratification (McCarthy et al., 2008). The extent to which the distribution is inflated can be expressed in a statistic called the genomic inflation factor, λ (lambda), which is calculated as the median χ^2 of the observed distribution, divided by the median χ^2 of the expected distribution. Ideally, λ should approach a value of 1. On the

basis of the value of λ, the test statistic can be rescaled to correct it for inflation. This procedure is called *genomic control* (Devlin & Roeder, 1999).

Meta-Analysis

GWA studies have shown to be effective and associations have been successfully identified for quite a number of human traits, such as Crohn's disease (Barrett et al., 2008), Type 2 diabetes (Zeggini et al., 2008), bipolar disorder (Ferreira et al., 2008), and obesity (Lindgren et al., 2009). For most complex traits, however, the observed effects are small and therefore very large samples are needed. Visscher (2008) estimated that to detect a variant that explains 0.1% to 0.5% of the variance in a quantitative trait (which may be a realistic effect size for genes affecting complex traits), tens of thousands of individuals are necessary for sufficient power. Because no single study has the budget to collect these enormous amounts of data, it is a necessity to combine GWA studies. For this reason, large consortia have been formed in recent years to enable meta-analyses of GWA results (e.g., Barrett et al., 2008; Lindgren et al., 2009; Zeggini et al., 2008). In a meta-analysis, the results of multiple individual studies are combined into one overall test statistic. Two types of meta-analysis can be distinguished: Methods that assume fixed effects and those that assume random effects (Kavvoura & Ioannidis, 2008). Fixed effects methods assume there is one common effect in all studies (homogeneity) and that between-study variability is due to chance. Two frequently used fixed-effects methods are the inverse-variance weighted method and the pooled z-score method. The inverse-variance weighted method pools the betas and standard errors from all studies, weighting each study by the inverse of the variance of beta. The outcome is an effect estimate for each SNP, pooled across all studies. This method is most suitable when the phenotype is measured on the same scale in all studies, so that beta can be interpreted the same way for all samples. The pooled z-score method does not pool effect sizes but z scores, weighted by sample size. It provides information on the direction and significance of the pooled effect but not about the effect size. This method is more appropriate when the phenotype is not measured on the same scale across studies and hence the effect sizes are not directly comparable.

In cases in which different genetic effects are expected across studies (*heterogeneity*), for instance, because the populations have a different genetic background, random effects methods are more appropriate. Various metrics are available to assess the presence of heterogeneity, such as Cochran's Q statistic or I^2 (Kavvoura & Ioannidis, 2008). The main drawback of random effects methods, however, is that they are more conservative and thus have low power compared with fixed-effects models. A useful practical guideline for meta-analysis of GWA studies has been provided by de Bakker et al. (2008).

HapMap and Imputation

One problem in meta-analysis of GWA results is the fact that different studies use different SNP chips, which tend to be largely nonoverlapping. As a consequence, the number of SNPs genotyped in all studies is limited. This can be overcome by imputing the genotypes of SNPs that were not measured, using data generated by the International HapMap Consortium (2003). The HapMap project was launched in 2002 with the purpose of creating a *haplotype map* of the human genome that describes common patterns of genetic sequence variation. In Phases I and II of the project, 270 individuals from four populations (European, Nigerian, Japanese, and Han Chinese) were genotyped to obtain information on more than 3.1 million SNPs. In Phase III, the project was expanded to include data from another seven populations.

The HapMap data can be used to infer a missing genotype at one marker from available genotypes at other markers. This is possible because due to the presence of LD, only a limited number of haplotypes frequently occur in the population, even though theoretically much more variation would be possible. To infer missing genotypes, a genotyped individual is compared with a HapMap reference sample. Because the LD structure in the HapMap samples is known, it can be determined, given the available genotypes, what the most likely genotype is for the missing SNP. For instance, if all reference individuals with a certain haplotype have a C allele at SNP X, and SNP X is in high LD with this haplotype, an individual with

the same haplotype but a missing genotype at SNP X is highly likely to also have a C allele. A detailed description of how the HapMap data can be used to infer missing genotypes can be found in Marchini, Howie, Myers, McVean, and Donnelly (2007). For a review of methods used for genotype imputation, see Marchini and Howie (2010).

There is some uncertainty involved in determining the most likely genotype for a missing SNP. For this reason, imputation programs calculate a probability for each possible genotype and provide a quality measure that indicates how reliable the imputation is for each SNP, so that in the analysis stage, the researcher can decide to remove SNPs that were poorly imputed. In addition, the probability scores for the different genotypes can be used to account for the uncertainty of the imputations.

One limitation of the HapMap is that it covers only common variation. Therefore, if a trait is primarily influenced by rare alleles, associations will not be detected using the HapMap SNPs. The aim of the more recently started 1000 Genomes Project (http://www.1000genomes.org) is to provide coverage of the rarer variants as well and to provide a more detailed map of the human genome. To do this, whole genomes of approximately 1,200 individuals will be sequenced (i.e., their entire DNA sequence will be determined). See Exhibit 36.1 for a selection of some widely used programs for SEM, linkage, GWA, imputation, and other types of analysis.

PART III: BEYOND GENE-FINDING

A person's phenotype depends on more than simply the genetic code. Genes exert their effects through their products, usually proteins. For proteins to be produced, a gene has to be expressed. The main steps in gene expression are *transcription* and *translation*. During transcription, the DNA molecule serves as a template to construct an RNA copy of itself (an RNA molecule resembles DNA but contains uracil [U] instead of thymine [T] bases and is single stranded). The RNA codes for a sequence of amino acids together, forming a protein. The construction of a protein on the basis of the RNA code is called *translation*.

The expression of genes is affected by various factors, such as epigenetic modifications (see the section Epigenetics) and regulation by other genes or *transcription factors* (proteins that bind to DNA, thereby controlling the expression of genes). In this last section, we discuss the effects of epigenetic modification on gene expression and the use of genomewide expression data in gene-finding studies. Finally, a closely related area of research is the study of interactions between genes in biological networks and pathways. Identifying these pathways is an important step from statistical linkage or associations to understanding the biology underlying human traits and diseases.

Epigenetics

Epigenetics is the study of heritable changes in gene expression that are unrelated to changes in the DNA sequence (Feinberg, 2007; Heijmans, Tobi, Lumey, & Slagboom, 2009). Epigenetic changes are caused by chemical modifications that affect the expression of genes. Two types of modification cause epigenetic changes: DNA methylation and histone modification. *DNA methylation* is the addition of a methyl group to a cytosine base that is followed by guanine (a so-called CpG site, where the "p" refers to the phosphodiester bond that connects two bases). CpG sites tend to occur in large repetitive sequences, which are highly methylated, or in short CpG-rich DNA stretches called CpG islands, which are mostly unmethylated. CpG islands frequently overlap with the promoter region of genes (i.e., a region close to the gene where the transcription process is initiated). It is thought that methylation affects gene expression by controlling whether proteins that affect transcription can bind to the DNA (Jaenisch & Bird, 2003).

The second type of alteration is *histone modification*. *Histones* are the proteins around which DNA molecules are wrapped. There are various types of chemical modification of histones, including methylation and modifications affecting how densely the DNA is "packed." A tightly packed structure of the DNA prevents gene expression, whereas in relaxed DNA gene expression is active.

One might say that the *epigenome* has a life cycle. After fertilization, most of the DNA is demethylized and a new wave of methylation occurs. This methylation pattern is inherited from parent to daughter cells during cell division, providing what might be called an *epigenetic memory*. Later in development, tissue-specific changes in methylation occur, which aid the differentiation of different cell types. At present, not much is known about how these changes occur (Feinberg, 2008). An interesting aspect of this phenomenon is that epigenetic changes are easier to reverse than genetic mutations, which may offer possibilities for the treatment of disease with drugs (e.g., Smith, Otterson, & Plass, 2007).

An additional factor that influences methylation patterns during the life span is the environment. Diet, for instance, has been suggested as an environmental factor that influences epigenetic processes. Diet-mediated epigenetic effects have been implicated in a variety of conditions, such as cancer and cardiovascular disease as well as depression and other psychiatric disorders (Van den Veyver, 2002). In recent years, it has become clear that epigenetics may explain part of the differences observed in genetically identical MZ twins. These differences will be part of the nonshared environmental component in a twin study. An interesting study in MZ twins showed that twins who were older, had more different lifestyles, and spent less of their lifetimes together displayed greater differences in their epigenetic profiles than younger twins who shared most of their environment and lifestyle (Fraga et al., 2005). On the other hand, Heijmans, Kremer, Tobi, Boomsma, and Slagboom (2007), who combined an epigenetic study with a classical twin design, found that most of the variation across individuals in DNA methylation at the locus they investigated (IGF2/H19) could be attributed to heritable factors. The influence of environmental factors did not increase with age, suggesting at least some loci are relatively unaffected by age-related changes in methylation.

Gene Expression

The genomewide study of gene expression is a rapidly developing area of research. To measure gene expression, the transcript (RNA) content of a tissue sample is analyzed to determine which genes are being transcribed and in which quantities. One application of gene expression analysis is to combine it with the regular GWA approach. In this type of study, gene transcript abundance is treated as a phenotype and can be mapped to genomic loci, called *expression QTLs* (eQTLs). This approach identifies markers that are associated with the expression of a gene and identifies genetic variants that regulate the expression of other genes (Gilad, Rifkin, & Pritchard, 2008). An example of how this might work is the situation in which a strong association signal is found with an area that contains no genes (a so-called *gene desert*), a phenomenon that is regularly observed (Manolio & Collins, 2009). This region may harbor some regulatory sequence that influences the expression of a gene located at some distance from the associated SNP. An expression study might reveal this mechanism by detecting an association between the SNP in the gene desert and the expression level of the distant gene, which would otherwise go unnoticed.

A complicating factor in the collection of expression data is that expression levels differ depending on the type of tissue. Ideally, gene expression is measured in the tissues involved in the disease or trait of interest; however, in many cases (e.g., brain disease), it is not an easy task to obtain the right tissue samples in sufficient quantities. One possible solution could be to use more easily accessible tissues as a surrogate for the tissue of interest. For instance, Sullivan et al. (2006) compared gene expression in whole blood and 16 different tissues from the central nervous system (CNS) to assess the feasibility of using whole blood samples as a surrogate for brain tissue samples. They concluded that, although imperfect, there is a correlation between CNS and whole blood gene expression (with a median around .5) and that in some situations the cautious use of whole blood gene expression data could be a useful proxy measure of CNS gene expression.

To investigate the feasibility of large-scale expression data collection, a pilot project called the Genotype-Tissue Expression project (GTEx; http://nihroadmap.nih.gov/GTEx/) was recently undertaken. The aim of this project is to develop a database containing expression data from approximately 1,000 donor individuals in 30 different types of tissue. These individuals will also be genotyped at high density. It is hoped that with these data a comprehensive database of human eQTLs can be developed.

Pathway Analysis

Variation or disruptions in different genes can have similar phenotypic consequences if the genes are involved in the same pathway. Disruptions at different stages of a pathway might all, independently or in interaction, lead to an increased risk of disease or expression of a complex trait. *Pathway analysis* investigates whether a number of genes that have been found in a genetic association study are more often involved in a certain biological pathway than expected by chance (Wang, Li, & Bucan, 2007).

Studies that have employed GWA and pathway analysis have reported some promising results (Ritchie, 2009). For example, Vink et al. (2009) searched for genes that may be involved in smoking behavior, both initiation and persistence. Genes that showed an association with smoking behavior in multiple samples were analyzed in terms of biological function, cellular location, and possible interactions of the gene products. Using this approach, they identified several groups of genes of similar function that may affect smoking behavior. Several other phenotypes have been investigated using similar approaches, including multiple sclerosis (Baranzini et al., 2009), Type 1 and Type 2 diabetes, and bipolar disorder (Torkamani, Topol, & Schork, 2008). Many others will undoubtedly follow. This type of analysis may be an important new step toward understanding the biological mechanisms underlying a trait.

The introduction of genomewide SNP arrays initiated many rapid developments in the field of gene-finding, and this may only be the beginning. New approaches such as the gene network and pathway-based analyses are only just starting to be developed. Although there have been many successes, plenty of challenges remain, especially in terms of the management and analysis of the huge amounts of data that are available and the even larger amounts of new data that are being collected, such as whole genome sequence data. Given the promising results published in recent years, we can only expect more to come.

References

Abecasis, G. R., Cardon, L. R., & Cookson, W. O. (2000). A general test of association for quantitative traits in nuclear families. *American Journal of Human Genetics, 66*, 279–292. doi:10.1086/302698

Abecasis, G. R., Cherny, S. S., Cookson, W. O., & Cardon, L. R. (2002). Merlin—Rapid analysis of dense genetic maps using sparse gene flow trees. *Nature Genetics, 30*, 97–101. doi:10.1038/ng786

Akaike, H. (1987). Factor analysis and AIC. *Psychometrika, 52*, 317–332. doi:10.1007/BF02294359

Almasy, L., & Blangero, J. (1998). Multipoint quantitative-trait linkage analysis in general pedigrees. *American Journal of Human Genetics, 62*, 1198–1211. doi:10.1086/301844

Amos, C. I. (1994). Robust variance-components approach for assessing genetic linkage in pedigrees. *American Journal of Human Genetics, 54*, 535–543.

Anguelova, M., Benkelfat, C., & Turecki, G. (2003). A systematic review of association studies investigating genes coding for serotonin receptors and the serotonin transporter: I. Affective disorders. *Molecular Psychiatry, 8*, 574–591. doi:10.1038/sj.mp.4001328

Balding, D. J. (2006). A tutorial on statistical methods for population association studies. *Nature Reviews: Genetics, 7*, 781–791. doi:10.1038/nrg1916

Baranzini, S. E., Galwey, N. W., Wang, J., Khankhanian, P., Lindberg, R., Pelletier, D., . . . Polman, C. H. (2009). Pathway and network-based analysis of genome-wide association studies in multiple sclerosis. *Human Molecular Genetics, 18*, 2078–2090. doi:10.1093/hmg/ddp120

Barrett, J. C., Hansoul, S., Nicolae, D. L., Cho, J. H., Duerr, R. H., Rioux, J. D., . . . Daly, M. J. (2008). Genome-wide association defines more than 30 distinct susceptibility loci for Crohn's disease. *Nature Genetics, 40*, 955–962. doi:10.1038/ng.175

Bartels, M., van den Oord, E. J., Hudziak, J. J., Rietveld, M. J., van Beijsterveldt, C. E., & Boomsma, D. I. (2004). Genetic and environmental mechanisms underlying stability and change in problem behaviors at ages 3, 7, 10, and 12. *Developmental Psychology, 40*, 852–867. doi:10.1037/0012-1649.40.5.852

Boomsma, D. I., de Geus, E. J., van Baal, G. C., & Koopmans, J. R. (1999). A religious upbringing reduces the influence of genetic factors on disinhibition: evidence for interaction between genotype and environment on personality. *Twin Research, 2*, 115–125. doi:10.1375/136905299320565988

Browne, M. W., & Cudeck, R. (1993). Alternative ways of assessing model fit. In K. A. Bollen & J. S. Long (Eds.), *Testing structural equation models* (pp. 136–162). Newbury Park, CA: Sage.

Bruder, C. E., Piotrowski, A., Gijsbers, A. A., Andersson, R., Erickson, S., Diaz de Stahl, T., . . . Dumanski, J. P. (2008). Phenotypically concordant and discordant monozygotic twins display different DNA copy-number-variation profiles. *American Journal of Human Genetics, 82*, 763–771. doi:10.1016/j.ajhg.2007.12.011

Carey, G., & Williamson, J. (1991). Linkage analysis of quantitative traits: increased power by using selected samples. *American Journal of Human Genetics, 49*, 786–796.

Caspi, A., Sugden, K., Moffitt, T. E., Taylor, A., Craig, I. W., Harrington, H., . . . Poulton, R. (2003). Influence of life stress on depression: moderation by a polymorphism in the 5-HTT gene. *Science, 301*, 386–389. doi:10.1126/science.1083968

Colson, N. J., Fernandez, F., Lea, R. A., & Griffiths, L. R. (2007). The search for migraine genes: an overview of current knowledge. *Cellular and Molecular Life Sciences, 64,* 331–344. doi:10.1007/s00018-006-5592-y

de Bakker, P. I., Ferreira, M. A., Jia, X., Neale, B. M., Raychaudhuri, S., & Voight, B. F. (2008). Practical aspects of imputation-driven meta-analysis of genome-wide association studies. *Human Molecular Genetics, 17,* R122–R128. doi:10.1093/hmg/ddn288

Devlin, B., & Roeder, K. (1999). Genomic control for association studies. *Biometrics, 55,* 997–1004. doi:10.1111/j.0006-341X.1999.00997.x

Distel, M. A., Rebollo-Mesa, I., Willemsen, G., Derom, C. A., Trull, T. J., Martin, N. G., & Boomsma, D. I. (2009). Familial resemblance of borderline personality disorder features: genetic or cultural transmission? *PLoS ONE, 4*(4), e5334. doi:10.1371/journal.pone.0005334

Dolan, C. V., & Boomsma, D. I. (1998). Optimal selection of sib pairs from random samples for linkage analysis of a QTL using the EDAC test. *Behavior Genetics, 28,* 197–206. doi:10.1023/A:1021423214032

Dudbridge, F., & Gusnanto, A. (2008). Estimation of significance thresholds for genomewide association scans. *Genetic Epidemiology, 32,* 227–234. doi:10.1002/gepi.20297

Elston, R. C., & Stewart, J. (1971). A general model for the genetic analysis of pedigree data. *Human Heredity, 21,* 523–542. doi:10.1159/000152448

Falconer, D. S. (1965). The inheritance of liability to certain diseases estimated from incidence among relatives. *Annals of Human Genetics, 29,* 51–76. doi:10.1111/j.1469-1809.1965.tb00500.x

Falconer, D. S., & Mackay, T. F. (1996). *Introduction to quantitative genetics* (4th ed.). Harlow, England: Longman.

Falk, C. T., & Rubinstein, P. (1987). Haplotype relative risks: an easy reliable way to construct a proper control sample for risk calculations. *Annals of Human Genetics, 51,* 227–233. doi:10.1111/j.1469-1809.1987.tb00875.x

Feinberg, A. P. (2007). Phenotypic plasticity and the epigenetics of human disease. *Nature, 447,* 433–440. doi:10.1038/nature05919

Feinberg, A. P. (2008). Epigenetics at the epicenter of modern medicine. *JAMA, 299,* 1345–1350. doi:10.1001/jama.299.11.1345

Ferreira, M. A. (2004). Linkage analysis: principles and methods for the analysis of human quantitative traits. *Twin Research, 7,* 513–530. doi:10.1375/136905 2042335223

Ferreira, M. A., O'Donovan, M. C., Meng, Y. A., Jones, I. R., Ruderfer, D. M., Jones, L., . . . Craddock, N. (2008). Collaborative genome-wide association analysis supports a role for ANK3 and CACNA1C in bipolar disorder. *Nature Genetics, 40,* 1056–1058. doi:10.1038/ng.209

Fischer, R. A. (1918). The correlation between relatives on the supposition of Mendelian inheritance. *Transactions of the Royal Society of Edinburgh, 52,* 399–433.

Fraga, M. F., Ballestar, E., Paz, M. F., Ropero, S., Setien, F., Ballestar, M. L., . . . Esteller, M. (2005). Epigenetic differences arise during the lifetime of monozygotic twins. *Proceedings of the National Academy of Sciences of the United States of America, 102,* 10604–10609. doi:10.1073/pnas.0500398102

Fulker, D. W. (1982). Extensions of the classical twin method. In B. Bonne-Tamir (Ed.), *Human genetics: Part A. The unfolding genome* (pp. 395–406). New York, NY: Alan R. Liss.

Fulker, D. W., Cherny, S. S., Sham, P. C., & Hewitt, J. K. (1999). Combined linkage and association sib-pair analysis for quantitative traits. *American Journal of Human Genetics, 64,* 259–267. doi:10.1086/302193

Gilad, Y., Rifkin, S. A., & Pritchard, J. K. (2008). Revealing the architecture of gene regulation: the promise of eQTL studies. *Trends in Genetics, 24,* 408–415. doi:10.1016/j.tig.2008.06.001

Hamer, D., & Sirota, L. (2000). Beware the chopsticks gene. *Molecular Psychiatry, 5,* 11–13. doi:10.1038/sj.mp.4000662

Haseman, J. K., & Elston, R. C. (1972). The investigation of linkage between a quantitative trait and a marker locus. *Behavior Genetics, 2,* 3–19. doi:10.1007/BF01066731

Heath, A. C., Eaves, L. J., & Martin, N. G. (1998). Interaction of marital status and genetic risk for symptoms of depression. *Twin Research, 1,* 119–122. doi:10.1375/136905298320566249

Heijmans, B. T., Kremer, D., Tobi, E. W., Boomsma, D. I., & Slagboom, P. E. (2007). Heritable rather than age-related environmental and stochastic factors dominate variation in DNA methylation of the human IGF2/H19 locus. *Human Molecular Genetics, 16,* 547–554. doi:10.1093/hmg/ddm010

Heijmans, B. T., Tobi, E. W., Lumey, L. H., & Slagboom, P. E. (2009). The epigenome: Archive of the prenatal environment. *Epigenetics; Official Journal of the DNA Methylation Society, 4,* 526–531. doi:10.4161/epi.4.8.10265

Hirschhorn, J. N., Lohmueller, K., Byrne, E., & Hirschhorn, K. (2002). A comprehensive review of genetic association studies. *Genetics in Medicine, 4,* 45–61. doi:10.1097/00125817-200203000-00002

International HapMap Consortium. (2003). The International HapMap project. *Nature, 426,* 789–796.

International Human Genome Sequencing Consortium. (2004). Finishing the euchromatic sequence of the human genome. *Nature, 431,* 931–945. doi:10.1038/nature03001

Jaenisch, R., & Bird, A. (2003). Epigenetic regulation of gene expression: how the genome integrates intrinsic and environmental signals. *Nature Genetics, 33(Suppl.),* 245–254. doi:10.1038/ng1089

Joutel, A., Bousser, M. G., Biousse, V., Labauge, P., Chabriat, H., Nibbio, A., . . . Tournier-Lasserve, E. (1993). A gene for familial hemiplegic migraine maps to chromosome 19. *Nature Genetics, 5,* 40–45. doi:10.1038/ng0993-40

Jung, J., Weeks, D. E., & Feingold, E. (2006). Gene-dropping vs. empirical variance estimation for allele-sharing linkage statistics. *Genetic Epidemiology, 30,* 652–665. doi:10.1002/gepi.20177

Kavvoura, F. K., & Ioannidis, J. P. (2008). Methods for meta-analysis in genetic association studies: a review of their potential and pitfalls. *Human Genetics, 123,* 1–14. doi:10.1007/s00439-007-0445-9

Lander, E. S., & Green, P. (1987). Construction of multilocus genetic linkage maps in humans. *Proceedings of the National Academy of Sciences of the United States of America, 84,* 2363–2367. doi:10.1073/pnas.84.8.2363

Lander, E. S., & Kruglyak, L. (1995). Genetic dissection of complex traits: Guidelines for interpreting and reporting linkage results. *Nature Genetics, 11,* 241–247. doi:10.1038/ng1195-241

Li, Y., & Abecasis, G. R. (2006). Mach 1.0: Rapid Haplotype Reconstruction and Missing Genotype Inference. *American Journal of Human Genetics, S79,* 2290.

Liang, F., Holt, I., Pertea, G., Karamycheva, S., Salzberg, S. L., & Quackenbush, J. (2000). Gene index analysis of the human genome estimates approximately 120,000 genes. *Nature Genetics, 25,* 239–240. doi:10.1038/76126

Ligthart, L., Nyholt, D. R., Penninx, B. W., & Boomsma, D. I. (2010). The shared genetics of migraine and anxious depression. *Headache, 50,* 1549–1560.

Lindgren, C. M., Heid, I. M., Randall, J. C., Lamina, C., Steinthorsdottir, V., Qi, L., . . . McCarthy, M. I. (2009). Genome-wide association scan meta-analysis identifies three Loci influencing adiposity and fat distribution. *PLoS Genetics, 5*(6), e1000508.

Manolio, T. A., & Collins, F. S. (2009). The HapMap and genome-wide association studies in diagnosis and therapy. *Annual Review of Medicine, 60,* 443–456. doi:10.1146/annurev.med.60.061907.093117

Marchini, J., & Howie, B. (2010). Genotype imputation for genome-wide association studies. *Nature Reviews: Genetics, 11,* 499–511. doi:10.1038/nrg2796

Marchini, J., Howie, B., Myers, S., McVean, G., & Donnelly, P. (2007). A new multipoint method for genome-wide association studies by imputation of genotypes. *Nature Genetics, 39,* 906–913. doi:10.1038/ng2088

Martin, N., Boomsma, D., & Machin, G. (1997). A twin-pronged attack on complex traits. *Nature Genetics, 17,* 387–392. doi:10.1038/ng1297-387

Martin, N. G., Boomsma, D., & Neale, M. C. (1989). Foreword. *Behavior Genetics, 19,* 5–7. doi:10.1007/BF01065880

McCarthy, M. I., Abecasis, G. R., Cardon, L. R., Goldstein, D. B., Little, J., Ioannidis, J. P., & Hirschhorn, J. N. (2008). Genome-wide association studies for complex traits: consensus, uncertainty and challenges. *Nature Reviews: Genetics, 9,* 356–369. doi:10.1038/nrg2344

Middeldorp, C. M., Sullivan, P. F., Wray, N. R., Hottenga, J. J., de Geus, E. J., van den Berg, M., . . . Martin, N. G. (2009). Suggestive linkage on chromosome 2, 8, and 17 for lifetime major depression. *American Journal of Medical Genetics: Part B, Neuropsychiatric Genetics, 150,* 352–358. doi:10.1002/ajmg.b.30817

Moffitt, T. E., Caspi, A., & Rutter, M. (2005). Strategy for investigating interactions between measured genes and measured environments. *Archives of General Psychiatry, 62,* 473–481. doi:10.1001/archpsyc.62.5.473

Munafò, M. R., Durrant, C., Lewis, G., & Flint, J. (2009). Gene × Environment interactions at the serotonin transporter locus. *Biological Psychiatry, 65,* 211–219.

Neale, M. C., Boker, S. M., Xie, G., & Maes, H. H. (2003). *Mx: Statistical modeling* (6th ed.). Richmond: Virginia Commonwealth University, Department of Psychiatry.

Neale, M. C., & Cardon, L. R. (1992). *Methodology for genetic studies in twins and families.* Dordrecht, The Netherlands: Kluwer.

Nyholt, D. R. (2008). Principles of linkage analysis. In B. M. Neale, M. A. Ferreira, S. E. Medland, & D. Posthuma (Eds.), *Statistical genetics: Gene mapping through linkage and association* (pp. 111–134). New York, NY: Taylor & Francis.

Ophoff, R. A., Terwindt, G. M., Vergouwe, M. N., van Eijk, R., Oefner, P. J., Hoffman, S. M., . . . Frants, R. R. (1996). Familial hemiplegic migraine and episodic ataxia type-2 are caused by mutations in the Ca2+ channel gene CACNL1A4. *Cell, 87,* 543–552. doi:10.1016/S0092-8674(00)81373-2

Ott, J. (1999). *Analysis of human genetic linkage* (3rd ed.). Baltimore, MD: Johns Hopkins University Press.

Pe'er, I., Yelensky, R., Altshuler, D., & Daly, M. J. (2008). Estimation of the multiple testing burden for genomewide association studies of nearly all common variants. *Genetic Epidemiology, 32,* 381–385. doi:10.1002/gepi.20303

Plomin, R., DeFries, J. C., McClearn, G. E., & McGuffin, P. (2008). Nature, nurture, and behavior. In *Behavioral Genetics* (5th ed., pp. 59–91). New York, NY: Worth.

Posthuma, D., & Boomsma, D. I. (2000). A note on the statistical power in extended twin designs. *Behavior Genetics, 30*, 147–158. doi:10.1023/A:1001959306025

Purcell, S. (2002). Variance components models for gene-environment interaction in twin analysis. *Twin Research, 5*, 554–571. doi:10.1375/136905202762342026

Purcell, S., Neale, B., Todd-Brown, K., Thomas, L., Ferreira, M. A., Bender, D., . . . Sham, P. C. (2007). PLINK: A tool set for whole-genome association and population-based linkage analyses. *American Journal of Human Genetics, 81*, 559–575. doi:10.1086/519795

Risch, N., Herrell, R., Lehner, T., Liang, K. Y., Eaves, L., Hoh, J., . . . Merikangas, K. R. (2009). Interaction between the serotonin transporter gene (5-HTTLPR), stressful life events, and risk of depression: A meta-analysis. *JAMA, 301*, 2462–2471. doi:10.1001/jama.2009.878

Ritchie, M. D. (2009). Using prior knowledge and genome-wide association to identify pathways involved in multiple sclerosis. *Genome Medicine, 1*(6), 65. doi:10.1186/gm65

Sawcer, S., Jones, H. B., Judge, D., Visser, F., Compston, A., Goodfellow, P. N., & Clayton, D. (1997). Empirical genomewide significance levels established by whole genome simulations. *Genetic Epidemiology, 14*, 223–229. doi:10.1002/(SICI)1098-2272(1997)14:3<223::AID-GEPI1>3.0.CO;2-6

Schwarz, G. (1978). Estimating the dimension of a model. *Annals of Statistics, 6*, 461–464. doi:10.1214/aos/1176344136

Sham, P. C., Purcell, S., Cherny, S. S., & Abecasis, G. R. (2002). Powerful regression-based quantitative-trait linkage analysis of general pedigrees. *American Journal of Human Genetics, 71*, 238–253. doi:10.1086/341560

Smith, L. T., Otterson, G. A., & Plass, C. (2007). Unraveling the epigenetic code of cancer for therapy. *Trends in Genetics, 23*, 449–456. doi:10.1016/j.tig.2007.07.005

Spielman, R. S., McGinnis, R. E., & Ewens, W. J. (1993). Transmission test for linkage disequilibrium: the insulin gene region and insulin-dependent diabetes mellitus (IDDM). *American Journal of Human Genetics, 52*, 506–516.

Sullivan, P. F., Eaves, L. J., Kendler, K. S., & Neale, M. C. (2001). Genetic case-control association studies in neuropsychiatry. *Archives of General Psychiatry, 58*, 1015–1024. doi:10.1001/archpsyc.58.11.1015

Sullivan, P. F., Fan, C., & Perou, C. M. (2006). Evaluating the comparability of gene expression in blood and brain. *American Journal of Medical Genetics: Part B, Neuropsychiatric Genetics, 141*, 261–268.

Terwilliger, J. D., & Ott, J. (1992). A haplotype-based "haplotype relative risk" approach to detecting allelic associations. *Human Heredity, 42*, 337–346.

Torkamani, A., Topol, E. J., & Schork, N. J. (2008). Pathway analysis of seven common diseases assessed by genome-wide association. *Genomics, 92*, 265–272. doi:10.1016/j.ygeno.2008.07.011

Van den Veyver, I. B. (2002). Genetic effects of methylation diets. *Annual Review of Nutrition, 22*, 255–282. doi:10.1146/annurev.nutr.22.010402.102932

Vink, J. M., & Boomsma, D. I. (2002). Gene finding strategies. *Biological Psychology, 61*, 53–71. doi:10.1016/S0301-0511(02)00052-2

Vink, J. M., Smit, A. B., de Geus, E. J., Sullivan, P., Willemsen, G., Hottenga, J. J., . . . Boomsma, D. I. (2009). Genome-wide association study of smoking initiation and current smoking. *American Journal of Human Genetics, 84*, 367–379. doi:10.1016/j.ajhg.2009.02.001

Visscher, P. M. (2008). Sizing up human height variation. *Nature Genetics, 40*, 489–490. doi:10.1038/ng0508-489

Wan, Y., Cohen, J., & Guerra, R. (1997). A permutation test for the robust sib-pair linkage method. *Annals of Human Genetics, 61*, 77–85. doi:10.1017/S0003480096005957

Wang, K., Li, M., & Bucan, M. (2007). Pathway-based approaches for analysis of genomewide association studies. *American Journal of Human Genetics, 81*, 1278–1283. doi:10.1086/522374

Wright, S. (1934). The method of path coefficients. *Annals of Mathematical Statistics, 5*, 161–215. doi:10.1214/aoms/1177732676

Zeggini, E., Scott, L. J., Saxena, R., Voight, B. F., Marchini, J. L., Hu, T., . . . Altshuler, D. (2008). Meta-analysis of genome-wide association data and large-scale replication identifies additional susceptibility loci for Type 2 diabetes. *Nature Genetics, 40*, 638–645. doi:10.1038/ng.120

Zwijnenburg, P. J., Meijers-Heijboer, H., & Boomsma, D. I. (2010). Identical but not the same: The value of discordant monozygotic twins in genetic research. *American Journal of Medical Genetics: Part B, Neuropsychiatric Genetics, 153B*, 1134–1149.